SCHIZOPHRENIA
Current Concepts
and Research

SCHIZOPHRENIA
Current Concepts and Research

Edited By

D. V. Siva Sankar Ph. D.

Associate Research Scientist, Creedmoor State Hospital
N. Y. State Department of Mental Hygiene
Adjunct Professor of Chemistry, Adelphi University
Adjunct Professor of Biology and Chemistry, Long Island University

The contents of this book are based upon the papers delivered at a Symposium on "Schizophrenia: Current Concepts and Research" held at the Waldorf Astoria Hotel, New York, on November 14, 15 and 16, 1968. The Symposium was sponsored by Eastern Psychiatric Research Association, and Psychiatric Research Foundation, New York.

PJD PUBLICATIONS LTD. BOX 581, HICKSVILLE, N.Y. 11802

P R E F A C E

Some of the aspects of the Biology of Schizophrenia have been presented in a previous volume (Annals of the New York Academy of Sciences 96) in 1962. Since then more controversy has been added to the subject. This monograph purports to portray the difficulties involved. Some newer areas of research have come to be important in a concept of the diversity and heterogeneity of schizophrenia. It is with this purpose, especially the biological diversity in mind, that I have attempted to bring together the several contributors of the present monograph. This would have been well neigh impossible but for three factors : (i). The enthusiasm, patience and the understanding of the contributors, (ii). The cooperation given to me by Dr. David Impastato and the Eastern Psychiatric Research Association Inc., and (iii). The cooperation given to me by Dr. Nathan S. Kline and the Psychiatric Research Foundation. A contribution from Endo Laboratories partly defrayed my personal expenses. I owe my gratitude to one and all of these persons and organizations.

My indebtedness extends also to my several associates who have been painstakingly understanding of the difficulties. I thank my wife, D. Barbara Sankar, and Miss Gail Weiner and Mr. Mark Snyder for helping me in the preparation and production and publication of this monograph. Some of the defects of this book have been unavoidable in view of the decision to produce it by the photo offset process in order to keep down the production costs.

It is with the fervent hope that the next seven years will be fat for research on the psychobiology of schizophrenia and its basic neurobiology, that I invite the reader to peruse this present monograph.

New York
May, 1969   D. V. Siva Sankar

i

TABLE OF CONTENTS

iii

v

THE GROWTH PROCESS AND SCHIZOPHRENIA: A HOLISTIC PSYCHODYNAMIC APPROACH

JACK L. RUBINS

It is becoming increasingly evident at present that hitherto held concepts about the psychogenesis of the Schizophrenias in general and the psychodynamics of many clinical symptoms in particular, are inadequate and must be modified. Such evidence is accruing from three groups of observations.

The first group points to a greater need to take into account the influence of sociocultural factors on this form of pathological development. The incidence of these psychoses seems to be increasing. During the decade 1940-50 (prior to the widespread use of psychotropic drugs), the number of admissions to New York State Hospitals for such conditions rose 32%. Since then, the rate seems to be further rising, considering the number being seen in clinics or privately. The number of cases has been found greater in city centers than in suburbia; and higher in the low socio-economic, culturally-underprivileged groups. In addition, many transcultural studies show that not only do the various endogenous schizophrenic-like psychoses throughout the world result from, and get their form and content from characteristic local cultural practices, beliefs and values, but even the incidence and form of the classic diagnostic syndroms may vary culturally. For instance, there is a higher incidence and special form of Schizophrenia in Japan as compared with other subcultures in the region. There is a lower incidence of paranoid symptoms and higher rate of catatonic and confusional states among primitive African peoples compared to a higher paranoid rate among the whites living among them. This has been attributed to a preoccupation with witchcraft and magic beliefs of the former, and "Europeanization" of the latter. A comparative study of Italian and Irish schizophrenics in New York showed significant differences. The former showed more overt homosexual activity, less guilt over sex, more somatization, overactive affective reactions, poorly controlled impulses, weaker interpersonal attachments and fewer, less systematized delusions. The latter showed strong feelings of guilt and sin, constricted affects, a rich fantasy life, rather fixed persecutory delusions with feelings of grandiosity, and suspiciousness.

Furthermore, just as the "popular" form of neurosis has been changing from the "grande hysterie" of 1900 to the character neurosis, so too have the predominant forms of schizophrenia been changing. The fulminating hebephrenias, the severe waxy catatonics, the refusal to eat are becoming infrequent today, and are being replaced by the undifferentiated or symptomatically mild or borderline cases. In fact such is the symptomatic variety seen today, that our presently held diagnostic categories are inadequate to describe them. In addition to the four Bleulerian types, we now describe latent, prepsychotic, masked, non-psychotic, pseudo-neurotic, schizo-affective, undifferentiated, late-onset forms, as well as related non-psychotic character disorders. Yet even this variety, however comprehensive, does not do justice to the manifold syndromes seen today. Symptoms may be manifest, clear-cut and objective or subtle, imprecise and subjective; or one form may change to another. Borderline forms may extend on a continuum from the apparent symptom-neurosis through the neurotic personality disturbance to the character disorder. Sometimes a definite diagnosis of schizophrenia cannot be made on the basis of "typical" symptoms alone; yet the experienced clinician is left with what seems to be a vague, intuitive feeling that his patient is psychotic.

Added to this, we are now becoming aware that such commonly held classical diagnostic criteria as type of onset, evolution and outcome are no longer tenable. The exception is as frequent as the rule. Many cases of so-called "nuclear" childhood schizophrenia, considered inevitably progressive toward deterioration, have been found to improve in adolescence. Some cases of acute, situational psychotic reactions, with a supposedly good prognosis, develop into intractable chronic forms. Many schizophrenic-like episodes during adolescence turn out to be simply adolescent identity crises which clear up on entering adulthood and do not recur. Although we still look for a "typical" prepsychotic personality (withdrawn, dreamy, unagressive, suspicious) we now often find acute psychotic episodes in patients who have previously been relatively healthy, well-adjusted and functioning. The distinction between so-called benign and malignant forms has become much less certain today. Acute benign forms may improve spontaneously or on medication or with short-term psychotherapy or on long-term analysis; or this may happen following another apparently traumatic event like the illness or death of a parent or spouse. But such acute cases may also prove resistant to any form of treatment and become progressively worse. Even among long-term chronic hospitalized patients, there is a surprising rate of remission (about 80%) as M. Bleuler has recently reported.

The relationship of the psychotic episode to some apparently precipitating event or situation is another question involving external versus internal factors, which we now recognize as being much more complex than previously thought. Such episodes are seen following every kind of situation: the first menstrual period, marriage, the first sexual intercourse, childbirth, the loss of someone close, an argument or frustration, a frightening experience, a real or imagined rejection, an operation or illness, an alcoholic or drug intoxication, etc. We are then inclined to consider the emotional reaction as acute or chronic stress or anxiety. And we might then say that the tolerance-threshhold has been exceeded, so there is decompensation. However, sometimes the predominant emotion is not anxiety, but some other feeling like guilt, humiliation, anger or sorrow. In fact, it need not be a so-called negative one, but a positive one like affection, relief or joy. So that the concept of stress or anxiety being the etiological agent by itself is an oversimplification.

We can no longer consider this group simply as "reactive states" or maladjustive ways of coping with society; nor simply as "social problems", therefore to be treated primarily by environmental manipulation or by explanations of the correct way to react or even by behavior-changing medication, so that the patient "fits in" better, conforms, without consideration for resolving his underlying attitudinal conflicts that are constantly generating his symptomatic pathology.

The second group of observations are those relating to our analytic concepts of, and therapeutic experience with the schizophrenias. Until recently, relatively few analysts had experience with such psychotic patients. The psychotic patient was less frequently referred than the neurotic, a lingering effect of the traditional analytic position. Some analysts were reluctant to accept such patients even when they were referred because their analytic tools were thought inapplicable, and technical difficulties were felt insuperable. Some analysts were purists and reluctant to "dilute" their theories or techniques, since certain modifications were required for treatment of these psychoses. Others were deterred by difficulties supposedly inherent in the psychoses themselves: the prevailing pessimism as to results with analytic psychotherapy, the notion of an inevitably poor prognosis, the length of time required for treatment, the acting out, the intense emotional swings or the lack of emotionality, the idea that unconscious material could not be dealt with, the tremendous demands and claims on the therapist, and the alleged difficulty in making a relationship.

However, these conditions and prejudgements have been changing in recent years. More psychotics are now coming into analysts offices under pressure for therapy by the large, hitherto neglected lower-income group; more psychotics are being treated as ambulatory rather than hospitalized; and financial means for such therapy is becoming available through third party payment. Other analysts are giving up their insistance of the purity of psychoanalysis, and realizing that modifications both in theory and technique are feasible without doing damage to essential principles. And changing notions about the schizophrenic process itself are permitting the use of newer analytic concepts.

The third group of assumptions now being questioned are inherent in the pathogenetic concepts of the classical Freudian approach. Without going into detail, according to this theory the central process of these psychoses is a regression to the earliest infantile libidinal stage; this is said to occur as psychic defenses collapse under the impact of overwhelming conflictive instinctive demands from within. The adult schizophrenic is thus supposedly experiencing the same intense narcissism and omnipotence as during his infancy. From the viewpoint of ego psychology, the regression is to a stage when the ego is unformed, archaic, undifferentiated from the outside world, therefore weak and without boundaries. Some of the pathological symptoms are said to result directly from this regression, others to be an overcompensatory reaction against it, and still others are restitutive in substituting false perceptions for the lost objects of reality.

I believe that this concept of regression is questionable on both theoretical and clinical grounds. It assumes that symptomatic schizophrenic behavior which resembles that of an infant is in reality infantile. The adult has supposedly returned to his infantile period, or conversely, the infantile state is repeated (repetition-compulsion). The adult is thus considered merely a grown child, is infantilized. A simple similarity is taken for actuality, when the behavior may really be quite different in its total form, etiology, motivation and meaning. A second objection is that the similarity or procedence is often based on the retrospective reconstruction from memory of the adult's infantile experience. As is well known analytically, the patient's remembering is overdetermined by the defensive coloring derived from his pathological attitudes, by his subjective misinterpretation of past situations or relationships, and by his selection for recall of some events and repression of others. Nevertheless, such recalled memories and reconstructions of early environment or parental attitudes are often taken for truth. Although this methodological error is being somewhat corrected now by the more frequently used direct observation of schizophrenic infants, this method too is subject to pitfalls. For instance, when behavior is noted, corresponding feelings of the infant are interpolated; those described by the adult observer may be projections of his own experience. The infant is "adultomorphized". Finally, even where feelings or attitudes are expressed in behavior, they may be explained on the basis of theoretical assumptions which are taken for truth and the only possible explanation. Childhood narcissism or omnipotence ascribed to an instinctive investment of self with libido may really be due to a faulty parental attitude; infantile clinging, instead of being a universal psychosexual phase may equally well be a reactive attitude to parental rejection or motivated by anxiety.

Previous interpersonal analytic approaches have made many contributions to understanding these psychoses. Schizophrenia is generally described as a distorted way of life, having its genesis in a non-specific infantile maladjustment that grows out of disturbed relationships with parents. This is predominantly a struggle for status as experienced through the appraisals of others. Psychosis breaks out at a point of "disaster to self-esteem" usually related to the eruption of sexual impulses, with its required "resymbolization of ideals and purposes". The process is described as a failure of security operations by the self-dynamism, so that a state of conflict is universalized and the dissociated conflict-provoking systems accorded independent personality, with power greater than that of the self. This state is said to be primarily manifested by regression from adult to childhood modes of interpersonal living and genital activity; from higher to lower orders of thought in the developmental sense; and by the erection of defensive barriers between the patient and others.

The holistic approach being presented here goes further in the direction already taken by this shift in viewpoint, namely from schizophrenia as disease-entity to symptom-clusters to way of life or social practice, and now to a distorted growth process; from libidinal plus ego to interpersonal alone, to interpersonal plus intrapsychic factors. But it differs from these above theories in that schizophrenia is not seen to be simply a chronological or phylogenetic regression whereby the adult symptom is a re-enactment of either a childhood behavior pattern or a primitive archaic behavior. Nor that the symptom expresses a collapse of psychological defenses, a "surrender to the unconscious". On the contrary, I would suggest that the adult schizophrenic symptom is different from any childhood behavior in its complexity, its motivations and its meanings; the resemblance is only apparent, to the extent that complex acts are made up of simpler bits, and there are only a limited number of ways of expression available to the human being. Furthermore, I feel the symptom is always defensive, albeit perhaps in a distorted form; and far from being a simpler form of defense, is generally a more complex form, expressing many levels of meaning and/or communication at once. In this pathological growth process, predispositional (temperamental-physical), developmental, intrapsychic and external (sociocultural) forces interact dynamically.

This analytic approach is an extension and modification of the theories of Horney, and is based therefore on four underlying principles: the holistic, the functional, the dynamic and the individualistic. According to the holistic principle, the individual is seen as an integral totality, a gestalt, acting on, interacting with and being acted upon by his external milieu and internal processes, both at any here-and-now moment as well as from past into future. In the functional sense, the personality (or self) is a sum total of lived attributes: biological and social needs, behavioral traits, feelings and sensations, acts, attitudes toward self and others, self-image and self-concepts, social values and self-evaluations, expectations and demands, conflicts and inhibitions. These qualities exist in a constantly changing functional (not a structural or static) organization. Some are more experienced and conscious, some more unconscious: some more expressed in behavior than others; some more subjective and others more objective; some valued and admired, others depreciated and hated or held in contempt; some closely identified with and experienced as being self and subject and in the foreground, others experienced as being other than self, object and in background. The dynamic principle postulates that each of these attributes has a peremptory force, is simultaneously created by the person and acting upon him reflexively, demanding satisfaction or producing strivings, or pressing toward action or inaction; thus they may reinforce, enter into conflict, inhibit or modify each other. The total personality - healthy, neurotic or psychotic - is thus changing in observable ways, showing movement and patterns and process, in definite directions and with definable rhythms, at various psychic levels. Although specific attributes may be experienced, may appear in behavior, may be expressed as a symptom, or may be focussed upon in therapy, this accent is an artificial isolation. In therapy, therefore, the symptom is of less importance than the underlying dynamic forces producing it; emphasis is placed on changing the existing pathological dynamic constellation of personality traits into a healthier direction of growth. Finally, the individualistic view stresses the uniqueness of one patient as distinct from every other, and the need to account for such differences.

Although the psychoses are, like the neuroses, seen as dis-ordered forms of growth, there are both similarities and differences between the two general groups of disorders. There exists a continuum from the least to the most sick in terms of pathological process (normal to neurotic to psychotic) but the difference between extremes is both of form and kind.

The schizophrenias, which are temporary and changing manifes-tations through symptoms of a disordered (psychotic) growth process, can best be understood by comparing this process with the neurotic and normal one. The growth process consists of two part-processes or aspects: emotional or personality development and maturational devel-opment. These two processes are simultaneous and parallel, continuing throughout life at varying rates for different age periods. Each impli-cates and modifies the other, and distortions in one may produce charac-teristic psychopathological symptoms depending on its interaction with the other.

Clinical observation shows that in spite of being biologically de-pendent on its parents, the normal child can psychologically relate to them in various ways: with compliance, submission and dependency; with opposition and self-assertion; with withdrawal and self-sufficiency. Such attitudes will normally be spontaneous, flexible and appropriate to the situation when the infant develops in a healthy parental atmos-phere. By this I mean where his healthy needs and demands are satis-fied, his given temperamental qualities accepted and respected, warm emotional interaction expressed, healthy friction allowed and rational limitations imposed. By contrast, pathological development occurs when the infant is confronted by various distorted parental attitudes such as overprotection, overindulgence, smothering love, emotional coldness or distance, harsh domination, excessive expectations, overt or covert rejection, sexual seductiveness, extreme friction between parents, emotional ambivalence, etc. He must then modify his healthy given attitudes so as to conform to the conscious or unconscious needs and demands of his parents, so as to procure for himself the optimal se-curity, safety and care in this potentially hostile (as he experiences it) environment. We know that this child-parent attitudinal relationship is not a simple direct one. It is rather a complex interaction, wherein the infants' traits influence the particular parental reaction, reacting back on the child, then back to the parent, in a circular fashion. The net re-sult of the adoption of such artificial attitudes, and subsequently of the directing of energies toward maintaining this defensive personality structure or facade, is a loss of the capacity to fulfil his healthy poten-tials, and a distancing from, or deadening of his genuine, normal inner experiences.

Many studies have attempted to delineate the "typical" schizo-phrenigenic mother or father or parental relationship, namely to blame the childs disturbance on specific parental attitudes. In the literature we find the mother described in different studies as compulsive and per-fectionistic, demanding and righteous: aggressive or domineering; over-solicitous, indulgent or overprotective which hinders the childs separation; excessively anxious and fearful; ambivalent or double-binding; disapproving, non-accepting or actively rejective, consciously or unconsciously; cold, unemotional or distant; mechanical or imper-sonal; overtly psychotic or with other severe pathology. Fathers have been found overtly rejective; tyrannical or sadistic; excessively de-manding or obsessive-perfectionistic; highly intelligent and preoccu-pied; ambitious for success or prestige; self-centered or grandiose; inconsistent or shifting in attitude; passive, undemanding, dependent, weak, ineffectual; withdrawn, emotionally absent or non-existent; mechanical or impersonal. The parental inter-relationship has been described as showing severe conflict and opposition; full of anxiety, anger, mutual criticism and destructiveness; or passive acceptance by one of the others pathology so that the difficulty is masked (pseudo-mutuality). I have studied a fair number of such parents, and have indeed found any or several of such attitudes present. Such a multiplicity of attitudes, often inconsistent, even contradictory, that have been found in these studies, leads to the conclusion that it is difficult if at all possible to correlate a specific parental attitude or environment to any specific form of schizophrenia. Such attitudes are, in fact, the same as found in parents of neurotic patients. One is hard put to explain why relatively healthy children may develop with the same kind of parents - even with schizophrenic siblings - except that we know there are subtle differences in parental attitudes toward each child in a family.

Yet in spite of this variety of specific attitudes, I have observed certain general personality attributes in most parents of actually psychotic or preschizophrenic children. These are an <u>apparent intensity</u> of attitude or emotion, an <u>inconsistency</u>, a <u>spuriousness</u>, and an <u>intangible lack of contact</u>. In overt behavior and on short contact, such parents may show a high degree of some particular major neurotic attitude - be this chronic anger, domination, repressiveness, overaffection, excessive demands, distance, fearfulness, deadness or other. The expressed attitude or feeling seems to be extremely intense at any moment, and habitual. But mere intensity of attitude is not enough to produce psychosis. The child who is totally rejected, harshly maltreated, neglected or abandoned, or smothered by love, may not become schizophrenic if such an attitude is consistent, although other emotional pathology may develop. In such cases, the child can usually develop some defensive stance with some form of inter-relatedness. However, on closer and longer observation of such parents, one finds that this intensity is only apparent; something is not genuine about the way they seem to be.

Often there is an inconsistency between attitudinal reaction and situation. A certain reaction is not always present, cannot be counted upon even with the same kind of situation or provocation; often an opposite reaction to the anticipated one may be forthcoming. Or there may be a shift from one to another attitude without apparent reason. This change may be sudden or slow, obvious or subtle, conscious or unconscious, and sometimes accompanied by felt conflict, anxiety or guilt, or helplessness. At times the inconsistency and shifting may go over into an actual disorganization, manifested in many activities of the parent.

Very often, even when such an attitude or emotion is intensely expressed or acted out in behavior, it is not full-felt or meant. Many such parents say that they do not know how to be or do with the child, must ask someone else, consult a book, think of what others would expect, or do what is proper, regardless of the childs needs. This form of attitude has variously been described as an "as-if" or other-directed personality, "living through reflected appraisals" or simply as vicarious or externalized living. One aspect of this is that appropriate and healthy limitations cannot be given; they are either excessive and arbitrary or poorly defined.

Another element often found in the spuriousness is the coexistence of several differing, even contradictory conscious or unconscious attitudes at the same time. Apparent concern may overlay unconcern; affection, rejection; emotionality, deadness; aggressiveness, compliance. This form of ambivalence (or duplicity) can be transmitted through contradictory verbal, emotional or behavioral messages at the same time, the double-bind condition.

A further quality, and partly resulting from the above, is an impairment of contact between parent and child. Close emotional relationships may be inhibited, impersonal or deadened. The parent may complain of not knowing how to communicate with the child. At times this may be primarily physical: there is little touching, fondling or picking up the child, or it is in a stiff, mechanical, unnatural way.

Of course, these four qualities are not present to the same degree in all such parents; one or other may predominate. But they are observable to a greater extent than in the case of the neurotic child.

Observations of preschizophrenic or psychotic children also reveal characteristic emotional responses to such parental attitudes.

The neurotic form of response would be the development of a major, compulsive expressed attitude through trial-and-error, with repression of those attitudes incompatible to this. But in the face of such over-intensity, inconsistency or disorganization, spuriousness and lack of contact, such form of response is inadequate or impossible. The child cannot define or determine how to react optimally. He may in turn overreact to the manifest parental attitude, only to find it does not produce a satisfying situation. He may try to placate by complying to every changing emotion, and develop then a severely compulsive compliance and other-directedness. With such spuriousness, he may try desperately to fathom the "real" meaning or feeling of the parent, and may learn to do so; such children can develop an uncanny way of knowing the unconscious feelings of others. Faced with much shifting or disorganization, he may in turn show a similar chaotic organization or excessive alternating of behavioral traits. At times these swings in the child may be an attempt to produce some, any, emotional response from neurotically deadened or alienated parents. If no clear-cut reactive attitude permits a relationship, withdrawal, resignation and repression of all emotion may result. In some cases, the fear of experiencing anger or hostility that might increase the parental rejection, the inability to find any security-producing response, and the greater degree of conflict resulting from contradictory yet more volatile attitudes, may all generate a severe, chronic infantile anxiety. Secondary defensive manoeuvers, which will be discussed later, can then aggravate the schizophrenic process.

The second aspect of the growth process, maturational development, involves three elements: the body-image, the self-concept and identity. The formation of an adequate body-image -- including conscious and unconscious physical details, dimensions and limits -- depends on many internal and external factors. Inner factors include physical defects or abilities, forms of perceptivity, degree of reactivity to stimuli, sexual drives, intelligence, innate likes or dislikes, etc. External factors may include parental values, peer influences, or cultural symbols. The self-concept (of which the body-image is part) includes such other attributes as forms of behavior, attitudes and personality traits, emotions, wants or needs, which develop in keeping with the particular growth pattern, family role and sociocultural milieu. Some of these are present from birth, others are adopted by imitation, through identification with others, through trial-and-error experimentation, or through usefulness to satisfy needs or to serve purposes of communication. The earliest physical self-image expands gradually into the more total and conceptual self-concept with the development of the capacity for focal attention and then for reflective abstract thought; with the ability to differentiate external objects from each other and from the self; with the capacity for symbolic representation; and with the appearance of communication, which helps delimit other selves from ones own. Organization of all these disparate percepts, stimuli and concepts into an arranged self and outside world also requires a learned awareness of temporal sequence, of cause-effect relations, of movement, positioning, spatial orientation and boundaries. Such learning is a complex phenomenological process of interaction between the infant and environment. Identity-formation is the last state of this psychological process; this involves the transformation of the self-concept into a self-identity. Identity provides an emotional assimilation or an experiencing of descriptive attributes of self ("what am I" becomes "who am I"), a constancy and continuity of the self into the past and future (while the self-concept may be continually changing), and an active placing of the self into the social environment.

I believe that this maturational process, which is normally harmonious and sequential throughout life, is most vulnerable to distortion by schizophrenigenic influences. Selective distortions may occur at any point of this process and affect any of the aspects noted above. Adding their effects to distortions in the concurrent emotional developmental process, they can specifically contribute to the form and severity of the symptomatic schizophrenic pathology, in the child, adolescent and adult.

To cite a few examples, "soft" constitutional impairments in motility, vision, hearing or physical growth can deform the body-image. A high innate threshhold of reaction to stimuli can cause the infant to be relatively insensitive to its environment; then faced with neurotically deadened parents, he will show a paucity of inner emotional experiences, so facilitating the creation of autistic or dereistic phenomena. With a low threshhold and increased sensitivity to stimuli, the infant faced with overstimulating or disorganized parents, may be overwhelmed and experience an overabundance or disorganization of inner reactions. He may show a hypersensitivity to stimuli and excessive distractibility; this can result in a withdrawal from contact with the environment or building up an insulating barrier. A high level of intelligence may favor an overemphasis on intellectualization and importance of the head; a high development of a single intellectual ability may produce the scattering of performance often found. Failure to develop adequate body-image boundaries may produce the need to cling, to merge with another person, found in the symbiotic psychotic child.

The self-concept may be impersonalized, inadequate or irrationally subjective, contributing thus to some of the depersonalization syndromes. Defective identity-formation (which normally provides constancy of time flow) may result in syndromes of time confusion, the inability to distinguish past, present and future. Disturbances in specific areas of identity, such as gender, can contribute to later sexual anxieties such as homosexual fears, ideas of reference. A deformed self-concept or identity, combined with non-accepting, critical or depreciating parental attitudes, may produce intensified feelings of being defective and loathsome, self-hate or self-destructiveness.

The outbreak of schizophrenic episodes during adolescence are also explainable on this basis. Both processes are subject to much stress during this period of rapid change; the quasi-normal adolescent turmoil and identity-crises give evidence of this. An excessively stressful change in the maturational development -- such as rapid physical growth, secondary sexual characteristics, acne or awareness of intellectual slowness -- may act as a decompensatory distortion. Increase in pressures, expectations and demands from parents, peers or society -- for sexual socializing, for intellectual performance, for self-sufficiency, for career-choices -- may bring awareness that the neurotic defensive attitudes toward others and the idealized image of self, are inadequate and cannot be maintained; this can act as the decompensatory distortion in the emotional developmental process.

Since the functional constellation of personality and its patterns of reacting, relating and changing become more established during adulthood, then such distortions of these two part-processes are likewise aggravated. The adult schizophrenic's symptoms are expressions of the dynamic interaction between such underlying factors. Similar dynamic factors may produce differing symptoms, and different factors may result in the same symptom. There may be great discrepancy between the degree of <u>dynamic</u> pathology, and the <u>symptomatic</u> disturbance; the former may be intense and the latter minimal, and vice-versa.

This is shown, for example, in the relationship between anxiety and the clinical picture, which is most complex. I have found the intensity of anxiety -- as an experienced affect, whether free-floating or in fixated forms -- to be most variable and not proportionate to the severity of the manifest condition. This disagrees with some authors who implicate anxiety as the major element in precipitating and maintaining the psychotic state. The schizophrenic is hypersensitive to its presence, often seems to follow an all-or-none law in his tolerance. This type of reaction is explainable for several reasons: (1) The <u>extensity</u> of possible areas of intrapsychic conflict is greater. Since a larger number of <u>ad hoc</u> defenses are needed to provide a feeling of security, stability and unity, there is more chance of inner contradiction or frustration. (2) The intensity of emotional needs and defensive atti-tudes are greater, therefore the reaction to their frustration by others or from within, is greater. (3) The total defensive psychotic personality structure is more fragile, therefore more easily threatened, i. e. by relatively minor situational or inner experiences. A threat to one de-fensive attitude may threaten the whole self. (4) With the inner disor-ganization and fluidity, there is a need to maintain sameness. Thus, any change per se, inner or external, is threatening. Anxiety is a threat not only as an experienced affect in itself, but as a change in status quo. (5) A particular defensive reaction is concreteness, in emotion, thought and behavior. This is specifically threatened by any dynamic shift or conflict that can be experienced as movement; by any emotion that can be felt as abstract; by expansion or lack of limits or control, from within or without. (6) Since during prepsychotic development there is a greater removal from real inner experiences and from relatedness to external reality, anxiety is engendered whenever the extent and intensity of this distancing-deadening comes into awareness. This may follow any increase or awareness of some specific feeling or emotionality in general.

For these reasons, minimal anxiety must immediately be de-fended against. And if this cannot be done, then it quickly may be mag-nified excessively, requiring secondary defensive movements. However, paradoxically, (7) secondary defenses may increase rather than still the anxiety in that they can threaten previous primary solutions to conflict. For example, the externalizing expressed in hallucinations or delusions may bring some awareness of the lack of contact with reality (therefore of the identity impairment and alienation from self). The illogicality of associations used to avoid painfully emotionally-charged ideas, may increase the lack of communication and distance from others, and so forth.

The need for sameness is acute in most schizophrenics and manifests itself in anxiety on even minor changes in routine, order, time and space. Firstly it results from the disorganized impulses and experiences arising within the self. We have seen that the prepsychotic usually develops an impaired body-image and self-concept, with diffi-culty in distinguishing inner from outer experiences, and in arranging these in time and space. In addition his neurotic-type emotions and compulsive attitudes toward others are more intense yet more rapidly changing, therefore more conflictual, even chaotic; but they are less stabilized by his identity and contact with reality. Much energy must be expended to stilling such inner experiences. This may show itself simply as an unwillingness to discuss or experience any change, move-ment, active initiative or conflict, within or without. In severe cases, the catatonic immobility, the waxy flexibility, the repeated stereotypic movements, are all evidence of this tendency to still or limit movement.

It is secondly an attempt to maintain a stable external frame of reference. Since the boundaries of the body-image are also impaired, many schizophrenics relate to the environment in a peculiar fluid way, feeling impelled to merge with other persons. A break in consistency of their external framework is often experienced as a defect or impair-ment of their own selves. Since identity is also impaired, they may lack the feeling of constancy in time and of actively being part of the social milieu. The constant and familiar external setting furnishes the needed feeling of solidity for orienting themselves. They may experi-ence a feeling of being adrift, of unrelatedness, of disorientation, of fluidity or falling apart, when it changes. The same need to staticize affects how other persons are experienced too. Instead of being able to experience others as live, emotional, interacting with himself, they may transform them into solid, unchanging objects. Or they may seek out others who are sensed to be as alienated, or who may show a rela-tively fixed, static, one-sided personality, or who are healthy enough to remain unaffected by their own shifting.

Another attitude often observed is grandiosity, varying from mild egocentricity to delusional megalomania. The theoretical notion of this being simply the regressive reactivation of an infantile instinctive narcissism-omnipotence is contradicted by clinical studies of children. Instead we find that such a state in a child is a complex combination of perceptual self-centeredness (before differentiation of self from outside); of conceptual egocentricity (before recognition of others' individuality); of attitudinal exploitativeness and self-importance (fostered by neurotic attitudes of parents); and finally of self-glorification (through neurotic development). In the adult, according to our holistic approach, excessive and irrational self aggrandizement is the core of pathological emotional growth. Although beginning in infancy to avoid basic anxiety and conflict of threatening relationships with parents, in the adult it becomes an unconscious self with which he is driven to identify and live up to. It is thus a defensive movement required to avoid the intrapsychic conflict between contradictory but compulsive repressed interpersonal attitudes; in addition it satisfies neurotic needs, avoids painful feelings or other attributes of self, transforms weaknesses into virtues, promises fulfillment of imagined capacities, and provides a feeling of inner unity. It involves such general feelings as being special, unique, perfect, privileged, superior, invulnerable; and also specific attributes according to the persons own favored needs, attitudes, standards, values and goals. In the schizophrenic, this irrationally grandiose self-image is more extreme and needed for a number of reasons. The inner conflict between opposing attitudes (compliance-closeness-dependency versus expansiveness-domination-aggressiveness versus detachment-freedom-resignation) is greater, since these are reinforced by needs arising from maturational defects. The resulting anxiety is also greater, and such attitudes are more volatile and fluid, and less effective in furnishing a feeling of security or unity; and the need to avoid it is equally greater. The feeling of incompleteness and deficit in identity, often with added self-hatred, requires compensatory measures. And the emotional detachment of parents which deprives the child of human models for identification, plus the childs own withdrawal, favors autistic preoccupation and flight into fantasy and self-glorification. This grandiose self is therefore less rooted in and related to the reality of self and the environment.

Its effects are experienced in the forms of pressures, of demands on the self ("shoulds") or as expectations of others in keeping with such grandiose self attributes. The pride invested therein is so great that it is much more vulnerable and fragile; thus the self-hate and self-contempt is much greater when claims on others are frustrated or the image is threatened or disproved. The inordinate acute schizophrenic rages are usually such hurt pride reactions. Likewise, the greater pressure from inner shoulds renders such patients exceedingly sensitive to external authority, at the same time that their impaired identity and need for control or limits makes them overdependent on such authority.

The content of delusions will thus depend on which specific attitudes or values are involved in this process so becoming available for further externalization. The messianic delusion will result from an unconsciously idealized saintliness, meekness, omniscience; the Napoleonic from an idealized arrogance, manipulativeness, need for power; the erotic delusion from an unconscious seductiveness, and so on. Or the patient may identify not with his idealized self, but with his despised self. He may then feel he is being laughed at, talked about, accused of being abnormal, dirty, homosexual, promiscuous, etc. Paranoid feelings may result when there occurs a frustration of some excessive claim on others, which then produces a severe threat to the underlying grandiose self and hurt pride. The consequent self-hate/self-contempt is then defensively externalized on to some pre-existing person or object, or to an hallucinated one created through the use of concretization and symbolization. The hostility, malevolence, persecution, poisoning or coercion felt to be emanating from others is thus an experience of ones own repressed hostility plus the particular form of intense self-hate.

The defensive mechanism of externalization has characteristic features in the schizophrenic patient. To experience inner events as outside, is a normal psychological tendency; and it is used defensively in neurosis to deny attributes which are conflictual, disruptive and emotionally painful or unacceptable to the artificially harmonious self-image. Its manifestations may vary from a simple hypersensitivity to ones own qualities seen in others (disliked or admired) to an excessive preoccupation with others and disinterest in ones own self, to a complete living vicariously through others. It may involve some limited attribute, affect, attitude, physical trait or value; or it may become a general and pervasive attitude of external living. It may be an acute avoidance manoeuver, namely blaming others for ones own weaknesses (the classic definition of projection) or a chronic attitude toward self and others.

Many schizophrenics use externalized living extensively and compulsively. Such a chronic state is necessitated by the need to avoid awareness or contact with a higher degree of painful inner experience such as chronic anxiety, conflict or self-hate. To this is added their conflictual way of relating to others, namely the need to merge with and define themselves by others, at the same time that the other persons emotional reactions may constitute a threat and necessitate the erection of a distancing barrier. As a result, this type of schizophrenic develops a special kind of emotional antennae, unconsciously over-focussing upon and trying to be aware of the attitudes of others, so as to foresee and forestall their possible reactions. Thus he is constantly experiencing both a tendency to move away from his inner experiences and a need to move toward and experience others. He comes to live vicariously in and through the emotions of other persons.

On top of this chronic baseline of externalized living, the paranoid patient also extensively uses projection as an acute manoeuver. Both defensive operations, the chronic and acute, are present in each such patient. It is the intensity and combination which makes the defensive system so impervious to direct interpretation of delusionary projections.

Although defensive externalization may use both space and time for removing present painful experiences from the self, spatial distance is most often used for hallucinations and time for delusions. For example, some paranoid patients may blame childhood events or persons for present difficulties. Whether the source of a delusion or hallucination is placed far away, in the next building, next room or within the head, and whether it is someone else's or ones own voice, is an indication of the intensity of the emotional "pain" or threat from within. Somatic delusions are simply the projection of the symbolized attitudes or emotions, distorted in keeping with the defensive need, on to the body-image acting as external framework.

Such symptomatic phenomena also involve two other disturbances of thinking, concretization and symbolization, which are considered by some authors to be pathognomonic of most schizophrenics. From this holistic viewpoint, concreteness is seen not as deficitary -- due supposedly to the impairment of figure-ground discrimination or loss of the ability to symbolize -- but as an active process, and one aspect of the more general defensive measure of making-still and maintaining constancy. To explain it, I would postulate that any form of inner experience may be transformed through symbolization into other forms of experience, i. e. feelings into images, perceptions into thoughts, feelings or thoughts into sensations, and (in the psychotic) attitudes into hallucinations. The selection of a particular channel of experience at any time is determined by various factors like the need to avoid emotional pain, to decrease or increase self-awareness, to disguise, or to communicate better. Concretized, symbolized representations can then be projected outside or on to the body-image. Even where a patient may personalize abstract proverbs instead of giving concrete interpretations, he is concretizing nonetheless, using his own self as the concrete object.

These same principles explain schizophrenic illogicality or incoherence in associations. This has been explained traditionally as being due either to a defective capacity to symbolize, and therefore selection of ideas or events which have been actual past experiences; or (in the classical psychoanalytic view) to a regressive re-emergence of unconscious, id-related, disorganized thought (primary process thinking) when a supposed collapse of defenses occurs. But the variations in clinical syndromes of associative looseness casts doubt on these explanations. Most patients are found to personalize and concretize as well as symbolize; neither process excludes the other. Some are concretistic only in an immediate and limited defensive way, avoiding the loose or disordered prelogical associations which may threaten a need for order or control; others are consistently loose and illogical; others are logical with occasional disjointedness, and accept a certain looseness; and others are logical in expression but have an almost uncanny awareness of other patients' bizarre communications and of the therapist's unconscious feelings. This does not seem to be simply a failure of defenses, with a flooding of the psyche by unconscious material. It would rather seem to be another form of logic, following definable associative patterns, forms of symbolization and levels of psychic function, which only appears to be distorted.

To understand these clinical phenomena, I would first define the process of associating (and communicating them) as based on several dynamic principles. First is the process of symbolizing as noted above, and the possibility of using interchangeable channels of expression, e.g. feelings, images, ideas, past or present time, near or far distance, subject or object experience, somatizations. Secondly, any expression may be derived from different levels of psychic function, such as the reality level, the interpersonal level or the totally intrapsychic level, from conscious to unconscious. Any one expression may have one meaning or be at one level at that moment, or may be communicating several at the same time. Thirdly, any one emerging personality trait or feeling is identified with or experienced only in a larger context, is embedded in a total sphere of other traits being experienced then as comprising the background. Fourthly, the most significant use or function and relatedness of any association or communication is determined by this dynamic constellation of intrapsychic attributes emerging into experience at the moment; and whether this element is experienced as positive, acceptable and therefore expressible, or negative, painful, unwanted or threatening and therefore to be repressed.

Even during the completest free association, the non-schizophrenic patient still exerts a degree of direction on his associations at an unconscious level. Although one sequence of ideas is expressed consciously, other consistent themes or movements can usually be found at some deeper level of psychic functioning, of which the self has also a kind of awareness. The schizophrenic, however, fearful of most of his inner experiences, attempts to prevent the emergence of all unconscious content; he feels it dangerous to let go into abstractness, or to make communicative contact at any level. But even with this form of more total control, his associations are still directed by mixtures of conscious-unconscious defensively-avoided or positively-related thoughts, concepts and images. So that even though expressions may seem illogical, a connecting theme is present in which the links are related but more distantly -- perhaps three or more associations removed from each other, and derived from different levels of experience. This extremely rapid inner associating, using the various defensive manoeuvers of repression, projection, concretization, symbolization, occurs at each step in the chain of thoughts, emerging feelings and actions. In addition, such shifting may be directed against parts of thoughts or sentences, so that phrases may not be completed, objects or words placed in other contexts, and expressed emotions related to repressed ideas resulting in the incongruity of affect. Furthermore, the irrelevancy may be due to the multiplicity of meanings and experiences simultaneously attached to any one specific expression. In other words, any expression may be disguising as well as uncovering, may be an attempt to obfuscate communication as well as a positive attempt to communicate that which is otherwise uncommunicable. The need to avoid the pain of communicative contact is in conflict with the desperate need to make contact; and the patient may be trying to do both at the same time.

In conclusion, although I have selected only certain dynamic phenomena for consideration, this holistic approach can be applied to explain any of the symptoms of the schizophrenias.

In summary, this holistic view allows for and explains the influence of social and cultural factors upon the personality so as to produce psychopathological changes at the same time that it sees the schizophrenias as an ongoing distorted process of growth. Such factors include parental relations for the child, peer relations for the adolescent and environmental conditions for the adult. It takes into account the possible effects of predisposing constitutional (physical or temperamental) factors as these can modify the maturational process. It postulates a concurrent pathological process of emotional development, beginning in disturbed parent-child relationships but becoming self-perpetuating by the erection of defensive movements within the personality. The mutual interactions of these two part-processes of growth produce characteristic symptoms. It does not exclude the possible role of biological part-mechanisms in contributing to the symptomatology, since emotional reactions may be mediated by metabolic-chemical processes; but these are considered secondary. Long therapeutic experience has now shown that clinical application of these theoretical principles can bring about an amelioration of the schizophrenias through resolution of the underlying emotional conflicts and defensive movements. This consists not only of a symptomatic improvement, but a change in the direction of growth from the schizophrenic to the more normal insofar as it emphasizes the inherent potential tendency toward constructive growth and the healthy aspects of the personality of every patient.

DISCUSSION BY LOTHAR B. KALINOWSKY M. D.

There are some clinical facts that cannot be ignored and have to be incorporated into any acceptable concept of schizophrenia. There are still typical syndromes corresponding to the long known subtypes of schizophrenia. Prognostic features like acute onset of illness as a favorable sign, and insidious onset as an unfavorable sign, do exist. Furthermore, we cannot ignore the accumulated genetic evidence in this illness. A holistic view of schizophrenia is desirable, but such view cannot disregard clinical, genetic and other findings.

J. L. Rubins, M.D., 82-15 234th Street, Queens Village, N.Y. 11427

OBSESSIONAL STATE AND SCHIZOPHRENIA

LEON SALZMAN

In our quest for specific determinants and etiologic factors in mental illness there has been a tendency to by-pass clinical data except as it relates to nosology. Clinical material has been used almost exclusively as a means of identifying the disorder, for example, whether it is or is not schizophrenia. One serious obstacle in all research in schizophrenia, I believe, has been the tendency to deal with the disorder as if it were a single diagnostic entity with a specific etiology in accordance with the traditional medical model of illness. Such a view assumes a consensus of what schizophrenia is and how it comes about. Clearly, neither of these assumptions is valid.

In relation to this problem Sir Aubrey Lewis commented on this situation in 1935. He said: "The need for clarification (in speaking of obsessional illness) is first in the area of definition, or, if one likes to call it so, diagnosis". This is particularly apt when he considers the relationship of obsessionalism to schizophrenia. What ever these illnesses may be, it has been clear to many clinicians including Freud, Kraepelin, Sullivan, and many others that there is a clear relationship between them. Aubrey Lewis said that "the surprising thing is not that some obsessionals become obviously schizophrenic, but that only a few do so. It must be a very short step, one might suppose, from feeling that one must struggle against thoughts that are not one's own, to believing that those thoughts are forced upon one by an external agency".

Since I visualize mental illness not as a group of etiologically distinct and separate disorders, but rather as a variety of adaptive defenses to anxiety, my report will develop the notion that some defenses may be ineffective to cope with a particular problem and there-by require more powerful defenses.

The obsessional defense structure attempts to exert maximal control over oneself and the environment, in order to guarantee absolute security and safety. It does this by attempting to know all that is to be known (perfectionism, omniscience) in order to foresee and forestall all eventualities. In addition, it avoids the knowledge of one's deficiencies and limitations by never acknowledging error or weakness. This is done by avoiding commitments of all kinds so that the failure of an enterprise or activity need not be viewed as a personal failure. Similarly, the maintenance of a state of doubt and indecision prevents one from taking a firm stand and thus possibly being caught on the wrong side of an issue. In addition to avoiding the discovery of one's weakness, the obsessive individual exerts direct control through ritual and magic, whether it is the magic of verbal devices or of ritualistic behavior. Emphasis on the intellectual and avoidance of the emotional is a way of being that is coupled with activities which can be controlled, while the emotional life is largely outside of one's conscious control.

This is, of course, a very abbreviated picture of the extensive devices which constitute the obsessional disorder. All the obsessional's defenses are efforts to adapt to a situation in which he feels endangered and uncertain about his ability to control himself or other elements in his living. The neurotic developments give him an illusion of strength which increases his feelings of security. If these devices fail to ensure or guarantee his security, then he may develop a phobia which will produce an absolute avoidance of those situations or places where he fears he many go out of control. This again guarantees control by not permitting him to confront those areas or issues which might get him "out of control".

What happens when this defense, which ordinarily is quite successful in maintaining an illusion of control, fails? Such a development may be produced by unexpected or accidental circumstances or by major cataclysms of death, physical injury or other events beyond human control. It may force the individual to acknowledge his limitations and weaknesses. This can also happen during particularly stressful developmental areas, such as adolescence or menopause.

If lustful needs are very great, and the person's skill in making contact with the opposite sex is not adequate, the youth may experience a good deal of difficulty unless he can control such needs. Obsessional defenses are most commonly utilized to control these desires and to keep the person's anxieties to a minimum. His ability to do so will depend upon his own capacities and on the availability and quality of sex partners. Therefore we may find that in some adolescents a minor event may produce a major breakdown, while in other individuals the most traumatic events seem to be handled with considerable ease. The capacity is directly related to the experience and self-esteem which has been established prior to adolescence. The success of obsessional patterns will depend upon the extent to which they have been needed to support the security structure prior to adolescence - so that the increased strain will not cause the structure to collapse. Harry Stack Sullivan developed this point of view most effectively and demonstrated how the breakdown of obsessional defenses may result in a schizophrenic disintegration of the personality structure.

In such circumstances a number of possible outcomes are available. One fortunately uncommon development is an increase in psychomotor activity accompanied by agitated efforts to restore a feeling of security through grandiose or paranoid elaborations. This often leads to panic and schizophrenic disintegration. At such times the previously peculiar behavior which was adaptive, eccentric, but still socially acceptable becomes so excessive as to focus community attention on the individual. The behavior becomes so aberrant and confused that the requirements of social intercourse breakdown. Ordinarily it is now called a psychosis, while only a short time previously, and perhaps again later on, it is labeled simply as peculiar behavior or a neurosis.

The description above stems from the view that mental illness is a holistic phenomenon, extending from normality (so-called) at one end of the spectrum to neurosis and psychosis at the other. It sees the problem in terms of the whole individual and his relationship to himself and others rather than as a collection of symptoms. Even so, some symptomatic changes such as the increasing preoccupation with somatic problems and the exaggerated concerns about losing control of these functions often herald the threatening complications of a psychotic development. Examination of the manifest and covert symptoms of schizophrenia can reveal the relationship to the previously obsessional defenses. For example, the grandiosity of the obsessional and his quest for omniscience and omnipotence often becomes a reality in his psychosis. He assumes he has achieved his omniscient or omnipotent state and may have delusions of being Christ or Caesar. The avoidance tendencies which may have been represented by multiple phobias, his lack of commitment and involvement with others may be manifested in total withdrowal and isolation. The alienation of thought and feeling which has always been high lighted in descriptions of schizophrenia, was already in evidence in the obsessional in his emphasis on the intellectual and cognitive elements and the almost complete avoidance of the emotional issues in living. In the obsessional state this was called emotional isolation or displacement.

Similarly, the pervasive feeling of danger and insecurity is expressed in multiple delusions of a paranoid nature. The resorting to magical thinking, the ritualized behavior or compulsions and the ritualized thoughts or obsessions are manifested in the schizophrenic state as magical operations of various kinds. It is such a transition of symptoms that gives credence to the psychological etiological theories of schizophrenia and the possibility of comprehending the disorder via a psychodynamic theory.

The types of defenses used may be related to the severity of the attack and indirectly may be a reflection of the potential personality disintegration. However, this is not always so. Denial may be utilized in a largely intact personality structure or it may play a dominant role in a totally disintegrated schizophrenic or lobotomized person. Similarly, the obsessional patterns are regular accompaniments of normal, everyday, adjusted living as well as being the prominent defenses in a severely schizophrenic state. The obsessional substitutions of magic ritual are designed, as stated before, to foster illusory strength and power by partially denying the realities of existence. When reality is absolutely denied we are dealing with the psychotic process. Psychosis becomes a process then, rather than a state.

While the severity of a mental illness is often closely related to the major defensive technique employed, there is nevertheless no hierarchy of illness extending from hysteria, the least pathological, to schizophrenia, the most pathological. An hysterical illness may be completely disruptive and incapacitating, while an ambulatory schizophrenic may be functioning effectively.

Is there a particular kind of obsessional neurosis which tends to regress into schizophrenia? While there is little support for the notion that certain kinds of obsessions are more likely to precede schizophrenia, it has been noted by some that when somatic preoccupations are prominent or hypochondriasis is extreme there is a greater likelihood for schizophrenia to supervene. A shift in the patient's preoccupation with dirt or feces to his bowels and its activities can be the center around which psychotic delusions may develop. These delusions may involve the feeling of being poisoned, or of having no intestines because they were destroyed by some malevolent influence. A variety of delusions may focus around the feces. Or the obsessional's preoccupation with his heart and its functioning, and his uneasy vigilence lest the cardiac rate change, maybe the prelude to a delusion concerning the heart. The intense anxiety surrounding this matter may actually alter the cardiac action, which may presage a psychosis.

In the transition from obsessionalism to schizophrenia, many features of these two syndromes can be noted and identified and it can be seen that they seem to serve the same purposes. The obsessional distractions of obfuscation and other complicated verbal operations can be recognized in the schizophrenic in his neologisms, autistic activity, and alienation of thought and feeling. The prevailing feeling of danger, threat, and anticipated humiliation and rejection is often translated as a paranoid system when a psychosis develops.

Often the resulting psychosis appears to be an extreme extension of the previous obsessional symptoms. The individual can no longer manage, and what was previously odd but functional now appears to be "crazy" and totally unacceptable, maladaptive, and disruptive.

Under certain circumstances an extension of the obsessional patterns can lead to paranoid development which, in turn, may become delusional and be part of a schizophrenic development. The uneasy, uncertain, obsessional person who scrutinizes every individual and event for evidence of criticism, contempt, or rejection sees every contact as a possible source of danger. He is set for attack and it is no wonder he often sees it coming. Since he must always be on tap, correct and omniscient, every minor failure will be viewed with alarm and be accompained by his feelings that the community will be pleased at his failure and will humiliate him. This is an ideal setting for the development of paranoid ideas - particularly when feelings of anger and hostility are also involved. The development of paranoid feelings which include expectations of malevolence from others inevitably follows the tendency to distort events and experiences so that one is always a victim. When one expectantly scrutinizes the behavior of others for evidences of reassurance, approval, or criticism, one does not take sufficient account of the possibility that the other person may be in some distress and may be focused on his own needs. This can mistakenly be interpreted as displeasure with or disapproval of the obsessional. Such a capacity for distortion arises from the obsessional's excessive need for approval and assumption that everything that happens has relevance for him.

Grandiosity - the ultimate effect of striving for omniscience, omnipotence, and the fulfillment of superhuman ideals - is an integral part of the obsessional disorder. While the obsessional proclaims his modesty and readiness to be satisfied with small achievements, his strivings and behavior belie this position. It is clear that he can be satisfied only with superhuman achievements. This is grandiosity in action -even though there is some embarrasment and denial when the obsessional is confronted with the full implication of such demands. The grandiosity of the paranoid state, on the other hand, is unashamedly expressed and aggressively defended - even though it consists of precisely these elements present in the obsessional state. Obsessional rituals and preoccupations are often indistinguishable from psychotic ritualistic performances, and they appear to serve the same purpose. While the obsessional ritual may be explained as silly and meaningless, but necessary, the schizophrenic makes no explanation for such behavior.

In spite of these similarities there is no direct continuum of obsessional neurosis into schizophrenia or vice versa, even though the schizophrenic may have an underlying obsessional personality structure. This situation was demonstrated by a young man whose life was filled with obsessive ritualistic practices involving Yoga-like exercises and hand-washing rituals as well as word games. He was immersed in "doing good" for all, while neglecting many essentials in his life. Perioically, however, under the stress of criticism at the job or difficulties with his wife or friends, he would express delusions of being God and plan to carry out some dangerous mission to prove this. The effect was only to produce damage to his professional standing. Instead of carrying out the dangerous missions, he would either admit himself or permit himself to be admitted to a mental hospital where, after a brief period of psychotherapy, he would temporarily abandon his delusions and return to the community. While such events might suggest an obsessional moving in and out of schizophrenia, the picture is essentially that of a psychotic individual who manages to keep his psychosis in control. This person demonstrates the close relationship of the obsessional defense with the schizophrenic illness, rather than the notion that one disorder regularly moves into the other.

It is this notion of hierarchies that has produced fears that the improperly handled obsessional individual may become schizophrenic, or that the resolution of a schizophrenic disorder must go through an obsessional state before complete restitution. As I have indicated, this is true to a certain extent, and therefore offers some clues about the tendencies of certain disintegrating obsessionals to become schizophrenic. On the other hand, it is invalid to say that the obsessional disorder represents a pre-schizophrenic state. The obsessional pattern of living rarely disintegrates and becomes worse, and only with the utmost skill and intelligence can it be altered, either for better or worse. It is usually a very stable structure which is affected, only under extreme circumstances. The very nature of the defense, with its capacity for distraction, denial, emotional isolation and grandiosity, makes it unlikely that change will occur unless it can be demonstrated that such change will offer more security to the individual. This is extremely difficult, since we can demonstrate this only in a long-term sense. In addition, the obsessional's tendency toward paranoid ideation is so great that it is often an insurmountable task to get close enough or be trusted enough to be able to influence him.

L. Salzman, M.D., 1610 New Hampshire Avenue, Washington 9, D.C.

THE PROBLEM OF UNDIAGNOSED SCHIZOPHRENIAS

IN PRISONERS

HOWARD DAVIDMAN

This brief, informal paper reports the high incidence of undiagnosed and unreported schizophrenia in prisoners incarcerated in New York City prisons. It derives from work done over an eight year period as a psychiatric teacher and consultant for the professional staffs of the New York City Prisons, and from teaching done as Training Program Coordinator of the Special Curriculum in Correctional Psychiatry of Criminal and Delinquent Behavior (2). This curriculum was offered for graduate psychiatrists by the New York School of Psychiatry in cooperation with the New York City Department of Correction and was sustained by a Federal training grant. The author also served as a psychiatrist on a federally supported research study headed by Mr. Edward Preble, anthropologist and street worker, which led among its publications to our co-authored paper, "Schizophrenia Among Adolescent Street Gang Leaders".

During these years of work the author conducted several hundred demonstration psychiatric interviews and observed many others. These interviews, largely with city prisoners, but also with some out patients, were searching in nature and were used to demonstrate the emotional resources and difficulties of the patients to other professionals. After some years the impression grew and was confirmed that the incidence of schizophrenic states was far greater than generally perceived in briefer and less dynamic interviews. The high incidence was often unreported even when perceived, and repeatedly, pervasive anxiety, guilt, shame (1), confusion, thought disorder and overtly psychotic symptomatology could be elicited in patients in whom their presence had previously been unsuspected or denied (4). The suspicion arose that the prisoners being seen might not be a representative sample of the prison population; our informal clinical check suggested that this was not the case. A formal as yet unpublished research study was undertaken by Dr. Emmasue Snow (10), while she was one of the graduate psychiatrists studying in The New York School of Psychiatry's Special Curriculum. She performed thorough diagnostic interviews on all prisoners arriving on six different but not consecutive week days at the Womans House of Detention. Forty five of the 105 women interviewed, roughly 43 %, were found to be overtly psychotic - "based upon definitive symptoms of disturbed, inappropriate affect, disorders of production and progression of thought, referential and delusional content of thought, and gross perceptual disorders such as hallucinations". Twenty of the women had an elicitable history of previous hospitalizations for psychosis. She excluded questionable or borderline cases among the remainder of the women studied. Our clinical impression among the male prisoners in the city prisons is that the incidence of symptomatic and gross schizophrenias, and cases with histories of prior hospitalization for psychosis is almost as high as that reported among the women. If one includes cases in which there is an outbreak of schizophrenic decompensation while imprisoned, and included the inmates who demonstrate submanifest schizophrenias or meet the criteria described by Rado as evidence of "schizotypal organization" (3, 8, 9), and cases whose underlying schizophrenia has been controlled by the drug addicted way of life, then the impression is that this would comprise a good majority of the prisoners.

This prison population consists largely of minor criminal offenders, those guilty of misdemeanors, those who have pled guilty to lesser offenses and those in detention. They come over-whelmingly from minority groups, from economically, socially and educationally deprived backgrounds, many from severely disordered families. They have a high incidence of drug use and the complications of the drug addicted way of life in urban slums. There are few white collar or successful criminals among them; this is a population of lesser offenders who are repeatedly arrested. At present there are about 12, 200 people in New York City prisons; in a year the New York City prison system houses about 65, 000 persons for varying periods of time.

This report only deals at first hand with New York City prisoners, but it is believed as a result of informal discussions that similar results could be deomonstrated in many other "big city" prison populations and prison systems in the United States.

The high incidence here reported is unusual; official statistical reports and psychiatric papers customarily provide figures varying from 1/2 to 10 % of prisoners who show evidence of psychosis. No gross social change in recent years is likely to have caused a recent increase in the frequency. There are, however, many references in the literature to underlying or concealed schizophrenias in populations of detected offenders without reference to frequency (5, 7). There are many reasons for the lower incidence usually reported in the literature.

Many professionals are unwilling to make the diagnosis of schizophrenia even when aware that the prisoner is grossly psychotic. There are administrative, institutional, dispositional and court room consequences they may prefer to avoid. Confidentiality of written reports is poor, details leak into the inmate populations as well as among correctional staffs, and occasionally prisoners have been abused as a result. Knowledge of the prison society is needed to be fully appreciative of its influence on official diagnoses.

Professional careers in prison systems are ill-paid and carry low professional prestige; more than the usual proportion of ill-trained and maladjusted professionals are attracted to the jobs as a result. The education of professionals in this area is often poor; people who are criminals, drug users, violent persons who are educational dropouts, inarticulate, hostile, sexually aberrant, irresponsible, often minority group members, are commonly rejected for study and therapy in training programs. The huge majority of the prison population can be described in the above terms. Senior and respected teachers have been known to make definitive but erroneous pronouncements about "psychopaths", despite, as one of them once told me, having "never examined one in the last thirty years - and then it was in another country". Poor training and personal difficulty often leave middle class prejudices unchallanged, with resultant inadequate psychodiagnostic performance in the prison setting.

Overt psychoses frequently, then, are officially diagnosed as "Transient Situational Personality Disturbance" and Sociopathic Personality Disturbance", and similar conditions (6) despite the often obvious irrelevance of these labels to the patients' real condition.

The socio-medical implications of this high incidence of severe mental illness in persons whose care, custody, and discharge are primarily under legal authority are disturbing.

These findings add emphasis to the continuing concern over the clash of priorities in the social care of criminal offenders. At present they are adjudged as primarily mentally normal, legally responsible and subject to punishment for their wilful misdeeds; these latter being determined by interpretations of law in a court of law. Our prison systems are organized as institutions for punishment and segregation in the interest of public safety. Only secondarily do prison systems attempt to provide rehabilitative and psychotherapeutic programs. Institutional programs, precedures and decisions in prison institutions are finally subject to legal authority and decision. Decisions and planning along therapeutic lines are not in the hands of medical leadership. While our public mental hospitals are far from ideal, they are run by professional personnel for the care and treatment of patients. Mental health care in prisons is inferior to that provided for the non-criminal patient. Prison hospital ward care is inferior to general ward care, units for the isolation of the most disturbed prisoners provide grossly inadequate, at times, scandalous, care for the severely mentally ill.

At the same time, our public hospitals have special difficulty in dealing with this group of offenders. Custodial staffs in prisons do provide simple effective routines of life in a drug free environment to a far greater degree than our hospitals do. Specialized institutions, under medical direction, are needed for this population, which would combine the best of the custodial procedures present in better prisons with more effective psychotherapeutic programs and direction. It is true that at present psychoterapeutic effectiveness with prisoners is poor in most settings - I believe this is not really due to any lack of knowledge - but rather to the gross inability of our society to apply what we know to the actual care of lower economic classes of patients and prisoners. Our society is changing however; at the present writing there is some hope for a reduction in war budgets and greater investment in the care of our own people.

A recent United States Supreme Court Decision (11) concerning alcoholism decided that while it is not "cruel and unusual punishment" and therefore not unconstitutional to incarcerate alcoholics for public drunkenness if they have a home to be drunk in, that it may well be unconstitutional -"cruel and unusual punishment" to criminally charge and incarcerate a homeless alcoholic for public drunkenness. The justices, while recognizing that alcoholism is either a symptom or a disease, noted that at present there are no adequate treatment procedures, staffs and institutions to care properly for any large new group of people suffering from alcoholism. Obviously, alcohol is also a drug addicton albeit artificially segregated under law from the problem of addictions to other drugs. Scientifically speaking, all drug addictions are symptoms and not diseases in themselves; although an addiction once established involves definable distinctive consequences determined by the nature of the drug and the nature of social attitudes and procedures in the addict's social environment. The Supreme Court decision possibly presages an increasing social demand for proper medical treatment rather than punishment for offenders who are mentally ill.

It behooves the psychiatric profession and the community at large to be concerned with the improvement of the care of the mentally ill in our community; and accurate diagnosis is essential to explicit and public socio-therapeutic planning to help with actual problems in the lives of this so called "criminal minority".

REFERENCES

(1). Bilmes, M.: Shame and delinquency. J. of Contemporary Psychoanalysis. 3, No. 2, 113-133 (1967).

(2). Davidman, H.: Psychiatrie Correctionelle de Comportement Criminel et Delinquant: Developpement d'um cours special pour psychiatres Diplomes. Med. et Hyg. 23, 680 (1965).

(3). Davidman, H.: The contributions of Sandor Rado to psychodynamic science. Science and Psychoanalysis. 7 Grune and Stratton, New York. 1964.

(4). Davidman, H. and Preble, E.: Schizophrenia among adolescent street gang leaders. Psychopathology of Schizophrenia. Paul H. Hoch and Joseph Zubin. 372-383. Grune and Stratton, New York. 1966. Reprinted in Approaches to Deviance; Theories, Concepts, and Research Findings. Ed. by Mark Lefton, James K. Skipper Jr. and Charles H. McGaghy, 189-199. Meredith Corporation. 1968

(5). Dunaif, S. L. and Hoch, P. H.: Pseudopsychopathic schizophrenia in psychiatry and the law, 169-195. Ed. by Hoch, Paul H. and Zubin, Joseph. Grune and Stratton. New York. 1955.

(6). Hoch, P. H. and Polatin, P.: Pseudoneurotic forms of schizophrenia. Psychiat. Quart. 23, 248 (1949).

(7). Loftus, T. A.: Meaning and Methods of Diagnosis in Clinical Psychiatry. 29 - 30. Lea and Febiger;Phila. 1960.

(8). Rado, S.: Dynamics and classification of disordered behavior. Psychoanalysis of behavior: collected papers. 268-285. Grune and Stratton, New York. 1956.

(9). Rado, S.: Schizotypal organization - Preliminary report on a clinical study of schizophrenia. Psychoanalysis of behavior: collected papers. 1-10. Grune and Stratton. New York. 1962.

(10). Snow, E.: Incidence of psychosis among arrested women at the time of arrival at the House of Detention for Women, New York City. (unpublished).

(11). Supreme Court Reporter.: Powell vs State of Texas No. 405 88 S. Ct. 2145 pp. 2145-2173 (1968).

H. Davidman, M.D., The New York School of Psychiatry, Ward's Island, N.Y. 10035

A HYPOTHESIS OF GENERAL AND SPECIAL FACTORS IN THE MULTITHEMIC ETIOLOGY OF SCHIZOPHRENIC BEHAVIOR AND THEIR RELATION TO THE COURSE AND PROGNOSIS OF THE DISEASE

D.V. SIVA SANKAR

Behavior (both in humans and animals) has been of great interest and importance to human societies since the evolution of man. Emotion, anxiety, vegetative needs, and their proper control and gratification have been choice subjects of many philosphers and even prophets. Patterning of behavior is controlled by biological assets and sociological and environmental observations and learning. Abnormal behavior is but only one indication of the inner inequilibrium in the psychobiologic domain of the living organism. Along with the manifestiation of abnormal behavior, molecular biological deficiencies will aslo be exhibited. The problem then revolves around the question: "Is the biological lesion associated with this abnormal behavior, the same one in all abnormal individuals and/or is it the same one in a given individual at all times"? A more important point about the elucidation of the molecular biological defect is that it should be studied in a dynamic operant state of the subject and not when the subject is in a static state of apparent psychobiological idling. This is comparable to the concept which holds that testing of a jet-plane in actual flight is much more important than turning its motors on while it is in the hangar.

The next important question is, "While the descriptive details of metabolism may vary in a given individual exhibiting abnormal behavior, can there be a single, monoetiological, monogenic molecular lesion in the CONTROL and REGULATION of metabolism"? Equally important is the concept that with breakdown of behavior there is a breakdown of patterning of metabolism. There is simply what may amount to waywardness and/or chaos in metabolism, and in its regulation. The biochemical, pharmacological, electrophysiologic patterns, so important in the normal cell, are disorganized to different extents and levels. Along with these there is a breakdown of concept of space and time, self and environment, appropriateness of required behavior patterns, immunological behavior, circadian rhythms, conception, perception, replication and of flight or fight systems.

An important question is "What constitutes abnormal behavior and how do we define its severity"? The war syndrome in our master civilizations, the amok syndrome in Papua and New Guinea, the breast feeding of a guest by the host's wife in some aboriginal societies, are all examples of accepted behavior in different societies.

Normalcy of behavior has been defined by Karl Menninger as: "adjustment of human beings to the world and to each other with a maximum of effectiveness and happiness. Not just efficiency, or just contentment, nor the grace of obeying the rules of the game cheerfully. It is all of these together. It is the ability to maintain an even temper, an alert intelligence, socially considerate behavior and a happy disposition".

Abnormality of behavior may be manifested in recognition, perception, interpretation, analog formation, contemplation, intellectual function, conceptualization and interrelations of space and time, self and environment, feelings of ability, insecurity, anxiety, guilt, anger, jealousy, love, impulse, hate, kindness, lust, needs, satisfaction, contentment, goal-directed functioning, avoidance behavior, ability to participate and share in the group activities, communication and equally important in the pursuit of "pleasure". Breakdown of behavior may signal the over-flow of the psychobiological elements beyond the limits of biological control. Testing for breakdown and/or deficiences in any few of the above areas yields information that can be, often correctly, extrapolated to the psychiatric state of the living organism, because the processes of life amalgamate, unify and regulate the psychobiology of self. A formalized definition of schizophrenia may not serve as much our present purpose as a definition of schizophrenic behavior outlined above.

A distinction can, perhaps, be made of two kinds of breakdown: (a) Intellectual functions (b) Vasovegetative function. A noted psychiatrist, whom I respect greatly, has once stated that in certain cases, schizophrenia may help towards the further evolutionary progress of man. This apparently untenable statement has value in it if one "digs" into some of the abnormalities in intellectual functioning. But, it is the lack of control of impulse, mood and emotions mediated through the psychopathology of anxietey, that characterizes schizophrenic behavior as a pathological syndrome and makes it an undesirable human trait. Schizophrenia may thus be a set of behavioral syndromes either accompanied with or resulting from metabolic waywardness, or several types of biochemical anormalities.

The psychobiology of anxiety in many ways is the progenitor of schizophrenic behavior. Behavior can be apparently classified into patterns while the etiology of generation and the channeling and control of anxiety may depend on several molecular biological events and accidents, and on the anxiety-generating quality of the environment and community.

Several great men have upheld the freedoms of man and several have deplored what man has done to man. It is now hightime that man should enjoy another freedom that should be at least partly safeguarded by the society. This is the freedom from Anxiety. The modern community is moving at a fast rate towards denying this to its most important possession, Man. Some of the stresses that modern society imposes on the growing and grown-up man maybe listed here:

1) The problems of competition and survival in fast motion on our long and narrow battlefields of breadwinners clad in iron, plastic, and gasoline.

2) The problem of heterogeniety of communities (mess pots instead of melting pots).

3) The disappearance of overt biological illness leaving a vacuum to be occupied by psychobiological illness.

4) The lack of feelings of adequacy and security in our "liquor, smoke and looks, beards and breasts, behavior and breath", and in our lives ,as highlighted, popularized, broadcast, pinpointed and reinforced by our television and other mass communication media. (How would a child react to a reassuring statement from a strong wonderful person that "life is full of --- headaches", or "before you reach the end of the rope, reach for ---").

5) The championing and provision for the material success of the capable, competetive and greedy by the free enterprise system.

6) The undue emphasis on success rather than on goodness by our modern cultures.

7) The lack of philosophy in our education, the lack of of civilization in our technology, the lack of holiness in our religion, the lack of "unselfish devotion" in our politics, the lack of humanism in our interpersonal relations, the lack of emotional depth in our neighborliness.

8) The common assembly in public places, intended for psybiological entertainment, of distrusting strangers, (men are biologically gregarious).

9) The modern failure of the classical concepts that held so-

cieties and families together.

10) The emphasis on commercialism and legalism etc.

11) The "mythless myth" of our belief in the "arrogant ration-ality" of a conspiracy of computerized technology in human existence. (I owe the underlined words, put out of context by me, to Rollo May and Michel Crozier, respectively). In our present era, we have a huge wealth of knowledge and technology, but insufficient philosophy.

Our culture threatens man's right to freedom from anxiety. The time is ripe now for our society to make some changes so that the guilt engendered by abnormal behavior, feelings, and abilities may be lessened and thus produce less anxiety.

Let us look at a few aspects of the possibility of quantifying the relations between anxiety and reaction (stimulus response). Let us define "Anxiety Quotient" as dA/dS where dA is the change in anxiety content in response to a change in stimulus dS. Similarly, the Response Quotient (RQ) dR/dS is the differential of Response with respect to stimulus S. dA/dS is a function of dR/dS. However, if we divide dA/dS by dR/dS, we obtain a new differential dA/dR. Let us examine what these terms, not unfamiliar to many of us, signify: (a) dA/dS indicates the susceptibility of the individual to generate anxiety within himself. High dA/dS may signify high vulnerability to psychobiological deviation unless compensated otherwise. This compensation is part of the differential dR/dS. (b) dR/dS, the Response Quotient, indicates the intensity of response. Since the total response R is a sum of different responses, R may be pictured as $R_1 + R_2 + R_3 \ldots$ up to the nth term. High dR/dS may be accompanied by high dA/dS. If we define compensation as C, the terms dC/dR and dC/dA also enters the picture. R and C are not mutually exclusive. (c) There is a normal range for dA/dS, dA/dR, dR/dA, dC/dR and dC/dA. Some apparent translations and conclusions are possible :

  i) High dR/dS indicates hyperactivity and vice versa.

  ii) High dA/dS indicates instability of personality structure and of metabolic regulation, possibly mediated through the biogenic amines.

  iii) High dR/dA with low dC/dA may indicate a maniac tendency.

  iv) Low dR/dA with low dC/dA may end in depression and/or autism.

  v) (dR/dS), (dA/dS), (dC/dS) are all dependent variables, controlled by psychobiological mechanisms, and also vary with sex, age, race, genetics, social and family culture etc.

vi) An abnormality in these variables may lead to neurosis and/or psychosis, depending on the depth of the lesion.

vii) An abnormality in these variables may be either:

    a. a direct result of a transient psychobiological lesion

    b. an indirect result of same.

    c. a direct result of a permanent biological lesion (or leseions) (an example here may be malignant carcinoma with alterations in the metabolism of serotonin).

THE EFFECTS OF STRESS

Stress may be defined in the classical sense as any agent that may attempt to, or may actually alter the state of equilibrium of a system, in this case the psychobiology of man. The intensity and direction of stress are subject to extreme variations. The target systems are also variable. Further, in a psychobiological system, the stress may be actual or imaginary, and may originate in the environment or endogenously from the system itself. Stress may be exogenously exerted as is exemplified by shock, surgery, sun stroke or infection (biological stress) or examinations, job security (psychosocial stress) etc. The endogenous stress is illustrated by birth process, puberty, pregnancy, climacteric etc. Further, the mode of reaction to stress may be partly learned from the environment. Drs. Smoyak and Peplau will perhaps discuss more of this under the concept of "pattern perpetuation". The effect of the stress is the strain on the system itself. The strain has the characteristics as mentioned earlier, of dA/dR, dC/dA, dC/dR etc.

The characteristic effects of stress may be subdivided into four broad, main groups:

I) The exertion of dS, dA, dR, and dC are altered appropriately and there are no special marks of strain left on the system even at the time of stress. In other words, the system has adequately weathered and emerged successfully through the stress. Depending on the nature of dA/dS, dR/dS and dC/dA . . even large scale changes in dS may be nullified. This system is in the "normal" state of psychobiologic health.

II) The system may develop acute and/or chronic psychophysiologic aberrations. The aberrations, which are part of dC and dR, may include the aberrant effects of biogenic amines and may be manifested as (a) ulcers of the GI tract (b) cardiac dys-function (c) immunological intolerances (d) defects of smooth muscle systems

(e) abberrations of lipid and glucose metabolism (f) neurotic compensations etc. Some of these effects may not affect the classical geno-type but will affect the biological milieu in which gene replication will take place and may thus have extraordinary congenital effects on the phenotype of the progeny. There is a predisposition to this kind of reaction to stress. The subject benefits highly from therapy, including psychotherapy, which is so often being covertly adminis-tered nowadays by GPs and internists.

III) The system may, under the effect of stress, undergo a psychotic breakdown. This breakdown is accompanied with biologi-cal lesions and is also facilitated through congenital predisposition. However, while the biological lesion is there, it may be different in different persons. The only similarity is that there is a lesion. How it is manifested and the severity of pathology may vary. The involvement of biogenic amines and of other regulators of muscle and metabolism is most probably intimately associated with the breakdown.

There are no overt genetic malformations in these subjects. There may be abnormal plasticity in embryonic maturation. The acute breakdown in these cases may also be modified by age, sex of subject and nature and duration of stress. However, in view of congenital lack of overt malformations the subject is amenable to therapy, including psychotherapy. The prognosis is good. More de-mographic studies are needed on the occurrence of nonpsychiatric illnesses including psychosomatic illnesses like ulcers of the stomach and CVA in this group, as well as in the next group.

IV) The effect of stress is most marked in this group, because there is a basic biological congenital lesion of either generalized adevelopment or of specialized defects like aminoacidemias, or ch-romosomal aberrations. The subject is comparable in many respects to a house that is ill-built in the foundation, the plumbing, electrical wiring, in the very brick and woodwork etc. This group, as a result, abounds in bio-pathology, and may display the disease from a very young age. There is a multiplicity of histories of hospitalization and even mental retardation in the relatives. However, besides this gene-tic history, some of these subjects may have suffered damage in utero, compounded at times by the effects of their genetically schi-zophrenic lineage.

The addage, "once a schizophrenic, always a schizophre-nic" is poignantly supported by observations on this group. The prog-nosis is not encouraging. Reinforcement of the autonomic system, as has been practiced by Bender, is one of the better modes of therapy. Psychotherapy is of little or no value, the etiology being a congenital biological adevelopment. Perhaps a third to a fourth of the total population of schizophrenics belong to this group. In other words, the occurrence of this form of schizophrenia may be expected to be approximately one in four to five hundred in the general population. This figure may be compared to other congenital malformations in the general population.

The first three reactions to stress may be looked upon as generalized factors, which may be found in most individuals in the population, lead to an average psychotic breakdown calculated to be about seven in a thousand. The fourth and last category has special biological lesions and may be compared to chromosomal (Turner's Syndrome etc.) and genetic (PKU etc.) aberrations in mental retardation. The distinction between the second and third groups, on one hand and the fourth, on the other hand, may be one of inadequacy vs incompleteness of the systems that maintain a balance between dA, dR, and dC.

In the foregoing discussion, four main groups have been characterized through their reaction to what may be stressful to the individual. There are a few other factors which may complicate the picture and the final out-come. These are described below:

(a) Culture - Modern culture, as highlighted by that of midtown Manhattan (and the bug is spreading far and deep in the world), is highly non-gregarious. The demands and aspirations, from within and without, are no match to the exogenous and endogenous psychobiological potential. This culture has to be modified to accept with grace and humanism the inadequacies and individualities of psychobiological outcasts. There is reason why man should be good, there is no reason why man must be great, powerful or even successful. Man must live to be happy, but not necessarily to achieve. Man must learn to decrease his needs, but not necessarily to increase his productions both technologically and psychobiologically.

(b) Race - Race, as a group of individuals, has no meaning in psychobiology, except as an expression of their cultures and in some instances biology. If defined this way, the white American is of a different race from the European to-day. The differences in culture are far more important in their "schizophrenogenicity" than the differences in race.

(c) Age - The age of the organism undergoing the stress is important because stress placed on an untempered (unlearned) system is apt to induce broad changes. Again the first incidence of breakdown may occur early or late depending on the severity of the pathology of inadequacy or incompleteness. The similarity and comparableness of childhood and adult schizophrenia is implied in this definition. Further, the biological inadequacy or incompleteness may be less widespread but more severe in the childhood form, if we eliminate the psychopathic behavioral deviations, which are so commonly found in urban civilizations.

(d) Sex - The male is always more vulnerable, both because of biology and cultural behavior patterning. This is well illustrated in the number of boy babies that die and in the occurrence of psychophysiologic illnesses. Thus, there will be a proportionally larger number of schizophrenic males at a younger age. However, this disproportion will not be so manifest at adult and older ages. Two equalizing factors are the undue stress on wives in American suburbia and the biological sequale to pregnancy and menopause. More adult men may belong to the Group II while more adult women may belong to Groups I and III.

(e) Globality of the Disease - While one of the key factors in schizophrenia may be the breakdown of the systems that regulate metabolism (biogenic amines, hormones etc.), the disease itself is global. This can be partly explained through the global nature of the role of biogenic amines, which are involved in carbohydrate metabolism, smooth muscle function, blood pressure, respiration, cardiac function, electrophysiology, pregnancy, immunological reactions, mood, body temperature, headaches, etc. The globality of the diseases manifested in Groups II and III are most possibly mediated through aberrant metabolism of biogenic amines and/or their regulators. The disease in the fourth group, however, is much broader and the result is due to a multiplicity of biological adevelopments, independent of the psychosociology of the environment. The globality in Group IV is due to incomplete structure but not limited primarily to inadequate biodynamics.

(f) Genetics- This is a global word, since almost everything about us, is genetically related. The concepts of biochemical genetics hold what is known as a "one gene--one peptide" hypothesis. It is perhaps the overutilization and high expectations from devoted molecular biologists (who may have no laboratories in the midst of psychiatric wards) of this hypothesis that placed in the wrong light the multiple etiology of schizophrenic behavior. Concordant monozygotic to dizygotic ratios have been reported in genetic studies on tuberculosis and poliomyelitis. Genetic factors play a role in resistance

to disease and perhaps in resistance to "stress" also. The predis-
postion to biodynamic equilibrium (Groups I) or its lack (Groups
II and III) or to overt biological defect (Groups IV) including in utero
accident, are all affected by genetic make up. The reverse, namely
an event that is affected by genetics may be governed by one gene,
is perhaps untenable in schizophrenia.

(g) Hospitalization- Hospitalization may have several important effects on the course and outcome of the disease. The factors
involved are:

    (a) The age at hospitalization

    (b) Duration of hospitalization

    (c) Nature of the hospital

    (d) Number of multiple hospitalizations

An early age of hospitalization may indicate a decreased ability to
successfully nullify the effects of stress. This perhaps indicates
a greater deficiency in the biological milieu. Long periods of hospitalization are usually required in cases which are less amenable
to therapy and/or return to the community. The nature of the hospital is very important as the involvement and the life processes of
the schizophrenic can be modified to a large extent by the economi-
cal aspects of the hospital. Thus, the highly skilled private hospital
may differ from a public hospital. Multiple hospitalizations are indicative of a greater inability to nullify the stress of life and may
again indicate deeper biological defects. The experience in the hospital ward, the inter-personal relationships with the other patients,
the cross currents of contagious elements and the emotional, social
and biological aspects of the hospital are all important factors which
may modify the outcome of the disease.

(h) Biochemical typing - (I owe this expression to Dr. C. C.
Pfeiffer)- It is becoming increasingly apparent that several biochemical aberrations reported in some patients could not be found in other
patients. Does this mean that the biochemical expression of the disease varies waywardly from individual to individual or even in the
same individual at different periods of his life time? Are there different schizophrenias that belong to different types of biochemical
abnormalities? - for example - pellagra psychosis, psychoses accompanied with abnormalities of uric acid metabolism, electron transport mechanisms etc. Instead of seeking one biochemical lesion in
schizophrenia, should we seek a psychiatric abnormality in a given
biochemical type of lesion?

(i) Miscellaneous factors - One that comes to mind readily

is the stress of cyclic variations, which put a stress on our equilibrium of circadian rhythms. These cyclic variations may include such apparently unrelated factors like cyclic variations in standard and daylight savings times, stock market variations, blue Mondays etc., or may be more closely related to events like weather or change of seasons. An exogenous or endogenous change causes a crisis of stress which may magnify or precipitate endogenous biological inadequacy or incompleteness. A more stable society and world will protect, conciliate and immunize the individual against schizophrenic behavior.

In summary, a classification of humans into four groups depending on their reaction to stress is possible. The ability to handle stress depends upon generalized biodynamic capacities and/or specialized aberrant biological adevelopment processes. The generalized factors are common to all humans who are endowed with them to different extents. Inequilibrium in these generalized biodynamic abilities by stress may result in neurotic and/or psychotic breakdown. This kind of breakdown is amenable to treatment, the milder forms being amneable to psychotherapy. The special biologic aberrations are congenital. Effects of stress in these cases precipitates an earlier disintegration of the biodynamic completeness. The organism can hardly make adequate responses in view of its incompleteness. Therapy is not promising, one of the best therapies being comparble, superficially, to kicking the television set into temporary operation. History of multiple hospitalizations is found abundant in the subjects of this group and in their relatives.

Further, the biological etiologies, including the fundamental biological crisis, can vary even in individuals exhibiting comparable modes of schizophrenic behavior. The main distinction from the biological view-point is inadequacy vs incompleteness. Future research in the biology of schizophrenia may find it more beneficial to study the system in a biodynamic operant condition but not in a state of "idling".

D. V. Siva Sankar, Ph.D., Creedmoor State Hospital, Queens Village, N.Y. 11427

HISTORICAL AND SOCIOCULTURAL FACTORS RELATED TO THE PHENOMENOLOGY OF SCHIZOPHRENIA

JOHN E. OVERALL

In research where the focus is on understanding the nature of schizophrenia, little can be learned from acceptance of current diagnostic practices to define the entity. In addition to familiar problems regarding unreliability and lack of uniform operational definition, the use of clinical diagnosis poses special problems for research concerned with the relevance of background variables. The diagnostician takes into consideration historical, etiological and sociocultural factors in reaching a diagnostic decision. It is not surprising, in view of diagnostic practice, that patients in different categories tend to have different background characteristics. In spite of these problems, much of the research concerned with background factors in schizophrenia has depended upon clinical diagnosis as a criterion.

Primary difficulties can be avoided by adopting a more restricted phenomenological definition of schizophrenia. The "schizophrenia" about which I will talk today is defined solely in phenomenological terms. The research that I am going to discuss has been concerned with the phenomenology of schizophrenia and its relationship to background characteristics.

> Schizophrenia is a functional psychotic disorder
> distinguished from other functional psychotic
> disorders by prominence of thinking disturbance
> in the relative absence of pervasive disturbance
> in mood.

Three types of empirical evidence have led to adoption of this phenomenological definition of schizophrenia. They include investigations of clinical diagnostic stereotypes (1, 2, 3), investigations of phenomenological differences among groups of clinically

1. This work was supported in part by grants DHEW 1 RO 1 MH 14675 (01) and MYP 5144.

diagnosed patients (4, 5), and results from factor analyses which have, disregarding clinical diagnoses, consistently revealed a distinct thinking disorder syndrome that corresponds closely to the clinical conception of schizophrenia (6). The phenomenological approach permits us to define schizophrenia in quantitative, rating-scale terms and then to employ empirical methods to investigate dependence of the phenomenology of schizophrenia on historical, social and cultural background variables.

A consistent methodological approach has been employed in studying relationships between phenomenology and background variables in sample from several patient populations. In view of the limited time available, I will discuss only one study to provide representative results and to illustrate the general approach that has been taken. A sample of 372 newly admitted male patients with clinical diagnoses of schizophrenia or depression was obtained from a series of drug evaluation projects conducted under direction of Dr. Leo E. Hollister in Six Veterans Administration hospitals.[2] (It will be noted that clinical diagnosis was employed for preliminary screening, but was not relied upon as a criterion in the study of relevance of background variables.) The psychopathology manifested by each patient was rated by two professional observers who recorded observations on the Brief Psychiatric Rating Scale (BPRS) (7). A standard coded history form was also completed for each patient.

A "schizophrenia index" was computed for each patient from the BPRS ratings. In this particular heterogeneous patient sample, the schizophrenia index represented a contrast between symptoms of thinking disturbance and anxious depression. Each of the six symptoms included in the contrast was rated on a 7-point scale of

2. Clinical investigators responsible for the studies in the six hospitals were Drs. Isham Kimbell, Jr. (Houston), Veronica Pennington (Jackson, Miss.), John Prusmack (Menlo Park), Merlin Johnson (Seattle), Jack Shelton (Palo Alto), George Katz (Denver).

severity and the S-D contrast function was computed as follows. [3]

$$S-D = \text{Conceptual Disorg} + \text{Hallucinatory} + \text{Unusual}$$

$$\text{Thought Content} - \text{Anxiety} - \text{Guilt}$$

$$- \text{Depress Mood}$$

Two different statistical models were employed to examine differences in the S-D index related to differences in background characteristics. First, simple analysis of variance was used to test the relevance of each background variable disregarding all others. Next, a complex least squares analysis of variance was employed to test the significance of the independent contribution of each background variable over and above others included in the analysis.

The results from analyses of differences in the level of S-D index for each background variable separately are presented in Table 1. Positive or higher scores on the S-D index represent an imbalance in the symptom profile pattern in the direction of schizophrenia, while negative or lower scores represent an imbalance in the direction of depression. It has been stressed that we are concerned here with a simple contrast between clinical symptom ratings and not with clinical diagnoses.

A glance at the results presented in Table 1 will confirm that most of the variables, which were selected initially because of hypothesized relevance, did in fact relate significantly to the level of the S-D index. A relatively high schizophrenia component was apparent in young patients and patients in the single marital status group. Psychiatric history including early onset, previous hospitalization and absence of recognized precipitating factors was associated with a positive schizophrenia index.

---

3. A discriminant function analysis was run on these data to verify the adequacy of the contrast function against the criterion of clinical diagnosis. Utilizing four higher order factor scores as discriminant variables, a chi-square of 1302.4 with 4 df was obtained to indicate less than 10 per cent overlap. The contrast between factors of thinking disturbance and anxious depression carried essentially all of the weight.

Table 1

Summary of Separate Analysis for Each Background Variable

Age	Mean	MS		d f	F
18–25	9.7	Between	3662.9	2	18.2
26–45	-0.2	Within	201.0	366	
46+	-6.7				

Age of Onset	Mean	MS		d f	F
0–45	2.4	Between	7512.4	1	37.8
46+	-7.4	Within	198.6	361	

Duration Episode	Mean	MS		d f	F
< 1 yr.	-0.8	Between	49.6	2	0.2
1-2 yrs.	-2.4	Within	213.9	352	
2 +	-1.9				

Previous Hosp	Mean	MS		d f	F
No	-5.8	Between	2443.3	1	11.4
Yes	0.5	Within	213.9	361	

Education	Mean	MS		d f	F
0–12	-0.1	Between	461.4	1	2.1
12 +	-2.7	Within	222.3	359	

Marital Status	Mean	MS		d f	F
Single	8.4	Between	6015.6	2	31.9
Married	-5.1	Within	188.7	366	
Other	-3.4				

Course of Illness	Mean	MS		d f	F
Chronic	-1.0	Between	238.3	2	1.1
First Acute	-3.5	Within	212.9	352	
Recur Episodic	-0.4				

Precipitating Event	Mean	MS		d f	F
No	2.0	Between	4973.3	1	24.3
Yes	-6.1	Within	204.6	322	

Alcohol Prob.	Mean	MS		d f	F
No	-0.1	Between	673.2	1	3.1
Yes	-3.4	Within	217.3	353	

Religious Att	Mean	MS		d f	F
Negative	-0.5	Between	1203.5	2	5.5
Moderate	-2.2	Within	217.5	340	
Zealous	6.9				

Race	Mean	MS		d f	F
White	-2.7	Between	4401.2	1	22.2
Negro	9.2	Within	198.5	341	

Work Level	Mean	MS		d f	F
Unskilled	4.2	Between	6062.3	1	30.2
Skilled and Other	-4.8	Within	200.5	358	

Significant elevation in the S-D index was associated with low work achievement. The observed S-D index was higher for the low education group, although this difference was not statistically significant. (Patients whose psychopathology interferred with early educational achievement were likely to have been eliminated from the VA population through screening for military service.) Finally, negro patients evidenced markedly higher average S-D index than did white patients in the sample.

Brief consideration should perhaps be given variables which did not appear to relate significantly to the prominence of schizophrenic symptom profile characteristics. Although duration of current episode might be expected to be greater for patients with schizophrenic profile patterns, this effect was possibly mitigated by selection of only new hospital admissions for inclusion in the sample. Higher levels of depression (negative S-D index) were observed among patients classified as having alcohol problems, but this relationship failed to reach statistical significance. Previous studies had led us to hypothesize greater proneness toward depressive pattern among patients with alcohol problems and thus a reduced proneness toward schizophrenic pattern. Had a one-tailed test been employed to test this directional hypothesis, the results would have been judged to be statistically significant in this study.

The negative result of perhaps greatest importance has to do with previous course of illness. Recurrent episodic course of illness is likely to be thought of in connection with cyclic depressive disorders. The fact that schizophrenic-type illness is equally likely to be characterized by episodic course is verified by the present results, as well as in other sets of data that we have examined. Recurrent episodic schizophrenia is a fact and appears to represent an illness with distinct therapeutic indications.

A final complex least squares analysis of variance was undertaken to test the significance of the independent contribution of each background variable over and above others included in the analysis. This type of analysis is especially important with regard to psychiatrically complex variables such as racial differences. Most of the previous research concerned with racial differences in psychopathology has been rationalized in terms of differences in social class. The complex least squares analysis can be used to partial out or to correct for social class differences in evaluation of race effects. Similarly, age and marital status tend to be confounded so that a complex analysis is required to determine whether each represents an independent source of variance.

Results from the least squares analysis of variance are summarized in Table 2. Age, previous hospitalization, marital status, religious zeal, race and work level each appeared to contribute independently to variation in the schizophrenia index. As judged from the magnitudes of variance accounted for, marital status and race appeared to be the most potent independent factors. Age of onset, which was highly significant when considered separately, did not provide significant information over and above that carried by other variables and was not significant in the complex analysis.

In summary, the investigation which has been discussed revealed significant empirical relationships between patterns of clinical symptoms and a variety of historical and sociocultural characteristics. Having established that such relationship exist, independently of current clinical diagnostic concepts and practices, it seems appropriate that such information should be taken into consideration for purposes of diagnostic classification. Schizophrenia is a functional psychotic disorder distinguished from other functional psychotic disorders by prominence of thinking disturbance in the relative absence of pervasive disturbances in mood, by early onset in individuals having histories of reduced social interaction and low achievement. The course may be either chronic or episodic, and repeated hospitalizations are common. Race may be a relevant factor, since the clinical syndrome is proportionately more frequent among negro psychiatric patients than it is among white psychiatric patients.

Table 2

Complex Least Squares Analysis of Variance Testing
Independent Contribution of Each Background Variable

Source	SS	df	MS	F
Age	935.9	2	467.9	2.9*
Age of Onset	181.9	1	181.9	1.1
Duration Episode	2.9	2	1.4	0.0
Previous Hosp.	686.4	1	686.4	4.2**
Education	216.8	1	216.8	1.3
Marital Status	3476.9	2	1738.5	10.6***
Course of Illness	6.9	2	3.4	0.0
Precipitating Factor	501.1	1	501.1	3.1
Alcohol Problem	124.2	1	124.2	0.8
Religious Zeal	1181.3	2	590.7	3.6**
Race	1983.2	1	1983.2	12.1***
Work Level	1089.4	2	544.7	3.3**
Error	57777.7	353	163.7	

*   Significant $p < .10$

**   Significant $p < .05$

***   Significant $p < .01$

43

References

1. Overall, J.E. and Gorham, D.R. A pattern probability model for classification of psychiatric patients. Behavioral Science, 1963, 8, 108-116.

2. Overall, J.E. A configural analysis of psychiatric diagnostic stereotypes. Behavioral Science, 1963, 8, 211-219.

3. Pichot, P., Bailly, R. and Overall, J.E. Les stereotypes diagnostiques des psychoses chez les psychiatres frabcais. Collegium International Neuropsychopharmacologicum: Proceedings V International Congress, 1966.

4. Gorham, D.R. and Overall, J.E. Dimensions of change in psychiatric symptomatology. Diseases Nervous System, 1961, 22, 1-5.

5. Patrick, J., Overall, J.E. and Tupin, J.P. Multiple discriminant analysis of clinical diagnosic groups. Proceedings, 76th Annual Convention, Am. Psychol. Asso., 1968.

6. Overall, J.E., Hollister, L.E. and Pichot, P. Major Psychiatric disorders: A four-dimensional model. Arch. Gen. Psychiatry, 1967, 16, 146-151.

7. Overall, J.E. and Gorham, D.R. The brief psychiatric rating scale. Psychol. Reports, 1962, 10, 799-812.

J. E. Overall, Ph.D., The University of Texas Medical Branch, Galveston, Texas 77550

AN INTERACTIVE VIEW OF CHILDHOOD SCHIZOPHRENIA

STELLA CHESS

There is increasing evidence that the schizophrenic child is a neurologically impaired youngster. As our techniques improve, and as follow-up studies and post-mortem examinations multiply, we find that a decreasing proportion of schizophrenic children appear to be organically intact. Even in those cases where organic damage cannot be identified, one may suspect that this inability testified more to the limitation of present techniques than to the non-existence of defects. After all, we have barely begun the biochemical and neurological investigation of childhood schizophrenia.

An organic etiology, however, does not in itself explain the clinical picture. The effect of the organic factor is not simple and direct, as when a severed sensory nerve leads to the loss of a specific sensation in a given area. What makes childhood schizophrenia a unified concept is the descriptive similarity of behvior in a group of children whose basic defects may be quite different. Among youngsters diagnosed as schizophrenic, some have later been found to have degenerative neurological disease leading to death; others, metabolic diseases such as phenylketonurea; still others have developed clinical convulsions years after the diagnosis of schizophrenia was made.

We characterize all these children as schizophrenic, not because of unified etiology, but because of a particular type of social behavior. The effect of the organic factor is determined by interaction with the environment and can be demonstrated only in its social expression.

To understand the specific features of the pathological behavior, one must examine in detail the simultaneous and interactive operation of environmental and organismic components. If a child with a defective capacity to learn socially flexible patterns of behavior meets environmental demands that he cannot respond to appropriately, these demands will evoke bewilderment and further behavioral deviations, which in turn add to the non-adaptive, repetitive, withdrawn or explosive actions.

Let us consider the common finding that the schizophrenic child is unable to make meaningful interpersonal relationships, an incapacity that may be noted in early infancy. A purely organic view might postulate that the interpersonal problem is due to the child's biochemical or neurological defect, or perhaps to a maturational lag. An environmentalist might attribute the fault to a pathological maternal attitude; that is, the child cannot form an object relationship because of defective mothering.

The interactionist hypothesis requires an examination of both factors. On the organic side is the infant's defective capacity to organize and integrate incoming stimuli, on the basis of biochemical or neurophysiological pathology. On the environmental side is the fact that, to an infant, a human being is a vastly complex and variable set of stimuli. The defective baby, who may perhaps be capable of responding appropriately to a simple auditory, visual, tactile, or thermal cue has his basic difficulty intensified by the great demands for processing novel and multiple stimuli. Thus the pathological behavior represents his limited capacity to respond to a given environmental situation.

As the schizophrenic child moves from infancy to the pre-school age, environmental demands become more complex and are responded to through his partial or distorted capacities. The schizophrenic three-year-old who is given a toy telephone may dangle the receiver from its cord and swing it endlessly; at five years of age he limits his play with toy cars to repetitious rolling of the wheels. In both cases the organic defect demonstrates itself in respect to the environmental expectation that the toy objects be responded to as social representations. The schizophrenic youngster responds only to a portion of the stimulus in a simplified manner. The limited nature of the child's play may be the only demonstrated symptom if there is no attempt to interfere by removal of the toy, scolding, or activity intended to elicit his interest in other aspects of the toy.

When the same youngster has arrived at school age, however, the manifest behavior may be more conspicuously pathological in response to the specific organization of the milieu with its many cues and behavioral expectations. In a classroom he may become upset at a change in routine or in seating arrangement. He may ask repetitious questions. As his age increases, so also does the complexity of the expectations. People now expect him to respond to individuals in a differentiated manner, to use complicated materials,

to make judgements leading to varied responses based on minor va-
-riations of environmental cue.

The schizophrenic behavior demonstrates itself in the inappropriate response, the repetition of an habitual and stereotyped activity,
the response to a tangential and hence irrelevant, loosely associated
aspect of the ongoing social situation. Not only is the youngster incapable of responding to an organized manner, but, in addition, his
distorted responses to these demands may evoke rebuke or taunting.
Anxiety may then be added to the already manifest symptoms.

Anxiety may now attach itself to a very specific circumstance
linked fortuitously to some event. One child has been warned about
bees. He is endlessly preoccupied with the possibility that bees may
sting him, and he repetitiously checks on the precautionary measures
he has been taught. Another may become fearful of a social situation,
such as school or parties. In other children the expression of anxiety
is diffuse and free-floating; it appears to be triggered whenever circumstances vary in the lightest degree from the familiar, circumscribed set.

The patterns of behvavior in schizophrenic children show a striking individuality. After one has noted the general characteristics of
such children -the way they look at people, their manner of handling
objects, their speech patterns and motor behavior- one can observe
that the behavioral acts themselves, especially those acquired after
infancy, bear the mark of individual life experiences. In two children
with the same type and degree of organic damage, environmental
differences paly a major role in determinaing the total behavior, particularly the content of each youngster's actions, which influence the
reactions of other people. These reactions, in turn, play a part in
shaping the child's habit patterns.

Let us postulate that two boys have identical basic pathology.
As infants, both manifest the same behavior; both are irritable, do
not respond to caretakers with personal recognition, show pronominal
reversals until the age of four years or later, exhibit peculiar tiptoe
walking and hand-shaking rituals, and evince no interest in playing
with other children.

One of the boys, Carl, belongs to a family that stresses good
manners. By age six, Carl has learened to let ladies into the elevator
first and to remove his hat indoors. At the table he waits for every-
one to be seved before starting to eat, says "Please" and "Thank
you", and chews with his mouth closed. He does all these things in
a mechanical fashion, and not always at appropriate moments. When

a guest visits, he makes the same stereotyped polite inquiries, whether to a stranger or to his aunt. His behavior evokes stares and raised eyebrows, but no animosity.

The other boy, Jack, comes from a permissive family that expects the niceties will take care of themselves. By age six, Jack pushes his way around, unaware that he may be shutting the door in someone's face; at the dinner table he grabs his food, stuffs his mouth full, chews with mouth open and spits out whatever he decides he doesn't want. Whereas Carl's behavior brings stares, Jack's conduct evokes angry disapproval. While Carl goes about his distant stereotyped routine, Jack develops anxieties about situations in which he has been scolded. He refuses to go visiting, and he adds name-calling to his routine.

At a later age, Carl may be a model pupil, answering when called upon, memorizing his lessons even if he is unable to discuss their meaning. Jack's classroom behavior has earned rebukes from the teacher and reprisals from his classmates. By adolescence, the youngsters present very different behavioral pictures.

Schizophrenic youngsters tend to carry out actions that would be appropriate at an earlier developmental stage or in an earlier environmental context. The acts remain a stereotyped and repetitive portion of the behavioral repertoire, once elicited by specific stimuli and still occurring despite the greatly altered social meaning and context of the stimuli. As the child grows older, his general physical and cognitive devolopment reaches a higher level of organization, and the environmental situation that confronts him becomes more complex. As a result, both the defective perception of the environment and the child's characteristic responses are more striking. It becomes increasingly difficult to understand the child in terms of organic or environmental factors alone. Only the interaction of these factors can illuminate the clinical picture.

The question has been raised about the relationship between childhood schizophrenia and schizophrenia in adulthood. Usually, in dealing with pediatric and adult illnesses, it is assumed that if the same diagnostic term is used, the identical pathogenic organism or disease process is involved. But the situation is more complicated in schizophrenia, since an etiology has not been firmly established in either age period. There are arguments about causation in both childhood and adult schizophrenia. Just as Bleuler referred to "the schizophrenias" of adult life, Kanner speaks of "the schizophrenias" of chilhood. Infantile autism has been distinguished discriptively from childhood schizophrenias in which the syndrome of infantile autism is not present. Thus, the question of unity between childhood schizophrenia and adult schizophrenia presents itself in a rather murky light.

In my own clinical experience, I have been able to follow perhaps a dozen schizophrenic patients from early childhood to adolescence and adulthood. The patients were seen initially at ages two through eight. The early history and observation definitely indicated infantile autism or had very strong suggestions of autistic qualities. The outcomes have had a wide range, as in the cases of Carl and Jack that I have just described. In the most severly disturbed patient, a young man who is now 19 years of age, the clinical picture is that of an adult hebephrenic schizophrenic. The least disturbed is a 24-year-old male who has completed graduate school with high academic standing.

The latter patient comes across as a stiff individual. He speaks in a monotone, and his language pattern is characterized by stereotyped phrases and cliches. He does not meet the eye of the person with whom he is talking. Because of the poor impression he makes in personal interview, this young man did not succeed in getting a job in the field of his training. However, he has obtained another position in which his skill can be of use. Though he has an appropriate attachment to his family he has not made personal friends. He is dejected and dissatisfied with his life style.

In the group who are clearly identifiable as schziophrenic on superficial contact, a number of characteristics are worth noting. Stereotypy of ideas and speech is prominent. Ideas and phrases that come up in current interview are the same as those that appeared when the patient was seen as a child. One 19-year-old runs through a repertory of little speeches associated with earlier visits. He will giggle as he calls me "Doctor Chest", and then say, "If I tell you that I masturbate, will you be mad? Will you hit me if I tell you that I masturbate, Dr. Chest"? After repeating this question a dozen times, he moves on to reports of other transgressions with similar giggling and mock expressions of apprehension. When I attempt to bring the discussion around to current matters, he assumes a serious expression, answers a few queries appropriately, then moves back to his pre-occupation of the moment: a magazine report about flying saucers and visitors to earth from outer space. He says, "Its in the magazine, Doctor Chest, so you have to believe it, you believe it, don't you .... "?

Another patient, a 20-year-old woman, whom I saw first when she was three years old, reports her current preoccupation with Eskimos and all facets of Eskimo life. While she knows that she must not let this intrude into her functioning on her job, she finds herself daydreaming and asking her fellow employees their opinions on the matter. Yet this girl was getting grades in the 90's up to her second year in high school. At this point her functioning deteriorated and she dropped out of school. She is pretty, her facial expression is jovial, her voice is pleasant. Distressed at her compulsive preoccupation, she is aware of the peculiar impression she gives with the limited and odd-ball ideas that she cannot keep out of her conversations. This patient has had auditory hallucinations, and at times talks to the voices.

Another patient is an 18-year-old boy who is now in his first year at college. Throughout his high school career he rarely received a mark below the high nineties. He could not let an assignment remain unstarted the very day he got it, even though it was not due for weeks. His inability to function in this compulsive manner in college has thrown him into a panic. He constantly runs to his instructors to ask their opinion of his work. His voice is a monotone, and his topics of conversation are limited virtually to three: his academic progress, an admired performer with whom he corresponds actively and whose public appearances he attends without fail, and the young child of a cousin to whom he is closely and appropriately attached. In earlier chilhood and adolescence, this boy had no motivation for examining and changing his own behavior. He was distressed by the negative attention he received, but kept hoping that children would cease teasing him. He was heartened by the increasingly benign attitude of his classmates in the high school years. Now he is concerned lest his cousin's child begin to imitate his own peculiar mannerisms. The degree of modification he has been able to effect does not appear to give him much hope that he will be able to change his strikingly odd appearance.

One could cite many similar examples.

Dr. Jacques Gottlieb has remarked that in his follow-up studies of Dr. Rabinovitch's childhood schizophrenic patients who are now, as young adults, chronically hospitalized, the diagnosis of schizophrenia is maintained. He remarks that these patients do not have the burned-out appearance of other chronically hospitalized schizophrenics with onset after the childhood period. If I understood his remarks correctly he found an interpersonal quality and affective

50

capacity in the grown-up childhood schizophrenics that does not appear in the other patients. On the basis of the cases that I have followed up from childhood to adolescence and adulthood, I tend to agree with this observation.

The final word in this controversy may indeed be biochemical in nature, and I await with interest the reports on the follow-up biochemical studies described by Dr. Gottlieb.

S. Chess, M.D., New York University Medical Center, 550 First Avenue, N.Y., N.Y. 10016

CHANGES IN THE SEVERITY OF SOCIAL ALIENATION-PERSONAL DISORGANIZATION IN CHRONIC SCHIZOPHRENIC PATIENTS: PSYCHOMETRIC AND PSYCHOPHARMACOLOGICAL FACTORS. PHENOTHIAZINE WITHDRAWAL IN CHRONIC SCHIZOPHRENICS

GOLDINE C. GLESER, LOUIS A. GOTTSCHALK, WALTER N. STONE AND JOHN CLEGHORN.

The study to be reported here was begun in 1964 to determine the effect of a phenothiazine derivative on speech content; particularly on scores for social alienation-personal disorganization derived from speech samples. [1, 2, 3] Our original intention was to study the fluctuations in the severity of schizophrenic symptomatology as measured by this verbal content scale over an eight-week period and to search for predictors of differential rate of improvement using independent measures of personality and symptomatology. These goals had to be modified somewhat when we found that the majority of newly-admitted patients to the State Hospital where we planned to carry out our study were already taking various dosages of phenothiazine derivatives as prescribed by referring physicians. We decided, therefore, to modify our plans to include a study of the effects of phenothiazine withdrawal over a four-week period on the severity of schizophrenic symptomatology in chronic patients, followed by a controlled study of the effect of thioridazine. Drug withdrawal seemed worth investigating in its own right since most clinicians believe that the schizophrenic patient's symptoms will return soon after the drug is completely eliminated from his system.

The scale that we proposed using as a criterion of the severity of schizophrenic symptomatology in this investigation has undergone extensive development over the past decade. It consists of a set of weighted categories of content which can be applied to speech samples recorded verbatim. The content that is scored covers a broad range of positively and negatively weighted categories referring to interpersonal and intrapersonal references, desire for control, disorientation, repetition, and bizarre or inaudible remarks. Our studies have shown that the content categories of this scale can be scored reliably and the resulting scores are relatively stable over time. The validity of this scale for determining intraindividual variations in severity of the schizophrenic syndrome[1] as well as interindividual variations[2] has been demonstrated. A further study[3] compared the distribution of scores obtained by applying this scale to groups of schizophrenic and non-schizophrenic individuals. It was found that the scale is capable of differentiating known schizophrenics from non-schizophrenic psychiatric patients, general medical patients, and non-hospitalized individuals employed in an industrial corporation. However, it did not differentiate schizophrenics from brain-damaged patients. As a result of that study some changes in category weights were made to improve differentiation between scores of schizophrenic and brain-damaged patients while maintaining the validity of the scales for ascertaining individual differences in the severity of schizophrenic illness of the previously studied samples. The findings in this report are based on the latest content category weights of the social alienation-personal disorganization scale.

METHODS AND PROCEDURES

A group of 74 chronic schizophrenic patients at Longview State Hospital (35 males and 39 females) was selected from the schizophrenic inpatient population on the following basis: (a) the patient had no complicating medical or neurological illness other than chronic schizophrenia; (b) he was receiving a phenothiazine derivative but no antidepressant medicament of any kind; (c) he was not mute and was capable of cooperating with the procedures used in the measurements of change. The group of patients selected had, in addition, the following other characteristics: They had been hospitalized from six months to 25 years on the present admission, with a median of 11 years. Those hospitalized for the shortest periods had had one to four previous admissions. All patients had been on some one of the phenothiazine drugs continually for at least six months. Approximately 37% were on Stellazine, 19% on Prolixin, 19% on Trilafon, and the other 25% on other drugs such as Thorazine, Compazine, Mellaril, or Vesprin. Patients were considered to be functioning sufficiently well within the hospital setting to cooperate with testing and interview procedures. They were all Caucasians and in the age range from 24 to 54, with an average age of 42.9.

For the initial assessment of these patients, several procedures were carried out. Five-minute verbal samples were obtained from each patient, two or three times the initial week, using the Gottschalk-Gleser method of asking each patient to tell an interesting or dramatic life experience.[1,2,3,4,5,6,7]

During the week each patient was seen by a psychiatrist or third-year psychiatric resident who administered a standardized interview from which he filled out the Mental Status Schedule devised by Spitzer and his colleagues.[8,9,10,11] Next, the 16 PF test, Form A[12], was administered by a psychologist and assistant to groups of 6 to 12 patients at any one session. Directions were read aloud and repeated when necessary to make sure that each patient knew what he was to do. In addition, individual attention was given to each person at some point during the time he was answering the test to make sure he was recording answers correctly and in some cases items were read to him if he was having difficulty reading or understanding the statements. By this means complete test results were obtained on 35 females and 34 males or 69 of the 74 patients.

On completion of initial psychological evaluations, all patients had their phenothiazine medication changed ostensibly to a new drug which was actually a placebo of identical appearance to thioridazine. None of the hospital personnel (doctors, nurses, or attendants) was told that a placebo was substituted for the psychoactive drug.

Five-minute speech samples were obtained twice weekly by the same "interviewer" whenever possible from each patient throughout the next eight weeks of the study. Four weeks after the patients had been taking the placebo one-half of the group, randomly selected, was started on thioridazine in doses comparable to the amount they had been receiving individually in the form of this or any other phenothiazine derivative at the onset of this study (300-1000 mg./day). The other half of the group of patients was continued on the placebo. At this four-week point of the study, all patients were reevaluated on the Mental Status Schedule. A third evaluation by this measure was done at the end of the eighth week of the study. Different raters were used each time.

Thus, half of the patients were on a placebo for eight weeks and the other half received a placebo for four weeks and then the phenothiazine derivative, thioridazine, for four weeks. During the course of this study, if patients became disturbed they were administered only chloral hydrate (8 cc) or a placebo by mouth or sodium phenobarbital (0.1 gm) intramuscularly. A few patients became difficult to manage during the first four weeks and had to be dropped from the study.

Typescripts of the five-minute verbal samples were scored independently and blindly by two content analysis technicians for anxiety, hostility outward, hostility inward, ambivalent hostility, and social alienation-personal disorganization. The findings on the affect scales are reported elsewhere[13] and will not be dealt with here.

The Mental Status Schedules that were completed during the initial, fourth, and eighth weeks contain a set of 248 items describing symptoms of behavior to which the psychiatrist responds true or false on the basis of a structured interview. The authors of this schedule have collected data on over 2,000 patients throughout the United States and at the time of this study were in the process of determining scales by means of factor analysis. In particular, a verimax rotation of the first three principal component factors yielded scores for neuroticism (feelings and concerns), psychoticism (delusions, hallucinations, grandiosity), and disorientation (confusion, retardation).[10] In addition, some 42 subscales have been derived as more specific and circumscribed symptom clusters. The Mental Status Schedules were scored for these factors and subscales.

RESULTS

Group Trends in Social Alienation-Personal Disorganization ("Schizophrenic" Scale)

Of the 74 patients placed on placebo at the beginning of the study, only four (two males and two females) were discontinued at the end of the first four weeks because of clinical considerations for their well-being. These four had required sedatives and had become assaultive or suicidal about the third week on placebo so that it was considered unwise to expose them to the risk of continuing another four weeks on placebo if they should happen to be assigned to that group. All four patients decreased steadily in the average number of words they spoke in the five-minute sessions and all but one was mute throughout the third or fourth week. Furthermore, their scores on the scale for social alienation-personal disorganization increased steadily, obtaining a total average rise of about 10 points in the four weeks. These data, which corroborate the clinical observations, add additional evidence to the validity of the verbal scale for assessing the severity of schizophrenic disorder.

One major problem which we encountered in analyzing the data was the large number of occasions for which verbal scores were not available. In some cases data were missing because patients were working or out on pass at the time of some of their scheduled sessions. More usually scores were missing because the patient refused to speak or spoke less than the minimum of 45 words needed to obtain a score on the "schizophrenic" scale. (At least 70 words are needed to score the affect scales with even a minimum of reliability.) From our previous study[2] we were able to make an estimate of the average score on social alienation-personal disorganization that would be obtained by patients equally disturbed clinically, but who did speak. On this basis we assigned a score of 8.0 to samples of up to 45 words and a score of 11.6 to samples in which the subject was completely mute. These estimates helped considerably in obtaining more regular trends. However, five patients spoke so seldom after the first week or two that they were dropped from consideration in analyzing overall longitudinal trends.

Table 1

Average Weekly Social Alienation-Personal Disorganization Scores and Number of Words (per Verbal Sample) from Chronic Schizophrenic patients

Time of Verbal Sample	Group A (Placebo for eight weeks, N = 32)				Group B (Thioridazine last four weeks, N = 32)			
	No. of Words (per sample)		Social Alienation Scores		No. of Words (per sample)		Social Alienation Scores	
	X̄	s.d.	X̄	s.d.	X̄	s.d.	X̄	s.d.
Pre-placebo	502.0	258.7	1.9	3.5	526.0	223.6	2.0	4.0
Week 1	407.4	247.7	1.4	4.6	438.6	221.8	2.9	4.8
2	411.2	258.8	2.4	5.0	429.9	243.6	2.6	5.4
3	416.3	282.4	2.5	4.8	392.7	189.0	4.6	7.4
4	410.3	282.3	3.7	5.0	364.8	238.6	3.7	7.7
Slope (Wks. 0-4)	-17.6	53.0	0.48	1.10	-36.6	47.3	0.50	1.41
5	405.5	288.5	3.6	5.7	394.3	246.5	4.3	6.1
6	404.0	287.2	3.4	5.6	437.8	261.2	3.5	5.8
7	437.8	301.0	3.7	5.6	450.9	268.1	3.2	6.6
8	436.4	294.0	3.9	5.6	459.6	258.5	3.6	6.1
Slope (Wks. 4-8)	6.2	18.7	0.07	0.68	25.5	34.0	-0.14	1.19

The average weekly social alienation-personal disorganization scores of the 64 patients who were followed
throughout the study are given in Table 1. Separate
averages are provided for these patients who were maintained on placebo throughout and those who received
thioridazine the last four weeks. The slopes of the
best-fitting linear trend lines for the first and second
four-week period were calculated and the average slopes
are indicated in Table 1. These slopes can be interpreted as average weekly rates of change. The average
slopes for the first four-week placebo period do not differ significantly between the two groups. The combined
average slope of 0.49 is significant at the .01 level ,
indicating an increase in severity of symptomatology
during the four-week placebo period.

In the second period the average scores on the "schizophrenic" scale continued to increase for those on placebo
but at a much slower rate. In fact, almost as many of
the patients improved as regressed so that the average
slope of .07 was not significant. Clinically also there
were no further patients who, because of severely disturbed behavior, had to be dropped from the study. The
patients who were placed on thioridazine showed some improvement on the average, but again the average slope of
-0.14 was not significant. Neither was the difference
significant between this average slope and that for
patients on placebo. These results are illustrated
graphically in Figure 1.

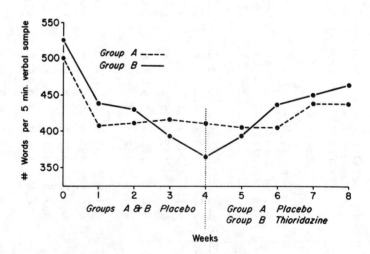

Figure 1. Average weekly scores on Social Alienation-Personal Disorganization Scale for two groups of
chronic schizophrenic subjects on two different experimental regimens.

The number of words spoken each week on the average are also given in Table 1 and graphically in Figure 2. The decrease with placebo during the first four weeks (Slope = -27.1 words/week) is very significant (p < .001). The difference in slope for the two groups in the placebo period is not significant. In the second four-week period the patients receiving the active drug (Group B) increased their speech at the average rate of 25.5 words per week, a highly significant increase. The placebo group (A) also showed a small rise, but this increase was not significant. Furthermore, the difference in slope for the two treatment groups was highly significant (T = 2.68, p = .01).

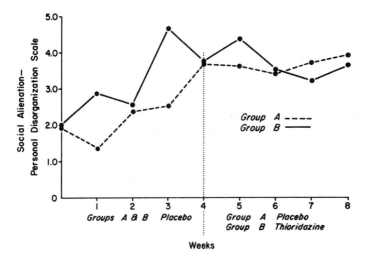

Figure 2. Average number of words spoken per verbal sample per week by two groups of chronic schizophrenics.

Prediction of Individual Difference in Response to Phenothiazine Withdrawal

From Figures 1 and 2 it is evident that on the average patients became increasingly disturbed during the first four weeks that they were on placebo as judged by both the amount and content of their speech samples. However, some patients showed almost no deterioration in their behavior, and, if anything, seemed to improve during the first four weeks on placebo. Even after eight weeks of placebo these patients seemed as well or better off than when they started. One of our major interests in this study was in trying to find some indicators in the initial data by which one could predict which patients would do well when taken off phenothiazines, and which would not.

In order to find predictors of response to phenothiazine withdrawal it was necessary to derive some measure to characterize the general trend of scores on the scale of social alienation-personal disorganization for each individual. For this purpose the slopes of the linear trend line for the first four weeks and for weeks 4 to 8 were computed separately for each individual. This method of computing the rate of increase or decrease results in a more reliable rate of change measure than would simple difference scores.

In Table 2 are presented the correlations between the personality factor scores of the 16 PF, the initial score on social alienation-personal disorganization, and the algebraic slope of the trend line for social alienation-personal disorganization scores during the first four weeks. For completeness, correlations between 16 PF scores and slope in the last four weeks for patients given placebo and separately for those on thioridazine are also included. (For additional information on 16 PF scores in this study see Gleser and Gottschalk, 1967.[14]) From the 16 PF it appears that patients with emotional warmth (A), high emotional stability (C), enthusiasm (F), conscientiousness (G) and shrewdness-sophistication (N) and those who are not particularly insecure (O-) or free-thinking (Q^-_1), tend to have negative or small positive slopes. However, none of these zero order correlations are significant at the .05 level. A multiple regression equation was obtained so as to maximize the multiple correlation using a minimum number of predictors according to the technique suggested by DuBois.[15] Using the six scales A, C, F, N, O, and Q_1 from the 16 PF a multiple correlation of .389 was obtained. The weights ranged from .08 for insecurity (O) to -.17 for enthusiasm (F). (Note that the predictor scores are such that a high value corresponds to a high rate of increase in social alienation-personal disorganization after phenothiazine withdrawal.)

Table 2

Correlations of 16 PF Factors with Initial Scores and Average Rate of Change in Social Alienation-Personal Disorganization

16 PF Scale	Initial Score (N=69)	Average Rates of Change		
		First 4 weeks (N=69)	Last 4 weeks placebo (N=30)	drug (N=28)
A. Warmth	-.10	-.20	-.22	.00
B. Intelligence	-.25	-.04	-.01	.20
C. Emotional Stability	-.17	-.21	.37	.24
E. Assertiveness	.08	.04	-.10	-.28
F. Enthusiasm	-.16	-.22	.04	-.17
G. Conscientious	-.39	-.17	.04	.35
H. Venturesome	-.10	-.10	.10	.22
I. Sensitivity	-.10	.04	-.07	.21
L. Distrustfulness	.01	-.05	.25	-.13
M. Autism	.30	.10	-.22	-.01
N. Sophistication	-.30	-.18	-.08	.42
O. Insecurity	.08	.21	.08	-.37
Q$_1$. Free-thinking	-.02	.15	-.21	.25
Q$_2$. Self-sufficiency	.07	-.10	.29	.12
Q$_3$. Self-sentiment	-.32	-.01	.06	.31
Q$_4$. Drive tension	.11	.11	-.32	-.06
Rate of change 1st 4 weeks			-.18	-.55

Intercorrelations among the three principal factor scores and selected factor analytically-derived cluster scores from the Mental Status Schedule, initial scores on social alienation-personal disorganization and rate of change of these scores over the first four weeks are shown in Table 3. Disorientation is the only one of the three principal component factors that is significantly correlated with rate of change scores. Among the cluster-scores disorientation, apathy-retardation, and silly disorganization each significantly predicted rate of change scores. The first two of these are highly correlated

with the primary disorientation scale,however, and hence-
are simply giving more specific symptom information.

Table 3

Intercorrelations among Initial Principal Factor and Selected Subscale Scores Derived from the Mental Status Schedule and Initial Scores and Average Rate of Change in the First Four Weeks for Social Alienation-Personal Disorganization (N = 74)

	b.	c.	d.	e.	f.	g.	h.	i.	Rate of Change
a. Neuroticism	.39	.22	.38	.02	.32	.08	.16	.19	.01
b. Psychoticism		.12	.80	.17	.07	.37	.52	.41	.19
c. Disorientation (primary)			.04	.77	.85	.22	.29	.43	.31
d. Delusions-Hallucinations				.12	-.06	.33	.34	.31	.20
e. Disorientation					.39	.17	.17	.35	.30
f. Apathy-Retardation						.07	.20	.31	.23
g. Silly Disorganization							.55	.38	.31
h. Elated Excitement								.36	.18
i. Initial score Social Alienation-Personal Disorganization									.11

Using the principal factors a multiple R of .350 was
obtained for the weighted sum of psychoticism and disorientation. The cluster scores yielded a multiple correlation of .422 for the weighted sum of scores for disorientation, apathy-retardation, silly disorganization
and delusions-hallucinations. Thus the more specific
symptom scores appeard to be considerably better pre-

dictors than the factor scores. However, it should be remembered that these scores are probably not as reliable as the more general factor scores and also that there is more opportunity for error to inflate the multiple.

The correlation was obtained between the two sets of predictor scores, i.e., the one from the 16 PF and the one from the symptom clusters, to determine to what extent they overlapped. The correlation between them was only .33, which while significant indicated considerable independence of prediction. The two scores combined predicted the average rate of change in social alienation-personal disorganization scores with an R of .497.

Looking again at Table 2 it is evident that individual differences in response to placebo during the second four-week period are not generally predictable from the same set of 16 PF factors as are individual differences in the first four weeks after drug withdrawal. The correlation between rates of change for the two periods is -.18, which is not significantly different from zero. Furthermore, many of the zero order correlations between the 16 PF scales and rate of change are markedly different for the two periods. Thus the more emotionally stable (C) and self-sufficient (Q_2) patient became increasingly socially alienated during the second four weeks while patients who were more free-thinking (Q_1) and tense (Q_4) in the baseline period show some improvement. However, the lack of significance of any of the correlations makes interpretation dubious.

The correlation between rates of change of social alienation-personal disorganization scores in the first four weeks and those in the last four weeks for subjects on drug is -.55 which is highly significant and indicates that these may be complementary processes. Thus subjects who showed the greatest increase in social alienation-personal disorganization when they were taken off phenothiazines tended to show the greatest improvement when given an active drug, whereas those who did well on placebo tended to lose any gains they had made when they were put back on drugs. This is further borne out by the fact that the linear equation from the combined Mental Status and 16 PF predictors of slope for the first period is also correlated -.218 with the slope in the second period for those on thioridazine. (The corresponding correlation for the placebo group is .002.)

On examination, the multiple regression equations from the Mental Status Scales, the 16 PF, or the two combined appeared to be yielding inflated multiple correlations as the result of the correspondence of a few extreme

values. Many intermediate sized changes were being
missed. Furthermore, the regression equations did not
seem to select those persons who continued to deteriorate with placebo during the second four weeks. Since it
was hoped that a simple rule could be found for possible
use in decisions to terminate drug therapy, and such a
decision does not entail a continuous variable, it was
decided to examine the possibility of making the prediction by the use of cut-off scores on the principal
factors. By trial and error it was determined that a
score of less than seven on both the psychoticism and
disorientation factors selected patients who did not
get worse when drug was withdrawn. On the other hand a
score of seven or greater on either scale indicated a
poor prognosis for drug withdrawal. This decision rule
actually provided a better separation of patients who
did and did not deteriorate with placebo than did the
linear regression predictor as measured by a phi coefficient.

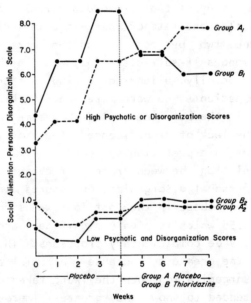

Figure 3. Social Alienation-Personal Disorganization
scores for drug and placebo groups classified on the basis of their initial Mental Status Factor scores.

Figure 3 shows the scores on the social alienation-
personal disorganization scale average over successive
two-week periods for patients classified according to the
multiple cut-off criterion and their assignment to drug
or placebo group at the end of the fourth week. Those
patients who became mute are not included in these averages. Some interesting features are evident in this
figure. First of all, it may be noted that the patients
who had high psychotic or disorientation scores on the
initial Mental Status score (N=29) tended to be somewhat
more socially alienated to begin with and remained so

throughout the study. This might have been anticipated from the fact that psychotic and disorientation scores are positively correlated with scores on social alienation-personal disorganization in the base period.[7] The average rate of change of scores on the social alienation-personal disorganization scale during the first four weeks was 1.0. Those patients who had low scores on the psychotic and disorientation scales of the Mental Status (N = 35) had low average social alienation-personal disorganization scores on their verbal samples and they continued to have low scores over the entire eight weeks of the study provided they were in the placebo group. If they were put back on drug (N=17) at the end of four weeks they actually showed a slight (non-significant) increase in social alienation. Another point of interest is the dip in scores in the first two weeks after drug withdrawal for the low symptom group. This drop has a p value of .10 by a sign test.

It will be remembered that over the total sample there was no difference in rate of change scores in the second period for those on drug as compared to placebo. The trend scores in the second period for patients who had scores of seven or higher in psychoticism or disorientation differ much more markedly depending on whether they were given drug or placebo, although the difference still has a probability of approximately .12 of arising by chance.

Since the average number of words spoken in a verbal sample had been noted to decrease when patients were on placebo and increase when they were again given a psychoactive drug, the question arose as to whether individual differences in these trends were also related to the dichotomy of high versus low psychotic and disorientation Mental Status scores. The high symptom group showed an average decrease in the first four weeks of -42.3 words per week whereas the decrease for the low symptom group was only -15.2 words per week, a difference significant at the .05 level. Furthermore, those having high scores who were given psychoactive drugs the second four weeks increased an average of 31.2 words per week as compared to only 0.4 words per week for the placebo group; again a significant difference. For the low symptom groups the corresponding values were 17.5 for those on drug and 11.3 for those on placebo the last four weeks, a non-significant difference.

Discussion

In general the verbal sample technique for assessing behavior appears to offer a fruitful method for following

longitudinal changes in the magnitude of the schizophrenic syndrome and in finding predictors of trend with
various types of therapy. The many kinds of problems
involved when assessing change in psychiatry and the
behavioral sciences have been well documented.[16, 17]
The use of repeated measures through which one can pass
a best-fitting trend line and determine its slope for
each subject offers an improved technique for dealing
with change, provided the task involved is one that can
be performed frequently without carry-over effects.
Verbal samples are well suited to this requirement.

Considerable evidence that the therapeutic effects of
phenothiazines are not maintained following drug withdrawal has been reported in the literature.[18,19] These
studies have been reviewed recently by Kamano[20] who points
out the need to find an effective method of predicting
which patients can tolerate long periods without drugs
and which cannot. The present study is a contribution
in this direction. Our findings indicate that on the
average chronic schizophrenic patients speak progressively fewer words and obtain higher social alienation-
personal disorganization scores in the first four weeks
after the phenothiazines they are taking are replaced by
a placebo. However, looking further we find that if the
psychoactive drug on which the chronic patient has been
maintained has not succeeded in eliminating the more
florid schizophrenic symptoms such as delusions and
hallucinations or the "withdrawal" symptoms of disorientation, apathy and retardation, then drug treatment
should be continued. Chronic patients who are relatively
free of such symptoms while on tranquilizing drugs can
go at least eight weeks without such medication with no
exacerbation of schizophrenic symptoms. In fact, they
may actually show some symptomatic improvement, possibly
because of a decrease of undesirable side-effects.

It is interesting that the number of words spoken in
the five-minute interview is so sensitive to pharmacological intervention. Thus a significant difference
was found in average rate of change in number of words
spoken for patients on thioridazine as compared to
placebo. One reason for the sensitivity of this measure
lies in its objectivity and reliability and in its availability for all subjects. Psychologically, however, its
importance lines in the fact that it is one of the "withdrawal" signs that Goldberg et al[21] have noted to be
among the first symptoms to disappear when patients are
put on phenothiazines. These withdrawal symptoms usually

abate to their maximum extent by the end of five weeks. At the end of four weeks on thioridazine, speech returns almost to the baseline rate, a finding which is consistent with those of Goldberg and his colleagues. The content measure of social alienation-personal disorganization is not only related to disorientation and withdrawal symptoms but also to other schizophrenic symptoms such as delusions, hallucinations, belligerence and memory deficit which Goldberg et al found continued to abate up to 13 weeks after the start of phenothiazine treatment. In this respect it is unfortunate that our patients weren't followed for a longer period of time.

The present study reemphasizes the difficulty of using chronic patients in state hospitals for the evaluation of new drugs. Almost all such patients are on some kind of phenothiazine medication. If they are not it is very likely they constitute a different population with regard to drug response than those who are continuously maintained on drugs. The latter again consist of two types: those who become more floridly psychotic after discontinuing medication and those who remain unchanged or even improve slightly. Experimental results would vary according to the relative proportions of each type of patient in the sample and the length of time elapsing between medications.

Many further questions are stimulated by the results of this investigation. It would be interesting to know, for example, how long the patients characterized as having a good prognosis with drug withdrawal could function reasonably adequately without drugs. Also, are such patients those who have always functioned marginally with or without drugs or have they had symptoms of disorientation and psychoticism at some prior time which were reduced when drug was administered? In this respect it may be that the high and low symptom groups are characterized by differences in the metabolic handling of phenothiazine drugs which would be reflected in differences in the blood levels and/or excretion rates of the phenothiazines. Again, they may differ with respect to the prior course of the disease process and/or the premorbid personality characteristics. In this respect there are some correlates of this dichotomy among the 16 PF scores although the differences are not very great. (See Gleser and Gottschalk.[14]). Also, the patients with the more severe symptoms had been hospitalized slightly longer (12.5 versus 9.5 years) but the lengths of stay overlap greatly so that this does not appear to be a crucial factor. Finally, this study raises the possibility that phenothiazines might be compared fruitfully with respect to the length of time they remain effective after medication is discontinued. While no contrasts among phenothiazines were evident for the groups studied here, the number of patients in each group who had been taking any one phenothiazine derivative was rather small. Obviously, further research studies are needed in these areas.

SUMMARY

Social alienation-personal disorganization scores of chronic schizophrenic patients were obtained from five-minute verbal productions elicited twice a week over an eight-week period. For the first four weeks all patients were on placebo, while during the next four weeks half were on placebo and half were on thioridazine. The chronic schizophrenic patients were 74 state-hospitalized Caucasians of both sexes in the age range 24-54, who were able, initially, to cooperate with testing and interviewing procedures. Each had been on some one phenothiazine derivative for at least the previous six months.

Patients were assessed initially using the standardized Spitzer-Burdock Mental Status Interview and the Catell 16 PF test. In addition, two or three five-minute verbal samples were obtained from each patient in the initial week by asking the patient to tell an interesting or dramatic life experience. Additional mental status interviews were obtained at the end of four and eight weeks.

The folowing results were obtained:

1. Average scores for social alienation-personal disorganization increased significantly over the first four weeks.

2. Those patients who continued on placebo showed little further increase in score in the second four weeks, whereas those patients who were given thioridazine showed a small, non-significant decrease.

3. The average number of words spoken in a verbal sample decreased significantly for the first four weeks while patients were on placebo. Patients having thioridazine drug the second period showed a significant increase in number of words spoken.

4. Using multiple correlation techniques with scores obtained during the initial testing period it was possible to predict individual differences in response to phenothiazine withdrawal. A multiple correlation of .39 was obtained using six of the 16 PF factor scales. A

multiple correlation of .42 was obtained using four "narrow" factor scales of the Mental Status Schedule. Using both sets of predictors the correlation was .50.

5. Using the general principal factor scores of psychoticism and disorientation from the Mental Status Schedule a multiple cut-off criterion of 7 or more in either scale divided the patients into those who gave verbal samples with increasingly high schores in social alienation-personal disorganization when on placebo from those who showed practically no change on this verbal score measure.

The same multiple cut-off differentiated those who showed a significant decrease in number of words spoken in the first period. The theoretical and practical implications of these findings were discussed.

Acknowledgements

Supported in part by grants from the Foundations Fund for Research in Psychiatry (T 57-74) and from the National Institute of Mental Health (MH-08282 and MH-K3-14,665.) We wish to express our appreciation to Dr. John Toppen, Superintendent, for his permission to use the facilities of Longview State Hospital, to the resident psychiatrists and research technicians who assisted in gathering and processing the data, and particularly to Mrs. C. Winget for accomplishing the monumental task of coding all verbal samples.

REFERENCES

1. Gottschalk, L. A., Gleser, G. C., Daniels, R. S., and Block, S. The speech patterns of schizophrenic patients: a method of assessing relative degree of personal disorganization and social alienation. J. Nerv. & Ment. Dis. 127, 153-166, 1958.

2. Gottschalk, L. A., Gleser, G. C., Magliocco, B., and D'Zmura, T. L. Further studies on the speech patterns of schizophrenic patients: Measuring inter-individual differences in relative degree of personal disorganization and social alienation. J. Nerv. & Ment. Dis. 132, 101-113, 1961.

3. Gottschalk, L. A. and Gleser, G. C. Distinguishing characteristics of the verbal communications of schizophrenic patients. In Disorders of Communication A.R.N.M.D. Vol. 42, pp. 400-413. Baltimore. William and Wilkins, 1964.

4. Gottschalk, L. A. and Hambidge, G. Jr. Verbal behavior analysis: a systematic approach to the problem of quantifying psychologic processes. J. Proj. Techn. 19, 387-409, 1955.

5. Gleser, G. C., Gottschalk, L. A., and Springer, K. J. An anxiety measure applicable to verbal samples. Arch. Gen. Psychiat. 5, 593-605, 1961.

6. Gottschalk, L. A., Gleser, G. C., and Springer, K. J. Three hostility scales applicable to verbal samples. Arch. Gen. Psychiat. 9, 254-279, 1963.

7. Gottschalk, L. A. and Gleser, G. C. The Measurement of Psychological States Through the Content Analysis of Verbal Behavior. Berkeley, Los Angeles: U. of Calif. Press, 1969.

8. Spitzer, R. L. Immediate available record of mental status examination. Arch. Gen. Psychiat. 13, 76-78, 1965.

9. Spitzer, R. L., Fleiss, J. L., Burdock, E. I., and Hardesty, A. S. The mental status schedule: rationale, reliability, and validity. Compr. Psychiat. 5, 384-395, 1964.

10. Spitzer, R. L., Fleiss, J. L., Endicott, J., and Cohen, J. Mental Status Schedule: properties of factor analytically derived scales. Arch. Gen. Psychiat. 16, 479-493, 1967.

11. Spitzer, R. L., Fleiss, J. L., Kernohan, W., Lee, J. D., and Baldwin, I. T. Mental Status Schedule. Arch. Gen. Psychiat. 13, 448-455, 1965.

12. Cattell, R. B. and Eber, H. W. Handbook for the Sixteen Personality Factor Questionnaire. Champaign, III. Institute for Personality and Ability Testing, 1957 (1964 supplementation).

13. Gottschalk, L. A., Gleser, G. C., Cleghorn, J. A., and Stone, W. N. Language as a measure of change in schizophrenia: effect of a tranquilizer (phenothiazine derivative) on anxiety, hostility, and social alienation-personal disorganization in chronic schizophrenic patients. Presented at the Symposium on Language and Thought in Schizophrenia, Newport Beach, Calif., Nov. 21-24, 1968.

14. Gleser, G. C. and Gottschalk, L. A. Personality characteristics of chronic schizophrenics in relationship to sex and current functioning. J. of Clinical Psychology 23, 349-254, 1967.

15. DuBois, P. H. Multivariate Correlational Analysis. New York. Harper & Brothers, 1957.

16. Group for the Advancement of Psychiatry, Committee on Research. Psychiatric Research and the Assessment of change. Vol. VI, Report No. 63, 357-478. New York. Group for the Advancement of Psychiatry (GAP), 1966.

17. Worchel, P. and Byrne, D. (Eds.) Personality Change. New York. John Wiley & Sons, Inc., 1964.

18. Blackburn, H.L., and Allen, J.L. Behavioral effects of interrupting and resuming tranquilizing medication among schizophrenics. J. Nerv. & Ment. Dis. 133, 303-308, 1961.

19. Diamond, L. S. and Marks, J. B. Discontinuance of tranquilizers among chronic schizophrenic patients receiving maintenance dosage. J. Nerv. & Ment. Dis. 131, 247-251, 1960.

20. Kamano, D. K. Selective review of effects of discontinuation of drug treatment, some implications and problems. Psychol. Rep. 19, 743-749, 1966.

21. Goldberg, S. C., Schooler, N. R., and Mattsson, N. Paranoid and withdrawal symptoms in schizophrenia: differential symptom reduction over time. J. Nerv. & Ment. Dis. 145, 158-162, 1967.

22. Green, D. E., Forrest, I. S., Forrest, F. M., and Serra, M. T. Interpatient variation in chlorpromazine metabolism. Exp. Med. and Surg. 23, 278-287, 1965.

G. C. Gleser, Ph.D., and W. N. Stone, M.D., University of Cincinnati, College of Medicine, Cincinnati, Ohio

Louis A. Gottschalk, M.D., University of California, College of Medicine, Irvine, California

J. A. Cleghorn, M.D., McMaster University Medical School, Hamilton, Ontario, Canada

SCHIZOPHRENIA AND ITS IMPROVEMENT: NECESSARY AND SUFFICIENT CONDITIONS FOR THE DIAGNOSIS OF SCHIZOPHRENIA: AND CRITERIA FOR IMPROVEMENT

DOUGLAS GOLDMAN

Nosology is defined in the Oxford dictionary as "a classification or arrangement of diseases; systematic classification or investigation of diseases, that branch of medical science which deals with this." It has been part of the mental processes of those human beings who are involved in the treatment or management of illness to classify such illness in categories according to various systems. Ancient physicians classified illness according to bile color, usually hypothetically determined. Phrenology was a classification of emotional traits with psychiatric overtones. Such systems historically seemed to have the purpose of assigning certain kinds of treatment (ostensibly) expected to relieve the illness, but the development of classification seems to have served the purpose more of producing the intellectual satisfaction of orientation and recognition in the physician than the relief of suffering in the patient.

In the development of modern medicine as we know it today, nosologic differentiation began in the eighteenth and nineteenth centuries. The earliest criteria were anatomic and were further elaborated by the cellular pathology of Virchow. Physiologic and chemical criteria in relation to the anatomic systems, developed in the nineteenth century under many historically important men among whom could be mentioned VonMehring and Claude Bernard. Etiologic considerations became important particularly with the important microbiologic discoveries of individuals like Koch and Pasteur. Nosology in our present science of medicine is clearly the elaboration and differentiation to a more advanced degree of the findings of our pioneer forebears.

Psychiatry, however, has been somewhat deviant and
retarded in the development of a nosologic matrix. It is
not much more than one hundred years since important
discriminations in psychologic and emotional illness began to be made. The present psychiatric concepts clearly
date to Kraepelin and his younger contemporary Eugen
Bleuler. Their classification of the illnesses assigned to
psychiatric interest still form the basis of present-day
psychiatric activity.

Certain illnesses characterized by psychologic and
emotional changes and deviant behavior were clearly
found to be related to pathologic changes in the brain
structure. The separation of these was an important aspect of the development of modern psychiatry. Particular note must be made of the separation of neurosyphilis
with reasonably satisfactory determination of infectious
etiology, and the subsequent development of appropriate
physical and chemical treatment to eliminate the causative agent. It was probably the example of neurosyphilis
which kept alive the hope that other kinds of mental illness not so clearly "organic" in origin, would be clarified by more meticulous examination of chemistry, physiology and anatomy of the victims.

The important group of functional psychoses classified
now as the affective psychoses and schizophrenia together
form a large part of the burden of psychiatric practice,
and have to a great extent resisted elucidation along classic etiologic, anatomic and physiologic lines. However, it
is amazing that Kraepelin's classification of the functional
psychoses particularly, developed in the central European
culture of the turn of the century still finds applicability in

all human groups regardless of cultural and geographic distribution. The term schizophrenia introduced by Bleuler to
replace Kraepelin's term dementia praecox is sufficiently
euphonious, and intellectually obscure, to be satisfying as a
name without committing the profession to any nosologic
decision.

In the last three or four decades, there has been a considerable erosion of the original concepts of Kraepelin and
Bleuler which were entirely clinical in origin. Under the
influence of the fascination with the ego psychology of Freud
with which Bleuler himself was unquestionably to some degree involved, the concepts of Bleuler and Kraepelin have
become somewhat obscure and diffuse, so that sharp categorization of clinical manifestations has to some degree
been lost and communication between psychiatrists garbled.

The development of psychopharmacology in the last
fifteen years particularly, has given new impetus to the motivation of those who sense the possibility of clearer recognition of entities for which chemical treatment is appropriate.
Amazingly, the initial use of such treatment has corroborated
the clinical acuity of those psychiatrists of more than one-
half century ago whose concepts and thinking were brought
to application by Kraepelin.

An interesting historical analogy is presented by neurosyphilis. With Von Jauregg's effective fever treatment as
an impetus, the diagnosis of paresis became much more
exact, both clinically and by the development of suitable
laboratory methods. In the management of the schizophrenic and depressive psychoses, good clinicians are now
motivated to achieve sharper distinctions and differentiations so that more effective therapy can be carried out. The

adequate diagnosis has social and economic as well as individual benefits.

CRITERIA FOR DIAGNOSIS

In the absence of associated or concomitant physiologic and chemical manifestations susceptible to recording and measurement, psychiatric nosology is dependent in the functional psychoses upon careful clinical observation and reasoning. The variability and highly individual characteristics of many manifestations of the illness schizophrenia as it confronts us, makes it difficult even for seasoned observers to separate and reassemble the manifestations into coherent nosologic entities. The seduction of words has apparently lured psychiatry off the course of careful clinical relatedness to patients with such illness, and the application of good inductive logic to clinical observation. The lure of words can be seen in a definition found in Bellak's Compendium:

" [Schizophrenia]... ...may range from a relatively purely psychogenic weakness of the ego to afflictions of ego functioning by disturbances brought about by infections, arteriosclerotic, enzymatic, toxic or by traumatic, constitutional or genetic factors; in short by any number of chemogenic, histogenic, genogenic or psychogenic factors, or by any combination thereof. "

Bleuler, shows a somewhat closer relationship to the clinical manifestations, but these are so varied and often elusive that even the master was hard put to recognize, define and classify the clinical evidence of schizophrenia. Bleuler divided the manifestations into fundamental symptoms and accessory symptoms, but in careful perusal of his defining and description, it is evident that the boundaries between fundamental and accessory were diffuse and overlapping.

With modern psychologic testing programs such as the formal intelligence tests (the Stanford-Binet and that of Wechsler) and projective tests (such as Rorschach's and others in common use), the present-day psychiatrist finds it difficult to make clinical manifestations of schizophrenia follow the lines of discrimination suggested by Bleuler's scheme, yet unquestionably his observations continue to have validity and are fundamental to the further development of understanding of the syndrome of schizophrenia.

More recent clinical observations, the extensive experience with psychologic testing programs, and the last decade of experience with psychopharmacologic treatment, have led to a sharper understanding by some psychiatrists of what they mean by the term schizophrenia.

Application of classic inductive logic to development of nosologic entities, requires discrimination between observed factors (parameters) mandatory (necessary) for diagnosis, and those irrelevant or even contraindicative to a diagnosis; and the recognition of such factors, single or in combination, which are conclusive (sufficient) for diagnosis of any given illness. At least the elementary form of the algebra of "sets" and "classes" (Boolian Algebra, symbolic logic) is necessary to clarify and systematize observation and thinking to establish schizophrenia as a nosologic entity. This presentation will avoid meticulous detail, but will apply the related visual diagrams according to the English mathematician, Venn.

In medical science other than psychiatry, factors from anatomy (including x-rays), physiology, chemistry and microbiology, furnish the necessary and sufficient conditions for nosologic determinations (diagnoses). In psychiatry, the development of ego psychology and the attention given to environmental influences, has obscured and brought confusion to the development of nosologic concepts in the definition of schizophrenia and affective psychoses. Philosophic verbal manipulations of the concepts of ego psychology and the supposed identification of certain environmental factors, have been used to re-define the meaning of the word schizophrenia and force the concept into a kind of procrustean "psychodynamic" matrix. An attempt will be made here to revert to the application of simpler, readily recognizable manifestations, psychologic, emotional and behavioral, in the construction of a practical nosologic concept by application of inductive logic along more modern lines.

In modern psychiatry, the diagnosis schizophrenia is applied under two somewhat different but over-lapping conditions. First, in the daily clinical practice of psychiatric medicine, and second in discriminate diagnostic determination of mental illness for research effort involving studies of prognosis, drug effect, neurophysiology, etc. Hopefully, the same differentiation would apply in both circumstances.

The proper separation of patients in the general class "schizophrenia" would not hinder but only promote further useful sub-groupings or total separations of new kinds of groups by more exact methods. A tabulation of diagnostic criteria as generally used at present in the establishment of the diagnosis of schizophrenia is presented in Table 1.

SCHIZOPHRENIA

DIAGNOSTIC CRITERIA

1. THOUGHT DISORDER

   Perception - auditory, tactile, olfactory, visceral

   Cognitive function - delusions, hallucinations
   (not visual)

   Associative function - autism, "concrete" thinking, etc.

   Memory function - delusions, hallucinations

2. AFFECT DISORDER

   Diminution - withdrawal, diminished attention span,
   non-involvement, etc.

   Distortion - euphoria, depression (delusional)

3. MOTOR DISORDER

   Catatonia

   Mannerisms, rituals

   Speech changes - muteness, neologisms, "tongues"

4. BEHAVIOR DISORDER RESULTING FROM OR ASSOCIATED
   WITH ABOVE

   Withdrawal, excitement, religious aspects, assaultiveness,
   sexual aspects, etc.

5. ABSENCE OF ORGANIC PSYCHOTIC (SENSORIAL) AND
   NEUROLOGIC DEFECTS

6. ABSENCE OF PURE AFFECT DISTURBANCE AS IN MAN-
   IA AND DEPRESSION

7. ABSENCE OF BEHAVIORAL MANIFESTATIONS NOT RE-
   SULTING FROM 1, 2, and 3 (AS IN PERSONALITY DIS-
   ORDERS)

There are positive and negative aspects to the diagnosis.
Central to the diagnosis of schizophrenia is thought disorder
which involves perceptive, cognitive, associative and memory
functions. Detailed description and elaboration of each of these
occupies much text-book space. Affect disorder is probably
the fundamental basis of Bleuler's concept of the "split" of
mental function; distortion, diminution and inappropriateness
are the chief characteristics of schizophrenic affect. Motor

disorder occurs variously in the forms of (1) catatonic rigidity that seems to have become a clinical rarity in recent decades, and (2) complicated mannerisms, rituals and speech changes which do not in and of themselves represent behavioral disturbance. The behavioral disorder characteristic of schizophrenia is associated with disorders of thought, affect and motor functioning indicated in the first three categories.

The negative aspects of the diagnosis schizophrenia, have to do with absence of organic sensorial and neurologic defects, absence of pure affect disturbance and absence of behavioral manifestations that do not result from the first three categories. It may be considered that the positive clinical aspects here outlined, represent the necessary conditions for the diagnosis of schizophrenia, but in and of themselves may occur in the normal or non-schizophrenic individual. The negative parameters are the extension of the positive parameters not in the schizophrenic zone.

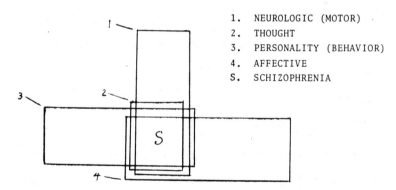

1. NEUROLOGIC (MOTOR)
2. THOUGHT
3. PERSONALITY (BEHAVIOR)
4. AFFECTIVE
S. SCHIZOPHRENIA

VENN DIAGRAM INDICATING COMPONENTS OF CLINICAL SCHIZOPHRENIA

To clarify this concept, Figure 1, a Venn diagram, indicates how these sets fit together to form the sufficient condition for the diagnosis schizophrenia. The intersection of thought disorder, affect disorder, motor disorder and behavior disorder produces the nuclear condition which satisfies the clinical concept of the diagnosis schizophrenia in both positive and negative sense. The areas of organic neurologic defect that do not intersect with thought disorder, affect disorder and the other specific kinds of disorder seen in schizophrenia, may be considered to be associated with the brain syndromes. The pure affect disorder outside the area of intersection can be considered to represent the psychoses of affect, manic-depressive and other depressive reactions, as well as normal fluctuations of affect. The pathologic behavioral manifestations not associated with schizophrenia, represent the disorders of personality. The borderland in which thought disorder does not intersect with the other manifestations may be considered the borderland in which diagnosis is difficult and art is long.

In research applications of the diagnosis schizophrenia, criteria for inclusion of patients should be such that only patients in whom the intersection of these factors is clear and complete would be included. In daily clinical practice, it is of course perfectly justifiable for diagnosis to be something less than perfect as long as careful maintenance of the patient's interest and welfare in the course of treatment is maintained.

CRITERIA FOR IMPROVEMENT

In certain kinds of investigation of drug effect in schizophrenic psychoses, it has become fashionable to use "rating scales" as a means of determining change in patients. The rating scales are lists of manifestations of illness grouped in generally coherent categories. Patients are scored for various characteristics in a quasi-quantitative way according to the intensity of the pathologic manifestations, both before treatment and at varying intervals after. Even though it has generally been found that there is good agreement, as determined by statistical arithmetic, between different raters, it has also generally been found that the "global" rating of a patient's improvement presents a more consistent and reliable assessment of change. The reason for this is probably that the global assessments are chiefly made by nurses and attendants who have a more intimate and continuous relationship with patients, and the formal rating scales are recorded by uninvolved individuals. Rating scales may seem to be a more objective means of assessment of patients, but may well represent as much a measure of the training and indoctrination of the rater as of the symptoms in the patient. Since this presentation is not primarily a critique of rating scales, this subject will not be pursued further. Suffice it to say that the rating scales have been able to indicate some degree of change in patients treated by various means, particularly with pharmacologic agents, but this assessment of change does not represent fulfillment of clinical requirements for assessment of restoration of useful life patterns.

Over the years, the author has applied certain criteria for determining and rating improvement in patients treated for schizophrenic psychoses. This can be called the A B C D system of rating treatment results. The criteria have, in a number of publications, been given in narrative form.

IMPROVEMENT CRITERIA

(A)   Patients who have recovered from all active psychotic
manifestations, particularly have lost all delusions
and hallucinations; have insight into previous delusions and hallucinations; have adequate affect, social
and industrial adaptive capacity, equal at least to the
premorbid level; and have no overt hostility, particularly to the hospital or its staff.

(B) Individuals who have recovered from most psychotic
manifestations but may not have lost belief in previously present delusional experience, who are able to
make a satisfactory social and industrial adaptation
away from the hospital or in the hospital under privileged conditions, whose improvement may be summarized as "a good social remission".

(C) Patients who have improved from the initial condition
in significant ways, particularly in ability to communicate verbally, in diminution or absence of assaultiveness, incontinence, denudativeness, and other gross
manifestations of psychosis, and in some diminution
of psychopathologic manifestations such as delusions
and hallucinations without actual resolution of these.

(D) Patients who have improved only slightly or not at all.

The same material in tabular form is presented in
Table 2 which indicates the relative simplicity of the criteria
for everyday use.

IMPROVEMENT CRITERIA

CRITERION / GRADE	A	B	C	D
Social adaptation	++	+	±	0
Work capacity	++	+	±0	0
"Insight"	++	±	0	0
Ability to communicate	++	+	0	0
Hostility (suspiciousness, assaultiveness)	0	±	+	+
Delusions	0	±0	+	++
Hallucinations	0	0	+	++
Incontinence, denudativeness	0	0	±	++

Patients who have improved to a useful degree, clearly
are segregated from those who have not, with minimal or
absent confusion at the border between groups.   Many of
these characteristics, particularly ability to work, agreeable
relating, and hostility, can be recognized without professional
training.   Certain manifestations such as delusions and hallucinations, and insight, require not only professional competence, but clinical intimacy with the patient.   The material
of Table 2 lends itself readily to the application of the symbolic logic of classes.

There has been, particularly in the formally organized
"controlled" investigations of drug effect, inability to discriminate between drugs which, to most careful clinical observers, show differences in anti-psychotic and other
effects.   The relatively brief periods, usually not more than
twelve weeks, of treatment that have been used in these investigations, give insufficient time for discrimination between

drugs, particularly between phenothiazines. In some previously reported work, the author has indicated certain kinds of
difference between drugs on one hand, and equivalence of
drugs with differences in patients on the other.

Table 3
Series Treatment

A.   Two Series Each Over 1 Year

1st Drug
Chlorpromazine

2d Drug
Triflupromazine, Prochlorperazine, Perphenazine,
Trifluoperazine or Fluphenazine

Result	A	B	C	D
1st Drug	58	151	299	48
2d Drug	71	154	298	33

B.   Two Series Each Over 1 Year

1st Drug
Prochlorperazine, Perphenazine or Triflupromazine

2d Drug
Prochlorperazine, Perphenazine, Triflupromazine,
Trifluoperazine or Fluphenazine

Result	A	B	C	D
1st Drug	5	20	71	17
2d Drug	3	22	77	11

Table 4
Treated 6 Months Or More Each Drug

A.	A	B	C	D
1st Treatment Trifluoperazine	2	7	27	4
2d Treatment Fluphenazine	2	12	25	1
2d Treatment Fluphenazine C and D results of first treatment	1	4	25	1

B.				
1st Treatment Fluphenazine	0	9	24	5
2d Treatment Trifluoperazine	2	9	24	3
2d Treatment Trifluoperazine C and D results of first treatment	1	3	22	3

These findings are illustrated in Tables 3 and 4 which clearly indicate that chlorpromazine is less effective in treating chronic psychotic patients over long periods than more intensely active phenothiazines such as trifluoperazine and fluphenazine. However, differences between patients probably determine whether trifluoperazine or fluphenazine would be most effective in relieving psychotic manifestations. The possibility of time being an important determining factor for these two drugs is not ruled out. It may well be that treatment for two years regardless of drug change, is capable of lifting a patient from the C and D to the A or B level of improvement.

It may be indicated at this point that necessary conditions for rating improvement from treatment in psychotic states, should avoid to the greatest degree possible, subjective and doctrinal bias of the rater, that the criteria for rating should represent practical, readily recognizable parameters (ability to work, carry out satisfactory social relationships, maintain grooming, etc.), and that resolution of gross psychopathology (delusions, hallucinations, etc.) must be determined at a professional level. The components of these factors (A, B, C, D) may be considered sufficient for valid recognition of improvement from the psychotic state.

SUMMARY

Criteria for establishment of the diagnosis schizophrenia as a nosologic entity by application of the logic of classes, have been described. Criteria for the determination of improvement in which "global" characteristics readily subject to clinical observation, are applied, have been described and tabulated. Use of such diagnostic and therapeutic criteria will help to make investigations more reproduceable and results less debatable.

D. Goldman, M.D., 179 East McMillan Street, Cincinnati 19, Ohio

LONG-TERM PROGNOSIS IN SCHIZOPHRENIA BASED ON RORSCHACH FINDINGS: THE LTPTI

ZYGMUNT A. PIOTROWSKI

One major function of clinical practice is the predicting of the course and outcome of illness. The usual assumption is that short term prognosis is easier and more valid than long term prognosis. Short term prognosis in general is less likely to be thrown off by unforeseen and unforeseeable factors. Long term test prediction of the course of schizophrenia seems to be one exception to the usual rule. The marked fluctuations in behavior and achievement which frequently occur after the onset of the manifest psychosis account for the difficulty in short-term prognosis in the early years of the psychosis. In the first years of schizophrenia the patient's behavior reflects not only the crippling effects of the psychosis but also his attempts at self cure which may be as maladaptive as the disease. It is very difficult to differentiate reliably and accurately between the effects of the chronic personality change and the effects of the

- --

This study was supported, in part, by a grant from the Research Council, Thirty-third Degree, Scottish Rite Freemasonry, Northern Jurisdiction.
- -

patient's transient disturbance associated with his re-
alization that the personality change he has experienced
threatens his survival. The awareness of the deep personality change as well as the ability to do something
about it, successfully or not, decrease gradually as the
emotional and intellectual impoverishment caused by the
psychosis increases or becomes chronic. Marked personality
changes become rare three to five years after the onset,
and then the lasting personality change can be more easily
and accurately evaluated[1].

Psychiatric clinical diagnoses of incipient
schizophrenia are notoriously unreliable with the result
that 40% to 50% of incipient schizophrenics are diagnosed
neurotic or manic-depressive, and the correct diagnosis
is given only years later[2]. Thus research findings may
be obscured for want of adequate independent criteria for
differential diagnosis. There is a way out: basing
one's conclusions on findings obtained from patients who
have been followed for more than three years after the
onset of symptoms. The LTPTI (Long-term Prognostic Test
Index) was developed in this way. Only cases with verified follow-up diagnoses of schizophrenia were included
in the standardization group of 33 patients, male and female. Dr. Nolan D. C. Lewis re-diagnosed these patients
at the end of the follow-up interviews and anamnesis.
The patients' ages varied between 16 and 36 years at the
time of the first pre-follow-up Rorschach examination.
Each patient was hospitalized for three to four months
at the time of the first pre-follow-up examination. The
intellectual level varied from low average to superior.
No patient with a suspected or demonstrated organic brain

disorder was included. Schizophrenia was not recognized in all cases at the time of the initial testing, but had to be unmistakable at the time of the last follow-up psychiatric interview [3]

In order to be classified as improved, the patient had to improve in all three of the following criteria: (a) Feeling about self. To be considered improved, the patient had to feel much more comfortable, less anxious, more self-confident, more hopeful, more relaxed;

(b) Thinking. His thought processes had to have become more realistic and/or less autistic, more consistent and relevant to his life problems; (c) Work output. The patient had to demonstrate an ability to achieve more with less effort or at a faster pace compared with his functioning preceding and immediately following the onset of the psychosis.

The patient had to improve in all three of these areas to be classified as improved; otherwise he was considered unimproved. Some patients remained "essentially the same" in the sense that they were free from obvious psychotic symptoms between periods of delusional or regressive behavior during the follow-up period. They were included in the unimproved group because they had these psychotic attacks during the follow-up period. A minority of patients became noticeably worse. The number of patients however was too small to sub-divide them into more than just two groups: improved and unimproved. In evaluating the LTPTI and its application to clinical practice, it is necessary to keep in mind our criteria of improvement and the manner in which the diagnosis was established: at the end of a follow-up period of more than three but

less than ten years, to assure validity. A validly established diagnosis of schizophrenia is a prerequisite for a
relevant application of the LTPTI to a Rorschach test record.

THE LONG-TERM-PROGNOSTIC-TEST-INDEX FACTORS

The Rorschach records of the improved schizophrenics were compared with the records of the unimproved
ones. The analysis produced 14 signs [4,5] which were
subsequently reduced to 12 by combining four of them into two. Four validation studies were done. Two of them
were "blind"; this means that those who scored the test
records for LTPTI signs did not know which of the patients
were improved and which were not; also the scorers did not
classify the patients as improved or unimproved. The Med-
field Foundation group of 18 male and female schizophrenics was one of the two for whom the LTPTI predictions
were written "blind". The LTPTI placed 83 percent of them
into the correct classification. The other "blind" group
consisted of the 68 Lyons VAH patients all of whom were
male with a large proportion of chronic cases; 75 percent
of them were correctly classified on the basis of their
LTPTI scores. The two remaining validation studies were
of patients known to some of the scorers and both yielded
percentages of correct classification of over eighty [6]
For every patient with an LTPTI score of 2 points or more
the prediction was made that he had remained unimproved,
while it was predicted in the case of those who scored
no more than +1 point on the LTPTI that he had improved
during the follow-up period.

The 12 LTPTI signs can be divided into two
groups. One contains indicators of personality impoverishment, i.e., a significantly reduced psychosocial re-

sponsiveness to the environment and reduced inner mental living. Absence of human content, low percentage of sharply perceived forms, paucity of movement and color responses are signs of the personality impoverishment. The other group consists of signs which reflect defective reasoning. This group of signs has diagnostic as well as prognostic significance.

The LTPTI signs as well as the reliability and validation studies are described in detail in "Evaluation of outcome in schizophrenia"[6]. Eight of the 12 LTPTI signs have a weight of plus two points. The exceptions are: Sign 1 with +3 points, signs 9 and 10, each with a +1 point; and sign 12 with a -2 point weight. The LTPTI score is the algebraic sum of the weights of the individual signs found in a test record. Each sign has been scored once regardless of how frequently it occurred in the test records. Refinements of calculating the total LTPTI score have been suggested[7].

Altogether 259 schizophrenics were followed for at least three years with an average follow-up period of six and one-half years. The first available Rorschach test records of all 259 patients were scored for the presence or absence of each of the 12 signs and then a correlation matrix of phi-coefficients was computed and an orthogonal factor analysis was made by means of the varimax method[7]. Four factors, statistically well differentiated, emerged. For conceptual clarity each test sign was scored only on one factor, using the loading criterion of .30 or above. Only three signs had a loading of over .30 on two factors, and none on more than two. In these three instances the sign was assigned to the factor with the higher loading. When combined, the four factors accounted for 53 percent of the total variance contained in the 12

signs. It is worth pointing out that there was no significant association between any of the 12 signs or the entire LTPTI scale and such emotional attitudes as degree
of cooperation and paranoid hostility. On the other hand,
there was significant association between the LTPTI or its
parts and the quality of thinking and work output. A description of the four LTPTI factors and the indication of
the degree to which each sign is associated with its factor follows.

FACTOR A: CONSTRICTION. - This factor is
indicated by signs 11 (.77), 7 (.76), 10 (.76) and 9 (.65).
It accounts for 39 percent of the variance. It is measured
by four signs. Sign 11 is said to be present when the
test record contains no human movement responses (8, p.136)
Adults without any human movements are unimaginative and
do not understand differing styles of relating to others
in personally vital matters. Such individuals are not
concerned with communication with others. Sign 7 is scored
when there is a complete absence of responses with human
content, whole human beings or parts of them, regardless
of whether or not movement is seen. Sexual responses,
secondary as well as primary, and anatomical responses,
i.e., parts of the body visible only as a result of dis-
section, are not considered human content but constitute
separate content categories. Absence of human content reveals indifference to the motivation of others and lack of
interest in the subjective experiences of others, usually
associated with strong hostility toward people.

Sign 10 is scored when there are no more than
five different content categories (8, p.340) represented
in the record. Sign 9 is scored when the record contains

no more than five of the 11 possible basic determinants
(8,p.402). Human movements, color, and form responses
are the most important determinants. Every determinant
is counted only once and the frequency with which it appears in the record is disregarded. Such a marked reduction
in content and determinant variety reflects a reduced
emotional and intellectual responsiveness to the environment, with a subsequent marked reduction in the capacity
for active and effective handling of problems of adjustment and survival. Most schizophrenics with a dominant
Factor A complain of somatic illnesses, displacing the
causes of their regression, thus alleviating their anxiety
but seeking the wrong type of cure. These schizophrenic
patients usually have regressed gradually, at least in
the last years before examination, and have moderate chronic
depressions. Those who score high on Factor A tend to be
withdrawn and apathetic. Factor A is not pathognomonic
of schizophrenia but occurs also in patients deteriorated
as a result of confirmed organic brain disorders.

FACTOR B: DOUBTFUL PERCEPTION OR INTERPRETATION.
This factor is indicated by signs 3 (.68) and 5 (.51). It
accounts for 22 percent of the variance. Patients scoring
high on Factor B have a conspicuously defective sense of
reality. Both perceptual and conceptual functioning are
inadequate and peculiar. Factor B patients have great
difficulty in differentiating both perceptually and conceptually between imagination and sensation. In the early
or mild phase of the psychosis, these schizophrenics have
periods during which they experience three kinds of cognition.

They can tell the difference between sensation and imagination but perceive as well a third type of reality in
which the two are confused and inseparable. This distortion of reality is apprehended as something half real
and half unreal and frightens the patients because they
cannot decide what it is they are perceiving. At the
same time these patients usually feel that they have undergone an undesirable and uncontrollable personality change
which further stimulates doubt regarding their own existence and the identity of others. These states of fusion
of·imagination and sensation are sporadic in the incipient
phases of the psychosis and tend to become chronic as the
psychosis advances. The rarity of the episodes, however,
only adds to the patient's horror because he can still
tell the difference and appreciate the threat.

The essential feature of Sign 3 is the vagueness
and tentativeness with which the patient sees the percept
(i.e., the visual image projected onto a specific blot
area). One aspect of this sign is the difficulty which
the patient experiences when he is asked to show how his
image fits the respective blot area. Sometimes the patient
spontaneously expresses surprise at his own percepts. The
difficulty in locating the image on the blot and the perplexity which the patient verbalizes resemble similar reaction patterns in cerebral organic cases [6,p.315]. At times
the patient is conceptually confused. He does not know
then what kind of image he is trying to convey. Contami-
nations which are pathognomonic of schizophrenia when defined strictly [8,p.74], also belong in the sign 3 category. It is impossible to tell what defies the patient's
comprehension of his own response beside his own vagueness of perception, imagination, or thought. All three

mental functions are mixed and confused in test responses
which qualify under sign 3. The inability to reach a final decision or create a good percept is very different
from the reaction of a hypercritical obsessive neurotic
who may also find it difficult to commit himself to a percept. In the obsessive it is the very clarity of the distinction he makes between perception and imagination which
creates the problem. The neurotic with normal reasoning
knows what he is doing. The sign 3 schizophrenic gropes
in the dark.

Sign 5 indicates what might be described as "onto-
logical mixup". Different types of reality, empirical and
conceptual, concrete and abstract, are treated as if they
were equivalent. Sign 5 reflects a significant breakdown
of interpretive attitude. This may or may not puzzle the
patient. It reflects also a more serious defect in the
sense of reality than indicated by sign 3. The main
difference between sign 3 and sign 5 can be described as
follows. Sign 5 responses are given with apparent self-
confidence; the patient seems to know what he is doing
and approve of it. By contrast, the most characteristic
feature of sign 3 responses is the uncertainty displayed
by the patient; he does not seem to know what he is perceiving or saying. It is possible that the sign 5 responses
reflect a more regressed type of perceiving and reasoning
since they are free of doubt and self-criticism. The two
signs are statistically associated. An example of a
sign 3 response is this: "Some sort of insect. Looks
kind of poisonous, does not look attractive to the eye.
Looks like some frog. I don't know what it looks like exactly. Such things I don't know" (gray areas of pl. III).

A characteristic sign 5 response is this one: "There are the men's hearts (middle red) meeting together; their chests are frayed where the hearts got out" (men, grays of pl. III).

Patients with high Factor B scores are relatively rare. Factor B responses tend to appear at the onset, usually acute, of a chronic paranoid form of schizophrenia. It may be associated with intensified interests in varied intellectual problems and pursuits which of course are handled inadequately. Such patients are attracted by what is new to them and sometimes feel that their psychotic state constitutes an expansion rather than a regression of the personality and its capacities. Factor B seems to be pathognomonic of schizophrenia and therefore can be used as a diagnostic as well as a prognostic indicator. It reveals an escape from the external, empirical reality into the world of fantasy.

FACTOR C: INAPPROPRIATELY APPLIED ENERGY. - This factor consists of signs 2 (.62), 6 (.57), 1 (.55) and 12 (-.43). Twenty-two percent of the accounted-for variance can be assigned to this factor. Patients scoring high on Factor C use their energy inappropriately and ineffectually. They are under-controlled. The great majority of patients with much Factor C appear helpless and incapable of alleviating the effects of the psychosis. The psychotic personality defects are manifest in thinking, feeling and acting. Sign 2 is credited when there is intellectual perseveration. (Rpt or repetition). This sign frequently occurs also in the cerebral organic cases and less frequently in unimproved schizophrenics. It consists of repeating a visual image which had been used at least twice before in the same test instead of a more appropriate visual image. Rpt indicates that imagination has been markedly reduced, thus making the patient more helpless against the environment. Perseveration with color response content or sexual imagery is not considered Rpt.

Sign 6 refers to an absurdly inconclusive explanation given in a matter-of-fact tone to at least one percept. The patient characteristically is unconcerned whether the examiner has understood him. One variety of sign 6 behavior is to repeat the response expecting the repetition to be accepted as a logical and satisfactory explanation. Sometimes the explanations are quite irrelevant; asked what was unusual about the "strange human being" the patient "saw", he answered "sick from birth," and could say no more about it. Sign 6 can be scored only when the patient's reasoning is logically inadequate. Such inadequacies rarely appear without an inquiry. The patients may get quite confused perceptually. Asked how the whole of pl. VII resembled an elephant, the patient went into a long, complicated and ineffectual explanation of how the plate would have to be changed and complemented to make an elephant. If every change suggested by the patient had been made, the resulting image would not resemble an elephant or any other known creature. Sign 1 is scored when the sum of weighted color responses exceeds the sum of human movements by at least 3 points and there is no more than one human movement in the test record. This combination of test components reveals great responsiveness to environmental stimulation combined with a reduced capacity for adequate adaptation.

Sign 12, producing at least five human movement responses, is the only one which is positively correlated with improvement, and negatively with all four LTPTI factors. Its highest negative correlation is with Factor C. Intellectual and general personality deterioration is smallest in schizophrenics and brain disorder cases who produce many human movement responses.

Schizophrenics with a high Factor C are clinically conspicuous through their hyperkinetic and peculiar behavior. They are restless and have no persistent purpose. Their associations are bizarre and are readily verbalized. Many of these acute cases improve up to one year, although the eventual outcome is unfavorable in at least 80% of the cases if the LTPTI score is high. The outstanding trait of Factor C schizophrenics is the excessively high arousal level which has disruptive effects.

FACTOR D: SPORADIC ARBITRARINESS. - This factor is positively correlated with sign 4 (.78) and negatively with sign 8 (-.57). This factor accounts for 18 percent of the variance. Patients scoring high on Factor D display from time to time an extraordinary arbitrariness in making statements or decisions usually without being able to explain adequately or justify their conclusions. In fact, they are not even concerned with the validity of their thoughts or decisions as viewed by others. Sign 4 is scored when the patient has given at least one indeterminate form response with apparent self-confidence. Such responses have some definite meaning for the patient even though he cannot communicate it. Moreover, he treats his response with utter lack of concern for adequacy of fit between image and blot area. This uncritical attitude toward the response is an essential requirement for sign 4.

If an indeterminate response, given with self-confidence, is deliberate, in order to create a humorous effect, perhaps, it is not scored as sign 4. Similarly, deliberate punning is not a manifestation of schizophrenia although the logical form of puns resembles schizophrenic thinking; the essential difference lies in the intention and control of reality which the normal individual displays when punning. The schizophrenic "puns" despite himself and without knowing it. The arbitrariness associated with sign 4 responses is illustrated in the following: "A prehistoric animal that nobody knows anything about". The patient claimed that he recognized this animal of no known shape in one of the ink-blots. An even more distinctly indeterminate response is

this: "Half of nothing". The patient implied that he "saw" something definite. More frequent but less extreme examples of sign 4 are: "A bat. Not exactly, but of course it would have to have horns", referring to the whole of pl. V which has **horn-like** extensions in the center of the upper edge. "That's a city, but I don't recognize it". The indeterminateness of the image must be accompanied by behavior which reflects the patient's feeling that he has produced something acceptable and specific.

There is a negative correlation between Factor D and sign 8 which is credited when the percentage of sharply conceived forms falls below 60. The following test components are used in calculating the F+%: F, Fc and Fc'; when these three categories total less than 10, it is advisable to include the animal and inanimate movements for the sake of reliability [8,p.104]. The negative correlation between low percentages of sharply conceived forms and sporadic arbitrariness has two implications. One is that patients who score high on Factor D usually have high quali-

ty form responses, or in other words,their thinking is usually realistic [8,p.100]. The other implication is that the
arbitrary indeterminate responses are conspicuous because of
the usually adequate reasoning. The disregard for accuracy
and validity is a sporadic event.

Schizophrenics with high Factor D scores show
relatively least thought disorders. Their delusional
states are relatively rare. They are likely to explain
their sporadic unrealistic behavior as a result of emotional
stress or environmental influences. One can have good
rapport with such patients, for, on the whole, they themselves try hard to regain the pre-morbid level of functioning.

DISCUSSION

The four LTPTI factors represent four different
ways in which the patient can handle schizophrenia. These
four ways of coming to grips with the psychosis provide
a meaningful classification of schizophrenics with practical implications both for understanding the patient and
for psychotherapy. This is more meaningful than sub-divid-
ing the patients according to their symptoms which often
change and which in addition have very little prognostic
significance. A symptom is always a sign of a disease process, but frequently it reflects more about what the patient
does about his disease than about the severity and course of
the disease itself. Which of the alternatives for handling
the psychosis is selected will depend on the degree of damage already caused, the pre-morbid assets of the personality
and the effectiveness with which the adjustment diminishes

the resultant subjective (mainly anxiety) and objective (maladaptation) handicaps.

The proportion of schizophrenics who eventually improve to those who were found to be unimproved on long-term follow-up is almost the same as the proportion of schizophrenics with low LTPTI scores (+1 point or less) to those with high LTPTI scores (at least +2 points). The 259 patients in our validation studies were divided into 77 improved (29.7%) and 182 (70.3%) unimproved on the basis of clinical psychiatric evaluations at the time of the follow-up. Of the same patients, 83 (32.0%) had LTPTI scores of +1 point or less, and 176 (68%) had LTPTI scores of at least +2 points. These percentages agreed very well with those found in other large scale long-term follow-up clinical investigations [6]. Schizophrenia is debilitating for life in about 70% of patients. The personalities even of those who eventually improve continue to show effects although the patients may not suffer any longer from primary thought disorders. Apparently the struggle with delusional thinking and emotional withdrawal which characterizes schizophrenics in acute psychotic states leaves a lasting mark. All who have experienced a schizophrenic psychosis change in a characteristically similar manner. The concern with what is real as opposed to mere appearance remains with them. This explains why it is frequently possible to make a clinical diagnosis of schizophrenia which will be confirmed with time without knowing the content of the patient's subjective experiences; the patient's attitudes about thought processes and feeling, both in himself and others, betray a peculiar deviation characteristic of schizophrenia.

Actually, specific symptoms are of little value in evaluating the degree of intellectual and emotional regression and in making prognostic predictions, with the exception of primary thought disorders occurring in a state of clear consciousness and no apparent emotional stress. [1] E. Bleuler observed that both the mildest and the most disturbed schizophrenics can perform the same overt acts, both innocuous and dangerous. Further, he made a remarkable statement which does not seem to have been quoted or commented on in the literature. He said that schizophrenic deterioration can be measured by the percentage of time the patient is delusional rather than by the severity of symptoms. The LTPTI signs 3, 4, 5 and 6 pertaining to delusions and other thought disorders confirm this observation. The reason for lack of comment on this important Bleulerian measure of schizophrenic deterioation probably is lack of experience. Only when one follows many schizophrenics over many years, can one acquire the evidence which makes it possible to submit the Bleulerian principle to validation.

Two of our patients, each of whom was followed for more than fifteen years, illustrate Bleuler's principle well. One of them, a married, childless man, was a fastidious ladies' custom tailor with a wealthy clientele. His manner was impeccable. He never touched the ladies, but had female assistants do the fitting under his direction. During one fitting, he heard suddenly a vulgar male voice laughing at him sarcastically and making gross homosexual proposals. The patient reacted with fear and amazement, but shrugged it off as an illusion. The frequency of this auditory hallucination increased from several times a week to several times a day and drove the patient to seek psychiatric treatment for the first time in his life, in his late thirties. The patient was discharged as an obsessive-compulsive neurotic. The following observations were used as arguments against schizophrenia: the patient experienced the hallucination as something absurd and foreign to him, and not as an integral part of his personality; he had some control over the hallucinatory experience since he had reported being able to ignore the voice and even working rapport with his psychotherapist. The patient returned within 8 months after discharge with unmistakable signs of schizophrenia. The voice had became more frequent and more insistent, disturbing the patient more than ever. A commitment to a state hospital followed. During the last years of the follow-up the patient was continually hallucinating; he wrote letters to the superintendent of the hospital asking to be placed in a building without voices. He had become unable to carry on an emotionally meaningful and rational conversation. Another patient, also in his thirties, married, childless and also obsessive-compulsive and also diagnosed as a neurotic at first, sought admission because despite his cleanliness, he felt lice crawling on his hands and was compelled to remove them with great care, making sure they fell into a waste basket. He too, was committed within a year and at the end of the follow-up period could not talk sensibly and rationally, automatically performing his ritual except for meal times.

In the incipient phase of the psychosis which may precede the manifest phase by many years, the delusional states may be rare and mild. It is very difficult to meas-

ure the increase of these states through occasional interviews until they influence overt behavior conspicuously.
The Rorschach technique, which consists in free associations

to indefinite and ambiguous visual stimuli, is an extremely sensitive instrument. It reveals the quality of thinking, goal direction, emotional attitudes and - which is of
greatest importance for diagnosis and prognosis in schizophrenia - the functioning of the sense of reality. The
sensitivity of the Rorschach even to slight disturbances
of the sense of reality has proved to be one of the techniques' greatest assets. The Rorschach, properly interpreted, can indeed be compared to an x-ray of mental functions
relevant to the individual's intellectual as well as psychosocial behavior.

CONCLUSIONS

Predictions of human behavior fail unless potential as well as actual behavior is considered. Since many
actions are mutually exclusive, overt behavior is necessarily simpler and more consistent than potential behavior.
Visual imagery provides one way of tapping this reservoir
of potential. The imagination is not limited to what is
physically or even logically possible. Thus it reveals
more about psychological complexities and especially dereistic motivation than action. Predictive power increases
when this tool is used in addition to other available information. However definitions of schizophrenia differ,

all include disorders of thinking and of the sense of reality. The basic empirical data of Rorschach perceptana-
lysis are free associations to indeterminate visual stimuli.

The ambiguity of the stimuli, the freeing effect of the
unstructured task, the absence of clear criteria for evaluating the adequacy of responses - all facilitate the manifestation of the subject's actual feelings and thought
processes. Schizophrenic thought disorders appear with
relatively greatest frequency during the Rorschach examination when the patient, in complying with the task of making
something definite out of an inkblot, cannot help being
creative and self-revealing. Thus his responses reflect
the individual's habitual ways of reacting and the range
of his potential actions. The interpretations of the ink-
blots vary in the degree to which the projected images corres-
pond to their referents in the physical world. This evaluation of goodness of fit provides the Rorschach test with
a built-in measure of the sense of reality, and explains
why it is so sensitive even to the mildest forms of schizophrenia and to personality traits relevant for prognosis.

The LTPTI predictions depend almost exclusively
on personality liabilities, especially intellectual ones,
rather than assets. In general, Rorschach records of schizophrenics who failed to improve resembled records of patients
with confirmed organic brain damage [9]. There were also
differences, the main one being an occasional response on
a higher imaginative level, or with a bizarre or much more
unusual content, than organic patients produce or are
capable of producing. The LTPTI thus differentiates
between two groups of schizophrenics, those who eventually
improve and those who do not, to a high degree of accuracy.
These two groups may have different etiologies and they
certainly require different treatment programs.

REFERENCES

1. Bleuler, E. <u>Dementia Praecox or the Group of Schizophrenias</u>. Intern. U. Press, New York, 1950 (Ist ed., 1911).

2. Piotrowski, Z. A. and Lewis, N. D. C. An experimental Rorschach diagnostic aid for some forms of schizophrenia. Amer. J Psychiat. <u>107</u>, 360, 1950.

3. Lewis, N. D. C. and Piotrowski, Z. A. Clinical diagnosis of manic-depressive psychosis. In <u>Depression</u>. P. Hoch and J. Zubin, eds. Grune & Stratton, New York. P. 25, 1954.

4. Piotrowski, Z. A. and B. Bricklin. A long-term prognostic criterion for schizophrenics based on Rorschach data. Psychiat. Quart. Suppl. <u>32</u>, 315, 1958.

5. Piotrowski, Z. A. and Bricklin, B. A second validation of a long-term Rorschach prognostic index for schizophrenic patients. J. Consult. Psychol. <u>25</u>, 123, 1961.

6. Piotrowski, Z. A. and Efron, H. Y. Evaluation of outcome in schizophrenia: The Long-Term-Prognostic-Test-Index. In <u>Psychopathology of Schizophrenia</u>. P. Hoch and J. Zubin, eds. Grune & Stratton, New York. P. 312, 1966.

7. Efron, H. Y. and Piotrowski, Z. A. A factor analytic study of the Rorschach prognostic index. J. Proj. Techn. <u>30</u>, 179, 1966.

8. Piotrowski, Z. A. <u>Perceptanalysis: A Fundamentally Reworked, Expanded and Systematized Rorschach Method</u>. 2nd print. Ex Libris, Philadelphia, 19103 (2217 Spruce St), 1965.

9. Piotrowski, Z. A. The prognostic possibilities of the Rorschach method in insulin treatment. Psychiat. Quart. <u>12</u>, 679, 1938.

Z. A. Piotrowski, Ph.D., The Jefferson Medical College of Philadelphia.

1025 Walnut Street, Philadelphia, Pennsylvania 19107

THE DIAGNOSIS OF SCHIZOPHRENIA BY QUESTIONNAIRES AND OBJECTIVE PERSONALITY TESTS

RAYMOND B. CATTELL

1. The Direction of Development of Psychological Tests

Although no psychiatrist or psychologist would be content to make a diagnosis by psychological tests alone, there is no doubt that every year new devices in this area continue to offer a more powerful addition to certainty of diagnosis. Every far-sighted person, no matter what the scientific discipline in which he works, must subscribe to the view that scientific progress moves upon a foundation of more exact measurement, and psychiatry is no exception to this need to acquire instruments. Let us hope that test devices will be increasingly applied, for every science can point to some major break-through which has followed upon, and been made possible by, a major advance in capacity to measure.

Unfortunately, not all psychological testing is measurement in the true sense. Anyone who looks at Buros' Yearbook of Mental Measurement cannot help being overcome by the immense variation in test instruments offered to him. He may justifiably ask, however, how many of these are necessary, how many are, in any sense, effective, and whether it might not be possible to settle on a minimal set of measurement instruments that would give maximum information upon the personality of any given individual. The school of psychological measurement which has given greatest attention to this problem of economy may be called

the structural measurement approach. The aim of structural

measurement is first to find the functional unities in the per-

sonality, and then to aim test specifically at these targets, vali-

dating each test by the degree to which it demonstrably measures

the natural trait or function intended.

The means by which these natural functional unities are found

may initially be either clinical or correlational. However, final

demonstration normally requires precise correlations of a variety

of observations to check that the component behaviors "go together",

as if by an underlying unitary influence. Factor analysis, when used

with sufficient skill and insight, has provided the chief avenue to

the more precise discovery of these functions. It showed its power

first in the early part of this century in the discovery of the primary

abilities by Thurstone, and the definition of general mental capacity

by Spearman, as well as in the recent demonstration of two distinct

powers in the intelligence, through the work of Horn (1966), of

Hebb (1942), of Cattell (1963), and others. However, it has been

the systematic application of these methods, in programmatic re-

search over the last twenty years, by Cattell (1957), Eysenck (1953),

Guilford (1959), and others to personality and motivational data as

such, which has provided us with the kind of knowledge most use-

ful to the psychiatrist.

Before seeing just how this structured measurement helps

the clinician, let us take the briefest possible overview to see

what twenty years of progress has done to the measurement of

traits in the normal individual. The historical development in

this field has been, first, from abilities to personality and motiv-

ation traits, as just mentioned, and, secondly, from the normal

to the abnormal. The latter may or may not be an ideal order,

since it can be argued that some of the features of the normal personality are better understood in their exaggerated expression in pathological behavior. On the other hand, any psychiatrist who wishes to go beyond the mere docketing of individuals in diagnostic syndrome classifications has the need to refer abnormal developments to normal processes, common to all humanity, though perhaps carried to extreme values in the patient. Certainly, the trend in psychiatry appears to have been in the direction of understanding pathology as a functional disorder, which means in terms of measurement, that the abnormal condition needs to be understood as unusual combinations and patterns of essentially normal functions.

The new, structured measurement, however, has a more diagnostic purpose rather than merely a descriptive one. It aims to understand the pattern and balance of forces which "explain" the particular pathological development. It cannot be claimed at the present moment that the measurement of personality factors has gone as far as it should in the direction of producing such explanations, but it has every hope of doing so if psychiatrists and psychologists apply themselves with a greater regard for the possibilities in such measurement than many have yet shown. In any case as a general scientific principle, we must expect that the laws and explanatory principles are more likely to emerge from a firm basis of systematic measurement than from merely qualitative clinical impressions, and certainly we shall not get far by approaches which merely apply a collection of psychological "tests" unrelated to demonstrated unitary structures. Let us, therefore, see what measuring devices are available and what preliminary conclusions have been reached, notably in regard to the present topic of schizophrenia.

2. The Findings by Questionnaire Scales

Psychological measurement can be pursued broadly through two media: (1) questionnaire data, in which the patient tries to report his own problem, as in the consulting room, and (2) objective tests, by which we mean tests in which the patient responds with certain actual performances in miniature situations and receives a diagnosis made in terms of the behavior itself. Projection of misperception tests were an early form of such devices, as in the Rorschach and the TAT, but a far more extensive development has occurred through the 300 or 400 types of tests developed by Cattell and Warburton recently (1967). Brief descriptions of the design and properties of these two kinds of media, with respect to structural research in both personality and motivation measurement, is given in the recent Comprehensive Textbook of Psychiatry by Freedman and Kaplan (1967, page 388). In the present section, an attempt will be made very briefly to designate the results in the questionnaire medium, leaving to the next section the discussion of objective findings.

Extensive factor analyses of varieties of questionnaire items, primarily normal in their range, have yielded about a dozen factors in the case of the Guilford Questionnaire and sixteen in the case of the present writer's 16 Personality Factor Questionnaire (Cattell, Eber, and Tatsuoka, 1969). The 16 P. F. yields an anxiety measurement and an extraversion measurement, as in the scales of Eysenck, but by the more precise route of compiling what are called second-order factors. Thus, one administration of the 16 P. F. is enough to yield both the primary factors, e.g., ego strength, intelligence, super-ego strength, and the second-order derivatives, e.g., anxiety (Cattell, 1963). These sixteen normal dimensions are, of course, not exhaustive of all that is necessary to describe a personality, but they cover most of the dimensions for adequate description of the individual differences among normal people. The 16 P. F., and its adaptation to high school ages, the HSPQ, have been extensively used in clinical work, educational prediction, and industrial selection. They cover such dimensions as ego-strength vs. ego-weakness, dominance vs. submissiveness, affectothymia vs. sizothymia, surgency-desurgency (which is an important dimension among the extraversion dimensions), guilt proneness, ergic tension or level of drive frustration, etc. These factors are briefly set out with explanatory phrases in Table 1. Their unitary nature has also been brought out in parallel researches in France, Germany, Italy, Japan, etc. From these cross cultural studies there seems little doubt that they are functional unities of almost universal application in analyzing personality, though their mode of expression necessarily alters slightly from culture to culture.

Recently, Cattell and Specht (1968), and Delhees and Cattell (1969) extended these analyses from the normal into the abnormal domain of behavior in two main directions. First, they factor analyzed the Minnesota Multi-Phasic Personality Inventory by items, which had not previously been done (only the syndrome scales had been so treated) and made the interesting discovery that it con - tained the sixteen personality dimensions of normal people (projected and modified somewhat in the form of abnormal expressions) plus some five further factors that are strictly pathological and which have not previously been found in items concerned with normal behavior. These pathological dimensions concern hypochondria, schizophrenia, paranoia, etc. and in this respect seem to have correspondence to the usual clinical syndromes, though in the Clinical Analysis Questionnaire, they are not syndromes but underlying source traits Secondly, the work of Delhees (1969), of Cattell (1967), of Bjerstedt (1967), of Friedman et. al. (1963), of Cropley (1966), Weckowicz et. al. (1967), and others has led to a more precise factor analytic definition of the unitary influences in the depression and anxiety area. This work confirms the earlier findings of Cattell and Scheier (1961) on the unitary nature of anxiety and the questionnaire set up to measure it (Scheier and Cattell, The IPAT Anxiety Scale, 1962), and has shown that there

TABLE I A

Brief Descriptions of Some Primary Source Traits Found by Factor Analysis*

Normal Dimensions

Low Score Description	Technical Labels		Standard Symbol	High Score Description
	Low Pole	High Pole		
Reserved, detached, critical, cool	Sizothymia	Affectothymia	A	Outgoing, warmhearted, easygoing, participating
Less intelligent, concrete thinking	Low general mental capacity	Intelligence	B	More intelligent, abstract thinking, bright
Affected by feelings, emotionally less stable, easily upset	Lower ego strength	Higher ego strength	C	Emotionally stable, faces reality, calm
Phlegmatic, relaxed	Low excitability	High excitability	D	Excitable, strident, attention-seeking
Humble, mild, obedient, conforming	Submissiveness	Dominance	E	Assertive, independent, aggressive, stubborn
Sober, prudent, serious, taciturn	Desurgency	Surgency	F	"Happy-go-lucky," heedless, gay, enthusiastic
Expedient, a law to himself, bypasses obligations	Low superego strength	Superego strength	G	Conscientious, persevering, staid, rulebound
Shy, restrained, diffident, timid	Threctia	Parmia	H	Venturesome, socially bold, uninhibited, spontaneous
Tough-minded, self-reliant, realistic, "no nonsense"	Harria	Premsia	I	Tender-minded, dependent, overprotected, sensitive
Trusting, adaptable, free of jealousy, easy to get on with	Alaxia	Protension	L	Suspicious, self-opinionated, hard to fool
Practical, careful, conventional, regulated by external realities, proper	Praxernia	Autia	M	Imaginative, preoccupied with inner urgencies, careless of practical matters, Bohemian
Forthright, natural, artless, sentimental	Artlessness	Shrewdness	N	Shrewd, calculating, wordly, penetrating
Placid, self-assured, confident, serene	Untroubled adequacy	Guilt proneness	O	Apprehensive, worried, depressive, troubled
Conservative, respecting established ideas, tolerant of traditional difficulties	Conservatism	Radicalism	Q1	Experimental, critical, liberal, analytical, free thinking
Group-dependent, a "joiner" and sound follower	Group adherence	Self-sufficiency	Q2	Self-sufficient, prefers to make decisions, resourceful
Casual, careless of protocol, untidy, follows own urges	Weak self sentiment	Strong self sentiment	Q3	Controlled, socially precise, self-disciplined, compulsive
Relaxed, tranquil, torpid, unfrustrated	Low ergic tension	High ergic tension	Q4	Tense, driven, overwrought, fretful

* In ratings and questionnaires, and now embodied in the Clinical Analysis Questionnaire.

TABLE I B

Brief Descriptions of Some Primary Source Traits Found by Factor Analysis*
Dimensions of Pathology

Low Score Description	Technical Labels		Standard Symbol	High Score Description
	Low Pole	High Pole		
Happy, mind works well, ill health is not frightening	Low hypochondriasis	High hypochondriasis	Hyp	Overconcern with bodily functions, health, or disabilities
Contented about surroundings, no death wishes	Zest	Suicidal disgust	Su	Disgusted with life, thoughts or acts of self destruction
Avoids dangerous and adventurous undertakings, little need for excitement	Low adventurous discontent	High adventurous discontent	Dis	Seeks excitement, restless, frustrated, takes risks, tries new things
Poised, confident about surroundings, enjoys meeting people	Low, agitated, depression	High, agitated depression	Agt	Loses temper easily, pacing, fidgeting, disturbing dreams
Relaxed, friendly and cheerful with people	Low, uncaring, hopeless withdrawal	High, uncaring, hopeless withdrawal	Wi	Avoidance of contact and involvement with people, isolation, discomfort with people
Zest for work, energetic, bursting, sleeps soundly	High energy, euphoria	Low energy depression	Lo	Feelings of weariness, worries, cannot get enough sleep
Satisfied with himself, not troubled by guilt	Low guilt and punishment	High guilt and punishment	Gu	Feelings of guilt, dissatisfied with himself, easily angry
Not bothered by unwelcome impulses or ideas	Low psychasthenia	High psychasthenia	As	Insistent repetitive ideas and impulses to perform certain acts
Trusting, not bothered by jealousy or envy	Low, paranoia	High, paranoia	Pa	Believes he is being poisoned, controlled, spied on, mistreated
Avoids engagement in illegal acts or breaking rules	Low psychopathic deviate	High psychopathic deviate	Pp	Complacent attitude towards own or others' antisocial behavior
Considers himself as good and smart as most others	Low general psychosis	High general psychosis	Ps	Timid, shy, feelings of inferiority and unworthiness
Realistic appraisal of himself, emotional harmony, absence of regressive behavior	Low schizophrenia	High schizophrenia	Sc	Hears voices or sounds without apparent source outside himself; claims implausible knowledge, power, or status; retreat from reality

* In ratings and questionnaires, and now embodied in the Clinical Analysis Questionnaire.

appear to be no fewer than seven distinct dimensions of depression .

On the basis of this and other factor analytic work on questionnaire scales, Delhees and Cattell (1969) have set up the most
extensive set of unitary scales yet available for clinical work,
namely, the Clinical Analysis Questionnaire which includes the
sixteen normal dimensions in their somewhat less normal expressions, the five factors of principal concern in psychotic pathology,
and the seven depression factors (the anxiety factor is included
additionally as the second-order 16 P. F. measure). The complete
set of scales, as shown in Table 1 is being tried out in several
mental hospitals and clinics to reach a more adequate description
of profiles which have already for some years been known in
terms of the normal factors only.

The main empirical findings by these measuring devices turn
out to be in good accord with general psychiatric theory. Deviations
on the normal dimensions of personality seem to be sufficient to
recognize, as distinct profiles, the various types of neurosis,
and to give statistically significant separation of neurotics from
normals. On the other hand, these scales alone have proved insufficient for diagnosis of psychotics, and it is evident that the
diagnostic separation of psychotic syndromes is going to require
the inclusion of the five new psychoticism dimensions and the
seven depression dimensions, which are, therefore, now included
in the CAQ, as indicated in Table 1.

Nevertheless, although the normal dimensions in the 16 P. F.
are not sufficient for full description of true pathology yet it is
an experimental fact that there are highly significant differences on
some of these "normal" personality factor scores between groups
of simple schizophrenics, paranoid schizophrenics, and others,
in relation to normals, as shown, by the work of Cattell, Tatro,

and Komlos (1967). Thus on a group of 125 schizophrenics, taken off drugs to insure unbiased measurement, the schizophrenics were found to differ from the normals at the $P < .01$ level in showing <u>lower</u> ego strength (C Factor), <u>lower</u> dominance (E Factor), <u>lower</u> surgency, <u>higher</u> threctia (H Factor, autonomic susceptibility to threat), <u>higher</u> guilt proneness (O Factor), and so on. It may be of interest to compare these deviations with those of patients classified as having affective disorders, in Table 2. There it will be seen that the affectives differ (from normals) in having decidedly higher super-ego strength, and in tending to be above average rather than below average in intelligence, and so on. Both psychotic groups share, however, deviation from the normal in the higher score on the Q_3 Factor, which indicates greater concern with the self, as commonly called the self-sentiment.

If these differences in Table 2 are viewed in terms also of second-order factors, it will be seen that the schizophrenics are decidedly above normal on anxiety, and the affectives only slightly so. The tendency of the affectives to be more "extraverted" is clearly but moderately evident, while the tendency of schizophrenics to be decidedly "introverted" is very apparent. (The factors which make up the extraversion pattern are A, E, F, and $Q_2(-)$, i.e., negatively). The schizophrenics are decidedly below normal on E, dominance; on F, surgency; and are above average on Q_2, self-sufficiency. However, the psychometric futility of depending too much on gross conceptions such as "extraversion" i.e., on factors at the second-order level is shown by the fact that the schizophrenics are actually above normal on Factor A, i.e., they have an odd "introversion" pattern, that would be missed by a single second-order extraversion-introversion scale.

Since the CAQ has only become finally available this year, no research results are yet available giving checked findings comparable to the above with the 16 P.F. But from preliminary results

Table 2

Questionnaire Scale Differences of Schizophrenics and Affectives from Normals

| Source Trait | | Combined Schizophrenics N=125 | | | | Combined Affectives N=43 | | | |
| | | Raw scores | | P* value of Difference from Normals | | Raw scores | | P* value of Difference from Normals | |
		Mean	Sigma	Matched	General	Mean	Sigma	Matched	General
Affectothymia	A	10.97	3.35	+.001	(+)	11.00	3.09	+.05	(+)
Intelligence	B	5.98	1.92	-.01	(+)	6.51	1.99	(+)	+.01
Ego Strength	C	13.75	3.80	(-)	-.001	13.62	4.82		
Dominance	E	10.43	3.65	-.001	-.001	11.23	4.13		
Surgency	F	12.10	4.01	-.01	-.001	13.79	4.47		
Super Ego Strength	G	12.97	2.95	+.05	-.05	13.39	3.16	+.001	(-)
Parmia	H	11.01	4.50	(-)	-.001	12.79	5.90		
Premsia	I	10.38	3.14			10.11	3.42		
Protension	L	8.50	3.32			8.30	2.86		
Autia	M	12.21	3.02			12.16	2.95		
Shrewdness	N	10.66	2.71	+.05	-.05	10.56	2.36		
Guilt	O	11.88	4.19	(+)	+.001	12.48	4.40		
Radicalism	Q1	8.70	2.56	(-)	-.001	8.42	2.37		
Self Sufficiency	Q2	10.84	3.04	(+)	+.05	10.76	2.78		
Self Sentiment	Q3	11.87	3.04	+.001	(+)	12.02	2.65	+.001	(+)
Ergic Tension	Q4	12.70	5.22	-.01	(+)	13.34	5.73		

* The sign by the P (+ or -) shows the direction of deviation from the normal.

now being analyzed, it is clear that the schizophrenics are highly deviant on more than one of the pathological dimensions. This being the case, the question arises whether their above noted deviations on the normal personality demensions have anything to do with the psychotic deviation as such, or whether they are merely the characteristic pattern of the pre-psychotic personality of the schizophrenic. The repeated findings of introverted behavior in the latter, by other surveys, suggest that we may be dealing with those features of the general personality which add to the particular conflict or inadequacy problems leading, along with the biochemical changes, to the schizophrenic conditions as such.

Since there is now a High School Personality Questionnaire (Cattell, Nuttall, and Cattell, 1969) measuring, in the adolescent period, the same personality factors as are measured by the 16 P. F. for adults, it should be possible soon to settle this question of whether the pattern in Table 2 is on the one hand a pre-psychotic pattern or on the other, a product of the psychosis. For the HSPQ is so quickly administrable that in some localities, it might be possible to measure all children in the last year of high school and preserve the results for some years. Thus, the results could be available to help mental breakdown in those patients who turn up at clinics or mental hospitals later, and also to answer statistically the question posed here. It would require the testing of several thousand normal children at high school age to yield enough cases for statistical statement akin to that of Table 2, for the small minority who become patients. But since absolutely no dependable information by actual measurement instruments has hitherto existed regarding pre-psychotic personalities, it would surely be worthwhile to add a simple questionnaire to some broad medical and mental health survey at the time of school leaving.

3. <u>The Findings From Objective Personality Dimension Measures</u>

The demonstration of functional unities in actual measured <u>behavior</u> (objective tests) rather than questionnaires, and the development of suitable batteries for measuring these factors, has been a much slower process than the development of <u>questionnaires,</u> However, in 1965, Hundleby, Pawlik, and Cattell were able to present an average of about ten experimental replications of each of some twenty personality factors in the objective test medium. Batteries have since been set up by Hundleby at the adult level and by Schuerger and Dielman at the high school level, whereby each of these person-ality factors can be measured. Each dimension is sampled by some six, seven, or eight subtests, precisely as an intelligence factor measurement is obtained by a similar number of diverse subtests. The validity, of course, is established by correlating the single subtests with the factor involved in the whole battery.

The nature of the personality factors discovered in objective test behavior is, in several cases, still in need of intensive research. That is to say, the patterns themselves have been found, recorded, and replicated, but the interpretation of the underlying influence in each source trait which produces the pattern is still a matter for theoretical speculation. The chief consistency that is appearing in relation to questionnaires is that the objective test factors seem to be second-order factors in relation to the primaries as seen in the questionnaires. Thus, a single battery (indexed U.I. 24 in the universal index series of objective test personality factors) can be set up for the anxiety factor, such as has been used by Rickels and his associates (1965, 1966 Cattell and Rickels, 1964, 1966, 1968) in investigating drug effects, and a single battery (U.I. 32) can be set up for extraversion, for ego strength (U.I. 16), and, apparently, also for a super-ego pattern (U.I. 29). Thus, in the end, the objective test batteries and the questionnaire scales must be regarded as alternative ways of measuring the same personality structures.

Parenthetically, it is somewhat to be regreted that the majority of psychologists in practice have concentrated on the questionnaire measurements of these source traits rather than upon the objective test batteries. The latter, of course, require more skill and instrumentation for their administration, and take more of the patient"s time, but like the questionnaires they can be administered to small groups as well as to individuals, and eventually, with improvement, they will probably be cut down in length to something not so different from the questionnaire. Obviously, questionnaires are vulnerable to distortion and "social desirability" effects, so the objective tests, if used more widely, would yield more reliable conclusions. But the required improvements in the convenience and streamlining of these batteries will, after all, only come about through increased clinical use.

Meanwhile, however, basic research has proceeded with objective batteries, undeterred by the time-demands which harass the practitioner, and has shown that such measures intrinsically have solid value for clinical diagnosis. The findings are very clear, namely, that with both neurotics and psychotics decided differences can be found from normals on at least a third of the dimensions. The work of Scheier, of Hundleby, of Swenson, of McQuarrie, of White, and others with these batteries (See Cattell and Scheier, 1961) are to the effect that groups of neurotics can be separated almost without overlap from non-neurotics by a combination of some six of these factor measures.

The profile for neurotics may be seen in the book indicated (Cattell and Scheier, 1961), but the profiles found more recently for psychotics are not so well known. The researches of Cattell and Tatro (1966) and of Cattell and Killian (1967) in different mental hospitals and diverse syndrome groups are shown in Table 3 as they concern schizophrenics.

Table 3

Objective Test Personality Factor Differences of Schizophrenics and Others from Normals

O-A factor / Title	Non-paranoid* Schizs. vs. Normals** (N=58)* (N=96)** Cattell & Tatro.		Paranoid* Schizs. vs Normals** (N=24)* (N=96)** 1966		Non-paranoid* Schizs. vs. Normals** (N=32)* (N=36)** Cattell & Killia.		Char DS* vs. Normals** (N=20)* (N=36)** 1967	
	t	p	t	p	t	p	t	p
U.I. 16 Developed ego (+) vs. Unassertiveness (-)	-7.23	.01	-6.41	.01				
U.I. 17 Timid distrust (+) vs. Trustingness (-)	+2.10	.05	+2.64	NS	+4.06	.0005	+2.20	.05
U.I. 18 Smartness (+) vs. Passiveness (-)	.49	NS	1.84	NS				
U.I. 19 Independence (+) vs. Subduedness (-)	-4.91	.01	-4.40	.01	-3.36	.005	.95	NS
U.I. 20 Comention (+) vs. Objectivity (-)	.72	NS	.28	NS				
U.I. 21 Exuberance (+) vs. Restraint (-)	-6.05	.01	-5.44	.01				
U.I. 22 Corteria (+) vs. Objectivity	1.18	NS	.56	NS	-7.22	.001	.56	NS
U.I. 23 Mobilization (+) vs. Regression (-)	-3.12	.01	.59	NS				
U.I. 24 Anxiety (+) vs. Adjustment (-)	.90	NS	.72	NS				
U.I. 25 Realism (+) vs. Tensidia (-)	-2.56	.05	.87	.05	-2.46	.01	-2.94	.01
U.I. 26 Self-realization (+) vs. Homespunness (-)	.10	NS	.35	NS				
U.I. 27 Unmovedness (+) vs. Involvement (-)	1.33	NS	.93	NS	1.61	NS		
U.I. 28 Super-ego asthenia (+) vs. Rough assurance (-)	.68	NS	.56	NS			-2.45	.05
U.I. 29 Determined responsiveness (+) vs. Lack of will (+)	.98	NS	1.74	NS				
U.I. 30 Mature stolidness (+) vs. Dissofrustance (-)	-8.50	.01	-5.86	.01				
U.I. 31 Wary steadiness (+) vs. Impulsive variability (-)	1.04	NS	1.26	NS				
U.I. 32 Exvia (+) vs. Invia (-)	.34	NS	.91	NS				
U.I. 33 Reactive dismay (+) vs. Sanguine poise (-)	+2.10	.05	1.32	.05				
U.I. 1 Intelligence	.55	NS	+3.32	.01				

A minus by the t means the pathological group is lower; a plus by the t means the pathological group is higher than the normal.

For exactness of reference, as well as to avoid premature theoretical labelings, the factor patterns in objective tests have been identified by being given universal index (U. I.) numbers, as indicated above. (Tentatively, they are also given brief descriptive terms, as shown). By the objective tests it will be seen that schizophrenics are more anxious (U. I. 24) but not significantly so, lower in the independence factor (U. I. 19), higher in the inhibition factor (U. I. 17), lower in the cortical alertness factor (U. I. 22), and lower in the realism factor (U. I. 25). They do not significantly differ on U. I. 27 and several other general personality factors. For contrast (rather than because they are of any intrinsic interest in a paper on schizophrenia), results for a set of character disorder cases are set out on the second row of Table 3 where it will be seen that the differences are not really significant except in regard to U. I. 25, in which particular dimension the character disorders resemble the schizophrenics in showing less realism than the normals. The U. I. 25 pattern, which has tentatively been called realism vs. inner tension is one which Eysenck and Eysenck (1956) have called (normality vs.) psychoticism. In our hypothesis, it is not the "psychoticism factor" but only one determiner within the psychotic picture. And since it also distinguishes the character disorders, it is surely better regarded as some component breaking down reality contact, and which, by hypothesis, would also be high in psychopaths. One must, in short, take issue with Eysenck's claim that it is the essence of psychoticism. This is part of the whole issue between the present Illinois and the London (Eysenck) schools as to whether clinical differences can be explained by three factors as Eysenck supposes, or, alternatively, hinge on as many as six to ten specific source traits, as we have long maintained (Cattell and Scheier, 1961).

The above findings of Killian are supported by the extensive studies of Tatro (1966), where the objective test battery for some eighteen primary personality factors was applied to nearly 200 patients and about the same number of controls. Good confirmation was obtained that non-paranoid schizophrenics deviate significantly in the direction of lesser reality contact (U. I. 25 minus), greater inhibition (U. I. 17), lesser independence (U. I. 19 minus), and greater pathemia, i. e., lower cortertia (U. I. 22, minus). In this case, however, with a longer hospitalized group, no deviation was found on the anxiety factor, U. I. 24.

4. Summary

What structured personality measurement, i. e., the use of scales and batteries for measurement of unitary personality factors, can offer to the diagnosis of schizophrenia at present can be summarized under the following three headings.

(1) In the realm of normal personality dimensions as measured by the 16 P. F., the HSPQ, and similar factor-structured questionnaires, it has been found that the schizophrenic tends to have a distinct profile from the patient with affective psychoses, paranoia, etc. and from the normal. He differs significantly in abnormally reduced ego strength (C-), higher submissiveness (E-), desurgency (F-), higher guilt proneness (O), and in higher susceptibility to. threat (H). In rough second-order terms, this amounts to saying that the schizophrenic tends to be more introverted and also more anxious. However, the more specific analysis of these concepts in terms of primary factors is more important than this coarse second-order generalization, since, for example, affectothymia (A Factor) which commonly belongs to extraversion, is a factor also on which the "introvert" schizophrenic is unduly high.

However, with present evidence, we are inclined to believe that this pattern is a description of the pre-psychotic personality rather than an indicator of changes in the actual disease process.

Nevertheless, the information from such a profile makes some contribution, at least statistically, to the probability of correctness of a schizophrenic diagnosis.

(2) The recent discovery of four or five distinct psychotic process factors in such questionnaire material as that of the MMPI (when fully factored) which can be demonstrated to be extra to the 16 P. F. factor dimensions (which also exist in the MMPI) opens up the possibility of measurement of the disease process itself by pathology scales. The Clinical Analysis Questionnaire (Delhees and Cattell, 1969) which contains new items constituting the most valid measures of these new dimensions yet available (along with the normal 16 P. F. dimensions and seven dimensions of depression, etc.) is now being applied to the diagnosis of schizophrenic groups, and it is likely that within a year or two, we shall have firm evidence regarding the pattern of deviations on these disease process dimensions that is peculiar to the schizophrenic.

(3) Going outside the questionnaire mode of measurement, which has certain obvious limitations, we get into objective personality tests, which also have now been factored to reveal some twenty independent dimensions, many of which are of a normal character. Measurements of various kinds of clinical groups on batteries of about six subtests set up for each of these factors show that neurotics can be separated from normals with a high degree of certainty by an unusual pattern on the normal personality traits, just as is the case with the questionnaire. In this case, however, a more powerful degree of "sorting out" is obtained also for psychotics. The factors which showed differences specifically for schizophrenics at the $P < .01$ level are general inhibition (U. I. 17) higher ; ego strength (U. I. 16) lower; independence (U. I. 19) lower; restraint (U. I. 21 minus) higher; pathemia (U. I. 22 minus) higher; realism (U. I. 25) lower; regression

(U. I. 23 minus) higher; and dissofrustrance, i.e., tendency to splitting under frustration (U. I. 30) higher.

Deeper understanding of what this means in terms of "explaining" schizophrenia is not yet possible. The personality factors here described have been repeatedly replicated and in both questionnaires and objective test forms, have been found to hold up in other cultures as well as in our own. Consequently, there can be no doubt about their reality as unitary causal influences in personality. Unfortunately, since the factor analysis have been busy on the structure and measurement itself, and communication with clinicians has been poor (See Cattell, 1968), so little clinical research has been done on these factors (relative, for example, to the amount of time expended on the Rorschach and TAT) that it is not possible at the present moment to avail ourselves of the explanatory power that is undoubtedly potential at this point. Nevertheless, through the knowledge of these factors which we already possess Cattell (1964), Cattell (1957), Cattell and Howarth (1962), it is clear that the deviations are meaningful in terms of clinical concepts of schizophrenia. They tell us that the schizophrenic is a person of very low ego strength (in the psychoanalytic sense, but now as measured by objective tests) who shows high tendency to split dynamic systems under frustration (dissofrustrance), who is in process of losing reality touch (U. I. 25 minus), who is constitutionally very susceptible to threat, in terms of autonomic responsiveness (H Factor), and whose inhibitory tendencies (U. I. 17, F minus, E. minus) have gained such ascendency as to upset the normal balance of expression and inhibition.

Two hopeful prospects open up for the clinician from this area of research. (a) The degrees of sheer statistical separation possible by these tests is considerable, so that regardless of the degree of understanding we have yet gained, the tests can

122

at least add considerably to the certainty of diagnosis, and (b)
The research now going on by various leading psychologists
toward the further understanding of the nature of these casual
influences, e.g., by Delhees, Eysenck, Horn, Howarth, Hundleby,
Nesselroade, Schneewind, Schuerger, and others, should soon
lead from diagnosis to the insightful understanding necessary
for treatment of the individual case (See Cattell, 1966). For
if these factors are distinct influences, as seems to be certain
on methodological grounds, then each patient will need to be
understood (in addition to his description by syndromes and surface traits) in terms of the quite specific combination of normal
personality and disease influences operative in his case as
shown by the factor profile. The profile of deviations on the
primary structures, obtainable by this test approach thus becomes
a guide to the etiology, the prognosis and the most effective
treatment in the individual case, once research has made due
progress regarding the meaning of these source trait factors.

Bibliography

Cattell, R. B. Personality and motivation structure and measure-
    ment. New York: World Book, 1957.
Cattell, R. B. Theory of fluid and crystallized intelligence: a
    critical experiment. Journal of Educational Psychology,
    1963, 54, 1-22.
Cattell, R.B. The nature and measurement of anxiety. Scientific
    American, 1963, 208, 96-104.
Cattell, R. B. The parental early repressiveness hypothesis for
    the authoritarian personality factor, U. I. 28. Journal of
    Genetic Psychology, 1964, 106, 333-349.
Cattell, R. B. The scientific analysis of personality. London:
    Penguin Books, 1965.
Cattell, R. B. The value of measurement approaches to psy-
    chiatric and behavior problems in children of lower
    classes. Mental Health and the Lower Social Classes, 1966,
    Florida State University Study No. 49.
Cattell, R. B. Quantitative personality theory. In A. M. Freedman
    and H. I. Kaplan (Eds.), Comprehensive textbook of psychiatry.
    Baltimore: Williams and Wilkins, 1967.
Cattell, R. B. Progress in clinical psychology through multivariate
    experimental designs. Multivariate Behavioral Research,
    Special Issue, 1968, 3, 4-8.

Cattell, R. B. and Bjerstedt, A. The structure of depression, by factoring Q-data, in relation to general personality source traits. Scandinavian Journal of Psychology, 1967, 8, 17-24.

Cattell, R. B., Eber, H. W., and Tatsuoka, M. M. The sixteen personality factor questionnaire. Champaign, Illinois: Institute for Personality and Ability Testing, 1602 Coronado Drive, 1962.

Cattell, R. B. and Howarth, E. Hypotheses on the principal personality dimensions in children and tests constructed for them. Journal of Genetic Psychology, 1962, 101, 145-163.

Cattell, R. B. and Killian, L. R. The pattern of objective test personality factor differences in schizophrenia and the character disorders. Journal of Clinical Psychology, 1967, 23, 3, 343-348.

Cattell, R. B., Komlos, Endre, and Tatro, Donald F. Significant differences of affective, paranoid, and non-paranoid schizophrenic psychotics on primary source traits in the 16 P. F. Multivariate Behavioral Research, Special Issue, 1968, 3, 33-54.

Cattell, R. B., Nuttall, R. L., and Cattell, M. D. L. The high school personality questionnaire. Champaign, Illinois: Institute for Personality and Ability Testing, 1602 Coronado Drive, 1969.

Cattell, R. B. and Rickels, K. Diagnostic power of IPAT objective anxiety neuroticism tests. Archives of Genetic Psychiatry. 1964, 11, 459-465.

Cattell, R. B. and Rickels, K. The relationship of clinical symptons and IPAT-factored tests of anxiety, regression, and asthenia: a factor analytic study. The Journal of Nervous Mental Disease, 1968, 146, 147-160.

Cattell, R. B., Rickels, K., Weise, C., Gray, B., and Yee, R. The effects of psychotherapy upon measured anxiety and regression. American Journal of Psychotherapy, 1966, 20, 2, 261-269.

Cattell, R. B. and Scheier, I. H. The meaning and measurement of neuroticism and anxiety. New York: Ronald Press, 1961.

Cattell, R. B. and Scheier, I. H. The IPAT Anxiety Scale. Champaign, Illinois: Institute for Personality and Ability Testing, 1602 Coronado Drive, 1962.

Cattell, R. B. and Specht, L. L. Comparison of the factor domains of the 16 P. F. and the MMPI--as conventionally scale scored and as content scored. Laboratory of Personality Analysis Advanced Report, No. 12, 1968, University of Illinois, Urbana.

Cattell, R. B. and Tatro, D. F. The personality factors, objectively measured, which distinguish psychotics from normals. Behavioral Research Theory, 1966, 4, 39-51.

Cattell, R. B. and Warburton, F. W. Objective tests of personality and motivation. Champaign, Illinois: University of Illinois Press, 1967.

Cropley, A. J. and Weckowicz, T. E. The dimensionality of clinical depression. Australian Journal of Psychology, 1966, 18, 1, 18-25.

Delhees, K. H. The abnormal personality: neurosis and delinquency In R. B. Cattell (Ed.), Handbook of Modern Personality Theory. Chicago: Aldine Press, 1969.

Delhees, K. H. and Cattell, R. B. The clinical analysis questionnaire. Champaign, Illinois: Institute for Personality and Ability Testing, 1602 Coronado Drive, 1969.

Eysenck, H. J. The structure of human personality. London: Methuen, 1953.

Eysenck, H. J. and Eysenck, S. B. G. Neurosis and psychosis: an experimental study. Journal of Mental Science, 1956, 97, 441-465.

Friedman, A. S., Cowitz, B., Cohen, H. W., and Granick, S. Syndromes and themes of psychotic depression: a factor analysis.

Archives of Genetic Psychiatry, 1963, 9, 504-509.

Guilford, J. P. Personality. New York: McGraw-Hill, 1959.

Hebb, D. O. The effect of early and late brain injury upon test scores, and the nature of normal adult intelligence. Proceedings of the American Philosophical Society, 1942, 85, 275-292.

Horn, J. L. and Cattell, R. B. Refinement and test of the theory of fluid and crystallized general intelligences. Journal of Educational Psychology, 1966, 57, 5, 253-270.

Hundleby, J. D., Pawlik, K., and Cattell, R. B. Personality factors in objective test devices. San Diego: R. Knapp, 1965.

Rickels, K. and Cattell, R. B. The clinical factor validity and trueness of the IPAT verbal and objective batteries for anxiety and regression. Journal of Clinical Psychology, 1965, 21, 257-264.

Rickels, K., Cattell, R. B., Weise, C., Gray, G., Yee, R., Mallin, A., and Aaronson, H. G. Controlled psychopharmacological research in private psychiatric practice. Psychopharmacologia, 1966, 9, 288-306.

Tatro, Donald F. The interpretation of objectively measured personality factors in terms of clinical data and concepts. Urbana, Illinois: Submitted in partial fulfillment of the requirements for the degree of Doctor of Philosophy in the Graduate College of the University of Illinois, 1966.

Weckowicz, T. E., Muir, W., and Cropley, A. J. A factor analysis of the Beck inventory of depression. Journal of Consulting Psychology, 1967, 31, 1, 23-28.

R. B. Cattell, Ph.D., D.Sc., University of Illinois, 907 South Sixth Street, Champaign, Illinois 61820

PATTERN PERPETUATION IN SCHIZOPHRENIA

SHIRLEY A. SMOYAK and HILDEGARD E. PEPLAU

Since human beings are socialized within family systems to play their future societal roles, it is necessary to seek an understanding of the various styles and workings of these intricate systems, as they affect the cognitive and emotional development of their members. The study of families as systems, however, departs radically from the historical trend of psychiatry and psychology, where the focus has been predominantly on intrapsychic processes and where, often, the family has been viewed variously as disruptive, irrelevant or benign. Handel provides an apt summary of the situation:

"Many clinical investigators are coming to believe, or at least to adopt as a working assumption, that mental illness is a function of the bonds operative in a family as a whole. While this view may thus far be no more than an article of faith, it is an article of faith whose tenability merits extended scrutiny through research, for it cannot be said that any competing view of the origins of mental illness has established itself beyond reasonable doubt" (1).

As a beginning, families, as systems, might be described in terms of life styles or usual operating modes. They might be more finely categorized in terms of their operating values for the total system and operating values for the individual family members. Hess and Handel phrase this idea a bit differently. They say that, "The ways in which a family is a unit and the ways it provides for being a separate person are, in one sense, what every family's life is about" (2). A crucial family issue is that of confronting and handling the exigencies surrounding separateness and connectedness. The family defines acceptable ways for its members to be separate individuals and also as members contributing to family cohesion and solidarity. Research data concerning how this issue is handled among many kinds of families is as yet lacking. This paper will provide a theoretical interpretation of how in one family a recurring pattern, namely threat, was originally set off as a solution to this problem of defining the limits of separateness and connectedness.

Threat as a Solution to Separateness/Connectedness

Families are not sufficient unto themselves. They are forced to adapt and to integrate with other families and with the larger societal system. Family responses to their environing others can be categorized as generally friendly and trusting or as generally unfriendly and to be avoided. In the former case, an individual family member would probably be allowed more room to experiment outside of the family system, with interpersonal relationships. In the latter case, family connectedness would be stressed and there would be severe admonitions against any behavior which might lead to "too much" separateness. In other words, when families perceive the environment as unfriendly, they also perceive efforts at separateness by individual members as threats to dissolution of the connectedness and ultimately of the family.

Granted, as yet there are no substantive confirming research data, but from non-systematic empirical evidence it does seem to be a fact that the view families hold of the outside and what it's like and how it is to be managed is a crucial variable affecting the determination of its intrafamily definitions of the proper or normative amounts of separateness and connectedness. The more a family anticipates the impact of a hostile world, the less autonomous, creative or self-directed any individual member may be. Under the conditions of perceived assault or destruction from the outside, the individual member is more likely to be expected to direct his energies toward family preservation rather than toward self-realization. A kind of "We'll-all-be-saved-or-perish-together" ideology seems to operate. This system survival phenomenon can be shown to exist in other areas than family. The same pattern may hold true for corporations, states and countries. System survival is given top priority.

Besides the value attached to separateness (i.e., whether families see it as something to be encouraged or discouraged as an occurrence) the style of achieving separateness varies from family to family. On the one hand, there may be the aloof, detached, totally isolated and private, autistic style. Or there is the autonomous, creative, active, individualistic style of separateness. Connectedness, too, may be played in various ways. On the one hand, connectedness may mean mutually conceived and shared pleasureable pursuits which, for a specified time, binds all members together. Or, on the other hand, connectedness might have a pervasive, far-reaching "forever" quality about it. Wynne describes this latter style as pseudomutuality (3). In pseudomutual families, the members are preoccupied with fitting together into formal, narrowly-defined roles at the expense of any one individual's identity. Divergence is forbidden. The authors contend that "... the pseudomutual relation involves a characteristic dilemma: divergence is perceived as leading to disruption of the relation and therefore must be avoided; but if divergence is avoided, growth of the relation is impossible" (4).

Hess and Handel (5) note that some families at the same time desire closeness and intimacy, but are afraid of it. "A family of this kind may be able to approach its desire only through much formalized or ritualized action, such as giving gifts, celebrating birthdays and holidays, making excursions."

Threat: A Mechanism to Support System Survival

Threat is a technic employed by a family to produce and maintain (or to re-institute) connectedness, to decrease efforts at separateness and hence to insure the survival of the family as a group against the outside. It is interesting to note that poverty groups, lower class or minority groups perceive a hostile world, use threat to control their family members' behavior and also have higher rates of mental illness than other groups.

Threat as a control technic may be operationalized as follows:

1. The family system perceives its surrounding environment as hostile.

2. Family values of connectedness thus come strongly into the foreground.

3. One (or more) family members acts in a "separateness" fashion, (i.e., acts autonomous, individualistic, self-directed).

4. Another family member(s) takes action to bring the separating individual "into line" by:

   a. threatening to leave the family system, (including suicide)

   b. threatening to forbid re-entry of the separating individual into the system

   c. threatening an aggresive act (either verbal or phsyical or both, e.g. bodily harm) against the separating individual or another family member

   d. threatening a withdrawal of affection and support

5. The "deviant" family member comes "into line" by stop-

ping the separateness action and again espousing connectedness values.

6. Equilibrium is temporarily restored. However, the member in this instance who is acted upon and who actively experiences being threatened also learns to use this technic. In a subsequent incident, he may become the active threatener, inducing another family member, who is temporarily moving toward separateness, to return to connectedness behavior.

In families where the outside world does not loom so darkly as the environing system of the family, the threat technic does not seem to work so effectively, or is not used to the extent that it is in troubled families. However, there are individuals, who are members of families of origin where threat is a constant theme, who somehow are able to withstand the threats and still value separateness so strongly that they succeed in separating themselves from the pathology. What is not known with any certainty is what enables them to do that, while others succumb to the threats and incorporate threat as an operative pattern. (Some use concealment of all attempts at separateness, for example).

A Clinical Example

The ideas about threat as outlined above were generated from contact with disturbed families in several clinical settings (6). In a private psychiatric hospital a psychiatrist admitted a teen-ager who had recently made a suicide attempt. He suggested to the family that family therapy was the treatment of choice. He and the senior author functioned as co-therapists. All the sessions were tape-recorded and typescripts produced; these serve as the source for the following clinical illustration.

The Alba's, a lower class family living in the Southwest United States, will be used to illustrate threat, as operationalized above. Mr. Alba, in his middle 50's, is of middle European extraction, and had been raised by a widowed, chronically bed-ridden mother and two older, phsyically abusive brothers. His boyhood is one long tale of misery -- leaving school before completing the eighth grade in order to go to work and help support the family, having to succumb to orders and abuses from his older brothers and his bosses and in early marriage, financially struggling to make ends meet. His wife, slightly younger than he, did not finish high school and was presently working in a bakery part time. While she was not as willing to talk about her early childhood, she said many times, "My story's the same as his. I can't remember anything good ever happening. I'm so ashamed." The two daughters completed this family system. Laura, in her mid-twenties, amidst much protest from her parents, had left home temporarily to come to New York and earn a Master's degree in a professional field. Linda, age 16, was the hospitalized family member, whose presenting symptoms included self-destructive acts and catatonic-like behavior. On a previous admission to the hospital, she had spent much time sitting in a closet and holding onto a stuffed animal.

Threat, as suggested before, is a technic used in response to a felt disruptive impact originating in a hostilely-perceived environment and triggered off by an individual family member's acting separate or autonomous. One learns, in a cognitive sense, how to threaten others from the experience of having been the deviant member and having experienced threat. The learning is also reinforced by watching the interaction as it is played among other family members. Mr. Alba's boyhood is replete with tales of his experiences with threat. In one particularly emotionally-charged family session, he told of his refusing to turn over his paycheck one Friday afternoon to his sister-in-law, who, at the moment, was the extended family treasurer and financier. In graphic detail, in a thick, halting, guttural voice not very acquainted with English grammar, he spoke of walking past his sister-in-law in the narrow, dimly-lighted hallway of a three-story frame house and proceeding up the steep stairs to the top floor where he lived with his mother. His brother threatened to come up after him and kill him. Mr. Alba responded by hurling furniture down the stair-case at him. This was just one instance of what happened when a member acted separately and was brought back toward the connectedness end of the continuum. Mr. Alba also experienced another kind of threat, that emitted by his mother. Although the situation with his brother was almost intolerable, he said he could not leave, because, "It would have killed my mother if I did. I had to stay and just go on as best I could with the way things were." Regrettably, data were not obtained on just how Mr. Alba knew that his leaving would produce her death. There were no clues to the mother's messages about how she would interpret his leaving. After her death, he did leave the family house and severed ties with his brothers.

While Mrs. Alba never offered any specific instances, there was the distinct impression that she, too, had experienced being threatened. In their relationship as man and wife, and as parents they used threats and counter-threats repeatedly and unwittingly as the following instances show. That is, the impression was that the threatener did not interpret his actions as threatening, but instead, as efforts to solve a problem or to communicate. Further, when the older daughter in one of family session pointed out their frequent, loud, threatening interchanges, the father said, "Why, honey, that shouldn't have bothered you. It was nothing. Parents have to talk, you know." Then the younger girl said the threatening talk had given her "chills", too. To this he said, shaking his head in a puzzled way, "I don't get it. You mean to sit there and tell me after all these years that you're all tied up in knots because Mama here and me said a few things now and then? This younger generation beats me. They don't know what real trouble is."

When a family argument gained full storm, Mrs. Alba would cry, withdraw to the bedroom and not eat for days. Mr. Alba would threaten suicide or homicide or both, or say he was leaving forever. Both occasionally packed their suitcases. In the family therapy sessions, both girls said that their earliest recall of their parents was of their battles and threats of leaving or of killing themselves or each other. Although the parents never acted on these threats (unless not eating is seen as a kind of sucide) Linda did act, and has made several suicide attempts.

In this family, the deviant member and the active threatener are rotating roles. Often the switching of roles occurs with lightning rapidity. Consider the following account of such an interchange told by the father in one of the sessions. "Well, it's news to me but maybe now I can see that them two (meaning the girls) didn't like it much when I worked a lot and didn't come home or when I went off in my little corner and read the news. Anyhow, one day I came into the room and there's Laura all red-eyed and there's Linda in that don't-touch-me mood she gets (describing the onset of a catatonic period) and where's the mother? She's in bed. They had her all worked up. So I says, O.K., if that's the way you guys want it, I'll take a gun and shoot all three of you and turn it on myself! I didn't really mean it, but at least that brought them to their senses."

Interestingly, Laura did leave the family for a while to study in New York, but was unable to maintain the separateness and returned home to live with the family again, saying, "I guess you might say the pull was so strong I could feel it all the way in New York. Oh, don't look at me so funny, Dad. Those letters were enough to bring me back. Anyway, here I am. And crazy as you all -- we all are, it's my family and I'll stick with them." Thus the pull she refers to is toward family connectedness.

This family also used accusations as a kind of subversive threat in a preventive vein. The mother occasionally, out of the blue, would accuse one or both of the girls of being ashamed of her and their father. The accusation would be denied, and some proof offered. For instance, at one point, Laura said, "Now Mother, even though you didn't graduate from high school, you know you're the best speller in our family. (turning to therapist) I'll bet she can spell words you'd miss."

The Alba's are excellent illustrations of family connectedness without warmth -- of closeness and intimacy, but being fearful of overt expression. Mr. Alba said that he loved his daughters and that they should know that without his having to tell them. Laura pleaded with him to just try saying it once, instead of giving gifts that he couldn't afford. To that he answered, "Well, honey, that's not my nature." They used ritual extensively to prove their family bonds. For instance, there was much discussion about whether Linda could have an extended pass from the hospital so that she and Laura could go to the opera, which was described as a "family tradition". Also, the father reported that his girls had given him a birthday party. When he was telling this to the therapist, he was very tearful, and then said, "Geez, look at me. A grown man. I don't know why I just can't say it when people are nice to me. Maybe I don't expect it."

In the family session, Laura was the first one to suggest that threat was an operative pattern with them and to make the generational connection. She put it this way. "Don't you see? Linda and I have been doing just what we see you do. Dad, you left your family and now you think that when I go off to school that I'm leaving you and that we'll all fall apart. I think Linda does what she does to make you two stick together when I'm not around. She's afraid when I'm gone." Earlier, Laura and Linda had told of a pact that they made when they were pre-schoolers. They swore that even if mother and father left, as they often threatened to do, that the two of them would stick together "forever".

Summary

It has been suggested that a profitable route to understanding families is to consider them as systems. One system problem is coping with the definitions of the acceptable limits of separateness and connectedness. Threat is one pattern employed by parents and perpetuated by their children to insure connectedness and to control family members who move too near separateness values and behaviors. Clinical data have been used for illustration.

Footnotes

1. Gerald Handel: "Introduction" in Gerald Handel, (Ed.) The Psychosocial Interior of the Family, Aldine Publishing Co., Chicago 1967, p. 5

2. Robert Hess and Gerald Handel, The Family as a Psychosocial Organization" in Gerald Handel, (Ed.) The Psychosocial Interior of the Family, Ibid. p. 10.

3. L. C. Wynne, I. M. Rycoff, J. Day, and S. I. Hirsch, "Pseudomutuality in the Family Relations of Schizophrenics". Psychiatry 21, 205-220 (1958)

4. I. Boszormenyi-Nagy and J. Framo quote Wynne in their introduction to Ivan Boszormenyi-Nagy and James Framo, Intensive Family Therapy (New York: Hoeber Medical Division, Harper and Row Publishers) 1965, 13.

5. Hess and Handel, Op. Cit. p. 13.

6. Families seen in therapy were located in a variety of clinical settings -- county psychiatric hospital, State hospital, Veteran's Administration and several out-patient health centers.

S. A. Smoyak, R.N., Ed.D., and H. E. Peplau, R.N., Ed.D., Rutgers — The State University.

91 Halsey Street. Newark. N.J. 07102

RESEARCH STRATEGY IN SCHIZOPHRENIA

MONICA D. BLUMENTHAL

There are times in the development of knowledge when it becomes necessary to ask oneself if one is really going in the right direction, and I am moved to write this essay about basic science and psychiatry, not so much because I understand the relationship, but to strike some sort of a balance. A great deal has been written about the mind and mental processes lately by people who are biochemists, neurophysiologists, and specialists in the ultrastructure of the cell, in short, the molecular biologists. They have called on the synapse, desoxyribonucleic acid and protein metabolism to solve the riddle of memory, or learning, which has become the focus of the molecular neurophysiologist. And inherent in much of the writing is the happy thought that this approach will solve, or at least make workable, the complex problems of psychology and psychiatry. If this approach will not solve these problems, then at least it is necessary to solve the "basic" molecular problems of central nervous system function before truly useful work can be done in areas as complex as psychiatric illnesses. We do not know enough, the argument goes, about fundamental processes in the central nervous system to begin working on anything as complex as psychiatric illness and human behavior.

Is this in fact the case? This is the question which I propose to examine, and I wish to state at the outset

that I believe the argument to be unsound. The idea
that there is a relatively straightforward relationship
between biochemical processes and behavior is an interesting one which probably represents an extrapolation
from the great wave of enthusiasm accompanying populari-
zation of human inborn errors of metabolism. The dramatic association between certain known metabolic defects and mental retardation seemed to present a clear
and readily comprehended demonstration of the relationship between metabolism and behavior. It seemed a simple step to extrapolate from mental retardation to mental illness, and so the challenge was rung, that for
every crooked thought there must be a crooked molecule.

At the time interest in inborn errors of metabolism
was gaining momentum, it seemed reasonable to feel con-
fident that it would be relatively simple to pinpoint
the exact biochemical mechanism producing mental retardation in those genetic diseases where mental retardation was associated with a well understood primary
metabolic error. But, in spite of the influx of an
enormous number of competent workers into the field, we
have yet to discover the immediate, biochemical mechanism responsible for mental retardation in any inborn
error of metabolism. There is a great deal to be learned
from the human inborn errors in respect to biochemical
behavioral relationships, but the lessons should be
focused on problems complicating the research since
these indicate the types of difficulty which the biological behaviorist can expect. One set of difficulties results from the endless ramifications the organism produces as it transcribes a single metabolic defect in

terms of varying organ systems and metabolic pathways.
Like a pebble dropped into an irregular body of water,
ripples echo and re-echo until the pattern on the surface can hardly be related to the focus from which it
began.

Phenylketonuria, the best studied inborn error of
metabolism, is an excellent case in point. The disease
itself is due to a recessive autosomal gene leading to
extremely low phenylalanine hydroxylase activity.(1)
Secondarily, large amounts of phenylalanine accumulate
and are metabolized along alternate pathways, leading
to excessive excretion and tissue accumulation of
phenylpyruvic acid. Both phenylalanine and its metabolites then secondarily inhibit a host of enzymes which
are not primarily involved in the genetic defect. For
example, it has been demonstrated that phenylpyruvic
acid can inhibit Dopadecarboxylase, leading to a deficiency in norepinephrine metabolism.(2) Phenylpyruvic
acid also competitively inhibits tyrosine hydroxylase
which leads to a defect in melanine formation.(3) This
is reflected clinically by lighter skin and eye pigmentation. Interestingly enough, skin pigment will increase if the patient is placed on a diet which reduces
the blood phenylalanine and consequently the phenylpyruvic acid, reflecting the reversibility of the biochemical mechanism producing the defective pigmentation.
Many other enzymatic reactions have been demonstrated to
be inhibited by phenylalanine including several pathways
important in neurohumeral metabolism. So, in this disease, we find an inhibition of serotonin formation,(4)
and must also consider that gama-aminobutyric acid

formation may be hindered due to the competitive inhibition of brain glutamic acid decarboxylase by phenylalanine.(5) However, it seems unlikely that the mental defect is due to any such secondary, competitive inhibition since in this case the retardation should be reversible, which it is not. The possibility of such an inhibition playing a major role in the development of retardation can only be considered in terms of some interaction with the developing organism, for example the absence of some substrate necessary to the development of an essential structure at a critical time during maturation. Similarly, excessive phenylpyruvate in brain may act to reduce the formation of glutamine and alanine in brain from glucose,(6) possibly leading to amino acid deficiencies during maturation. There is also evidence suggesting phenylalanine may inhibit the transport of other amino acids across the blood-brain barrier.(7)

In addition to inhibitory effects discussed above, it has been shown that phenylketonuric patients produce excessive amounts of such pharmacologically active substances as phenylethylamine.(8) The effects of such compounds could also interact with maturation. And, as if these were not ramifications enough to keep the researcher busy, some defect in lipid metabolism must be postulated to account for the defective myelin found in the brains of these patients.(9) I should like to point out that the secondary abnormalities defined above are only a few of those which have been reported. It should come as no surprise to the reader at this point to find that intelligence in phenylketonuric patients cannot be

correlated with simple biochemical measures, such as
serum phenylalanine, which might be expected to relate
relatively directly to the primary enzymatic defect.
In fact, there are phenylketonuric persons with IQ's in
the normal range who show the same high levels of serum
phenylalanine as do the most severe retardates. So,
it seems that even in a system where a known biochemical defect is obviously causally related to a clear cut
behavioral syndrome, there is no clear pathway from the
biochemistry to the behavior.

Other problems are generated by the fact that the mental retardation produced in the phenylketonuric child
is probably a result of an interaction between the developing organism and a particular biochemical environment. Study of the results of treatment of the disease
helps demonstrate these difficulties. So, it is possible to greatly reduce the degree of mental retardation
in phenylketonuric patients by reducing dietary phenylalanine during infancy. However, the later the diet is
begun, the more severely the child is apt to be retarded,
and most workers agree that there is very little likelihood of increasing the IQ after age three by dietary
means.(10) In addition, patients removed from their low
phenylalanine diets after four years of age do not appear to suffer from intellectual deterioration. When a
biological researcher begins a study of a group of patients who have passed the critical age, obvious biochemical measures do not discriminate between patients who
have been treated for the disease and those who have not.
In predicting the IQ of a group of phenylketonurics the
biochemist is able to make a very accurate prediction on

the basis of the fact that he can identify the disease,
if he knows whether or not the patient has received
treatment, and when in the patient's lifetime treatment
has occurred. If this additional piece of information
is not available to him, his prediction becomes far less
accurate. A study of biochemistry of mental disorders
in which attempts are made to correlate behavior with
chemical variables may very well require information
analogous to the information required in the case of
phenylketonuria for the accurate prediction of IQ. The
additional problems created by the fact that mental retardation in phenylketonuria is probably the result of
interactions with maturational events have to do with
the irreversibility of such events, a situation which
makes experimental manipulation extremely difficult.
These problems are not what the first wave of enthusi-
asts envisioned. Nevertheless it seems likely that
phenylketonuria is an example indicative of the complexity characterizing the system.

Having considered the complexity of the relationship
between behavior and biochemistry in a molecular disease, it is reasonable to ask whether it will be fruitful to investigate a mental illness such as schizophrenia as though it were a molecular disease. There is
probably no simple answer to this question. To begin
with, it is unlikely that schizophrenia is a single disease entity. A variety of biological conditions can
produce behavior that leads to a diagnosis of schizophrenia by experienced clinicians. For example, both
myxedema and temporal lobe epilepsy can produce such a
picture.(11) It also seems likely that an excess of

persons with extra X chromosomes will be found among populations of schizophrenics.(12) It is possible but not likely that these three diverse conditions mentioned produce a single molecular lesion. It seems more probable that schizophrenia represents a behavior pattern which is the final common response to a variety of stimuli and conditions.

Simple systems exist which provide clear examples of behaviors representing final common responses to a variety of stimuli, for example, some behaviors of Daphnia magna. These plankton crustaceans perform color dances which are statistical behaviors leading to food. Under red lights (6,000 A and over) the population appears calm, dancing in an upright direction, with only a small horizontal vector in their locomotion. Under blue light (5,000 A or shorter) the population is distinctly agitated, individuals leaning well forward in their dance and roaming about with a large horizontal vector in their locomotion.(13) When, however, these organisms, who have been adapted to 25° C, are cooled to 10° C or less, the blue response disappears. On the other hand, if the animals are hungry, the red dance will disappear and the Daphnia magna will blue dance in all wave lengths of the visible spectrum. Conversely, if food in the form of photoplankton is added to the hungry population, all blue dancing will disappear and red dancing will occur in all incident wave lengths. Other behaviors of Daphnia magna such as vertical migration, are found to be variously affected by various factors such as gravity, light intensity or wave length, pH, redox poisoning compounds, temperature and pressure. In any case, the

behavior produced is not specific to a given stimulus,
but can be produced by a host of apparently unrelated
stimuli. It seems likely that analogous stimuli-
response relationship exists in the case of schizophrenia, and in most of the other so-called "functional"
mental illnesses. A moment's reflection makes it clear
that it would be difficult, if not impossible, to study
the relationship between light and motion of the crus-
tacean described above if the investigator were not
aware of what was the temperature of his aquaria or
whether his animals had had access to food prior to his
experiments. In fact, the investigator studying _Daphnia_
color dances is observing the results of an interaction
between the effect of incident wave lengths and a variety of other variables. While the nature of the interactions does not cause any particular difficulty when
the experimenter is investigating animals' behavior in
aquaria where the environment can easily be controlled,
prediction of behavior under field conditions would require knowledge of the state of all the relevant variables.

Predicting the behavior of _Daphnia_ in ponds probably
represents the prototype of the problems which must be
faced in investigations of mental illness. The most
reasonable speculation on the nature of the functional
mental illnesses is that the abnormal behavior is a
resultant produced by the interaction of a variety of
vectors. In the case of schizophrenia, a reasonable
guess as to the nature of the interaction might be that
it is a function of biological mechanisms, learned patterns (the result of the individual's past psychological

and sociological experiences), and environmental stresses. There is considerable evidence to support this view. On the one hand, it seems likely that there is a genetic component in schizophrenia. On the other hand, the age of onset and severity of the disease do not appear to be genetically determined.(14) In addition, concordance rates in monozygotic twins do not approach the 100 percent which would be expected if the disease could be completely accounted for in terms of genetic factors. These data indicate the importance of non-genetic modifying factors in determining the disease of schizophrenia. Such modifying factors might include the impaired mother-child relationship which has been postulated as productive of schizophrenia.(15) Parenthetically, if this impaired relationship is truly a modifying factor, it may be analogous to diet in phenylketonuria. Since it is theorized that the crucial relationship occurs early in childhood, one could guess that the effect of the relationship on the individual interacts with the developing organism during a critical time during maturation. Other vectors acting to contribute to the production of schizophrenia might be very different, e.g., social class or environmental stress.

If it is indeed the case that mental illnesses represent *interactions* between biological, social and environmental components then it follows that studying one of these components at a time without attention to the others will not produce meaningful information. Let us suppose that schizophrenia is truly the result of an interaction of three or more vectors. Suppose also that the magnitude of each vector is distributed along some continuum and that that this magnitude can vary independently for each factor. In addition, suppose that no one vector can ever be the sufficient factor in the production of the disease, but that some vectors can approach sufficiency in the causation of disease as their magnitude increases. If this situation were indeed the case, then it seems likely that experimenters would recognize the importance of individual factors without being able to prove their hypotheses experimentally, as long as only one variable was studied at one time. Speculations concerning individual vectors would most likely arise from observations of groups of patients where the magnitude of one vector was such that it could be easily observed. When, however, the investigator seeks to test his hypothesis in another population, or another investigator seeks to test the hypothesis, it is likely that the second experiment will deal with a situation where the vectors are distributed more equitably, i.e., the interactions between two or more vectors of similar magnitude will predominate. In this population, the investigator looking at a single vector is likely to be unable to demonstrate any significance for that factor because of his failure to recognize the interactions. This becomes likely, if the disease is the result of interactions, since the factor under observation is apt to be found also in control groups, the interactions being the difference between the ill and the control patients. For example, in the case of schizophrenia, let us suppose that the investigator is studying a relevant biological variable

which does indeed contribute to the interaction producing schizophrenia. However, development of the disease also requires the presence of environmental stress
and can act only if the patient has been subject to maternal deprivation. Unfortunately, the investigator is
interested in the biological factor per se. One might
guess our imaginary investigator to be dealing with a
schizophrenic population somewhat as follows: one group
of patients has a high magnitude of biological factor
and a small amount of current stress and maternal deprivation; one group of patients suffers from a high degree of maternal deprivation and a small amount of biological factor or environmental stress, while the third
group suffers from high environmental stress and low biological factor and maternal deprivation; a fourth group
suffers from moderate biological factor and moderate
maternal deprivation, little current stress, and so on.
It can readily be seen that the control group might very
well contain persons who were high on biological factor
but who did not have maternal deprivation or suffer from
environmental stress, etc. This situation is difficult
enough to imagine when one is only considering three
factors; still there is a good likelihood that more than
three factors actually contribute to such interactions
in the development of schizophrenia. It has been pointed
out that no engineer dealing with linear systems would
attempt to predict performance in a three variable system on the basis of experience and intuition.(16) How
much more unlikely then is the chore of developing behavioral, biological associations in a situation where
there is no evidence that the interactions are linear,

and the number of variables contributing to the interactions cannot be calculated. Moreover, the fact that
interactions may exist is almost never taken into account by the experimenter. If schizophrenia, or other
mental illnesses, does indeed represent a final common
behavior which is the result of an interaction in which
a larger number of components may be necessary, then
the only sensible way to investigate these conditions is
by either controlling or measuring all relevant variables
at once in the same population. Since it is impossible
to control patients' past lives, we must measure.

If these speculations about the nature of the psychiatric disease processes are correct, it seems reasonable
to suppose that the most fruitful scientific approach to
psychiatric problems would occur if scientists concerned
with the major areas of presumed interaction were to
approach the problem jointly. If relevant variables
could be measured, then statistical manipulation could
correct the defects in nature's experiments by appropriate co-variant techniques. It seems reasonable to
guess that if joint studies involving the major areas
of relevant interaction were to be conducted, these
would be most productive if the scientists in the diverse fields were at approximately the same level of
proficiency and sophistication when such studies were
begun. High orders of precision in the biological sciences would be wasted if the psychiatrist could do no
better than to make rude approximations. If this is
the case, it is clear that there is a tremendous need
to increase the amount of basic clinical research in
psychiatry in the immediate future. Research psychiatry

is still without fundamental definitions and agreements on terminology which other sciences take for granted. There are available only the most primitive, impressionistically based tools, and the field is plagued by a lack of reliable measures, not to mention a lack of measures. Only recently, a few small voices have begun to plead for the replication of results, the necessity for reproducing data having largely passed research psychiatry by. It is a discouraging fact that only a small proportion of research in clinical psychiatry can in any way be interpreted to conform to the rules of evidence, and at the same time, energetic young men who might bring some order into this discipline are discouraged from entering the field because it is too "soft." It may very well be too "soft" but in that case it is time to begin more thorough investigations aimed at improving the general methodology. I believe the study of interactions between components may very well prove to be the fruitful approach to psychiatric illness; but in that case, work in clinical research psychiatry must begin to move promptly, since it is clear that the field has a long way to travel before it can take its place in joint efforts with its molecularly oriented friends.

BIBLIOGRAPHY

1. Knox, W.E. and Hsia, D.Y.-Y. Pathogenic problems in phenylketonuria. Am. J. Med. 22, 687, 1957.
2. Fellman, J.H. Inhibition of DOPA decarboxylase by aromatic amino acids associated with phenyl-pyruvic oligophrenia. Proc. Soc. Exp. Biol. and Med. 93, 413, 1956.

3. Undenfriend, S., Zaltmann-Nirenberg, P. and Nagatsu, T. Inhibitors of purified beef adrenal tyrosine hydroxylase. Biochem. Pharmacol. 14, 837, 1965.

4. Pare, C.M.B., Sandler, M. and Stacey, R.S. 5-hydroxy-tryptamine deficiency in phenylketonuria. Lancet 1, 551, 1957.

5. Tashian, R.E. Inhibition of brain glutamic acid decarboxylase by phenylalanine, valine, and leucine derivatives: a suggestion concerning the etiology of the neurological defect in phenylketonuria and branched-chain ketonuria. Metabolism 10, 393, 1961.

6. Itoh, T. Effect of sodium phenylpyruvate on amino acid formation in brain. Canad. J. Biochem. 43, 835, 1965.

7. Undenfriend, S. Factors in amino acid metabolism which can influence the central nervous system. Am. J. Clin. Nutrition 12, 287, 1963.

8. Oates, J., Nirenberg, P., Jepson, J.A., Soerdsma, A. and Undenfriend, S. Conversion of phenylalanine to phenylethylamine in patients with phenyl-ketonuria. Proc. Soc. Exp. Biol. and Med. 112, 1078, 1963.

9. Malamud, N. Neuropathology of phenylketonuria. J. Neuropath. and Exp. Neurol. 25, 254, 1966.

10. Baumeister, A.A. The effects of dietary control on intelligence in phenylketonuria. Am. J. Med. Deficiency 71, 840, 1967.

11. Freedman, D.A. Various etiologies of the schizo-phrenic syndrome. Dis. Nerv. Sys. 19, 108, 1958.

12. Judd, L.L. and Brandkamp, W.W. Chromosome analysis

of adult schizophrenics. <u>Arch</u>. <u>Gen</u>. <u>Psychiat</u>. <u>16</u>, 316, 1967.

13. Baylor, E.R. and Smith, E.E. Diurnal migration of plankton crustaceans. In <u>Recent</u> <u>Advances</u> <u>of</u> <u>Invertebrate</u> <u>Physiology</u>, Scher, B.T. (Editor), University of Oregon Publications, Eugene, 1957.

14. Rosenthal, D. The offspring of schizophrenic couples. <u>J</u>. <u>Psychiat</u>. <u>Res</u>. <u>4</u>, 169, 1966.

15. Weiner, H. Schizophrenia. III: etiology. In <u>Compre-hensive</u> <u>Textbook</u> <u>of</u> <u>Psychiatry</u>, Freedman, A.M. and Kaplan, H.I. (Editors), p. 603, William and Wilkins Co., Baltimore, 1967.

16. Horvath, W.J. The systems approach to the national health problem. <u>Management</u> <u>Sci</u>. <u>12</u>, B-391, 1966.

M. D. Blumenthal, M.D., Ph.D., Mental Health Research Institute,

The University of Michigan, Ann Arbor, Michigan 48104

PHARMACOLOGICAL ANALYSIS OF THE PATHOBIOLOGY OF SCHIZOPHRENIA

EDWARD F. DOMINO

Psychopharmacology is now on a plateau regarding the chemotherapy of schizophrenia. The initial breakthrough with chlorpromazine and haloperidol as useful antipsychotics prompted a search for more active drugs of similar pharmacological properties. To a large extent this goal has been achieved. Our present therapeutic armamentarium consists of many brands of antipsychotics of different spectra of side effects. There is no doubt that some of these congeners are quite valuable and have advanced the chemotherapy of this disease. However, nothing chemically or pharmacologically new has become available since the initial accidental discoveries of the prototype antipsychotic compounds. Clinical psychopharmacology suffers from the lack of additional unique chemicals with which to treat our seriously mentally ill.

It is obvious that any successful approach to this problem will come only with an increase in knowledge of the pathobiology of mental disease. From a pharmacological point of view we need to conceive, synthesize and test chemicals which modify known or postulated biochemical, physiological and psychological abnormalities in this disease. Drugs which either exacerbate or alleviate specific clinical symptoms are of interest. If the mechanisms of action of such drugs are known, one can postulate specific biochemical systems as normal or abnormal in schizophrenia.

Biogenic Amines and Schizophrenia

A pharmacological clue that some schizophrenic symptoms involve adrenergic and serotonergic mechanisms is based on the fact that some substituted phenothiazines and butyrophenones are antipsychotic. The primary effect of the antipsychotic phenothiazines and butyrophenones is to antagonize some of the central actions of endogenous adrenergic agents like dopamine and norepinephrine, and synthetic adrenergic agonists like amphetamine. Furthermore, serotonergic agonists including tryptamine and 5-hydroxytryptamine are antagonized by the same antipsychotic drugs.

Supported in part by grant MY-11846, USPHS.

These findings support the now widely held belief that there is a relationship between "amines and schizophrenia" as evidenced by the recent symposium on this subject[1].

DaPrada and Pletscher[2-4] have shown that antipsychotic drugs increase markedly the content of brain homovanillic acid (HVA), one of the metabolites of dopamine, without affecting brain dopamine levels in most species. However, in both the cat[5] and dog[6] these compounds decrease dopamine levels in certain brain areas possibly by preventing the neuronal uptake of this amine or by enhanced turnover and utilization of the amine in the presence of receptor blockade. The action of these compounds on cerebral norepinephrine is less clear but appears to be similar to dopamine. There is evidence that chlorpromazine blocks the excitatory effects of norepinephrine and enhances the inhibitory effects of this biogenic amine on brainstem neurons[7].

It is generally recognized that one of the best models of schizophrenia is amphetamine-induced psychosis. This usually occurs after chronic amphetamine use[8,9]. It has long been known that amphetamine not only induces a general increase in motor activity but also abnormal motor behavior in animals. Randrup et al.[10] have made an extensive study of amphetamine-induced stereotyped abnormal behavior. It includes constant sniffing, biting and walking backwards. Of special importance, this stereotyped behavior is independent of general motor activity[11]. Amphetamine-induced stereotyped behavior depends upon brain dopamine[12,13]. Evidence for this is based upon the results of various complex drug interactions. For example, the compound disulfiram, a dopamine-β-hydroxylase inhibitor, which decreases the synthesis of norepinephrine[14,15] prevents amphetamine-induced general motor activity, but not the stereotyped behavior. Furthermore, a synthetic amino acid precursor of norepinephrine, threo DOPS, does not restore amphetamine stereotypic behavior in reserpine treated animals, but DOPA, the amino acid precursor of dopamine, does. These findings in animals have direct relevance to schizophrenia for Heath et al.[16] have shown that disulfiram administration to schizophrenics exacerbates their illness markedly in contrast to its effects in normals. After disulfiram schizophrenics show extreme mental and physical changes. Auditory hallucinations, delusional thinking, autism and depersonalization are increased. Patients show confusion, forgetfulness, and impaired ability to calculate. In addition they become hypertensive, weak, pale, have tightness in their legs, chest pains, shortness of breath and obvious anxiety. Both the schizophrenics and normals show mild EEG slowing. However, the normal subjects do not show any delusions or hallucinations. They do have some difficulty concentrating, impaired calculating ability and recall, and some deficiency in memory. After disulfiram there are minimal physical changes in the normal subjects with only a slight increase in blood pressure. These findings indicate that inhibition of dopamine-β-hydroxylase in schizophrenics is especially critical and suggests that a shift in catechol amine metabolism toward dopamine and its metabolites exacerbates this disease. In view of the fact that dopamine is found in high concentrations in the basal ganglia, it is pertinent to inquire what the role of these brain structures is in this disease.

There is evidence that the basal ganglia are one of the important sites of action of antipsychotic drugs both from a biochemical as well as an electrophysiological point of view[17,18,19]. It is therefore of interest that Mettler[20], on the basis of lesion studies, suggested that one anatomical substratum underlying the schizophrenic process is dysfunction of this subcortical area. However, he and Kline[21] have emphasized that although extrapyramidal mechanisms are disturbed in advanced schizophrenia, any hypothesis suggesting a causal relationship between this anatomical area and schizophrenia is unsophisticated. Most investigators are in agreement that extrapyramidal system side effects and antipsychotic activity are unrelated[22]. Yet, it is a fact that the most potent antipsychotics are also the most likely to produce extrapyramidal symptoms. Janssen[23] has pointed out that in animal screening tests catalepsy is a predictor of extrapyramidal side effects, but antagonism of amphetamine-induced stereotypes a predictor of antipsychotic activity. Janssen et al.[24] and Janssen[25] have shown that antipsychotic drugs inhibit amphetamine-induced stereotypes in rats in doses which correlate well with the doses used clinically in man for antipsychotic effects. The fact that Randrup and Munkvad[26] have shown that destruction of striatum prevents amphetamine-induced stereotypes causes one to reexamine the basal ganglia, their functions and probable chemical transmitters. Dopamine and acetylcholine are the two major transmitter candidates in the basal ganglia. However, a role for serotonin and histamine also must be considered.

Classically the basal ganglia are involved in diseases of motor function such as Parkinson's disease, where an imbalance between dopamine and acetylcholine exists[27]. The opposite imbalance may exist in schizophrenia if the pharmacological model being developed is valid. Amphetamine-induced stereotypes are enhanced by cholinergic antagonists[28, 29]. Tryptamine and 5-hydroxytryptamine also induce stereotypic behavior[26]. Curiously, reserpine has been reported to induce "paradoxical" stereotyped activity[30] similar to amphetamine. Reserpine is known to affect biogenic amines in a complex manner, reducing total brain levels of 5-hydroxytryptamine, dopamine, norepinephrine and increasing brain acetylcholine. The turnover of some of these amines is enhanced. There is also evidence of reserpine-induced denervation sensitivity. Thus, reserpine produces a very complex functional imbalance of brain neurotransmitters[31]. It is of interest, therefore, that Luby[32] in a recent review of the literature concluded that reserpine is not a clinically reliable antipsychotic.

Using the pharmacological model of amphetamine induced abnormal stereotypic behavior of schizophrenia, as proposed by Munkvad, Randrup and their coworkers, one would predict that schizophrenics have a multiple disturbance of neurotransmitters including too much functional dopamine or related amines, too much serotonin or related amines like tryptamine and too little acetylcholine. Inasmuch as most neurotransmitters, either in deficiency or excess, produce opposite effects to optimal levels, the problem obviously becomes very complex from both a pathobiologic and a therapeutic point of view.

Faurbye[33] very recently has reviewed the role of amines in the etiology of schizophrenia from the point of view of the mescaline, amphetamine, phenylalanine, tryptophan and the methylated metabolite hypotheses. The fact that some antidepressants such as MAO inhibitors and tricyclic antidepressants that prevent neuronal amine uptake, methyl donors like methionine and betaine, and a β-hydroxylase like disulfiram make schizophrenics worse indicates that in this disease a shift in amine metabolism is very critical. As shown below there are three major pathways for the biotransformation of biogenic amines.

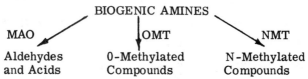

BIOGENIC AMINES

MAO	OMT	NMT
Aldehydes and Acids	0-Methylated Compounds	N-Methylated Compounds

The major oxidative pathway utilizes monoamine oxidase (MAO) to form aldehydes and acids. For example, serotonin is oxidized to 5-hydroxyindoleacetic acid. Of course, lesser known pathways of metabolism do exist such as the formation of the corresponding alcohol, etc. (See Feldstein in this Symposium.) In the case of catecholamines both the MAO pathway and the O-methyltransferase pathway (OMT) are utilized to form as end products homovanillic acid (HVA) and vanillylmandelic acid (VMA). Recently an intermediate 3-methoxy-4-hydroxyphenylglycol (MHPG) has been implicated as an important brain metabolite of norepinephrine and its low levels related to symptoms of mental depression[34]. The N-methyltransferase pathway (NMT) of biotransformation of some amines such as serotonin leads to compounds which have psychotomimetic properties including bufotenine and dimethyltryptamine. Histamine is also methylated to the corresponding N-methylhistamine via an analogous pathway. It is obvious that if the oxidative pathway for deamination is blocked by MAO inhibitors metabolism will shift to the other two pathways. When clinically suitable OMT inhibitors become available, it will be important to know if they too will make schizophrenics worse. On the other hand, selective NMT inhibitors should improve schizophrenics, as is already true of chlorpromazine, a known inhibitor of this enzyme system[35].

Presently available antipsychotic substituted phenothiazines have a wide spectrum of pharmacologic activity. These include actions on the central nervous system, peripheral nervous system and metabolic effects as outlined below.

MAJOR PHARMACOLOGICAL ACTIONS OF SUBSTITUTED PHENOTHIAZINES

I. Central Nervous System
   A. Sedative but not soporific
   B. Depress conditioned avoidance and approach behavior
   C. Antiemetic (block apomorphine which may act on dopaminergic receptors in the chemoreceptor trigger zone)
   D. Alter temperature regulation
   E. Alter skeletal muscle tone
   F. Antipruritic
   G. Analgesic (only certain derivatives)
   H. Facilitate seizure discharge (especially in limbic system)
   I. Induce neuroendocrine changes (pseudopregnancy, etc.)
II. Peripheral Nervous System
   A. Alpha adrenergic blockade
   B. Prevent retention of exogenous adrenergic amines (Antiadrenergic uptake, adrenergic potentiation)
   C. Antiserotonergic
   D. Antihistaminic

      E. Anticholinergic

      F. Inhibit as well as activate cholinesterase

      G. Potentiate d-tubocurarine and antagonize decamethonium

      H. Local anesthetic

III. Metabolic Actions

      A. Potentiate various drugs

          1. Central action

          2. Alter biotransformation

             Inhibition of alcohol dehydrogenase, inhibition of methylation

             of histamine, serotonin, etc.

      B. Widespread biochemical and enzymatic effects

          1. Selective uncouplers of oxidative phosphorylation

          2. Increase NAD levels after nicotinamide

          3. Inhibit brain Na^+ - K^+ activated ATPase

      C. In low concentrations stabilize biological membranes and high

          concentrations the reverse

The problem of the pharmacologist is to decide which of these diverse pharmacological effects are epiphenomena and which are related to antipsychotic effects. To help one decide the pharmacology of other classes of antipsychotics such as the thioxanthines and especially the butyrophenones is most helpful. For purposes of brevity as well as to stimulate discussion and research in this area, the following are suggested as the principal central nervous system actions most closely related to antipsychotic effects.

      1. Competitive blockade of adrenergic agonists. This would include

          dopamine especially in the basal ganglia and hypothalamus and

          possibly the excitatory effects of norepinephrine in the reticular

          formation, both ascending and descending.

      2. Competitive blockade of serotonergic and tryptaminergic receptors

      3. Membrane stabilization

      4. N-methyltransferase inhibition

      5. Na^+, K^+ ATPase inhibition

Sleep and Schizophrenia

In the past 10 years it has become very clear that sleep consists of at least two basic states: a) slow wave (Stage II-IV) and b) fast wave (dream sleep, "D" state, Stage $I_{REM})^{36-41}$. Most research in man, until recently, has dealt with dream sleep because of the importance of dreaming in current psychoanalytic theory. However, there is now an active interest in slow wave sleep as well[42]. Apparently, both are necessary[43]. Although dream sleep may vary markedly in acute schizophrenics, it is remarkably normal in chronic schizophrenic adults[44-47] and children[48-50]. Our own research with adult schizophrenics[47] confirmed the finding of normal dream sleep, but also called attention to a peculiar deficit of slow wave sleep, particularly Stage IV. Although almost all schizophrenics studied had a marked decrease in the voltage of delta waves during Stage IV[51], there were marked individual differences in the amount of time spent in Stage IV on the basis of percent of total sleep. Thus, some schizophrenics spent a relatively normal amount of time sleeping in Stage IV whereas others spent almost no time in this stage.

Gottlieb[52] suggested that there are at least two groups of clinically homogeneous chronic schizophrenics, and a third group of clinically different childhood schizophrenics who mature to adulthood. Evidence for the multiple group hypothesis is extensive based upon biochemical, psychological and neurophysiological research conducted on the same population of drug-free schizophrenics at the Lafayette Clinic. Of special interest is the fact that Frohman[53] reported that tryptophan uptake by chicken erythrocytes is enhanced by plasma from schizophrenics which show the least amount of Stage IV sleep. This negative correlation has been discussed recently by Caldwell[54]. Although data in man with tryptophan and 5-hydroxytryptophan suggests a role of these indoles in dream sleep[38, 55, 56], animal data indicate that 5-hydroxytryptophan in particular promotes slow wave sleep. In fact, the evidence that serotonin plays a critical role in slow wave sleep is impressive[40, 41]. Doses of 5-hydroxytryptophan given to man to date have been small, in view of its marked gastrointestinal effects, so that further data on the central effects of larger doses needs to be obtained.

Assuming that the chemical models of slow wave sleep in animals are valid, one could suggest again that schizophrenics have a deficiency or an excess of serotonin. This old hypothesis of Woolley and Shaw[57, 58] and Gaddum[59] should, of course, be extended to include the metabolites of tryptamine as well as serotonin, especially the methylated compounds. Our own unpublished studies on the dose-effect relations of 5-hydroxytryptophan in promoting slow wave sleep in animals indicate an important and critical inverted "U" shaped function in that small doses enhance slow wave sleep, but large doses have the opposite effect.

It is not our purpose to review the extensive biochemical studies on serotonin and its metabolites in schizophrenia. This will be done by Feldstein and others at this Symposium. However, sleep research does implicate this amine or possibly some of its metabolites in schizophrenia.

155

It should be emphasized that reduction of Stage IV sleep is not specific
for schizophrenia. A similar decrease has been reported in old people[42],
patients with mental depression[60-62], hypothyroidism[63], and asthma[63].
A recent report by Jus et al. [64] suggests that drug free schizophrenics
have a decrease in Stage II as well as Stage IV of slow wave sleep but a
paradoxical increase in Stage I and III. The alterations were not related
to clinical subtype. No significant differences were found between catatonics and paranoids, hallucinating and non-hallucinating patients or those
with and without symptoms of anxiety. Large doses of antipsychotic phenothiazines given chronically normalized Stages I and IV. Although the time
spent in Stages II and III shifted toward normal following medication, they
were still not normal. Before medication the duration of Stage I REM did
not differ significantly from normal. However, REM was interrupted frequently by bursts of EMG potentials and gross body movements which were
less frequent after phenothiazine medication. The mean duration of REM
sleep was higher during treatment, but this was not statistically significant. However, rapid eye movements were very intense, resembling
REM storms.

SUMMARY

In general, drugs which alleviate the symptoms of schizophrenia are
antagonists of adrenergic and serotonergic amines, are N-methyltransferase inhibitors and act to stabilize biologic membranes. Chemicals which
exacerbate schizophrenia increase the availability of certain brain amines
and cause shifts in their biotransformation in part toward methylated compounds. Amphetamine-induced psychosis in man and amphetamine repetitive behavior in animals may serve as useful models for studying antipsychotic drugs and for delineating chemical and anatomical mechanisms which
relate adrenergic and serotonergic amines to schizophrenia. A role of
acetylcholine must still be considered. It appears that multiple neurotransmitters are involved in this disease. Data from sleep studies again
implicate the biogenic amines, especially serotonin and its metabolites,
since Stage IV sleep is decreased in chronic schizophrenics. However,
this disturbance in sleep is not specific to schizophrenia. There appear to
be at least two biologic subtypes of adult schizophrenia on the basis of
these and related studies.

REFERENCES

1. Himwich, H.E., Kety, S.S. and Smythies, J.R. (Editors) Amines and Schizophrenia, 290 p. Pergamon Press, Oxford, 1967.

2. Da Prada, M. and Pletscher, A. Acceleration of the cerebral dopamine turnover by chlorpromazine. Experientia 22, 465, 1966.

3. Da Prada, M. and Pletscher, A. On the mechanism of chlorpromazine-induced changes of cerebral homovanillic acid levels. J. Pharm. Pharmac. 18, 628, 1966.

4. Pletscher, A. and Da Prada, M. Mechanism of action of neuroleptics. In Neuro-Psycho-Pharmacology, Brill, H. (Editor), p. 304, Excerpta Medica Foundation (Excerpta Med. Int. Congress Ser. No. 129) Amsterdam, 1966.

5. Laverty, R. and Sharman, D.F. Modification by drugs of the metabolism of 3,4-dihydroxyphenylethylamine, noradrenaline and 5-hydroxytryptamine in the brain. Br. J. Pharmac. Chemother. 24, 759, 1965.

6. Himwich, W.A. and Glisson, S.N. Effect of haloperidol on caudate nucleus. Int. J. Neuropharmac. 6, 329, 1967.

7. Bradley, P.B., Wolstencroft, J.H., Hosli, L., Avanzino, G.L. Neuronal basis for the central action of chlorpromazine. Nature 212, 425, 1966.

8. Connell, P.H. Amphetamine Psychosis, 133 p., Chapman & Hall, Ltd. Publishers, London, 1958.

9. Rockwell, D. Amphetamine use and abuse in psychiatric patients. Arch. Gen. Psychiat. 18, 612, 1968.

10. Randrup, A., Munkvad, I. and Udsen, P. Adrenergic mechanisms and amphetamine abnormal behavior. Acta Pharmac. tox. 20, 145, 1963.

11. Munkvad, I. and Randrup, A. The persistence of amphetamine stereotypes of rats in spite of strong sedation. Acta psychiat. scand. Suppl. 191, 178, 1966.

12. Randrup, A. and Scheel-Krüger, J. Diethyldithiocarbamate and amphetamine stereotype behaviour. J. Pharm. Pharmac. 18, 752, 1966.

13. Scheel-Krüger, J. and Randrup, A. Stereotype hyperactive behaviour produced by dopamine in the absence of noradrenaline. Life Sci. 6 1389, 1967.

14. Goldstein, M., Anagnoste, B., Lauber, E. and McKereghan, M.R. Inhibition of dopamine-β - hydroxylase by disulfiram. Life Sci. 3 763, 1964.

15. Musacchio, J., Kopin, I.J. and Snyder, S. Effects of disulfiram on tissue norepinephrine content and subcellular distribution of dopamine, tyramine and their β -hydroxylated metabolites. Life Sci. 3, 769, 1964.

16. Heath, R.G., Nesselhof, W., Bishop, M.P. and Byers, L.W. Behavioral and metabolic changes associated with administration of tetraethylthiuram disulfide. Dis. Nerv. System 26, 99, 1965.

17. Domino, E.F., Hudson, R.D. and Zografi, G. Substituted Phenothiazines: Pharmacology and Chemical Structure. In Drugs Affecting the Central Nervous System, Vol. 2, Burger, A. (Editor), p. 327, Marcel Dekker, Inc., New York, 1968.

18. Domino, E.F. Substituted phenothiazine antipsychotics. In Psychopharmacology-Review of Progress 1957-1967, Efron, D.H. (Editor). U.S. Government Printing Office, P.H.S. Pub. No. 1836, Washington, D.C., 1968.

19. Janssen, P.A.J. Applied pharmacology of the butyrophenones. In Psychopharmacology-Review of Progress 1957-1967, Efron, D.H. (Editor), U.S. Government Printing Office, P.H.S. Pub. No. 1836, Washington, D.C., 1968.

20. Mettler, F.A. Perceptual capacity, functions of the corpus striatum and schizophrenia. Psychiat. Q. 29, 89, 1955.

21. Kline, N.S. and Mettler, F.A. The extrapyramidal system and schizophrenia. In Extrapyramidal System and Neuroleptics, Bordeleau, J.M. (Editor), p. 487, Editions Psychiatriques, U. of Montreal, 1961.

22. Bordeleau, J.M. (Editor). Extrapyramidal System and Neuroleptics, 574 p., Editions Psychiatriques, U. of Montreal, 1961.

23. Janssen, P.A.J. The evolution of the butyrophenones, haloperidol and trifluperidol from meperidine-like 4-phenylpiperidines. Int. Rev. Neurobiol. 8, 221, 1965.

24. Janssen, P.A.J., Niemegeers, C.J.E. and Schellekens, K.H.L. Is it possible to predict the clinical effects of neuroleptic drugs (major tranquilizers) from animal data? I. "Neuroleptic activity spectra" for rats. Arzneimittel-Forsch. 15, 104, 1965.

25. Janssen, P.A.J. Questions and Comments-Antipsychotics. In Psychopharmacology-Review of Progress 1957-1967, Efron, D.H. (Editor) U.S. Government Printing Office, P.H.S. Pub. No. 1836, Washington, D.C., 1968.

26. Randrup, A. and Munkvad, I. DOPA and other naturally occurring substances as causes of stereotypy and rage in rats. Acta psychiat. scand. Suppl. 191, 193, 1966.

27. Costa, E., Côté, L.J. and Yahr, M.D. (Editors) Biochemistry and Pharmacology of the Basal Ganglia. 238 p. Raven Press, Hewlett, New York, 1966.

28. Schelkunov, E.L. The technique of "phenamine stereotypy" for evaluating agents on the central adrenergics. Farmak. Toxs. (Moskva) 27, 633, 1964.

29. Fog, R.L., Randrup, A. and Pakkenberg, H. Aminergic mechanisms in corpus striatum and amphetamine-induced stereotyped behaviour. Psychopharmacologia 11, 179, 1967.

30. Schiørring, E. and Randrup, A. "Paradoxical" stereotyped activity of reserpinized rats. Int. J. Neuropharmac. 7, 71, 1968.

31. Domino, E.F. Human pharmacology of tranquilizing drugs. Clin. Pharmac. Therap. 3, 599, 1962.

32. Luby, E. Clinical efficacy of reserpine-like drugs. In Psychopharmacology-Review of Progress 1957-1967, Efron, D.H. (Editor). U.S. Government Printing Office, P.H.S. Pub. No. 1936, Washington, D.C., 1968.

33. Faurbye, A. The role of amines in the etiology of schizophrenia. Compreh. Psychiat. 9, 155, 1968.

34. Maas, J.W., Fawcett, J. and Dekirmenjian, H. 3-Methoxy-4-hydroxy phenylglycol (MHPG) excretion in depressive states. A pilot study. Arch. Gen. Psychiat. 19, 129, 1968.

35. Axelrod, J. The enzymatic N-methylation of serotonin and other amines. J. Pharmac. exper. Ther. 138, 28, 1962.

36. Wolstenholme, G.E.W. and O'Connor, M. (Editors), The Nature of Sleep, 416 p. Little, Brown and Co., Boston, 1960.

37. Foulkes, D. The Psychology of Sleep, 265 p. C. Scribner's Sons, New York, 1966.

38. Hartmann, E. The Biology of Dreaming, 206 p. C.C. Thomas, Springfield, 1967.

39. Kety, S.S., Evarts, E.V. and Williams, H.L. (Editors), Sleep and Altered States of Consciousness. Res. Publ. Ass. nerv. ment. Dis. 45, 591 p. Williams and Wilkins Co., 1967.

40. Koella, W.P. Sleep - Its Nature and Physiological Organization,
    199 p. C.C. Thomas, Springfield, 1967.

41. Jouvet, M. Neurophysiology of states of sleep. Physiol. Rev. 47,
    117, 1967.

42. Feinberg, I. and Carlson, V.R. Sleep variables as a function of age
    in man. Arch. Gen. Psychiat. 18, 239, 1968.

43. Williams, R.L., Agnew, H.W. and Webb, W.B. Effects of Prolonged
    Stage four and I-REM Sleep Deprivation. USAF School of Aerospace
    Medicine Publ. SAM-TR-67-59, July, 1967.

44. Dement, W. Dream recall and eye movements during sleep in schizo-
    phrenics and normals. J. Nerv. Ment. Dis. 122, 263, 1955.

45. Koresko, R., Snyder, F., and Feinberg, I. "Dream time" in hallu-
    cinating and non-hallucinating schizophrenic patients. Nature 199,
    1118, 1963.

46. Feinberg, I., Koresko, R., Gottlieb, F. and Wender, P. Sleep elec-
    troencephalographic and eye movement patterns in schizophrenic
    patients. Compreh. Psychiat. 5, 44, 1964.

47. Caldwell, D.F. and Domino, E.F. Electroencephalographic and eye
    movement patterns during sleep in chronic schizophrenic patients.
    Electroenceph. clin. Neurophysiol. 22, 414, 1967.

48. Onheiber, P., White, P., Demyer, K. and Ottinger, D. Sleep and
    dream patterns of child schizophrenics. Arch. Gen. Psychiat. 12,
    568, 1965.

49. Ornitz, E., Ritvo, E. and Walter, R. Dreaming sleep in autistic and
    schizophrenic children. Amer. J. Psychiat. 122, 419, 1965.

50. Brané, A., Caldwell, D.F. and Beckett, P.G. EEG sleep patterns in
    psychotic children. Report to the Midwestern Psychological Assoc-
    iation, May, 1968.

51. Caldwell, E., Frost, M.K. and Domino, E.F. Analog computer
    analysis of EEG patterns during sleep in normal and chronic schizo-
    phrenic subjects. Electroenceph. clin. Neurophysiol. In press, 1969.

52. Gottlieb, J.S. The biologic correlates of the serum factor in schizo-
    phrenia. In Molecular Basis of Some Aspects of Mental Activity,
    Walaas, O. (Editor), 2, 347, Academic Press, New York, 1967.

53. Frohman, C.E., Warner, K.A. and Barry, C.T. Amino acid trans-
    port and the plasma factor in schizophrenia. Report to the Soc. Biol.
    Psychiat., Washington, D.C., June, 1968.

54. Caldwell, D.F. Differential levels of Stage IV sleep in a group of clinically similar chronic schizophrenic patients. Report to Soc. Biol. Psychiat., Washington, D.C., June, 1968.

55. Oswald, I., Berger, R., Evans, J. and Thacore, V. Effects of l-tryptophane upon human sleep. Electroenceph. clin. Neurophysiol. 17, 603, 1964.

56. Mandell, M., Mandell, A. and Jacobson, A. Biochemical and neuro-physiological studies of paradoxical sleep. Rec. Adv. Biol. Psychiat. 7, 115, 1964.

57. Woolley, D.W. and Shaw, E. Some neurophysiological aspects of serotonin. Brit. med. J. II, 122, 1954.

58. Woolley, D.W. The Biochemical Basis of Psychoses, John Wiley and Sons, New York, 1962.

59. Gaddum, J.H. Drugs antagonistic to 5-hydroxytryptamine. In Ciba Foundation Symposium on Hypertension. Wolstenholme, G.E.W., Cameron, M.P. (Editors), p. 75 Little, Brown and Co., Boston, 1954.

60. Diaz-Guerrero, R., Gottlieb, J.S. and Knott, J. The sleep of patients with manic-depressive psychosis, depressive type. Psychosom. Med. 8, 399, 1948.

61. Gresham, S., Agnew, H. and Williams, R. The sleep of depressed patients. Arch. Gen. Psychiat. 13, 503, 1965.

62. Zung, W., Wilson, W. and Dodson, W. Effects of depressive disorders on sleep EEG responses. Arch. Gen. Psychiat. 10, 439, 1964.

63. Kales, A., Heuser, G., Jacobson, A., Kales, J.D., Zweizig, J.R. and Hanley, J. Changing sleep patterns in hypothyroidism. Psychophysiol. 4, 392, 1968.

64. Jus, K., Kiljan, A., Wilczak, H., Kubacki, A., Rzepecki, J. and Jus, A. Polygraphic studies on sleep in never previously treated schizophrenic patients before and during psychotropic drug treat-ment. In Proc. Sixth Internat. Cong. Neuropsychopharmacology. Excerpta Medica Foundation, In press, 1969.

E. F. Domino, M.D., Department of Pharmacology, University of Michigan, Ann Arbor, Michigan 48104

DRUG RESPONSES IN SCHIZOPHRENIA[*]

**RICHARD I. SHADER, LESTER GRINSPOON, JACK R. EWALT, and
DOUGLAS A. ZAHN**

In earlier papers we have reported our findings on the relative
merits of regimes of psychotherapy and milieu therapy versus psychotherapy, milieu therapy, and pharmacotherapy in the treatment of
chronic schizophrenic patients.[1,2] Our findings along with those
of May and Tuma in acute schizophrenic patients,[3,4] seriously
challenge the utility of psychotherapy in schizophrenia while at
the same time strongly suggesting that phenothiazine therapy is
one of the most useful approaches now available to this illness.
The present report is the first of our studies of acute schizophrenia,
and it is focussed exclusively on the pharmacotherapy; subsequent
reports will deal with other aspects of these studies.

Methods

The study reported here was carried out in a small specially
built research ward at the Massachusetts Mental Health Center. The
subjects were acute schizophrenic patients who satisfied the following criteria for admission:

1. That the patient be between the ages of 17 1/2 and 35.

2. That there was no psychiatric hospitalization during
   the twelve months prior to the current episode.

3. That the current episode must be
   a. acute rather than insidious in onset, and
   b. of no longer than two month's duration.

4. That there be some evidence present of both thought
   disorder and disturbance of affect.

5. That there be no evidence of the following clinical
   disorders:
   a. childhood autism or childhood schizophrenia,
   b. chronic or acute brain syndrome,
   c. mental deficiency with I.Q. below 70,
   d. alcoholism a significant feature of clinical history,
   e. epilepsy,
   f. drug addiction,
   g. toxic or metabolic psychoses,
   h. manic depressive psychoses.

[*]Supported by USPHS Grant 5P01 MH 12556.

These patients received no medication upon arrival, and only after they were legally cleared as research subjects did they begin to receive "project medication" capsules. The first week after clearance,* hereafter referred to as "week zero", all patients received placebo. Thereafter, each was randomly assigned to one of the three drug regimes and continued to receive that drug for a minimal period of eight weeks. All capsules were identical in appearance and contained either thioridazine, haloperidol, or placebo. Upon arrival all patients began carefully supervised psychotherapy with a first year resident in psychiatry at the Massachusetts Mental Health Center.

The measures used in this study were as follows:

1. Educational Status: At the time of admission each patient was assigned a value one through seven as determined on the Alba Edwards Education Scale. [5]

2. Prognosis: An Assessment of Prognosis form was completed by the therapists on each of their patients. This scale consists of 12 items, which have been reported to correlate with outcome in schizophrenia. A score of 30 or below correlates with poor prognosis, and one above 30 with good prognosis. [6]

3. Clinical Assessment: This assessment was arrived at by three people not involved in other assessments (the head nurse, the chief resident, and the project director). They each judged whether at the end of the eight week period a patient was markedly, moderately, or slightly improved, showed no improvement at all, or was worse. A consensus of their opinions determined the patient's ultimate rating.

Values for the above three scales were obtained once, whereas the data for the scales which follow were obtained on at least a weekly basis from the time of the patient's admission to the ward:

1. The Hospital Adjustment Scale: [7] This scale (HAS) is a list of statements about behavior which is used to provide a quantitative estimate of the hospital adjustment of psychiatric patients. It is not meant to provide a measure of degree of pathology, but rather to indicate the extent to which the patient is incapacitated in the context of his hospital environment as a function of his illness. The scale was completed weekly on all patients by two members of the nursing staff. While there are three subscales, analyses presented in this paper deal only with the total score.

2. Behavioral Disturbance Index: [8] This index (BDI), developed originally as a device for coding nursing notes, was modified and adapted on the Clinical Research Center ward for use as a rating scale to assess the behavioral disturbance level of schizophrenic patients as

---

*In order for patients to participate as subjects in this research it was necessary for each to have a court appointed guardian. This process took from two days to two weeks, and its completion marked the beginning of the "week zero".

viewed by the nursing staff. It is a 54 item scale which
reflects the degree to which a patient's behavior, thinking
processes, and affect are disturbed. Each patient is rated
twice daily by two members of the nursing staff. While
there are five subscales, analyses presented in this paper
deal only with the total score.

3. The Inpatient Multidimensional Psychiatric Scale: [9] This
is a 75 item scale (IMPS) designed to measure manifest
psychopathology of psychiatric patients. The items are
divided into ten clusters, each corresponding to a different
dimension of psychopathology.

Lorr 1 (excitement)
Lorr 2 (hostile belligerence)
Lorr 3 (paranoid projection)
Lorr 4 (grandiose expansiveness)
Lorr 5 (perceptual distortion)
Lorr 6 (anxious intropunitiveness)
Lorr 7 (retardation and apathy)
Lorr 8 (disorientation)
Lorr 9 (motor disturbances)
Lorr 10 (conceptual disorganization)

The ten cluster scores may be combined into the following
morbidity scores:

EXC + HOS - RTD = excitement versus retardation pattern
PAR + GRN + PCP = distortion of thinking and perception
RTD + DIS + MTR + CNP = schizophrenic disorganization

This scale was completed on each patient on a weekly basis
by their therapist and also by two trained attendents.

4. Likeability Scale: [10,11] The likeability scale contains
six items which assess the nursing staff's conscious
responses toward the patient. In answer to such questions
as "How likeable is this patient?" and "How much did you
like being with this patient?", the staff member responded
by checking minimally, moderately, quite a bit, extremely,
or not at all. The form was completed twice a week by
each of the ward staff on all in-patients.

5. Quantified Mental Status Exam: [12] This exam (QMS) is used
to measure the degree and nature of psychotic symptomatology.
It consists of 16 continua grouped under the three main
categories: "General Appearance and Manner," "Affect and
and Mood," and "Content of Thought and Thought Processes."
It provides a reflection of the clinical judgements and
impressions of the therapists, each of whom completed the
form on a weekly basis on their patients. Analyses presented
in this paper deal only with the total score from this exam.

Data Analysis and Results

I. Comparisons of the Three Treatments: The basic unit of assessment
employed in this study was a change score. This score was obtained by
subtracting the values obtained on all scales in week eight from
values obtained on those same scales in week zero, the pretreatment
placebo week. This procedure was reversed for the HAS since on
this particular scale improvement is associated with a larger score.
The first aim of this study was to compare the efficacy of the three
treatments, thioridazine, haloperidol, and placebo, as measured by

the battery of assessment procedures which have been described above.
One usual approach to this type of research question involves an
analysis of variance in which mean change scores for the three treatment
groups are compared to one another. This approach does not take
into account the initial level from which patients begin their change.
In order to take this important parameter into account, it was our
decision to employ an analysis of covariance in which the initial
scores would be employed as a covariate. It also seemed important,
however, to adjust the treatment groups along other parameters as
well, particularly education and prognosis, in order to take into
account pretreatment differences that might exist. Therefore, we
undertook a series of covariance analyses which utilized initial
or week zero scores, education and prognosis as covariates. Fifteen
individual analyses were completed. The scales employed were the
BDI, HAS, QMS; ten Lorr (IMPS) subscales; the third morbidity score
from the Lorr (IMPS) scale (schizophrenic disorganization); and
the total Lorr (IMPS) score. The results of the analyses of covariance
are given in the following table:

TABLE 1

Covariance Analysis of Change Scores on Three Treatment Groups*
(thioridazine, haloperidol, placebo)

Treatment	Thioridazine	Haloperidol	Placebo	Thioridazine	Haloperidol	Placebo		
Unadjusted and Adjusted Means	Unadjusted Means			Adjusted Means			F_A	p
Variables								
HAS Total	44.7	12.0	19.0	39.2	13.4	22.4	3.29	<.05
BDI Total	19.8	4.5	11.6	19.9	3.4	12.5	3.72	<.05
QMS Total	33.2	16.5	10.4	30.6	16.4	12.8	3.57	<.05
Lorr 1 (excitement)	18.2	9.2	1.5	16.9	5.7	5.8	7.98	<.005
Lorr 2 (hostile belligerence)	9.0	2.8	0.4	6.9	2.5	2.4	0.53	n.s.
Lorr 3 (paranoid projection)	10.9	7.0	6.8	10.1	8.5	6.2	0.81	n.s.
Lorr 4 (grandiose expansiveness)	3.8	1.7	2.9	3.7	2.1	2.6	1.74	n.s.
Lorr 5 (perceptual distortion)	4.3	0.8	1.7	4.3	2.3	0.4	3.13	<.10
Lorr 6 (anxious intropunitiveness)	4.0	-1.2	6.6	5.4	-1.3	5.5	2.01	n.s.
Lorr 7 (retardation and apathy)	9.7	-4.3	-0.1	8.7	-2.1	-1.1	2.90	<.10
Lorr 8 (disorientation)	0.5	0.2	0.4	0.4	0.4	0.3	0.83	n.s.
Lorr 9 (motor disturbances)	17.8	8.2	3.1	15.1	8.1	5.5	6.52	<.005
Lorr 10 (conceptual disorganization)	8.2	8.1	4.3	8.1	7.5	4.9	3.12	<.10
Lorr Total	86.5	32.5	27.6	79.6	33.7	32.6	6.12	<.01
Lorr M3 Morbidity score	36.2	12.2	7.7	32.4	14.2	9.2	5.14	<.025

*The covariates used were educational level, prognosis, and zero week scores on the given variable.

Approximately 13 subjects were available for each of the treatment
groups, and each analysis of covariance involved approximately 40
subjects. On occasion change scores were not available for a given
subject on a given scale, as either a week zero or a week eight score
might be missing. Therefore, the groups were not consistently 13, and
the total number of subjects available ranged from 37 to 41. It can
readily be seen, both from the unadjusted and adjusted mean scores,
that large differences exist among the three treatment groups on the
change scores in the majority of the scales used. Significant differences among the three treatment groups at the 5 per cent level were
found for the HAS, BDI, QMS; schizophrenic disorganization factor of
the Lorr (IMPS); Lorr (IMPS) total; and the subscales of the Lorr
IMPS) 9 (motor disturbances); and 1 (excitement). In addition,
borderline statistical significance was obtained on Lorr (IMPS) subscales 5 (perceptual distortion); 7 (retardation and apathy); and 10
(conceptual disorganization). In all but one of the remaining scales,
Lorr (IMPS) 6 (anxious intropunitiveness), similar, although non-significant, trends were observed. On the seven scales in which significant differences were obtained, thioridazine was consistently superior
to at least one of the remaining two treatments. In no instance was
haloperidol significantly better than placebo. The lack of improvement
on haloperidol may, in part, be accounted for by the presence of side
effects which resulted in proportionately lower doses of haloperidol
being used. This will be discussed below.

II. Who Gets Better?: Although on several variables the covariance
analyses indicated that thioridazine does produce significantly larger
changes than haloperidol or placebo, it is also true that some haloperidol and placebo patients did significantly improve. It, therefore,
seemed of interest to determine what pretreatment characteristics of
patients are associated with response and non-response in this particular
ward setting. In order to accomplish this we needed to be able to
define cohorts of responders and non-responders. This was accomplished
according to the following procedure. The analysis was limited to those
32 patients having complete data on all three scales (BDI, HAS, and QMS)
as well as a clinical assessment rating. As the first step, the

clinical assessments, which were referred to under the methods section, were examined. Patients were dichotomized on the basis of the clinical assessments into two groups, improvers (those rated marked or moderate) and non improvers (those rated slight, none, or worse).[*] This split generated cohorts of 17 improvers and 15 non-improvers. A second step involved the conversion of individual patient change scores on the BDI, HAS, and QMS into standard (z) scores which were then added algebraically to achieve a resultant sum for each patient. These sums were then ranked and dichotomized into groups of 17 and 15 to match the group sizes yielded by the clinical assessment dichotomy. The cohorts so defined by the z scores were considered to be "changers" and "non-changers", respectively. The patient cohorts defined by these two procedures were then examined to determine the degree of agreement between the two procedures. The resulting two by two contingency table is given below.

TABLE 2

Classification of the 32 Patients by Clinical and
Scales Assessment of Improvement

		Clinical Assessment		
		Improvers	Non-improvers	Total
Scales Assessment	Changers	11	6	17
	Non-changers	6	9	15
		17	15	32

A total of 20 patients were similarly defined by these two assessment procedures. The eleven patients who both improved and changed will hereafter be referred to as responders, and the nine who showed less improvement and less change will hereafter be referred to as non-responders. Of the 11 responders who were defined this way, five received thioridazine, three received haloperidol, and three received placebo. Of the nine non-responders, five received placebo, three received haloperidol, and one received thioridazine.

On the basis of a preliminary, step-up regression analysis, eight pretreatment variables were selected for study as discriminants of response and non-response. These eight variables are as follows: education; patient likeability; Lorr (IMPS) 1 (excitement); Lorr (IMPS)

---

[*] The improver cohort consisted of six thioridazine patients, six haloperidol patients, and five placebo patients. The non-improver cohort consisted of five thioridazine patients, three haloperidol patients, and seven placebo patients.

2 (hostile belligerence); Lorr (IMPS) 3 (paranoid projection); Lorr
(IMPS) 5 (perceptual distortion); Lorr (IMPS) 7 (retardation and apathy);
and Lorr (IMPS) 10 (conceptual disorganization). A discriminant function
analysis was then performed using these eight variables. The results
are summarized in the following table:

TABLE 3

Discrimination Between Responders and Non-responders Using

Eight Initial Scores

Variables*	Lorr 1 (excitement)	Lorr 3 (paranoid projection)	Educational Status	Likeability Rating	Lorr 2 (hostile belligerence)	Lorr 10 (conceptual disorganization)	Lorr 7 (retardation and apathy)	Lorr 5 (perceptual distortion)
b weights	.02	.08	-.91	-.37	,06	-.10	.04	.08
Responder Mean	36.18	19.36	3.55	1.69	28.64	16.73	20.55	4.64
Non-responder Means	10.22	9.33	4.33	2.74	11.33	5.89	25.33	4.67

Responder Mean Score on the Discriminant Function = -0.40

Non-responder Mean Score on the Discriminant Function = -2.67

*Variables are listed in the order in which they entered into the step-up regression equation.

Using the weights and cut-off points developed in this analysis, it
was possible to accurately assign 18 of the 20 patients, as can be seen
in the following table. Ten of the 11 responders were accurately
assigned, as were eight of the nine non-responders. In brief, responders can be described as those patients who were initially highly
excited, were described as having paranoid projection, were more
highly educated, and were relatively less liked by the nursing staff.
It should be remembered that this is a post hoc analysis in which the
discriminant function has been applied to the same patients from whom
it was constructed. Further validation of these variables would require
the application of this discriminant function procedure to an independent
sample of similarly studied subjects.

TABLE 4

Results of Applying the Discriminant Function
to the Sample of 20 Patients

| | | Predicted Classification | | |
		Responder	Non-responder	Total
Actual Classification	Responder	10	1	11
	Non-responder	1	8	9
		11	9	20

III. Is Each Treatment Associated With Specific Patterns of Change?: The discriminant function analysis given above was based on week zero scores. In order to answer the question posed in this section, discriminant function analyses employing change scores were carried out. Thirty-two patients were again available for study. Since we are now discriminating between three treatment groups, it is possible to improve our ability to discriminate by constructing two orthogonal discriminant functions and to base our evaluation of specific treatment associated patterns on a pair of discriminant function scores rather than on a single score, as was done in the previous section. On the basis of a preliminary, step-up regression analysis, eight change score variables were selected for study. These eight variables are as follows: BDI, Lorr (IMPS) 1 (excitement); Lorr (IMPS) 3 (paranoid projection); Lorr (IMPS) 4 (grandiose expansiveness); Lorr (IMPS) 6 (anxious intropunitiveness); Lorr (IMPS) 7 (retardation and apathy); Lorr (IMPS) 9 (motor disturbances); and Lorr (IMPS) 10 (conceptual disorganization). A discriminant function analysis based on two discriminant functions was then performed using these eight variables. The results are summarized in the following table.

TABLE 5

Discrimination Among Thioridazine, Haloperidol, and Placebo Using

Two Orthogonal Discriminant Functions

(based on eight change score variables)

Variables*	Lorr 1 (excitement)	BDI	Lorr 10 (conceptual disorganization)	Lorr 4 (grandiose expansiveness)	Lorr 9 (motor disturbances)	Lorr 6 (anxious punitiveness)	Lorr 3 (paranoid projection)	Lorr 7 (retardation and apathy)
b weights for discriminant function 1	0.34	0.32	-0.81	0.20	0.02	0.03	-0.05	0.30
b weights for discriminant function 2	-0.25	0.29	-0.15	0.85	-0.30	0.11	-0.13	0.01
Thioridazine Mean	18.55	20.32	8.55	3.82	17.73	2.64	9.64	8.91
Haloperidol Mean	10.78	6.97	9.44	2.22	12.22	-0.56	9.56	-4.00
Placebo Mean	2.67	10.77	4.50	3.58	6.33	8.00	8.08	-0.67

Discriminant Function Means for the Three Treatment Groups

	Mean Score on Discriminant Function 1	Mean Score on Discriminant Function 2
Thioridazine	9.24	-3.03
Haloperidol	-2.81	-5.24
Placebo	1.18	2.67

*Variables are listed in the order in which they entered into the step-up regression equation.

Using weights and cut-off points developed in this analysis, it was then possible to accurately assign seven of the 11 patients taking thioridazine, six of the nine patients taking haloperidol, and nine of the 12 patients taking placebo. In other words, 69 percent of the patients were accurately assigned to their actual treatment cell by their patterns of change on the eight variables studied. These results are summarized in the following table.

TABLE 6

Results of Applying the Treatment Group Discriminant Functions
to the Sample of 32 Patients

| | | Predicted Treatment Group | | | Total |
		Thioridazine	Haloperidol	Placebo	
	Thioridazine	7	0	4	11
Actual Treatment Group	Haloperidol	1	6	2	9
	Placebo	3	0	9	12
		11	6	15	32

The first discriminant function seemed to separate the thioridazine group from haloperidol and placebo. It weighted heavily the variables on which thioridazine was distinctly superior to both haloperidol and placebo. These were Lorr (IMPS) 1 (excitement); Lorr (IMPS) 7 (retardation and apathy); and the Behavioral Disturbance Index score. Thus, the thioridazine treatment group can be characterized as one in which considerable behavioral change was observed. The second discriminant function, on the other hand, seemed to separate the placebo group from the two active drug groups, thioridazine and haloperidol. The haloperidol treatment group showed less improvement than the thioridazine and placebo groups on the BDI; no change in Lorr (IMPS) 6 (anxious intropunitiveness); and a slight increase in psychopathology on Lorr (IMPS) 7 (retardation and apathy). The placebo treatment group tended to show less improvement than the other two groups. However, on the dimension measured by Lorr (IMPS) 6 (anxious intropunitiveness), the placebo treated patients demonstrated more improvement than either of the two active drug groups. These results tend to be comparable to the covariance analyses results.

Discussion

Our results suggest that psychotherapy combined with thioridazine,

a piperdine phenothiazine, tends to be a significantly better treatment
for young acute schizophrenic patients than psychotherapy combined with
haloperidol, a butyrophenone, or placebo. The criteria for treatment
efficacy involved an assessment of change over an eight week period as
measured by a number of standard rating scales. These findings were
consistent with the length of hospitalization data for the three groups.
Thioridazine patients had a mean hospital stay of 116 days, while
haloperidol and placebo patients had mean stays of 123 and 131 days,
respectively. These findings are particularly striking when we consider
that the statistical procedures used enabled us to adjust for any pretreatment differences that might have occurred, on initial level of
illness, education level, and prognosis, despite the randomization process followed in treatment assignments.

Since haloperidol is accepted as a potent antipsychotic agent, we
must try to understand why it did not appear to be efficacious in this
study. Several factors can be considered, such as assessment procedures,
dosage, and side effects. It is always possible that the assessment
procedures used in a study are more sensitive to the type of change
produced by one drug rather than another. The scales used covered a
broad range of areas including disturbances in behavior, thought, and
affect. It seems unlikely that the differences observed were merely a
function of rating scales artifact.

Dosages may have been an important factor. Physicians were allowed
to prescribe a range of dosages on a four times per day schedule. The
particular range varied from required minium dose of four units per day
to maximum of 12 units per day. Most placebo subjects reached the upper
limits of dosage by the end of the study, although the mean daily dose
was 6.6 units per day. For the thioridazine group, each unit contained
75 mg. of thioridazine resulting in a minimal dose of 300 mg. per day
and a maximum dose of 900 mg. per day. The mean daily dose for the
thioridazine group was 6.9 units or 517.5 mg. Only one patient briefly
received over ten units, receiving a total daily dose of 825 mg. for
only one week of the study. Thus, the thioridazine dosage schedule used
was within manufacturer's specified recommendations (maximum 800 mg. per
day) except for the one, brief exception. For the haloperidol group,
one unit contained 1 mg. of halperidol, which converts to a range of

from 4 mg. to 12 mg. per day. The mean daily dose was 5.7 units, or 5.7 mg. per day. None of the haloperidol patients received over 10 mg. per day. These data suggest that perhaps the dose of haloperidol was proportionately low. Manufacturer's recommendations suggest that haloperidol should be limited to 15 mg. per day. This dose limitation was not reached in our study, and high dosages might have yielded results more comparable to those of thioridazine.

The haloperidol doses remained low because of the extrapyramidal effects of this drug. The syndrome which appeared in most of the haloperidol patients was one of akinesia. It was mainly apparent in slowness of speech, immobility of the face, and slowness in voluntary movements. All three of these items are contained in Lorr (IMPS) 7 (retardation and apathy), and this is undoubtedly the reason for the increase in psychopathology manifested by the haloperidol patients on this subscale. Haloperidol patients also complained of motor restlessness and tremor, and anti-parkinsonian drugs were used when indicated. Most other side effects tended to be comparable between the two active drug groups, with the exception that drowsiness, fatigue, epigastric distress, and postural hypotension were more often reported by the thioridazine patients.

It would appear then that for this group of young, relatively well-educated acute schizophrenic patients that thiordazine was a well tolerated and effective treatment at the dosage used. Since the patients who were found to improve, regardless of treatment assignment, tended to show initial higher levels of overactivity, press of speech, and lack of restraint in their behavior, all aspects of Lorr (IMPS) 1 (excitement), they may have responded better to the sedative properties of thioridazine as compared to haloperidol. Haloperidol was effective in these areas in some instances, but symptom reduction often overshot the mark because of the production of akinesia (i.e. slowed speech or slowed movements).

Many psychopharmacologists are now aware that it may be possible to circumvent the extrapyramidal syndrome by giving much higher levels of drug. It now appears that extrapyramidal effects, which may be prominent when dosages are gradually raised, may be minimized by using higher initial dosage schedules. It should also be noted that Goldstein and Clyde in a study of similarly selected patients, except that their age range covered ages 21 to 55, found that 10 mg. to 22 mg. of haloperidol was the daily dosage level achieved by their patients.[13] They concluded that the effective daily dose for haloperidol was 16 mg. to 20 mg., a range higher than that used in our study, and higher than manufacturer's suggested maximum of 15 mg. per day.

It is also of interest to note that the trend of the findings in this study, to associate improvement with the use of thioridazine, is further mirrored in the analysis which focussed on the patterns of change associated with each treatment. All three placebo patients who were mis-classified as thioridazine patients were placebo patients who could also be defined as responders. The one haloperidol patient misclassified as a thioridazine patient was also a responder.

Summary

Psychotherapy was combined with either thioridazine, haloperidol, or placebo in this double-blind study of newly-admitted, young acute schizophrenic patients. Psychotherapy combined with thioridazine was found to be superior to the other two treatment regimens.

The authors would like to acknowledge the valuable assistance of Miss Linda Twing in the preparation of this manuscript.

1. Grinspoon, L., Ewalt, J.R., and Shader, R. Long-term treatment of chronic schizophrenia: A preliminary report. Int. J. Psychiat. 4:116-128, 1967.

2. Grinspoon, L., Ewalt J.R., and Shader, R. Psychotherapy and pharmacotherapy in chronic schizophrenia. Amer. J. Psychiat. 124:1645-1652, 1968.

3. May, P.R.A. Treatment of Schizophrenia. New York, Science House. 1968.

4. May, P.R.A., and Tuma, A.H. Treatment of Schizophrenia. Brit. J. Psychiat. 3:503-510, 1965.

5. Hollingshead, A.S., and Redlich, R.C. Social Class and Mental Illness. New York, John Wiley and Sons, pp. 398-407, 1958.

6. Stephens, J., Astrup, C., and Mangrum, J. Prognosis in schizophrenia. Arch. Gen. Psychiat. 16:693-698, 1967.

7. McReynolds, P., and Ferguson, J., Clinical Manual for the Hospital Adjustment Scale. Palo Alto: Consulting Psychologists Press, 1946.

8. Framo, J., and Alderstein, A.A. A behavioral disturbance index for psychiatric patients and ward disturbance. J. Clin. Psych. 17:260-264, 1961.

9. Lorr, M., Klett, J.C., and McNair, D.M. Syndromes of Psychosis. London, Pergamon Press, 1963.

10. Shader, R., Binstock, W.A., and Scott, D. Psychiatrists' biases: Who gets drugs? Soc. Sci. and Med. 2:213-216, 1968.

11. Shader, R., Binstock, W.A., and Scott, D. Rational and irrational determinants of treatment allocation. Hospital and Community Psychiat. Jan., 1969. (in press).

12. Rockland, L.H., and Pollin, W. Quantification of psychiatric mental status. Arch. Gen. Psychiat. 2:23-28, 1965.

13. Goldstein, B.J., and Clyde, D.J. Haloperidol in Controlling the Symptoms of Acute Psychoses. Part II : A Double-Blind Evaluation of Haloperidol and Trifluoperazine. Current Therapeutic Research, 18:236-240, 1966.

R. I. Shader, M.D., L. Grinspoon, M.D., J. R. Ewalt, M.D., and D. A. Zahn, Harvard Medical School, Department of Psychiatry, 74 Fenwood Road, Boston, Mass. 02115

A RESEARCH TACTIC FOR EVALUATION OF DRUG SPECIFICITY IN SCHIZOPHRENIA

EUGENE I. BURDOCK and ANNE S. HARDESTY

Behavioral characteristics of schizophrenia are commonly assessed on rating scales in which judgments of behavioral pathology are made concomitantly with a diagnosis by psychiatrists or others concerned with diagnosis. Such ratings are likely to be biased because when diagnosis is in the center of the rater's attention, he is naturally inclined to look more diligently for behaviors that confirm his diagnostic conclusion. Similarly, sensory, perceptual or conceptual defects which accompany schizophrenia are usually inferred from experimental studies of subjects already diagnosed as schizophrenics. It is thus difficult to determine whether the characteristics studied reveal underlying features of the process of schizophrenia or merely reflect the diagnostic biases present during selection of the sample.

Assessment of behavioral characteristics for evaluation of process or change of psychopathology requires independent professional personnel uninvolved with diagnosis and free of responsibilities for treatment. Behavior must be evoked in a standardized situation and those elements relevant for psychopathology rated in explicit rather than global terms.

Zubin has told of a study in which he collaborated with a distinguished genetic psychiatrist who was often critical of the work of others. This study required the psychiatrist to interview the patients for diagnosis and then later to make an independent assessment of constitutional type. The biometric analysis of the data indicated a relation between the constitutional types in the sample and diagnosis. In particular, a correlation was found between leptosomic physique and schizophrenic diagnosis. The geneticist was delighted. But when Zubin cautioned him that since he, the geneticist, had both made the diagnosis and subscribed to the hypothesis, he might have to consider the results an artifact of his investment, the scholar became angry. "I interviewed them," he said, "I didn't look at them."

The technique of the STRUCTURED CLINICAL INTERVIEW which couples a standard interview with an inventory of psychologically significant molecular units of behavior makes possible a uniformly explicit description of behavior which is amenable to statistical treatment and which can consequently be assessed for reliability and used for comparison of diagnoses, for grouping of patients with similar behavioral characteristics and for evaluation of changes in response to treatment. A detailed description of the SCI together with evidence for its reliability and validity has been presented elsewhere (Burdock & Hardesty, 1968).

This investigation was supported in part by United States Public Health Service Grants Nos. MH-04669 and MH-08618 from the National Institute of Mental Health.

Figure 1 illustrates the method of quantifying data obtained through use of such a technique.

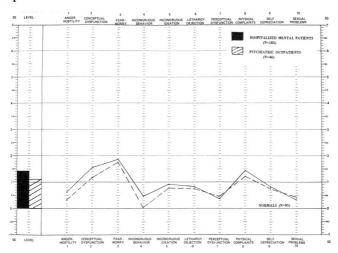

Fig. 1. Comparison of mean scores of inpatients and outpatients.

On the left side of the figure the bar graphs show the mean level of psychopathology, which can be thought of as a measure of overall intensity. This serves as a kind of thermometer which varies with the severity, or acuteness of symptoms. The detailed profile of psychopathology is shown by the 10 subtests whose points have been connected for easier visualization. The 10 subtests, arranged in alphabetical order, are:

1. Anger-Hostility--which may be reflected either in verbalization or in behavior;
2. Conceptual Dysfunction--disturbances of orientation, attention, memory, communication and concentration;
3. Fear-Worry--reports or displays of apprehensiveness, nervousness or anxiousness;
4. Incongruous Behavior--unusual or bizarre gestures or actions;
5. Incongruous Ideation--delusions or ideas of reference;
6. Lethargy-Dejection--sadness, apathy or psychomotor retardation;
7. Perceptual Dysfunction--evidences of hallucinations;
8. Physical Complaints--reports of somatic problems;
9. Self Depreciation--feelings of guilt, inferiority or worthlessness;
10. Sexual Problems--difficulties stemming from sexual attitudes or sexual behavior.

The figure contains the profiles of three groups. The first group of 95 normals in the community is represented by the zero line extending horizontally across the graph. The mean scores of the normals represent for each subtest the zero point of pathology. About 80% of normals can be expected to score below 1 sigma. Scores higher than 1 sigma can thus be regarded as significantly deviant from the norm. The higher the score, the more deviant it is. Deviations in a negative direction simply indicate absence of pathology. Variation below minus one sigma did not occur in the normal group. The solid bar and profile present the average scores of 183 consecutive admissions to a psychiatric hospital, whereas the dashed line and bar indicate the corresponding values for 46 consecutive admissions to an outpatient clinic. The three chief indicators of pathology in both groups are Subtest 3, Fear-Worry, Subtest 2, Conceptual Dysfunction and Subtest 8, Physical Complaints. In each of these subtests the outpatients (dashed line) show less pathology than the inpatients. Because of the heterogeneous composition of the two groups both of which include neurotics together with psychotics, mild cases as well as severe, both profiles tend to be less elevated than those commonly obtained from individuals or groups with severe pathology. Figure 2, illustrates contrasting profiles of small homogeneous groups who were interviewed on admission to a research ward.

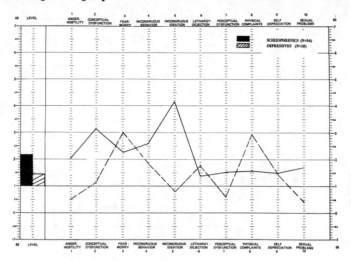

Fig. 2. Comparison of mean SCI scores of depressives and schizophrenics.

Diagnosis was not available to the interviewer and no case records were read by him. The zero line represents the same normal reference group as in Figure 1. This time, however, the solid bar and line show the mean level and profile of a group of clearcut carefully diagnosed inpatient schizophrenics. Their mean level is more than two deviation units above that of normals and the whole profile is elevated above the range of random variation. The highest scores for this group are in Subtest 5, Incongruous Ideation, Subtest 2, Conceptual Dysfunction, Subtest 4, Incongruous Behavior, Subtest 3, Fear-Worry, and Subtest 1, Anger-Hostility. Moreover, the significant elevation of Subtest 7, Perceptual Dysfunction, is almost pathognomonic for schizophrenia. The dashed bar and profile of the Depressives, a group independently diagnosed for the research ward with the same careful procedure as that used for the schizophrenics, show a lower mean level of pathology than the schizophrenics in the bar at the left of the figure, but nevertheless a significantly elevated level. The peak points in their profile are Subtest 3, Fear-Worry, Subtest 8, Physical Complaints, Subtest 6, Lethargy-Dejection, and Subtest 9, Self Depreciation. Unlike the Schizophrenics, the Depressives are with the normal range for Anger-Hostility (Subtest 1), Incongruous Ideation (Subtest 5), Perceptual Dysfunction (Subtest 7) and Sexual Problems (Subtest 10).

They show a comparable amount of Self Depreciation (Subtest 9) and significant but lesser amounts of Incongruous Behavior (Subtest 4) and Conceptual Dysfunction (Subtest 2).

In Figure 3 the same 34 Schizophrenics are shown whose mean scores were compared with those of a group of 18 Depressives in Figure 2, but now divided among the three treatment groups to which they were randomly assigned at admission. As these profiles make clear, pretreatment differences among the three groups are not marked either in level of pathology (bar graphs on the left of the figure) or in the configuration of the subtests, although the placebo group tends to be somewhat higher than the others.

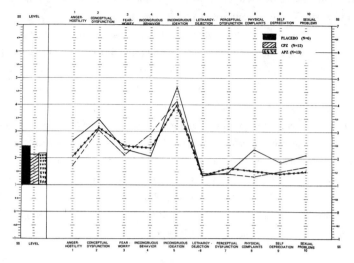

Fig. 3. Pretreatment profiles of newly admitted acute schizophrenics subsequently assigned to three different drugs.

In Figure 4 the solid bar and line once again depict the pretreatment level and profile of the combined groups. The other three profiles show the relative statuses of the three treatment groups after one month. The placebo group (dotted bar and line) shows no improvement; on the contrary, severity of symptoms has increased in almost all areas. The other two treatment groups, acetophenazine (dashed bar and line) and chlorpromazine (X's), both show approximately equal declines in level of pathology to nearly normal. In both groups, Incongruous Behavior (Subtest 4), Perceptual Dysfunction (Subtest 7) and Self Depreciation (Subtest 9) have come within the normal range.

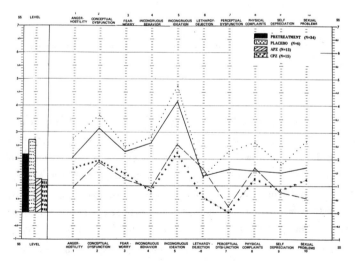

Fig. 4. Follow-up profiles of acute schizophrenics after one month on three different treatments.

178

The acetophenazine group drops to within the normal range in Anger-Hostility (Subtest 1) and in Sexual Problems (Subtest 10), while the chlorpromazine group shows a less significant decline on these two subtests. On the other hand, the chlorpromazine group shows a unique drop in Lethargy-Dejection (Subtest 6) whereas the acetophenazine group shows no improvement at all on this rubric. This finding runs counter to the usual expectation that piperazine phenothiazines are more effective than chlorpromazines in reducing apathy and retardation. A report by Goldberg and Mattsson (1968) provides some independent corroboration for this result. They too found that "apathy and retardation predicts improvement...in chlorpromazine treated patients (contrary to) the general folklore on drug specificity... ."

A recurrent problem in psychiatric diagnosis is that of distinguishing Schizoaffectives from Manics. In Figure 5 the solid line (and bar) of our already twice-used Schizophrenic sample is again reproduced, but now it is contrasted with a dashed line profile of a sample of 12 Manics and an X-ed line profile of a group of 8 Schizoaffectives.

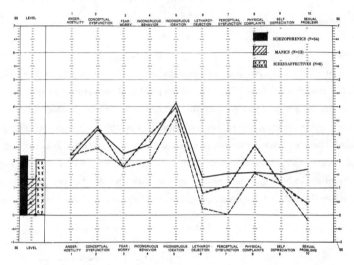

Fig. 5. Comparison of mean scores of schizoaffectives with those of manics and depressives.

Corresponding bar graphs for level of pathology appear on the left side of the figure and show the Manics, as a group, to be at a slightly lower level of pathology than the other two groups. All SCI assessments reflect admission status and were made independently of diagnosis, the separation into diagnostic groupings being made subsequently. In contrast to the Schizoaffectives whose profile follows that of the other Schizophrenics fairly closely, the Manics show no evidence of Sexual Problems (Subtest 10), Lethargy-Dejection (Subtest 6) or Perceptual Dysfunction (Subtest 7). This latter rubric, as pointed out earlier, is almost pathognomonic for Schizophrenia, and thus for Schizoaffectives.

Responses of the Schizophrenics to drug treatment have already been presented. Figures 6 and 7 show the Before-and-After profiles of the Schizoaffectives who were divided into two groups, treated with Chlorpromazine and Lithium respectively.

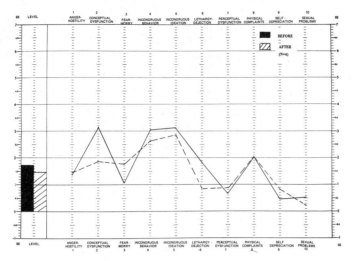

Fig. 6. Profiles of schizoaffectives treated with CPZ.

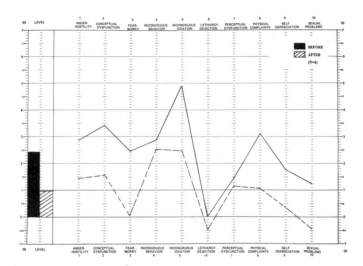

Fig. 7. Profiles of schizoaffectives treated with lithium.

The chlorpromazine treated group shows, after two weeks, a light diminution in level, a drop in Conceptual Dysfunction (Subtest 2), which, however, remains elevated above the normal range, and a decline in Lethargy-Dejection (Subtest 6), to within the normal range, as was found in the case of Schizophrenics treated with CPZ. The Schizoaffectives treated with lithium, though sicker on admission, 2½ deviation units above normal level as compared with 1¾ units for the CPZ group, show a more marked drop, almost to normal level. Perhaps they had more room to travel. Fear-Worry (Subtest 3), Self Depreciation (Subtest 9) and Sexual Problems (Subtest 10) appear to be dissipated and Anger-Hostility (Subtest 1) and Conceptual Dysfunction (Subtest 2) drop nearly to the normal range. Significantly, Perceptual Dysfunction (Subtest 7) remains high, apparently impervious to treatment. Despite similar diagnoses the two treatment groups show certain pretreatment differences which might account for differences in response to treatment: the CPZ group starts with a significant amount of Lethargy-Dejection (Subtest 6) whose reduction by treatment is accompanied by a rise in Fear-Worry (Subtest 3), while the lithium group starts and ends with no evidence of Lethargy-Dejection (Subtest 6), but retains its initial Perceptual Dysfunction (Subtest 7).

In Figures 8 and 9 the Manics previously shown in Figure 5 are divided into the same two treatment groups as the Schizoaffectives. The two Manic groups start at about the same level of pathology. Both treatments are accompanied by a decline to the normal range, although the CPZ group shows a somewhat greater drop.

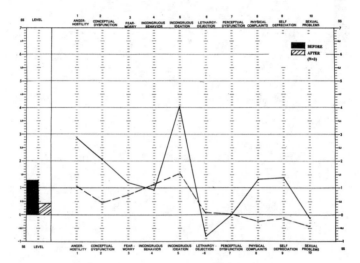

Fig. 8. Follow-up profiles of manics treated with CPZ for 2 weeks.

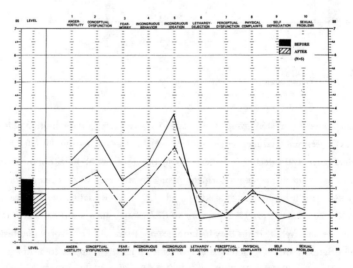

Fig. 9. Follow-up profiles of manics treated with lithium for 2 weeks.

With respect to schizophrenia, the data presented here indicate that individuals classified as schizophrenics can be characterized in explicit and quantifiable terms by those behavioral elements which are critical for the diagnosis. The data also indicate that improvement in schizophrenics treated by phenothiazines tends to be represented by a general downward drift in psychopathology, i.e. a decline in level of pathology rather than a change in the specific characteristics of the illness. In manic-depressive psychosis, on the other hand, the behaviors at opposite ends of the cycle seem like mirror images of one another.

This paper has described a technique which is aimed at obtaining reliable, objective and comparable data in the investigation of psychopathology. Such assessments will be useful to clinicians who seek independent corroboration of their judgments of improvement, as well as to the research psychiatrist who is seeking clues to the determinants of psychopathology and to the relation between the organic and functional components of illness. In the study of manics and of schizoaffectives from which the data presented above is drawn, the SCI profiles will be compared with chemical analyses of urine, blood and saliva to determine the relation between lithium, electrolyte balance and behavior. In the study of the three schizophrenic groups the search for drug specificity is approached in the behavioral realm in a somewhat more objective manner than is the case when the therapist fills in a rating scale. When judgments are made by neutral observers, they can provide corroboration of the psychiatrist's judgment or call attention to alternative interpretations if disagreement occurs.

References

Burdock, E. I. & Hardesty, Anne S. A psychological test for psychopathology. Journal of Abnormal Psychology, 1968, 73, 62-69.

Goldberg, S. C. & Mattsson, N. B. Schizophrenic subtypes defined by response to drugs and placebo. Diseases of the Nervous System, 1968, 29, 153-158.

E. I. Burdock, Ph.D., and A. S. Hardesty, Ph.D., Department of Psychiatry, New York University Medical Center, School of Medicine, 550 First Avenue, New York, N.Y. 10016

PERCEPTUAL AND NEUROPHYSIOLOGICAL ANALOGUES OF "EXPERIENCE" IN SCHIZOPHRENIC AND LSD REACTIONS

JULIAN SILVERMAN

The basic premise of this paper is that experiential reports of schizophrenic and LSD-drugged individuals are extremely significant data. The failure to consider these reports seriously has served to limit our understanding of mental disorder. In the following pages, an evaluation of this area of inquiry is presented. The information derived from the approach is systematically related to important perceptual and neurophysiological researches.

"Scientific" Biases Regarding Experience in Schizophrenic and LSD-Drugged Subjects.

Most research psychologists and psychiatrists do not realize the scientific value of studies of the subjective world of schizophrenic and LSD-drugged individuals. Among the factors which can be cited as reasons for this are the following:

1) Most laboratory studies of behavior are evaluated in terms of effectiveness of performance criteria (adequacy, accuracy, efficiency). Typically the performances of schizophrenic and LSD-drugged subjects on psychological laboratory procedures are less adequate, accurate, and efficient than "normal" subjects. Individuals who evidence such generally ineffective behavior usually are presumed to be unreliable informants regarding their experiences during laboratory testing (e.g. Silverman, 1967, pg.234).

2) Clinical studies of schizophrenic and LSD-drugged subjects are evaluated traditionally in terms of appropriateness of behavior and of degree of reality testing criteria. Often, these subjects do not behave according to standards of personal and social appropriateness and evidence a reduced degree of reality testing. If they make comments, which are indicative of keen awareness, the comments are regarded by the average clinician as extra-ordinary and accidental. All too often, individuals evidencing indications of mental and emotional disorder are presumed to be unreliable informants regarding their experiences during clinical interviews. A monumental example of how such an attitude has affected our conceptualizations in this

field NEGATIVELY is found in Eugen Bleuler's
(1950) famous (and in almost all respects excellent) monograph on the schizophrenias:

> "Sensory response to external stimulus is
> quite normal. To be sure the patient will
> complain that everything appears to be dif-
> ferent and frequently we can observe the ab-
> sence of the "feeling of familiarity" with
> known things. However, this strangeness is
> usually attributable to a deficit in cus-
> tomary associations and particularly to an
> alteration in emotional emphasis, not to
> disturbances of sensation (pg.56) [My Ital-
> ics]."

Bleuler's subsequent remarks regarding this
issue also were to the effect that what the
patient says is one thing and what really is
happening within him is quite another. How
wrong he was!

3) Most ordinary "normal" people (including scientists) experience contact with schizophrenic
and LSD-drugged subjects as mildly-to-moderate-
ly stressful. Manfried Bleuler (1963) has written on this issue as follows: "Something in us
reacts to this experience [of encountering an
insane person] as a serious threat to our own
existence." Sullivan (1927) wrote of the aver-
sion of the "normal" for the "insane." In order
to protect himself from this stressful experience,
the average clinician acquires distance-taking
techniques. (M. Bleuler, 1963; H. Wiener, 1967,
III). These techniques necessarily interfere
with personal communications between patient and
clinician. Thus, rather than effecting open and
direct contact with a schizophrenic or LSD-drugged person, the person is "treated." One consequence of this at-arms-length approach is that
essential signs of disorganization are not uncovered in soon-to-become psychotics (McGhie and
Chapman, 1961; Wiener, 1967, II) and erroneous
and often ineffable signs are relied upon (Temerlin, in press; Wiener, 1967, III).

OVERVIEW

Attempts to obtain detailed information about experiences of schizophrenic and LSD-drugged subjects have
yielded a number of interesting and reliable findings
(e.g. Bowers, 1968; Bowers and Freedman, 1966; Chapman,
1966; Hoffer and Osmond, 1966; McGhie and Chapman, 1961).

Examined in relation to perceptual and neurophysiological researches in this area, these findings indicate that sensory behavior and sensory experience are
fundamental considerations in any explanation of altered psychological states (Silverman, 1968).

Incipient schizophrenic and LSD-drugged subjects
experience stimulation of ordinary-range intensities
more strongly than others. They also report unusual
sensitivities to low intensity stimuli (e.g. Bowers
and Freedman, 1966; McGhie and Chapman, 1961). Sights
and sounds are experienced as brilliant, intense, more
alive, vivid, rich, full of energy, compelling. Inputs
to the other senses also are experienced as being more
acute. Apparently because of this hypersensitivity,
the sensory attributes of meaningful stimuli (e.g. intensity, magnitude, color) often are responded to more
strongly than perceptual and ideational attributes of
stimuli (e.g. configuration, quality, quantity). In
effect, attention is "captured" by the compelling sensory attributes of stimulus configurations. Distract-
ability is markedly increased. Even normally stable
and automatic aspects of perception, such as body-bound-
aries are affected by this new way of experiencing sensory input. Pronounced increases in responsiveness to
sensory events, inside and outside of the body, also
are associated with decreases in attention to other aspects of the environment, including the fundamental self-
environment differentiation. The dedifferentiation of
body boundaries makes it difficult to distinguish between
external sensory events and sensations which have their
origins within the body. Thought-images and feelings
may be experienced as external sensations (realities).
For example, it literally becomes possible to perceive
a person as a figure of ice if he or she is experienced
as cold and not understanding (e.g. Sechehaye, 1951,
pgs.27-30). (This translation of emotion or feeling into sensory experience, is a highly common report). The
extraordinary vividness and strangeness-of-feeling-and-
thoughts may have the quality of revelation and often
is experienced as coming from outside. It is as if
"boundaries" which enable one to differentiate inner
and outer sensations no longer function properly. For
example, an individual under the influence of LSD was
asked his associations to an idea (Savage, 1955). "Instead of producing verbal associations, he had an hallucination of two men carrying in a heavy box, the plastic

representation of the idea he was seeking. So real was the hallucination that he said aloud: "O.K., boys, you can set it down right here," (pg.13).

Norma McDonald (1960) a one-time schizophrenic patient, explained such experiences in the following way:

> "the mind must have a filter which functions without our conscious thought, sorting stimuli and allowing only those which are relevant to the situation in hand to disturb consciousness... What had happened to me...was a breakdown in the filter and a hodge-podge of unrelated stimuli were distracting me from the things which should have had my undivided attention (pg.218). By the time I was admitted to the hospital I had reached a stage of "wakefulness" when the brilliance of light on a window sill or the color of blue in the sky would be so important it could make me cry. I had very little ability to sort the relevant from the irrelevant. The filter had broken down. Completely unrelated events become intricately connected in my mind (pg.219)."

It is most interesting to compare McDonald's interpretation of her breakdown, derived primarily from her experiences, with neurophysiology theorist Donald Hebb's (1960) explanation of a comparably awesome experience:

> "The normally complete dichotomy of self from other depends entirely on the efficacy of the distinguishing sensory cues (pg.743)."

A number of abnormal perceptual phenomena:

> "can be accounted for by the failure of an inhibition which is normally present and necessary for the integration of higher processes... The integration of the thought process, the attainment of veridical perception, and a unified control of response, evidently depends as much on the suppression of some central activities as on the excitation of others (pg.743)."

In this paper, the experience, control, and inhibition of sensory stimulation are considered as the primary variables. Other characteristics of incipient schizophrenic and LSD reactions are derived strictly from these considerations. Part I of this presentation is elaborated primarily from the point of view of the individual who is going "out of his mind." Part II is concerned with the integration of these experiential reports with important behavioral researches.

I. THE SUBJECTIVE-WORLD

1. Heightened Sensory Experience - The Key
   Characteristic

> The usual boundaries which struc-
> ture thought and perception become
> fluid; awareness becomes vivid...
>
> Bowers and Freedman, 1966

Heightened sensitivity to stimulation is a primary characteristic of incipient schizophrenic and LSD reactions. More than fifty years before Bleuler's monograph on the "Group of Schizophrenias" appeared, Conolly (1849) wrote of "a sensible excitement of the mind, more or less partial" in psychotic patients; their "senses become disturbed." The famous schizophrenic Judge, Daniel Schreber, whose autobiography was so extensively studied by Freud, was evaluated by a well known medico-legal expert of the time, G. Weber, as follows:

> "I have in no way assumed a priori the patholog-
> ical nature of these ideas, but rather tried to
> show from the history of the patient's illness
> how the appellant first suffered from severe
> hyperaesthesia, hypersensitivity to light and
> noise, how to this were added massive hallucin-
> ations and particularly disturbances of common
> sensation which falsified his conception of
> things, how on the basis of these hallucinations
> he at first developed fantastic ideas of in-
> fluence which ruled him to such an extent that
> he was driven to suicidal attempts and how from
> these pathological events, at last the system
> of ideas was formed which the appellant has re-
> counted in such detail and so vividly in his
> memoirs...(Macalpine and Hunter, 1955, pg.319)."*

More recently McGhie and Chapman (1961), Chapman (1966), and Bowers and Freedman (1966), employing specially designed interview techniques, reported that alterations in color and sensory quality precede other perceptual disturbances. Most schizophrenic individuals experiencing these changes report that for a time, everything around them looks "fascinating, objects standing out vividly in contrast to the background;" "noises all

---

* This quote is the most incisive summary statement of
  the development of a schizophrenic reaction that the
  present writer has ever read.

seem to be louder...It's as if someone had turned up
the volume." These initial changes in sensory experiences often are regarded as pleasant and a number of
patients, at this stage go through a period of mild-
to-marked elation.

> "One night I woke up and started feeling good
> again...I felt alive and vital, full of energy.
> My senses seemed alive, colors were very bright,
> They hit me harder. Things appeared clear-cut.
> I noticed thing I had never noticed before
> (Bowers, 1968, pg.350)."

Patients report that they regarded everything during
this period with a new significance. "There was a
general tendency for interest to be directed to rumin-
ating about the world and life in general, religion,
philosophy, art, and literature (Chapman, pg.240)."

Identical kinds of observations are documented in the
literature on subjective reactions to psychedelic drugs
(e.g. Cohen, 1964; Savage, 1955). The citation of a
unique case study reported by Bowers and Freedman (1966)
is appropriate here. Two years prior to hospitalization,
their patient had taken LSD. During his admission interview he judged his LSD and schizophrenic reactions to
be essentially the same.

> "I feel my tactile senses are enhanced as well
> as my visual ones, to a point of great power.
> Patterns and designs begin to distinguish them-
> selves and take on significance. This is true
> for the LSD-25 experience also. It's the same
> now as it was with the drug, only then I knew
> I was coming back (pg.242)."

In all cases the individual is acutely aware that
he has stepped beyond the bounds of his usual state of
awareness. Sensory impressions are awesome and attention is directed, in large measure, by them. This
"openness" to stimulation often is associated with a
fear of being swamped by sensations and images. Laing
(1960) terms this the "implosion" of reality -- the
danger of losing all control, of being hurt, of being
obliterated. The natural tendency is to engage in psychological and physical maneuvers which the overwhelmed
individual thinks will restore sensory control.* From
a clinical viewpoint, these defensive maneuvers are
familiar symptoms of early schizophrenia and of LSD reactions -- distractibility, blocking, withdrawal, loss

---

* An experienced LSD-guide usually has no difficulty
  in guiding a subject through such disturbances by
  encouraging him to "engage in the experience and
  surrender to it" (Kast, 1967). It is conceivable
  that comparable techniques will be used widely with
  incipient schizophrenic reactions, in the not-too-
  distant future.

188

of spontaneity in movement and speech. From the viewpoint presented here, their initial purpose is to reduce the overwhelming intensity of, ordinarily regarded, minimal-to-moderate intensity stimulation (Silverman, 1968).

2. Distractibility and Figure-Ground
Disorders

> In psychotic states, where the
> fate of the whole universe may
> be at stake, awareness of ma-
> terial objects and of trivial
> events can be heightened to an
> extent that is outside the range
> of sane experience.

Coate, 1965

The sensory attributes of complex information exert a particularly strong influence on highly sensitive individuals. The term "stimulus-bound" describes
this effect well (Silverman, 1967). The experience of
this effect is one of being "caught," or being "com-
pelled-to-attend" to irrelevant, and otherwise innocuous events in unpredictable ways. Furthermore, it may
be especially difficult for the schizophrenic or LSD-
drugged person to stop attending to incidental stimuli.
The consequences of this failure in inhibition of attention range from annoyance and perplexity all the way to
fragmentation of perceptual configurations.

e.g. "Everything seems to grip my attention although I am not particularly interested in
anything. I am speaking to you just now but
I can hear noises going on next door and in
the corridor. I find it difficult to shut
these out and it makes it more difficult for
me to concentrate on what I am saying to you.
Often the silliest little things that are going on seem to interest me. Thats not even
true; they don't interest me but I find myself attending to them and wasting a lot of
time this way (McGhie and Chapman, 1961,
pg.104)."

e.g. "If something else is going on somewhere, even
just a noise, it interrupts my thoughts and
they get lost (ibid, pg.105)."

Small details like paint brush markings on a wall,
dirt, or slight imperfections in furniture may be experienced forcefully and in effect, temporarily exclude
other stimuli from awareness (e.g. Cohen, 1964; McGhie
and Chapman, 1961; Savage, 1955). "The way one walks,
the rubbing of the nose, the crossing of the knees, the

arrangement of the chairs on the ward and of the
knives and forks on the table, the smoking of a cigarette, the color of a necktie, are all supposed to
have meaning... (Boisen, 1942, pg.25)." Hyperattentiveness to details of stimulus configurations also
results in pronounced perceptual changes. Under the
effects of LSD, in which attention to sensory events
shifts unpredictably from moment to moment, these perceptual changes may occur with amazing frequency:

> e.g. "I feel like I don't have a head, just my
> mouth is moving... My mouth or my lips feel
> very dry. I feel very squished now, sort of
> narrow (Pollard and Uhr, 1965, pg.50)."

Arieti (1961) describes an effect, termed "awholism,"
in which extreme perceptual disorganization is associated with hyperattentiveness to ordinarily disregarded
aspects of a stimulus configuration.

> "For instance, a patient looking at the nurse
> could not see or focus on her as a person but
> perceived only her left or right eye or her
> hand or her nose, etc. Another patient who,
> while she was in a state of dangerous excite-
> ment was put in a seclusion cell, remembered
> that she could not look at the whole door of
> the cell. She could see only the knob or the
> keyhole or some corner or the door (pg.8)."

Chapman (1966) and McGhie and Chapman (1961) cite ex-
cerpts from interviews which are in accord with Arieti's
report.

> e.g. "I have to put things together in my head. If
> I look at my watch I see the watch, watchstrap,
> face, hands and so on then I have got to put
> them together to get it into one piece (Chap-
> man. 1966, pg.229)."

Hyperresponsiveness to details and hyporesponsive-
ness to organizational aspects of the perceptual field
(involving abstracting and relating) are underlying determinants of so-called "thought disorder."

3. Thought Disorder

> In the abstract attitude we trans-
> gress the immediately given specific
> aspects or sense impression...We de-
> tach ourselves from the given impres-
> sion and the individual thing repre-
> sents to us an accidental sample or
> representative of a category...
>
> Goldstein, 1954

Marked increases in the strength and significance with which sensory stimuli are experienced are associated with decreases in the immediate significance of meaningful symbols. Attention becomes passively directed; that is, it is controlled to a greater extent by the compelling aspects of stimulus configurations than by concentration (Bleuler, 1924). Difficulties in differentiating salient from irrelevant stimuli in problem-solving situations occur. Anticipation and logical organized thinking are interfered with. Thinking is "Stimulus-bound." In the extreme, stimulus-boundedness may result in dissolution of the ordinary experience of continuity from moment to moment; goal-directed thinking may be impossible.

   e.g. "It's like being a transmitter. The sounds
         are coming through to me but I feel my mind
         cannot cope with everything (McGhie and Chap-
         man, 1961, pg.104)."

   e.g. "I can hear what they are saying all right,
         it's remembering what they have said in the
         next second that's difficult -- it just goes
         out of my mind. I'm concentrating so much on
         little things, I have difficulty in finding an
         answer at the time (Chapman, 1966, pg.237)."

   e.g. "Everything is in bits. You put the picture
         up bit by bit into your head. It's like a
         photograph that's torn in bits and put together
         again (Patient 3, McGhie and Chapman, 1961,
         pg.106)."

   e.g. "I get fogged up with all the different bits
         and lose the important things in the picture
         (Patient 6, ibid, pg.108)."

Under the effect of LSD, these experiences usually are not unpleasant and often there is little concern about the fragmented ways in which thinking goes on.

4. Blocking

> The most extraordinary formal element
> of schizophrenic thought processes is
> that termed "blocking." The associa-
> tive activity often seems to come to
> an abrupt and complete stand-still.
>
> Bleuler, 1911

In his excellent paper on "The early symptoms of schizophrenia," Chapman (1966), observed that hyper-responsiveness to sensory input is closely linked to the occurence of blocking phenomena ("trances," "blank spells," "thought-deprivation," "dazes"). Blocking phenomena are regarded as transient disturbances in

consciousness which are associated with a failure to
exclude irrelevant stimulation. Many of the patients
interviewed by Chapman stated that they had experienced
some kind of blocking effect on countless occasions and
that this effect was associated with being overstimulated.

e.g. "I just get cut off from outside things and
go into another world. This happens when the
tension starts to mount until it bursts in my
brain. It has to do with what is going on
around me -- taking in too much of my surroundings -- vital not to miss anything. I can't
shut things out of my mind and everything
closes in on me. It stops me thinking and
then the mind goes a blank and everything gets
switched off... I can't control whats coming
in and it stops me thinking with the mind a
blank."

e.g. "I don't like dividing my attention at anytime
because it leads to confusion and I don't know
where I am or who I am. When this starts I
just go into a trance and I just turn off all
my senses and I don't see anything and I don't
hear anything."

This extraordinary statement regarding a kind of all-
or-none control of sensory input actually is quite consistent with recent neurophysiological researches by
Petrie (1967); Buchsbaum and Silverman (1968), and
others and will be considered in detail, at a later
point.

e.g. "You can very easily go into a trance --
it goes on as soon as the mind stops and then
you realize you are not actually seeing anything
or hearing anything. It's a delight -- you
don't feel anxious until you come out of it."

e.g. "My mind goes blank when I listen to somebody
talking to me -- telling me a story and my eyes
just stare and I'm not aware of anything... I
go into a daze because I can't concentrate long
enough to keep up the conversation and something
lifts up inside my head and puts me into a
trance or something but I always wake up later."

Chapman (1966) also reported a blocking effect which
he observed first hand. If the interviewer talked a lot,
and particularly if the communication was conceptually
difficult, the patient would become confused, distracted , and be unable to maintain his line of thought.

When this occurred, the patient lost his initial composure and became manifestly anxious. A perceptible increase in the pressure of the patient's talk was noted at this time. Also, the patient nearly always continued or initiated talk at this point. With further increases in distractibility, there occurred a sudden cessation of talk and/or an apparent lack of attention to what the interviewer was saying. These episodes ranged from a few seconds to one or two minutes in patients "within the first two years of the illness," and for much longer periods of time in longer-term patients and in patients with "additional catatonic symptoms." During these episdoes,

> "the patient does not move, speak, or respond
> to verbal stimulation. Eye-blinking is either
> infrequent or absent and the patient looks fix-
> edly at some point in the room, usually the
> floor. The observer may deliberately introduce
> new stimuli at this stage, such as questions,
> noises, movements, etc.; but the patient fails
> to attend to them (Chapman, 1966, pgs.232-233)."

Blocking phenomena also are common during LSD intoxication. Often words and thoughts are totally inadequate for describing the intense kaleidoscope of feelings and visions.

> "When you ask a psychedelic subject what is
> happening, he can't tell you. He looks at
> you blankly or he gasps: "WOW"! (Leary, 1966,
> pg.71)."

5. Withdrawal

> The most striking aberration of be-
> havior of the schizophrenic patient
> is his tendency to retreat from real-
> ity: not a surprising reaction with
> nerves made raw by warped input...
> Wiener, 1967

The hypersensitive person's avoidance of other people is part of an overall effort to reduce his intake of sensory stimulation. Sensory input may be reduced by minimizing conversation, voluntarily maintaining fixed gaze, closing ones eyes, and in more severe cases, plugging ones ears, or hidding in a corner. Note that some of the illustrations of the blocking phenomenon, cited above, involve other people being a prominent source of overstimulation. The desire to avoid others certainly is a "sensible" one. It is no wonder that some schizophrenic and LSD-drugged individuals interpret their difficulties in controlling sensory input as being due to other people exercising the control.*

6. Loss of Spontaneity in Movement and Speech

> Loss of spontaneity in moving and
> speaking...is associated with a
> heightened awareness of mental and
> bodily processes and flooding of
> consciousness with excess sensory
> data.
> Chapman, 1966

Kinesthetic and proprioceptive responses are reduced in schizophrenic and LSD reactions. Apparently they have to be because they are experienced as over-stimulation. McGhie and Chapman (1961) cite some very good examples.

e.g. "I can't move if I am distracted by too much noise. I can't help stopping to listen. That's what happens when I am lying in bed. If there's too much noise going on I can't move."

e.g. "I get stuck, almost as if I am paralyzed at times. It may only last for a minute or two but it's a bit frightening...Say I am walking across the floor and someone suddenly switches on the wireless, the music seems to stop me in my tracks and sometimes I freeze like that for a minute or two."

e.g. "If I could walk slowly I would get on alright. My brain is going too quickly. If I move quickly I don't take things in. My brain is working alright but I am not responding to what is coming into it. My mind is always taking in little things at the side."

e.g. "When I move quickly it's a strain on me. Things go too quick for my mind. They get blurred and it's like being blind. It's as if you were seeing a picture one moment and another picture the next. I just stop and watch my feet. Everything is alright if I stop, but if I start moving again I lose control."

---

* Sullivan (1953), Boisen (1942) and others have discussed withdrawal from a different perspective -- the absorption of the individual with awesome, cosmic and profoundly serious events. Since the concern here is primarily the defensive character of withdrawal, consideration is not given to withdrawal in terms of the self-absorption of the individual with his inner world. The reader is referred to such sources as Sullivan (1953), Boisen (1936) and Cohen (1964).

Examples of speech difficulties due to overstimulation are the following:
  e.g.   "My brain is not working right -- I can't
            speak properly -- the words won't come."
  e.g.   "If people talk to me about anything -- say
            the weather -- my mind feels no response and
            I have difficulty in finding an answer at the
            time. There's nothing there and I can't get
            the ideas quick enough."
Retardation of movement and speech is characteristic
of most individuals while under the effects of LSD (e.g.
Klee, 1963). The association of heightened sensitivity
to stimulation with reduction in motor responsiveness
also is characteristic of day-dreaming and so-called sensory deprivation. Fischer (1969) emphasizes that in
all of these conditions there is a high sensory to motor
ratio; that is, there is a predominance of the sensory
over the motor component of behavior. The prototypic
example of this is in the catatonic hallucinatory state
with its very high sensory involvement and no motor
performance.

7. Changes In Space Perspective

> Immediate-raw and uninterpreted, i.e.,
> a-logical, sensations are the content
> of experience in non-Euclidian hyper-
> bolic sensory space-time, whereas
> survival space-time is the realm of
> active waking experience, a modified
> sensory space constructed by and re-
> flecting life experience.
>   Fisher, 1969

During schizophrenic and LSD, reactions, attention
to visual stimuli is captured by dominant objects in
the field. Relatively minimal attention is payed to
less impressive stimuli. This has the effect of changing the way in which objects are perceived in space
(Silverman, 1968). In nearby space, objects are experienced as even larger than they are ordinarily, whereas distant objects are experienced as smaller. Events
are perceived "in a world-space...from which the actors
suddenly emerge much larger nearby than in ordinary
(learned) life (Fischer, 1968)" Considered in relation to changes which occur in the experienced intensity
of stimulation, it is no wonder that schizophrenic
and LSD-drugged individuals report that things appear
"strange," "unfamiliar," "different." They are indeed
strange, unfamiliar and different.
The strange and unstable quality of depth perspective also contributes to the loss of spontaneity

in coordinating body movements in space.

    e.g.   "I am not sure of body movements anymore. It's very hard to describe this but at times I am not sure about even simple actions like sitting down (McGhie and Chapman, 1961, pg. 107)."

    e.g.   "The things I look at seem to be flatter as if you were looking just at a surface. Maybe its because I notice so much more about things and find myself looking at them for a longer time (ibid, pg. 105)."

Similar behaviors are reported by normal-state subjects who have been given the hypnotic suggestion that there is no depth to space (Aaronson, 1968). Under this condition, subjects may evidence such symptoms as disturbances of gait, movement, and posture, dysphoria, blunted affect and withdrawal. Movement in a world which may appear "as though painted on a glass window (Savage, 1955, pg. 11)" is beyond the empathic comprehension of normal-state individuals. When no reasonable explanations are available as to how this can be, hidden explanations may be sought by the schizophrenic or LSD-drugged subject.

    8.   Stimulus Intensity Reduction

> For the living organism, protection against stimuli is almost a more important task than reception of stimuli.

          Freud, 1920

There is a paradoxical quality to sensory experience which is exemplified in some of the experiential reports of schizophrenic and LSD-drugged individuals. On the one hand, hypersensitivity is reported in response to ordinary range stimulation. On the other hand hyposensitivity is reported to extremely strong stimulation (Silverman, 1968). (The perceptual and neurophysiological bases for this paradoxical effect will be elaborated upon in Part II of this presentation). Feelings of numbness and paresthesias of the entire body are common (e.g. Klee, 1963). Despite this kind of subjective experience, registration and differentiation of minimum intensity sensations is not lost. An example of this superficially contradictory state is provided by a patient examined by Bowers and Freedman (1966). The subject reported that during the week prior to his hospitalization "My senses were sharpened;" several sentences later he stated in regard to this same period of time: "There was a fog around me in some sense* and

---

* Italics mine.

I felt half asleep (pg.241)."

Paradoxical complaints of blurred vision and a fuzziness in the quality of sensory input also are common (e.g. Savage, 1955). The metaphor of the "trance" is used by a number of patients interviewed by Chapman (1966) and McGhie and Chapman (1961). In many individuals the experience of nonfeeling becomes pronounced.

> e.g. "I am starting to feel pretty numb about everything because I am becoming an object and objects don't have feelings (McGhie and Chapman, 1961, pg.109)."

In it's extreme form, the feeling commonly reported is one of having died (Chapman, 1966; Cohen, 1964; Savage, 1955).*

It is most interesting to note that when schizophrenic and LSD-drugged individuals are placed in reduced sensory-input situations (e.g. sensory isolation) they evidence less pronounced indications of being in an altered state of consciousness (Chapman, 1966; Cohen, S. I., et al., 1963; Pollard, Uhr, and Stern, 1965; Wiener, 1967). This suggests that indications of markedly reduced responsiveness to stimulation are compensatory responses to the experience of being overstimulated. In physiological terms, they are the result of an "attempt" by the sensory control apparatus of the central nervous system to reduce the experienced intensity of sensory stimulation. Unfortunately, this type of sensory adjustment has disruptive effects on other sensory, perceptual and cognitive functions. When overstimulated individuals are placed in a sensory-isolation situation the degree of aberrant behavior and experience is lessened, apparently, because exaggerated sensory-input-reduction responses are evoked to a lesser extent (see Silverman, 1968).

II. PERCEPTUAL AND NEUROPHYSIOLOGICAL ANALOGUES OF EXPERIENCE

In Part I of this paper a relationship was elaborated between the experience of being hypersensitive to stimulation and various aspects of incipient schizophrenic and LSD reactions. Gross alterations in perception and thinking were ascribed to a sensory input modulating system which does not dampen (as it formerly

---

* Other aspects of the experience of having died probably relate to the perception of space-time as being different from moment to moment and of one's self as being "discontinued" or diffused.

did) the intensity of ordinary-range stimulation.
Perceived much more intensely than normally, this
stimulation serves to "bind" behavior and experience
to the immediate here-and-now.* Inhibitory responsiveness in the sensory nervous system (sensory input reduction) has little affect in attenuating the overwhelming experience of ordinary-intensity stimulation.
Feelings of "nonfeeling" co-occur with feelings of
being overstimulated. The overall result is a radically different-than-normal way of experiencing one's self
and one's environment.

Part II of this presentation is concerned with
a discussion of the experimental literature relevant
to these issues. Hypersensitivity in schizophrenic
and LSD-drugged subjects is found in the laboratory.
Paradoxically, reduction of the experienced intensity
of strong stimulation also is found in the same types
of subjects. For example, very unpleasant stimulation
is tolerated less well by nonpsychiatric subjects than
by schizophrenic and LSD-drugged subjects. Additional
researches indicate a neurophysiological basis for the
paradoxical association of feelings of being hypersensitive to minimal-intensity stimulation and feelings
of anesthesia. Because a good deal of this evidence
has already been integrated elsewhere (Silverman, 1967,
1968), this discussion is concerned primarily with up-
dating the review of the experimental literature and
with a consideration of some important issues relevant to research with nonreality-oriented subjects.

1. Sensitivity to Low-Intensity
Stimulation

Until recently, results of experiments on the
sensitivity of schizophrenic and LSD-drugged individuals
were inconsistent with the subjective reports of these
subjects. Hence, statements about extraordinary sensitivity were regarded by most scientists merely as exaggerations and distortions. After all, the experimental evidence indicated that, at most, sensory responsiveness was within normal limits and all too often was
"impaired" just like cognitive and emotional responsiveness was impaired. However, within the past
several years a number of researchers have reported

---

* "Immediate experience, that is, the accomodation
  of thought to the surface of things, is simply
  empirical experience which considers, as objective
  datum, reality as it appears to direct perception
  (Piaget, 1954, pg.381)."

laboratory performances indicative of hypersensitivity
in these nonreality-oriented subjects (Fischer and
Kaelbling, 1967; Fischer, Ristine, and Wisecup, 1968;
Henkin, et al., 1967; Hill, Fischer and Warshay, 1968;
Keeler, 1965; Lapkin, 1962; Maupin, 1963; Rockey and
Fischer, 1967). In contrast with earlier laboratory
reports these studies are consistent with the subjective
report literature; they indicate that during a schizophrenic reaction and under the influence of psychedelic
drugs, 1) ordinary-intensity stimuli are experienced
more intensely than normally and 2) less sensory information is necessary in order to report that a stimulus
is present. Previous failures to demonstrate hypersensitivity in the laboratory quite likely occurred for
several reasons. To begin with, it is very difficult
for an experimenter to control the stimuli to which individuals in an altered psychological state are responding. Considering that these subjects disattend to re-
quests or communications when demands are made on them
(e.g. Chapman, 1966) and, that they are extra-ordinarily
distractible (Silverman, 1968), it should not be at all
surprising if their laboratory performances did not reflect their stimulus-detection capacities. Secondly,
a strong presumption on the part of the experimenter
that subjects would perform in an abnormally inefficient
manner actually may have contributed to the outcomes
of some of the earlier experiments (see Rosenthal, 1966).
Katz, Waskow and Olsson (1968), commenting on such
issues in regard to research with psychedelic-drugged
subjects wrote:

> "The available research literature does not
> indicate that the psychological states which
> are produced have been as carefully and un-
> emotionally described or analyzed as they
> could be, or that the appropriate methods
> for their study have generally been applied...
> (pg.2)."

Finally, the problem of individual differences has undoubtedly contributed confusion to the sensitivity
issue. This problem probably has been less in psychedelic drug studies. Thus, Fischer, et al., (1968)
and McGlothlin, Cohen, and McGlothlin (1967) have found
that many volunteers for psychedelic drug studies tend
to be of a similar personality type in which hypersensitivity to stimulation is common. Nevertheless, considerable personality and perceptual style differences
have been found in individuals who respond differently
under the effects of psychedelic drugs (Fisher, et al.,

1968; Silverman, in press). In laboratory studies of
schizophrenic subjects, the problem is more pronounced.
Performances of heterogeneous groups of schizophrenics
tend to define the extremes of behavior on several basic
sensory response dimensions, including hypersensitivity
and hyposensitivity to stimulation (e.g. Fischer, et al.,
1968; Silverman, 1967). Contrary to popular clinical
impression, the paranoid type of schizophrenic is not
hypersensitive to minimal intensity stimulation. Rather,
the essential or nonparanoid, schizophrenic (Sullivan,
1953), who maintains a perceptually undifferentiated
orientation toward his environment, is the one who is
hypersensitive to stimulation (Silverman, 1968). Indeed,
in studies of normal subjects by Allison (1963), Kaswan,
Haralson and Cline (1965), and others, the maintenence
of a perceptually undifferentiated orientation to input
is associated with greatest sensitivity to low intensity
stimulation. In accord with these findings Sullivan
(1953), has noted that the development of a differentiated delusional system (characteristic of the paranoid
type) has the effect of toning down the intensity of an
acute schizophrenic reaction. Apparently a delusional
system functions as a buffer, which somehow lessens the
impact of sensory stimulation. It is interesting to
note that Sullivan considers this to be an abortion of
the schizophrenic process and a poor-prognosis sign.

> "The patient, caught up in the spread of mean-
> ing, magic, transcendental forces, suddenly
> 'understands' it all as the work of some other
> concrete person or persons. This is an omin-
> ous development in that the schizophrenic
> state is taking on a paranoid coloring. If
> the suffering of the patient is markedly dimin-
> ished thereby, we shall observe the evolution
> of a paranoid schizophrenic state. These con-
> ditions are of relatively much less favorable
> outcome. They tend to be permanent distortions
> of the interpersonal relations, though the un-
> pleasantness of the patient's experience grad-
> ually fades and a quite comfortable way of life
> may ultimately ensue...(pg.153). A paranoid
> systematization is therefore, markedly benefi-
> cial to the peace of mind of the person chief-
> ly concerned, and its achievement in the course
> of a schizophrenic disorder is so great an im-
> provement in security...(Sullivan, 1953, pg.157)."

Laboratory sensitivity studies have not differentiated
between schizophrenic subjects in terms of degree of systematized delusional activity. No doubt consideration

of this aspect of behavior will shed further light on
the nature of hypersensitivity in schizophrenic states.*
At present it appears that in incipient schizophrenia
(and under the effects of psychedelic drugs) hypersensitivity and, associated with it, undifferentiated perceptual and cognitive activity are fundamental response
characteristics; they emerge earlier in time than "paranoid coloring," and "paranoid systematization." At
least, in part, paranoid adjustments may be considered
as attempts to free oneself from the hypersensitive,
high excitation state, from the "implosion" of reality.
In this context, a delusional construction is literally
an attempt at making NONSENSE out of intense SENSE
experience.

 2. Hypersensitivity, Overstimulation and
 Paradoxical Reduction Responsiveness

 Individuals, who are hypersensitive to low intensity
stimulation react strongly to ordinary sensory events in
the here-and-now. Experimental studies indicate that
these subjects have difficulty in inhibiting responsiveness to irrelevant, contextual stimuli when the stimuli
are of low-to-moderate intensity (Palmer, 1966; Silverman, 1967). However, inhibition of response is observed
in hypersensitive individuals when the intensity of stimulation presented is "very strong" (Silverman, 1967).
Pavlov (1957) suggested an explanation for such findings.
He observed that organisms who are hypersensitive to
stimulation are most likely to become overstimulated.
If overstimulation occurs, he hypothesized that a generalized state of "protective inhibition" is induced in order
to protect the nervous system from further stimulation.
If further strong stimulation is registered in this state,
more protective inhibition is generated; the organism
now is observed to evidence reduced responsiveness to
strong stimuli. Thus, hypersensitivity and overstimulation are among the basic precursors of reduced responsiveness to strong stimulation and reduced responsiveness to strong stimulation is characteristic of
schizophrenic and LSD-drugged subjects. Excellent illustrations of this kind of response to strong stimulation
are provided by Donoghue (1964) and Kast (e.g.1966).**

---

 * In any case it will always be a noteworthy report
 when hypersensitivity is demonstrated in nonreality
 oriented subjects. Obviously other laboratory
 techniques for inferring hypersensitivity need to
 be developed, e.g. Silverman et al., submitted for
 publication.

 ** For a more extensive survey of the literature in this
 and related areas see Silverman, 1967, pgs.229-235
 and pgs. 239-243.

201

Donoghue (1964), using the psychophysical method
of single stimuli, recorded the judgments of sounds
of different intensities by sixty schizophrenic subjects
and thirty nonpsychiatric control subjects. (I. Q.
scores and years of education were not significantly
different in the two groups; mute and uncooperative
patients were excluded from the study). Sound intensity ratings were made by subjects on a six point
scale ranging from pleasant to unpleasant. Median values (in decibels) of the sound intensities rated
"slightly unpleasant" and "very unpleasant" were computed for each subject. Schizophrenic subjects were
found to require a significantly more intense stimulus
than nonschizophrenics in order for them to rate a
stimulus as "slightly unpeasant." An intensity which
was rated as "very unpleasant" among control group subjects was likely to be rated as only "slightly unpleasant" by schizophrenic subjects (Fig. 1). The results

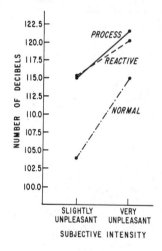

FIG. 1. Degree of unpleasant-
ness ratings of a 440 cps.
tone presented at different
intensities to normal subjects and to process and reactive schizophrenics (from
Donoghue, 1964).

of a number of pain reactivity experiments also have
indicated the occurrence of reduced responsiveness to
strong stimulation in schizophrenic subjects (Silverman,
1967). Investigations of pain tolerances in individuals
under the influence of LSD have yielded similar results.
Kast and Collins (1964) studied the pain reactions of
50 gravely ill medical patients before and after the
administration of 100μ of LSD. Pain reaction scores for
LSD were compared with pain reaction scores obtained
while subjects were under the effects of two other established and potent analgesics, meperidine (Demerol)

and Dilaudid. "When compared with LSD-25, both drugs
fell short in their analgesic action, although the onset of therapeutic action of LSD-25 was somewhat slower
(pg.290)." In a subsequent study of 128 terminal cancer
patients (Kast, 1967), 100µ dosages of LSD were found
to provide substantial relief from pain with a minimum
of medical and psychiatric side-effects. Marked relief
from pain occurred about 2-3 hours after LSD administration and lasted approximately 12 hours. Compared with
pain scores obtained before LSD administration, pain
scores after LSD administration remained lower for a
three week period (Figs. 2 and 3).

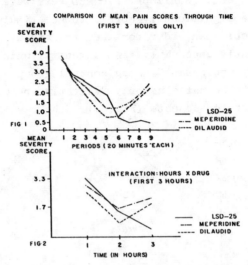

FIG. 2. Comparisons of the
effects of three analges-
ics (From Kast and Collins,
1964).

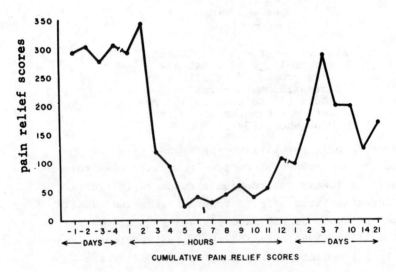

FIG. 3. Pain relief scores
following administration
of 100µ of LSD (Kast,1967).

203

Recent electroneurophysiological studies by Buchsbaum and Silverman (1968) and others (Blacker, Jones,
Stone and Pfefferbaum, 1968; Silverman, Buchsbaum and
Henkin, submitted for publication) have indicated that
reduced responsiveness to strong stimulation occurs on
the electroencephalographic averaged evoked response
(AER) procedure. By averaging electrical potentials,
recorded from the scalp, for long series of stimuli,
such as light flashes, an averaged evoked response waveform is produced. For a given individual, the amplitudes of certain peaks of the waveform change systematically with changes in stimulus intensity. In the mod-
erate-to-high range of stimulus intensities, amplitudes
of one particular peak of the waveform (Peak 4) are
found to change in different ways for individuals with
different perceptual judgment characteristics. In
brief, subjects who reduce the sizes of tactile judgments of width, following a period of tactile stimulation, evidence quite different AER patterns than subjects who augment the sizes of tactile judgments following stimulation. Size judgment "reducers" evidence
relatively decreased AER amplitudes at the higher stimulus intensities. Size judgment "augmenters" evidence
increases in AER amplitudes with increases in stimulus
intensity (Fig. 4). This effect is found in normal

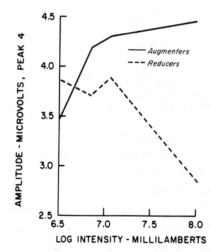

FIG. 4. Amplitudes of averaged
evoked responses to four intensities of photic stimulation
for normal size-judgment-aug-
menter and normal size-judgment-
reducer subjects' (from Buchsbaum and Silverman, 1968).
Note: Peak 4 designation is
based upon numbering system of
Kooi and Bagchi (1964). Light
values in lumen seconds range
from 32 to 980 lumen seconds.

subjects and in various psychiatric patient and medical
patient groups.

The AER reduction curve was found to be pronounced
in a small group of college-age, reducer, essential
schizophrenic males (Buchsbaum and Silverman, 1968). A
comparable AER reduction curve was reported by Blacker
and his collegues (1968) for habitual LSD users who had
not ingested LSD within 48 hours of the EEG recording
(Fig. 5). Other studies of LSD-drugged subjects, employing rather different AER procedures, yielded results

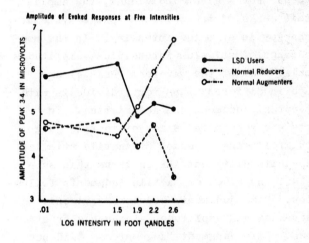

FIG. 5. Amplitudes of averaged evoked responses to
five intensities of stimulation for three groups of
subjects (from Blacker, et
al., 1968).
Note: Light intensities 1.5
to 2.6 in foot candles are
similar to the light intensities employed by Buchs-
baum and Silverman, 1968,
measured in millilamberts.

which are consistent with the hypothesis of reduced
responsiveness to strong stimulation (Chapman and
Walter, 1964; Rodin and Luby, 1966).

Most recently, it has been observed that an AER
reduction curve also occurs among normal, male subjects
whose performances on traditional sensory threshold
procedures are indicative of greater sensitivity to low
intensity stimulation (Silverman, Buchsbaum and Henkin,
submitted for publication). Individuals with augmenter
AER curves tend not to be as sensitive to low intensity
stimulation. Consistent with this finding are others
which indicate that administration of phenothiazines
to schizophrenic subjects changes baseline AER reduction
to AER augmentation (Singer, et al., in press), and that
phenothiazines also cause individuals to be less sensitive to low intensity stimulation (Fischer and Kaelbing,

1967). Thus, the hypersensitivity formulation elaborated here receives considerable support. Experimental studies turn out to be consistent with subjective reports.

Taken together these researches indicate that the study of the sensory nervous system is of fundamental importance for our understanding of schizophrenic and LSD reactions. Furthermore, the value of carefully listening to and examining the subjective reports of our nonreality oriented subjects is confirmed; they do have substantive things to teach us about altered psychological states.

REFERENCES

1. Aaronson, B. S. Hypnotic alterations of space and time. In Proceedings of an International Conference on Hypnosis, Drugs, Dreams, and PSI, 1967. Garrett Press Inc., New York, 1968.

2. Allison, J. Cognitive structure and receptivity to low intensity stimulation. J. abnorm. soc. Psychol. 67, 132-138, 1963.

3. Arieti, S. The loss of reality. Psychoanal. Rev. 3, 3-24, 1961.

4. Blacker, K. H., Jones, R. T., Stone, G. C. and Pfefferbaum, D. Chronic users of LSD: The "Acidheads." Amer. J. Psychiat. 125, 341-351, 1968.

5. Bleuler, E. Textbook of Psychiatry. Macmillan, New York, 1924.

6. Bleuler, E. (Orig. publ. 1911). Dementia Praecox or the Group of Schizophrenias. (Translated by Zinkin, J.) International University Press, New York, 1950.

7. Bleuler, M. Conceptions of schizophrenia within the last fifty years and today. Proc. Roy. Soc. Med. 56, 945-952, 1963.

8. Boisen, A. T. The Exploration of the Inner World. Harper, New York, 1936.

9. Boisen, A. T. The form and content of schizophrenic thinking. Psychiat.5, 23-33, 1942.

10. Bowers, M. B. Pathogenesis of acute schizophrenic psychosis: an experimental approach. Arch. Gen. Psychiat. 19, 348-355, 1968.

11. Bowers, M. B. and Freedman, D. X. "Psychedelic" experiences in acute psychoses. Arch. Gen. Psychiat. 15, 240-248, 1966.

12. Buchsbaum, M. and Silverman, J. Stimulus intensity control and the cortical evoked response. Psychosom. Med. 30, 12-22, 1968.

13. Chapman, J. The early symptoms of schizophrenia. Brit. J. Psychiat. 112, 225-251, 1966.

14. Chapman, L. F. and Walter, R. D. Actions of lysergic acid diethylamide on averaged human cortical evoked responses to light flash. In Recent Advances in Biological Psychiatry, VII, Wortis, K., (Editor), Plenum Press, New York, 1964.

15. Coate, M. Beyond All Reason, Lippincott, New York, 1965.

16. Cohen, S. The Beyond Within: The LSD Story. Athenium Press, New York, 1964.

17. Cohen, S. I., Silverman, A. J. and Shmavonian, B. M. Psychophysiological studies in altered sensory environments. J. Psychosom. Res. 6, 259-281, 1963.

18. Conolly, J. The Croonian Lectures, 1849. Reprinted from the Lancet by C. B. Birnie, St. Bernard's Hospital, Southall, England, 1960.

19. Donoghue, J. R. Motivation and conceptualization in process and reactive schizophrenia. Unpublished doctoral dissertation, University of Nebraska, 1964.

20. Fischer, R. Space-time coordinates of excited and tranquilized states. In Psychiatry and Art, Jakob, I. (Editor) S. Karger, Basel, New York, 1968.

21. Fischer, R. On creative, psychotic and exstatic states. In Proceedings of the American Society of Psychopathology of Expression, Jakob, I. (Editor) Karger, Basel, 1969.

22. Fischer, R. and Kaelbling, R. Increase in taste acuity with sympathetic stimulation: The relation of a just-noticeable taste difference to systemic psychotropic drug dose. Recent Advances in Biological Psychiat. 9, 183-195, 1967.

23. Fischer, R., Marks, P. A., Hill, R. M., and Rockey, M. A. Personality structure as the main determinant of drug induced (model) psychoses. Nature, 218, 296-298, 1968.

24. Fischer, R., Ristine, L. P. and Wisecup, P. Increase in gustatory acuity and hyperarousal in schizophrenia. Soc. Biol. Psychiat., in press.

25. Freud, S. Beyond the Pleasure Principle. (Originally published in 1920). The Complete Works of Sigmund Freud. Standard Ed. 18, London, 1955.

26. Goldstein, K. "Methodological approach to the study of schizophrenia. In Language and Thought Schizophrenia. Kasanin, J. S. (Editor), University of California Press, Berkeley, 1954.

27. Hebb, D. The American Revolution. Amer. Psychol. 15, 735-745, 1960.

28. Henkin, R., Buchsbaum, M., Welpton, D., Zahn, T., Scott, W., Wynne, L., Silverman, J. Physiological and psychological effects of LSD in chronic users. Presented at the Eastern Meeting of the American Federation for Clinical Research, December, 1967.

29. Hill, R. M., Fischer, R. and Warshay, D. Effects of psychodysleptic drug psilocybin on visual perception: changes in brightness preference. Submitted for publication, Experientia, 1968.

30. Hoffer, A. and Osmond, H. Some psychological consequences of perceptual disorder and schizophrenia. Int. J. Neuropsychiat. 2, 1-19, 1966.

31. Kast, E. C. LSD and the Dying Patient. Chicago Med. School Quarterly, 26, 80-87, 1966.

32. Kast, E. C. Attenuation of anticipation: A therapeutic use of lysergic acid Diethylamide. Psychiat. Quart., 41, 1-12, 1967.

33. Kast, E. C. and Collins, V. J. Lysergic Acid Diethylamide as an Analgesic Agent. Anesthesia and Analgesia, 43, 285-291, 1964.

34. Kaswan, J., Haralson, Sally and Cline, Ruth. Variables in perceptual and cognitive organization and differentiation. J. Pers., 33, 164-177, 1965.

35. Katz, M.M., Waskow, I.E. and Olsson, J. Characterizing the psychological state produced by LSD. J. Abnorm. Psychol., 73, 1-14, 1968.

36. Keeler, M.H. The effects of psilocybin on a test of after-image perception. Psychopharm., 8, 131-139, 1965.

37. Klee, G.D. Lysergic acid diethylamide (LSD-25) and ego function. Arch. Gen. Psychiat., 8, 461-474, 1963.

38. Kooi, K.A. and Bagchi, B.K. Visual evoked responses in man: Normative data. Ann. N.Y. Acad. Sci., 112, 254, 1964.

39. Laing, R.D. The Divided Self. Tavistock, London, 1960.

40. Lapkin, B. The relation of primary-process thinking to the recovery of subliminal material. J. Nerv. Ment. Dis., 135, 10-25, 1962.

41. Leary, T. The experiential typewriter. Psychedelic Rev., No. 7, 70-85, 1966.

42. Macalpine, Ida and Hunter, R. A. Daniel Paul
    Schreber-Memoirs of my Nervous Illness. W.
    M. Dawson and Sons, Ltd., London, 1955.

43. Maupin, Barbara A. M. The Effect of Altered
    Ego States on the Utilization of Subliminal
    Registrations of Color, unpublished disserta-
    tion, University of Michigan, 1963.

44. McDonald, Norma. Living With Schizophrenia. Canad.
    Med. Assoc. J. 82, 218-221, 1960.

45. McGhie, A. and Chapman, J. Disorders of attention
    and perception in early schizophrenia. Brit.
    J. Med. Psychol. 34, 103-116, 1961.

46. McGlothlin, W., Cohen, S. and McGlothlin, M. S.
    Long lasting effects of LSD on normals. Arch.
    Gen. Psychiat. 17, 521-532, 1967.

47. Palmer, R. D. Visual acuity and excitement. Psy-
    chosom. Med. 28, 364-374, 1966.

48. Pavlov, I. P. General types of animal and human
    higher nervous activity. In I. P. Pavlov's
    Experimental Psychology and Other Essays. Phil-
    osophical Library, New York, 1957.

49. Perry, J. W. Reconstitutive process in the psycho-
    pahtology of the self. Annals New York Acad.
    Science 96, 853-876, 1962.

50. Petrie, Asenath. Individuality in pain and suf-
    fering, Chicago. University of Chicago Press,
    1967.

51. Piaget, J. The construction of reality in the
    child. Basic Books, New York, 1954.

52. Pollard, J. and Uhr, L., and Stern, Elizabeth.
    Drugs and Phantasy, The Effects of LSD, Psilocy-
    bin, and Sernyl on College Students. Little,
    Brown and Company, Boston, 1965.

53. Rockey, M. and Fischer, R. An interpretation of
    the aesthetic experience of non-artists under
    psilocybin. Proceedings of the Fifth Inter-
    national Congress on Psychopathology of Expres-
    sion, 1967, in press.

54. Rodin, E. and Luby, E. Effects of LSD-25 on the
    EEG and photic evoked responses. Arch. Gen.
    Psychiat., 14, 435-441, 1966.

55. Rosenthal, R. Experimenter effects in behavioral
    research. Appleton-Century-Crofts, New York,
    1966.

56. Savage, C. Variations in ego feeling induced by
    D-Lysergic Acid Diethylamide (LSD-25). Psycho-
    anal. Rev. 42, 1-16, 1955.

57. Sechehaye, M. Autobiography of a schizophrenic
    girl. Gruen and Stratton, New York, 1951.

58. Silverman, J. Variations in cognitive control and psychophysiological defense in the schizophrenias. Psychosom. Med. 29, 225-251, 1967.

59. Silverman, J. The study of individual differences in the effects of LSD-25 on sensory-perceptual functioning. A report of a pilot study. In Proceedings of the Conference on Adverse Reactions to LSD, 1967. NIMH Publication, in press.

60. Silverman, J. A paradigm for the study of altered states of consciousness. Brit. J. Psychiat. 114, 1201-1218, 1968.

61. Silverman, J., Buchsbaum, M. and Henkin, R. Stimulus sensitivity and stimulus intensity control. Perceptual and Motor Skills, 28:71-78, 1969.

62. Singer, M., Borge, G., Almond, R., Buchsbaum, M., Silverman, J. and Wynne, L. C. Correlation between phenothiazine administration, clinical course and perceptual (neurophysiological) measures. Clinical Res., 17:133, 1969.

63. Sullivan, H. S. The common field of research and psychiatry. Psychiatric Quart. 1, 276-291, 1927.

64. Sullivan, H. S. (Originally written in 1940). Conceptions of Modern Psychiatry, New York, 1953.

65. Temerlin, M. K. Suggestion effects in psychiatric diagnosis. J. Nerv. Ment. Dis., in press.

66. Wiener, H. External Chemical Messengers. I. Emission and Reception in Man, New York State J. Med. 66, 3153-3170, 1966.

67. Wiener, H. External Chemical Messengers. II. Natural History of Schizophrenia, New York State J. Med. 67, 1144-1165, 1967.

68. Wiener, H. External Chemical Messengers. III. Mind and Body in Schizophrenia, New York State J. of Med. 67, 1287-1310, 1967.

J. Silverman, Ph.D., Agnews State Hospital, San Jose, California

QUANTITATIVE ANALYSIS OF "MOTOR PATTERN" IN SCHIZOPHRENIA

TURAN M. ITIL

Morphological and biochemical studies have failed to answer some of the basic questions concerning schizophrenia. One of these basic questions relates to the problem of nosology. There is recognized dissatisfaction with present-day nomenclature in the diagnosis of this illness and more so in the classification of the subgroups. The lack of objective measurements hampers the evaluation and the treatment of schizophrenia. The manifest psychopathology is the main variable on which diagnosis and subclassification depend. Because the psychopathology of schizophrenic patients is determined almost exclusively on the basis of "verbalized mental aberrations," in recent years attempts have been made to develop "objective" assessment devices in the form of rating scales.[1-4] Although this type of psychopathological evaluation is superior to overall psychopathological judgment for research purposes, it still has limited value. The symptoms included in these scales are usually arbitrarily selected, their evaluation as absent or present is subjective or interpretative, their definitions are variable, and their explanations are abstract.

Since the introduction of classical psychotropic drugs in psychiatry, the need for objective methods to evaluate human behavior has become more obvious. Like other investigators, we have developed rating scales to evaluate psychopathology in wards and during occupational therapy for use in our psychopharmalogical research.[5,6]

Seeking more objective fundamental data to evaluate behavioral patterns of schizophrenic patients, we attempted to develop a new method which is primarily focused on the motor aspects of behavior rather than the psychopathology. Based on the discoveries of Whitman[7] and Heinroth[8] that certain motor coordinations are just as reliable and widely spread taxonomic characters as any morphologic properties, we began

Supported, in part, by USPHS grant MH-11381 and the Psychiatric Research Foundation of Missouri.

collecting behavioral information using cinematographic techniques. We were interested in analyzing various spatio-temporal
patterns of muscular contractions (kinetic pattern) in an effort to maximize the objectivity of behavioral observations
and permit a more precise and sensitive measure of the "degree
of manifestation" of the variables.

Work of this nature is not new. Description of the
observable behavior from the point of view of causation, survival value, and evolution was introduced in animal behavior
research by Lorenz,[9] who used the term of _ethology_ to describe
this approach. Lorenz[10] defined ethology as the application
of orthodox biological methods to the problems of behavior.
An ethologist, like a psychologist, is interested in studying
"behavior phenomena" wherever they are found.[11] The methods
used, however, have not been spared criticism.[12] Based on the
concept that the underlying causes of man's behavior do not
qualitatively differ from the causes of animal behavior,[13]
ethological methods have already been applied in human behavioral research. Kretschmer[14] described the role of the
motor pattern in relation to normal and pathological life
processes. We reported that a variety of hyperkinetic movements are distinct "motor patterns" associated with characteristic neurological and psychopathological syndromes during
gradual deterioration of cerebral organic patients.[15]

Proceeding on the principle expressed by Hinde[16] that
"behavior is mediated by the nervous system and every particular pattern of behavior is mediated by a particular nervous
system mechanism or pattern of nervous activity," we utilized
the basic empirical approach of an ethologist for the assessment of the motor behavioral alterations of schizophrenic
patients during drug treatment. Our first aim has been to
provide a descriptive analysis of the types of spontaneous
behavior present in the behavioral repertoire of an individual patient and explore the interrelationships among the

various behavioral categories. This presentation will be
limited to an outline of our method and some of the preliminary results. The detailed study will be reported elsewhere.[17]

MATERIAL AND METHOD

Investigations have been carried out primarily on hospitalized chronic schizophrenic patients during placebo and
active drug treatment periods.

Environmental considerations. Each patient was brought
into a room (which was called a visiting room) and was told
that he was "free to do as he pleased." To avoid complicating
external stimuli in terms of potential interaction with other
persons or observers, the subject was placed in the room by
himself and was observed without his knowledge through a one-
way mirror running along one wall of the room. Since we wanted
the setting per se to be as "natural" as possible, we furnished
it as a typical living room with the usual accoutrements. In
addition to the standard furnishings, papers, pencils, drawing
supplies, magazines, and a radio were made available to the
subject and a table on which he could work was placed in one
corner of the room. Thus, although the setting was simple,
unstructured, and standardized, it retained a degree of complexity that would facilitate the emitting of a variety of
behavioral responses (depending on the patient's inclinations).

Behavior categories. The behavior categories to be
observed and assessed in this environmental setting were developed purely on an empirical basis after many months of
observing schizophrenic patients on the hospital ward. Sixty
motor behavior characteristics that most frequently occurred
on the ward were listed. After patients were studied in the
experimental setting, these were reduced to 37 by deleting infrequently occurring categories and combining several categories
under a general label based on certain motor syndromes known to

neurologists (Fig. 1). These 37 motor behavior characteristics were divided into 9 clusters, for example, behavior of eyes, mouth, and face, task orientation, motor orientation, and various types of motor activity.

A major problem we had to deal with in developing some of the categories was the degree of "abstractness" or generality of the descriptive labels placed on the responses. For example, the items of spontaneous laugh, facial mannerism, meaningless task, etc. involve what can be considered the bizarre and abnormal behavioral responses so typical of the schizophrenic process and are relatively easy to score. We found, however, that despite the "abstract" qualities and subjectivity of certain labels, designations such as "simple vs. complex," "rhythmic vs. nonrhythmic," and "unusual" are very useful for characterizing certain motor behavior syndromes. Similarly, we classified the subject's interactions with objects in the environment (putting out a cigarette, playing solitaire, etc.) according to the degree of concentration or attention given to the task, a general characteristic along which all environmental interactions can be dimensionalized and a relevant dimension in terms of the subject's contact with reality or, conversely, his degree of internal preoccupation. Thus, putting out a cigarette would be a level I task (little concentration, short attention span), whereas playing solitaire would constitute a level III task (sustained attention and concentration). This is probably our most subjective scoring category in terms of deciding at what level to place the behavior. There is, however, never any question as to whether the behavior belongs in this general category, i.e., the observers can always agree that the subject is interacting with his environment. There may be some disagreement as to the degree of the interaction (but never more than one level).

Assessment. To assess the behavioral pattern, we again

214

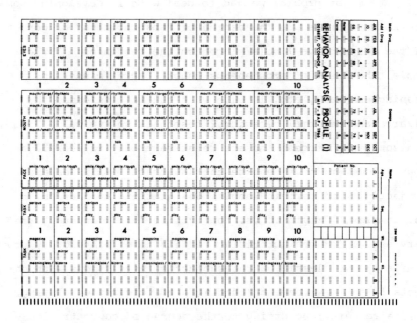

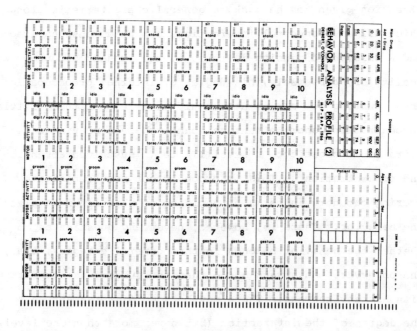

FIG. 1

used the ethologist's method and attempted to count the frequency of the occurrence of the behavioral responses. A
difficulty arises, however, when one is trying to assess
several behavioral responses at one time. It is impossible
for one or two observers to score all simultaneous responses
accurately. In addition, many of the categories we scored
were not amenable to frequency counts. Sitting, walking, and
task orientation are continuous motor postures that cannot be
counted. We decided, therefore, that a "time-sampling" procedure would be the best means of coping with this problem,
facilitating an evaluation of both types of responses at the
same time. In the case of a continuous behavior (sitting),
it would give us an accurate measure of the "amount of time"
it occurred. In the case of discrete, repetitious motor
responses, it would provide a relatively accurate estimate
of frequency, for one would expect that, in general, the more
frequently an individual performs a response the greater the
probability that it will occur at the moment the behavioral
sample is taken. Hence, it should reflect a "frequency"
dimension.

In order to facilitate this procedure we devised
scoring sheets to permit us to take a 10-minute time sample
of the patient's behavior, scoring every 15 seconds. The
categories to be scored are listed and spaces are provided
for scoring their presence at the time the sample was taken.
Thus, at the end of 10 minutes we have a profile of the "stream
of behavior" that the subject emitted or engaged in during
that period. Patients are scored twice during each session
for a 10-minute period. The recording of the subjects during
2 X 10 minutes observation time on a video tape system permits
the raters to reassess their scores.

RESULTS AND DISCUSSION

Although this research is still in the developmental
phase, some of our preliminary findings are encouraging
enough to justify continuing our investigations. In a double-
blind study, we observed surprisingly stable baseline values
of some motor behavior patterns in chronic schizophrenic
patients. It seems that the frequency of some behavioral
categories relates to the psychopathology of the subject.
With the decrease of psychopathology during the drug treatment,
a reduction of certain motor patterns was observed. For
example, eye behavior underwent systematic alterations during
P-5227* (a dibenzoxepin) treatment (Fig. 2). Before drug
treatment, this patient has normal eye movement only 35% of
the observation time (20 minutes), whereas at the 7th week of
P-5227 treatment the patient demonstrated normal eye behavior
90% to 100% of the observation time. When the drug was discontinued, normal eye movements decreased and stare and scan
behavior recurred. With the decrease of psychopathology, the
reduction of various types of nonrhythmical and/or unusual
motor patterns were observed. On the other hand, the rhythmi-
cal motor phenomena increased, particularly after major tranquilizers (neuroleptics). This is probably due to extrapyramidal side effects of the neuroleptic compounds. After discontinuation of treatment, these changes also decreased.

It would appear that this technique is quite sensitive
for determining the changes in behavior induced either by drugs
or occurring spontaneously. Based on the evaluation of some
of our data, it seems that the motor behavior categories vary
for different schizophrenic subgroups.

Of the 37 categories scored, 4 showed striking differences in patients classified as paranoid and another group
classified as chronic undifferentiated (CUT). These 4 categories are eyes-scan, eyes-closed, talk/smile, and bizarre motor

---

*Chas. Pfizer Co., Groton, Conn.

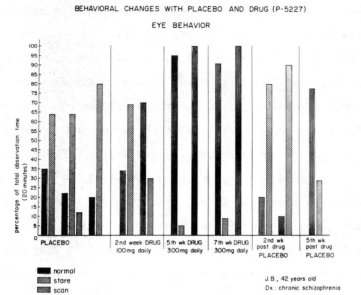

BEHAVIORAL CHANGES WITH PLACEBO AND DRUG (P-5227)

EYE BEHAVIOR

■ normal
▨ stare
▧ scan

J.B., 42 years old
Dx.: chronic schizophrenia
MIP/272

FIG. 2

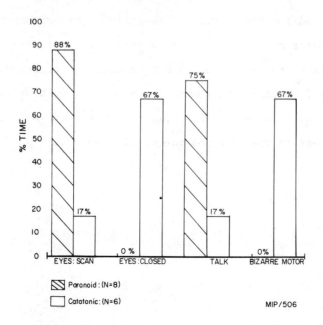

MOTOR PATTERN IN PARANOID AND CATATONIC SCHIZOPHRENICS

▨ Paranoid : (N=8)
☐ Catatonic: (N=6)

MIP/506

FIG. 3

behavior (Fig. 3). Those patients classified as paranoid schizophrenics exhibited more scanning eye behavior and closed their eyes less often than the group classified as chronic undifferentiated. Paranoids had higher talk/smile ratings than the CUT group. The paranoids showed no evidence of bizarre motor behavior, while two-thirds of the CUT group did.

These are only superficial observations on rather gross dimensions and are not particularly impressive or conclusive at this early stage of investigation. However, with the accumulation of more data from greater numbers of subjects of more heterogeneous composition, greater objectivity in selecting behavioral categories, and application of on-line computer techniques, more statistically sophisticated analyses on more complex relationships are possible. Of course, even with the improvement of the methodology this technique will not solve the problem of classification of schizophrenia, but it may be a potentially useful adjunct to the evaluative techniques presently employed in psychiatry, and particularly in psycho-pharmacology.

SUMMARY

A method for the quantitative analysis of behavior in terms of "motor pattern" has been described. This method has some similarity to the "ethological" evaluation of behavior, with some modification from the viewpoints of neurological and psychiatric symptoms. The preliminary results suggest its usefulness in psychopharmacological research.

219

REFERENCES

1. Wittenborn, J. R.: Manual: Wittenborn psychiatric rating scales. The Psychological Corporation, New York, 1955.

2. Hamilton, M. A.: Rating scale for depression. J. Neurol. Psychiat. 23:56, 1955.

3. Lorr, M.; Klett, C. J.; McNair, D. M. and Lasley, J. J.: Inpatient multidimensional psychiatric scale. Consulting Psychologists Press, Palo Alto, 1963.

4. Overall, J. E. and Gorham, D. R.: The brief psychiatric rating scale. Psychol. Rep. 10:799, 1962.

5. Itil, T. and Keskiner, A.: Psychopathological and psychosomatic rating scale. Psychiatric Research Foundation of Missouri, Publication No. 12, 1966.

6. Kimes, M.; Holden, J. M. C.; Keskiner, A. and Itil, T. M.: Occupational therapy rating scale. Psychiatric Research Foundation of Missouri, Publication No. 11, 1967.

7. Whitman, C. O.: Animal Behavior. Biol. Lectures, Marine Biol. Lab. Wood's Hole, Boston, 1899.

8. Heinroth, O. Verhandl. v. Intern. Ornithol. Kongr. Berlin, 1911.

9. Lorenz, K. Vergleichende Bewegunsstudien an Anatien. J. Ornithol. 89:119, 1941.

10. Lorenz, K.: Methods of Approach to the Problems of Behavior. Harvey Lectures, Academic Press, London, 1960.

11. Russel, R. W.: The Comparative Study of Behavior. Oxford Press, London, 1952.

12. Lehrman, D. S.: A critique of Konrad Lorenz's "Theory of Instinctive Behavior." Quart. Rev. Biol. 28:337, 1953.

13. Tinbergen, N.: The Study of Instinct. Oxford Press, London, 1951.

14. Kretschmer, E.: Der Begriff der motorischen Schahlonen und ihre Rolle in normalen und pathologischen Lebensvorgangen. Arch. Psychiat. 190:1, 1953.

15. Wieser, S. and Itil, T.: Die Aufbaustufen der primitiven Motorik. Arch. Psychiat. 191:450, 1954.

16. Hinde, R. A.: Changes in responsiveness to a constant stimulus. Brit. J. Anim. Behav. 2:41, 1954.

17. Deibert, A.; O'Connor, E. and Itil, T.: Unpublished data, 1968.

T. M. Itil, M.D., Section of Psychopharmacology, University of Missouri School of Medicine.

5400 Arsenal Street, St. Louis, Missouri

EVOKED RESPONSES IN SCHIZOPHRENIA.

CHARLES SHAGASS, DONALD A. OVERTON and GIAMPIERO BARTOLUCCI

Our studies of evoked response characteristics in mental disorders have been in progress for nearly a decade. Throughout this time, rapid advances in instrumentation and progressively greater awareness of factors which require careful control have necessitated constant revision of conclusions and rendered psychiatric research with evoked response methods increasingly complicated. Nevertheless, many investigators seem to be entering the field. In work already reported, the schizophrenias have probably received more attention that other psychiatric disorders, and it seems likely that this will continue.

This paper has a twofold purpose: (1) to provide a brief review of previous evoked response findings in schizophrenic disorders; (2) to present preliminary results obtained in schizophrenic patients in our most recent study. It is hoped that the recent data will provide some indication of the vast, and as yet untapped, research possibilities opened up by evoked response methods.

BRIEF REVIEW OF LITERATURE

Evoked response studies of schizophrenic disorders have generally employed brief, simple stimuli in either the somatic or visual sensory modalities. In early studies of the somatosensory response, we measured the variations in amplitude of its initial negative-positive component to different stimulus intensities[1] and also measured the recovery function of this component[2]. The intensity-response data indicated that, for any given strength of stimulus, responses were larger in schizophrenic patients than in nonpatient controls or psychoneurotic disorders characterized by dysphoria. However, the intensity-response amplitude differences between schizophrenic patients did not differ with those of patients with psychotic depressions or personality disorders[1, 3]. Unfortunately, later data bearing on somatosensory response amplitude differences between schizophrenic patients and nonpatients did not confirm the earlier findings[4]. One possible explanation of the discrepancy is that the earlier results were influenced by unsuspected interactions between clinical condition and age. Initially[3], we did not find significant age relationships within the total subject sample for our amplitude measures, but they have been demonstrated subsequently and they are not uniform from one clinical group to another.[4]

In a study of visual evoked responses, we found only one significant difference between schizophrenic patients and nonpatients, namely, a shorter latency of the initial positive peak occurring at about 46 msec after the flash.[5] More encouraging results were obtained by Rodin et al.[6] They found statistically significant differences between schizophrenic patients and nonpatients when the patients were subdivided on the basis of energy metabolism. In patients with abnormally high lactate-pyruvate ratios, visual evoked responses were generally smaller than normal, and instead of one negative peak at 80 msec there were two such peaks occurring at 70 and 100 msec, respectively. In contrast, schizophrenics with normal lactate-pyruvate ratios had a larger positive peak at 135 msec than the normals. Rodin et al pointed out that, if they were to group all of their schizophrenic patients together, the average evoked response of the group would be very similar to that of the normals. In additional studies, Rodin et al found evidence suggesting that the intercorrelation of response curves between the two hemispheres or between the right occipital and the right parietal areas, were lower than such intercorrelations in normals. This suggests less synchrony in response between different brain areas in the patients. They also obtained evidence to suggest that the right hemisphere is more involved in the pathological process than the left. They found some correlations between evoked response amplitude and a number of psychopathological characteristics, such as "nonverbal accessibility".

The heterogeneity of evoked responses in schizophrenic patients is further supported by observations of Speck et al[7, 8], who stated that there were at least three major patterns in their population: (1) "amorphous" type with low amplitude and broad deflections; (2) a group resembling the "average normal"; (3) a group with very high voltage oscillating deflections. Speck et al, however, failed to find significant differences between schizophrenics and normals in responses to the unpaired flash stimuli, although the patients did tend to have higher amplitudes, a finding similar to that obtained by us.[5]

Our study of visual evoked responses did reveal one very interesting, statistically signi-ficant difference between patients and nonpatients. The late after-rhythm, or "ringing", por-tion of the visual response was significantly less well developed in the psychiatric patient group as a whole than in normals, and the least amount of "ringing" was found in the schizophrenic group. In acute and chronic deliria[9, 10], we also found "ringing" to be virtually abolished and it disappears with drowsiness and sleep.[11] However, although "ringing" is abolished in states of impaired awareness, it also tends to disappear with hyperalertness, possibly due to de-synchronization brought about by irregular and excessive input. Such irregular and excessive input could be facilitated by undue attention to random aspects of the stimulus situation. This suggestion would be compatible with the results of Callaway and his co-workers.[12, 13, 14] They compared the evoked responses elicited by two auditory tones of different frequency, and found that the responses were more dissimilar in schizophrenic patients than normals and that the measurements were related to the acuteness of the disorder and some of its clinical charac-teristics.

More recently, however, Callaway[15] has obtained findings suggesting that the lower auditory evoked response correlations of schizophrenics in his two-tone test can be attributed to greater variability of their evoked responses rather than to differential effects of the stimuli. The reduced "ringing" found by us could also be due to greater variability, at least of the la-ter portions of the evoked response. The findings of Goldstein et al[16] showing reduced EEG amplitude variability in chronic schizophrenic patients, even though total electrical output is not changed, seems incompatible with the concepts of response variability suggested by our findings and those of Callaway. Both EEG and evoked responses need to be studied in the same subjects before we can be justified in distinguishing evoked response variability from EEG vari-ability.

The recovery function is measured by administering pairs of stimuli separated by vary-ing intervals. The size of the second response, relative to the first, indicates the extent to which responsiveness has recovered after a given interval. All of our studies of somatosensory recovery functions have shown significant differences between schizophrenic patients and non-patients.[1, 2, 4, 17] In the earlier studies, only the initial negative-positive deflection was measured; the recovery of this component, particularly during the first 20 msec, was significantly reduced in the schizophrenic patients compared with normals. However, the finding was not specific, since reduced recovery was also observed in patients with psychotic depressions and personality disorders.[18, 19] In the most recent study[4], six additional peaks in the evoked response were measured; the data in schizophrenic patients were similar, showing reduced recovery. However, the additional measurements provided no increase in specificity, since other patient groups gave similar findings. The times of occurrence of peaks after stimulation (latencies) were also measured. Latency recovery of several peaks differed in schizophrenia in that it was earlier. There thus appeared to be a dissociation between amplitude and latency recovery.

Fig. 1 shows data from our last study of somatosensory recovery functions in schizophrenics, there were 18 patients and 18 nonpatients, matched for age and sex. The data are treated in a somewhat different manner from the plotting of the relative amplitudes of the response to

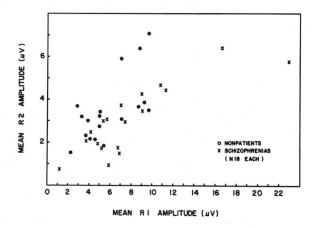

Fig. 1   Scatterplot relating mean somatosensory response amplitudes to first (R1) and second (R2) stimuli of the pair at 8 interstimulus intervals in equal steps from 2.5 to 20 msec. Measurements were made by hand on the initial negative-positive deflection (peaks 1 and 4[4]). Eighteen schizophrenic patients matched for age and sex with 18 nonpatients. Note that for any given value of R1, R2 tends to be greater in nonpatients. Differences would be even greater if age and sex matching were taken into account.

the first and second stimuli over time (R2/RI ratio). Only eight intervals, from 2.5 to 20 msec, are used and the amplitude is that for the initial negative-positive component. It is seen that the mean value of R2 is rather strongly correlated with that of RI, but that the R2 value for any given value of RI tends to be greater in the nonpatients than in the patients.

A study of visual recovery functions in psychiatric patients yielded disappointing results, since the patients did not differ significantly from nonpatients.[5] However, these negative findings for visual recovery functions differ from those of Speck et al and Floris et al,[20, 21] who did find reduced recovery in schizophrenic patients compared with nonpatients. Speck et al focussed their attention on recovery at the interval of 35 msec while Floris et al found their differences mainly between 100 and 180 msec.

It seems clear that deviant recovery has been the most consistent evoked response finding in schizophrenic disorders as well as other major psychiatric illness. The lack of specificity for schizophrenia is troubling. Greater specificity might be established by following the suggestion of Rodin et al[6] to subdivide schizophrenic patients according to other criteria. For example, the classification of patients by behavioral tests of stimulus intensity control has yielded interesting results in the hands of Buchsbaum and Silverman.[22] Another approach is to introduce greater diversity into the evoked response data by varying stimulus conditions in the hope of sifting out additional response factors. The experimental results presented below were obtained by this latter approach.

PRELIMINARY ANALYSIS OF RECENT DATA

The data to follow are from a study which is still in progress, and which involves two experimental questions concerning recovery functions. Measurements of recovery imply that they indicate the degree of restoration of neuronal aggregates to their responsiveness status existing before the conditioning stimulus. The reduced recovery found in psychiatric syndromes would suggest some kind of interference with these restorative functions. If a single conditioning stimulus produced detectable interference, it was reasoned that several conditioning stimuli (a train) would accentuate the differences. Consequently, one aspect of the present experiment involves the use of trains, as well as single conditioning stimuli, for the study of recovery functions.

In the second aspect of the study, the intensity of conditioning stimuli or trains was manipulated. In nearly all previous work, intense conditioning stimuli were used; these tended to suppress, or "inhibit" test responses. In contrast, weak conditioning stimuli often increase, or "facilitate" test responses.[4, 23] By varying conditioning stimulus intensity, we hoped to obtain measures of both "inhibitory" and "facilitatory" cortical response tendencies.

METHODS

Recording and stimulating electrodes were chlorided silver discs, attached with collodion. The recording leads were placed 6 cm apart in the left parasaggital plane, 7 cm from the midline; the posterior lead was 2 cm behind a line from the vertex through the external auditory meati. Stimulating leads were applied over the right median nerve at the wrist 3 cm apart (anode distal). Two constant current stimulators, whose intensity settings can be independently varied, were connected to the common pair of stimulating electrodes. The constant current stimulators were driven by the two outputs of a Grass S8 stimulator. In turn, the initiation of single stimulus pulses or trains of pulses by the S8 was controlled by the address register of the Mnemotron CAT 1000. Amplification was with a Grass Model 7 polygraph with time constant of 0.45 sec and upper frequency limit set at 3 Kc.

Each stimulus sequence contained five stimulus configurations presented in pseudorandom order by means of a programming device. In a sequence containing 250 stimuli at a repetition interval averaging about 1 sec, there were 50 each of the following five configurations: unpaired test stimulus; unpaired conditioning stimulus; paired conditioning and test stimulus; train of nine conditioning stimuli; train of nine conditioning and one test stimulus. The interstimulus interval for paired stimuli or trains was 10 msec. This interval was selected on the basis of pilot studies in which eight subjects were tested repeatedly so that the full recovery functions with differing conditioning stimulus intensities could be obtained. These pilot trials showed that 10 msec was the most representative single interval.[23] Using the 10 msec interval alone in order to make the duration of the test procedure practical, the following intensities were applied: (a) for conditioning stimuli -- 0.5 ma below sensory threshold, threshold, 2, 5 and 10 ma above threshold; (b) for test stimuli -- 5 and 10 ma above threshold. Nine of the ten possible stimulus intensity combinations were employed.

The evoked responses displayed are illustrated in Fig. 2: RI test; R2 test; RIO test; and RI conditioning. R2 was obtained by subtracting RI from RI+R2, and RIO was obtained by sub-

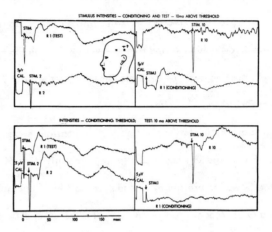

Fig. 2 Somatosensory evoked responses with varied conditioning stimulus intensities and application of trains of 9 as well as single conditioning stimuli. Upper tracings: conditioning and test stimuli, all 10 ma above sensory threshold; this is reflected in virtually identical RI test and conditioning responses. R2 is average of 50 (RI+R2) minus 50 RI. RIO is average of 50 (RI-IO) minus 50 (RI-9). Note suppression of R2 and RIO. Lower traces: conditioning stimulus at sensory threshold values, test stimulus 10 ma above threshold. Note augmentation of R2 in comparison with RI at test intensity. RIO is still somewhat suppressed but larger than above. Square wave calibration at left inserted in series with input leads.

tracting RI-9 from RI-IO. The four evoked responses illustrated in Fig. 2 were stored for each stimulus sequence on digital magnetic tape for later automatic quantification by a large general purpose computer. Although the computer amplitude quantification program employed by us yields a fairly large number of values, our preliminary analysis was confined to one, namely, the average deviation from the mean during the epoch from 15 to 31 msec after the stimulus. This average deviation measure has been found highly correlated with computer derived peak-to-peak measurements and with hand measurements of the initial negative-positive component (r about 0.90). The results were further restricted to the five stimulus sequences in which the test intensity was 10 ma above threshold.

Our preliminary analysis was made by selecting all patients with available printed computer outputs who were diagnosed as schizophrenic and had been free from drugs for five days or more at time of testing. For comparison, nonpatient subjects and patients who were not considered schizophrenic, were not psychotic when tested, and who had not received psychoactive drugs for about the same time as the schizophrenics were selected. Table I gives some descriptive data concerning the subject groups. It will be noted that the schizophrenic patients were

TABLE I

Description of Subject Groups

Group	No.	Male	Age Range	Median Age	No Drugs*	Remainder Off Drugs
Schizophrenics	11	5	18–47 yrs.	27 yrs.	4	5–14 days
Nonpsychotic patients	11	6	17–42 yrs.	23 yrs.	0	5–29 days
Nonpatients	10	5	15–22 yrs.	18 yrs.	10	---

*No drugs indicates no known psychoactive drug intake for at least 3 months.

somewhat older than the nonpsychotic patients or nonpatients, but that the sex distribution was about equal. Schizophrenic subtypes were: chronic undifferentiated, 4 cases; paranoid, 3; acute undifferentated, 3; schizoaffective, 1. In three cases, current symptoms had begun from 4 days to about one months before hospitalization; in two of these, illness durations were four days and three weeks. In the remaining cases, clear symptoms of illness or previous psychotic episodes had occurred from one to ten years before testing. The nonpsychotic group was heterogeneous with respect to diagnosis; there were two psychoneuroses with compulsive features, four personality trait disturbances, one with mental retardation, three sociopathic personality disturbances involving the use of drugs or alcohol; one adolescent adjustment reaction and one inadequare personality pattern disturbance. Four of these patients had a history of previous psychotic reactions induced by LSD, marihuana, or alcohol withdrawal.

RESULTS

Fig. 2 illustrated the general finding that the initial negative-positive component of both R2 and R10 tended to be "inhibited", or reduced in amplitude when the conditioning stimulus was intense and that it tended to be as great as, or greather than, the unconditioned test response (RI_T) when the stimulus was at threshold level. In the nonpatient group, this relationship between R2 and R10 and conditioning stimulus intensity was quite regular, but regularity was less in the patient groups. The significance of group differences was, therefore, tested. A non-parametric procedure was used because of the rather large individual variations in evoked response amplitude and the small number of subjects. For each subject, the amplitudes of the responses associated with the five conditioning stimulus intensities were ranked so that I indicated the greatest and 5 the least amplitude. Mean ranks for each group are shown in Fig. 3 for RI test, RI conditioning, R2 and RIO. It will be seen that for both R2 and RIO the gradient

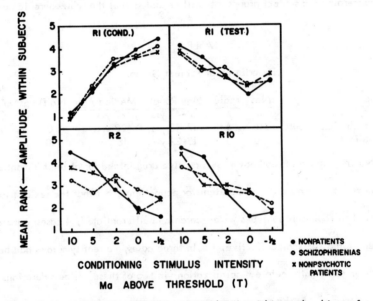

Fig. 3 Mean ranks for variations of amplitude within each subject of RI test, RI conditioning, R2 and RIO with respect to differing conditioning stimulus intensity. Rank I indicates highest amplitude; rank 5, lowest.

for the nonpatients was steeper than that for the schizophrenic patients. Particularly for R2 the responses following conditioning stimuli of threshold intensity in the schizophrenics were often no larger than those following stimuli of highest intensity. To provide a numerical index of deviation from regularity, differences between the actual and predicted ranks, ranging from I when conditioning stimulus intensity was 0.5 ma below the threshold, to 5 when it was 10 ma above threshold, were summed for each subject. Table 2 shows the distribution of these deviation values about the median.

TABLE 2

Distribution of Deviations of R2 and RIO
Amplitude Ranks from Prediction

Rank Deviation Sum	R2*		
	Nonpatients	Schizophrenics	Nonpsychotics
4 or less	9	3	6
5 or more	1	8	5
	RIO**		
3 or less	6	4	4
4 or more	4	7	7

*   Chi square 8.04; df 2; $p < .05$
**   Chi square 1.56; ns

For R2 most of the nonpatients had a low deviation value, whereas most of the schizophrenic patients had a high one, with the nonpsychotic patients intermediate; a median chi square test showed a significant difference between groups ($p < .05$). The trend for RIO was not significant. Fig. 3 also shows a definite trend for the amplitude of the unconditioned RI test response (RI_T) to increase with lower conditioning stimulus intensity values, suggesting that the conditioning trains may exert a persistent suppressing influence between individual stimulus applications within a sequence. However, this effect was similar in the three groups, so that variations in R2 between groups cannot be attributed to it. The gradients for the RI conditioning responses, reflecting the experimentally manipulated variations in intensity, were also steep and similar between groups.

Fig. 4 shows scatterplots relating the mean values of R2 and RIO obtained for the five stimulus sequences to the mean value of RI_T. For the entire group of subjects, the correlations

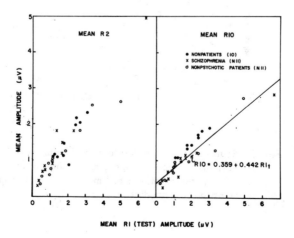

Fig. 4   Scatterplots relating mean R2 and RIO amplitudes to mean RI (test) amplitude. Note absence of group difference trends for R2 whereas for RIO most nonpatient subjects fall above regression line computed for the entire group.

between RI_T and R2 or RI0 were very high.   Since the plot for R2 suggested that the groups were completely intermingled, no further analysis for R2 was performed.   The plot for RI0 suggested that, for any given value of RI_T, the RI0 values of the nonpatients were higher than those of the patients.   To test for a possible group difference in RI0 amplitude with the influence of RI_T amplitude equated, the following procedure was employed.   First, the equation for the linear regression of RI0 on RI_T was computed.   This was:

$$RI0 = 0.359 + 0.442 \ RI_T$$

Then, for each subject, the value of RI0 predicted from the actual RI_T was determined and the difference between the actually observed RI0 and the predicted one was calculated. An analysis of variance, performed on these difference values, yielded an F ratio of 12.89 (df 2, 29), indicating a statistically significant difference between groups (p < .01). Comparison of the individual group means by "t"-test showed that the nonpatients differed significantly from both patient groups (p <.01), but that the patient groups did not differ from one another.

Fig. 5 shows scatterplots relating mean RI0 to the mean R2 values. The RI0 values for any given R2 for the nonpatient subjects appeared to be higher than those for the patients;

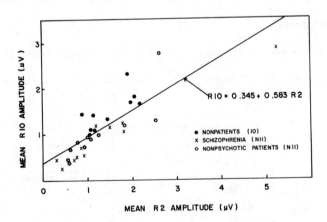

Fig. 5   Scatterplot relating RI0 to mean R2 values. Note that nonpatients fall above the regression line for the entire group, schizophrenic patients fall most below and nonpsychotic patients are intermediate.

there was also an indication that the nonpsychotic patients were intermediate between the nonpatients and the schizophrenics. The same statistical analysis was carried out for deviations of RI0 from the value predicted from R2. Analysis of variance yielded a significant F ratio of 7.61 (p <.01). Individual group comparisons showed the nonpatients to be significantly different from schizophrenic patients (p <.01) and from the nonpsychotic patients (p <.05), but the difference between nonpsychotics and schizophrenics was not quite significant (p = 0.11, two-tailed).

Because the groups were not completely equated with respect to age and sex, two additional analyses were carried out on the deviation values of RI0 predicted from R2 to determine whether the data would support the possibility of a difference between schizophrenics and nonpsychotic patients. In one of these, it was possible to match five subjects from each group for sex and for age within one year, except for one nonpsychotic patient who was five years older than the nonpatient and four years older than the schizophrenic patient matched to her. Table 3 shows the individual deviation values for each of these subjects.

TABLE 3
Deviation of Actual Mean RI0 Values
from those Predicted from Total Group
Regression of RI0 on R2
(Subjects Matched for Age and Sex)

Matched Triplet	Sex	Deviation Values		
		Nonpatient	Nonpsychotic	Schizophrenic
1	F	.013	.888	-.050
2	F	.280	-.188	-.551
3	F	.577	-.030	-.146
4	M	.219	-.072	-.341
5	M	.104	.030	-.066

It will be seen that, except for one instance in which the nonpsychotic patient had a very high positive deviation value, those of the nonpatients were most positive, those of the schizophrenics most negative, and those of the nonpsychotics intermediate. This suggests that the intermediate position of the nonpsychotics, although not verified as statistically significant for the group as a whole, may be the true state of affairs for properly matched groups. This possibility was checked further by matching nine schizophrenic and nine nonpsychotic patients for sex and age within two years except for one pair in which the age difference was four years. In eight of nine instances, the deviation value was more negative for the schizophrenics. A "t"-test for matched pairs yielded a significant difference (p <.05).

DISCUSSION

These preliminary data indicated two ways in which schizophrenic patients deviated from normal: (I) variations in amplitude of their test responses following single conditioning stimuli bore a less regular relationship to conditioning stimulus intensity; (2) they showed greater than normal response decrement after a conditioning train of nine stimuli. The data also suggested that nonschizophrenic patients deviated from normal with respect to these indicators, but less than the schizophrenics.

Considering the small size of the subject groups, and the fact that only a portion of data for each subject were analyzed, the positive results seem encouraging. However, the negative findings with respect to group differentiations by R2 disagree with the results of most previous studies, as exemplified in Fig. I. Some possible explanations may be suggested. Previous results were based on a number of determinations of R2, with one conditioning stimulus intensity, the strongest one employed here, and varying interstimulus intervals. Since the peak of recovery can occur at different intervals, the present standard 10 msec interval may have been inadequate to reveal consistent R2 differences. The influence of varying conditioning stimulus intensities could also be important. The major "inhibitory" effect of the most intense conditioning stimuli could be largely lost in a mean derived from five R2 values in which most of the conditioning stimuli were weak. However, the one sequence in which conditioning and test stimuli were both 10 ma above threshold did not reveal any consistent R2 discrimination between groups. Another possible explanation of the divergent R2 results could be inadequacy of the sample due to small size, variation in age, and clinical heterogeneity of the patient groups. Since all of these factors could have led to the negative R2 results, it is noteworthy that the RIO results, which could be similarly influenced, were still positive. This suggests that differential responsiveness may be brought out more consistently by a train than by a single conditioning stimulus. The direction of the group difference, i.e., smaller RIO in patients, is in accord with the idea that psychopathology is associated with greater "inhibitory" effects.

Since four of the II patients labelled "nonpsychotic" had a history of previous psychotic episode of presumed toxic origin, their results were examined to determine whether they differed from the rest of their group in any outstanding way. Although two of the four had the most extreme RI0 values, these were in opposite directions, so that elimination of these subjects would not greatly affect the results. Another intragroup observation of interest, which can be seen in Fig. 4, is that about half of the schizophrenic group had very small responses (RI_T). Since amplitude trends in previous samples were, if anything, in the opposite direction, an attempt was made to discern whether the low amplitude group differed clinically from the other schizophrenic patients, but no distinguishing features were found. It is also noteworthy that the four schizophrenic patients with no history of psychoactive drug intake did not differ from the rest of the group with respect to the measures which differentiated schizophrenics from nonpatients.

The less regular relationship between R2 and conditioning stimulus intensity among the schizophrenic patients than among nonpatients suggests a different balance of "inhibitory" and "facilitatory" reaction tendencies. This may be related to the differences in stimulus intensity control considered by Buchsbaum and Silverman.[22] It does not appear to be due simply to greater variability of response amplitude in the patients, since no differences were found for concomitantly measured single responses (Fig. 3).

In addition to measurements of the later portions of the evoked response, and for additional stimulus sequences, data remaining to be analyzed in this study include EEG amplitude and frequency measures. Since EEG-evoked response amplitude relationships have recently been found to be correlated with perceptual performance[24], it seems hopeful that the addition of EEG parameters to the evoked response data may yield interesting clinical differentiations.

SUMMARY

The first part of this paper presented a brief review of the literature on evoked responses in schizophrenic disorders. This indicated that the most consistent deviant finding has been reduced recovery function, although this is not specific for schizophrenics. Other findings suggest that the yield of evoked response correlates may be increased by proper subtyping of schizophrenic patients on such parameters as energy metabolism.

234

The second part of the paper described preliminary results obtained with a new experimental procedure. This involves the measurement of recovery functions following trains, as well as individual, conditioning stimuli; conditioning stimulus intensities are also varied. The available data indicated that schizophrenic patients show less regular effects of varying conditioning stimulus intensities and less recovery after a conditioning train than nonpatients. A heterogeneous group of nonschizophrenic patients tended to be intermediate between nonpatients and schizophrenics. The results are taken as encouraging for further study. The experimental procedure is only one example of new avenues for psychiatric research provided by evoked response methods.

REFERENCES

1. Shagass, C. and Schwartz, M.: Cerebral responsiveness in psychiatric patients. Arch. Gen. Psychiat., 8: 177–189, 1963.

2. Shagass, C. and Schwartz, M.: Excitability of the cerebral cortex in psychiatric disorders. In Physiological Correlates of Psychological Disorder, Roessler, R. and Greenfield, N.S. (Editors), p. 45, University of Wisconsin Press, Madison, 1962.

3. Shagass, C. and Schwartz, M.: Psychiatric disorder and deviant cerebral responsiveness to sensory stimulation. In Recent Advances in Biological Psychiatry, Vol. V, Wortis, J. (Editor), p. 321, Plenum Press, New York, 1963.

4. Shagass, C.: Averaged somatosensory evoked responses in various psychiatric disorders. In Recent Advances in Biological Psychiatry, Vol. X, Wortis, J. (Editor), p. 205, Plenum Press, New York, 1968.

5. Shagass, C. and Schwartz, M.: Visual cerebral evoked response characteristics in a psychiatric population. Amer. J. Psychiat., 121: 979–987, 1965.

6. Rodin, E., Grisell, J. and Gottlieb, J.: Some electrographic differences between chronic schizophrenic patients and normal subjects. In Recent Advances in Biological Psychiatry, Vol. X, Wortis, J. (Editor), p. 194, Plenum Press, New York, 1968.

7. Speck, L.B., Dim, B. and Mercer, M.: Visual evoked responses of psychiatric patients. Arch. Gen. Psychiat., 15: 59–63, 1966.

8. Heninger, G. and Speck, L.: Visual evoked responses and mental status of schizophrenics. Arch. Gen. Psychiat., 15: 419–426, 1966.

9. Brown, J.C.N., Shagass, C. and Schwartz, M.: Cerebral evoked potential changes associated with the Ditran delirium and its reversal in man. In Recent Advances in Biological Psychiatry, Vol. VII, Wortis, J. (Editor), p. 223, Plenum Press, New York, 1965.

10. Straumanis, J.J., Shagass, C. and Schwartz, M.: Visually evoked cerebral response changes associated with chronic brain syndromes and aging. J. Gerontology, 20: 498–506, 1965.

11. Shagass, C. and Trusty, D.: Somatosensory and visual cerebral evoked response changes during sleep. In Recent Advances in Biological Psychiatry, Vol. VIII, Wortis, J. (Editor), p. 321, Plenum Press, New York, 1966.

235

12. Callaway, E., Jones, R.T. and Layne, R.S.: Evoked responses and segmental set of schizophrenia. Arch. Gen. Psychiat., 12: 83-89, 1965.

13. Jones, R.T., Blacker, K.H., Callaway, E. and Layne, R.S.: The auditory evoked response as a diagnostic and prognostic measure in schizophrenia. Amer. J. Psychiat., 122: 33-41, 1965.

14. Jones, R.T., Blacker, K.H. and Callaway, E.: Perceptual dysfunction in schizophrenia: Clinical and auditory evoked response findings. Amer. J. Psychiat., 123: 639-645, 1966.

15. Callaway, E.: Diagnostic uses of the averaged evoked potentials. Presented at Symposium on "Current Research Problems in the Study of Evoked Potentials", San Francisco, September, 1968 (in press).

16. Goldstein, L., Sugerman, A.A., Stolberg, H., Murphree, H.B. and Pfeiffer, C.C.: Electro-cerebral activity in schizophrenics and nonpsychotic subjects: Quantitative EEG amplitude analysis. Electroenceph. clin. Neurophysiol., 19: 350-361, 1965.

17. Shagass, C. and Schwartz, M.: Psychiatric correlates of evoked cerebral cortical potentials. Amer. J. Psychiat., 119: 1055-1061, 1963.

18. Shagass, C. and Schwartz, M.: Observations on somatosensory cortical reactivity in personality disorders. J. Nerv. Ment. Dis., 135: 44-51, 1962.

19. Shagass, C. and Schwartz, M.: Somatosensory cerebral evoked responses in psychotic depression. Brit. J. Psychiat., 112: 799-807, 1966.

20. Floris, V., Morocutti, C., Amabile, G., Bernardi, G., Rizzo, P.A. and Vasconetto, C.: Recovery cycle of visual evoked potentials in normal and schizophrenic subjects. In The Evoked Potentials, Cobb, W. and Morocutti, C. (Editors), Electroenceph. clin. Neurophysiol., Suppl. 26, p. 74, Elsevier, Amsterdam, 1967.

21. Floris, V., Morocutti, C., Amabile, G., Bernardi, G. and Rizzo, P.A.: Recovery cycle of visual evoked potentials in normal, schizophrenic and neurotic patients. In Computers and Electronic Devices in Psychiatry, Kline, N.S. and Laska, E. (Editors), p. 194, Grune and Stratton, New York, 1968.

22. Buchsbaum, M. and Silverman, J.: Stimulus intensity control and the cortical evoked response. Psychosom. Med., 30: 12-22, 1968.

23. Shagass, C. and Overton, D.A.: Measurement of cerebral "excitability" characteristics in relation to psychopathology. Presented at Conference on Objective Indicators in Psychopathology, Sterling Forest, New York, February, 1968 (in press).

24. Shagass, C., Haseth, K., Callaway, E. and Jones, R.T.: EEG-evoked response relationships and perceptual performance, Life Sciences, 7: 1083-1092, 1968.

ACKNOWLEDGEMENTS

Research supported (in part) by a grant (MH12507) from the National Institute of Mental Health, USPHS.

C. Shagass, M.D., D. A. Overton, M.D., and G. Bartolucci, M.D., Temple University,

Eastern Pennsylvania Psychiatric Institute, Henry Avenue and Abbotsford Road, Philadelphia, Pennsylvania, 19129

QUANTITATIVE ELECTROENCEPHALOGRAPHIC CORRELATES OF THE PSYCHOLOGICAL STATUS IN SCHIZOPHRENICS

LEONIDE GOLDSTEIN and CARL C. PFEIFFER

The statistical finding that signal variance was lower in the base-line quantitated EEG of unmedicated chronic male schizophrenics than in non-patient, was first reported in 1963 (Goldstein et al[1]) on a small group of subjects (25). Later on it was extended to a larger sample of both normals and patients (over 100) with similar results (Goldstein et al[2]). Using a related measurement method of the EEG (modulus voltage integrator rather than global amplitude integrator), a confirmation of these data was obtained by Marjerrison et al[3] and by Callaway[4]. With a different method of analysis of the EEG, Volavka et al[5] also found the between individual variances to be smaller, in the 9.5 to 12.5 Hz band in schizophrenics than in non-patients.

A further indication of the validity of this concept was obtained in a year long study of the quantitated EEG correlates of behavioral changes, as produced by different drug therapies. Sugerman et al[6] reported highly significant correlations between psychological-based judgments of improvement in behavior and increases in EEG variability. The IMPS (Lorr[7]) items which were most prominently changed were: excitement, hostility, paranoid projection, retardation and apathy, motor disturbances, conceptual disorganization and schizophrenic disorganization. In the PRP Dimension scale (Lorr et al[8]) the 3 items of withdrawal, thinking disorganization and paranoid belligerence, as well as the global score, were significantly correlated with increases in EEG variability. These data have been recently reviewed by Goldstein and Sugerman.[9]

Marjerrison and Keogh[10] reported a few months ago on quantitated EEG changes in relation to drug effects in acute schizophrenic patients. The study was performed on 34 unmedicated, newly admitted patients. Following a single week of therapy with neuroleptic agents (randomized double-blind, cross-over design), changes were detected in EEG variability which correlated significantly with improvements in the two scales of perceptual distortion and motor disturbance scores of the IMPS.

The present study is also concerned with acute patients. However, these were not hospitalized. They were seen as outpatients over periods of time varying from 3 to 18 months. The comparisons to be reported were restricted to the differences between EEG variability levels and the different scores of the Experiential World Inventory ("EWI", El-Meligi and Osmond[11]). Based on the EWI scores, the patients were classified as being improved ("Therapeutic success") or non-improved ("Therapeutic failure"). What was looked for was whether EEG variability increased in cases of success and did not change (or decreased) in cases of failure. The therapies used are not relevant to such an analy- sis and will not be listed or discussed as to their relative merits. Suffice it to say that they included neuroleptics, lithium, vitamins and other drugs.

METHODS

The EWI test, in either of its two forms, was administered to 51 subjects, 27 females and 24 males. The age range was 18-60 for the fe- male patients and 18-68 for the male patients. The median age was 32 for the males and 29 for the females. The scores were computed directly and their distribution normalized by means of T-score transformations.

The EEG (left and right occipital leads recorded monopolarly in supine, eyes closed, subjects) was directly monitored and processed at the same time, through electronic integrators. The on-line quantitated data were computed so as to yield, for each patient-session, an estimate of the time-course variability of the EEG, as manifested in 30 successive "epochs" each of 20 seconds duration. The coefficient of variation ("CV": standard deviation expressed as a percentage of the mean was used throughout to express the levels of EEG variability. Significance levels, in case of change, were ascertained from F-ratios of the variances. The methodological and practical aspects of such an approach to EEG quanti - tation have been discussed in a number of publications (Goldstein et al[2], Goldstein and Beck[12], Pfeiffer et al[13]).

RESULTS

The results obtained up to the time this paper was written are list- ed in Tables I and II. As can be seen (Table I), successful therapy was based on a significant decrease in the scores of the 8 scales of the EWI. Unsuccessful therapy was claimed when no significant changes occurred in either one of these scales.

It should be noted that the base-line EWI scores were not different in patients found to improve and/or not affected by the therapies. There were no differences between male and female patients, both for the initial or the final scores provided, of course, the improved and non-improved groups are considered separately insofar as the last measurements are concerned.

TABLE I

Mean EWI Scores ± Standard Deviation (T-transformation)

		1	2	3	4	5	6	7	8
FEMALES									
Success N = 14	Initial	54 ± 11	49 ± 6	54 ± 9	55 ± 9	54 ± 9	55 ± 12	54 ± 8	51 ± 12
	Final	41* ± 7	46 ± 6	45* ± 6	44* ± 9	47* ± 7	44* ± 7	46* ± 10	43* ± 10
Failure N = 13	Initial	59 ± 7	53 ± 5	56 ± 9	60 ± 7	57 ± 5	62 ± 8	56 ± 9	58 ± 7
	Final	55 ± 11	50 ± 7	57 ± 12	57 ± 9	55 ± 9	61 ± 11	57 ± 10	56 ± 10
MALES									
Success N = 16	Initial	53 ± 10	52 ± 3	54 ± 8	55 ± 6	57 ± 7	58 ± 7	55 ± 11	55 ± 11
	Final	43* ± 8	47* ± 4	46* ± 6	45* ± 6	46* ± 9	46* ± 9	44* ± 9	47* ± 9
Failure N = 8	Initial	59 ± 13	48 ± 10	63 ± 8	58 ± 16	58 ± 13	63 ± 14	62 ± 10	59 ± 11
	Final	57 ± 17	53 ± 6	64 ± 14	62 ± 14	62 ± 16	61 ± 15	64 ± 13	58 ± 16

*Statistically significant difference (t-test) p < .05.

**The 8 EWI scales (1 to 8) permit to measure respectively: Sensory perception, Time perception, Body perception, Self perception, Perception of others, Ideation, Dysphoria and Impulse regulation.

EEG data (Table II) revealed clearly, and to a highly significant degree that there were changes in EEG variability related to the EWI scores. When improvement was obtained, there occurred a 38 per cent increase in this parameter in male patients, and a 45 per cent increase in female patients. In case of therapeutic failure no changes in EEG variability were found. It is interesting to note that comparable to the EWI data, the EEG base-line values did not reveal any difference between patients who later on improved and those who did not improve. Again, male and female patients had similar initial values.

TABLE II

EEG and EWI data for all the subjects
involved in the study

Outcome of Therapy	N	Global EWI Scores (average of 8 scales)	EEG Data	
			MEC[1]	CV[2]
Successful				
Initial	27	54. 1	94. 4	10. 7
Final		44. 9**	90. 2	15. 2
Unsuccessful				
Initial	35	58. 3	84. 4	10. 5
Final		58. 2	91. 2	10. 8

*Statistically significant difference (F-ratios) p : 0.02

**Statistically significant difference (t-test) p : 0.05

[1] Mean energy content (Average integrated amplitude) of the left occipital brain waves.

[2] Coefficient of variation computed from the standard deviation of the distribution of 30 successive MECs on each patient at each session.

DISCUSSION

This report is necessarily limited in breadth and scope, since it is based on measurements obtained on a fluctuation population. The cut-off point, namely EWI-based evidence of improvement or absence of such, should not be taken to mean that this is a final outcome for the patients in these groups. Both relapse in improved patients and improvement in therapeutic failures can be expected. Therefore, this is, at best an arbitrarily selected period in which comparisons between behavioral and EEG data have been made.

As the data now stand, they confirm, in acute ambulatory patients, the findings obtained on hospitalized chronic and acute schizophrenics. Any possible biasing of the data produced by the very process of hospitalization is thereby eliminated. Therefore the finding that schizophrenics have a low variability EEG, which shifts towards normal range when behavior improves, is confirmed. It is extended to a lack of change when behavior does not improve.

The most often advanced objection to this characterization of the EEG is that it defeats its own purpose in revealing hypovariability in patients known to be hypervariable in their behavior. However, as pointed out previously (Goldstein et al[2], Goldstein and Sugerman[8]), this is only an apparent contradiction. As shown by Ashby[14], loss of variability in regulating potencies cannot but lead a homeostatic system to a disruption of its adaptive capacities.

We pointed out (Goldstein et al[1], Goldstein et al[15]) that decreases of EEG variability can be obtained in normal subjects by drug induced excitation or hyper-arousal. The similarities of the EEG under such conditions and those found to exist spontaneously in chronic schizophrenics has led us to hypothesize that these patients were in a sustained state of hyper-arousal. From the data presented in this paper, as well as that recently collected by Marjerrison and Keogh[10], it now appears that we can extend this concept to certain ambulatory acute schizophrenic patients. The possible reason (or reasons) for this hyper-arousal remain to be found.

BIBLIOGRAPHY

1. Goldstein, L. , Murphree, H. B. , Sugerman, A. A. , Pfeiffer, C. C. and Jenney, E. H. Quantitative electroencephalographic analysis of naturally occurring (schizophrenic) and drug-induced psychotic states in human males. Clin. Pharmacol. and Therap. 4, 10, 1963.

2. Goldstein, L. , Sugerman, A. A. , Stolberg, H. , Murphree, H. B. and Pfeiffer, C. C. Electro-cerebral activity in schizophrenics and non-psychotic subjects: Quantitative EEG amplitude analysis. Electroenceph. and clin. Neurophysiol. 19, 350, 1965.

3. Marjerrison, G. , Krause, A. E. and Keogh, R. P. Variability of the EEG in schizophrenia: Quantitative analysis with a modulus voltage integrator. Electroenceph. and clin. Neurophysiol. 24, 35, 1967.

4. Callaway, E. Personal communication.

5. Volavka, J. , Matousek, M. , and Roubicek, J. EEG frequency analysis in schizophrenia. Acta Psychiat. Scand. 42, 237, 1966.

6. Sugerman, A. A. , Goldstein, L. , Murphree, H. B. , Pfeiffer, C. C. and Jenney, E. H. EEG and behavioral changes in schizophrenia. Arch. gen. Psychiat. 10, 340, 1964.

7. Lorr, M. Measurement of the major psychotic syndromes. Ann. N. Y. Acad. Sci. 93, 851, 1962.

8. Goldstein, L. , and Sugerman, A. A. EEG correlates of psychopathology. Paper read at the Annual Meeting of the American Psychopathological Association 1968.

10. Marjerrison, G. , and Keogh, R. P. Integrated EEG variability: Drug effects in acute schizophrenics. Paper read at the 18th Annual Meeting of the Canadian Psychiatric Association, 1968.

11. El-Meligi, A. M. and Osmond, H. An attempt to measure various aspects of the phenomenal world of schizophrenics, alcoholics and neurotics. Paper read at the meeting of the Eastern Psychological Association, 1966.

12. Goldstein, L. , and Beck, R. A. Amplitude analysis of the electroencephalogram. Review of the information obtained with the integrative method. Intern. Rev. Neurobiol. 8, 265, 1965.

13. Pfeiffer, C. C. , Goldstein, L. , and Murphree, H. B. Effects of parenteral administration of haloperidol and chlorpromazine in man. J. Clin. Pharmacol. 8, 79, 1968.

14. Ashby, W. R. Requisite variety and its implications for the control of complex systems. Cybernetica 1, 83, 1958.

15. Goldstein, L. , Murphree, H. B. and Pfeiffer, C. C. Quantitative electroencephalography as a measure of CNS stimulation. Ann. N. Y. Acad. Sci. 107, 1045, 1963.

L. D. Goldstein, D. Sc., and C. C. Pfeiffer, M.D., Ph.D., Bureau of Research in Neurology and

Psychiatry, New Jersey Neuro-Psychiatric Institute, Box 1000, Princeton, N.J. 08540

COMPUTER TIME-SERIES FREQUENCY ANALYSIS OF THE ELECTROENCEPHALOGRAMS OF MALE NONPSYCHOTIC AND CHRONIC SCHIZOPHRENIC SUBJECTS

H.B. MURPHREE and R.E. SCHULTZ

Earlier, we have reported[1,2] that the integrated electrical energy of the scalp electroencephalogram of male chronic schizophrenic patients is typically less variable than that of nonpsychotic volunteer subjects. We have also reported[3,4] that adequate pharmacotherapy of these patients causes an increase in variability of the electrical energy of their electroencephalograms. This is correlated with behavioral improvement as assessed by psychiatric rating scales. These findings have raised the possibility that schizophrenics are in a sustained state of over-arousal, because stimulant drugs given to nonpsychotic subjects produce similar findings. This work employed the integrative method of Drohocki[5] which is entirely concerned with total electrical energy in a given lead of electroencephalogram without consideration of the frequency components of that energy.

Another previous paper[6] summarized this earlier work and reported a newer analytic method which takes into account both the amplitude characteristics of the total electroencephalogram and the discrete frequency characteristics. The present report presents comparisons of the electroencephalograms of psychotic patients with those of nonpsychotic subjects, as derived through the newer method. A review of methodological considerations has been published recently.[7]

METHODS

The patients were male chronic schizophrenics housed in the Investigative Psychiatry ward of the Bureau of Research, New Jersey Neuropsychiatric

Institute. The criteria for selecting these patients
were as follows: age 21-45, diagnosis of schizophrenic
reaction, little or no response to usual somatic
therapies, and no abnormalities by neurological examination or clinical electroencephalogram. A further
restriction was that the patients had to be cooperative enough that adequate electroencephalographic
recordings could be made. These patients all had been
hospitalized three or more years and had long histories of chronic psychosis, usually with onset in adolescence. All had poor premorbid psychiatric histories.
All had been treated with electroconvulsive therapy
and with one or more phenothiazine derivatives. Some
had been treated with insulin. None of these therapies
had proved effective enough in any of these patients
to make hospitalization unnecessary. For this work,
the patients were divided into three groups, depending
on how long they had been off treatment. The first
group had been drug free for a minimum of three months
and were considered for the purposes of this study to
be "untreated." The other two groups were in phases
of withdrawal from medication, which in this case was
perphenazine, 16 mg per day. One group had been off
medication for 7 weeks, the other for 9 weeks.

There were two groups of nonpsychotic volunteer
subjects. One was composed of prerelease inmates of
New Jersey Reformatory, housed on the grounds of New
Jersey Neuropsychiatric Institute. The other was
composed of laboratory staff personnel. These persons
ranged in age from 21-54 years. Although the range
of ages of the reformatory group was smaller, no
statistically significant differences in the ages of
the groups was demonstrable. The nonpatients were
within normal limits by medical history and physical
examination and had unremarkable clinical electroencephalograms. Although the reformatory inmates

typically had evidences of mild personality or character disorders on intensive psychological testing, none had any evidence of psychosis.

All recordings were monopolar from the left occipital area with both ears as reference and a ground in the middle of the forehead. The subjects were supine during the recording, in a partially sound-attenuated room, with eyes closed. Paper records were made on a clinical electroencephalograph. Simultaneous recordings were made on a magnetic tape data recorder. The latter were then played back into the analyzer which was built in our laboratory and which was described in earlier reports.[6,8] Total, unfiltered energy was integrated over 20-second intervals, and simultaneously, the energy of 28 narrow frequency bands was integrated. These bands had center frequencies from 1.0 to 36 cycles per second. At least 30 successive 20-second intervals were processed (ten minutes of recording time) for each subject. The data were then punched on 80-column cards, after which they were processed on a digitial computer.

The computer can give a number of processed

	T.0	1.0	2.0	3.0	4.0	5.0	6.0	7.0	8.0	8.5	9.0	9.5	10.0	10.5	11.0	12.0	14.0
T 01	25.0	12.5	9.5	8.5	5.5	9.0	6.5	5.0	3.0	7.0	6.5	5.5	5.0	7.5	9.5	5.0	3.0
T 02	26.0	11.0	10.0	7.5	5.5	7.5	6.5	5.0	3.5	7.0	6.0	5.5	5.0	7.0	6.5	4.5	3.5
T 03	32.0	17.5	10.5	9.5	8.0	9.0	7.5	7.0	5.0	9.0	8.0	7.5	7.0	9.0	9.0	5.5	4.5
T 04	29.0	11.0	10.0	9.0	7.0	8.5	8.0	8.0	5.5	8.0	6.5	5.5	5.0	7.5	8.5	5.0	4.0
T 05	30.0	10.0	7.5	11.0	8.5	9.5	9.5	9.0	6.5	9.5	8.0	8.0	7.5	10.0	9.5	6.5	5.0
T 06	29.0	12.0	7.5	10.5	8.0	8.5	9.5	8.5	6.5	9.5	7.5	6.5	6.5	8.5	11.0	6.0	4.0
T 07	29.0	9.5	10.5	8.5	8.0	8.5	8.5	7.0	5.0	8.5	7.0	6.5	6.0	8.5	6.0	6.0	4.5
T 08	27.0	10.5	8.5	8.5	7.0	9.0	8.5	7.0	4.5	8.0	7.0	6.5	6.0	8.5	6.5	5.5	4.5
T 09	31.0	11.5	9.0	10.5	9.0	10.5	9.0	7.5	5.0	8.5	7.5	7.0	7.0	9.0	9.0	6.0	4.5
T 10	33.0	12.0	12.5	8.5	10.5	11.5	8.5	7.5	6.0	8.5	6.5	6.0	5.5	8.0	8.5	6.0	5.0
T 11	33.0	13.0	8.5	9.5	9.0	10.0	9.0	8.0	5.5	9.5	9.0	8.5	8.5	10.0	11.5	7.0	5.0
T 12	37.0	17.0	12.0	9.5	10.0	12.0	11.0	9.0	6.5	8.0	7.0	7.0	9.0	10.0	9.0	7.0	5.5
T 13	44.0	14.0	17.0	12.5	18.0	15.0	12.5	10.5	7.5	9.5	8.0	7.5	7.5	10.0	11.0	8.0	7.0
T 14	36.0	16.0	12.0	11.0	9.0	11.5	11.5	10.0	8.0	10.5	9.0	7.5	6.5	8.5	9.5	6.0	5.0
T 15	36.0	13.5	12.5	11.5	9.5	12.0	10.0	9.0	6.0	8.5	7.5	6.5	6.0	10.5	6.5	5.0	5.0
T 16	47.0	14.5	17.0	15.0	14.5	13.0	12.5	10.5	8.0	11.0	10.5	10.0	10.0	12.0	15.5	8.5	7.5
T 17	37.0	14.0	11.5	12.0	10.0	10.5	9.0	8.0	7.0	10.5	10.0	9.5	9.5	11.5	11.5	9.0	8.0
T 18	37.0	12.0	12.5	12.0	10.5	10.0	10.0	9.5	7.0	10.0	9.0	8.0	7.5	9.5	10.0	7.0	6.0
T 19	39.0	10.5	11.0	15.0	12.5	11.0	10.5	10.0	8.5	10.5	9.0	7.5	7.0	9.0	9.5	7.0	8.0
T 20	33.0	12.0	10.5	7.0	6.5	9.5	8.0	9.5	8.0	11.5	10.5	10.0	10.0	11.5	13.0	8.0	7.5
T 21	36.0	13.0	12.0	12.0	12.5	12.5	11.0	9.5	6.5	10.0	8.5	8.0	8.0	10.5	12.0	9.0	8.5
T 22	38.0	13.5	13.0	13.5	10.0	11.5	11.0	10.5	9.0	11.5	10.5	10.0	10.0	11.5	10.0	8.0	6.0
T 23	43.0	13.5	13.5	14.0	12.5	12.5	12.5	9.5	6.5	10.0	8.5	8.0	8.0	10.5	10.0	8.5	9.5
T 24	44.0	11.5	13.0	11.0	12.5	14.0	13.0	12.0	8.5	11.0	9.5	8.5	8.0	10.5	12.0	10.0	14.5
T 25	48.0	11.0	13.0	13.0	15.0	15.0	13.5	12.0	11.5	14.5	13.0	12.0	11.5	13.5	19.5	11.0	10.5
T 26	32.0	13.0	12.5	8.0	7.0	11.0	9.0	8.0	5.5	9.0	8.5	7.5	7.0	9.0	9.0	6.0	5.0
T 27	34.0	14.0	9.5	9.0	6.5	8.5	8.5	8.0	6.5	10.5	9.5	9.0	9.0	11.5	9.0	8.5	6.5
T 28	31.0	13.0	11.0	7.5	7.0	8.5	8.5	7.5	5.5	9.5	9.0	8.5	8.5	12.5	10.5	6.5	5.5
T 29	30.0	10.0	8.0	8.0	7.5	7.5	7.0	7.0	5.0	9.0	8.0	7.5	7.5	9.5	9.0	6.5	5.0
T 30	34.0	10.0	9.0	7.5	5.5	8.0	6.5	6.5	5.5	9.0	7.5	7.0	6.5	9.0	7.5	5.5	4.5
MEAN	34.7	12.6	11.2	10.4	9.4	10.5	9.6	8.5	6.4	9.6	8.5	7.8	7.5	9.7	10.2	7.0	6.1
VARIANCE	35	4	5	5	9	4	3	3	2	2	2	2	2	2	6	2	5
STAND. DEV.	5.9	2.0	2.3	2.3	3.0	2.1	1.9	1.7	1.7	1.5	1.5	1.5	1.6	1.5	2.5	1.5	2.4
C. V.	17.0	15.9	20.5	22.1	31.9	20.0	19.8	20.0	26.6	15.6	17.6	19.2	21.3	15.5	24.5	21.4	39.3
VON NEUMANN	28	6	7	7	13	3	3	2	3	3	3	3	4	3	10	2	4
RATIO D/V	0.78	1.48	1.25	1.31	1.41	0.66	0.76	0.65	1.02	1.30	1.33	1.32	1.53	1.24	1.56	0.81	0.69

Fig. 1. Part of computer output for EEG of subject without prominent alpha activity.

data outputs some of which were illustrated in the earlier reports.[6,8] Of these outputs, two were used in the present studies. Figure 1 presents a sample of the first kind of output. These are data from one subject for one 10-minute recording, that is, 30 20-second integration intervals. The left hand column, labeled T.O. presents from the top downward the successive determinations of integrated electrical energy for the successive 20-second intervals. The columns to the right of this present the determinations for the separate frequency bandwidths. At the bottom, the computer has calculated for each column the mean, variance, standard deviation, coefficient of variation, mean square successive difference (von Neumann), and the ratio of the latter to variance. Note that this subject has no peaking of activity in the alpha (8-12 per second) band. Figure 2 shows the record from a subject with prom-

	T.O	1.0	2.0	3.0	4.0	5.0	6.0	7.0	8.0	9.0	10.0	11.0	12.0	13.0	14.0	15.0	16.0
T 1	98.0	5.7	5.3	6.3	5.7	7.7	8.3	12.0	23.3	30.0	40.0	27.0	18.0	10.0	7.3	3.7	6.3
T 2	113.0	5.0	6.3	6.0	6.0	8.0	11.0	17.0	24.3	32.0	53.0	34.0	19.0	11.0	7.3	4.7	7.3
T 3	140.0	2.7	6.0	5.7	10.7	9.3	14.3	17.0	30.0	43.0	72.0	34.0	22.0	12.0	9.3	6.0	12.3
T 4	148.0	14.7	6.3	13.0	9.3	13.7	13.7	19.0	31.7	41.0	66.0	41.0	22.0	13.0	10.3	6.7	10.3
T 5	109.0	6.7	6.0	9.0	7.3	11.0	14.4	11.7	25.3	31.0	58.0	27.0	20.0	11.0	8.7	5.0	7.7
T 6	118.0	7.7	4.7	8.3	5.0	7.3	8.7	12.0	18.3	36.0	64.0	39.0	24.0	13.0	8.3	6.0	7.3
T 7	96.0	6.0	5.3	5.3	3.0	6.7	10.0	12.0	10.7	31.0	57.0	29.0	17.0	9.0	7.0	7.3	5.7
T 8	106.0	5.3	4.7	3.3	5.3	8.0	11.0	12.3	21.0	30.0	55.0	35.0	18.0	9.0	7.0	9.0	7.3
T 9	101.0	5.7	6.0	8.0	6.3	10.3	12.0	12.0	24.3	25.0	48.0	35.0	22.0	11.0	8.7	8.3	6.3
T 10	99.0	3.7	3.0	7.7	5.7	7.3	11.0	11.3	20.0	26.0	50.0	36.0	21.0	11.0	8.3	7.7	6.0
T 11	103.0	4.7	5.0	6.0	6.3	8.0	7.3	10.3	17.3	27.0	57.0	34.0	21.0	10.0	4.7	6.3	7.0
T 12	113.0	7.7	5.3	8.7	7.0	11.7	14.0	20.3	25.7	28.0	48.0	36.0	22.0	11.0	9.3	10.3	9.7
T 13	91.0	4.3	2.3	6.3	4.3	10.3	10.7	11.0	20.7	23.0	48.0	33.0	25.0	12.0	8.3	8.3	6.0
T 14	125.0	4.7	8.7	9.0	12.3	18.3	14.0	15.0	27.3	31.0	58.0	32.0	22.0	12.0	8.7	11.7	9.3
T 15	111.0	11.3	8.3	7.0	10.0	8.7	10.3	16.0	21.3	28.0	61.0	29.0	18.0	10.0	8.7	10.0	7.7
T 16	113.0	7.3	5.0	6.0	6.3	7.0	10.0	12.3	25.0	32.0	60.0	37.0	19.0	10.0	6.3	10.0	6.7
T 17	102.0	5.7	5.7	6.7	3.3	8.3	10.7	9.7	25.3	37.0	53.0	26.0	19.0	9.0	7.3	8.0	5.3
T 18	93.0	5.0	3.3	6.7	3.3	6.7	9.7	10.7	20.0	26.0	49.0	33.0	18.0	10.0	7.0	10.7	6.3
T 19	114.0	9.7	7.0	13.3	8.0	11.0	12.7	17.7	32.3	24.0	54.0	28.0	21.0	11.0	8.7	11.3	8.0
T 20	59.0	4.0	2.7	4.3	3.7	4.3	5.3	7.7	11.3	17.0	38.0	18.0	14.0	7.0	5.7	7.7	4.0
T 21	56.0	4.0	4.0	5.0	6.3	4.3	6.7	8.7	15.7	12.0	32.0	12.0	10.0	6.0	5.0	7.3	3.0
T 22	109.0	5.7	11.3	13.3	11.0	11.7	14.3	20.0	27.7	27.0	43.0	27.0	19.0	10.0	8.7	8.3	7.0
T 23	59.0	3.7	3.3	4.0	4.3	6.0	8.3	9.0	14.0	16.0	35.0	17.0	13.0	6.0	5.7	7.7	4.7
T 24	55.0	6.7	5.0	6.0	8.0	3.7	6.0	9.0	13.3	10.0	32.0	13.0	11.0	7.0	5.7	7.7	4.3
T 25	37.0	5.7	2.7	4.0	4.7	5.0	8.0	8.0	8.7	8.3	26.0	9.0	7.0	3.0	4.0	7.0	2.3
T 26	63.0	4.7	4.0	6.3	6.7	7.3	8.0	9.7	15.7	15.0	31.0	14.0	9.0	5.0	5.7	7.7	4.3
T 27	92.0	6.7	9.7	7.0	7.0	13.7	11.0	13.7	19.0	18.0	44.0	17.0	14.0	9.0	7.0	9.3	6.0
T 28	66.0	6.3	6.0	6.0	8.3	6.3	12.0	10.7	12.7	13.0	33.0	13.0	12.0	8.0	6.0	7.7	4.0
T 29	95.0	12.7	8.0	10.3	10.0	11.0	13.3	18.7	20.3	18.0	35.0	17.0	14.0	9.0	6.7	9.0	6.0
T 30	46.0	6.0	4.7	3.3	4.7	4.0	6.3	6.7	10.3	8.0	29.0	14.0	10.0	5.0	4.7	6.7	4.0
T 31	86.0	6.7	4.7	7.7	4.7	8.0	9.7	11.3	22.0	19.0	40.0	16.0	13.0	9.0	7.0	9.0	7.0
T 32	96.0	8.7	8.3	10.7	10.3	7.7	15.7	15.0	24.0	25.0	49.0	15.0	12.0	7.0	7.3	10.0	5.3
T 33	109.0	9.3	9.0	7.0	9.0	8.3	14.0	16.7	28.0	37.0	49.0	16.0	13.0	9.0	7.7	10.0	6.3
MEAN	94.58	6.50	5.73	7.27	6.78	8.50	10.68	12.88	20.70	24.88	47.48	25.55	16.94	9.24	7.22	8.06	6.36
VARIANCE	693.25	6.94	4.73	7.10	6.13	9.81	7.88	14.01	40.57	90.11	138.82	92.51	23.06	5.81	2.35	3.54	4.24
STAND. DEV.	26.33	2.63	2.18	2.67	2.48	3.13	2.81	3.74	6.37	9.49	11.78	9.62	4.80	2.41	1.53	1.88	2.06
C.V.	27.84	40.54	37.95	36.66	36.51	36.83	26.29	29.07	30.77	38.16	24.81	37.65	28.35	26.09	21.24	23.32	32.35
VON NEUMANN	681.84	14.81	10.51	17.57	11.03	18.25	13.49	30.61	60.86	50.41	68.16	44.84	12.78	5.28	3.38	2.95	4.74
RATIO D/V	0.98	2.13	2.22	2.47	1.80	1.86	1.71	2.18	1.50	0.56	0.49	0.48	0.55	0.91	1.44	0.83	1.12

Fig. 2. Part of computer output for EEG of subject with prominent alpha activity.

inent alpha activity, a pronounced peak at 10 per second. Of interest is the fact that his ratio D/V is 0.44 indicating a highly significant trend. (See Murphree et al.[9] for discussion.) Looking at the column, we see that the values first increase, then decrease, then return to about initial values. We

will come back to consideration of this later. The
second kind of computer output employed in these
studies is a histogram of class interval of electrical energy versus frequency of occurrence which
the computer plots automatically for total energy
and any selected separate frequencies. These outputs from the computer for individual subjects are
easily compiled for groups by clerical methods.

RESULTS

Table 1 shows the mean total electrical energies
and coefficients of variation for the various groups
of subjects and patients. Although the mean for the

Table 1. Mean EEG Electrical Energies (E)

Coefficients of Variation (C)

All records

Nonpsychotic Subjects	N	E	C
All	68	72.77	18.34
Reformatory only	43	74.23	20.30
Staff only	25	70.24	14.92
Patients			
"Untreated"	18	62.77	10.82
7 weeks posttreatment	14	77.57	12.79
9 weeks posttreatment	15	74.38	11.22

untreated patients is suggestively smaller than the
means for the other subjects and post-treatment
patients, the difference is not statistically significant. But the coefficients of variation of the
three patient groups are significantly different
from those of the reformatory subjects and those of
all nonpsychotic subjects together. The probabilities are less than 0.005 and 0.001 respectively.
Reformatory and staff volunteers do not differ significantly from each other, nor do staff and patients.
That is, the staff occupy an intermediate postion
between the reformatory and patient groups.

In considering why some of these apparent dif-

ferences lack significance, the question occurs
whether the data were normally distributed. Figure 3

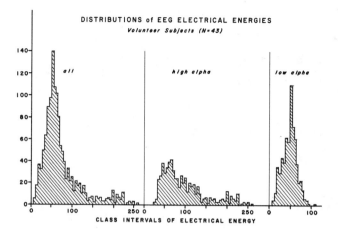

Fig. 3. Histograms of distributions of EEG
electrical energies of reformatory subjects.

shows on the left the distribution of total electrical energies in the reformatory sample. This
histogram, which was simply an aggregation of the
individual histograms presented by the computer,
plainly is not symmetrical, and probit transformation confirms this. Careful study of the records
suggested that the extended upper tail was due to
the alpha activity in those subjects who had prominent alpha. Separate histograms were then plotted,
shown at the center and at the right of Figure 3,
for subjects who had above average electrical energy
in their alpha activity and those who had below
average alpha energy. This was done by calculating
the percent of total electrical energy which each
subject had in his alpha peak, computing the mean
percent for each group, then rating each subject
as high-alpha or low-alpha according to whether he
was above or below the 50th percentile for his group.
When the high-alpha group is removed, the remainder,
the low-alpha group has a very tidy normal distribution. The same general picture occurred with the

other groups of subjects and patients.

Table 2 shows the mean electrical energies and coefficients of variation of the high-alpha subject of each group of volunteers and patients. Despite

Table 2. Mean EEG Electrical Energies (E)
and Coefficients of Variation (C)
High alpha records

Nonpsychotic subjects	N	E	C
Reformatory only	21	100.70	26.30
Staff only	15	78.69	17.25
Patients			
"Untreated"	8	69.73	11.11
7 weeks posttreatment	8	95.84	12.68
9 weeks posttreatment	6	94.00	9.88

the apparently striking differences in the means of total electrical energy, these are not significantly different. The reason is that the variances are very large, so that there is great overlap. The differences in the coefficient of variation, however, are highly significant. All groups differ from each other except the three patient groups, among whom there are no significant differences.

Table 3 shows the same data from low-alpha subjects and patients. By inspection, the differences appear non-significant, and by statistical

Table 3. Mean EEG Electrical Energies (E)
and Coefficients of Variation (C)
Low alpha records

Nonpsychotic subjects	N	E	C
Reformatory only	22	48.98	14.59
Staff only	10	57.56	11.46
Patients			
"Untreated"	10	57.26	10.59
7 weeks posttreatment	6	53.22	12.95
9 weeks posttreatment	9	61.30	12.12

test, this turns out to be true. So far, this makes a rather nice story for the differences in the volunteers and the patients being due entirely to differences in the constancy of their alpha activity. Now, some other work with time-serial statistical analysis has shown that volunteers tend to have greater incidences of trends in their records. Table 4 shows this. Here we have another evidence of invariance in the patient's electroencephalograms, namely a smaller tendency to change in time. In-

Table 4. Chi-square analysis for signficant trends in EEGs at nonpsychotic subjects and schizophrenic patients.

δ^2/S^2	P	Nonpsychotic	Patients
≥ 1.47	> 0.05	15	23
< 1.47	< 0.05	25	11

$x^2 = 5.53$ (with Yates); $P < 0.02$

spection of the records suggests that the volunteers have a greater tendency toward developing drowsiness during the course of the recording. If the patients have a greater likelihood of remaining fixedly awake, this would fit with their observed electroencephalographic stereotypy, and with the idea that they are somehow "overalerted." The latter is also supported by studies such as that of Kornetsky and Mirsky,[10] as well as clinical observations, suggesting that chronic schizophrenics are highly resistant to sedative drugs.

SUMMARY

Electroencephalographic recordings from nonpsychotic subjects were compared with those from chronic schizophrenic patients. The comparisons were made by means of integrative determinations of total electrical energy in one lead of the electroencephalogram and simultaneous determinations of energy in discrete portions of the spectrum from 1.0 to 36 cycles per second in the same lead. The patients tended to have significantly less variability in the electrical energy of their electroencephalograms. Examination of the frequency characteristics of the records revealed that the differences were related in part to differences in the amount of electrical energy in the alpha range. Patients with above average energy in the alpha range were significantly less variable than nonpsychotics with above average alpha energy. Patients with below average energy in the alpha band did not differ significantly from nonpsychotics with below average alpha energy. A further difference was that the patients had less likelihood of change during the time-course of the recordings. This could be an aspect of an unyielding state of arousal.

CONCLUSIONS

From these studies, it is concluded that:

1. The previous observations that male chronic schizophrenic patients tend to have smaller than normal variability in the mean electrical energy of their electroencephalograms are confirmed.

2. The observed differences in variability of electroencephalographic energies between schizophrenic patients and nonpsychotic subjects is due in large part to differences in the variability of alpha activity. Patients and nonpsychotic subjects who have low alpha activity do not differ from each other. Patients and nonpsychotic subjects who have greater alpha activity do differ from each other. The differences in alpha activity cannot be reliably detected by visual inspection of the records.

3. The observed differences may be due to a tendency for the nonpatients to become drowsy while the patients remain fixedly awake.

REFERENCES

1. Goldstein, L., Murphree, H. B., Sugerman, A. A., Pfeiffer, C. C., and Jenney, E. H. Quantitative electroencephalographic analysis of naturally occurring (schizophrenic) and drug-induced psychotic states in human males. Clin. Pharmacol. Therap. 4:10-21, 1963.

2. Goldstein, L., Sugerman, A. A., Stolberg, H., Murphree, H. B., and Pfeiffer, C. C. Electro-cerebral activity in schizophrenics and nonpsy-chotic subjects: quantitative EEG amplitude analysis. Electroenceph. clin. Neurophysiol. 19:350-361, 1965.

3. Murphree, H. B., Sugerman, A. A., Jenney, E. H., and Schultz, R. E. Quantitative EEG effects in male chronic schizophrenics of phenothiazines and deanol. Fed. Proc. 22:510, 1963.

4. Sugerman, A. A., Goldstein, L., Murphree, H. B., Pfeiffer, C. C., and Jenney, E. H. EEG and behavioral changes in schizophrenia. Arch. Gen. Psychiat. 10:340-344, 1964.

5. Drohocki, Z., L'intégrateur de l'électroproduction cérébrale pour l'électroencephalographie quantita-tive. Rev. Neurol. 80:619-624, 1948.

6. Murphree, H. B., Goldstein, L., Pfeiffer, C. C., Schramm, L. P., and Jenney, E. H. Computer analysis of drug effects on the electroencephalograms of normal and psychotic subjects. Int. J. Neuro-pharmacol. 3:97-104, 1964.

7. Murphree, H. B. Electroencephalographic tech-niques for studying drug effects. Chapter 31 in Siegler, P. E., and Moyer, J. H., III, eds., Animal and Clinical Pharmacologic Techniques in Drug Evaluation, Volume II, Chicago, 1967, Year Medical Publishers, Inc.

8. Murphree, H. B., and Price, L. M. Electro-

encephalographic changes in man following smoking. Ann. N.Y. Acad. Sci. 142:245-260, 1967.

9. Murphree, H. B., Pfeiffer, C. C., Goldstein, L., Sugerman, A. A., and Jenney, E. H. Time-series analysis of the effects of barbiturates on the electroencephalograms of psychotic and nonpsychotic men. Clin. Pharmacol. & Therap. 8:830-840, 1967.

10. Kornetsky, C., and Mirsky, A. F. On certain psychopharmacological and physiological differences between schizophrenic and normal persons. Psychopharmacologia 8:309-318, 1966.

ACKNOWLEDGMENTS

This work was supported by a grant from the American Medical Association Education and Research Foundation. Our thanks to Dr. A. A. Sugerman, Chief of Investigative Psychiatry, Bureau of Research in Neurology and Psychiatry, Princeton, New Jersey, who allowed us to study patients on his ward.

H. B. Murphree, M.D., and R. E. Schultz,

Rutgers University Medical School, New Brunswick, New Jersey

EEG PATTERNS AND SCHIZOPHRENIA: SHORT CRITIQUE

J. RUBICEK

I have, of course, no intention to discuss in these short remarks the problem of the possible etiology of schizophrenia. In Prague we tried to be eclectic on the view of etiology, but schizophrenia is mostly considered to be in a broad sense an organic brain disease with up to now an unknown biochemical substrate. Genetic factors are accepted as a possible basis for these biochemical constellations which are responsible for the disease and the psychogenetic factors and psychodynamic influences are considered to be one of the possible stimulating factors for development of schizophrenic disease. We were concerned about the heterogeneous nature of the schizophrenic group. While it could be shown that the schizophrenic group as a whole could be statistically differentiated from normal it is not easy to distinguish this from various other mental states.

I expect that you will agree that in Europe the diagnosis of schizophrenia is not as frequent as on the American continent. Some of the patients diagnosed here as schizophrenic would be diagnosed as neurotics or character disorders (psychopaths) in Europe.

We did not succeed in our studies to successfully discover the origin of schizophrenia. We could not find any leading points in the EEG. As one part of our experimental studies directed to the problem of schizophrenia we worked from the year 1952 for several years in the field of experimental psychotic states. It is well known now that LSD, mescaline, psylocybin and other hallucinogenic drugs do not produce experimental schizophrenia but clinically these experimental states have more the character of toxic, acute exogenous reaction types (Bonhoeffer). The term "experimental schizophrenia" is inadmissible, as it is contrary to the basic psychopathological findings. In this area we found very different results of EEG studies. There is no typical EEG for schizophrenia. Both in recent, acute states and also in chronic cases we see frequently normal frequency patterns with well modulated alpha activity and correct reactions on various activations. The toxic experimental psychosis on the other hand produce a typical EEG with intensive desynchronization. The rate of the alpha rhythm increases, sometimes by as much as four cycles per second, its amplitude decreases and the amount of fast beta waves increases.

While we were not able to come directly nearer to the etiology of schizophrenia, we have focussed our effort to make the territory, the field of schizophrenia, narrower. We have chosen an indirect approach and in these efforts we found again important help in the EEG examination. We found that many so called schizophrenics in our country are, after very careful studies of case histories, after biochemical and electrophysiological exams in reality temporal lobe epilepsies or some of them postencephalitic states with schizophrenia-like symptomatology. We were able to find larger groups of such pathologic states in the clinics and various hospitals in our country. We do not think, as for example Gibbs, that there is a significant positive relationship between schizophrenia and temporal lobe paroxysmal activity and epilepsy, but on the other hand, that positive EEG findings in temporal regions very often exclude diagnosis of schizophrenia and that it is necessary to treat these patients as epileptics. We have seen relatively good results in these type of patients previously sometimes for years treated as schizophrenics when we have given them anti-epileptic drugs especially Tegretol. I feel that this differential diagnosis is very important for practical reasons for therapy of our patients. In general, we think that larger EEG abnormalities speak against the diagnosis of schizophrenia.

In the last years we compared with Dr. Matousek and Dr. Volavka a group of 42 schizophrenics without any medication with a group of 42 controls carefully matched as to their age and sex. Routine visual evaluation showed that schizophrenics have significantly more non-normal curves than the controls. Abnormalities were mostly diffuse and non-specific. Occurrence of sleep modification did not differentiate significantly schizophrenics from controls. Frequency analysis of the right temporo-parietal regions showed the schizophrenics to have a significantly higher amount of theta and alpha activity than the control. We worked with broad band Kaiser-Peterson frequency analyzer. Differences in the beta bands were not significant. In schizophrenics variance between individuals in the output values of frequency analyzer was significantly higher in the delta and alpha bands. On the other hand the coefficient of variance of the dominant alpha activities was higher in the controls.

Schizophrenics were ranked according to the age and divided

into younger and older groups. Means and variances of the frequency analysis ouput of the two groups were again mutually compared. Data of the control group were processed in the same manner.

Younger control subjects had significantly more slow activity than the older ones. Differences between younger and older schizophrenics were insignificant. These findings may support the theory that EEG abnormalities of schizophrenics are a manifestation of a maturation defect.

J. Rubicek, M.D., Psychiatric Institute, Prague, Czechoslavakia

THE ELECTRODERMAL ORIENTING RESPONSES IN CHRONIC SCHIZOPHRENIA: MANIFEST CONFUSION AS A SIGNIFICANT DIMENSION

ALVIN S. BERNSTEIN

From the time the syndrome was first defined, confusion and disorganization, manifested in such things as disorientation, incoherent and rambling speech, tangential or irrelevant behavior, inappropriateness, etc., have been described as central features of the schizophrenic process. More recently, factor analytic studies by Lorr and his associates[1,2] have described a similar "Thinking Disorganization"[1] or "Schizophrenic Disorganization"[2] dimension which "defines a broad parameter probably central to schizophrenia"[1] (p. 243). However, controlled study of such disorganization, particularly of its attentional-perceptual correlates, is made difficult by the very nature of the schizophrenic pathology. Patients who are apathetic, uncommunicative or unintelligible, cannot provide the descriptive reports often required in perceptual studies. The orienting response (OR) offers a more fruitful avenue of approach, allowing direct study of such inaccessible patients.

I wish to present briefly several such OR studies, each examining the responsiveness of chronic schizophrenics to novel stimuli—that is, to the availability of external information. So far only simple, objectively innocuous stimuli have been studied. In each instance the primary emphasis was on determining the responsiveness of the chronic schizophrenic who showed confusion in comparison with that of his fellow chronic patient who did not, as well as with that of the general population. The electrodermal component of the OR was used to gauge such responsiveness. In a normal population Voronin and Sokolov[3] showed the electrodermal response to be the most reliable individual OR component. Additional OR measures are being used in subsequent studies, but more of that later.

All the work reported here was carried out with chronic, long-hospitalized, male schizophrenics all of whom were free of known organic defect, and with normal control groups largely drawn from the hospital's nonprofessional personnel and of similar age and background to the patients. Patients were dichotomized into Confused, and nonconfused, or Clear, subgroups. In these initial studies the difference was kept broad: chronic patients selected for study either displayed very much confusion or virtually none. In selecting patients, each ward psychiatrist and psychologist was first asked independently to list those of his patients who were markedly confused, disorganized, and disoriented, as well as those who were markedly free of such disorder, omitting those in the intermediate range. All patients on a given ward who were not similarly listed by both raters, or in whom brain damage or other significant physical disability were suspected, were eliminated. The psychiatrist and psychologist were then asked independently to complete the Montrose Rating Scale (MRS) (Rackow, et al.[4])

on each remaining patient. The MRS rates the patient's current level of function from zero to 4 in each of 7 areas, including manifest overt behavior, communication, reality testing, emotional appropriateness, intellectual functioning, human relationships, and aspirations towards recovery. $\underline{S}s$ were then selected from either end of the MRS distribution to yield non-overlapping samples of "Confused" and "Clear" patients.

In the first study, 48 Controls, 60 Clear and 60 Confused patients were examined. The patient samples were subdivided into a drug group (currently receiving one of the phenothiazines) and a nondrug group (free of drugs at least 30 days before testing). In every study the Confused patients showed a longer mean total hospitalization than did the Clear patients. In this first study, for example, mean total hospitalization was 14.4 years for the Confused samples and 8.9 years for the Clear ones (p<.01).

The stimuli have always been either brief, repetitive lights or tones. In the first study half the $\underline{S}s$ in each group saw a square of white light at 5 ft.c., and half at 25 ft.c. The square was 6-5/8 inches on a side and was seen at eye level on a screen 3 feet in front of $\underline{S}$. The stimulus was repeated at irregular intervals between 15-60 seconds for 10 trials. The intensity was then switched and another 10 trials given. An assistant always sat in the test chamber with a clear view of $\underline{S}$'s face, and signalled the instrument room so that stimuli were given only when $\underline{S}$ had both eyes open and was directly addressing the screen.

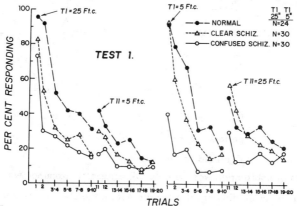

<u>Fig. 1</u>   Frequency of OR in the first visual study among normal Controls, combined drug and nondrug Clear schizophrenics and combined Confused schizophrenics.

The phasic, GSR OR was defined as a resistance drop of at least 500 ohms within 1-3 seconds of signal onset. Each record was scored by 2 independent judges and the few instances of disagreement resolved by a third judge.

Fig. 1 reveals the frequency of response in each group. Drug and nondrug patients are combined here since there were no drug-associated differences (see Fig. 2). Two important facts are illustrated in Fig. 1. First, when initially presented with a novel external stimulus (i.e., on Trial 1 (T1)), chronic schizophrenics <u>as an entity</u> are not necessarily hyporesponsive. Rather, it is particularly those chronic schizophrenics who display confusion who are often nonresponsive. Second, reactivity among such Confused patients is dependent to a considerable degree on the intensity of the stimulus applied. Significantly fewer Confused patients responded to a 5 ft.c. light than did either Clear patients or Controls. However, when a 25 ft.c. light was shown initial OR frequency rose sharply among Confused

patients reaching a level similar to the Clear patients and of only borderline difference
(p = .07) from Controls. Among those in each sample who did respond on T1 there was no
difference in T1 OR amplitude between Clear patients and Controls while Confused patients who were responsive gave smaller OR's than either. Raising signal intensity here
therefore brought a response from a greater proportion of the Confused sample without
improving the amplitude of that response (Bernstein[5]).

The presence of a phenothiazine regimen was not associated with any significant alteration of phasic OR. In Fig. 2 response frequencies are collapsed across stimulus intensities and plotted for each of the four patient-samples in this study and in its retest. Similarities are evident between the two Clear and between the two Confused samples rather
than along the drug dimension. As expected, these similarities (and differences) are greatest immediately following the appearance of novelty—i.e., T1, T2, T11, and T12. The
same pattern is true with regard to OR amplitude and speed of habituation.

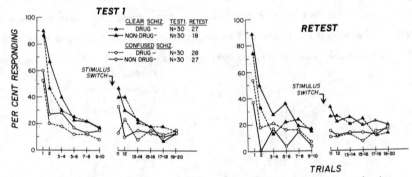

Fig. 2   Frequency of OR in both visual studies showing separately the
performances of drug and nondrug samples within the Clear and
Confused patient groups.

Speed of habituation was the only OR parameter examined where presence or absence
of marked confusion did not differentiate within the chronic schizophrenic population.
Whether habituation was defined as the first appearance of 2, or of 3, consecutive nonresponsive trials the various chronic samples reacted here as a homogeneous entity, and
all showed faster habituation than the Controls, regardless of signal intensity (Bernstein[5]).

Approximately two months after this first test Ss were recalled and the study was repeated. Retest data support the original findings in virtually all respects. That support
is illustrated in the similarity of retest response frequency curves in Fig. 3 to those of the
initial test in Fig. 1. The retest also provided information concerning the stability over
time of the particular OR (or lack of OR) shown by the individual Ss. T1 was examined on
both tests to see if those who did or did not respond on first testing would exhibit the same
characteristic on retest. In all, 142 Ss were retested, of whom 108 had initially given an
OR. On retest, 88 of this 108 again gave a T1 OR. Thirty-four had not responded on the
initial test and 25 of them again failed to respond on retest. A X^2 contingency test (p<.01)
showed that individuals do, in fact, show significant consistency in being (GSR) OR "responders" or "nonresponders". The results were similar when the major subject-groups were

separately analyzed (Bernstein[6]).

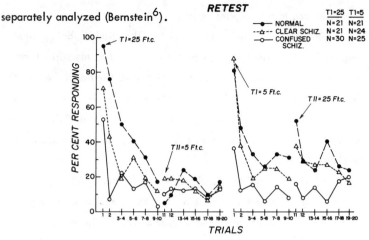

Fig. 3   Frequency of OR in the retest visual study among normal Controls,
combined drug and nondrug Clear schizophrenics and combined
Confused schizophrenics.

A series of product-moment correlations were calculated to evaluate the degree of consistency shown in response amplitude (in log conductance units), speed of habituation in the first 10 repetitive trials, and total number of responses over the 20 trials. Pooling samples by z' transformation the correlation coefficients were significant (save for one group with a small n, (Bernstein[6]) and moderate; .46 for T1 OR amplitude; .63 for total number of OR's; and .65 for trials to habituation, all p<.01. Actually, these figures probably underestimate the true values (Bernstein[6]).

The rearousal of OR on Trial 11 (T11) immediately following the stimulus change also deserves comment (Figs. 1 and 3). While the T1 differences described earlier are supported by the fact that T11 rearousal frequency is lowest among Confused patients, this support is compromised by the somewhat higher OR frequencies on Trials 9 and 10 among the Clear and Control groups. However, when OR frequency on T9 and 10 is subtracted from that of T11, rearousal is still lowest among Confused patients, although the differences fall short of conventional significance levels (using 2-tailed tests).

These rearousal data do illustrate another fact about the OR—namely, that the direction in which a stimulus change occurs is also an important determinant of response to that change. Thus in Figs. 1 and 3, Ss experiencing a 20 ft.c. increase in intensity showed more frequent OR than did those experiencing a 20 ft.c. decrease. These 2 studies and, more significantly, a third in which all Ss responded to a single common stimulus on the crucial rearousal trial (Bernstein[7]) demonstrated the same "directional bias" in both chronic schizophrenics and in the general population.

The OR correlates of manifest confusion in chronic patients were then explored further; first, to determine whether similar impairment would be found following stimulation of a non-visual sense modality, and second, to learn whether impairment would be found in the relatively enduring tonic OR as well.

Auditory stimuli were selected for study because it has been shown that auditory signals are more effective than visual ones as arousal stimuli (e.g., Bernhaut, et al[8]), and because some writers (e.g., McGhie[9]) have suggested that schizophrenics may be particularly poor in processing visual as compared to auditory information.

Two to 2-1/2 years after the visual studies all subjects still available, both patient and Control, were recalled. New clinical judgments were obtained on the patients and additional new Ss were selected as before to produce samples of 48 Controls (of whom 23 were recalls), 72 Clear (14 recalls), and 72 Confused patients (40 recalls). An increase in the use of ataractic drugs in this hospital made it impossible to obtain sufficient drug-free samples. Only 10 Clear and 9 Confused Ss were free of drugs; the remainder were receiving one of the phenothiazines.

The procedure was similar to that of the visual studies except that a 1000 cps tone was repeated 15 times at irregular intervals (Bernstein [10]). One sample in each subject-group received the tone at 60db, one at 75db, and another at 90db. Fig. 4 shows frequencies of response to each stimulus intensity in the various subject groups, and Fig. 5 the response amplitudes, square-root transformed to reduce skewness.

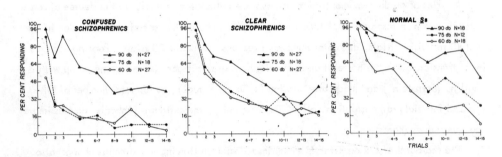

Fig. 4   Frequency of OR at each tone intensity.

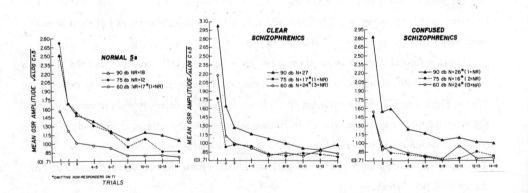

Fig. 5   Mean OR amplitude at each tone intensity, eliminating Ss who failed to respond on Trial 1. Scores are in log conductance units, square-root transformed.

As you see in Fig. 4 only 52% of the Confused patients respond when first hearing a tone at 60db, significantly fewer than among either Controls ($x^2 = 7.262$, 1df, p<.01) or Clear patients ($x^2 = 7.194$, 1df, p<.01). In this instance, however, there were no significant differences in T1 OR amplitude among responsive $\underline{S}$s in each group (Fig. 5). When a moderately louder 75db tone is ued there is again a significant rise in the incidence of initial response among Confused patients ($x^2 = 5.104$, 1df, p<.05). With 89% responding to a 75db tone Confused OR frequency no longer differs from Clear patients or Controls. Despite this marked increase in response frequency, however, T1 OR amplitude to 75db among Confused patients is the same as that to 60db and smaller than that shown by the Controls. Therefore, just as in the visual study, a modest increase in stimulus intensity appears to make a greater number of Confused patients responsive although the average amplitude of such response remains small. (The Clear patient's nonsignificant decrease in T1 OR amplitude at 75db is rather puzzling.) Further, the improvement in response frequency at 75db is short-lived. On T2 there is a steep fall-off in OR frequency among Confused patients who again show fewer instances of response than either Controls ($x^2 = 9.381$, 1df, p<.01) or Clear patients ($x^2 = 2.812$, 1df, .05>p<.10). It is only when there is a more substantial increase in the intensity of the impinging stimulus—here, to 90db, that Confused schizophrenics are able to make and sustain significant levels of response. There are no significant differences in either frequency or amplitude of T1 OR to a 90db tone. As in the visual studies, however, Controls do show more responses overall as stimuli of any intensity are repeated. Thus, whether habituation is defined as either 2 or 3 consecutive nonresponsive trials Confused patients do not differ from Clear ones, and both habituate faster than Controls at all 3 auditory intensities.

Virtually identical results emerged when these analyses were repeated using only the newly-selected $\underline{S}$s in each group. In addition, none of the within-group comparisons between recalled and new $\underline{S}$s revealed significant differences. The Clear-Confused distinction is thus both meaningful and replicable.

In both sensory modalities the intensity of the stimulus being applied proved important in determining whether Confused chronic schizophrenics would show a GSR OR. I can cite a final bit of data to illustrate this. Among the recalled $\underline{S}$s were 20 Confused patients all of whom had been phasic OR nonresponders in the previous visual study. They were distributed 8 each to the 60 and 90db groups, and 4 to the 75db group. Seven of 8 still did not respond when given a 60db tone; all 4 responded at first to 75db, but 3 did so only on T1; while all 8 responded to the 90db tone and gave a mean of 8.4 OR's over the 15 trials.

It thus turns out that the pattern of phasic OR (at least in its GSR component) is indeed quite consistent across sense modalities. In all major respects the auditory data confirm the visual ones. We can now turn to an examination of the tonic electrodermal OR.

Two different aspects of the OR have been described—a phasic OR and a tonic OR (Sharpless and Jasper[11]; Sokolov[12]). The phasic response has a short latency and a brief duration, is relatively slow in habituating but recovers quickly after habituation. The tonic OR has a longer latency and relatively long duration. It habituates more quickly and recovers more slowly afterward. Phasic OR is a more specific, differentiated response mediated by the more rostral, thalamic portion of the reticular system while the tonic OR, relatively diffuse and undifferentiated, is mediated through the more caudal, brain stem portion. In terms of electrodermal measurement, the phasic OR is represented by the familiar GSR and the tonic response by such things as shifts in baseline levels.

The groups examined in this study were similar to those of the phasic visual ones—28 normal Controls, 40 Clear and 40 Confused schizophrenics, each divided into 20 drug and 20 nondrug patient-samples. The same 1-second lights were used, with half of each group receiving 5-, and half 25 ft.c. beginning after 5 minutes of adaptation in semidarkness and continuing at irregular 15-60 second intervals for at least 6 minutes. Mean base admittance level (BAL) (an a.c.-type instrument was used) were scored over 10-second periods at 4 different points: a) at the end of the adaptation period immediately preceding onset of the first flash, b) 2 minutes later, c) 2 minutes after that, when the intermittent lights had been viewed for 4 minutes, and d) 2 minutes after that, following 6 minutes of such observation. The results are illustrated in Fig. 6 (Bernstein[13]).

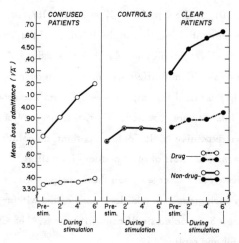

Fig. 6   Mean base admittance levels at rest, and at successive 2-minute intervals during intermittent visual stimulation. BAL is square-root transformed.

In the nondrug samples there were no differences between Confused patients and Controls in prestimulus, or "resting" BAL while Clear patients were significantly higher than either. The onset of intermittent stimulation after the adaptation period was expected to produce a tonic arousal, signified here by heightened base levels (e.g., Lader[14]). In the present study such tonic response was analyzed as a difference score: BAL 2 minutes after onset of intermittent stimuli minus prestimulus BAL (Bernstein[13]). Among nondrug patients both Clear and Confused schizophrenics clearly demonstrated such tonic OR (Fig. 6). In fact, there were no differences between Controls and either nondrug patient-sample in such 2-minute tonic response. The differences shown in Fig. 6 suggest hyperresponsiveness in both nondrug patient-samples. Thus, while BAL among Controls leveled off at 4 minutes and began the expected decline by 6 minutes, both Clear and Confused nondrug samples showed a consistent heightening of BAL throughout.

This means that the nonresponsiveness often seen in Confused patients is limited to the phasic OR. It also suggests a considerable degree of independence between the tonic and phasic components. This was supported by a series of product-moment correlations obtained between the 2-minute tonic difference score and 2 measures of phasic response—amplitude of T1 OR, and the number of phasic responses made to the first 5 stimuli (every $\underline{S}$ saw at least 5 during these first 2 minutes). The coefficients were generally significant (Bernstein[13]) but consistently of small magnitude, ranging between .240 and .484. They do not, therefore, support Sokolov's assumption of an "intimate" association between tonic and phasic OR (Sokolov[12], p. 117). No more than about 20%, at best, of the variance in tonic electrodermal OR appears to be associated with variance in phasic response.

Tonic OR differed from the phasic response in another way as well. While the phenothiazines exerted no differential effect on phasic OR, Fig. 6 illustrates a significant damping effect on tonic response and on BAL generally. While some caution is necessary here since the drug-samples consisted of patients for whom the drugs had already been prescribed by their physicians, there were no differences between drug and non-drug samples in such variables as diagnosis, age, race, sex, MRS rating, total time in hospitals, and general state of health.

Such a difference in apparent drug-effect within the OR is consistent with the literature. For example, using radioactive phenothiazine S^{35}, Tadros and Wahab[15] reported the greatest drug concentration in the brain stem reticular formation with least in the thalamic nuclei. Rothballer[16] found that chlorpromazine blocks the adrenergic mesencephalic (tonic) response without affecting the cholinergic, more rostral (phasic) system. See also the brief review here by Lynn[17] (pp. 31-2).

In sum, I think all these data add up to the following picture. Perception among chronic schizophrenics in general is more diffuse and undifferentiated than among the general, normal population. In such patients there is a faster but less detailed assimilation of information from the environment. Chronic patients who are confused superimpose on this an often marked attenuation of certain inputs from the environment. Such "input dysfunction" (Venables[18]) is peculiarly characteristic of confused schizophrenics within the chronic population and presumably serves a protective or defensive function, shielding them from the full impact of tension-provoking external stimuli. However, this confusion-associated "stimulus barrier" is neither perfect nor permanent: it becomes increasingly penetrable as signals of increasing intensity are applied. As stronger stimuli are applied, confused patients lose their distinctiveness and begin to respond as do other chronic patients. In addition, such attenuation is apparently employed only against specific, discrete signals from the environment. Chronic patients generally, including those who are confused, remain highly sensitive toward the general demand characteristics of their environment, and may even be hypervigilant in this respect.

Let me try to specify those aspects of the data on which these working hypotheses are based. First, relatively undifferentiated perception is suggested by the consistently faster habituation shown by all chronic samples. According to Sokolov[12] OR habituation depends on a restructuring of the internalized model at every point of mismatch until the model again becomes redundant with current input. The judgment of redundancy is that of the observer himself. Thus, habituation would proceed more quickly where any or all of several conditions held; where the model itself is characterized by fewer (per-

haps broader) stimulus dimensions; where stimulus input is categorized into fewer (perhaps broader) determinants; and where a looser fit is acceptable in judging match/mis-
match between model and input. In turn, these properties characterize less differentiated perception. Chronic schizophrenics as a group therefore appear to absorb information from their environment quickly, perhaps sacrificing detail for speed.

Further, it was only the Confused patients who consistently displayed a marked
lack of phasic response. Others have also reported that the greatest loss of phasic OR
occurs among deteriorated chronic patients (see, e.g., Lynn's[17] review of Russian research). Working with acute schizophrenics, Stern, Surphlis, and Koff[19] similarly
found that the least electrodermal OR occurred among those patients who demonstrated greater pathology and were more severely ill. In addition, my data show that phasic OR among Confused patients consistently increased markedly when stimulus intensity was raised. When stimuli are sufficiently strong phasic OR in the Confused becomes indistinguishable from the Clear patients. Similar stimulus-intensity effects in
schizophrenics have been described by others, e.g. Levitt[20] who suggested that more
intense stimuli are effective because they redirect the schizophrenic's attention onto
the otherwise nonattended external stimuli.

The evident fact is that GSR's in Confused chronic schizophrenics are singularly
dependent on stimulus intensity. This fact, however, can be interpreted in either of
2 mutually antagonistic ways. One, essentially the hypothesis offered above, maintains that there is simply a rise in the phasic OR threshold associated with confusion in
chronic schizophrenics. The other is that such patients give relatively little phasic OR
at any intensity and show substantial GSR to more intense stimuli only because they
have begun to produce defensive responses (DR's). Soviet writers make an important
distinction here, and report that OR gives way to DR as stimulus intensity increases and
finally becomes sufficient to pose a potential threat (Sokolov[12]). Where the OR is a
positive feedback system (Lynn[17]) facilitating stimulus input and assimilation, the DR
involves negative feedback and the attenuation of input. The consequences for perception and learning would therefore be very different depending on which explanation is correct.

Cardiovascular measures have been used to distinguish OR from DR. Russian authors have relied largely on measurement of blood flow in the skin of the finger and
the forehead, with a simultaneous pattern of finger constriction and forehead dilation
indicating an OR, and constriction at both sites a DR (Sokolov[12]). Based primarily on
the work of John Lacey and his associates in this country, cardiac deceleration following sensory stimulation has been described as an OR, with acceleration here defined as
a DR (Graham and Clifton[21]). In the studies reported here only the electrodermal response was recorded, so such information had to be sought elsewhere. One distinction
between OR and DR is that, unlike the OR, DR's do not readily habituate (Sokolov[12]).
I therefore examined the number of Ss in each group that failed to reach even the 2-
trial habituation criterion. Such "nonhabituators" particularly might be giving DR's.
Table 1 shows that except for the 90db auditory sample, there were few such Ss in any

of the groups and particularly few in the Confused samples where this comparison is especially important.

TABLE 1.   THE FREQUENCIES OF "HABITUATORS" AND "NONHABITUATORS" AT EACH STIMULUS INTENSITY, USING THE 2-TRIAL HABITUATION CRITERION

		Normal Controls		Clear Schizophrenics		Confused Schizophrenics	
	Stimulus Intensity	No. of Habit.*	No. of Nonhabit.*	No. of Habit.*	No. of Nonhabit.*	No. of Habit.*	No. of Nonhabit.*
First Visual Study	25 ft.c.	18	5	24	1	19	3
	5 ft.c.	17	5	26	2	11	1
Retest Visual Study	25 ft.c.	17	3	13	2	16	0
	5 ft.c.	14	3	20	1	8	1
Auditory Study	60db	16	1	22	2	14	0
	75db	9	3	16	1	16	0
	90db	8	10	22	5	18	8

* Omitting Ss who were nonresponsive on T1.

There are no differences in either visual study between 25- and 5 ft.c. intensities in the proportion of "nonhabituating" Ss, nor between the 60 and 75db intensities in the auditory one. Since there was a significant increase in OR frequency among Confused patients to the 25 ft.c. light as well as to the 75db tone, the lack of any increase in the proportion of "non-habituators" here supports the increased threshold interpretation.

At 90db, however, there is a marked increase in such "nonhabituation" relative to any of the other intensities in either modality. This was investigated further by plotting OR amplitude over trials separately for "habituators" and "nonhabituators" (Fig. 7).

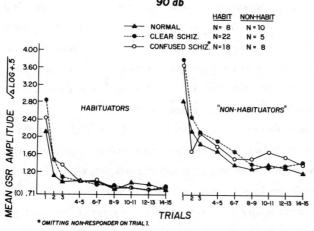

Fig. 7   Mean OR amplitude to the 90db tone for those Ss within each group who do not reach the 2-trial habituation criterion ("Nonhabituators") and for those who do (Habituators). Ss not responsive on Trial 1 are eliminated, and amplitudes are log conductance, square-root transformed.

The fact that habituation occurs in every sample is obvious on inspection of Fig. 7 and was supported by statistical analysis. The regression of GSR OR amplitude was plotted over log trials, to produce linearity. Regression coefficients were negative and significant for all groups in both "habituator" and "nonhabituator" samples ($\underline{b}$ ranged between -.769 and -1.271 for the former, and between -1.220 and -.779 for the latter, all $p<.01$). "Nonhabituators" are thus only <u>slower</u> habituators and the evidence again suggests that the GSR's obtained were not defensive reflexes in <u>any</u> of the groups.

Fenichel[22] and other psychoanalytic theorists have long suggested that confusion may serve a defensive function in schizophrenia by effectively damping contact between the patient and a threat-filled environment. The fact that impaired phasic OR was found particularly in Confused patients is consistent with such an interpretation. Equally supportive was the fact that 'resting' base admittance levels in such Confused, phasic-OR-impaired patients were significantly lower than in the phasic-OR-unimpaired Clear patients. Corroborative data have recently been presented by Goldstein and Acker[23]. Among their chronic patients those displaying "high-thought-disturbance" also showed lower base conductance levels than either normal controls or low-or-moderately-thought-disturbed patients, together with possibly reduced reactivity to the film-stimuli used.

The data also demonstrate that OR impairment in Confused patients involves only the phasic response. While additional work is needed to define fully the functional or behavioral significance of the phasic-tonic distinction there is evidence that they are separately mediated within the central nervous system. Phasic reactions are believed to be responsive to relatively specific, discrete signals from the environment signifying particular, possibly rapidly changing events (e.g., Sharpless and Jasper[11]). Tonic response, however, defined by shifts in base levels or rate of spontaneous electrodermal discharge (which was also examined in the tonic study, Bernstein[13]) is thought responsive to the organism's general perception of the demands of his environment and the likely need for response on his part (see, e.g., Berlyne[24]; Lacey and Lacey[25]). It thus appears that Confused patients attenuate only specific signal-input (if these are of low-to-moderate intensity). The steady increase in BAL shown only by both groups of nondrug patients (Fig. 6) indicates that their vigilance concerning the nature of their environment is maintained for prolonged periods (Malmo[26]). Similar phenomena have been reported in schizophrenics by Cohen and Patterson[27] and Zahn[28], and in neurotics as well (Lader and Wing[29]; Malmo, Shagass and Heslam[30]).

These several studies make it apparent that the Clear-Confused dichotomy (which may, perhaps, prove to be a meaningful continuum with more sensitive measurement) is a significant one within the chronic schizophrenic population. Unrecognized it would simply have contributed to error variance, and thus might help account, in part, for the high within-group variability so often encountered in research into schizophrenia. Further, these data make it plain that the practice of studying only coherent, cooperative patients and generalizing to the entire chronic population is invalid.

Since all the patients in these studies were chronic, and virtually all in the process, poor premorbid categories, the Clear-Confused distinction appears to be largely independent of these dimensions. As shown in Table 2, however, there were significantly more paranoids among Clear patients, and more hebephrenics among the Confused. This raises the possibility that the Clear-Confused dimension may be only a restatement of the familiar paranoid-nonparanoid, or paranoid-hebephrenic (Shakow[31]) distinction. In addition, Confused patients were consistently hospitalized longer than Clear ones, and we must consider also the extent to which the Clear-Confused dimension may be reflecting variance due to differences in hospitalization.

TABLE 2. THE FREQUENCY OF OCCURRENCE OF VARIOUS SCHIZOPHRENIC SUBDIAGNOSTIC GROUPS IN THE CLEAR AND THE CONFUSED SAMPLES*

Subdiagnostic Groups

	Paranoid	Catatonic	Hebephrenic	Undifferentiated	Mixed	Simple
First Visual Study						
Clear Pts.	39	6	1	10	2	2
Confused Pts.	17	8	22	10	1	2
Auditory Study						
Clear Pts.	34	6	3	24	0	5
(**)	(27)	(4)	(2)	(19)	(0)	(4)
Confused Pts.	27	9	21	12	2	1
(**)	(12)	(5)	(7)	(6)	(1)	(1)

* Subdiagnosis in the visual retest study was the same as in the first study; Subdiagnosis was not recorded in the tonic study.

** These N's refer only to newly selected patients in each group.

The studies of phasic OR consistently indicate that the Clear-Confused differences here are not simply due to differences in the proportion of paranoid or hebephrenic patients. While Clear-Confused differences in T1 OR were present in each phasic study, paranoid-nonparanoid and hebephrenic-nonhebephrenic comparisons were consistently nonsignificant. The distribution of hebephrenic and nonhebephrenic patients was similar across intensities among Confused patients, as were those of paranoid-nonparanoid patients within the Clear groups (except in the visual retest where patient discharges and transfers somewhat upset the balance). Table 3 presents the frequency of T1 OR shown by hebephrenic and by nonhebephrenic patients among the Confused samples in each phasic study as well as the frequencies shown by paranoids and nonparanoids among the Clear.

TABLE 3. FREQUENCY OF <u>OR</u> OR ABSENCE OF <u>OR</u> ON T1 IN EACH PHASIC <u>OR</u> STUDY AMONG KEY DIAGNOSTIC SUBGROUPS WITHIN THE CLEAR AND CONFUSED SAMPLES. DATA ARE COLLAPSED ACROSS INTENSITIES WITHIN EACH STUDY.

	Confused Pts.			Clear Pts.		Controls	
First Visual Study	T1 OR	T1 No OR		T1 OR	T1 No OR	T1 OR	T1 No OR
Hebephrenic	10	12	Paranoid	32	7	45	3
Nonhebephrenic*	24	14	Nonparanoid**	21	0		
Retest Visual Study							
Hebephrenic	7	14	Paranoid	20	7	37	5
Nonhebephrenic*	18	16	Nonparanoid**	16	2		
Auditory Study							
Hebephrenic	16	5	Paranoid	32	2	47	1
Nonhebephrenic*	40	11	Nonparanoid**	32	2		

* Includes paranoids

** Includes hebephrenics

Confused patients are less responsive than either Controls or Clear patients on T1 whether these Confused patients are hebephrenic or not. In the first visual study hebephrenic Confused Ss were less frequently reactive than either the Control or the combined Clear samples: $X^2 = 14.304$, and 18.129, respectively, with $p<.01$ in both (1df). However, the nonhebephrenic Confused patients <u>also</u> showed significantly fewer T1 OR's: nonhebephrenic Confused patients vs. Controls, $X^2 = 7.326$, $p<.01$; vs. combined Clear patients, $X^2 = 4.898$, $p<.05$. On visual retest comparison of hebephrenic Confused with Controls and Clear patients gave respective $X^2 = 17.417$, and 13.279, each $p<.01$. The same comparisons for nonhebephrenic Confused patients gave $X^2 = 9.921$, $p<.01$, and $X^2 = 6.527$, $p<.02$. Finally, in the auditory study, the Confused hebephrenics vs. Controls, $X^2 = 8.103$, $p<.01$; vs. Clear patients $X^2 = 5.732$, $p<.02$. Additional analyses of variance involving the Clear-Confused classification, paranoid-nonparanoid diagnosis, and stimulus intensity showed no differences between diagnostic subgroups in T1 amplitude or speed of habituation in any study. Thus it is the presence of manifest confusion itself that appears to be the significant variable here in determining initial phasic response among chronic schizophrenics.

Some caution is necessary in interpreting these last data because diagnoses were taken from the patient's current clinical folder. However, it seems unlikely that whatever diagnostic error may be present would be of sufficient magnitude to overturn these results.

Product-moment correlations were obtained in each phasic OR study between length of hospitalization and T1 amplitude, trials to habituation using both 2- and 3-trial criteria, and total number of OR's across all trials. In addition, correlations were obtained in the tonic OR study between prestimulus, "resting" BAL and hospitalization because Clear and Confused patients differed here too. All correlations were determined separately in each patient-sample, compared and pooled by z' transformation because there were no group differences. The evidence indicates that the Clear-Confused difference in total hospitalization time did not itself affect these scores. In the initial visual study the respective correlations for T1 OR amplitude, habituation 2-trial, habituation 3-trial and total number of OR's were: -.054; -.109; -.118; and .059. Similar correlations for retest were, respectively: -.042; -.037; -.011; and -.114. In the auditory study these correlations were: .082; -.015; .071; and .104. Finally, in the tonic OR study the correlation between hospitalization and "resting" BAL was -.173. All are low and nonsignificant.

There is, however, a relationship suggested between total hospitalization and occurrence of phasic OR within the Confused sample. In both the first visual study and in the auditory study, those Confused patients who failed to show an OR on T1 had been hospitalized longer than those who did: $t = 2.863$, $p<.01$, and $t = 2.135$, $p<.02$, respectively. The biserial correlation between total length of hospitalization and presence or absence of T1 OR in these Confused subgroups is .439 in the visual, and .553 in the auditory study. A similar difference existed in the visual retest but fell short of conventional (2-tailed) significance: $t = 1.395$, $p>.10$, and $r_b = .218$.

Despite this, the Clear-Confused difference in T1 phasic responsiveness is not simply due to differences in hospitalization. When subgroups in each were equated for total hospitalization (by dropping all patients hospitalized less than 70 or more than 270 months) Confused patients still consistently showed fewer T1 OR's in both the initial visual ($X^2 = 3.990$, $p<.05$) and auditory studies ($X^2 = 4.140$, $p<.05$).

It is difficult to assess the significance of this relationship between T1 OR and hospitalization among Confused schizophrenics. First, it is not clear why OR incidence should be affected but not amplitude or habituation. However, it should again be noted that the present patients were long-hospitalized (consistently at least 75% were hospitalized over 5 years). The first 2-3 years may be more significant here. But beyond this, any apparent "hospitalization-effect" raises a question that cannot be answered by these data: is this effect due to some influence of institutionalization itself (as, e.g., Silverman, Berg and Kantor[32] suggest), or simply to the gradual unfolding of some internal "schizophrenic" process (as, e.g., Johannsen and O'Connell[33] suggest)? While this broader question remains unanswered, the present studies do indicate that (a) any hospitalization-associated changes in phasic GSR OR are limited in scope, and (b) differences in phasic OR between Clear and Confused chronic schizophrenics go beyond any difference between them in total hospitalization.

These studies therefore indicate that chronic patients who are long-hospitalized and who carry a hebephrenic diagnosis are more likely to be confused. However, it is the fact of such confusion itself, rather than these correlated variables, that appears to be significant in determining electrodermal responsiveness.

All of these studies have used only simple, innocuous stimuli. Whether the picture is the same with regard to more complex, or more socially, personally, or biologically relevant stimuli remains to be seen. In addition, only the electrodermal OR was examined. Other components must also be studied, not only because of the OR-DR issue raised earlier, but also in order to learn whether impairment is general across the entire range of the OR. Individual differences in the responsivity of particular physiological channels are commonplace. Despite the reliability of the electrodermal OR component, demonstrated in normal groups by Voronin and Sokolov[3] and by Dykman, et al.[34] such more extensive study is clearly indicated.

REFERENCES

1. LORR, M., O'CONNOR, J. P., and STAFFORD, J. W. The Psychotic Reaction Profile, J. Clin. Psychol., 16, 241, 1960.

2. LORR, M., KLETT, C. J., and CAVE, R. Higher-level psychotic syndromes. J. Abnorm. Psychol., 72, 74, 1967.

3. VORONIN, L. G., and SOKOLOV, E. N. Cortical mechanisms of the orienting reflex and its relation to the conditioned reflex. In The Moscow Colloquium on Electroencephalography of Higher Nervous Activity, H. H. JASPER and G. D. SMIRNOV (Eds.), Supplement No. 13, The EEG Journal, Montreal, 1960.

4. RACKOW, L., NAPOLI, P., KLEBANOFF, S., and SCHILLINGER, A. A group method for the rapid screening of chronic psychiatric patients. Amer. J. Psychiat., 109, 561, 1953.

5. BERNSTEIN, A. S. The galvanic skin response orienting reflex among chronic schizophrenics. Psychon. Sci., 1, 391, 1964.

6. BERNSTEIN, A. S. The orienting reflex as a research tool in the study of psychotic populations. In Mechanisms of the Orienting Reaction in Man, I. Ruttkay-Nedecky, L. Ciganek, V. Zikmund, and E. Kellerova (Eds.), Slovak Academy of Sciences, Bratislava, 1967.

7. BERNSTEIN, A. S. The orienting response and direction of stimulus change. Psychon. Sci., 12, 127, 1968.

8. BERNHAUT, M., GELLHORN, E., and RASMUSSEN, A. T. Experimental contributions to problems of consciousness. J. Neurophysiol., 16, 21, 1953.

9. McGHIE, A. Psychological studies of schizophrenia. Brit. J. Med. Psychol., 39, 281, 1966.

10. BERNSTEIN, A. S. The phasic electrodermal orienting response in chronic schizophrenics: II. Response to auditory signals of varying intensity. In press.

11. SHARPLESS, S., and JASPER, H. Habituation of the arousal reaction. Brain, 79, 655, 1956.

12. SOKOLOV, E. N. Perception and the Conditioned Reflex, New York, Macmillan, 1963.

13. BERNSTEIN, A. S. Electrodermal base level, tonic arousal and adaptation in chronic schizophrenics. J. Abnorm. Psychol., 72, 221, 1967.

14. LADER, M. H. The effect of cyclobarbitone on the habituation of the psychogalvanic reflex. Brain, 87, 321, 1964.

15. TADROS, F., and WAHAB, F. The site of action of phenothiazine S^{35} in the central nervous system. J. Ment. Sci., 108, 816, 1962.

16. ROTHBALLER, A. Studies on the adrenalin-sensitive components of the reticular activating system. EEG clin. Neurophysiol., 8, 603, 1956.

17. LYNN, R. Attention, Arousal and the Orientation Reaction, New York, Pergamon, 1966.

18. VENABLES, P. H. Input dysfunction in schizophrenia. In Progress in Experimental Personality Research, Vol. I., B. Maher (Editor), New York, Academic Press, 1964.

19. STERN, J., SURPHLIS, W., and KOFF, E. Electrodermal responsiveness as related to psychiatric diagnosis and prognosis. Psychophysiol., 2, 51, 1965.

20. LEVITT, H. Performance deficit and auditory inefficiencies in schizophrenia. J. Nerv. Ment. Dis., 140, 290, 1965.

21. GRAHAM, F., and CLIFTON, R. Heart-rate change as a component of the orienting response. Psychol. Bull., 65, 305, 1966.

22. FENICHEL, O. The Psychoanalytic Theory of Neurosis. New York, W. W. Norton, 1945.

23. GOLDSTEIN, M., and ACKER, C. W. Psychophysiological reactions to films by chronic schizophrenics: II. Individual differences in resting levels and reactivity. J. Abnorm. Psychol., 72, 23, 1967.

24. BERLYNE, D. Conflict, Arousal and Curiosity. New York, McGraw Hill, 1960.

25. LACEY, J., and LACEY, B. The relationship of resting autonomic activity to motor impulsivity. In The Brain and Human Behavior; Proceedings of the Association for Research in Nervous and Mental Diseases, Baltimore, Williams and Wilkins, 1958.

26. MALMO, R. B. Physiological gradients and behavior. Psychol. Bull., 64, 225, 1965.

27. COHEN, L., and PATTERSON, M. Effect of pain on the heart rate of normal and schizophrenic individuals. J. Gen. Psychol., 17, 273, 1937.

28. ZAHN, T. Autonomic reactivity and behavior in schizophrenia. Psychiat. Res. Rep., 19, 156, 1964.

29. LADER, M., and WING, L. Habituation of the psychogalvanic reflex in patients with anxiety states and in normal subjects. J. Neurol., Neurosurg., and Psychiat., 27, 210, 1964.

30. MALMO, R., SHAGASS, C., and HESLAM, R. Blood pressure response to repeated brief stress in psychoneurosis: A study of adaptation. Canad. J. Psychol., 1951, 5, 167.

31. SHAKOW, D. Psychological deficit in schizophrenia. Behav. Sci., 8, 275, 1963.

32. SILVERMAN, J., BERG, P., and KANTOR, R. Some perceptual correlates of institutionalization. J. Nerv. Ment. Dis., 141, 651, 1966.

33. JOHANSSEN, W., and O'CONNELL, M. Institutionalization and perceptual decrement in chronic schizophrenia. Percept. mot. Skills, 21, 244, 1965.

34. DYKMAN, R., REESE, W., GALBRECHT, C., and THOMASSON, P. Psychophysiological reactions to novel stimuli: measurement, adaptation, and relationship of physiological variables in the normal human. Ann. N. Y. Acad. Sci., 79, 43, 1959.

A. S. Bernstein, Ph.D., State University of New York, Downstate Medical Center, 450 Clarkson Avenue, Brooklyn, N.Y. 11203

LOBOTOMY IN SCHIZOPHRENIA: A REVIEW

SIDNEY MALITZ, VIRGINIA LOZZI and MAUREEN KANZLER

Since the publication of Moniz' monograph in 1936, in which he described improvement in 20 chronic psychotic patients after cutting their frontal lobe white matter, the surgical procedure known as lobotomy has been performed for the relief of severe mental illness. At first it was met with great enthusiasm only to fall into later disrepute. Today, the pendulum has swung back to center and the operation is seen as a desirable procedure for certain classes of patients. The purpose of this paper is to present a review of lobotomy as a therapeutic technique in schizophrenia. Case studies from a recent follow-up project at Psychiatric Institute will be used to illustrate some of the more salient points.

Lobotomy

In lobotomy a variable number of the white frontothalamic fibres are sectioned. Developments in the operational procedure have been in the direction of reducing the number of fibres cut to the minimum consistent with improvement and of greater precision in selecting the location of the cut. The most radical procedure was the earliest--a full lobotomy anterior to the plane of the coronal suture. Other variations included the bimedial lobotomy, in which the medial half of the frontothalamic radiation was severed, and the transorbital lobotomy, in which the frontothalamic fibres were sectioned by a leukotome inserted supra-or-

bitally. Orbital-medial undercutting of the frontal
lobe cortex was introduced by Scoville. Knight modified this technique so as to restrict further the undercutting.

In addition to the lobotomy strictly defined,
there are other psychosurgical procedures aimed at
accomplishing the same result. These include topectomy or the ablation of part of the frontal lobe cortex, cingulectomy, in which the anterior part of the
cingulate gyrus is removed, and thalamotomy, in which
the frontothalamic connections are interrupted at the
level of the dorso-medial nucleus by electrocoagula-
tion. In this paper we shall expand the topic to include topectomy as well as lobotomy.

Follow-Up Studies

A number of follow-up studies have been summarized in Table 1 which appears on the following pages.
FREEMAN[1] reported concerning the progress of the first
200 patients in the Freeman-Watts series, who had been
followed for 10 years since operation. Of these patients, the schizophrenic group did not do as well over
the 10 years as they had seemed to be doing in the beginning. There was a general reduction in the usefully occupied group from 54 per cent to 39 per cent,
while the number requiring hospitalization rose from
14 per cent to 39 per cent. Those patients who had
not been hospitalized for prolonged periods before operation were found to have had the best results.

FREEMAN, et al.,[2] reported results of 602 transorbital lobotomies performed from 1952 through 1954 in
West Virginia state hospitals. The patients were, for

TABLE 1. SUMMARY OF FOLLOW-UP STUDIES OF PSYCHOSURGERY

Reported by	Date of publication	Dates of operations	No. of cases Schiz.	No. of cases Non-Schiz.	Type of operation	Results in schizophrenic patients
Freeman	1953	Pre 1943	200		Prefrontal lobotomy	Ten years later % usefully occupied dropped from 54% to 39% and % hospitalized rose from 14% to 39%.
Freeman, et al.	1954	1952-1954	602		Transorbital lobotomy	Fair response in schizophrenics; failures (21%) were mostly chronic schizophrenics with hallucinations.
Pippard	1955	1948-1952	31	201	Rostral leucotomy	Schizophrenics: Improved 29%; Unimproved 71%
Tooth	1961	1942-1954	6634	3731	Usually standard	Discharged: Schizophrenics 36%; affective disorders 67%; other diagnoses 63%
Nicholas	1967	1944-1956	25	--		Discharge rate for lobotomized patients lower than for controls in severely ill patients.

TABLE 1. SUMMARY OF FOLLOW-UP STUDIES OF PSYCHOSURGERY (continued)

Reported by	Date of publication	Dates of operations	No. of cases Schiz.	No. of cases Non-Schiz.	Type of operation	Results in schizophrenic patients
Miller	1967	1948-1952	85	31	Prefrontal lobotomy	Schizophrenics: 39% out of hospital; 21% intermittent- ly hospitalized; 40% hos- pitalized permanently.
Hoch, et al.	1955	1949-1954	40	--	Medial lobotomy 10 Precoronal 9 Topectomy 21	65% improved
Hirose	1966	1947-1966	327	167	Various	Satisfactory results in atypical schizophrenia. Poor results with chronic, deteriorated schizophrenia.
N.Y.S. Brain Research Project	1956	1948-1949	66	--	Topectomy	Overt schizophrenia 22% improved; pseudoneurotic 83% improved.
Sykes and Tredgold	1964	1951-1961	13	337	Restricted orbital undercutting	Improvement in schizophrenics with marked tension. Poor results in other schizo- phrenics.

the most part, long-term severely ill psychotic patients with an average duration of hospitalization of
5.7 years. The majority were suffering from various
types of schizophrenia. Two-thirds of them were management problems. In May 1954, 38 per cent of the patients who survived the operation were out of the hospital. Schizophrenics responded fairly well if they
were operated on within the first two years of hospitalization. The failures, 21 per cent of the operated
group, were usually patients who had chronic schizophrenia and whose hallucinations persisted after lobotomy.

The results of rostral leucotomy in 240 cases,
including 31 schizophrenics, were reported by PIPPARD[3].
Of the schizophrenic patients, the operative results
were good in 13 per cent, fair in 16 per cent and poor
in 71 per cent. PIPPARD concluded that rostral leucotomy was useful when the prepsychotic personality was
good, when affective response was strong, particularly
with tension and depression with aggression directed
toward the self rather than to the outside, when the
duration of illness was less than 4 years or fluctu-
ated according to environmental events. He found that
late paranoid and atypical schizophrenics did better.
No simple, catatonic or hebephrenic schizophrenics did
well. He recommended a lobotomy in which a blind in-
cision was made below the superior frontal cortex, isolating part of Brodmann's areas 8, 9 and 10 or a little
posterior to this plane. With this type of operation,
intellectual deficits had been less serious. He
stressed the importance of the environment to which
the patient would return as an important factor in his
recovery.

A large follow-up study[4] surveyed 10,365 lobotomized patients who had been operated on between 1942 and 1954 in England and Wales. Of these, 6,634 were schizophrenics and 3,731 fell into other diagnostic categories. After surgery the discharge rate for schizophrenic patients was lower than for the other diagnostic categories. In the latter, more than 60 per cent were discharged as opposed to the schizophrenic patients, of whom only 36 per cent had been discharged.

NICHOLAS[5] followed 25 lobotomized schizophrenic patients and compared them with a control series of 192 unleucotomized schizophrenic patients. In the moderately ill group of 20 lobotomized patients, 35 per cent were still hospitalized several years after surgery. Of 163 controls, 38 per cent were still hospitalized. Of severely ill lobotomy patients, 5 in number, 60 per cent were still hospitalized and of 29 control patients, 55 per cent were still hospitalized. In this group, the operation would seem to have had no advantage as treatment.

Pre-frontal lobotomies were performed on 150 patients with chronic mental illness in Toronto, Canada. A 10-year follow-up was made by MILLER[6]. Included in the group were 85 schizophrenics, subdivided as follows: catatonic 18; paranoid 20; schizo-affective 7; undifferentiated 40. Schizophrenic patients tended to show slightly poorer results than other diagnostic categories. On the average the patients had been in the hospital 5 years before operation. When followed a decade later, 61 per cent of the total group were liv-

ing out of the hospital whereas only 39 per cent in
the schizophrenic subgroup had been able to remain
out of the hospital. Of the remaining schizophrenics,
21 per cent were intermittently hospitalized and 40
per cent permanently. The symptoms which were reliev-
ed were those of persistent anxiety, fear, tension,
preoccupation with guilt, failure and inadequacy,
while marked autism, fragmented thinking, emotional
flattening, and bizarre ideation were not significantly influenced by the operation. It is noteworthy that
the latter symptoms are those which are particularly
characteristic of schizophrenia.

Limiting the patients to the diagnostic category
of pseudoneurotic schizophrenia, HOCH et al.[7,8] reported concerning 40 such patients who were treated with
three types of operations: Topectomy in 21 patients,
medial lobotomy in 10 patients, precoronal lobotomy in
9 patients. Of the 37 patients who were living at the
time of follow-up, 65 per cent had improved significantly. Furthermore, it was found that gains continued to accrue over 2½ to 3 years after operation. Significant improvements occurred in alleviation of disabling anxiety without change in the basic structure
of personality or evidence of impairment of depth of
emotional feeling. It was also found that if the illness began before the age of 15, the prognosis was
poor. The point was made that in pseudoneurotic schizophrenia, psychotherapy is effective in only 20 to 25
per cent of patients. Therefore, the improvement rate
of 65 per cent following psychosurgery represented a
substantial gain.

In Japan, HIROSE[9] performed various kinds of lobotomy on 494 patients, of whom 327 were schizophrenic. Before 1955, 72 per cent of the patients on whom
he operated were schizophrenic. Since 1955, the proportion of schizophrenic patients has dropped to 43
per cent with a corresponding increase in surgery for
patients suffering from affective disorders, neurosis,
epilepsy and personality disorders. From 1947 to 1956,
HIROSE performed closed, blind lobotomies. During
1956 to 1957 he used a modification of Scoville's undercutting, and after July of 1957, he adopted orbi-
tal-ventromedial undercutting. Over the course of the
years, the work of HIROSE has moved in the direction
of modification of operative procedures so as to minimize destruction of brain tissue and to improve selection of candidates for psychosurgery. Within the schizophrenic group, he came to prefer patients whom he
named "atypical" schizophrenics, with whom he had a-
chieved good results, rather than chronic deteriorated
schizophrenics in whom the results were poor. "Atypical" schizophrenics he defined as patients with recurring catatonic episodes or with periodic delusional
states with affective coloring or with chronic neurosis-like states or with paraphrenia. Patients whom he
defined as suffering from chronic neurosis-like states
would appear to be similar to those named pseudoneurotic schizophrenics by HOCH and POLATIN.[10]

Typical of research on topectomy was the work of
the New York State Brain Research Project[11] which was
related procedurally to Columbia-Greystone projects of
a similar nature. In the New York State Brain Research

Project, 66 schizophrenic patients received a bilateral frontal topectomy. The basic criteria for the
selection of patients for the operation required that
the patient be confined to the hospital for at least
three years without remission, that he have no obvious medical complications and no family history of
functional psychosis, that he have no gross psychopathic traits, that he be sufficiently cooperative for
psychological testing and that a satisfactory home environment be available to which he might return. Of
the 66 patients, 59 manifested overt schizophrenia,
the other 7 belonged to the pseudoneurotic category.
There was a marked difference in results between the
two groups. The overt schizophrenic group showed only
22 per cent of any improvement at all and only 6.8 per
cent significant improvement, whereas the pseudoneurotic group had an improvement rate of 83 per cent. It
was found that topectomy did not eliminate basic psychotic features in the sense of primary symptoms of
schizophrenia but rather reduced emotional response to
delusions and hallucinations and increased accessibility and contact with the environment. It was concluded that 30-35 grams of cortex had to be removed on
each side, that less than this amount was not sufficient for relief, but that removal of more than 35
grams did not help schizophrenic patients if the removal of the 35 grams had not already helped. Since
the bilateral frontal topectomy in this project was
inadequate for chronic deteriorated schizophrenics,
the project report recommended that a prefrontal lobotomy remain the operation of choice in such chronic
deteriorated patients.

282

The decreased use of psychosurgery for schizophrenic patients in the 1950's was manifested in a
study by SYKES and TREDGOLD[12] of 350 patients on whom
a restricted orbital undercutting was performed between 1951 and 1961. Of these patients, only 13 were
diagnosed as schizophrenic. They found that schizophrenics with marked tension improved to a fair degree
but that other schizophrenics had a poor operative outcome. Of the thirteen patients, four left medical
care, 4 had partial improvement and 5 were unchanged.
This striking shift away from schizophrenics as candidates for psychosurgery reflects not only the poor results obtained with the chronic patients but also the
increasing recourse to chemotherapy as a preferred
treatment for schizophrenia.

Multiple Lobotomies

The result of second leucotomies were reported by
PIPPARD[13] for 27 cases. Analysis of the results of
surgery showed that while a more extensive pre-frontal
cut than rostral leucotomy might relieve symptoms, personality deficits might be extremely serious, especially in younger and vulnerable personalities. PIPPARD
suggested that if rostral leucotomy failed in cases
which appeared to have been suitable for it, it was
unlikely that a standard operation would have produced
better results.

FREEMAN[14] reported concerning 414 patients who
have undergone multiple lobotomies and who were followed over an average period of 12.4 years after the
first operation. The objective in second lobotomies
was the extension of previous incisions into basal

portions of the frontal lobes. FREEMAN claimed that second operations more frequently produced successful results in affective and psychoneurotic disorders as against schizophrenic illnesses. With schizophrenic illness, better results were obtained in early stages of the disorder, and FREEMAN cautioned against long delay before resorting to surgery.

Patient Selection

In the early years of the period surveyed by the studies described above, lobotomy was used most frequently for chronic deteriorated schizophrenics who had been hospitalized for long periods of time. The operation was in most cases the measure of last resort so that any improvement at all was considered an operative success. As techniques were refined and operative mortality reduced, other classes of patients were treated psychosurgically and it was found that affective disorders responded better than did schizophrenia. Nevertheless, within the broad diagnostic of schizophrenia, some schizophrenics responded better than others. Table 2 lists the symptoms which can be

TABLE 2. SYMPTOMS PROGNOSTIC OF OPERATIVE RESULTS

Symptoms likely to respond	Symptoms likely not to respond
Anxiety (Cattell[15]; Freeman[16])	Anergia (Cattell[15])
	Sociopathy (Cattell[15])
Obsessions and compulsions (Cattell[15])	Deterioration (Hoch[18])
Phobias (Cattell[15])	Hallucinations and delusions (Freeman[17])
Depression (Cattell[15])	
Self-directed violence (Freeman[17])	Externally directed violence (Freeman[17])
Fear (Miller[6])	Scattered thought processes (Freeman[17])
Tension (Miller[6])	Marked autism (Miller[6])
Preoccupation with guilt, failure, and/or inadequacy (Miller[6])	Emotional flattening (Miller[6])
	Bizarre ideation (Miller[6]

considered prognostic of good and poor operative results. It will be noted that the symptoms which have
been found most likely to respond well to psychosurgery are those which have a strong affective charge of
anxiety, fear or depression with strong obsessive-compulsive traits. Symptoms which have been found to be
unresponsive to surgery are characterized by a lack
of this affective charge or by a disorder of thought
or perception. Sociopathy, as well, has been found
not to respond well to psychosurgery.

In addition to the symptoms listed in Table 2,
the age of the patient and the duration of illness affects prognosis. CATTELL[15] found that patients under
20 years of age had a poorer prognosis than those a-
bove that age. FREEMAN[16] pointed out that chronicity
of illness was one of the most important considerations.
Observing that duration of illness over 5 years was a
poor prognostic sign, FREEMAN urged that the operation
not be delayed for patients who show the symptoms likely to respond well to surgery.

Within the diagnostic classification of schizophrenia, subgroups show a differential response to
psychosurgery. Table 3 summarizes the conclusion of

TABLE 3. RESPONSE TO PSYCHOSURGERY
OF SUBGROUPS OF SCHIZOPHRENICS

Good response	Poor response	Questionable response
Paranoid (Cattell[15], Freeman[20], Pippard[19], Hirose[9])	Hebephrenic (Cattell[15], Freeman[20])	Catatonic Good — (Cattell[15], Hirose[9]) Poor — (Pippard[3])
Pseudoneurotic (Hoch[18], Pippard[19])	Simple (Cattell[15], Pippard[3]) Unclassified (Freeman[20])	

various investigators regarding good and poor response

according to kind of schizophrenia manifested by the patients. In general, the paranoid and pseudoneurotic schizophrenics have responded well; the hebephrenic, simple and unclassified schizophrenics do poorly. There is a divergence of opinion regarding the response of the catatonic patient, CATTELL[15] and HIROSE[9] claiming good results and PIPPARD[3], poor results.

An attempt to develop systematic selective procedures was described by FREEMAN[17]. The Malamud rating scale was applied to the preoperative state of 1,120 patients who afterwards submitted to one form or another of lobotomy. The scale consisted of 19 categories of behavior, such as appearance, motor activity, responsivity, socialization, etc. For each of these behaviors, 8 descriptive adjectives were supplied and the investigator was to choose the one which most closely characterized the patient's behavior. For each category of behavior the number of patients described by each adjective was computed for in two groups of patients separately--one group (144) who made a good adjustment and the other group (576) who made a poor adjustment. Chi-square methods were used to see which aspects of behavior differentiated the preoperative condition of the groups representing the two kinds of postoperative adjustment. It was found that favorable indications were obsessive manifestations, anxiety and self-directed violence while unfavorable indications included disorganization of thought processes, hallucinations, delusions and externally directed violence. It was concluded that the Malamud rating scale was of some prognostic value in selecting patients for psychosurgery.

In general, it can be said that there are three key factors to be considered in deciding the suitability for psychosurgery: 1) pre-morbid personality; 2) degree of affective distress; 3) suitability of the environment to which the patient is to return. With regard to the first of these, it may be observed that the operation will not supply personality deficiencies. It cannot supply what the patient has never had. With regard to the second issue, a significant degree of patient distress appears to be important--of anxiety, fear, depression, or guilt. With regard to the third factor, it has been found that the patient must have a supportive environmental situation to which to return. There must be a niche available to him both for the postoperative recovery **period**, which requires 8-15 months, and in subsequent months and years while the patient is learning how to adjust his altered state to the demands of the environment. As VOSBURG[21] has said, "Sustained recovery is a reading on the equilibrium struck by the social environment and the patient."

Rationale of Operation

Speculation about how psychosurgery achieves positive results has been concerned with two processes --physiological and psychological. In the early 1950's it was thought that the quantity of the destroyed pathways regulated the effect of the operation rather than what part of the frontal lobe was cut. (KALINOWSKY[22]; HOCH[18,23,24,25]) This view was a reaction to the belief that Brodmann areas 9, 10 and 46 were the centers for emotional functioning. Both KALINOWSKY and HOCH spoke against the idea of specific localization of emotional functioning in the frontal lobe in favor of a more generalized localization. KALINOWSKY, for example, held that if delusions and hallucinations remained after lobotomy, they must therefore have originated in deeper parts of the brain. HOCH pointed out that Brodmann areas 9, 10 and 46 were important, not as a localization center for emotions but as the assemby point for fibres to the thalamus.

STRÖM-OLSEN[26] remarked, "All the neuropathological studies emphasized the importance of the area in front of the tip of the anterior horn and below the genu of the corpus callosun. We may ask ourselves if one or all these lesions are required to produce a therapeutic effect. In other words, interruption of the afferent fibres may diminish to a very large extent the number of impulses influencing consciousness and so provide relief from a state of tension, or the severing of the efferent tracts may diminish emotional reaction and vegetative symptoms associated with depression or anxiety. We may argue that both are in volved but at present it must be conceded that this is largely speculation."

HIROSE[9] postulated that psychosurgery, operating within the limitations set by the pre-morbid personality of each patient, re-regulated the autonomic functions of the limbic system and the hypothalamus so as to stabilize pre-existing excessive defense mechanisms, both psychological and biological, in such a way as to block the vicious circle.

Accenting more the psychological after-effects of the operation, HOCH[23,27] made use of the concept of primary and secondary awareness, primary awareness referring to the awareness of a stimulus and secondary awareness to a modification of the primary sensory perception into a caring or a not caring. This mental process of attachment or detachment he saw as a function of the ego, to the end that after surgery the patient might still have a specific symptom but did not care about it and, therefore, was not disorganized by it. The pre-operative affective component was reduced (HOCH, et al.[28]).

Summary

Surgical treatment for schizophrenia has gone through many stages during the past 30 years. Originally seen as the operation of last resort for chronic, deteriorated schizophrenics, the operation has come to be recognized as being much more effective for other psychiatric diagnostic categories, particularly those with strong affective and disabling neurotic symptoms. The advent of chemotherapy in the early 1950's has played a large part in the shift away from surgical treatment of schizophrenia to an emphasis on drug therapy. Within the broad diagnostic category, the subgroup of pseudoneurotic schizophrenics has been found to be the most likely candidates for lobotomy.

The operative techniques have become more restricted in the direction of the minimal destruction of tissue consistent with desired behavior change. Interruption of fibres connecting the frontal lobe and the thalamus has been the key factor in all techniques. The selection of a suitable patient involves consideration of three important factors--the pre-morbid personality, the existence of a strong and distressing affective component to the illness, and the availability of an environment to which the patient may be returned and in which he can function.

REFERENCES

1. FREEMAN, W.   Late results of prefrontal lobotomy.
   Act. Psychiat. Neurol. Scand. 27, 3-4, 1953.
2. FREEMAN, W., DAVIS, H. W., EAST, I. C., TOUT, H.
   S., JOHNSON, S. G. and ROGERS, S. G.   West
   Virginia lobotomy project. J. Am. Med. Ass.
   156, 939-943, 1954.
3. PIPPARD, J.   Rostral leucotomy: A report on 240
   cases personally followed up after 1 1/2 to 5
   years. J. Ment. Sci. 101, 756-773, 1955.
4. TOOTH, G. C. and NEWTON, M. A. Leucotomy in England and Wales, 1942-1954. H.M.S.O., London,
   1961.
5. NICHOLAS, J.   The rehabilitation of long stay
   schizophrenic patients who have had leucotomy.
   Brit. J. Psychiat. 113, 153-156, 1967.
6. MILLER, A.   The lobotomy patient a decade later.
   Canad. Med. Ass. J. 96, 1095-1103, 1967.
7. HOCH, P. H., POOL, L., RANSONHOFF, J., CATTELL,
   J. P., and PENNES, H. H.   Case presentation of
   pseudoneurotic schizophrenic patients treated
   with psychosurgery. J. Nerv. Ment. Dis. 120,
   102-103, 1954.
8. HOCH, P. H., POOL, J. L., RANSONHOFF, J., CATTELL,
   J. P., and PENNES, H. H.   The psychosurgical
   treatment of pseudoneurotic schizophrenia. Am.
   J. Psychiat. 111, 653-658, 1955.
9. HIROSE, S.   Present trends in psychosurgery. Fol.
   Psychiat. Neurol. Jap., 20, 361-373, 1966.
10. HOCH, P. H. and POLATIN, P.   Pseudoneurotic forms
    of schizophrenia. Psychiat. Quart. 23, 248-
    276, 1949.
11. LEWIS, N. D., LANDIS, C. and KING, H. E.   (Eds.).
    Studies in Topectomy. Grune & Stratton, New
    York, 1956.
12. SYKES, M. K. and TREDGOLD, R. F.   Restricted orbit-
    al undercutting. Brit. J. Psychiat. 110, 609-
    640, 1964.
13. PIPPARD, J.   Second Leucotomies. J. Ment. Sci.
    101, 788-793, 1955.
14. FREEMAN, W.   Multiple lobotomies. Am. J. Psychiat.
    123, 1450-1452, 1967.
15. CATTELL, J. P.   Some observations on the selection
    of patients for psychosurgery and psychotherapy
    after operation. Am. J. Psychother. 7, 484-
    491, 1953.
16. FREEMAN, W.   Review of psychiatric progress 1959.
    Psychosurgery. Am. J. Psychiat. 116, 601-604,
    1960.
17. FREEMAN, W.   Prognosis in frontal lobotomy by use
    of the Malamud Rating Scale. Am. J. Psychiat.
    109, 595-602, 1952.
18. HOCH, P. H.   Personality changes after topectomy.
    Psychiat. Quart., 25, 402-408, 1951
19. PIPPARD, J.   Leucotomy in Britain today. J. Ment.
    Sci., 108, 249-255, 1962.
20. FREEMAN, W.   Level of achievement after lobotomy.
    A study of one thousand cases. Am. J. Psychiat.
    110, 269-276, 1953.

21. VOSBURG, R. L. Lobotomy in Western Pennsylvania: Looking backward over ten years. Am. J. Psychiat. 119, 503-509, 1962.

22. KALINOWSKY, L. B. Cerebral localization and the contributions of psychosurgery and shock therapy. Archs. Neurol. Psychiat. 69, 582-586, 1953.

23. HOCH, P. H. Psychosomatic problems: Methodology, research material and concepts. Psychoanal. Rev. 39, 213-221, 1952.

24. HOCH, P. H. Some psychic manifestations in relation to brain function. Proc. Rudolf Virchow Med. Soc. in City of New York. 11, 108-114, 1952.

25. HOCH, P. H. Progress in psychiatric therapies. Am. J. Psychiat. 112, 241-247, 1955.

26. STRÖM-OLSEN, R. The importance of the orbital cortex in psychiatry. Act. Psychiat. Scand. 41, 274-285, 1965.

27. HOCH, P. H. Theoretical aspects of frontal lobotomy and similar brain operations. Am. J. Psychiat. 106, 448-453, 1949.

28. HOCH, P. H., CATTELL, J. P., PENNES, H. H., and GLASER, G. H. Theoretical and practical observations on patients subjected to topectomy. J. Nerv. Ment. Dis. 112, 545-546, 1950.

The following case history illustrates a patient who underwent two pre-coronal lobotomies and sustained a gradual improvement with ultimate limited but satisfactory social adjustment within the framework of a sympathetic environment affording her the opportunity to function as a housewife:

Patient F. T., a 22-year-old female, diagnosed originally as suffering from schizophrenia, pseudoneurotic type, was admitted to P.I. in 1954 with a 10-year history of illness. Prior to admission, she had had extended psychotherapy, 32 E.C.T. and insulin therapy without benefit. Her symptoms were pan anxiety, obsessive thinking, somatic preoccupation to the point of delusions, unreality feelings and ideas of reference. At P.I., she was treated for 11 months with intensive psychotherapy without improvement. In March 1955, at the age of 23, the patient underwent a pre-coronal lobotomy. Her clinical progress was erratic for a year but despite fluctuations in symptoms, there was a definite diminution in anxiety and tension. Approximately 10 months after surgery, she was started on an experimental phenothiazine, NP-208 and Ritalin, 10 mgm three or four times a day. In June 1956, a year and two months after surgery, she obtained a clerical job and was sent home three months later, considered improved. Seven months later she was readmitted because of overwhelming anxiety and obsessional thinking. Diagnosis at the time of this admission was schizophrenia, mixed type. In April 1957, approximately two years after the first operation, a revision of a precoronal lobotomy was performed. Her anxiety diminished and 9 months later she was able to take a job as a receptionist. Shortly after becoming employed she began to take Trilafon, 8 mgm q.i.d., and six months later was discharged from the hospital as improved. She married shortly after discharge and continued to work for several years on temporary jobs or was employed by her family. Her slowness at work was a problem. She was in a car accident in 1959 and has had headaches ever since. She bore a child in 1963, at which time she stopped working. She has had no psychiatric care since her discharge in 1958. She takes Miltown and phenobarbital when necessary. She claims that the first operation had no effect but that she gradually improved for about 2½ years after the second operation until 1960 when she reached a plateau. In a recent interview, she appeared as a well-dressed woman, with slow speech who was somewhat tangential and complained of mild to moderate anxiety and tension. She showed a blunted affect, mild obsessional thinking, and mild impairment of remote memory. She claims that she is more outspoken since surgery, occasionally yelling or screaming at her husband or mother. She leads a restricted life but one in which she functions adequately as a housewife.

This case history illustrates a good result with prefrontal lobotomy in a patient with pseudoneurotic schizophrenia who had some degree of satisfactory adjustment earlier in life. Her predominant symptomatology was anxiety and depression. Her sustained improvement was probably related to the fact that she had a niche in life to return to in which she was greatly needed:

G. M., a female, diagnosed as a pseudoneurotic schizophrenic, was admitted to P.I. in June 1955 at the age of 42. She was a married housewife with children. She had a 12 year history of anxiety, depression and cancerphobia. She had been in therapy privately for two years prior to admission, during which her anxiety and depression had increased. She seemed to have had a life-long history of anxiety, withdrawn behavior and hypochondriasis. A prefrontal lobotomy was performed several weeks after admission. Her post-operative course was uneventful. Gradually she became more able to function and to handle difficulties with her children without panic attacks. She was discharged home in January 1956, about six months after surgery on Dilantin 100 mgm t.i.d. and Dexamyl 5 mgm b.i.d. She continued on Dexamyl and NP-208, an experimental phenothiazine, 50 mgm daily, for two years post-operatively. When interviewed recently, her only symptoms appeared to be mild obsessional thoughts. There was no deterioration. She seemed well-balanced, energetic, and happy, with no specific complaints. She has handled family crises, such as a schizophrenic reaction in her daughter-in-law, in a competent manner, and acted as

surrogate mother for her grandchildren. She runs her
own household and has held a part-time secretarial job
for the past eight years. She has good interpersonal
relationships, particularly with her husband. She
still has intercourse with orgasm, and her enjoyment
of life in general is good.

The following case is an example of two operations, topectomy followed by lobotomy with minimal improvement over many years, in a hospital setting. The
early onset of illness presaged a poor prognosis.

H. D., a 29-year-old unemployed male, suffering
from schizophrenia, mixed type, was admitted to P.I.
at the age of 20 in 1949. He was single, with a history of tension, restlessness and difficulty in social
and school situations all his life. In the two years
prior to admission, he had become increasingly withdrawn. Two months before admission, he became agitated, obsessive, and paranoid, with bizarre preoccupations about his body. In April 1951, after a year
of unsuccessful treatment including 9 E.C.T., he underwent a bilateral lateral lobotomy (partial lobotomy
with section of the lateral half of each frontal lobe).
After several weeks of quiescent behavior, he again
became disturbed and assaultive with auditory hallucinations. Two months after surgery, he was transferred
to Rockland State Hospital. When evaluated four and
one half years later, in 1956, he was considered unimproved. He was interviewed in September 1968 and
he appeared to be in good contact, relevant and coherent but with a tendency to withdrawal. His insight
and judgment were impaired. He was well oriented and

free of hallucinations but not of paranoid delusions.

He appeared to be able to care for himself and per-

formed domestic chores for the hospital. He is re-

ceiving Dilantin and phenobarbital and has been on

these medications since his operation. In addition,

he has received Mellaril and Cogentin since 1966.

According to the hospital record, his behavior

seems to have improved since 1960. Credit for his

slight improvement cannot be ascribed clearly to any

one factor although psychotropic drugs may play a

role.

The following case illustrates the inability of

some patients to withstand the stress of life out of

the hospital, in spite of, in this instance, two psy-

chosurgical procedures.

Patient I. N., a 31-year-old female patient diag-

nosed as suffering from schizophrenia, mixed type with

catatonic and depressive features, was admitted to

P.I. in 1952 with symptoms of blankness in the head,

memory loss, withdrawal, confusion, depression with

suicidal thoughts, visual and auditory hallucinations.

The onset of her illness began 3 years prior to ad-

mission during her second pregnancy. She had also had

a postpartum depression 6 years prior to that. Pre-

ceeding her admission to P.I., she had been in a pri-

vate hospital for 2 months and had received 11 E.C.T.,

45 insulin comas and out-patient psychotherapy for 9

additional months. At P.I., prior to surgery, she

received 5 E.C.T. and 35 insulin comas. A medial lobotomy was performed in May 1952. Recovery was uneventful with gradual improvement, although the patient still complained of blankness and auditory hallucinations which interfered very little with her activities. She was discharged five months after operation and remained out of hospital for a year, at the end of which time she was readmitted with auditory hallucinations, withdrawal, anxiety, depression and confusion. A coronal lobotomy was performed six months later, an interval of 2 years and one month after the first operation. Again, there was gradual improvement with no further complaints of hallucinations. She was discharged 5 months postoperatively. She remained at home only two months when she had to be readmitted to another state hospital with ideas of reference, paranoid ideation and anxiety. Her subsequent history was marked by alternating periods of hospitalization, convalescent care and family care until 1952 when she was permanently hospitalized at Pilgrim State. At present she is reported to be disinterested in personal hygiene, evasive, irrelevant with a lackadaisical attitude, withdrawn, but apparently not hallucinating or delusional in the hospital. She has been receiving Stelazine and Tofranil, along with anti-depressant medication for the last 8 years.

The following patient is presented as an example of moderate delayed improvement in social adaptation after a second more extensive surgical procedure when the first procedure had failed. It is interesting to note that many of his original symptoms are still present after 18 years but are of insufficient intensity to dominate him or prevent him for holding a job.

F. D., a 35-year-old pseudoneurotic schizophrenic, underwent a bilateral frontal topectomy in 1949 after 20 months of hospitalization at P.I. He had been ill for 12 years and unable to work. Among his symptoms were severe anxiety, multiple phobias, obsessive thoughts and ritualistic acts to the point of total incapacitation. Improvement was minimal after surgery. Therefore, 9 months after the first operation, the patient underwent a bilateral pre-frontal lobotomy. He was again reported as slightly improved but not sufficiently to be discharged. He was, therefore, transferred to Rockland State Hospital where he remained until 1956. When interviewed recently, the patient reported that he remembered some improvement in his anxiety and phobias about two years after the second operation in 1951 at which time he started working at the hospital. After his discharge in 1956, the patient had two unsuccessful job experiences within the first year. However, in 1957 he secured a position as a clerk typist which he is still holding after 11 years. He married that year and had successful sexual relations for a few years after which time he became impotent. When interviewed in March, 1968, 18 years after his last operation, he presented the following symptoms in

slight to moderate degree: anxiety, obsessional thinking involving fear of ceilings falling on him, of
heights, of crossing bridges (which he is able to
cross anyway), a phobia for airplanes, somatic concerns and a moderate degree of compulsive behavior
such as checking the gas stove three or four times a
night. When last seen, the patient was well dressed
but obese, opinionated, rigid and very circumstantial.
He describes feeling somewhat slowed down and leads
a restricted anhedonic life, without friends. He has
developed seizures--the first occurring just before
the second operation. He had a second seizure in 1962
and a third two and a half years ago. He receives
Dilantin regularly.

The following case history illustrates the poor
prognosis of early onset which persisted in spite of
two lobotomies:

Patient M. C., an 18-year-old male, diagnosed as
suffering from pseudoneurotic schizophrenia, underwent
a precoronal lobotomy after having been ill since 14.
His symptoms were severe pan-anxiety, depression with
suicidal thoughts, a neurodermatitic skin rash covering his entire body complicated by compulsive scratch-
ing, bizarre ideation, seclusiveness, aggressiveness,
drinking, homosexual behavior and inability to hold a
job. He had been hospitalized for 9 months pre-opera-
tively and treated with an experimental phenothiazine,
NP-207, which was discontinued when he developed a
retinitis pigmentosa-like picture. He was discharged

as somewhat improved a year after operation. After
leaving the hospital, he underwent private psychotherapy for four years during which time he held a job.
Subsequent to the private psychotherapy, his symptoms
worsened, and he was re-hospitalized on separate occasions at P.I. Between hospitalizations, Trilafon helped him to function somewhat better. He worked intermittently in the post office but engaged in fist
fights which led to further damage to one of his eyes
(detached retina). He was finally hospitalized for the
fifth time at P.I. at age of 31 with the same symptoms
as on the first admission with the addition of homi-
cidal thoughts and paranoid ideation. After unsuccessful trials on various phenothiazines and haloperidol,
he underwent a second pre-coronal lobotomy in February
1968, five months after admission and 12 years after
his first operation. He remained in the hospital following surgery for two months and then signed out
against medical advice. He was described as markedly improved in anxiety, depression and billigerence
but still was unable to function successfully out of
the hospital and signed himself into another state
hospital several months later.

The following case illustrates the ineffective-
ness of multiple procedures in a severly ill schizophrenic patient:

S. I., a female paranoid schizophrenic, was operated on at the age of 41 in the first of five surgical procedures. The patient was a housewife, married
12 years. She was first admitted to P.I. in 1947 at

age 38, manifesting hypochondriacal complaints, irritability, chronic fatigue, anxiety, paranoid delusions, and inability to function as a housewife for the three years prior to admission. She was treated with insulin comas and psychotherapy and discharged as unimproved. Eleven months later she was readmitted and a transorbital lobotomy was performed. Her mood changed, she was less anxious and tense and the delusions no longer dominated her. Improvement lasted 10 days and then the patient relapsed. Ten weeks after the first operation, a second transorbital lobotomy was performed. Again there was a short improvement and again the patient relapsed. Four and a half months later the patient underwent a bilateral prefrontal circumsection (not a complete topectomy). Postoperatively, she was more polite but there was no change in paranoid ideation. Seven months later a bilateral topectomy (orbital-frontal) was performed. After this operation, the patient was still paranoid but not as much concerned with her delusions. Four months after this operation, she was sent home on convalescent care, rated as "slightly improved" to "improved." After a month, she was rated as having lost some of the gains she had made. She was readmitted with a mild deterioration, having remained out of the hospital 6 months. A prefrontal lobotomy was performed approximately 11 months after the fourth operation. Postoperatively, her behavior was described as haughty, rigid, bizarre and irritable. She died two months later of acute infectious hepatitis and cardiovascular collapse due to cholemia, having had five surgical procedures in two years. Between operations, she had been treated with E.C.T., insulin coma and psychotherapy with no lasting effect.

The following patient also underwent two operations with a poor result, probably related to the very early onset of her illness.

H. N., a female, diagnosed as suffering from schizophrenic reaction, hebephrenic type, entered P.I. in 1952 at age 15, having had a history of mental illness since age 12 at which time she developed ideas of reference, became inappropriate, manneristic and preoccupied with auditory hallucinations. Before coming to P.I., she had had two state hospital admissions and a course of 20 E.C.T. without improvement. A medial lobotomy was performed in January 1952. She improved slightly in that she was more alert, outgoing, less tense and fearful, but two months later relapsed, becoming occasionally assaultive. Two months later she underwent a lateral lobotomy and was returned to a state hospital where she has remained ever since. For four years, she was rated as unimproved. When interviewed for this follow-up study, she appeared minimally improved in that she had become more manageable and able to dress and feed herself. However, she remained referential, occasionally hallucinating, irrelevant and demonstrated a severe thought disorder. She has been maintained on phenothiazine medication for several years.

S. Malitz, M.D., Psychiatric Institute, 722 West 168th Street, New York, N.Y. 10032

V. Lozzi, M.D., Vanderbilt Clinic, Presbyterian Hospital, New York

M. Kanzler, Ph.D., N. Y. State Psychiatric Hospital, New York

Discussion by Lothar B. Kalinowsky :

There has been recently a very definite revival of psychosurgery. Applying what both Dr. Malitz and I have learned from
the material studied in late Dr. Hoch's Department, we can
today better prognosticate the outcome of operations than the
outcome of other treatments in psychiatry. Among the schizophrenia groups, the pseudoneurotic form ranks highest as indication for surgery. Other schizophrenics with good response
to this method are those with somatic delusions, hypochondriacal
ideas, and some non-deteriorating chronic paranoids. Depressed patients can be good candidates if they are chronic, anxious depressions without deep affect, and unresponsive to
ECT or drugs. Of the obsessive-compulsives, those with some
degree of depression respond best. Although psychosurgery
has been wrongly abandoned, it gives most gratifying results
in many chronic and otherwise untreatable patients, who often,
after years of suffering, are again able to live a useful life.

A REAPPRAISAL OF GENETIC STUDIES IN SCHIZOPHRENIA

JOHN D. RAINER

In a report a year or two ago, Erik Strömgren said that what might be needed in schizophrenia research today was not more studies but the time to sit down or better lie down and think about the information already collected. I believe myself that reappraisal is good, not because the knowledge is all there if only it were properly organized, but because such reflection may suggest some directions for future research by delineating the areas of ignorance, and unearth some hypotheses for further exploration.

There are four themes that seem to come out of appraising the present situation in the study of the genetics of schizophrenia. The first is the need to look more closely for what are the significant genetic and environmental variables; the second is to find better ways to describe their interaction; the third is that even at the roughest level, it is becoming clear that certain severe forms of schizophrenia have greater genetic determination than less severe forms; and the fourth is the emergence of studies either prospective or retrospective which are longitudinal in nature and explore the nature of the development of the growing person in psychobiological context.

Regarding the first of these themes, in genetics one no longer operates with crude and oversimplified concepts; one is rather involved and sometimes overwhelmed by the complexities of the genetic code and DNA translation, and the important though yet unclear mechanisms of control and feedback in this molecular system, by the intricacies of cellular structure and ultrastructure and the effects of chromosomal variations, by the sophistication of modern statistical theory and population genetic methods. At which level and with which tools to explore possible genetic transmission and possible pathways, to find out what is transmitted and how it is observed clinically, is not at all obvious and not at all established. Much interchange is necessary with persons concerned with problems of diagnosis and classification and of biochemical correlates, topics amply discussed by other contributors to this symposium.

When it comes to specifying the environmental or exogenous factors which are germane to the pathogenesis of schizophrenia, there have been many proposals, ranging from nutrition, pre- or post-natal, to early communication patterns in the family; the specificity of any of these, with or without a genetic predisposing constellation, has yet to be established.

The second theme concerns interaction; much attention is being given to this concept, which presumably is more than co-action, the need established statistically for two or more forces to combine, but rather a dynamic process with mutual feedback, spiral development, and critical stages. There are models for this process at the levels of molecular biology, hormonal physiology, and for that matter, sociology; by some general systems approach, a refined and usable frame of reference is badly needed to replace the nature-nurture dichotomy in schizophrenia. Former adherents of both sides of the debate are finally agreeing on acceptable scientific data regarding both genetic and non-genetic factors, but the language does not yet exist to describe their dynamic interworking.

My third observation is one which has become clear both on re-analyzing some of the earlier genetic studies in schizophrenia and on repeating these on wider samples, namely that even when considering only the crude frequency of schizophrenia in twins or families of authenticated patients, concordance rates have been generally higher for twins of more severely affected cases, often with higher incidence in their families as well. These observations more than anything else mark the transition from the dichotomous approach, which has always been so inconclusive, to the search for new data and new frameworks described above.

It is the fourth trend which I describe in the study of the genetics of schizophrenia, the longitudinal family and case study approach, that promises to yield the richest store of observations, to answer the most penetrating kind of questions and to produce the most complete synthesis of genetic, chemical, familial and social forces. Retrospective studies of families either with twins or other special circumstance can reveal more of the details of pathogenesis than frequency counts, while prospective designs allow also for experimentation, testing, and measuring in an interdisciplinary approach.

That the trends about which I speak are not entirely new can be proved by returning to the history of the genetic study of schizophrenia, where much valuable material may be found, if only as approximations to the better formulations to follow. Ending the "dark ages" of genetics – and of psychiatry – the early investigators established methods and worked hard to obtain data which still yield new insights on careful review. I would like to turn to such a review of older and more recent studies of
various kinds, trying to trace the threads of the four themes I have discussed, and to
include some of the current work and thought of our staff at the Psychiatric Institute.
There have recently appeared a number of excellent surveys [1,2,3] which present in
detail tables and figures, both old and recent; I shall refer to these here and avoid
repeating them.

Nineteenth century notions were as primitive genetically as they were psychiatrically; in their extreme, they could be typified by the conception of hereditary degeneration, manifesting itself in more severe form in successive generations. The re-
discovery of Mendel's quantitative approach to genetics and the Kraepelinian description of dementia praecox set the stage by the turn of the century for more precise
measurements of hereditary factors. Ernst Rüdin [4] in 1916 published his examination of
the families of a series of almost 1000 patients from the Munich psychiatric clinic; in
their sibs, he found a schizophrenia rate ranging from 4.48 per cent where neither
parent was schizophrenic to 22.72 per cent where both were psychotic or alcoholic.
Despite the heterogeneity of diagnosis, Rüdin was concerned with possible hereditary
models, and advanced theories either of two recessive genes or of genes on both sides
of the family. The details of the various hypothesized modes of inheritance interest
us here only because they epitomize the problems, even in the early days of careful
genetic research, of choosing and dealing with the many interactive factors that were
found. Another pioneer, Bruno Schulz, [5] in 1932 was one of the first to consider differences in heredity in various clinical types of schizophrenia. Studying 660 of
Rüdin's cases with acceptable diagnoses, he found higher sib frequencies for index
cases with no precipitating cause (8.3%) than for those with an acute outset and benign
course (4.0%) thus anticipating a key trend in all subsequent research.

Studies of twins soon became a prominent instrument of research. Excellent historical and methodological discussions may be found in the chapter by Gottesman and Shields[6] as well as in the monographs by Kringlen[7] and Tienari.[8] The first systematic investigation of twins, reported by Luxenburger[9] in 1928, foreshadowed problems of sampling which bear closely on distinctions of severity. Luxenburger included resident Bavarian hospital patients plus new admissions, comparing his lists with birth registers and finally obtaining a complete and unselected series of 65 twin index cases with a restricted, classic type of schizophrenia. Using similar clinical criteria for schizophrenia in the co-twins, he found concordance rates in the range of 50 to 60 per cent for monozygotic twins, the rates varying according to decisions regarding diagnosis and zygosity. There were no concordant dizygotic pairs in his material.

Of great interest because of the wealth of clinical description is the study conducted in Sweden and reported in 1941 by Essen-Möller.[10] His twins were obtained by comparing consecutive admissions with birth registers, thus providing a complete and representative series, but Essen-Möller was more interested in the detailed clinical descriptions of the co-twins than in definite concordance rates. He described schizophrenic symptoms and schizoid character, though no clearcut schizophrenia, in all the co-twins of his seven monozygotic index cases at the time of his report, and 15 years later one did show a typical psychotic picture. While people have attributed anything from zero to 71 per cent concordance to the monozygotic twins in this series with 8 to 17 per cent for the 24 dizygotic pairs, the study is cited here because of its drive to distinguish between the varied clinical manifestations in the genetically identical pairs and to consider the environmental factors which might correlate with or account for the differences.

It was Kallmann and Slater who conducted three of the largest and most carefully planned family and twin studies in the pre- and early post-World War I years. While their use of hospitalized index cases as well as their strict diagnostic criteria focussed their studies on more seriously ill patients, these investigators by the thoroughness of their research and the expertness and maturity of their psychiatric commitment, did much to establish the validity as well as the limits of the genetic component in schizophrenia.

Kallmann organized his first family study[11] while a fellow in the clinic of the eminent Bonhoeffer and the research institute of Rüdin after training and experience in clinical psychiatry, forensic psychiatry, psychoanalysis, neuropathology and genetics. The material for that 1938 report consisted of 1087 index cases making up the total number of schizophrenic case records available in the Herzberge hospital in Berlin for the years 1893 to 1902. These cases were chosen after the charts of all admissions were personally reviewed and the diagnoses were made without reference to the hospital's diagnosis or to any notes on hereditary conditions in the family of the patient. Omitting patients developing symptoms only after the age of 40, as well as those with neurological symptoms associated with syphilis or alcohol, Kallmann divided the index cases into hebephrenic, catatonic, paranoid and simple categories and proceeded to trace their sibs and descendants, both direct and collateral. Some of the more detailed breakdown of the data he obtained is not as well known as the general findings of this study, and yet it bears directly on the currently highlighted trends. For children of index cases, the overall schizophrenia rate corrected for age distribution was 16.4 per cent, but it ranged from about 20 per cent each for hebephrenic and catatonic cases to about 10 per cent each for paranoid and simple ones; Kallmann bracketed the first two types as the nuclear group and the last two as the peripheral group. For sibs the overall rate was 11.5 per cent, with about 13 per cent in the nuclear group and about 9 per cent in the peripheral. Case descriptions of all secondary cases were provided. A steep rise in mortality from tuberculosis was found for the schizophrenic patients as well as for their sibs and children, while the marriage and fertility rates of the nuclear but not of the peripheral group were greatly reduced.

In its discussions of these findings, the book The Genetics of Schizophrenia[12] deals with many theoretical and methodological implications. Paramount is the fundamental implication that while a genetic factor is necessary for schizophrenia, it is not sufficient, and that both the penetrance and the phenotypic manifestation depend on dispositional factors; as stated in the volume, "the mode of manifestation... depend on the result of the individual interplay among genetic, constitutional, and environmental factors." Like his contemporary Essen-Möller and many researchers to the present time, Kallmann was not ready or able to pinpoint any consistent environmental factors; his discussion of constitutional factors in terms of an impaired reactivity of the reticulo-endothelial system furnished hypotheses which are still very much alive. But the lack of manifestation in about 30 per cent of the children of two schizophrenic parents in his own study, as well as a similar rate of discordance in those twin studies at that time in the literature, led directly to Kallmann's own large scale study of twins in New York State. With much sanguinity, he said that the main purpose of the twin study was "not to show concordance but to study those pairs that differ in onset or production, in order to prevent or to heal the condition," and that curability and inheritability were not incompatible.

In the study of twins and their families itself, reported first by Kallmann [13] in 1946, trends so important in the appraisal of current research were further foreshadowed. The general results are among the most widely known data in psychiatric genetic research and have served as the stimulus for research in wide fields extending from biochemistry to psychodynamics, as well as the baseline for much critical evaluation. In brief, the overall concordance rates uncorrected for age distribution included about 10 per cent for full sibs and dizygotic twins and about 70 per cent for monozygotic twins; with the Weinberg correction, these become about 14 per cent for the sibs and dizygotic twins, and about 86 per cent for the monozygotic twins. Index cases, to be sure, were obtained by reports from hospitals of resident patients and new admissions; consistency of diagnostic criteria was indicated by the fact reported later, [11,14] that the co-twins diagnosed as schizophrenic had almost all themselves been in psychiatric institutions, and that this held for the dizygotic as well as the monozygotic ones.

While Kallmann did not succeed in achieving his main purpose, the delineation of environmental and constitutional factors involved in the clinical expression of schizophrenia, his study of twins provided a number of formulations whose import has still to be explored. Kallmann liked to consider the interacting but non-specific factors as protective to various degrees, but was only able to report negative findings. Concordance did not seem to be related to prematurity, instrumental delivery or left-handedness; it was related to a small degree with environmental similarity, living apart for a time, or like or unlike sex in the non-identical pairs, and to a high degree with severity. Indeed analysis of some of the severity data shows a concordance rate of as little as 26 per cent for the monozygotic co-twins of cases with little or no deterioration and as much as 100 per cent for those with extreme deterioration, with a similar spread of from 2 per cent to 17 per cent for the dizygotic pairs, a breakdown which is hidden by considering only the overall figures of 69 per cent versus 10 per cent. It was left for later investigators to dig more deeply toward the solution of the basic problem formulated by Kallmann in the following words: "in future twin studies...emphasis should be placed on clarifying the intricate interplay of gene-specific biochemical dysfunctions, general constitutional (adaptational) modifiers and precipitating outside factors arising from the effect of certain basic imperfections in the structure of modern human societies."[15]

At about the same time that the study just described was started in New York State, Eliot Slater with the assistance of James Shields undertook a similar study in London.[16] In this study as well, a resident population was combined with new admissions, principally to psychiatric hospitals but also to a clinic. The overall concordance figures for the 156 pairs of twins ascertained through schizophrenic index cases are of the same order of magnitude as those in the previously mentioned studies; 76 per cent for monozygotic pairs, 14 per cent for dizygotic. The rate for sibs was only 5 per cent; the discrepancy between the sib and dizygotic twin rates was attributed by Slater largely to the more thorough investigation in the case of twins. In this study there were somewhat higher concordance rates for female pairs than for male pairs, and a lack of family history in the discordant pairs - points which have been selected for comment in more recent critical reviews.[17,18] There were notable similarities within the concordant pairs with respect to course of illness and type of onset, including such clinical features as catatonic symptoms, passivity feelings, positive affective symptoms, depersonalization, organic signs and tendencies to suicide and self injury. In discordant or dissimilar pairs, some distinguishing features were indeed suggested by Slater's ample and careful case histories; the more sick twin tended to be the one to have had a more difficult birth, a more submissive childhood, and a more unstable occupational history, while order of birth, breast feeding, early physical development, physique and health, handedness, and intelligence seemed to make no difference. In the overview of this distinguished

British psychiatrist, "genetical causes provide a potentiality for schizophrenia, per-haps an essential one, though environmental factors play a substantial role which may be decisive in the individual case. Those environmental factors which affect personality and constitution appear to be the most important."

Other studies could be added to the above to extend the essential expectancy and concordance rates to other parts of the world. Inouye's study of a collection of 72 twins in Japan [19] showed very similar concordance figures – 60 per cent for mono-zygotic versus 12 per cent for dizygotic, or with age correction, 76 per cent versus 22 per cent – and variation in concordance rates with severity, with the mild, chronic, or transient cases providing only 39 per cent concordance. Mitsuda [20] divided his cases clinically into typical and atypical forms and found some genetic confirmation of this nosological distinction. In Geneva, an extensive family study by Garrone [21] of almost 4000 index cases and their families, all known cases of schizophrenia in Geneva between 1901 and 1950, yielded a 14.7 per cent sib rate with figures for parents and children also similar to the German, British, and American results already described.

While these older, some of them classic, investigations set the framework and posed the questions that must still be answered, they suffered from certain methodo-logical defects, mostly unavoidable at the time. In the past decade, a new crop of reports on twin and family research attempted to refine these methods. Their results are occasionally surprising, usually however in direct line with the earlier ones, their formulations tend to show more sophistication in the use of psychodynamic vari-ables, but vary in the success of their attempt to conceptualize the transmission and interaction of genetic mechanisms as biological forces. In the main, the newer twin studies tried to start either with all twins in the population, searching out afterwards those that had psychiatric illness, or at least with a consecutive clinic population of patients rather than a static hospital one. In either case, less severe index cases now had the chance to enter the study along with the chronic ones. At the same time, more refined methods of zygosity analysis using blood groups made it possible to re-duce even further any errors here, although it has been established that such errors must have been rare and could not have been crucial even in the older work.

Thus Gottesman and Shields [22] picked up all twins treated at the Maudsley in London, either as outpatients or short-stay inpatients, between 1948 and 1964; 57 pairs constituted the series in which at least one was a schizophrenic patient. In this series, the overall concordance for hospitalized schizophrenia was 42 per cent for monozygotic pairs, 9 per cent for fraternal (65% versus 17% with age correction); a concordance rate was found higher for female monozygotic pairs than for the male, but the difference was not statistically significant; however there were striking differences in concordance when severity in the index cases was taken into account. Rates of 67 per cent and 20 per cent for monozygotic twins were found where the index case had been in a hospital more than or less than one year respectively; if one makes the division at two years in the hospital, the rates are 77 per cent and 27 per cent with 10 per cent and 15 per cent for the dizygotic pairs. Thus on a very rough basis of clinical evaluation, this study confirmed results implicit in some of the earlier ones. The investigators do not intend to stop there, but plan to employ various rating scales and psychometric measures to obtain finer quantitative and more meaningful qualitative data, thus using the twins and their families to look for more specific noxious factors which can influence the manifestation or even the presence of schizophrenia.

A second recent study [7] reported by Einar Kringlen in 1967 is in the tradition of the best Scandinavian epidemiological research, starting as it does with all 25,000 pairs of twins born in Norway between 1901 and 1930 as ascertained in the Central Birth Registry. Since it was possible to check these against the Central Register of Psychosis, a large and unselected sample of 342 pairs of psychotic twins was obtained, including 233 pairs within the schizophrenic group. To obtain data on these, Kringlen journeyed up and down the country, a hard but rewarding task described with much charm in his monograph. His overall concordance rates for schizophrenia are what would be expected - 25 per cent to 38 per cent for monozygotic pairs, 4 per cent to 10 per cent for dizygotic, variations depending on whether the figures were based on hospitalized cases or on personal investigation,and on the strictness of diagnostic criteria. The rates are lower than the overall ones in previous studies based on hospital-reported index cases, similar to those for less severe cases extracted

from those older studies, and in line with those in the current Maudsley project.
Nevertheless the difference in concordance rates for monozygotic and dizygotic
twins remains significant. A relationship between severity of illness and concordance
in monozygotic twins was found; though not meeting the criteria of statistical significance; the pattern is familiar, ranging from 25 per cent for the co-twins of more
benign index cases to 60 per cent for the most severe group. Unlike the case in some
other reports, no difference was found between concordance in female or male identical pairs, and a great variation was found in the clinical syndromes within pair
members with little positive correlation between clinical types, other diagnoses, or
severity of illness. Some of the significant factors found in the schizophrenic and
not in the non-schizophrenic co-twins were submissiveness, reserve, loneliness and
dependence, sensitivity and obedience, fewer friends, unmarried status and lower
social status, while there was a tendency to difficult relations with fathers, and
overprotective mothers. Birth order, birth weight, difficulty of birth, physical
strength and psychomotor development in infancy seemed to have no consistent relevance.

Kringlen's discussion of his carefully obtained data bears close examination,
since his italicized summary statement has been quoted a great deal in an oversimplified context: - "A genetic factor in the etiology of schizophrenia has to be recognized. However, the genetic factor does not play as great a role as (or seems to be
weaker than) has been generally assumed." Since there is no simple way to quantify
the role or the strength of genetic factors, it might be better to look at Kringlen's
more detailed discussion. Here he considers the questions of what is inherited, how
it is inherited and what the significant environmental factors are. Since schizophrenia
as such is not inherited, he conceives of potentials for certain psychological and
physiological response patterns as likely candidates for the role of genetically determined correlates with clinical psychiatric variables. In this framework, Kringlen
interprets his data as indicating a graduated series of disorders and personality patterns in the co-twins of schizophrenic patients, ranging from a duplication of the
psychosis to neurosis and clinical normalcy; this observation in turn he considers to
be in line with the theory of a non-specific predisposition to mental illness, rather

than a specific one to schizophrenia as such. It is consistent with this viewpoint that he feels the genetic factors are polygenic; he then concludes that the environmental ones must be social, rather than biochemical. This conclusion is important of course in suggesting the direction of further research; it may be commented then that step-wise biochemical mechanisms have been described in other areas of medicine with a polygenic determination (e.g. penicillin sensitivity or hyperuricemia - gout) and a unimodal distribution of phenotypes does not rule out the operation of a single major gene if the traits measured do not reflect the action of the mutant gene directly.

The twin study whose results seem to be most at variance with a necessary role for genetic factors is the one carried out in Finland by Tienari.[8] Here one's attention is focussed on 16 schizophrenic patients with monozygotic co-twins; all of these pairs are said to be discordant, although most of the co-twins are said to display "unmistakable schizoid features." The pairs are all male and were obtained by investigating the psychiatric cases found among the group of all same-sexed pairs of male twins born in Finland in the years 1920-1929 who were alive at the beginning of the study and both resident in Finland. Tienari considers that previous studies over-estimated concordance rates due to methodological biases; others have pointed out sources of possible bias in the Finnish study such as the loss of identical pairs due to death or migration and the absence of female pairs. It has also been pointed out that some of the index cases in this study appear to have organic features and might not be legitimately classifiable as schizophrenic. On the other hand the co-twins - admittedly borderline or schizoid - may include a number whom others would consider in the psychotic range. In a group of dizygotic twins, Tienari found from 10 per cent to 15 per cent concordance, but unlike the monozygotic group, the index cases here were limited to those who had been in hospital treatment. It has been pointed out that twin studies are of most use in defining the nature of the non-genetic components.[23] Aside from the problems concerning the concordance rate, Tienari's study provides a carefully described group of dissimilar identical twin pairs and in this connection his observations on their earlier differences are of great value; considering all pairs, neurotic and psychotic, as a continuum of mental illness, Tienari finds that the more seriously ill twin in each pair has been more submissive

in the twins' mutual relationship, has had more somatic illness, has left the home
later and has married later; and there is a tendency also for him to have weighed
less at birth, to have been physically weaker, to have done worse at school and to
have been less active socially.

Similar differences, with birth weight the most consistent one, were found in a
series of discordant identical pairs carefully studied by Pollin, Stabenau and their
coworkers at the National Institute of Mental Health;[24] in the formulation of this
research team, the actual physiological incompetence of the smaller twin is reflected
in a reduced sense of effectiveness and the difference between the twins is reinforced
continuously by their parents' conceptions of them, the roles they assigned to them
and their emotional transactions with them. The contribution of Pollin to the present
symposium will certainly present the most up-to-date version of this investigation and
may have something to say about whether the process described is specifically related to schizophrenia or operates in the development of psychopathology in general.
Other intensive studies of discordant pairs, such as the one by Rainer, Kolb, Mesnikoff, and Carr related to homosexuality,[25] indicate that the findings may be more
general in application. In any event, the development of twins would certainly appear to be an area which calls for longitudinal studies from infancy. In all these
family and twin studies, with their differences in sampling techniques and diagnostic
standards, there has been a search for answers to the persistent questions of what are
the significant genetic and environmental variables and how may one conceive of
their interaction. Other research designs which have been used to explore hypothesis concerning genetics of schizophrenia have related to one or another of the key
themes under consideration here. For example a population of persons deaf since
birth or early childhood afforded the opportunity to some of us at the Psychiatric
Institute to assess the role of communication barrier and maturational lag as a stress-
provoking or as a protective factor. Actually the schizophrenia expectancy rate
in this group was found by Rainer and Kallmann[26] to be something over 2 per cent,
higher than some but equal to other estimates for the general population. Considering the sibs, 331 in number, of 138 deaf schizophrenic patients, the corrected
risk figure for schizophrenia in all the sibs was found by Altshuler and Sarlin to be

11.6 per cent,for hearing sibs alone, 11.2 per cent and for deaf sibs alone, 15.8 per cent. These rates are not significantly different from each other, nor from the 14.3 per cent rate found in Kallmann's study of sibs of schizophrenic index cases in New York without a hearing loss. The authors of the report of this study concluded that the severe and varied stresses associated with early total deafness apparently do little to increase – and it should be added, to decrease – the chance of developing clinical symptoms of schizophrenia.

Some of the most promising investigations completed or reported as in progress by various research groups consist of the study of high-risk groups, of longitudinal observations, or of a combination of both of these approaches. Mednick and Schulsinger[28] have reported on an ongoing longitudinal study of children with a high risk for schizophrenia, namely prospective observations planned for 15 to 20 years of a group of adolescent children of chronically schizophrenic mothers in Denmark together with a matched control group of children. The eventual development of schizophrenia in some of these offspring, the differentiation into "process" and "reactive" types, [29] and, in the meantime, experiments related to autonomic responsiveness conducted on the entire group, are aimed at exploring hypotheses on significant psychophysiological characteristics of the pre-schizophrenic.

Separation of family interaction and genetic determinants has been attempted by this Danish investigation as well as by others who have considered schizophrenic patients reared in adoptive homes. Preliminary findings by Wender, Rosenthal·and Kety[30] on a group of 10 adopted schizophrenic patients and 10 reared by their parents demonstrated a considerable increase in severity of psychopathology among the biological as compared with the adoptive parents, affording support for genetic transmission; repetition with a more representative group is under way. The converse of this study is to look at persons who have been taken as children from schizophrenic mothers and reared in foster, nursing, or adoptive homes; Heston[31] found a high rate of schizophrenia (5 out of 47) in such a group with no schizophrenics in a control group of similarly reared children of non-schizophrenic mothers.

Among other retrospective studies of a longitudinal nature, the one by Pollock and his co-workers[32] found that a group of psychiatric patients, all young adults, had been more irritable, shy, dependent and non-affectionate in childhood and had

poorer social adjustment and poorer school performance than their sibs. These

patients included 33 schizophrenics, but also 4 with personality trait disturbance, 5

with organic syndromes and 2 with psychoneurosis. Finally, the multidisciplinary

volume edited by Rosenthal [33] representing a case study of a set of quadruplets

with schizophrenia of varying severity and outcome is a storehouse of observation

and thought and a taking-off point for many directions of future hypothesis and ex-

perimentation.

Before leaving this discussion of the genetic and environmental variables in

schizophrenia - their detection, the estimation of their absolute and their relative

roles and the attempt to find the language or the mathematical model with which to

describe their interaction - some space should be given to the low-key but intriguing

work related to cellular and immunological mechanisms, foreshadowed by Kallmann's

early thoughts about the reactivity of the reticulo-endothelial system. Maricq,

Jarvik and Rainer [34] compared rates of lymphocyte division in vitro for two groups

of chronic schizophrenic patients and a normal sample; the patients were divided ac-

cording to nailfold plexus visualization score, shown by earlier reports to distin-

guish clinically homogeneous groups. Those with high score were clinically more de-

teriorated and showed more mental illness in the immediate family; they also showed

the lowest mitotic indices, measures of in vitro lymphocyte response to stimulation

by foreign antigen. Vartanian, on the other hand, [35] considering possible lymphocyte

response to endogenous antigens, found increased blast cell transformation, character-

istic of immune response, in the cultured cells of schizophrenic patients without the

addition of foreign antigen, and some correlation of such transformation with titer

of antibrain antibodies in the blood. He observed a similarly increased response in

identical twins of patients, while other normal relatives formed two distinct groups,

one resembling normal controls, the other the schizophrenic patients. The nature

of possible defects - hypo or hyperreactivity - of the cellular defense system in

schizophrenia needs more study; it may have some relation to the diminished resis-

tance to tuberculosis on the one hand or the increased resistance to some other in-

fections, summarized in a paper by Huxley, Mayr, Osmond and Hoffer. [36]

In another aspect of cytogenetic research, the determination of the karyotype or chromosomal constitution, no significant or constant chromosomal anomalies have been found in schizophrenic patients, although a small proportion of patients with sex chromosomal aberrations or mosaicism have been reported by various investigators to have schizophrenic or schizophrenia-like symptoms. [37,38,39] Automated methods of chromosome analysis will make it possible to screen larger populations and may delineate sub-groups marked by defects at this level; such results in turn may provide further handles for the investigation of genetic mechanisms and pathways.

The complexity of productive research into the genetics of schizophrenia seemed not too long ago to have limited its pursuit to a dedicated few. Now however it seems not to deter a new generation of scientific workers, with varied disciplines and orientation, who are likewise ready to discard as neither necessary or meaningful their allegiance to one or another side of the old nature-nurture controversy. There are still some protagonists and a larger number of publicizers who exalt the head-count type of statistical presentation, and headlines still perpetuate the battle of the numbers with many of the implications of a Gallup poll of popularity. There is no reason to demand a different level of rigor of genetic theories than of environmental or to place all of the burden of proof on the former; if it is presently easier to hold the phenotype constant than the environment, more work is required on defining equivalences in environmental stimuli and transactions. Curt Stern [40] pointed out that while genetic theories are to some degree susceptible to non-genetic interpretation, the hereditarian has had to be more open minded, since his bias has always been counteracted by the presence of discordant identical twins, while the environmentalist encounters no intrinsic check to a non-genetic interpretation, so that he may "remain unchallenged in the premise that lack of final proof for genetic causation is equivalent to its exclusion." Going beyond Stern, I hope that open-mindedness can be taken for granted among all scientists and in the planning and operation of future research.

Meanwhile there are some matters which cannot and need not await the data and the formulations to be supplied by those programs of the future. In our department, studies by Erlenmeyer-Kimling and co-workers [41] have indicated that schizophrenic patients, both male and female, have increased their marital rate, their rate of fertile marriages and their overall reproductive rate between the mid 1930's and the mid 1950's, both absolutely and relative to the general population. The risk for schizophrenia as well as other behavioral deviations is higher in the children of schizophrenic than those of non-schizophrenic parents, whether or not interpreted in a context which includes some form of genetic transmission. These facts taken together call for the availability of responsible and sound advice, clinically oriented, in the areas of genetic counseling, family planning, child rearing, adoption and foster care, to go along with improvements in treatment, in homes where schizophrenia is present.

In the broad area of social psychiatry, as well, there are questions which cannot be put off. [42] As pointed out in a series of papers by Erlenmeyer-Kimling and associates, [43,44] the selective disadvantage of schizophrenia as measured by lower reproductivity of patients may be offset by compensatory factors – she has found indications of higher infant survival of the offspring of schizophrenic patients. In any event the disadvantage is reduced, perhaps eliminated, by the increasing reproductivity referred to above. There is much debate about tampering with genetic variables, either through changes in marriage and parenthood patterns, or in the science-fiction realm of the not-too-distant future where sperm banks, ovum implants and DNA substitution form a successive bridge to control over human heredity. The psychiatrist with his understanding of motivation and dynamics must assume his proper responsibility for the humanitarian aspects of these concerns and proposals as they are discussed and debated and decided in the coming years.

REFERENCES

1. Strömgren, E. Psychiatrische genetik. In Psychiatrie der Gegenwart, Gruhle, H. W., Jung, R., Mayer-Gross, W. and Müller, M. (Editors), p. I, Springer, Berlin, 1964.

2. Rosenthal, D. An historical and methodological review of genetic studies of schizophrenia. In The Origin of Schizophrenia, Romano, J. (Editor), p. 15, Excerpta Medica Foundation, Amsterdam, 1967.

3. Shields, J. The genetics of schizophrenia in historical context. In Recent Developments in Schizophrenia, Cooper, A. and Walk, A. (Editors), p. 25, Headley Bros., Ltd., London, 1967.

4. Rüdin, E. Zur Vererbung und Neuenstehung der Dementia Praecox, Springer, Berlin, 1916.

5. Schulz, B. Zur Erbpathologie der schizophrenia. Z. ges. Neurol. Psychiat. 143, 175, 1932.

6. Gottesman, I. I. and Shields, J. Contribution of twin studies to perspectives on schizophrenia. In Progress in Experimental Personality Research, Maher, B. A. (Editor), p. 1, Academic Press, New York, 1966.

7. Kringlen, E. Heredity and Environment in the Functional Psychoses, Universitetsforlaget, Oslo, 1967.

8. Tienari, P. Psychiatric Illnesses in Identical Twins, Munksgaard, Copenhagen, 1963.

9. Luxenburger, H. Vorläufiger Bericht über psychiatrische Serienuntersuchungen an Zwillingen. Z. ges. Neurol. Psychiat. 116, 297, 1928.

10. Essen-Möller, E. Psychiatrische Untersuchungen an einer serie von zwillinger, Munksgaard, Copenhagen, 1941.

11. Rainer, J. D. The contributions of Franz J. Kallmann to the genetics of schizophrenia. Behav. Sci. 11, 413, 1966.

12. Kallmann, F. J. The Genetics of Schizophrenia, J. J. Augustin, New York, 1936.

13. Kallmann, F. J. The genetic theory of schizophrenia: An analysis of 691 schizophrenic twin index families. Am. J. Psychiat. 103, 309, 1946.

14. Shields, J., Gottesman, I. I. and Slater, E. Kallmann's 1940 schizophrenic twin study in the light of fresh data. Acta. Psych. Scand. 43, 385, 1967.

15. Kallmann, F. J. The genetics of psychoses. In Proceedings, First International Congress of Psychiatry, Section VI, Hermann & Co., Paris, 1950.

16. Slater, E. (with the assistance of Shields, J.) Psychotic and neurotic illnesses in twins. Med. Res. Coun. Spec. Rept. Ser. No. 278, His Majesty's Stationery Office, London, 1953.

17. Rosenthal, D. Sex distribution and the severity of illness among samples of schizophrenic twins. J. Psychiat. Res. 1, 26, 1961.

320

18. Rosenthal, D. Some factors associated with concordance and discordance with respect to schizophrenia in monozygotic twins. J. Nerv. Ment. Dis. 129, 1, 1959.

19. Inouye, E. Similarity and dissimilarity of schizophrenia in twins. In Proceedings, Third World Congress of Psychiatry, Vol. 1, p. 524, Univ. of Toronto Press, Montreal, 1961.

20. Mitsuda, H. Clinical Genetics in Psychiatry: Problems in Nosological Classification, Igaku Shoin, Tokyo, 1967.

21. Garrone, G. Étude statistique et génétique de la schizophrénie à Genève de 1901 à 1950. J. Genet. Hum. 11, 89, 1962.

22. Gottesman, I. I. and Shields, J. Schizophrenia in twins: 16 years' consecutive admissions to a psychiatric clinic. Brit. J. Psychiat. 112, 809, 1966.

23. Allen, G. Twin Research: Problems and Prospects. In Progress in Medical Genetics, Vol. IV, Steinberg, A. G. and Bearn, A. (Editors), p. 242, Grune and Stratton, New York, 1965.

24. Pollin, W., Stabenau, J. R., Mosher, L. and Tupin, J. Life history differences in identical twins discordant for schizophrenia. Am. J. Orthopsychiat. 36, 492, 1966.

25. Rainer, J. D., Mesnikoff, A., Kolb, L. C. and Carr, A. Homosexuality and heterosexuality in identical twins. Psychosom. Med. 22, 251, 1960.

26. Rainer, J. D. and Kallmann, F. J. Genetic and demographic aspects of disordered behavior in a deaf population. In Epidemiology of Mental Disorder, Pasamanick, B. (Editor), p. 229, AAAS, Washington, 1959.

27. Altshuler, K. Z. and Sarlin, M. B. Deafness and schizophrenia: Interrelation of communication stress, maturation lag and schizophrenic risk. In Expanding Goals of Genetics in Psychiatry, Kallmann, F. J. (Editor), p. 52, Grune and Stratton, New York, 1962.

28. Mednick, S. A. and Schulsinger, F. A longitudinal study of children with a high risk for schizophrenia: A preliminary report. In Methods and Goals in Human Behavior Genetics, Vandenberg, S. G. (Editor), p. 255, Academic Press, New York, 1965.

29. Higgins, J. The concept of process-reactive schizophrenia: Criteria and related research. J. Nerv. Ment. Dis. 138, 9, 1964.

30. Wender, P. H., Rosenthal, D. and Kety, S. S. A psychiatric assessment of the adoptive parents of schizophrenics. In The Transmission of Schizophrenia, Rosenthal, D. and Kety, S. S. (Editors), Pergamon Press, Oxford, in press.

31. Heston, L. L. Psychiatric disorders in foster home reared children of schizophrenic mothers. Brit. J. Psychiat. 112, 819, 1966.

32. Pollack, M., Woerner, M. G., Goodman, W. and Greenberg, I. M. Childhood development patterns of hospitalized adult schizophrenic and non-schizophrenic patients and their siblings. Am. J. Orthopsychiat. 36, 510, 1966.

33. Rosenthal, D. (Editor) The Genain Quadruplets, Basic Books, New York, 1962.

34. Maricq, H. R., Jarvik, L. F. and Rainer, J. D. Chronic schizophrenia, lymphocyte growth and nailfold plexus visualization score. Dis. Nerv. System, in press.

35. Vartanian, M. E. Biochemical and immunological changes in schizophrenia and their relation to inheritance. In Proceedings, IV World Congress of Psychiatry, López-Ibor, J. J. (Editor), p. 3030, Excerpta Medica Foundation, Amsterdam, 1968.

36. Huxley, J., Mayr, E., Osmond, H. and Hoffer, A. Schizophrenia as a genetic morphism. Nature 204, 220, 1967.

37. Raphael, T. and Shaw, M. W. Chromosome studies in schizophrenia. J. Am. Med. Assoc. 183, 1022, 1963.

38. Judd, L. L. and Brandkamp, W. W. Chromosome analysis of adult schizophrenics. Arch. Genet. Psychiat. 16, 316, 1967.

39. Kaplan, A., Cotton, J. E. and Powell, W. High incidence of chromosomal mosaicism among hospitalized schizophrenic patients. In Proceedings, Twelfth International Congress of Genetics, Tokyo, 1968.

40. Stern, C. Genes and people. In Proceedings, Third International Congress of Human Genetics, Crow, J. F. and Neel, J. V. (Editors), p. 507, Johns Hopkins Press, Baltimore, 1967.

41. Erlenmeyer-Kimling, L., Nicol, S., Rainer, J. D. and Deming, W. E. Changes in fertility rates of schizophrenic patients in New York State. Am. J. Psychiat., in press.

42. Rainer, J. D. Genetic counseling, social planning and mental health. Res. Publ. Ass. Nerv. Ment. Dis. 47, Williams and Wilkins, Baltimore, in press.

43. Erlenmeyer-Kimling, L. and Paradowski, W. Selection and schizophrenia. Am. Naturalist 100, 651, 1966.

44. Erlenmeyer-Kimling, L. A tentative lead to the problem of selection and schizophrenia. In Proceedings, Twelfth International Congress of Genetics, Tokyo, 1968.

J. D. Rainer, M.D., Psychiatric Institute of New York State, 722 West 168th Street, New York, N.Y. 10032

CHROMOSOMES, MOSAICISM, AND SCHIZOPHRENIA

ARNOLD R. KAPLAN

Modes of Postulated Gene Transmission in Schizophrenia

The nature-nurture controversies, today, have little more than historical value. The experiencing of any environmental factor varies with the constitutions of the individuals who do the experiencing. Constitutional differences, which affect perceptions of experiences, result from experiential or environmental differences, genetic differences, and different combinations of both kinds of factors. The same trait or characteristic may result, in different affected individuals, from different combinations of different factors. A particular factor which tends to be etiologically associated with a particular effect in some contexts may not manifest the same association in other contexts. No behavioral trait is 'genetic' in the simple and direct sense that many specific biochemical and morphological traits may be described as 'genetic', because there are no specific genes for behavior. The genes affect functional and/ or structural characteristics which, interacting with other aspects of the biological and psychosocial context, affect behavoral characteristics.

Vast quantities of accumulated data have demonstrated that predisposition to, and etiology of, schizophrenia involves both genetic and environmental variables. The theories of Böök (1953) and Slater (1958) associate predisposition with presence of a single gene. The theory of Kallmann (1946) associates predisposition for schizophrenia with presence of a pair of recessive genes. In addition to variable penetrance of the genotype as a result of environmental variables, Kallmann (1953) postulated the involvement of an ancillary pair of "modifier genes." Accordingly, penetrance of the primary pair of genes in predisposing an individual to schizophrenia was hypothesized to depend upon presence or absence of one or both of the modifier genes as well as numerous environmental variables. Karlsson (1966) hypothesized the primary etiological involvement of two genetic loci -- i.e., two pairs, four genes.

Accordingly, different combinations structure different constitutional predispositions to schizophrenia. Odegard (1963) hypothesized the
involvement of multiple genetic loci and many different genes acting
cumulatively to affect different degrees of predisposition to schizophrenia. Mitsuda (1968) has described schizophrenia as a group of
several specific disorders with each one of the group being associated with one of several different modes of genetic transmission.

Each of the cited genetic theories specifies the major etiological
involvement of nongenetic factors, and each of the theories therefore
specifies incomplete penetrance of the schizophrenogenic genotype.
The occurrence of incomplete penetrance means only that there is
less than a one-to-one relationship between incidence of the genotype
and its associated phenotype or trait. Complete penetrance of a particular genotype may occur only when no other factors are relevant to
etiology of the trait or disorder. Since environmental etiological factors are not ignored, but are included in each of the cited genetic
hypotheses, only incomplete penetrance of the respective postulated
genotypes are appropriate to the hypothesis. The available data, at
the present time, may be fit equally well into each of the several genetic hypothesis involving different modes of genetic transmission. This
fact represents a principal weakness of each of the hypotheses.

Kety (1967) has suggested that the great range of schizophrenic manifestations, observed even in close biological relatives, indicates that
schizophrenia is not a single or unitary disorder. According to this
viewpoint, the hereditary diatheses relevant to schizophrenia do not involve only a single genotype. A possible alternative hypothesis might
involve multiple genetic loci and heterogeneous polygenic factors. M.
Bleuler (1967) has also described the etiology of schizophrenia as involving combinations of inherited predispositions and life experiences.
He rejects any single simple general concpet, however, including any
concept which generally involves one specific genotype or one specific
psychological condition or one specific environmental stress. Thus,
according to Bleuler, an infinite number of different combinations of
different genotypes and different environments and different life experiences may facilitate development of schizophrenic psychoses. The
lack of any established specific medical or somatic or biochemical
basis for schizophrenia, and the enormous variations in schizophrenic
manifestations and prognoses, are consistent with the suggestions of
multiple etiologies, as well as the hypotheses involving multiple genetic
loci and heterogenic polygenes.

324

Chromosomal Aneuploidies

The normal human chromosome number, 46, was first clearly demonstrated by Tjio and Levan in 1956. Since then, numerous chromosomal anomalies have been described. Numerical abnormalities of chromosome number, aneuploidies, most commonly result from nondisjunction or nonseparation of a pair of chromatids during cell division. The occurrence of meiotic nondisjunction during gamete development results in gametes with abnormal chromosome complements -- i.e., each affected gamete contains a haploid number of chromosomes plus or minus the nondisjoined member. Fertilization with such a gamete produces an abnormal zygote in which all of the cells have the same anomalous chromosomal complement. A mitotic nondisjunction during embryogenesis, however, produces mosaicism -- i.e., at least two distinct cell populations or lines in the tested tissue of the affected individual. Mosaicism, in rare cases, may also result from double fertilization (Corey, et al., 1967). This may occur through fertilization with two independent spermatozoa, each one combining with one of the two (i.e., already divided) nuclei within an undivided oocyte.

Aneuploidies in general, and trisomies (i.e., aneuploidies involving three homologous chromosomes instead of only a pair) in particular, do not occur as strictly random events. Their incidences have been associated with numerous pathological, physiological, and environmental variables (Kaplan, 1966). The familial recurrence of chromosomal anomalies may sometimes be related to familial exposure to a common mutagenic agent and/or to familial constitutional predisposition for occurance of the chromosomal anomaly.

Aneuploidies involving the X and Y chromosomes and the smaller autosomes, as well as deletions and duplications involving small chromosomal segments, tend to be viable, whereas duplications and deletions involving larger amounts of autosomal material are generally inconsistent with viability and cause gross morphological abnormalities. Thus, the most common chromosomal anomalies observed in the living involve aneuploides of the sex chromosomes (i.e., the X and Y chromosomes), aneuploides of the smallest autosomes (i.e., the 'G' group, as in Down's syndrome), deletions and duplications of small autosomal sections. The chromosomal anomalies involving autosomes or autosomal segments are, in general, associated with syndromes which include gross morphological anomalies and severe mental retardation (Kaplan, in press). Morphological and mental aspects of the chromosomal anomalies, however, are inconsistent and vary from the normal

to the grossly malformed and defective in mosaics -- i.e., depending
upon which tissues are involved and the extent of involvement, as well
as the kind of chromosomal anomaly. Anomalies of the X and Y chromosomes, however, are not associated with severe congenital morphological anomalies and severe mental retardation. Relationships between abnormal sex-chromosome (i.e., X and/or Y) complements in
humans and mental disorders have been explored, and some of the
findings appear to be relevant to etiologies of mental disorders, as
discussed below.

X-monosomy, Turner's syndrome.

The X chromosome exists normally in the monosomic or hemizygous
condition in the male (i.e., XY), whereas effects of deletion of one member of any autosomal pair are generally lethal or semilethal. The one-X
condition is present in patients having Turner's syndrome with a count
of 45 chromosomes (Ford, et al., 1959). A variant of this chromosomal
syndrome occurs, in which the female has one normal X chromosome
and the other one partially deleted (Jacobs, et al., 1960; Lindsten, 1963).
Many of the symptoms which characterize Turner's syndrome have been
observed in affected individuals with X isochromosomes -- i.e., anomalous structures involving deletion of the short arm and duplication of the
long arm in some, deletion of the long arm and duplication of the short arm
in others (Morishima and Grumbach, 1967). Thus, factors on both the
short and the long arm are needed in duplicate for normal female development. Mosaics have been described, whose tissues include cells with
more than one genotype -- e.g., both one-X and XX cells. An extensive
Scottish survey has indicated that the incidence of one-X genotypes among
live-born females is about 0.4/¹,000 (MacLean, et al., 1964). Surveys
of institutionalized mental retardates have indicated very similar frequencies of one-X females (MacLean, et al., 1962), supporting the impression that this genotype is not associated with severe mental retardation.
The distribution of I.Q. scores of one-X females has indicated no significant deviation from those observed in XX females (Lindsten, 1963). The
possibility of there being an association between the genotype and mental
subnormality has not yet been definitely settled. The most characteristic stigmata found in one-X females include short stature, little or juvenile mammary development, amenorrhea, broad chest with widely-spaced
nipples, neck webbing, and peripheral lymphedema. The streak-like gon-
ads may be represented by only collections of Leydiglike cells imbedded
in bundles of stroma. Congenital cardiovascular anomalies are common
in this syndrome, and the occurrence of aortic coarctation has often
been observed. Many affected girls are not sufficiently peculiar, however,

to have been examined and diagnosed for presence of this chromosomal anomaly and syndrome. Very often, only when puberty fails to occur normally does a real suspicion occur: the breasts fail to develop and the external genitalia remain infantile, there is sparseness or absence of pubic and axillary hair, and menstruation does not occur. One investigator has observed that affected X-monosomic females are characteristically lacking in ambition, timid, dependent, easily influenced, and with frequently reduced libido (Valentine, 1966)

KLINEFELTER'S SYNDROME

The occurrence of more than a single X chromosome in association with a Y chromosome is most commonly known as Klinefelter's syndrome, testicular dysgenesis, and chromatin-positive microorchidism. The XXY karyotype is the most usual variety associated with this syndrome. Combinations involving other multiples of X chromosomes with one or more than one Y chromosome have also, but relatively rarely, been observed (Polani, 1964; Eggen, 1965). Mosaics involving cells with normal karyotypes and cells with characteristic Klinefelter's karyotypes, as well as mosaics involving more than one kind of Klinefelter karyotype, have been described (Polani, 1964; Eggen, 1965). Generally, no clinical abnormalities are observed in affected boys prior to puberty. Relatively long limbs have been described in many affected individuals, and enlarged brest development (i.e., gynecomnastia) has been described in at least 25 to 30 percent of those diagnosed as affected with Klinefelter's syndrome, but there is no consistent pattern of stigmata and many affected individuals are known to be normal in appearance. The outstanding clinical feature is the presence of small testes (Ferguson-Smith, et al., 1957), which is generally detected only after puberty when the testes have failed to enlarge. MacLean et al., (1964) found that the incidence of sex-chromatin positive individuals among unselected newborn males was about 2.0/1,000. Nearly three-fourths of the observed group had simple XXY karyotypes, and all but one of the remaining one-fourth in the Scottish survey were XY/XXY mosaics. Among male inmates of institutions for the mentally retarded, the incidence of Klinefelter's syndrome is about 8.0/1,000; and among the mentally retarded male inmates with I.Q. scores over 50, the incidence of Klinefelter's syndrome exceeds 1.0 percent (Valentine, 1966). Evidently, a relatively mild degree of mental retardation is associated

with the chromosomal anomaly. Forssman and Hambert (1963)
studied 760 males in three hospitals for criminal or hard-to-manage
males of sub-normal intelligence and found that 2.0 percent were sex-
chromatin positive and apparently affected with Klinefelter's syndrome
and chromosomally characterized by two X chromosomes plus at least
one Y. Approximately 25 percent of observed individuals affected with
Klinefelter's syndrome have manifested some degree of mental retardation, and most have exhibited personality traits of dependency and submissiveness (Valentine, 1966).

MULTIPLE-Y MALES

The incidence of XYY individuals is not definitely known, but is much
lower than that of XXY individuals, and is quite rare in the general population (MacLean, et al., 1964). Jacobs, et al. (1965) determined karyotypes of 197 male mental patients who were mentally subnormal and
showed "dangerous, violent or criminal propensities." Eight of the
patients, nearly 4.0 percent of their sample, had XYY chromosome
complements. Casey, et al. (1966) reported a relatively high frequency
of XXYY males among mental hospital patients. Previous studies indicated a very low frequency of multiple-Y males in institutions for the
mentally retarded (MacLean, et al., 1964). Prince and Whatmore (1967)
found nine XYY males, a frequency of 3.0 percent, among males at a
British institution for mentally disordered patients with "dangerous, violent, or criminal propensities." The XYY patients were found to suffer
characteristically from severe personality disorder, in most cases (i.e.,
six out of nine) associated with mild mental retardation. The reports reviewed above indicate that the XYY chromosome complement tends to be
associated with antisocial, especially aggressive, behavior; and, also,
with mild mental retardation and very tall stature.

TRIPLE-X FEMALES

The XXX or triple-X female has a total of 47 chromosomes (Jacobs,
et al., 1959). Mosaics have been observed, whose cell lines include
more than a single genotype -- eg., XX and XXX cells (Jacobs, et al.,
1960). Phenotypic females with three instead of two X chromosomes, and
two instead of one nuclear sex-chromatin bodies, differentiate psycho-
sexually as females and are not characterized by manifestations of gross
morphological abnormalities. The reported clinical observations are
variable, and most of the observed affected individuals are phenotypical-
ly normal females, with pubescence, ovulation, and fertility. Incidence of the XXX syndrome is greater than that of the one-X syndrome in
females, being approximately 1.2/1,000 among live-born females (MacLean,
et al., 1964). The XXX genotype is evidently the most common sex-chromo-

some abnormality observed in newborn females. There is evidence that this chromosomal anomaly has a higher incidence among mentally retarded populations, indicating an association between the genotype and mental deficiency (MacLean, et al., 1962); Fraser, et al., 1960; Johnston, et al., 1961). The available material on XXX females, however, suggests that mental subnormality is not a consistent and characteristic feature of the genotype. The relatively few affected individuals who have been studied were mostly located in institutions for the mentally retarded or in mental hospitals and may not be considered representative of XXX females in general. A Scottish study (Kidd, et al., 1963) showed that the diagnostic distribution of XXX patients located in mental hospitals, who were not mentally subnormal, were broadly typical of the mental hospital populations from which they were drawn. This was not the case, however, for the XXX females located in institutions for the mentally retarded, in whom the most outstanding feature was "super-imposed psychosis" (Kidd, et al., 1963). Primary mental subnormality accounts for about 80 percent of cases in British institutions for the mentally retarded (Curran and Partridge, 1957), but only two of the 12 XXX females located in their institutions for the mentally retarded (i.e., 16 percent) were so diagnosed (Kidd et al., 1963). The incidence of mental subnormality combined with psychosis, observed in the Scottish XXX patients, was markedly different from the general observations based on the Scottish mental hospital patients in general, or on patients in Scottish institutions for the mentally retarded. The unusually high incidence observed for coexistence of mental retardation and schizophrenia in triple-X patients has also been suggested by observations in U.S. studies (Money and Hirsch, 1963; Raphael and Shaw, 1963). Female patients diagnosed as schizophrenics and institutionalized in state mental hospitals appeared to include significantly higher incidence of the XXX genotype than that in the general population (Raphael and Shaw, 1963; Kaplan, 1967). More recent studies (Kaplan and Cotton, 1968; Kaplan, Cotton, and Powell, 1968), however, have indicated that the incidence of non-mosaic XXX females among institutionalized schizophrenic patients is not significantly different from the general population incidence -- but, rather, than schizophrenics may include a significantly higher incidence of mosaics than the general population.

MOSAICISM AND SCHIZOPHRENIA : Studies of Mosaicism Involving X-Chromosome Aneuploidies in Female Ohio State Hospital Patients with Diagnosis of Schizophrenia.

Buccal smears were obtained bilaterally from 1,061 female patients who had been diagnosed as schizophrenics and were confined in state mental hospitals in Ohio. The smears were fixed on coded slides in ether-alcohol, and then stained with 1.0 percent acetic orcein solution. Specimens were examined 'blind' and patients, whose buccal smears indicated abnormal sex-chromatin complements were selected for detailed chromosome studies.

Karyotype analyses were based on cultured leukocytes from peripheral blood. Sterile techniques were used, and approximately 0.25 ml. of blood was collected in a heparinized capillary tube from a finger stab in each subject under study. Each blood sample was then transferred to a culture flask containing 1.5 ml. of fetal calf serum, 3.5 ml. of TC-199 solution (containing 3.3 mM penicillin and 3.4 mM streptomycin) and 4 drops of phytohemagglutinin. Incubation at 36 degrees C was maintained for each culture for a period of 72 hours. Two hours prior to harvesting the cultured cells, colchicine was added as a mitotic-arresting agent. Afterwards, the cultured cells were placed in a hypotonic solution; then they were fixed, air-dried on slides, stained with carbol fuchsin, and examined with a light microscope. The well spread metaphase plates were photographed and then analyzed by cut-out karyotyping.

A previously-reported group of 986 female schizophrenic patients included five patients who showed X-chromosome aneuploides (Kaplan and Cotton, 1968). This included one triple-X female and four mosaics with chromosome counts, respectively, of: 45/46 (XO/XX); 45/46 (XO/XX); 45/46/47 (XO/XX/XXX); and 46/47/48 (XX/XXX/XXXX). The previous study (Kaplan and Cotton, 1968) has been continued, and several previously-implicated patients with abnormal buccal smears have recently been karyotyped. An additional 75 patients were screened and several of them have also been karyotyped. Two more mosaics have been found, who show chromosome counts, respectively, of: 46/47 (XX/XXX) and 45/46/47 (XO/XX/XXX). Table 1 shows the distribution of chromosome counts for the seven patients with abnormalities.

Patient	Buccal Smear Sex Chromatin	Numbers of Plates with the Following Chromosome Counts			
		45	46	47	48
V.R.	?-Negative	3	19		
A.H.	?-Negative	4	20		
B.M.	Some Double	7	7	18	
C.V.	Some Double		16	55	3
M.S.	Some Double			30	
S56	Some Double	1	29	8	
S57	?- Negative	7	28	2	

Table 1. The first five of the above seven patients were previously
described (Kaplan and Cotton, 1968). The numbers of metaphase plates observed to include 45, 46, 47, and 48 chromosomes are tabulated.

Sex-chromatin or Barr bodies occur in interphase nuclei of some female mammalian cells (Barr and Bertram, 1949). The maximum number in any particular nucleus is one less than the number of X chromosomes in that nucleus. The patients in our sample whose buccal smears
indicated possible sex-chromatin pecularities included only one with consistent triple-X karyotypes and six mosaics. Each of the Barr-negative-?
patients showed at least two cell lines, one of which contained only a
single X chromosome among a total of only 45 chromosomes (i.e., one
X chromosome and a normal complement of 44 autosomes). Each of the
patients whose buccal smears showed multiple sex-chromatin bodies included cells with more than the normal female complement of two X
chromosomes.

The overall incidence of females who were found to be affected with
X-chromosome abnormalities, in our study, of 1,061 patients is 7/1061
or 0.66 percent. This includes one generally triple-X female and six
mosaics. The mosacism incidence is 6/1061 or 0.57 percent of the
sample. Karyotypes were studied only from females whose buccal
smears indicated sex-chromatin abnormalities, thus screening out
only those patients with X-chromosome aneuploides manifested in the
buccal cells. Subsequent karyotype analyses were based only on peripheral blood leukocytes. The occurrence of chromosomal mosaicism
in other tissues was not investigated, and only patients with aneuploid
anomalies affecting their buccal cells and their leukocytes were indicated in our studies. Thus, our observed incidence of X-chromosome abnormalities represents a minimal estimate of those who may be similarly affected. The occurrence of chromosomal mosaicism in other tissues

was not investigated. The occurrence of cytologically less discernible mutations -- e.g., involving duplications and/or deletions of
only segments of X chromosomes -- was not investigated. The possibility that chromosomal mosaicisms in general -- i.e., not only
mosaicisms involving X-chromosome aneuploidies -- may be associated with the complex of disorders involved in schizophrenia has
not been specifically investigated. The present study has been confined to X-chromosome aneuploidies in females because buccal-smear
evaluation studies of sex chromatin facilitated a simple method for
screening such abnormalities.

The actual incidence of mosaicism in the general population is
not known, and such determination awaits future accumulations of
relevant data. The incidences of mosaicism observed among individuals affected with specific chromosomal syndromes, however, have
been found to involve only small minorities of those observed to be
affected (Brown, et al., 1966; Lindsten, 1963; Makino, 1964).

Previous investigators have discussed schizophrenics affected with
mosaicism involving X-chromosome aneuploidies (Slater and Zilkha,
1961; Brown, et al., 1966; Judd and Brandkamp, 1967; Nielsen and
Thomsen, 1968). The present data suggest an association between
schizophrenia and chromosomal mosaicism. The present study has
indicated an incidence of the general triple-X genotype -- i.e., non-
mosaic only -- in schizophrenic females which is consistent with the
expected incidence for the general female population. The overall incidence of females affected with X-chromosome anomalies, including
the mosaics, appears to be about five or six times the expected general female population incidence. The various hypotheses regarding
nature and mode of transmission of constitutional differences relevant
to different predispositions for schizophrenia are still open for debate
(Kaplan, 1967 a). The observed incidence of mosaicism in female
schizophrenic patients, which is low but very much higher than the
presumed general-population incidence, suggest that chromosomal
mosaicism may be etiologically relevant to the schizophrenic disorders.
The observations also imply the suggestion that more subtle mosaicisms
-- i.e., not involving such easily discernible anomalies as X-chromosome aneuploidies specifically involving and observable in the buccal
cells and the peripheral blood leukocytes -- may be relevant to constitutional variables associated with predisposition for the schizophrenic

disorders. Thus, genetic mosaicisms are suggested as possible etiological factors in a minority of schizophrenic cases. Genetic mosaicisms, if established as significant by additional data, might be etiologically manifested either as primary factors or as secondary evocative factors.

SUMMARY

Genetic hypothesis of schizophrenia etiology, and relevant aspects involving aneuploidies of the X and Y chromosomes, have been reviewed. Recent observations have been discussed, of a relatively high incidence of mosaicisms involving X-chromosome aneuploidies among hospitalized female patients with diagnoses of schizophrenia. Possible implications of such observations have been considered, relevant to etiology of the schizophrenic disorders.

REFERENCES

Barr, M.L. and Bertram, E.G. A morphological distinction between neurones of the male and female, and the behavior of the nuclear satellite during accelerated nucleoprotein synthesis. Nature, 163, 676, 1949.

Bleuler, M. Natural history of schizophrenia: a 20-year longitudinal study of 208 schizophrenics. Paper presented at Conference on The Transmission of Schizophrenia, sponsored by the Foundations' Fund for Research in Psychiatry, Dorado, Puerto Rico, 1967. Proceedings, edited by D. Rosenthal, to be published.

Böök, J. A genetic and neuropsychiatric investigation of a North-Swedish population, with special regard to schizophrenia and mental deficiency. Acta Genet. Stat. Med., 4, 1, 1953.

Brown, W.M.C., Buckton, K.E., Jacobs, P.A., Touch, I.M., Kuenssberg, E.V., and Knox, J.D.E. Chromosome Studies on Adults. London: Cambridge University Press, 1966.

Casey, M.D., Segall, L.J., Street, D.R.K., and Blank, C.E. Sex chromosome abnormalities in two state hospitals for patients requiring special security. Nature, 209, 641, 1966.

Corey, M.J., Miller, J.R., MacLean, J.R., and Chown, B. A case of XX/XY mosacism. Amer. J. Hum. Genet., 19, 378, 1967.

Curran, D. and Partridge, M. Psychological Medicine, Fourth Edition. Edinburgh: Livingstone, 1957.

Eggen, R.R. Chromosome Diagnostics in Clinical Medicine. Springfield: Thomas, 1965.

Ferguson-Smith, M.A., Lennox, B., Mack, W.S., and Stewart, J.S.S. Klinefelter's syndrome: frequency and testicular morphology in relation to nuclear sex. Lancet, 2, 167, 1957.

Ford, C.E., Polani, K.W., de Almeida, J.C., and Briggs, J.H. A sex-chromosome anomaly in a case of gonadal dysgenesis (Turner's Syndrome). Lancet, 1, 711, 1959.

Forssman, H. and Hambert, G. Incidence of Klinefelter's syndrome among mental patients. Lancet, 1, 1327, 1963.

Fraser, S.H., Campbell, J., MacGillivray, R.G., Boyd, E., and Lennox, B. The XYY syndrome: frequency among mental defectives and fertility. Lancet, 2, 626, 1960.

Jacobs, P.A., Baikie, A.G., Court-Brown, W.M., MacGregor, D.N., MacLean, D.N., MacLean, M., and Harnden, D.G. Evidence for the existence of a human "super female." Lancet, 2, 423, 1959.

Jacobs, P.A., Brunton, M., Melville, N.M., Brittain, R.P., and McClemont, W.F. Aggressive behavior, mental subnormality, and the XXY male. Nature, 208, 1351, 1965.

Jacobs, P.A., Harnden, D.G., Court-Brown, W.M., Goldstein, J., Close, H.G., MacGregor, T.N., MacLean, N., and Strong, J.A. Abnormalities involving the X chromosome in women. Lancet, 1, 1213, 1960.

Johnston, A.W., Ferguson-Smith, M.A., Handmaker, S.D., Jones, H.W., and Jones, G.S. The triple-X syndrome: clinical, pathological, and chromosomal studies in three mentally retarded cases. Brit. Med. J., 2, 1046, 1961.

Judd, L.L. and Brandkamp, W.W. Chromosome analyses of adult schizophrenics. Arch. Gen. Psychiat., 16, 316, 1967.

Kallmann, F.J. The genetic theory of schizophrenia: an analysis of 691 schizophrenic twin index families. Amer. J. Psychiat., 103, 309, 1946.

Kallmann, F. J. Heredity in Health and Mental Disorder. New York: Norton, 1953.

Kaplan, A.R. Introduction. Paper presented at Conference on Leukocyte Chemistry and Morphology Correlated with Chromosome anomalies, sponsored by the N.Y. Academy of Sciences, New York, 1966. Proceedings, with A.R. Kaplan and M.A. Kelsall consulting editors, to be published in Ann. N.Y. Acad. Sci. (in press).

Kaplan, A.R. Sex chromatin variations in institutionalized females. I. Sex chromosome anomalies in hospitalized schizophrenics, adult prisoners, confined juvenile offenders, and noninstitutionalized volunteers. Recent Advances in Biological Psychiatry (New York: Plenum Press) 9, 21, 1967.

Kaplan, A.R. Genetics and schizophrenia. Eugen. Quart., 14, 296, 1967 a.

Kaplan, A.R. The use of cytogenetical data in heredity counseling. Amer. J. Ment. Defic., in press.

Kaplan, A.R. and Cotton, J.E. Chromosomal abnormalities in female schizophrenics. J. Nerv. Ment. Dis., 147, 402, 1968.

Kaplan, A.R., Cotton, J.E., and Powell, W. High incidence of chromosomal mosaicism among hospitalized schizophrenic patients. Paper presented at XII International Congress of Genetics, Tokyo, 1968. Abstract in Proceedings of the XII International Congress of Genetics, Vol. I: 218. Tokyo: Science Council of Japan, 1968.

Karlsson, J.L. The Biologic Basis of Schizophrenia. Springfield, Thomas, 1966.

Kety, S. The types and frequencies of mental illness in the biological and adoptive families of adopted schizophrenics. Paper presented at Conference on the Transmission of Schizophrenia, sponsored by the Foundations' Fund for Research in Psychiatry, Dorado, Purerto Rico, 1967. Proceedings, edited by D. Rosenthal, to be published.

Kidd, C.B., Knox, R.S., and Mantle, D.J. A psychiatric investigation of triple-X chromosome females. Brit. J. Psychiat., 109, 90, 1963.

Lindsten, J. The Nature and Origin of X Chromosome Aberrations in Turner's Syndrome. Stockholm: Almquist & Wiksell, 1963.

MacLean, N., Harnden, D.G., Court-Brown, W.M., Bond, J., and Mantle, D.J. Sex-chromosome abnormalities in newborn babies. Lancet, 1, 286, 1964.

MacLean, N. Mitchell, J.M., Harnden, D.G., Williams, J., Jacobs, P.A., Buckton, K.A., Baikie, A.G., Court-Brown, W.M., McBride, J.A., Strong, J.A., Close, H.G., and Jones, D.C. A survey of sex-chromosome abnormalities among 4514 mental defectives. Lancet, 1, 293, 1962.

Makino, S. Chromosomal studies in normal human subjects and in 300 cases of congenital disorders: Parts I, II, and III. Cytologia, 29, 13, 125, and 233, 1964.

Mitsuda, H. Clinical Genetics in Psychiatry. Tokyo: Igaku Shoin Ltd., 1968.

Money, J. and Hirsch, S.R. Chromosome anomalies, mental deficiency, and schizophrenia. Arch. Gen. Psychiat., 8, 242, 1963.

Morishima, A. and Grumbach, M. Human sex chromosome abnormalities and function of sex chromosomes. Paper presented at Sixth Conference on Mammalian Cytology and Somatic Cell Genetics, Asilomar, California, 1967.

Nielsen, J. and Thomsen, N. A psychiatric-cytogenetic study of a female patient with 45/46/47 chromosomes and sex chromosomes XO/XX/XXX. Acta Psychiat. Scand., 44, 141, 1968.

Ödegård, O. The psychiatric disease entities in the light of a genetic investigation. Acta Psychiat. Scand., 167-169, 94, 1963.

Polani, P.E. Sex chromosome anomalies in man. Chap. 7 in Chromosomes in Medicine, ed. by Hamerton, J.E. London: Heineman, 1964.

Price, W.H. and Whatmore, P.B. Behavior disorders and pattern of crime among XYY males identified at a maximum security hospital. Brit. Med. J., 1, 533, 1967.

Raphael, T. and Shaw, M.W. Chromosome studies in schizophrenia. J. Amer. Med. Assn., 183, 1022-1028, 1963.

Rosenthal, D. Critical summary of research design, problems, and present status of the field. Paper presented at Conference on the Transmission of Schizophrenia, sponsored by the Foundations' Fund for Research in Psychiatry, Dorado, Puerto Rico, 1967. Proceedings, edited by D. Rosenthal, to be published.

Slater, E. The monogenic theory of schizophrenia. Acta Genet., 8, 50, 1958.

Slater, E. and Zilkha, K.A. A case of Turner mosaic with myopathy and schizophrenia. Proc. Roy. Soc. Med., 54, 674, 1961.

Tjio, J.H. and Levan, A. The chromosome number of man. Hereditas, 42, 1, 1956.

Valentine, G.H. The Chromosome Disorders. London: Heineman, 1966.

A. R. Kaplan, Ph.D., Cleveland Psychiatric Institute, Cleveland, Ohio 44109

THE PATHOGENESIS OF SCHIZOPHRENIA: II CONTRIBUTIONS FROM THE NIMH STUDY OF 16 PAIRS OF MONOZYGOTIC TWINS DISCORDANT FOR SCHIZOPHRENIA

JAMES R. STABENAU and WILLIAM POLLIN

One research strategy of the NIMH Twin Study has consisted of the investigation, in a hospital setting, of a series of 16 pairs of monozygotic twins in which only one of each pair had been diagnosed as having been schizophrenic.[1,2,3,4] This group provided a sample of schizophrenics and a matched sample of non-schizophrenics, with factors of genetic difference, age, sex and dietary variables controlled to a varying extent, which offered collaborative investigators an opportunity to blindly evaluate their biochemical variables in this unique sample by their method at NIMH or in their own laboratories. Additionally, the NIMH investigators, through intensive interviews with the parents and twins, were able to explore possible psychological and biological "markers" of schizophrenia, pre-schizophrenia, or the antecedents of the development of schizophrenia. These could be noted and compared within and between families. The assessment of psychologic "markers" of schizophrenia obtained from the life history review for the 16 pairs studied to date suggests that in discordant pairs, biologic defects or vulnerability, real or feared, apparently contributed to a faulty self-image and reduced self-esteem which later was associated with a schizophrenic break. The pre-schizophrenic twins experienced more fearfulness, dependence, compliance and frustration; were less competent, dominant, open, differentiated and related. The early parental view of the schizophrenic-twin-to-be as defective, weaker and vulnerable based on birth weight and early physical defect differences appeared to have led to the different and distinct pattern of parent-child relationship with this twin as compared to his co-twin. Unresolved parental conflict displaced onto him also appeared to have contributed to the more varied and stressful interaction with him.

A review of published early life data from 86 additional pairs of monozygotic twins discordant for schizophrenia and the NIMH twin series has yielded the following: 1) Nine behavioral traits were characteristic of the pre-illness twin submissive; sensitive; serious-worrier; obedient-gentler; dependent; well behaved; quiet-shy; stubborn; and neurotic as a child; and 2) six physical traits were found to distinguish the pre-schizophrenic twin: having had a central nervous system illness as a child; any birth complications; neonatal asphyxia; weaker, shorter; and lighter at birth.[4] The criterion employed here was that the designated trait was present for the index twins by a ratio of 2 to 1 or greater.

DIFFERENTIATING CHARACTERISTICS: MZ TWINS DISCORDANT FOR SCHIZOPHRENIA (100 pairs)

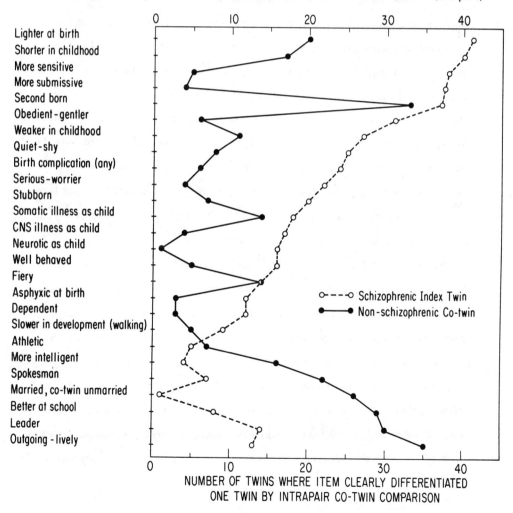

NUMBER OF TWINS WHERE ITEM CLEARLY DIFFERENTIATED
ONE TWIN BY INTRAPAIR CO-TWIN COMPARISON

Figure 1 graphically demonstrates the relative differences for these and other characteristics among the twin pairs.

Two items which appeared most consistently in the 14 sources for these data were the pre-illness developmental description of the schizophrenic twins as more submissive (9.3:1) and more sensitive (7.6:1) as compared to their co-twins.[4] Such early psychobiologic "markers" may play a significant role within pathogenic families in the selection of one twin as the more vulnerable and the one whose life course could be most seriously pathologically altered. For 12 of the 16 pairs studied at NIMH there was significantly lower birth weight for the schizophrenic twins (8% as compared to their co-twins); for three of the four higher birth weight twins who developed schizophrenia, there was suspected physical defect in the first three years of life.

The power of cultural expectancy may be more clearly seen in twins than in singletons. In Western culture, being first born in a twin pair is associated with being physically stronger, more often the dominant and the leader in childhood as compared to the second born twin. However, if the expectancies associated with being the first born for twin pairs in the Western culture are placed on the second born as they are in the Eastern cultures, there is a reversal of the picture. In Japan the second born is considered the elder because he was mature enough to let the other twin enter the world first. Being the oldest, he has all the rights and obligations accorded to his station. He tends to take charge in the twinship, being more dominant and aggressive in initiation.

The work of Robert Rosenthal[5,6] has suggested to us that the role of expectancy may promote or limit normal psychological growth or development which could result in deviancy in one child within a family, while other children develop relatively "normally." In one study children in a primary grade school were tested as part of a research study of intellectual capacity. The experimenter randomly selected 20% of the children from 18 classrooms. Their teachers were then told that they were showing unusual potential for intellectual gains, thus marking them for an expectation of different performance as compared to their peers. Testing eight

months later demonstrated significant increases in IQ for those children
so marked as compared to their peers. Perhaps this favorable outcome
expectancy effect is a partial factor in the rate of change found in
high nutriment environment studies such as the Headstart Program.

Expectancy can work in the opposite direction as the same experimenter
demonstrated with graduate students and the white rat.[7] Rats who were litter
mates of similar genetic and early maternal environment were given to graduate students with the statement that certain of these rats were "less intelligent" than the others. The students testing these marked "dumb" rats found
significantly poorer maze performance and the prophesy had been fulfilled.

Scott[8] has described the effect of the shadow of insanity which hangs
over families where a member in a previous generation has been psychotic.
He describes how this shadow influences the life course of a child whom the
family feels is bearing out this legacy and thus one child may become directed toward the fulfillment of the development of psychosis.

In the NIMH comparative family study, a beginning has been made
toward delineating whether such expectancy may exist within a family.[9,10]
Two groups of families were compared. In one group each family had a
schizophrenic child and a same-sexed non-schizophrenic child. The other
group was of families with non-schizophrenic "normal" children. They were
all tested on their first visit to NIMH. Each family member made a description by checklist of himself, his ideal, and each of the other family members.
In six of 11 families of schizophrenics, the parents' self-ideal image was
negatively correlated with the view of the index child while it was positively correlated with the view of the control child. For the five families
of "normals" all correlations were positive except for one control sibling.[10]
This suggested a negative-positive split in the view of the index and control
sibling for the parents of schizophrenics.

If there is indeed such a selective sorting and selective expectancy
for psychologic failure in some families, what are the necessary characteristics which constitute the psychonoxious family effect.

Thus far families of schizophrenics have been blindly differentiated
from families of normal children by differences in parental Rorschach pro-

files[11], characteristics of parental TAT stories[9,12] and Object Sorting Tests [9,13]. However, other groups of parents with children with psychologic disorder such as neurosis or delinquency have shown disturbance in these measures almost as great as in families of schizophrenics.[9] All of the above studies, including the NIMH Check List Study, have been subjected to the effects of a pathogenic child on the family itself, which may to a greater or lesser degree account for differences found.

The relative role of the genetic component to the development of schizophrenia has already been stated.[14,15] Genetic influence offers an alternative hypothesis to explain sibling differences. Existing data, however, suggest environmental influences are of substantial importance in determining a schizophrenic outcome in not only monozygotic twins, but also in adopted singletons born to parents who have had schizophrenia.

In an attempt to assess possible biological "markers" of schizophrenia, a study was made of the lactate/pyruvate (L/P) ratio, the rabbit red cell agglutination titer, serum S_{19} macroglobulin, serum protein bound iodine (PBI), and urine 3,4-dimethoxyphenylethylamine (DMPEA) in this series of monozygotic twins discordant for schizophrenia.[16]

Lactate-pyruvate Ratios

Frohman et al[17] have reported a series of studies which suggested that individuals with the diagnosis of schizophrenia, as compared with non-schizophrenic controls, had a serum factor which produced higher lactate/pyruvate ratios in an incubated chicken erythrocyte preparation. The results of the blind analysis of the L/P ratio in 14 of the 16 pairs of monozygotic twins discordant for schizophrenia demonstrate consistent intrapair differences in the L/P ratio. For 12 of 14 pairs, the L/P ratio was greater for the schizophrenic twin than for his co-twin.

Table 1

Lactate-Pyruvate Ratio (L/P)

Paired Comparison: Schizophrenic Index and Cotwin Control

Code No.	Observed L/P Ratio[†]		"Normalized" L/P Ratio[††]		d[†††]
	I	C	I	C	
1	1.76	1.31	+0.20	-0.63	+0.83
2	0.32	0.32	-1.15	-1.12	-0.03
5	11.35	1.62	+2.22	-0.53	+2.75
6	9.92	7.13	+0.47	-0.16	+0.63
7	2.47	1.54	+1.47	+0.05	+1.42
8	0.82	0.30	+1.63	-1.02	+2.65
9	0.75	0.56	-0.43	-0.68	+0.25
10	3.91	1.23	+0.26	-0.72	+0.98
13	22.86	16.63	+1.72	+0.80	+0.92
14	15.50	8.57	+0.37	-0.25	+0.62
17	64.73	22.91	+0.42	-0.30	+0.72
18	66.52	76.93	+0.30	+0.72	-0.42
22	163.13	40.52	+2.97	+0.13	+2.84
23	22.99	8.59	+1.93	-0.56	+2.45
Mean	28.00	13.44			
S.D.±	43.48	20.77			
S.E.±	11.62	5.55			

N = 14   N = 14

t = 1.62   t = 4.13

p = .10   p = <.001

† I = Index schizophrenic twin, C = non-schizophrenic monozygotic cotwin control. Mean L/P ratio from before and after exercise blood samples. For all above pairs both twins were simultaneously studied. Where two cotwins were not studied the ratios for the schizophrenic indexes were 3.84 for #3 and 28.15 for #4.

†† Plus or minus standard deviation from the substudy mean.

††† d = "normalized" ratio for Index minus "normalized" ratio for cotwin control.

The split duplicate measures for reliability were moderate (r=0.49). The day-to-day variability in range of observed L/P ratio limited its reliable usefulness in this series. For example, intrapair t-test comparison of the observed L/P ratios for each twin pair yielded a non-significant value. The use of the statistical procedure of normalization within the sub-studies made the sub-series of studies in the entire sample more comparable. When this statistical technique was used, the intrapair differences in L/P ratio between schizophrenic twin and non-schizophrenic co-twin became significant (p<.001). Extreme caution must be taken in directly relating these higher values with the schizophrenic condition since all schizophrenic subjects had at some time prior to admission received phenothiazine drugs in varying amounts and for varying duration. In this series there was a direct correlation between high positive normalized L/P ratio values and recentness of phenothiazine drug intake. Those individuals who had never had phenothiazine predominantly had L/P ratios less than the mean in each sub-study. The schizophrenic subjects who most recently had received phenothiazines had the highest normalized L/P ratios (r=0.56,p<.05). Frohman has noted, from studies done in his laboratory, that "Patients on phenothiazine show higher L/P ratios than those without phenothiazines, but four days off phenothiazine was sufficient to negate this effect."[16]

Anti-rabbit Heterophyle Hemagglutinin

Turner and Chipps[18], using a technique of measuring hemolysis of rabbit red cells, demonstrated a significantly higher degree of hemolysis for sera from schizophrenics as compared to non-schizophrenics and "normals." In the current blind study those investigators employed a hemagglutinin method.[16] In this small sub-sample the titers did not discriminate significantly between the sera sample from the schizophrenic twins and their non-schizophrenic co-twins.

Table 2

Serum Titers of Anti-Rabbit Heterophile Hemagglutinin

Paired Comparison: Index and Cotwin Control

Code No.	Observed % Agglutination		d†
	I	C	
5	79.6	6.1	73.5
10	81.3	65.3	16.0
13	75.8	29.4	46.4
14	9.7	18.2	-8.5
17	74.9	27.8	47.1
18	8.5	3.1	5.4
22	9.5	17.3	-7.8
23	6.1	12.6	-6.8
Mean	43.17	22.47	
S. D.	±34.78	±18.37	
S. E.	±12.33	± 6.51	
	N = 8		
	t = 1.87		
	p = .10		

I = index schizophrenic, C = cotwin control

†d = index - control

Recent replication studies done in Turner's laboratory, using the hemolysis method, have not been able to discriminate between schizophrenic and non-schizophrenic sera.[19]

S_{19} Macroglobulin

The work of Fessel et al[20,21] indicates that psychotics, especially schizophrenics, had higher serum levels of S_{19} macroglobulin as compared to control subjects. Paired intrapair t-test comparison revealed no significant difference between schizophrenic and non-schizophrenic co-twins.

Table 3

Serum S_{19} Macroglobulin

Paired Comparison: Index and Cotwin Control

Code No.	S_{19} Observed (gm%)		d[†]
	I	C	
1	.27	.27	.0
2	.33	.29	.04
5	.22	.16	.06
6	.27	.18	.09
7	.31	.26	.05
8	.17	.19	-.02
9	.21	.27	-.06
10	.33	.34	-.01
13	.43	.43	.0
14	.29	.34	-.05
17	.33	.37	-.04
18	.21	.18	.03
Mean	0.281	0.273	
S. D.	±0.069	±0.082	
S. E.	±0.020	±0.024	

$$N = 12$$

$$t = 0.55$$

$$p = N.S.$$

† d = Index - Control

For the schizophrenic group and a larger control group, which included parents of the twins, females had a significantly higher mean value for S_{19} macroglobulin as compared to males (0.305 and 0.303 for females versus 0.233 and 0.241gms.% for males).[22] The data from this report demonstrate that S_{19} macroglobulin elevation is more clearly related to being a female than to the diagnosis of schizophrenia.

Serum Protein Bound Iodine

Neither a hypothesis nor observed relationship between PBI and schizophrenia diagnosis was being tested when PBI samples were initially obtained.
For the 15 pairs where paired comparison was possible, PBI's were significantly lower for the schizophrenic index twins (mean 4.89μg%) as compared to
the values for the non-schizophrenic co-twins (mean 5.75μg%, p<.01).

Table 4

Serum Protein Bound Iodine (PBI)

Paired Comparison: Index and Cotwin Control

Code No.	Observed P B I (μg%)		d†
	I	C	
1	5.0	6.3	-1.3
2	3.5	5.1	-1.6
3	6.0	6.0	0
4	4.2	5.0	-0.8
5	5.3	5.7	-0.4
6	5.0	6.5	-1.5
7	5.3	8.6	-3.3
8	4.9	5.1	-0.2
9	4.3	6.0	-1.7
10	4.3	5.8	-1.5
13	4.9	4.8	0.1
14	5.0	6.0	-1.0
17	5.2	4.1	1.1
18	5.5	6.0	-0.5
23	5.0	5.3	-0.3
mean	4.89	5.75	
S. D.	±0.59	±0.98	
S. E.	±0.152	±0.25	

N = 15

t = 3.23

p = <.01

† d = Index - Control

In this series the twin who subsequently became schizophrenic was significantly lighter at birth (mean 2165 ± 507gms.) as compared to his non-schizophrenic co-twin (mean 2362 ± 588gms., p<.05, 12 of 16 pairs). When the PBI data for these pairs and additional "normal" control monozygotic twins were examined in relation to the birth weight of the twins, it was observed that the twins who were lighter in weight at birth had significantly lower PBI values as compared to their higher birth weight co-twins (p<.001).[23] The direct relation between PBI and birth weight is significant with or without these schizophrenic subjects (r=0.58 and 0.65 respectively). No relationship was found between sex, age of the subject, drug history, or duration of hospitalization or illness.

DMPEA

Friedhoff and co-workers[24,25] found 3,4-DMPEA was present in the urine of schizophrenics and was absent from the urine of non-schizophrenics. The possible occurrence and significance of the "pink spot" or 3,4-DMPEA in the urine of schizophrenic patients has stimulated considerable interest and a large number of investigations. The results reported are not uniform. Factors which may influence variability include differences in: diagnosis and clinical conditions; methodology (including techniques employed for isolation and detection of DMPEA, as well as criteria for defining the DMPEA-like substance); dietary artifact; and the presence or absence of phenothiazine drug intake. In this small sample of monozygotic twin pairs discordant for schizophrenia, the blind analysis by Friedhoff and associates of urine samples obtained under controlled conditions to date demonstrates no significant difference for excretion of DMPEA in the urine of schizophrenic twins (4 of 11) as compared to the non-schizophrenic co-twins (4 of 6).[16]

Table 5

Urine DMPEA (3,4, dimethoxyphenylethylamine)

Paired Comparison: Index and Cotwin Control

Code No.	Index		Control	
1	Neg+	Neg	*	*
2	Neg		*	*
3	Tr	Tr	*	*
5	M.Pos.		*	*
7	Tr	Tr	Unsat.	Unsat.**
8	Neg	Neg	S.Pos.	S.Pos.
9	0	0	25†	43††
10	M.Pos.	M.Pos.	M.Pos.	
	52	88	35	65
13	0	0	0	0
17	0	0	0	0
18	0	0	8	9
Total	11		6	
Pos	4		4	
Neg	7		2	

+ Neg = negative, Tr - trace, M.Pos. = moderate positive, S. Pos =
strong positive. Determination by paper chromatography method.[24]
The second statement represents a retest value for this method.

* Urine for #2, #3, lost in freezer failure; #1, #6 not collected;
#5, #14, #22, #23 analysis pending.

† First figure for subject = μg DMPEA/gram creatinine; †† Second
figure for subject = μg DMPEA/total sample.   Determination by
paper and gas chromatographic method.[25]

** Unsatisfactory separation.

However, one must exercise caution in the interpretation of these data.
Three factors which may influence the findings to varying and as yet
undefined degrees are present: genetic factors, phenothiazine modification factors; and illness duration variables.

If the urinary presence of DMPEA is related to schizophrenic symptoms,
but largely controlled by genetic factors, it should not be expected to be
differentially present in pairs discordant for schizophrenia. With respect

to phenothiazine, it has been variously reported that chlorpromazine results
in the appearance of false positive "pink spot" (DMPEA-like substance) in
the urine;[26,27] and on the other hand, that administration of clinical doses
of chlorpromazine results in the disappearance of DMPEA from the urine of
excretors.[25] None of the non-schizophrenic twins had received any phenothiazine medication, while all of the schizophrenic twins had taken these drugs
at sometime prior to study. A possible relationship between the length of
illness and excretion of DMPEA may be suggested by these data. The mean duration of illness for the four schizophrenic twins who were found to excrete
the DMPEA is 1.25 years. The duration of illness in the seven schizophrenic
twins found not to excrete DMPEA was 3.1 years. Although the relationship
is not significant (p=1.5, Mann Whitney U) the direction is consistent
with the report that the incidence of excretors among chronic patients is
lower than among acute subjects.

Comments

The sample population reported in this paper is thus far quite small.
It consists only of one-egg twins; is heterogeneous as to diagnosis of
schizophrenia and to duration of illness, hospitalization and somatic treatment; and was selected on a non-random basis. Thus, any extrapolation of
these findings to the larger sample of non-twin, singleton schizophrenics
must be made with caution and reservation. On the other hand, the control
of genetic differences, similarity of diet for index and control subjects,
control for drug intake, and the blind analytic technique are important in
evaluating the relative value of these data.

Summary

By comparing concordance rates for schizophrenia in monozygotic and
dizygotic twins in the NRC twin panel[15] and in the recent large-scale
European twin studies,[14,28] the role of a genetic factor in schizophrenia
is demonstrated. However, since the discordance rates for monozygotic pairs
in these studies exceed concordance rates, environmental factors appear to
be more important in deciding who it is that becomes ill with schizophrenia.

Within pair comparison of several biologic variables in 16 pairs of
monozygotic twins discordant for schizophrenia studied at NIMH, has shown

that: high L/P ratio significantly differentiates schizophrenic twins, but was also related to phenothiazine drug intake; differences in rabbit red cell hemagglutination, serum S_{19} macroglobulin, serum protein bound iodine, and urinary DMPEA were not significantly related to the diagnosis of schizophrenia in this sample.

REFERENCES

1. Pollin, W., Stabenau, J.R., and Tupin, J. Family studies with identical twins discordant for schizophrenia. Psychiat. 28, 60, 1965.

2. Pollin, W., Stabenau, J.R., Mosher, L. and Tupin, J. Life History differences in identical twins discordant for schizophrenia. Amer. J. Orthopsychiat. 36, 492, 1966.

3. Pollin, W., and Stabenau, J.R. Findings from the intensive study of a series of identical twins discordant for schizophrenia, and their relevance to a theory concerning the etiology of schizophrenia. Excerpt. Med. Int. Cong. Proceedings of the IV World Congress of Psychiatry, 150, 1107, 1966.

4. Stabenau, J.R., Pollin, W. Early characteristics of monozygotic twins discordant for schizophrenia. Arch. Gen. Psychiat. 17, 723, 1967.

5. Rosenthal, R. and Jacobson, L. Teachers' expectancies: determinants of pupils' I.Q. gains. Psychol. Rep. 19, 115, 1966.

6. Conn, L.K., Edwards, C.N., Rosenthal, R. and Crowne, B. Perception of emotion and response to teachers' expectancy of elementary school children. Psychol. Rep. 22, 27, 1968.

7. Rosenthal, R. and Fode, K.L. The effect of experimental bias on the performance of the albino rat. Behavioral Sci. 8, 183, 1963.

8. Scott, R.D. Perspectives on the American family studies in schizophrenia. Confin. Psychiat. 8, 43, 1965.

9. Stabenau, J.R., Tupin, J., Werner, M. and Pollin, W. A comparative study of families of schizophrenics, delinquents and "normals." Psychiat. 28, 45, 1965.

10. Stabenau, J.R. and Pollin, W. Comparative life history differences for families of schizophrenics, delinquents and "normals." Am. J. Psychiat. 124, 11, 1968.

11. Singer, M.T. Family transactions in schizophrenia: I. Recent

research findings. In <u>The Origins of Schizophrenia</u>, Romano, J. (ed.),
p. 147, Excerpta Medica Foundation, New York, 1967.

12. Werner, M., Stabenau, J. and Pollin, W. A TAT method for the differentiation of families of families of schizophrenics, delinquents and
"normals." <u>J. Abn. and Soc. Psychol.</u> (In press, 1968)

13. Wild, C., Singer, M., Rosman, B., Ricci, J. and Lidz, T. Measuring
disordered styles of thinking. <u>Arch. Gen. Psychiat.</u> 13, 471, 1965.

14. Stabenau, J.R. Heredity and environment in schizophrenia, the contribution of twin studies. <u>Arch. Gen. Psychiat.</u> 18, 458, 1968.

15. Pollin, W., Stabenau, J.R. and Hoffer, A. The pathogenesis of
schizophrenia: I Contributions from varied types of twin studies.
Preceding paper in this volume.

16. Stabenau, J.R., Pollin, W., Mosher, L.R., Frohman, C., Friedhoff, A.,
and Turner, W. A study of monozygotic twins discordant for schizophrenia:
Some biologic variables. (Lactate-pyruvate; 3,4-dimethoxyphenylethylamine;
S_{19} macroglobulin; anti-rabbit red cell hemagglutinin; protein bound
iodine). <u>Arch. Gen. Psychiat.</u> (In press, 1968).

17. Frohman, C., Czajkowski, N., Luby, E., Gottlieb, J. and Senf, R.
Further evidence of a plasma factor in schizophrenia. <u>Arch. Gen. Psychiat.</u>
2, 263, 1960.

18. Turner, W. and Chipps, H. A heterophile hemolysin in human blood.
<u>Arch. Gen. Psychiat.</u> 15, 373, 1966.

19. Turner, W. J. and Turano, P. Anti-rabbit heterophile hemolysin and
agglutinin in human serum. <u>Arch. Gen. Psychiat.</u> 19, 616, 1968.

20. Fessel, W. Blood proteins in functional psychoses. <u>Arch. Gen.
Psychiat.</u> 6, 1932, 1962.

21. Kurland, H.D. and Fessel, W.J. Distinctive protein patterns in
functional psychoses. <u>Proc. Soc. Exp. Biol. Med.</u> 113, 244, 1963.

22. Stabenau, J.R., Pollin, W. and Mosher, L. Serum macroglobulin
(S_{19}) in families of monozygotic twins discordant for schizophrenia.
<u>Amer. J. Psychiat.</u> 125, 147, 1968.

23. Stabenau, J.R., Pollin, W. Adult protein-bound iodine and maturity at
birth in monozygotic twins. <u>J. Clin. Endocrin. and Metab.</u> 28, 693,

24. Friedhoff, A. and Van Winkle, E. Isolation and characterization of a
compound from the urine of schizophrenics. <u>Nature</u> 194, 897, 1962.

25. Friedhoff, A.J. Metabolism of dimethoxyphenethylamine and its
    possible relationship to schizophrenia. In The Origins of Schizo-
    phrenia in Roman, J. (ed.) p 27, Excerpta Medica Foundation, 1967.

26. Closs, K., Wad, N. and Ose, E. The "pink spot" in schizophrenia.
    Nature 214, 483, 1967.

27. Steinberg, H.R. and Robinson, J. Nor-2-chlorpromazine sulfide and
    3,4-dimethoxyphenethylamine. Nature 217, 1054, 1968.

28. Stabenau, J.R. Schizophrenic and affective psychosis: twin and
    family studies. Presented at Third International Conference,
    Manfred Sakel Foundation, New York Academy of Medicine, New York
    City, N. Y. May 2, 1968. Conference Proc. (In press, 1968).

J. R. Stabenau M.D., and W. Pollin M.D., National Inst. of Mental Health, Bethesda, Md.

THE HIGH INCIDENCE OF PSYCHIATRIC MORBIDITY IN PARENTS AND SIBLINGS OF SCHIZOPHRENIC CHILDREN WITH IMMATURE EEG PATTERNS

KARL ANDERMANN

For the last 6 years, the author was reading and interpreting the E. E. G. tracings of thousands of disturbed children in the Childrens' Unit of Creedmoor State Hospital. He was impressed by the large proportion of immature activities in their E. E. G. and by the high incidence of mental illness of parents and siblings of those children whose E. E. G. was immature.

By immaturity of the E. E. G. one usually understands (for the age group) a gross excess of slow waves, of background amplitude, that do not increase with hyperventilation. These are found in the posterior regions. Gibbs and Gibbs (11) in their Atlas of Electroencephalography established rough norms for each age group, and the illustrations can be used as helpful, if crude, standards of reference.

In addition, the author was observing certain specific posterior slow wave forms, which he named "serrated delta waves" and which, as he found later, resembled closely the "alpha variants" of Aird and Gastaut (1). These were slow waves of delta frequency which rose sharply at one end, descended sharply at the other end and were connected by an elevated serrated plateau.

They usually occurred scattered in between alpha waves, were of alpha amplitude and did not increase with hyperventilation. They disappeared or were blocked when the patient opened his eyes. The "serration" on the plateau was often of alpha frequency, and the delta waves were of 1/3rd, 1/4th or 1/5th alpha frequency. Occasionally, there were odd serrated delta waves which seemed to split into an "aberrant" alpha wave. To sum up, the author got the impression that these "serrated delta waves" represented clusters of poorly differentiated coalescing alpha waves which, so to say, had not separated from each other. Similar "serrated delta waves" occur in normal children below the age of 5 years. Being easily recognized by their form, they were used in this study as a kind of tracer element for immaturity.

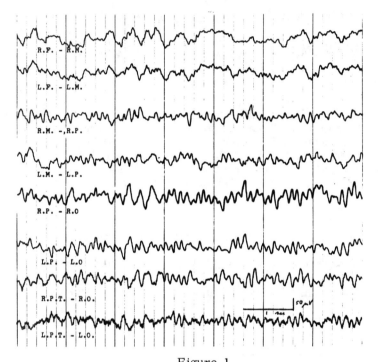

Figure 1.
Excess of posterior slow waves that do not increase
with hyperventilation in an 11 year old boy.
R.F.: Right Frontal, L.F.: Left Frontal, R.M.: Right Motor
L.M.: Left Motor, R.P.: Right Parietal, L.P.: Left Parietal
R.O.: Right Occipital, L.O.: Left Occipital, R.P.T.: Right
Posterior Temporal, L.P.T.: Left Posterior Temporal.

There were several disturbed siblings in the Childrens' Unit, and the author observed that if one sibling had three "serrated delta waves", the other sibling had them too. In eight children with "serrated delta waves", at least one of the parents also had them.

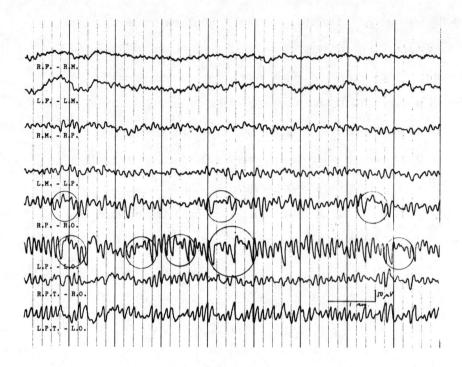

Figure 2.
"Serrated Delta Waves" marked by circles in a 12 year old boy.
R.F.: Right Frontal, L.F.: Left Frontal, R.M.: Right Motor,
L.M.: Left Motor, R.P.: Right Parietal, L.P.: Left Parietal,
R.O.: Right Occipital, L.O.: Left Occipital, R.P.T.: Right Posterior Temporal, L.P.T.: Left Posterior Temporal.

HYPOTHESIS

The hypothesis is that disturbed children with "serrated delta waves" and/or gross excess of slow waves that do not increase with hyperventilation, have significantly more mentally sick or deviant parents or siblings than those without.

METHODOLOGY AND FINDINGS

A survey of E.E.G. tracings of 609 newly admitted verbal disturbed children, aged 6-15 years, was made in 1964-1966. The bipolar tracings were recorded on an 8 channel Medcraft Machine. The pen deflection was 6 mm per 50 microvolt. The tracings were scrutinized and examined in relation to their age group for the presence of "serrated delta waves" and/or gross excess of slow waves that do not increase with hyperventilation, hereafter called "immature E.E.G. patterns".

Sixty four of the records had grossly abnormal or desynchonized patterns or artifacts which could have masked the underlying background activity that may have included "immature E. E. G. patterns". These were excluded from the study.

Table 1.

Psychiatric Diagnosis and Immature E. E. G. Patterns in 545 Disturbed Children

	Presence of Immature E. E. G. Patterns	Absence of Immature E. E. G. Patterns	Total
Childhood Schizophrenia	187 (49%)	195 (51%)	382 (100%)
Epileptic and Orgnnic Psychosis of Children	33 (40%)	50 (60%)	83 ('00%)
Environmentally conditioned Behavior Disorder in Children	15 (19%)	65 (81%)	80 (100%)
	235 (43%)	310 (57%)	545 (100%)
Adult Schizophrenia	43 (52%)	39 (48%)	82 (100%)

Of the remaining 545 disturbed children, 235 (43%) had the above described "immature E. E. G. patterns", and 310 (57%) had not. Of the 382 schizophrenic children, 187 (49%) had "immature E. E. G. patterns" and 195 (51%) had not. Of the 83 epileptic and organic psychotic children, 33 (40 %) had "immature E. E. G. pat-patterns" and 50 (60%) had not. Of the 80 children with essentially environmentally conditioned behavior disorders, 15 (19%) had "immature E. E. G. patterns" and 65 (81%) had not.

Thus, the highest proportion (49%) of "immature E. E. G. patterns" was found in schizophrenic children, less so (40%) among epileptic and organic psychotic children, and least (19%) among children with environmentally conditioned behavior disorders.

Of the 545 children investigated, we found medical hospital charts of 223 of them that contained "adequate" informations on the mental conditions of the parents and siblings. By "adequate" is meant that the psychiatrist who had examined and investigated the children, had obtained information from a relative about each member of the family, and that the informant was considered to be reliable. This information was often verified from the psychiatric agencies and mental institution which had contact with these families. In addition, the author excluded from this study the group of children diagnosed as epileptic or organic psychosis in order to avoid conceptual difficulties. Of the remaining 202 disturbed children, 185 were diagnosed as schizophrenic and 47 as disturbed by environmental circumstances only. At this stage, the 202 disturbed children were reconsidered as to the reliability of the diagnosis at a meeting of the attending psychiatrists and whenever there was the slightest doubt, the children were dropped from the study. Thus we were left with 181 children of whom 161 were diagnosed as schizophrenic and 20 as having environmentally conditioned behavior disorders.

Table 2.
Psychiatric Family Morbidity of Disturbed Children in the Unit.
Schizophrenic Children

At least one parent or sibling	Number	Percent
In Mental Institution	36	22
Mentally Deviant	78	48
Functioning adequately within their community	47	30
	161	100

Environmentally Conditioned Disturbed Children

At least one parent or sibling		
In Mental Institution or mentally deviant	9	45
Functioning adequately within their community	11	55
	20	100

As can be seen in the above table, out of 161 schizophrenic children, 36 (22%) had at least one parent or sibling who had been in a mental institution, 78 (48%) had at least one mentally deviant (see table 4) parent or siblings and 47 (30%) had parents or siblings who functioned adequately within their community. The incidence of psychiatric family morbidity in our sample of 161 schizophrenic children is high (70%).

As for the 20 children with environmentally conditioned behavior disorders, 9 (45%) had psychiatric family morbidity, and 11 (55%) had not. As, however, the number was too small to represent the whole group, it was dropped from further evaluation at this time.

Table 3

Presence of Absence of Immature E. E. G. Patterns in Schizophrenic Children with Parents or Siblings in Mental Institutions.

Parents or Siblings in Mental Institution for	"Immature E. E. G." "Patterns"	"Mature E. E. G." "Patterns"
Schizophrenia	9	4
Psychopathic Personality	1	0
Pregnancy Psychosis	1	0
Depression or Suicide	1	2
Psychoneurosis	1	0
Alcoholism	2	0
Unknown Causes	11	4
	26 (72%)	10 (28%)
and Parents and Siblings Functioning Adequately Within their Community	8 (17%)	39 (83%)

Chi Square is 20.33   P is less than .001

The above table shows that out of 36 children whose parents or siblings had been in a mental institution, 26 (72%) had "immatute E. E. G. patterns" and only 10 (28%) had not. In the control group of 47 children whose parents or siblings were not considered to be mentally ill or deviant, only 8 (17%) had "immature E. E. G. patterns" and the great majority (83%) had not. Statistical evaluation of this correlation shows a p value of less than .001. Of some interest is that psychopathy, pregnancy psychosis, severe psychoneurosis and severe alcholism occurred only in relatives of schizophrenic children with "immature E. E. G. patterns". About twice as many close relatives of schizophrenic children with "immature E. E. G. patterns" were also schizophrenic as in those without.

358

Table 4.

Presence or Absence of Immature E. E. G. Patterns in Schizophrenic Children with Mentally Deviant Parents or Siblings

	"Immature E. E. G." "Patterns"	"Mature E. E. G." "Patterns"
Parent Diagnosed as Psychotic during Interview with Psychiatrist	2	1
Parent had Psychiatric Treatment	2	2
Parent seems to have Psychotic History	3	1
Parent Depressed or Attempted Suicide	4	4
Sibling attempted Suicide	0	1
Parents are "nervous"	8	4
Siblings had "Nervous Breakdown"	1	1
Parent is Mentally Unstable	3	1
Problem Siblings	6	3
Parent Alcoholic and Mentally Unstable	7	4
Parent has Childlike Behavior	0	1
Parent is Irresponsible	4	3
Parent is Violent or in Jail	3	2
Parent is Alcoholic	0	4
Parent is Drug Addict	1	2
	44 (61%)	34 (39%)
Parents and Siblings Functioning Adequately Within their Community	8 (17%)	39 (83%)

Chi Square is 18.73.   P. is less than .001.

Out of 78 children whose parents or siblings were described
as being mentally deviant, and some mentally ill as well, 44 (61%)
had "immature E. E. G. patterns" compared to only 8 (17%) in the
control group of 47 schizophrenic children whose close family mem-
ers had no obvious mental deviation. Also in this group, statistical
evaluation shows that the correlation has a p value of less than .001.
One should note that the following conditions occurred more often
among close family members of schizophrenic children with "immature E. E. G. patterns" than in those without: 1) Parents diagnosed
as psychotic during interview with the psychiatrist, 2) Parents who
had a psychotic history, 3) parents who were "nervous" or mentally
unstable or irresponsible, 4) parents who had a history of violence
or had been to jail, 5) parents who were alcoholics as well as
mentally deviant, 6) problem siblings. However, attempted suicide occurred equally in both categories.

The findings indicate that schizophrenic children with "immature E.E.G. patterns" have about 4 times higher psychiatric family morbidity than schizophrenic children without "immature E.E.G. patterns". This is statistically highly significant.

Clinical Evaluation of Procedures leading to Findings:

One might wonder whether the exclusion of 428 of the initially 609 newly admitted disturbed children had introduced a bias into the composition of the remaining 181 children tested, and has led to spurious findings.

Checking up on the first 64 excluded E.E.G. records that were grossly abnormal or desynchronized or had major artifacts, the proportion of the vaguely discerned "immature E.E.G. patterns" was found to be a close to that observed in the non-excluded E.E.G. records. The proportion of psychiatric family morbidity of these 64 children lay between those for children with "immature E.E.G. patterns" and those without. All this suggests that the children as well as the family correlations belonged to approximately the same kind of populations.

Further, 322 children were excluded on whom no "adequate" information on the psychiatric family background was available in the hospital charts. This was mainly due to the fact that the investigating clinical psychiatrist had not asked detailed questions on the life history of each member of the family of the disturbed children, or had noted that the informant was not reliable. Only in some cases was the child adopted and the whole family unknown. This exclusion is not likely to have affected to any significant extent the nature of the child population tested. Certainly, the association of the "immature E.E.G. pattern" with the existence of psychiatric family morbidity would not be affected.

The reliability of the information on the family background could be still questioned. However, apart from the investigating psychiatrist making a note to the effect that the informant gave an impression of reliability, whatever information on a mentally ill patient that was available was checked up in the respective mental institution that furnished it, and it was always found to be correct. Existing psychiatric family morbidity may have been denied, but the number of socalled "normal" families was only 30% which suggests that there was not much denial. Moreover, the social workers having contact with all family members at one time or another usually confirmed it.

The children with and without "immature E. E. G. patterns" were nearly matched as to their age and sex.

The final reduction to 181 children with an unequivocally certain diagnosis is also not likely to have affected the quality of the child population. The approximately 50% of children with"immature E. E. G. patterns" in the sample of 161 children is consistent with the "immature E. E. G. patterns" of the initial sample of 382 schizophrenic children and 82 schizophrenic adults (table 1).

Discussion and Psychiatric Implications:

(1) Earlier in the paper, the author defined as "immature E. E. G. pattern" of children a gross excess of slow waves that did not increase with hyperventilation and the presense of peculiar slow waves of "serrated delta" shape. But this is not quite correct. Strictly speaking, the words "immature E. E. G. patterns" imply that the whole E. E. G. pattern belongs to a younger than chronological age group. This is, however, difficult to establish, for there are great variations within each age group. In addition, the "immaturity" of the E. E. G. can not be quantitatively measured, except perhaps by a count and computation of the whole spectrum of the slow wave population. Also, there sometimes occurred a concentration of the excess of slow waves in one area of the brain that was usually not found in normal younger children. There was also the possibility that the excess of slow waves, although not increasing with hyperventilation, could be associated with some organicity and had nothing to do with immaturity.

Table 5

	Sharp waves and bursts of slow waves in the E.E.G. are related to paranatal brain damage		Immature wave patterns are not related to para- natal brain damage	
	Sharp waves or bursts of slow waves present	Sharp waves or bursts of slow waves absent	"Immature wave pat- tern" present	"Immature wave pat- tern" absent
History suggestive of brain damage	80	6	6	16
History not suggestive of possible brain damage	8	16	16	34

In the past, the author (3) found evidence that medium voltage fast waves, sharp waves, and local bursts of slow waves in the E.E.G. were associated with long-standing, mainly parantal, brain damage. The above table, however, does not suggest that our "serrated delta waves" and gross excess of slow waves, are associated with paranatal brain damage.

There exists a large volume of literature on the physiological significance of what the author called "excess of posterior slow waves" that do not increase with hyperventilation. The majority of the workers think that these are manifestations of immaturity of electrical brain function (1, 13, 14, 15). Some think that they re- flect constitutional or biochemical defects of the brain (20), and one (18) speculated on the possibility of their being psychosomatic manifestations. The author found that in a longitudinal E.E.G. study on several of these children over a period of five years, there was a decrease of "serrated delta waves" in only a few of them. Nevertheless, Kiloh and Osselton (20) summarizing the litera- ture wrote, "There is general agreement that a substantial pro- portion of records show evidence of immaturity.... there has been a lag of the development of the appropriate neurological E.E.G. features...."

(2) The author observed in his schizophrenic children with

"immature E. E. G. patterns" that they are easily crying, clinging, thumbsucking and emotionally immature, much more so than the children with "mature E. E. G. patterns".

Ellingson (8) summarizing the literature reports on apparent agreement that the "immature E. E. G. patterns" are associated with emotional immaturity.

Several workers, (1, 7, 13, 14, 15, 16, 21) report that many psychopaths have in their E. E. G. what they regard as "immature" features, mostly slow activity in the posterior brain areas.

Other workers report that a significant proportion of enuretic children have immature E. E. G. patterns (12, 22).

Kennard (19) mentions that many more of her schizophrenic children had "immature E. E. G. patterns" and a greater E. E. G. evidence for drowsiness and sleep (associated with excess of slow waves) than non-schizophrenic children.

The author observed that schizophrenic children with "immature E. E. G. patterns" had also a greater tendency for poorly organized visual-motor pattern drawings (Bender Gestalt Test) and poorly organized speech (cluttering) than schizophrenic children with "mature E. E. G. patterns".

(3) As previously mentioned, the author found the "immature E. E. G. patterns" in some schizophrenic children, and in at least one sibling or in one of the parents. This in fact, stimulated him to undertake this study.

Several workers (13, 20, 21) suggest that genetic factors may involve the E. E. G. as well as the incidence of psychiatric family morbidity, particularly in subjects with "immature E. E. G. patterns". Only Kennard (18) argues in some cases for environmental stress as a possible cause for the similarity of E. E. G. patterns.

In this connection it was of interest to notice that the "immature E. E. G. patterns" in our schizophrenic children (and in schizophrenic adults) was consistently near 50% whatever sample we took in this study. Thus, one wonders whether the "immature E. E. G. patterns" in our schizophrenic children at least, is a dominant genetic feature.

(4) If the sample of 161 schizophrenic children is really a reflection of all our schizophrenic children, the incidence of mental illness of their parents and siblings is extraordinarily high, more than 22%, and of gross mental deviation about 48%. That is, in 70% of these children, there is marked psychiatric family morbidity. The figure approximately corresponds to the personal experience of the author when dealing with the families of schizophrenic children.

The findings of very high incidence of psychiatric family morbidity, particularly of true mental illnesses, brings up the problem of the etiology of schizophrenia; is it the result of environmentally interpersonal malfunction within the family, or is it of a hereditary nature, or both? Can our seemingly conclusive findings give any clue in the controversy?

When trying to interpret the findings, one has, of course, to keep in mind that human behavior is largely culturally conditioned and dependent on social and economic factors; what may appear not to be mentally deviant in one culture may be so in another. In order to evaluate the findings one has to view them against the background of behavior of the same population outside the hospital. Unfortunately, the author was not able to conduct a study on such control children for administrative reasons.

(5) The author felt that our findings and those reported by others, can perhaps be best understood by using the frame work supplied by Dr. Lauretta Bender on the nature of schizophrenia (4, 5, 6, 7, 8). Her observations led her to believe that schizophrenia is the result of immature brain function and that this lag of maturation is essentially of a hereditary nature (6, 8, 17). She also holds that the maturational lag can be aggravated by brain damage in children and possibly also by environmental stress factors in-

volving the family relationship (6). A child having the syndrome of childhood schizophrenia may, according to the development of various defence mechanisms, evolve to the adult form of schizophrenia, or pseudo-psychopathic schizophrenia, or pseudo-neurotic schizophrenia, or autistic schizophrenia, or to a comparatively "normal" though slightly compulsive schizoid personality(7).

This would give a meaningful structure to our bewildering and seemingly unconnected findings. It would explain the hereditaty nature of the high incidence of schizophrenia, pseudo-psychopathy, pseudo-neurosis, schizophrenic instability and irresponsable behavior of the near relatives of our schizophrenic children with "immature E. E. G. patterns", because all these features may be related to each other by a common underlying hereditary lag of maturation of brain function.

The author is aware that much more work is required to demonstrate unequivocally the significance of the "immature E. E. G. patterns" of schizophrenic children. Investigations have still to be made on control groups of nonschizophrenic children and E. E. G. studies have to be extended to a great number of families in both schizophrenic and non-schizophrenic children and adults before any final assessment can be made.

SUMMARY:

1) The readable E. E. G. tracings of 545 newly admitted disturbed children to the Childrens' Unit of Creedmoor State Hospital were scrutinized for the presence of gross excess of slow waves that did not increase with hyperventilation, and for "posterior serrated delta waves" both of which were called "immature E. E. G. patterns". These patterns were evaluated in relation to the age group of the children.

2) In this group, there were 382 schizophrenic children, 49% of whom had "immature E. E. G. patterns", 87 epileptic and organic psychotic children, 40% of whom had "immature E. E. G. patterns",

and 80 children whose behavior disorder was thought to be the result of interpersonal conditions in the family, 19% of whom had "immature E. E. G. patterns".

3) Of the 545 children, there was adequate information available in 181 on the psychiatric conditions of their parents and siblings as well as an unequivocally certain psychiatric diagnosis.

Out of these 181 children, 161 were diagnosed as schizophrenia (childhood type). Of the latter 78 (48%) had "immature E. E. G. patterns" and 83 (52%) had not.

4) Of the 78 schizophrenic children with "immature E. E. G. patterns", 26 (33%) had at least one parent or sibling in a mental institution, 44 (57%) had at least one mentally deviant parent or sibling, and only 8 (10%) of them had close relatives who seemed to function adequately.

In contrast, of the 73 schizophrenic children with "mature E. E. G. patterns" 10 (12%) has parents or siblings in mental institutions, 34 (41%) had mentally deviant parents or siblings, and 39 (47%) of the close relatives seemed to function adequately.

These findings indicate that schizophrenic children with "immature E. E. G. patterns" have about 4 times (p is less than .001) more psychiatric morbidity in the family than schizophrenic children with "mature E. E. G. patterns". (Critical evaluation of the procedure does not suggest that the findings are affected by the selection of the children).

6) The psychiatric morbidities that were encountered more often in parents or siblings of schizophrenic children with "immature E. E. G. patterns" than in those without, are in order of frequency: schizophrenia, "instability" of parents, "psychotic" parents, "neurotic" or "nervous" parents, problem siblings, psychopathic personality and pregnancy psychosis.

7) This is followed by a critical discussion on the nature of "immature E. E. G. patterns", and on their suggested positive correlation with emotional immaturity, psychopathic personality,

enuresis in children, tendency to sleep in schizophrenic children, poorly organized and variable visual-motor gestalt drawings (Bender Gestalt Test) and poorly organized speech ι (clutter). There is also a suspicion that the "immature E.E.G. patterns" are genetically determined, and the author wondered whether the findings of these "immature E.E.G. patterns" in nearly 50% of the schizophrenic children (and adults) could be an expression of some genetic mechanism.

8) The theory formulated by Dr. Lauretta Bender (6, 8) on a hereditary form of lag of maturation of brain function in schizophrenia, as well as the development from childhood schizophrenia to nearly adequate compensation, or to pseudo-neurotic and pseudo-psychopathic personalities or to adult forms of schizophrenia, were found to be a useful frame for a possible explanation of the relationship between "immature E.E.G. patterns" and schizophrenia.

9) Further investigations into the E.E.G. and psychiatric morbidity on the general child and adult populations are still required to obtain a rounded picture, but could so far not be undertaken by the author.

REFERENCES

1) Aird, R.B., and Gastaut Y. Occipital and posterior Electroencephalographic Rhythms' Defect. Electroenceph. clin. Neurophysiol. 11:637-656, 1959.

2) Andermann, Karl. The high incidence of mental disturbance in the family of schizophrenic children with excess of immature slow waves in the E.E.G. Presented at the Eastern Association of Electroencephalographers, Nov. 1966. Synopsis publ. in, Electroenc. clin. Neurophysiol, 23: 494, 1967.

3) Andermann, Karl. Interpretation of sharp waves and bursts of slow waves in the electroencephalograms of mentally disturbed children. Recent Advanc. Biol. Psychiat. 8 257-268, 1966.

4) Bender, L. The schizophrenic child, in pediatric problems in clinical practice. Michael-Smith, Grune and Stratton, New York, 1954.

5) Bender, L. Childhood schizophrenia. Symposium 1955, Amer. J. Orthopsychiat., July 1956.

6) Bender, L. Organicity in Schizophrenic Children. Proc. London scient. study. Ment. Def. 2: 411-416, 1962.

7) Bender, L. Childhood Schizophrenia: Its Genesis and Course. Congress report of the 2nd International Congress for psychiatry Zurich. Vol. IV September 1957.

8) Bender L. Genetic data in evaluation and management of disordered behavior in children. Diseases of the nervous system, monograph supplement, vol. XXI, February 1960.

9) Cohn, R., and Nardini, J.E. The correlation of Bilateral Occipital slow activity in the human E.E.G. with certain disorders of behavior. Amer. J. Psychiat. 115: 44-54, 1958.

10) Ellingson, R.J. Brain waves and problems of psychology. Psychol. Bull. 53: 1-34, 1956.

11) Gibbs, F.A., and Gibbs, E. Atlas of Electroencephalography. Addison-Wesley publishing, Inc., Reading, Massachusetts and Palo Alto, and London vol. 1. 1951.

12) Gunnarson, S. and Melin, K.A. The electroencephalogram in enuresis. Acta Pediat. (Uppsala) 40: 496-501, 1951.

13) Gottlieb, J.B., Ashby, M.C., and Knott, J.R. Primary behavior disorder and psychopathic personality: I. Correlations of the electroencephalogram with family history and antecedent illness or injury. Arch. Neurol. Psychiat. 56: 381-400, 1946.

14) Hill, D. Psychiatry. In: Electroencephalograph, D. Hill and Parr (Editors) MacDonald and Co., Ltd. pp 319-363, 1950.

15) Hill, D. E.E.G. in episodic psychotic and psychopathic behavior. A classification of data. Electroenceph. clin. Neurophysiol. 4: 419-442, 1952.

16) Hill, D., and Watterson, D. Electroencephalographic studies on psychopathic personalities. J. Neurol. Psychiat. 5: 47-65, 1942.

17) Kallmann, F.J., and Roth, B. Genetic Aspect of preadolescent schizophrenia, Amer. J. Psychiat. 112: 599-606, 1956.

18) Kennard, M.A. Inheritance of electroencephalographic patterns in children with behavior disorder. Psychosom, Med. 11: 151-157, 1949.

19) Kennard, M.A. The E.E.G. in schizophrenia. In: Application of Electroencephalography in Psychiatry, Duke University Press, Durham, North Carolina, p. 177, 1965.

20) Kiloh, L.E. and Osselton, J.W. Clinical E.E.G. Butterworth, London, p. 101, 1961.

21) Knott, J.R., Platt, E.B., Ashby, M.C., and Gottlieb, J.S.A. A familial evaluation of the electroencephalogram of patients with primary behavior disorders and psychopathic personality. Electro. clin. Neurophysiol. 5: 363-370, 1953.

22) Turton, E.C. and Spear, A.B. E.E.G. findings in 100 cases of severe enuresis. Arch.Dis. Child. 28: 316-320, 1953.

K. Andermann, M.D., Child Psychiatry, Creedmoor State Hospital, Queens Village, N.Y. 11427

BIRTH FACTORS IN SCHIZOPHRENIA

ELAINE MURA

The significance of various birth factors in the occurrence and development of many forms of human deviance has long been of interest. Recently, researchers have been able to demonstrate that one or another of these factors seems to correlate with specific physical and/or mental pathology.

This paper shall discuss the relationship between many birth factors and the incidence and course of psychosis--especially schizophrenia. Only studies which are probably or definitely unrelated to purely genetic elements or in which these play a minor role will be evaluated.

To establish some order in this broad field, birth factors have been subdivided into two areas--central and peripheral. The former will cover research into some predominantly organic questions: pregnancy difficulties, unfavorable fetal environment associated with maternal factors, paranatal complications, prematurity, and weight at birth. The latter will deal with circumstantial occurrences surrounding the event of birth:

1. Order of birth and other familial predictors

2. Sex

3. Season of birth

4. Social factors

       a. Race
       b. Migration
       c. Intelligence
       d. Culture
       e. Social class

CENTRAL FACTORS

The fact that individuals can be affected by occurrences and cir-

cumstances in their fetal life has been well demonstrated. Jackson

(1960) describes a number of such cases:

Nutrition

Fetal rickets among the offspring of starving Chinese mothers
showing up at one month in X-Rays despite breast feeding (Maxwell, Hu, Turnbull, 1932)

Altered oxygen supply

Mongolism being associated with hemorrhage and resultant
threatened abortion (Ingalls, 1947)

Increased fetal movkement of arms and legs in severe hemorrhage
and premature separation of placenta with its hemorrhage (Preyer,
1885)

Endocrine system

Insulin content in pancreases of fetuses of diabetic mothers being
twenty-four times that of normals (Gray and Feemster, 1926)

Fetal goiter possibly resulting from maternal inadequately functioning thyroid (Patterson, 1939)

Pseudo-hermaphroditic female infants being born to women who
were administered progestins in their pregnancies (Wilkins,
Jones, Holman, and Stempfel, 1958)

Placental barrier

Increased incidence of congenital deafness in children whose
mothers were heavy users of quinine during malarial season
(Taylor, 1934)

Increase in fetal heart rate comparable to that of many adult
cigarette smokers when the mother smoked during the last three
months of pregnancy. Byproducts of tobacco were found in the
fetal bloodstream (Sontag and Wallace, 1935)

To measure fetal reactivity, Sontag and Richards (1938) placed

a block of wood on the mother's abdomen and struck it with a doorbell

vibrator; they got what was probably a startle reflex in the fetus.

Jackson (1960) noted what looked like fetal learning when he stimu-

lated the fetus at one minute intervals and measured changes in the

heart rate; he found both negative adaptation and recovery.

In contrast to the foregoing physiological effects, Plum (1962)

felt that subnormal intelligence in spastic cerebral palsy was less related to pregnancy or birth factors than to family history (like palsies, subnormal intelligence, psychosis, or epilepsy among close relatives). Previously, in surveying 543 cases of cerebral palsy, Plum (1956) found that, except for toxemia and metrorrhagia, pregnancy factors seemed to be of little etiological significance. However, he did find that birth complications occurred more frequently than normal with certain types of problems related to different varieties of the disease. Observing only birth trauma in 35 children, Schachter (1950) uncovered some personality correlates related to whether or not the individual experiences birth abnormalities, with deviance appearing in adulthood in one-third to one-half of the afflicted group (particularly alcoholism and subsequent neuropsychiatric disorders). He found that asphyxia did cause some retardation compared to a control group of one hundred normal children. When Ucko (1965) investigated two groups of 29 boys each longitudinally for five years, he found no differences in either intellectual or emotional development between the asphyxiated and normal group. However, he did discover some significant differences in temperamental characteristics, with the asphyxiated being unusally sensitive, overreactive, having a tendency to "disequilibrium" when their normal routine was broken.

When Pasamanick and Knobloch (Chapter 4 in Caplan, 1961) found pregnancy difficulties to be associated with cerebral palsy, epilepsy, mental deficiency, behavior disorders, reading disabilities, and tics, they distinguished between prolonged or difficult labor and employment of operative procedures (like Caesarian, forceps, breech) and stated that, the association occurred rather with prolonged anoxia, producing complications of pregnancy like toxemia and maternal bleeding. Weidon (1954) also found toxemia to be significantly higher (46. 4% in schizophrenic patients and 22. 2% in controls). Pre-eclamptic toxemia is known to produce a thrombosis of part of the vascular system of the placenta that becomes fibrosed, thus cutting off the oxygen supply to the fetus. It is not unusual for one-third or more of the placental tissue to be destroyed by long-standing toxemic pregnancy.

These studies, as Jackson (1960, p. 183) suggests, "offer further evidence of the importance of fetal environment as a determinant of behavior postnatally, perhaps, as well as prenatally."

Certain women are reported to be vulnerable to pregnancy complications and produce abnormal offspring with behavior disorders. In studying families with two or more hospitalized for psychiatric illnesses, Lucas, Rodin, Simson (1965) found a very high incidence of paranatal complications. This concurs with world-wide epidemiological studies which have shown that whenever disturbed children are studied, there is a much higher percentage of them who have had a typical birth experiences (Pasamanick, Rogers, and Lilienfeld, 1956).

The majority of studies relating birth and pregnancy complications to psychosis and schizophrenia have been carried out with children. Analysis of five studies discussing childhood schizophrenics by Pollack and Woerner (1966) revealed a significant association between complications of pregnancy and psychosis in children; they ascribed the ambiguity of findings regarding birth complications to differing categories used by the authors. A summary of this study illustrates the type of study, methodology, and findings typical of this area.

Comparing 43 psychotic children and their 66 siblings, Whittam, Simon, and Mittler (1966) found that the psychotic group contained a significantly higher proportion of children (67%) with one or more abnormalities in the pre-, peri-, or early post-natal period than the sibling group (33%). Interestingly, the patients had a lower incidence of toxemic history suggested by some authors to be the crucial factor than either their siblings or the general population. They also found that children with retarded motor milestones tended to be those with a history of abnormal delivery (highly significant). None of the psychotic children showed normal speech development--true for 12% of the sibling group, which is also an unusually high proportion. Besides complications of pregnancy and birth, health of the psychotic children in

TABLE I

Year	Author	Subjects	Controls	Methodology	Results	Abn	Norm
1960	Vorster	15 schiz. children (10 M, 5 F) 4-14 seen at guidance clinic—no organic problems	33 normal sibs (19M, 14 F) 2-25	Retrospective questionnaire, maternal interview, hospital records in 2/3 cases	Preg. comp. Birth & neonat comp. including prematurity Infantile ill. Abortion just pre or post	.05 NS .01 NS	
1962	Knobloch and Pasamanick	50 early infant autism in Ohio (34 M, 16 F) 11 weeks–9 years some organic problems	1. 50 abnorm without autism but some organic disorders (23 M, 27 F) 2. 50 norm lower socio-ec status (27 M, 23 F)	Retrospective maternal interview	Preg. comp. Abnorm del. Premat (BW) Neonatal abnorm.	NS .05 NS NS	.01 .05 NS NS
1963	Hinton	62 psychotic out-patients in Ontario 46—evidence of or-ganic brain dis-order 10 mean age (39 M, 23 F)	62 consecutive admissions to children's hosp. for tonsillectomy 6.1 mean age (29 M, 33 F)	Retrospective parental interview, hospital records	Preg. comp. Birth and neonat compl. including prematurity Prematurity (BW) Severe infantile illness or feed-ing difficulties		NS NS NS .01
1964	Taft and Goldfarb	29 schiz. inpat. NYC 6-11 (21 M, 8 F)	1. 39 sibs (20 M, 19F) 2. 34 pub sch ch socio-ec, age matched (17M,17F)	Retrospective maternal interview physician and hospital records	Preg. comp. Boys .05 Girls .05 Birth and neonat comp. incl. Prem. Boys .001 Girls .10		
1964	Terris and Lapouse Monk	463 schiz. ch. Bellevue 2-12 (372 M, 91 F)	463 matched ch. NYC	Retrospective maternal interview Hospital records	Abnorm del. Premat (BW) History of prev-ious stillbirths or abortions	NS NS .02	

the first year of life was also poorer, suggesting higher risk dis-
posing to a handicapping condition. Gittelman and Birch (1967) also
found excessive perinatal complications in 97 schizophrenic children
attending a day school for disturbed children, particularly characterizing those children with subnormal mentality. Twenty-five per cent
of that group, as a matter of fact, was subsequently rediagnosed as
mentally subnormal and/or chronically brain damaged. In the entire
group, central nervous system pathology was evident in 80 per cent,
revealing that neurologically damaged may also be encountered outside
an institution. By contrast, Osterkamp and Sands (1962) found that
birth difficulties alone did not differentiate schizophrenic and neurotic
children--but that when a patient had experienced both birth difficulties
and feeding difficulties (especially a difficult and short period of breast
feeding), he was more likely to fall into the schizophrenic group. This
is consonant with Osterkamp's finding (1962) that mothers of schizophrenics more often try breast feeding unsuccessfully (both frequency
and lack of success characterizing the group). Investigating 286 psychotic children (including hospital admissions, outpatients in both a
child guidance clinic and consulation with a private psychiatrist), Bender
and Faretra (1962) found that a significantly high number had pregnancy
and birth complications. They especially found maternal illness, bleeding, and toxemia in the period of pregnancy and delivery and respiratory
disturbances related to anoxia in the period of birth to be most frequent
among schizophrenics. In disagreement, Patterson, Block, Block and
Jackson (1960) found no significant differences between schizophrenic,
non-schizophrenic but disturbed, and normal children on this axis.
The findings specifically related to autistic children have been inconclusive, with Kanner (1957) showing significantly increased rates of
pregnancy complications, Lotter (1967) showing significantly fewer
than non-autistic but handicapped controls, and Rimland (1964) showing no significant difference between autistics and normals. He did,

however, find that many mothers had experienced bleeding and had a history of previous miscarriage and stillbirth, reminiscent of Terris Monk and Lapouse's finding of a definite association between childhood schizophrenia and previous fetal loss (1964).

In deviant adolescents, Pollack (1967) found a significant incidence of pre- or peri-natal abnormalities, especially in the group with a history of learning defects and behavior disorders in childhood. Pollack, Levenstein, and Klein (1968) also found that early minimal brain damage of a pre- or para-natal origin may be the significant factor in the development of adult psychopathology in some patients. Those in this category had a poorer prognosis: as the severity of their damage increased, almost one hundred per cent of their hospitalized schizophrenic patients fell into the "very poor" group of chronics. In a third study, Pollack and Greenberg (1966) also found a significant relationship between paranatal complications and psychosis, with the highest incidence of such complications being significantly correlated with personality disorders and almost none appearing in the history of affective disorders. In their 71 consecutively admitted patients, they also found that onset was significantly associated with birth abnormalities, with those having severe complications also having a lower age of onset. In fact, twice as many in the severe group (as compared to none or moderate) were treated in adolescence. Specifically in schizophrenia, a younger onset was noted for those with both moderate and severe paranatal abnormalities; 78 per cent in the moderate and 89 per cent in the severe group were treated under the age of 18 compared to 14 per cent who had no birth complications.

When comparing monozygotic twins discordant for schizophrenia, Stabenau and Pollin (1967) found that birth complications differentiated the index from the health--specifically neonatal asphyxia. They suggested that this might be due to the index twin's often being second born, thus being more likely to experience periods of anoxic cyanosis during delivery or respiratory distress thereafter. Rosenthal (1963) also reported severe pregnancy and birth complications in quadruplets concordant for schizophrenia; however, this might have been an artefact of a multiple birth of this size in an older woman.

Studies discussing the association between pregnancy and birth factors and psychosis using adult subjects have been few--suggesting either that their being farther away from the event of birth causes researchers to think less in terms of these factors and more in terms of psychological stresses in developing theories of etiology or simply that fewer significant correlations have been drawn in this population. The foregoing empirical evidence suggests the former possibility.

Prematurity

If a correlation could be drawn between prematurity and psychosis, this would also tend to support an organic etiology in schizophrenia, the rationale being that either more fetal complications have resulted in birth before full term or more fetal complications have caused a premature birth. Pasamanick and Knobloch (Chapter 4 in Caplan, 1961) found that prematurity was probably involved in brain injury, especially when precipatated by toxemia or bleeding. If this is considered as lowering the threshhold to stress in an individual already predisposed to schizophrenia, then the incidence of mental illness should be higher.

Studies have found prematurity to be related to several other subsequent events. Graham, Ernhart, Thurston, and Craft (1962) found that 16.7 per cent of a group of premature children performed abnormally on one or more tests of cognitive functioning compared to 6.9 per cent of the normal full-term group. Cutler (1965) also found depressed intellectual functioning in premature Negro babies which she attributed to the high incidence of neurologic damage, especially among males. However, even without neurological abnormalities, she found depressed IQ and gross motor scores in comparison with full-term matched controls.

In mental deficiency, Lilienfeld, Pasamanick, and Rogers (1955) noted significantly more retarded Negro children to be premature even with no significant difference in pregnancy complications. They also concluded that complications of pregnancy and prematurity were significantly associated with epilepsy, behavior disorders, reading disabilities, and cerebral palsy. Studying cerebral palsy, Plum (1962) also found a large number of prematures, especially girls who were also smaller. Pasamanick and Knobloch (Chapter 4 in Caplan, 1961) attempted to separate the effects of prematurity and birth weight -- often confused in these studies since, of course, premature infants are usually lighter in weight --and found that 44 per cent with a birth weight under 1500 grams had abnormal conditions of serious magnitude, compared to 8.6 per cent in the rest of the premature group and 2.6 per cent in full-term controls. They also designated more prematures as having "minimal damage."

The majority of studies investigating the variable of prematurity found significantly higher rates of prematurity in schizophrenics. Lane and Albee (1966) noted that in 52 schizophrenic adults, five were premature at birth compared to five in a control group of 115 siblings; this represents a significant difference which they felt might even be larger in future since some of the siblings might also become schizophrenic. Three studies investigating children also were relevant. For the autistic child, Kanner (1957) found very significantly higher rates of prematurity when organic entities were removed from the sample; these were, however, similar to children who were organically impaired but without autism. Keeler (1957) pointed out the same for autistic children as well as a lack of movement before birth in most of them. Bender and Faretra (1962) also concluded that prematurity was a significant factor in schizophrenic children. Terris Monk and Lapouse (1964), on the other hand, found no significant differences between 463 children diagnosed as schizophrenic and matched controls (9. 2 per cent rate for cases and 8. 4 per cent for controls).

In twins, Rosenthal (1963) found no increase in rate of schizophrenia despite their high incidence of prematurity (even making them, he adds, a deviant sample in this respect). In a sample of 10,000 cases of premature monozygotic twins, in fact, he found only seven who were said to be schizophrenic. On the other hand, Pasamanick and Knobloch (Chapter 4 in Caplan, 1961) found twinning to be more common among cases of neuropsychiatric disorders--possibly relating, they feel, to the significantly higher incidence of prematurity. Havelkova (1967) commented on the unusually high number of twins in 29 families with schizophrenic children.

The empirical data reveals a possible but still ambiguous relationship between prematurity and schizophrenia. Of interest is the number of studies utilizing children which reached significance, possibly suggesting that prematurity effects are more readily discernible in children, with adults compensating--or simply that researchers interested in childhood psychosis tend to analyze birth data like this more closely.

Birth Weight

For those interested in establishing a relationship between organic damage or physiological weakness (leading to high risk) and incidence of psychosis, the question of birth weight is especially important. If birth weight could be shown to be lower for the mentally ill than for normal siblings or the general population, some link inferring organic causation would appear plausible. Studies which have been carried out have illustrated that birth weight is in fact lower for those afflicted with cerebral palsy (Plum, 1956). Knobloch, Rider, Harper, and Pasamanick (1956) have also found that the rate of neuropsychiatric abnormalities increased as birth weight decreased.

Several explanations have been offered to explain the existence of a correlation between birth weight and psychosis. One is, of course, the organic theory which suggests either a higher risk for a lighter baby or simply that a less adaptive baby is born smaller. Another theoretical possibility is that birth weight is really reflecting the lower class membership of the mother. When comparing 377 high income mothers with 1019 low income mothers, Baird (1945) found that smaller women in the lower wage group had a higher proportion of light babies than women of the corresponding size in a well-to-do group. He explained this as being reflective of the poorer diets of the low income group who were undernourished in their youth and grew about three inches shorter on the average --and shorter women tend to have lighter babies. The fact that maternal diet may affect birth weight has been suggested by the finding that children born in the summer are significantly lighter (Pasamanick and Knobloch, Chapter 4 in Caplan, 1961), when maternal dietary intake (especially protein) decreases. The relationship of diet to birth weight has also been studied by Ebbs, Tisdall, Scott, Moyle, and Bell (1942) who followed babies from pregnancy through six months of age for three groups of mothers: a poverty group with poor diets, a poverty group whose diets had been liberally supplemented, and a middle class well-nourished group. Surprisingly, they found that the heaviest babies (averaging seven pounds ten ounces) were born to the unsupplemented poorly fed women, while the other two groups were almost the same (seven pounds seven ounces). However, two weeks later the babies in the unsupplemented poverty group were judged to be generally poorer in condition compared to the other two--with the supplemented diet babies being in the best condition! Six months later the influence of a well-nourished mother apparently finally became noticeable when this group of babies was found to have significantly fewer illnesses--of course, this may reflect differential class hygienic standards or postnatal care. Paffenbarger et.

_al._'s study (1961) noted that alive infants born to women suffering from post-partum psychosis weighed less than average; perhaps the mother's attitude or her physiological condition might affect the weight of the child. Paffenbarger found more hypertension and headaches during pregnancy--but suggested that this might reflect organic dysfunctions which he hypothesizes as etiological in post-partum psychosis.

Drawing an empirical correlation between birth weight and schizophrenia has yielded ambiguous results. Some studies uncover no significant differences between cases and controls (Terris, Lapouse and Monk, 1964; Pollack and Woerner, 1966, analyzing studies by Vorster, 1960; Knobloch and Pasamanick, 1962; Hinton, 1963; Terris, Lapouse and Monk, 1964; Taft and Goldfarb, 1964 with only the latter yielding significance for boys). Some studies have shown birth weights for schizophrenics to be significantly lower. Lane and Albee (1966, 1967) found a significant difference: 52 schizophrenic adults with 115 siblings were found to have an average mean difference of six ounces less with schizophrenics averaging seven pounds and siblings averaging seven and one-half pounds Seventy per cent weighed less than the average for siblings, while 61 per cent weighed the least in the family at birth no matter what the number of siblings. Whittem, Simon, and Mittler (1966) similarly noted that a higher proportion of psychotic children weighed five and one-half pounds or less (but this just failed to reach significance at .06).

In multiple births, the twin lighter at birth has been found to be the schizophrenic one in later life (Pollin, Stabenau, Mosher, and Tupin, 1965; Stabenau and Pollin, 1967). A single case of quadruplets (Rosenthal, 1963) concordant for schizophrenia revealed that the two lighter at birth became in later life the chronic, sicker patients, while the heavier two achieved a more satisfactory (although minimal) life adjustment. The Stabenau-Pollin twin study also found the schizophrenic one to be shorter and weaker, comparable to Simon and Gillies study (1964) which noted that when the physical characteristics of 34 psychotic children were compared to the normal standard, the psychotics were significantly below their peers in weight (above and below the fifth percentile), bone age (over half below the 25 percentile and one-third below the tenth), and height (the majority below the tenth percentile). Although controversial, the empirical findings lean slightly in the direction of no significance. In contrast, the results in prematurity studies show a more frequent association, interesting in light of the fact that some analyses seem to have defined prematurity in terms of lighter-than-average birth weight.

Maternal Factors

Many relationships have been documented between the physiological and mental state of the pregnant woman and the fetus. Masland (Chapter 3 in Caplan, 1961) mentions empirical links drawn between a number of maternal factors and the outcome of pregnancy:

1. Nutrition
2. Physical activity (like heavy manual labor)
3. Maternal immune reactions
4. Physique
5. Heart volume
6. Illness or infections
7. Massive X-Ray
8. Toxin intake (like abortive agents, tobacco)
9. Hormones (like cortisone and insulin)
10. Electrophoretic pattern of blood proteins
11. Emotional status

The relationship between emotional states and fetal reactions is probably largely an endocrinological event--for example, blood sugar and ultimately epinephrine being liberated by emotional excitement, passing through the placental barrier, and affecting the endocrine balance in the fetus. In the study at Fells Research Institute, Jackson (1960, p. 184) observed both pre- and post-natal effects of maternal emotional stress. In a group of 300 children, the pregnancies of five women were traumatic (that is to say, husbands died or abandoned their wives, etc.) In each, fetal heart rate increased by 20-25 beats a minute--this phenomena lasting over weeks. After birth, all five babies were also found to be hyperactive, irritable and restless; they cried more, had more interruptions in sleep, had more hyperactive gastrointestinal tracts so that they experienced more bowel movements, a greater intolerance for food, and more spitting up. Stott (cited in Bender and Faretra, 1962) found a significant association between frequency of emotional shock and other psychosomatic stress in pregnancy and defective children--suggesting other abnormalities resulting from maternal emotional state.

It, therefore, seems reasonable to assume that maternal factors might enter into the production of psychotic offspring. In fact, some studies have shown a relationship between emotional stress and schizophrenia. Ricks and Nameche (1965 cited in Lane and Albee, 1966) found that traumatic pregnancies (defined as "crises levels of mental disorder in the mother during pregnancy or immediately thereafter, extreme disruption of family life at the time of pregnancy, serious physical illness in the mother, and illegitimacy") differentiated mothers whose infants later became schizophrenic adults from a group of controls. They suggest that since the birth was associated with a period of tension that exceeded other pregnancies of the same mother, she was less well organized and able to cope with the child--clearly a different interpretation of the data strongly leaning to a psychological etiology. Similarly, a psychological attitude has been shown to have little effect on offspring. Patterson, Block, Block, and Jackson (1960) found that mothers with unplanned pregnancies had more physical symptoms than those who had planned pregnancies, but that these probably psychosomatic complaints were not correlated to later schizophrenia, psychosis, or normality in the infant.

The mental status of the mother could also affect the offspring. Paffenbarger, Steinmetz, Pooler, and Hyde (1961) found that mothers who later suffered from post-partum psychosis tended to complain of headaches and manifested hypertension during the pregnancy. They also had more respiratory illnesses and dystocia. This might be linked to the lower birth weight of their infants and their tendency to be premature. As a matter of fact, although this seems at first glance to be an association based on emotional factors, Paffenbarger hypothesizes that this is in fact a physiological disorder associated with hormonal imbalance due to pregnancy. Actual physical increase in ovarian insufficiency has also been found in hebrephrenic and catatonic patients (Elasser and Subke cited in Bellak, 1958). Perhaps a factor of this nature might ultimately explain the higher incidence of schizophrenia in offspring of schizophrenic mothers or at least their deviance. Fish (1962) described such a difference in the children of hospitalized schizophrenic mothers, with children showing some evidence of disturbance in the functioning of the nervous system; they were described as either excessively quiet or excessively irritable. Fish hypothesizes a similarity between this behavior and the motility, excitability, and perceptual disturbances she has observed in older schizophrenic children.

Even the moment of conception has been linked to psychosis in the offspring. Heuyer, Lebovici, and Roumajon (cited in Caplan, 1955) suggested that an association might exist between the fact that a woman was intoxicated at the moment of conception and her son's psychosis. However, Caplan dispels this connection "adduced to hide our ignorance."

Table 2

CENTRAL FACTORS: Survey of Studies Cited in this Section

Factor	Significant	Not Significant
Pregnancy Complications	M and F--7	M and F--1 1 fewer
Birth Complications	M and F--12 M only -- 1	M and F--3 F only -- 1
Prematurity	M and F--4 M only -- 1	M and F--5 F only -- 1
Birth Weight	M and F--3 M only -- 1	M and F--5 F only -- 1
Infantile Illness	M and F--2	
Abortion or Stillbirth	M and F --1	M and F--1
Neonatal Abnormality		M and F--1

Theories

Several organic theories have evolved from the work on birth and pregnancy factors and psychosis which are similar but have a different emphasis. The first will be referred to as the genetic-precipitation theory. The major proponent of this view has been Lauretta Bender. In essence, schizophrenia is described as being initially an inherited predisposition decompensated by an intrauterine or para-natal noxious or traumatic event. This brain damaged or otherwise defective or traumatized infant who might have had only a marginal handicap will suffer more from deprivation, hospitalization, and separation from the mother, even for shorter periods, than the potentially normal child. Recently, Bender (1955) has defined schizophrenia as "a maturational lag at the embryonic level in all areas which integrate biological and psychological behavior; an embryonic primitivity or plasticity characterizes the pattern of the behavior disturbances in all areas of personality functioning. It is determined before birth and hereditary factors appear to be important. It may be precipitated by a physiological crisis which may be birth itself, especially a traumatic birth." Stabenau (1968) states a similar view: "There is evidence to postulate a genetic component to the etiology of schizophrenia; however, detailed family study of monozygotic twins discordant for schizophrenia suggests there are pre- and/or post-natal experiential environmental components necessary for schizophrenia to emerge in a given individual."

Pollack also postulates an organic theory which will be referred to as the cognitive disorganization theory. In contradistinction to the former theory, which based much importance on the genetic component in schizophrenia, he describes a model based on the interaction of cerebral dysfunction, childhood social deviancy, and increasing stress of changes created by advancing age. A crucial factor in his hypothesis is the presence of early minimal brain damage of a pre- or para-natal origin. While this is not especially radical, he goes on to suggest that "neurological as well as psychiatric dysfunctions in the child originate from organic disorders in central nervous system integration." (Pollack and Gittelman, 1964) "The critical factor seems to be cognitive disorganization, not paranatal complications per se, and the temperamental patterns resulting from interference with normal brain development." (Pollack and Greenberg, 1966)

In discussing infantile autism, Rimland (1964) postulates a similar problem in conceptual impairment; however, he more specifically suggests a malfunction of the reticular formation as the direct cause since this portion of the brain "provides the driving force in facilitating cortical activity and is felt to be the site at which sensory input is integrated and converted to a code which makes it compatible with the retrieval system used in making available a wide range of content of memory." Hyperoxia, he specifies, is a possible factor in the malfunction of the reticular formation. He also cites the biological law which states that organisms destined to reach higher states of development are most vulnerable to damage by adverse environmental conditions. "Austistic children were genetically vulnerable as a consequence of inborn capacity for high intelligence."

Pasamanick and Knobloch (Chapter 4 in Caplan, 1961) have hypothesized the existence of a continuum of reproductive assault, with abortions, stillbirths, and neonatal deaths on one end and varying degrees of neuropsychiatric disability (like cerebral palsy, epilepsy, and child behavior disorders) at the other. They base their model on the theory that maternal and fetal factors causing anoxia, toxemia, hemorrhage, and prematurity result in either lethal damage to the fetus or sublethal damage to the brain. They mention that the continuum is at least partially socio-economically determined and suggest preventive programs in the prenatal and even pre-conception period.

Another theoretical conception might be termed polycausal. Jackson (1960) suggests that although nutritional, endocrinological, toxic, and emotional factors in the fetal environment bear no known relationship to the etiology of schizophrenia, they do indeed bear a relationship to constitution. "... Such modification of a constitutional character in the biochemical and physiological nature of the brain cells may be influenced adversely by fetal environment, and that at a later date they may be responsible for grave behavioral deviation. " (p. 185) "It seems to me, therefore, that it is only rational to think of schizophrenia as a somatopsychic disease, one in which the cerebral physiology, determined and modified as it may be by genic inheritance and by prenatal and postnatal environment, that is adverse at least to that individual, to create psychological defense mechanisms that may be both physiologically and psychologically inappropriate and inadequate for the organism's protection. " (p. 186)

In contrast to most of the foregoing theories, Brackbill and Fine (1956) clearly differentiate two different etiologies, depending on whether the patient is diagnosed process or reactive schizophrenic. They suggest that the former is reflective of central nervous system involvement (the result of infection or trauma) while the latter might be primarily psychological. This might explain the different course and functioning observed in the two groups.

In summary, most authors investigating pregnancy and birth factors in the etiology of schizophrenia suggest that in an individual predisposed to the illness such assaults seem to raise the risk for the emergence of schizophrenia. In combination with unfavorable social factors, the disease entity we know as schizophrenia emerges.

Critique

The birth and pregnancy factor studies may be criticized severely on several counts The first problem is in the selection of the subjects. If hospitalized patients are used, the assumption is that their psychopathology is serious enough to warrant institutionalization. Since more than half of schizophrenics are out patients (Rosenthal, 1963), this may not make generalization over the entire population feasible. Diagnosis is another difficulty, since diagnoses are usually subjective and often change in the course of treatment or with the change of expectations accompanying the increase of age. Definition of the defect can also be difficult because some conditions (like mental deficiency or behavior disorders) are not entities but symptom complexes related to a variety of etiologies. Lumping them together may invalidate results. Specifically in twin studies (considered especially enlightening when discordance is present since genetic similarities are erased as a variable), some glaring problems are present. According to Rosenthal (1963), same sexed twins may live in the same geographic area (contributing to a sampling error). Males may migrate more (bringing the later to be described variable of migrant disposition into play), while females may stay and be maintained at home. Furthermore, the healthy-unhealthy ratio may be disturbed by later onset of psychosis in the "normal" twin. Two physiological factors may enter into the interpretation of findings: monozygotic twins, who share maternal circulation, may be differentially affected, with one being disadvantaged. Twins are anyway a deviant sample, being more prone to both prematurity and fetal death than singletons. Especially in this field of central factors, the inclusion of so many children and so few adults in studies might lead one to question the generality of the findings.

Another problem is in the collection of relevant data. Hospital records are notoriously unreliable (Masland in Caplan, 1961). In Oppenheimer et. al.'s 1957 report, hospital records were often found to be incomplete; the following percentages of completeness suggest the unreliability of such data:

Table 3

Data	Hospitals			
	1	2	3	4
Rh Factor	32	13	84	93
Serology	78	13	83	99
Anaesthesia	64	5	100	100
Weight of Infant	89	90	100	100
Infant Physical Exam	93	51	100	55

As is readily obvious from even cursory examination, the quality of hospital reports varied considerably. The retrospective interview (usually maternal) also has serious drawbacks. Wenar (1963) summarized his investigations into this area of recall as follows:

1. Information on pregnancy and delivery
   Good for overall gestation and delivery
   Poor for health during pregnancy, duration of delivery, maternal injuries during delivery, use of instruments, immediate difficulties with neonate

2. Factual development data
   Good for motor development
   Poor for weight after first year

3. Illnesses
   One third of major and one half of minor forgotten (including pneumonia and tuberculosis!)

4. Child rearing practices
   Good for breast feeding
   Poor for thumb-sucking, toilet training, personal and social independence encouragement

5. Interpersonal relationships
   Poor in all areas

Wenar also found that the passage of time did not matter: what a mother remembered was well-remembered; the forgotten was forgotten forever. Boys' mothers recalled better than girls'. Social class did not affect the frequency of errors, but rather the type. Robbins (1963) studied this problem with similar results. In 47 upper middle and upper class Jewish families with mothers and fathers both being well educated (most college plus) and many holding advanced degrees in medicine, law, or even psychology, the inaccuracy of recall was striking. Even with frequency of interviews (they were in a longitudinal study), they did not improve. Their inaccuracies were greatest in items dealing with age of weaning and toilet training, occurrence of thumbsucking, and demand feeding; they tended to be in the direction of the recommendations of experts. In contrast to the evident unreliability of retrospective reports, Pollack and Greenberg (1966) suggested that parental reports may be less distorted than one is led to believe, since in their study one group (personality trait disturbances) reported such difficulties and one (affective disorders) did not. Clearly they saw no reason to assume a differential bias in one mother over another.

Another important problem is the formulation and interpretation of results. Dependent variables are built right into the studies: for example, authors have shown prematurity to be correlated significantly with lower social class and height of the mother. The danger of focussing on a specific factor (like toxemia) might well result in ignoring the other important variables which might be interrelated or independent.

With the many difficulties existing in carrying on these studies and interpreting the results, it is surprising that the data seems to hold in so many of the pregnancy and birth studies.

Problems specifically related to birth weight and prematurity findings are similar--however, a few added difficulties present themselves. Birth weight and prematurity are often pooled or confused in these studies. Some use the two interchangeably, with prematurity being defined as lower birth weight. When authors have attempted to divide the two, they have often found no significance where it existed before. Another ambiguity in interpretation is present. Perhaps, these are not the important variables at all, but merely causative of later poorer adjustment due to differential maternal treatment-- with the mother tending to overprotect the smaller and weaker. In the case of the Genain quadruplets, the opposite was found to be true; the fact that the two smallest and lightest became the sickest might have reflected their mother's rejection, this pair constantly being shoved aside in favor of the other. Social class variables are apparently important as well. For example, Pasamanick, Knobloch, and Lilienfeld (1956) discovered that prematurity and social class seemed significantly correlated. In their sample, five per cent were upper class whites, 14. 6 per cent were lower class white, and a whopping 50. 6 per cent were lower class Negroes--suggesting as well a confounding racial variable. Baird (1945) found the same overrepresentation of prematurity in lower class English mothers, with 8.38 per cent in this group as compared to five per cent in an upper class group. The latter were also almost always for the usual medical reasons (85 per cent) while the former were often unexplained (52 per cent). If such strong class effects show up, it should not be surprising that significant differences are often found in child psychotics who have been found to reflect this variable more than adults (von Brauchitsch and Kirk, 1967).

PERIPHERAL FACTORS

Birth Order

A relationship between ordinal position in the family constellation and incidence of psychosis has been the topic of serious investigation since the 1950's. When in 1959 Schachter formulated some hypotheses regarding the psychological effects of being born first or last in the family, he renewed interest in this subject. Briefly, Schachter's position was that first-born children are more affiliative-- that is to say, they prefer social outlets for their anxieties and prefer to be with others when in stressful situations. His rationale was that first-born children spend more of their earlier life with adults and are more dependent on them (their parents have sufficient time to lavish attention on them and the inexperience to pay doting and overprotective heed to every untoward movement they make). On the other hand, later-born children get little parental attention and tend to spend more time alone, thus becoming more self sufficient and tending to handle their problems in an asocial manner. If in fact such differences in personality (the gregarious vs. the withdrawn approach to anxiety) do exist, then birth order should have an effect on the occurrence, course, and treatment of psychosis. The organic approach to psychosis would postulate a similar tendency for the later-born to show more deviance; however, the reason would stem instead from the less favorable intrauterine environment to which the later-born is subjected. In support of this prediction, Pasamanick and Knobloch (in Caplan, 1961) found that increasing birth order increased the risk for mental deficiency. The implication of heightened fetal and neonatal risk of damage could have ramifications in the occurrence of psychosis, but thus far most of the studies have theorized regarding the psychological rather than the physiological possibilities. A third interpretation might be cultural: since expectations and stresses differ (especially in non-Western cultures) different family position could affect adjustment. Generally, the prediction has been in the direction of more breakdown among the more stressed group, the first-born children.

Some early studies into this question investigated the relationship of ordinal position and deviant behavior. For example, Bakan (1949) found that later-born siblings were significantly overrepresented in the alcoholic population--the likelihood of becoming alcoholic increasing as the number of older siblings increased, so that younger children in larger families had the highest probability of becoming alcoholic. The psychological causality of this fact was evolved by Schachter (1959), who suggested that having fewer social outlets, the younger in the family would turn to an isolated means of facing problems--alcohol--rather than to talking them out or seeking therapy (Wiener and Stieper in Schachter, 1959). However, a physiological explanation might be inferred from Schachter's study (1950), which found that one-third of a group of individuals who had suffered a serious birth trauma became alcoholics in adulthood (among other defects including 47 per cent retardation and 42 per cent neurologic manifestations). As the alcoholic group was correlated with subsequent appearance of neuropsychiatric disorder, one might question whether the appearance of alcoholism and psychiatric disturbance both might not be a function of undetected or minimal paranatal damage occasioned by later birth. Both Bakan's and Schachter's studies could be criticized for possibly presenting data confounded by social class variables; however, Schachter (1959, p. 71) found that the birth order effect held in duration of therapy even when the increased size of the family suggested increased lower class participation. The evidence linking ordinal position and other behavior deviances is con- tradictory. While Sletto (1934) noted more early-born siblings and Burt (1925) more only boys to number in the ranks of the delinquent, Baker, Decker, and Hill (1929) and Slawson (1926) found no relationship what- ever. The same seems true for childhood behavior disorders, where Rosenow and Whyte (1934) and Bender and Faretra (1952) found first or second-born children to preponderate, while Levy (1932) also uncovered no relationship. Earlier Rosenow and Whyte (1931) found that the middle child in the three-sibling family was more often treated in guidance clin- ics. Measuring for psychological problems by the Taylor Manifest Anx- iety Scale was attempted by Schachter (1959, p. 66), who administered this test to 298 undergraduates; he found no significant relationship or systematic trends between birth order and disturbances. However, this author's reanalysis suggests sexually differentiated trends in the direction of more middle-born males manifesting anxiety, compared to females, who seem more anxious if the oldest in a large family or the later-born in a small family. Neurosis has also been empirically found to occur significantly more often in all position in the family con- stellation (Spiegel and Bell in Arieti, 1959) or to be insignificant (Caudill, 1963).

With inconclusive findings such as the above in the birth order literature, it is not surprising that research linking order of birth and psychosis has been controversial.

The typical study has utilized male and/or female hospitalized patients--primarily adults and often chronic. It has generally been carried out in countries with Western European culture (although re- cently a few studies have appeared from Asiatic countries). Numbers have varied from sparse (32) to huge (2227), with occasional use of control groups. Many times, however, birth order effects have been tangential findings either thrown in to fill space or pulled in to explain confusing results. Most U. S. studies after 1959 have relied on Schachter's retionale if at all possible, while cross-cultural results have been explained in terms of traditionalism. Some researchers have examined the first or last ordinal positions. Others have suggested that first half and last half findings are statistically stronger due to the increased number. The research abounds in both types of analysis; some authors, in fact, use both to achieve significance.

The following studies illustrate the type of research and findings in the field.

A summary of the results of studies carried out in the last twelve years reveals the following patterns: some studies have shown schizophrenic males to be first born (Caudill, 1963; Schooler, 1964; Rao, 1964; Sundraraj and Rao, 1966); others have shown them to be later or last born (Wahl, 1954, 1956; Granville-Grossman, 1966). One study (Nowicki, 1967) stresses the deviance of the middle born, and several studies qualify their findings: first-born males in small (2-3) families or upper-class families (Barry and Barry, 1967; Solomon and Nuttall, 1967). First-born males have also been found to be more socially isolated (chronic hospitalized patients) by Schooler, 1964.

For schizophrenic females, results are somewhat more confirmatory. Most studies found that they are more often last or later born (Schooler, 1961; Farina, Barry and Garmezy, 1963; Caudill, 1963; Paffenbarger, 1964). Two studies found no significance but were in the direction of last (Smith and McIntyre, 1963) and first (Sundararaj and Rao, 1966), while one uncovered no significant trend at all (Granville-Grossman, 1966). Schooler and Scarr (1962) and Schooler (1964) found first-born females hospitalized for schizophrenia to be more sociable and later born to be less sociable (with only children, in contrast to Schachter, being the least sociable of all).

Table 4

Author	Year	Subjects	Family Size	Results
Wahl	1956	568 schiz. in Navy compared to 100,000 Naval recruits and 392 schiz. from his 1954 study	Significantly larger than average (4+)	Later-born slightly predominated
Schooler	1961	25% of all hospitalized female schiz. in 1959 from 17-65 at Springfield State Hospital, L Bldg. more than 18 mths.	2-4	Significantly more patients in last half; in several studies she analyzed, later-born sig. but difference due entirely to 4+ families. In this sample similar but N.S.
Caudill	1963	All admissions in 1958 to 3 private and 1 public hosp. in Tokyo (psychot, neurotic, and sch)	All sizes only children excluded	In schiz. and psychot. eldest son and youngest daughter overrep'd, esp. unmarried males in traditional families. N.S. for neurotics
Schooler	1964	Female schiz. admitted in Maryland 1942-49; All male schiz from 18-40 in 2 state hosp. in 1958	2-3 show effects; not 4+	First-born in lower class males; last born in middle class males; Sig. more last-born females but class N.S.
Granville-Grossman	1966	1244 schiz. (562 males, 682 females) in U.K.	All sizes	Later-born and last-born overrep'd in males N.S. for females. N.S. when both sexes pooled
Barry and Barry	1967	1009 schiz. (320 males, 689 females) in Pa.	2-3 group 1 4+ group 2	In group 1 sig. more first-born males. In Group 2 sig. more born in second half
Solomon & Nuttall	1967	291 male schiz. in 5 mental hosp. in Mass.	2, 3, 5 sig. for chronicity	First-born for high socio-ec. class. Earlier-born recover more quickly and are more likely to have an acute onset; later-born more likely to become chronic and manifest undesirable ward behavior after an insidious onset.
Nowicki	1967	1400 psychot. patients in U.S. V.A. hosp. over 7-yr. period.	small (4+ excluded)	Middle-born group also deviant; all groups differed sig.

Two investigations uncovered birth order effects which held for both male and female schizophrenics--the prevalence of first born (Bender and Faretra, 1952) and first half (Rao, 1964). Interestingly, the former study investigated children and the latter Indians. In a large family (4+) Barry and Barry (1967) found that schizophrenics tend to be in the second half, while Lotter (1967) found no significant trends at all in autistic children but Phillips (1957) did with the autistic child tending to be a first-born male.

Table 5

	Male	Female	Both
First Born	4 (plus 1 aut., 1 small family, 1 upper class, 1 socially isolated)	1 N. S.	2
Middle Born	1		
Last Born	3	4 1 N. S. 2 less sociable	1 large family
N. S. (and no trend)		1	1 aut.

In analyzing previous data, Barry and Barry (1967) found early-born children to be generally overrepresented in large families in non-Western cultures (India), but later-born children to be overrepresented in large families with Western culture (England and U. S.), especially for women. Only in small families in the U. S., they found first-borns to be more common. Apparently, they did not look comprehensively enough into available data, since this author's investigations yielded questionable results. The birth order effect appears to hold most (according to the empirical data cited in this paper) for schizophrenic females, who seem to be more often later or last born. In schizophrenic males, all ordinal positions seem to be overrepresented, depending on the study. Numerically, the data favor first-born as being overrepresented; however, the bulk of these are qualified by family size, social class, culture, etc. At least the smaller number of studies relating later birth to psychosis in males is more clean-cut. For schizophrenics in general, the evidence is completely useless in formulating a hypothesis, except to say that the birth order effect seems to be very closely related to sex and that pooling data flattens or totally negates most significance.

Family Size

One cannot speak of ordinal position in the family without investigating the effect of family size on incidence of psychosis. Schooler and Scarr (1962) suggest that small families may be less cohesive than large, with the parents of the large having at least stayed together long enough to produce more children. They feel that this may be a crucial factor in the development of schizophrenia, whereas in normals it may be trivial. Wahl (1954, 1956) found that the families of his schizophrenics were larger than average (4+ compared to the national norm of 2.2) with the youngest overrepresented. Farina, Barry, and Garmezy (1963) and Barry and Barry (1967) noted that when families were larger than average (4+), a significant number of patients came from the second half. Generally, when the use of large families is specified, later-born siblings tend to preponderate; on the other hand, the use of small families results in ambiguous findings--either not significant or equal occurrence of all ordinal positions. Perhaps small family constellations tend to flatten effects which appear as number of siblings increases. Furthermore, incidence of schizophrenia might not be the relevant factor in family size. Farina, Barry, and Garmezy (1963) suggested instead that recoverability is related to large family size: the larger the number of older siblings, the more likely the patient was to be hospitalized for schizophrenia and the less likely he was to recover; the same was true for only children. In their sample of 167 schizophrenic patients admitted to two state hospitals (82 male and 85 female), they also found that females had more older siblings--perhaps offering an explanation for the greater number of female chronic patients present in mental hospitals, perhaps also throwing a statistical monkey wrench into their data. As mentioned earlier, an obvious criticism regarding large family findings is that this may be a social class related factor (especially in state hospital and chronic populations) with lower classes tending to have larger families. It may also be a valid correlation and supportive of both Schachter's psychological view and an organic view of schizophrenia.

Maternal Age

Another variable which is difficult to separate from birth order effects is the age of the mother. If mothers of schizophrenics could be shown empirically to be older than the average, the implications for physiological causation would be enormous, indicating less favorable fetal environment, greater biological stress, etc. Interestingly, maternal birth rank has a greater effect in producing fraternal twins than her increasing age or the presence of older siblings in the family she has mothered (Schooler, 1961), suggesting that her own birth order may actually affect her physiological process of conception. This does not rule out the relevance of maternal age to psychological factors as well (for instance, how might this affect the child rearing practices she employs). The results nicely uphold the suggestion that maternal age is greater for mothers of schizophrenics--that is to say, they confirm this finding until one peruses the studies which have included maternal age data and finds that practically every study mentioning older mothers also found an overrepresentation of mental illness in later or last born siblings. A study which only used three-sibling families (Grosz, and Miller, 1958) found no significance in psychosis or neurosis. However, in some specifically organically related difficulties, mothers were found to be older. Ucko (1965) found that when comparing 29 boys asphyxiated at birth with 29 boys not asphyxiated, the mothers of the asphyxiated boys were significantly older. This was an especially powerful finding since first born children in both groups were compared (erasing the effects of family size), although when all ranks were pooled, significance disappeared. Of course, it might also represent a statistical artefact created by the small number. Paffenbarger, Steinmetz, Pooler, and Hyde (1961) noted that rates increased with age in para-partum psychosis. Since they suggested that at least post-partum psychosis may have an organic etiology, this seems to suggest that increased age renders women more vulnerable to physiological difficulties relating to birth. As age has also been found to be significantly related to mental deficiency and mongolism (MacMahon and Sowa, 1961), there seems to be some justification for expecting older women to experience more pregnancy and birth difficulties, which in turn may lead to more neuropsychiatric disorders. By contrast, Pasamanick and Knobloch (1958) found that very young or older women had a significantly higher risk of producing mental defectives, but this is not necessarily inconsistent with organic causation theories if one sees both extremes as a typical or higher risk ages. In studying parental (rather than maternal) age, Dennehy (1966) found a slightly higher than average age for parents of all groups he investigated (depressives, schizophrenics, alcoholics, combined) except drug addicts. Granville-Grossman (1966), on the other hand, found a similar but not significant trend for parents of schizophrenics but concluded that parental age --especially paternal age--was not a factor.

Familial Factors

Perhaps searching for birth order effects in order to predict incidence or course of schizophrenia is an attempt to oversimplify a complex family constellation with innumerable individual variations. Both genetic-organic factors and social factors seem to enter into the picture. The former cites the higher incidence of schizophrenic offspring when the mother is schizophrenic herself (16 per cent probability as compared to one per cent without a psychotic parent, Rosenbaum, 1968). When a group of children with such a family were compared with children with a normal background, Heston (1966) found that the children who did not become schizophrenic showed a higher incidence of emotionally labile neurotics and psychopaths--but also individuals living a more interesting, varied, and creative life than the controls. Perhaps Huntington's finding (1938) that more great men are born in the same season as more schizophrenics reflects the fine line between constructive and destructive creativity. These might be particularly relevant findings today when schizophrenics have been found to be experiencing relatively greater increases in marriage and total reproduction than the general population--particularly in the case of schizophrenic women (Goldfarb and Erlenmeyer-Kimling, 1962). Social factors are many and complex, but suggest that the mother-father-child triad might be the relevant one with siblings playing a very minor role in the process, certainly quite contradictory to ordinal position theories, especially in the case of later-born siblings (Jackson, 1960, p. 364). Clausen and Kohn noted in the Hagerstown study (cited in Jackson, 1960, p. 298-304) that schizophrenic families differed from controls in that there was more often a strong maternal and weak paternal figure (particularly among paranoids); they also found that males said that they felt closer to their mothers and females to their fathers. When comparing schizophrenic and neurotic children, Block, Patterson, Block, and Jackson (cited in Jackson, p. 237, 1960) found that the mothers of schizophrenics tended to be hostile, distrustful and manipulative, while fathers were more direct in expression of hostility than mothers and were assertive to the point of being counterphobic. By contrast, Creak and Ini (1960) noted that the parents of 102 psychotic children were heterogeneous, representing the full range of emotional warmth, which they consider evidence of a constitutional or pathogenic etiology. Similarly, Bender and Grugett (1956) found that the emotional climate of the family of the schizophrenic child was not unfavorable but considerably more favorable than that of the non-schizophrenic behavior disorders in terms of cohesion, stability, interest in children, etc. The latter may represent the clear-cut diagnosis of middle class children as schizophrenic when compared to lower class children, who are usually difficult to differentially diagnose (von Brauchitsch and Kirk, 1967). The findings of Lowe (1966), Levine and Olson (1968), Lotter (1967) and Rimland (1964) that autistic children have parents who are better educated and intelligent, in a higher socio-economic class, and more stable might also reflect the class difference or possibly that (as Rimland and Sankar suggest) autistic children are in fact different from schizophrenic children. Interestingly, Lotter (1967) did find that while there was no greater incidence of psychotic illness in relatives, there was a greater incidence of other serious mental illness in the families of autistics when compared to her normal controls.

Occurrence of other mental illness in the family, not being married, and having an absent father appear at first glance to predict significantly better hospital adjustment for schizophrenics (Schooler and Parkel, 1963). However, these authors feel that such negative qualities do in fact merely characterize chronic patients or militate against their being discharged from the hospital. They suggest that other mental illness in the family merely prepares the patient early for life among deviants and dulls the distinction between being inside and outside the hospital. Some studies have attempted to correlate religion and psychosis, but these investigations have yielded little, with religion simply reflecting the composition of the particular population (Wahl, 1954, 1956; Bender and Grugett, 1956). Schooler (1964) found significantly more schizophrenics to be Catholic and Jewish compared to Protestant even though guessing ethnic background by name showed all to be equally represented.

Criticisms of birth order findings are usually made because of the lack of control for many of the familiar factors described above. Of course, some of these variables are difficult to control for, since maternal age and larger family size must almost certainly be correlated, as must ordinal position and birth rank (the first born must also be the oldest). Some statistical artefacts also enter the picture--for example, does larger family size really increase the likelihood of schizophrenia or does it increase the likelihood that a statistical significance will be obtained? And what about studies which have not found first born but have found first half significant? Is this a legitimate statistical manipulation as Schooler (1961) suggests or does it cast doubt on the validity of the findings? A further question has been asked which casts doubts on interpreting the results at all. Couldn't it be, as Sundararaj and Rao (1966) suggest, that the patients admitted to hospitals are not representative of schizophrenia in general who do not seek admission? For instance, in the rural population, deviants are more readily assimilated in India. They go on to ask whether in fact early born individuals (more frequently psychotic in their population) might not only have a better chance of hospital admission while other disturbed siblings are kept at home. Perhaps a family is ashamed or discouraged after one hospitalization and maintains other family ill at home. Since a U.S. sample (Abe, 1966) found, however, that younger siblings seem to have an earlier onset of disease (as measured by hospital admission), this might not be a tenable hypothesis in this country. This is also suggested by the finding that the closer the blood relationship in the family, the smaller the age difference between onsets. Schooler (1964) also suggests that birth rank might not reflect incidence, but rather symptomatology--with the last born female being less competent socially and prone to bizarre or self-destructive behavior.

The implications of birth order data to the two major theoretical entities are interesting but inconclusive. When postulating an organic etiology in schizophrenia, the sex differences which seem to enter into most of the results could reflect the variable occurrence of fetal and paranatal injury with later born females less able to withstand the increased risk but all males (in any ordinal position) more susceptible to damage. If as the slight trend suggests, schizophrenic males tend to be first born, could this be consistent rather with a psychogenic explanation (with first born siblings being more subject to reactive stress or react violently to the inability of the environment to stand their overassertiveness) while the evidence showing high incidence of later born schizophrenics especially among chronics could be consistent with Brackbill and Fine's theory that process schizophrenia is organic or biochemical in etiology with later borns being exposed to more biological stress (Solomon and Nuttall, 1967). However, if order of birth (at least in females) is relevant, why has it been found that all siblings of schizophrenics including those who develop normally have been found to have more pregnancy and birth complications (Bender and Faretra, 1962)? Moreover, if cultural differences seem to affect data (Caudill, 1963; Rao, 1964) how can physiology be causally involved?

Birth order effects may be related to several psychological variables postulated by Schachter. In terms of sex role in greater dependency and need to verbalize and interact socially may be more acceptable in the first-born female (these elements being consonant with the female role in the American culture) while the tendency to withdraw or be more self-sufficient and inner directed (characteristic of later born) may be less acceptable in the later born female, heralding at least the beginnings of poorer societal adjustment. On the other hand, the latter constellation would be more acceptable for the male in our culture while the former would not--suggesting greater adjustment problems for the first-born male. However, the inability to verbalize could also get him into more "hot water" in this society, as could the exaggerated need for self-sufficiency. Thus the male might be prone to more difficulties no matter what his mode of adjustment or ordinal position. If childhood treatment does in fact influence ability to withstand later assaults, then females--especially first born--who experience greater approval and attention in the family should be healthier.

On the other hand, greater interest in the first-born male may be coupled with more demands and responsibilities--again tempering a positive with a negative aspect. This has been postulated in both the Japanese (Caudill, 1963) and the Indian (Rao, 1964; Sundararaj and Rao, 1966) cultures in traditional families. The additional finding by Caudill that the youngest female is more poorly adjusted due to enforced dependency and responsibilities to the father suggests the power of parental expectations and attitudes in developing stress situations. If birth order then does have an effect in the social sphere, why do schizophrenics tend to have more poorly adjusted siblings (including marital discord, mental defectives, delayed speech, schizophrenia), the conclusion of Havelkova (1967). And why have normal siblings been found at least to suffer from marked constriction of personality (Jackson, 1960, p. 340). Schooler (1961) suggests that environmental factors related to birth order have a transitive effect--that is to say, either the number of schizophrenics is highest for the first born and decreases steadily thereafter or is highest for the last born and steadily increases, nicely taking all results into account, explaining family size variables, and getting rid of genetic explanations since this would assume a random distribution.

The variety of findings regarding birth order factors in the occurrence of schizophrenia suggest that something is going on--but no consistent pattern has emerged and at present the results must be considered inconclusive.

Sexual Factors

Whether an individual is born a male or a female appears to have a definite correlation with the probability of his becoming psychotic and even the course of his psychosis. Even before birth, in fact, this factor has an influence. The varieties of such effects run the gamut from predispositions to actual incidences of all manner of deviances.

Very few serious organic diseases have been found to be more common in females. Most diseases of the gastro-intestinal tract, respiratory tract, blood vessels, heart, bones, joints, and urinary

tract have much higher frequency in males, while some are limited

to males alone (thromboangiitis obliterans). On the other hand, fe-

males are more subject to functional diseases like hypertension,

migraine, hysteria, and chronic nervous exhaustion (possibly sub-

substantiating the finding that females are more prone to experience anx-

iety and react to stress made by Sontag in 1947). This apparent in-

herent sex-linked weakness in the male even holds true for the animal

kingdom, where the male is shorter lived (Boyd, 1961).

In terms of pregnancy, birth, and maladjustment, males have

been found to be more prone to:

1. Pregnancy difficulties in utero (Pasamanick and Knobloch cited
   Caplan, 1961; Gittelmen and Birch, 1967)
2. Paranatal complications (Gittelmen and Birch, 1967; Pollack and
   Gittelman, 1964)
3. Fetal death (Bellack, 1962)
4. Higher infant mortality (Bellack, 1962; Birch, 1964)
5. Higher mortality from childhood diseases (May, 1956)
6. Higher mortality rates at any age (Bellack, 1962; Boyd, 1961;
   Gruenberg in Birch, 1964)
7. Cerebral palsy (Lilienfeld, Pasamanick, 1955; Asher and
   Schonell, 1950)
8. Epilepsy (Lilienfeld and Pasamanick, 1954)
9. Mental deficiency (Pasamanick and Lilienfeld, 1955; Canadian
   Department of National Health and Welfare Report cited by
   Taft and Goldfarb, 1964)
10. Reading disabilities (Kawi and Pasamanick, 1958
11. Behavior disorders (Pasamanick, Rogers, and Lilienfeld, 1956)
12. Neuropsychiatric disorders (Lilienfeld, Pasamanick, and Rogers,
    1955; Gittelman and Birch, 1967)
13. Higher suicide rates both in adulthood (3:1) and old age (10:1)
    Dublin, 1963

In incidence of psychosis, males also seem to have the edge--at

least until the adult years. Males are more likely to be psychotic in

infancy (Rutter and Lockyer, 1967; Whittam, Simon, and Mittler, 1966),

autistic (Lotter, 1966), and hospitalized for psychosis (and schizophrenia)

in childhood (Whittam, Simon, and Mittler, 1966; Taft and Goldfarb, 1964).

In fact, up to the age of 12, males outnumber females in ratios variously

quoted as 5:1, 4:1, 3:1, or 2:1 with the former larger ratios predominating

(Bender and Grugett, 1956). Pollack, Levenstein, and Klein (1968) found

that male adolescents also outnumber females in schizophrenia. However,

during the child-bearing years, Jaco (1960) and Pugh and MacMahon
(1962) both found that mental illness is higher for females than males.
Pollack (1967) suggested a ratio around 3:2 (F:M). Of course, this
increase in females may be reflecting three diagnostic categories
other than schizophrenia--parapartum psychoses and involutional
melancholia (to which only females are obviously subject) and manic-
depressive psychosis, which Malzberg (1935) and Spiegel and Bell (cited
in Arieti, 1959) found to be more prevalent among females. In schizophrenia Erlenmeyer-Kimling, Rainer, and Kallmann (cited in Hoch
and Zubin, 1966) found that in New York State from 1934-6 and 1954-6
at approximately age 35 the prevalence of males was reversed and females thereafter consistently outnumbered males. Malzberg (cited in
Arieti, 1959) cautioned that in New York State this might be due to the
use of state hospital populations in the figures; more males were probably being admitted to Veteran's Administration hospitals and not state
hospitals after World War II. With advancing age, more females are
found in the ranks of the chronic patients (Rosenthal, 1962); their rate
of hospitalization also increases until they definitely lost any advantage
and catch up with males (Spiegel and Bell in Arieti, 1959). One could
argue, naturally, that with increasing age, life expectancy, which is
higher for females, begins to enter the picture. The higher ratio of
F:M senile psychotics tends to corroborate this impression (Ferraro
in Arieti, 1959; Malzberg, 1955).

Rosenbaum (1968) noted other sex-linked probabilities in schizophrenia by investigating twins and relatives of schizophrenics. In the
primary family group, an individual of the same sex as the patient is
more likely to become schizophrenic. This is especially true if the
patient is a female. Rosenthal (1962) found that brother pairs of twins
exceeded by more than one-half number of all brother-sister pairs
when they were concordant for schizophrenia. Concordance rates
were higher, however, for female pairs compared to male pairs. In

dizygotic twins, he discovered that the female-male ratio was 4:1--
but cautioned that this might be a sampling error due to the greater
number of female chronics in hospitals which are used for such research.

In an attempt to understand the reason for the sex differences in
distribution and course of psychosis, researchers have formed a
number of hypotheses related to either biological or psychological
factors. The first of these attempts to causally link the well-known
fact that males are biologically less able to withstand physiological
assaults, both before and after birth. Thus they would be more apt to
sustain organic damage. In point of fact, a number of researchers
(Pollack and Gittelman, 1964; Taft and Goldfarb, 1964; Birch, 1964;
Cutler, 1965; Gittelman and Birch, 1967) have found that more males
than females are organically brain damaged.

For example, Taft and Goldfarb (1964) investigated the difference
between boy and girl schizophrenics (21 boys to 8 girls reflecting the
usual male:female ratio in childhood schizophrenia). They found that
boys outnumbered girl significantly in organic involvement (8:3), whereas
girls outnumbered boys significantly in nonorganic, functional etiology
(7:1). Rosenthal (1962) found a similar cluster when he compared male
and female twins who were schizophrenic. Four times more often than
females, males had a history of trauma or infection; females, on the
other hand, had a psychic etiology more often than males (the first
finding was highly significant while the second just fell short of significance but was in the right direction). The results might demonstrate,
as Stabenau (1968) suggests, that "there is evidence to postulate a
genetic component to the etiology of schizophrenia; however, detailed family study of monozygotic twins discordant for schizophrenia
suggests there are pre- and/or post-natal experiential environmental
components necessary for schizophrenic symptomatology to emerge in
a given individual."

Birch (1964) asks whether there could not be a connection between boys' significantly larger head sizes at birth and their higher incidence of the organoid syndrome. He also postulates a correlation between paranatal mortality and organicity: "If you want to find a high incidence of organic and organoid syndromes, look for a population with high paranatal mortality rates." (p. 125) He does, however, offer an alternate explanation to the usual which suggests biological weakness in the male, suggesting instead male strength. Males, Birch hypothesizes, might tolerate brain damage in fetal life better than females, who die in early pregnancy. Therefore, the preponderance of males with brain damage may be reflecting the fact that they tolerate damaging experiences fatal to females. The higher male birth rate also might be called into evidence for such a position. Actually, Record and Smith's Birmingham data (1955) on mongolism show that paranatal mortality rates are higher in female mongols than in male, whereas a few years later, male mongol death rates are higher than female.

Shearer and Davidson and Finch (1967) even postulated differential chemical reactions in the ova of schizophrenic women which prevented the development of males. They found that in women who had an onset of schizophrenic symptoms within one month before or after the theoretical date of conception, no males and 14 females were born. They postulated that perhaps some chemical substance interfered with the viability of the ovum to the Y chromosome carrying sperm or its development in the fertilized ovum which was not lethal at a later stage of development.

Sex Role

A second set of theories revolves about sex role factors. Several researchers (Gardner, 1967; Schooler and Iong, 1963; Schooler, 1963; McClellandand Watt, 1968; Schooler and Parkel, 1963; Barry and Barry, 1967; Sundararaj and Rao, 1966; Caudill, 1963; Murphy and Lemieux,

1967) have stated that sex role identification or expectations might account for differential sexual incidence and course of psychosis. For instance, Gardner (1967) suggests that sex role identification might account for the fact that girls who later became schizophrenic after being seen in a child guidance clinic for a period of time in their childhood had severely disturbed mothers significantly more often than those in the same group who became well-adjusted adults. On the other hand, this was not important for boys who became schizophrenic. Such a finding would also be consistent with Rosenbaum's conclusion (1968) that same sex (and especially female) primary family members had a higher probability of also becoming schizophrenic. By contrast, Costello, Gunn, and Dominian (1968) found that three background events seemed common in schizophrenic males absence of a father, early childhood single illness (perhaps consonant with Bowlby's theory (1951) of maternal deprivation), and less adolescent illness. It would appear, therefore, that having an unhealthy same sex person with whom to identify--or none at all--predisposes towards poor mental health later in life. Another possibility is cross-sexual identification, suggested by Clausen and Kohn (cited in Bellak, 1962) who noted in their Hagerstown study that schizophrenic males often said they felt closer to their mothers, while schizophrenic women often stated a preference for their fathers.

Schooler and Long (1963) divided a group of 144 regressed chronic schizophrenics (half male and half female) into three experimental conditions: benevolent, hostile, and control. In the first, the patient was told that a paired patient would receive a dime every time he correctly completed a task; in the second, a paired patient would lose a dime for every error; in the third, no money was involved. Analysis revealed no initial significant sex or condition differences between patients and controls but unexpected and interesting differences in sub-groups. Male catatonics were found to begin the task with hostility; then over time they became more benevolent. The same was true for female paranoids. Male paranoids, on the other hand, began more benevolently and over time became more hostile. This pattern was also found in female catatonics. The initial sex difference was explained by sexually determined defense mechanisms and sex roles (for instance, females being culturally conditioned to be less aggressive). However, the authors had to resort to "complexity" explanations when the behavioral changes described appeared over time. Schooler (1963) also found differences between schizophrenic males, schizophrenic females, and normal controls when investigating affiliation preferences. The higher the level of intellectual functioning, the more likely the schizophrenic male was to want to work with someone who would want to make friends and express both positive and negative opinions. Female schizophrenics, by contrast, preferred the co-worker to keep negative feelings hidden. Schooler explained this desire in females for harmony by denial to be a function of culture--the tendency for females to feel helpless in the face of aggression and to want to avoid it. On the other hand, McClelland and Watt (1968) found that female schizophrenics tended to react assertively like normal males, while male schizophrenics reacted sensitively like normal females. Since the same might be said for career women as schizophrenic women, they suggested that sex role alienation might not be the relevant explanation, but rather the self-image disturbance in schizophrenia. Schooler and Parkel (1963) also noted that male and female chronics differed qualitatively, with females being more ideationally disturbed, holding more implausible ideas, and showing greater conceptual disorganization--in other words, being better able to see both the real and unreal connections between phenomena. Possibly this is also a function of the greater sensitivity that this culture expects of a woman.

One obvious criticism of the studies disclosing differences between the sexes related to incidence of psychosis is that they have rarely been investigating that factor when they almost accidentally found it. Therefore, they often have been working with unequal numbers of each sex (weakening their statistical conclusions) or have not been following up their studies with interpretive discussion. Again has a looseness of diagnostic categories been applied, making understanding and generalization difficult. The use of hospitalized patients--usually chronic-- leads one to wonder if this might not be the reason for some "sex" differences. For example, might not the higher number of male hospitalized childhood disorders really be reflecting the fact that boys are harder to handle at home, or that families somehow feel more responsible for little girls? Of course, in all relationships between psychosis and sex, there must be weighed the inescapable fact that generally males experience most forms of neuropsychiatric disorder more frequently than females. Therefore, might not the higher incidences of psychoses (especially in childhood and adolescence) merely be reflecting this general tendency? In old age, might not the longer life span of females be the relevant variable?

At present the two explanations of sexual differences--level of biological risk and sex role factors--both seem to interact in the differential incidence (especially the former) and course (especially the latter) of psychosis.

Season of Birth

Since the late nineteenth century, researchers have exhibited an interest in a topic which has intrigued man since the dawn of recorded history: How does the month of birth effect the life of the individual? At first glance for today's scientists, this question smacks of pseudo-psychological or even magical flavor; after all, astrology has long passed from the realm of serious scientific pursuit into the nether world populated by charlatans and quacks. Yet is a relationship between time of birth and subsequent events entirely implausible? After all, the fetal and neonatal periods are highly sensitive ones in which vicissitudes of environment could conceivably have an effect--and a lasting one-- especial- ly if an unfavorable season coincides with a critical stage of development, such as the first three months of fetal life or immediately before or after birth. Already many authors have uncovered what appear to be definite links between physiological ailments or deviations and season or even month of birth. For example, Rutstein, Nickerson, and Heald, (1952) showed that the highest incidence of newborns with arteriosis was in the late autumn, logically following the spring prevalence of maternal rubella, often considered an antecedent factor if occurring in the early months of pregnancy. Barry and Barry (1961) also cite a seasonal cor- relation for anencephaly and congenital cranial osteoporosis, as does Plum (1956, 1962) for cerebral palsy. Pregnancy complications (Pasa- manick and Knobloch, 1958), perinatal mortality (Barry and Barry, 1961), and prematurity (Masland in Caplan, 1961) seem to occur most frequently in the winter, as do births later found to be mentally defi- cient (Knobloch and Pasamanick, 1958; Orme, 1962) or less intelligent (Orme, 1963). Possible connections between winter birth and social or personality deviance like criminal insanity or "the problem child" have even been suggested (Barry and Barry, 1961). It is therefore not surprising that some psychologists have attempted to investigate the possible relationship between psychosis and season of birth.

The typical study in this field--consisting of only about two dozen in over fifty years--had certain features in common. It was usually conducted in a country manifesting Western European culture and con- cerned statistics gathered for hospitalized psychotic patients (the major- ity diagnosed as schizophrenic or manic-depressive). The size of the sample was typically in the thousands (the range covering anywhere from 1453 to 23,000) but more often around two or three thousand. While both sexes were included, this was usually in random proportion in the year or years of the sample. Most studies have been conducted with adults and have included all patients newly admitted into a mental institution for a span covering from one to 25 years (the median being around seven years). Controls were average monthly birth rates taken from census statistics for the general population for one or more years (usually in the range of birth years for the subjects) for either a delimited area (like a particular state or city) or a nation (like Canada). The year was divided into 12 months, 4 seasons, or trimesters (1: January-April; 2: May-August; 3: September-December), with the latter predominating.

The following eight summarized studies are representative of some of the more important work done in the area. The results of these and other investigations are surprisingly confirmatory, each supporting the other with amazing accuracy. The majority found that schizophrenics are more often born in the winter (if the year was divided into four seasons) or in the first trimester (Tramer, 1929; Nolting, 1934, 1951, 1954; Petersen, 1934; Huntington, 1938; Knobloch and Pasamanick, 1958; Barry and Barry, 1961; Pile (1949) reanalyzed by Barry and Barry, 1961; Norris and Chowning, 1962). Others who found no statistically significant difference nevertheless discovered that the results were in the direction of the preceding studies (Lang, 1931; Orme, 1963; Barry and Barry for males, 1963). A few found no significant differences at all in the incidence of schizophrenia and season of birth (Pile, 1949; Norris and Chowning, 1962). On the other hand, Goodenough (1941) actually found that more schizophrenics were born in the spring and fewer in the winter.

When these results are compared with those for other behavioral deviances--for example, problem children--they yield similar findings: more individuals with severe personality problems are also born in the winter (cited by Barry and Barry, 1961). As a matter of fact, so are more great men--a positive personality deviation?--(Huntington,

Author	Year	Subjects	Country	Years under Study	Results
Tramer	1929	2100 schiz, psychot, alcoholics, paretics from private clinic	Switzerland	1871-80 1901-10	Significant difference Winter--Dec. to May smaller number in May
Lang	1931	3976 schiz; 1879 manic-depress. 17379 control psychiatric hospit. pats. Total monthly rate and total birth rate in Bavaria, 1905-14 All S's in public hospitals	Bavaria	1905-14	Somewhat higher for schiz. from Jan to Feb and lower in Aug and Nov, but N.S. N.S. for sibs, manic-depressives, or psychopaths compared to general population
Petersen	1934	3467 schiz; 691 manic-depress. in public hospitals; Control monthly birth rate in U.S., 1917-29	U.S.	1917-1929	Winter--Dec and Jan higher for schiz. Summer--June to Sept. lower for schiz. Manic-depress. above controls in March-May.
Huntington	1938	10420 schiz; 3683 manic-depress. Control total monthly birth rate for Mass, 1885-1914	U.S. Ind., Md., NY, Mass., Mich., Ohio, Pa.	1885-1914	Both schiz and manic-depressives higher in Winter (Feb-April) and lower in Summer (June-Sept)
Nolting	1934 1951 1954	2589 schiz; 1556 manic-depress. 2090 schiz; 1228 manic-depress. 3253 schiz. Controls for all birth rates for Neth. in years studied	Netherlands	1920-53	Winter (Dec-March) higher for schiz; Summer (June-Sept) lower; N.S. difference between manic-depressives and controls
Barry and Barry	1961	1453 schiz (pub. hos.) from N.J. & Mass; Controls 1-1/2 million from general population in Mass.	U.S.	1883-90 1903-10 1923-30	Jan-April highest for schiz; May-Aug Lowest; Sept-Dec intermediate; N.S. for manic-depressives but similar to schiz.
Norris and Chowning	1962	3617 schiz. in pub. hosp.; Controls total Canadian birth rate for 1923, 34, 37, 40 (randomly selected)	Canada	1959 (S's born 1919-44)	Jan-May higher for schiz; June-Sept lower but N.S. for other randomly selected years in span of 1919-44
Barry and Barry	1963	6751 schiz from 2 private hosp. (2416 males, 3261 females--1907; 455 males, 619 females--1931) Controls monthly birth rate for total years	U.S.	1907-62	N.S. but suggested sex difference with males highest in Jan-April and females highest in May-Aug; also suggested that the higher the social class, the closer to the norm.

1938), less intelligent men (Orme, 1963) and retardates (Orme, 1962; Knobloch and Pasamanick, 1958). More pregnancy difficulties are also noted by the latter authors to occur in the winter. In fact, the only deviations which appeared to more often correlate with the third trimester were those which might be termed neurological (Rutstein, Nickerson, and Heald, 1952; Barry and Barry, 1961; Plum, 1956, 1962).

The following gives an overview of the season of birth-psychosis findings.

Table 7

Finding	Number of Studies
Winter or first trimester	10
N.S. but in the direction of above	3
N.S.	2
Spring	1

A variety of hypotheses for the observed season of birth-psychosis connection have been proposed by authors interested in the question.

Parental Considerations

Many of these theories have tried to relate cultural, subcultural, and socio-economic class behavior of the parents to season of birth. One such theory suggests that parental mating habits may account for the greater number of deviant individuals born in the first trimester. As Hollingshead and Redlich (1958) have clearly demonstrated, different cultural groups do in fact have different seasonal mating habits. Therefore, Barry and Barry (1961) ask if parents of psychotics might not comprise a subgroup with atypical mating habits. Thus far no studies have investigated this possibility. Huntington (1938) suggested that the favorable and pleasant climate of spring would appeal to procreation among basically unfit and impulsive people and cited material showing the large number of illegitimate births in the winter; he generalized unfit and impulsive to include criminals and psychotics who would in turn have less than fit offspring. Barry and Barry (1961) point out, however, that unstable parents also offer the poorest home environment and often come from the lowest socio-economic classes. In fact, they found that psychotic patients do come predominantly from the lowest socio-economic strata and suggested that the lower class may have a different seasonal distribution of birth which is being reflected in the supposed season-psychosis correlation. When studies have attempted to control for this variable, some of the striking correlations found between winter and mental illness have disappeared (Barry and Barry, 1963), although a few authors have found that class differences do not affect the results which are the same for all groups (Knobloch and Pasamanick, 1958; Goodenough, 1941). Other authors have simply concluded that lower classes show greater deviation from the norm (Pasamanick, Dinitz, Knobloch, 1960; Barry and Barry, 1963). Still, Pasamanick and Knobloch (1957) have found that neuropsychiatric disorders are more common among lower classes. Perhaps, as Barry and Barry (1963) suggest, the middle and upper classes are better able to modify the deleterious effect of climate and feed and care for their pregnant women. In fact, Pasamanick, Dinitz, and Knobloch (1960) virtually ruled out the postulated increased rate of lower class births in winter when they found that both Negroes and whites included in all social classes had fewer deliveries in winter in a five-year period in Baltimore.

Fetal Environment

Other hypotheses have attempted to show the connection between fetal environment and season of birth. A relationship between weather and time of conception has been shown in a study by Pasamanick, Dinitz, and Knobloch (1959). They found that when all 1955 births in the U.S. were compared by month and geographic distribution, certain patterns became clear: in the South, there was a marked decline during the spring; in the Midwest and Northeast, there was only a slight trough in the spring; in the Northwest (Washington and Oregon), there was no spring trough; in fact, births were slightly higher in the spring than expected. Thus summer conception would appear to be less likely in the hotter South than in either the Midwest and Northeast, whereas it would seem that in the cooler summers of the Northwest conception was actually more likely. Although the obvious criticism could be leveled that this was found to be true only in 1955 and that the results could be an artefact of that particular year, the study is still suggestive of the types of investigations which are possible and the type of inferences which have been drawn.

One of the leading theories has related this idea of summer heat to deviant development. A lowered threshhold to stress through the hypothalamico-pituitary-adrenal-cortical axis serving as an additional organic precursor in an individual already genetically predisposed has been postulated by Pasamanick and Knobloch (in Caplan, 1961). In fact, Knobloch and Pasamanick (1958) did find a significant increase in the rate of both schizophrenia and mental deficiency in individuals born in years following hot summers as compared to cool.

A second effect of summer heat might be nutritional reflecting maternal diet. Knobloch and Pasamanick suggest a possible protein deficiency caused by decreased dietary intake (inferred from their discovery that in one year all children born in the summer were significantly lighter in birth weight and such weight is largely accumulated by the fetus during the last three months of pregnancy--Pasamanick, Dinitz, and Knobloch cited in Caplan, 1961). Nolting (1934) suggested a Vitamin C deficiency was the crucial factor. He stated that winter birth is related to schizophrenia since in this critical period when normal mental development is taking place (a few weeks before or after birth) Vitamin C is lacking. In a later study among mental defectives, Nolting (1951) found that the highest birth rate was during June and July, when he rapidly changed the critical period of Vitamin C deficiency to the last three months of prenatal development. Pasamanick, Dinitz, and Knobloch (cited in Caplan, 1961) state that summer conception would seem to have some effect on twinning--possibly due to the teratogenic effect of heat stress on the embryo--since the peak season of twin births (which show significantly higher infant mortality, prematurity, and neuropsychiatric disorders) was in the spring. Males (usually considered more susceptible biologically) have lower birth rates just prior to and during the descending curve of the spring depression as well as increased pregnancy complications. Again these events coincide with summer conception as does the neonatal death peak in spring (Pasamanick, Dinitz, and Knobloch, 1959).

Pasamanick, Rogers, and Lilienfeld, 1956, also found that more births in the first trimester were preceded by complications of pregnancy (specifically eclampsia or preeclampsia, uterine bleeding, and heart disease). Pre-maturity has also been found to occur most frequently in the winter (Masland in Caplan, 1961). Many of these birth and pregnancy complications have been linked to schizophrenia. Petersen (1934) also stresses the importance of season of conception--the critical period, however, being spring, when the fetus is overstimulated and fatigued by meteorological instability.

One investigator (Orme, 1963) even suggested that the increased incidence of winter births found among schizophrenics really reflected differential intelligence. More intelligent patients were born in the second and third trimesters and less intelligent in the first: since more patients were found to be born in the first, this must reflect the inferior level of performance of most schizophrenics.

In summary, the hypotheses regarding reasons for a correlation between season of birth and psychosis have grown out of many studies linking season of birth and other atypical or generally deviant subsequent events like brain damage or mental deficiency. These theories have considered the parents (especially the mother) in terms of mating habits and social class. Fetal environment--including climate, nutrition, pregnancy difficulties, and complicating factors of birth--have also been cited in explanation. At present not enough uncontested data is available to select a probable hypothesis; however, theories revolving about fetal environment seem to offer the most promise if in fact a relationship between season of birth and psychosis exists.

The whole area of study is open to severe criticism, especially on methodological grounds. This was perceived and actually investigated statistically by Norris and Chowning (1962), whose original study is presented in the Table preceding. After finding significant results in the usual direction (more schizophrenics born in the first trimester), they compared prior research and their own study and found that almost none of them had controlled for variables which could turn out to be relevant: geographic area, socio-economic class, yearly differences in control census figures. The use of representative years taken from the range of birth dates of the subjects was questioned. Their initial study, which found significant differences between schizophrenics and normals when the years of 1923, 1934, 1937, and 1940 (randomly selected) were averaged to give a monthly birth rate, yielded different results when different randomly selected years were compared. For instance, the results were not significant for the years 1925, 1935, 1937, and 1945--but they were significant for 1922, 1934, 1944, 1939; 1922, 1929, 1931, and 1944 also was not significant. Neither was a monthly birth rate based on all the years of the study, 1921-1946. Norris and Chowning then compared several pairs of years randomly and found that 1922-1940 and 1935-1946 differed significantly, while 1935-1944 and 1935-1941 did not. In fact, fifty per cent of monthly birth rates in Canada differed significantly from each other in any year and/or from themselves in different years. As the most common control in nearly all the studies in the field has been figures from randomly selected years, this criticism may negate many of the conclusions found. They also found that the birth rate for one province could differ significantly from another province and/or itself from year to year; as the control for patients in one hospital or clinic has often been the national norms, a geographic artefact might interfere with interpretation of results. They also found that most studies did not control for social class, a possible significant variable, although the few that have executed this control have not found it important, except for Barry and Barry, whose 1963 study was published after Norris and Chowning's and found that the higher the social class the less deviation from the norm.

In this study Barry and Barry criticized Norris and Chowning on several counts: as they used months rather than trimesters, they felt that the number per month might have been too small to be valid. They also questioned whether the difference in Canada's climate (where summers are relatively cool) might not have explained their absence of significant differences, especially when compared to American studies. Finally, they suggested that Norris and Chowning's cases probably had fewer lower socio-economic representatives since they included both public and private hospitals. If social class does play a significant role in the statistics of prior studies, this could explain the different results. This study also found a non-significant but clear tendency for psychotic males to be born in the first trimester and psychotic females in the second. This could be due to the fact that in the general population fewer male births occur in the spring (Pasamanick, Dinitz, and Knobloch, 1959) and more neonatal death (to which males are more subject than females). Still, sex is a possible relevant variable which has rarely been controlled for.

Another possibly relevant variable is intelligence. The only study which controlled for this (Orme, 1963) revealed a connection between spring and summer birth and more intelligent patients and winter birth and less intelligent patients. This data is somewhat substantiated by studies showing that mental defectives are also more often born in the winter (Knobloch and Pasamanick, 1958).

In fact, might not the whole area really be reflecting deviance in general rather than psychosis, one subheading in this broad topic. The many previously mentioned investigations relating all types of deviations from the norm to season of birth certainly enhance this possibility.

The two criticisms which could be leveled at nearly all birth factor studies might be confounding the findings further: Does the inclusion of hospitalized patients only effect the results? Do the diagnostic categories (and the considerable looseness with which they are applied to seasonal studies) influence the results? In other words, can results found for "psychotics" be generalized to schizophrenia? Can results found for schizophrenics be accurately ascribed to all schizophrenics or only those in a particular geographic area, year, hospital?

Social Factors

A number of social factors have been found to be relevant when investigating the problem of birth in psychosis. These include such elements as race, migratory tendencies, functioning level in society, culture, and social class.

Race

Most postulated racial differences appearing in birth factor-psychosis studies have discussed the Negroid and Caucasoid, particularly in terms of their relative positions in U.S. society. Other "racial" differences have been interpreted as due to different norms rather than skin color. These will be discussed in the section related to culture.

Generally, Pasamanick (1946) found that Negro babies matched the Gesell norms set up for white children in almost all areas except two: language and gross motor behavior. Comparison of Negro premature babies and Negro full-term babies at 30 months (Cutler, 1965) revealed similar findings. However, Pasamanick and Knobloch (in Caplan, 1961) found that when comparing white and Negro babies at 40 weeks and again at three years a significant difference appeared. At 40 weeks both groups showed no disparity in a general development quotient; at three years, on the other hand, they found that the white mean was 110.9, while the Negro mean was 97.4.

Negroes have been found to differ from Caucasians in the occurrence of some deviant physical events. For example, they have been noted to have a higher incidence of:

> Pregnancy abnormalities (Lilienfeld and Pasamanick, 1956)
> Prematurity (Pasamanick, Knobloch, and Lilienfeld, 1956)
> Cerebral palsy (Lilienfeld and Pasamanick, 1955)
> Mental deficiency (Pasamanick and Lilienfeld, 1955)
> Behavior disorders (Pasamanick, Rogers, and Lilienfeld, 1956)
> Neuropsychiatric disturbances (Pasamanick and Knobloch, 1957)
> Epilepsy (not significant but in the right direction)
> (Lilienfeld and Pasamanick, 1954)
> Postnatal injuries like head injury, lead intoxication, and infection
> (Pasamanick and Knobloch in Caplan, 1961)

In hospitalization for psychosis, diagnosis and course of illness, Negroes have also been found to differ. Malzberg (1953) discovered that Negro rates of hospitalization in New York state hospitals from 1939 to 1941 were twice as high as rates of admission for white patients in the same period. Upon investigating further, he found that the two most common diagnostic categories for Negroes were paresis and alcoholic psychosis When comparing Negro and white male and female schizophrenics, Lane (1968) found that significantly more Negro males were diagnosed process schizophrenics, while significantly more white females were diagnosed reactive schizophrenics, with Negro females and white males falling into intermediate positions. She hypothesized that if process was defined as withdrawal and turning against others, this might often in fact fit the Negro male patient; if reactive was defined as reacting by turning against oneself, this might often in fact describe the white female patient. When comparing the two extremes, she also suggested that the white female might encounter enough childhood acceptance to alter the inexorable course of schizo-phrenia, while the Negro male might be the most rejected of the four groups. Furthermore, culturally, the white female would be encour-aged to repress aggressive behavior and introject, in the process be-coming more self-critical. On the other hand, the Negro male tends to be both more aggressive due to positive cultural sanctions and more isolated. The white middle or upper class mental health worker would certainly be more comfortable with the former mode of behavior than the latter and so would be more disposed to diagnosing the white fe-male in the less severe and more hopeful diagnostic category.

Basically, two different approaches have evolved in the attempt to explain the differences connected with race in birth factor-psychosis studies. The first cites organic etiology; the second, social.

Organic theories stress the preponderance of pregnancy abnor-malities and prematurity complications in the Negro group. Lilien-feld, Pasamanick, and Rogers (1955) have hypothesized a relationship between such physiological factors of birth and any number of neuro-psychiatric disorders, including cerebral palsy and childhood behavior disorders. Such disorders have, in fact, been found to be more pre-valent in the Negro group. These theories also point out that Negroes do in fact have a more chaotic physical history after birth, with in-fections and injuries more common and thus more likely to traumatize the individual.

The major criticisms to this line of reasoning come under the heading of the second type of theory: social factors. Such theories stress the different family life and social environment to which Negroes have been exposed. For instance, Kardiner and Ovesey (1951) found the Negro home to be mother dominated, with a lack of respect for the father, who was usually either absent or if present passive and remote (except for occasional violence). If process schizophrenics come from mother-dominated homes, as Chapman and Baxter (1963) suggest, could this not explain Lane's results (1968) cited above? However, Kohn and Clausen (1956) have noted that mother-dominated homes also correlate with other deviances, including ulcers, anorexia nervosa, juvenile delinquency, and drug addiction. They suggest that the inclusion of this factor in schizophrenic etiology may be premature. Perhaps the absence or passivity of the father is the important variable, as Costello, Gunn, and Dominian (1968) suggest. Since these subjects were white male schizophrenics, however, this flattens rather than heightens the racial difference. Bender and Grugett (1956) feel that parents of Negro children seem less sensitive to childhood problems, another environmental variable which could be relevant in explanation. Malzberg (1956) suggests that the migratory habits of many New York State Negroes (who float back and forth between North and South, often with little economic stability) might explain the high incidence of mental illness. Socio-cultural deprivation might also account for the inflated inclusion of Negroes in the ranks of the deviant. Intellectual functioning, for example, is often found poorer among Negroes . However, when Lilienfeld and Pasamanick (1956) investigated mental deficiency among Negro and white patients, they uncovered some interesting differences. Below the I. Q. of 50, Negroes and whites alike were found to have experienced one or more pregnancy or paranatal abnormalities. Above 50, however, this ceased to be true for Negroes but remained significant for whites, who had such abnormalities equally at all I. Q. levels. The results strongly suggest that atypical birth factors are operating in the occurrence of mental deficiency for all whites but only those Negroes termed most retarded. The authors state that the "less retarded" Negroes may in fact be suffering from socio-cultural deprivation. Finally, Malzberg (1953) suggests that both paresis and alcoholic psychosis, the two categories with the majority of Negroes, are really socially-determined illnesses stemming from an unstable and unhealthy environment.

When evaluating the studies which have found significant differences between the races, several critical problems arise. The first
of these is the bias imposed by testing instruments and individual
items. For instance, Lane (1968) questions the use of items relating
to aggression, which she feels impose negative bias on the Negro,
whose subculture sanctions amounts of violence intolerable to the
middle-class white, as well as on the male, who can be acceptably
more aggressive, especially among Negroes of the lower class.
Carlson (1966) also found a cultural bias on the Bender-Gestalt test.
When she administered it in Alabama to two groups of 31 each (one
Negro schizophrenic and one white schizophrenic), she found that
although the Negroes were better educated than the white, they did
more poorly--both on Designs 4, 6, 7, 8 and in total time.

A second problem is an examiner bias. Lane (1968) suggests
that in her study the interviewers offering the diagnoses might have
felt more antipathy towards Negro males than any other group, consonant with findings by Hollingshead and Redlich (1958). Paffenbarger
(1964) found that female Negroes were more apt to be diagnosed psychotic than female whites when both were suffering from parapartum
psychoses. Consistent underrecording of Negro symptomatology was
discovered by de Hoyos and de Hoyos (1965), which they attributed to
status differences between Negro patients and white therapists in the
direction of overcompensation. Pasamanick (1946) questioned his own
finding that Negro children are less verbally responsive because of
their possible inhibition in speaking to a white examiner.

A third problem seems to be the almost constant confounding of
two separate but interrelated variables, race and social class. So
many of the findings related to Negroes seem to be related as well
to inclusion in the lower class that it is difficult to separate the two
or to decide which is in fact the relevant factor. For example, prematurity is more common among Negroes (Pasamanick, Knobloch,

and Lilienfeld, 1956). However, as there is a significant correlation between size of mother and prematurity and as undernourished women from the poverty classes tend to be smaller in adulthood, might not prematurity really be related to lower class membership? This was, in fact, what Baird (1945) found. A variation of the same argument can be applied, as a matter of fact, to all of the organic deviances described above.

In summary, studies relating race to psychosis leave much to be desired, primarily because of the many relevant variables which are not controlled for and because of the ambiguity of interpretation possible.

Migration

Although only a handful of researchers have delved into the relationship between migratory groups and psychosis, some relevant findings have emerged. Several authors (Tietze, Lemkau, and Cooper, 1942; Malzberg, 1936; Odegaard, 1932; Wedge, 1952; Faris and Dunham, 1939; Dunham, 1947; Clausen and Kohn, 1947) have found that mobile populations had a disproportionately high incidence of psychosis. Specifically in schizophrenia, Faris and Dunham (1939) found this rate to be highest in the areas of highest mobility and social disorganization. When they divided the city of Chicago into a number of differing neighborhoods, they found that the rate of schizophrenia varied from a low of 111 per 100,000 in outlying wealthier suburban districts to a high of 1195 per 100,000 in central city areas devoted to housing transients (rooming houses, for instance). The drift hypothesis has been formulated to explain this fact--that is to say, people in poorer mental health tend to drift into the slum and transient neighborhoods of the city. Of course, others have asked if in fact the stressful situation of living in these areas did not result in poorer mental health or an actual psychotic break. Dunham and Faris (in Jackson, 1960) suggest that social isolation--prevalent in the slums--is a necessary precursor to schizophrenia, especially in the child. The phenomena of higher rate of psychosis and living in the central city seems limited to the megalopolis. By contrast, Clausen and Kohn (in Jackson, 1960) found this to be untrue in the Hagerstown, Maryland, study. They concluded that the small size of the city explained the difference and suggested that poorly adjusted individuals tended to leave (to the very large cities nearby?)

Malzberg (1956) uncovered similarly high rates among migrants hospitalized in New York State. Upon investigating further, he found that the psychosis was not always manifested immediately after the move, but might be delayed for extended periods of time. He also felt that the high rate of native born Negro admissions might be par- tially explained as a drift function of their migratory habits.

Comparisons of native born and foreign born hospitalized psy- chotic patients have usually shown that a relatively larger number were foreign born. For example, Malzberg in 1936 found that a higher percentage of immigrants numbered in the ranks of hospitalized schizo- phrenic patients than the comparable rate for natives (2:1). In a later study, Malzberg (1962) found that when comparing foreign born Norwe- gians and the later generations with the same Norwegian origin, the natives had a lower rate than their migratory forbears. Wedge (1952) also found that migrant Okinawans in Hawaii had a far higher rate than would be expected from their small numbers and their rate of schizo- phrenia reflected in hospitalization on Okinawa (their native environ- ment).

Some significant differences were also found in diagnostic cate- gories when looking at foreign born admissions to U.S. hospitals. For instance, Malzberg (1962) found that the Norwegian patients (foreign born and later generations both) had a lower rate of inclusion in all categories except paresis and alcoholic psychosis. He found the same to be true for Negroes (1956) in even higher percentages--so much so, in fact, that this group outnumbered all others. Opler and Singer (1956) also uncovered some significant qualitative differences in hospitalized schizophrenics in New York City with Irish and Italian backgrounds (37 of the former and 40 of the latter). Alcoholism was found more important to the Irish, while the Italians tended to sublimate their problems in hypochandriasis and somatization in general. Irish tended to exhibit latent homosexuality, were more quietly anxious and paranoid, and were more prone to defenses like fantasy and withdrawal. On the other hand, Italians tended to exhibit overt homosexual behavior more frequently, were more excited and confused (generally in the schizo-affective category), and were more prone to poor control.

Various rationales have been cited by these quthors in the attempt to explain their results. Odegaard (1932) hypothesizes that the individual psychology of the patients is the important factor, with schizoid personalities tending to emigrate. A more anthropological explanation was attempted by Wedge (1952), who investigated mothering practices and found no differences between the two groups. Therefore, he postulated vulnerability to schizophrenia despite positive mothering practices (like breast feeding) and described the two types of Okinawan patients he had encountered in Hawaii, one matching the schizoid designation of Odegaard (shy, suspicious, and withdrawn) and one being evaluated as aggressive and overcompensating. Both, he states, are probably reactions to the status of Okinawans in Hawaii--that of a despised minority. The latter position of the migrant is consonant with the third theory regarding the causality of such a high incidence of psychosis: the lower social status of the migrant.

Malzberg reanalyzed his 1936 data on 15704 native-born white patients and 10987 foreign-born white patients admitted to New York State mental hospitals from 1928 to 1931 in an attempt to ascertain whether such factors could account for the fact that foreign-born patients outnumbered native-born two to one. When he corrected for the different age composition of the two groups (with foreign-born immigrants tending to be older), he found that the ratio of 1.2 to 1 (F.B. : N.B.) was reduced by twenty percent. When he corrected for the different level of urbanization (with immigrants tending to be more highly urbanized), and socio-economic environment (with immigrants tending to belong to a more indigent economic and occupational class), he found that ratios became insignificant. The total reanalysis revealed no important difference between native and foreign groups, who only exceeded the natives by eight percent when the above variables were taken into account. He also found no significant differences between them in representation in different diagnostic categories.

Braatoy (1937) noted that migrants also had a higher total mortality and a higher suicide rate than native-borns and concluded that unfavorable living conditions imposed upon the immigrants were in fact responsible for their higher rates of schizophrenia.

It seems plausible to suggest that some relationship exists between place of birth, tendency to move, and psychosis when one looks at the available figures regarding incidence of psychosis and migratory behavior. However, the present quantity of investigation seems to leave enough doubt regarding what is happening to make the formulation of hypotheses premature. The major criticism of the literature is the lack of control of what might eventually turn out to be crucial variables.

Intelligence

The relationship of birth factors and psychosis cannot be complete without at least a brief look at the research regarding intelligence and level of functioning. Much of the relevant research in the area of pregnancy and birth complications and their subsequent effects has been related to the later functioning of those so damaged in the fetal or neonatal periods. For instance, studies have revealed a correlation between both mental deficiency (Pasamanick and Lilienfeld, 1955) and reading disabilities (Kawi and Pasamanick, 1958) and such abnormalities--the former a generalized deficit in functioning and the latter a more specific decrement. As such complications are also associated with neuropsychiatric disorders (Lilienfeld, Pasamanick, and Rogers, 1955), one would be tempted to look for lower intellectual abilities in those so afflicted. In fact, using the 1916 form of the Stanford-Binet, Roe and Shakow (1942) found a significantly lower mental age for schizophrenics (141 months compared to 164 for a control group). Similar findings were made by Kendig and Richmond (1940) and Shakow (1946). The major criticism of these studies has been that no premorbid I. Q. 's were available--leaving unanswered the obvious question: Are schizophrenics in fact less intellectually able or is their functioning being impaired by the onset of the disease? Winder (in Jackson, 1960) suggests that "... for organic theories, the implication is that dementia or deterioration begins well before the time of overt psychotic symptoms and introduces the possibility that often there is no significant decrease in intellectual performance during a large part or even all of the psychotic period. "

In studying childhood school records of adult schizophrenic patients, Lane and Albee (1967) found that future schizophrenics scored significantly lower than their own siblings, while a control group of neighborhood children and their siblings did not differ significantly. In a suburb study of 114 middle and upper class schizophrenics, they discovered that when the patients were compared with their own siblings, the crucial variable in terms of premorbid intellectual functioning seemed to be the later type of schizophrenia which developed. In process schizophrenics, she found a lower I. Q. even in childhood, but in reactive schizophrenics, she found no such decrement and the patients scored as well as their health siblings. Other researchers have noted that diagnostic category is important in assessing intellectual functioning. Kendig and Richmond (1940) found that paranoids scored the highest of the schizophrenic group, as did Harper (1950). In fact, Mason (1956) found that when comparing army induction I. Q. 's for normals and individuals who later became schizophrenic, paranoids did not at that time differ from normals. Neither, he also found, did catatonics. Manic-depressives, as a matter of fact, were to be above the control group in I. Q. Taken together, the deviant group (schizophrenics, alcoholics, neurotics, manic-depressives and character disorders) did not differ from the normals. Roe and Shakow (1942) found catatonics to function slightly above the normal group; by contrast, Kendig and Richmond found them to be similar to paranoids but slightly lower. All researchers found hebrephrenic and simple schizophrenics to have the lowest level of intellectual functioning even before onset of illness. Pollack and Greenberg (1966) found that a group of schizophrenics with paranatal abnormalities scored lower than those without. On the V. I. Q. those with complications scored significantly lower (including those with moderate or severe dysfunction). Generally, schizophrenics with "minimal brain damage" have been found to score less on tests of cognitive functioning. The implication is, of course, that some schizophrenics (perhaps those with particular diagnoses) might be functioning less efficiently due to physiological damage occasioned by irregularities of pregnancy or birth.

A number of criticisms have been leveled at theories which relate less adequate intellectual functioning with psychosis. The majority of the studies utilized hospitalized patients--usually chronic. Miner and Anderson (1958) found that chronics do in fact score lower than less chronic patients. This could be considered supportive of Lane's findings as well, since chronics would be largely classified as process schizophrenics. Another criticism must be acknowledged when perus-ing the literature--the lack (especially in some of the early studies) of adequate controls of such variables as social class, sex, age, and education. As a matter of fact, some studies have equated educational level and intelligence, although the correlation between the two have yielded a weak correlation. Shakow (1946) noted that among 723 schizo-phrenics admitted to a Massachusetts State hospital, the educational levels were almost exactly comparable with the general population at that time (66 per cent grammar school, 29 per cent high school). How--ever, in college attendance he found that schizophrenics only had a six per cent rate, while normals had a ten per cent rate. Of course, many reasons might exist to explain this difference, including less ability among schizophrenics, interruptions in education among schizophrenics occasioned by the onset of the disease, or even the tendency for state hospital patients to be from lower socio-economic classes (and thus less likely to seek a college education). Another difficulty in meas-uring intellectual functioning is the tests themselves. These may im-pose a number of biases: 1) a negative bias for socio-economic de-privation, 2) a design which specifically attempts to minimize sex differences, 3) a bias favoring cooperative subjects (or those with-out organic difficulties, since organics will doggedly try and try but never succeed).

The literature regarding relationships between intellectual factors and psychosis reveals some enlightening intra-schizophrenic differences; however, these may in fact be a function rather of differ-ential reality contract. Unless studies are undertaken which attempt to compare non-hospitalized schizophrenics with normals, many of the effects noted must be taken very cautiously. In terms of birth factors affecting intellectual functioning, investigations revealing deficits should be reanalyzed to determine how much of the lowered functioning might be due to specific organic defects like impaired verbal or perceptual abilities and how much might be due to actual generalized poorer functioning. Furthermore, instruments differ-entiating between sexes and races should be developed so that the "I. Q. " difference might be understood apart from other variables.

Culture

There is evidence that schizophrenia or schizophrenic-like re-actions occur in all the known cultures of the world (Bellak, 1958) The apparent paucity of mental illness in primitive societies could be explained in terms of their not being hospitalized as often as Europeans or Americans (Benedict in Bellak, 1958) and by the abi-lity of these societies, often organized around much magic and mysti-cism, to assimilate those we would term psychotic into acceptable and even highly desirable roles like shaman (Benedict and Jacks, 1954). Of course, the lack of complexity in these societies when they are compared to the Western culture could be cited to show that in fact less mental illness does exist in the primitive world; however, re-searchers have found that the rate of hospitalization increases with the decrease of tribalization and increase of acculturation (Benedict in Bellak, 1958). In fact, the major difference seems to be qualitative rather than quantitative, with depressive features in psychosis being rare in native primitive patients. Lemkau and Crocetti (in Bellak, 1958) estimate the range in occurrence of schizophrenia to be con-servatively 50-60 per 100,000 per year minimally and 250 per 100,000 maximally. In the U.S., Lemkau, Tietze, and Cooper (1943) found that in 1943 there were approximately 290 schizophrenics per 100,000 with 147 of these actually hospitalized. Most present estimates of true incidence cluster about the maximal point of 250 per 100,000 and of hospitalization rate from 160 to 200 per 100,000.

Cultural factors have often been cited in studies first investigated in the U. S. to account for divergent results. For example, Barry and Barry (1967) explained the reversal of expected birth order effects due to differently culture-determined parental expectations or attitudes. They felt that the fact that more first-born or early-born siblings were represented in the ranks of the schizophrenic in India (investigated by both Rao in 1964 and Sundararaj and Rao in 1966) could be understood in light of the Indian family constellation, in which these positions were more stressful than later due to the national custom of expecting family responsibilities to be handled by the older children (particularly the male). Caudill (1963) made similar comments about his finding the same pattern in Japan, adding that the cultural set-up also placed the youngest daughter in a responsible and dependent role in relation to her father--and so the oldest male and youngest female in the family tended to be overrepresented. These authors also suggested that in tradition-bound families this was especially true. Caudill postulates that this is because modern homes follow Western customs more commonly--and in Western cultures the eldest and youngest both occupy different positions without the added stresses and strains of family responsibility. This added difficulty in sex role was cited in the study by Murphy and Lemieux (1967), who investigated three French-Canadian communities notable for their traditionalism in an effort to discover why the incidence of schizophrenia was so high there. They found that the inflated numbers were actually females in these societies and suggested that the ambiguity of their actual vs. nominal sex role accounted for their maladjustment.

The main problem in evaluating cross-cultural studies is that one must be completely versed in the customs involved, often difficult for the observer not of the culture and often impossible for the member observer to fully explain to the outsider. In fact, some of the variables studied by the researcher in one culture may not even be remotely relevant to the second culture; therefore, investigations might yield spurious results and confound rather than clarify understanding. In other words, is it relevant to compare a country like India--where large families are the rule--with England and the U.S.--where they are the exception (except for certain subcultures)--in terms of birth order? Or, for example, when authors cite the more problems accruing to belonging to a traditional culture, are they not ignoring the sociological research which has stressed the crippling difficulties in Western "modern" society like anomiet? In the Japanese study, could not one question the effect of the loss of the greater stability and security of the traditional family or the more conflicts it faces in the changing world, possibly not yet reflected in the statistics? And particularly relevant to physiological factors surrounding pregnancy and birth, the different attitudes and procedures of various cultures have not been investigated to uncover a possible connection in this area between cultural practices and psychosis.

Social Class

Speaking of social factors has been nearly impossible without constantly making reference to social class. In every area covered--race, culture, migration, intelligence--social class has been so completely interrelated that it begins to assume important proportions in a final theory of etiology of schizophrenia. As a confounding variable alone in a huge volume of study it becomes crucial. For example, Hollinghead and Redlich (1958) noted a marked inverse relationship between rates of treated schizophrenics (mostly hospitalized) and social status. Clearly, therefore, the majority of hospitalized patients (on whom the majority of studies are run) are from the lower classes. Von Brauchitsch and Kirk (1967) found the same for adult schizophrenics, but the opposite for children. This factor might account for the repeated reference to class variables found in many of the studies cited in this entire paper.

A brief review of the interrelated quality of social class variables and some of these general topics will serve to make this clear. Central studies on birth factors have often postulated a rather direct correlation between pregnancy and birth abnormalities and later neuropsychiatric disorders. However, most of the studies showing this have been conducted using hospitalized subjects, who are usually lower class members. Therefore, it is not surprising that researchers have found neuropsychiatric disorders (Pasamanick and Knobloch, 1957), pregnancy abnormalities and complications (Knobloch and Pasamanick, 1956; Pasamanick, 1956), and prematurity (Ebbs, Tisdall, Scott, Moyle, and Bell, 1942 cited in Barcroft, 1947; Baird, 1945; Pasamanick, Knobloch, Lilienfeld, 1956) significantly more common in the lower than upper class. Gruenberg (in Birch, 1964) also found that a disproportionately large number of mental retardates came from the relatively small group with the lowest living standards. Differential nutritional standards might also account for some of the birth differences in lower class babies. When Ebbs et. al. (in Barcroft, 1947) compared three groups of mothers (one poverty group poorly nourished, one poverty group being fed supplemental rations, and one well nourished middle class group) they found that the condition of the babies during the first and second week of life was significantly poorer for the poorly nourished unsupplemented group. They found, furthermore, that the illness record in the first six months was better for those with better nourished mothers. To their surprise, they found that in some ways the babies whose mothers were fed supplemental vitamins were in better condition and healthier than even the middle class babies, interpreted as suggesting that even the diets of middle class women were sometimes less than perfect. Similar nutritional deficits were used by Baird (1945) in explaining why lower class mothers had more premature babies. He suggested that smaller mothers tend to have premature babies--and lower class women poorly nourished from birth themselves tend to be smaller. He found that even the mature babies from the low income group were more feeble as judged by increased incidence of intrauterine death and asphyxia during pregnancy or labor. He also discovered that the cause of half of the mothers in premature labor in his low income group (8.38 per cent of 1019 women) was inexplicable (and therefore deviant) while only 15 per cent of the causes of the high income mothers' prematurity was deviant, the other 85 per cent being for the usual medical reasons (5 per cent deviant of 377). Baird also found a higher incidence of stillbirths and neonatal mortality in the lower class group (3:1). Gruenberg (in Birch, 1964) found that the lower class has more brain damage with or without a positive family history, while Masland (in Caplan, 1961) suggested that prenatal injury has a less favorable outcome in this class. Schachter (1950) compared 35 children with birth trauma and 100 normal children and found that the traumatized group had a history notable for alcoholism (one-third, correlated with later neuropsychiatric disorders), retardation (47 per cent), and neurological manifestations (42 per cent). Since 93 per cent of the traumatized group came from poor homes, this might be yet another finding really correlated with lower class membership.

Seasonal studies have also been linked to social class in many instances. Barry and Barry (1963) suggested that membership in the lower class is characteristic of any subpopulation with an elevated birth rate in the first trimester, although Pasamanick, Dinitz, and Knobloch (1959) found that both lower and upper classes had fewer births in the winter. Later Pasamanick, Dinitz, and Knobloch (1960) even suggested a dip in the lower classes in the winter with little or no birth variation throughout the year for the upper class. The theory of less protection from bad effects of the hot summer for the lower classes has been suggested to deal with the dip and lower classes' twin rate being less frequent in the winter and most frequent in the spring.

Some of the most striking findings regarding racial differences in the U. S. have been questioned due to the preponderance of Negroes in the lower class. The only study which seems to show a consistent Negro difference which is not flattened by studying social class membership was by Knobloch, Pasamanick, and Lilienfeld (1956). They found that prematurity occurs at the rate of five per cent in the white upper class, 14. 6 per cent in the white lower class, and 50. 6 per cent in the Negro lower class. While both lower class groups have greater numbers of premature births Negroes clearly outnumber whites; this may, of course, reflect biological differences in race or a lower living standard among Negroes, even when compared to lower class whites.

Regarding social class and sex, Rosenberg (1964) and Kohn (1959, cited in Schooler, 1964) both found social class to be extremely relevant when dealing with males and generally irrelevant when dealing with females. This might have reflected the form of measure they used to determine the class membership.

Schooler (1964) noted a social class difference in birth order correlations with psychosis; she found that significantly more first-born psychotics were from the lower class and significantly more last-born were from the middle class.

Social class has also entered in the interpretation of why migratory groups apparently have poorer mental health. Both the drift hypothesis and those regarding slum stress, etc., emphasize the lower living standards and class of these migrants and transients, as do theories regarding foreign-born immigrants and their status in their new countries.

When von Brauchitsch and Kirk (1967) analyzed 141 hospitalized mentally ill children according to diagnosis, social class, age, sex, race, place of residence, family background, and duration of hospitalization, they noted that most of the variables were either directly or indirectly related to social class. For example, they found that the diagnosis of schizophrenia was more frequent in hospitalized children from the upper socio-economic classes. These were easier to identify and cases with this diagnosis were usually unanimous since they were often "classic" in symptomatology. Their prognosis was poor and they usually became chronic patients. On the other hand, the rate of schizophrenia decreased as the social standing decreased, so that in lower class children diagnoses were more equivocal with doubts arising among schizophrenia, neurosis, character disorder, and adjustment reaction of childhood. In contrast to adult schizophrenia, there was a positive correlation between social class, family background, and incidence rates for childhood schizophrenia. Bender (1955) also found that non-schizophrenic, lower class children seemed to have a more favorable prognosis and adjusted somehow in adulthood.

Clausen and Kohn (cited in Jackson, 1960) also found some interesting correlations between social class and incidence of mental illness in the Hagerstown, Maryland, study (p. 298-304). There was only one significant finding: manic-depressive psychosis occurred three times as often in the upper two strata as in the lower three. Two findings which were not significant were of interest in light of prior research: first, they uncovered no difference in average rates of first hospital admissions for schizophrenia in districts of varying socio-economic status; and second, they found that rates did not vary in occupational groups. Both findings seem to lessen some of the importance of social class membership in psychosis.

When discussing social class, mobility cannot be ignored. The evidence regarding social class change, however, is ambiguous. Before hospitalization, schizophrenics have been found to be upwardly mobile in New Haven (Hollingshead, 1954), downwardly mobile in

Chicago (Schwartz cited in Jackson, 1960) and New Orleans (Liptad, 1957) and neutral in Buffalo (La Pouse, 1956). This evidence is particularly relevant when evaluating the drift hypothesis; certainly upward mobility casts doubt on its validity.

Several criticisms have been leveled on studies measuring the effect of social class. The statistics presented may be misleading, since they are offered as though they represented an average length of hospitalization for all schizophrenics. However, as more than half of all patients are returned home in less than a year, they represent instead an at least moderately chronic population. These may of course also be the sickest of all schizophrenics. Especially relevant to social class studies is the fact that families must agree to participate in them--particularly if social history is required. The families that agree may in fact be a special group, which is atypical. Investigation of one variable may also result in forgetting about others-- for example, everything may be related to a broken home if the investigator is single-mindedly searching this sector to the exclusion of others. Finally, so many variables must be correlated and explained that the task becomes a monumental one, especially if the major source of information is interview and other subjective measures. Many biases also may be interfering with the results, including the bias imposed by the upper or middle class interviewer on the lower class patient (Hollingshead and Redlich, 1958) and the test items and norms (usually formulated for the middle and upper classes) imposing a negative bias on lower class performance or values.

The bulk of evidence seems to strongly suggest a definite relationship between social class and many variables related to schizophrenia. Perhaps the crucial element will ultimately turn out to be the cluttering effect of this component rather than any true relationship. In other words, if social class can be controlled for and its effects teased out, some clear connections between psychosis and other factors, especially birth factors, may emerge.

SUMMARY

The literature linking birth factors and schizophrenia has some significant and some ambiguous findings to contribute to the study of psychosis.

Birth and pregnancy complications appear to be associated with the occurrence of schizophrenia, while material linking prematurity and birth weight is ambiguous.

Season of birth appears to be correlated with psychosis, although recent methodological inconsistencies throw some question on many previous conclusions.

Order of birth seems to be related to schizophrenia in a sexually differentiated manner, but the present literature has failed to establish reliable correlations.

Sex differences are certainly related to frequency and type of disease category.

Various social factors are definitely interrelated with many of the findings in all birth factor literature. The dependence or independence of such variables is yet to be determined with clarity.

The present state of the literature does not differentiate between crucial and intervening variables, so that the areas under investigation may be the major ones or merely secondary in relationship to a possible new variable or combination of variables as yet untested. These findings may be chance variations or relevant when taken with currently unknown factors or sets of factors. A great deal of further investigation and interpretation is needed to clarify the myriad conclusions which have already been suggested.

REFERENCES

Abe, K. Susceptibility to psuchosis and precipitating factors: A study of families with two or more psychotic members. Psychiatria et Neurologia, 1966, 151 (5), 276-290.

Arieti, S. (ed.) American Handbook of Psychiatry. New York: Basic Books, Inc., Publishers, 1959, Volumes I, II.

Asher, P. & Schonell, R. E. Survey of 400 cases of cerebral palsy in childhood. Archives of Diseases of Childhood, 1950, 25, 360.

Baird, W. Social class and birth weight. Journal of Obstetrics and Gynecology, 1945, 52 (4), 339-366.

Bakan, D. The relationship between alcoholism and birth rank. Quarterly Journal of Studies on Alcoholism, 1949, 10, 434-440.

Baker, H. J., Decker, F. J. & Hill, A. S. A study of juvenile theft. Journal of Educational Research, 1929, 20, 81-87.

Barcroft, J. Researches on Prenatal Life, Vol. I. Springfield, Ill.: Charles C. Thomas, Publishers, 1947.

Barry, H. & Barry H., Jr. Birth order, family size, and schizophrenia. Archives of General Psychiatry. 1967, 17 (4), 435-440.

Barry, H. & Barry, H., Jr. Season of birth. Archives of General Psychiatry, 1961, 5, 292-300.

Barry, H. & Barry, H., Jr. Season of birth. Archives of General Psychiatry, 1963, 7, 385-391.

Bellak, L. (ed.) Schizophrenia: A Review of the Syndrome. New York: Logos Press, 1958.

Bender, L. Theory and treatment of childhood schizophrenia. Acta Paedopsychiatrica, 1967, 34, 298-307.

Bender, L. & Grugett, A. E. A. study of certain epidemiological factors in a group of children with childhood schizophrenia. The American Journal of Orthopsychiatry, 1956, 26 (1), 131-143.

Bender, L. & Laretra, G. Pregnancy and birth histories of children with psychiatric problems. Reprinted from Proceedings of the Third World Congress of Psychiatry, 1962, 1329-1333.

Benedict, P. K. & Jacks, G. Mental illness in primitve societies. Psychiatry, 1954, 17, 377-389.

Birch, H. G. (ed.) Brain Damage in Children. New York: Williams and Wilkins Co, 1964.

Bowlby, J. Maternal Care and Mental Health. New York: Schocken Books, 1951.

Boyd, W. The influence of sex. In A Textbook of Pathology. Philadelphia: Lea and Febiger, 1961.

Braatoy, C. Is it probable that the sociological situation is a factor in schizophrenia? Acta Psychiatria Scandinavia, 1937, 12, 109-138.

Brackbill, G. A. & Fine, H. J. Schizophrenia and central nervous system pathology. Journal of Abnormal and Social Psychology, 1956, 52, 310-313.

Burt, C. The Young Delinquent. New York: Appleton, 1925.

Caplan, G. (ed.) Emotional Problems of Early Childhood. New York: Basic Books, Inc., 1955.

Caplan, G. (ed.) Prevention of Mental Disorders in Children. New York: Basic Books, Inc., 1961.

Carlson, L. A comparison of Negro and Caucasian performance on th Bender-Gestalt test. Journal of Clinical Psychology, 1966, 22 (1), 96-98.

Caudill, W. Sibling rank and style of life among Japanese psychiatric patients. Proceddings of the Joint Meeting of the Japanese Society of Psychiatry and Neurology and the American Psychiatric Association, May, 1963, Tokyo, Japan. Supplement to Psychiatria et Neurologia Japonica, 35-40.

Chapman, L. J. & Baxter, J. C. The process-reactive distinction and patients"s subculture. Journal of Nervous and Mental Disorders, 1963, 136, 352-359.

Clausen, J. A. & Kohn, M. L. The ecological approach in social psychiatry. American Journal of Sociology, 1947, 60, 140-151.

Costello, A. J. & Gunn, J. C. & Dominian, J. Aetiological factors in young schizophrenic men. British Journal of Psychiatry, 1968, 114 (509), 433-441.

Creak, M. & Ini, S. Families of psychotic children. Journal of Child Psychology and Psychiatry, 1960, 1, 156-175.

Cutler, R. The effects of prenatal and neonatal complications on the development of premature children at age $2\frac{1}{2}$ years. Journal of Genetic Psychology. 1965, 107 (2), 261.

de Hoyos, A. & de Hoyos, G. Symptomatogogy differences between Negro and white schizophrenics. International Journal of Social Psychiatry 1965, 11 (4), 245-255.

Dennegy, C. M. Childhood bereavement and psychiatric illness. British Journal of Psychiatry, 1966, 112 (491), 1049-1069.

Dublin, L. I. Suicide. New York: Ronald Press, 1963.

Dunham, H. W. The current status of etiological research in mental disorder, Sociological Focus, 1947, 25, 321-326.

Ebbs, J. H., Tisdall, F. F., Scott, W. A., Moyle, W. J., & Bell, M. The influence of prenatal diet on the mother and child. Canadian Medical Association Journal, 1942, 46 (1).

Elasser, G. & Subke, H. Ovarian fuction and body constitution in female inmates of mental hospitals. Archives Psychiatria Nervenberank. 1954, 14, 561-566.

Farina, A., Barry, H. & Garmezy, N. ·Birth order of recovered non-recovered schizophrenics. Archives of General Psychiatry, 1963, 9, 224-228.

Faris, R. E. L. & Dunham, H. W. Mental Disorders in Urban Areas. Chicago: Chicago University Press, 1939.

Fish, B. & Alpert, M. Abnormal states of consciousness and muscle tone in infants born to schizophrenic mothers. American Journal of Psychiatry, 1962, 119, 439-445.

Gardner, G. G. Role of maternal psychopathology in male and female schizophrenics. Journal of Consulting Psychology, 1967, 31, 411-413

Gittelman, M. & Birch, H. G. Childhood schizophrenia: Intellectual, neurological status, perinatal risk, prognosis, family pathology. Archives of General Psychiatry, 1969, 17 (1), 16-25.

Goldfarb, C. & Erlenmeyer-Kimling, L. Mating and fertility trends in schizophrenia. Expanding Goals of Genetics in Psychiatry, Kallman, F. J. (ed.) New York: Grune and Stratton, 1962.

Graham, F. K., Ernhart, C. B., Thurston, D., and Craft, M. Development three years after perinatal anoxia and other potentially damaging newborn experiences. Psychology Monographs, 1962, 76 (3),

Granville-Grossman, K. L. Birth order and schizophrenia. British Journal of Psychiatry, 1966, 112 (492), 1119-1126.

Granville-Grossman, K. L. Parental Age and schizophrenia, British Journal of Psychiatry, 1966, 112 (490), 899-905.

Gray, S. H. & Feemster, L. C. Compensatory hypertrophy and hyperplasia of the islands of langerhans in the pancreases of children born of diabetic mothers. Archives of Pathology and Laboratory Medicine, 1926, 1, 348-355.

Grosz, H. J. & Miller, I. Sibling patterns in schizophrenia. Science, July 4, 1958, 128, 30.

Harper, A. E., Jr. Discrimination of the types of schizophrenia by the Wechsler Bellevue Scale. Journal of Consulting Psychology, 1950, 14, 290-296.

Havelkova, M. Abnormalities in siblings of schizophrenic children. Canadian Psychiatric Association Journal, 1967, 12 (4), 363-369.

Heston, L. L. Psychiatric disorders in foster home reared children of schizophrenic mothers. British Journal of Psychiatry, 1966, 112, 819-825.

Hinton, G. G. Childhood psychosis or mental retardation: A diagnostic dilemma. II. Pediatric and neurological aspects. Canadian Medical Association Journal, 1963, 89, 1020-1024.

Hoch, H. & Zubin, J. Psychopathology of Schizophrenia. New York: Grune and Stratton, 1966.

Hollingshead, A. B. Social mobility and mental illness. American Sociological Review, 1954, 19, 577-584.

Hollingshead, A. B. & Redlich, F. C. Social Class and Mental Illness: A Community Study. New York: Wiley, 1958.

Huntington, E. Season of Birth: Its Relation to Human Abilities. New York: John Wiley and Sons, Inc., 1938.

Ingalls, T. H. Etiology of mongolism: Epidemiologic and teratologic implications. American Journal of Diseases of Childhood. 1947, 74, 147-165.

Jackson, D. D. The Etiology of Schizophrenia. New York: Basic Books, Inc., 1960.

Jaco, E. G. The Social Epidemiology of Mental Disorders: A Psychiatric Survey of Texas. New York: Russell Sage Foundation, 1960.

Kanner, L. Child Psychiatry. Springfield, Illinois: Thomas, 1957.

Kardiner, A. & Ovesey, L. The Mark of Oppression: A Psychosocial Study of the American Negro. New York: W. W. Norton, 1951.

Kawi, A. & Pasamanick, B. The association of factors of pregnancy with the development of reading disorders in childhood. Journal of the American Medical Association, 1958, 166, 1420.

Keeler, W. R. Discussion. Psychiatric Reports of the American Psychiatric Association, 1957, 7, 66-88.

Kendig, I. & Richmond, W. V. Psychological Studies in Dementia Praecox. Ann Arbor: Edwards, 1940.

Knobloch, H. & Pasamanick, B. A developmental questionnaire for infants 40 weeks of age: An evaluation. Monograph 61, Society of Research in Child Development. Yellow Springs: Antioch Press, 1956.

Knobloch, H. & Pasamanick, B. Etiological factors in early infantile autism and childhood schizophrenia. Paper presented at the International Congress of Pediatrics, Lisbon, Portugal, 1962.

Knobloch, H. & Pasamanick, B. Seasonal variation in the births of mentally deficient. American Journal of Public Health, 1958, 48, 1201.

Knobloch, H., Rider, R., Harper, P., & Pasamanick, B. The neuro-psychiatric sequelae of prematurity: A longitudinal study. Journal of the American Medical Association, 1956, 161, 581.

Kohn, M. L. & Clausen, J. A. Parental authority, behavior, and schizo-phrenia. American Journal of Orthopsychiatry, 1956, 26, 297-313.

Lane, E. A. The influence of sex and race on process-reactive ratings of schizophrenia. Journal of Psychology, 1968, 68 (1), 15-20.

Lane, E. A. & Albee, G. W. Comparative birth weights of schizophrenics and their siblings. The Journal of Psychology, 1966, 64, 227-231.

Lane, E. A. & Albee, G. W. Intellectual and perinatal antecedents of adult schizophrenia. Grant M5186 from National Institute of Mental Health. Read at Conference on Life History Studies in Psychopath-ology, 1967.

La Pouse, R. The drift hypothesis and socio-economic differentials in schizophrenia. American Journal of Public Health, 1956, 46, 978-986.

Lemkau, P. V., Tietze, C. & Cooper, M. A survey of status studies on the prevalence and incidence of mental disorder in a sample population. Public Health Reports, 1943, 57, 1909-1924.

Levine, M. & Olson, R. P. Intelligence of parents of autistic children. Journal of Abnormal Psychology, 1968, 73, 215-217.

Levy, J. A quantitative study of behavior problems in relation to family constellation. American Journal Psychiatry, 1931, 10, 637-654.

Lilienfeld, A. M. & Pasamanick, B. Association of maternal and fetal factors with the development of epilepsy. I. Abnormalities in the prenatal and paranatal periods. Journal of the American Medical Association, 1954, 155, 719.

Lilienfeld, A. M. & Pasamanick, B. A study of variations in the frequency of twin births by race and socio-economic status. Journal of Human Genetics, 1955, 7, 401.

Lilienfeld, A. M. & Pasamanick, B. The association of maternal and fetal factors with the development of mental deficiency. II: Relationship to maternal age, birth order, previous reproductive loss, and degree of mental deficiency. American Journal of Mental Deficiency, 1956, 60, 557.

Lilienfeld, A. M., Pasamanick, B. & Rogers, M. E. The relationship between pregnancy experience and the development of certain neuropsychiatric disorders in childhood. American Journal of Public Health, 1955, 45, 637.

Lotter, V. Epidemiology of the autistic condition in young children. II: Some characteristics of the parents of children. Social Psychiatry, 1967, 1 (4), 163-173.

Lowe, L. H. Families of children with early childhood schizophrenia: Selected demographic information. Archives of General Psychiatry, 1966, 14 (1), 26-30.

Lucas, A. R., Rodin, E. A., Simson, C. B. Neurological assessment of children with early school problems. Developmental Medicine and Child Neurology, 1965, 17, 145-156.

MacMahon, B. & Sowa, J. M. Physical Damage to the Fetus in Causes of Mental Disorders: A Review of Epidemiology and Knowledge. New York: Milbank Memorial Fund, 1961.

Malzberg, B. Mental disease among native and foreign born whites in New York State. American Journal of Psychiatry, 1936, 93, 127-137.

Malzberg, B. Mental disease among Negroes in New York State. Mental Hygiene, 1953, 37, 450.

Malzberg, B. Mental illness among Norwegian born and native born of Norwegian parentage in New York State 1949-51. Acta Psychiatria Scandinavia, 1962, 38, 48-75.

Malzberg, B. Migration and mental disease in New York State 1939-41. Human Biology, 1956, 28, 350.

Malzberg, B. Trends in mental disease in New York State 1920-50. Proceedings of the Association of the Philadelphia Society, 1955, 99, 176.

Mason, C. F. Intelligence and mental illness. Journal of Consulting Psychology, 1956, 20, 297-300.

Maxwell, J. P., Hu, C. H. & Turnbull, H. M. Foetal rickets. Journal of Pathology and Bacteriology, 1932, 35, 419.

May, J. M. Discussion. The American Journal of Orthopsychiatry, 1956, 26, 144.

McClelland, D. C. & Watt, N. F. Sex role alienation in schizophrenia. Journal of Abnormal Psychology, 1968, 73, 226-239.

Miner, J. B. & Anderson, J. K. Intelligence and emotional disturbance: evidence from Army and Veterans Administration records. Journal of Abnormal and Social Psychology, 1958, 56, 75-81.

Murphy, H. B. & Lemieux, M. Some considerations on the high rate of schizophrenia in the French Canadian community. Canadian Psychiatric Association Journal, 1967, 12, 71-85.

Norris A. S. & Chowning, J. R. Season of birth and mental illness. Archives of General Psychiatry, 1962, 7, 206-212.

Nowicki, S., Jr. Birth order and personality: Some unexpected findings. Psychological Reports, 1967, 21 (1), 265-267.

Odegaard, S. Emigration and insanity. Acta Psychiatria Scandinavia, 1932, Supplement 4.

Opler, M. K. & Singer, J. Ethnic differences in behavior and psychopathology: Italian and Irish. International Journal of Social Psychiatry, 1956, 2, 11-23.

Orme, J. E. Intelligence and season of birth. British Journal of Medical Psychology, 1962, 35, 233-234.

Orme, J. E. Season of birth, psychosis, and intelligence. Diseases of the Nervous System, 1963, 24, 489.

Osterkamp, A. & Sands, D. J. Early feeding and birth difficulties in childhood schizophrenia: A brief study. Journal of Genetic Psychology, 1962, 101 (2), 363-366.

Paffenbarger, R. S., Jr. Epidemiological aspects of parapartum mental illness. British Journal of Preventative and Social Medicine, 1964, 18, 189-195.

Paffenbarger, R. S., Jr., Steinmetz, C. H., Pooler, B. G. & Hyde, R. T. The picture puzzle of the postpartum psychosis. Journal of Chronic Diseases, 1961, 13 (2), 161-173.

Pasamanick, B. A comparative study of the behavioral development of Negro infants. Journal of Genetic Psychology, 1946, 59, 3.

Pasamanick, B., Dinitz, S., & Knobloch, H. Geographic and seasonal variation in birth rates. Public Health Report, 1959, 74 (4), 285.

Pasamanick, B. , Dinitz, S. , & Knobloch, H. Socioeconomic and seasonal variation in birth rates. Millbank Memorial Fund Quarterly, 1960, 38, 348.

Pasamanick, B. & Knobloch, H. Seasonal variation in complications of pregnancy. Journal of Obstetrics and Gynecology, 1958, 12, 110.

Pasamanick, B. & Knobloch, H. Some early organic precursors of racial behavioral differences. Journal of the National Medical Association, 1957, 49, 372.

Pasamanick, B. , Knobloch, H. , & Lilienfeld, A. M. Socioeconomic status and some precursors of neuropsychiatric disorders. American Journal of Orthopsychiatry, 1956, 26, 594.

Pasamanick, B. & Lilienfeld, A. M. Association of maternal and fetal factors with the development of mental deficiency. I: Abnormalities in the prenatal and paranatal periods. Journal of the American Medical Association, 1955, 159, 155.

Pasamanick, B. , Rogers, M. E. , & Lilienfeld, A. M. Pregnancy experience and the development of childhood behavior disorders. American Journal of Psychiatry, 1956, 112, 613.

Patterson, W. B. Congenital factors in thyroid disease. Western Journal of Surgery, 1939, 47, 273-276.

Patterson, V. Block, J. , Block, J. , & Jackson, D. D. The relation between intention to conceive and symptoms during pregnancy. Psychosomatic Medicine, 1960, 22, 373-376.

Petersen, W. F. The Patient and the Weather. In Mental and Nervous Diseases, Vol. 3. Ann Arbor, Michigan: Edwards Bros. , Inc. , 1934.

Phillips, E. E. Contributions to a learning theory account of childhood autism. Journal of Psychology, 1957, 43, 117-125.

Pile, W. J. A study of the correlation between dementia praecox and the month of birth. Virginia Medical Monthly, 1951, 78, 438.

Plum, P. Cerebral palsy: A clinical survey of 543 cases. Danish Medical Bulletin, 1956, 3 (4), 99-108.

Plum, P. Early diagnosis of spastic paraplegia. Spastic Quarterly, 1962, 11 (3), 4-11.

Pollack, M. Early "minimal brain damage" and the development of severe psychopathology in adolescence. Journal of Orthopsychiatry, 1967, 37, (2), 23-214.

Pollack, M. & Gittelman, R. K. The siblings of childhood schizophrenics: A review. The American Journal of Orthopsychiatry, 1964, 34 (5).

Pollack, M. & Greenberg, M. Paranatal complications in hospitalized schizophrenic and nonschizophrenic patients. Journal of Hillside Hospital, 1966, 15 (3-4), 191-204.

Pollack, M., Levenstein, S., & Klein, D. F. The 3 year post hospital follow-up of adolescent and adult schizophrenics. American Journal of Orthopsychiatry, 1968, 38 (1), 94-109.

Pollack, M. & Woerner, M. G. Pre and perinatal complications and "childhood schizophrenia": A comparison of 5 controlled studies. Journal of Child Psychology and Psychiatry, 1966, 7 (3-4), 235-242.

Pollin, W., Stabenau, J. R., Mosher, L. & Tupin, J. Life history differences in identical twins discordant for schizophrenia. Presented at the 42nd annual meeting of the American Orthopsychiatric Association, New York, 1965.

Preyer, W. Spezielle Physiologie des Embryo. Leipzig: Grieben, 1885.

Pugh, T. F. & MacMahon, B. Epidemiologic Findings in U. S. Mental Hospital Data. Boston: Little, Brown, 1962.

Rao, B. S. Birth order and schizophrenia. Journal of Nervous and Mental Diseases, 1964, 138, 87-89.

Record, R. G. & Smith, A. Incidence, mortality, and sex distribution of mongoloid defectives. British Journal of Preventative and Social Medicine, 1955, 9, 10-15.

Rimland, B. Infantile Autism. New York: Appleton Century Crofts, 1964.

Robbins, L. C. The accuracy of parental recall of child development and child rearing practices. Journal of Abnormal and Social Psychology, 1963, 66, 261-270.

Roe, A. & Shakow, D. Intelligence in mental disorder. Annals of the New York Academy of Sciences, 1942, 42, 361-400.

Rosenbaum, C. P. Metabolic, physiological, anatomic, and genetic studies in the schizophrenias: A review and analysis. The Journal of Nervous and Mental Disorders, 1968, 146 (2), 103-123.

Rosenow, C. & Whyte, A. H. The ordinal position of problem children. American Journal of Orthopsychiatry, 1931, 1, 430.

Rosenthal, D. Familial concordance by sex with respect to schizophrenia. Psychological Bulletin, 1962, 59, 401-421.

Rosenthal, D. The Genain Quadruplets. New York: Basic Books, 1963.

Rosenthal, D. Problems of sampling and diagnosis in the major twin studies of schizophrenia. Journal of Psychiatric Research, 1963, 1, 116-134.

Rutstein, D. D., Nickerson, R. J. & Heald, F. P. Seasonal Incidence of patent ductus arteriosus and maternal rubella. American Journal of the Diseased Child, 1952, 84, 199.

Rutter, M. & Lockyer, L. A 5 to 15 year follow-up study of infantile psychosis. I: Description of sample. British Journal of Psychiatry, 1967, 113 (504), 1169-1182.

Sankar, D. V. Siva. Multiple biochemical deviations in childhood schizophrenia (Autism). Annual Convention of the Society of Biological Psychiatry, May 1969. In Press. Biological Psychiatry.

Schachter, M. Observations on the prognosis of children born following trauma at birth. American Journal of Mental Deficiency, 1950,
54, 456-463.

Schachter, S.   The Psychology of Affiliation. Stanford, California:
Stanford University Press, 1959.

Schooler, C. Affiliation among schizophrenics: Preferred characteristics of the other. Journal of Nervous and Mental Disease, 1963,
137 (5), 438-446.

Schooler, C. Birth order and hospitalization for schizophrenia. Journal
of Abnormal and Social Psychology, 1964, 69, 574-579.

Schooler, C. Birth order and schizophrenia. Archives of General Psychiatry, 1961, 4, 91-97.

Schooler, C. & Long, J.   Affiliation among chronic schizophrenics:
Factors affecting acceptance of responsibility for the fate of another. The Journal of Nervous and Mental Diseases, 1963, 137 (2),
173-179.

Schooler, C. & Parkel, D.   The overt behavior of chronic schizophrenics
and its relationship to their internal state and personal history. Reprinted with permission by the U. S. Department of Health, Education, and Welfare, Public Health Service, 1963.

Schooler, C. & Scarr, S.   Affiliation among chronic schizophrenics:
Relation to intrapersonal and birth order factors. Journal of Personality 1962, 30 (2), 178-192.

Shakow, D. The nature of deterioration in schizophrenic conditions.
Nervous and Mental Disease Monographs, 1946, No. 70.

Shearer, M. L., Davidson, R. T. & Finch, S. M.   The sex ratio of
offspring born to state hospitalized schizophrenic women. Journal
of Psychiatric Research, 1967, 5 (4), 349-350.

Simon, G. B. & Gillies, S. M.   Some physical characteristics of a
group of psychotic children. British Journal of Psychiatry, 1964,
110, 104.

Slawson, J. The Delinquent Boy.   Boston: Gorham Press, 1926.

Sletto, R. F. Sibling position and juvenile delinquency. American
Journal of Sociology, 1934, 39, 657-659.

Smith, C. M. & McIntyre, S.   Family size, birth rate, and ordinal
position in psychiatry. Canadian Psychiatric Association Journal,
1963, 8, 244-248.

Solomon, L. & Nuttall, R.   Sibling order, premorbid adjustment,
and remission in schizophrenia. Journal of Nervous and Mental
Disorders, 1967, 144 (1), 37-46.

Sontag, L. W. & Richards, T. W.   Studies in fetal behavior: I. Fetal
heart rate as a behavioral indication. Child Development Monograph,
1938, 3 (4).

Sontag, L. W. & Wallace, R. F.   The effect of cigarette smoking during pregnancy upon the fetal heart rate. American Journal of Obstetrics and Gynecology, 1935, 29, 77-82.

Stabenau, J. R.   Heredity and environment in schizophrenia: The contribution of twin studies. Archives of General Psychiatry, 1969, 18 (4), 458-463.

Stabenau, J. R. & Pollin W.   Early characteristics of monozygotic twins discordant for schizophrenia. Archives of General Psychiatry, 1967, 17 (6), 723-734.

Sundararaj, N. & Rao, B. S.   Order of birth and schizophrenia. British Journal of Psychiatry, 1966, 112 (492), 1127-1129.

Taft, L. & Goldfarb, W.   Prenatal and perinatal factors in childhood schizophrenia. Developmental Medicine and Child Neurology, 1964, 6 (1), 32.

Taylor, H. M.   Prenatal medication as a possible etiologic factor of deafness in the newborn. Archives Otolarynx, 1934, 20, 790-803.

Terris, M., LaPouse, R. & Monk, M.   The relation of prematurity and previous fetal loss to childhood schizophrenia. The American Journal of Psychiatry, 1964, 121 (5).

Tietze, C., Lemkau, P. & Cooper, M.   Personal disorder and spatial mobility. American Journal of Sociology, 1942, 48, 29.

Ucko, L.   A comparative study of asphyxiated and nonasphyxiated boys from birth to 5 years. Developmental Medicine and Child Neurology. 1965, 7 (6), 643.

von Brauchitsch, H. K. & Kirk, W. E.   Childhood schizophrenia and social class. American Journal of Orthopsychiatry, 1967, 37 (2), 400.

Vorster, D.   An investigation of the part played by organic factors in childhood schizophrenia. Journal of Mental Science, 1960, 106, 494-522.

Wahl, C. W.   Some antecedent factors in the family histories of 392 schizophrenics. American Journal of Psychiatry, 1954, 110, 668-676.

Wahl, C. W.   Some antecedent factors in the family histories of 562 male schizophrenics of the U. S. Navy. American Journal of Psychiatry, 1956, 113, 201-210.

Wedge, B.   Occurrence of psychosis among Okinawans in Hawaii. American Journal of Psychiatry, 1952, 109, 255-258.

Weidon, W. S.   Toxemia of pregnancy and schizophrenia. Journal of Nervous and Mental Disorders, 1954, 120, 1-9.

Wenar, C.   The reliability of developmental histories. Psychosomatic Medicine, 1963, 25, 505-509.

Whittam, H., Simon, G. B. & Mittler, P. J.   The early development of psychotic children and their siblings. Developmental Medicine and Child Neurology, 1966, 8 (5), 552-560.

Wilkins, L. W., Jones, H. W., Holman, G. H. & Stempfel, R. S., Jr.   Masculinization of the female fetus associated with administration of progestine during gestation. Journal of Clinical Endocrinology, 1958, 18, 559-588.

E. Mura, M.A., Child Psychiatry, Creedmoor State Hospital, Queens Village, N.Y. 11427

DEMOGRAPHIC STUDIES ON CHILDHOOD SCHIZOPHRENIA:

PRELIMINARY REPORT ON SEASON OF BIRTH, DIAGNOSIS, SEX,

I.Q. AND RACE DISTRIBUTION

D.V. SIVA SANKAR

SECTION I: STUDIES ON SEASON OF BIRTH

Several important aspects of the relationship of the season of birth to mental illness have been reviewed in the preceding paper by Mura. We have carried out several demographic studies on children admitted to the Children's Unit at Creedmoor State Hospital from 1956-1967. Our results regarding the season of birth are presented in Tables I, II and Figures 1-5. There were a total of 3,377 cases analyzed in these studies. The results on the distribution of the month of birth in these children are compared to those of the total New York City population (Queens, Brooklyn, Richmond, Bronx, Manhattan) for the years 1952-1967. These results are shown in Table I.

TABLE I
DISTRIBUTION OF THE MONTH OF BIRTH IN CHILDREN ADMITTED FROM 1957-1967

Month	Child Psychiatric Unit 1957-1967 inclusive (Data for 11 years)			New York City (per year data) from 1952-1967		
	No. of Births	% of yearly births	Births per day	No. of Births	% of yearly births	Births per day
January	260	7.70	8.39	13486	8.25	435.0
February	259	7.70	9.18	12719	7.78	451.0
March	315	9.30	10.13	13895	8.56	448.2
April	290	8.58	9.67	12978	7.94	432.6
May	250	7.40	8.06	13601	8.38	438.7
June	307	9.09	10.23	13675	8.37	455.8
July	297	8.79	9.58	14431	8.82	465.5
August	289	8.56	9.32	14182	8.67	457.5
September	274	8.11	9.13	13928	8.52	464.3
October	272	8.05	8.77	13977	8.55	450.9
November	269	7.96	8.97	13157	8.04	438.6
December	296	8.76	9.55	13411	8.31	432.6
Average	281	8.33	9.25	13620	8.33	447.6

Further, the number of births in any given month are evaluated as a percent of the total births for the year. Table I also presents the number of births per day in the total population at the children's unit and in New York City. The average number of births per day for the whole year are taken as 100%, with a view to normalize the number of births per day in any given month, for eg., the average number of births per day in the population of the children's unit is 9.25. Out of this is 100% the number of births in January are 8.39 or 90.7 is a normalized value. The normalized figures for both the child psychiatric population and the New York City population are·shown in Figure 1.

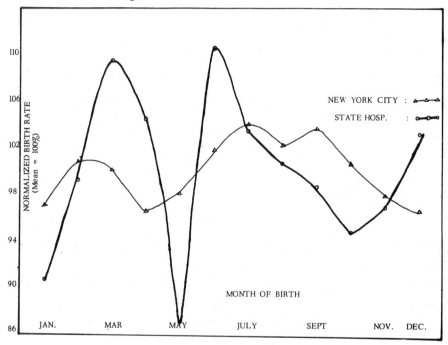

Fig. 1 - Normalized Curves for daily birth rates presented for the 12 months of the year for Child Psychiatric Patients vs. Total N.Y.C. births.

It may be seen from Figure 1 that there is a distinct increase in the number of births of the subjects in the child psychiatric patients, whereas the New York City birth rate does not show an increase in the months of March and April. This increase in the number of births is offset by decrease in the months of May, September and October.

If the number of births in the child psychiatric population are high in March and April (this corresponds to conception in June and July) the first trimester of the pregnancy will then coincide with the months of June, July and August. It is conceivable, but by no means the only etiological argument, that the heat in the first trimester or the unusual summer activities of the first trimester, or the poor nutritional habits (does this include drinking large amounts of sweetened or artificially sweetened sodas!) may be responsible for the larger number of psychiatrically anormal children. With the evidence that we have it is not possible to evaluate the relative validity of the different etiologies. It will be of interest to compare these data with data obtained from south of the equator eg., Argentina, Australia etc. In Figure 2 we have presented the data, by the season. For this purpose the year was divided into Winter (consisting of December, January, February, March), Spring (consisting of April, May), Summer (June, July, August), Fall (September, October, November). In this mode of presentation many of the months that show individual differences are amalgamated with those that may not show a difference. However, it can still be seen that there is a higher

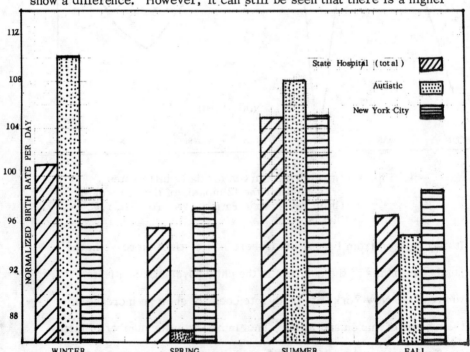

Fig. 2 - Normalized births per day by the season. Average
number of births per category = 100% for that category
only.

453

number of births in winter in the child psychiatric population than
in the New York City population. From the results presented in the
following pages it is felt that the births occurring in winter especially
the months of March, April and May possess a larger amount of

TABLE   II
MONTH OF BIRTH DISTRIBUTION BY DIAGNOSIS

	Total Births	Births Per Day	Normalized
TOTAL NEW YORK CITY			
Winter	535,115	4415	98.8
Spring	265,792	4357	97.3
Summer	422,880	4596	105.1
Fall	410,621	4512	100.9
TOTAL CREEDMOOR STATE HOSPITAL			
Winter	1,129	9.33	100.9
Spring	540	8.85	95.7
Summer	893	9.70	104.9
Fall	815	8.95	96.7
SCHIZOPHRENIA (TOTAL)			
Winter	701	5.79	101.4
Spring	329	5.29	94.4
Summer	570	6.19	106.5
Fall	506	5.56	97.4
SCHIZOPHRENIA (AUTISTIC)			
Winter	41	0.34	111.0
Spring	16	0.26	87.0
Summer	30	0.33	108.0
Fall	26	0.29	95.0
PRIMARY BEHAVIOR DISORDERS			
Winter	234	1.93	100.5
Spring	129	2.11	109.9
Summer	147	1.59	82.8
Fall	186	2.04	106.2
PSYCHOSIS			
Winter	116	0.96	103.3
Spring	48	0.77	83.0
Summer	99	1.07	115.3
Fall	83	0.91	98.2
MENTALLY DEFECTIVE			
Winter	78	0.64	114.0
Spring	34	0.55	98.6
Summer	57	0.62	109.6
Fall	40	0.44	77.7

Winter - Dec., Jan., Feb., March; Spring - Apr., May;
Summer - June, July, Aug.; Fall - Sept., Oct., Nov.

neurological damage resulting in either mental deficiency or psychosis or in autism. Figure 2 also shows the normalized birth rates for autistic children in our population at the Child Psychiatric Unit. It can be clearly seen that there is a much higher percent of autistic children born in winter compared with the other populations. Similarly the results from Table II show that the highest number of births in winter are to be found again in the diagnostic categories of psychosis and mental deficiency. There is no prominent increase in the winter births for the diagnostic categories of primary behavior disorders.

Autistic children have been shown by our several studies (cf: also "Recent Advances in Biological Psychiatry" Conference held in May, 1969, In Press) to be clinically different, biologically and biochemically, from other child psychiatric patients. The difference lies not only in several biological parameters but also in a higher number of breaks (independent of pharmacological treatment) in the leucocyte chromosomes (D. V. Siva Sankar et al. Clinical Research XVII, p. 317, April 1969).

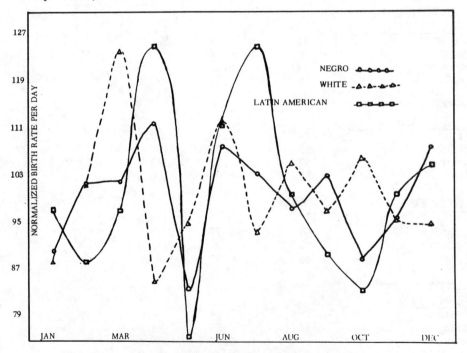

Fig. 3 - Normalized rates of births per day distributed according to race. Data on child psychiatric patients

The number of births were also normalized with respect to race, and are presented in Figure 3. It may be seen from these figures that the largest number of white children in our population were born in the month of March, whereas the largest number of Negro and Latin American children were born in the month of April. The next largest number of births occur in the months of June and July in our population. Here again the larger number of births in the months of March and April in the psychiatric population corroborate our previous finding of higher conception rates of the psychiatric population in June and July. This may also be due to the fact that a larger number of matrimonies occur in the month of June. The results in Figure 4 show the normalized distribution according to sex. Here again the highest number of births take place in March. While it can be seen that our results show an increase in the number of births in March and June, there is no similar increase of births in these months in the general population of New York City from 1952-1967 (cf. Figure 1).

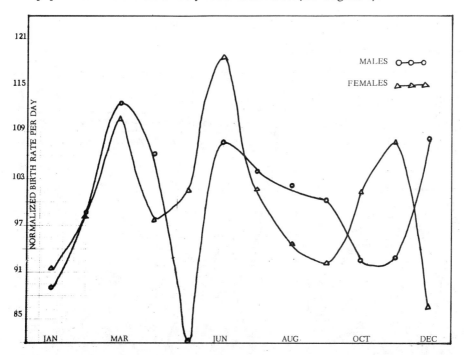

Fig. 4 - Normalized rate of births per day distributed
according to sex. Data on child psychiatric patients.

The births were distributed according to psychiatric diagnosis
and the normalized values for this are presented in Figure 5. It
may be seen from these data that the largest increases in the month
of March are shown by the diagnostic categories, psychosis and
mental deficiency. It was for this reason that we have hypothesized that the fetus conceived in summer months may have a
higher amount of neurological damage. The question of assessing
neurological damage in psychiatric child populations is very difficult. The two may, at times, be the two sides of the same coin.
If we are looking for a biological defect in psychiatric illness it is
hard to conceive of a psychological biological defect which may not
have its own neurological counterpart also. The normalized values
for the different psychiatric groups have been calculated according
to the four seasons (winter, spring, summer, fall) and are presented
in Table II. These results indicate a slightly larger amount of births
in winter for the diagnostic group of childhood schizophrenia. Birth
rates in the categories of autism, psychosis and mentally deficient
are highest in the winter season.

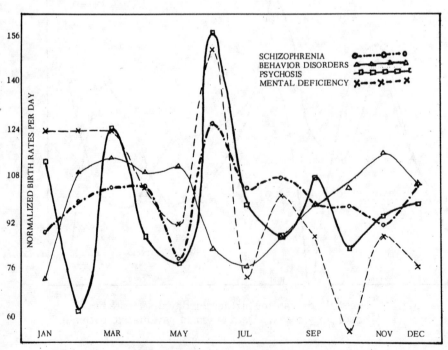

Fig. 5 - Normalized rates of births per day distributed
according to diagnosis. Data from child psychiatric
patients.

In summary our several data do show an increase in birth rate in March and April, among the patients hospitalized in our unit. This increase is not to be found in overall New York City birth rates for the years 1952-1967 inclusive. There seems to be a fairly larger increase of births in winter that carry a diagnostic label in later life that may involve neurobiological damage. The question looms as ever, can we distinguish neurological defect from psychiatric defect in schizophrenia, especially childhood schizophrenia.

SECTION II: RACE DISTRIBUTION

Our results on the distribution of the child patients admitted to the Children's Unit of Creedmoor State Hospital in 1956-1967, according to race are shown in Table III. It may be seen that there is a distinct majority of Negro children in this population. The percent of Negroes in the general population of New York City was 14.3% in 1960, while in our child population the Negro patients account for 46.7% of the patients. This is a much larger percent than in the general population and may be due to the fact that many Negro children may have been admitted to the unit for various reasons. Some of these reasons may be due to sociopathological behavior which may at times be undifferentiated from schizophrenia.

It is also intriguing to compare the percent of Negro patients in child psychiatric and adult populations. If we assume, with some justification that the percentage of Negro adults in adult psychiatric patients is not as high as that of Negro child patients in total child psychiatric patients, the question may be asked, "What is happening to the Negro child patient after his release from the child psychiatric hospital?"

458

TABLE III

TOTAL NUMBER OF PATIENTS

FIRST ADMISSIONS TO CREEDMOOR

CHILDREN'S UNIT

3406

DIAGNOSTIC DISTRIBUTION	NUMBER OF SUBJECTS	% OF TOTAL
Schizophrenia	2125	62.38
Primary Behavior Disorders	716	21.02
Psychosis	352	10.33
Mental Deficiency without psychosis	213	6.25

SEX DISTRIBUTION		
Males	2527	74.19
Females	879	25.81

RACE DISTRIBUTION		
Negro	1591	46.71
White	1258	36.93
Latin American (Includes Puerto Ricans)	557	16.35

The sex distribution in the race is presented in Tables IV and V. It can be seen from Table IV that there is a higher ratio of Negro female to male patients. This may reveal the greater protection afforded to females in the non-Negro segments of the population.

TABLE IV

SEX AND RACE DISTRIBUTION

	NEGRO	WHITE	LATIN AMERICAN
MALE (TOTAL 2527)			
Number of Subjects	1153	942	432
As % of Total Males	45.6	37.3	17.1
FEMALE (TOTAL 879)			
Number of Subjects	438	316	125
As % of Total Females	49.8	36.0	14.2
(M/F) RATIO (Overall = 2.87)	2.63	2.98	3.45
FEMALES PER 100 MALES (Overall = 34.8)	38.0	33.5	29.0

TABLE V

SEX, RACE AND CLINICAL DIAGNOSIS

	Total	Number of Subjects			
		Clinical Diagnosis and No. of Subjects			
Total		S	PBD	PSY	MD
Male	2527	1569	527	297	134
Female	879	556	189	55	79
(Male/Female) Ratio		2.82	2.79	5.40	1.70
NEGRO					
Male	1153	726	2.57	118	52
Female	438	299	97	15	27
(Male/Female) Ratio	2.63	2.43	2.65	7.87	1.93
WHITE					
Male	942	578	173	133	58
Female	316	169	70	32	45
(Male/Female) Ratio	2.98	3.42	2.48	4.16	1.29
LATIN AMERICAN					
Male	432	265	97	46	24
Female	125	88	22	8	7
(Male/Female) Ratio	3.46	3.01	4.01	5.75	3.43

The distribution within the race according to diagnostic categories is shown in Table VI. It may be seen from this table that 64% of the Negroes are diagnosed as schizophrenics while only 59% of the White are diagnosed schizophrenic. The diagnosis of behavior disorders accounts for 22% of the Negroes and 19% of the Whites. This may indicate a larger amount of sociopathology in the Negro child patient. This may be a result of the systems ("Les systems") of our culture. On the other hand, under the diagnostic category of psychoses and mental deficiency, one finds a much larger number of White than Negro patients. These two diagnostic categories have distinct and recognizable neurobiological components in terms of EEG and IQ. Again the results in Table VII show that the population of White to Negro children in 113 autistic children is 80 to 29. The preponderance of White children under this category may be either genetically determined or may be due to the simple possibility

TABLE VI

RACE AND CLINICAL DIAGNOSIS

Number of Subjects in Each Category

	S	PBD	PSY	MD
Total				
Number	2125	716	352	213
As % of Total	62. 3	21.0	10. 3	6. 3
Negro				
Number	1025	354	133	79
As % of Negro Cases	64. 4	22. 2	8. 4	5. 0
White				
Number	747	243	165	103
As % of White Cases	59. 4	19. 3	13.1	8. 2
Latin American				
Number	353	119	54	31
As % of Latin American Cases	63. 4	21. 4	9. 7	5. 6

that an autistic Negro child has a higher probability of mortality or may not be brought to the hospital. While these data represent in general all cases admitted from 1956-1967, the data on the autistic children represent only those (by no means all austistic children admitted) that were studied for biochemical deviations.

TABLE VII

MONTHLY DISTRIBUTION OF BIRTH IN AUTISTIC CHILDREN

RACE	WHITE		NEGRO		LATIN AMERICAN		TOTAL	
SEX	M	F	M	F	M	F	M	F
MONTH OF BIRTH								
January	5	1	3	0	1	0	9	1
February	12	0	1	0	2	0	15	0
March	3	3	1	0	1	0	5	3
April	8	1	0	0	0	0	8	1
May	4	2	1	0	0	0	5	2
June	8	0	6	0	0	0	14	0
July	4	0	4	0	0	0	8	0
August	5	1	2	0	0	0	7	1
September	5	0	1	0	0	0	6	0
October	4	0	3	0	0	0	7	0
November	8	0	5	0	0	0	13	0
December	5	1	2	0	0	0	7	1
TOTAL	71	9	29	0	4	0	104	9

SECTION III: SEX DISTRIBUTION AND SEASON OF ADMISSION

Our data with respect to sex distribution, diagnosis and race are shown in Tables VIII and IX. Out of a total of 3,406 patients, 74. 2% are males whereas 25. 8% are females.

TABLE VIII

SEX, RACE AND CLINICAL DIAGNOSIS

| | Clinical Diagnosis and Number of Subjects | | | |
	S	PBD	PSY	MD
MALES				
Total Number	1569	527	297	134
Negro	726	257	118	52
White	578	173	133	58
Latin American	265	97	46	24
As % of Clinical				
Group Total	100	100	100	100
Negro (45. 6%)	46. 27	48 . 77	39. 73	38. 81
White (37. 3%)	36. 84	32. 83	44. 78	43. 28
Latin American (17. 1%)	16. 89	18. 40	15. 49	17. 91
FEMALES				
Total Number	556	189	55	79
Negro	299	97	15	27
White	169	70	32	45
Latin American	88	22	8	7
As % of Clinical				
Group Total	100	100	1 00	100
Negro (49. 8%)	58. 78	51. 32	27. 27	34. 18
White (36. 0%)	30. 39	37. 03	58. 18	56. 96
Latin American (14. 2%)	15. 83	11. 64	14. 55	8. 86

TABLE IX

SEX AND RACE DISTRIBUTION

| | Number of Subjects | | |
	Female	Male	Total
NEGRO			
Number	438	1153	1591
As % of Total Negro Cases	27. 5	72. 5	100
As % of Total Cases	12. 86	33. 85	46. 67
WHITE			
Number	316	942	1258
As % of Total White Cases	25. 1	74. 9	100
As % of Total Cases	9. 28	27. 66	36. 90
LATIN AMERICAN			
Number	125	432	557
As % of Total Latin American Cases	2 2. 4	77. 6	100
As % of Total Cases	3. 67	12. 68	16. 34

The ratio of males/females is interesting and may reveal two possibilities. One of them is that more male children are prone to childhood schizophrenia than female children. From other data, shown in
Table XI (cf: Male/Female ratio), the male child is admitted to the hospital earlier in life, starting especially at the sixth to seventh year of
age, whereas the female child is admitted at a later age, at about eleven
years of age. Again, the length of stay in the hospital is higher in the
males than in the females. The other possibility in the uneven distribution of the sex of the child psychiatric patient population may be that
female childhood schizophrenia is better tolerated and protected in our
cultures. The distribution of the sexes in the races are presented in
Table IX.

The sex distribution in the different diagnostic categories is shown
in Table X.

TABLE X

SEX AND CLINICAL DIAGNOSIS

	Number of Subjects		
	Male	Female	Total
SCHIZOPHRENIA			
No. of Cases	1569	556	2125
As % of Cases of Same Sex	62.09	63.2	
As % of Total Cases	46.07	16.32	62.39
PRIMARY BEHAVIOR DISORDERS			
No. of Cases	527	189	716
As % of Cases of Same Sex	20.89	21.5	
As % of Total Cases	15.45	5.55	21.00
PSYCHOSIS			
No. of Cases	297	55	352
As % of Cases of Same Sex	11.75	6.26	
As % of Total Cases	8.72	1.61	10.33
MENTAL DEFICIENCY			
No. of Cases	134	79	213
As % of Cases of Same Sex	5.30	9.0	
As % of Total Cases	3.93	2.32	6.25

Of the total female patients admitted 63.2% have been diagnosed schizophrenic whereas in the males 62.1% have been diagnosed. The male-
female ratio is approximately 2.88 in the total population and 2.82 in
the patients diagnosed schizophrenic and 2.79 in patients diagnosed
as preliminary behavior disorders. However, in the diagnostic category
referred to as psychosis due to known and/or unknown causes, the male-
female ratio is 5.4 showing a larger number of males (cf: Table V).
This may include a larger and more prominent occurrence of neurologica
damage in male children. Again in our population the ratio of males to
females in the diagnostic category of mental deficiency is only 1.79 showing a larger occurrence of female patients in this group. The diagnostic
categories of psychosis and mental deficiency may at times border each
other with neuro-and electro-biological components.

The age at admission varies with sex. These data are shown in
Table XI.

TABLE XI

AGE AT ADMISSION AND SEX: Number of Subjects

Age In Years	Male	Female	M/F
3	5	2	2.50
3-1/2	11	2	5.50
4	24	6	4.00
4-1/2	14	8	1.75
5	41	14	2.93
5-1/2	41	9	4.44
6	52	8	6.50
6-1/2	79	16	4.94
7	69	12	5.75
7-1/2	103	17	6.06
8	117	20	5.85
8-1/2	138	24	5.75
9	150	28	5.36
9-1/2	161	32	5.03
10	167	34	4.91
10-1/2	156	29	5.38
11	167	32	5.22
11-1/2	140	45	3.11
12	117	51	2.29
12-1/2	109	61	1.80
13	130	83	1.57
13-1/2	119	93	1.28
14	160	90	1.77
14-1/2	129	84	1.54
15	106	68	1.56
15-1/2	20	7	2.86
16	2	3	0.67
TOTAL	2527	879	2.88

The overall ratio of the sexes is 2.88 males per each female case in the Unit. However, at the younger ages, the ratio of males to females is much higher. Up to six years of age, the M/F ratio is 3.8, while it soars to 5.35 between six and half and eleven years. However, from eleven and on, this ratio decreases. Actually, between 11 and 16 years, the ratio M/F is 1.76 only. Below six, the subjects have probably distinct and deeper neurobiological and psychobiological lesions, and the males may have either more of it or begin to suffer from it at a younger age. It has also been pointed out to the author that the demands of school work are heavier on males and their roles as males in the younger set is more demanding at this age in American culture. This is a debatable point. However, it is unmistakable that the manifestation of this 'psychobiological entity' begins at a younger age in males. The sex ratio of 5.35 between the ages of six and half to eleven is very significant. With the onset of puberty, however, the number of females admitted seems to increase. It is possible that the demands on the female can produce more stress at this age. Further, there may be sociocultural reasons also, inasmuch as the female is less rapidly hospitalized even in an industrial civilization (and less so in a more feudalistic or less industrialized culture). It is possible that the female does not exert as much a disruptive influence on the family as the male does. These, and I am sure there are several others, are some of the plausible explanations for the discordance in the M/F ratios in hospitalized children. Greater discussion and a more critical evaluation of these data is planned in future.

There is a pattern in the monthly rate of admissions also. These data are shown in Table XII.

Not only is the season of birth significant, but even the seasonal variations in the admission rates seem to be important. Similar findings for first consultations with physicians have been reported by several

TABLE XII

MONTH OF ADMISSION AND SEX DISTRIBUTION

MONTH	TOTAL ADMISSIONS	MALES No.	As %	FEMALES No.	As%
January	277	220	79. 4	57	20. 6
February	295	235	79. 7	60	20. 3
March	406	294	72. 4	112	27.6
April	357	268	75. 1	89	24. 9
May	327	236	72. 2	91	27.8
June	339	240	70. 8	99	29. 2
July	288	209	72. 6	79	27. 4
August	235	175	74. 5	60	25. 5
September	153	117	76. 5	36	23. 5
October	216	165	76. 4	51	23. 6
November	204	148	72. 5	56	27. 5
December	283	206	72. 8	77	27. 2
TOTAL	3380	2513	74. 3	867	25. 7

others. The available data shows that there is an increase in the mortality rates in January and February in Bristol (U. K.) and in June and July in LaPlata and Santiago in South America. Illustrative data on the month of initial consultation (from Report on National Morbidity Survey, Australian National Health and Medical Research Council; part 1, p. 66, 1962-63) are shown below:

MONTH OF INITIAL CONSULTATION IN AUSTRALIA

Month	Psychoses	Psychoneurotic	Diseases of Character, behavior, intelligence
January	27	504	102
February	43	711	128
March	41	795	142
April	31	558	118
May	26	578	101
June	42	588	105
July	37	620	132
August	34	605	108
September	39	511	102
October	33	681	116
November	51	637	101
December	21	481	91
TOTAL	425	7, 269	1, 346

From our data, the largest number of children are admitted in the month of March, the next highest months are April and June. The lowest admission rates can be found in September and November. The largest proportion of males can be found in February and the lowest proportion of males in June. The importance of these data can again be analyzed either from a psycho- and neurobiological view or from a sociocultural standpoint. The admission to school is highest in the month of September, and this may explain why the admission rates are lowest in September. After one term of school, the teacher tries to help the potential psychiatric patient without much success and then by the beginning of the next term in February the child is referred to a psychiatrist. This may explain the higher admission rate in March. Further, after a limited amount of day time (and perhaps natural light) and the stresses of winter, the child may either succumb to the stress with a crisis in March of may 'become more fanciful in Spring'. Our additional data, not shown here, also indicate seasonal fluctuations in the official discharge dates. All these data have been analyzed with respect to sex, age, I.Q., psychiatric diagnosis, race, length of hospitalization, initial consultation etc., and will be published elsewhere.

S E C T I O N   IV: STUDIES ON I.Q. DISTRIBUTION

Our results on the distribution of I.Q. in 1362 patients are shown in Tables XIII and XIV.

TABLE   XIII

I.Q. IN FIRST ADMISSION

Overall I.Q. = 81 (No. of Subjects 1362)

Category	No. Ss	I.Q.
Males	1035	81
Females	327	79
Schizophrenic	852	83
PBD	282	87
PSY	130	75
MD	98	58

These results show that the average I. Q. of the hospitalized child psychiatric patient is 81 and is lower than in the general population. We do not have a large enough population in our I. Q. studies. This may give rise to a certain element of statistical vulnerability.

The results with respect to age at admission, I. Q. and diagnosis are shown in Table XIV.

TABLE XIV

AGE AT ADMISSION, DIAGNOSIS AND WISC FULL SCALE I. Q.

AGE IN YEARS	S No.	S I. Q.	PBD No.	PBD I. Q.	PSY No.	PSY I. Q.	MD No.	MD I. Q.
4	3	54	1	92	1	69	2	52
4-1/2	3	40	0	--	1	76	5	52
5	10	73	2	84	0	--	4	61
5-1/2	7	67	5	97	3	86	1	70
6	17	77	1	81	1	53	2	37
6-1/2	19	76	7	85	3	71	5	60
7	23	76	0	--	3	75	6	50
7-1/2	38	81	7	83	5	68	4	55
8	43	81	14	88	4	78	2	60
8-1/2	50	88	9	86	8	72	2	60
9	48	82	18	89	11	72	11	61
9-1/2	38	84	14	89	7	72	6	58
10	56	81	17	85	7	73	11	62
10-1/2	47	88	21	88	7	76	5	60
11	47	84	24	86	6	79	6	51
11-1/2	51	87	13	87	9	68	5	66
12	49	84	20	82	3	77	5	61
12-1/2	55	84	9	82	3	73	2	64
13	62	82	18	83	12	79	3	66
13-1/2	39	81	24	87	11	83	4	49
14	63	85	15	84	11	75	2	49
14-1/2	43	84	21	88	6	66	1	53
15	36	82	20	91	4	83	4	52
15-1/2	4	69	2	86	4	71	0	--
16	1	75	0	--	0	--	0	--
Total	852	82. 6	217	86.6	113	74. 4	98	57. 5

The distribution of the different diagnostic categories within the ranges of I. Q. are shown in Table XV. The largest number of pa- tients are in the I. Q. range of 50-110 in the overall population (1363) that we studied as shown in Table XV. However, in the schizophrenic group a large number of subjects are in the I. Q. group 91-110, whereas in the PBD group the largest number of children are found in the 81-110 group. In the diagnostic category of psychosis, the largest number of children are in the I. Q. range of 50-80, whereas in the mentally defective group the largest number are in the groups of 70 and below. These results show that while the I. Q. of the schizophrenic and behavior disorder patient is not comparable to that of the general population, they are comparable to each other. The I. Q. of the psychosis and mentally defective groups are comparable.

TABLE XV

NO. OF PATIENTS AND I. Q. RANGE

I. Q.	S No.	%	PBD No.	%	PSY No.	%	MD No.	%	Total No.	%
50 & below	28	49.12	0	0	6	10.53	23	40.35	57	100
50-70	153	50.50	35	11.55	44	14.52	71	23.43	303	100
71-80	193	65.87	61	20.82	34	11.60	5	1.71	293	100
81-90	212	66.46	86	26.96	21	6.58	0	0	319	100
91-110	237	67.71	89	25.43	24	6.86	0	0	350	100
110 & over	29	70.73	11	26.83	1	2.44	0	0	41	100
Total	852	62.51	716	20.69	130	9.54	99	7.26	1363	100
Total Admission	2125	62.4	716	21.0	352	10.3	213	6.3	3406	100

S U M M A R Y : Our present demographic studies show that there is a seasonal variation in the birth rates of the several psychiatric patients admitted to the Child Psychiatric Unit of Creedmoor State Hospital over the years 1956-67. The diagnosis of schizophrenia may be accompanied with more neurobiological damage in the whites and in the females and with more sociopathology in the Negro child. The question can be raised as to the basic differences between what is called "schizophrenia" among the different racial groups of New York City. Depending on the depth of psychobiological and sociobiological damage (starting from in utero), childhood schizophrenia (which has been designated as a psychobiological entity by Bender) can perhaps also be subdivided into good prognosis categories and bad prognosis categories.

There are definite age related patterns in the admission of males and females. Further, the diagnosis varied with the age at admission The age of admission is lowest in the patients with most marked biological pathology, and also the length of hospitalization is longest in these cases. There are seasonal variations in the month of birth, month of admission and even in the month of discharge of child psychiatric patients. The average I.Q. of these patients is 81 and is lower than in the general population.

D. V. Siva Sankar, Ph.D., Child Psychiatry, Creedmoor State Hospital, Queens Village, N.Y. 11427

THE INTERACTION OF STRESS AND HALLUCINOGENIC DRUG ACTION: IMPLICATIONS FOR A PATHOPHYSIOLOGICAL MECHANISM IN SCHIZOPHRENIA.

WAGNER H. BRIDGER

Most studies on the role of heredity and environment in the etiology of schizophrenia suggest that while heredity factors may be necessary, they are by no means sufficient. There must be environmental factors that lead to the production of a schizophrenic illness. The possibility that the heredity factor may be an abnormal biogenic amine has received increased emphasis in recent years primarily because of FRIEDHOFF's[1] finding of 3,4 dimethoxyphenethylamine in the urine of schizophrenic patients. Since this compound is similar in structure to the known hallucinogenic drug mescaline, the role of environmental factors on the action of hallucinogenic drugs would appear to be relevant since this information would be useful in leading to the possible understanding of the interaction of heredity and environmental factors in schizophrenia. The clinical effect of mescaline is very variable both between different subjects and in the same subject at various times. KLERMAN[2] has shown in a double-blind study that anxious subjects react in a far more psychotic manner to mescaline than do non-anxious subjects. In an unpublished study from the U. S. Army Department of Chemical Warfare, it was reported that soldiers who were administered mescaline unknowingly in their drinking water showed much more evidence of psychotic-like behavior than subjects who were aware that they were being submitted to an experimental procedure. It appears that the lack of understanding of what was causing their change in consciousness produced a stress that enhanced the drug effect. Clinical observations confirm that stress and anxiety play a crucial role in hallucinogenic drug action.

Studies on the effects of hallucinogenic drugs on animal behavior support this interpretation. Most studies dealing with the effect of hallucinogenic drugs on animal behavior utilize either a technique of producing catatonia by the administration of large doses of these compounds to naive animals[3], or by the study of the effects of these drugs on the continued performance[4] or extinction of a well-learned operant

*This research was supported by USPHS grants K5-MH4177 and 5TI-MH-6418.

response[5]. The latter studies on well-established operant behavior indicate that hallucinogenic drugs produce disruption or inhibition of the conditioned response. However, some recent electrophysiological studies comparing classical and instrumental conditioning have suggested that these two types of behavior differ in respect to the neuroanatomic structures which mediate them. Both JOHN[6] and HEARST et al[7] have shown that when the classical conditioned response is established there continued to be bioelectrical activity as recorded from the depth electrodes in the hippocampus. When an operant avoidance conditioned response is well established, the electrodes in the hippocampus reveal no bioelectrical activity. In previous research, we[8,9] and others[10,11] have described experiments in which mescaline produces an excitatory effect on classically conditioned behavior. In a recent study[12], we have shown that both 3,4 dimethoxyphenethylamine DMPEA and mescaline have an excitatory effect on classical conditioning in rats as measured by the potentiated startle response. This suggests that hallucinogenic drugs have inhibitory effects on operant conditioning and excitatory effects on classical conditioning. It would also support the concept that operant and classical conditioning are basically different. However, SMYTHIES and SYKES[13] have recently reported that mescaline has a biphasic effect on the performance of a well-established operant avoidance response in rats. The initial effect of the drug was one of inhibition followed by a later excitatory effect. In the Smythies and Sykes experiment, the initial inhibition of the behavior leads to longer latencies in a shuttle box avoidance procedure and this eventually causes the animal to receive many electric shock reinforcements. After this initial disruption of behavior the animals begin to show excitation as measured by latencies that are less than the matched saline trials. Smythies and Sykes interpret this data as indicating that the main effect of mescaline is one of inhibition and that the later excitatory effects are probably due to the chemical degradation of mescaline to other compounds or decreasing amounts in the central nervous system. However, our own studies on the effects of mescaline on classical conditioning suggest that there may be another mechanism involved to explain this biphasic phenomenon. In his comparison of operant conditioning John[6] reported that during the acquisition of the operant response while the animal is still receiving many shock reinforcements, it appears very agitated and shows increased bioelectric potentials in the hippocampus. This is similar to what he observed in classical conditioning. When the operant response was well established these similarities to classical conditioning disappeared. It seems likely that the acquisition of an operant response may be equivalent to classical conditioning especially in regard to emotionality or stress.

Since mescaline is excitatory in a classical conditioning procedure, we performed experiments to test the hypothesis that mescaline would be excitatory during the acquisition of an operant avoidance response. The apparatus used was a two-compartment grid floor shuttle box with a center hurdle. The CS was a compound auditory and light stimulus. The US was an electrical shock delivered to the grid floor. The CS-US interval was 5 seconds. A jump during the time terminated the CS and prevented the US. The latencies of the response were automatically recorded on a print-out counter. The four groups of 15 hooded rats were tested on day one after having received either saline, 12 1/2, 25, or 50 mg/kg of mescaline, and on day two after having received saline. There were one hundred trials on each day. The results upheld our hypothesis by clearly demonstrating that when mescaline is given to rats prior to the acquisition of a conditioned avoidance response, the drug has dose dependent excitatory effects that facilitate the performance, but not the learning, of a conditioned avoidance response. The performance facilitation was evident in the inverse relation between drug dose and response latency on day one. That this facilitation was a performance but not a learning effect was demonstrated on day two by the failure to find a difference between the saline control and the drug groups.

These results are quite different than the results of experiments dealing with the effects of mescaline on either the performance or extinction of a well-learned conditioned response. In the Smythies and Sykes[13] experiment it was reported that 25 mg/kg of mescaline produced a peaked inhibitory effect producing long latencies at approximately 26 minutes after injection. In our experiment, an analysis of the latencies of the trials occuring approximately 26 minutes after injection indicated that the mescaline group had a significantly lower mean latency than did the saline controls. In our experiment mescaline had an excitatory effect at the same time after drug administration that Smythies described peak inhibition. Thus, it seems likely that the finding of either excitatory or inhibitory effects of mescaline is not dependent on a secondary drug effect but rather on the experimental conditions. In classical conditioning where the animal continues to receive the stressful electrical shock reinforcement, the effects of mescaline are purely excitatory. During acquisition of the avoidance response, the animal receives many stressful electrical shocks and as we have shown, the effects of mescaline are excitatory at this time. When the animal has a well-established avoidance response and is not receiving the stressful electrical shock reinforcement, the effects of mescaline are inhibitory. In the Smythies experiment the initial inhibitory effect of mescaline was seen when the animals were performing a relatively non-stressful behavior, i.e., the animals were showing continued performance of a successful avoidance response. Since this was a continued performance paradigm, the inhibition was manifested by increasing response latency which eventually caused the animal to receive stressful electrical shocks. These repeated shocks changed the reinforcement contingency from non-stress to stress, similar to our acquisition conditions. These stressful contingencies permitted the excitatory aspects of mescaline to be manifested. In summary, it appears that there is an important interaction between stress and hallucinogenic drug action. When stress is present in the experimental procedures, either in operant or classical conditioning one finds an excitatory effect. If stress is not an important component of the experiment, the main effect of the hallucinogenic drug is inhibition.

Smythies et al[4] have reported some interesting findings in regard to studies of tolerance to these chemicals. They found that with the repeated administration of both mescaline and 3,4 dimethoxyphenethylamine, the initial inhibitory effects decreased and the later excitatory effects became more apparent. If an abnormal biogenic amine is present in schizophrenic patients and is responsible for the symptomatology, the apparent lack of tolerance to this amine would have to be explained. However, as it was just mentioned, tolerance develops to the inhibitory drug non-stress interaction, but not to the excitatory drug stress interaction. It would appear that the inhibitory effects of hallucinogenic drugs are not as important as the excitatory effects in respect to their relevance to our understanding of the schizophrenic process. One can assume that the schizophrenic would become tolerant to the inhibitory effects of an abnormal biogenic amine on non-emotional behavior but not to the excitatory effects of this chemical on emotional behavior. By paying attention to the role of stress in the production of psychotic symptoms, one can deal with an important objection to the abnormal biogenic amine hypothesis, namely, the problem of tolerance. The role of stress in producing the excitatory effects of hallucinogenic drugs in animal behavior and the demonstration that animals do not become tolerant to these excitatory effects allows one to formulate a pathophysiological mechanism in schizophrenia which allows for the role of the environment in its etiology. Thus, an individual with an abnormal biogenic amine predisposition to schizophrenia would become tolerant to the inhibitory effects of this compound and not manifest any excitatory effects unless sufficient environmental stress was present. This could explain why there are many monozygotic twins who are discordant for schizophrenia[14].

The exact mechanism underlying the interaction between stress and hallucinogenic drug effects has not yet been elucidated. Stress increases central adrenergic activity and this in turn may act on some biochemical mechanism related to the metabolism of the hallucinogenic drug. Another approach deals with the fact that stressful behavior produces different bioelectrical potentials in subcortical and limbic structures as compared to non-stressful behavior. Since it has been shown[15] that hallucinogenic drugs effect these structures the different effects of these compounds on stressful and non-stressful behaviors may be explained by the presence or lack of activity in these structures. For example, if mescaline produces activation in limbic structures but the behavior is not accompanied by activity in these limbic structures, mescaline may not show any effect. If these limbic structures are involved in mediating the stressful behavior, then mescaline will show an excitatory effect. Another important reason for emphasizing the role of stress in hallucinogenic drug activity is that the excitatory effects of these compounds appear to be more ammenable in terms of formulating a model for the production of schizophrenia. The excitatory effects of mescaline produce increased resistance to extinction in classical conditioning and facilitate the acquisition of operant avoidance behavior. If the animal responds to the conditioned stimulus in a manner similar to his response to the unconditioned stimulus, he would show increased resistance to extinction and faster acquisition. The excitatory effects of mescaline may be due to the animal's inability of differentiating the CS from the UCS.

If one assumes that the conditioned stimulus is a signal for the unconditioned stimulus and that this is analogous to symbol-object relationship in human behavior one can speculate that the schizophrenic has an inability of differentiating the symbol from the object symbolized, and this could lead to hallucinations, delusions, and paralogical thinking. In this way the excitatory effects of hallucinogenic drugs can be related to the production of psychotic like behavior. However, the excitatory effects of these drugs occur only with stress. Applying this model to schizophrenic symptomatology, the schizophrenic will only show psychotic symptoms in situations which are emotionally meaningful and stressful. As is well known, most schizophrenic patients do not show a global disturbance in behavior but show psychotic symptoms in relation to certain aspects of their personality and their environment. In conclusion, recent experiments on hallucinogenic drug activity indicate that environmental stress is a crucial factor in determining the behavioral effects of these drugs. These findings allow one to formulate a mechanism whereby environmental stress can play a crucial role in the etiology and underlying mechanism of schizophrenic illness.

REFERENCES

1. Friedhoff, A. J. and Van Winkle, E. (1962): Isolation and characterization of a compound from the urine of schizophrenics. Nature, 194, 897.

2. Klerman, G. L. (1961) In: Trans. Sixth Res. Conf. on Cooperative Chemotherapy Studies in Psychiatry and Broad Research Approaches to Mental Illness. Washington, 339.

3. Ernst, A. M. (1962): Phenomena of the hypokinetic rigid type caused by O-methylation of dopamine in the para-position. Nature, 193, 178.

4. Smythies, J. R., Sykes, E. A. and Lord, C. P. (1966) Structure–Activity relationship studies on mescaline. Psychopharmacologia, 9, 434.

5. Chorover, S. (1961): Effects of mescaline sulfate on extinction of conditional avoidance response (CAR). J. comp. physiol. Psychol., 54, 649.

6. John, E. R. (1958): Electrophysiological correlates of avoidance conditioning in the cat. In: The Central Nervous System and Behavior, p. 334. Trans. First Conf., Josiah Macy, Jr. Foundation, New York.

7. Hearst, E., Beer, B., Sheatz, G. and Galambos, R. (1960): Some electro-physiological correlates of conditioning in the monkey. Electroenceph. clin. Neurophysiol., 12, 137.

8. Bridger, W. H. and Gantt, W. H. (1956): The effect of mescaline on differential conditional reflexes. Amer. J. Psychiat., 113, 352.

9. Bridger, W. H. (1960): Signal systems and the development of cognitive functions. In: The Central Nervous System and Behavior, p. 425. M.A.B. Brazier, editor. Trans. Third Conf. Josiah Macy, Jr. Foundation, New York.

10. Swadjian, J. (1934): Etude pharmacologique d'un reflex condionee, C. R. Acad. Sci., Paris 199:884.

11. Courvoisier, S. (1956): Pharmacodynamic basis for the use of chlorpromazine in psychiatry, J. Clin. Exp. Psychopath. 17:25.

12. Bridger, W. H. and Mandel, I. J. (1967) The effects of dimethoxyphenylethylamine and mescaline on classical conditioning in rats as measured by the potentiated startle response. Life Sciences, 6, 775-781

13. Smythies, J. R. and Sykes, E. A. (1964) The effect of mescaline upon the conditioned avoidance response in the rat. Psychopharmacologia, 6, 163-172.

14. Pollin, W., Stabenau, J. R. and Tupin, J. (1966): Life history differences in identical twins discordant for schizophrenia. Amer. J. Orthopsychiat., 36, 492.

15. Monnier, M. (1958) In: Neurological Basis of Behavior, Ciba Foundation.

W. H. Bridger, M.D., Albert Einstein College of Medicine. New York, N.Y.

EXPERIMENTAL OBSERVATIONS ON THE PROBLEM OF SCHIZOPHRENIA

HERMAN C.B. DENBER and DAVID N. TELLER

Medical research on human illness has either concerned the disorder itself or a model which simulated the disease. Psychiatric illness has not lent itself to this approach for a wide variety of reasons in which the psychogenic versus organic dichotomy has been most prominent. A series of papers proposed a theoretical formulation concerning schizophrenia, [Denber and Teller (1-2), Denber (3), Teller and Denber (4), Denber and Teller (5), Denber and Teller (6)], describing the data and hypothesis, and the present paper summarizes this information. *

Schizophrenia is defined as a biochemical genetic disorder, cyclical in its time course, probably due to a defective enzyme in the synaptic membrane and based on an abnormal protein structure, (Teller and Denber (4), Denber and Teller (5). The endogenous disorder is susceptible to exogenous influences, familial or environmental, with the actual clinical syndrome being the final common pathway of all factors. Our data** indicate that the mescaline-induced state is similar to acute schizophrenia and effective antipsychotic drugs inhibit the behavioral and biochemical changes produced by this drug. This represents the experimental model for our studies. Arguments concerning nosological or differences between endogenous and drug-induced states will not contribute materially to a better understanding of either condition, [Denber (7)].

The sequence of clinical symptoms due to mescaline and their variations have been described extensively, [Denber, Merlis and Hunter (8), Denber and Merlis (9), Merlis and Denber (10), Denber and Merlis (11, 12), Denber (13-15)]. Neuroleptics block the mescaline-induced state when administered before, and the symptoms disappear when they are given after mescaline. A close relationship exists between clinically effective neuroleptic drugs and their ability to inhibit the fall in total serum amino

---

*Extensive bibliographies are available in the references cited herein.
 **See bibliographic references below.

acids (ninhydrin positive substances) when given before mescaline to human subjects, [Denber (16), Denber, Teller and Kauffman (17)]. On the other hand, when given one hour after intravenous mescaline, the fall in ninhydrin positive substances was unaffected. We inferred that drugs such as chlorpromazine and thioperazine were exerting some protective action on the cell, perhaps at the membrane level inhibiting the psychotomimetic effect. This was supported by studies of others, [Guth and Spirtes (18) (a review), Seeman (19),] concerning the effects of phenothiazines on cell membranes. Thus, it would be important to know: 1) The time course and localization of mescaline in the brain or other tissues, particularly for comparison with neuro-leptics, 2) the subcellular localization of mescaline, 3) how these are affected by neuroleptic drugs, 4) if there is a relationship between cerebral mescaline concentration and symptoms. Inferences then could be drawn regarding human behavior.

If a subcellular mechanism of action is implicated for the neuroleptic drugs, the results should be subject to study and replication in simple models. Experiments were designed and techniques developed using flu-orescence to determine: 1) If the drugs were protein or membrane-bound, and 2) what the effects were of binding on structure, enzyme activity and other physiological parameters, [Teller, Goldberg and Denber (20), Teller (21)].

Materials and Methods

Procedures for the determination of radioactivity, protein and sep-aration of subcellular fractions have been reported, [Denber (3), Denber and Teller (5), and the details of fluorimetric methods and equipment described [Teller, Levine and Denber (22)].

Radioactive mescaline was injected intravenously or intraperitone-ally in Wistar female rats, weighing 175-250 grams, while neuroleptic drugs were given intramuscularly, [Denber (3), Denber and Teller (23)]. The animals were sacrificed, the brain and other organs removed, and homogenized. The subcellular fractions were separated and radioactiv-ity determined in the liquid scintillation spectrometer (Nuclear Chicago).

Results

The uptake of mescaline-8-^{14}C into rat brain was less than 0.2 of the amount injected. The drug was distributed uniformly between hemis-pheres, concentrated in the cortical fraction, descreasing progressively caudad. The average uptake (intravenous) was dose and time dependent, being linearly proportional to dose but logarithmically related to time after 30 minutes. For intraperitoneal mescaline, the average uptake increased linearly with dosage between 0.5 and 40 mg./kg.

A peak concentration was reached at 30 minutes, being highest in kidney and more vascular organs (liver and lung). The blood concentration was invariant with time, and proportional to dose with either route of administration. The brain concentration rose rapidly to a peak at 30 minutes (0.14%), and at 120 minutes was 0.17% of the injected amount.

The prior administration of phenothiazines (chlorpromazine and thioperazine) reduced brain mescaline content. The inhibition was more marked with amobarbital sodium and amphetamine than with the phenothiazines. A brain concentration of mescaline between 0.363 ug./gm. and 0.646 ug./gm. was necessary to produce a beha-vioral reaction in rats. We have observed some variability in behavioral response of rats to mescaline even at higher doses, which may depend on local environmental conditions. Prior administration of chlorpromazine or thioperazine inhibited the behavioral reaction, although the quantity of brain mescaline was well above 0.646ug./gm, [Denber and Teller (23)].

In vitro, mescaline binds loosely to, or is only adsorbed by cell fraction fragments and is washed off, appearing in the microsomal supernatant. A small and specific binding was shown for mitochondria with a peak for 45 minutes. The total uptake of mescaline was low in the myelin-microsomal soluble supernatant, with a maximum at 30 minutes. The nerve ending fraction had the highest concentration of any subcellular particles at 45 minutes. In this organelle, mescaline content rose abruptly after 30 minutes, and fell again in 60 minutes, with minute amounts present at 120 minutes.

The prior administration of chlorpromazine before mescaline increased mescaline content in the nerve ending fraction by a factor of 2.6, while the increase after thioperazine was 1.3.

The localization of radioactive chlorpromazine was studied at two hours in rat brain in different cell fractions. The greatest radioactivity was found in cortex, while thalamus and basal ganglia had an isotope concentration equal to that in midbrain and pons. The cerebellum, medulla and spinal cord had the lowest radioactivity. The subcellular localization of chlorpromazine in cortical grey matter in order of concentration was: microsomes, nerve ending particles, microsomal supernatant, mitochondria and myelin-microsomal soluble supernatant, with the highest radioactivity being found in the pure microsomal fraction.

In another series of experiments, pairs of rats were injected with 10 mg./kg. i.m. chlorpromazine 9-^{3}H. After 15, 30, 60 and 120 minutes, they were killed and the brains removed, sectioned, homogenized and placed in the liquid scintillation spectrometer for counting, as previously described. The concentration of chlorpromazine in each anatomical section did not vary by more than 20% from the total brain concentration. The uptake of ^{3}H chlorpromazine was 0.35% of the injected dose within 15 minutes, but the CNS concentration became linear with time thereafter, rising at the rate of 0.30% of the dose/hour. When the animals were treated daily with chlorpromazine at the same, or one-half the dose (5 mg./kg. i.m. for 8-15 days, this linear increase after the first uptake was abolished, suggesting that there are two compartments for chlorpromazine uptake, one of which becomes saturated rapidly. Concurrent treatment with a new antiparkinson agent*, [Denber and Mohr (24)] during acute and chronic experiments or with procyclidine, did not significantly alter chlorpromazine uptake.

When mescaline was injected intraperitoneally 30 minutes before chlorpromazine, the rapid uptake of chlorpromazine increased, while the later linear increase disappeared. However, when mescaline was injected 60 minutes before chlorpromazine, the phenothiazine uptake was reduced by more than 50%.

In one experiment, [Teller, Denber and Charipper (25)], it was found that chronic injections of mescaline substantially increased the amount of phenothiazines bound _in vitro_ by subcellular particles from liver and brain, with differences depending upon tissue source, fraction composition and type of neuroleptic.

At low concentrations, neuroleptic drugs may produce a facilitation of electron transport and photochemical reactions, while at a concentration greater than 10^{-4}M, inhibition is found, [Teller and Denber (26-28)]. It was possible to show adsorption kinetics and stoichiometry of neuroleptic binding to soluble proteins and subcellular fractions, such as mitochondria, [Teller, Wackman and Denber (29), Teller, Levine and Denber (22)]. However, all of these studies were _in vitro_ and it was

*Mefexamide, (ANP 297), Laboratores Anphar, Paris.

apparent that the concentration range of drug used (10^{-6} to 10^{-4}M) was still much above that to be found in the central nervous system after a single human equivalent dose.

At very low concentrations, the neuroleptics changed protein structure both in membranes, [Teller, Levine and Denber (22)] and soluble proteins, [Teller, Levine, Wackman and Denber (30)]. These structural changes occurred at concentrations (10^{-7}M) comparable to those found in the central nervous system after single human dose equivalent injections and produced marked changes in the enzymatic capabilities of the proteins, [Levine, Teller, and Denber (31)].

A series of experiments were performed with model proteins to study thermodynamic and equilibrium forces involved in phenothiazine-protein binding. In all cases (i.e., holoenzymes, apoenzymes, enzymes not requiring coenzymes, plasma proteins), there was evidence of a structural change caused by phenothiazines*. However, even with a relatively inert protein (albumin), there were major changes in drug binding due to cooperative effects of protein concentration and structure changes. Therefore, conclusions concerning the effects of drug binding must account for the high probability of this binding causing structural changes in the substrate.

In a proteolipid fraction isolated from synaptic membranes of bovine hypothalamus, thioperazine at 3×10^{-6}M produced total inhibition of the effects of atropine. This was equivalent to a blockade with 10^{-4}M dimethyltubocurarine. Thus, these drugs may have much more specific effects on specialized proteins in the central nervous system than on substrates from other areas of the body.

Discussion

The symptoms of the mescaline-induced state reached their maximum between 30 and 60 minutes in human subjects, correlating well with the findings of maximum localization in nerve ending particles in rat at 45 minutes. Our evidence does not suggest a "mescaline protein" as the causative factor, [Block and Block (32)], since the microsomal concentration was low and mescaline binding very loose. Rather, the data are consistent with a synaptic site of action, [Denber (3)]. Calculations indicate that infinitesimal amounts of the drug (250 molecules/cell) will produce the alterations in the central nervous system leading

---

*A more complete report concerning binding of prochlorperazine and thioperazine to serum albumin will be published elsewhere.

to the behavioral and physiological symptoms.

Interference with synaptic transmission in the human cerebral cortex could conceivably initiate the train of events recognized as schizophrenia. If the psychotomimetic drug penetrates the intersynaptic cleft reaching the presynaptic membrane to produce a transitory reversible structural defect, [Denber (3), Teller, and Denber (4)], a rapid discharge of catechol amines could take place. Under these circumstances, a persistent state of depolarization would develop leading to uncontrolled information transfer. The symptoms would subside only after a neuroleptic stabilized the defect, or after the operation of some as yet unknown endogenous mechanism. If this uninhibited flow of transmitter across the synaptic barrier takes place after the proposed change due to mescaline, the study of Dairman, Gordon, Spector, Sjoerdsma and Udenfriend (33) is relevant. They have reported an increase in catechol amine synthesis following administration of alpha-adrenergic blocking agents. Since mescaline may be a central alpha-adrenergic agent, [Clemente and Lynch (34)], a "circus rhythm" would be set up. The initial catechol amine discharge would be followed by increased synthesis and subsequent discharge. The clinical symptoms and their duration are in agreement with such a hypothesis. Although most of the mescaline has disappeared from the rat central nervous system within two hours, symptoms still are present, and in the human persist as long as eight hours. Furthermore, increased blood and pulse pressure as well as tachycardia during the human mescaline-induced state, [Denber and Merlis (35)], might very well be due to a high level of circulating amines.

The issue at present resolves itself into the following: Does mescaline act at the post-synaptic membrane producing a prolonged depolarization, or is the site of action pre-synaptic giving rise to a persistent catechol amine discharge through membrane leakage. There is reason to believe that the second is more probable.

As the spectrophotofluorimetric techniques are improved, it may be possible to demonstrate changes in protein structure induced by psychotomimetics. Certainly this exists with neuroleptics. It is probable that the latter are repairing an initial structural defect produced endogenously on the one hand, and experimentally (mescaline) on the other hand. If our reasoning is correct, analysis of the experimentally induced synaptic protein defect whose existence we are postulating may yield information of interest with regard to schizophrenia.

Summary

Clinical and biochemical studies with mescaline and different phenothiazines have been reviewed with particular emphasis on the subcellular findings. The localization of mescaline in the nerve ending fraction suggests that an alteration of synaptic transmission may be related to the observable behavioral phenomena. Theoretical formulations based on the findings have been discussed.

References

1. Denber, H.C.B., and Teller, D.N. A biochemical genetic theory concerning the nature of schizophrenia. Dis. Nerv. Syst., 24, 106, 1963.

2. Denber, H.C.B., and Teller, D.N. Molecular biology and psychiatry. In: Neuropsychopharmacology, (Eds.: Brill, H., et al.) New York, Excerpta Medica Foundation, ICS 129, pp. 1199, 1967.

3. Denber, H.C.B. Intracellular localization of psychotomimetic and psychotropic drugs. Ph.D dissertation. Graduate School of Arts and Science, New York University, 1967.

4. Teller, D.N., and Denber, H.C.B. Defining schizophrenia with the techniques of molecular biology. Dis. Nerv. Syst., 29, 93, 1968.

5. Denber, H.C.B., and Teller, D.N. Studies on mescaline XIX: A new theory concerning the nature of schizophrenia. Psychosomatics, 9, 45, 1968.

6. Denber, H.C.B., and Teller, D.N. Nouvelles considerations sur le de la biologie moleculaire en psychiatrie. Comptes rendus du Congres de Psychiatrie et de Neurologie de Langue Francaise, LXV Session, Dijon, Masson et Cie, pp. 436-440, 1967.

7. Denber, H.C.B. Clinical considerations of the mescaline-induced state. In: Chemical Concepts of Psychosis, (Ed.: Rinkel, M., and Denber, H.C.B.), New York, McDowell, Oblensky Inc., pp. 120-126, 1958.

8. Denber, H.C.B., Merlis, S., and Hunter, W. The action of mescaline on the clinical and brain wave patterns of schizophrenic patients before and after electroconvulsive treatment. Proc. Third Internat. E.E.G. Congress, pp. 30, 1953.

9. Denber, H.C.B., and Merlis, S. A note on some therapeutic implications of the mescaline-induced state. Psychiat. Quart., 28, 635, 1954.

10. Merlis, S., and Denber, H.C.B. The etiological significance of certain brain wave patterns in non-epileptic psychiatric disorders. Proc. Third Internat. E.E.G. Congress, pp. 52, 1953.

11. Denber, H.C.B., and Merlis S. Studies on mescaline I: Action in schizophrenic patients. Psychiat. Quart., 29, 421, 1955.

12. Denber, H.C.B., and Merlis, S. Studies on mescaline VI: Therapeutic aspects of the mescaline-chlorpromazine combination. J. Nerv. Ment. Dis., 122, 463, 1955.

13. Denber, H.C.B. Chlorpromazine et mescaline. L'Encephale, 4, 440, 1956.

14. Denber, H.C.B. Studies on mescaline Vl: The Role of anxiety in the mescaline-induced state and its influence on the therapeutic result. J. Nerv. Ment. Dis., 124, 74, 1956.

15. Denber, H.C.B. Studies on mescaline VIII: Psychodynamic observations, Amer. J. Psychiat., 115, 239, 1958.

16. Denber, H.C.B. Studies on mescaline XI: Biochemical findings during the mescaline-induced state with observations on the blocking action of different psychotropic drugs. Psychiat. Quart., 35, 8 18, 1961.

17. Denber, H.C.B., Teller, D.N., and Kauffman, D. Studies on mescaline XIV: (Comparative biochemical effects of different drugs.) Dis. Nerv. Syst., 24, 302, 1963.

18. Guth, P.S., Spirtes, M.A. The phenothiazine tranquilizers: Biochemical and biophysical actions. In: International Review of Neurobiology (Ed.: Pfeiffer, C. and Smythies, J.R.), New York, Academic Press, 231, 1964.

19. Seeman, P. The erythrocyte as a model for studying membrane stabilization by tranquilizers, anesthestics and steroids. Ph.D. dissertation. Rockefeller University of New York, 1966.

20. Teller, D.N., Goldberg, B., and Denber, H.C.B. Methods of early drug evaluation --1. Leucocytic motility and succinic dehydrogenase activity. Int. J. Neuropharmacol., 2, 241-247, 1963.

21. Teller, D.N. Kinetics of binding and inhibition of enzymatic activity by phenothiazine compounds, Ph.D. dissertation. Graduate School of arts and Schince, New York University, 1964.

22. Teller, D.N., Levine, R.J.C., and Denber, H.C.B. Binding of chlorpromazine and thioproerazine in vitro 11. Fluorometric measurement of stoichiometry and alteration of protein structure. J. Agressol, 9, 167, 1968.

23. Denber, H.C.B., and Teller, D.N. Studies on mescaline XVIII: Effect of phenothiazines, amphetamine and amobarbital sodium on uptake into brain and viscera. J. Agressol, 9, 127, 1968.

24. Denber, H.C.B., and Mohr, C. Mefexamide as an antiparkinson drug: Preliminary report of a double blind study. Dis. Nerv. Syst., in press.

485

25. Teller, D.N., Denber, H.C.B., and Charipper, H.A. Studies on mescaline XVI: Effect of chronic injections on binding of neuroleptics to mouse mitochondria, *in vitro*. Fred. Proc., 24, 301, 1965.

26. Teller, D.N., and Denber, H.C.B. Phenothiazine binding and oxidation by subcellular organelles. Fluroescence methods. Abstr. Proc. III Internat. Pharmacol. Cong., Sao Paulo, July, 1966.

27. Teller, D.N. and Denber, H.C.B. Binding of psychotropic drugs to soluble proteins. In: Neuropsychopharmacology, (Eds.: Brill, H., et al.), New York, Excerpta Medica Foundation, ICS 129, 1177, 1967.

28. Teller, D.N., and Denber, H.C.B. Fluorescence of leuco-N-methylphenazinium methylsulfate (Phenazine methosulfate) as a measure of succinic dehydrogenase (SDH) activity. Abstracts, Amer. Chem. Soc., 152nd Mtg., Sept., 1966 C114.

29. Teller, D.N., Wackman, N.J., and Denber, H.C.B. Fluorometric measurement of thioproperazine binding to rat brain mitochondria, *in vitro*. Abstracts, Amer. Chem. Soc., 152nd Mtg., Sept., 1966.

30. Teller, D.N., Levine R., Wackman, N.J., and Denber, H.C.B. Alterations in protein structure and enzymatic activity: By phenothiazine tranquilizers. Abstracts, Seventh Internat. Cong. Biochem., Vol. 5, 1031, 1967.

31. Levine, R.J.C., Teller, D.N., and Denber, H.C.B. Binding of chlorpromazine and thioproperazine in vitro 111. Fluorometric measurement of changes in Limulus polyphemus (Horseshoe crab) myosin B structure and enzyme activity after treatment with phenothiazine drugs. Mol. Pharmacol. 4, 435, 1968.

32. Block, W., and Block, K. Tierversuche mit ^{14}C- radioaktiven mescalin und sein einbau in das eiweiss des leber. Ange. Chem. 64, 166, 1952.

33. Dairman, W., Gordon, R., Spector, S., Sjoerdsma, A., and Udenfriend, S. Increased synthesis of catecholamines in the intact rat following administration of alpha-adrenergic blocking agents. Mol. Pharmacol. 4, 457, 1968.

34. Clemente, E., and Lynch, V.C. In vitro action of mescaline: Possible mode of action. J. Pharmaceutical Sci. 57, 72, 1968.

35. Denber, H.C.B., and Merlis, S. A note on some therapeutic implications on the mescaline-induced state. Psychiat. Quart., 28, 65, 1954.

H. C. B. Denber, M.D., Ph.D., and D. N. Teller, Ph.D.,

Manhattan State Hospital, Research Division, Ward's Island, N.Y. 10035

THE BIOCHEMICAL LESION IN SCHIZOPHRENIA

J. R. SMYTHIES, F. BENINGTON and R. D. MORIN

In spite of fifty years of intensive research into the nature of the
presumed biochemical lesion in schizophrenia, it can hardly be said
that much progress has been made.   However, there are some promising leads that are being followed, although it is as yet still too early
to make out if they are likely to disappoint as so many such leads have
done in the past.   Two centers of current interest are the biogenic
amines and transmethylation processes.   Himwich and his co-workers
have shown that exacerbations of the psychosis are accompanied by an
increase in the excretion of tryptamine.   Abnormally methylated tryptamines have been reported to be present in schizophrenic urine but
this still remains a matter of controversy.   Kety and his group were
the first to report that methionine and tryptophan appear to exacerbate the symptoms in a few cases of schizophrenia.   This has been confirmed by several other groups but it is not yet clear whether the effect is not merely a non-specific psychosis of the toxic variety.   Furthermore the biochemical mechanism involved remains totally obscure.
There are hints that the proportion of tryptophan metabolised via the
kynurenine pathway is altered and Ashcroft has reported that the levels
of 5HIAA in the cerebrospinal fluid are low in schizophrenia.   The 'pink
spot' has fragmented into a large number of constituents none of which
has yet been shown to have any connection with the illness.   One of the
best attested findings is that schizophrenics appear to be remarkably
resistant to histamine.   Pfeiffer and his group have reported associated
abnormalities of certain polyamines in certain types of schizophrenia.
Meltzer has reported that the levels of creatine kinase and aldolase
are raised to a marked degree and this rise may occur a day or so before the psychosis manifests itself.   This suggests that the schizophrenic
process may be related to changes in the permeability of membranes.
The Lafayette group have reported that schizophrenic plasma causes a

change in the uptake of certain amino acids by cells, notably glutamate, dopa and tryptophan. There have in addition been many reports over the years that schizophrenic serum is 'toxic' to a variety of biological systems.

Thus the evidence to date obtained from a direct study of the schizophrenic metabolism does not give any very clear picture of what the basic fault may be. A study of what agents are therapeutic in the illness - e.g. the phenothiazines - leads to a possible implication of central adrenergic mechanism - Bradley's work having shown that chlorpromazine has a fairly specific antagonist effect against norepinephrine in the brain stem.

The main difficulty of all this work is that it is difficult to find an abnormal compound or process in the organism, if one has no idea what kind of thing one is looking for. An optimist can hope for the lucky chance observation that led to the discovery of the etiology of such disease as phenylketonuria and other inborn errors of metabolism but the odds against this are long. It is, of course, possible that the defect may lie in the operation of an, as yet, undiscovered mechanism. In fact our ignorance about the brain is so vast that this is very likely. Thus the problem of the most promising strategy to employ in schizophrenia research is becoming pressing. Fifty years of nearly fruitless empirical search has led to a pessimistic outlook amongst certain psychiatrists who have directed their main attention to the social and psychological determinants of the illness. Basic neuroscientists prefer to investigate basic problems most of which are not connected in any recognizable way with schizophrenia. They are content to lay the ground work of knowledge that may become relevant for our understanding in the future. However, the art of this type of research lies in steering a middle course between these two extremes. It is inefficient to attempt million-to-one-against chances of finding the 'cause of schizophrenia' in one shot. It is highly unimaginative to hope that the answer will emerge out of the vast bulk of 'normal' biochemistry and other brain sciences not directed at answering this problem in any way. In this regard many people have felt that the most promising strategy to follow is to work out the mode of action of the hallucinogenic drugs. Endless ink has been wasted on the dispute as to whether the syndrome that these drugs cause is or is not equivalent to a schizophrenic syndrome. There are certainly differences but there are also sufficient similarities for the syndrome to act as a good model for the disease. The whole point about a model is that it should not be exactly like what it models - otherwise science would really be too easy. Thus it is perfectly legitimate to adopt the position that a better knowledge of the mechanism of action of these drugs should enable us to test the schizophrenic metabolism in a much more sophisticated manner than we can do at present.

In 1952 Osmond, Harley-Mason and Smythies suggested that schizophrenia might be related to an aberration of metabolism whereby abnormally methylated catecholamines resembling mescaline might be produced in the brain. Since then we thought for many years that the site of action of mescaline and other hallucinogens related to the catecholamines would be on the catecholamines themselves, for example on such reactions as uptake of metanephrine or on O-methylation. However the mode of action of a compound should be kept clearly distinct from its mode of production - which this theory did not do. Recently it has become clear that the hallucinogens all act on serotonin receptors and not on adrenergic receptors (vide Nature, 220, 961, 1968 and Wright et al, 1962). Thus abnormal toxic compounds may be produced by aberrations in catecholamine metabolism, or of course indoleamine metabolism, but they produce their behavioral effects by action on the serotonin mechanism. Of course, if the latter become severly disturbed, secondary disturbances may arise in catecholamine mechanisms due to homeostatic imbalance, but the key locus remains the serotonin receptor site.

Thus the problem of the mode of action of the hallucinogenic drugs become one of the nature of the serotonin recpetor site, what 5HT does when it binds there and how this site may be blocked by the drugs. Serotonin in the brain is very largely confined to the cells of the raphe nuclei. However, their axons are very widespread in the brain and are thought to release 5HT at their synapses. This system is thought to be involved in slow-wave sleep and it may be concerned in other functions such as affect, learning and memory formation. Recent data by Flexner and Flexner (1967), Barondes and Cohen (1968) and Hyden and Lange (1968) have clarified to some extent the role of protein synthesis in learning. It now appears that permanent memory formation depends on the initiation of protein synthesis within a very few minutes of the presentation of the learning situation. The experiments of Rappoport and Daginawale (1968) suggest in addition that RNA synthesis may be concerned in olfactory sensory discrimination over and above learning.

It has commonly been assumed that information processing in the brain is purely a function of electrochemical events, such as action potentials, EPSPs, IPSPs, DC potentals etc. The sole means of communication between neurones has been thought to be by transmitters whose sole function has been assumed to be to depolarize or hyperpolarize membranes. However, as Costa (1959) and Weiss (1960) have pointed out, this may reflect nothing more than the fact that our only means of recording the activity of neurones up to now has been electrical. It is also theoretically possible that one neurone can transmit information to another by other chemical means. That is to say neural transmitters may be able to do more than just alter ionic conductance through membranes. Kety (1969) and others have suggested that the biogenic amines in the brain may be concerned somehow in modulating the protein synthesis associated with learning. There is evidence that they are concerned with affect (Kety, 1969) and with reinforcement mechanims (Poschel and Ninteman, 1963) on which so much of learning depends. Costa (1959) postulates that 5HT has an important intracellular site of action.

If protein synthesis is linked to synaptic events there must be some messenger from the synapse to the DNA/RNA system of the cell. Electrical stimulation and raising Na levels inhibits RNA synthesis in neurones and raising K levels has the opposite effect. These effects are probably mediated via ATP snythesis, but clearly they suggest mechanisms whereby protein synthesis is modulated by synaptic activity. In this case, the The function of the biogenic amines (signalling reinforcement) may be to counter this habituation and to initiate the synthesis of particular proteins (e. g. by uptake in adjacent non-aminergic terminals) that alter synaptic resistance, latency, etc. In this way learning takes place. Siegal and Salinas (1968) have reported that 5HT is a potent inhibitor of RNA polymerase and interacts strongly with nucleic acids. Neuhoff (1968) reports that LSD (300 ug/day for 4 days) causes a change in rabbit RNA base ratios in hippocampal neurones (11% increase in cytosine, 4% decrease in guanine) as well as an overall increase in nucleoproteins and of tryosine containing proteins in the cell. Since DNA and RNA are present in the synaptosome, presumably these changes could occur at the presynaptic level. It is also possible that the biogenic amines, or their metabolites, could cross into the post-synaptic site and modulate post-synaptic protein synthesis. Schmitt (1967) has written: "The action of transmitters may not be limited to topochemical reactions on the external membrane of the neurone, as pictured in conventional receptor theory: they in fact may exert their effect intracellularly by repression or activation of gene expression."

It is therefore of interest to note that the activated form of mitomycin (Fig. 1) is a close structural relative of 5HT. This

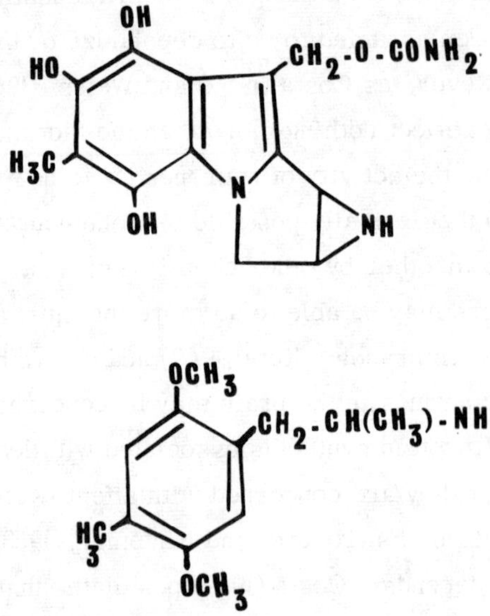

Figure 1.   Formulae of activated mitomycin and DOM.

antibiotic acts by forming covalent cross links between base pairs of DNA and RNA. The number of cross-links is always very low (not more than one per 10^6 or 10^7 daltons (Waring, 1968)). This suggests that there is something special about the site it does attack.   Another antibiotic - violacein - is an even closer analogue of 5HT and quinine, chloroquine and quinacrine are all quite similar in their stereochemical properties to d-LSD. Mitomycin has in addition the basic bonding struc- ture of DOM, the most potent hallucinogen in the amphetamine series. (fig. 1)

Serotonin has three groups capable of forming hydrogen bonds or ionic attachments - its ring hydroxyl, indole N and the positively charged (protonated) amine group. It also has a very energetic π cloud and is capable of forming charge transfer complexes. Thus the site at which it attaches should contain three atoms appropriate for its three active groups to bind and it should be very lipophilic. The hallucinogens should block the site by close but inappropriate patterns of bonding. Synder and Merrill(1966) have presented evidence that all hydrogen bonds that these compounds form are in the plane of the ring. They were referring specifically to internal hydrogen bonds but their arguments apply as well to external bonds. A more detailed stereochemical analysis that we have presented elsewhere (Smythies et al, 1969) supports this view. In which case a detailed consideration of the molecular consitutions of all the hallucinogens known to act at this site reveals that there is no possible single collection of three fixed atoms that can fulfill these criteria, i.e. to which molecules as diverse as the methoxylated amphetamines, dialkylated tryptamines, LSD and THC can all bind in such a way as to block the bonding of 5HT. One possible solution we worked out in some detail is based on the concept of a movable atom in an allosteric site but this did not prove very satisfactory.

If a model of DNA or helical RNA is examined to see how 5HT and its antagonists could bind, one can note firstly that these molecules can intercalate between base pairs. After intercalation they could bond to the two ring oxygens of deoxyribose (ribose for RNA) that present into the site as shown in figure 2 (Fuller and Waring, 1964). These are too

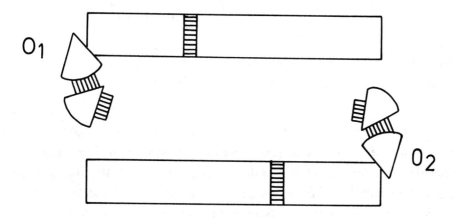

Figure 2. Possible receptor site in the intercalation site in nucleic acid: both ring oxygens are shown hydrated.

far apart to bond directly to serotonin but as they are located in the hydrophilic region of the nucleic acid molecule, it is likely that they would normally be hydrated. If a water molecule H-bonds to each in a particular orientation, the position shown in figure 2 will be obtained with horizontally oriented hydrogen bonds with a wide range of horizontal rotation. The minimum interbond distance would be approximately 7.5 A, the distance of one such bond to the water-ribose bond of the other side is approximately 9.0 A and the distance between the two water-ribose bonds would be about 10.5 A. Experiments with the model indicated that serotonin could bond very well in this site with maximum cloud interaction, bonding to one ribose oxygen (O1) directly by an ion-dipole interaction with its amino group displacing the water molecule of hydration, and with its hydroxyl group via a hydroxyl ion to the other ribose ring oxygen (O2) (Fig. 3).

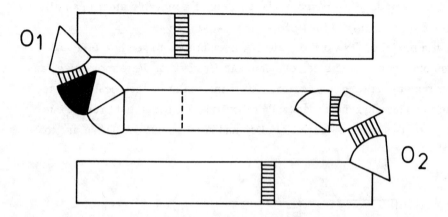

Figure 3. Postulated mode of binding of serotonin in the site. The amine group displaces one water molecule at O2.

The indole N is now freely exposed between the base-pairs bonded perhaps to a site (O3) in some protein wrapped around the nucleic acid molecule. The function of 5HT in the site might be to stabilize the helix and so inhibit RNA polymerase; or, in the case of a possible site in helical RNA, charge transfer mechanisms may become important (see further Smythies et al, 1969). It is of course also possible that the 5HT receptor site may be in membrane protein. Nevertheless the steric and energetic properties that we have detailed would hold here as well with respect to the nature of the site. In otherwords it is likely that it would also be an intercalation site, only between two molecules of e.g. tryptophan rather than between two base pairs, (for reasons detailed elsewhere) with three negatively charged atoms located as specified. These two can be combined since it is now thought possible that RNA occurs in the synaptic membrane (Morgan and Austin, 1969). Thus a portion of helical RNA could present on the external surface of the post-synaptic neurone, and the occupation of this site by serotonin might have important effects on the charge distribution in the membrane. Nucleic acids are normally insulators, but, when acted upon by molecules such as 5HT in the presence of an external electric field orientated parellel to the molecule, nucleic acids become conductors by virtue of π electron migration. If the RNA molecule consists of a helical portion in the membrane and an unpaired portion in the subsynaptic region this charge transfer reaction might have important functional consequences in the initiation or inhibition of protein synthesis.

We can now specify the nature of serotonin agonists and antagonists at the site. An agonist would be any molecule with the right steric and energetic properties that can bond to 01, 02, and 03. There would appear to be two types of antagonist. (A) Compounds bonding to 03 but lacking the proper groups to bond to 01 and/or 02, and (B) compounds bonding to 01 and 02 (but not to 03) and so preventing the entry into the site of 5HT. The hallucinogenic tryptamines are class A antagonists. In these di-alkylation of the amino group prevents proper attachment to 01. DMT lacks the ring hydroxyl to bond to 02, psilocin has it in the wrong place, and 5-methoxy-N, N-DMT must bond via the weak methoxy O via water to 02 rather than the strong hydroxyl H via an hydroxyl ion. The order of potency of these compounds exemplifies the rule that the closer the inappropriate binding the stronger the antagonism.

The methoxylated amphetamines are class B antagonists. These fall into two main classes. One (B1) exemplified by 4-methoxy amphetamine could bond with its methoxy group via water to 02 and with its amino group directly to 01. The other (B2) exemplified by 2, 5-dimethoxy-amphetamine could bond using only its two methoxy groups via two water molecules to 01 and 02. A detailed consideration of the invaluable structure-activity relationship data compiled by Shulgin et al (1969) indicates that the model accounts very well for the quantitative as well as the qualitative data. The hypothesis can also explain the mode of action of d-LSD and the active ingredient of hashish, THC. They both would appear to block the site by a mixture of π cloud interaction, hydrogen bonding and a very close steric fit which gives a strong bonding due to the accumulation of many weak van der Waals type of interactions. LSD has a very energetic π cloud due to the extra double bond in the D ring and if it is placed in the intercalcation site in helical RNA (or DNA) its "waist" gets nipped by the two water molecules on 01 and 02, with the possibility of hydrogen bonds forming direct to the   cloud. The tilted diethylamide side chain (in its energetically preferred position) lies neatly along the backbone of the helix in close van der Waal's contact with two ribose molecules and there is the steric possibility of a water mediated H-bond between the amide O and a site on the upper base pair. THC can also make a close steric fit with its complex tilted ring structure acting as the homologue of the di-ethylamide side chain of d-LSD and its benzene ring is intercalated with good H-bonds to O1 and O2 (both hydrated). Space does not permit the full development of the stereochemistry of this interaction (which is presented in our forthcoming papar already referred to).

If mitomycin is bonded in the site in the manner of DOM which it resembles(Figure 1) this locates its two reactive groups directly under the H-bond between guanine O and cytosine N that it is thought to attack. Thus 5HT and LSD should protect nucleic acids against attack by mitomycin.

Summary

This paper commences with a review of what is known of the pathological physiology of schizophrenia. It is concluded that nothing is known but that a few promising leads are being pursued. A section then discusses the preferred strategy for schizophrenia research in view of our great ignorance about the chemistry of the brain. It is proposed that attention should be concentrated on determining the mechanism of action of the hallucinogenic drugs. Recent progress in this field is presented. The paper concludes with a brief summary of a recent stereochemical analysis of the interaction of hallucinogenic drugs and serotonin on the serotonin receptor site in the brain that the authors have conducted. This involves a new hypothesis that specifies the requirements for the central 5HT receptor. The hypotheis can explain for the known facts and suggests several experiments to test it. Once the precise mode of action of these drugs is known we should be able to subject the schizophrenic metabolism to more sophisticated tests than we can at present.

Acknowledgements

We are most grateful to Professor Francis O. Schmitt for his encouragement and for the NRP Work Session that triggered these ideas.

REFERENCES

Barondes, S.H. and Cohen, H.D. Science, 160, 556, 1968
Costa, E. Int. Rev. Neurobiol., 2, 175, 1959
Flexner, L.B. and Flexner, J.B. Science, 159, 330, 1968
Fuller, L.B. and Waring, M.J. Ber. Bunseges. Physik. Chem., 68, 805, 1964
Hyden, H. and Lange, P.W. Science, 159, 1570, 1968
Kety, S.S. in Beyond Reductionism, Macmillan, in press, 1969
Morgan, I.G. and Austin, L. J. Neurochem., 15, 41, 1968

Neuhoff, V. Umsch. Wissensch. Technik., 17, 1968

Poschel, B.P.H. and Ninteman, F.W. Life Sci., 10, 782, 1963

Rappoport, D.A. and Daginawala, H.F. J. Neurochem., 15, 99, 1968

Schmitt, F.O. in The Human Mind, Amsterdam, North Holland, 1967

Shulgin, A.T. Sargent, T. and Naranjo, C. Nature, 221, 537, 1969
Siegal, F.L. and Salinas, A. Fed. Proc., 27, 464, 1968

Smythies, J.R., Benington, F. and Morin, R.D. Int. Rev. Neurobiol. 12, in press

Snyder, S.H. and Merril, C.R. in Amines and Schizophrenia, Oxford, Pergamon Press, 1966

Waring, M.J. Nature, 219, 1320, 1968

Weiss, P. Arch. Neurol., 2, 595, 1960

Wright, A.M., Moorhead, M. and Welsh, J.H. Brit. J. Pharmacol. 18, 440, 1962

NOTE ADDED IN PROOF : Yielding and Sterglanz (Proc. Soc. Exp. Biol. Med. 128, 1096, 1968) have reported that LSD-25 binds to native (helical) DNA but not to RNA or denatured DNA.

J. R. Smythies, M.D., University Department of Psychiatry, Edinburgh 10 U.K.

F. Bennington, M.D., and R. D. Morin, M.D., Dept. of Psychiatry, University of Alabama

AN N, N-INDOLE TRANSMETHYLATION THEORY
OF THE MECHANISM OF MAOI-INDOLE AMINO ACID LOAD
BEHAVIORAL ACTIVATION

ARNOLD J. MANDELL and CHARLES E. SPOONER

One of the major strategies used by researchers attempting to generalize work involving drugs and putative transmitters in animal brains and behavior to man has involved the use of loads of precursors of metabolic substances hypothesized to have central nervous system action in man (1, 2). The assumption made in such an approach is that by selectively increasing the amount of substrate available for a metabolic pathway, there will be an increase in the end product of interest in the brain and that this increase will result in an exaggerated expression of its normal behavioral effect. Frequently, this substrate load is preceded by treatment by an inhibitor of the major degradative pathway of the hypothesized transmitter which is assumed to combine with the load to more definitely produce an increase in the putative transmitter (1). The chemical concomitants of such manipulations in man are studied in various animals which permit the removal of the brain and other organs for direct analysis of "levels" of the substance of interest. Many of the problems in making these kinds of assumptions and deductions have been discussed at some length in a previous communication (2).

METHODS

In general, this study addresses itself to the chemical mechanism underlying the phenomenon of behavioral activation in animals and

This work was supported by NIMH Grants MH-14360 and MH-10836.

man when monoamine oxidase inhibitor pretreatment is combined
with an indole amino acid load (3, 5). These studies are particularly puzzling in view of other work demonstrating that the levels
of serotonin are unrelated to the state of activation of the animal
(6). This report suggests that this kind of inhibitor-load combination in addition to resulting in an increase in a "normal" or dominant metabolite such as serotonin, may also exaggerate the function of a usually minor side path, such as N, N-dimethylation.
This would result in the production of physiologically significant
amounts of a centrally activating "abnormal" metabolite, such as
bufotenine. This phenomenon seems possible in a number of species
including man following the work of Axelrod (7) demonstrating the
presence of an enzyme that can carry out this step in the lung.
Amino acid precursors of the major monoamines have been utilized
in many experiments to shed light on the function of the monoamines
in the brain. A consistent finding of many studies of the behavioral
alterations induced by the administration of the precursor amino
acid 5-HTP (5-hydroxtryptophan) is a dose-related biphasic response
in rabbits, cats and dogs (8, 10). In these species, 5-HTP produces
signs of sedation with low doses and a syndrome of muscular tremors,
motor excitement and alertness with higher doses. Mice and rats
demonstrate only sedation and reduced motility at all dose levels of
5-HTP, but after pretreatment with MAO inhibitors, much lower doses
of 5-HTP produce excitement, motor hyperactivity, muscular trembl-
ing, and preconvulsive twitches (11, 12). Several laboratories have reported that in the young chick, in which 5-HT (5-hydroxytryptamine)
does enter the CNS, systemically administered 5-HT produces behavioral and electrophysiological signs of sedation that are similar to
natural sleep, differing only in manifesting more muscular relaxation
(13, 16). The above findings suggested that 5-HT was not responsible
for the excitatory phenomena observed after 5-HTP was given in various doses in several species or after drug induced MAO inhibition.
In addition, the observation that pyrogallol (100 mg/kg) prevented the
appearance of the 5-HTP induced activation syndrome in chicks following pretreatment with the MAO inhibitor, pargyline, suggested that
5-HTP activation following MAOI (Fig. 1), was perhaps not due to 5-HT
but possibly due to a methylated indole product. Pyrogallol has been
reported to be a depletor of S-adenosylmethionine (17).

From our initial behavioral observations in the chick, studies were initiated in which the major metabolites of injected radioactive 5-HT and 5-HTP were determined and correlated with the behavioral

PYROGALLOL REVERSAL OF THE MAOI REVERSAL OF 5-HTP BEHAVIORAL DEPRESSION

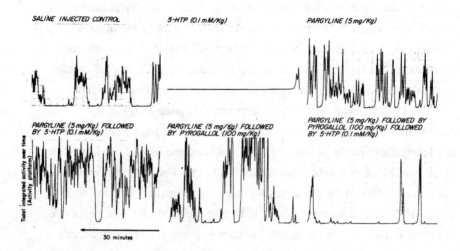

Fig. 1. Elapsed time for each recording goes from right to left. Comparisons of the effects of drug treatments on activity level starts at the upper left and goes to the lower right of the figure. Note that the MAOI reverses the behaviorally depressing effect of 5-HTP and pyrogallol pretreatment prevents this reversal.

responses observed in normal and pargyline pretreated chicks. In addition, behavioral responses were observed after intravenously administered bufotenine or serotonin as well as various mixtures of these agents in control and pargyline pretreated chicks. Finally, the effects of pyrogallol (100 mg/kg) were studied with regard to its influence on the metabolism of 5-HTP and on behavior.

PROCEDURE

Chemical studies were carried out on the whole brain and the blood content of labelled 5-HTP, 5-HT, BUFO (bufotenine), and 5-HIAA (5-hydroxyindolacetic acid) in 30 White Leghorn cockerels that received DL-5 hydroxytryptophan-3-C^{14} (0.93 millicuries/millimole) and in 10 animals that received 5-hydroxytryptamine-2-C^{14} (10.4 millicuries/millimole). Isotopes were obtained from the New England Nuclear

Corporation and unlabeled or carrier substances from Cal Biochem. Animals receiving 5-HT were sacrificed 3 minutes after injection and those receiving 5-HTP were decapitated 30 minutes after inject-ion. The radioactivity of the metabolites was determined using sol-vent extraction, ultracentrifugation, thin layer chromatography and scintillation counting. The brains were rapidly removed, weighed and homogenized in acidified enthanol (0.01% HCl) maintained at 4^OC. Blood was treated in a similar manner, and in addition, lung and liver tissue was collected in 4 animals. Ten mgms. of ascorbic acid and 10 to 30 micrograms of appropriate carriers (5-HTP + 5HT + BUFO + 5-HIAA) were added during the extraction procedure. An equal amount of water was added and the sample frozen for a brief period of time. The extracts were thawed and centrifuged at 75,000 xG 4^OC for 90 minutes. The supernatant was lyophilized and resolubilized in 0.5 ml. of cold acidified ethanol. A 10% aliquot of the concentrated extract was chromatographed bidimensionally on cellulose TLC using methanol - butanol - benzene - water - formic acid (40:30:20:10:1) in the first dimension and in the second dimension without the formic

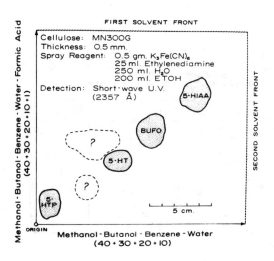

Fig. 2. A typical cellulose TLC separation of 5-HTP, 5 HT, BUFO, and 5-HIAA. Two additional areas of unidentified radioactivity were frequently found.

acid (Fig. 2). The compounds were visualized under ultraviolet light after ferricyanide oxidation and ethylenediamine condensation, or after spraying with a modified Erlich's reagent (10% p-dimethylamino-benzaldehyde). The areas of cellulose in which 5-HTP, 5-HT, BUFO, and 5-HIAA were located, were collected, and placed in vials containing PPO (2, 5-diphenyloxazole 0.5gm/100 ml. toluene) liquid scintillation medium and thixotropic gel powder (Cab-O-Sil, Packard), thoroughly mixed in a shaker and counted in a Beckman LS II liquid scintillation spectrometer with external standard quench corrections. CPM's recorded on data tape were converted to DPM's and the data further computed using the Beckman Omega Data Reduction System. In addition to the known indole metabolites, two additional areas on the chromatograms of blood and liver were occasionally found to contain low amounts of a C^{14} containing material. These spots are at present unidentified and not included in the chemical analyses.

RESULTS

Behavioral studies of the pharmacological effects of bufotenine and serotonin are summarized in Table 1. Bufotenine in the dose range of 10-80 uM/kg. i.v. produced an excitatory syndrome in which the

BEHAVIORAL EFFECTS OF
BUFOTENINE-SEROTONIN COMBINATIONS

RATIO BUFO:5-HT	μM DRUG/Kg I.V.		BEHAVIOR	
	BUFO	5-HT	UNMEDICATED	POST MAOI
1:0	10·00	0·00	EXCIT.	EXCIT.
0:1	0·00	10·00	DEPR.	DEPR.
1:1	10·00	10·00	EXCIT.	EXCIT.
1:2	6·66	13·32	EXCIT.	EXCIT.
1:4	4·0	16·00	EXCIT.	EXCIT.
1:8	2·22	17·78	DEPR.	EXCIT.

TABLE 1: The behavioral effects in chicks of the simultaneous administration of bufotenine-serotonin mixtures in various concentration ratios in control and pargyline pretreated chicks.

animals displayed spread wings, tremors, occasional running,
aimless lateral head movements, hyperventilation, and piloerection.
The hyperexcitation induced by bufotenine was potentiated by the prior
administration of an MAO inhibitor, pargyline, 5 mgm/kg i.v. given
one hour previously. Serotonin in the same dosage range induced a
state of lethargy and reduced muscle tone with the animal usually
assuming a sleeping posture. MAO inhibition induced a variable degree of potentiation of the 5-HT effect but much less than that observed
with bufotenine. Even in the presence of pargyline, serotonin at near
lethal doses (80 uM/kg.) produced only lethargy or depression. The
simultaneous administration of combinations of bufotenine and serotonin demonstrated a central pharmacological antagonism of the action
of 5-HT by bufotenine. This phenomenon has been reported previously
by Rauzzino and Seifter (18). The bufotenine effect dominated over 5-HT
and was selectively potentiated by MAO inhibition in molar ratios of BUFO
to 5-HT: 1:1, 1:2 and 1:4. However, when the combination of 5-HT was
8 times the BUFO, the animals displayed a serotonin-like lethargy.
Prior MAO inhibition converted this serotonin effect of the combination
into a bufotenine response demonstrating the selective potentiation of
the action of bufotenine by an MAOI. The behavioral responses of these
last two groups of animals were very similar to those animals administered 0.28 mM/kg., 5-HTP alone (depression) and 5-HTP with pargyline
(excitation). These studies suggest that in the presence of an MAOI,
relatively little bufotenine is required to counteract the depressant
effects of serotonin.

The major metabolic products 30 minutes after the administration
of 0.28 mM/kg. of 5-HTP-3-C^{14} were determined in 5 animals without pargyline and 5 with 5 mgm/kg. pargyline administered one hour
before. The increase in brain 5-HT between the groups (66.9+2.0
and 82.8+2.3; mean and standard error of the percent of total metabolic products) and the decrease in brain 5-HIAA (31.9+1.6 and
11.7+1.4) clearly reflected MAO inhibition. Bufotenine could be detected in the brains of both groups of animals with an increase in the
MAOI pretreated animals (2.8+0.8 and 6.7+2.1) but the difference
failed to reach significance. However, the behavioral differences between the two groups were marked in that the 5-HTP treated animals
were sedated while the pargyline plus the 5-HTP animals were hyper-
excited. One might be tempted to conclude that the change in 5-HT
could be related to the behavioral differences. This is unlikely how-

ever, since a comparable change in brain 5-HT was observed in animals receiving 5-HT-2-C^{14} (10 uM/kg. i.v.) alone and 5 mgm/kg. of pargyline prior to 5-HT-2-C^{14} (34.39$\pm$2.85 and 52.66$\pm$2.36) both of these groups displayed only behavioral depression. Smaller amounts of bufotenine could be detected in the brains after 5-HT-C^{14} (1.73$\pm$0.8) and after pargyline plus 5-HT-C^{14} (3.25$\pm$0.73), but presumably due to the short half-life of injected 5-HT (2-3 minutes for the 10 uM/kg. dosage used) amounts produced were too small to alter the 5-HT response. Pyrogallol (100 mgm/kg 30 min. pre-5-HTP) did not diminish the amount of bufotenine formed significantly even though it blocked the behavioral excitatory effect of 5-HTP in an MAO inhibited animal. This latter effect therefore, may be both a pharmacological as well as a biochemical antagonism in that we have subsequently found that pyrogallol alone could antagonize the excitatory effect of administered bufotenine in the chick.

Axelrod has reported that the lungs of rabbit and man contain a non-specific N-methyl transferase enzyme which can catalyze the methylation of a wide variety of naturally occurring amines, such as 5-HT, as well as foreign compounds(7). Fig. 3 demonstrates the marked increase

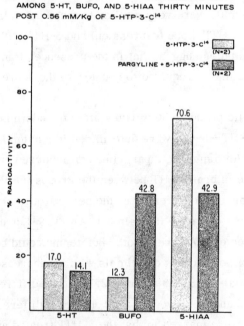

Fig. 3. The percent distribution of labelled 5-HT, BUFO, and 5-HIAA in lung tissue of control and pargyline pretreated chicks thirty minutes after the i.v. administration of 5-HTP-3-C^{14}, 0.56 mM/kg.

in bufotenine content in the lung following the administration of 5-HTP (0.56 mM/kg. i.v.) when the animal was pretreated with an MAOI. The lungs, blood, and liver consistently contained more bufotenine than the brain; the lung bufotenine levels were most markedly augmented by pargyline pretreatment. This probably means that the majority of the bufotenine found in the brain was transported to the CNS via the blood. With this thought in mind, the bufotenine content determined as DPM/tissue unit weight or volume of the brain and

SUBSTANCES ADMINISTERED DOSE/Kg I.V.	N	BUFOTENINE CONTENT AVERAGE DPM		BUFO BRAIN TO BLOOD RATIO	BEHAVIOR
		BRAIN DPM/GM	BLOOD DPM/ML		
5-HT-2-C^{14} 10μM	5	39·48 *(3·53)	3407·93 (304·5)	0·011	Lethargy-Hypotonia
PARGYLINE 5 mgm + 5-HT-2-C^{14} 10μM	5	101·98 *(9·08)	1591·86 (142·2)	0·064	Lethargy-Hypotonia potentiated in 3/5
5-HTP-3-C^{14} 0·28 mM	5	98·24	712·05	0·137	Lethargy-Hypotonia
5-HTP-3-C^{14} 0·56 mM	4	284·67	1917·70	0·148	Lethargy mixed with sporadic activity - Tremors - Spead wings.
PARGYLINE 5 mgm + 5-HTP-3-C^{14} 0·28 mM	5	225·39	1104·51	0·204	Hyperexcited - Spread wings - Tremors - Aimless head movements -
PARGYLINE 5 mgm + 5-HTP-3-C^{14} 0·56 mM	3	314·93	1856·97	0·169	Hyperventilation - Piloerection

*ADJUSTED EQUIVALENT OF 5-HTP PRODUCTS
(5-HT SPECIFIC ACTIVITY 11·2 x 5-HTP)

Table 2. Summary of the labelled bufotenine content of brain and blood, brain to blood ratios, and behavior in control and pargyline pretreated chicks after the administration of 5-HT-2-C^{14} and 5-HTP-3-C^{14}. See Text.

blood were tabulated as in Table 2. The C^{14} 5-HT animals were sacrificed 3 minutes after injection and the C^{14} 5-HTP animals were sacrificed 30 minutes after i.v. injection. Both of these times corresponded to the times of the peak behavioral effects. The pattern of brain C^{14} indole metabolites seem to relate to behavior biphasically. Serotonin treated animals with and without pargyline and those given the lower 5-HTP dose had relatively lower labelled bufotenine brain levels and manifested primarily serotonin-like lethargic behavior. The animals treated with higher doses of 5-HTP and pargyline evidenced higher brain levels of labelled bufotenine and showed partial or complete bufotenine-like behavior. This suggests that, especially in those animals receiving both pargyline and 5-HTP (the two bottom groups in Table 2), that the bufotenine excitatory effect was dominant. It may be that both the pargyline induced increase in central levels of bufotenine (increase in brain to blood ratio) and the pargyline potentiation of bufotenine excitation may combine to produce some aspects of

as portrayed in Fig. 4 may be partially responsible for these behavioral findings; that in addition to the accrual of normal indole
amines (such as serotonin or tryptamine) following indole amino acid
load and MAOI pretreatment, there is a shunting of a small, but physiologically significant amount of the amino acid into an N, N-dimethy-

DISCUSSION

The phenomenon of the reversal of 5-HTP induced behavioral depression with the use of MAOI pretreatment has been reported
widely in laboratory investigations in various animal species (3 5, 19).
In addition, a number of clinical studies in depressed or schizophrenic
populations in which tryptophan or 5-hydroxytryptophan was combined
with a monamine oxidase inhibitor have reported various kinds of behavioral activation, from "potentiation" of the antidepressant effect
of MAOI to the activation of the psychotic process in chronic schizophrenics (3, 4). Recently, Williams et al (20) have shown that whereas night time tryptophan loads alone either had little or no effect on
EEG sleep patterns in normal volunteers, when this load was preceded
by MAOI, it led to multiple arousals and a disturbed night sleep. When
this kind of data is taken in conjunction with the preliminary findings
reported here, it is tempting to speculate that a metabolic phenomenon

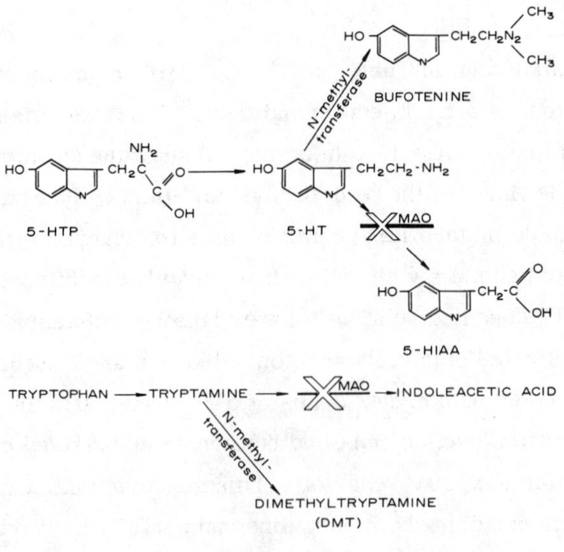

FIG. 4. A representation of the hypothesized chemical mechanism
resulting in the behavioral activation of man and animals following
MAOI-Indole amino acid administration.

this excitatory state. The above is prominent despite the fact that in the presence of pargyline, there is often a slight reduction in the production of total metabolic products from either 5-HT or 5-HTP.

lated indoleamine produce pool. Both of the compounds portrayed (bufotenine and dimethyltryptamine) have been shown to be centrally active. It would seem that since a "non-specific N-methyltransferase" which can carry out this kind of reaction has been described in the lung of man (7), such a mechanism for the behavioral activative effect of an MAOI Indole amino acid load is worthy of serious consideration.

SUMMARY

Many laboratories have reported the reversal of 5-hydroxytryptophan induced behavioral depression with monoamine oxidase inhibitor pretreatment in various species including man. The mechanism of this activation has not been established. Using behavioral and biochemical techniques we have gathered evidence that the reversal of 5-HTP induced lethargy appears to be related to the production and subsequent increase in the brain concentration of N, N-dimethylserotonin (Bufotenine). Pargyline, an MAO inhibitor increases the tissue levels of labelled bufotenine formed from 5-HTP-3-C^{14} as well preferentially potentiating the central excitatory action of bufotenine over the sedative action of its precursor, serotonin. The suggestion is made that the behavioral activation that has been reported following MAOI Indole amino acid load treatment of normal, depressed, and schizophrenic man may be due to the shunting of indoleamines through a usually minor pathway resulting in the production physiologically significant amounts of N-N, dimethylated indoleamines such as bufotenine or dimethyltryptamine.

REFERENCES

1. Kety, S.S. The precursor load strategy in Man. In Methods and Theory in Psychochemical Research in Man. Mandell, A. J. and Mandell, M.P. (Editors), Academic Press. In press.

2. Mandell, A. J. and Spooner, C.E. Psychochemical research strategies in man. Science. In press. N.Y., 1969.

3. Kline, N.S., Simpson, G., and Sacks, W. Amines and amine precursors combined with a monoamine oxidase inhibitor in the treatment of depression. In Neuropsychopharmacology Brill, H. (Editor), Excerpta Medica. N. Y., 1967.

4. Sprince, H., Parker, C.M., Jameson, D. and Alexander, F. Urinary indoles in schizophrenic and psychoneurotic patients after administration of tryanylcypramine and methionine or tryptophan. J. Nerv. Ment. Dis. 137, 256-251, 1963.

5. Montegazzini, P. Pharmacological actions of indolealkylamines and precursor aminoacids on the central nervous system. In Handbook of Experimental Pharmacology, XIX Erspamer, V. (Editor). N.Y. 1966.

6. Brodie, B.B., Spector, S., and Shore, P.A. Interaction of monoamine oxidase inhibitor with physiological and biochemical mechanism in brain. Annals N. Y. Acad. Sci. 80, 609-616, 1959.

7. Axelrod, J. The formation and metabolism of physiologically active compounds by N and O methyltransferases. In Transmethylation and Methionine Biosynthesis. Shapiro, S.K. and Schenk, F. (Editors). Univ. Chicago Press, Chicago, 1965. pp. 71-84.

8. Bogdanski, D.F., Weisbach, H., and Udenfriend, S., Pharmacological studies with the serotonin precursor, 5-hydorxytryptophan. J. Pharmacol. Exp. Ther., 122. 182-194, 1958.

9. Costa, E. and Rinaldi, F. Biochemical and electroencephalographic changes in the brain of rabbits injected with 5-hydroxytryptophan (influence of chlorpromazine premedication). Amer. J. Physiol. 194, 214-220, 1958.

10. Monnier, M. Actions électro-physiologiques des stimulants du systéme nerveux central. I systéme adrénergiques, cholinergiques et neurohumeurs sérotoniques. Arch. int. Pharmocodyn. 124, 281-301, 1960.

11. Chessin, M. Dubnick, B., Kramer, E.R., and Scott, C.C. Modifications of pharmacology of reserpine and serotonin by iproniazid. Fed. Proc. 15, 409, 1956.

12. Hess, S.M., and Diepfner, W. Behavioral effects and brain amine content in rats. Arch. int. Pharmacodyn 134, 89-99, 1961.

13. Hehman, K.N., Vonderahe, A.R., and Peters, J.J. Effect of serotonin on behavior, electrical activity of the brain, and seizure threshold of the newly hatched chick. Neurology 11, 1011-1016, 1961.

14. Kramer, S.Z., and Seifter, J. The effects of GABA and biogenic amines on behavior and brain electrical activity in chicks. Life Sci. 5, 527-537, 1966.

15. Spooner, C.E. and Winters, W.D. Evidence for a direct action of monoamines on the chick central nervous system. Experientia 21, 256-257, 1965.

16. Spooner, C.E., and Winters, W. D. Evoked responses during spontaneous and monoamine-induced states of wakefulness and sleep. Brain Res. 4, 189-205, 1967.

17. Baldessarini, R. J. Factors affecting S-adenosylmethionine levels in mammalian tissues. In Amines and Schizophrenia, Himwich, H. E. Kety, S.S., and Smythies, J.R. (Editors), Pergamon Press, New York, 1967, pp 199-208.

18. Rauzzino, F. J. and Seifter, J. Potentiation and Antagonism of Biogenic Amines. J. Pharmacol Exp. Therap. 157, 143-148, 1967.

19. Kety, S.S. Possible relation of central amines to behavior in schizophrenic patients. Fed. Proc. 20 4, 1961.

20. Williams, H.L., Lester, B.K., and Coulter, J.D. Paper presented at the annual meeting of the Association for Psychophysiological Study of Sleep, Denver, March, 1968.

A. J. Mandell, M.D., University of California, Department of Psychiatry School of Medicine, Los Angeles,

C. E. Spooner, Ph.D., Dept. of Neurosciences, University of California at San Diego, La Jolla, California

AMPHETAMINE INDUCED SCHIZOPHRENIFORM PSYCHOSIS

BURTON M. ANGRIST and SAMUEL GERSHON

One approach to the understanding and treatment of schizophrenia that has been undertaken in the past is the attempted induction of "model psychoses". Such an approach has several advantages: 1) A non schizophrenic subject can critically evaluate the subjective aspects of the experience and, if no amnesia is produced, report them to others. This could improve communication with those who suffer from this disease; 2) If the model is sound and truly mimics schizophrenia, then intense study of its mechanisms of pathogenesis would be justified, since such a study might lead to analogous mechanisms in the natu- rally occurring disease; 3) Even in the absence of an understanding of the fundamental mechanism, such a model might provide a useful pharmacologic screening system for the detection of agents that might have therapeutic use; 4) Such a system has the added advantage of convenience for the investigator.

Historically each time a drug has been discovered that was felt to produce behavioral effects analogous to schizophrenia there has been a resurgence of psychiatric interest in that compound. Thus, Moreau, in 1845, advocated that students of psychiatry experience the effects of hashish in order to better under- stand the experiences of psychotic patients. Similarly Lewin's work with pey- ote in 1888 generated widespread interest in mescaline, its active ingredient; and Hoffman's discovery of the effects of LSD in 1943 produced yet another wave of interest in psychotomimetic agents.

Some investigators have hypothesized that these or analogous substances may play a role in the actual pathogenic mechanisms of the endogenous disease. The potency of LSD suggested that the endogenous production of only minute

This paper was supported by U. S. P. H. S. Grant No. MH-04669 amounts might be sufficient for behavioral effects. The "transmethylation" hypothesis of Osmond, Smythies and Mason in 1952 indicated that altered methylation processes could account for the in vivo formation of such compounds[1] The activation of symptomatology observed in schizophrenic subjects to whom a methyl donor and monoamine oxidase inhibitor were administered [2], the discovery by Friedhoff of 3,4 DMPEA (0-dimethylated dopamine) in the urine of schizophrenics [3] and his subsequent confirmation of its identity [4], and the tentative demonstration of bufotenin in the urine of schizophrenics who had experienced exacerbation of symptoms after a monoamine oxidase inhibitor [5], all constituted important support for the hypothesis.

However, each of these findings has subsequently been disputed [6,7,8] and considerable controversy in this area still exists. Moreover, the demonstration of the rapid development of tolerance to the behavioral effects of LSD, psilocybin and mescaline suggest that it is unlikely that these compounds per se play a causal role in the production of the characteristically long-lasting symptomatology of schizophrenia.

Finally, a critical clinical evaluation of the states induced by these compounds indicates important phenomenological differences from naturally occurring schizophrenic illness. This is especially the case with regard to the type of hallucinatory experience induced and formal aspects of thinking.

The occurrence of paranoid and paranoid-hallucinatory syndromes in association with the ingestion of amphetamine was first noted in 1938 by Young and Scoville [9]. Subsequent reports [10] confirmed their observations and in 1954, the first sizable series of patients with amphetamine psychosis were reported [11]. This paper was also significant from another point of view, for whereas Young and Scoville had formulated their cases in terms of "precipitating of a latent paranoid psychosis", this report stressed that the patients involved appeared to have sociopathic, not overtly schizophrenic backgrounds and that they characteristically showed a rapid restitutio ad integram when the drug was withheld. This suggested that amphetamine might cause a paranoid hallucinatory psychosis in non-schizophrenic subjects.

In 1958, Connell's monograph[12], a detailed study of 42 patients with amphetamine psychosis was published. He confirmed that this was the case "apparently normal and well adjusted people can develop this reaction" and, on the basis of his study asserted, "the mental picture can be indistinguishable from acute or chronic paranoid schizophrenia."

Other investigators, however, have disagreed with his conclusions. Slater in reviewing Connell's monograph said:

> An experienced physician would probably suspect a toxic psychosis if he bore a possibility in mind. Features which tend to differ from a schizophrenic state are the past history of psychopathic traits, the rapidity of onset, the dreamlike quality of the experiences, the tendency toward visual hallucination, and the brisk emotional reaction usually in the direction of anxiety. Only the most hyper-acute of paranoid schizophrenic states will mimic this syndrome in all its peculiarities.[13]

A second author, Bell, has also suggested that these two entities can be distinguished on purely clinical grounds.[14] After comparing the symptomatology of patients with presumed diagnoses of schizophrenia and amphetamine psychosis he concluded that the patients with a true amphetamine psychosis tended to have visual and not auditory hallucinations and lack the characteristic schizophrenic thought disorder that was seen in the naturally occurring illness.

> The non-schizophrenic subjects had psychotic episodes that cleared within ten days after the withdrawal of amphetamine. They did not exhibit schizophrenic thought disorder and it was not uncommon for them to experience vivid visual hallucinations. The other group of subjects suffered psychoses that lasted for months and all the characteristics of their illness including the presence of thought disorder and the relative absence of visual hallucinations were typical of schizophrenia.

Most recently Griffith has administered amphetamine to toxicity under controlled conditions.[15] His observations under these conditions indicated that amphetamine produces a paranoid psychosis which more clearly resembles schizophrenia than any other drug induced state; but that formal thinking disorder and hallucinations are not seen. Thus while most investigators agree that amphetamine psychosis can to a certain degree, mimic schizophrenia the degree to which it exactly duplicates the clinical features of the naturally occurring disease remains debated.

Further evaluation of the clinical symptomatology of amphetamine psychosis especially as compared to schizophrenia is the purpose of this report. Data will be presented from two sources. First, the clinical features of patients with amphetamine related admissions to Bellevue Psychiatric Hospital will be presented. Data from 60 such patients will be reviewed.

Secondly, in an attempt to control for the role of possibly coexisting schizophrenia as a determinant of clinical outcome, a smaller group of patients was studied more intensively. In this study patients' symptomatology was rated in detail semiquantitatively. After clearing of acute symptoms the patients were seen by an independent rating team of psychiatrists and a judgment was made as to the presence of residual schizophreniform pathology of thinking and affect. The symptom scores of ten patients who showed such residual pathology was compared statistically with those of ten patients who did not. In these patients urine was also collected so that urinary amphetamine levels could be correlated with behavioral features.

METHODS

All admissions to Bellevue Psychiatric Hospital were reviewed daily for a period of approximately two years and those who gave a history of amphetamine ingestion prior to admission were interviewed by the research staff. In most cases at least two interviews were conducted, one as soon after admission as feasible, to document the presenting psychiatric symptomatology. The second , after clearing of symptoms was more prolonged and assessed the patient's past history. Data was collected with regard to demographic features, dose, early development, school adjustment and performance, childhood socialization patterns, evidence of past behavioral disorder, police record, family history of drug use or police problems, past psychiatric and medical history, and sexual , occupational, and military adjustment.

Patients selected for detailed study were transferred to a research ward for behavioral observation and urine collection. Phenothiazines were withheld during this time. Behavioral data were collected by means of a fifty item rating scale that parallels the format of the standard mental status examination but allows for semiquantitative evaluations of symptom intensity on a scale of zero to four plus. This format approximates but is not identical with those for which validity and reliability has previously been established [16]. The psychiatric profile thus obtained was assessed daily until acute symptoms subsided and the patient became organized and amenable to more prolonged interviews. At this point retrospective reconstructions of the acute episode were undertaken and past history was explored.

Urine was collected daily in 24 hour samples from the time of the patient's arrival on the ward. Amphetamine levels were assessed by gas chromatography. The method for this analytical procedure was, in brief, one which relied on the use of an internal standard, phenethylamine, a small amount of which was added to a 5 ml aliquot of each pooled 24 hour specimen. After extraction for amines, this fraction was acetylated and subjected to gas chromatic analysis. The amount of amphetamine present could then be calculated from the height of its peak as compared to that for a phenethylamine. In studies with known amounts of amphetamine this method provided linear reproducable results over a wide range of amphetamine concentrations. A detailed description of the method will be reported elsewhere.

This gas chromatographic method for assessing urinary amphetamine levels has two advantages: 1) It is more sensitive than other techniques and permits assessment of small amounts late in the clinical course; 2) It has high specificity for the amphetamine compound being assessed and unlike the methyl orange method will not give false positives when phenothiazines, ephedrine or anti-histamines or tricyclic antidepressants are being excreted concomitantly[17,18].

Behavioral observations and urine collections continued until discharge. After the patient's clinical course became stable and no further behavioral change was noted by the rater, the patient was seen, prior to discharge, in an independent diagnostic interview by two other psychiatrists of the research staff. These psychiatrists, by design, had minimal or no contact with the patient during the acute phases of his symptomatology and were kept unaware of the rating psychiatrist's diagnostic impression. On the basis of this interview the patient was assigned to one of two study groups, the first of these showed complete clearing of symptomatology and an apparent restitutio ad integram. A second group showed clearing of acute symptomatology but persistence of residual affectual blunting or incongruence, thought disorder, and in some cases, chronic delusional ideation. These features were clinically indistinguishable from those noted in chronic schizophrenic patients in relative remission. The decision to assign patients to study groups on the basis of an independent assessment after clearing was made to eliminate the bias that the rater might develop on the basis of his observation of the acute symptomatology or in the course of daily contact with the patient.

RESULTS

1. A review of 60 amphetamine related admissions

    a. Historical and Demographic Data

        The mean age for these 60 patients was 25.2 years; 43 were male and 17 female. Fifty-two were white, seven were Negro and one was Puerto Rican. Thirty-eight were single, ten were married, six divorced, and six separated. The reported duration of amphetamine use varied markedly. Three patients claimed that the episode leading to hospitalization was the first time they had tried the drug, and an additional three claimed less than a month's experience. On the other hand, six patients claimed over ten years of amphetamine use. The mean duration of use was somewhat over three and one-half years. The dosage could not be calculated for users of amphetamines that were obtained from black market sources as a powder because of questions as to purity and potency of the compound they obtained. Twenty-two patients, however, took amphetamine in the form of commercial preparations and dosages could be obtained for this sub group. These ranged from 20 to 800 mg. per dose with a mean of 165.7 mg per day. Source of the drug was given as black market "dealers" in over half of the patients (33). Ten patients, however, were given the drug on prescription by physicians.

        Occupational adjustment was poor in these patients. Forty-four were unemployed at the time of admission and only four had had skilled jobs. Approximately two-thirds(39) of these patients had police records. Offenses ranged from loitering and disturbing the peace to attempted homicide. Experience with other drugs was the rule. Forty-one had smoked marijuana more than 30 times. Twenty-two had taken LSD and an additional fifteen had used this drug over ten times. Eight had been heroin addicts at some time in the past and one was actively addicted at the time of admission. Barbiturates were used by fifteen patients, usually at the end of the amphetamine experience to avoid the "let down". A history of heavy drinking prior to drug use was reported by sixteen. Use of unusual drugs was reported by some; these included "STP"-4, morning glory seeds-4, cough syrups-3, and Mexican mushrooms, thyroid, anticholinergic compounds and amyl nitrite by one patient each.

The developmental histories of these patients were positive for temper tantrums(8) and prolonged nocturnal eneuresis(7). School adjustment had been poor. The mean number of years of school completed was 11.8 - for the mean high school was not completed. Eighteen patients had been severe behavior disorders and seven had been suspended. Seventeen had been truants. Ten described themselves as solitary with poor peer relationships. Sexual adjustment in these patients frequently showed severe pathology. Eleven of the forty-three males were active homosexuals. Eight males reported increased libido after taking amphetamine and four reported a concomitant delayed ejaculation. This combination of effects led to reports of "marathon" sexual relations (up to 18 hours with only one to two orgasms) in which they took great pleasure. Females frequently had a pre-existing history of sexual promiscuity and these usually reported an intensification of sexual feelings and behavior when amphetamines were ingested. Increased promiscuity , compulsive masturbation, prostitution, an intensification of sado-masochistic fantasies were all reported as consistent effects of amphetamine use. One female patient claimed that she had become orgastic only after using amphetamine. These findings are consistent with reports of other investigators [19].

The Family History was positive for alcoholism or drug use in a sibling in eleven cases. In twelve cases the father had been alcoholic.

b.   Symptomatology

Over half of these patients (32) showed acute paranoid (13) or paranoid-hallucinatory psychoses (19). In these patients the onset of symptoms was generally abrupt. During the period of acute symptomatology blunting or constriction of affect was frequently noted. In some cases who subsequently cleared ad integrum without residual pathology of thinking and affect, a formal thought disorder was noted during the acute phase. A typical case illustrates these features as well as a characteristic past history.

> The patient was an 18 year old single male who left high school in the eleventh grade. He had been in a reformatory because of refractory truancy in the past and had arrests for possession of marijuana and petty larceny. At the time of his hospitalization a trial was still pending for Sullivan Law violation (possession of a loaded pistol). He had sniffed glue and Carbona from ages 12 to 13, drunk heavily from ages 13 to 15, and had used amphetamines orally (5 to 10 capsules per day) and intravenously from the age of 16 onwards. He had been addicted to heroin for 3-4 months between the ages of 17 and 18. After leaving school he had worked in a pizza stand, a bicycle store and as a messenger but no job had lasted for more than 5 to 6 months.
>
> For the two weeks prior to admission he had stayed in his brother and sister-in-law's apartment and had taken 3 to 7 injections per day of a powder that he was told was methamphetamine. He had slept very little during this time. He suddenly heard his brother tell his sister-in-law that he had killed his mother and planned to kill him as well. He panicked and ran into the street without shoes or shirt. He still heard his brother's voice telling his wife of plans to kill him and in an attempt to escape, jumped on the rear fender of a passing mail truck. This led to his being taken to Bellevue Psychiatric Hospital by the police. In the hospital, he was frightened and apprehensive. It seemed that the staff and other patients were implying that he "knew something" that he refused to tell. When he was seen by the research staff two days after admission (a Monday) his affect was blunt and constricted and at times, incongruent. He became frightened and tearful when transferred, fearing that the new ward was a place where patients were sent to be punished and perhaps even killed. He showed a formal thought disorder some examples of which are as follows: On the day of his transfer, speaking of his brother's drug use, he said, "My brother has been playing with the fires of hell. " On the same day, when asked what "a stitch in time saves nine" meant, he said, "Hurry up with that date and don't be late " (laughs) "make that first stitch right and the rest will follow. " By the next day his persecutory ideation had diminished and was replaced by a diffuse referentiality - i. e., other patients on the ward were looking at him peculiarly.

Affect was still somewhat blunt, constricted and incongru-
ent to ideation expressed. On the following day (his third on
the research ward and fifth in the hospital) he responded to
the proverb about glass houses, thus "If you throw stones
you risk your life. Living in a glass house would shatter your
whole being. " He was apprehensive about a female patient on
the ward that he referred to as "the girl I call Bonnie" (after
the movie "Bonnie and Clyde"). These mental status features
then cleared rapidly. When seen in an independent diagnostic
interview by two research psychiatrists seven days after admission both felt that his mental status clearly indicated a
diagnosis of sociopathy and that there was no evidence to
suggest a schizophrenic illness.

2.   Comparison of Two Matched Patient Groups

The major points that emerged are as follows: Two groups
of ten patients each were compared. All had experienced acute psychotic
symptoms in conjunction with amphetamine abuse. One group showed complete clearing while the other cleared of acute symptoms only to show residual
pathology of thinking and affect. Symptomatology was scored daily on a zero
to four plus scale and mean symptom scores were compared for the two groups.
Results were as follows:

TABLE 1

Mean Scores (0 - 4+) for Initial Symptomatology of the Two Patient
Groups*

Symptom	Complete Clearing	Residual Schizophreniform Psychopathology
Behavioral Disturbance	3. 5	2. 6
Delusional Ideation	2. 6	2. 8
Hallucinatory Experience	2. 0	2. 55
Thought Disorder Schizophreniform	1. 2	1. 7
Manic Features	1. 6	1. 5
Affectual Blunting or Incongruence	1. 55	1. 65

*No significant differences between the two groups by "t" test.

1.   Demographic and historical features were the same for the two groups.
The group with residual schizophreniform psychopathology appeared to show a
greater tendency toward the use of sedative drugs (alcohol and barbiturates) in

the past.

2. There were no qualitative differences in the presenting symptomatology for the two groups. As to hallucinatory experience, five patients in each group experienced auditory hallucinations. Visual hallucinations were experienced by four of the patients who cleared completely and three of the patients who had residual pathology.

3. There was no significant difference in initial symptom intensity for the two groups (Table 1).

4. The group with residual schizophreniform pathology of thinking and affect required significantly longer to clear of behavioral disturbance and delusions than the group that did not show this residual pathology.

5. The clearing rate for hallucinations was not significantly different for the two groups. This appeared to be due to the fact that hallucinations cleared rapidly in both groups.

6. Initial pathology of thinking and affect was somewhat higher in the group in which these features remained pathological. However, these features were also noted in the group that showed total clearing; so much so, that no significant difference for initial scores emerged for these symptoms (See Table 1).

3. Biochemical Data

The following figure indicates the relationship between the symptoms of the case presented in detail and the 24 hour amphetamine excretion as determined by gas chromatography.

This case is typical of those patients in whom these relationships have been determined in two ways:

1. Hallucinations have generally cleared first, that is, prior to other symptoms. Hallucinatory experiences appear to be associated only with the highest points on the amphetamine excretion curve.

2. Clearing of delusions appears to parallel the urinary amphetamine excretion rather closely.

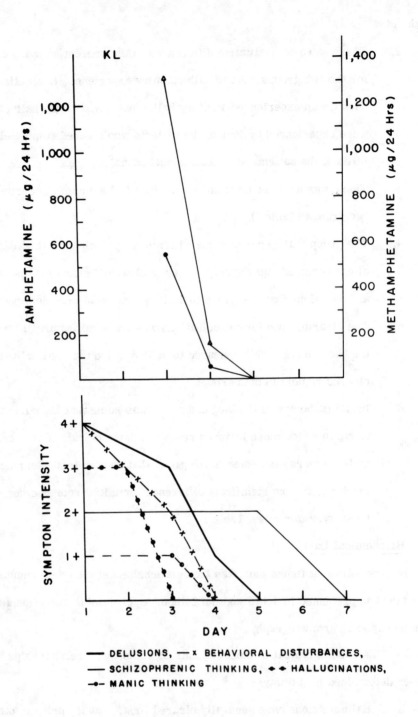

Further studies are currently being done to determine the consistency of these relationships.

DISCUSSION

This study indicates that the phenomenology of amphetamine psychosis is such as to make it the best available clinical model of naturally occurring schizophrenia, and represents support for Connell's original contention in this regard. Other investigators who have disagreed with these conclusions have cited clinical features which differentiate the two conditions. Our data support some of these but not others.

Slater has indicated five differentiating clinical parameters: 1) The past history of psychopathic traits; 2) The rapidity of onset; 3) The dream-like quality of the experiences; 4) The tendency toward visual hallucinations; 5) The brisk emotional reaction usually in the direction of anxiety.

Our study certainly confirms the first of these; psychopathic traits were the dominant features of our patients' past histories. Rapid onset of symptoms also was the rule. A dream-like quality to the experience was noted at times, but appeared quite variable from patient to patient. An unavoidable problem in evaluating symptomatology in drug abusers is the possibility of the concomitant use of drugs other than the one reported. Use of sedative drugs which cloud con- sciousness might alter the clinical features and impart a dream-like quality to the experience. As to the tendency toward visual hallucinations, this is con- firmed in part. Ten out of our sixty patients had visual experiences that are impossible to explain except on a hallucinatory basis, (purple shapes in cars, men turning into smokestacks, etc.), and many more had transient visual illus- ions, probably on the basis of hyperalert expectation. This incidence is probably significantly greater than would be noted in a series of sixty admissions for schizophrenia. The brisk emotional reaction usually in the direction of anxiety is confirmed only in that panic was a frequent basis for admission; but is not confirmed if "brisk emotional response" is meant to connote a healthy and congruent affectual display. In comparing the initial symptom scores of our two matched patient groups, the affectual blunting and incongruence of the group that showed complete clearing was almost as great on day 1 as it was for those who showed residual pathology of affect after clearing of acute psy- chotic mental status features.

Bell has suggested that parameters of hallucinatory experience and think- ing can be used to differentiate amphetamine psychosis from schizophrenia in the acute phase and to predict the rate of clearing, i.e., that patients with amphetamine psychoses tend to have visual hallucinations and no thought disorder while those with schizophrenia have a formal thought disorder and tend to have auditory hallucinations. While our data indicate that visual hallucinations do seem to appear more frequently in amphetamine psychosis than in schizophrenia, it should also be noted that once an amphetamine intoxication has occurred in the two types of patients the hallucinatory experience does not appear to have predictive value. In our two matched groups five in each group had auditory hallucinations. Visual hallucinations occurred in four of the patients who showed clearing and three of those who cleared to show residual schizophreniform pathology. Thought disorder was also noted in both groups initially and a statistically significant difference for the two groups was not attained. neither of these features, then, appears to be completely reliable parameters for sorting the two groups in the acute phase of intoxication.

Griffith's observations that neither a schizophrenic thought disorder nor hallucinations occur in the course of experimental amphetamine intoxication under controlled conditions is an important one because his represents the only investigation that has definitively controlled for the possible influence of concomitant ingestion of other drugs. However, administration of toxic dosages are associated with risks and deaths from amphetamine poisoning have occurred[20]. It is possible, therefore, that humane and ethical compunctions (which do not influence amphetamine abusers as regards their own dosages) intervened to prevent the induction of a more advanced syndrome of toxicity than other investigators have generally reported. Furthermore, the limited duration of administration and its cessation after the first psychotic features appeared could well account for this difference. Our own data regarding correlation of hallucinatory experience with urine levels suggest that hallucinatory experience is associated with higher points on the amphetamine excretion curve than other symptoms. This suggests that hallucinations occur only with more advanced toxicity. Griffith's observation of marked individual vulnerability to the psychotogenic effect of amphetamine is, however, totally consistent with the wide scatter noted in our patients' initial excretion rate.

Our data, therefore, suggest that amphetamine psychosis represents a rather strikingly close clinical approximation of schizophrenic illness. The mechanism of its pathogenesis, therefore, seems to deserve closer scrutiny; and in this area less definitive knowledge is available.

If one focuses on central adrenergic mechanisms it is known that amphetamine has four-fold effects on this system, i.e., it releases biogenic amines, prevents inactivation by their re-uptake, has a direct effect on the receptor and is a weak monoamine oxidase inhibitor. The fact that some substances with analogous effects, i.e., imipramine and monoamine oxidase inhibitors have induced symptom activation in schizophrenic patients [21,22] is inferential support for this approach.

Utena has suggested metabolic effects of amphetamine on brain tissue which should also be noted as possibly etiologically significant. These studies indicate a decrease in aerobic glycolysis in the brain of animals with chronic amphetamine intoxication and have shown similar trends in lobotomy specimens from chronic schizophrenics and patients stated to have "chronic methamphetamine psychosis" [23].

Finally, the possibility of a psychotoxic metabolite of amphetamine itself occurs. Tri-methoxy amphetamine has been shown to be hallucinogenic and to have an order of potency twice that of mescaline [24,25]. Axelrod has demonstrated para-hydroxylation of amphetamine in mamalian systems [26]; Subsequent methylation of this compound could produce para-methoxy-amphetamine, a compound which Smythies has tested in animal systems which are stated to parallel human psychotogenicity and found it to be the most potent of all compounds tested with the exception of LSD [25]. Moreover, a hypothesis as to the endogenous production of such a compound is totally consistent with the time course of the clinical effects of amphetamine. Users almost invariably report an initial confidence and euphoria and only later in the "trip", the development of psychotic or dysphoric experiences. This could be interpreted to suggest that these latter experiences are caused by a metabolite rather than amphetamine itself. Studies are now in progress at our center to document the presence of paramethoxy-amphetamine in the urine of patients who present with amphetamine psychosis.

REFERENCES

1. Osmond, H. and Smythies, J.: Schizophrenia: A new approach. J. Ment. Sci., 98, 309, 1952.

2. Pollin, W., Cardon, P. V. and Kety, S.: Effects of amino acid feeding in schizophrenic patients treated with iproniazide, Science, 133, 104, 1961.

3. Friedhoff, A. J. and Van Winkle, E.: Isolation and characterization of a compound from the urine of schizophrenics, Nature, 194, 897, 1962.

4. Friedhoff, A. J. and Van Winkle, E.: The characteristics of an amine found in the urine of schizophrenic patients, J. Nerv. & Ment. Dis., 135, 550, 1962.

5. Tanimukai, H., Ginther, R., Spaide, J., Bueno, J. R., and Himwich, H. E.: Occurrence of bufotenin (5-hydroxy-N, N-dimethyltryptamine) in urine of schizophrenic patients, Life Sciences 6, 1697, 1967, Pergamon Press, Ltd.

6. Kakimoto, Y., Sano, R., Kanozawa, A., Tsujio, T., and Kineko, Z., Metabolic effects of methionine in schizophrenic patients treated with a monoamine oxidase inhibitor, Nature, 216, 1110, 1967.

7. Pind, K., Faurbye, A.: Does 3,4 dimethoxyphenethylamine occur in the urine of schizophrenic and normal persons? Acta Psychiatrica Scand., 42, 246, 1966.

8. Faurbye, A. and Pind, K.: Occurrence of bufotenin in the urine of schizophrenic patients and normal persons. Nature, 220, 489, 1968.

9. Young, D. and Scoville, W. B.: Paranoid Psychosis in narcolepsy and the possible dosages of benzedrine treatment. Med. Clinics of North America, Boston, 22, 673, 1938.

10. Monroe R. R. and Drell, H. J. : Oral use of stimulants obtained from inhalers. JAMA 135 908 1947.

11. Herman M. and Nagler S. H. : Psychoses due to amphetamine. J. Nerv. & Ment. Dis. , 120, 268, 1954.

12. Connell, P. H. : Amphetamine Psychosis, Maudsley Monographs, No. 5 Oxford University Press, London, 1958.

13. Slater, E. : Book review of amphetamine psychosis by P. H. Connell. Brit. Med. J. , 488, Feb. , 1959.

14. Bell, D. S. : A Comparison of amphetamine psychosis and schizophrenia. Brit. J. Psychiat. , 3, 701, 1965.

15. Griffith, J. , Oates, J. and Cavanough, J. : Schizophreniform psychosis induced by large dose administration of d-amphetamine. Presented at APA Meetings, May, 1968.

16. Rockland, L. H. and Pollin, W. : Quantification of psychiatric mental status. Arch. Gen. Psychiat. , 12, 23, 1965.

17. Abenson, M. J. : An analysis of urinary amines on routine admissions to a mental hospital. Acta Psychiatrica Scand. , 41, 582, 1965.

18. Rockwell, D. A. and Ostwald, P. : Amphetamine use and abuse in psychiatric patients. Arch. Gen. Psychiat. , 18, 612, 1968.

19. Bell, D. S., Trethowan, W. H. : Amphetamine addiction and disturbed sexuality. Arch. Gen. Psychiat. , 4, 74. 1961.

20. Zalis, E. G. and Loren, F. P. : Fatal amphetamine poisoning. Arch. Int. Med. , 112, 822, 1963.

21. Pollack, M. , Klein, D. F. , Wilner, A. , Blumberg, A. , Fink M. : Imipramine induced behavioral disorganization in schizophrenic patients: Physiological and psychological correlates. Recent Advances in Biological Psychiatry, Vol. III. J. Wortis, M. D. (Ed.), Plenum Press, New York, 1964.

22. Pekkarinen, A., Rinne, U., Iisalo, E.: Prolonged decrease in vanilman-delic (3-methoxy-4 hydroxymandelic) acid by man during and after nialamide treatment. Acta Pharmacol. et Toxicol., 22, 331, 1965.

23. Utena, H., Ezoe, T., Koto, N. and Hodo, H.: Effects of chronic administration of methamphetamine in enzymic patterns in brain tissue. J. Neurochem., 4, 161, 1959.

24. Perelz, D. I., Smythies, J. R. and Gibson, W.: A new hallucinogen: 3,4,5 trimethoxyphenyl-B-aminopropane with notes on the stroboscopie phenomenon. J. Ment. Sci., 104, 317, 1955.

25. Smythies, J. R., Johnston, U. S. Bradley, R. J., Benington, F., Morin, R. D., and Clark, L. C.: Some new behavior - disrupting amphetamine and their significance. Nature, 216, 128, 1967.

26. Axelrod, J.: Studies on sympathomimetic amine II. The biotrans-formation and physiological disposition of d-amphetamine. d-p-hydroxy - amphetamine and d-methamphetamine. J. Pharmacol. & Exper. Therap. 110, 315, 1954.

B. M. Angrist, M.D. and S. Gershon, M.D., New York University School of Medicine, New York, New York

BASIC PRINCIPLES OF CNS PATHOGENIC MECHANISMS AT THE MOLECULAR LEVEL OF ORGANIZATION. (MEMBRANE SYSTEMS (VI) AND SYNAPSES (VII)

LEON ROIZIN

In a previous symposium on the Biology of Schizophrenia, organized under the auspices of the N. Y. Academy of Sciences, in our paper on "Histopathologic and Histochemical studies in Schizophrenia" (1), we concluded with a brief discussion on "Future perspectives." In the latter we indicated that new pathways for future research in neurocytological and histochemical fields are open which may advance our knowledge beyond that of the previous neuronal and neuroglial unit concept and, possibly, they may unveil the as yet unexplored precellular and ultramicroscopic (or molecular) homeokinetic reversible processes. These could be used as "biological subcellular structural-functional indicators" inasmuch as they appear to be more sensitive reacting gradient units or systems than the entire neuron maze. Consequently, we hope that such studies may be helpful in the understanding of neurogenic and eventually psychotogenic disorders or disease processes of the central nervous system.

The present paper is summarizing some of the most outstanding progress to date in the study of the ultracellular mechanisms.

The classical cellular (2) and recent molecular theories (3) represent the stepping stones in the evolution of pathogenic mechanisms of functional disorders and disease processes. Recent biophysical and biochemical investigations of operational principles of living matter seem to indicate that the molecules may be considered as the instruments of function, whereas the atoms are the basic chemical elements of the living system (4). However, the only way the molecules could

* Supported, in part, by the General Research Grant No. FR-05650-03

influence the tissue functions is to pass through the anatomo-functional "barriers" of the cell and to combine or penetrate its ultrastructural subunits. These are principally represented by membrane systems and specialized orgenelles (4).

Because of space limitation I will restrict my discussion only to some fundamental structural, functional and pathologic aspects of membrane systems and synapses of the CNS*, since in our previous papers we reported on mitochondria or pleomorphometabolosomes (PMS) (5), lysosomes (6), multivesicular bodies (MVB) and endoplasmic reticulum (7). We are investigating these organelles particularly in relation with their role as anatomo-functional and histometabolic gradients in the study of physiological and pathogenic mechanisms at the ultracellular level of organization (organellopathies).

Some basic structural-functional and pathogenic aspects of membrane systems

During recent years the study of the structure and function of cell membranes or membranology has become one of the most debated and stimulating research topics. This is reflected in the enormous amount of cytologic, electron microscope, biophysical, biochemical or physicochemical publications (8-10), etc. and symposia (11, 12), etc. In brief, the elaborate membrane systems consist of "repeating units" or unit membranes (13). Structurally the basic patterns of the cellular membrane organization consists of: a) single "lamellae" or "leaflets" which delineate the large variety of cytosomes such as lysosomes, MVB, Golgi's intermidiary or transitional structures, pinocytotic vesicles, etc. (Fig. 1) and b) "double lamellae" as for instance the nuclear membranes, the endoplasmic reticulum, the mitochondrial or PMS membranes, etc. (Fig. 1). The "unit membrane" concept proposed by J. D. Robertson (13) has evolved principally from the studies of the development of the myelin of the peripheral nerves and Davson-Danielli's model (10). According to this concept

---

* This paper was included in a Jubilee volume in honor of Prof. M. Gozzano

a unit membrane consists of a single bilayer of lipid with the nonpolar chains directed towards the center of the membrane and the polar pointing outward. The latter is covered by unimolecular leaflets or films of non-lipid or proteins. Thus the outer surface of each membrane differs chemically from the inner and, therefore, the membrane is chemically

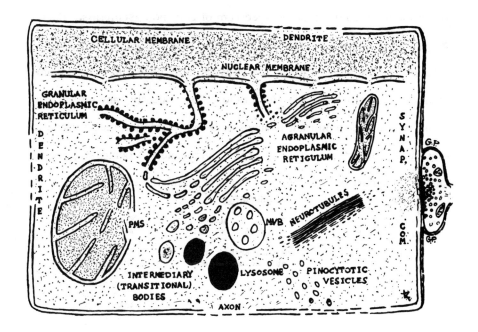

Fig. I: Schematic outline of various basic membrane systems of a neuron as described in the text. (The location, orientation and dimensions are arbitrary for illustrative purposes). Abbreviations: MVB=Multivesicular body; PMS=pleomorphometabolosomes or mitochondria; synap. com. =synaptic complex; G.P. =glial process.

an assymetric structure. For details on the structure and molecular organization of the membrane systems as estimated by recent biophysical, physico-chemical and electron microscope investigations, the interested reader should refer also to the following bibliographical references (8, 13) etc. While improved or newly developed techniques and elaborate research procedure are aiming at defining the finer molecular configurations, current knowledge seems to indicate (in a simplified manner) that: 1a) the membrane systems enclose the cell and its organelles, b) compartmentalize their interior, c) structurealize the orderly arrangement of the enzyme assemblies and d) channel the intermidiary metabolites (secretory product) or histometabolic processes; and 2) the properties of the membrane systems are expressed by the particular arrangement of the phospholipids (30%) and protein (50%) molecules. These are patterned in multiple species of "repeating units" (within a membrane system) and they serve as a miniaturized base for a characteristic spectrum of enzyme assemblies. Each enzyme in this membrane-bound metabolic process serves in a dual capacity: a) as one of a group of catalysts in a sequential process and b) as an integral part of the membrane. Consequently, any alterations would result in concomitant changes of both the original metabolic function and the structural integrity of the membrane. A demonstrative example in support of this concept is briefly summarized in Figs. 2 and 3

STRUCTURE	CHEMISTRY	FUNCTION
Outer and inner limiting membranes:	DPN, flavoproteins cytochromes, E.C.E.*	E.T.P., K inner membrane
Matrix:	Enzymes Krebs' and fatty ac.oxidation cycles	Oxidation Krebs' tricarboxylic ac. cycle; "respiratory assemblies", conversion of ADP in ATP; trans. H_2O and certain m.**
Cristae:	Stratified proteins and phospholipid molecules	E.T.P., fatty ac. and some NH_2-ac. oxidation; oxidative phosphorilation

Fig. II. Structural, chemical and functional interdependence of the PMS or mitochondrial organelle in physiological conditions.

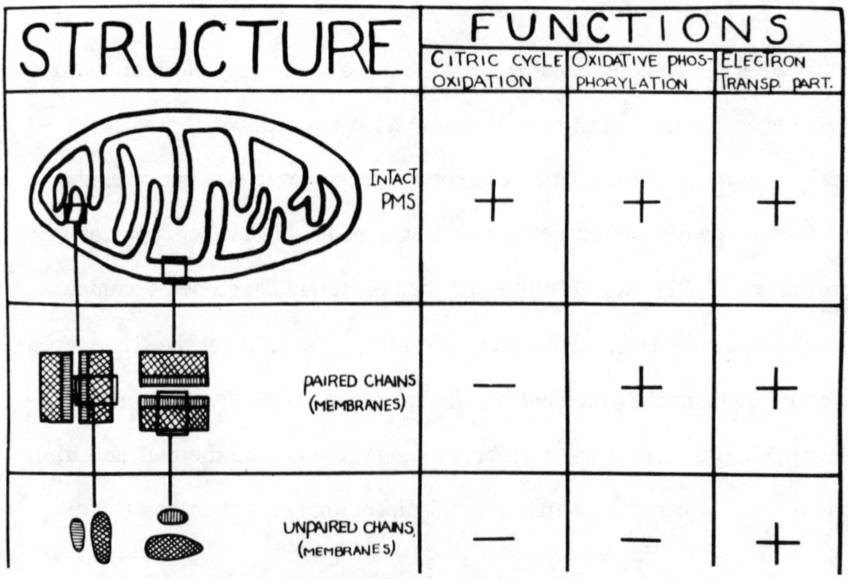

STRUCTURE	FUNCTIONS		
	CITRIC CYCLE OXIDATION	OXIDATIVE PHOSPHORYLATION	ELECTRON TRANSP. PART.
INTACT PMS	+	+	+
PAIRED CHAINS (MEMBRANES)	—	+	+
UNPAIRED CHAINS (MEMBRANES)	—	—	+

Fig. III. Structural and metabolic interdependence of PMS membrane in accordance with various investigations and as described in the text.

illustrating the structural, functional and histometabolic interdependency of mitochondrial subunits. It has been established that when the mitochondria or PMS are damaged or disrupted (14, 15) the enzyme assemblies of the citric cycle oxidations are apparently detached from the respective units and become water soluble. In these circumstances or when the fragmented organelles are composed principally of paired membranes the citric cycle oxidative functions are altered or lost.

With subsequent fragmentation of the fine structural unpaired (single) membranes, the original functions of the disintegrated organelle are reduced only to the electron transport mechanisms(Fig. 3). It is also of significance to note that drugs may exert strong effects on organelles in situ (tissue) or in vitro (16) and on particular membrane bound enzymes; but they may have non demonstrable effect on the same enzyme after these have been separated or extracted from the membrane (4). Thus, the membrane-enzyme associated systems represent the molecular basis of the histometabolism or the biological energy transformation in tissues. Their synergistic functions mediate the cybernetics (*) of the specialized histometabolic compartmentalized activities and regulate the flow of the living cellular energy. In association with these functions and, at times independently, some membrane varieties control the passage of electrolytic-colloidal systems and substrates; regulate the traffic of the intracellular metabolites or direct the flux of the specialized energy transformation processes. These biological cycles involve fixation, release, transfer (translocation) and use of energy for synthesis, mechanical, digestive, secretory, bioelectrical, etc. activities. Recent investigations have also revealed that various biophysical, biochemical and morbigenous agents could act as stabilizers or disorganizors of the membrane bound enzymes (4-6 18 19 etc.).

(*) "A set of principles underlying communication information and operation of self controlling mechanisms in either non-biological or biological systems" (19).

Some basic structural, histochemical
and functional aspects of CNS synapses

The gradual affirmation of the "contiguity" theory (20-22)

over reticular (23, 24) the assertion of the neuronal concept (25)

and dynamic polarization of the neuron (26) the demonstration of the

characteristic "boutons" (27-29) etc., the studies on neural conduc-

tion and transmission (30) and the investigations of the special prop-

erties of the reflex have(31)led to the development of the structural

and functional concept of the synapses. The subsequent microscopic

description of the neuromuscular junction of vertebrates, the various

types of the synapses in the CNS, sympathetic ganglia and neuropile

in vertebrates, the giant synapses in the squid stellate ganglion, etc.

have disclosed that these organelles consist of a remarkably diversi-

fied structural organization. However, more recent electro-physiologi-

cal, histochemical and particularly electron microscopic investigations

indicate that these different types of synapses have a specific ultrastruc-

tural and functional uniformity which is principally correlated with the

operation of the action potential of the nervous system (32, 33 etc.).

Because of space limitation I will restrict my discussion only to a few

basic aspects of the structural, functional and pathologic aspects of the

CNS synapses.

The synapses, in relation with their contacts with the neurons

(Fig. 1, Synap. Com.) and their processes, have been defined as ax-

osomatic (surface of the perikaryion), axo-dentritic and axo-axonic

respectively. Furthermore on the basis of current electron micros-

cope observations, the fine structural organization of the synaptic or-

ganelle or "complex" consists of a presynaptic terminal, synaptic cleft,

post-synaptic membrane, sub-synaptic web, and, in certain regions,

the synaptic "spine apparatus" (dendrite spines) (32-35 etc.).

The presynaptic terminal (axon terminal), which corresponds

to the old term "bouton", "bulb" or synaptic knob, contains principally

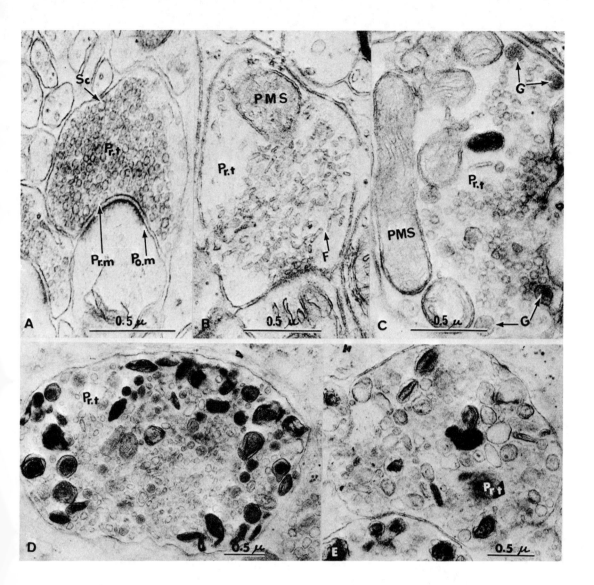

Fig. IV. Demonstrative examples of CNS synapses as described
in the text: A. (4, 652) Cerebral cortex, rat, magnification
60, 200 X; B. (5, 761) Spinal cord, rat, magnification 54, 288 X;
C. (5, 688) Brainstem, rat, magnification 54, 288 X; D. (6, 464)
Frontal biopsy, human, magnification 28, 375; E. (6, 465)
Frontal biopsy, human, magnification 36, 888.
Abbreviations : Prt. = presynaptic terminal; Pr.m. = presynaptic membrane; Po.m. = postsynaptic membrane; Sc. = synaptic
vesicle, circular type; F. = tubular or flat type of synaptic vesicles;
G. = granular type of synaptic vesicles; PMS = pleomorphometabolo-
somes or mitochondria.

synaptic vesicles which are frequently intermixed with tubules (neurotubules), vacuoles, mitochondria or PMS and multivesicular bodies (MVB). Among these ultrastructural components particular attention has been focused upon the synaptic vesicles (32-39). They are considered to contain the "transmitter substances" or the "neuro-chemical mediator." Although some finer details are still disputed, fundamentally there is common agreement, that in morphologic terms, the synaptic vesicles may vary in shape, size, concentration and distribution within the presynaptic terminal.

In accordance with the profiles of their shape, the synaptic vesicles have been classified (32-39) as: a) circular or spheroid or S type (Fig. 4A); b) tubular or flattened or F type (Fig. 4B) and c) granular type (Fig. 4C). The latter contains an electron dense material which biochemically has been identified with catecholamines. In functional terms it has been suggested (35) that the S types are of an excitatory or stimulating character and the F type inhibitory.

Furthermore, in biochemical terms the cholinergic containing vesicles have been named type C, whereas adrenergic and the catecholamine (as aforementioned) are called A type. Since there is no space available for a thorough discussion, it should be kept in mind that, at times, two and even three types of vesicles could be encountered in the same presynaptic terminal (40). The surface membrane of the presynaptic terminal has a triple layered structure (32) with a thickness of 50-70Å and in continuity with the axon membrane. This surface membrane in the CNS, is usually covered by a "glial membrane." (Fig. 1, G.P.). This, at the junctional contact, continues directly over the corresponding portion of the postsynaptic membrane. (*)

Usually, at the junction of the presynaptic membrane, "patches" or areas of higher electron density and increased thickness (32, 36) are present. The opposite postsynaptic membrane, at times, also appears

(*) Small glial processes interposed between two membranes with only some partial obstruction of the direct contact, have also been noted (41).

denser or of increased osmiophilia (**) as compared with either site. The synaptic vesicles cluster and make closer contact at this level. These are considered as morphological subunits of the synaptic membrane. It also has been suggested that they may be "active points" or "zones" (42) of the synapse where the transmission of the impulse occurs.

Additional electron microscope investigations (34, 32, 33) have described three types of denser "zones". Of these, two types are currently considered of functional significance. Type I is differentiated from type 2 (34) on the basis that its synaptic cleft is wider (300Å whereas that of type 2 is 200Å), the postsynaptic membrane is thicker and denser (this is much more extensive and occupying the greater part of the opposing synaptic membrane) and in the cleft there is a band of extracellular material which is nearer to the postsynaptic membrane. It is also of significance to note the selectivity in distribution and function of these two types of synapses (32-34 43-45).

The third type of membrane thickening is represented by a symmetrical density of the opposite membranes of an unchanged synaptic cleft.

The synaptic cleft (about 120Å-300Å) is the interspace between the pre- and postsynaptic membranes. Recent investigations have revealed also the presence of "intersynaptic filaments (about 50Å)" which form regular parellel patterns across the cleft at intervals of about 100Å. These macromolecular structures of extracellular appearance are assumed to provide an adhesive contact or special anchorage mechanism to the opposite membranes at the synaptic junction.

The "synaptic web" (32) consists of a web of fine filaments or cannaliculi of 80Å. They extend from the postsynaptic membrane for varying distance (1500Å or more) into the postsynaptic region.

(**) These electron microscope features seem to be very similar to desmomal contacts.

The width of this web may vary among synapses and even at different parts of the same synapse. The significance of the subsynaptic web is still in the stage of speculation. However, in view of the location in the subsynaptic region it is suspected of being a specialized "histo-chemical receptor" zone for the transmitter substances released at the presynaptic terminal. The "spine apparatus" is another characteristic subsynaptic unit which is located in the postsynaptic (34, 46, 47, 48) depths of dendritic spines in the neocortex and hippocampus of mammalians (43, 45). The significance of this specialized ultrastructure as in the case of the intersynaptic filaments and subsynaptic web, is uncertain. Some investigators suggest (44) that because of its very selective location (as afore mentioned) it may be related with processes of learning and memory.

Synaptic glial membrane. Several investigators have noted beyond the synaptic junction and over the presynaptic terminal glial processes (32, 41). This relationship is assumed to represent some kind of a "synaptic glial barrier" or "perisynaptic barrier". According to some authors (32) this barrier is mediated by astroglia similarly to the blood-brain-barrier (BBB) and the liquor-brain-barrier (LBB). Moreover it is assumed that it is a protective device for the diffusion of the transmitter substance and ionic flux of the synaptic cleft as well as shielding for the underlying subsynaptic receptor from pharmacologic agents applied in the vicinity of synapses.

From a functional point of view the electrical and chemical hypothesis of the transmission of the synaptic action across the synaptic membranes have been periodically disputed. Although the former mechanism appears to predominate, the latter has been also demonstrated for both (33, 49, 50) the inhibitory as well as the excitatory synapses.

From the review of the current literature it appears that, the physiological operation of the synapses is mediated or regulated by its ultrastructural subunits and histochemical correlates in the following manner (in brief): a) the nervous impulse or the action potential (bio-electrical current) induces the discharge, from the synaptic vesicles, of a transmitter substance or neurochemical mediator (acetylcholine, noradrenaline, gammabutyric acid and, possibly 5-hydroxy tryptamine) which moves across the presynaptic membrane (active zone); b) the quantum molecules of the transmitter substance by coupling (anchoring) to the specific chemoreceptor of the postsynaptic membrane causes an alteration of its polarization (depolarization or hyperpolarization); c) the consequent increase in ionic flux (electrochemical gradients) creates the synaptic potential across the postsynaptic membrane into the sub-synaptic region (web); and finally, d) the effects of the transmitter sub-stance is checked or terminated in the subsynaptic region (web) by the reaction of the correlated enzyme systems (acetylcholinesterase, mono-aminoxydases, etc.).

Pathologic aspects

Electron microscope alterations of the synapses and their res-pective subunits have been observed in some experimental conditions (51-58 etc.) and some human biopsies as for instance in a case of psy-chomotor retardation (58) and a presenile psychosis which clinically and histopathologically was consistent with Pick's type (60). Although no definite ultrastructural, electrophysiological and histochemical corre-lations have been established in the afore mentioned pathologic conditions, none the less the demonstration of qualitative and quantitative alterations of the synapses (59 69), the synaptic vesicles (57, 58), the pre-and postsynaptic as well as the perisynaptic glial membranes (58) and the cleft (57, 58) would also imply concomitant involvement of their res-pective molecular patterns of organization. Furthermore, these ini-tial pathologic observations, in the light of the previously discussed physiologic and biochemical activities of the synapses, seem to sug-gest that pathogenic mechanisms may occur as a result of malfunction-ing of individual or combined intermediary phases of the synthesis

(generation, development), storage, release and transmission of the
neurochemical mediator (transmitter substance), and/or propagation
of the action potential. On this basis the synapses, like the intracellular organelles, comply also with the "principle of the integrated anatomo-
functional synergism" (3). In the sense that: a) each component part
through their reciprocal relationship, contribute to the same specific
activity; b) the character of each part is expressed through the chemical
nature of constituent substances; c) the specific pattern of the arrangement of the parts is of greater functional significance than the chemical
nature of the individual components and d) the alteration of any structural component is synchronized with functional changes.

Conclusive Remarks

1) The diversified behavior or the cellular membranes stems not only
from the structural organization of the molecular configuration but
also from the interaction of their chemical components. 2) The organelles and the membrane units function as histochemical vectors
and gradient systems at the ultracellular level of organization. 3) The
physiological mechanisms of the organelles depend upon the maintenance of the integrity of the membrane and the molecular relationship
with its specialized structural architecture rather than upon a particular molecule. 4) Consequently, a "molecular disease or molecular
pathology" is not caused by a special pathologic molecule, but it is the
result of a mutation (genetic), disorder (biochemical and functional) or
disruption (morphologic or biophysical) of a specific molecular pattern
(arrangement) of the specialized structural organization; and 5) the
fine ultrastructural alterations of the synaptic subunits, in various experimental and pathologic conditions, demonstrate that pathogenic mechanisms in the CNS may result not only from intracellular abnormalities
but also from alterations or dysfunctions of the intercellular communication systems.

REFERENCES

1. ROIZIN, L., EROS, G. and WEINBERG, F.: Ann. N. Y. Acad. Sci. 96: 477-486, 1962.

2. ROIZIN, L.: Dis. Nerv. Syst. 21, 1-17, 1960.

3. ROIZIN, L.: J. Neuropath. & Exper. Neurol. 19, 591-621, 1960.

4. GREEN, D. E. & GOLDBERGER, R. F.: Molecular insights into the living process. Academic Press., New York, 1967.

5. ROIZIN, L.: J. Neuropath. & Exper. Neurol. 23, 209-252, 1963.

6. ROIZIN, L., KAUFMAN, M. A. & RUGH, R.: Acta Radiologica. 5, 161-176, 1966.

7. ROIZIN, L., NISHIKAWA, K., KOIZUMI, J. & KEOSEIAN, STEVEN: J. Neuropath. & Exper. Neurol. 26, 223-249, 1967.

8. LOEWRY, A. G. & SIEKEVITZ, Ph.: Cell structure and function. Modern Biology Series. Holt, Rinehart and Winston, New York, 1963.

9. The interpretation of ultrastructure. Symposia of the Int'l. Soc. Cell Biology. J. C. Harris (Ed.). Academic Press, New York, x: 438, 1962.

10. SNELL, F., SHULMAN, S., SPENCER, R. P. & MOOS, C.: Biophysical principles of structure and function. Addison-Wesley Publishing Co., Inc., Reading, Mass. 1965.

11. Properties of membranes and diseases of the nervous system. Symposium, Am. Neurol. and Am. Neuropath. Associations, Springer Publishing Co., Inc., New York, 1962.

12. Membrane structure and function. Biochemical Conf. St. Marguerite, Pub. Canada Review by J. H. Quastel. Science. 158 (3797) 147-161, 1967.

13. ROBERTSON, D. J.: The membrane of the living cell. In: The Living Cell. San Francisco, W. H. Freeman and Co., 45-52, 1962.

14. GREEN, D. E. and FLEISCHER, S.: On the molecular organization of biological tranducing systems. In: Horizons of Biochem. Kasha, M. & Pullman, B. (Eds.). New York, Academic Press, 1962.

15. LEHNINGER, A. L.: The mitochondrion; molecular basis of structure and function. New York, W. A. Benjamin (xx-263), 1964.

16. ROIZIN, L., WECHSLER-BERGER, M. & BROCK, D.: Trans. Am. Neurol. Assoc. 89, 247-248, 1964.

17. DE DUVE, C.: Fed. Proceed. 23, 1045-1049, 1964.

18. BITENSKY, L.: The Reversible activation of lysosomes in normal cells and effects of pathological conditions. In: Lysosomes, Ciba Fund, Symp. de Rueck, A. V. S. and Cameron, M. P., ED., Boston, Little Brown and Co., 362, 1963.

19. LEHNINGER, A. L.: Bioenergetics. The molecular basis of biological energy transformations. New York, W. A. Benjamin, 1905.

20. HIS, W.: Abh. Math. Physik., Kl. Akad. Wiss. 15, 311-372, 1889.

21. FOREL, A.: Arch. Psychiat. Nervenheilk. 18, 162-198, 1887.

22. CAJAL, S. R.: Anat. Anz. 5, 579-587, 1890.

23. GERLACH, J.: Von dem Ruckenmarke. In: Handbuch der Lehre von den Geweben. Bd. 2, Ed. Stricker. 1871.

24. GOLGI, C.: Anat. Anz. 5, 372-396, 1890.

25. WALDEYER, H. W. G.: Dtsch. med. Wschr. 17, 1213-12!8, 1891.

26. CAJAL, S. R.: Trab. Inst. Invest. Biol. (Madrid). 24, 1, 1934.

27. HELD, H.: Die Entwicklung des Nervengewebes. S. 378. Leipzig, 1909.

28. AUERBACH, L.: Neurol. Zbl. 17, 445-454, 1898.

29. CAJAL, S. R.: Les nouvelles idees sur la structure du systeme nerveux chez l'homme et chez les vertebres. Paris, Reinwald, 1895.

30. DU BOIS-REYMOND, E.: Gesammelte Abhandl. d. allgem. Muskel- und Nervenphysik 2, 700, 1877.

31. SHERRINGTON, C. S.: Integrative action of the nervous system. Yale Univ. Press. New Haven and London, 411, 1906.

32. DE ROBERTIS, E. D. P.: Histophysiology of synapses and neuro- secretion. Pergamon Press Book. The MacMillan Co., New York 1964.

33. ECCLES, J. C.: The physiology of synapses. Academic Press Inc. Pub., New York, 316, 1964.

34. GRAY, E. G. & GUILLERY, R. W.: Int'l. Rev. Cytol. 19, 111-182, 1966.

35. BODIAN, D.: Bull. Hopkins Hospital. 119, 16-45, 1966.

36. BAK, I. J.: Exper. Brain Res. 3, 40-57, 1967.

37. NATHANIEL, E. J. H. & NATHANIEL, D. R.: J. Ultrastruct. Res. 14, 540-555, 1966.

38. WHITTAKER, V. P., MICHAELSON, I. A. & KIRKLAND, A. J.: Bioch. J., 90, 293-303, 1964.

39. WESTRUM, L. E.: J. Physiol. 179, 4-5, 1965.

40. ROIZIN, L., KAUFMAN, M. A., GAVENESS, W. F. & CARSTEN, A. L.: J. Neuropath, & Exper. Neurol. 27, 150-151, 1968.

41. PALAY, S. L.: Exp. Cell. Res., Suppl. 5, 275-293, 1958.

42. COUTEAUX, R.: Exp. Cell. Res., Suppl. 5, 275-322, 1958.

43. PAPPAS, G. D. & PURPURA, D. : Exper. Neurol. 4, 507-530, 1961.

44. Van der LOOS, H. : Zeitschr. f. Zellforsch. 60, 815, 1963.

45. KOMORI, J. & SZENTAGOTHAI, J. : Exp. Brain Res. 1, 65-8, 1966.

46. WHITTAKER, V. P. & GRAY, E. G. : Brit. med. Bull. 18, 223-228, 1962.

47. HAMLYN, L. H. : J. Anat. (Lond.) 96, 112-120, 1962.

48. ANDERSEN, P., BLACKSTAD, T. W. & LOMO, T. : Exp. Brain Res. 1, 236-248, 1966.

49. DE LORENZO, A. J. : Science. 152, 76-78, 1966.

50. HAMA, K. : Some observations on the fine structure of the synapses. In: Intracellular membranous structure. Seno, S. & Cowdry, F. V., Ed., 539-548, 1965, Cell Biology, Okayama, Japan.

51. KIMURA, R. & WERSALE, H. : Acta Oto-Laryngol. 55, 11-32, 1962.

52. TAXI, J. : Compt. R. 252, 174-176, 331-333, 1961. Proceed. IV. Intr. Congr. Neuropath. II, 197-203. H. Jacob, Ed. Stuttgart, George Thieme, 1962.

53. COLONNIER, M. : J. Anat. 98, 47-53, 1964.

54. COLONNIER, M. & GUILLERY, R. W. : Z. Zellforsch. Mikroskop. Anat. 62, 333-335, 1964.

55. DAVIDOVA, T. V. : Proceed. of the U. S. S. R. Acad. of Sci. 155(4), 970, 1964.

56. WALBERG, F. : J. Comp. Neurol. 125, 205-222, 1965.

57. NISHIKAWA, K. & ROIZIN, L. : 6th Int'l. Cong. Electron Microscopists. Proc. 441-442, Kyoto, Japan, 1966.

58. ROIZIN, L. & SHADE, J. P. : V. Ultrastructural Findings. In: Pathogenesis of x-irradiation effects in the monkey cerebral cortex. Brain Research, 7, 87-109. 1968.

59. GONATAS, N. K., EVANGELISTA, I. & WALSH, G. O. : J. Neuropath. & Exper. Neurol. 26, 179-199, 1967.

60. ROIZIN, L., KAUFMAN, M. A., CAVENESS, W. F. & CARSTEN, L. A. : Proceed. 2nd Pan Amer. Cong. Neurol., San Juan, P. R., 1968.

L. Roizin, M.D., New York State Psychiatric Institute, 722 West 168th Street, New York, N.Y. 10023

SCHIZOPHRENIA: POSSIBLE RELATIONSHIP TO CEREAL GRAINS AND CELIAC DISEASE

F.C. DOHAN

The kinds and quantities of cereal grain products customarily eaten may be a major factor in the production of psychiatric symptoms in those with an inherited susceptibility to schizophrenia. This hypothesis is supported by: (1) clinical observations indicating that schizophrenia and celiac disease (gluten enteropathy) occur in the same person more frequently than expected by chance and have important features in common; (2) epidemiological evidence that the marked changes in first admissions for schizophrenia occurring during World War II were highly correlated with changes in wheat plus rye consumption and were not related to measured psychosocial variables; (3) experimental evidence that relapsed schizophrenics randomized to a milk and cereal-free diet improved almost twice as fast as those on a somewhat high cereal diet and that this effect disappeared when wheat gluten was secretly added to the diet.

PART 1: SCHIZOPHRENIA AND CELIAC DISEASE

Celiac disease occurs infrequently and is recognized more often in children than in adults. It is classically characterized by intestinal malabsorption of fat and other nutrients with resultant secondary effects in severe cases. Autonomic and behavioral disturbances (not dependent on the presence of chronic nutrient deficiencies) are frequent and are often present in the absence of the classical diagnostic features. The importance of the probable association of celiac disease and schizophrenia rests in the fact that wheat gluten and some of its analogues in other cereals have been demonstrated to evoke symptoms of celiac disease in those with an inherited susceptibility to it. Other foods (e.g. cows' milk), infections and psychological factors may also play a role in the production of symptoms.

Susceptibility to Schizophrenia and to Celiac Disease (gluten enteropathy) May Be Determined by Polygenic Inheritance.

The literature bearing on the possible etiology of schizophrenia has recently been summarized in a number of publications. (1-3) It is apparent that the pathogenic environmental factors are not established. An hereditary component is generally accepted but the mode of inheritance is not clear. Gottesman and Shields have recently suggested that polygenic inheritance may best explain the data for schizophrenia (4). The inheritance of celiac disease is also probably polygenic (5). The clinical evidence of association of schizophrenia and celiac disease and certain common features outlined below suggest (among other possibilities) that one or more genes may be common to both diseases and that some of the environmental determinants may be the same. Definitive investigation of these problems may be fruitful.

Evidence of Association of Celiac Disease and Schizophrenia.

Celiac disease and schizophrenia appear to occur in the same individual more frequently than expected from chance alone as judged by published and unpublished data originating in the Philadelphia and New York areas. Benson, Kowlessar and Sleisenger (then at New York Hospital) found 11 severely disturbed patients among their 32 well studied adult celiac patients (6). Of these three were considered to be schizophrenic (personal communication from M. Sleisenger). Among 12 adults diagnosed by symptoms and intestinal histology as having celiac disease (at the Hospital of the University of Pennsylvania) there was one with schizophrenia and another with a schizophrenic daughter (J. Cerda personal communication). G. Barbero, (then at Childrens Hospital, Philadelphia) has stated in a personal communication that one of the "possibly 35" celiac children seen by him had a schizophrenic episode at about age 17. Bossak, Wang and Adlersberg reported from Mount Sinai Hospital, New York, in 1957 that five of 94 patients with "idiopathic sprue" (celiac disease in adults) were also "psychotic" (7). Although some reports on relatively large numbers of celiac patients do not mention schizophrenia in the sample, case reports and several personal communications to me about individual celiac patients with diagnosed or probable schizophrenia support the belief that celiac patients are more prone than the general population to schizophrenia. In addition, I have become aware, by chance, of six families in the Philadelphia and New York areas, including the one noted above, in which one or more immediate members was reported to have or have had celiac disease and another (parent or sibling) has schizophrenia, (personal communications from J. Kremens, Haverford State Hospital; J. Ewing, University of Pennsylvania; J. Cerda, University of Pennsylvania; F. Flach, Cornell University, and 2 personal cases).

There is also some evidence of an increased frequency of celiac disease or a history of it in schizophrenics. This appears to be at least 30 times more frequent than the lifetime incidence of recognized celiac disease in the general population, which is possibly about 1 in 3,000 (8). Lauretta Bender (Creedmore State Hospital, Queens Village, N. Y.) reported in 1953, that the schizophrenic child was subject to celiac disease (9) and wrote me that she believed she had seen about 20 recognized celiac patients among well over 2,000 schizophrenic children. Barbara Fish (New York University) wrote me that she found possibly 3 celiacs in about 300 schizophrenic children. Graff and Handford reported that 4 of the 37 male schizophrenics admitted to The Institute of the Pennsylvania Hospital during one year had a history of celiac disease in childhood (10). Three others with extensive experience with psychotic children (C. Scott, Devereux Schools, Devon, Penna.; S. Nichtern, Hillside Hospital, Glen Oaks, N. Y., B. Rimland, San Diego) have written me that they have the impression that celiac disease is more frequent in schizophrenic than in non-psychotic children.

Some possible relationships between schizophrenia and celiac disease were noted before World War II. Menninger-Lerchenthal reported from Austria in 1938 (when cereal consumption was greater than after the war) on the symptoms of 20 schizophrenic patients who needed to be fed by tube (11). Sixteen were catatonic. One had steatorrhea, 9 had diarrhea and the other 10 were constipated (as may be true in some patients with celiac disease). He stated that these symptoms plus the evidence of vitamin deficiencies, skin pigmentation, edema, subcutaneous bleeding, and other changes were apparently identical with those of "endemic sprue" (celiac disease) described by Hansen and von Staa only two years before. A report from a German mental hospital during this period indicated that of 124 schizophrenic patients whose deaths were not due to tuberculosis, "a few" apparently died of "endemic sprue" (12). This frequency is many times that expected in a general hospital. The diet in this hospital was reported to have been mainly "bread, potatoes and coffee".

Some Similarities of Schizophrenia and Celiac Disease.

Obviously the usual present-day adult schizophrenic patient rarely has classical celiac disease. However, there are certain similarities. The behavioral abnormalities of the celiac child are well known and sufficiently severe to have induced one investigator to speak of a hypothetical "brain toxin" in gluten at a conference on celiac disease (13), and another to use the word "schizoid" (14). In fact, Haffter's description (15) of the schizophrenic child almost duplicates Asperger's description (16) of the celiac child: "encapsulated", "not integrated with his surroundings", "turns entirely inward", "reacts with inappropriate anxiety". Compulsive and ritualistic behavior, stereotyped movements, impaired speech development, peculiar voice, negativism and peculiarities of play and food habits are noted in both diseases (9, 13, 14, 15, 16). Rubin and his co-workers (17) have noted mood changes after administration of gliadin, and many authors have commented on the marked improvement in mood and behavior of celiac patients shortly after starting a gluten-free diet.

Autonomic nervous system abnormalities, vagaries of behavior, appetite, body weight, course of the disease and exacerbations apparently associated with psychic stress are characteristic of both diseases. The pattern of psychic stress affecting both diseases may be similar. Grant (18) reported that episodes of steatorrhea in celiac patients tolerating a gluten-containing diet were preceded by stressful situations which the patient considered as without solu -tion (resulting in a feeling of "giving-up") and that celiac patients on a gluten-free diet were prone to have ordinary diarrhea under these circumstances. Bruch (19), as well as others, has emphasized that the "feeling of being trapped in impossible contradictions" frequently occurs before the development of schizophrenic symptoms.

The increased urinary excretion of indoleactic acid and 5-hydroxy-indoleactic acid reported as occurring during longitudinal studies

of schizophrenics when symptoms were more severe than usual
(20) may be compared with the increased excretion of these substances by celiac patients eating a gluten containing diet (6), a
situation which is also associated with marked psychiatric symptoms as noted above.

Although the usual post mortem histology of the small intestines
of 15 schizophrenics dying in the past two years (B. Czernobilsky,
J. Daniels and F. C. Dohan--unpublished) did not show the "flat"
mucose characteristic of the untreated celiac patient, a few reports over 25 years ago described "atrophic changes" (21, 22, 23).
One, (a monograph on the gastro-intestinal disturbances in demetia
praecox) stated that "gastroenteritis" was the most constant somatic symptom (22). Another report from the same hospital indicated that about 20% of the 212 schizophrenics dying during 1923 to
1927 had "gastroenteritis" compared to about 1% of the 418 non-
schizophrenic patients dying during this period (24). K. Soddy
(University College Hospital, London) wrote me that he had noted
that "recurrent gastrointestinal upsets are a constant feature" of
autistic children and that, among other symptoms, the deteriorat-
ing autistic child often has acute diarrhea. Patients with Stauder's
lethal catatonia, particularly those who die, are likely to show purpura (also seen in severe celiac disease) and diarrhea, (D. Lask-
owska, Lodz, Poland, personal communication). This form of
schizophrenia and the less severe forms of catatonia have become
much less frequent in western countries than before World War
II (25). The possible relationship of this decrease in frequency
and the findings noted above to the changes in diet since that time
merit investigation. A high intake of wheat and rye was more
common before World War II in much of the western world and
I surmise that for economic reasons, it was probably especially
high in the mental hospitals.

COMMENT

There appears to be considerable suggestive evidence that celiac disease and schizophrenia have occurred in the same individual more frequently than expected from chance alone, and that the
two diseases exhibit many similarities. This suggests, among
other possibilities, that one or more genes may be common to these
two, probably polygenic, diseases and that at least some of the en-

vironmental factors apparently necessary for the production of symptoms in these possibly related genotypes may be similar. Cereal ingestion, and the effects of "insoluble" life situations and infections deserve attention. Systematic studies of these suggestive relationships appear to be warranted. Creamer's recent review of some of the problems involved in the study of celiac disease may be helpful (26).

PART 2: SCHIZOPHRENIA AND INGESTION OF CEREAL GRAINS

There are a number of reports of unexplained decreases in admissions to mental hospitals during wartime (27, 28). Since some were obviously associated with severe food shortages it seemed likely that a more systematic investigation might be of heuristic value.

High Correlation of Changes in First Admissions For Schizophrenia and Changes in Wheat Plus Rye Consumption.

Because of the probable relationship of celiac disease (gluten-enteropathy) and schizophrenia, I collected statistical information on wheat and rye "consumption" and hospital admissions of women with schizophrenia before and during World War II in Finland, Norway, Sweden, Canada and the United States (27-29). The experience during the first and last three years of the war were compared to the prewar averages. Admission data for Norway were available only as the 5-year periods: 1936-1940 and 1941-1945. The marked decrease in admissions for schizophrenia in the Scandina-viani countries were considerably greater than for all other psychoses (27). The data for men were similar to those for women. Data for women were analyzed because neither cereal consumption nor admission data for the large number of males in the mili :-tary services were available. Changes in first admissions of women for schizophrenia varied from a decrease of 45% in the second three war years in Finland to plus 15% in the same period in U.S.A. Variations in cereal consumption were comparable.

The relationship between the percentage change (Δ) from prewar in wheat (W) and rye (R) "consumption" and in first admissions of women for schizophrenia (S) is expressed (28) by the multiple regression equation: $S = 5\% + 1.04 (\Delta W) + 0.48 (\Delta R)$. Using these coefficients there is a high correlation ($r = 0.961$, 6 d.f., P 0.01) between the summed percent change in wheat and rye consumption and first admissions for schizophrenia. The correlation between percent change in first admissions for schizophrenia and wheat "consumption" alone is also high (r = 0.908, 7 d.f., P 0. 01). (27, 28).

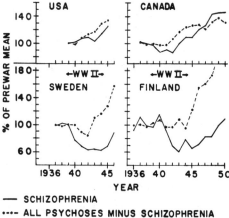

Fig. 1. Per cent changes in admissions to mental hospitals. Values for Finland are for first plus readmissions (see reference 28). All others are for first admissions only. First admissions of women for schizophrenia decreased 40% while all other psychoses increased during World War II in Norway.

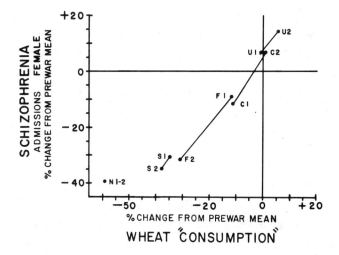

Fig. 2. Relationship of changes in first admissions for schizophrenia and changes in wheat plus rye consumption. Letters indicate the first and second three years of the war period, 1940-1945 inclusive.

The available data (27, 28) (discussed in detail in the references) on such variables as changes in numbers of mental hospital beds or physicians, alcohol consumption, unemployment and duration of symptoms prior to admission and apparent consumption of other foods were not related to changes in first admissions for schizophrenia nor was the war status of the country, (neutral, active war on home soil, occupied, overseas war). In addition, changes in first admissions of patients with other psychoses were not correlated with the changes in cereal consumption or changes in first admissions for schizophrenia.

Cereals and the "Lifetime Expentancy" of Developing Schizophrenia

Estimates from reported survey studies of the "lifetime expectancy" for schizophrenia indicate that the rank order of the likelihood of developing schizophrenia is roughly related to the kinds and quantities of cereal grains eaten (28). It appears that although individuals develop schizophrenia in societies not eating wheat or rye, the "lifetime-expectancy" in rice eating societies is about 56-60% of that in northern Europe, while in populations whose cereals are primarily maize or millet and sorghum, the estimates are only about 25% or less of that of wheat (and rye) consuming populations.

PART 3: EXPERIMENTAL EVIDENCE OF A BENEFICIAL EFFECT OF A MILK AND CEREAL-FREE DIET IN RELAPSED SCHIZOPHRENICS.

Because of the findings noted above and encouraging results in 6 relapsed schizophrenics studied individually during periods on and off a celiac type, milk and gluten-free diet, more systematic studies were performed.

Initial Study - Milk and Cereal-free Diet Versus High Cereal Diet: Relapsed Schizophrenics.

We have recently reported that a milk and cereal-free diet hastened the improvement of otherwise routinely treated relapsed schizophrenic men (30, 31). All men admitted to a locked psychiatric ward (Veterans Admininistration Hospital, Coatesville, Penna.) were assigned by social security number (odd or even) to either a milk and cereal-free diet or a somewhat high cereal diet (more wheat). Milk was omitted because some celiac patients on a gluten-free diet do not improve unless it is also eliminated. The effectiveness of randomization in regard to anti-schizophrenic medi-

-cation was examined. The median and range of the daily dose per man while on locked ward of chlorpromazine and separately of thioridazine did not differ between the two diet groups. The median age of each group was 38 years and the age distributions were similar

Of those schizophrenics during Period I (175 days) who remained on the locked ward more than one day, 55 had been assigned by the randomizing technic to the high cereal diet. Of these only 36% were released from the locked ward (i.e. to "full privileges") in less than the combined groups median of 7 days. In contrast, 62% of the 47 relapsed schizophrenics similarly assigned to the milk and cereal-free diet were released in less than 7 days, (P ≐ 0.0091, Fisher's Exact Probability Test). See Figure 3.

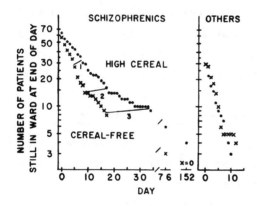

Fig. 3. Effect of randomization to either a milk and cereal-free diet (x) or a somewhat high cereal diet (o) on length of stay in a locked ward. The ends of the numbered lines indicate points at which approximately 50% (1), 75% (2) and 85% (3) of all the relapsed schizophrenics in each diet group had been released from the locked ward to "full privileges".

The proportions released by the end of day 5, 6, 8 and 9 were also significant by Fisher's Exact Probability test. When divided into subgroups by temporal or ordinal midposts or according to each of the 3 "modes" of admission to the locked ward (27 "first admissions", 33 "readmissions", 42 by intrahospital transfer from an open ward or return from "trial visit"), or by each of the 3 treating psychiatrists, 57 to 67% of the patients in the cereal-free subgroups were released by the end of day 7 compared to 32 to 41% of those on the high cereal diet. The mean length of stay on the locked ward was 30.6 days for the high cereal group of schizophrenics and 17.3 days for the milk and cereal-free diet group.

Secret Addition of Gluten to the Milk and Cereal-free Diet.

The absence of gluten (and analogues in other cereals) from the cereal-free diet was thought to be a possibile cause of the more rapid release from the ward. It was also considered possible that the ward staff may have been biased by knowing the diet of patients considered for release (this knowledge was consistently denied), or that psychological factors may have favorably affected the patients' behavior. Therefore, without the knowledge of the ward staff or patients, about 19 gm of wheat gluten/man/day were added to the cereal-free diet during Period II (143 days). During this period 19 of 39 relapsed schizophrenics randomized to the cereal-free plus gluten diet and 22 of 45 relapsed schizophrenics assigned to the high cereal diet were released on or before the median day of the combined groups. It thus seems unlikely that non-specific psychological effects on patients or staff accounted for the more rapid release of the cereal-free group.

Non-effect on Diet in Non-schizophrenic Patients.

Of the 50 non-schizophrenics (mostly depressive reaction, anxiety reaction, or chronic brain syndrome) randomized to the milk and cereal-free diet or high cereal diet during Period I, half of each group were released from the locked ward on or before the "median day" (see figure 3, "others"). There was also no signi-ficant difference (P approx. 0.15) during Period II in which 9 of the 23 non-schizophrenics randomized to the cereal-free plus gluten diet and 15 of the 25 randomized to the high cereal diet were released on or before the "median day".

Comment

These and subsequent (unreported) trials of diet appear to sup-port the hypothesis that cereals play a role in the pathogenesis of overt symptoms in those with an hereditary capacity to develop schizophrenia (28). Studies such as these obviously require independent testing. However, if confirmed, many non-specific (e.g. effect on phenothiazines), and specific effects, particularly those hypothesized for celiac disease, deserve consideration.

CONCLUSIONS

The data appear to support the hypothesis that ingestion of cereal grain products may be one of the factors evoking phenotypic psychiatric symptoms in those with the genotype for schizophre - nia. I believe, therefore, that carefully structured "blind" trials of the milk and cereal-free diet and also of the celiac type, milk and gluten-free diet are warranted. Unbiased psychiatric ratings and similar appearing and tasting control diets containing gluten (or gliadin) should be employed. There are many reports of the production of symptoms in celiac patients by small amounts of cereal under conditions that are not yet clearly defined. In addi -tion, the response of the celiac patient to a gluten-free diet and to the refeeding of gluten, although usually occurring within a few weeks, may not occur for many months. It is evident that com-plete and continuous control of the kinds of food eaten is absolute -ly necessary for valid interpretation of the results.

Acknowledgement: Supported in part by Schizophrenia Research Program, Scottish Rite, and National Association of Mental Health, Inc., J. Grasberger, F. Lowell, H. Johnston, Jr., and A. W. Arbegast were co-investigators in the experiments performed at the Veterans Administration Hospital, Coatesville, Penna.

REFERENCES

1. Recent Developments in Schizophrenia - A Symposium, (Coppen A. and Walk, A. (Editors) Headley Brothers, Ltd., Ashford, Kent, England, 1967.

2. Biological Psychiatry - a review of recent advances. Smythies, J. R. (Editor,) with the collaboration of Coppen, A.,Kreitman, N. Springer-Verlag, New York, 1968.

3. The Orgins of Schizophrenia, Internat. Congress Series No. 151. Romano, J. (Editor), Excerpta Medica Foundation, New York, 1967.

4. Gottesman, I. I. and Shields, J. A. polygenic theory of schizophrenia. Proc. Nat. Acad. Sci. 58, 199, 1967.

5. McConnell, R . B. The Genetics of Gastro-intestinal Disorders, p. 112 Oxford University Press, New York, 1966.

6. Benson, G. D., Kowlessar, O. D. and Sleisinger, M. H. Adult celiac disease with emphasis upon response to the gluten-free diet. Medicine 43, 1, 1964.

7. Bossak, E. T., Wang, C. I. and Adlersberg, D. I. Clinical aspects of the malabsorption syndrome (idiopathic sprue). In The Mal-absorption Syndrome, Adlersberg, D. I. (Editor) Grune and Stratton, Inc., New York, 1957.

8. Black, J. A. Possible factors in the incidence of coeliac disease. Acta paediat. 53, 109, 1964.

9. Bender, L. Childhood schizophrenia. Psychiat. Quart. 27 663, 1953.

10. Graff, H. and Handford, A. Celiac syndrome in the case history of five schizophrenics. Psychiat. Quart. 35, 306, 1961.

11. Menninger-Lerchenthal E. Chronische Darmkrankheit and Avitaminose bei Geisteskranken. Allg. Ztschr. f. Psychiat. 109, 245, 1938.

12. Materna, von A. Die Obduktionsbefunde bei der Schizophrenie. Munch. Med. Wschr. 85, 1875, 1938.

13. Multiple Authors. Beitrage zur Klinik der Coeliakie. Ann. paediat. (Basel) 197, 309, 1961, (p. 413)

14. Kaser, H. Diagnose und Klinik der Coeliakie. Ann paediat., Basel 197, 320, 1961.

15. Haffter, C. Schizophrenie im Kindesalter. Ann. paediat. (Basel) 196, 408, 1961.

16. Asperger, H. Die Psychopathologie des coeliakekraken Kindes Ann. paediat. (Basel) 197, 346, 1961.

17. Dobbins, W. D. and Rubin, C. E. Studies of rectal mucosa in celiac sprue. Gastroenterology 47, 471, 1964.

18. Grant, J. M. Studies on celiac disease--The interrelationship between gliadin, psychological factors and symptom formation. Psychosomatic Med., 21, 431, 1959.

19. Bruch, H. Studies in schizophrenia. Acta psychiat. et neurol. Scand. Suppl. 130, 34, 1, 1959.

20. Berlet, H. H., Bull, C., Himwich, H. E., Kohl, H., Matsumato K., Pscheidt, G. R., Spaide, J., Tourlentes, T. T., and Valverde, J. M. Endogenous metabolic factor in schizophrenic behavior. Science 144, 311, 1964.

21. Meyer, Fr. Anatomisch-histologische Untersuchungen an Schizophrenen. Monatschr. f. Psychiat. u. Neurol. 91, 185, 1935.

22. Reiter, P. J. Zur Pathologie der Dementia Praecox--Gastro-intestinale Storungen. Ihre Klinische und Aetologische Bedeu-tung. George Thiemes Verlag, Leipzig, 1929.

23. Buscaino, V. M. Patologia extraneurale della schizofrenia. Acta Neurologica, Napoli, 8, 1, 1953.

24. Beyerholm, O. Gastro-intestinale Forstyrrelser ved Dementiapraecox. Hospitalstidende 72, 193, 1929.

25. Lehman, H. E. Schizophrenia IV: Clinical Features. In Comprenhensive Textbook of Psychiatry, Freedman, A. M. and Kaplan H., I. (Editors), p. 128, Williams and Wilkins Company, Baltimore, 1967.

26. Creamer, B. Coeliac thoughts. Gut 7, 569, 1966.

27. Dohan, F. C. Wartime changes in hospital admissions for schizophrenia. Acta psychiat. Scand. 42 1, 1966

28. Dohan, F. C. Cereals and schizophrenia - Data and hypothesis, Acta psychiat. Scand 42, 125, 1966.

29. Dohan, F. C. Wheat consumption and hospital admissions for schizophrenia during World War II - A preliminary report. Am. J. clin. Nutrition 18, 7, 1966.

30. Dohan, F. C., Grasberger, J., Lowell, F., Johnston, Jr., H. and Arbegast, A. W. Cereal-free diet in relapsed schizophrenics. Fed. Proc. 27, 219, 1968.

31. Dohan, F. C., Grasberger, J., Lowell, F., Johnston, Jr. H., and Arbegast, A. W. Relapsed schizophrenics: More rapid improvement on a milk and cereal-free diet. Brit. J. Psychiat. To be published.

F. C. Dohan, M.D., Hospital of the University of Pennsylvania, William Pepper Laboratory,

3400 Spruce Street, Philadelphia, 19104

METHYLATION PROCESSES IN SCHIZOPHRENIA

ARNOLD J. FRIEDHOFF

The observation that anti-psychotic agents do not have therapeutic effect unless they also have potential for producing extrapyramidal disturbance is one of the most interesting findings of modern psychiatric research. This unusual correlation holds not only within a given chemical class but also among agents of widely diverse chemical structure. For instance, in a series of phenothiazines, only those which have extrapyramidal disrupting potential act as anti-psychotic drugs. Although clinical manifestations of Parkinsonism do not always develop when these drugs are given in therapeutic doses, this disturbance can invariably be produced if the dose is increased to a high enough level. Alpert in our laboratories, using a sensitive tremor measuring device, has succeeded in demonstrating Parkinsonian like changes in resting finger tremor at doses of tranquilizers which do not produce clinical manifestations of Parkinsonism (Fig.1) (1). It seems likely that these drugs exercise an effect on the extrapyramidal system even at doses which do not produce apparent toxicity. It was, therefore, with great interest that we viewed the work of Hornykiewicz (2), Barbeau (3), Bertler (4) and others who demonstrated that Parkinsonism was associated with low levels of dopamine in the extrapyramidal nuclei, since, from this finding, it could be considered that dopamine might be mediating some action of anti-psychotic drugs.

It has now been demonstrated quite definitively, that dopaminergic neurons have been destroyed or inactivated in patients with Parkinsonian disturbance. Reserpine (5), chlorpromazine (6) and other anti-psychotic agents interfere with biogenic amine uptake, storage or metabolism and this seems to account for the Parkinsonian effects of these drugs. The relationship between dopamine metabolism and Parkinsonism has been further demonstrated by the work initially carried out by Barbeau (3) and in our own laboratories (7) and more recently by Cotzias (8), showing that extra-pyramidial manifestations can be reserved by administering dopa,the precursor of dopamine.

That effective anti-psychotic agents all produce Parkinsonism,

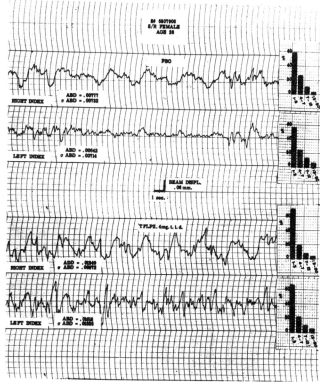

Figure 1. Resting finger tremor of right and left hands during placebo treatment and after treatment with trifluoperazine. Histograms at right show distribution of energy in each of four frequency ranges.

presumably by an effect on dopamine, has focused attention on dopamine as a possible factor in genesis of psychosis. Dopamine, is inactivated by two main metabolic routes. One involves the transfer of a methyl group and the other involves deamination and oxidation (Fig. 2). The methylation process produces a compound, methoxytyramine which has certain structural similarities to mescaline (Fig. 3) The fact that abnormal methylation processes might result in compounds with mescaline-like activity has led to the formulation of the so-called trans-methylation hypothesis of schizophrenia first proposed by Harley-Mason to Osmond and Smythies (9). This hypothesis states that schizophrenia results from an abnormality in the transfer of methyl groups to catecholamines resulting in the production of compounds with mescaline-like activity. This abnormality in transfer could result from an enzyme lesion of genetic origin or might reflect an excess of normal enzymatic activity. In 1961 we undertook to investigate the possibility that abnormal

metabolites of dopa were formed in schizophrenics and in 1962 we first
reported that dimethoxyphenethylamine (DMPEA) a di-O-methylated

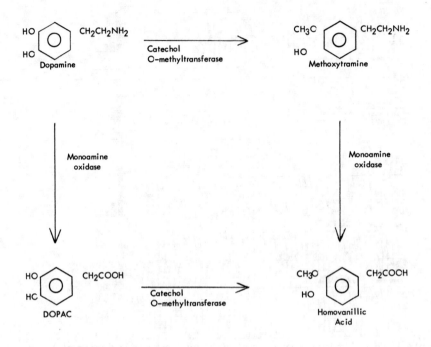

Figure 2. Metabolism of Dopamine

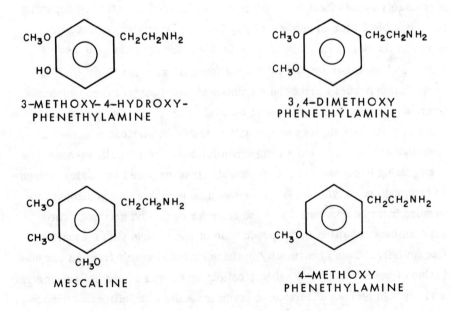

Figure 3. Mescaline and structurally related phenethylamine derivatives.

analogue of dopamine was excreted by schizophrenics, in their urine, but not by normals (10) (11). The idenity of this compound has been carefully verified by many methods including mass spectrometry (12). More recently we have identified a number of metabolites of DMPEA (Fig 4). It will be noted that the major pathways for inactivation of

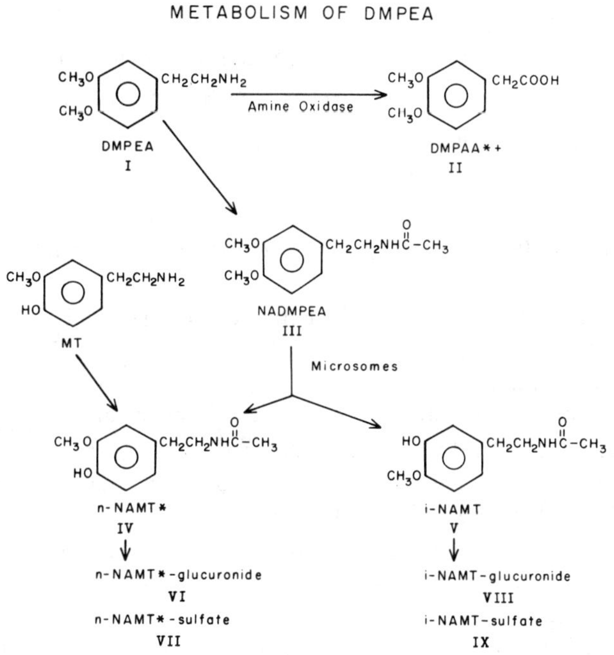

METABOLISM OF DMPEA

Figure 4. Metabolism of DMPEA

DMPEA involve deamination and acetylation. The deamination pathway results in the formation of dimethoxyphenylacetic acid. This acid has been identified in both normals and schizophrenic subjects in contrast to DMPEA itself which has been found only in association with schizophrenia. A disturbance in this pathway could result in backup and excretion of DMPEA in the urine of schizophrenics. However, investigation of this metabolic route by the administration of radioisotope labelled DMPEA to schizophrenics has failed to reveal any abnormalities. The possibility remains, however, that specific DMPEA oxidases are present in the brain of humans. Disturbances in these enzymes could be masked by the action of less specific monoamine oxidase which is present in high concentration in most tissues. In order to study this phenomenon it will be necessary to carry out experiments designed to demonstrate enzyme activity in the human brain.

The second pathway, the acetylation pathway, is interesting because it results in the production of NADMPEA which has mescaline-like activity in animals but is about five times more potent than mescaline itself. This pathway has been investigated in our laboratories to some extent and thus far appears to be normal. A new metabolite of DMPEA, N-acetyl hydroxy DMPEA has only recently been identified by Van Winkle, Schweitzer and myself (13) and its formation in schizophrenics has not yet been investigated.

This research was supported by Public Health Service Grant Nos. MH 08618 and MH 07961, and Research Scientist Award No. K3-MH-14,024 to Arnold J. Friedhoff.

1. Alpert, M.: In Psychopharmacology Service Center Bulletin, 3, 21, 1965.

2. Hornykiewicz, O.: Dopamine (3-hydroxytyramine) and brain function. Pharmacol. Rev. 18, 925, 1966.

3. Barbeau, A., Sourkes, T.L., and Murphy, G.F.: Les catecholamines dans la maladie de Parkinson. Monoamines et Systeme Nerveux Central. Symposium Geneva, 1961, 247, 1962.

4. Bertler, A.: Occurence and localization of catecholamines in the human brain. Acta physiol. scand. 51, 97, 1961.

5. Holzbauer, M., and Vogt, M.: Depression by Reserpine of the Noradrealine Concentration in the Hypothalamus of the Cat. J. of Neurochem. 1, 8, 1956.

6. Axelrod, J.: The Uptake and Release of Catecholamines and the Effect of Drugs. In: Himwich, H.E., and Himwich, W.A. Progress in Brain Research 8, 81, 1964.

7. Friedhoff, A.J., Hekimian, L., Alpert, M., and Tobach, E.: Dihydroxyphenylalanine in extrapyramidal disease. J. Amer. med. Assoc. 184, 285, 1963.

8. Cotzias, G.E., Van Woert, M.H., and Schiffer, L.M.: Aromatic Amino Acids and Modification of Parkinsonism. New Eng. J. Med., 276, 374, 1967.

9. Osmond, H., and Smythies, J.R.: Schizophrenia: a new approach. J. Ment. Sci. 98, 309, 1952.

10. Friedhoff, A.J., Van Winkle E.: Isolation and Characterization of a compound from the Urine of Schizophrenics. Nature 194, 867, 1962.

11. Friedhoff, A.J., and Van Winkle, E.: The Characteristics of an Amine found in the Urine of Schizophrenic Patients. J. Nerv. & Ment. Dis. 135, 550, 1962.

12. Creveling, C.R., and Daly, J.W.: Identification of 3,4-dimethoxyphenethylamine from schizophrenic urine by mass spectrometry. Nature 216, 190, 1067.

13. Van Winkle, E., Schweitzer, J.W., and Friedhoff, A.J.: Unpublished data.

A. Friedhoff, M.D., Department of Psychiatry, New York University Medical Center, 550 First Avenue, New York, N.Y.

SERUM POLYAMINE LEVELS IN SCHIZOPHRENIA AND OTHER OBJECTIVE CRITERIA OF CLINICAL STATUS

CARL C. PFEIFFER, VENELIN ILIEV, LEONIDE GOLDSTEIN, and
ELIZABETH H. JENNEY

Histamine and the polyamines Spermidine and Spermine have attracted less attention than other biogenic amines in the study as to the etiology of the schizophrenias. Until now a specific and sensitive chemical method for the determination of blood histamine was lacking.

The discovery of spermidine (1) (2) (3) as the interfering substance in the determination of blood histamine casts doubt on the reports of elevated serum histamine levels in schizophrenics (4) (5) (6). Furthermore, no longitudinal studies to determine the change in histamine levels with change in mental state have been reported. A better understanding of the role of histamine and histidine in the bio - chemical processes of the human body is necessitated by the hypothesis of Heath, et al., (7) (8) that brain auto-immune mechanisms are involved in schizophrenia. The several reports of lack of somatic allergic disorders (9) and hyporesponses to intradermal histamine (10) in schizophrenics also need biochemical clarification.

The accurate method for the determination of blood histamine plus the quantitative EEG method (11) for precise assay of the degree of brain arousal and the Experiential World Inventory (EWI) (12) to determine the degree of disperception and thought disorder now make possible the correlation of biochemical findings with the neurophysiological status and psychiatric state of the schizophrenic patient. With sufficient samples and patients the correlations can be made by the application of statistical methods to the large number of simultaneously collected numerical observations. In this study the simultaneous measurements were 15 in number as follows: mean energy content (MEC) of the occipital leads of the EEG, coefficient of variation (CV) of the EEG, EWI total score, the 8 subheadings of the EWI, blood histamine, spermidine, spermine and serum uric acid (SUA) levels. A computer program is now being tested to determine the correlation coefficients between 500 observations of these 15 variables. In this preliminary report standard statistical methods were used to reveal the significant relationships between blood histamine and changes in the psychiatric rating scale (EWI). Dr. Goldstein has reported at this conference on the coefficient of variation of the quantitative EEG as correlated with the psychiatric rating scales of this same group of patients.

The patients were out-patients most of whom had been hospitalized one or more times for schizophrenia. A few (six) were so severely ill as to require hospitalization during the 16 month period of the study. When patients without a previous hospitalization were admitted to the study the Minnesota Multiphasic Personality Inventory (MMPI) and EWI were used as aids to establish a diagnosis. The patients (Total of 72) were classified as follows: Male paranoid 16, male non-paranoid 23, female paranoid 11, female non-paranoid 22. Patients were seen at 1 to 4 week intervals for periods of at least 4 months. This study is based on those visits when blood histamine determinations and psychiatric ratings were obtained simultaneously.

The medications used to obtain improvement in these patients were numerous. Therefore, this report cannot be considered an evaluation of any specific or supportive antipsychotic therapy. Formal psychotherapy was deliberately avoided. The main purpose of the study was to ascertain correlations of the EEG and polyamine blood levels with psychiatric improvements. Future reports will deal with the individual effect of the specific medications used. The changes in spermidine, spermine and serum uric acid will also be reported in more detail elsewhere.

RESULTS:

Unpublished data from this laboratory Table 1 gives some background information for this study. From these early studies it is evident that chronic male schizophrenics have a lower mean blood histamine level than the non-hospitalized controls. More convincing, however, is the finding that antipsychotic drug therapy with P 5227 increases the mean blood histamine levels of the chronic male patients to a "normal" level.

TABLE 1

Whole Blood Histamine Levels in Man
Mean ± S.D.

Group	Number	Type	Histamine ng/ml
1 A	20	Schizophrenic males Aug. 1966	27.19 ± 23.54 Range (0.00 - 77.4)
1 B	20	Ditto, Sept. 1966	28.46 ± 12.06 Range (14.5 - 57.4)
2	23	Schizophrenic males After Rx with P-5227	47.94 ± 21.97[**] Range (17.7 - 93.4)
3	13	"Normal" males	44.56 ± 13.79[**] Range (21.1 - 68.5)
4	11	"Normal" females	46.65 ± 23.08[*] Range (12.8 - 93.9)

*Significant difference from 1A & B P < 0.05
**Significant difference from 1A & B P < 0.01

Table 2 summarizes similar data on 72 out-patients. Their mean histamine levels are between those of the hospitalized patients and normal controls. More important perhaps is the finding that in eight samples from 5 patients we found no detectable blood histamine.

TABLE 2
Initial Levels of Blood Histamine Schizophrenic Out-Patients

		Mean SD
Paranoids (27)	16 Male	32 ± 17.2
	11 Female	$44 + 29.0$
Non-Paranoids (45)	23 Male	$42 + 22.9$
	22 Female	41 ± 18.2
All Patients (72)	Both Sexes	39.8 ± 21.9

Table 3 summarizes the correlation coefficients between the pairs of blood histamine levels and the corresponding total EWI numerical reading for various groupings of the 72 patients. The therapeutic successes have a higher negative correlation coefficient than any other group although all groups show a good degree of biological significance.

TABLE 3
Correlation Coefficients Between Blood Histamines and Corresponding Total EWI Levels - Schizophrenic Out-Patients

	N	Pairs of Observations	r	Significance
Paranoids	27	109	-.24	0.05
Non-Paranoids	45	174	-.22	0.05
All Patients	72	283	-.23	0.05
Therapeutic Successes	22	136	-.28	0.01
Therapeutic Failures	50	147	-.20	0.05

Table 4 summarizes those patients who had more than four pairs of EWI and histamine observations with high significance. One should note that the last two patients show a positive correlation rather than the usual negative correlation. This group represents approximately 20% of the schizophrenic patients. Their inclusion in the overall study makes the histapenic syndrome less evident. These patients are extremely depressed and suicidal, have less disperception, do not have hallucinations, and their thought disorder is minimal. They present a greater treatment challenge since they respond mainly to ECT. They may represent a subtype or a developmental type of schizophrenia.

TABLE 4

Individual Significant Changes in Histamine and EWI

Patient	Sex	Class	Pairs	r	p
M. E. V.	F	U	5	-.84	.02
G. B.	M	S	10	-.81	.01
C. B.	M	S	5	-.88	.02
C. Be.	M	S	6	-.71	.05
N. K.	M	S	9	-.66	.05
S. P.	M	S	5	-.75	.05
L. B.	F	S	9	-.62	.05
A. K.	M	S	4	+.66	
P. G.	F	U	11	+.54	.05

DISCUSSION

The negative correlation between the blood histamine levels and the schizophrenic rating scales is significant for both paranoids and non-paranoids. When this measure is applied to the patients who are therapeutic successes then the negative correlation becomes highly significant. Thus, we can state unequivocally that with some schizophrenics the degree of schizophrenia decreases as the blood histamine rises. This observation is in accord with the clinical observation that in some patients allergies appear when the schizophrenic process abates.

Since the blood histamine is stored almost entirely (94%) in the basophilic granulocytes the actual levels of basophils in the schizo-phrenic before and after improvement becomes a pertinent requisite. Studies of the basophil response during treatment of selected schizo-phrenics is needed.

Two of the three previous studies wherein an elevated histamine level was found used blood serum rather than whole blood. The present study may not be in total disagreement since whole blood containing the basophiles was measured. The present findings are in complete accord with those of Le Blanc, et al. (13) who found a deficiency of tissue mast cells in the schizophrenic. This deficiency was corrected when chlor-promazine therapy was successful in decreasing the degree of schizo-phrenia.

That histapenia is only a sub-type of the schizophrenias, is indicated by the finding that 3 of the chronic male schizophrenics and 3 of the out-patient schizophrenics had blood histamines above 80. These patients must be studied individually to ascertain the possible significance of elevated histamine levels.

The observed histapenia does not correlate with any of the treatment medications. It is observed with equal frequency in out-patients who are with or without previous drug therapy. Furthermore, the "therapeutic successes" (with raised blood histamine) were accomplished by a variety of therapeutic measures such as electroconvulsive, niacinamide, lithium and anti-psychotic drug therapy.

The histapenia of late pregnancy is known to be caused by the diamine oxidase elaborated by the fetus. Since late pregnancy is only rarely accompanied by psychosis the biochemical mechanisms of pregnancy must in some mysterious fashion protect the brain. The post-partum psychosis, which occurs frequently, will be interesting to study as a possible histapenic state.

Any generalization at this time on the role of histamine in schizophrenia is obviously premature. One is tempted to suggest, however, that histamine may be important in neurohumoral transmission and that stores of histidine (as in the dipeptides, homocarnosine and homoanserine) may be depleted during stress in one of the subtypes of schizophrenics. Conversely, a smaller percentage and different subtype (perhaps one fifth of the patients) may have an elevated blood histamine with schizophrenic symptoms. Finally, the schizophrenias would appear to have several biochemical changes which may correlate with psychiatric improvement.

Histidine is not considered to be an essential amino acid for the adult human, although animals and the infant seem to require a regular dietary supply. Presumably adult man can synthesize histidine as needed. If this is true, then the lowered histamine levels in the schizophrenic may be owing to: 1) Increased utilization (as by stress); 2) Faulty decarboxylation of histidine; 3) Inadequate storage; 4) Inadequate synthesis; 5) Increased histaminase activiey; 6) Increased methylation of histamine or histidine; or 7) Deficiencies of folic acid or vitamin B-12. These and other possibilities need study and clarification. In regard to methylated histamine, we have found N,N dimethyl histamine to be more stimulant in the rabbit brain (14) than histamine. We have also found the Shiff's base addition product of acetaldehyde with histidine to be stimulant (15). Thus, both histidine and histamine may be unavailable because of abnormal alkylation of methylation processes.

SUMMARY:

A longitudinal study on out-patient schizophrenic patients which assayed the blood levels of polyamines and the degree of schizophrenia discloses a relative and sometimes absolute histapenia and shows a significant negative correlation between the degree of schizophrenia and the blood histamine levels. This may account, in part, for the absence of allergic disorders in some schizophrenics. The degree of involvement of histamine and histidine and their congeners in the actual schizophrenic process remains to be determined. This correlation of behavioral rating and blood levels of polyamines provides a new and potent tool for the study of the schizophrenias. Histamine or its precursor histidine may be utilized in an abnormal pathway such as methylation or alkylation.

REFERENCES

1. Kremzner, L.T., and Pfeiffer, C.C. Identification of Substances Interfering with the Fluorometric Determination of Brain Histamine. Biochem. Pharmacol. 14, 1189, 1965.

2. Michaelson, I A. Spermidine: A Contaminant in the n-Butanol Extracts of Brain in the Fluorometric Assay of Histamine. Eur. J. Pharmacol. 1, 378, 1967.

3. Medina, M. and Shore, P.A. Increased Sensitivity in a Specific Fluorometric Method for Brain Histamine. Biochem. Pharmacol. 15, 1627, 1966.

4. Lovett Doust, J.W., Husdan, H. and Salna, M.E. Blood-Histamine and Tissue-cell Anoxia in Mental Disease. Nature 178, 492, 1956.

5. Stern, P., Hukovic, S., Madjerek, Z. and Karabaig, S. The Histamine Level of the Blood of Schizophrenic Subjects. Arch. Int. Pharmacodyn. 109, 294, 1957.

6. Cassell, W.A., Newton, G. and Cho, M. Serum histamine concentrations in schizophrenic and non-schizophrenic patients. J. of Schizophrenia 1, 65, 1967.

7. Heath, R.G. Schizophrenia: Biochemical and Physiological Aberrations. Int. J. Neuropsychiat. 2, 597, 1966.

8. Heath, R.G. and Krupp, I.M. Schizophrenia as an Immunologic Disorder. Arch. Gen. Psychiat. 16, 1, 1967.

9. Ehrenthiel, O.F. Common Medical Disorders Rarely Found in Psychotic Patients. Arch. Neurol. Psychiat. 77, 178, 1957.

10. Lucy, J.D. Histamine Tolerance in Schizophrenia. Arch. Neurol. & Psychiat. 71, 629, 1954.

11. Goldstein, L. and Pfeiffer, C.C. Quantitative EEG in the Appraisal of Basal State and Drug Response in Schizophrenics. Report this Conference.

12. El-Meligi, A.M. The Scientific Exploration of the Worlds of the Mentally Ill. J. Med. Soc. N.J. (In Press).

13. Le Blanc, J. and Lemieux, L. Histamine and Mental Disease. Medical Experiments 4, 214, 1961.

14. Goldstein, L. Histamine and the Nervous System. Fed. Proc. 23, 1113, 1964.

15. Beck, R.A., Pfeiffer, C.C., Iliev, V., and Goldstein, L. Cortical EEG Stimulant Effects in the Rabbit of Acetaldehyde-Biogenic Amine Reaction Products. Proc. Soc. Exp. Biol. & Med. 128, 823, 1968.

ACKNOWLEDGMENTS

These studies were supported by the State of New Jersey, by USPHS grants MH-04229 and FR-05558 and by the Hoyt Foundation.

We are indebted to the following physicians for the referral of patients for this study: Robert E. Bennett, M.D., Alan Cott, M.D., Louis Fraulo, M.D., Granville L. Jones, M.D., Humphry F. Osmond, M.B., A. Arthur Sugerman, M.D., Jack L. Ward, M.D.

C. C. Pfeiffer, M.D., V. Iliev, M.D., L. Goldstein, D.Sc., and E. H. Jenney, M.D., Bureau of Research in Neurology and Psychiatry, c/o New Jersey Neuro-Psychiatric Institute, Box 1000, Princeton, N.J. 08540

METABOLIC ACTIONS OF THE ALPHA-2-GLOBULIN IN THE SERUM OF PATIENTS WITH SCHIZOPHRENIA

CHARLES E. FROHMAN and JACQUES S. GOTTLIEB

In the past the Lafayette Clinic laboratories have presented evidence for the presence of a higher concentration of an α-2-globulin in plasma from schizophrenic patients than in plasma from control subjects.[1] Several other groups have separated similar fractions from plasma from schizophrenic patients: Bergen and Pennell at the Worcester Foundation for Experimental Biology and the Protein Foundation;[2] Heath at Tulane University;[3] Ehrensvard at Lund University in Sweden;[4] Walaas at the University of Oslo, Norway;[5] and Krasnova of the Institute of Psychiatry of the National Academy of Science, U.S.S.R.[6] Table 1 compares the properties of the active fractions separated from plasma from schizophrenic patients by these various investigators. It can be seen that while

Table 1. Characteristics of Plasma Fractions in Schizophrenia

	INDICATOR	TYPE	LIPID	MOLECULAR WEIGHT	LABILITY
Bergen and Pennell (Boston)	Rat climbing	α-2	+	High	++++
Ehrensvard (Stockholm)	O_2 of an amine	α or β	?	High	++++
Frohman (Detroit)	L/P ratio	α-2	+	400,000 ±50,000	++++
Heath (New Orleans)	Monkey behavior	γ	?	?	-
Vartanyan (Moscow)	L/P ratio	α or β	+	?	++++
Walaas (Oslo)	CHO uptake	α or β	+	High	++++

different methods were used to assay activity of the fractions, in every instance the fraction was a protein in the α or β globulin range, with the exception of the fraction currently reported by Heath. Previously he had reported that an active fraction in plasma of patients with schizophrenia was either an α or β globulin.[7] The present fraction Heath is working with is a γ globulin. Four of the fractions reported in the table have been tested for lipid and it is present in all four. The other investigators have not reported data concerning lipid in their fractions. All investigators except Heath agree that the fraction is quite labile. Furthermore, all those who have measured the molecular weight find it to be quite high. Two investigators state that they have evidence of an active small molecule attached to the protein. Neither Krasnova nor Walaas as far as is known have tested for a small molecule while our laboratory has been unable to confirm its presence. From the similarities that exist among the various fractions it would appear that, with the exception of the most recent one identified by Heath, all of the various investigators probably are working with the same protein.

PREPARATION OF THE α-2-GLOBULIN IN OUR LABORATORY

A group of typical chronic male schizophrenic patients free of any discernible physical illness has been under study for 6 years at the Lafayette Clinic. Diet and physical activity have been carefully controlled for this entire period. The patients' average age is 37. They have been hospitalized for an average of 11 years and have been maintained on a drug-free regime for 6 years.[8]

The factor is prepared from plasma obtained from the subjects by plasmapheresis. The protein is isolated in several steps. Plasma from the patients or control subjects is dialyzed against distilled water to precipitate the euglobulin fraction. The euglobulin fraction is taken up in a 0.005 M phosphate buffer, pH 7.4. After 3 hours of stirring, the supernatant is placed on a column of DEAE cellulose (2 cm diameter, 80 cm long) in the phosphate form. The protein is eluted by a gradient buffer system made by siphoning 0.04 M phosphate buffer containing 0.15 M NaCl, pH 4.5, into 0.005 M phosphate buffer, pH 7.4. The fraction having activity is then placed on a Spinco C.P. curtain electrophoresis apparatus and separated in 0.04 M Tris buffer, pH 8.4, using 700 V, 35 milliamperes current. Further purification is accomplished by ultracentrifugation at 20,000 rpm for 36 hours, using a sucrose gradient ranging from 20 per cent to 5 per cent. To prevent destruction of the active substance during the separation all solutions are made 0.6 M with sucrose.

Throughout the separation the activity of the fraction is followed by its effect on cellular oxidation as measured by the ratio of lactic acid to pyruvic acid (L/P ratio) in chicken erythrocytes after 1 hour incubation with the fraction.[9] After the final purification, 10 μg of the resulting α-2-globulin has an activity equivalent to 100 ml of plasma. The purified α-2-globulin has a high molecular weight (approximately 400,000) and contains a high percentage of lipid (up to 80 per cent). This protein is probably present both in control subjects and in schizophrenic patients.[10] Approximately 60 per cent of these patients have a consistently higher level of the active α-2-globulin than the control subjects.[11]

Ryan and co-workers have reported that the change in L/P ratio when chicken erythrocytes are incubated with serum from schizophrenic patients is a result of an immune lysin.[12] It is true that such a lysin is present but it is a β-2-globulin (Table 2). Although the

Table 2. Means of 10 Determinations Using Fractions Separated by Curtain Electrophoresis

	PROTEIN TYPE	L/P RATIO WITHOUT COMPLEMENT	L/P RATIO WITH COMPLEMENT	HEMOLYSIS WITHOUT COMPLEMENT	HEMOLYSIS WITH COMPLEMENT
Schizo-phrenic	α-2-globulin	14.95	15.20	0.5%	1.3%
Control	α-2-globulin	6.47	6.56	0.2%	1.0%
Schizo-phrenic	β-2-globulin	7.21	7.32	2.0%	44.8%
Control	β-2-globulin	7.40	7.31	0.5%	12.2%

567

β-2-globulin responsible for hemolysis occurs with a high frequency
in patients characterized by a high L/P ratio, it can be electropho-
retically separated from the α-2-globulin. It is also very unlikely
that hemolysis resulting from the lysin raises the L/P ratio. In
fact, it has been shown that hemolysis lowers L/P ratios (Table 3).

Table 3. Effect of Rupture of Chicken Cell Membrane on Mean L/P
Ratios Following Incubation with Plasma from 28 Schizophrenic and
23 Control Subjects

	N	WHOLE CELLS L/P	HEMOLYZED CELLS L/P
Schizophrenic	28	26.58	7.43
S.D.		± 8.01	± 5.06
Control	23	14.26	8.06
S.D.		± 5.25	± 5.49

When the membranes of chicken erythrocytes were destroyed in the
hemolysis experiments, the α-2-globulin lost its ability to affect
oxidation by the cellular enzyme systems[13] (Table 3). This leads to
the hypothesis that the α-2-globulin may assert its effect on metabolism by selectively changing the permeability of the cell membrane.
It had previously been shown that this protein fraction does not
affect the permeability of the membrane to lactate and pyruvate.[14]
Measuring the distribution of sodium, potassium and chloride between
plasma and cells of schizophrenic patients demonstrated that membrane
permeability to these ions was not affected either.[11]

At about the same time, a study was being performed involving
the citric acid cycle in chicken erythrocytes. We incubated labeled
acetate with chicken erythrocytes in the presence of plasma from
schizophrenic patients and from control subjects and measured the
conversion of the acetate to citric acid cycle intermediates by the
cell.[11] The amount of radioactivity and the specific activity were
measured for citrate, α-ketoglutarate, succinate, fumarate, malate,
pyruvate and lactate. Table 4 shows several differences between the
effects of plasma from high-factor schizophrenic patients and plasma

from control subjects. The specific activity was significantly lower

Table 4. Mean* Specific Activities x 10^{-3} of Organic Acids Formed from Chicken Erythrocytes Incubated in a Medium Containing Either Plasma from Schizophrenic Patients or Control Subjects and Acetate-2C-14

ACIDS	CONTROL SUBJECTS		SCHIZOPHRENIC PATIENTS		SIGNIFICANT DIFFERENCES
	Mean	S.D.	Mean	S.D.	
Citrate	1780	1291	2907	1810	N.S.
Alpha-keto-glutarate	466	355	288	159	< .02
Succinate	2437	1505	2019	876	N.S.
Fumarate	1026	956	699	360	N.S.
Malate	2737	2339	1468	752	N.S.
Lactate	1404	62	780	17	< .001
Pyruvate	69	65	209	183	N.S.

* 11 subjects in each group

for lactate, and approached significance for α-ketoglutarate and malate. There were no effects on specific activity of any of the other acids in the cycle. Could plasma of schizophrenic patients block the utilization of α-ketoglutarate, lactate and malate? Examining the data further, one finds that this cannot be so (Table 5).

Table 5. The Mean* Levels of Lactic Acid and the Mean Total Counts per Minute of Acetate-2C-14 Incorporated Into Lactic Acid by Chicken Erythrocytes When Incubated in Plasma from Either Schizophrenic or Control Subjects

LACTIC ACID	CONTROL SUBJECTS		SCHIZOPHRENIC PATIENTS	
	Mean	S.D.	Mean	S.D.
Levels	1.12 mg%	0.72	208 mg%	1.23
Cpm	155,000	19,056	152,000	15,276
Sp. Act. x 10^{-3}	1,404	62	780	17

* 11 subjects in each group

Looking at total radioactive counts per min in lactic acid derived from acetate, one finds that in the case of control subjects there were 155,000 counts and for the schizophrenic patients there were 152,000 counts. This is not significantly different. However, the concentration of lactic acid differs, as has been noted in previous studies, being 1.12 mg/100 ml in the controls and 2.08 mg/100 ml in the schizophrenic patients. Consequently, specific activity of lactate differs in the two groups, being 0.78×10^6 for the patients and 1.404×10^6 for the control subjects. From this it seems that the difference in specific activity was due, not to a block in the conversion of acetate into lactate, but to isotope dilution. Some substance other than radioactive acetate was forming additional lactate at a much more rapid rate in the presence of plasma from the schizophrenic patients than in the presence of plasma from the control subjects and was diluting the labeled lactate.

Investigations were undertaken to determine if the dilution of radioactive lactate resulted from nonradioactive lactate being formed from amino acids. Labeled alanine was substituted for the labeled acetate in the previous experiments. The incorporation of labeled alanine into lactic acid in the presence of plasma from schizophrenic patients is shown in Table 6. Indeed alanine is incorporated more

Table 6. Incorporation of Alanine-C-14-ul into Lactic Acid by Chicken Erythrocytes when Incubated in Plasma from Schizophrenic Patients or Control Subjects: The Mean* Levels, Counts Per minute $\times 10^{-3}$, and Specific Activities $\times 10^{-6}$ of Lactic Acid

	CONTROL SUBJECTS		SCHIZOPHRENIC PATIENTS	
	Mean	S.D.	Mean	S.D.
Lactic Acid ** Level (mg%)	1.594	± 1.043	3.523	± 3.656
Cpm $\times 10^{-3}$	471	± 358	963	± 817
Sp. Act. $\times 10^{-6}$ (in millimoles)	27.3	± 8.8	28.0	± 15.5

* 11 subjects in schizophrenic group
  10 subjects in control group
**$P < 0.05$

rapidly in the presence of plasma from schizophrenic patients. This allowed us to speculate that plasma from schizophrenic patients causes amino acids to cross the cell membrane more rapidly.

The next series of studies determined the effect of the α-2-globulin on cellular permeability to amino acids. These studies compare the effect on amino acid uptake using plasma from three groups of subjects: 12 schizophrenic patients with elevated α-2-globulin, 12 schizophrenic patients with normal α-2-globulin, and 12 control subjects. Eight ml of saline-washed chicken erythrocytes and 12 ml of modified Krebs-Ringer solution[15] were incubated with 4 ml of plasma and 2 ml of a solution containing 4 μc of labeled amino acid. Enough carrier amino acid was also added to bring the level of the amino acid to (1) one-fifth that normally found in human plasma, (2) equal to that normally found in human plasma, or (3) five times that normally found in human plasma. The mixture was incubated at 37°C and aliquots were taken every 15 min for 2 hours. The cells were removed, washed, and a Folin-Wu filtrate prepared from them. An aliquot of this filtrate was counted in a Beckman C.P. 100 scintillation counter. The counts accumulated in the cell taken up by the time the mixture reached equilibrium are shown in Table 7. Note that apparently more of all 15 amino acids studied are accumulated by cells in the presence of schizophrenic plasma. However, the number of counts in the cells differed most significantly ($P < 0.001$) only when glutamic acid, tryptophan and 5-hydroxytryptophan were used. Aliquots of the filtrate from the cells were placed on the amino acid analyzer and the levels of tryptophan, 5-hydroxytryptophan and glutamic acid were measured. Samples were collected from the amino acid analyzer for counting so that the specific activity of the amino acid could be determined. Results are shown in Table 8. In the case of tryptophan and 5-hydroxytryptophan indeed these acids were entering the cell more rapidly in the presence of plasma from schizophrenic patients characterized by high levels of the α-2-globulin. However, no more glutamic acid entered the cell with plasma from these schizophrenic patients and therefore plasma from these schizophrenic patients apparently had no effect on the

Table 7. Radioactive Counts Accumulated at Equilibrium in
Chicken Erythrocytes Incubated with Labeled Amino Acids

	CONTROL		SCHIZOPHRENIC		
	Counts/ min x 10^{-3}	S.D.	Counts/ min x 10^{-3}	S.D.	Per cent of Normal with Schizophrenic Plasma
Glutamic acid	5	± 1	12	± 3	240.0**
5-Hydroxytryptophan	69	±17	119	±30	171.6**
Tryptophan	93	±20	142	±35	151.7**
Eroline	83	±31	126	±38	151.4*
Lysine	14	± 7	20	± 6	142.8
Alanine	116	±11	165	±15	142.0
Tyrosine	87	±17	116	±33	135.7*
Aspartic acid	6	± 2	8	± 3	135.0*
Methionine	25	± 4	20	± 5	127.9
Arginine	9	± 3	7	± 2	128.6*
Histidine	53	±19	64	±13	121.1*
α-Aminoisobutyric	20	± 4	24	± 5	120.6
Cystine	85	±20	103	±24	118.3
Phenylalanine	292	±33	317	±32	108.6
Serine	184	±42	197	±43	107.5

* $P < 0.05$
** $P < 0.001$

Table 8. Amino Acid in Cells after One Hour Incubation

	CONTROL		
	Nanomoles amino acid	Counts	Counts/min/ nanomoles
Tryptophan	42.9	93,000	2,160
5-Hydroxytryptophan	14.3	69,000	4,825
Glutamic acid	1.3	5,000	3,846
	SCHIZOPHRENIC		
	Nanomoles amino acid	Counts	Counts/min/ nanomoles
Tryptophan	53.5*	142,000*	2,654
5-Hydroxytryptophan	21.6*	119,000*	5,509
Glutamic acid	1.4	12,000*	8,571*

* Differed from control at 0.1% level of confidence

uptake of this substance. Since the intracellular/extracellular ratio of glutamic acid is so small, it was suspected that permeability to some trace impurity could be profoundly affected by plasma from these schizophrenic patients and could account for the apparent increase in glutamic acid uptake. Further investigation demonstrated that there was such an impurity and that it was 2-pyrrolidone 5-carboxylic acid (glutiminic acid),a cyclization product of glutamic acid.

Six other amino acids differed significantly at the 5 per cent level of confidence: proline, alanine, tyrosine, aspartic acid, arginine and histidine. None of the other amino acids differed significantly.

In the range studied, the addition of carrier had no effect on uptake of the labeled amino acid.

The importance of the carboxyl group of the amino acids was investigated by studying the effect of high α-2-globulin plasma from schizophrenic patients on the uptake of some biogenic amines. The results are shown in Table 9. Although tryptophan and 5-hydroxy-tryptophan entered cells more rapidly in the presence of plasma from

Table 9. Effect of Schizophrenic Plasma on Uptake of Some Amines

	CONTROL		SCHIZOPHRENIC		
	Counts/min x 10^{-3}	S.D.	Counts/min x 10^{-3}	S.D.	Per cent of Normal with Schizophrenic Plasma
Serotonin	16.8	±9.2	14.5	±9.4	88.3
Tryptamine	19.2	±5.1	18.8	±4.6	98.4
Dopamine	68.5	±11.3	61.6	±12.1	91.4

these schizophrenic patients, the decarboxylated analogues tryptamine and serotonin were not similarly affected. It would appear that the presence of the carboxyl group was essential for the increase in uptake of the amino acids. Likewise tyrosine entered cells more rapidly but dopamine did not.

Next the importance of the amino group on this difference in uptake was also studied. The results of studies of biologically important organic acids are shown in Table 10. Both citrate and

---

Table 10. Effect of Schizophrenic Plasma
on Uptake of Some Organic Acids

ACID	CONTROL		SCHIZOPHRENIC		
	Counts/ min x 10^{-3}	S.D.	Counts/ min x 10^{-3}	S.D.	Per cent of Normal with Schizophrenic Plasma
Acetic	90.0	±8.7	92.0	±9.0	102.7
Succinic	1.3	±0.3	2.0	±0.5	133.0*
Citric	0.9	±0.2	1.5	±0.4	189.2*

* Differs significantly from the control at the
1% level of confidence

---

succinate were taken up significantly faster, while acetate was unaffected. It would appear therefore that the amino group is not essential for the effect of the α-2-globulin.

Further characteristics of the amino acid uptake system affected by plasma from these schizophrenic patients were studied.

Effect of Temperature on Tryptophan Uptake

The above experiment using labeled tryptophan was repeated but with incubations at $1^{o}C$, $6^{o}C$, $13^{o}C$, $25^{o}C$, and $37^{o}C$. The results are shown in Figure 1. The slope of the curve for the effect of temperature on tryptophan uptake is quite different at lower temperatures than at higher temperatures. In addition, the uptake by cells did not differentiate between plasma from high-factor schizophrenic patients and plasma from control subjects at the lower temperatures but differentiated increasingly as the temperature approached $37^{o}C$.

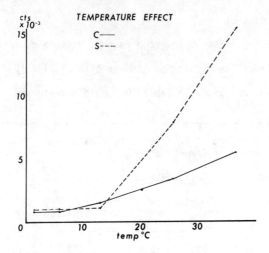

Effect of Ouabain on the Plasma Factor

Sufficient ouabain to make the concentration 10^{-3} M was added to the incubation mixture containing labeled tryptophan. Failure of ouabain to affect the uptake of tryptophan in the presence of the factor is shown in Figure 2.

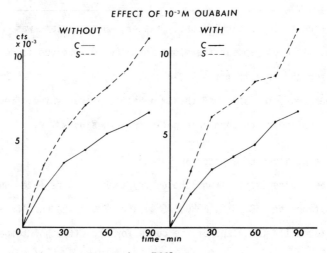

Effect of the Factor on Tryptophan Efflux

Forty-eight ml of washed chicken erythrocytes were added to a mixture of 72 ml of modified Krebs-Ringer solution, 24 ml of plasma from a control subject, and 12 ml of a solution containing 30 μc of labeled tryptophan per ml. The mixture was incubated at $37^{\circ}C$ for 100 min. At the end of the incubation, the tryptophan-loaded cells were removed by centrifugation at $4^{\circ}C$. They were then washed three times with cold saline. Twenty ml of cells loaded in this manner

were added to a mixture of 30 ml of modified Krebs-Ringer solution
and 10 ml of plasma from high-factor schizophrenic patients, or
plasma from control subjects, or an equivalent solution of purified
α-2-globulin. This mixture was incubated at 37°C. Aliquots were
taken at 0, 15, 30, 45, 60, 90, 120, 150, and 180 min. The cells
and medium were separated and amino acid measured as in previous
experiments. The results are shown in Figure 3. Plasma from these

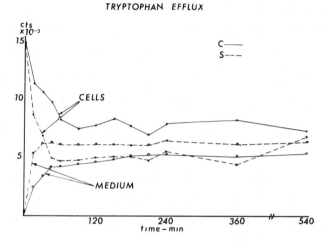

TRYPTOPHAN EFFLUX

schizophrenic patients caused more tryptophan to leave the cells than
plasma from the controls; however, the plasma did not have as great
an effect on tryptophan efflux as on influx.

Discussion

It is evident that the α-2-globulin or plasma rich in α-2-globulin
increases the rate of accumulation of tryptophan and 5-hydroxytryptophan
in cells. The question is: what is the mechanism of transport of the
two amino acids so affected by this substance? Since amino acids
probably can enter and leave the cell by means of simple diffusion,
it might be hypothesized that a change in the nature of the cell
membrane may permit material to diffuse in and out more rapidly.
Under these circumstances one would expect a significant change in
the rate of diffusion in all amino acids rather than to have only
a few of them affected (e.g., one would not expect the rate of
accumulation of tryptophan and 5-hydroxytryptophan to increase
while the rate of accumulation of phenylalanine remains relatively

unaffected). One would also expect that in diffusion the temperature coefficient would be considerably less than that in active
transport. Note in Figure 1 that the curve of the rate of accumulation of tryptophan in the cell has two different slopes. The
slope at the lower temperatures probably represents diffusion while
that at the higher temperatures probably represents active transport.
The difference between the effect of plasma from control subjects
and that of plasma from high-factor schizophrenic subjects is
apparent only at the higher temperatures. Therefore, it is very
unlikely that diffusion is the process affected by the plasma factor.

Since both the influx and the efflux of these amino acids are
affected by this substance, one might suspect that exchange is the
process that is affected. This process as described by Christensen
involves moving amino acids in and out of the cells at equal rates.[16]
Final levels of the acids in the cells are not affected. Since the
process is closely tied to the transport of sodium, it therefore
should have been inhibited by ouabain, a sodium transport inhibitor.
Failure of ouabain to inhibit the activity of the plasma factor
demonstrated that this activity is not dependent on sodium transport.
Also, there is a significant difference in the increase in equilibrium in levels of tryptophan in cells incubated in plasma from these
schizophrenic patients as compared with cells incubated in plasma
from control subjects. It was also found that influx of tryptophan
was affected more profoundly by the α-2-globulin than was efflux.
Because of these three observations (the failure of ouabain to
inhibit, the increased accumulation of tryptophan, and the differential effect on influx and efflux), it can be definitely stated
that exchange as defined by Christiansen is not affected by the
plasma factor. It appears at the present time that an active
transport system is involved. Structural requirements for the
substrate of this system are that a carboxyl group be present but
not necessarily an amino group. It also appears that, in general,
long chain acids are more profoundly affected than short chain

acids, that an aromatic ring further increases the effect and that the effect reaches a maximum when the aromatic ring contains a negative group. Further details of this transport system are still unknown.

Regardless of the mechanism, it remains a fact that two very important precursors of neurohumoral substances enter the cells more rapidly in the presence of plasma from high-factor schizophrenic patients than in the presence of plasma from control subjects. Tryptophan and 5-hydroxytryptophan are precursors of serotonin, an important neurohumoral transmitter. Recently serotonin has been shown to be involved in the production of sleep.[17] Administration of p-chlorophenylalanine (an inhibitor of serotonin production) in sufficient amounts prevents sleep in animals. Caldwell and Domino have reported that in patients with a high level of the α-2-globulin, stage 4 sleep either is decreased or is completely absent.[18] The level of α-2-globulin correlates with the amount of stage 4 sleep with a coefficient of -0.550 ($P < 0.05$). The uptake of tryptophan and the abnormal sleep patterns may be closely related to one another and could be related to a neural mechanism involved in the etiology of schizophrenia. The in vitro studies upon which this hypothesis is based are currently being tested in neural tissue in vivo.

REFERENCES

1. FROHMAN, C.E., LUBY, E.D., TOURNEY, G., BECKETT, P.G.S. and GOTTLIEB, J.S. Steps Toward the Isolation of a Serum Factor In Schizophrenia. Amer. J. Psychiat., 117, 401, 1960.

2. PENNELL, R.B. and SARAVIS, C.A. A Human Factor Inducing Behavioral and Electrophysiological Changes in Animals. I. Isolation and Chemical Nature of the Agent. Ann. N.Y. Acad. Sci., 96, 462, 1962.

3. HEATH, R.G., MARTENS, S., LEACH, B.E., COHEN, M. and FEIGLY, C.A. Behavioral Changes in Nonpsychotic Volunteers Following the Administration of Taraxein, the Substance Obtained from Serum of Schizophrenic Patients. Amer. J. Psychiat., 114, 917, 1958.

4. EHRENSVARD, G., LILJEKVIST, J. and HEATH, R.G. Oxidation of 3-Hydroxyanthranilic Acid by Human Serum. Acta Chem. Scand., 14, 2081, 1960.

578

5. HAAVALDSEN, R., LINJAERDE, O. and WALAAS, O. Disturbances of Carbohydrate Metabolism in Schizophrenics. The Effect of Serum Fractions from Schizophrenics on Glucose Uptake of Rat Diaphragm in Vitro. Conf. Neur., 18, 270, 1958.

6. KRASNOVA, A.I. Influence of Blood Serum from Schizophrenic Patients on the Carbohydrate Metabolism of Chicken Erythrocytes. Zh. Neuropat. Psikhiat. Korsakov (Moskva), 65, 1206, 1965.

7. LEACH, B.E., BYERS, L.W. and HEATH, R.G. Methods for Isolating Taraxein. A Survey of Results. In Serological Fractions in Schizophrenia, R. Heath (Editor), Hoeber Med. Div., Harper & Row, New York, 1963.

8. CRANDALL, R.G., DAY, H., BECKETT, P.G.S., CHEN, C., BROSIUS, C., FROHMAN, C.E. and GOTTLIEB, J.S. Conflict Between Treatment and Science on a Research Ward Investigating Schizophrenia. Can. Psychiat. Assn. Jour., 11, 306, 1966.

9. FROHMAN, C.E., CZAJKOWSKI, N.P., LUBY, E.D., GOTTLIEB, J.S. and SENF, R. Further Evidence of a Plasma Factor in Schizophrenia. A.M.A. Arch. Gen. Psychiat., 2, 263, 1960.

10. FROHMAN, C.E., LATHAM, L.K., WARNER, K.A., BROSIUS, C.O., BECKETT, P.G.S. and GOTTLIEB, J.S. Motor Activity in Schizophrenia: Effect on Plasma Factor. Arch. Gen. Psychiat., 9, 83, 1963.

11. FROHMAN, C.E. Biochemical Studies of a Serum Factor in Schizophrenia. In The Molecular Basis of Some Aspects of Mental Activity, Vol. 2, O. Walaas (Editor), Academic Press, New York, 1967.

12. RYAN, J.W., BROWN, J.D. and DURELL, J. Antibodies Affecting Metabolism of Chicken Erythrocytes: Examination of Schizophrenic and Other Subjects. Science, 151, 1408, 1966.

13. FROHMAN, C.E., WARNER, K.A., ARTHUR, R.E., BECKETT, P.G.S. and GOTTLIEB, J.S. Hemolysis by Schizophrenic Plasma and its Relationship to the Schizophrenic Plasma Factor. (In preparation).

14. LATHAM, L.K., LONCHARICH, K., WARNER, K.A., CRANDALL, R.G., BECKETT, P.G.S., FROHMAN, C.E., and GOTTLIEB, J.S. Effects of a Protein Factor Isolated from Schizophrenic Blood on Permeability. Vox Sang., 8, 491, 1963.

15. FROHMAN, C.E. Studies on the Plasma Factor in Schizophrenia. In Mind as A Tissue, C. Rupp (Editor), Hoeber Med. Div., Harper & Row, New York, 1968.

16. EAVENSON, E. and CHRISTENSEN, N. Transport Systems for Neutral Amino Acids in the Pigeon Erythrocyte. J. Biol. Chem., 242, 5386, 1967.

17. SNYDER, S.H. Catecholamines, Brain Functions, and How Psychotropic Drugs Act. In Principles of Psychopharmacology, W.G. Clark (Editor), Academic Press, New York, In press.

18. CALDWELL, D., and DOMINO, E. Electroencephalographic and Eye Movement Patterns During Sleep in Chronic Schizophrenic Patients. EEG and Clin. Neurophysiol., 22, 414, 1967.

C. E. Frohman, Ph.D., and J. S. Gottlieb, M.D., Lafayette Clinic, Detroit, Michigan 48207

DISCUSSION BY DR. FRITZ FREYHAN :

I have followed the work of Dr. J. S. Gottlieb and Dr. C. E. Frohman with very great interest. During the last 2 years I have had the opportunity to evaluate an investigation of the plasma factor in schizophrenic patients at St. Vincent's Hospital and Medical Center in New York. According to the evidence at this time, the plasma factor could not be detected in the greater majority of schizophrenic patients admitted to St. Vincent's Hospital. While these patients are clinically more acute, many have had multiple hospitalizations. We therefore obtained the kind approval of Dr. Herman Denber to extend the study to typical chronic schizophrenic patients at Manhattan State Hospital. Findings in these patients appear quite similar to those reported by Dr. Frohman.

The question now arises whether one can relate the protein factor to "schizophrenic plasma" as Dr. Frohman does, or to the plasma of some schizophrenic patients whose characteristics have yet to be defined. It is not clear to me why this factor should be absent in those more acute patients who are blatantly psychotic with every evidence of typical schizophrenic symptomatology. Why should a biochemical disturbance, assumed to be etiologically involved, be absent in the intensely acute stages and only emerge in patients with prolonged hospitalization? Recent work in the affective disorders indicates a close interdependence of biochemical findings and affective symptomatology regardless of length of illness. Is it conceivable that the protein factor is a secondary phenomenon reflecting functional maladaptation in prolonged illness and/or hospitalization?

F. Freyhan, M.D., St. Vincent's Hospital, New York, N.Y.

SCHIZOPHRENIA: EVIDENCE OF A PATHOLOGIC IMMUNE MECHANISM

ROBERT G. HEATH

The present concept of schizophrenia as an immunological disorder is based on the following experimental data, previously reported:

(1) Clinical manifestations of schizophrenia have been shown to be associated with focal physiologic abnormalities affecting principally the septal region and sometimes the hippocampus as well (1-4).

(2) By fluorescent antibody technics, globulin has been demonstrated principally on cells at focal sites in the septal region of brains of schizophrenic patients who died while displaying acute psychotic signs and symptoms (5). The extent of brain cells affected seemed, on gross inspection, to be roughly related to the intensity of psychosis before death. In contrast, globulin has not been detected with these technics in brain tissues of nonschizophrenic control subjects after death.

(3) Studies have shown that the unique globulin of schizophrenic serum, which has been named taraxein, is confined to the gamma G immunoglobulin (IgG) fraction. Its injection into Macaca rhesus monkeys induced aberrations in electroencephalograms (EEGs) focal in the septal region and, less consistently, in the hippocampus, and its intravenous injection into nonpsychotic volunteer-subjects induced acute psychotic signs and symptoms that persisted for one to two hours (6-9).

(4) Antibody produced against human and monkey septal tissues in sheep possessed the same characteristics as taraxein, inducing focal EEG abnormalities and associated behavioral changes in the rhesus monkey (10). When tissues were reacted with the relevant fluorescein-tagged antisera, both taraxein (schizophrenic IgG) and the sheep antibody (IgG) were noted on cells of the septal region of brains of recipient monkeys that were killed at the peak response to the serologic fractions.

(5) Taraxein and control serum fractions labeled with ferritin and fluorescein isothiocyanate were injected intravenously into monkeys that were killed at varying intervals five minutes to nine hours after injection. Ultraviolet microscopic examination of tissue sections showed the presence of globulin on cells of the brain parenchyma, principally of the septal region (9). Tissues examined under the electron microscope showed ferritin-labeled taraxein uniformly distributed through cytoplasm of oligoglial cells, principally of the septal region. These labeled molecules have been shown to pass freely through blood vessel walls and into oligoglial cells in the absence of structural changes (11,12). The molecules have not been noted in other cells or in intercellular spaces of the brain. Although the labeled taraxein (schizophrenic IgG) appears, by present technics, to be much more heavily concentrated in the brain than the labeled control globulins, more control studies will be required to establish the conclusion that this phenomenon is unique for schizophrenia.

From these data we have postulated that schizophrenia is an immunologic disorder in which patients produce a unique antibody, taraxein, against an unidentified antigen in brain cells principally of the septal region. We further postulate that in vivo combination of the antigen and unique antibody alters neural activity at focal sites, probably through impaired neurohumoral conduction, and that this physiologic abnormality is responsible for psychotic signs and symptoms.

The present study was designed to identify more precisely those brain sites at which electrical changes were induced by intravenous injection of taraxein to monkeys. In our standard test monkey, small ball electrodes are implanted into the septal region, caudate nucleus, hypothalamus, hippocampus, and thalamus, as well as over selected cortical sites (7). Injection of an active psychosis-inducing taraxein fraction induces focal spiking or slow-wave activity, or both, usually most pronounced in the anterior septal leads.

To determine more precisely the site of generation of the maximal EEG abnormality, we prepared two Macaca rhesus monkeys with 12 septal leads, 4 caudate leads, and 4 hippocampal leads, in addition to the usual hypothalamic and cortical electrodes. Electroencephalograms obtained after intravenous injection of schizophrenic IgG (taraxein) showed maximal abnormalities in the center of the septal region, (13) with lesser changes occurring in the most ventral medial aspect of the head of the caudate nucleus. The degrees of physiologic abnormality recorded from various sites in the rostral forebrain are shown in schematic drawings (Fig. 1), which represent cross-sections

ELECTRODE PLACEMENTS

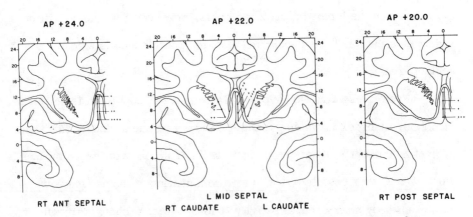

Fig. I : Schematic drawing of placements of septal-caudate leads. Degree of abnormal electroencephalographic activity induced by injection of taraxein into a monkey is indicated by plus (+) marks: one + indicates minimal abnormality and four + maximal abnormality.

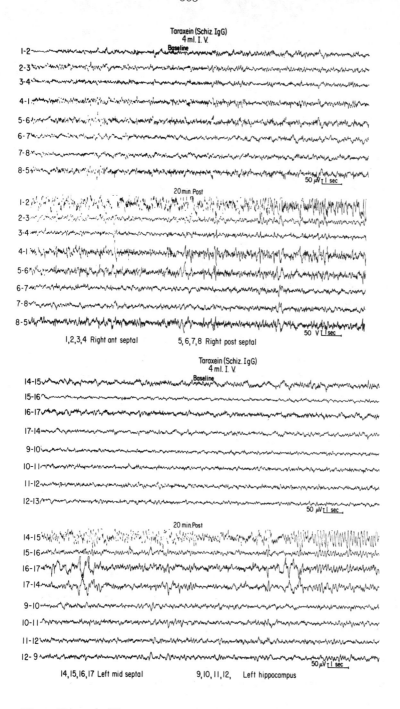

Fig. II and III. Sample electroencephalograms (from leads shown in figure I before and after taraxein administration. The serial numbers at the bottom of the figures indicate relative depths of the leads, the lowest number representing the most ventral of the four leads in each electrode array and the highest number, the most dorsal lead.

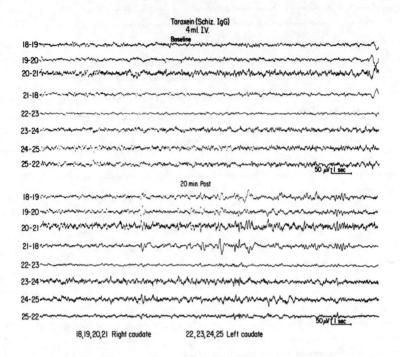

Fig. IV. Sample electroencephalograms as shown in Figs. II and III.

of various stereotaxic AP levels. Maximal changes were recorded from the nucleus acumbens septi, islets of Calleja, and nucleus of the diagonal band (Figs. II, III and IV).

It is at these sites of maximal EEG abnormalities that the largest concentrations of ferritin-tagged taraxein have been seen in brain tissues of monkeys killed after having received intravenous injections of ferritin-tagged taraxein (12). These observations support the concept that schizophrenia represents an immunologic disorder.

REFERENCES

1. HEATH, R. G., and the Department of Psychiatry and Neurology, Tulane University. Studies in Schizophrenia. Harvard University Press, Cambridge, 1954.

2. HEATH, R. G., and MICKLE, W. A. Evaluation of seven years' experience with depth electrode studies in human patients. In Electrical Studies on the Unanesthetized Brain, RAMEY, E. R., and O'DOHERTY, D. S. (Editors), p. 214, Paul B. Hoeber, New York, 1960.

3. HEATH, R. G. Developments toward new physiologic treatments in psychiatry. J. Neuropsychiat., 5, 318, 1964.

4. HEATH, R. G. Schizophrenia: Biochemical and physiologic aberrations. J. Neuropsychiat., 2, 597, 1966.

5. HEATH, R. G., and KRUPP, I. M. Schizophrenia as an immunologic disorder: I. Demonstration of antibrain globulins by fluorescent antibody techniques. Arch. Gen. Psychiat., 16, 10, 1967.

6. HEATH, R. G., MARTENS, S., LEACH, B. E., COHEN, M., and ANGEL, C. Effect on behavior in humans with the administration of taraxein. Amer. J. Psychiat., 114, 14, 1957.

7. HEATH, R. G., KRUPP, I. M., BYERS, L. W., and LILJEKVIST, J. I. Schizophrenia as an immunologic disorder. II. Effects of serum protein fractions on brain function. Arch. Gen. Psychiat., 16, 10, 1967.

8. HEATH, R. G., and KRUPP, I. M. Schizophrenia as a specific biologic disease. Amer. J. Psychiat., 124, 37, 1968.

9. HEATH, R. G. Schizophrenia: Studies of pathogenesis. In Biological and Clinical Aspects of the Central Nervous System, Symposium Monograph from a meeting held on October 16, 1967 to commemorate the 50th Anniversary of the Pharmaceutical Department of Sandoz Ltd., p. 189, Basle, 1967.

10. HEATH, R. G., KRUPP, I. M., BYERS, L. W. and LILJEKVIST, J. I. Schizophrenia as an immunologic disorder: III. Effects of antimonkey and antihuman brain antibody on brain function. Arch. Gen. Psychiat., 16, 24, 1967.

11. HEATH, R. G., FITZJARRELL, A., and KRUPP, I. M. Pathogenetic studies of schizophrenia: Ferritin and fluorescein labeling of IgG. In press. Presented at the Third International Conference of The Future of the Brain Sciences, sponsored by The Manfred Sakel Institute Inc., New York, May, 1968.

12. HEATH, R. G., FITZJARRELL, A., and KRUPP, I. M. Effect of taraxeon on blood-brain barrier: Passage of taraxein into septal oligoglial cells. Amer. J. Psychiat. In press.

13. HEATH, R. G. Definition of the septal region. In Studies in Schizophrenia. Harvard University Press, Cambridge, 1954, p. 1.

R. G. Heath, M.D., Department of Psychiatry & Neurology, Tulane University School of Medicine, 1430 Tulane Avenue, New Orleans, La. 70112

A SUMMARY OF THIRTY DIFFERENT BIOCHEMICAL TESTS IN CHILDHOOD SCHIZOPHRENIA

D.V. SIVA SANKAR

Extensive studies have been carried out on the biological aspects of schizophrenia in the adult, but little has been done on "childhood schizophrenia". Biogenic amines have received some attention and justifiably so in view of their involvement in the actions of psycho-active drugs (1-5), and in phenylketonuria (6, 7). Elevated levels of serotonin have been reported in autistic children by Schain and Freedman (8). Perry et al. (9, also cf.10) reported the occurrence of N-methylmetanephrine in the urines of three out of 18 juvenile psychotics. However, Shaw and his colleagues (11, 12) did not find any significant differences between schizophrenic and nonschizophrenic children with respect to the effect of tryptophan loading on the urinary excretion of indoles nor with respect to the urinary amino acid excretion patterns.

We have carried out several studies on children (boys) hospitalized at Creedmoor State Hospital. A summary of our biochemical findings is presented in Table I. While statistical considerations have been worked out for these several biochemical test parameters, these have not been presented here. These results show that in many of the tests the autistic schizophrenic child stands out on one end of the test results, and the nonschizophrenic child on the other end. The

TABLE I

Biochemical differences between schizophrenic and control children

Test Number	Biochemical Test	Diagnostic Category		
		Nonschizophrenic	Schizophrenic Nonautistic	Autistic
1)	Serotonin Uptake by platelets*			
	Expt. I	7. 62	5. 81	2. 63
	Expt. II	17. 2	15. 5	12.1
	Expt. III	18. 0	14. 5	12.8
2)	Norepinephrine Uptake by platelets			
	Expt. I	30.1	31.5	30. 4
	Expt. II	30. 0	38. 4	34. 5
	NE/S Ratio			
	Expt. I	1. 88	2. 00	3. 06
	Expt. II	1. 67	2. 65	2. 69
3)	Platelets +	147	152	228
4)	Plasma Inorganic Phosphorous (uM/ml)	1. 60	1. 50	2. 80
5)	Erythrocyte Inorganic Phosphorous (uM/g hemoglobin)	3. 02	2. 99	6. 53
6)	Plasma Lactic Dehydrogenase *	117. 8	120. 1	169. 8
7)	Plasma Alkaline Phosphatase **	5. 53	5. 69	6. 85
8)	Blood Aldolase #	1. 575	1. 575	1. 583
9)	Blood glucose-6-phosphate isomerase #	1. 363	1. 442	1. 463
10)	Hemoglobin (g/100ml blood)	11. 2	11. 9	11. 0
11)	Blood ATPase (A)	334. 7	360. 0	303. 1
12)	Blood Lysate ATPase (B)	1810	2033	2907
13)	Plasma Phospholipid Phosphorus (uM/ml)	1. 35	1. 80	2. 16
14)	Plasma sialic acid mg/100ml	38. 2	39. 7	44. 2
15)	Plasma Cholesterol mg/100ml	200. 2	289. 1	191.6
16)	Plasma tyrosine mg/100ml	1. 06	1. 12	1. 05

		Nonschizophrenic	Schizophrenic Nonautistic	Autistic
17)	Plasma PBI (ug/100ml)	6. 2	6. 2	6. 2
18)	Plasma Uric acid (ug/ml)	42. 2	39. 2	--
19)	Plasma creatinine (ug/ml)	14. 3	12. 3	--
20)	Erythrocyte Postassium mg/gHb)	14. 12	12. 90	9. 76
21)	Erythrocyte Magnesium ug/gHb)	155. 2	148. 6	126. 0
	Plasma Vitamins			
22)	Ascorbic Acid mg%	0. 91	0. 96	0. 76
23)	Folic Acid[1] ug%	1. 32	1. 55	1. 70
24)	Folic Acid (readily available to L. casei ug%	1. 08	1. 27	1. 23
25)	Vitamin B-6 (yeast assay) ug%	12. 60	11. 92	12. 75
26)	Riboflavin (L. casei assay) ug%	11. 21	9. 82	12. 13
27)	Plasma total amino acids as um glutamic acid per ml. plasma	5. 65	5. 50	5. 48
28)	RBC total amino acids as um glutamic acid/g. Hemoglobin	94. 31	80. 75	87. 78
29)	RBC Copper mg/g. Hemoglobin	11. 37	10. 68	10. 68
30)	RBC Zinc mg/g. Hemoglobin	75. 89	70. 84	73. 82

Expt. I is not a duplicate of II and III.
* Wroblewski Units.
** Bodansky Units.
+ Turbidity of platelet pellet suspended in saline.
1 Available to L. casei after incubation with hog kidney extracts.

schizophrenic nonautistic is usually in between. Our nonschizophrenic children are also gathered from the hospitalized population and have been clinically categorized as "primary behavior disorders". The usual number of children involved in these studies are approximately

as follows: schizophrenic (nonautistic): 60 to 80; schizophrenic
(autistic): 20 to 30; nonschizophrenic: 30. Not the same individual
children have been used from test to test. The several different
tests have been carried out on a total of 1, 000 children. Out of this
pool, a total of 100-140 subjects have been used for different tests
each time. The age of these children ranged from 5 to 15 years.

T A B L E   II

AGE AT ADMISSION AND SEX

Number of Subjects

AGE IN YEARS	MALE	FEMALE	M/F
3	5	2	2. 50
3-1/2	11	2	5. 50
4	24	6	4. 00
4-1/2	14	8	1. 75
5	41	14	2. 93
5-1/2	41	9	4. 44
6	52	8	6. 50
6-1/2	79	16	4. 94
7	69	12	5. 75
7-1/2	103	17	6. 06
8	117	20	5. 85
8-1/2	138	24	5. 75
9	150	28	5. 36
9-1/2	161	32	5. 03
10	167	34	4. 91
10-1/2	156	29	5. 38
11	167	32	5. 22
11-1/2	140	45	3. 11
12	117	51	2. 29
12-1/2	109	61	1. 80
13	130	83	1. 57
13-1/2	119	93	1. 28
14	160	90	1. 77
14-1/2	129	84	1. 54
15	106	68	1. 56
15-1/2	20	7	2. 86
16	2	3	0. 67
TOTAL	2527	879	2. 88

We have studied these data as affected by the age of the patients also.
These studies show that the schizophrenic (autistic) child compares to a
chronologically younger nonschizophrenic patient. This observation
gives biochemical support to the theory of "maturational plasticity"

usually manifested as a maturational lag in childhood schizophrenia.
The involvement of (a). serotonin uptake by the thrombocytes, (b).
differences in plasma electrolytes and (c). of plasma sialic acid levels
may indicate the possible role of a defect of neural functions of complex
lipids, biogenic amines and of electrolytes. These data seem to indicate
that autistic childhood schizophrenia may be associated with congenital
neurobiological damage, and perhaps lipidosis. If these autistic children belong to an educated and/or upper middle class family, they may
be brought to a clinic, whereas if they came from a lower socioeconomic
group, this would not have happened with high infant mortality rates in
the underprivileged groups.

T A B L E   III

SEX, RACE AND CLINICAL DIAGNOSIS

	TOTAL NO. OF SUBJECTS	CLINICAL DIAGNOSIS AND NO. OF SUBJECTS			
		S	PBD	PSY	MD
TOTAL					
Male	2527	1569	527	297	134
Female	879	556	189	55	79
(M/F) Ratio	2.88	2.82	2.79	5.40	1.70

That the permeability of the erythrocyte may be involved in
childhood schizophrenia is indicated by the observation (cf: Table I)
that the ratio of ATPase activities in the lysed blood and whole blood
(B/A) is much higher in the schizophrenic children. Lipo-protein
complexes are usually involved in permeability into cells. The differences in several enzymatic activities, especially lactic dehydrogenase and alkaline phosphatase, show that the autistic child is possibly comparable to less highly specialized types of tissues (eg:
embryonic or cancer tissues in the lag of development of biochemical
and metabolic ingenuities. However, none of these enzymatic activities
are of such a large extent as to indicate overt and primary muscular,

osseous or hepatic dysfunction.

Marked differences can usually be found between the autistic
and the nonautistic children. These differences are more consistent than the differences between schizophrenic and nonschizophrenic children. In our more recent and unpublished work we have
found a higher percentage of breakage in leucocyte chromosomes in
tissue culture in the case of autistic children than in the case of

T A B L E   IV

AGE AT ADMISSION AND DIAGNOSIS

Number of Subjects

AGE IN YEARS	S	PBD	PSY	MD	TOTAL
3	2	2	2	1	7
3-1/2	10	0	3	0	13
4	15	3	5	7	30
4-1/2	11	0	3	8	22
5	34	2	2	17	55
5-1/2	29	5	6	10	50
6	42	2	7	9	60
6-1/2	62	12	11	10	95
7	53	5	12	11	81
7-1/2	80	17	16	7	120
8	90	29	12	6	137
8-1/2	110	22	20	10	162
9	101	34	26	17	178
9-1/2	123	34	27	9	193
10	129	34	16	22	201
10-1/2	116	50	12	7	185
11	117	48	24	10	199
11-1/2	113	47	19	6	185
12	104	42	15	7	168
12-1/2	106	45	15	4	170
13	146	38	20	9	213
13-1/2	121	66	19	6	212
14	159	58	27	6	250
14-1/2	130	62	17	4	213
15	104	50	11	9	174
15-1/2	13	8	5	1	27
16	5	0	0	0	5
TOTAL					
No.	2125	716	352	213	3406
%	62.4	21.0	10.3	6.3	100

nonautistic children. These several findings indicate that the autistic
child differs from the nonautistic child in many ways. The autistic

child has more manifest biological deviations, perhaps dating back to embryonic development in utero. The lowest rate of variation of biochemical parameters with increasing age is to be found in the case of the autistic children. This may suggest a "biological freezing" of the autistic child in spite of increasing chronological age.

T A B L E IVa

AGE AT ADMISSION AND DIAGNOSIS

AGE IN YEARS	(Data shown as per cent of cases at each age)				
	S	PBD	PSY	MD	TOTAL
3	28.6	28.6	28.6	14.3	100.1
3-1/2	76.9	0	23.1	0	100.0
4	50.0	10.0	16.7	23.3	100.0
4-1/2	50.0	0	13.6	36.4	100.0
5	61.8	3.6	3.6	30.9	100.0
5-1/2	58.0	10.0	12.0	20.0	99.9
6	70.0	3.3	11.7	15.0	100.0
6-1/2	65.3	12.6	11.6	10.5	100.0
7	65.4	6.2	14.8	13.6	100.0
7-1/2	66.7	14.2	13.3	5.8	100.0
8	65.7	21.2	8.8	4.4	100.1
8-1/2	67.9	13.6	12.3	6.2	100.0
9	56.7	19.1	14.6	9.6	100.0
9-1/2	63.7	17.6	14.0	4.7	100.0
10	64.3	16.9	8.0	10.9	100.0
10-1/2	62.7	27.0	6.5	3.8	100.0
11	58.8	24.1	12.1	5.0	100.0
11-1/2	61.2	25.4	10.3	3.2	100.1
12	61.9	25.0	8.9	4.2	100.0
12-1/2	62.4	26.5	8.8	2.4	100.1
13	68.5	17.8	9.4	4.2	99.9
13-1/2	57.1	31.1	9.0	2.8	100.0
14	63.6	23.2	10.8	2.4	100.0
14-1/2	61.0	29.1	8.0	1.9	100.0
15	59.8	28.7	6.3	5.2	100.0
15-1/2	48.2	29.6	18.5	3.7	100.0
Average	60.6	17.9	12.1	9.4	

These studies indicate multiple biochemical deviations in the autistic child. However, with respect to the biochemistry of childhood schizophrenia, we interpret our data as biochemical profiles of schizophrenic children admitted to a state hospital setting and do not yet confess to a knowledge of a single monofactorial biochemical etiology of the disease. More complete and detailed discussion of these findings is planned in other publications (13).

Schizophrenia clinically manifests certain abnormal modalities of behavior and sensory functions. In this way it seems to be rather a limited number of abnormalities, which may have, to all apparent purposes, a common etiology. Factors like age of onset, subjection to (or protection from) stress-producing situations, compensation and decompensation, type of treatment etc., apparently seem to modify these abnormalities in behavior and sensory function. However, it cannot be ruled out that several biological abnormalities, including embryonic and genotypic deviations can give rise to the same apparent psychiatric abnormality in behavior and sensory functions. This way schizophrenic behavior, which is the most apparent clinical entity in schizophrenia, may be a byproduct of several different etiological biological abnormalities. It is this discrepancy and divergency of the biological etiology that may give rise to the good or bad prognosis in the clinical manifestations of schizophrenia. The disruption and way-wardness of inner homeostatic equilibrium which as we have pointed out in another part of this monograph can be caused either by bio-dynamic inequilibrium (with good prognosis) or a deeper biological lesion, perhaps congenital (with bad prognosis), would give rise to schizophrenias of a more limited number of clinical modalities. Bio-chemically, the schizophrenias may have a common funneling through the metabolism of biogenic amines. Robins and Guze have presented at this conference their ideas about good prognosis and bad prognosis schizophrenias being quite different types of diseases.

The problem of childhood schizophrenia is more complicated because social factors, problems of growth, maturation, develop-ment and learning weigh heavily on children. In our demographic studies, we find a higher number of Negroid children in the child psychiatric unit then in the general population. Further the average age of admission seems to vary with the sex of the patient (cf. Table II & III). The problem of neurological and EEG damage cannot be mini-mized in a diagnosis of childhood schizophrenia. Again the relevance

between neurological damage, behavior disorders and the diagnosis
of childhood schizophrenia is indeed very intricate. From our data
relating the age of admission of the children to the hospital (cf: Table
IV), and also on the basis of laboratory determinations, it is felt
that there was more neurobiological damage in children admitted
at a younger age than in those admitted at 11 years and after. Our
finding that children admitted at a younger age stayed longer on the
hospital records (cf: Table V) than children admitted at an older age,
further strengthens this view. The results in Table V do not take
into consideration weekend home visits and convalescent care outside the hospital, while the patient is not officially yet discharged.

T A B L E   V

Relation of Age at Admission to Total Time in Hospital

Age at Admission	No. of Subjects	Total Time in Hospital (in years)
3 to 6 years	134	2.32
6-1/2 to 8	273	1.85
8-1/2 to 10	500	2.12
10-1/2 to 12	556	1.86
12-1/2 to 14	699	1.36
14-1/2 to 16	372	0.971

Further, the autistic child is quite distinct and is admitted at
an early age (cf: Table VI). The autistic child differs most clearly
from all the other children both in psychosociological assets and
biochemical laboratory findings. Schizophrenia in these children
seems to be just one byproduct of a more serious congenital biological damage. While we have been unable to find any chromosomal
abnormalities comparable to aneuploidy in these children, (our having
studied a total of 35 autistic children) there seems to be a higher percentage of breakage in leucocyte chromosomes in the autistic children

(cf: D. V. Siva Sankar et al. Clinical Research XVII 317, April 1969).
This adds more strength to our concept that schizophrenia in the autistic
child is only a byproduct of a more severe biological problem, and also
to our concept that schizophrenia is a common psychiatric manifestation of possibly several different biological abnormalities. It is also
felt that the age of onset of pathology is lower with the deeper involvement of biological defect. Complicating factors have been discussed
in our previous article (13).

T A B L E   VI

Average Age at Admission and Psychiatric Diagnosis

Diagnosis	Average Age at Admission (Years)	Number of Children
Schizophrenia (Autism)	6. 5	113
Mentally Defective	8. 97	213
Schizophrenia (Total)	11. 6	2125
Psychosis	12. 0	352
Behavior Disorders	12. 9	716

These results have an important implication both in the nosology
of schizophrenia and the possible differences between adult and childhood schizophrenias. While schizophrenia is categorized by clinical
modalities of behavior, mood, space-time orientation, hallucinations,
etc. , its biochemical categorization is very complex. However, if one
subscribes to the idea that schizophrenia is one disease, one must not
forget that the biological lesions and the severity of the expression of
this disease are highly variable. This may depend, as we have mentioned earlier in this monograph, either on a biodynamic inequilbrium
(general factors) or on a biological defect (special factors). This may
give rise to a variety of modes of remission and expression of the disease at various ages. In view of this, while schizophrenia can possibly

be construed clinically as one disease, it is hard to accept it as one disease with one single gene-linked biochemical disorder. It is possible that there may be one centralized controlling factor lacking in the regulation of metabolism in schizophrenia. But, the nature and the genetic aspects of this central factor elude us. To invoke it at the present time is perhaps more unjustified than to deny it.

Many of our studies show a difference between adult and childhood schizophrenia. For example, in one of our previous publications (14) we noticed slightly lower levels of the Hopkins-Cole-reagent-positive materials in the urine of schizophrenic children. In adults higher urinary levels of this substance have been reported (15). Similarly in our studies, the plasma levels of sialic acid are higher in the autistic schizophrenic children, whereas lower levels have been reported in the plasma of adult schizophrenics (16, also cf. 17). Again, in our studies on the uptake of serotonin by platelets from schizophrenic children, especially autistic schizophrenic children, a similar lowered platelet uptake of serotonin cannot be found in the case of adult schizophrenics. In view of these above findings it is possible that childhood schizophrenia may have different biochemical expressions and lesions from adult schizophrenia. Support for this hypothesis comes from quite a different type of work (18) where significant differences in the dermatoglyphics in childhood schizophrenia and adult schizophrenia have been found.

In view of the above considerations, while it is difficult to be sure that schizophrenia has a monogenic etiology and a single biological lesion, at whatever level it may be, it is very probable that schizophrenia may have different biochemical and biologic expressions. We are further engaged in correlating the biological defect with psychiatric defect, besides in seeking a biological defect in known psychiatric diseases.

Autistic children display the largest amount of biological deviation from other children and are also admitted at an early age. Similarly, a higher percentage of children admitted at an early age belong
to the diagnostic categories of "psychosis" and "mentally defective".
The present results lead us to a hypothesis of general etiological
factors (biodynamic inequilibrium with good prognosis) and special
biological defects (with poor prognosis and history of multiple hospitalizations in the family) in both childhood and adult schizophrenia.
A larger percentage of childhood schizophrenics (especially from
socio-culturally better families) may belong to the latter group, and
may be termed as "burnt out" cases by the time they reach adult age.
In view of this "burning out", some biochemical and biological findings
may differ in the childhood schizophrenia from adult schizophrenia.

REFERENCES :

(1). Siva Sankar, D. V., Cates, N. R., Broer, H. H., and Sankar
D. B. Biochemical parameters of childhood schizophrenia(autism)
and growth. In "Recent Advances in Biological Psychiatry" (Ed.)
J. Wortis. 5, 76, Plenum Press, N. Y. 1963.

(2). IDEM. Studies on biogenic amines and psychoactive drug
actions, with special reference to lysergic acid diethylamide.
Trans. N. Y. Acad. Sci. Ser. II, 26, No. 3, p. 369 (1964).

(3). Cates, N. R., Goldsmith, E. D., and Siva Sankar, D. V.
Interrelations between the effects of endocrine organectomies and
of LSD-25. Federation Proceedings 23, 147 (1964).

(4). Siva Sankar D. V. Effect of psychoactive drugs on particulate
norepinephrine levels, plasma glucose and 17-hydroxycorticosteroids
and urinary excretion of biogenic amines and their metabolites.
Federation Proceedings 24, 195 (1965).

(5). IDEM. Tissue and intracellular binding and distribution of histamine, norepinephrine and serotonin. Clinical Research. XV, 471(1967).

(6). Nadler, H. L., and Hsia, D. Y. Epinephrine metabolism in phenyl
ketonuria. Proc. Soc. Exptl. Biol. Med. 107, 721 (1961).

(7). Perry, T. L. Urinary excretion of amines in phenylketonuria and
mongolism. Science, 136, 879 (1962).

(8). Schain, R. J., and Freedman, D. X. Studies on 5-hydroxyindole
metabolism in autistic and other retarded children. J. Pediatrics
58. 315 (1961).

(9). Perry, T. L. N-methylmetanephrine : excretion by juvenile
psychotics. Science 139, 587 (1963).

(10). Siva Sankar, D. V., Gold, E., Phipps, E., and Barbara Sankar, D. Biochemical studies on schizophrenic children. III World Cong. Psychiat. Proceedings. Univ. Toronto Press. p. 610, 1961.

(11). Shaw, C. R., Lucas, J., and Rabinowitch, R. D. Effects of tryptophan loading on indole excretion. A. M. A. Arch. Gen. Psychiat. 1, 366 (1959).

(12). Shaw, C. R., and Sutton, H. E. Metabolic studies on childhood schizophrenia. Ibid. 3, 519 (1960).

(13). Siva Sankar, D. V. Multiple Biochemical Deviations in Childhood Schizophrenia (Autism). Paper presented at the annula convention of the Society of Biological Psychiatry, Miami Beach, May 1969. Submitted for publication to the Society's Journal, Biol. Psychiat.

(14). Siva Sankar, D. V., Gold, E., Phipps, E., and Sankar, D. B. General metabolic studies on schizophrenic children. Annals of the N. Y. Acad. Sci. 96, 392 (1962).

(15). Yuwiler, A., and Good, M. H. Chromatographic study of "Reigelhaupt" chromogens in urine. J. Psychiat. Res. 1, 215 (1962).

(16). Bogoch, S. Nervous system glycoproteins in mental disorders. In " Biological Treatmant of Mental Illness", (Ed.) M. Rinkel, L. C. Page & Co., N. Y. 1966. p. 406.

(17). Mikhailova, Zh. Neuropatol. Psikhiat. 66, 1542 (1967). From Chem. Abstracts, 66, 1153 c (1967).

(18). Sank, D. Dermatoglyphics in childhood schizophrenia. Acta Genet. 18, 300 (1968).

ACKNOWLEDGEMENTS : The author wishes to thank Dr. L. Bender for her interest in the biology of childhood schizophrenia, Dr. Gloria Faretra for her careful scrutiny of diagnoses, and his several colleagues and assistants for help in various phases of this work. Mention may be made of the excellent assistance given by : Dr. N. R. Cates, A. Geisler, N. S. Kumar, Dr. R. Raikow, P. W. Rozsa, C. F. Saladino Jr., and J. Weidenbaum.

D. V. Siva Sankar, Ph.D., Child Psychiatry, Creedmoor State Hospital, Queens Village, N.Y. 11427

Is Schizophrenia a Disease ?

Eli Robins M. D.
and
Samuel B. Guze M. D.
Washington University, St. Louis, Mo.

It is possible to distinguish good prognosis schizophrenia from poor prognosis schizophrenia. When this distinction is made, bad prognosis cases have predominantly schizophrenia among the psychiatrically ill first - degree relatives, whereas good prognosis cases have predominantly affective disorders among the psychiatrically ill first - degree relatives. Therefore, apparent " schizophrenia " with a good prognosis is not a mild form of nuclear schizophrenia, but is a different illness. Research in this area, whether genetic, psychodynamic, clinical, sociological, chemical, physiological or therapeutic must take this distinction into account.

Pupillary Reactions in Schizophrenia

Gad Hakerem Ph. D.
Queens College and Biometrics Research

The pupillary reactions to light and other sensory stimuli were electronically recorded from a group of psychiatric patients and compared to normal controls. The initial diameter of the pupil of the dark adapted eye and the extent and speed of the contraction and dilation responses were obtained from averaged response curves. Significant differences between the groups on the initial diameter measure were found. More striking, however, was the finding that the extent of contraction of the pupil to a brief light stimulus differentiated the two groups with only 15% overlap.

An attempt was made to explain this phenomenon in terms of aberrations in the functioning of the autonomic nervous system in the patients.

BASAL BIOCHEMICAL MEASURES AND THEIR POSSIBLE INFLUENCE ON BIOCHEMICAL TESTS FOR SCHIZOPHRENIA.

ARTHUR YUWILER

Urine is the most accessible and most investigated human tissue and the source of much of our knowledge of human biochemistry. Gross abnormalities in urinary composition have lead to the characterization of maladies such as diabetes and pheochromocytoma and have even been remarkably successful in defining some mental diseases despite the physical and physiological distance between brain and urine. Diseases such as the aminoacidurias and the porphyrias have been characterized in this manner and important suggestions on the nature of the biochemical lesions have been obtained. Further, urinary excretion patterns have helped elucidate the gross metabolism of important centrally active compounds and of psychoactive agents.

Attempts to differentiate psychiatric populations by smaller quantitative differences in urinary composition have been less successful. In large part this can be attributed to such environmental complications as diet, concurrent medication and physical illness but in addition some of the conflicting results in this field may be related to more subtle methodological problems in the reporting of data.

During the course of a large multidisciplinary study on schizophrenia and psychopharmacology at the University of Michigan, psychiatric patients and hospitalized controls were compared in some 60 biochemical indices, as well as a combined 388 physiologic, psychologic, psychiatric, social and

This investigation was carried out as part of the Schizophrenia and Psychopharmacology Joint Research Project under the direction of Dr. R. W. Gerard, and supported by USPHS MY-1972, MY-4567 and MH-07293-01. Statistical analyses were carried out by Mr. N. Mattsson, anthropometric measures were made by Dr. C. Ingram, and psychiatric evaluations and ratings by Drs. K. B. Moore, E. A. Broder, J. Olariu, A. P. Dukay, Mrs. C. Gervais, R. N., and Mrs. V. M. Reuell, R. N. The author is grateful to Mr. T. Best, Mrs. M. Good, Miss I. M. Jenkins, and Dr. N. S. Ging for technical assistance, and Dr. R. W. Gerard for his helpful comments.

anthropometric variables. Portions of the resulting material have been presented elsewhere (1-4) and a detailed presentation of the full study is in preparation. The current presentation is limited to the interrelationship between and among some urinary variables and some anthropometric and psychiatric factors. Specifically, this paper is concerned with factors affecting urinary volume and creatinine concentration and their possible significance in attempted differentiation of diagnostic populations.

Methods

Subjects: Male patients between 18 to 50 years of age who were physically well and sufficiently mentally competent and cooperative to be tested in psychological tests were drawn from the hospital population at the Ypsilanti State Hospital. Subjects hospitalized for longer than 10 years were discarded from the research sample and the remainder diagnosed indepedently by three psychiatrists. Patients were included in the study only if the three independent diagnoses unanimously concurred on the major categories of schizophrenic or nonschizophrenic. Patients were excluded from the study if: body weight exceeded 100 kg; they were diagnosed as having acute brain disorders; chronic brain disorders associated with diseases or conditions due to prenatal constitutional influence; drug or poison intoxication other than alcoholism; circulatory disturbance; convulsive disorders; disturbance of metabolism growth or nutrition; operated tumors; diseases of unknown or unspecified etiology such as multiple sclerosis or Pick's disease; psychophysiologic skin reaction; speech disturbance; enuresis or somnanbulism; marked mental deficiency; or inability to speak, comprehend or read English. In addition, patients were excluded if medication could not be withheld for at least 8 weeks, if they had undergone lobotomy, or if they had undergone electroshock or similar treatments within 6 months preceding the study.

Of the 1670 schizophrenic and 1330 nonschizophrenic subjects in the Ypsilanti State Hospital at the time of this study, 235 schizophrenics and 165 nonschizophrenics fulfilled the selection criteria. The final sample consisted of 108 schizophrenics and 100 nonschizophrenics.

Application of these selection criteria prevented truly random selection of the population. Further, because of the need to obtain sufficient relatively acute subjects, the initial sample was randomly selected from the admissions ward and the residential wards separately with the result that admissions ward representation was higher in the final sample than would occur for true random sampling of the hospital. Nonetheless, selection was automatic within the set restrictions so that judgmental biases were excluded.

Ward Procedures. Upon selection subjects were admitted to a research annex ward. All medication was discontinued and patients were served regular hospital fare supplemented with multivitamin tablets. After 4 or more weeks, groups of 5 patients, alternately divided in 2 of one diagnosis and 3 of the other, were transferred to the research ward where they remained for an additional 4 weeks. The research ward was organized to provide continuous observation and close regulation of 25 patients. Once in the research ward, subjects were maintained on an unvarying diet with daily vitamin supplementation. The diet was prepared by University of Michigan dieticians to contain a constant amount of protein. Caloric requirements for the three weight groups (less than 65 kg, 65-75 kg and greater than 75 kg) were met by appropriate adjustments in sugar, jelly and oleomargarine content. Salt was adjusted to maintain a constant sodium intake by all subjects. Water was freely available.

Two 12-hour urine samples were obtained daily from each subject during his last 5 days on the research ward. An attendant was with patients at all times. All doors to toilet facilities were kept locked and reliable patients had to obtain the key from the attendant. Unreliable patients were toileted at frequent intervals under staff supervision. Urine was collected in gallon bottles kept refrigerated between collection periods. Determinations were made the morning after collection. Despite the precautions taken to assure complete and uncontaminated urine collections, there were occasional instances in which samples were suspect either because of ward impressions that cross-contamination may have occurred due to breakdown in the ward routine, because of aberrant volume, specific gravity, or pH of the urine, or because of gross evidence of contamination. Such samples were discarded. The values reported here are group means derived from individual means. For basal measures such as volume, creatinine, pH, and specific gravity, the individual means were averaged over five determinations; for others, such as urinary epinephrine or norepinephrine, they were the average of two determinations. Rejection of samples, therefore, decreased the number of samples averaged from these maximum numbers. Fortunately, sample rejection was relatively rare. Failure to void during the night was taken as a true zero and was used in computing individual means.

Creatinine was determined by a Jaffe reaction (5), sodium and potassium by flame photometry, 5-hydroxyindole acetic acid by the method of Udenfriend (6), epinephrine and norepinephrine by the procedure of Von Euler and Floding (7), and serum phosphorous by the method of Ging (8). Clinical assessment was made using the Lorr Scale (9) and the Gorham Scale (10).

Results and Discussion

The development of units is one of the simplest but most important steps in the evaluation of data. Data is invariably presented in association with units, generally in the form of a ratio between tested variable and some basal measure. The selection of the basal measure is of considerable importance for implicit in its choice is the assumption that it is related to the tested measure and that the ratio corrects for that relationship. This normalization permits uniform comparisons between sets of data and these comparisons, in turn, are really comparisons of the proportionality constants between tested and basal measures and of the stability of those constants.

Urinary constituents are generally quantified relative to urine volume (concentration), time (rate), or another urinary constituent. The use of these particular basal measures should be predicated upon their relevance to the excretion of the tested variable. Thus, concentration units assume a volume dependency in excretion, a rate assumes a time dependency, the use of creatinine as a basal measure implies that the tested variable is excreted in proportion to muscle mass, etc. Although the selection of an inappropriate basal measure may confound, rather than simplify, interpretation, remarkably little attention has been given to the selection of the baseline when urinary variables are examined. This stems partly from neglect of the significance of this measure and partly from insufficient data in the literature regarding relationships between variables.

Two of the more common basal measures are urine volume and urinary creatinine. As may be seen in Table I, diagnostic populations in this study had small but significant differences in excretion volumes.

TABLE I. URINE VOLUME EXCRETION BY DIFFERENT DIAGNOSTIC POPULATIONS

| | | Urine Volume (liters) | | |
| | | 24-hour | Night | Day |
	N	Mean ± S.D.	Mean ± S.D.	Mean ± S.D.
Schizophrenic	107	1.48 ± 0.64	0.49 ± 0.27	0.98 ± 0.46
Paranoid	42	1.68 ± 0.73	0.50 ± 0.28	1.17 ± 0.54
Nonparanoid	65	1.35 ± 0.55	0.48 ± 0.26	0.86 ± 0.35
Nonschizophrenic	83	1.75 ± 1.06	0.51 ± 0.39	1.26 ± 0.79
CBS*	29	1.92 ± 1.59	0.51 ± 0.50	1.40 ± 1.18
Non CBS	54	1.66 ± 0.66	0.50 ± 0.33	1.19 ± 0.49

Difference Comparisons

	Groups	F	P
24 hr:	Schiz. vs. Non Schiz.	5.09	<0.05
	Non Par Schiz. vs. Paranoid Schiz.	7.09	<0.01
	Non Par Schiz. vs. CBS Non Schiz.	6.78	<0.05
	Non Par Schiz. vs. Non Schiz. other than CBS	7.99	<0.01
Day Vol:	Schiz. vs. Non Schiz.	9.12	<0.01
	Non Par Schiz. vs. Paranoid Schiz.	12.99	<0.001
	Non Par Schiz. vs. CBS Non Schiz.	11.42	<0.001
	Non Par Schiz. vs. Non Schiz. other than CBS	17.50	<0.001

* Chronic brain syndrome.

This difference was largely attributable to a smaller urinary output, during the day, by non-paranoid schizophrenics and an elevated excretion by chronic brain syndrome subjects. The results raise questions of the diagnostic significance of the difference, the reasons for the difference, and the effect of the difference on other variables.

TABLE II. COMPARISONS OF FIRST AND SECOND HALVES OF STUDY

A. 24-hour Urine Volume (liters)

	1st Half Mean ± S.D.	2nd Half Mean ± S.D.
Schizophrenics	1.35 ± 0.60	1.56 ± 0.66
Paranoid	1.68 ± 0.62	1.67 ± 0.79
Nonparanoid	1.26 ± 0.58	1.46 ± 0.49
Nonschizophrencis	1.61 ± 0.99	1.90 ± 1.11
CBS	1.74 ± 1.40	2.33 ± 1.99
Non CBS	1.79 ± 0.43	1.49 ± 0.78

B. Day Urine Volume (liters)

	1st Half	2nd Half
Schizophrenics	0.90 ± 0.37	1.04 ± 0.51
Nonschizophrenics	1.19 ± 0.81	1.32 ± 0.76

Some measure of the consistency and diagnostic significance of the observed difference can be obtained by comparison of data derived from the first and second halves of the study. Such comparisons are particularly useful in multivariate studies where increased numbers of chance differences are to be expected in correspondence with the increased numbers of comparisons. The results in Table 2 show the general relationship held in both halves of the study, but only attained statistical significance when the combined data were analyzed. It is also clear that different diagnostic populations contributed to the 24-hour difference in each half. In the first half of the study urinary volumes of nonparanoid schizophrenics were decidedly lower than those of other diagnostic groups while in the second half, excretion by nonschizophrenics with chronic brain syndrome was decidedly higher. The diagnostic relevance of 24-hour urinary output, then, seems meager. On the other hand, schizophrenics and nonschizophrenics differed in day urine volumes in both the first half of the study (F 5.35; $P < 0.05$) and the second half (F 4.80; $P < 0.05$). Again, however, despite the greater consistency, values overlapped considerably both within and between halves so that this variable is also an unsatisfactory diagnostic measure. A subpopulation comparison was not carried out on day urine volume.

An examination of portions of the cross-correlation matrix presented in Table III suggests some explanations for the differences and for their possible relevance to other variables.

TABLE III. PARTIAL CROSS-CORRELATION MATRIX BETWEEN 24-HOUR
URINE VOLUME AND OTHER VARIABLES

	Schizophrenics			Nonschizophrenics		
	100r	df	P	100r	df	P
Urinary Variables 24 hr.						
Creatinine	48	105	.001	28	85	.01
Sodium	59	105	.001	63	85	.001
Potassium	54	105	.001	18	85	--
5-hydroxy indole acetic acid	40	61	.01	70	58	.001
Epinephrine	41	62	.001	34	54	.01
Norepinephrine	45	60	.001	71	52	.001
Serum Phosphate mgs %	-33	92	.01	3	74	--
Hospitalization	-19	105	.05	26	85	.05
Lorr A*	24	98	.05	7	82	--
Lorr D[t]	25	99	.05	0	81	--
Lorr 1[‡]	45	93	.001	-22	82	.05
Gorham 1[§]	25	104	.05	-11	85	--
Gorham 4[‖]	24	104	.05	-10	85	--
Gorham 5[¶]	-36	104	.001	30	85	.01
Reaction time (standard delay)	33	98	.001	-24	85	.05
Reaction time (variable delay)	37	98	.01	-17	85	--

* depression vs. excitement.
t activity.
‡ withdrawal (more to less).
§ activity (under to over).
‖ predominant mood (depression to euphoria).
¶ interpersonal relationship (less to more withdrawn).

It can be seen that 24-hour urine volume was negatively correlated with hospitalization for schizophrenics but positively correlated for nonschizophrenics. More than half (65 compared to 42) of the schizophrenics in this study were nonparanoid schizophrenics whose mean stay in the hospital was more than twice as long (68 months) as paranoids (33 months). Further, both of these schizophrenic groups had been hospitalized longer than either CBS nonschizophrenics (20 months) or other nonschizophrenics (14 months). This difference in correlations between urine volume and hospitalization could be interpreted as reflecting activity level rather than diagnosis, per se, with increased water consumption during hyperactive phases following admission, and decreased consumption during subsequent hypoactivity and physical deterioration. Analysis of the intercorrelation matrix for the entire patient population yielded little support for this (urine volume correlating neither with psychiatric measures of activity [Lorr and Gorham scales] nor with pertinent anthropometric measures). A similar analysis of the intercorrelation matrix for the separate diagnostic populations, however, revealed such correlations with Lorr A (depression vs. excitement); Lorr D (activity); Lorr I (withdrawal, more to less); Gorham activity (under to over); Gorham predominant mood (depression to euphoria); Gorham interpersonal relations (less to more withdrawn) reaction time standard delay and reaction time variable delay. On the other hand, nonschizophrenic urinary output correlated only with Lorr withdrawal; Gorham interpersonal relationship; and reaction time, standard delay; and in each instance the sign of the correlations was opposite to that for the schizophrenics. This sign reversal accounts for the absence of correlations within the total sample.

Psychiatric measures were compared between subjects having the lowest and highest Z scores for urine volume independent of diagnosis. On this basis large volume excretors (Z score 10-11) showed more manic excitement, overactivity, melancholy agitation, and belligerence; were more grandiose; had more anxiety; expressed more anger; and were less withdrawn than low excretors. The low excretors, as a group, had more perceptual distortion, more motor disturbance, more mental disorganization, and were more euphoric and withdrawn than high excretors.

These results certainly do not demonstrate that the diagnostic separation obtained on the basis of urine volume derives from a correlation with activity level rather than disease, but they do strongly suggest that such must be considered, and that studies involving volume dependent excretions of urinary constituents should take account of this possibility.

Urinary excretion during the day period even more consistently and successfully discriminated between schizophrenic and nonschizophrenic population in this study (cf. Table II). Again, day urine volume was significantly and negatively correlated with hospitlization among schizophrenics ($r = -0.22$; $p = -0.05$) and positively correlated among nonschizophrenics ($r = +0.40$; $p = +0.001$). The correlation between day urine volume and 24 hour urine volume was extremely high for both groups ($r = 0.94$; $p = 0.001$: $r = 0.96$; $p < 0.001$) and it is reasonable to assume that the various factors discussed with regard to 24 hour urine volume are also applicable here. For example, 62% of the subjects within the two lowest Z scores on 24 hour volumes are nonparanoid schizophrenics, and of these more than half also had the lowest day volume.

That these correlations with urine volume may be of importance in assessing diagnostic tests for schizophrenia is suggested by the upper portion of the correlation matrix in Table III. It can be seen that six urinary measures correlate with urine volume. When calculated as rates (24 hour value or day value) three of these differed significantly between diagnostic populations (Table IV); day excretion differentiating better than 24 hour excretion. When calculated as concentrations (amount/liter) the differences diminish and, in the case of epinephrine, even reverse. Serum phosphorous correlates negatively with urine volume and this is apparent in the relative values for the diagnostic groups.

Thus, the diagnostic significance of these measures resides at least partly in their correlations with urine volume and this relationship can be masked if another basal measure is employed.

TABLE IV. BIOCHEMICAL MEASURES DIFFERENTIATING DIAGNOSTIC POPULATIONS

Variable	Schizophrenics Mean ± S.D.	Nonschizophrenics Mean ± S.D.	F	P
Urine vol. 24 hr.	1.48 ± 0.64	1.75 ± 1.06	5.09	.05
Urine vol. day	0.98 ± 0.46	1.76 ± 0.79	9.12	.01
Sodium day	3.32 ± 1.24	5.09 ± 1.24	14.62	.001
Potassium ave. 24 hr	2.99 ± 1.15	3.41 ± 1.52	4.96	.05
Potassium day	2.62 ± 0.04	3.65 ± 1.37	5.36	.05
Epinephrine 24 hr	7.81 ± 5.08	10.11 ± 6.78	4.49	.05
Serum phosphate	3.57 ± 0.92	3.95 ± 1.04	6.16	.05

The diagnostic populations in this study differed only slightly in urinary creatinine excretion (Table V); the only statistically significant differences being between nonparanoid schizophrenics (low excretors) and non CBS nonschizophrenics (high excretors). Its diagnostic significance, per se, is thus very limited.

TABLE V. CREATININE EXCRETION BY DIFFERENT DIAGNOSTIC POPULATIONS

	Creatinine (gms)		
	24 hour Mean ± S.D.	Night Mean ± S.D.	Day Mean ± S.D.
Schizophrenic	1.50 ± 0.44	0.42 ± 0.34	1.02 ± 0.45
Paranoid	1.57 ± 0.51	0.41 ± 0.35	1.10 ± 0.50
Nonparanoid	1.45 ± 0.38	0.43 ± 0.32	0.97 ± 0.41
Nonschizophrenic (NS)	1.54 ± 0.37	0.42 ± 0.36	1.03 ± 0.41
CBS	1.44 ± 0.44	0.33 ± 0.29	0.86 ± 0.42
Non-CBS	1.61 ± 0.32	0.47 ± 0.39	1.15 ± 0.36

24 hr. creatinine
  Nonparanoid Schiz. vs. NS other than CBS $F = 5.67$ $P < 0.05$
Day creatinine
  Nonparanoid Schiz. vs. NS other than CBS $F = 6.49$ $P < 0.05$

The use of creatinine as a basal measure is predicated upon the assumption that it reflects muscle mass and is relatively constant within an individual and even between individuals. As can be seen in Table VI, at least the former assumption is partly true. Twenty-four hour urinary creatinine correlated quite well with many anthropometric measures; and correlations with those particularly relevant to muscle mass (lean body weight, muscle score, muscle biceps and calf girth) were somewhat, although not inordinately, higher. Despite these correlations, none of the anthropometric measures accounts for even 20% of the variance, suggesting that factors other than muscle mass, per se, play a role in creatinine excretion.

TABLE VI. 24-HOUR URINARY CREATININE CORRELATIONS WITH ANTHROPOMETRIC MEASURES

	All Subjects		Schizophrenics		Nonschizophrenics	
Variable	100r	P	100r	P	100r	P
Weight	35	.001	38	.001	27	.05
Height	18	.05	17	--	27	.05
Arm Length	21	.05	*		*	
Leg Length	24	.01	30	.01	27	.01
Shoulder Width	27	.01	30	.01	29	.01
Chest Width	27	.01	*		*	
Chest Girth	28	.01	35	.001	14	--
Waist Girth	22	.05	*		*	
Calf Girth	39	.001	38	.001	33	.01
Muscle Biceps	29	.01	*		*	
Muscle Score	20	.05	*		*	
Androgeny Score	26	.01	28	.01	29	.01
Lean Body Weight	38	.001	42	.001	32	.05

df = all patients 150–204; schizophrenics 88–105; nonschizophrenics 52–83.
*   not calculated.

Clinical state seems to be one of the factors involved despite the absence of diagnostic differentiation using this variable. Correlations with clinical state are given in Table VII and it is immediately apparent that significant correlations are largely limited to the schizophrenic population. A more detailed analysis reveals that paranoids contribute heavily to the correlations with the Lorr A (retarded depression vs. manic excitement r=0.349, P <0.05), and nonparanoid schizophrenics primarily contribute to the correlation with the Lorr B (compliance vs. resistiveness r = 0.349, P <0.05). Urinary creatinine from both groups contributed to the correlation with Lorr I (withdrawal; paranoids r = 0.474, P <0.01; nonparanoids F = 0.478, P <0.001) Lorr K (conceptual disorganization; paranoids r =-0.444, P <0.01; nonparanoids r = 0.299, P <0.05), Gorham 3 (mental disorganization; paranoids r = 0.467, P <0.01, nonparanoids r = 0.447, P <0.001) and Gorham 5 (interpersonal relationships --- less to more withdrawn; paranoids r = -0.335, P <0.01; nonparanoids r = -0.578, P <0.001). Of the nonschizophrenics, those other than CBS patients contributed heavily to the correlations with the Lorr I (r = 0.328, P <0.05).

These correlations appear to fall into two groups, a "deterioration" set consisting of decreasing creatinine correlating with increased compliance, withdrawal and retarded depression (Lorr A, B and I and Gorham 5) and a "disorganization" portion of less creatinine excretion with more conceptual disorganization (Lorr K and Gorham 3). The "deterioration" portion appears to primarily reflect the responses of the nonparanoid schizophrenics who had the lowest activity levels on the Lorr D and Gorham 1, were the most withdrawn (Lorr I and Gorham 5), most compliant (Lorr H), had the greatest motor disturbance (Lorr G) and were the most depressed (Gorham 4) of all the patients.

TABLE VII. 24-HOUR URINARY CREATININE CORRELATIONS WITH PSYCHIATRIC VARIABLES

Variable	All Subjects		Schizophrenics		Nonschizophrenics	
	100r	P	100r	P	100r	P
Lorr A						
depression vs. excit.	16	--	27	.01	4	--
Lorr B						
compliance vs. resist.	-25	.01	-27	.01	-20	.05
Lorr F						
perceptual distort.	-22	.05	-26	.05	-15	--
Lorr G						
motor disturb.	-20	.05	-27	.01	- 6	--
Lorr I						
withdrawal	33	.001	48	.001	22	.05
Lorr K						
concep. disorg.	-28	.01	-38	.001	-18	--
Gorham 1						
activity	18	--	22	.05	2	--
Gorham 2						
anxiety	-15	--	-21	.05	- 4	--
Gorham 3						
mental disorg.	-35	.001	-44	.001	-22	.05
Gorham 5						
interpersonal relations	-28	.01	-44	.001	- 5	--
Reaction time						
standard delay	35	.001	48	.001	4	--
Reaction time						
variable delay	33	.001	44	.001	7	--
Age	-20	.05	-25	.05	-15	--
Hospitalization	-25	.05	-34	.001	- 5	--

df = all patients 198-205; schizophrenics 98-105; nonschizophrenics 81-85.

On the other hand, the "disorganization" portion of these correlations seems mainly due to contributions from the paranoid schizophrenics although the nonparanoid schizophrenics move in a similar direction. These two portions, of course, are intercorrelated to some extent, mental disorganization (Gorham 3) correlating with both withdrawal (Lorr I, $r = -0.666$, $P < 0.001$ for schizophrenics and $r = -0.486$, $P < 0.001$ for nonschizophrenics) and depression (Lorr A, $r = -0.255$, $P < 0.05$ for schizophrenics and not significant for nonschizophrenics).

Urinary creatinine also significantly decreases with increasing age and increasing length of hospitalization. The age correlation might be expected on the assumption that creatinine levels follow muscle mass and that muscle mass declines with age. However, the age correlation was only statistically significant for schizophrenics and, indeed, only for nonparanoid schizophrenics ($r = -0.262$, $P < 0.05$) when subgroups were compared, although other groups showed a trend in the same direction. Further, groups did not differ in age (Table VIII), and muscle mass measures (lean body weight, calf girth, etc.) were not age correlated among the nonparanoid schizophrenics, so that the relationship between creatinine and age among nonparanoid schizophrenics is not due to a simple age-dependent decrease in muscle mass.

TABLE VIII. COMPARISONS OF AGE AND HOSPITALIZATION

	Age (yrs.)	Hospitalization (months)
	Mean ± S.D.	Mean ± S.D.
Schizophrenics	35.7 ± 8.2	54.4 ± 77.4
Paranoids	35.6 ± 7.8	32.9 ± 62.2
Nonparanoids	35.9 ± 8.6	68.3 ± 83.3
Nonschizophrenics	35.6 ± 10.1	15.8 ± 29.4
CBS	38.2 ± 10.9	19.8 ± 34.1
Non-CBS	33.8 ± 9.6	14.4 ± 2.7

Hospitalization
Nonparanoid schizophrenics vs. paranoids	$F = 5.5$ $P < 0.05$
Nonparanoid schizophrenics vs. CBS	$F = 9.1$ $P < 0.01$
Nonparanoid schizophrenics vs. nonschizophrenics other than CBS	$F = 20.7$ $P < 0.001$
Schizophrenics vs. nonschizophrenics	$F = 19.4$ $P < 0.001$

Although the groups did not differ in age, the nonparanoid schizophrenics were hospitalized longer than any other group and, again, this population accounted for most of the correlation between creatinine and hospitalization ($r = -0.353$, $P < 0.01$). It is of incidental interest that hospitalization and age were intercorrelated for both paranoid schizophrenics ($r = 0.382$, $P < 0.05$) and nonparanoid schizophrenics ($r = 0.460$, $P < 0.001$) reflecting the iceberg phenomenon in mental hospitals of a large static population block beneath a more rapidly overturning patient population.

Taken together, then, these results suggest a deterioration, particularly among the nonparanoid schizophrenics, which increases with hospitalization and age and which is accompanied by a declining excretion of creatinine without leading to significant changes or group differences in muscle mass measurements.

The possible significance of these findings to studies attempting to differentiate diagnostic group on the basis of urinary excretion of some product is indicated by the correlation matrix on Table IX.

TABLE IX. 24-HOUR URINARY CREATININE CORRELATIONS WITH BIOCHEMICAL VARIABLES

Urinary variables	All Subjects		Schizophrenics		Non-schizophrenics	
	100r	P	100r	P	100r	P
Volume 24 hr	35	.001	48	.001	28	.01
Sodium 24 hr	42	.001	51	.001	30	.01
Potassium 24 hr	21	.05	47	.001	- 4	--
5-hydroxyindoleacetic acid 24 hr	46	.001*	59	.001	32	.05‡
Epinephrine 24 hr	5	-- *	23	.05+	-12	-- ‡
Norepinephrine 24 hr	12	-- *	38	.01+	- 8	-- ‡
Serum phosphorous mg %	- 9	--	-32	.01	10	--

df for all patients 180-206; schizophrenics 92-105; nonschizophrenics 74-85 unless otherwise specified.

* df = 120-132
+ df = 60 and 62
‡ df = 52 to 58

It can be seen that a number of measures correlate with urinary creatinine, particularly among schizophrenics. Some of these, when expressed as a rate, differ between diagnostic populations, but when expressed on a creatinine basis, fail to do so. Perhaps the best example of this is urinary potassium. Schizophrenics and nonschizophrenics differed in 24 hour urinary excretion (Table IV) but the potassium creatinine ratio was 1.89 for schizophrenics and 2.04 for nonschizophrenics and these two numbers are not statistically different.

Comments

In its simplest terms the analysis of the relationship of urine volume and urinary creatinine to other variables seems an important step in separating primary phenomena from epiphenomena and in deciding upon the appropriate units for the expression of urinary constituents. Such an analysis does not obviate the findings, however, but rather helps in explaining them. To know that urinary epinephrine, for example, correlates both with urine volume and urinary creatinine and that expression of urinary epinephrine as a rate suggests differences between populations, expression in proportion to creatinine diminishes the diagnostic difference, and expression as a concentration eliminates it, suggests that urine volume is more likely to be the critical variable in the population difference than is epinephrine. Such an analysis also permits some reanalysis and, perhaps, reconciliation of conflicting reports in the literature, particularly where different basal units are employed. The difference in urine volume remains, however, and its cause may be as trivial as a relationship between water intake and activity or as profound as altered antidiuretic hormone secretion accompanying a pituitary disturbance.

The results also stress the need to characterize the populations examined. The correlations between creatinine excretion, age and hospitalization among nonparanoid schizophrenics, for example, suggest that a creatinine correction inappropriately applied to a compound excreted in a creatinine-independent manner might lead to misinterpretations when a chronic nonparanoid schizophrenic population is compared to controls. Again, the creatinine change may be the source of the difference rather than the compound tested. The basis for the group specific age correlation, however, is unexplained and may be of importance.

An attempt has been made to illustrate the importance of the basal measure in interpreting metabolite excretion and only those relationships pertinent to the role of time, urine volume and creatinine as basal measures have been presented. However, urine volume and creatinine are also variables in their own right. Although not directly relevant to the present topic, interesting and significant relationships between them and autonomic, psychological, social and psychiatric variables have been found and will be explicated elsewhere.

Summary

Cross-correlations between urine volume, urinary creatinine, and psychiatric and biochemical variables were examined to assess their relevance to the clinical disease and to determine appropriate units for expression of urinary variables. Schizophrenics and nonschizophrenics were found to differ in mean 24-hour urine volume and in day urine volume. Further, several urinary constituents appeared to be excreted in a volume dependent manner and diagnostic populations also differed in the 24-hour, or day excretion of some of these constituents. It was suggested that part of the population differences resulted from employing the units of rate rather than concentration in cross-comparisons of such volume dependent excretions, thereby reiterating the differences in urine volume in a more hidden form. The group differences in urine volume appeared to reflect activity level.

Schizophrenics and nonschizophrenics did not differ in urinary creatinine levels although some differences were found between subgroups. Despite the absence of strong diagnostic differentiation, urinary creatinine correlated with a number of psychiatric features among schizophrenics. Urinary creatinine also correlated with muscle mass measurements although the correlations only accounted for a fraction of the variance. Correlations between creatinine and other urinary constituents were found and the use of creatinine as a basal measure is discussed.

References

1. GERARD, R. W. The nosology of schizophrenia. Am. J. Psychiat. 120, 16, 1963.
2. GERARD, R. W. and MATTSSON, N. B. The classification of schizophrenia. In The Diagnostic Process, JACQUES, J. A., (Editor), The University of Michigan, Ann Arbor, Michigan, 1963.
3. GERARD, R. W. Nosology of Schizophrenia: a cooperative study. Behav. Sci. 9, 311, 1964.
4. YUWILER, A. Psychopathology and 5-hydroxyindoleacetic acid excretion. J. Psychiat. Res. 3, 125, 1965.
5. KINGSLEY, G. R. and SCHAFFER, R. R. Creatinine. In Standard Methods in Clin. Chem., Vol. 1, REINER, M. (Editor), p. 55, Academic Press, New York, 1953.
6. UDENFRIEND, S., TITUS, E. and WEISSBACH, H. The identification of 5-hydroxy-3-indoleacetic acid in normal urine and a method for its assay. J. Biol. Chem. 216, 499, 1955.
7. EULER, U. S. von, and FLODING, I. Fluorimetric estimation of noradrenaline (NA) and adrenaline (A) in urine. Acta Physiol. Scand. 33 Suppl. 118, 57, 1955.
8. GING, N. S. Extraction method for colorometric determination of phosphorous in microgram quantities. Analyt. Chem. 28, 1330, 1956.
9. LORR, M. Multidimensional scale for rating psychiatric patients. Vet. Admin. Technical Bulletin TB 10-507, 1953.
10. OVERALL, J. E. and GORHAM, D. R. The brief psychiatric rating scale. Psychological Reports 10, 799, 1962.

A. Yuwiler, Ph.D., Veterans Administration Center, Wilshire and Sawtelle Blvds.,

Los Angeles, California 90073

SYNOPSIS OF BIOLOGICAL AND CLINICAL DATA IN THE RESEARCH OF SCHIZOPHRENIA

O.H. ARNOLD and H. HOFF

INTRODUCTION: The last decade has brought us many new biological data in the research of Schizophrenia. The following groups have been set up (HOFMANN, 1963):

BIOLOGICAL DATA : Of carbohydrate and phosphate metabolism;
Of the biogenic amines and their metabolites;
Of hormone metabolism and of plasma proteins

PHARMACOPSYCHIATRIC DATA:

NEUROPHYSIOLOGICAL DATA.

The present difficulties to judge these results based on 1.the problem to control and copy new techniques. 2. The necessary congruence of the clinical material 3. The transposition of biological data into the clinical concept of schizophrenia.

There is no doubt that the pure collecting of data without potentially researchable hypothesis is unusable for research of schizophrenic illness process. Of course it is admissible in the first step to merely collect unprejudiced data, e.g. with the new technical methods. But the results remain meaningless or in the best case take the position of epiphenomena until the investigator takes a certain standpoint, thereby stating his working hypothesis. As an example of the possible arrangement of biological data in general clinical research we present the following table of the diagnostic process used for psychic disease.

It is hereby evident that in the taking of a case history not only the experience of the observer but also his evaluation, dependent on his standpoint, and finally his thought-mechanisms attributable to a certain psychiatric school of thought, already play a role in the first step of objective realisation of the patient. These factors will always colour the case history.

The process (with which the primary experience interacts thereby becoming a phenomenon) is on the other hand not unaffected by the observer. The manner in which the patient's manifest symptoms affect

the observer are naturally set back to the patient. Neither is the
co-action of simultaneous and often seen symptoms into a syndrome
a purely empirical achievement since subjective values of the observer
will also be incorporated. Only when biological laws can causally explain a syndrome, thereby denoting the syndrome as such, will the
subjective motive lease to play a role. Unfortunately, however, when
a group of symptoms must be expanded into a nosological entity, value
judgements, experiences and the school of thought of the observer will
play a role in the modus operandi of the diagnosis.

This table shows quite clearly how important biological data can be
in the research of a clinical presentation when they are properly rated.

Biological data: Because of this the collection of biological data
assumes such great importance in schizophrenia research. We have
shown, however, that the choice of data will always be primarily based
on a working hypothesis derived from single observation or multiple
experiences. For instance if we start from the classic observation
of possible toxic factors in the body fluids of certain schizophrenics,
our data will concern the composition of these body fluids. With the
development of the proper methods it is now in fact possible to achieve
agreement that the possible toxic factor is a certain protein fraction
(FROHMANN 1967, GOTTLIEB 1967, BERGEN 1967, PENELL 1967,
HEATH 1966, a.o.). Nevertheless, general criteria concerning the
gathering of these biological data are necessary: as in all gathering
of data we dare not forget that in picking single values out of a complete system we distort the system itself by the removal of that fact.
The better each unit of data fits into the system, the more each indivi
-dual unit is worth in itself. By way of example, by examining carbohydrate phosphate metabolism using isolated groups of ganglion cells
and the metabolically assoicated glia in the human (e.g. with the help
of bioptic techniques) the technically necessary operations will distort
the complete system to such an extent that we can only expect weak
data, even if we work with histo-chemical microtechniques. By contrast erythrocyte in a physiological milieu, with its relatively few
metabolic possibilities when compared to other body cells, presents
a smaller and more completely closed system, enabling us to gain
more consistent and meaningful data (ARNOLD a.HOFMANN, 1962,
1963, 1966, 1967, 1968).

With regard to the methods of collecting biological data about schizophrenia it has been found that spontaneously given data i.e. data given

without pharmacologic or neurophysiologic aid, have been of little
value over the years. On the other hand the comparison of spontaneous data with standardised (intentional and reproducible) data
has become very important. Noteworthy are e.g. inquiries with the
help of neurophysiological stimulation techniques,, sleep -wake
studies, the exploration of various sleeping states, and finally our
own method of standardised stimulation of the carbohydratephosphate
metabolism through succinate stress. There is no doubt that with
the refinement of techniques the collection of spontaneous data in
schizophrenia research will prove fruitful (the technique of the combined implantation of multiple electrodes and chemitrodes). DEL-
GADO, 1968).

The question of the constancy of the data on a single patient in a
longitudinal series gains increasing importance with both variations.
Only when the observer tests his data for constancy and variation as
well as the variation in the examination conditions can his results be
verified. We are obliged, however, to mention that the specialised
techniques in schizophrenia research have become increasingly complicated - perhaps because the gathering of spontaneous data was so
long fruitless. Therefore it must be remembered that not only the constancy of the variation of data must be analysed for verification, but
also individual instruction of the verifier in the specific techniques involved is often necessary in the laboratories of the first researcher.
The question of Materialkongruenz shall be dealt with below.

Our previous experience with biological data in the research of
schizophrenia generally show quite clearly that we are dealing in each
case with parameters of isolated systems which has been removed from
the whole complex. Therefore biological research of schizophrenia
can be classified as parameter research.

In the question of extraction of hard data we must remember this
fact, because parameters always signify merely isolated moments in
a steady state flux and are therefore indexes of modes of regulation
(BERTALANFFY, 1950). It is such a complex task to integrate the
regulation conditions, and thereby the regulation mechanisms and the
regulators themselves, that we may not a priori classify parameter
data as hard data. This is also true in effect for values won with
neurophysiological techniques, which of course are nothing more than
having recorded the electron flow as the observable concomitant mo--
lecular phenomena (ITIL, 1964). The application of specific theoretical principles "Regelkreisprinzip" (self conditioning and regulating
system, feedback system) have not simplified the use of parameter

data in schizophrenia research (this has, however, found limited
use in the depressive diseases). The naming of regulative processes as "Ablauf vegetativer Programme in eineme vermaschten
Netzwerk" points up the deficiencies of interpreting parameter
data quite clearly (SELBACH, 1963). Only where a cross over point
can be demonstrated in a steady state flux can the result be considered one step closer to the system of regulators and even to their here-
ditarily preformed form including their subsidiary enzyme system.
The previously (ARNOLD a. HOFMANN, 1962) found disposition factor in schizophrenics and their otherwise healthy families also represents a parameter, but on a cross over point. Therefore its value
is independent of prevailing conditions and completely independent of
any other regulatory factors. Necessary significance of data is based
on all of these partial aspects, but it should be mentioned that the significance of data is only evident after mathematical and/or statistical
analysis. On the other hand we dare not forget the pitfalls of mathematical or statistical analyses: logic will sometimes show us that
such analysis cannot be true.

When the above mentioned criteria of data gathering (consistency,
technical verification, parameter data)(und dazu Materialkongruenz
and Materialkonstanz) are not given to begin with, the results of statistical manipulation merely mean that the manipulation of the input
data is in itself significant, however, not the value thereof in conjunction with the expected results.

Clinical data: The cardinal problem in the collection of clinical
data is the diagnostic constancy of the material. If in schizophrenia
research one does not stand on the standpoint that one is dealing with
a homogeneous disease, i. e. , a qualitatively specific aberration of
life style, one is not freed of precise working hypothesis. It must
therefore be demanded that the biological data of the material be veri-
fiably in accord with a specific physical pattern of behaviour. This is
in fact the case when one says that one is examining the correlation between certain biological data and a certain social misanthropy, aggressive behaviour or general emotional disturbance. Here, however, one
distances oneself from the classic and also generally accepted modern
definition of schizophrenia. On the other hand such an inquiry is certainly experimentally interesting. To return to the theme at hand, the
collection of clinical data concerning the disease of schizophrenia per
se, we are confronted with a further important problem: are we confronted with one single, homogeneous biological modification or are
there multiple qualitatively different modifications. Recent research

into schizophrenia in Scandinavia, Central Europe, Russia and here
in Austria tends towards the acceptance of two basic types: Nuclear
schizophrenia and the so-called 'random types'. (STRÖMGREN,
1967) Among the many studies found in the literature we draw specific attention here to our own works where we show that many other
psychoses may mimic schizophrenic symptoms. To this end we have
used horizontal and longitudinal studies, plus hereditary factors in
order to differentiate the parameter of the disposition factor in our
biochemical system. The following table lists the nuclear groups of
schizophrenia and the 'synonym mimicking' ("phenokopierende")
psychoses based on our own studies. (ARNOLD a. HOFMANN, 1967)
The collection of clinical data should, with consideration of such experience, contain the following details:

1. Hereditary data, according to ascendancy, side chains of ascend-
   ance, siblings, collateral lines, direct and branched descendance.
   Here it is not enough to merely list the manifest psychic disease in
   each case, it is furthermore of importance to collect data on somatic
   illness, in addition to the collection of personality and social data.

2. Personality data. The collection of data from psychodynamic
   (psychoanalytic) aspects is only one part of the picture albeit an
   important part of a correct biographic picture. The somatic case
   history is every bit as important as personality development and
   social development.

3. Social data in the following descending hierarchy; family unit, social
   environment, Lebensraum, race, nationality.

4. Existential data, membership in a religious group and/or sect, to
   a political or philosophical group. Of special importance, however,
   are such subtle data, which only appear as the result of an existential analysis, such as the personal relationship to Dasein, to life and
   death, and to specific social and cultural problems, and the resulting
   side aspects of life, e.g. the question of secondary occupations,
   hobbies previous emotional experience, and affective relationships
   to certain data of social, cultural or political development.

The necessity of making a congruent and comparable material as the
bases for the harvest of biological data forces one at this point to a
'diagnosis-for-the-present', as a working label for the qualitative unity
of the material. From the collection of psychically abnormal symptoms
we arrive at first at the diagnosis of syndrome in the present profile.
The syndrome can, via the group of symptoms, be immediately translated into the nosological diagnosis, arriving finally at a profile diagnosis
of the disease.

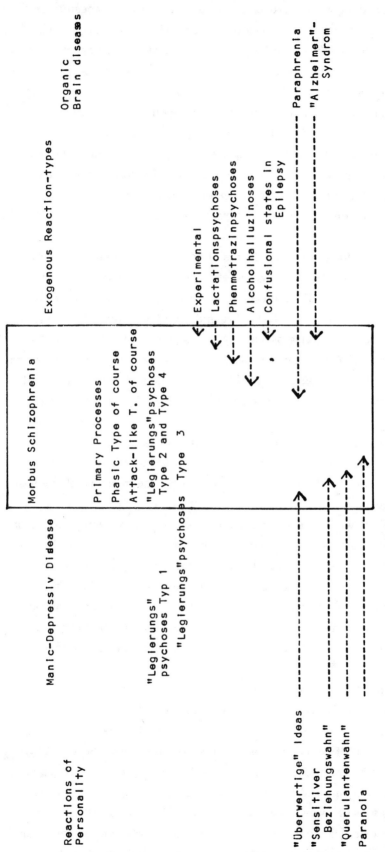

Paranoia a. Paraphrenia acc. BERNER 1967, "Leglerungspsychose" acc. ARNOLD, GASTAGER a. HOFMANN 1965
The hands stand for average frequency

In the same way a syndrome can be built up to the repeated profile studies first to a group of symptoms and then to a diagnosis.
We have now arrived at a longitudinal diagnosis. For example, our
own study of five hundred schizophrenics: The comparison of the profile diagnosis with a control examination made nine years later, and
the resultant longitudinal diagnosis, showed that six per cent of the
profile diagnoses differed from the longitudinal diagnoses. We believe this to be an optimum result which is in part explainable by the
fact that roughly two-thirds of the material at the time of the first
profile diagnosis had already been diagnostically recorded at an even
earlier date (an average of 7 years prior to the study). (ARNOLD, 1955,
1963)

From a study of random forms of schizophrenia using longitudinal
controls there was a divergenge of nineteen percent with a control
after five years. The method of case history taking and the translation of symptoms into data is always the decisive point. Middle Euro-
-pean, German talking psychiatry works predominantly with a "Merk-
malregister" (rating scale) based on classic psychopathology (Jaspers,
Bleuler, Kurt Schneider). Russian and Scandinavian psychiatry follows
the same pattern. American psychiatry generally uses other Merkmals-
kataloge. However, we would like to emphasise the impression which
we have received at international symposia: As far as the nuclear
groups of schizophrenia are concerned, it seems that experienced psychiatrists from all over the world are in a large measure of diagnostic
concordance. (HOFF, 1956)

The following exceptions are taken against the systematic usage of
the codification of symptoms: Position, rating, experience and school
of thought of the examiner all play an active role and lead to miss manipulations of selection of the material ("Auslesefreiheit"). Furthermore the selective process of "elements" (i.e. fictive constructed
parts) within the unreproductable "Ganzheit" of a certain personality
interferes into the structure and dynamic dimension of this personality.

A codification of symptoms has nevertheless prevailed, because this
method alone yields data which can automatically be further used. The
uncertainty factor in the Manipulationsprozess for the gathering of symptoms is nullified as much as possible by interviews. Several psychiatrists gather the information either independently or in a discussion
group. This method is either substituted by or supplmented through
a questionnaire which the patient himself fills out. Furthermore projective tests and achievement tests are used, behaviour observation is
carried out by people from the family circle, other groups, by trained

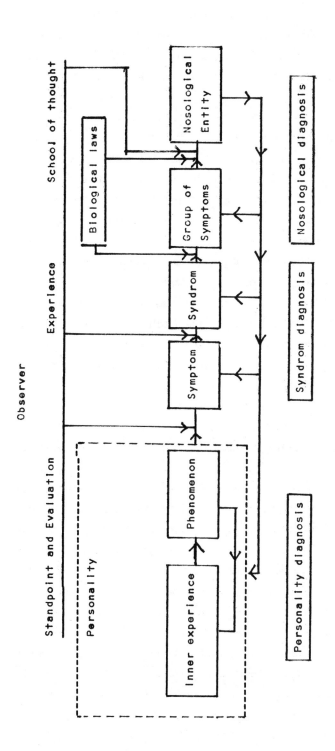

personnel of the clinic and the hospital and finally by doctors.

It is interesting to note that in countries where schizophrenia is a fairly narrow term (Scandinavia, Central Europe, Russia) priority is given to the unsystematic exploration by the experienced psychiatrist at the bedside; in places where 'schizophrenia' is a fairly mute term, the methods of Merkmalkataloge, questionnaire multiple diagnosis and group diagnosis as well as organised behaviour observation is more popular.

Discussion and Synopsis; Before any connection is made between biological and clinical data one must be sure of the meaning concerning the biological data. Only those biological figures that show heretically and constitutionally dispositions can be brought into connection with any type of courses or subgroups of schizophrenia as they must remain constant, independent of the actual cross- section of symptomatology. Even more than they must be related to the clinical data concerning healthy and ill members of family back-ground of the examined patients. In opposition all the other biological data have to be compaired separately with clinically well-defined actual manifestations of schizophrenia because they compair with values within parameters of regulative actions also. Here it definitely depends on symptomatology in time of examination, on syndrom time and type of course and finally on the special subgroup of schizophrenia. Therefore one should include all stages and types of courses as well as subgroups of schizophrenia in the examination-material. Furthermore it seems to be necessary to elect the material according to the spontaneous distribution of types of schizophrenia.

Making a connection between biological, clinical and psychopathological data we have to use all methods of modern statistics to find conditions (variation and correlation analysis, factor analysis, Cluster-method a.s.o.). The more data one can recognize in both separated series the more difficult the comparison becomes of course but the methods of statistical procedures are promising. On the other hand their capacity for archivment must not be overjudged as we would like to show with an example of our own work. Our material consists of 365 schizophrenics, family members of schizophrenics, normal control persons and representative of other psychiatric illness. 130 biological and clinical psychiatric data were picked up and examined using a computer on the type IBM 360-30 (K 32). This type of analysis was primarily not a great help. In fact certain adaptations of the rating program was necessary according to the various parts of results on time to time. This denotes above all that one is on new ground in the method of working out of biochemical

data and its correlation to psychiatric data. At the present time we
see a rapid development and therefore continuously demand corrections (ARNOLD a. HOFMANN, 1968). The logical interpretation of
these connections always remains difficult. Above all, we must
keep in mind that biological data from a system may not be explained principally by psychiatric data, just as the psychiatric data
may not be explained by the biological data.
The relations between both these systems can be interpreted at the
level of laws of structures (Ordnungsentsprechungen) only. Method-
ologically corresponding step for step interpretation should be aimed
for. Then the working hypothesis may be verified probably. An example of our own examination will show this: According to the old
clinical approach in hereiditary back-ground of schizophrenics there
must be schizothyme or schizoide personalities numbered in the foreground. Recently we found that a statistically significant correlation
exists between schizothyme personality structures and a certain regu-
lation-type within the carbohydrate metabolism: The so called asthenic
regulation type reigns. On the other hand we found that this regulation
type in no way shows a statistically significant relation to schizophrenia.
In fact we found that this high significancy applies only for our disposition factor demonstrable as the increase of concentration of ADP and
the decrease of ATP/ADP-quotient after succinate within a Erythrozyts-
plasma-system (p under 0, 0001). This disposition factor varies completely free and independent of the asthenic regulations type. The following correction of the hypothesis was necessary at this point: The schizo-
thyms in the hereditary back ground of schizophrenia are not the carriers of genetic dispositions but the following question results: How does
this possession of a certain regulation tendency interfere with manifestation and course of schizophrenia. In a group of 27 clinically and bio-
chemically examined families consisting of 104 members 95 had the disposition factor. With regard to manifest schizophrenia the percentage
of cykloids in this group was 12.7% of schizothymics though 52, 5%! Between schizothymic personality and asthenic regulation type on one hand
and the tendency of attack-like or continuous progressive type of schizophrenia on the other hand a statistically significant correlation existed
on a medium level. In the hypothesis the following question therefore
rises up: How can one imagine the connection between asthenic regulation and the possession of disposition factor with regard to the manifestation of schizophrenia. Therefore the relevant biochemic examinations
point to the fact, the human beings with asthenic regulation in carbohydrate

metabolism tend to a certain pathway within the distribution of energy-
processes. This is a tendency to shift the energy transport from glycolysis to HMP-shunt (Hexose-Monophosphat-Shunt) under stress situations. That can be interpreted as an inappropriate reaction, because
energy reserves in the energy low-run of the shunt disappear inspite
of a stress situation. At the present time the hypothesis is confronted
with experimental methods with the aim to test enzymatic equipments
and regulating mechanisms including their subsidary enzymes(ARNOLD
a.HOFMANN, 1968). At the same time the example shows how one
could proceed to put in biological data with a certain value (Stellenwert) in the pathogenesis of schizophrenia. Merely one must be satisfied to define single mechanisms which can not be seen on a specific
order within the general mode of action. This is exactly the meaning
of synopsis. Analysing the pathogenesis of schizophrenia,the often repeated confrontation of the results from time to time in both series of
biological and clinical data must be pointed out as the possible optimum.
As we were already able many years ago to say that the pathogenesis of
schizophrenia must be multifactorial, so we have to be content with an
outline (ARNOLDa.HOFF, 1958): hereditary disposition, personality,
psychodynamic and familial development and social milieu become in
the system the value of factors of partial causality. The synopsis between new biological and clinical data should be a new way of research
in schizophrenia not only for verification but also in interpretation of
specific relations within partial causality within the system of pathoge-·
nesis of schizophrenia. The obtainment of further data in both series will
be helpful only under exact conditions of operational criteria. The
method of synopsis seems to support us to realise further details of
pathogenesis of schizophrenia and therefore new therapeutic possibilities.

REFERENCES

Altschule, M. , Henneman, D. , Holliday, P. , und Goncz, R. Carbohydrate metabolism in brain disease. Arch. intern. Med. 99, 22 (1957).

Arnold, O. H. Untersuchungen zur Frage des Zusammenhanges zwischen Erlebnisvollzug und Kohlehydrat-Stoffwechsel Wien. Z. f. Nervenheilk. X, 1 (1954).

Arnold, O. H. Schizophrener Prozess und schizophrene Symptom-gesetze Wien, Maudrich (1955).

Arnold, O. H. An attempt to form a bridge from the schizophrenic manifestations to Heredogenetics. The Chemical Concepts of Psychosis, New York, Mc. Dowell-Obolensky (1958).

Arnold, O. H. Die Therapie der Schizophrenie Stuttgart: Hippo-krates (1963).

Arnold, O. H. Der Beitrag biochemischer Untersuchungen zum Stellenwert schizophrener Symptomatik, Kranz Ed. : Pharmako-psychiatrie und Psychopathologie, Stuttgart: Thieme (1967).

Arnold, O. H. Zur Theorie des Morbus Schizophrenia. Wien. Z. Nervenheilk. XXV 2-4 (1967).

Arnold, O. H. Ein Beitrag zur Frage: Alkoholhalluzinose und schizophrene Enzymopathie, Donau-Symposium, Wien, in press (1968).

Arnold, O. H. Untersuchungen zum Erbgang des Morbus Schizo-phrenia. Wien. Klin. Wschr. 80, 45-46 (1968).

Arnold, O. H. , Gastager, H. und Hofmann, G. Klinische, psychopath-ologische und biochemische Untersuchungen bei Legierungspsychosen. Wien, Z. Nervenheilk. XXII, 4 (1965).

Arnold, O. H. und Hoff, H. Synthese in der Schizophreniefrage. Med. Klinik 53, 1-3 (1958).

Arnold, O. H. und Hoff, H. Wie weit ist eine Untergruppierung der Schizophrenie noch aktuell. Folia Psych. Neur. Nerlandica 61, 2 (1958).

Arnold, O. H. und Hoff, H. Psychiatry in Germany and Austria Bellak Ed. : Contemporary European Psychiatry, New York· Grove P. I. (1961).

Arnold, O. H. und Hofmann, G. Ergebnisse einer biochemischen Untersuchungsmethode zur Diagnostik schizophrener Psychosen und ihres Erbkreises. III. Weltkong f. Psychiatrie 613-618, Montreal (1962).

Arnold, O. H. , Hoff, H. und Hofmann, G. Zur Multifaktoriellen Genese der Schizophrenie. Schweiz. Arch. N. Psych. 91, 1 (1963).

Arnold, O. H. und Hofmann, G. Ergebnisse einer biochemischen Untersuchungsmethode in der Schizophrenie und ihres Erbhintergrundes Wien. Wschr. 75, 33-34 (1963).

Arnold, O. H. und Hofmann, G. Korrelation klinischer und biochemi-scher Daten bei Schizophrenen, IV. World Congress of Psychiatry, pro-ceedings, Exc. Med. I. C. S. 150 (1966).

Arnold, O. H. und Hofmann, G. Results of biochemical investigation in schizophrenics, 381-396. Correlation between biochemical and clinical data in schizophrenics. Walaas Ed. The Molecular basis of some aspects of mental activity. London: Acad. Press (1967).

Arnold, O. H. und Hofmann, G. Psychopathologische und biochemische Untersuchungen zur Gruppe der Phenmetratinpsychosen. VI. Int. Kongr. C. I. N. P. , Tarragona, in press (1968).

Arnold, O. H. und Hofmann, G. Zur operationellen Technik der Gewinnung und Verarbeitung psychischer. Daten. Wien: Holinek (1968).

Bellak, L. Ed.: Schizophrenia. New York, Logos Press (1958).

Benedetti, E. , Bleuler, M. , Kind, A. , und Mielke, F. Entwicklung der Schizophrenielehre seit (1941) Basel: Schwabe (1960).

Bergen, J. Possible relationships of plasmafactors to schizophrenia. Walaas Ed.: London, Logos Press (1967).

Berner, P. Das paranoische Syndrom. Monograph. Ges. Gebiet Psych. Neur. 110, Berlin: Springer (1966).

Bertalanffy, L. The theory of open system in physics and biology; Lancaster 23 (1950).

Biological Research in Schizophrenia, Academy of Medical Sciences of the USSR, Institut of Psychiatry, MOSCOW 1967.

Conrad, K. Die beginnende Schizophrenie. Stuttgart: Thieme (1959).

Delgado, J. Recent advances in neurophysiology. General Lectures, VI. Int. Congr. C. I. N. P. , Tarragona (1968).

Frohmann, C. Biochemical studies of a serum factor in schizo-phrenia, Walaas Ed.: The molecular basis of some aspects of mental activity, London: Academic Press (1967).

Gottlieb, J. The biological correlations of the serum factor in schizophrenia. Walaas Ed.: The molecular basis of some aspects of mental activity, London: Academic Press (1967).

Heath, R. Schizophrenia: Biochemical and physiologic aberrations. Intern. J. Neuropsychiat. 2. (1966).

Hoff, H. Lehrbuch der Psychiatrie Basel: Schwabe (1956).

Hoff, H. und Hofmann, G. Biochemische Befunde bei Schizophrenen und deren Familienangehorigen und ihre Bedeutung fur die Schizophrenie. Arch. Psych. Z. N. 211 (1968).

Hofmann, G. Experimentelle Grundlagen der multifaktoriellen Genese der Schizophrenie. Wien: Springer (1963).

Hofmann, G. Biochemische Forschungsrichtungen und ihr Aussagewert fur die Klinik der Schizophrenie. Wien. Z. Nervenheilk. XXIV, 1 (1966).

Hofmann, G. Stoffwechseluntersuchungen zum Pathomechanismus des exogenen Reaktions typs. Arzneimittelforsch. 16. (1966).

Hofmann, G. Operationelle Denkmodelle in einer Stoffwechselforschung bei psychiatrischen Krankheitsgruppen. Wien. Z. Nervenheilk. XXV, 2-4 (1967).

Itil, T.   Elektroencephalographische Studie bei endogenen Psychosen . . . .
Achmed. Said Matbaasi, Istanbul (1964).

Kety, S.   Biochemical theories of schizophrenia Int. J. Neuropsychiat.
1 (1965).

Lozovski, D.   Biochemical theories of schizophrenia Int. J. Neuropsychiat. 1 (1965).

Penell, R.   Biological properties of the blood serum of schizophrenic
patients. Biological research in schizophrenia, Moscow (1967).

Selbach, H.   Die endogene Depression als Regulationskrankheit.
Schweiz. Arch. Neur. 94 (1964).

Stromgren, E.   Psychiatrische Genetik. Psychiatrie der Gegenwart
I, 1 a Berlin: Springer (1967).

Walaas, O.   Ed.: Molecular basis of some aspects of mental activity,
London: Academic Press (1967).

O. H. Arnold, M.D., and H. Hoff, M.D.,

University of Vienna, Vienna, Austria

BIOCHEMICAL ASPECTS OF SCHIZOPHRENIA

ABRAM HOFFER

Diseases, diagnosed and treated by physicians, have been classified clinically, that is, on the basis of symptoms and signs grouped into syndromes, etiologically when the main causes are known and by more objective laboratory tests after a consensus is reached that there is a clear and specific relationship. Laboratory diagnosis being the most precise is most often preferred and as more becomes known about a disease may replace clinical and etiological diagnosis. A classic example is syphilis which until its spirochaete was seen in the microscope was diagnosed clinically. Later it was diagnosed etiologically and today serologically.

A method seldom used is diagnosis on the basis of response to treatment. When an appreciable proportion of patients respond to a particular chemical then there is no theoretical reason why it should not be classed as a disease responsive to this chemical. Diabetes mellitus could be defined as an insulin responsive disease. Every chemotherapy which works even if only on a proportion of cases, must somehow restore to normal some biochemical system. When two entirely different chemicals have a curative effect upon a disease then it is reasonable to hypothesize that each chemical acts upon a component of the same system. Thus, every chemical which works directs ones attention to certain chemical possibilities. When enough markers are known the final task of identifying the specific chemical process will be simplified enormously. It is this approach I will examine.

For the purpose of developing a treatment classification of schizophrenia, there is no need to expect that each treatment should cure every schizophrenic. It is enough that it helps the majority of patients. Since the natural recovery rate of acute schizophrenia unchanged in over two hundred years, is about 35% it seems reasonable that a treatment should help twice as many or about 75% before it can be examined as a specific treatment.

Only a small number of chemicals have been used for treating schizophrenia with recovery rates of over 75%. But additional criteria should be used to ensure that most chemicals used or reported in the literature as being effective are in fact specific treatments. The additional criteria are (a) the chemicals must have been used by several independent groups with equivalent results (b) the treatment must not be evanescent - thus electroconvulsive therapy is an excellent therapy for acute schizophrenics if one judges the response one month after treatment has been given. The results drop off to natural recovery rates after a year or more. (c) There must be a close association between absence of illness and maintenance medication, that is, when treatment is stopped the illness will reappear and when medication is resumed will disappear. (d) The chemicals must be relatively non toxic; its therapeutic benefit must overwhelmingly overweigh its toxicity.

The chemicals which in my opinion meet these criteria are the tranquilizers phenothiazines, and the member components of the pyridine nucleotide cycle. Chemicals which should be considered are the butyrophenones but little is known about their mode of action in the body. Treatments which are excluded are insulin coma not because it is not effective but because the outcome of treatment several years later is not better than natural recovery. For the same reason ECT is excluded.

The use of tranquilizers and components of the pyridine nucleotide cycle for treating schizophrenia arose independently of each other. In Saskatchewan Dr. H. Osmond and I began to use mega-vitamin doses of nicotinic acid and nicotinamide early in 1952. By mid 1952 we were able to report to the Saskatchewan Committee on Schizophrenia Research that out of eight acute patients given 3 to 10 grams per day all had recovered.

We immediately started the first blind experiment in psychiatry. Our first research in the fall of 1952 was a triple blind experiment conducted at the Munro Wing, General Hospital at Regina. Every patient admitted to this treatment center if diagnosed schizophrenic by his psychiatrist and the director of the ward was included in the study. After they were diagnosed they were evaluated for a period of about one week by the research psychiatrist and by psychologists who used a battery of objective psychological tests which seem irrelevant today.

Nursing observations were carefully made and recorded. Then each patient was placed at random into one of three treatment groups, placebo, nicotinic acid, and nicotinamide. Nicotinamide was used as a hidden control. The nicotinic acid flush usually betrays it has been given and this would have broken the code. None of the evaluating or treating staff, or nurses knew about the nicotinamide control. In several briefings for the entire staff they were informed nicotinic acid and a placebo would be used. Thus observant staff would assume every patient who flushed would be on nicotinic acid and every non flusher on placebo while in fact one half of the non flushers were receiving nicotinamide. We also hoped to rule out the vasodilation (flush) as a therapeutic variable.

All the patients were seen at least twice each week for formal psychotherapy. They were also given the best chemotherapy of the day which consisted of barbiturates, and morphine and its derivatives. The decision to give electroconvulsive therapy was made individually by the treating physician. Patients were given 1 gram of the vitamin or placebo three times each day for thirty-three days. Patients were informed they might flush so they would not be frightened.

After thirty-three days the patients were again evaluated by the same team using identical methods. If the patients were sufficiently improved they were discharged. If not, they were kept for additional treatment or committed to a nearby mental hospital.

After discharge they were seen at three month intervals by a follow-up worker who was not informed of the treatment code. If in the opinion of the follow-up worker the patient was clearly sick again, then the patient was examined by a psychiatrist.

I have gone into this early study in some detail because many uninformed physicians have claimed that no controlled studies were run with these vitamins.

The results of this study are given in Table I.

Table I

Results of the first double blind study using placebo, nicotinic acid and nicotinamide.

Group	Number	Number on ECT	Follow-up after one year, well
Placebo	10	6	3
Nicotinamide	11	7	9
Nicotinic acid	9	7	7

One third from each group received only psychotherapy. From
the placebo group of the three on psychotherapy none were well for
any period after discharge. Of the three who received psychotherapy
plus nicotinic acid, one was still well two and a half years later, the
second after three years and the third well on discharge relapsed in
the community. Of the four on psychotherapy plus nicotinamide one
was committed to a mental hospital, and the other three were still
well three years later. None of this group received the vitamin after
discharge.

Encouraged by these results and wishing to avoid premature claims
of efficacy we began our second double blind experiment in 1953 which
was terminated in 1957 after eighty-two schizophrenics had been treated.
The results of this second study using only nicotinic acid and placebo
(but informing the staff a hidden nicotinamide control was being used)
are given in Table II.

Table II

Comparison of placebo and nicotinic acid therapy.

Group	Number	Age	Number on ECT	Past treatment evaluation improved
Placebo	43	31.9	21	18
Nicotinic Acid	39	30.3	15	31

$$X^2 = 14, P < .001$$

Based upon these double blind studies, upon my own personal experience on over 1000 schizophrenics treated since 1952, upon corroborative studies by MacLean (on 1000 cases since 1957), Hawkins and
his group (on 1000 cases since 1966), Cott (on over 400 cases since
1966), Ward (on over 400 cases since 1966), and on a combined total
group of nearly 6000 cases evaluated by the committee on Therapy,
American Schizophrenia Foundation, (1968), I have concluded that
nicotinic acid and nicotinamide in doses of 3 to 30 grams per day are,
if not specific, closer to being specific than any other medication.

Using criteria for improvement which included number of days in
hospital after treatment, number of readmissions, condition in the
community, suicide rates, and independent evaluation by other physicians it is clear that these vitamins work. However, they work best
for early cases and most often must be combined with ECT or tranquilizers. As a general rule they are more effective in keeping patients well (in preventing relapse) than they are in getting them well.

See bibliography for published reports of megavitamin B-3 therapy.

The only other member of the pyridine nucleotide cycle studied is nicotinamide adenine dinucleotide (NAD).

Hoffer and Osmond (1966) gave eighteen patients(two alcoholics) one to two grams of specially capsulated NAD. This was enteric coated and suspended in an oily base so that the NAD was dispersed after four hours. If released in the stomach, NAD is quickly hydrolyzed. The results are shown in Table III.

Using an entirely different group of patients who were chronic deteriorated incarcerated patients and a different preparation which was impure and not adequately prepared Kline et al (1967) gave 1 gram NAD per day to twenty. None were improved clinically; a few were better on the HOD test.

Gallant et al (1966) gave NAD capsules, prepared by the same company which had supplied me, to a series of very chronic patients. None were improved.

So far no studies using active NAD properly prepared on acute or non deteriorated cases have been reported. It is not easy to work with NAD. McComb and Gay (1968) compared four different commercial preparations and reported they differed considerably in physical and chemical characteristics. Pfeiffer (1967) used the sensitive quantitative EEG to compare the NAD I used, Kline et al NAD and some he prepared. The NAD I used had strong activity, the Kline et al material hardly any.

Thus there is some evidence NAD is therapeutic at least for some schizophrenics.

The tranquilizers were introduced in 1954 and by 1957 were in general use because their therapeutic effect was often very dramatic. But even though it is known they are effective there is no general consensus how they act. Although some psychotherapists still believe the tranquilizers tranquilize the transference and so make patients more accessible to psychotherapy, I am convinced that if all tranquilizers were removed from the market there would soon be a mass exoduses of patients from the community back into the mental hospital and the psychiatric wards.

One of the more interesting properties of phenothiazine tranquilizers is their ability to maintain high NAD levels in livers of animals given nicotinamide, Burton (1960) et al (1958, 1960). Perhaps this is the basis of their tranquilizing effect. Nicotinamide and nicotinic acid have sedative properties as does NAD. Greengard & Quinn (1962) reported a relation between sedation and elevation of NAD.

Gholson (1966) concluded that there are two natural sources of NAD. The de novo pathway begins from tryptophan, the amino acid following a complex series of reactions catalyzed by pyridoxine. NAD is then rapidly hydrolyzed into its components. The nicotinamide in turn is deamidated to nicotinic acid which in turn is reconverted into NAD. This later reaction is the second source of NAD.

If we postulate that the pyridine nucleotide cycle must remain intact to prevent or treat schizophrenia the major and minor chemotherapies for schizophrenia become rational. Nicotinic acid, nicotinamide, and perhaps NAD are therapeutic because they restore the main function of the pyridine nucleotide cycle. The tranquilizers are effective because they increase NAD levels in tissues. Apparently tranquilizers block the methylation of nicotinamide to N-methyl nicotinamide. This removes pyridine molecules from the cycle. Excessive methylation of nicotinamide reported to be the case in schizophrenic blood by Buscaino (1966) would lead to a decrease in NAD synthesis.

Pyridoxine is required for the conversion of tryptophan into NAD. In its absence pellagra may develop. Children develop convulsions. Pyridoxine and the metabolites of tryptophan are receiving careful examination in the etiology of some forms of mental retardation. Several childhood schizophrenics appeared much improved when pyridoxine was added to their program.

There are no published reports of the effects of tryptophan on schizophrenic patients. Normal subjects given 10 grams in one dose suffered psychological changes in areas of perception and mood. Chronic alcoholics were not aware of any changes, Olson, Gursey, and Vester (1961). However, protein deficient diets would fail to provide enough NAD and should aggravate schizophrenia. Faurbye (1968) reported that reducing dietary intake of tryptophan provoked a flare up of hallucinations and delusions in schizophrenic patients.

Pellagra, of course, produces a psychiatric condition indistinguishable from schizophrenia unless clear cut skin changes are produced. The fortification of flour with nicotinamide in vitamin doses thus has been one of the greatest single preventive measures and has removed from psychiatry a disease which once accounted for ten percent of the admissions to some mental hospitals, as well as 10,000 deaths per year. For these reasons and for others which cannot be listed here, Hoffer and Osmond (1968) suggested that schizophrenia is an NAD deficiency

disease, a form of cerebral pellagra as described by Pauling (1968).
This hypothesis economically accounts for therapeutic effects of
nicotinic acid, nicotimamide, and NAD, for the tranquilizing effect
of some phenothiazines, for the importance of high protein diets in
treating schizophrenia.

Table III   Effect of NAD on some patients.

Experimental Conditions	Well	Much Improved	Improved	Sick
Before NAD	0	6	2	10
During NAD	11	3	4	0
After NAD	0	5	3	9

If we are correct then it follows that schizophrenia can by prevented
by placing all first order relatives of schizophrenics (parents, children,
and siblings) on one to three grams of nicotinamide or nicotinic acid
per day. I have already placed several hundred relatives who were
referred to me for treatment but were not schizophrenic on preventive
doses. So far hardly any have become schizophrenic. On the contrary,
over 90% become normal. I have not placed entire families on this
program as I do not believe this is indicated, provided members who
become disturbed are examined and treated early.

A better method would be to increase the fortification of flour so
that the average person would receive 1 gram of nicotinamide per day.
This quantity in bread and cereal products would not be detectable.
This would not establish a new principal as some is already being
added. Our hypothesis predicts that this kind of fortification would
within a few years markedly reduce the incidence and prevalence of
schizophrenia.

This line of reasoning suggests that the pyridine nucleotide cycle
plays a very important role in maintaining mental health and when it
becomes deficient serious cerebral functional changes appear. Schizophrenia may be considered a particularly malignant form of an NAD
deficiency disease.

Bibliography

Hoffer, A. American Schizophrenia Foundation, Committee on Therapy. Meeting.September, 1968, Twin Pines Hospital, Belmont, California.

Beebe, W. E. Schizophrenia and Nicotinic Acid. Read at Amityville Conference, Brunswick Hospital, New York, January 21, 22, 1967.

Burton, R. M. Inhibition of the nervous system and gamma aminobutryic acid. Ed. E. Roberts. Pergamon Press New York 1960.

Burton, R. M., Kaplan, N. O., Goldin, A., Leitenberg, M. Humphreys, S. R., & Sood, M. A. Effect of reserpine and promazine on diphosphopyridine nucleotide synthesis in liver Science 127, 30-32, 1958.

Burton, R. M., Kaplan N. O., Goldin, A., Leitenberg, M., & Humphreys, S. R. Interaction of nicotinamide with reserpine and chlorpromazine. III. Some effects on the diphosphopyridine nucleotide content in the liver. Archives of International Pharmacodynamics, 128, 260-275, 1960.

Burton, R.M. Salvador, A., Goldin, A. & Humphreys, S. R. Interaction of nicotinamide with reserpine and chlorpromazine. II. Some effects on the central nervous system of the mouse. Archives of International Pharmacodynamics, 128, 253-259, 1960.

Buscaino, G. A., Spadetta, V. & Carella, A. In Vitro Methylation of Nicotinamide: A Biochemical Test for Schizophrenia. Madrid: International Congress Psychiatry 1966.

Cott, A. A. Treatment of Ambulant Schizophrenics with Vitamin B-3 and relative hypoglycemic diet. J. Schizophrenia 1, 189-196, 1967.

Cott, A. A. Treatment of Schizophrenic Children. Schizophrenia In press 1969.

Denson, R. Nicotinamide in the treatment of schizophrenia. Diseases of the Nervous System 23, 167-172, 1962.

Faurbye, A. Role of Amines in etiology of schizophrenia Comp. Psychiat. 9, 155-177, 1968.

Galambos, M. Use of Nicotinic Acid for Treatment of some Adult Mentally Retarded Patients. Read at Amityville Conference, Brunswick Hospital, New York, January 22, 1967.

Gallant, D. M., Bishop, M. P., & Steele, C. A. DPN (NAD oxidized form): a preliminary evaluation in chronic schizophrenic patients. Current Therapeutic Research 8, 542-543, 1966.

Gholson, R. K. The pyridine nucleotide cycle. Nature, 212, 933-934, 1966.

Greengard, P. & Quinn, G. P. Metabolic effects of tranquilizers and hypophysectomy. Annals of the New York Academy of Sciences 96, 179-184, 1962.

Hawkins, D. R. Treatment of Schizophrenia based on the medical model. J. Schizophrenia 2, 3-10, 1968.

Herjanic, M., Moss-Herjanic, B., & Paul, W.K. Treatment of schizophrenia with nicotinic acid. J. Schizophrenia 1, 197-199, 1967.

Hoffer, A. Five California Schizophrenics. J. Schizophrenia 1, 209-220, 1967.

Hoffer, A. Niacin Therapy in Psychiatry. C. C. Thomas, Springfield, Ill. 1962.

Hoffer, A. Laboratory tests for following progress of schizophrenia. Dis.Nerv.Syst. 27, 466-469, 1966.

Hoffer, A. Treatment of Organic Psychosis with nicotinic acid. Dis. Nerv. Syst. 26, 358-360, 1965.

Hoffer, A. Nicotinic Acid: An adjunct in the treatment of schizophrenia. Am J. Psychiat. 120,171-173, 1963.

Hoffer, A. The effect of nicotinic acid on the frequency and duration of re-hospitalization of schizophrenic patients: a controlled comparison study. Int. J. Neuropsychiat. 2, 234-240, 1966.

· Hoffer, A. Treatment of Schizophrenia with a therapeutic program based upon nicotinic acid as the main variable. Proc. NATO Advanced Study Institute. Oslo, 1965.

Hoffer, A. Enzymology of Hallucinogens. Proc. Carl Neuberg Society Meeting. J. B. Lippincott, Phil.1966.

Hoffer, A., & Osmond, H. The Chemical Basis of Clinical Psychiatry. C. C. Thomas, Springfield, Ill. 1960.

Hoffer, A., & Osmond, H. Some schizophrenic recoveries, Dis. Nerv. Syst. 23, 204-210, 1962.

Hoffer, A., & Osmond, H. Scurvey and Schizophrenia. Dis. Nerv. Syst. 23, 273-285, 1963.

Hoffer, A., & Osmond, H. Treatment of schizophrenia with nicotinic acid (A ten year follow-up). Acta Psychiat. Scand. 40, 171-189, 1964.

Hoffer, A., & Osmond, H. How to Live with Schizophrenia. Canada: Ryerson Press, 299 Queen Street W., Toronto, Ontario.

Hoffer, A., Osmond, H., Callbeck, M. J., & Kahan, I. Treatment of Schizophrenia with nicotinic acid and nicotinamide. J. Clin. Exper. Psychopath. 18, 131-158, 1957.

Kline, N. S., Barclay, C. L. Cole, J. O., Esser, A. H. Lehmann, H., & Wittenborn, J. R. Controlled evaluation of nicotinamide adenine dinucleotide. Brit. J. Psychiatry 11, 731-742, 1967.

Kowalson, B. Metabolic dysperception: Its diagnosis and management in general practice. J. Schizophrenia 1, 200-203, 1967.

MacLean J. Ross. Clinical experiences and general impressions in the treatment of schizophrenia with nicotinic acid. Read at Amityville Conference, Brunswick Hospital, New York, January 21, 22, 1967.

McComb, R. B., & Gay, R. J. A comparison of reduced NAD preparations from four commercial sources. Clin. chem 14, 754-763, 1968.

Meiers, Robert L. Relative hypoglycemia in schizophrenia reactions. J. Schizophrenia 1, 204-208, 1967.

Olson, R. E., Gursey, D., & Vester, J. W. New England J. Med. 263, 1169-1174, 1960.

Osmond, H. Background to the niacin treatment. J. Schizophrenia. 1, 125-132, 1967.

Osmond, H., & Hoffer, A. Massive niacin treatment in schizophrenia. Review of a Nine Year Study. Lancet, 1, 316-320, 1962.

Osmond, H. & Hoffer, A. A Comprehensive Theory of Schizophrenia. Int. J. Neuropsychiat. 2, 302-309, 1966.

Pauling, L. Orthomolecular Psychiatry. Science 160, 265-271, 1967.

Robie, T. R. Cyproheptadine: an excellent antidote for niacin-induced hypothermia. J. Schizophrenia 1, 133-139, 1967.

Tobin, J. M. Treatment of schizophrenia with nicotinic acid: an overview. J. Schizophrenia 1, 182-188, 1967.

Ward, J. L. Treatment of neurotics and schizophrenics using clinical and Hod criteria. J. Schizophrenia 1, 140-149, 1967.

A. Hoffer, M.D., Ph.D., 800 Spadina Crescent East, Saskatoon, Canada

LONGITUDINAL STUDIES OF PERIODIC CATATONIA

LEIV R. GJESSING

In his textbook of Psychiatry of 1909 Kraepelin (1) gives an excellent description of periodic catatonic excitement.

"At shorter or longer intervals, often very few weeks, sometimes only every few years, there occur sudden confused states of excitement.....

The excitement is usually very abrupt in onset. After very slight warning signs - groundless laughter, glazed eyes, restless wandering - the patient from one day to the next, often in the middle of the night, becomes violently excited. Sometimes this may be limited to increased irritability, mood swings, restlessness and pressure of talk, but usually the condition gradually worsens, and may reach acute mania, accompanied often by delusions and hallucinations. There is a sudden fall in weight, sometimes 5 to 8 pounds in 24 hours (Fürstner). The excitement often lasts only a few days or weeks, more rarely, it continues for months and is then interrupted by a few days of calm. Generally the intervals are longer - a few weeks or months. The duration of the attacks may increase with time.

In women they are often associated with menstruation, the attack beginning simultaneously with the menses or shortly before, and lasting one or two weeks, usually followed by a somewhat longer period of freedom from symptoms ("menstrual insanity").

The period of calm usually begins as suddenly as the phase of excitement, although towards the end of the attack there is generally a slight lessening of confusion and restlessness. Recovery is instantaneous, though the patient is noticeably quiet, indifferent and dull, and as a rule does not have full insight into the nature of this illness; although he may remember many details quite well, he is inclined rather to view his disturbance as something quite innocuous, brought on by his environment, by his detention in hospital, etc. On the first day of tranquility he considers himself quite cured and presses for his discharge. Physically he seems to recover quickly, although during this interval his weight often remains lower than it was before he fell ill.

After a good many attacks there often occurs a fairly long, or lasting, remission. On the other hand the attacks may grow longer and be interrupted only by short periods of remission. A small number of cases eventually come to fluctuate regularly, over decades, between short periods of severe excitement and intervals of calm".

One of Kraepelin's patients showed a very regular, daily fluctuation between socially completely acceptable behavior and violent excitement, and this continued for at least ten years. "As a rule, however, it develops into a genuine mental illness, sometimes presenting more the features of simple feeblemindedness, with poverty of ideas, lack of judgment, apathy and weak will, or sometimes accompanied by lability and mannerism. In contrast to other forms, in which there was a preponderance of men, two-thirds of these patients were women, in whom the periodicity of sexual life obviously favors this kind of development". Kraepelin continues:

"I used to regard these cases as a form of manic-depressive insanity. There is no doubt that there are some manic-depressives whose attacks are of similarly short duration. However, the states of excitement now described, which occur at short intervals, often form only part of the course of an illness which otherwise clearly belongs to the dementia praecox group: moreover the condition that finally develops has the characteristic features of the disorder. These considerations have led me to change my mind. In addition the states of excitement, with their uniformity, their instinctive nature, and their poverty of ideas, are much nearer to dementia praecox than to mania. It should also be mentioned that periodic excitement is frequently seen in the final stages of dementia praecox. Finally one might argue that there are hereditary relationships between this and other forms of dementia praecox. One might therefore say that in the cases under discussion a feature of the illness, that generally does not appear until much later, here dominates the picture at a particularly early stage and to a particularly strong degree".

The first description of periodic catatonic stupor on the other hand was done by R. Gjessing in 1932 (2). The stupor cases are very rare compared to the excitement cases. The frequency of both types of periodic catatonia within the groups of schizophrenias is about 2-3 percent according to both Kraepelin and R. Gjessing.

In some periodic catatonic patients the pathophysiological picture synchronized with the clinical one. Changes in various functions investigated are in complete syntony. This type is called the synchronous-syntonous type (SS-type) and encompasses the nuclear group of regularly recurring periodic catatonic excitement of stupor.

Around this SS-type there are cases with less pronounced symptomatology and less sharp beginning and ending of the catatonic phases, but where the metabolic picture is similar. This type has been called dys-synchronous-dys-syntonous (dd). In addition there are also cases which are progressively more a-synchronous-a-syntonous (aa) in character. In this paper only the SS-type will be considered as they constitute the most regular and classical cases.

After a thorough clinical investigation and removal of any focal or general infection, the patients were trained to live in a metabolic ward on constant fluid diet and under constant environmental conditions. Daily recorded were mental state, pulse, temperature, weight and sleep. In additon the movements in the bed were registered by a seizmograph and the behavior of the patient through day and night was recorded by especially trained nurses. This represented the clinical background for pathophysiological studies.

In periods over weeks, months and even years different physiological and chemical investigations were carried out in 20 SS-types, 10 dd-types and 8 aa-types from 1925-1968. The following parameters were studied:

In urine: Total volume and specific gravity, total N in urine, urea, NH_3, SO_4, PO_4, Cl, Na, K, -CNS, creatinine, uric acid, urobiline, amino acids, phenolic acids and phenolic amines. Total N was also determined in feces, hair and nails in order to study the N-balance.

In blood: Urea, total N, blood sugar, hemoglobin, sedimentation rates, white cell count, differential count, protein-bound iodine, fatty acids and amino acids. In the cerebrospinal fluid also the amino acids.

Further on: blood pressure, basal metabolic rate, respiratory quotient, electro-encephalography, -cardiography, -myography, caloric nystagmus, pupilometry, Achilles tendon reflex time and reaction time on visual and auditory stimuli as well as liver tests, water loadings and loads with different vitamins and drugs, protein and sugar.

In the interval both the stuporous and the excited periodic catatonias are awake, fully orientated, able to help in the ward and read a little. They appear normal, but they lack in self-judgment and have no insight into their disease.

Somatically in the interval they are predominantly in a cholinergic vegetative state with low pulse frequency, low combustion, leucopenia and lymphocytosis and low fasting blood sugar. Towards the end of the interval cholesterol is increasing (3).

The transition into stupor may be instantaneous or last some hours, into excitement a day or two. Somatically the patients show vegetative lability with changing pulse frequency and varying width of the pupils. After a day or two the patients are stabilized in an adrenergic state.

The catatonic excitement is characterized by psychomotoric "catatonic" excitement together with a decreasing ability to concentrate and regression into infantile and primitive reactions. The excitement usually reaches its maximum in the first part of the psychotic phase and lessens thereafter gradually without a sharp ending.

In complete stupor the patient lies completely mute, negativistic and immobile in his bed in a petrified stiff position with no ability to get in contact with his surroundings.

Somatically both the excited and the stuporous patient are in an adrenergic phase with increased pulse frequency, increased blood pressure, moderate rise in temperature, changing mydriasis, increased BMR and protein bound iodine (4), increased fasting blood sugar, decreased diuresis and very low sedimentation rate. EEG and EKG are markedly changed (5). There is loss of appetite, constipation and retention of urine. The sleep is absent or very poor and the weight goes down. All the somatic manifestations are more pronounced in stupor than in excitement, but similarly present in both.

Balance studies disclosed a periodic retention and over-excretion of nitrogen. The peak of retention and over-excretion was independent of the psychotic phase. The over-excretion of N was mainly due to increased excretion of urea.

All the changes repeat themselves with nearly photographic accuracy from one period to another indicating a chain reaction. Most of the changes in the somatic field are within the normal limits but they are varying from one extreme to the other, from the highest to the lowest normal values.

All the signs and symptoms within the vegetative system varies synchrounously with the mental state. The psychotic symptoms begin at nearly the same time as the vegeatative state switches over from the cholinergic into the adrenergic phase. R. Gjessing emphasized that "Where the reversal is accomplished in a few hours, close and constant observation of the patient is most instructive. By bedside observation changes in the pupils, salivation, pulse, complexion, blood pressure, muscletone, humidity and temperature of the arms and feet can easily be followed and recorded.

It is as if an unseen hand were playing on the keyboard of the vegetative nuclei in the hypothalmus: First, as the prelude, single notes or simple two-note chords are played softly and from time to time fuller chords are coming from the cholinergic base register. Then the composition moves more towards th adrenergic-atonal, grouping, or florid and weighty - the two contrasting autonomic registers sound together or alternate until finally the individual melody of the reaction phase is established. It may all stem from stimulation of the autonomic centers, it may be humoral in nature, but from where remains an open question ..... Whether the stimulus which causes the autonomic reversal ends in excitement or in stupor may depend chiefly on the state of the end-organs and the intensity of the stimulus".

Today many different amines are in the focus of attention. Especially the phenolic and indolic amines are of special interest since some of their derivatives like dimethoxyphenylethylamine and bufotenine have hallucinatory properties. Several publications indicate their presence in the urine of schizophrenic patients.

We have studied the urine from periodic catatonia, both in stupor and excitement phases, and both without and with monoamineoxidase inhibitor, but we were unable to detect the above mentioned two amines (6).

We also studied the urinary excretion of metanephrine and nor-metanephrine. They were within normal limits in the interval but pathologically elevated during catatonic phases. The metanephrine had a marked peak during the first week of stupor whereas the nor-metanephrine was over-excreted during the whole psychotic phase which lasted 3-4 weeks with a maximum in the middle of the stupor period (7).

On monoamineoxidase inhibitor (MAO), however, the nor-metanephrine excretion increased even more in the interval than it did in the stupor without MAO, but without precipitating a psychotic phase. These findings are difficult to interpret. Is the increased excretion of normetanephrine mainly a result of the increased adrenergic state in the psychotic phase and only a symptom just as the psychotic manifestations?

If so, some other amines, peptides or other compounds, may be the stimuli which put the patient into this adrenergic and psychotic

state. MAO would elevate many amines, and among them normetanephrine, but probably not norephinephrine.

On the other hand we have found that reserpine and haloperidol
suppress or abolish the psychotic phase as well as over-excretion
of normetanephrine (8). Is this effect due to interference with the
storage function of catecholamines or does it interfere with the storage or function of some unknown disturbing compound?

Thyroxine given at the peak of N-retention mobilizes nitrogen
and causes a large over-excretion of nitrogen. If the patients are
kept on thyroid substance, after this thyroxine load, keeping the oxygen consumption slightly elevated, on + 10 to 15 %, many of them
recover completely as all the psychotic and pathophysiological symptoms disappear. The reason why is unknown.

Curt P. Richter (9) at Johns Hopkins University has created periodic behavior in rats by subtotal thyroidectomy, antithyroid drugs,
hypophysectomy or lesion in hypothalamus. This periodic running,
eating and drinking behavior was also abolished by thyroxine or thyroid substance.

This means that thyroxine or thyroid medication abolishes the
synchronized periodicity both in man and rats and they return to normal behavior. Withdrawal of thyroxine causes new periodic behavior.
In man this seems to indicate that the psychosis is latent and only
compensated by thyroxine.

References

1. Kraepelin, E.: Psychiatrie, Ein Lehrbuch fur Studierende und Arz-
te, Bd. 2, S. 234. 8. Aufl. I.A. Barth, Leipzig. (1909)

2a. Gjessing, R.: Beitrage zur Kenntnis der Pathopysiologie des katatonen Stupors. I. Mitteilung. Uber periodisch rezivierenden kataton-
en Stupor, mit kritischem Beginn und Abschluss. Arch. Psychiat. Nervenkr. 96, 319 (1932)

2b. Gjessing, R.: Beitrage zur Kenntnis der Pathophysiologie der katatonen Stupors. II. Mitteilung. Uber aperiodisch rezidivierend verlau-
fenden katatonen Stupor mit lytishem Beginn und Abschluss. Arch. Psychiat. Nervenkr. 96, 393 (1932)

2c. Gjessing, R.: Uber die Atiologie und Pathogenese der Schizophrenie.
Acta Psychiat. (Kbh.), 8, 373 (1933)

2d. Gjessing, R.: Beitrage zur Kenntnis der Pathophysiologie der katatonen Erregung. III. Mitteilung. Uber periodisch rezidivierende ka-
tatone Erregung, mit kritischem Beginn und Abschluss. Arch. Psychiat. Nervenkr. 104, 355 (1935)

2e. Gjessing, R.: Disturbances of somatic functions in catatonia with
a periodic course, and their compensation. J. Ment. Sci. 84, 608
(1938)

2f. Gjessing, R.: Beitrage zur Kenntnis der Pathophysiologie periodisch katatoner Zustande. IV. Mitteilung. Versuch einer Ausgleichung
der Funktionsstorungen. Arch. Psychiat. Nervenkr. 109, 525 (1939)

2g. Gjessing, R.: Biological investigation in engenous psychoses. Acta Psychiat. (Kbh.), Report on the VIII Congress of Scandinavian Psychiatrists, 93, (1947)

2h. Gjessing, R.: Mental Hospital Problems. In: Perspectives in Neuropsychiatry. Ed. by Derek Richter. H.K. Lewis and Co., London (1950)

2i. Gjessing, R.: Beitrage zur Somatologie der periodischem Katatonie. V. Mitteilung. Verlaufstypen B. Arch. Psychiat. Nervenkr. 191, 191 (1953a)

2j. Gjessing, R.: Beitrage zur Somatologie der periodischen Katatonie. VI. Mitteilung. Umweltfaktoren, die sich nicht beseitigen lassen. Arch. Psychiat. Nervenkr. 191, 220 (1953b)

2k. Gjessing, R.: Beitrage zur Somatologie der periodischen Katatonie. VII. Mitteilung. Wertung der Befunde I. Arch. Psychiat. Nervenkr. 191, 247 (1953c)

2l. Gjessing, R.: Beitrage zur Somatogolie der periodischen Katatonie. VIII. Mitteilung. Wertung der Befunde II. Arch. Psychiat. Nervenkr. 191, 297 (1953d)

2m. Gjessing, R.: Beitrage zur Somatologie der periodischen Katatonie. IX. Mitteilung. Die periodische Katatonie in der Leteratur. Ed. by Leiv Gjessing and R. Jung. Arch. Psychiat. Nervenkr. 200, 350 (1960a)

2n. Gjessing, R.: Beitrage zur Somatologie der periodischen Katatonie. X. Mitteilung. Pathogenetische Erwagungen. Ed. by Leiv Gjessing and R. Jung. Arch. Psychiat. Nervenkr. 200, 366 (1960b)

2o. Gjessing, R.: Prinzipielle Erwagungen uber Forschungswege und Ergebnisse in der Gruppe der Schizophrenien. In: Memorial Research Monographs Naka. Ed. by Leiv Gjessing. Committee on the Celebration of 60th Birthday of Professor S. Naka, Osaka. (1960c)

3. Maeda, M., Borud, O. and Gjessing, L.R.: Investigation of Cholesterol and Fatty Acids in Periodic Catatonia. Brit. J. Psychiat., in press.

4. Gjessing, L.R.: Studies of periodic catatonia. I. Blood levels of protein-bound iodine and urinary excretion of vanillyl-mandelic acid in relation to clinical course. J. Psychiat. Res. 2, 123-134 (1964)

5. Gjessing, L.R.; Harding, G.F.A, Jenner, F.A. and Johannessen, N.B.: The EEG in Three Cases of Periodic Catatonia. Brit. J. Psychiat. 113, 1271-1282 (1967)

6. Nishimura, T. and Gjessing, L.R.: Failure to detect 3, 4-Dimethoxyphenylethyamine and Bufotenine in the Urine from a Case of Periodic Catatonia. Nature 206, 963-964 (1965)

7. Gjessing, L.R.: Studies of Periodic Catatonia. II. The urinary excretion of phenolic amines and acids with and without loads of different drugs. J. Psychiat. Res. 2, 149-162 (1964)

8. Gjessing, L.R.: Effect of thyroxine, pyridoxine, orphenadreine-HCl, reserpine and disulfiram in periodic catatonia. Acta Psychiatrica Scandinavica 43, 376-384 (1967)

9. Richter, C.P.: Biological Clocks in Medicine and Psychiatry. Charles C. Thomas, Springfield, Ill. (1965)

L. R. Gjessing, M.D., Dikemark Hospital, Asker, Solberg p.a. Norway

PERIODIC CATATONIA — SOME ENDOCRINE STUDIES

PER VESTERGAARD

Periodic psychoses as mentioned by Menninger-Lerchenthal in his monograph about periodicity in psychopathology[1], were already recognized by Aristotle. The clinical subdivision of periodic psychiatric disorders were discussed in the latter part of the nineteenth century by French and German psychiatrists but it was not until Kraepelin's and Bleuler's classification systems that periodic catatonia was separated as a distinct clinical subgroup.

Although a few biochemical studies of periodic catatonics were undertaken in the early part of the century, the systematic biochemical investigation of the disorder was initiated by the truly monumental studies of metabolism in periodic catatonics undertaken by the Norwegian psychiatrist Rolv Gjessing. This pioneer in biological psychiatric research introduced controlled long term biochemical investigations of individual periodic catatonics as his preferred approach to psychiatric research methodology. In 1960[2] he summarized and discussed the overview of his work. He and his collaborators over a period of approximately 30 years investigated a total of 32 periodic catatonic patients, studying them longitudinally, following and correlating changes in a number of biochemical indices with changes in psychiatric status. The findings have been repeatedly reviewed and surveyed together with other biochemical and metabolic data from periodic catatonics by Stokes[3], Rey[4], Minde[5], Jenner[6], and most recently, by L. R. Gjessing[7].

Rolv Gjessing's studies in the endocrine area were mostly concentrated around indices related to thyroid function. He did a few steroid analyses, but did not perform longitudinal studies in the area of adrenocortical function as evaluated from longitudinally collected steroid excretion data: the focus of our own work.

Other groups have, however, centered their interest on steroid excretion and this facet, besides nitrogen balance, mineral metabolism and thyroid function is among the best studied areas of

metabolism in periodic catatonics. Because of the complexity of the
work involved, the total number of patients followed longitudinally
remains small. Worldwide about a dozen female and two male patients
have been studied. The small number of male patients investigated is
particularly unfortunate because of the uncertainties in the evaluation
of the results introduced by the menstrual cycle in females. We have
studied only male patients in our investigations to eliminate the
endogenous periodicity from the data.

The first to report steroid excretion data in periodic catatonia
was Ashby[8] who could find no correlation between psychic state and reducing cortins and 17-ketosteroids in a female patient. An increase in
sugar-active cortins a few days into the excited phase was ascribed to
the electro-shock treatment given. Rowntree and Kay[9] gave as their
findings in two female patients followed longitudinally that preceding
and during the early stages of an attack there is a preponderance of
electrolyte-controlling factor; at the height of an attack, a preponderance of androgenic substance; and during recovery and remission, a
preponderance of "sugaractive cortins." The same patients and an additional third patient were studied by Rey et al.[10] some years later.
They found, in agreement with Rowntree's and Kay's observations, that
the excretion of 17-ketosteroids was higher in the reaction phase, but
observed an increased glucocorticoid excretion during the attack while
it was low during remission contrary to Rowntree's and Kay's previous
findings.

Gornall et al.[11] did longitudinal steroid investigations in two of
three periodic catatonics studied. In one male patient with excitement
phases there was a tendency for the 17-ketosteroids to decrease. In a
female patient with periodic stupor phases, 17-ketosteroids and corti-
coids increased markedly in the disturbed phases. This patient responded normally to ACTH, whereas the male patient responded poorly to a
challenge with this hormone.

Plasma 17-hydroxycorticosteroid levels were found to vary synchronously with the psychic state in a male case of periodic catatonia
studied by Gunne and Gemzell.[12] There was a strong increase in the

steroid level during the first few dysphoric days of each psychotic
episode followed by a sharp drop when the period turned into its
catatonic excited phase later on. The urinary 17-ketosteroids were
found decreasing in the psychotic phase.

From Japan comes the most extensive endocrine study in periodic
catatonia. Hatotani and collaborators[13] give data for longitudinal
studies on 17-ketosteroid excretion and corticosteroid excretion in
four women out of eight periodic catatonics studied. There was no systematic change in these indices in any of the patients studied. These
authors also examined the excretion of individual 17-ketosteroid fractions and report as their most consistent findings changes in the androgen index that is the ratio between androsterone and etiocholanolone
which falls to low levels in the periodic psychotics during the psychotic episode. Whereas with their method an androgen index of over 1.5
is always found in normal individuals it often drops to below 1.0 in
the reaction phase in the periodic catatonics due to a fall in androsterone excretion. This finding was ascribed to a changed metabolism of
testosterone and it was shown that injected testosterone was metabolized
differently in periodic catatonics when compared with normal controls.

In a study of a single female periodic catatonic Cookson et al.[14]
found increases of both 17-ketosteroid and 17-corticosteroid excretion
during stupor phases.

OUR OWN INVESTIGATIONS

CASE HISTORIES

Case 1. PERIODIC CATATONIA, Periodic stupor phases.

S.S., born 1911, was first admitted to Rockland State Hospital in
1938. He is caucasian. The patient has three sisters and brothers.
There are no known cases of mental disease in the family. The mother
is described as "nervous and high strung." The father left the family
to return to Austria when the patient was an infant, leaving the mother
with four children to care for and two of the children were sent to an
orphan asylum. The patient and the younger sister remained home while
the patient's mother worked as a cook in a restaurant. The patient was
considered a good student in school. He got a chauffeurs license at age
18 and from then on worked as a cab driver. He was married at the age
of 25.
The patient's psychosis started about half a year before admission
to the hospital and appears to have been gradual in onset, starting with
persecutional ideas. He was being spied on. A neighbor was trying to
broadcast in order to drown out his and other people's voices. There
were delusions: he once said that his whole family were doctors. His
wife was supposed to be Jeanette McDonald. He told his wife some months

before admission that he spoke to God and that God told him it was going to rain. He had suddenly, a month before admission, gotten out of bed and gone to the bathroom to drink from a bottle of iodine.

He was brought to Bellevue Hospital after he had threatened to strangle his mother. He also stated that the whole house was wired so that people could spy on him. At Bellevue, the patient was at times very noisy, disturbed and agitated. At times would laugh without reason. His affect was flat. His speech was monotonous and low.

After transfer to Rockland, he was found to be quiet and cooperative with occasional silly laughter. He told the interviewer that he had been doped and that blood was drawn from him by his wife, acting on orders from the government to produce babies. He said he had made a suicide attempt in response to hallucinations. He was diagnosed as dementia praecox, paranoid type. It was noticed during his 6-month stay at the hospital, that he would show occasional withdrawn behavior with good social contact in interphases. The diagnosis was changed to dementia praecox, hebephrenic type. He was paroled to his wife and father-in-law. He left them after some months to live with his mother, working occasionally as a cab driver.

He was readmitted in 1941 having shown frequent "moody" periods in which he would eat poorly, become increasingly more irritable and somewhat disturbed. He was found, on readmission, to be in periods surly, underproductive, seclusive and practically idle. One of these episodes lasted 2 1/2 months and it was noted that this was unusually long for such an episode as the patient otherwise would "recover" from his episodes in a week or ten days. The diagnosis was dementia praecox, paranoid type, but was changed to dementia praecox, catatonic type when the patient was paroled to his mother. The clinical director wrote on this occasion: "This case illustrates the difficulty and arbitrariness in classifying many schizophrenic cases by type. At different times, this patient was thought to exhibit hebephrenia, paraphrenia and finally, catatonia, and these diagnoses were all made by competent and experienced psychiatrists."

The patient lived on welfare with his mother until he was readmitted to the hospital in 1953. It was now fully established that he showed episodic catatonic states and he continued to have intermittent stuporphases during this stay. He was transferred to the Research ward in 1958 after electroshock treatment followed by insulin coma treatment had been tried without effect. Marsilid was also given without lasting effect on his status. The patient, while in the Research ward, showed regular changes alternating between somewhat longer mute, withdrawn phases lasting about a month in which he would sit by himself, refusing to answer any questions and appearing extremely hostile, and somewhat shorter phases of approximately three week's duration in which he would be friendly, overtalkative and somewhat hyperactive, in good contact, a good worker, television fan and ward organizer.

Case 2. PERIODIC CATATONIA, Periodic stupor phases.

M.B. born in 1914. He is caucasian. He grew up as the fourth of six children. There are no known cases of schizophrenia or manic-depressive psychosis in the family. He seems to have made a normal adjustment as a child and was characterized from this period as being friendly, good natured and generous although, at times, stubborn and willful. He left high school at 15 and then spent two years in a trade school. When 16 years old, he had a "nervous breakdown." He became quiet and refused to eat and talk. After a period of inactivity, he went through a period of increased psychomotor activity. He was cared for at home during this episode. From 17 until admitted to a mental hospital at 19, he helped in his father's iron shop.

His first hospitalization (in 1933) was due to a sudden, unprovoked attack on a visitor to his father's shop followed by profuse crying. He was, on admission to hospital, completely disoriented and restless. His productions were rambling, incoherent, disjointed and irrelevant. His conversation consisted of rhyming and occasional neologisms. He said he heard people's voices talking to him at all times. He showed a certain amount of muscular negativism and automatic obedience.

He was diagnosed as dementia praecox, catatonic type and released--much improved--to his father's care. He helped out in the store, but did very little elsewhere, had few outside interests or activities. Some months before his second hospitalization, he became more excitable and disturbed. On the day before his admission, he jumped on the stage of a theater and returned home without hat and coat.

He was readmitted to the receiving hospital in 1940 after another sudden unprovoked attack, this time on a newsstand attendant. On admission he expressed auditory and visual hallucinations. He had ideas of reference. Emotionally he was shallow and inadequate. On admission to Rockland, he was overactive, disturbed and assaultive. He was impulsive, manneristic and silly. His speech disjointed and schizophasic. Emotionally he was silly and rigid. He admitted that he constantly heard voices. They repeated his thoughts and sometimes spoke his thoughts for him. People followed him in the streets. They called him a masturbator.

Subsequently he quieted down. He continued silly and manneristic. It was difficult to follow him from one idea to the next. Allusions were very frequent. He constantly was heard recognizing his friends or some famous people on the ward. Auditory hallucinations were almost constant. The patient was completely without insight. His silliness was a rather marked feature. He was summed up clinically as follows: "His present admission was brought about by a sudden and impulsive rage attack. The mental picture has been marked by auditory hallucinations, ideas of mind control, schizophasia and a rather marked emotional and personality deterioration with a tendency towards silliness. At the same time his sensorium had been clear." The diagnosis offered: Dementia praecox, hebephrenic type.

During the next year or so in the hospital he deteriorated further, showing in particular a marked degree of emotional deterioration. He became seclusive, idle, dull, listless, self-absorbed, apathetic, manneristic, grinning and was lying around on benches most of the time.

Nevertheless, on the family's insistence, he was released in their care where he seemed to get along fairly well, although he still continued sick. He was married for a time, although his marriage was annuled. He was readmitted to the hospital in 1947 because he had followed a woman whom he thought was his former wife and had annoyed her. On readmission to the hospital he was, for a while, a custodial problem. He frequently threw things around and assaulted patients and attendants. Hallucinations continued. Emotionally he continued very silly and showed continuous evidence of personality disintegration.

From then and until his transfer to the Research unit in 1954 it is somewhat difficult to trace developments. The yearly notes from 1950, 1951 and 1952 describe him as rather seclusive, silly, inappropriate, passively cooperative but generally disinterested in his surroundings. He is often hallucinated and admits that in interviews, "sometimes they send out telepathic powers, it is really imagination though." Nowhere in records or ward notes is there anything recorded about periodic changes in behavior.

On transfer to the Research ward, it was noted that this patient showed marked periodic changes in behavior. The changes between the two phases have, as for Case 1, generally been rapid, often occurring within hours. In the withdrawn phase, he will sit most of the time unoccupied, often glaring at the wall or through a window, in his most withdrawn state, answering only with a shrug of the shoulder when talked to. He is often observed laughing silly and unmotivated in this period and appears, at times, to have auditory hallucinations. There is some mannerism in this period. In his hyperactive period there seems, very generally speaking, to be three phases. He is quite active both physically and mentally immediately after coming out of the stuporous phase, will talk incessantly and show increased motor activity. However, he appears in this first phase of the hyperactivity period to be in better contact than in the last part of the period where he also is quite hyperactive, but may direct his constant talk, for example, towards autistic patients who in the first part of the phase, he does not approach. He generally quiets down in the middle of his hyperative phase and is then nearest to a normal state. He will however, when interviewed in this phase, show a marked emotional shallowness and some tendency to perseverance. However, he is in his best phase quite social, eager to make contacts, plays the piano, plays bridge and table tennis, paints and is easily the most normal in behavior of the patient group at this time.

Case 3. SCHIZOPHRENIA with alternating catatonic and excitement states.

J.L. born 1927. This patient is a negro from a large family. His mother has been married twice, the first time when she was 13 years old. There were seven children born of this marriage. She married J.L.'s father in 1919 and there were eleven children in this marriage, six of whom survived. Three of his sisters were characterized as mentally retarded and were sent to a state school. His father died in 1940, after being separated from the mother for three years. He was committed by his mother to Wassaic State School because he had threatened shortly after to kill his younger brother, had broken windows and destroyed his mother's prized possessions. His behavior was looked upon by the staff as a psychotic episode from which he apparently recovered and he was returned on parole to his mother.

In 1941, a psychometric examination at the State School showed an intelligence quotient of 78. Diagnosis: mental deficiency, borderline-familial. He went to public school and to junior high school and worked for a short time as a messenger boy at Bellevue Hospital prior to his admission as a patient to that hospital.

His psychosis started some months before his admission to Bellevue. The patient acted queer. He talked about voices annoying him day and night. Said the voices were making derogatory remarks about him. Claimed people were after him. They seemed to check up on him wherever he went. He decided to stay home to avoid any contact if possible. He went from one room to another in order to trace the origin of the voices. When admitted to Bellevue, the patient was tense and anxious. Talked spontaneously of his hallucinations and delusions and was preoccupied with them. On transfer to Rockland State Hospital, the patient was found to be quiet, withdrawn, preoccupied, with intact sensorium but hallucinating and with delusions. He remained hallucinated after admission, became rather tense, extremely agitated and hallucinated and had to be transferred to a disturbed ward where he displayed assaultiveness, impulsiveness and was actively hallucinated.

He showed a slight improvement after a full course of 25 electroshock treatments, but was still hallucinating at times and now and then violent and assaultive. He continued from 1945 until his transfer in 1956 to the Research ward on a chronic ward, and in this period is described as an idle, seclusive patient who, at times, becomes disturbed, irritable and assaultive and requires care during such periods either in camisole or seclusion. He collects food and rubbish which he carries around in his shirt.

After transfer to the Research ward, it was noted that he showed very marked excitement phases at irregular intervals alternating with catatonic phases.

In his excitement phases, this patient is in almost perpetual aimless motion. His actions consist of, for example, collecting all magazines everywhere on the ward and redistributing and recollecting them ad infinitum. He continuously arranges and rearranges the chairs in the room. His shoelaces are knotted and unknotted many times through the day. He paces back and forth in the hallway compulsively touching everything and carrying anything he can put his hand on hither and dither. He will grab other patients and staff and walk arm-in-arm or hand-in-hand with them down the hallway and sometimes pulls them along whether they are willing or not. Most of his verbal output is jibberish and he keeps repeating the same sentences many times during the day sounding like a record being played over and over. He sleeps little in his excited phases, three or four hours per twenty-four hour period.

In the catatonic phases in between, he shows various degrees of withdrawal, ranging from mixed phases with some motor activity to periods when he is completely withdrawn, mute except for some grunty sounds in the back of the throat. He sits in a corner all day, sleeping at times, biting his nails and hiding his face now and then with his hands. He appears at times to be hallucinating in this phase.

BIOCHEMICAL METHODS

Creatinine in urine has been determined with our micromodification of the Folin method.[15] Urinary 17-ketosteroids (17 KS) and urinary 17-ketogenic steroids (17 OHCS) were estimated with methods developed in this laboratory.[16,17] Individual 17-ketosteroids (Dehydroisoandrosterone (DHIA), androsterone (A), etiocholanolone (E), 11 keto androsterone (OA), 11 keto etiocholanolone (OE), 11 hydroxy androsterone (OHA) and 11 hydroxy etiocholanolone (OHE) were initially determined with the method of Lakshmanan & Lieberman.[18] Later, our own method using multicolumn chromatography on alumina and gradient elution chromatography was used.[19] Gonadotropins in urine were assayed with the bio-assay method of Johnsen.[20]

All determinations were done in duplicate except for the complicated chromatographic determinations. A second set of duplicate analyses were done for the - very few - steroid determinations from low concentration urines, where the coefficient of variation for the assays rise to above 10%, as illustrated in Figure 1, that shows coefficient of variation (standard deviation in per cent of the mean) as a function of the concentration in urine of 17 hydroxycorticosteroid (17 OHCS), 17 ketosteroids (17 KS) and creatinine.

Analyses were also repeated if the duplicate analyses differed by more than 3 standard deviations for any of the methods at a given concentration.

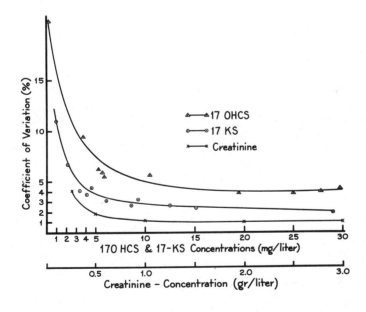

Figure 1.

Coefficient of variation as a function of concentration of steroids and creatinine. Each point gives the mean for a batch of 12 analyses plotted against the coefficient of variation.

WARD PROCEDURES

Behavior rating.

In the initial phase of the study, different behavior rating scales were tried out. They were all quite cumbersome and time consuming and they did not seem to offer any distinct advantage over simpler ratings based on nurses and attendants daily observations.

The patients have been observed by:
1. The ward psychiatrist, making daily notes.
2. The nurses, keeping a special logbook on each patient and entering their overall impression of him for the period they worked on the ward.
3. The attendants keeping an hour-by-hour log of the patients behavior and the trivial happenings. This included a simple rating on a five point scale of motor activity and speech besides notes on sleep periods.

On the basis of these ratings and observations, an arbitrary scale was constructed for each patient assigning a -4 rating to the deepest degree of stupor in that patient and a +4 rating to the highest degree of excitement observed in the patient.

This type of rating, although obviously less desirable than a completely objective rating system, was considered adequate because the patients showed such marked and mostly sudden changes in behavior and the basic question whether the patient was in a marked stupor phase or a marked excitement phase has never been in doubt to any observer. At the lower ratings, the +1 and -1 areas, different observers have often differed somewhat in their judgment of the patient's condition and these intermediate scale ratings must be taken with the necessary grain of salt.

Drugs: The patients had, with the exception of the cortisone used experimentally in one patient, been taken off drugs for the duration of the experiments.

Physical check-up: The patients were thoroughly examined by hospital consultants and found without signs of somatic disease. A battery of standard laboratory tests were performed all giving normal values.

Urine collections.

Great care was taken with the urine collections. The attendants were trained over years in these procedures. The water section was kept locked so that the patient had to be taken there by the attendant to prevent "unauthorized" urination. Nevertheless, in spite of all precautions, losses unavoidably occurred now and then in disturbed periods.

Diet.

The diet for the two of these patients who maintained an adequate intake in their stupor phases, was standard hospital food.

In the third patient who stopped eating or had a very low caloric intake for the first days of a stupor phase, a controlled diet was introduced for a three-month period. This diet consisted of the commercially-available "Metrecal" powder mixed with water and served refrigerated. The total caloric intake had been figured out in advance to be 2200 calories per day for this patient and he maintained his weight on this intake. Total liquid intake was standardized at 2 1/2 liters per day liquid food and drinking water.

Ward measurements.

Resting morning temperatures (rectal) and pulse rate were recorded daily. The weight was recorded once a week.

RESULTS

Case 1. Patient S.S.

This patient showed, as can be seen from Figure 2, quite regular phase swings between somewhat longer lasting stupor phases and somewhat shorter excitement phases. Both his 17-ketosteroid excretion and his 17-hydroxycorticosteroid excretion dropped markedly in the stupor phases. The lower limit for 48 year old men -- the age of the patient at the time of the studies -- is with our methods for 17-ketosteroids 5 1/2 mg per 24 hours, and for 17-hydroxycorticosteroids 5 mg per 24 hours, It can be seen that the excretion in this patient consistently, and for considerable periods of time, falls below this lower limit in the stupor phase.

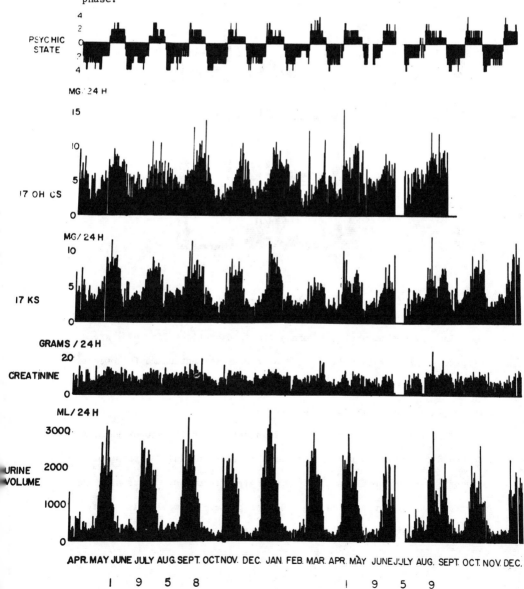

Figure 2.
Steroid and creatinine excretion data for patient S.S.

The upper normal limit of 17 mg/24 hours for 17-ketosteroids and 16 mg/24 hours for 17-hydroxycorticosteroids is not exceeded at any time for this patient.

We felt that it would be interesting to take a look at changes in pituitary hormones in periodic catatonia since so many of the findings in this disorder seem to point towards disturbances in the hypothalamic/ pituitary system. The only hormones we, at the time, could determine were the urinary gonadotropins.

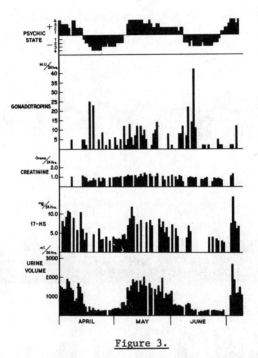

Figure 3.

Changes in urinary gonadotropins, 17-ketosteroids and creatinine in patient S.S.

The changes occurring in gonadotropin excretion (Figure 3) are a drop to low levels towards the end of the excitement phase followed by an increase to high levels some days into the stupor phase and a drop to low levels later in the stupor phase.

This patient was definitely undernourished in the stupor phase. He would often refuse food for several days in the initial phase of the stupor period and would eat only sparingly afterwards. He usually lost several pounds of weight during a stupor phase. He would also restrict his fluid intake to a minimum and his urinary output would fall to mini-

mum values of 200-300 ml per 24 hours. It is known from the studies of
Huseby et al.[21] of the effects of semistarvation and water deprivation
on adrenocortical function in normal volunteers that reduced caloric
intake and water deprivation may bring about a pronounced fall in steroid
excretion, in their study over a two-week period on an average to about
50% of baseline values. This has later been confirmed for individual 11
desoxy 17-ketosteroids by Hendrikx et al.[22] in studies of obese women
being treated by starvation followed by low caloric diets. These authors
also found very low values for 11 desoxy 17-ketosteroids in anorexia
nervosa with marked increases when the caloric intake was normalized.

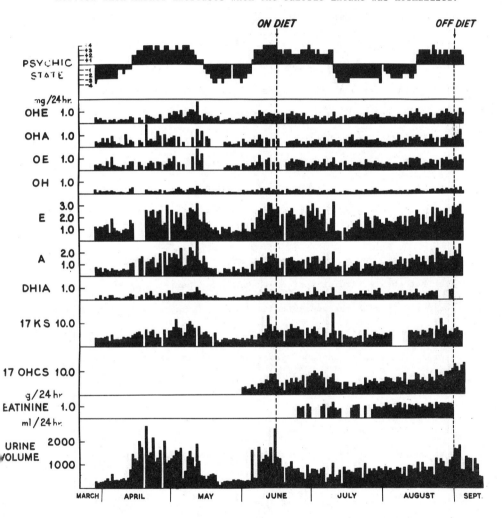

Figure 4.

Effect of controlled diet and constant fluid intake on the
excretion of individual 17-ketosteroids, total 17-ketosteroids
and 17-hydroxycorticosteroids. Patient S.S.

Since the steroid excretion data quite possibly in this patient were explainable as an undernutrition and low fluid intake phenomenon, it was obviously necessary to undertake a study of steroid excretion with the patient on an adequate caloric intake and with an adequate and constant fluid intake.

The effect of the constant diet on steroid excretion can be seen to be pronounced (Figure 4). A number of the individual 17-ketosteroids that are supposed to derive from the adrenal cortex namely the 11 oxy-genated 17-ketosteroids (OA, OE, OHA and OHE) and dehydroisoandrosterone (DHIA) varied quite markedly, dropping to low levels when the patient was on a free diet, however no significant change is seen in these compounds when the patient is on a constant diet. This is somewhat difficult to get to agree with the finding that the corticosteroids (17 OHCS) in the diet period still are falling in the stupor phase. It may indicate that some metabolic pathways for the corticosteroids are also still inhibited when diet is controlled. Two other steroids that are still clearly lowered in the diet period in the beginning of the stupor phase are androsterone and etiocholanolone. Since these steroids are derived both from the adrenal cortex and from the testicles, the fact that the other 17-ketosteroids derived from the adrenal cortex only are unaffected on a controlled diet by the stupor condition might indicate that the testicular part of these fractions is suppressed. This would fit in with the gonadotropin data from Figure 3. that shows an increase in gonadotropins at about the time in the stupor phase when the androsterone and etiocholanolone values are at their lowest, indicating a possible feedback increase because of lowered testosterone production.

Case 2. Patient M.B.

At the time we studied him, this patient was clinically very simi-lar to patient S.S., probably presenting as similar behavior patterns as one is likely to meet in two patients on a chronic psychiatric ward.

They both had stupor phases of about the same relative duration and presented the same clinical picture interrupted by excitement phases in which they both would be in good contact, quite sociable and with only a few residual symptoms.

Nevertheless, their steroid excretion patterns were very different. Patient M.B. (Figure 5) shows in contrast to the marked drop in levels seen in Patient S.S., marked increases in both corticosteroid and 17-ketosteroid excretion in his stupor phases to well about the highest normal levels for his age (17 mg/24 hours for 17-ketosteroids and 16 mg/ 24 hours for 17-hydroxycorticosteroids).

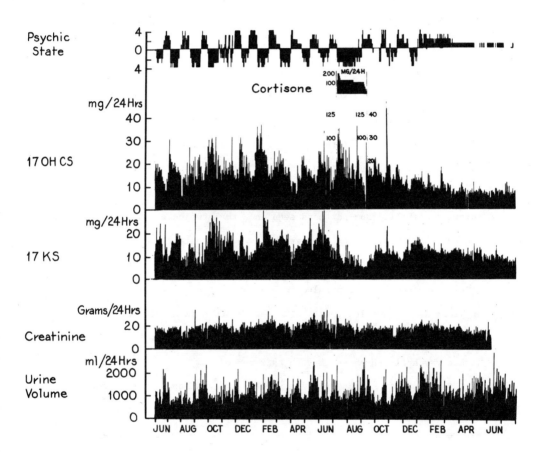

Figure 5.

Steroid patterns in Patient M.B. and the effect of cortisone.

We felt that such high excretion values consistently through much of the stupor phase pointed towards a strong central stimulation of the adrenal cortex. We decided, therefore, after we had studied him through a number of phase swings, to see if we, by giving cortisone, could suppress this hypothetical central stimulation and perhaps this way influ-

ence the condition. We thought we had to give large dosages of cortisone to achieve a good suppressant effect and started out with a dosage
of 200 mg of cortisone per 24 hours, lowered stepwise to 125 mg, and
then to 100 mg/24 hours, We found, as has Gornall et al.[11] in one case,
and Cookson et al.[14] in their case, that the psychotic phase was prolonged
by cortisone treatment. However, the patient, while still on cortisone, did pull out of the stupor and went into an excitement phase.
The cortisone had the usual effect on 17-ketosteroid excretion of suppressing the 17-ketosteroids and, of course, the corticosteroids went
up to high values as can be seen from the chart. The cortisone had a
marked lasting effect, however, on the cyclic variation in steroid excretion. It broke the cyclic pattern. Only for two days after the cor-
risone had been given did the steroids reach abnormally high values although the patient went through two stupor phases and two excitement
phases. The steroid excretion patterns, however, continued to become
more and more normalized and flattened after some months out to become
indistuinguishable from patterns seen in normal subjects. At the same
time this occurred, the patient gradually pulled out of his last excitement state and after he had been without recurrence of the stupor phases
for eight months, he was paroled to his family. A check with the family
two years later revealed that he had been able to make a living as a
junk dealer in another state and as far as the family knew he had been
without psychotic episodes through this period.

Of course, it can be argued that this was a spontaneous recovery
occurring fortuitously at the time when these experiments were conducted.
Such recoveries are statistically rare in chronic patients hospitalized
continuously for 16 years as this patient had been, but manifestly it is
impossible as long as one has only one case to exclude the possibility.
We believe, however, that it is more probable that the cortisone
given somehow interferred with the underlying pathological process,
stopped the metabolic cyclicity and, in consequence, also changed the
psychic state.

In this patient, we compared chromatographic patterns of individual
17-ketosteroids in an excitement phase with similar patterns from a stu-

por phase. We estimated, in this case, the glucuronide fraction separate from the fraction released by continuous extraction at pH 1 (steroid sulfates) and small amounts of other steroids released by boiling. The striking finding in these studies were (Figure 6).

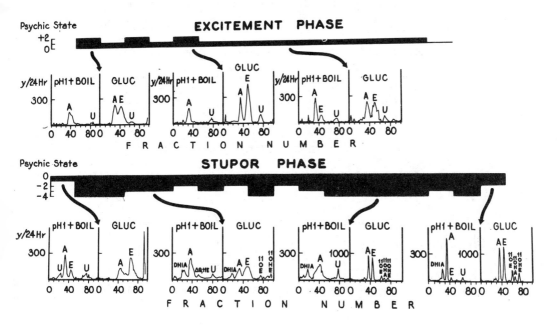

Figure 6.

Chromatographic patterns for individual 17-ketosteroids in an excitement and a stupor phase. Patient M.B.. Abbreviations as under "BIOCHEMICAL METHODS." "U" Signifies unidentifiable by infrared spectroscopy. The other steroids were identified by this method.

that we could find no dehydroisoandrosterone in the excitement phase and not enough of the 11 oxy. 17-ketosteroids to allow identification by infrared spectroscopy. This is difficult to interpret, but could perhaps be ascribed to exhaustion of the adrenal cortex in the stupor phase. The only abnormality in the stupor phase, apart from generally elevated values, were the low excretion of 11 hydroxy androsterone relative to 11 keto and 11 hydroxy etiocholanolone, indicating possible inhibition of some of the enzymatic pathways for corticosteroid metabolism in this phase.

Case 3. Patient J.L.

This patient is similar to the two previous patients in that he alternates between stupor phases and excitement phases. He is different, however, from these patients and all other patients called periodic catatonics in the publications about this disorder in that he has no non-psychotic intervals. His swings between severe excitement phases and stupor phases occur within a general psychotic condition. The diagnosis mental retardation - borderline case was considered when he first came to Rockland State Hospital. The receiving psychiatrist at the time was, however, struck by his knowledge of current events and questioned him about American History. He found him quite knowledgeable with good recall of dates and events and questions the validity of the borderline mental retardation diagnosis, based mainly on the I.Q. value of 78 from Wassaic State School. The notes from this school call him one of the most intelligent pupils in the school. It seems likely, therefore, that we are not confronted with a poorly defined psychosis in a mental deficient. This patient is a chronic psychotic that for the twelve years prior to his transfer to the Research ward had shown dissociated thinking with marked perseveration and frequent neologisms, complete emotional blunting and pronounced autism -- all the classical Bleulerian symptoms besides chronic hallucinations. He is undoubtedly a schizophrenic as this diagnosis is generally used.

His steroid excretion longitudinally followed (Figure 7) does not show any systematic changes as seen in the other two patients. There are odd sudden spurts in steroid excretion lasting only for a day; they occur mostly in the 17-hydroxy corticosteroids. There is no obvious pattern to them. Six out of eight of these spurts of 17 hydroxycorticosteroids, with the higher increases going past the 20 mg/24 hour mark, occur in excitement phases -- two however, in stupor phases.

The rhythmicity in urine volume noted at the end of the study was due to the installation of a water fountain on the Research ward. This patient developed, as part of his behavior during the excited periods, constant stops at the water cooler for a short drink. This, of course, can secondarily affect any biochemical data sensitive to urine volume, but did not seem to have any effect on our data.

Chromatographic studies of individual 17-ketosteroids in this patient were not done on a longitudinal basis. Single studies in an excitement phase and in a stupor phase did not reveal any abnormality.

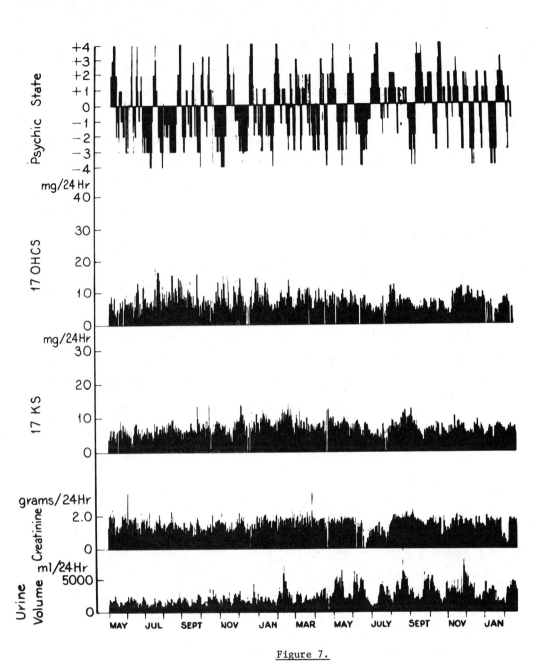

Steroid excretion patterns in Patient J.L.

DISCUSSION

It has been much discussed what the patients labeled periodic catatonics are and how they fit into current diagnostic categories. At a
Scandinavian round table conference discussing, "some somatic problems"[23]
in schizophrenia, at which Rolv Gjessing was present, two of the clinicians, Strømgren and Lunn, emphasized the diagnostic difficulties. Some

of the patients described by Gjessing might just as well have been diagnosed as somewhat atypical manic-depressives. They felt that it was
dangerous to make any generalizations from Gjessing's findings in periodic catatonia to schizophrenia as a whole.

Gjessing responded by agreeing that he did not consider periodic
catatonia in any way representative of "schizophrenia as such". He felt
it was worth emphasizing that many psychoses appear to represent borderline cases between the manic-depressive psychosis and the so-called
schizophrenia. Periodic catatonia may, according to Gjessing, be visualized as standing somewhere between the two poles, some of the patients having a larger share from the manic-depressive side and some
being more related to hebephrenics. Minde[5] makes the point that periodic catatonia probably is a "schizophreniform" psychosis and not related
to the group of "process schizophrenia" as defined by Langfeldt.[24] This
is certainly a valid comment, the trouble is though that nobody in the
final analysis knows whether "process schizophrenics" is a homogenous
group when it comes to etiology or whether they represent a response
form in a group of patients that well might react in a similar way to
different etiological factors.

Of our own patients, the two we have labelled periodic catatonics
with stupor phases seem to fit quite well the definition given by R. &
L. Gjessing[25] for the synchronous/syntonous type of periodic catatonia
with stupor phases.

To discuss in much detail whether these cases are atypical schizophrenics or atypical manic-depressives, mixed psychoses, the same psychotic process changing from a schizophrenic to a manic-depressive manifestation or a unique periodic psychosis unrelated to either of the main
psychoses seems, at this time, futile as long as nobody knows what schizophrenia, or the groups of schizophrenias, are.

What is important, however, is that this type of patient should be
identified because of the relatively good prognosis and response to treatment.
If, as has been claimed from Kraepelin to Gjessing, 2% of all patients
labelled schizophrenics belong in the periodic catatonic group, then of
a conservatively estimated 300,000 schizophrenic patients in the U.S.A.,

6,000 may be periodic catatonics and no excuse should be necessary to
study this kind of patients as a group per se.

As emphasized over and over again by R. Gjessing, it would seem important that this be done as longitudinal studies in individual patients.
Certainly our studies bear this out. Our findings emphasize that two
patients presenting with clinically very similar pictures may show quite
different endocrine changes in response to the stuporous condition. Even
if we assume a common etiology in these two patients -- and one can in
no way be sure of that -- then obviously the same factors influencing,
over years, two organisms will not necessarily produce the same conditions in both. Two diabetics followed longitudinally over ten years or
studied ten years after the outbreak of the disease are not very likely
to show identical metabolic pictures. Only if the individual patient is
metabolically described as comprehensively as possible can one hope in a
rational way, eventually, to treat such patients.

When longitudinal data from an individual patient are available, a
rational basis for attempts of therapy can be established. Our own
treatment experiment in Patient M.B. was built on a working hypothesis,
however primitive, that a hypothetical central stimulation from the hy-
pothalamic/pituitary area can be suppressed by peripheral hormone if
there are signs of stimulation of the peripheral gland. Only further
experimentation in other cases of periodic catatonia with similar metabolic patterns can show whether this in some periodic catatonics may be
so or not. The very high dosages of thyroid preparations used by
Gjessing, Dantziger,[26] Mall,[27] and others in the effective treatment of
a high precentage of periodic catatonics would certainly be compatible
with an effect through suppression primarily of the production of pituitary hormones secondarily producing effects in diencephalic areas
that well may be the hypothetical central localisation of the disorder
as suggested by Gjessing and other investigators.

Since the metabolic findings were so completely different in Patient
S.S., we had in this case planned to attempt combined ACTH and gonadotropin therapy late in the excitement phase in an attempt to rectify
the endocrine abnormalities and perhaps to delay or abolish the stupor

phase. However, the patient left the hospital without consent in a protest against the monotonous diet used in the studies. He objected vig-
orously when he got back to further experimentation and could not be
persuaded to go on with the investigations.

We are, after our experiences with this patient, firmly convinced
that we, in future studies involving diet control, must introduce much
more sophisticated food preparation from a special diet kitchen with
reasonable variety and choice of food. Less than that will, we feel,
in many patients, be less than morally defensible.

We feel that our findings in Patient J.L. are of considerable interest. Most observers would probably list this particular patient as
belonging to Langfeldt's[24] group of "process schizophrenics". No systematic endocrine changes synchronous with or related to the marked
swings in psychic state occurred. This patient, being continuously
psychotic, was in his behavior very different from the other two who
showed integrated personalities with only slight residual symptomatology
in interval phases.

Jenner[6] quotes an "authority" as stating that, "no field has been
more overworked," than the periodic psychoses. This is obvious nonsense. Certainly in the endocrine field the surface has only been
scratched and most investigations such as ours have been performed to a
large degree with quite crude group assays because longitudinal studies using refined biochemical methodology have been prohibitively complex and expensive. We have, in an effort to circumvent this problem,
under development high resolution multi-column automated and computerized chromatographic systems.[28,29] We believe that such methods will
make it possible to greatly expand the scope of what any one laboratory
can perform of biochemical studies in periodic catatonia and other mental disorders. With such methods, a far more sophisticated evaluation
of a periodic catatonic's endocrine status, for example, becomes possible. The development of practical methods for the assay of pituitary
hormones in body fluids by radio-immunoassay methods also opens great
new vistas for endocrine research in periodic catatonia.

It is quite clear from ours and others rhapsodic findings of hormonal changes in periodic catatonia that what is called for in future work in this area is a comprehensive study of the endocrine status of these patients longitudinally followed including above all pituitary hormone assays besides a broad-spectrum analysis of peripheral hormonal status.

The periodic catatonics appear a most promising research object for the psychoendocrinologist because of the frequent and marked changes observed in endocrine indices and the effect endocrine treatment seems to have in many of these cases.

SUMMARY

Some endocrine longitudinal studies have been performed in two periodic catatonics with stupor phases and one schizophrenic with periodic excitement and stupor phases.

(1) Quite dissimilar steroid excretion patterns were obtained in the two periodic catatonics who, at the time of study, presented very similar behavior patterns. One showed marked increases in both 17-ketosteroid and 17-hydroxy corticosteroid excretion in stupor phases, the other marked decreases.

(2) The patient with the increased steroid excretion in the stupor phases was treated with cortisone on the working hypothesis that peripheral hormones, if there are signs of stimulation of the peripheral glands may exert their effect on the condition by suppressing hormonal production in the anterior pituitary. This will then secondarily, through unknown mechanisms, stop a hypothetical central process in the diencephalon. The cortisone, while prolonging the stupor phase, broke the cyclicity of the steroid excretion patterns in this patient and he gradually stopped showing alternating psychic phase swings.

(3) The effect of maintaining a controlled constant diet and fluid intake on steroid excretion was shown clearly in the other periodic catatonic who was undernourished when on an ordinary hospital diet in his stupor phases. A constant diet normalized the excretion of some steroids while others still showed low values in the stuporous state.

(4) Gonadotropin studies in this patient showed cyclic changes related to psychic phase changes.

(5) The schizophrenic patient with alternating catatonic and excitement phases did not show any cyclicity in his excretion patterns.

ACKNOWLEDGEMENTS

This work could not have been performed without the constant interest and vigilance shown by the ward staff under the direction of Amparo Chamberlain, R.N. The studies were supported by grant MH-01953 and institutional grants, MH 07292 and FR 05651 from the National Institutes of Health, U.S. Public Health Service. We want to thank Sidney Bernstein for the photographic illustrations.

REFERENCES

1. MENNINGER - LERCHENTHAL, E. Periodizität in der psychopathologie, Maudrich, Wien, 1960.

2. GJESSING, R. Beiträge zur somatologie der periodischen katatonie. X. Mitteilung. Arch. Psychiat. Zeitschr. Neur. 200, 366, 1960.

3. STOKES, A.B. Critical Review. Somatic research in periodic catatonia. J. Neur. Psychiat. 2., 243, 1939.

4. REY, J.H. Metabolism in recurrent schizophrenia. In: Schizophrenia somatic aspects, RICHTER, D. (Editor) p. 147 Pergamon Press, New York, 1957.

5. MINDE, K. Periodic catatonia, a review with special reference to Rolv Gjessing. Can. Psychiat. Ass. J. 11, 421, 1966.

6. JENNER, F.A. Studies on periodic catatonia. In: Amines and schizophrenia. HIMWICH, H.E., KETY, S.S. and SMYTHIES, J.R. (Editors) p. 115 Pergamon, New York, 1967.

7. GJESSING, L.R. A review of the biochemistry of periodic catatonia. In: Proceedings of the IV world congress of psychiatry, Excerpta Medica Int. Congr. Ser. No. 150, p. 516.

8. ASHBY, W.R. Adrenal cortical function and response to convulsive theraphy in a case of periodic catatonia, J. Ment. Sci. 98, 81, 1952.

9. ROWNTREE, D.W. and KAY, W.W. Clinical, biochemical, and physiological studies in cases of recurrent schizophrenia, J. Ment. Sci. 98, 100, 1952.

10. REY, J.H., WILLCOX, D.R.C., GIBBONS, J.L., TAIT, H. and LEWIS, D.J. Serial biochemical and endocrine investigations in recurrent mental illness. J. Psychosom. Res. 5, 155, 1961.

11. GORNALL, A.G., EGLITIS, B., MILLER, A., STOKES, A.B. and DEWAN, J.G. Long-term clinical and metabolic observations in periodic catatonia. Am. J. Psychiat. 109, 584, 1953.

12. GUNNE, L.M., and GEMZELL, C.A. Adrenocortical and thyroid function in periodic catatonia. Acta psych. Scand. 31, 367, 1956.

13. HATOTANI, N., ISHIDA, C., YURA, R., MAEDA, M., KATO, Y., NOMURA, J., WAKAO, T., TAKEHOSHI, A., YOSHIMOTO, S., YOSHIMOTO, K., and HIRAMOTO, K., Psycho-physiological studies of atypical psychoses - Endocrinological aspects of periodic psychoses. Folia Psychiat. Neur. Jap. 16, 248, 1962.

14. COOKSON, B.A., QUARRINGTON, B., and HUSZKA, L. Longitudinal study of periodic catatonia, J. Psychiat. Res. 5, 15, 1967.

15. VESTERGAARD, P. and LEVERETT, R. Constancy of creatinine excretion. J. Lab. & Clin. Med. 51, 211, 1958.

16. VESTERGAARD, P. Rapid micro-modification of the Zimmermann/Callow procedure for the determination of 17-ketosteroids in urine. Acta endocr. 8, 193, 1951.

17. VESTERGAARD, P. and SAYEGH, J.F. Semi-automated assays for urinary 17-ketogenic steroids. Clin. Chim. Acta. 14, 247, 1966.

18. LAKSHMANAN,T.K. and LIEBERMAN, S. An improved method of gradient-elution chromatography and its application to the separation of urinary ketosteroids. Arch. Biochem. & Biophys. 53, 258, 1954.

19. VESTERGAARD, P.   Gradient elution chromatography of urinary 17–
     ketosteroids.   Acta. Endocr.   Suppl. <u>64</u>, 3, 1962.

20. JOHNSEN, S.G.   A clinical routine method for the quantitative
     determination of gonadotropins in 24–hour urine samples.   Acta.
     Endocr. <u>28</u>, 69, 1958.

21. HUSEBY, R.A., REED, F.C. and SMITH, T.E.   Effects of semi–starva-
     tion and water deprivation on adrenal cortical function and
     corticosteroid metabolism.   J. Appl. Physiol. <u>14</u>, 31, 1959.

22. HENDRIKX, A., HEYNS, W., STEENO, O. and DEMOOR, P.   Influence of
     bodysize, changes in body weight and/or food intake on urinary
     excretion of 11–desoxy–17–ketosteroids.   In: Androgens in normal
     and pathological conditions.   Excerpta Medica Foundation, Amsterdam,
     1966, p. 63.

23. MUNKVAD. I. & SCHOU, M.   Symposium on "some somatic problems in
     schizophrenia".   Acta. psych. Scand. <u>30</u>, 687, 1955.

24. LANGFELDT, G.   Some points regarding the symptomatology and diag-
     nosis of schizophrenia.   Acta psych. Scand. Suppl. <u>80</u>, 7, 1952.

25. GJESSING, R. and GJESSING, L.R.   Some main trends in the clinical
     aspects of periodic catatonia.   Acta psych. Scand. <u>37</u>, 1, 1961.

26. DANZIGER, L. and KINDWALL, J.A.   Treatment of periodic relapsing
     catatonia.   Dis. Nerv. Syst. <u>15</u>, 35, 1954.

27. MALL, G.   Beitrag zur Gjessingschen thyroxinbehandlung der period-
     ischen Katatonien.   Arch. Psych. Ztschr. Neur. <u>187</u>, 381, 1952.

28. VESTERGAARD, P., WITHERELL, C., and PITI, T.   Magazine fed fraction
     collector for multi-column liquid chromatography.   J. Chromat.
     <u>31</u>, 337, 1967.

29. VESTERGAARD, P., HEMMINGSEN, L. and HANSEN, P.W.   High capacity
     multi–channel computerized read-out system for multi–column
     chromatography.   (in press).

P. Vestergaard, M.D., Rockland State Hospital, Orangeburg, N.Y. 10962

6-HYDROXYLATION AND SCHIZOPHRENIA

ARTHUR SOHLER and JOSEPH NOVAL

The relationship of indoles to schizophrenia is still uncertain and it is a good example of the difficulties involved in the search for abnormalities in body fluid constituents. This state of affairs is not surprising when one considers the complexity of tryptophane metabolism and the number of factors such as stress, vitamin deficiency, microbial population and physical activity which may influence the amount of various metabolites found in the urine. Added to these difficulties is the heterogeneity of the patient population referred to as schizophrenic.

The hydroxylation of indoles in the six position may be of special significance with regard to schizophrenia in view of the findings of Szara[1] that 6-hydroxylation produces psychoactive metabolites in the case of N-alkylated tryptamines. In man the major 6-hydroxylated indole metabolite found in urine is the sulfate conjugate of 6-hydroxyskatole. This compound, 6-skatoxylsulfate has been found to be excreted in elevated amounts by a number of groups since it was originally reported by Leyton[2-6]. Studies have also shown a fairly high correlation between excretion level and duration of institutionalization[7], that excretion may be characteristic of a particular family environment[8], and that high levels of 6-skatoxylsulfate excretion persist despite changes in diet[9].

Nakao and Ball[10] and Dohan et al.[11] have fairly clearly demonstrated that 6-skatoxylsulfate arises from skatole produced by bacterial action in the intestinal tract which is subsequently hydroxylated and conjugated with sulfate.

Although it appears quite improbable that 6-skatoxylsulfate has a direct relationship with schizophrenia there is the possibility that it might be of some diagnostic use as a measurement of 6-hydroxylation potential. In order to evaluate its significance in this vain a series of studies were undertaken with acute patients and the effect of a number of extraneous factors such as stress were evaluated not only in regard to 6-skatoxylsulfate excretion, but also in regard to the excretion of other indole metabolites. A study was also carried out of indole excretion in chronic patients.

6-Hydroxylation and Schizophrenia

METHODS

6-Skatoxylsulfate was determined as described by Sohler et al.[7]. Indican was determined by the method of Curson and Walsh[12]. 3-Indolylacetic acid was determined as described by Weisbach et al.[13] and 5-hydroxyindolyl acetic acid was determined by the procedure of Udenfriend et al.[14]. Plasma cortisol levels were determined by a modification of the isotope dilution method of Peterson and Wyngaarden[15].

Fecal indole and skatole levels were determined after isolation by steam distillation and extraction into chloroform, by absorbtion at 282 mμ to give total indole and skatole. The percent indole in the mixture was determined by taking advantage of the rate and intensity of color formation when the mixture is reacted with p-dimethylaminobenzaldehyde and measuring absorbtion at 558 mμ.

Bowel habits, physical activity, dietary factors and history of medication where applicable, were ascertained by means of an appropriate questionnaire and the cooperation of the nursing staff. Diagnostic information was obtained from the referring psychiatrist.

RESULTS AND DISCUSSION

Earlier studies have shown that elevated 6-skatoxylsulfate excretion levels are characteristic of hospitalized chronic schizophrenic patients and other chronically hospitalized patients. The first table presents some of this data. Both the chronic schizophrenic group and the epileptic group showed elevated levels. Both groups of patients had been hospitalized for extensive periods.

Table 1. 6-Skatoxylsulfate excretion levels

Group	6-Skatoxylsulfate	
	n	M ± S.D. mg/24 hr.
Hospital Personnel	20	2.7 ± 1.5
Alcoholics	23	2.3 ± 2.1
Epileptics	19	5.2 ± 2.9
Chronic Schizophrenics	20	8.4 ± 5.3

In order to evaluate the significance of 6-skatoxylsulfate and other indole metabolites in the urine of schizophrenic patients it was decided to use patients who were not hospitalized and to use other members of their family as control subjects. The confound-effects of hospitalization were clearly evident in the studies we carried out on chronic patients.

To date we have studied nine such families comprising a total of forty individuals. A total of nine patients were in these families.

6-Hydroxylation and Schizophrenia

Five of the nine families studied had a history of mental illness. The patients were for the most part young adults, mean age, 24.9. The patients had a diagnosis of schizophrenia or were showing a schizoid reaction.

The families were comprised for the most part of four to five individuals. Eight members were children under 12 years of age. Of the forty individuals examined 19 were males, 21 were females. Six of the patients were males.

Table 2 gives the means and standard deviations of a number of indole urinary metabolites for both the patient group and non-patient family members. No significant differences were found in the excretion of the following indole metabolites: 3-indolylacetic acid, 5-hydroxyindolyl acetic acid, indican, and 6-skatoxylsulfate.

Table 2. Indole metabolite excretion in acute patients
(mg per gm creatinine)

	Indican $\overline{M} \pm S.D.$	3-Indolyl-acetic acid $\overline{M} \pm S.D.$	5-Hydroxy-indolyl-acetic acid $\overline{M} \pm S.D.$	6-Skatoxyl-sulfate $\overline{M} \pm S.D.$
Patients	54.9 ± 26.7	6.8 ± 2.1	6.2 ± 1.8	2.7 ± 2.0
Controls	59.5 ± 24.2	5.9 ± 3.3	6.1 ± 2.3	2.0 ± 1.7
t	.207	.360	.016	.660
P	N.S.	N.S.	N.S.	N.S.

The 6-skatoxylsulfate levels in these patients are not elevated as compared to other family members. In general we have found that 6-skatoxylsulfate levels are not elevated in acute patients. What then accounts for the elevated levels in the chronic patients?

6-Skatoxylsulfate levels were not significantly elevated in the patients living at home. Elevated levels were found in some male control subjects who were in their late fifties or sixties.

Figure 1 presents a scatter plot of 6-skatoxylsulfate values in chronic patients and control subjects.

Chronic patients below the age of 40 have in general higher skatoxylsulfate levels as compared with control subjects. The increased levels are therefore not as definitively correlated with age in the case of the patient population. In the case of the non-patient population there is a highly significant correlation with age (Table 3). Elevated 6-skatoxylsulfate levels are found with increasing frequency in older subjects.

Previously we have shown that there is a fairly good correlation between duration of institutionalization and 6-skatoxylsulfate levels.

6-Hydroxylation and Schizophrenia

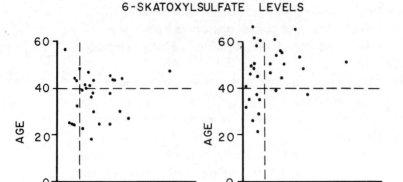

Fig. 1   Scatter plot of 6-skatoxylsulfate levels in relation to age
in chronic schizophrenic patient and control subjects.

Table 3.   Age as a factor in 6-skatoxylsulfate excretion in male
subjects

Group	n	Age $\overline{M} \pm$ S.D.	6-Skatoxyl-sulfate mg/gm creatinine $\overline{M} \pm$ S.D.	r	P
Non-schizophrenic	70	37. 2 ± 14. 0	2. 5 ± 2. 0	0. 74	. 001
Schizophrenic	31	36. 4 ± 19. 6	4. 2 ± 2. 3	0. 43	. 02

Table 4 presents a comparison between indole   and   skatole
levels in feces with the urinary excretion of 6-skatoxylsulfate, 3-
indolylacetic acid, indican, and 5-hydroxyindolyl acetic acid in a
group of chronic schizophrenic patients as compared with a control
group of laboratory personnel.   The results of this study indicate
a correlation between fecal skatole levels and 6-skatoxylsulfate excretion in a general way although a direct correlation in each   instance was not observed.

Skatole levels in the chronic patient group were   significantly
higher but indole levels were not when compared to the control
group.

In addition to elevated 6-skatoxylsulfate levels the 3-indolyl-
acetic acid level was elevated in the patient group.   Urinary indican was not elevated.

From this data and that of other investigators it would appear
that elevated 6-skatoxylsulfate excretion is due partly to increased

Table 4. Indole factors in chronic schizophrenia

Compound	Control (N=8)	Chronic Schizophrenia (N=6)	t	P
Skatole (feces)	180±108 µg/g	320±114 µg/g	2.14	0.10
6-Skatoxylsulfate (urine)	2.3±1.0 mg/24 hr.	7.4±5.2 mg/24 hr.	2.50	0.05
Indole (feces)	130±116 µg/g	105±40 µg/g	0.46	N.S.
Indican (urine)	62±23 mg/24 hr.	57±29 mgs/24 hr.	0.35	N.S.
3-Indolylacetic acid (urine)	5.8±1.8 mg/24 hr.	9.1±3.0 mg/24 hr.	2.40	0.05
5-Hydroxyindolylacetic acid (urine)	9.7±4.2 mg/24 hr.	13.0±9.8 mg/24 hr.	0.85	N.S.

levels of skatole in the intestinal tract and in part to malfunction-
ing of the intestinal tract allowing for greater skatole absorbtion.

The hydroxylation of skatole appears to be a general hydroxylation reaction as elevated levels of 5-hydroxyskatole can also be
detected (Table 5). A number of factors were assessed for a possible influence on 6-skatoxylsulfate. No significant effects were
found with such dietary factors as drinking tea or coffee, and eating tomatoes, banana, citrus fruit, legumes or meat. No effect
was noted due to cigarette smoking.

Table 5. Five and 6-sulfatoxyskatole excretion levels measured
as hydroxyskatole

Group	n	6-Hydroxyskatole µg/100 mg creatinine M ± S.D.		5-Hydroxyskatole µg/100 mg creatinine M ± S.D.	
Control	9	49 ± 39		Not measurable	
Schizophrenic	7	153 ± 48		33 ± 16	

Another factor which was examined for its effect on 6-skatoxyl-
sulfate excretion was stress or fatigue. The influence of non-
specific stress or fatigue on the excretion of indole metabolites
was investigated in collaboration with other members of the department and the Naval Air Development Center, Johnsville, Pennsylvania. The experiment involved subjects who were taking part in
human centrifuge studies. Urine samples were taken during twenty-
four hours which included an acceleration run. Later control
samples were obtained from the same subjects. Plasma cortisol
and other steroid levels were measured and the subjects were divided on this basis into those which showed a stress response and
those that did not. Urinary 6-skatoxylsulfate, indican, 3-indolyl-
acetic acid, 5-hydroxyindolyl acetic acid, and creatinine were
determined.

The data from the acceleration study on the human centrifuge
has been analyzed on the basis of which subjects showed a stress
response as indicated by an elevation in their plasma cortisol levels.

Table 6 presents the mean and standard deviation of the parameters measured in terms of excretion in mg/24 hours. No significant difference was noted between control and acceleration
levels of 6-skatoxylsulfate, indican, 3-indolylacetic acid (3IAA)
and 5-hydroxyl acetic acid (5HIAA). There was a tendency however for these values to be generally higher in the stress response
group as compared to the non-responsive group. The stress responsive group was excreting more metabolites in a general way
indicating that we are dealing with a general physiological phenomena having nothing to do specifically with indole metabolism.

Table 6. Urinary indole excretion in acceleration subjects showing stressed levels of cortisol as compared to subjects showing no increase in cortisol

	6-Skatoxylsulfate mg/24 hr. $\overline{M} \pm$ S.D.	Indican mg/24 hr. $\overline{M} \pm$ S.D.	3IAA mg/24 hr. $\overline{M} \pm$ S.D.	5HIAA mg/24 hr. $\overline{M} \pm$ S.D.	Blood Cortisol μg/100 ml $\overline{M} \pm$ S.D.
Subjects Showing a Stress Response					
A) Control period	3.0±1.4	99.3±57.1	9.0±3.2	8.8±2.7	13.8±3.6
B) Acceleration period	2.7±1.4	78.7±34.4	9.2±3.9	9.1±1.2	19.2±2.0
Subjects Not Showing Stress Response					
C) Control period	1.6±0.9	61.4±34.3	6.8±2.3	8.5±3.0	11.2±2.0
D) Acceleration period	1.7±1.1	67.7±31.1	6.5±2.8	8.2±2.8	10.6±2.2

	t	p	t	p	t	p	t	p	t	p
A vs B	0.385	N.S.	0.817	N.S.	0.103	N.S.	0.296	N.S.	3.31	0.01
C vs D	0.192	N.S.	0.324	N.S.	0.207	N.S.	0.191	N.S.	0.571	N.S.
A vs C	2.16	0.05	1.50	0.2	1.24	0.3	0.198	N.S.	1.75	0.10
B vs D	1.45	0.2	0.564	N.S.	1.48	0.2	0.790	N.S.	7.54	0.001

6-Hydroxylation and Schizophrenia

The fact that 6-skatoxylsulfate, indican and 3-indolylacetic acid are primarily of intestinal origin would seem to indicate differences in indole metabolism.

SUMMARY

There appears to be a tendency for 6-skatoxylsulfate levels to increase with age at least in the male population examined. 6-Skatoxylsulfate excretion levels were not significantly elevated in non-hospitalized acute patients but elevated levels were character- istic of several hospitalized populations such as epileptic and chronic schizophrenics. 6-Skatoxylsulfate levels are influenced by skatole levels in the intestinal tract but other factors related to in- testinal function play a modifying role. An example of this may be how responsive an individual is to stress. No evidence was obtained to indicate that there might be a difference in the rate of 6-hydroxyl- ation in schizophrenic subjects.

It would appear that 6-skatoxylsulfate excretion would be a poor measure of 6-hydroxylating ability of an individual since fac- tors primarily involving intestinal function account for the observ- ed elevation levels in chronic schizophrenic patients. Factors such as increasing age, stress responsiveness and physical acti- vity act as major factors in influencing 6-skatoxylsulfate levels.

ACKNOWLEDGEMENT

The authors wish to express their appreciation to Dr. Theodore B. Post for carrying out the cortisol determinations and to Mr. Paul Pellerin for technical assistance.

REFERENCES

1. Szara, S. and Rockland, L.H. Psychological effects and me- tabolism of N,N-diethyltryptamine, an hallucinogenic drug. Proceedings of the Third World Congress of Psychiatry, 1:670 1961.
2. Leyton, G.B. Indolic compounds in the urine of schizophrenics. Brit. Med. J., 2:1136, 1958.
3. Acheson, R.M. and Hands, A.P. 6-Sulphatoxyskatole in human urine. Biochim. Biophys. Acta, 51:579, 1961.
4. Sprince, H., Houser, E., Jameson, D. and Dohan, F.C. Dif- ferential extraction of indoles from the urine of schizophrenic and normal subjects. Arch. Gen. Psychiat., 2:268, 1960.
5. Forrest, A.D. Indoluria in schizophrenia: II. Chromatogra- phic study on 40 schizophrenic and 10 normal subjects. J. Ment. Sci., 105:685, 1959.

6. Reigelhaupt, L.M. Investigation of the urinary excretion pattern in psychotic patients. J. Nerv. Ment. Dis., 127:228, 1958.

7. Sohler, A., Noval, J.J., Renz, R.H. 6-Hydroxyskatole sulfate excretion in schizophrenia. J. Nerv. Ment. Dis., 136:591, 1963.

8. Dohan, F.C., Ewing, J., Graff, H. and Sprince, H. Schizophrenia, 6-hydroxyskatole and environment. Arch. Gen. Psychiat., 10:426, 1964.

9. Rodnight, R. Body fluid indoles in mental illness. In Int. Rev. Neurobiol., Pfeiffer, C.C. and Smythies, J.R. (Editors), 3:25, Academic Press, New York, 1961.

10. Nakao, A. and Ball, M. The appearance of a skatole derivative in the urine of schizophrenics. J. Nerv. Ment. Dis., 130:417, 1960.

11. Dohan, F.C., Durkin, J., Kulick, A., Rosenblum, M. P., Bachrach, D.L., Grassberger, J., Lynch, F.A., and Sprince, H. Arch. Gen. Psychiat., 9:520, 1963.

12. Curson, G. and Walsh, J. A method for the determination of urinary indoxylsulphate (Indican). Clinica. Chimica Acta., 7:657, 1962.

13. Weisbach, H., King, W., Sjoerdsma, A. and Udenfriend, S. Formation of indole-3-acetic acid and tryptamine in animals: method for estimation of indole-3-acetic acid in tissue. J. Biol. Chem., 234:181, 1959.

14. Udenfriend, S., Weissbach, H. and Titus, E. The identification of 5-hydroxy-3-indole acetic acid in normal urine and a method for its assay. J. Biol. Chem. 216:499, 1955.

15. Peterson, R.E. and Wygaarden, J.B. The visible pool and turnover rate of hydrocortisone in man. J. Clin. Invest., 35:552, 1956.

A. Sohler, Ph.D., and J. J. Noval, Ph.D.,

Neurochemistry Section, Bureau of Research in Neurology and Psychiatry,

c/o New Jersey Neuro-Psychiatric Institute, Box 1000, Princeton, N.J.

SOME COMMENTS ON THE STATUS OF 6-HYDROXYLATION AND SKATOLE IN SCHIZOPHRENIA

HERBERT SPRINCE

Dr. Sohler is to be commended for persevering with research on 6-hydroxy-skatole sulfate (6 HSKS) in an era when high fashion dictates otherwise. Before further comment, I should like to set the record straight concerning the finding of 6 HSKS in schizophrenic urine. The first published reports identifying 6 HSKS to occur as such more frequently in the urine of schizophrenia were those of H. Sprince et al. (March, 1960)[1] and A. Nakao and M. Ball (May, 1960)[2]. The latter also observed 6 HSKS to be abolished by antibiotics (tetracycline). In our experience, 6 HSKS occurred in the urine of about 70% of the schizophrenics and about 30% of normal controls[1, 3, 4]. According to R. Rodnight[5], 6 HSKS excretion is related primarily to bacteria in the small intestine from whence it may be absorbed, but not to diet, indican output, constipation, and large intestine function. There is now general agreement that skatole originates from intestinal bacteria, but is transformed into 6 HSKS by body tissues. With these findings, interest in 6 HSKS became limited to its possible value as a metabolic indicator of the 6-hydroxylation of indoles to form psychoactive metabolites. Such interest stemmed from the work of Szara and associates[6, 7, 8] (with N-alkylated tryptamines) which suggests that 6-hydroxylation of the indole nucleus results in increased psychotropic activity. Dr. Sohler's present report would seem to devaluate the importance of 6 HSKS as a metabolic indicator of the 6-hydroxylation of indoles. Recently, however, the whole relation of 6-hydroxylation of indoles to psychotropic activity has also been questioned[9]. On the other hand, the 6-hydroxylation of catecholamines in relation to psychotropic activity may now begin to command attention in view of the recent findings with 6-hydroxy-dopamine, i.e. its destructive action on postganglionic sympathetic nerve endings[10, 11, 12].

A few final words about skatole and its 6-hydroxylation in relation to mental disease may yet be in order. Despite all research done thus far, the direct effect of a test dose of skatole or 6-hydroxyskatole on the mental state of schizophrenic patients and normal controls remains yet to be tested and is still unknown. In preliminary, unpublished experiments with skatole, we have observed depressant (catatonic-like) activity on swimming behavior of guppies and exploratory behavior of rats. Conversely, indole gave rise to excitatory activity (frantic, darting movements in the fish and gasping convulsions in rats). Most provocative, however, are the recent studies by R. H. McMenamy and associates[13, 14, 15] who have shown that (amongst other factors) the indole ring, and more specifically the 6-position of the indole ring, is involved in the highly stereospecific binding of tryptophan by human serum albumin. Skatole and other tryptophan analogues give evidence of being bound at the same site on serum albumin, but with some thermodynamic differences. Skatole binding is uniquely atypical in that a large loss of entropy is involved which is presumably due to the loss of freedom (i.e. arrest in torsional movements) of key hydrophobic groups on the protein molecule. The serum albumin molecule heavily laden with bound skatole (or indole) might conceivably be so altered as to possess psychotogenic properties (my own speculation). When one recalls that skatole is a major indole metabolite found in the human body and was claimed many years ago (about 1907) by C. A. Herter to pass more readily into the blood stream of the mentally-ill (due to a possible breakdown in an "intestinal-blood barrier"), the elegant physicochemical findings of McMenamy and associates suggest a new approach. The future of skatole research in mental illness would now appear to lie: (a) in comparison measurements of the skatole or 6-hydroxy-skatole binding power (i.e. uptake of skatole or 6-hydroxyskatole) by serum albumin from schizophrenic patients compared with normal controls; and (b) in tests to determine whether human serum albumin saturated with bound skatole or 6-hydroxyskatole possesses psychotogenic properties; and (c) in careful reevaluation as to whether skatole can arise in vivo from indoleacetic acid by tissue decarboxylation especially under stress, as well as from the metabolism of intestinal bacteria. We are contemplating the initiation of such experiments to test these ideas in the not too distant future.

REFERENCES

1. SPRINCE, H., HOUSER, E., JAMESON, D., and DOHAN, F. C. Differential extraction of indoles from the urine of schizophrenic and normal subjects. Arch. Gen. Psychiat. 2, 268-270, March 1960.

2. NAKAO, A. and BALL, M. The appearance of a skatole derivative in the urine of schizophrenics. J. Nerv. Ment. Dis. 130, 417-419, May 1960.

3. SPRINCE, H. Indole metabolism in mental illness. Clin. Chem. 7, 203-230, 1961.

4. SPRINCE, H. Biochemical aspects of indole metabolism in normal and schizophrenic subjects. Ann. N. Y. Acad. Sciences 96, 399-418, 1962.

5. RODNIGHT, R. Body fluid indoles in mental illness. Internat. Rev. Neurobiol. 3, 251-292, 1961.

6. SZARA, S. Hallucinogenic effects and metabolism of tryptamine derivatives in man. Fed. Proc. Am. Soc. Exp. Biol. 20, 885-893, 1961.

7. KALIR, A. and SZARA, S. Synthesis and pharmacological activity of fluorinated tryptamine derivatives. J. Medicinal Chemistry 6, 716-719, 1963.

8. SZARA, S. Hallucinogenic amines and schizophrenia (with a brief addendum on N-dimethyltryptamine). In Amines and Schizophrenia (H. E. Himwich, S. S. Kety, and J. R. Smythies, Eds.) pgs. 181-197, Pergamon Press, 1967.

9. TABORSKY, R. G., DELVIGS, P., and PAGE, I. H. 6-Hydroxylation: Effect on the psychotropic potency of tryptamines. Science 153, 1018-1020, 1966.

10. TRANZER, J. P. and THOENEN, H. An electronmicroscopic study of selective, acute degeneration of sympathetic nerve terminals after administration of 6-hydroxydopamine. Experientia 24, 155, 1968.

11. THOENEN, H. and TRANZER, J. P. Chemical sympathectomy by selective destruction of adrenergic nerve endings with 6-hydroxydopamine. Naunyn-Schmiedebergs Arch. Pharmak. Exp. Path. 261, 271-288, 1968.

12. MUELLER, R. A., THOENEN, H., and AXELROD, J. Adrenal tyrosine hydroxylase: Compensatory increase in activity after chemical sympathectomy. Science 163, 468-469, 1969.

13. McMENAMY, R. H. and ONCLEY, J. L. The specific binding of L-tryptophan to serum albumin. J. Biol. Chem. 233, 1436-1447, 1958.

14. McMENAMY, R. H. and SEDER, R. H. Thermodynamic values related to the association of L-tryptophan analogues to human serum albumin. J. Biol. Chem. 238, 3241-3248, 1963.

15. McMENAMY, R. H. The binding of indole analogues to defatted human serum albumin at different chloride concentrations. J. Biol. Chem. 239, 2835-2841, 1964.

H. Sprince, Ph.D., Department of Biochemistry, Veterans Administration Hospital, Coatesville, Pennsylvania

THE CLINICIAN VS STATISTICIAN CONTROVERSY

NATHAN S. KLINE

There is no more certain way of arousing the distrust of a practicing physician than to tell him that something has been "statistically
proven". His reflexes then alert him to the probability that whatever
it is, it must be contrary to medical experience and resort is being had
to some arithmetic manipulation to try to persuade him.

In beautiful reciprocity, one way to send a statistically trained
researcher straight up the wall is to speak with conviction of something
that has been "clinically demonstrated".

This deep distrust is not without its justifications. At a superficial level there is the problem that some minor factor or some small
difference may exist at a high order of statistical significance - there
being a confusion in the minds of the clinician between the degree of a
difference and the degree of its statistical significance.

Much more basic is the clinician's orientation toward the individual
case. It is well and good that e.g. 75% of patients react in a particular manner. The practicing physician has need to know whether his case
is the 1 in 4 that will react differently and if so, how. The same is
true in respect to side effects, probable clinical course, and a number
of other factors. The clinician feels he can intuit - albeit not always
too clearly - how events will proceed in the individual case he is treating and that experience will aid him in making the judgment.

Even where "statistically proven" information is available on all
the separate elements of his concern the clinician has less information
than he needs. Is the patient who responds with reaction X the one who
will also have a course Y, a side effect Z, and so on? Did the patient's
prior reaction to J mean that drug K should be avoided in combination
with L and M? Knowledge of probabilities for each item separately will
not suffice.

The statistician's academic-theoretical position is not nearly so kind. From his point of view the clinician's tedious and practically endless inclusion of apparently irrelevant details is obviously a manifestation of premature anecdotage. The material is simply not organized in a fashion that is amenable to evaluation and it is usually (as far as he can tell) a completely atypical example which most strikes the vulnerable impressionable clinician.

Not only is there deep distrust of each other but there is overt and covert evidence that the two protagonists are anything but secure in their own convictions. Despite any voiced skepticisms the clinician scans with avidity the statistical data and if he writes a paper himself will try to handle his own data in a statistically acceptable fashion.

If the statistician becomes ill he does not seek out the medical researchers whose statistical data is the most validly presented but will turn to the man whose clinical experience and reputation seem most reassuring.

In the brief period of its existence (compared with medicine) statistics has depended heavily on the methods originated by Fisher for large populations with a normal distribution. An approach centering on very few or rare cases seemed almost a contradiction in terms. Yet fortunately the mathematical basis for such an approach was developed some 200 years ago by the Reverend Bayes. This is not the occasion, nor do I have the requisite skill, but the "prior probability" of this method meeting the needs of the clinician in a scientific fashion seems extraordinarily high. This makes feasible the study of a relatively smaller number of individual cases.

With a few rare exceptions the physician is interested in the longitudinal history of his patient. Viewed from one point of view it becomes increasingly evident that an important part of this history involves periodicity. Every competent physician asks "Have you ever had this condition before?" and if it recurs in anything like a regular fashion wants all the details. The mathematical competence to handle such data adequately for individual patients has not been fully developed and as yet only a handful of medical researchers (e.g. Halberg in the U.S.A., Reinberg in France) are fully committed to the problem.

Such an approach naturally leads to a broader appreciation of inter-disciplinary concerns. It has long been evident that a variety of "fields" of study are inter-connected but the absence of a suitable methodology has severely limited such investigations. The fact that some of the relations are probably phasic makes such a longitudinal approach almost mandatory. Conceptualizing the problem is probably the most difficult part now that high speed data processing makes feasible the testing of hypotheses. Compartment models are only a first beginning.

Greater precision also is required in the definition of such terms as base-line, variability, normality[1].

In a high speed professionally mobile universe there is a real emotional block against undertaking 5, 10 or 20 year studies of individual patients. In addition the practical difficulties, including the cost, at first glance seem horrendous. However the type of information to be obtained is unique.

Although the study must start with individual patients it is to be hoped that new patterns of response will emerge which permit us to detect recognizable longitudinal patterns. The ability to formalize and subject to critical mathematical evaluation the clinician's traditional method should immensely broaden the entire field of biological investigation.

During the past 10 years we have undertaken precisely such an investigation* and a report covering the first 7 years of the study which stresses the effect of drugs on endocrome factors in chronic schizophrenics is now in print[2]. Our report stresses the deficiencies which we ourselves observed (and there are probably others which we overlooked); the practical problems; the failure to anticipate and think through some of the conceptual needs; the absence of adequate mathematical and computer soft-ware. All of these should be of use to others and hopefully even to ourselves if we are able to find support for a second "go" at the problem.

Not all was negative since we did develop some important apparatus, techniques and methodology. I will mention only two of the substantive findings that are of prime importance to anyone doing cross-over studies: 1) the Latin Square design we used was modified to the extent that the first of the three medications successively given each patient was re-

peated before proceeding. In a substantial number of patients in a substantial number of the 37 variables studied <u>the patient responded differ-</u>
<u>ently to the second administration of a drug although the dose and route</u>
<u>of administration were identical and no other drug was given during the</u>
<u>placebo interval between the two periods of drug administration</u>. Since
cross-over studies are based on the assumption that had the first drug
been given a second time the results would have been identical, we have
exposed a most unpleasant possibility.

2) Another disconcerting discovery (which may be related to the
first) is that <u>some of the responses to medication persist for as long</u>
<u>as 9 months before the former base-line is restored or a new one estab-</u>
<u>lished</u>. The usual study which allows a 2 week or even 2 month interval
between drugs is in part still involved with the action of the prior
medication.

In my youth I was much impressed by the theoretical justifications
for multidisciplinary longitudinal studies. A group of us have spent 10
years in a first attempt to actually carry out such a study. Our results
are reported elsewhere. It is important and inevitable that in the end
the competence to do such studies effectively be developed. We believe
the mistakes of our first attempt even more than the actual achievements
can help point the way that future studies may follow.

References

1. Kline, N.S.: "The Nature of Normality". In: Evans, W. and
    Kline, N.S. (Eds.), <u>The Psychopharmacology of the Normal Human</u>,
    Charles C. Thomas, Fort Lauderdale, Florida.

2. Kline, N.S.; Blair, J.; Cooper, T.B.; Esser, A.H.; Hackett, E.,
    & Vestergaard, P.: Problems of Interdisciplinary Longitudinal
    Research on Psychiatric Patients: A Controlled Seven Year Study
    of Endocrine and Other Indices in Drug Treated Chronic Schizophre-
    nics. <u>Acta Psychiatrica Scandinavica</u>.

with the assistance of NIMH grants MHO 3031, MHO 7292 and FRO 5651

N. S. Kline, M.D., Rockland State Hospital, Research Center, Orangeburg, N.Y. 10962

OVERALL CORRELATIONS OF BIOLOGICAL FINDINGS IN SCHIZOPHRENIA

ELIZABETH HACKETT

The longitudinal study of chronic schizophrenic patients entailed collections of data relevant to questions raised within each of several disciplines. All the measurements of what might be considered the patients' subsystems provided partial views of the total organism. If there were any consistent relationships among the subsystems some might be made evident by the existence of statistically significant correlations among the variables measured. Pearson product moment correlational values provided a statistical description of simultaneous direct or inverse relationships of the study data.

A prior publication (1) discussed the interrelationships among 13 variables measured in 24 patients over the course of 2 years. Data used in the above analysis were pooled to include samples obtained during placebo periods as well as those from drug periods. The 13 variables analyzed were chosen from the 37 in the study; computer limitations had necessitated eliminating almost two-thirds of the information available. A more powerful computer has provided matrices of the intercorrelations for all possible dyadic combinations of the 37 variables. An additional refinement was that of separating drug and placebo periods and using data only from the 13 weeks that were the second half of a 26 week period when a patient was on a specific drug or on placebo.

In subdividing the data into drug and placebo periods there had been included a post-drug placebo period which was the last 13 of 26 weeks following placebo

substitution for active medication. However, for
each patient with more than one drug period a post-
drug placebo period was in most instances identical
with a pre-drug placebo period. Owing to this overlap of roughly 80% consideration of the 37 variable-
by-37 variable intercorrelation matrices has been limited here to pre-drug placebo periods and drug periods.
The data are those from the first four years of the project.

There was a separate 37 by 37 matrix for each patient's data for each pre-drug and each drug period he
completed while on the study. Thus, although 18 patients contributed all the data correlated there were
39 pre-drug placebo matrices and 39 drug matrices. Of
the latter 19 were perphenazine, 11 were phenelzine and
9 were reserpine matrices.

The 37 variables were:

1. Fergus Falls Rating Scale

2. Weight

3. Systolic blood pressure

4. Diastolic blood pressure

5. Erythrocyte sedimentation rate

6. White blood count

7. Zinc sulfate

8. Total serum protein

9. Albumin

10. Globulin

11. Alkaline phosphatase

12. Urine volume

13. Creatinine

14. 17-ketosteroids

15. 17-hydroxycorticosteroids

16. Dehydroisoandrosterone

17. Androsterone

18. Etianolone

19. 11-ketoandrosterone

20. 11-ketoetianolone

21. 11-hydroxyandrosterone

22. 11-hydroxyetianolone

23. Low polar steroids of unknown composition

24. Total mg. 17-ketosteroids

25. Gonadotropins

26. Cholesterol

27. Protein-bound iodine

28. Red cell uptake

29. Volume of expired air

30. Volume of inhaled oxygen

31. Kilocalories per square meter per hour

32. Lean body mass

33. Walking as a percentage of four 3-minute samples
    per day

34. Stereotyped or idiosyncratic behavior as a percen-
    tage of four 3-minute samples per day

35. Sperm count

36. Semen volume

37. Sperm motility

The matrices were individually examined to determine which correlational values were sufficiently high
to be statistically significant at the 5% level. A
scoring sheet was used to tally the number of statistically significant values for each correlation in the

37-by-37 matrix. There were four sheets completed.
Significant correlations were totalled for: 1) the 39
pre-drug placebo matrices; 2) the 19 perphenazine matrices; 3) the 11 phenelzine matrices; and 4) the 9
reserpine matrices.

Theoretically a 37-by-37 intercorrelation matrix
ought to contain 666 cells. This would mean 666 correlational values per matrix for each of the 78 matrices
here discussed. But not all variables were obtained or
available for measurement at all times for all patients.
Therefore a number of matrices had empty cells. Furthermore, when 13 regular weekly measures had been made
for two variables being correlated the 5% significance
level was attained by a value of 0.55; but if, for example, owing to any of a variety of mischances, only 4
of the 13 weeks' measures on any variable were available
for analysis then any correlation involving that variable would require a value of 0.95 to reach the 5% significance level. If the gaps in the matrices could have
been filled, and if each value could have been arrived
at by comparing 13 weekly measurements of each variable
the results might have been different from those obtained
under existing circumstances.

A significant correlation between etianolone and
total milligrams of 17-ketosteroids was about the most
frequently found relationship among the 37 variables
under the 3 drug and the placebo conditions. Only in
the perphenazine matrix total was another correlation
found more frequently -- that of systolic and diastolic
blood pressure. (See Table 1.)

Table 1

Number of Significant Correlations Among 37 Variables
(Highest Frequencies Only)

	Placebo (39 matrices)	Perphena- zine (19 matrices)	Phenel- zine (11 matrices)	Reser- pine (9 matrices)
Total mg. 17-ketosteroids & Etianolone	28	9	8	6
Total mg. 17-ketosteroids & Androsterone	25	8	7	4
Systolic blood pressure & Diastolic blood pressure	23	11	4	4

The single obvious finding is that of the statistically strong interrelationships expressed as positive correlations of the various 17-ketosteroids. This was seen under placebo conditions and logically it could be expected. It is interesting, though, that none of the three drugs seems to alter these relationships. Equally, there is no discernable difference between the three drugs in regard to the interrelationships of the 17-ketosteroid measures. It must be remembered that these data were gathered before the year-long placebo period between drugs had been instituted.

The paucity of reportable findings is in part probably a function of completely or partially missing data. However, there exists a possibility that among the variables there are relationships which cannot be detected by correlations of contemporaneously obtained data. It is generally considered that biological functions have rhythmicity. Only concurrent rhythms in two functions

689

would demonstrate a significant correlation in such
data. Even with a regular time lag interspersed between the data for one variable and the data for another -- this is to account for lack of simultaneity
of rhythm -- there is presupposed by this technique an
equality of rhythmic frequency. Perhaps some method
of introducing into the computations comparing variables a non-constant factor would make it possible to
learn which biological functions bear some relationships to others; further, it would enable us to learn
the pattern or, more likely, patterns of these various
interrelationships and the manner in which the patterns
are altered by exogenous factors such as drugs. The
information basic to deriving any hypothesized varying
factor though can come only from observations made longe-
tudinally on individuals under no-drug or under placebo
conditions to establish for each his personal rhythm
for every variable to be considered.

Reference

1. Kline, N. S., Blair, J., Cooper, T., Esser, A. H.,
   Hackett, E., and Vestergaard, P. Problems of Interdisciplinary longitudinal Research on Psychiatric
   Patients: A Controlled Seven Year Study of Endocrine
   and Other Indices in Drug Treated Chronic Schizophrenics. Acta Psychiatrica Scandinavica, 44, Suppl.
   206, 1968

E. Hackett, Ph.D., Rockland State Hospital, Orangeburg, N.Y. 10962

INVESTIGATIONS OF MODELS OF THE THYROID AT ROCKLAND STATE HOSPITAL

THOMAS B. COOPER, JACK R. GRADIJAN, CAROLE SIEGEL, and MORRIS J. MEISNER

A LONGITUDINAL investigation of the effects of psychotropic drugs on the endocrine system was initiated nine years ago at this center. An interim report of the first years of this study has been reported elsewhere.[1] Briefly, four medications were tested on patients in a double blind study, comprising three months drug free, three months active medication and three months placebo periods. It is the purpose of this paper to describe the development and application of mathematical models and simulation techniques to the data derived from the radioisotope studies of thyroid function carried out as part of the aforementioned investigations.

The problems of data analysis and interpretation were extremely complex. Regulations stipulated that each patient was to receive not more than 12 diagnostic doses of $Na^{131}I$ and that each administration must be separated by at least three months. It was decided that the only solution to the above would be to carry out the isotope studies during the last week of each three month period to detect any cumulative effect of the medication. The inherent weakness of this design was that any short term changes which occurred and for which subsequent physiological compensations were made may not have been observed, and biphasic responses would not have been detected.

In 1958 Clynes and Cranswick[2] at this center simulated a five compartmental model of the thyroid system on an analog computer. Data was fitted by adjusting the "pots" (inputs to amplifiers) until the closest visual fit was obtained.

Taking the previous work of the group at Rockland State Hospital as a starting point we investigated the feasibility of the following experimental techniques. Using analog-digital simulation techniques and a fixed compartmental model, can we determine the rate constants for each of these compartments, and, with these simulate the whole

This work was supported, in part, by National Institutes of Mental Health Grant Numbers MH 12955, MH 07292, MH 02740 and FR 00268.

experiment, not by turning dials intuitively, but by setting "pots" (rate constants) from empirically derived data? If this be possible, to determine the shortest possible time interval, after the injection of the isotope, in which these rate constants can be determined such that their accuracy is in no way impaired. As the last sentence is crucial to this whole concept this will be expanded. We have stated previously that with present techniques in our longitudinal studies, we are unable to demonstrate short term drug induced changes. If we were able to simulate the kinetics of an isotope experiment over a 14 day period a few hours after the injection of the isotope, then we could give the medication under investigation and compare the subsequent experimental data with the simulated data. Any consistent difference or differences outside the limits of experimental error, would be indicative of a short term drug induced change. To go one step further, if we could determine these rate constants using $Na^{132}I$ (half life 2.3 hrs.) then after the rate constants were determined with ^{132}I we could give the medication simultaneously with the injection of $Na^{131}I$ and measure the changes which take place in the first few hours of the experiment.

METHODS OF INVESTIGATION AND RESULTS

<u>Simulation</u>

1. <u>PACTOLUS</u>. The simulation of the model in Figure 1 was developed and tested using the PACTOLUS program for the IBM 1620 computer.[3] This digital analog simulation program provides a complement of functional elements comparable to, but more extensive than, an analog computer, and a block oriented language for describing the simulation configuration. The 1620, a small scientific computer, permitted an on-line conversational mode of operation comparable to setting "pots" on the analog computer. The simplicity of this digital simulation language and the operational flexibility it provided were particularly attractive to us in our initial attempts to model the thyroid system.

Several preliminary approaches were taken to test the model in terms of its ability to produce standard curves. The primary source in the literature was the rate constant data presented in the classical paper by Riggs.[4]

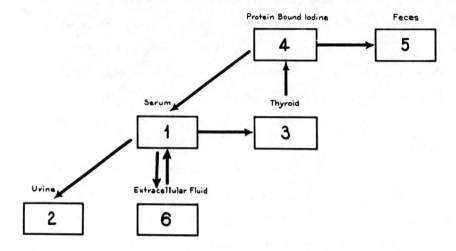

FIG. 1. Compartment model used in PACTOLUS simulation.

This data was presented as the expected theoretical rate constants for typical subjects in three categories: normal, chronic iodine deficiency, and thyrotoxic. The computer-generated curves were in keeping with the three categories.[5]

Since this model could be described by a linear system of ordinary differential equations, an exact solution of the model was possible. The agreement between the analytic solution and the PACTOLUS results indicated little loss of accuracy due to numerical integration.

An analysis of the effect of errors in the rate constants upon the accuracy of the solution of the fixed model are attached (Appendix 1). Of main interest was the effect of these variations upon the amount of iodine in an individual compartment. However because of complex linkage between compartments this particular type of result was unobtainable. It was possible to obtain an error bound on a quantity representing the sum of the individual compartment variations at each fixed time point. The error bound obtained varies linearly with the maximal error in the rate constants. Further, this bound was shown to grow exponentially in time.

2. _Stochastic elements_. It seems reasonable to assume since many of the underlying quantities are irregular in behavior that the process of thyroid functioning is stochastic. A natural generalization of the deterministic compartment model has been suggested by the work of Weiss and Zelen[6] in their application of a semi-Markov model to leukemia.

In this approach the role of the rate constants is assumed by conditional probabilities. Thus molecules leaving a compartment having more than one outward direction of flow determine their path according to probabilities - referred to as conditional transition probabilities. The numerical determination of these conditional probabilities is a difficult problem. We have used as a first approximation the normalized rate constants. The duration time of a molecule in a compartment which we refer to as "sojourn time" need be determined for the serum, thyroid, and protein bound iodine (PBI) compartments (see Figure 2). In each of these compartments we initially chose gamma sojourn times, S_i with distinct parameters.

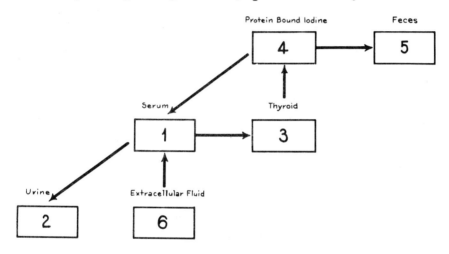

FIG. 2.   Compartment model used in stochastic simulation.

The aim of this semi-Markov model was to obtain an expression for the probability of a particle (or transaction) to be in compartment i at time t . A comprehensive description of the techniques for calculating this probability are given elsewhere.[7] This allows the estimation of the average amount of iodine in a compartment at a given time. Although analytical results were possible, the form of the solution proved intractable. Accordingly a stochastic simulation technique was utilized for this model.

    3. General Purpose Systems Simulator (GPSS). The most suitable language available is the IBM GPSS III.[8] This language is particularly useful for systems in which the flow of transactions as well as the duration time of the transactions in various locations are probabilistically determined. Our application considers a "transaction" as a

molecule of radioactive iodine and we consider a "location" as a compartment. In our GPSS program we have created 100 transactions (34 of which begin in the serum and the remaining 66 in the extra-cellular compartment). This division corresponds to the real-life phenomenon of an almost immediate flow of iodine from the serum into the extra-cellular compartment so that within a short period of time the ratio of iodine in these two compartments is 2 : 1. Our simulation causes each departure of a molecule from the blood serum to result in a departure of two molecules from the extra-cellular into the serum, as long as the extra-cellular compartment is non-vacuous.

In our first run of the simulation we chose exponential sojourn times

$$P\{S_i \leq t\} = 1 - e^{-\lambda_i t}, \qquad t \geq 0$$

The choice of the proper values of the parameters λ_i for each of these compartments is difficult. As a first approximation we have chosen

$$\lambda_i = \frac{\log 2}{T_i}$$

where T_i is the half-life of the compartment, i.e. the time it takes for half the contents of the compartment to empty. This choice of λ_i makes T_i the median sojourn time for the compartment, namely

$$P\{S_i \leq T_i\} = \tfrac{1}{2}.$$

(The average sojourn time is $T_i / \log 2$ which is larger than T_i.)

The program tabulates the number of molecules in each compartment as a function of time. We print out the contents of each compartment at suitable time intervals. A sampling of this output is contained in Appendix 2. In addition, the program prints out summary statistics, e.g. average time a molecule spends in a compartment for the run of the program. However if at the termination of the program the current contents of a compartment is non-zero this average is not to be interpreted as average sojourn time.

4. <u>Continuous System Modeling Program (CSMP)</u>. A digital simulation of an analog representation of the four compartment thyroid model (Figure 3) was constructed using the CSMP[9] which is an adaptation for the IBM 1130 of the 1620 PACTOLUS program. The program has been further adapted for the IBM 360, and a number of modifications have been made at Rockland State Hospital, including the addition of

a versatile graphical output utilizing the Calcomp 565 digital plotter (all curves shown in the present paper were plotted using this device). A CSMP simulation, although considerably slower than an equivalent analog computer simulation, offers greater accuracy and can simulate more complex systems than can most analog computers.

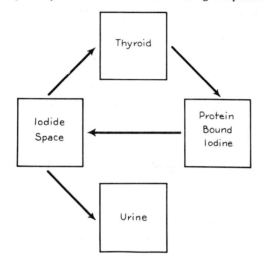

FIG. 3.   Compartment model used in CSMP simulation.

Rate constants for the thyroid compartment model are calculated from empirical neck, urine, and blood data during the first few hours of the experiment. Using these estimates of the rate constants, a CSMP digital simulation of the compartment model is run, calculating the distribution of ^{131}I in the thyroid, urine, PBI, and iodide space for the full duration of the experiment (15 days) and plots of these

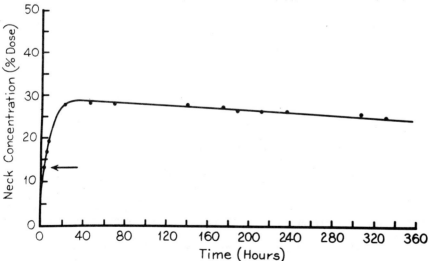

FIG. 4.   CSMP simulation of neck data. Smooth curve computer generated from first four hours data (arrow indicates prediction point). Dots indicate experimental data points.

distributions are generated. Examples of such plots of ^{131}I concentration in the neck region and in the urine, as compared with the actual empirical data, are given in Figures 4 and 5.

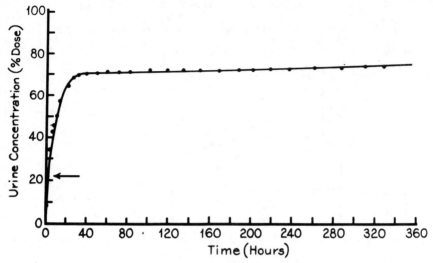

FIG. 5. CSMP simulation of urine data. Smooth curve computer generated from data in first four hours of experiment (arrow indicates prediction point). Dots indicate experimental data points.

Sensitivity analysis

In studying the thyroid system and in examining the model, it becomes evident that the various parameters involved exert their influences on the system at different times. For example, since the concentration of the isotope in PBI is not quantifiable during the first few hours, the transfer from PBI to plasma during this initial period is negligible, and consequently the value of the PBI-plasma rate constant is relatively unimportant as far as the simulation of the first few hours is concerned. On the other hand, the neck coefficient, which represents the proportion of the neck reading contributed by the isotope present in the plasma, is most important during the first few hours when the neck reading is mainly due to the plasma concentration.

To determine the dynamic effects of the model parameters upon a given variable, such as neck concentration, a set of parametric sensitivity functions was calculated. The sensitivity function, $\eta^{(k)}$ is defined as
$$\eta^{(k)} = \frac{\partial Y}{\partial P_k}$$
where Y is the variable of interest (e.g. neck concentration), and P_k is the k-th parameter (e.g. PBI-plasma rate coefficient). Thus, $\eta^{(k)}$ represents the sensitivity of the variable Y, to the value of the k-th

parameter and is a function of time, since Y is a function of time and p_k may be a function of time.

In the case of the thyroid model, the function Y is not known explicitly, although a set of differential equations defining Y is given. For this type of situation, King[10] has developed an analog computer technique for calculating the sensitivity functions. The technique is not restricted to linear time-invariant systems.

King's analog computer technique was simulated by means of CSMP, and the sensitivity functions for neck concentration with respect to the five model parameters were calculated. Plots of these five sensitivity functions are given in Figure 6.

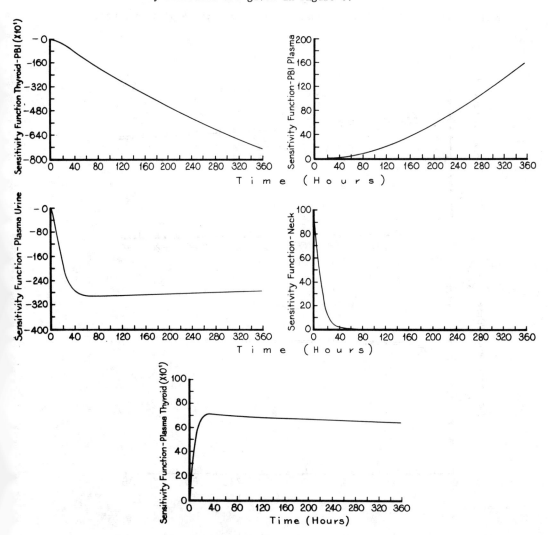

FIG. 6. Sensitivity functions for neck concentration with respect to the five model parameters.

Parameter estimation

A least-squares parameter estimation program has been developed[11] that is applicable to refining the values of the parameters of the thyroid compartment model. This program, when given the set of differential equations defining the model, an initial estimate of the model parameters, and a set of equations evaluating the sensitivity functions for the parameters of interest, will produce a new set of parameter values such that the curve generated by the model will be a least-squares fit to the empirical data over any given region of the independent variable. The program solves the set of differential equations by means of CSMP and utilizes King's analog technique to evaluate the sensitivity functions. An iterative process is involved,

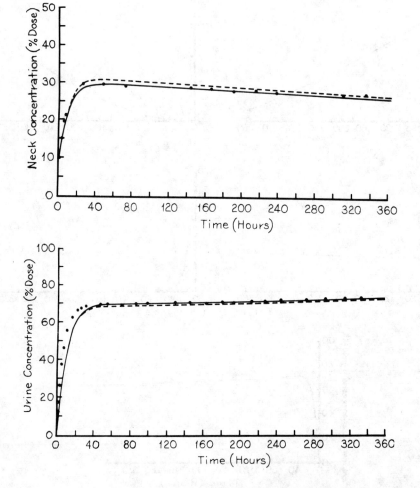

FIGS. 7 and 8. CSMP simulation (neck and urine) plus least squares fitting of data using iterative technique. Broken line represents original computer generated curves using initial rate constants (see Table 1). Smooth line shows final computer generated curve using altered rate constants (see Table 1). Dots indicate experimental data points.

and the program will handle nonlinear, time-variant systems.

Using initial estimates of rate constants and neck coefficients derived from the empirical data, the parameter estimation program was applied to produce a least-squares fit to the neck data for one subject. Figures 7 and 8 show the resulting curves of neck and urine concentrations, compared to the data and to the curves resulting from the use of the initial estimates of the parameters. In Table 1 the initial estimates of the model parameters are compared to those produced by the parameter estimation program.

TABLE 1. COMPARISON OF RATE CONSTANT ESTIMATES BEFORE AND AFTER LEAST SQUARES FITTING TECHNIQUE

	Initial Estimate	Final Estimate
21 (Plasma-Thyroid)	0.0335	0.0313
41 (Plasma-Urine)	0.0731	0.0717
13 (PBI-Plasma)	0.0091	0.0082
32 (Thyroid-Plasma)	0.000647	0.000550
Neck coefficient	0.0930	0.0992

Data collection

In our normal population study we used the following procedure for data collection. An intravenous plastic catheter* is placed in a suitable vein in the antecubital fossa. This is connected to a manifold similar to that described by Kety et al.[12] for cerebral blood flow measurements and 2.5 ml of heparin is injected to flush all blood from the catheter and to heparinize the patient. This manifold enables the operator to add small increments of heparin to prevent small clots forming in the catheter and yet be able to collect representative samples from the vein when required, i.e. the blood sample is from that actually flowing through the vein, it is not diluted by the blood-heparin mixture already in the catheter.

The patient is positioned between the three scintillation detectors by means of a sliding bed (this system was constructed to enable this type of study to be carried out and has been described elsewhere.[13] The isotope ($Na^{131}I$ carrier free and thyroxine ^{125}I is injected in the

---

* Intracath (large) available from C.R. Branch Inc., Murray Hill, New Jersey.

opposite arm. The detection systems are activated at the mid point of injection (t_o) and the count rate is monitored over the thyroid region of the neck by two systems:

(1) A rate meter set at a suitable time constant (the shape of the bolus passing the detectors was a good indication of the presence, or lack of extravasation of the dose).

(2) Integral counting at one minute intervals. The integral counting is facilitated by using the A-D equipment from our automatic gamma counting system, thus after activating, the technician is then free for other work on the experiment.

Blood samples are collected at 1, 2, 3, 5, 7, 10, 15, 20, 25, 30, 40, 50, 60, 70, 80, 120, 240, 360 minutes and 1 through 14 days after injection. Blood samples are collected by means of the "intracath" until the 80 minute sample and thereafter by normal venipuncture techniques. Total iodide levels ^{131}I and ^{127}I are determined on all specimens and $PB^{131}I$ and $PB^{127}I$ estimations are then carried out on the day 1 - 14 samples.

Urine samples are collected at 10 minutes, 30 minutes, and 1, 2, 4 and 6 hours, and as many samples as possible during the following 14 days. We have found that the patient can get up from the bed and collect a urine sample when required without any undue discomfort with the "intracath" in situ. The patients are given plastic containers to collect all urine during the 14 days following the initial experiment day.

All samples are counted twice and until acceptable statistical accuracy is obtained. Programs have been formulated for the calculation and correction of all of the data, including time intervals, mid point of time intervals, amount of activity present either as %/dose/liter, or %/dose in the sample, rate/hours (in urine the cumulated excretion is also calculated). All data is corrected for residual counts remaining in the syringe after injection.

When labelled thyroxine is injected simultaneously, counting of blood and urine samples is done using a channel analyzer. All the necessary correction for ^{131}I counts registered in the ^{125}I window are done using a program written at this center.

PBI levels are determined in all blood samples and free thyroxine levels in two of the samples (using a modified dilution technique first described by Oppenheimer et al.[14]). Stable iodine concentration in urine is also determined in all samples. All of these determinations are done in duplicate.

Our approach to patient data collection was modified because of the problems associated with a psychotic population. We did not use the "intracath" for blood collection but collected samples by standard venipuncture technique. The modified experimental design is as follows: the patient is injected with the isotope and four one minute neck counts are obtained between two and six minutes after injection. Urine samples and neck counts are collected at 1, 2, 4 and 6 hours after injection, blood samples at 1½, 4 and 6 hours after injection. Daily neck counts and blood samples are collected during the subsequent 14 day period. We have found that we can run six patients simultaneously with the above approach and that we have had better than 70% success in our attempts with this experimental design. Collection of urine during the subsequent 14 days posed a major problem which we have overcome in the following manner. It is impossible to collect all urine from a psychotic population unless a tremendous investment in terms of manpower (24 hours continuous observation) is made and even then one can never be certain of complete collection. Rather than attempt total urine collection we decided that it would be better to collect urine over a timed period (ca. 2 - 3 hours) at the same time each day and then to express this excretion as a rate. The program can be easily instructed to print out operation rates rather than cumulative excretion and thus little is lost. We have also continued to collect all urine and attempt analysis of this, but with few exceptions urine collections were found to be incomplete.

Rate constant determination

A first step in this investigation was to determine whether one could estimate the rate constants for each compartment in the early hours of the experiment with sufficient accuracy so that the computer generated curves and the experimental data were in close agreement. To this end we carried out 20 (15 day) experiments on normal male volunteer subjects (age range 21 - 47, without family history or clinical signs of thyroid disorder). The rate constants were determined by the methods described below and the experiment allowed to run without any drug challenge being presented to the system.

This way we could compare our predicted data and our experimental
data. It requires but a moments thought to realise that certain of
these rate constants cannot be determined in a matter of hours, e.g.
the thyroidal turnover is a matter of weeks in a euthyroid, iodine
replete population such as we have at this center[15], and the
thyroxine turnover is a matter of days. Therefore other methods are
required to determine these rate constants. Several possibilities
presented themselves. We could, using T_4 ^{125}I, determine the thyroxine
degradation rate in the days prior to the experiment and then give the
Na ^{131}I injection. Riggs observed that the proportion of hormone in
the tissues turned over per unit time increases when the concentration
of hormone increases. He concluded from the available experimental
evidence and his mathematical derivation that the absolute quantity of
thyroxine disposed of each day is a function of the second power of
the thyroxine concentration. Since this article was published the
introduction of techniques of measuring free thyroxine levels in
plasma[14] and the specific method for bound thyroxine[16] encouraged
us to investigate the possibility of determining this rate constant
using Riggs' formula

$$B^2 = \frac{H}{000122 V_B}$$

where B = concentration of organic iodine in plasma

H = rate of secretion of hormonal iodine

V_B = volume of distribution of organic iodine in B
referred to its concentration in plasma

Using this formulation and the specific estimation of thyroxine we
have found that this rate constant can be determined with reasonable
accuracy. We have calculated V_B from body size[17] and also in recent
experiments using double isotope injection of Na ^{131}I and T_4 ^{125}I,
from the actual experimental data.

Assuming steady state in the thyroxine compartment then the hormone
degraded per unit time must be replaced and thus we have a measure of
the quantity of hormone released by the thyroid per unit time. To
determine the rate constant for thyroid to PBI requires knowledge of
the absolute amount of iodine in the gland and this is most difficult
to overcome. To date we have used (a) the biological half life of
the gland determined in previous studies to form this estimate

(b) taken a mean value of 8.5 mg iodine as the content of the gland
(average of data from our patient population) with either one of these
methods reasonable fit of the data is obtained. It is surprising
that such a crude method should yield satisfactory results in the
patients tested so far, especially as the parameter sensitivity
analysis shows after the first days of the experiment the sensitivity
of the system to this single rate constant increases markedly and
continuously throughout the remaining period of data collection. It
may be that fluctuations in the iodine content of the gland in
different populations may make the second method for this parameter
estimation impracticable. It is for this reason that we are
conducting a controlled study in an iodine deficient population at
this time. Renal clearance and thyroid clearance, iodide and
thyroxine space, specific activities, plasma inorganic iodide are
estimated by a number of techniques.[18,19,20,21] The respective rate
constants are derived from these measures.

DISCUSSION

Several reports have appeared in the literature on compartmental
analysis of the thyroid system both for the total system[22,23,24,25]
and for specific compartments within the entire system.[26,27,28]
Certainly the most exhaustive study of the former has been and is being
carried on by Berman and his various colleagues throughout the world.
They state in a recent publication[29] that their aim is to build a
model of the thyroid system which will fit all data (normal and
pathological) no matter what its source. This approach is a rewarding
one in that it sheds some light on the physiology of the system and
indicates areas which would be of interest to investigate, e.g. the
iodide "leak" from the thyroid has been the subject of much controversy
and experimental work[30,31,32] and is an integral part of the Berman
model.

Our aim is to fit the experimental data from patients without
clinical symptoms of thyroid pathology, with a model containing only
observable and measurable parameters. It is for this reason we have
restricted our model to 4 - 6 compartments. Due to the experimental
errors we feel that the addition of further compartments will not

improve the inherent accuracy of the simulation.

We are at present collecting data on a population which has a markedly different dietary intake of iodine than our hospital population (ca. 50 mcgs/day as opposed to ca. 400 mcgs/day) to check the validity of the present model.

Future efforts will utilize the flexible and general capability of CSMP to handle nonlinear and time-varying systems, which cannot be solved by conventional and analytical techniques. For example, the initial diffusion of the isotope following injection may be simulated by making the plasma-thyroid and plasma-urine rate coefficients functions of time rather than constants. This will certainly help the early data fitting, inspection of the curves in Figures 4, 5, 7, and 8 shows that the actual data is always higher than the predicted data by varying amounts, the variability being a function of several parameters.

The curves generated by the data of the GPSS model should compare well with the investigators data. To this end an iteration scheme varying the input parameters, i.e., conditional transition probabilities and sojourn time distributions, need be searched for.

Our latest mathematical approach is motivated jointly by our experimental desires and a series of papers by Bergner.[33,34,35] Bergner formulates the problems of tracer theory in a probabilistic setting and utilizing ergodic theory obtains estimates for mean sojourn times, turnover rates and pool sizes. In this approach the time mean is used in obtaining these estimates. If we measure drug effects on thyroid activity in terms of these parameters, the problem suggested by our experimental procedures is to estimate the total area under the curve after observing the curve for a short period of time. More precisely, we will consider the following problem:

Let $X_i(t:u)$ denote the indicator function of compartment i at time t with respect to a fixed particle u. That is $X_i(t:u)$ assumes the value one if u is in compartment i at time t, and it assumes the value zero otherwise. The mean sojourn time of compartment i (say θ_i) is given by the following expressions:

$$\theta_i = \int_o^\infty E[X_i(t:u)]dt = \int_o^\infty R_i(t)dt$$

where $R_i(t)$ is the percent of tracer in compartment i at time t.

Accordingly we need observe $R_i(t)$, $t \leq T_i$ and then estimate $\int_0^\infty R_i(t)dt$. The desired goal is then to simultaneously obtain good estimates of θ_i and minimize T* the maximum observation time i.e. $T* = \max T_i$.

The combination of Berman's technique and our own may prove to be a very powerful tool in the investigation of drug related effects in the thyroid system. As soon as a modified program suitable for our computer is available we intend to investigate this possibility.

The longer term aims are to apply this approach to a study of the various subgroups of schizophrenia both in acute and chronic states and in the affective disorders. The plethora of data for and against this glands role in these disorders is, to say the least, confusing.[36]

APPENDIX 1

ERROR BOUNDS OF PERTURBED SYSTEMS OF DIFFERENTIAL EQUATIONS

Herman Hanisch
City University of New York and
Research Center, Rockland State Hospital

I.   General Theorems

Theorem 1. Let $u(x)$ and $v(x)$ be continuous in $[a,b]$ and have right hand derivatives in $[a,b]$ i.e.

$$u'_+ (x) = \lim_{\substack{h \to 0 \\ h > 0}} \frac{u(x+h) - u(x)}{h}$$

and satisfy the inequality

$$u'_+ \le v'_+ .$$

Then for all $a \le x_1 \le x_2 \le b$,

$$u(x_2) - u(x_1) \le v(x_2) - v(x_1)$$

Proof: We set

$$w(x) = v(x) - v(x_1) - (u(x) - u(x_1)) , \; x \, \varepsilon [a,b]$$

where $x_1 \, \varepsilon [a,b]$ and show $w(x) \ge 0$ for $x \, \varepsilon [x_1,b]$ which is obviously equivalent to our assertion.

We immediately have that

$$w(x) \, \varepsilon \, C \qquad x \, \varepsilon \, [a,b]$$

$$w'_+ \text{ exists} \qquad x \, \varepsilon \, [a,b]$$

and hence $w'_+ \ge 0$ since $v'_+ \ge u'_+$.

Let $x_2 \, \varepsilon (x_1,b]$ and $\varepsilon > 0$ be any arbitrary positive number. Hence there exists a $\delta > 0$ such that

(1) $\dfrac{w(x)}{x-x_1} - w'_+(x_1) = \dfrac{w(x) - w(x_1)}{x-x_1} - w'_+(x_1) \ge -\varepsilon$

for $0 < x - x_1 < \delta$, since $w(x_1) = 0$, and since also $w'_+(x_1) \ge 0$, $x - x_1 > 0$, we get from (1)

(2) $w(x) \ge -\varepsilon(x-x_1)$. Let c be least upper bound of all right intervals such that (2) is true for $x \le x_2$ i.e.

$$c = \sup \{x: w(t) \ge \varepsilon(t-x) , \; x_1 \le t \le x\}$$

$$x_1 \le x \le x_2$$

In fact $c = x_2$ because the continuity of w insures that (2) holds for $x = c$

(3) $w(c) \geq - \varepsilon \, (c-x_1)$, and if $c < x_2$ then just as before with

c in place of x_1, there exists an interval to the right of c

such that

(4) $w(x) - w(c) \geq - \varepsilon \, (x-c), \quad 0 \leq x - c \leq \alpha \, , \, \alpha > 0$

adding inequalities (3) and (4) we get

(5) $w(x) \geq - \varepsilon \, (c-x_1) - \varepsilon \, (x-c) = - \varepsilon \, (x-x_1), \quad x \varepsilon [c,c+\alpha]$ and thus

(2) is valid for all $x \, \varepsilon [x,c+\alpha]$ which contradicts the definition

of c as a $\ell.u.b.$ Thus $c = x_2$, and so (3) is really

(3)' $w(x_2) \geq - \varepsilon \, (x_2 - x_1)$ for all $\varepsilon > 0$.

Let $\varepsilon \to 0$ in (3)', we obtain

$$w(x_2) \geq 0$$

and since x_2 is any arbitrary number in $(x_1,b]$ our proof is

completed.   This leads to the following

Theorem 2.   Let $u\,(x) \, \varepsilon \, C$ in $[a,b]$ and have right hand derivatives

in $[a,b)$, and satisfies the inequality

(A) $| u'_+ (x) | \leq m | \, u(x) \, | + n \qquad x \varepsilon [a,b)$ where $m > 0, \, n \geq 0$.   Then

for any numbers x and c in $[a,b]$,

$$| u(x) | \leq | u(c) | \, e^{m | x-c|} + \frac{n}{m}(e^{m | x-c|} - 1)$$

Proof: Set $v(x) = | \, u(x) \, |$, and clearly v is continuous in $[a,b]$.

Also v'_+ exists in $[a,b)$ because, for $x \, \varepsilon [a,b), \, h > 0 \quad x+h \, \varepsilon [a,b]$,

(1) $\dfrac{v(x+h)-v(x)}{h} = \dfrac{| u(x+h) | - | u(x) |}{h}$

Note that if $u(x) > 0$ then $u(x+h) > 0$ for sufficiently small h   by

continuity.   Likewise if $u(x) < 0$, then $u(x+h) < 0$ for small enough h.

Hence in the case $u(x) \neq 0$ at point x , the right hand side of (1)

becomes

$$\frac{u(x+h) - u(x)}{h} \qquad \text{if } u(x) > 0$$

or $- \dfrac{u(x+h) - u(x)}{h} \qquad \text{if } u(x) < 0$

so that

(2) $v'_+(x) = u'_+$ if $u(x) > 0$

$- u'_+$ if $u(x) < 0$

$| \, u'_+ \, |$ if $u(x) = 0$

Observe, this is where in case $u(x) = 0$, we used the hypothesis of

right hand derivative, i.e. $h > 0$ in $\lim\limits_{h \to 0} | \frac{u(x+h)}{h} | = u'_+(x)$.   Thus,

$v'_+(x)$ exists in $[a,b]$ and

(2) shows that

(3) $|v'_+| = |u'_+|$. Therefore the inequality (A) of the hypothesis becomes (B) $|v'_+| \leq mv+n$ or

(4) $v'_+ + mv \geq -n$

(5) $v'_+ - mv \leq n$

Note that $(e^{mx}v)'_+ = e^{mx}(v'_+ mv)$ so we can write (4) in the form

(6) $(e^{mx}v)'_+ \geq -ne^{mx} = (\frac{-n}{m} e^{mx})'_+$ and applying Theorem 1 to equation (6) we obtain,

for $a \leq x \leq c \leq b$

(7) $e^{mc}v(c) - e^{mx}v(x) \geq \frac{-n}{m} e^{mc} + \frac{n}{m} e^{mx}$

Similarly multiplying (5) by e^{-mx} and applying Theorem 1 in $a \leq c \leq x \leq b$, we get

(8) $e^{-mx}v(x) - e^{-mc}v(c) \leq \frac{-n}{m} e^{-mx} + \frac{n}{m} e^{-mc}$

It follows from (7) and (8) that solving for $v(x)$,

(9) $v(x) \leq v(c) e^{m(c-x)} + \frac{n}{m} (e^{m(c-x)}-1)$, $x \leq c$

(10) $v(x) \leq v(c) e^{m(x-c)} + \frac{n}{m} (e^{m(x-c)}-1)$, $c \leq x$

that is (9) and (10) are equivalent to

(11) $|u(x)| = v(x) \leq |u(c)| e^{m|x-c|} + \frac{n}{m} (e^{m|x-c|} -1)$ which proves

our theorem.

We can generalize Theorem 2 as follows:

Corollary 1   Let $u_i(x) \in C$ in $[a,b]$, $i=1,2,\ldots,n$ be n right hand differentiable functions in $[a,b]$ which satisfy the inequality

(A) $\sum_{i=1}^{n} |u'_{i,+}(x)| \leq M \sum_{i=1}^{n} |u_i(x)| + N$

where $M > 0$, $N \geq 0$. Then for any two, x and c, points of the interval $[a,b]$,

(B) $\sum_{i=1}^{n} |u_i(x)| \leq \sum_{i=1}^{n} |u_i(c)| e^{M|x-c|} + \frac{N}{M} (e^{M|x-c|} -1)$

for $x \in [a,b]$

Proof: Set $u(x) = \sum_{i=1}^{n} |u_i(x)|$, $x \in [a,b]$ $v_i(x) = |u_i|$

Then as before we have, x and $x+h \in [a,b]$, $h > 0$,

709

(1) $\dfrac{u(x+h) - u(x)}{h} = \sum_{i=1}^{n} \dfrac{|u_i(x+h)| - |u_i(x)|}{h}$

$= \sum_{i=1}^{n} \dfrac{v_i(x+h) - v_i(x)}{h}$

and so as $h \to 0$ in (1),

(2) $u'_+ = \sum_{i=1}^{n} v_{i,+}'(x)$, and

(3) $|u'_+(x)| \le \sum_{i=1}^{n} |v_{i,+}'(x)| = \sum_{i=1}^{n} |u_{i,+}'(x)|$

Using inequality (A), (3) becomes therefore,

(4) $|u'_+(x)| \le M \sum_{i=1}^{n} |u_i(x)| + N = M u(x) + N$

Thus for any two points x and $c \in [a,b]$, we have by Theorem 2

$\sum_{i=1}^{n} |u_i(x)| = u(x) \le u(c) e^{m|x-c|} + \dfrac{n}{m}(e^{m|x-c|} - 1)$,

which is inequality (B).

We can now apply our results to obtain estimates on solutions of differential equations.

Theorem 3. Let $f_i(x,y_1,y_2,\ldots y_n)$, $i=1,2,\ldots n$ be continuous and bounded and satisfy a Lipschitz condition in a domain D, i.e.

$|f_i(x,y_1,y_2,y_n)| = |f_i| \le B$

$|f_i(x,\bar{y}_1,\bar{y}_2,\ldots\bar{y}_n) - f_i(x,y_1,y_2,\ldots y_n)| \le M \sum_{i=1}^{n} |\bar{y}_i - \bar{y}_i|$

$i = 1,2,3,\ldots n$, and $(x,y_1,y_2,\ldots y_n) \quad \epsilon \ D$

$(x_1,\bar{y}_1,\bar{y}_2,\ldots\bar{y}_n) \quad \epsilon \ D$ where

B and $M>0$ are constants independent of the points of D.
Furthermore let $\phi_i(x)$ and $\psi_i(x)$ be continuous and have right hand derivatives in (a,b), $i=1,2,\ldots n$. Let $(c,b_1,b_2,\ldots b_n)$ and $(\bar{c}, \bar{b}_1, \bar{b}_2, \ldots \bar{b}_n) \epsilon \ D$. Suppose

$\phi_i(c) = b_i$

$\psi_i(\bar{c}) = \bar{b}_i$

(A) $|\phi'_{i,+} - f_i(x, \phi_1, \phi_2, \ldots, \phi_n)| \le \epsilon_1$

(B) $|\psi'_{i,+} - f_i(x, \psi_1, \psi_2, \ldots, \psi_n)| \le \epsilon_2$

and

$$(x, \phi_1(x), \ldots, \phi_n(x)) \; \varepsilon \; D$$

$$(x, \psi_1(x), \ldots, \psi_n(x)) \; \varepsilon \; D \quad \text{for } x \; \varepsilon \; (a,b)$$

Then, for $x \; \varepsilon \; (a,b)$

$$\sum_{i=1}^{n} | \phi_i(x) - \psi_i(x) | \leq \frac{\varepsilon_1 + \varepsilon_2}{M} (e^{nM|x-c|} - 1) +$$

$$[n(B + \varepsilon_1 + \varepsilon_2) | c - \bar{c} | + \sum_{i=1}^{n} | b_i - \bar{b}_i | e^{nM|x-c|}] .$$

Proof: We have by the Lipschitz condition since all points belong to
D, when $x \; \varepsilon \; (a,b)$

$$(1) \quad | f_i(x, \phi_1(x), \phi_2(x), \ldots, \phi_n(x)) - f_i(x, \psi_1(x), \ldots, \psi_n(x)) |$$

$$\leq M \sum_{i=1}^{n} | \phi_i(x) - \psi_i(x) | , \quad i = 1, 2, \ldots, n .$$

Hence, $x \; \varepsilon \; [a,b)$

$$(2) \quad \sum_{i=1}^{n} | \phi'_{i,+}(x) - \psi'_{i,+}(x) | \leq \sum_{i=1}^{n} | \phi'_{i,+}(x) - f_i(x, \phi_1, \ldots, \phi_n) | +$$

$$+ \sum_{i=1}^{n} | \psi'_{i,+}(x) - f_i(x, \psi_1, \ldots, \psi_n) |$$

$$+ \sum_{i=1}^{n} | f_i(x, \phi_1, \ldots, \phi_n) - f_i(x, \psi_1, \ldots, \psi_n) |$$

$$\leq n(\varepsilon_1 + \varepsilon_2) + nM \sum_{i=1}^{n} | \phi_i(x) - \psi_i(x) |$$

by inequalities (A), (B) and (1). Let $x \varepsilon (a,b)$: choose a_1 and b_1 such
that $a < a_1 < b_1 < b$ and x and $c \; \varepsilon [a_1, b_1]$. Applying corollary 1
to (2) in the interval $[a_1, b_1]$, we obtain

$$(3) \quad \sum_{i=1}^{n} | \phi_i(x) - \psi_i(x) | \leq \sum_{i=1}^{n} | \phi_i(c) - \psi_i(c) | e^{nM|x-c|} +$$

$$\frac{(\varepsilon_1 + \varepsilon_2)}{M} (e^{nM|x-c|} - 1)$$

But,

$$(4) \quad | \phi_i(c) - \psi_i(c) | \leq | \phi_i(c) - \psi_i(\bar{c}) | + | \psi_i(\bar{c}) - \psi_i(c) | .$$

We recall now a theorem in analysis which states that if $f(x) \epsilon C$, $x \epsilon [a,b]$ or (a,b) then all the following functions have the same $\ell.u.b.$ and $g.\ell.b.$

$$I(x_1, x_2) = \frac{f(x_1) - f(x_2)}{x_1 - x_2} \quad , \quad x_1 \neq x_2$$

$$D^+ f(x) = \overline{\underset{\substack{h \to 0 \\ h > 0}}{\ell im}} \quad \frac{f(x+h) - f(x)}{h} \text{ , or for } h > 0$$

$$D^+ f(x) = \overline{\underset{h \to 0}{\ell im}} \quad I(x+h, x)$$

$$D^- f(x) = \underset{\overline{h \to 0}}{\ell im} \quad I(x+h, x)$$

$$D^- f(x) = \overline{\underset{h \to 0}{\ell im}} \quad I(x-h, x)$$

$$D_- f(x) = \underset{\overline{h \to 0}}{\ell im} \quad I(x-h, x)$$

and as a consequence we get a generalized form of the law of the mean of the differential calculus

$$f(b) - f(a) = (b-a) \, I \, (a_1, b) = (b-a) \, I \, (a, b) = (b-a) \, M$$

where M is a number between $g.\ell.b.$ and $\ell.u.b.$ of any one of the derivatives of $f(x)$. Consequently it follows that if any one of the derivatives of $f(x)$ is bounded say by K, then

$$|f(x_1) - f(x_2)| \leq K |x_1 - x_2|$$

for any x_1, $x_2 \, \epsilon \, [a,b]$.

From (B) and the bound on f_i, it follows

(5) $\quad |\psi'_{i,+} (x)| \leq |f_i(x, \psi_1, \psi_2, \ldots, \psi_n)| + \epsilon_2 \leq B + \epsilon_2$.

Thus by the above with $K = B + \epsilon_2$, we have

(6) $\quad |\psi_i(\bar{c}) - \psi_i(c)| \leq |\bar{c} - c|(B + \epsilon_2) \leq (B + \epsilon_1 + \epsilon_2)|\bar{c} - c|$

and so (4) becomes

(7) $\quad |\phi_i(c) - \psi_i(\bar{c})| \leq |\phi_i(c) - \psi_i(\bar{c})| + (B + \epsilon_1 + \epsilon_2)|\bar{c} - c| =$

$$|\bar{b}_i - b_i| + (B + \epsilon_1 + \epsilon_2)|\bar{c} - c|$$

which when substituted in (3) gives the estimates of the theorem (to be proven).

The next theorem will give an estimate of the manner in which the solutions of the initial value problem $y'_i = f_i$ will change when we alter f_i slightly. More precisely

Theorem 4.   Let $f_i(x,y_1,\ldots,y_n)$ and $g_i(x,y_1,\ldots,y_n)$ be continuous in a domain D, $i=1,2,\ldots,n$. Suppose

(A) $\left| f_i(x,y_1,\ldots,y_n) - g_i(x,y_1,\ldots,y_n) \right| \le \varepsilon$ in D, and

$$\left| f_i(x,\bar{y}_1,\ldots,\bar{y}_n) - f_i(x,y_1,\ldots,y_n) \right| \le M \sum_{i=1}^{n} \left| \bar{y}_i - y_i \right|, \quad M>0$$

(B) $\phi_i'(x) = f_i(x,\phi_1,\phi_2,\ldots,\phi_n)$

(C) $\psi_i'(x) = g_i(x,\psi_1,\psi_2,\ldots,\psi_n)$

$$\phi_i(c) = \psi_i(c) = b_i, \quad i = 1,2,\ldots,n$$

$(x,\phi_1,\ldots,\phi_n)\ \varepsilon D,$

$(x,\psi_1,\ldots,\psi_n)\ \varepsilon D, \qquad x\ \varepsilon(a,b)$

$(c,b_1,b_2,\ldots,b_n)\ \varepsilon D$

then

$$\sum_{i=1}^{n} \left| \phi_i(x) - \psi_i(x) \right| \le \frac{\varepsilon}{M} (e^{nM\left| x-c \right|} -1)$$

Proof: Note that if D is bounded then the Lipschitz condition implies the f_i are bounded. Here we do not assume $\left| f_i \right| \le B$ as in theorem 3 which was used to estimate $\left| \phi_i(c) - \psi_i(\bar{c}) \right|$ in 4. Here we have the following correspondence in theorem 3.

I.C. $\bar{c} = c$

$\bar{b}_i = b_i$

$\left| \phi_i' - f_i \right| = 0 = \varepsilon_1$ from (B)

$\left| \psi_i' - f_i \right| = \left| \psi_i' - g_i + g_i - f_i \right|$ from (C)

$= \left| g_i - f_i \right| \le \varepsilon = \varepsilon_2$ from (A)

and so also

$\left| \phi_i(c) - \psi_i(\bar{c}) \right| = \left| b_i - \bar{b}_i \right| = 0$, $i=1,2,\ldots,n$, $x\ \varepsilon(a,b)$.

Theorem 3, therefore, gives us

$$\sum_{i=1}^{n} \left| \phi_i(x) - \psi_i(x) \right| \le \frac{\varepsilon}{M} (e^{nM\left| x-c \right|} -1) \ .$$

II. Application to linear systems of the first order

Suppose $a_{ij}(\varepsilon), i,j = 1.2.,,,.n$ are constants depending on a parameter ε such that

$$|a_{ij}(\varepsilon) - a_{ij}| \leq \delta$$

$$a_{ij}(0) = a_{ij}, i,j = 1,2,\ldots,n$$

$$|a_{ij}| \leq M .$$

Let

$$\phi'_{i,\varepsilon}(x) = \sum_{j=1}^{n} a_{ij}(\varepsilon) \phi_{j,\varepsilon}(x), j = 1,2,\ldots,n$$

$$\phi_{i,\varepsilon}(c) = b_i, \quad i = 1,2,\ldots,n .$$

$x, c \in (a,b)$, and we identify the following

$$f_i(x,y_1,\ldots,y_n) = \sum_{j=1}^{n} a_{ij} y_j , \quad i = 1,2,\ldots,n$$

$$g_i(x,y_1,\ldots,y_n) = \sum_{j=1}^{n} a_{ij}(\varepsilon) y_j$$

$$\phi_i = \phi_{i,0}$$

$$\psi_{i,\varepsilon} = \phi_{i,\varepsilon}$$

so that

$$\left| f_i(x,\bar{y}_1,\ldots,\bar{y}_n) - f_i(x,y_1,\ldots,y_n) \right| \leq \left| \sum_{j=1}^{n} a_{ij}(\bar{y}_j - y_j) \right|$$

$$\leq M \sum_{j=1}^{n} |\bar{y}_j - y_j|$$

$$\left| f_i(x,y_1,\ldots,y_n) - g_i(x,y_1,\ldots,y_n) \right| \leq \delta \sum_{j=1}^{n} |y_j| \leq \delta B$$

$$\varepsilon = \delta B$$

where we take D to be a bounded domain and so $\sum_{j=1}^{n} |y_j| \leq B$. Thus

$$\text{(I)} \quad \sum_{i=1}^{n} |\phi_i - \phi_{i,\varepsilon}| \leq \frac{\delta B}{M} (e^{nM|x-c|} - 1)$$

Now let us suppose that we can solve explicitly the above differential equation

$$\frac{dy_i}{dx} = f_i(x, y_1, y_2, \ldots, y_n) \qquad i=1,2,\ldots,n$$

$$= \sum_{j=1}^{n} a_{ij} y_j$$

for some of the functions y_i , say for convenience in writing (one can always reorder the system) for the

$$y_i = \phi_i(x) \ , \ n \geq i \geq m+1$$

Our system becomes

D.E. $\quad \dfrac{dy_i}{dx} = \sum_{j=1}^{m} a_{ij} y_j + \sum_{j=m+1}^{n} a_{ij} \phi_j(x), \quad i=1,2,\ldots,m$.

I.C. $\quad y_i(c) = b_i \ , \ i=1,2,\ldots,m$

$$\phi_i(c) = b_i \ , \ i=m+1, m+2, \ldots, n$$

Thus in this case, we get

$$f_i = \sum_{j=1}^{m} a_{ij} y_j + \sum_{j=m+1}^{n} a_{ij} \phi_j(x)$$

$$g_i = \sum_{j=1}^{m} a_{ij}(\epsilon) y_j + \sum_{j=m+1}^{n} a_{ij}(\epsilon) \phi_j(x), \ i=1,2,\ldots,m$$

so that the Lipschitz condition becomes

$$\left| f_i(x, \bar{y}_1, \ldots, \bar{y}_n) - f_i(x, y_1, \ldots, y_n) \right| = \left| \sum_{j=1}^{m} a_{ij}(\bar{y}_j - y_j) \right|$$

$$\leq M \sum_{j=1}^{m} \left| \bar{y}_j - y_j \right|$$

and

$$\left| f_i(x, y_1, \ldots, y_n) - g_i(x, y_1, \ldots, y_n) \right| = \left| \sum_{j=1}^{m} (a_{ij} - a_{ij}(\epsilon)) y_j + \right.$$

$$\left. \sum_{j=m+1}^{n} (a_{ij} - a_{ij}(\epsilon)) \phi_j \right| \leq \delta \left(\sum_{j=1}^{m} |y_j| + \sum_{j=m+1}^{n} |\phi_j| \right) \leq \delta B .$$

Our estimate becomes,

II $\quad \displaystyle\sum_{i=1}^{m} \left| \phi_i(x) - \phi_{i,\epsilon}(x) \right| \leq \frac{\delta B}{M} (e^{mM|x-c|} - 1)$

Note that in both systems ϕ_i, $i=1,2,\ldots,m$ are the same by uniqueness theorems while obviously $\phi_{i,\epsilon}$,$i \leq m$ are most probably different. Comparing II and I we observe the improved estimate since $m < n$.

APPENDIX 2

SAMPLE GPSS OUTPUT (EDITED)

RELATIVE CLOCK	N R	VALUE	N R	VALUE	N R	VALUE	N R	VALUE
0	1	34					6	66
1	1	37	2	2	3	1	6	60
2	1	41	2	5	3	2	6	52
10	1	41	2	50	3	9		
20	1	11	2	74	3	15		
40	1	1	2	82	3	17		
100			2	83	3	17		
1000			2	92	3	5	4	3
3000			2	94	3	6		

STORAGE	AVERAGE CONTENTS	AVERAGE UTILIZATION	ENTRIES	AVERAGE TIME/TRAN	CURRENT CONTENTS	MAXIMUM CONTENTS
1	.290	.002	114	7.912		65
2	87.817	.878	94	2897.968	94	94
3	10.892	.108	20	1689.399	6	17
4	.906	.009	14	200.928		3
6	.060	.000	66	2.848		66

LEGEND

RELATIVE CLOCK	– Time in hours.
N R	– Refers to compartment number, where labelling of compartment is given in Figure 2 in the text.
VALUE	– Number of molecules (transactions) in the compartment.
STORAGE	– Same as N R, above.
AVERAGE CONTENTS	– Average contents of each compartment during the course of the simulation.
AVERAGE UTILIZATION	– Average contents divided by 100. (100 is the capacity of each compartment.)
ENTRIES	– Total number of molecules entering this compartment.
AVERAGE TIME/TRAN	– Average length of time a molecule remained within this storage compartment.
CURRENT CONTENTS	– Contents at 3000 hours, end of simulation.
MAXIMUM CONTENTS	– Maximum number of molecules in the compartment during the course of the simulation.

REFERENCES

1. KLINE, N.S., BLAIR, J., COOPER, T.B., ESSER, A.H., HACKETT, E. and VESTERGAARD, P. Problems of interdisciplinary longitudinal research on psychiatric patients: A controlled seven year study of endocrine and other indices in drug treated chronic schizophrenics. Acta Psychiatrica Scandinavica, Supplement, 1968.

2. CLYNES, M. and CRANSWICK, E.H. Dynamic analysis: An analog computer study of thyroid functions. In Psychopharmacology Frontiers, Kline, N.S. (Editor), p.515, Little, Brown & Co., Boston, Mass., 1959.

3. BRENNAN, R., SANO, H. "PACTOLUS" A digital analog simulator program for the IBM 1620. Proceedings 1964 Fall Joint Computer Conference. AFPIS, Vol. 26, p.299.

4. RIGGS, D.S. Quantitative aspects of iodine in man. Pharmacol. Rev. 4, 284, 1952.

5. BRENNAN, R.D., COOPER, T.B. and LASKA, E.M. Investigation of thyroid metabolism by digital simulation. Presented at American Simulation Council Meeting December 3, 1965, Las Vegas, Nevada.

6. WEISS, G. and ZELEN, M. A semi-Markov model for clinical trials. Math. Res. Ctr., Madison Wisconsin. Technical Note #BN312 March, 1963.

7. SIEGEL, C., COOPER, T.B. and MEISNER, M. Mathematical models of the thyroid: Deterministic and stochastic. In Computers and Electronic Devices in Psychiatry, Kline, N.S. and Laska, E. (Editors), p.100, Grune & Stratton, Inc., New York, 1968.

8. General Purpose System Simulator III of IBM Technical Publications Department.

9. 1130 Continuous System Modeling Program. 1130-CX-PX IBM Manual H20-0282-0.

10. KING, R.E. Parametric sensitivity of physiological systems - prognostic analyses. IEEE Transactions on Bio-Medical Engineering. Vol. BME-14, 1967, p.209.

11. GRADIJAN, J.R. Manuscript in preparation.

12. KETY, S.S. Quantitative determination of cerebral blood flow in man. In Methods in Medical Research, Potter, V.R. (Editor), p. 204, Year Book Medical Publishers, Chicago, Ill., 1948.

13. CRANSWICK, E.H. and McFADDEN, P.L. Improved equipment design for studies on thyroid uptake. Amer. J. Med. Electronics, 1, 108, 1962.

14. OPPENHEIMER, J.H. and SURKS, M.I. Determination of free thyroxine in human serum, a theoretical and experimental analysis. J. Clin. Endocr. 24, 785, 1964.

15. SIMPSON, G.M. and COOPER, T.B. Thyroid indices in chronic schizophrenia: III. J. Nerv. Ment. Dis. 142: 1, 1966.

16. MURPHY, B.E.P. and PATTEE, C.J. Determination of thyroxine utilizing the property of protein binding. J. Clin. Endocr. 24, 187, 1964.

17. ODDIE, T.H., FISHER, D.A., WATT, J.C. and NEWTOWN, B.
     Radioiodide space in human subjects without edema. J.
     Clin. Endocr. 24, 54, 1964.

18. VEALL, N. and VETTER, H. Radioisotope techniques. In
     Clinical Research and Diagnosis, Veall, N. and Vetter, H.
     (Editors), p.289, Butterworth, London, 1958.

19. BERSON, S.A., YALOW, R.S., SORRENTINO, J. and ROSWITT, B.
     The determination of thyroidal and renal plasma ^{131}I
     clearance rates as a routine diagnostic test of thyroid
     dysfunction. J. Clin. Invest. 31, 141, 1952.

20. ODDIE, T.H., MESCHAN, I. and WORTHAM, J. Thyroid function
     assay with radioiodine I, II. J.Clin. Invest. 34, 95, 1955.

21. FISHER, D.A. and ODDIE, T.H. Comparison of thyroidal iodide
     accumulation and thyroxine secretion in euthyroid subjects.
     J. Clin. Endocr. 24, 1143, 1964.

22. ODDIE, T.H. Analysis of radio-iodine uptake and excretion
     curves. Brit. J. Radiol. 22, 261, 1949.

23. BERMAN, M. Application of differential equations to the study
     of the thyroid system. In Proceedings of the Fourth Berkeley
     Symposium on Mathematical Statistics and Probability.
     Neyman, J. (Editor), p.87, University of California Press,
     California, 1961.

24. BERSON, S.A. and YALOW, R.S. Quantitative aspects of iodine
     metabolism. The exchangeable organic iodine pool, and the
     rates of thyroidal secretion, peripheral degradation and
     fecal excretion of endogenously synthesized organically bound
     iodine. J. Clin. Invest. 33, 1533, 1954.

25. RIVIERE, R., COMAR, D. and KELLERSHOHN, C. A comparative analysis
     of the curves of the iodine specific activity determined in
     man throughout long-period studies, in the different
     compartments of the thyroid metabolic system. In Current Topics
     in Thyroid Research, Cassano, C. and Andreoli, M. (Editors),
     p.112, Academic Press, New York, 1965.

26. BROWNELL, G.L. Analysis of techniques for the determination of
     thyroid function with radioiodine. J. Clin. Endocr. 11, 1095,
     1951.

27. WOLLMANN, S.H. and REED, F.E. Kinetics of accumulation of radioiodine
     by thyroid gland. Am. J. Physiol. 202 (1), 182, 1962.

28. HAYS, M.T. and WEGNER, L.H. A mathematical and physiological
     model for the early distribution of radioiodine in man.
     J. Appl. Physiol. 20, 1319, 1965.

29. BERMAN, M., HOFF, E., BARANDES, M., BECKER, D.V., SONENBERG, M.,
     BENUA R. and KOUTRAS, D.A. Iodine kinetics in man - a model.
     J. Clin. Endocr. 28, 1, 1968.

30. WERNER, S.C. and RADICHEVICH, I. Presence of iodine-127
     iodotyrosines in extracts of normal human serum. Nature, 197,
     877, 1963.

31. WEINER, J.D. Functional heterogeneity of the thyroid and possible
     presence of iodotyrosine-like compounds in normal serum.
     Acta Endocr. 48, 199, 1965.

32. DEGROOT, L.J. Kinetic analysis of iodine metabolism. J. Clin. Endocr. <u>26</u>, 149, 1966.

33. BERGNER, P.E.E. Tracer dynamics. I. A tentative approach and definition of fundamental concepts. J. Theor. Biol. <u>1</u>, 120, 1961.

34. BERGNER, P.E.E. Tracer dynamics. II. The limiting properties of the tracer system. J. Theor. Biol. <u>1</u>, 359, 1961.

35. BERGNER, P.E.E. On ergodic properties of the tracer system. (Personal communication.)

ACKNOWLEDGEMENTS: We wish to acknowledge the advice and help of Drs. G.M. Simpson, L. Krakov, L. Deutsch and J.S. Angus in the experimental procedures, Dr. E. Laska for contributing a great deal of effort in the early phases of this work and to the Thyroid Unit staff for their expert technical assistance.

T. B. Cooper, F.I.M.L.T., J. R. Gradijan, M. J. Meisner, Rockland State Hospital, Orangeburg, N.Y.

Carole Siegel, New York University, New York, N.Y.

THE ESSENTIAL MORPHOLOGICAL NORMALITY OF SCHIZOPHRENICS' SEMEN

JOHN H. BLAIR, JOHN MACLEOD, and GEORGE M. SIMPSON

Mental illness, particularly schizophrenia, has often been related to ill-defined and as yet unproven biochemical, cytological and physiological abnormalities. The continuous hospitalization or institutionalization of patients must also be considered a possible source of enhanced abnormality.

Our own interest in the field of physical involvement accompanying schizophrenia started with the reports[1,2] that the testes of schizophrenic patients were histologically abnormal. We were able to show, however[3] that there were no abnormalities particular to this disease; a finding that was confirmed shortly by others[4].

In recent years, with the advent of many psychoactive medications with endocrinological and neurological side effects, another aspect of reproduction remains to be investigated, i.e. the possible effects of the drugs on various qualitative aspects of reproduction. Although we have reported certain alterations in seminal and reproductive reflexes, it is now necessary to determine the degree of functional normality, by means of semen analysis, of the testes of chronic schizophrenic patients. This step is necessary before definitive statements regarding drug induced changes may be made.

Despite the fact that the hospital populations receive relatively large dosages of medication, it is hoped that information on drug induced seminal changes would provide information on the effect of these drugs in lesser dosages on the large number of non-hospitalized patients when used by their general practitioners or psychiatrists.

In order to accurately assay the degree of normality, the morphological character of the semen is a factor of greatest importance.

It is the purpose of this report to point out the essential normality of the semen of otherwise healthy chronic schizophrenic patients, with particular emphasis on the morphological aspects of their semen.

This study was supported in part by Grants MH-08240 and MH-07292 from the National Institute of Mental Health

METHODS

The subjects were a group of 22 schizophrenics who have been well studied in many other connections, and, most unusually, have been drug-free for at least six months. These have been on a research ward at least two years and have had weekly medical examinations throughout this period. Some have been subjects of experimental investigations involving the thyroid and/or adrenal gland, some for cerebral metabolic studies, and some for routine drug evaluation. All subjects were considered free of physical ailments. They have had regular dental check-ups and routine clinical examinations. Most maintain their weight on the hospital diet. Their mean age is 44 (range 27 - 57) and length of hospitalization 19 years (6 - 42 years).

The morphological readings were determined by one of us (J. MacL) using the standards established in his laboratory. Only one sample from each subject was investigated as it has been shown[5,6,7,8] that an individual's morphological characteristics remain virtually unchanged under conditions of health.

RESULTS

The results of the morphological classification are shown in Table 1 and the averages are compared with the MacLeod prison population. The striking similarity of the two groups is evident. As the prisoner group is superior in all respects it is used by MacLeod as a standard reference[9].

DISCUSSION

We have seen in the literature only two references to seminal characteristics in chronic schizophrenic subjects. Both were published in 1937 and were concerned entirely with morphological characteristics, although different systems of classification were used. Generales[10] compared the semen of an unstated number of males with congenital defects (including chronic alcoholism) with an undefined "normal" group, and the chief changes appear to be in change of head size and with increase in both large and small heads. However, his schizophrenic samples were the most normal of all the defective males listed (53.8% abnormal cells compared with his normal group with 19% abnormal cells).

The type of abnormalities specifically for schizophrenics were not
indicated.

Williams[11] also described the semen of schizophrenics (15 patients
- diagnosis, age and chronicity unstated) as compared with an undefined
normal group and found 64.5% abnormal cells. Again the head size, both
large and small, caused the greatest increase in abnormal forms. His
normal group averaged 26.7% abnormal cells.

The fact that patients receiving certain of the psychoactive drugs
may have a pronounced alteration of the reproductive reflexes[12,13,14,15]
and that, with certain drugs necrospermia, oligospermia, polyspermia
and grossly observed abnormal forms have been observed give cause for
concern. In our series of 22 patients only one (#1) had true oligospermia (less than 20 million per ml[16]), as compared with one out of
three reported by Shader et al[17]. However, their patients were drug-
free for three months while ours were drug-free for a minimum of six
months and in some cases one year. This particular sample from patient
#1 was obtained just six months post-drug. In 10 samples obtained
during the three previous months, five samples were oligospermic, but
with an average value of 21.6 million/cc. This and other evidence
prompted us to use the criterion of six months drug-free before
obtaining baselines for any drug studies. Hartman[18], in comparing
spontaneous infertility in the male with drugs known to have an adverse
effect on sperm motility states "these considerations make one wonder
whether some of the infertile males may not, prior to their visit,
have ingested drugs deleterious to the sensitive spermatogenic
mechanism."

It is now evident that the semen of drug-free hospitalized schizophrenic patients must be accepted as superior in quality when examined
by these methods and that they are therefore suitable subjects for
studies of psychoactive drugs on testicular function.

SUMMARY

Twenty-two schizophrenic patients, drug-free for a period of six
months, were studied with regard to their semen morphology. The
general picture was a normal one, with the group as a whole showing

no differences from a prison population previously studied by MacLeod. The essential normality of these subjects makes them suitable subjects for the study of the effect of psychoactive drugs on semen morphology.

TABLE 1. SPERM DATA ON SCHIZOPHRENIC PATIENTS, 6 MONTHS DRUG FREE

Pat. No.	Vol.	Count/ cc	Tot.	% Motile	Oval	Large	Small	Tapered	Amor- phous	Dup.	Imma- ture
1	1.0	13	13	45	70	6	16	6	2	0	0
2	1.0	65	65	30	70	3	12	3	5	1	0
3	2.0	400	800	35	90	0	5	2	3	0	0
4	1.0	196	196	60	78	4	10	4	4	0	0
5	5.0	84	420	60	64	0	23	2	10	1	0
6	6.5	72	468	40	48	7	2	24	18	1	0
7	1.5	270	405	25	62	2	2	19	10	5	1
8	2.0	255	510	70	73	3	2	19	3	0	0
9	6.0	100	600	45	74	4	4	11	7	0	0
10	2.0	264	528	40	74	1	8	5	12	0	0
11	2.0	104	208	80	69	0	21	3	6	1	0
12	2.5	42	105	20	72	2	22	4	0	0	0
13	2.0	29	58	70	70	4	6	10	9	1	0.5
14	8.0	102	816	50	89	1	4	4	2	0	0
15	4.5	68	306	25	62	11	2	19	5	1	0
16	3.0	128	304	75	62	6	7	13	11	1	2.5
17	1.5	128	192	40	87	0	9	3	1	0	0
18	8.0	23	184	20	67	0	9	17	5	1	0
19	2.0	346	692	30	68	3	5	16	7	1	1
20	8.0	23	184	20	50	12	6	15	16	1	1
21	1.0	100	100	15	65	3	10	15	5	2	0
22	2.0	82	164	80	70	2	18	2	8	0	1
Ave.	3.3	131	336	44	70	3.4	9.2	9.8	7.0	0.7	0.3
St. Dev.	2.5	109	243	22	10	3.3	6.7	7.1	4.4	1.1	0.06
MacLeod Prison Population				73	3.5	8.5		6.0	8.7	1.0	.40

REFERENCES

1. HEMPHILL, R.E., REISS, M. and TAYLOR, A.L. A study of the histology of the testis in schizophrenia and other mental disorders. J. Ment. Sci. 90: 380, 1944.

2. HEMPHILL, R.E. The significance of atrophy of the testis in schizophrenia. J. Ment. Sci. 90: 380, 1944.

3. BLAIR, J.H., SNIFFEN, R.C., CRANSWICK, E.H., JAFFE, W. and KLINE, N.S. The question of histopathological changes in the testes of schizophrenics. J. Ment. Sci. 98: 464, 1952.

4. TOURNEY, G., NELSON, W.O. and GOTTLIEB, J.S. Morphology of the testes in schizophrenia. Arch. Neurol. Psychiat. 70: 240, 1953.

5. JOEL, C.A. Studien am Menschlocken Sperma. B. Schwabb & Co., Basel, 1953.

6. HOTCHKISS, R.S. Fertility in man. Lippencott, Philadelphia, 1944.

7. WILLIAMS, W.W. The germ plasma factor of sterility. New England J. Med. 217: 946, 1937.

8. MacLEOD, J. A possible factor in the etiology of human infertility. Fertil. and Steril. 13: 29, 1962.

9. MacLEOD, J. The clinical implications of deviations in human spermatogenesis as evidenced in seminal cytology and the experimental production of these deviations. Excerpta Medica International Congress, Series No. 133, Stockholm, June 16-22, 1966.

10. GENERALES, K.D.J. Mikropathologie der spermatozoen bei erbranken. Zeitschrift fur induktive Abstammungs-und Vererbungslehre. 1937 Bd. LXXIII Heft 3/4.

11. WILLIAMS, W.W. Spermatic abnormalities. New England J. Med. 217: 946, 1937.

12. BLAIR, J.H., KLINE, N.S. and SIMPSON, G.M. Monoamine oxidase inhibitor and sperm production. J.A.M.A. 181: 172, 1962.

13. SIMPSON, G.M., BLAIR, J.H., IQBAL, J. and IQBAL, F. A preliminary study of trimiprimine in chronic schizophrenia. Curr. Therap. Res. 8: 225, 1966.

14. SIMPSON, G.M., BLAIR, J.H. and AMUSO, D. Effects of anti-
    depressants on genito-urinary function. Dis. Nerv. Syst.
    26: 787, 1965.

15. BLAIR, J.H. and SIMPSON, G.M. Effect of antipsychotic drugs
    on reproductive functions. Dis. Nerv. Syst. 27: 645, 1966.

16. MacLEOD, J. The semen examination. Clin. Obstet. Gynec. 8:
    115, 1965.

17. SHADER, R.I. and GRINSPOON, L. Schizophrenia, oligospermia
    and the phenothiazines. Dis. Nerv. Syst. 28: 240, 1967.

18. HARTMAN, C.G., SCHOENFELD, C. and COPELAND, E. Individualism
    in the semen picture of infertile men. Fertil. and Steril.
    15: 231, 1964.

J. Blair, M.A., and G. M. Simpson, M.B., Ch.B., Rockland State Hospital, Orangeburg, N.Y. 10962

J. MacLeod, Ph.D., Cornell University Medical College, New York Career Scientist,
Health Research Council of the City of New York.

The research of this author supported in part by Grant 5-RO1-HDOO 481-09
from the National Institutes of Health.

CLINICAL STATE AND CATECHOLAMINE EXCRETION WITH DRUG TREATMENT OF CHRONIC SCHIZOPHRENICS

ARISTIDE H. ESSER

ABSTRACT

As part of a longitudinal research design presently in its tenth year, data were collected on a total of 46 chronic schizophrenic patients housed on a special research ward. Of these patients 32 remained in the study long enough to be reported on for this purpose. Their average age at admission to Rockland State Hospital was 23.9 years (range 17-36), at arrival in the research ward they were 32.5 years old (range 22-50), and the average length of their participation in that ward was 3.2 years (range 1-9).

The patients were subjects in a double-blind placebo study of four psychoactive drugs, in which the treatment periods were 12-26 weeks and the placebo period 12-52 weeks long. Clinical ratings and behavioral and biochemical measurements were made with sampling frequencies of 1-28 times per week. For the purpose of this presentation, all data were averaged to weekly values and then analyzed for drug-induced changes, using the patient as his own control. To minimize carryover effects of previous drugs, only those weekly data were used that were obtained after at least 12 weeks of placebo; similarly, in some instances, treatment data were used obtained after 12 weeks of drug administration.

As expected the results show both consistent and statistically significant differences in values obtained during placebo and drug treatment. Surprisingly, however, there were many variables that did not react in a predictable manner to drug treatment, even when the same drug was repeatedly given to the same patient. Also, changes in the values of variables persisted, sometimes long after a drug was withdrawn. These inconsistent findings point to the necessity for reevaluating results obtained in psychopharmacological research utilizing cross sectional designs.

INTRODUCTION

This report can only highlight some of the clinical findings of our on-going study, now in its tenth year, of a group of chronic schizophrenic patients. A description of the over-all findings during the first 5 1/2 years of the project has been presented before (1). I refer to this publication for a more general and systematic discussion of the patient material and the procedures. Here, I will only indicate briefly the enlarged, and simultaneously more restricted scope of the present data.

In the first place, for the past 3 1/2 years of the project we have introduced amitriptyline treatment, additional to the medication used in the first 5 1/2 years (perphenazine, phenelzine and reserpine). All these drugs are presently administered in standarized dosages predicated on weight, and given in once-a-day capsule form. These capsules are identical, and barium tagged to enable us to check on their actual ingestion (2)*.

In the second place, the word "cases" refer to medication episodes; where the same medication has been repeated in a patient, he represents two cases. The variables selected for this study were the ones on which we had most complete data and for various reasons were considered interesting. The choice, in part, may seem arbitrary, but I think that the data allow us to draw the same general research conclusions as would any other variable presently studied in schizophrenia.

In the third place, for this report only 12-13 week data blocks obtained after at least 12 weeks of placebo were analyzed. This explains the fact that some of the patient data used in our first publication had to be deleted here, the remaining material is divided according to the following criteria:

1. Cases in which the preceding placebo period was 12-26 weeks and those on which it was 39 weeks or longer.

2. Cases in which the medication data represented the 12 week treatment period (short-term medication) and those in which the data used came from the last 13 weeks in a treatment period of 6 months or more (longterm medication).

The following patient groups therefore emerged (see also Table 1 and Figure 1):

a) Placebo period between 24-39 weeks, medication period 12-24 weeks (n=29).

*We wish to acknowledge Ciba; Merck, Sharpe and Dohme; Schering Company; and Warner Chilcott for the supply of respectively reserpine, amitriptyline, perphenazine and phenelzine. I wish to thank Dr. M. Thorner and Schering Company for their contribution in tagging and custom packing our capsules.

Table 1	Characteristics of Study Patients						
			Rockland State Hospital		Research Project		
Pt. #	Pt. Abbv.	Birth Date	Date Admitted	Diagnosis (Type)	Age at Admission	Weeks on Project	Classif.
002	KL	1928	1952	Paranoid	30	400	
003	Ms	1929	1948	Paranoid	30	400	Completed
004	Bk	1916	1938	Hebephrenic	43	430	Completed
007	Ro	1922	1954	Catatonic	37	132	
008	Mg	1934	1955	Mixed	25	138	
009	El	1097	1940	Catatonic	52	200	Completed
010	Fd	1928	1951	Paranoid	31	350	Completed
011	Pl	1909	1941	Paranoid	50	200	Completed
013	Rz	1926	1951	Mixed	33	132	
014	Jb	1933	1956	Mixed	28	140	
015	Fn	1925	1947	Hebephrenic	36	46	
016	Sv	1938	1957	Mixed	23	42	
017	Mn	1920	1949	Paranoid	42	112	Completed
018	Rd	1934	1958	Mixed	27	72	
019	Ga	1932	1959	Catatonic	30	56	
020	Cp	1929	1951	Paranoid	33	90	
022	St	1924	1953	Catatonic	38	110	
025	Kr	1938	1955	Mixed	25	234	Completed
027	Pk	1939	1959	Mixed	25	65	
029	Bu	1939	1957	Mixed	25	209	Completed
030	Dl	1926	1952	Paranoid	38	207	Completed
031	En	1924	1957	Paranoid	41	68	
032	Gr	1935	1957	Mixed	30	80	
033	Vi	1939	1957	Mixed	26	116	
034	Ba	1938	1957	Paranoid	27	170	Completed
035	Bt	1935	1953	Catatonic	30	155	
037	Lo	1934	1951	Catatonic	31	157	Completed
039	Gu	1939	1961	Mixed	26	143	
041	Os	1926	1962	Mixed	39	96	
043	Wh	1927	1950	Mixed	38	96	
044	Dv	1931	1958	Mixed	35	105	Completed
057	Fr	1936	1957	Mixed	26	271	

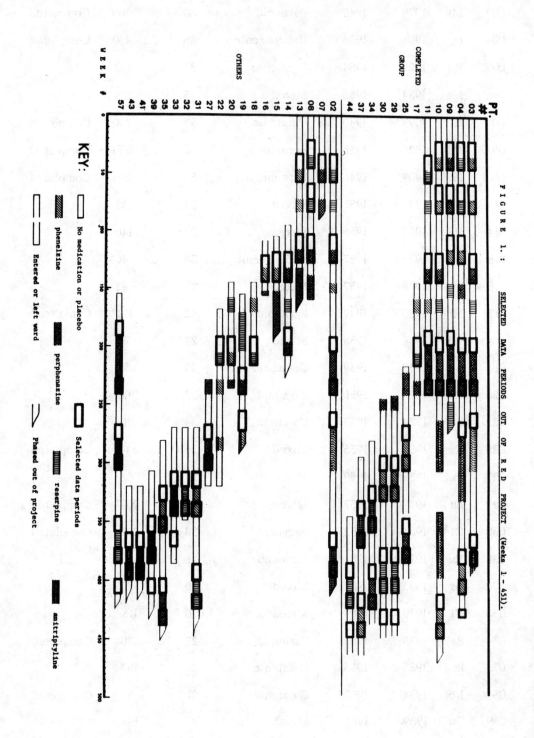

FIGURE 1.: SELECTED DATA PERIODS OUT OF R.E.D. PROJECT (Weeks 1 - 451).

KEY:

☐ No medication or placebo

▨ phenelzine

▣ perphenazine

☐ Selected data periods

▥ reserpine

▤ amitriptyline

☐ Entered or left ward

⟍ Phased out of project

b) Placebo period more than 39 weeks, medication period 12-24 weeks, (n=3).

c) Placebo period between 24-39 weeks, medication period more than 24 weeks. (n=9)

d) Placebo period more than 39 weeks, medication period more than 24 weeks (n-24).

Patient groups a and c will be distinguished as short-term placebo, while b and d are called longterm placebo. Likewise groups a and b will be called short-term treatment, and c and d longterm treatment. Also, in each medication group I have tried to contrast patients who belonged to what can be termed the "completed" group (i.e. patients who were able to stay on the ward without interruption of their pre-arranged medication schedule (3) and "others", patients who did not complete the design for various reasons, mostly because they could not be maintained on placebo for a full year.

In our previous publication we reported on 6 of such "complete" patients, and 14 others. The completed patients were older, had been hospitalized longer, and were more often initially diagnosed as paranoid, than the others (3). The same holds true for the 12 "completed" patients of the present study as compared to the 20 others (Table 2)

Table 2 : Summary of Table 1

	Completed Pts. n=12	Other Pts. n=20
Average age at RSH admission	23.5	24.1
Average age at Project admission	34.8	30.9
Average No. of weeks in Project	217	122
Diagnosis: Paranoid	6	3
Hebephrenic	1	1
Catatonic	2	4
Mixed	3	12

I have selected those patients in each medication group on whom we have data before, during and after a minimum of 6 months drug administration. The reactions of these patients are described under the heading "ideal cases". Of such ideal cases a few in each medication group were monitored for their uninary catecholamine secretion. The data presented here can only be a summary of a planned report (4), but they permit us a more comprehensive basis for the discussion of the implications of our research.

In the fourth place, the data for this report cover 9 years of the project; the additional years are important because they provide us with patients who have had 52 week placebo periods between 26 week medication periods. Since we initially had a minimum of 12 week medication periods interspersed with 12 week placebo, the new design allows us two comparisons:

1. The effects of short-term (3-6 months) vs. longterm (1 year) placebo periods. This is important since we want to know how long a period is needed between medications to "return to baseline", i.e. to avoid interaction of sequentially given drugs.

2. The effects of short-term (3 months) vs. longterm (6 months) medication periods. This is important in determining which of the expected drug actions not observed in our previous study period, would be seen if only the drug is administered long enough.

Here something should be said about the statistical signficance of the results. As we have explained before, no adequate statistical methods for dealing with our longterm material have been found (1). The results are given for the trends they reveal, only in the "ideal cases" when I talk about return to the baseline was .01 value of the t-tests used as a criterion to declare pre- and post-medication placebo values different.

RESULTS

Perphenazine: We have had more experience with this drug than with any of the others. In the present study I analyzed 27 cases. Table 3 shows the results according to length of the premedication placebo period, the length of medication, and the type of patient.

Table 3 : Per Cent Reaction to Perphenazine

Variable	n	Placebo condition n=16 short	n=11 long	Medication n=12 short	n=15 long	Patient Type n=11 complete	n=16 other
Clinical rating improved	21	75	81	75	86	63	87
Weight increased	16	43	81	25	86	54	64
Blood pressure decreased	14	50	54	50	54	54	50
Alkaline phosphatase decreased	15	75	63	50	60	45	64
Total proteins decreased	14	68	63	58	48	45	56

A short placebo period and a short medication period both seem to lead to less weight gain than would be the case in longterm treatment. Also, the completed patients do not react as favorably in clinical improvements as the others. There seems to be an overall tendency for the patients to react better if they had not received another drug recently and if they received perphenazine for 6 months. This tendency also appears in table 4, where the ideal cases are shown.

Table 4

Ideal Cases: Reaction to perphenazine

	Increase	Decrease	No. of cases back to baseline with 6 months placebo
Clinical rating	7	-	7
Weight	6	1	0
Blood pressure	6	1	2
Alkaline phosphatase	5	2	1
Total protein	5	2	2

The most important observation in the "ideal" case is that apart from the clinical rating the drug influence mostly persists for longer than three months. In one case with more than 9 months of placebo following perphenazine, I could still not find that all variables had gone to premedication levels, e.g. the weight never completely reversed.

Phenelzine: I can report on only 18 cases of this drug, table 5 provides the breakdown.

There seem to be few differences between the groups. The weight increased more in the patients who had been longer on placebo or who received the drug for a long time, much as this occurred with perphenazine. In contrast to perphenazine, however, the completed patients seem to increase in weight and improve in clinical rating more than the others. There are 6 "ideal cases" of which 5 had a post medication period of one year (table 6).

Table 5

Per cent Reaction to Phenelzine

Variable	n	Placebo condition n=12 short	n=6 long	Medication n=10 short	n=8 long	Patient Type n=11 condition	n=7 other
Clinical rating improved	9	48	66	50	50	63	28
Weight increased	12	58	84	50	88	72	56
Blood pressure decreased	10	58	50	60	50	63	42
Alkaline phos-phatase de-creased	9	50	50	70	24	45	56
Total protein decreased	13	75	66	70	75	81	56

From these results it is clear that phenelzine administration has longer lasting effect on clinical behavior rating and shorter lasting effect on total protein than perphenazine. Just as is the case with perphenazine, phenelzine effects wear off very slowly, in the five cases of 1 year post-medication placebo, the data obtained in the 9th to 12th placebo month still show significant differences compared to pre-medication baseline in 3 cases for weight, and one case each of blood pressure and alkaline phosphatase.

Table 6

Ideal Cases: Reaction to phenelzine

	Increase	Decrease	No. of cases back to baseline without 6 months placebo
Clinical rating	4	2	4
Weight	5	1	0
Blood pressure	4	2	4
Alkaline phos-phatase	4	2	1
Total protein	1	5	4

Reserpine: There are 15 cases of administration of this drug, as analyzed in table 7. In all cases where the placebo treatment had been shorter than 9 months the medication period also had been short, so that no separate analysis for placebo conditions and medication was needed. The only difference between short term medication after a short placebo period and longterm medication after a year of placebo seems to be in the latter's definite improvement in clinical rating. There also seems to be a more general decrease in alkaline phosphatase and total protein during the short medication period.

Table 7

Per cent Reaction to Reserpine

Variable	n	Placebo condition		Patient Type	
		n=9 short	n-6 long	n=7 Completed	n=8 Other
Clinical rating improved	11	55	100	72	75
Weight increased	14	100	84	86	100
Blood pressure decreased	13	88	84	72	100
Alkaline Phosphatase decreased	11	88	50	72	75
Total protein decreased	8	77	16	42	62

There are 4 "ideal cases", whose post-medication placebo data were derived from the 3rd to 6th months (table 8).

Table 8

Ideal Cases: Reaction to reserpine

	Increase	Decrease	No. of cases back to baseline with 6 months placebo
Clinical rating	4	0	2
Weight	3	1	1
Blood pressure	1	3	3
Alkaline phosphatase	3	1	0
Total protein	3	1	3

Again for all variables except perhaps the clinical rating a six month period seems not long enough to undo the effects of longterm administration of reserpine.

Amitriptyline: Since there are only 5 (with two "ideal") cases of this drug in the present analysis, the data are presented in one table, (cf: Table 9).

Table 9

Reactions to amitriptyline

	Increase	Decrease	No. of cases back to baseline with 6 months placebo
Clinical rating	4	1	2
Weight	4	1	0
Blood pressure	3	2	2
Alkaline phos- phatase	4	1	0
Total protein	2	3	2

Even though the number of cases followed for their post medication placebo reaction is small, it is again evident that longterm effects of amitriptyline exist. Even after one year placebo the weight of one patient had still not returned to baseline.

Catecholamine excretion in 24 hour urines: The results of our analyses of "ideal cases", summarized in table 10, are only intended to provide an impression of the direction of the changes brought about by the study drugs. These data are averages of urinary values obtained at the end of one year placebo (before), after 3-6 months of drug administration (during), and after 3-6 months of post-medication placebo (after).

Only the norepinephrine excretion is affected with phenelzine and reserpine medication, the apparent drop with perphenazine in the example in the table does not occur generally in our data on perphenazine treated patients. In all cases it seems that the catecholamine values are back to baseline after six months placebo.

Table 10

Effects on Urinary Catecholamines of Drug Administration

Patient n		Norepinephrine				Epinephrine			
		F*	C*	M*	Total	F*	C*	M*	Total
Drug used: Perphenazine									
	Before	42.7	65.3	288	396	7.1	7.7	184	199
1	During	28.1	70.6	154	252	4.4	15.6	136	156
	After	82.5	173.5	354	610	15.1	16.3	360	258
Drug used: Phenelzine									
	Before	40.5	193.5	332	566	5.8	19.9	232	258
3	During	44.3	199.0	887	1130	7.3	20.0	261	288
	After	41.9	146.3	214	302	10.0	17.3	187	214
Drug used: Reserpine									
	Before	42.5	184.5	352	579	7.0	20.0	279	306
1	During	23.0	80.2	127	230	13.4	11.0	260	284
	After	53.2	166.3	231	450	10.1	23.7	217	251
Drug used: Amitriptyline									
	Before	37.2	118.8	218	374	10.3	21.7	253	285
1	During	44.8	88.2	206	339	7.0	8.9	218	334
	After	53.0	62.0	284	399	9.4	5.4	267	282

*F=Free   *C=Conjugated   *M=Methylated

DISCUSSION

It is a sobering thought that 9 years of labor with a total of 46 carefully selected "therapy resistant" schizophrenic patients residing under strict control on a specially designed research ward, have provided us with results which were essentially well known before. That is what our studies seem to indicate as far as the positive findings are concerned: perphenazine improves the behavior as well as increases weight in all types of chronic schizophrenic patients, so does reserpine. One could also find an explanation for the tendency of the "completed" patients to improve with phenelzine and amitriptyline; psychic energizers are better than no medication at all in such apparently "burnt-out" cases.

It is informative, however, to look at some of the negative data in our studies, those results that can be considered contrary to expectation. Such unexpected findings have implications for three broad aspects of schizophrenic research.

In the first place: the patients. I have shown earlier that the patients in the completed groups differ from the others in that they on the average are older, longer hospitalized, and more often initially diagnosed as paranoid. Also, at the time of that writing, the completed group seemed to react more favorably to reserpine, the others to perphenazine (3). With the present data reserpine seems to affect all patients to the same extent, but for the completed patients perphenazine and phenelzine both seem equally favorable, in marked contrast to the other patients, who react better to perphenazine, and far worse to phenelzine. Here then, one might say that for the older chronic, paranoidly integrated schizophrenic, a tranquillizer and an energizer produce equal results, any medication is bound to unhinge their condition, and in so doing make them more socially influencable. For the younger, disorganized schizophrenic, activation with an MAO inhibitor seems disastrous, tranquillization on the other hand gives him an opportunity to become socially tractable. Our results therefore underline the need to define subgroups in reporting on results of drug research in schizophrenia.

In the second place, results only tend to become consistent after long-term (at least 6 month) medication, this certainly applies for the two tranquillizing drugs. However, even then, such reliable physiological variables as weight and blood pressure may react in an unexpected manner. This observation, together with the knowledge that none of the variables affected consistently can be expected to return to baseline even after one year post-medication placebo, should make us cautious in the interpretation of the results of short term drug studies, especially if these are not preceded by adequate placebo periods. It is as yet impossible to say what a minimum placebo period for drug studies in schizophrenia is, but even if one only looks at changes in clinical ratings a three month placebo and a 6 month medication period seem necessary to obtain reliable (and valid) results.

In the third and final place there is a reassuring point. The time-honored clinical question "What does he do", and "How does he look", are still most reliable indicators of a patient's reaction to medication. Of all the variables studied only the clinical ratings and the weight, inconsistent as they occasionally may be, are indispensable for a total drug evaluation. The catecholamine excretion changing reliably as it does (and should do) with phenelzine and reserpine, is irrelevant for the evaluation of total drug effect. The changes in excretion values did not correlate with changes in behavior, or even blood pressure.

In summary: this project in its clinical aspects has shown that results of drug research in chronic schizophrenia have to be interpreted with extreme caution. The fact that this statement has been so well documented in this patient group, together with the fact that availability of our patients for research on testable claims in schizophrenia research and treatment has crucial value (e.g. 5, 6, 7), provides us with continuing motivation for this unique longterm approach.

ACKNOWLEDGEMENT: This investigation was supported in part by "Clinical Research Center Grant #MH-07292" and "General Research Support Grant #FR-05561".

REFERENCES

1. Kline, N.S., Blair, J., Cooper, T., Esser, A.H., Hackett, E., and Vestergaard, P.: A Controlled Seven Year Study of Endocrine and Other Indices in Drug Treated Chronic Schizophrenics, Acta Psychiatrica Scandinavica, supplement, 1968.

2. Esser, A.H., Kline, N.S. and Vestergaard, P.: "Custom-packed once-a-day medication with barium-sulphate tracer for use in drug research", accepted for publication in International Journal of Neuro-Psychiatry.

3. Esser, A.H.: "Clinical data" in (1), pages 11-29.

4. Kahane, Z., and Esser, A.H.: "Psychotropic Drugs and Catecholamine Excretion", in preparation.

5. Ryan, J.W., Steinberg, H.R., Green, R., Brown, J.D. and Durrell, J.: Controlled Study of Effects of Plasma of Schizophrenic and Non-Schizophrenic Psychiatric Patients on Chicken Erythocytes. J. Psychiatric Research, In Press, 1968.

6. Kuehl, F.A.: "Occurrence of 3,4-dimethoxyphenylacetic acid in urines of normal and schizophrenic individuals", Nature, 211:606-608, 1966.

7. Kline, N.S., Barclay, G., Esser, A.H., Cole, J., Lehman, H., and Wittenborn, J.D.: "Controlled Evaluation of DPN(NAD) in the treatment of chronic schizophrenic patients", British Journal of Psychiatry, 113:731-742, 1967.

A. H. Esser, M.D., Rockland State Hospital, Orangeburg, N.Y. 10962

RECENT SLEEP RESEARCH: FINDINGS IN SCHIZOPHRENIA AND SOME POSSIBLE IMPLICATIONS FOR THE MECHANISM OF ACTION OF CHLORPROMAZINE AND FOR THE NEUROPHYSIOLOGY OF DELIRIUM

I. FEINBERG

The notion that dreaming and psychosis are related processes is an ancient one. Aristotle, for example, suggested that the hallucinations of madness result from a derangement of the mechanisms normally involved in dreaming (1). Subsequent observers of human behavior have repeatedly emphasized similarities between psychosis and dreaming. In addition to hallucinations, there occur in both conditions peculiarities of thinking, intense and bizarre fluctuations of affect and, perhaps most importantly, a suspension of critical faculties and an inability to reject bizarre ideas and experiences. The 1952 discovery by Aserinsky and Kleitman of rapid eye movement (REM) or paradoxical sleep (2) -- a physiological correlate of remembered dreaming (3,4) -- made it possible to apply modern techniques of psychophysiological investigation to many of these ancient questions. Although this application was somewhat delayed at first, the number of reported studies is by now too great to permit a complete review in the space allotted. The interested reader will find a general review of the implications of sleep research for psychiatry elsewhere (5).

In what follows, I shall focus on those studies which seem to me either of historical interest or else whose results appear particularly promising with respect to the problems of schizophrenia and hallucination. I shall first review the evidence pertinent to REM* processes in schizophrenia, considering studies of both the basal level and of the response of these systems to the stress of deprivation. I shall then consider evidence regarding disturbances of non-REM (NREM) sleep in schizophrenia. Finally, I shall present some new findings from my own laboratory which may prove pertinent to the mechanism of action of chlorpromazine and to the mechanisms which underlie the occurrence of hallucinations in delirium.

A. REM Sleep

Dement (6) carried out the first EEG study of sleep in schizophrenic patients, monitoring the sleep of 17 chronic patients, four of whom had undergone recent somatic treatment. He found the amount and pattern of REM sleep in this group to be similar to that found in ten medical students. In 1963, Fisher and Dement (7) reported more positive results. They studied a single "borderline" patient within one day of the onset of a florid psychosis characterized by visual and auditory hallucinations and paranoid delusions. However, on the first night of study, this patient was treated acutely with a massive dose (20 mg.) of "Stelazine" (trifluoperazine).

---

*The Dement and Kleitman (4) nomenclature for the EEG stages of sleep is employed here. REM sleep refers to rapid eye movement or paradoxical sleep generally. NREM sleep refers to slow-wave sleep including both the sustained high voltage delta phases (stages 3 and 4) and the lower voltage activity with spindles and K-complexes (stage 2).

The sleep record was interpreted as showing 50% REM sleep (measured as emergent stage 1 EEG) and, on this basis, several hypotheses were advanced regarding the relationship of REM sleep to psychosis. However, subsequent work (see below) has demonstrated that early schizophrenia is associated with low rather than with high REM levels. The findings in the patient of Fisher and Dement have been reproduced by administration of a similar dose of Stelazine to a schizophrenic patient with a normal baseline sleep pattern (8,9).

Koresko, Snyder and Feinberg (10) compared the physiological sleep pattern of seven hallucinating schizophrenic patients with that of four non-hallucinating patients. Total sleep time was similar in the two groups, as was the amount of REM sleep measured by both emergent stage 1 EEG and rapid eye movement activity. Expanding this work, Feinberg, Koresko, Gottlieb and Wender (11) and Feinberg, Koresko and Gottlieb (12) investigated the sleep patterns of 22 schizophrenic patients of whom 18 were actively ill and four in states of remission. Nine of the actively ill patients were classified as short-term (ill less than one year) and nine as long-term (continuously ill for over two years). Ten of the 18 were experiencing hallucinations at the time of study. The results obtained were compared with those found in a control group (N=10) consisting of four hospitalized patients suffering from character disorders and six non-hospitalized control subjects. All subjects in this investigation were studied for at least four consecutive nights, care being taken to prevent day-time sleep. The subjects were drug-free during the period of study, and with the exception of four patients, had received no medication during the preceding three weeks. It was found that the total sleep time of the actively-ill schizophrenic group did not differ from that of the control subjects, although sleep latency was significantly longer for the patients. Absolute and percentage stage 1 EEG did not differ in the two groups. However, the patients showed significantly lower values for another index of REM sleep, the amount of rapid eye movement activity. This difference was due to low values in the short-term subgroup of patients. Latency to the first eye movement was significantly more variable in the schizophrenic subjects as a result of values which were both longer and (more frequently) shorter than those found in control subjects. In addition, there was a tendency for hallucinating patients to show a higher density of eye movement activity during REM periods. Feinberg and associates concluded that the neurophysiological mechanisms underlying dreaming sleep were fundamentally normal in schizophrenia. The fact that recent onset of illness appeared associated with a slight diminution of REM sleep was interpreted as indicating that this stage of sleep, already known to be reduced under the initial stress of laboratory recording, is generally sensitive to disturbed states of the organism. In a later review of these data, taken in association with further study of both schizophrenic and control subjects, Feinberg noted that the variability of REM onset was attributable mainly to the occurrence of very short latencies in some schizophrenic subjects* and that the previously noted tendency of hallucinating patients to show a higher density of eye movements during REM sleep did not receive further support (9). It was concluded that REM mechanisms were fundamentally intact in schizophrenia

---

*Since REM and NREM sleep are in dynamic interaction, it should be noted that the early onset of REM sleep in some schizophrenic subjects may reflect an abnormality of the first NREM period rather than an abnormality of REM processes themselves. I shall return to this point later.

and that there was no evidence to implicate a disturbance of these mechanisms in the waking hallucinations of schizophrenic patients.

Subsequent studies have corroborated the conclusion that basal REM levels are within normal limits in schizophrenia (13-15). The observation that early stages of illness are associated with a reduction rather than an increase in the proportion of REM sleep has also received some further support (16,17). However, in contrast to the results of Feinberg, et al. (11), who found normal sleep patterns in four recovered acute schizophrenic patients, Gulevich, Dement and Zarcone (18) reported that a group of 13 chronic schizophrenic patients "at or approaching a state of clinical remission" showed significantly higher values in amount and percentage of REM sleep when compared with seven nonpsychotic controls. This discrepancy may be due to the differences in the nature of the patients studied, to previous drug treatment, or to other, unknown variables.

Physiological systems whose basal levels are within normal limits may nevertheless reveal aberrant function when placed under stress. The glucose tolerance test represents a familiar clinical example of this phenomenon. Attempts have now been made to stress REM systems in schizophrenic patients in an attempt to detect pathological function not otherwise apparent. Azumi, et al. (19) compared the effects of four to five nights of REM deprivation (accomplished by awakenings at the onset of REM periods) in three chronic schizophrenic patients and four normal control subjects. The patients had been without somatic therapy during the previous year, although one patient had had a previous course of insulin and another, a course of ECT. No exacerbation of psychotic symptoms was noted during the period of REM deprivation. On recovery nights, when sleep was permitted without interruption, two of the three patients showed compensatory increases in REM smaller than those found in the control group. These results are difficult to interpret because of the high baseline values in two of the patients. Thus, although their increment was less, the mean percentage of REM sleep on the first recovery night was greater for the schizophrenic patients than for the three control subjects who underwent the same deprivation procedure (29.2% vs. 27.8%). Since the schizophrenic patient with the lowest baseline values showed the highest increment, the difference between schizophrenic and control subjects in this study may have been a function of the differences in initial values. The interpretation of these findings is further complicated by the uncertain consequences of previous somatic therapy and by the fact that two of the three schizophrenic subjects (aged 45 and 55 years) were older than the oldest control subject (36 years).

Zarcone, Gulevich, Pivik and Dement (20), carried out deprivation of REM by repeated awakenings in six schizophrenic patients in remission, three actively ill patients, and four control subjects suffering from character disorders. These investigators found that, compared with the control group, compensation of REM after the two-night deprivation period was greater for the patients in remission and smaller for the actively ill patients. On the basis of these observations, the authors concluded that "at the very least ... we have demonstrated a dramatic association between a physiological variable (the REM deprivation-compensation response) and clinical state." In addition, they suggested that "the CNS changes associated with REM sleep deprivation may directly underlie psychotic disintegration."

In the paper presented at this symposium, Dement and Zarcone extend this interpretation (21). They suggest that the failure of schizophrenic subjects to show the usual rebound response to deprivation results from the fact that the excess REM activity has been discharged during waking. They further propose that such discharge is characteristic of schizophrenia and is directly responsible for schizophrenic symptoms. Data from animal studies are cited as lending additional support to this conclusion. Dement and Zarcone report that parachlorophenylalanine (PCPA) produces a "psychotic" state in cats, including apparent hallucinations. In addition, under chronic administration of this drug, compensatory rebounds do not occur after REM deprivation. The absence of such rebounds under PCPA is taken as supporting the view that the behavioral disturbance induced by this drug in cats is similar to schizophrenia. Furthermore, during both waking and NREM sleep, Dement and Zarcone have found sharp electrical transients in the pons, geniculate, and occipital areas (P-G-O spikes) of the brain. Such spikes are usually restricted to REM sleep. Their occurrence in other behavioral states is interpreted as evidence that REM processes are indeed intruding into waking under these pathological conditions.

On the basis of the available data, I find myself unconvinced by these interpretations. First, one wishes that measurement of eye movement or of some other index of REM intensity had been included in Dement and Zarcone's REM deprivation studies. It is possible that some patients compensate for deprivation by an increase in the intensity rather than in the duration of REM processes. Second, the drugs administered to the schizophrenic patients undergoing deprivation may have affected their responses to this procedure. It is true that remitted schizophrenics in this study were receiving similar drugs and yet still showed adequate rebound responses. However, the possibility remains that patients in different clinical states will respond differently to the same drugs.

Anxiety also constitutes a potentially crucial variable in REM deprivation studies. Anxiety acts to diminish REM sleep. The intense anxiety of actively-ill schizophrenic patients may well permit only some limited amount of REM which fulfills a minimal biological requirement. Such a limitation might preclude the observation of extensive rebound effects.

According to the Dement and Zarcone hypothesis, one should have expected an increase in schizophrenic symptoms during the period of deprivation since more REM activity should then have been discharged during waking. The failure to observe such exacerbations by Dement and Zarcone themselves, as well as by others who have carried out similar studies, casts further doubt on the validity of their hypothesis. It must also be noted that an investigation specifically aimed at detecting the occurrence of physiological correlates of REM during waking in severely ill schizophrenic patients has proved negative (22).

It is difficult to interpret the data from animal studies which Dement and Zarcone present in support of their hypothesis. One wishes to know the precise nature of the behavioral disturbance induced by PCPA. Did this syndrome resemble delirium, schizophrenia or some other condition? On what evidence was the interpretation that the animals hallucinated based? Did the hallucinations appear to be auditory or visual? It is not helpful to know only that an "obvious psychotic state" was produced. I would also question the enormous burden placed upon the P-G-O spike. Can one justify seizing a single physiological feature of REM sleep and attributing to its occurrence all of the subjective phenomena of dreaming, including hallucinations, "thought disorder" and "delusions"? Such an interpretation is especially difficult to accept in the face of the extensive and profound changes in brain physiology associated with REM sleep (23).

Finally, it must be noted that Vogel and Traub (24) have carried out a careful study of the REM deprivation response in schizophrenic patients and have obtained results opposite to those of Dement and Zarcone. Vogel and Traub observed entirely normal rebound responses in a group of patients who, while apparently less anxious and less agitated than the subjects of Dement and Zarcone, were nevertheless indisputably schizophrenic at the time of study.

In closing this section on REM sleep in schizophrenia, I should like to cite two of the conclusions reached by Vogel (25) on the basis of a thoughtful and detailed review of the potential relations between REM sleep and psychopathology. First, Vogel found that the claim that deprivation of REM sleep produces psychopathology in normal adults is not supported by compelling evidence. Second, Vogel found that the data available argue strongly against the hypothesis that REM sleep systems function aberrantly in schizophrenia.

B. NREM Sleep

Abnormalities of the NREM sleep systems of schizophrenics have been consistently noted and consistently ignored. They have been ignored in spite of the fact that, quantitatively, they far exceed any changes detected thus far in REM sleep variables. The reasons for this cavalier neglect appear to be psychological rather than scientific. They have to do with the glamour of dreaming and with the novelty of REM sleep rather than with any rational assessment of the relative importance of the two sleep mechanisms (if such an assessment were possible). Until quite recently, I have been as guilty of such bias as anyone.

Stubborn and insistent facts have now compelled us to reconsider our neglect of NREM sleep. Thus, Caldwell and Domino (15) reported last year that values for stage 4 EEG in 25 chronic schizophrenic patients were 50% lower than those found in 10 medical student control subjects. Since these controls were younger (mean age=24 yrs.) than the patients (mean age=32 yrs.) and since stage 4 EEG is quite sensitive to age (26) the interpretation of these findings remained somewhat in doubt. However, recent data (27) from my laboratory strongly support the findings of Caldwell and Domino. Fig. 1 shows the frequency-distributions for percentage stage 4 EEG in 17 actively ill schizophrenic patients and 17 age-matched controls. The distribution of the patients' scores is clearly shifted to the left and their mean percentage stage 4 (6.3%) was exactly half the value (12.6%) found in the controls (p <.01). Fig. 2 shows the distribution of stage 4 EEG by successive NREM periods across the night. The greatest part of the difference between the two groups was found in the first NREM period. It was noted above that early REM onset occurs occasionally in schizophrenia and that this phenomenon could as well represent an abnormality of the first NREM as of the first REM period. The present data show that the first NREM period is indeed abnormal in its stage 4 content. This finding lends support to the view that early REM onset in schizophrenia may result from decreased intensity or "pressure" of NREM sleep.

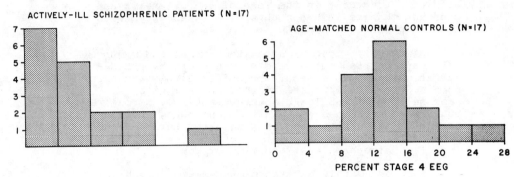

Fig. 1 - Percentage stage 4 EEG in
schizophrenic and control subjects

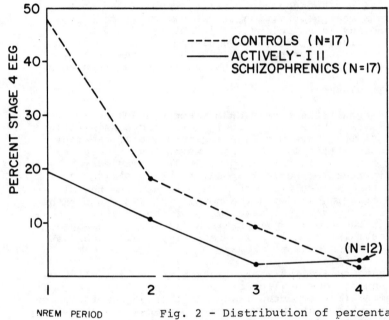

NREM PERIOD

Fig. 2 - Distribution of percentage
stage 4 EEG by successive NREM periods

How should the low stage 4 sleep in schizophrenia
be interpreted? Certainly, this abnormality is not
specific. Stage 4 sleep is reduced to a similar extent in depression (28,29). It remains possible that
the reduction of stage 4 sleep -- the deepest stage of
sleep -- is simply a manifestation of increased arousal
levels secondary to anxiety.

However, a recent finding in my laboratory raises
the possibility that reduction of stage 4 EEG in schizophrenia is of greater interest than it initially seemed
(30). Fig. 3 shows some of the relevant data. Chlorpromazine (200 mg. h.s.) tends to increase stage 4 sleep
although phenobarbital, in the same dosage, exerts the
opposite effect. This action of chlorpromazine takes
place with relatively little inhibition of the phasic
(eye-movement) activity of REM sleep. Since schizophrenic patients have low stage 4 sleep, and since chlorpromazine appears to promote a specific increase in this
sleep variable, the possibility is raised that the antipsychotic action of chlorpromazine, and perhaps of other
major tranquilizers as well, is associated with the capacity to increase stage 4 sleep without at the same

time suppressing the phasic activity of REM sleep.

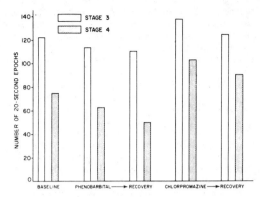

Fig. 3 - Opposing effects of phenobarbital and
chlorpromazine on stage 4 sleep. Both drug effects persisted into the recovery periods. However, by the fourth night after withdrawal, stage
4 values were at or near baseline levels.

C. Delirium

     I should like now to turn to the problem of delir-
ium. It was noted above that the hypothesis that the
hallucinations of madness result from a derangement of
the normal hallucinatory mechanisms of dreaming, is
quite ancient. In 1964, I suggested (9) that this hypothesis was more plausible for delirium than for any
of the other major psychiatric syndromes. The relevant
evidence at that time consisted of an apparent relation
between REM sleep and nocturnal delirium in patients
with chronic brain syndrome (31) and the high levels of
REM sleep observed in a small number of patients with
delirium tremens (32,33) and in a single patient with
an apparent "chronic delirium" (34). I noted also that
certain clinical data pointed in the same direction.
Thus, the frequent, vivid visual hallucinations which
occur in delirium might be the counterpart of visual
dreaming associated with REM sleep (35,36). In addition,
the regularly-occurring nocturnal exacerbation of symptoms in delirium suggested that symptoms were most severe at that time when the diurnal cycle might be expected to produce maximal pressure for REM activity.

     Recently E. V. Evarts and I (5) proposed a model
for drug-withdrawal delirium. We noted that increased
REM pressure was, in itself, insufficient to cause an
intrusion of REM processes into the waking state. For
example, hallucinations and delirium do not occur with
the increase in REM pressure associated with selective
REM deprivation (37,38) or amphetamine withdrawal (39).
A second factor (in addition to REM suppression-compen-
sation) seemed required, one which permitted the intrusion of REM processes into waking. We suggested that
it was this factor which was associated with the increase
in brain excitability and the impairment of cognitive
processes of delirium.

     Recent data, taken in association with our own
findings, suggest this second factor may prove to be a
change in the mechanisms which govern stage 4 sleep.
Thus, Gross and Goodenough found that repeated administration of large dosages of alcohol suppressed stage 4

sleep* and they suggested that this aspect of its action
might be implicated in delirium (40). Kales and co-
workers observed extremely low values of stage 4 EEG in
an addict ingesting enormous daily doses of phenobarbital (41). Our own data now show that stage 4 EEG is reduced to quite low levels with moderate dosages of
phenobarbital within three days of repeated administration (Fig. 3). Kales, et al. (42) have also found that
at least one non-barbiturate hypnotic reduces stage 4
sleep. On the basis of these observations, we would
propose the following hypotheses:

1. All drugs which produce delirium upon withdrawal
   (note that opiates are not included in this group
   (cf. 43)) act initially to suppress both the
   mechanisms responsible for the phasic activity of
   REM sleep and the mechanisms which govern stage 4
   EEG. With chronic administration (i.e., during
   the addiction period), REM activity returns to
   near-normal levels but stage 4 EEG remains suppressed.** Upon withdrawal, "hypertrophied" REM
   mechanisms, rather than previous REM deprivation,
   produce high levels of REM activity.

2. The probability of addiction is directly proportional to the intensity and duration of both drug
   actions. In addition, this probability is enhanced when the temporal sequences are such that
   REM rebound occurs while stage 4 EEG mechanisms
   have not yet recovered.

3. The inadequate function of stage 4 mechanisms is
   specifically correlated with the increase in brain
   excitability (44) and the cognitive disturbances
   (45) of delirium.***

---

*Gross and Goodenough administered massive doses of
alcohol to their patients -- an amount sufficient to produce semi-coma. We think it likely that acute administration to the point of coma of any potent central nervous system agent would act to obliterate the physiological constituents of normal sleep, especially including
eye movements, spindles and stage 4 sleep. Indeed, we
have seen these changes as the result of single large
dosages of phenothiazines (8). It was essentially this
phenomenon which Fisher and Dement (7) observed in a
schizophrenic patient treated acutely with 20 mg. of
trifluoperazine. They interpreted the flattened EEG
tracing which resulted as representing stage 1 EEG and
hence increased REM sleep.

**Stage 4 sleep is associated with certain types of
nightmares (46). If the present hypothesis regarding the
effects of hypnotic drugs on stage 4 sleep is correct, it
would suggest that the nightmares which occur on withdrawal of these drugs (42) might involve altered stage 4
as well as altered REM mechanisms.

***Evans and Lewis have recently suggested that
chlorpromazine will prove a useful agent in the treatment of delirium (47,48). If this view is confirmed, we
suspect that the value of the drug would lie more in its
ability to stimulate stage 4 sleep than in its capacity
to suppress eye movement activity.

These hypotheses have many points of similarity with the views of others, especially including, in addition to those cited above, Dr. Ian Oswald (49). However, their present formulation differs from previous interpretations and suggests certain new experiments. While obviously quite speculative, at present, these hypotheses are put forward because they are readily testable and because they deal with urgent clinical problems.

Summary

A review of studies of physiological sleep patterns in schizophrenia reveals that basal REM activity is normal in this condition. While it has been claimed that the response of schizophrenic patients to REM deprivation is abnormal and that this abnormality is linked to the pathophysiological mechanism of the illness, the available data seem largely inconsistent with this view.

In contrast to the relatively slight changes in REM sleep, recent studies show clearly that the stage 4 component of NREM sleep is reduced by about 50% in groups of schizophrenic patients. It is recognized that reduced stage 4 sleep is not specific to schizophrenia (it occurs as well in depression) and may ultimately be shown to be secondary to anxiety and unrelated to psychosis itself. However, the abnormally low stage 4 values in schizophrenia become of greater interest in light of recent data which indicate that chlorpromazine can stimulate stage 4 sleep without suppressing the phasic aspects of REM sleep. The hypothesis was therefore advanced that the anti-psychotic activity of chlorpromazine, and perhaps of other major tranquilizers as well, is related to the capacity to stimulate stage 4 sleep without suppressing phasic REM processes.

Finally, additional data were presented which are relevant to the problem of drug-withdrawal delirium. According to the model presented, the probability of such delirium is directly proportional to the ability of addicting drugs to suppress both the phasic aspects of REM sleep and the mechanisms which govern stage 4 sleep. It was predicted that the likelihood of delirium is enhanced if the temporal relations during withdrawal are such that stage 4 mechanisms remain suppressed when the REM sleep rebound occurs. It was further suggested that the impairment of stage 4 sleep during the withdrawal period was responsible for the increased brain excitability which occurs in this state.

Acknowledgements: This research was supported, in part, by USPHS Research Grant MH 10927. Many colleagues, especially Richard L. Koresko, Father Joseph A. Piehuta, and Drs. F. Gottlieb and P.H. Wender, contributed to the studies from our laboratory which are summarized here.

References

1. ARISTOTLE. De Somnis. In The Basic Works of
    Aristotle. McKEON, R. (Editor), New York,
    Random House, 1941.

2. ASERINSKY, E. and KLEITMAN, N. Regularly occurring
    periods of eye motility, and concomitant phenome-
    na, during sleep. Science, 118, 273, 1953.

3. ASERINSKY, E. and KLEITMAN, N. Two types of ocular
    motility occurring in sleep. J. Appl. Physiol.,
    8, 1, 1955.

4. DEMENT, W.C. and KLEITMAN, N. Cyclic variations in
    EEG during sleep and their relation to eye-move-
    ments, body motility and dreaming. Electroenceph.
    Clin. Neurophysiol., 9, 673, 1957.

5. FEINBERG, I. and EVARTS, E.V. Some implications of
    sleep research for psychiatry. In Neurobiological
    Aspects of Psychopathology. ZUBIN, J. (Editor),
    New York, Grune and Stratton, in press.

6. DEMENT, W. Dream recall and eye movements during
    sleep in schizophrenics and normals. J. nerv.
    ment. Dis., 122, 263, 1955.

7. FISHER, C. and DEMENT, W. Studies on the psycho-
    pathology of sleep and dreams. Amer. J. Psychiat.,
    119, 1160, 1963.

8. FEINBERG, I., WENDER, P.H., KORESKO, R.L., GOTTLIEB,
    F. and PIEHUTA, J.A. Current studies of sleep and
    dreaming in psychiatric patients. Paper read at
    Ass. Psychophysiol. Study Sleep, Palo Alto, 1964.

9. FEINBERG, I. Sleep electroencephalographic and eye-
    movement patterns in patients with chronic brain
    syndrome and with schizophrenia. Paper read at
    Ass. Res. Nerv. Ment. Dis., New York, 1964. In
    Sleep and Altered States of Consciousness, KETY,
    S.S., EVARTS, E.V. and WILLIAMS, H.L. (Editors),
    pp. 211-240, Williams and Wilkins, Baltimore, 1967.

10. KORESKO, R.L., SNYDER, F. and FEINBERG, I. 'Dream
    time' in hallucinating and non-hallucinating schizo-
    phrenic patients. Nature, 199, 1118, 1963.

11. FEINBERG, I., KORESKO, R.L., GOTTLIEB, F. and WENDER,
    P.H. Sleep electroencephalographic and eye-movement
    patterns in schizophrenic patients. Comp. Psychiat.,
    5, 44, 1964.

12. FEINBERG, I., KORESKO, R.L. and GOTTLIEB, F. Further
    observations on electrophysiological sleep patterns
    in schizophrenia. Comp. Psychiat., 6, 21, 1965.

13. ONHEIBER, P., WHITE, P.T., DeMYER, M.K. and OTTINGER,
    D.R. Sleep and dream patterns of child schizo-
    phrenics. Arch. gen. Psychiat., 12, 568, 1965.

14. ORNITZ, E.M., RITVO, E.V. and WALTER, R.D. Dreaming
    sleep in autistic and schizophrenic children. Amer.
    J. Psychiat., 122, 419, 1965.

15. CALDWELL, D. and DOMINO, E.F. Electroencephalographic
    and eye-movement patterns during sleep in chronic
    schizophrenic patients. Electroenceph. Clin. Neuro-
    physiol., 22, 414, 1967.

16. LAIRY, G.C., BARTE, H., GOLDSTEINAS, L. and
    RIDJANOVIC, S. Sommeil de nuit des malades
    mentaux: etude des bouffees delirantes. In
    Le Sommeil de Nuit Normal et Pathologique:
    Etudes Electroencephalographiques, p. 353,
    Masson & Cie., Paris, 1965.

17. SNYDER, F. Disturbance of sleep in relation to
    psychosis. Paper read at a Symposium, "Schizo-
    phrenia: Current Concepts and Research," New
    York, 1968, to be published.

18. GULEVICH, G.D., DEMENT, W.C. and ZARCONE, V.P.
    All-night sleep recordings of chronic schizo-
    phrenics in remission. Comp. Psychiat., 8, 141,
    1967.

19. AZUMI, K., TAKAHASHI, S., TAKAHASHI, K., MARUYAMA,
    N. and KIKUTI, S. The effects of dream depriva-
    tion on chronic schizophrenics and normal adults:
    a comparative study. Folia Psychiat. Neurol.
    Japonica, 21, 205, 1967.

20. ZARCONE, V., GULEVICH, G., PIVIK, T. and DEMENT,
    W. Partial REM phase deprivation and schizo-
    phrenia. Arch. gen. Psychiat., 18, 194, 1968.

21. DEMENT, W.C. and ZARCONE, V.P., JR. REM sleep
    processes and psychosis. Paper read at a Sym-
    posium, "Schizophrenia: Current Concepts and
    Research," New York, 1968, to be published.

22. RECHTSCHAFFEN, A., SCHULSINGER, F. and MEDNICK,
    S.A. Schizophrenia and physiological indices
    of dreaming. Arch. gen. Psychiat., 10, 89, 1964.

23. JOUVET, M. and JOUVET, D. A study of the neuro-
    physiological mechanisms of dreaming. Electro-
    enceph. Clin. Neurophysiol. Suppl. 24, 133, 1963.

24. VOGEL, G.W. and TRAUB, A.C. REM deprivation. I.
    The effect on schizophrenic patients. Arch. gen.
    Psychiat., 18, 287, 1968.

25. VOGEL, G.W. REM deprivation. III. Dreaming and
    psychosis. Arch. gen. Psychiat., 18, 312, 1968.

26. FEINBERG, I. and CARLSON, V.R. Sleep variables as
    a function of age in man. Arch. Gen. Psychiat.,
    18, 239, 1968.

27. FEINBERG, I., BRAUN, M., KORESKO, R.L. and GOTTLIEB,
    F. Stage 4 sleep in schizophrenia. Arch. Gen.
    Psychiat., in press.

28. GRESHAM, S.C., AGNEW, H.W. and WILLIAMS, R.L. The
    sleep of depressed patients. Arch. Gen. Psychiat.,
    13, 503, 1965.

29. MENDELS, J. and HAWKINS, D.R. Sleep and depression.
    Arch. gen. Psychiat., 16, 344, 1967.

30. FEINBERG, I., WENDER, P.H., KORESKO, R.L., GOTTLIEB,
    F. and PIEHUTA, J.A. Differential effects of
    chlorpromazine and phenobarbital on EEG sleep pat-
    terns. (Unpub. ms.)

31. FEINBERG, I., KORESKO, R.L. and SCHAFFNER, I. Sleep
    electroencephalographic and eye-movement patterns
    in patients with chronic brain syndrome. J. Psy-
    chiat. Res., 3, 11, 1965.

32. GROSS, M.M., GOODENOUGH, D., TOBIN, M., HALPERT, E.,
    LEPORE, D., PEARLSTEIN, A., SIROTA, M., DIBIANCO,
    J., FULLER, M. and KISHNER, I. Sleep disturbances
    and hallucinations in the acute alcoholic psycho-
    ses. J. nerv. ment. Dis., 142, 493, 1966.

33. GREENBERG, R. and PEARLMAN, C. Delirium tremens and dreaming. Am. J. Psychiat., 124, 133, 1967.

34. FEINBERG, I., KORESKO, R.L., HELLER, N. and STEINBERG, H.R. Unusually high dream time in an hallucinating patient. Amer. J. Psychiat., 121, 1018, 1965.

35. FOULKES, W.D. Dream reports from different stages of sleep. J. Abn. Soc. Psychol., 65, 14, 1962.

36. RECHTSCHAFFEN, A., VERDONE, P. and WHEATON, J.V. Reports of mental activity during sleep. Can. Psychiat. Ass. J., 8, 409, 1963.

37. DEMENT, W.C. The effect of dream deprivation. Science, 131, 1705, 1960.

38. KALES, A., HOEDEMAKER, F.S., JACOBSON, A. and LICHTENSTEIN, E.L. Dream deprivation: an experimental reappraisal. Nature, 204, 1337, 1964.

39. OSWALD, I. and THACORE, V.R. Amphetamine and phenmetrazine addiction: physiological abnormalities in the abstinence syndrome. Brit. Med. J., 2, 427, 1963.

40. GROSS, M.M. and GOODENOUGH, D.R. Observations and formulations regarding REM and other disturbances of sleep in the acute alcoholic psychoses and related states. Paper read at Sleep Research Symposium, 1st. Int. Psychosomatic Week, Rome, 1967.

41. KALES, A., MALMSTROM, E.J., RICKLES, W.H., HANLEY, J., LING TAN, T., STADEL, B. and HOEDEMAKER, F.S. Sleep patterns of a pentobarbital addict: before and after withdrawal. Psychophysiology, 5, 208, 1968. (Abstract)

42. KALES, A., LING TAN, T., SCHARF, M.B., KALES, J.D., MALMSTROM, E.J., ALLEN, C. and JACOBSON, A. Sleep patterns with sedative drugs. Paper read at Ass. Psychophysiol. Study Sleep, Denver, 1968.

43. ESSIG, C.F. Addiction to barbiturate and non-barbiturate sedative drugs. In The Addictive States, WIKLER, A. (Editor), p. 188, Williams and Wilkins, Baltimore, 1968.

44. VICTOR, M. The pathophysiology of alcoholic epilepsy. In The Addictive States, WIKLER, A. (Editor), p. 431, Williams and Wilkins, Baltimore, 1968.

45. WOLFF, H.G. and CURRAN, D. Nature of delirium and allied states: the dysergastic reaction. Arch. Neurol. Psychiat., 33, 1175, 1935.

46. BROUGHTON, R.J. Sleep disorders: disorders of arousal? Science, 159, 1070, 1968.

47. EVANS, J.I. and LEWIS, S.A. Drug withdrawal state. Arch. gen. Psychiat., 19, 631, 1968.

48. EVANS, J.I. and LEWIS, S.A. Sleep studies in early delirium and during drug withdrawal in normal subjects and the effect of phenothiazines on such states. Electroenceph. Clin. Neurophysiol., 25, 508, 1968. (Abstract)

49. OSWALD, I. Sleep and dependence upon amphetamine and other drugs. In The Physiology and Pathology of Sleep, KALES, A. (Editor), to be published.

I. Feinberg, M.D., State University of New York, Downstate Medical Center.

450 Clarkson Avenue, Brooklyn, N.Y. 11203

DISTURBANCE OF THE EEG SLEEP PATTERNS IN RELATION TO ACUTE PSYCHOSIS

FREDERICK SNYDER

Like many over the centuries who have mused about the idea of special kinship between sleep and psychosis, when I first approached this topic in a paper published just six years ago (1) my speculative flight was blissfully unburdened by crucial evidence, for virtually no precise, objective information then existed concerning vicissitudes of sleep in relation to any form of mental illness.* Nothing discouraged conventional wisdom that troubled spirits had troubled sleep, that troubled sleep could predispose to troubled minds, or that psychosis might be a 'waking dream'---but neither was there any but the most meager evidence to test these assumptions. Although impressive beginnings have been made in the collection of such evidence since then, this brief presentation is simply to indicate that many important questions about the relationship of sleep disturbance to psychosis are still not finally answered.

If, in any sense, psychosis were a 'waking dream', six years ago it seemed very plausible that it might be connected, somehow, with that newly recognized biological condition associated with nocturnal dreams, the Rapid Eye Movement or REM state. But thoughts about the exact nature of such possible connections (or the evidence that might test them) were then, and still are, exceedingly

---

*An exception was the pioneering study of Diaz Guerra and his associates in 1946 (2) pointing to marked abnormalities in the EEG sleep patterns of depressed patients, but no similar effort was made for the next decade and a half.

vague and tentative. Therefore, the study of EEG sleep in psychiatric populations has proceeded largely on the basis of sheer empiricism---initial reconnaisance of previously virgin terrain in search of any deviations from the predictable nightly patterns of normal persons. Among the innumerable aspects of EEG sleep that might be examined it is not surprising that REM has been the focus of most prominent attention thus far, as it will be in this discussion. But that intriguing phenomenon has stimulated general awakening of scientific interest in all facets of sleep, and it would now be highly premature to predict what relationships ultimately may be considered most significant for clinical psychiatry.

The predominant theme of most studies thus far has been quantitative comparison of that proportion of EEG sleep occupied by REM in various psychiatric groups by comparison with that of normals, an approach initiated by the early report of extremely high REM percentage in a single patient fortuitously studied at the onset of an acute paranoid psychosis (3).* Yet, almost simultaneous study of all-night EEG sleep patterns in a group of schizophrenic patients failed to find any consistent abnormalities of REM percentage (4), and that conclusion is now supported by more than a half dozen subsequent studies of adult and childhood schizophrenics (5-11). Within the broad category of schizophrenic patients thus far studied not only is there nothing very remarkable about the REM proportion of sleep, but even the total duration of EEG documented sleep appears scarcely affected. Contrasting in that respect, but in keeping with the usual clinical impression, is the general finding of reduced total sleep in EEG studies of hospitalized depressed patients, but within that category there is much less agreement regarding the typical

---

*That observation has now been retracted by one of its authors (12) who now concludes that REM was actually reduced.

proportion of REM. Some studies have found it reduced (13), others have found it like that of normals (14-17) and still others have found it elevated (18).

Thus, there appears to be no striking or consistent abnormality in the REM proportion of sleep typical of all patients identified as schizophrenic or depressed, but it is by no means established that the same is true in terms of all other characteristics of EEG recorded sleep or even of REM sleep. Moreover, there is very suggestive evidence of important variations between different stages in the natural history of these illnesses.

Several recent studies find that if there is any-thing characteristic of sleep of schizophrenics it is the low percentages of those high voltage, slow, 'delta' wave patterns comprising EEG stages 3 and 4 (9, 11), but that feature would not distinguish schizophrenics from depressed patients, in whom it has been repeatedly noted (2, 13, 15, 16, 19, 20). Since there is every reason to interpret delta wave patterns as indicators of relatively 'deep' or sound sleep,* their deficiency in these patient groups confirms that troubled spirits do have troubled sleep, or at least under the conditions imposed by these studies.

Regardless of the percentage of sleep occupied by REM, marked individual variations are found in the density or intensity of rapid eye periods across the night. Greater densities of REM eye movement have been found in hallucinating than in non-hallucinating schizophrenics (25) and a similar observation has been made of schizophrenics in remission as compared to normals (26). The interval from sleep onset to the

---

*Delta sleep is associated with the highest arousal thres-holds (21), is greatly enhanced by sleep deprivation (22) or by strenuous exercise (23) and is reduced by transient psychological stress even in normals (24).

first REM period, 'REM latency', has been noted to be both unusually short and unusually long in actively ill schizophrenics (25), while remitted schizophrenics were found to have short REM latencies (26). In relation to stage of illness, slightly lower REM percentages have been found in schizophrenics ill for less than one year than in those ill for two years or longer (5), while relatively high REM proportions have been reported both in borderline patients (3) and in remitted schizophrenics (26).

Probably the most significant shortcoming of most psychiatrically oriented sleep studies thus far is that they have included extremely few examples of the most turbulent phase of schizophrenic illness, that of acute onset or exacerbation, or of the most severe condition of depressive illness, that associated with overt psychosis. Yet, general clinical experience is that these are the situations in which sleep disturbances assume their most extreme forms. Lairy and her colleagues found greatly reduced REM percentages in ten patients at the onset of what were described as transient delirious psychoses (27), but the patient group covered a wide age span and apparently was diagnostically mixed, and the conclusion was based upon just single nights of recording at psychosis onset.* Similarly, among the many depressed patients in whom EEG sleep has been studied extremely few have been explicitly identified as 'psychotic' at the time of study, and conclusions concerning these are conflicting (28, 29). Therefore the nature of EEG sleep records associated with those psychiatric situations in which sleep might be of most crucial importance is least known, and the remainder of this

---

*REM proportions are typically reduced even in normals on first nights of recording.

paper will focus upon recent studies specifically
concerned with the sleep disturbances of psychotic
depression and acute onset or exacerbation of
schizophrenic psychosis.

SLEEP OF PSYCHOTIC DEPRESSIVES

Over the past four years or so we have slowly
accumulated a series of EEG sleep observations upon
patients who were not only severely depressed, but
also frankly psychotic at the time of study, i.e.,
unquestionably delusional and sometimes hallucinating.
That group now numbers sixteen patients, and is
compared with the same number of nonpsychotic hospitalized depressives as well as age matched normal controls.
All subjects were studied for sampling periods of at
least three or more consecutive nights and at times
when they were free of all medication effects. For the
most part they were studied in their own beds on their
own ward, and the data compared was collected only
after they had become very accustomed to the recording
procedure.

Since the findings from these studies have been
described at earlier stages (30, 17, 20) and will be
reported at length and in detail when finally completed,
they will be merely summarized and illustrated here.

The degree or nature of sleep disturbance found
in patients hospitalized with diagnoses of depression is
as variable as the kinds of patients so designated. This
ranges from those who could be better described as very
'unhappy' in particular life situations (who often show
little or no abnormalities of sleep after ensconced in
the protective environment of the hospital), to the
profoundly depressed and psychotic persons who are the
main concern of this discussion. As shown diagrammatically
in the examples of Fig. 1 the most outstanding and

consistent characteristic of sleep in psychotic depressives
is its tenuousness and fragmentation by intermittent
awakenings throughout the night. Deeper EEG phases (stages
3 and 4) are virtually non-existent in the records of
these patients. Delayed sleep onset or early final
awakening do frequently occur, but in our experience they
are much less consistent than the overall lightness and
intermittency of sleep. It might seem questionable to
compare the sum of these shallow fragments of sleep to the
total duration of sustained sleep in normals. Nevertheless,
all intervals of sleep added together average hardly more
than three hours in our psychotic depressive sample as
compared with roughly twice that duration in age matched
controls.* Not included in that reckoning and not
exemplified here are nights of total insomnia, occasionally experienced by any depressed or anxious person,
but very common in the most severe states of psychotic
depression. Therefore, when our severely depressed
patients complain that they have not slept for months,
their conviction probably is not without very significant basis in subjective experience.

Our impression of the tortured quality of sleep
in these patients is entirely in keeping with that from
the smaller psychotic sample of Mendels and Hawkins
(1968), but we would also stress some additional
features which were not emphasized in their report.
The most striking of these is how quickly the first REM
period occurs after sleep onset, the REM latency. Note
that many of these patients display intense and prolonged
REM periods almost immediately after sleep onset, and
this occurs night after night. Yet some of these same
patients occasionally have nights of such minimal sleep

*The characteristics of psychotic depressive sleep so far
described are marked exaggerations of tendencies also
apparent in sleep of many depressed persons, as well as of
trends correlated with age itself. By comparison with
sleep of young normals, sleep of our older controls is
conspicuously shallow, broken and abbreviated.

757

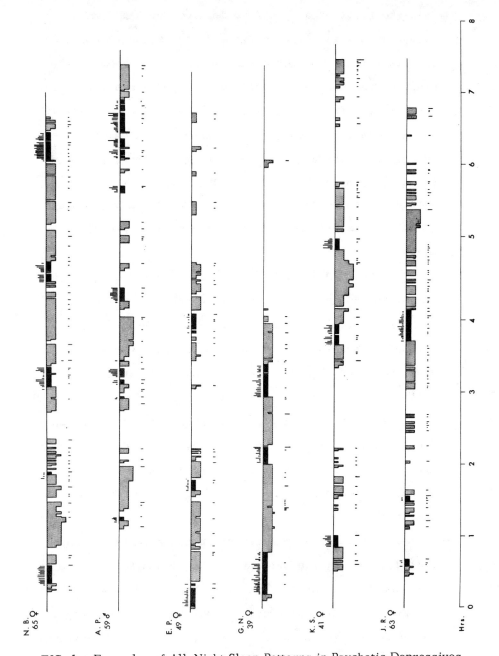

FIG. 1. Examples of All-Night Sleep Patterns in Psychotic Depressives.

These are diagramatic examples of all-night sleep patterns found in
psychotic depressives. Solid bars represent REM periods and marks
above them stand for intensity of eye movement each minute; the
width of the gray bars indicates EEG stage of non-REM sleep in
steps from 1 to 4; open portions are periods of spontaneous walking;
and the dashes below each graph symbolize frequency and intensity
of body movements within sleep.

that the first sign of REM is delayed for many hours
after the initial sleep onset. Hence, although the mean
of this measure for our psychotic sample is about forty
minutes, the median is less than ten (vs roughly seventy-
five minutes for both in normal controls). A corollary
of the prompt appearance of REM after sleep onset at the
beginning of the night is that there are frequent abrupt
transitions between waking and REM throughout the night.
If these denote transitions between waking and dreaming
consciousness, perhaps this in itself might greatly
burden such individuals' grasp of reality.

Another REM characteristic occasionally encountered
in non-psychotic depressives but very prominent among
the psychotics is a dramatic heightening of REM eye
movement intensity. This too is unusually variable in
the psychotics, being especially low in the presence of
the most disturbed sleep, yet the average for the psychotic
group is about one-third greater than that of the normals.
Many individual nights are marked by extraordinary eye
movement such as has been described as 'REM' storms in
alcoholic psychotics (31, 32) as well as in remitted schizophrenics (26).

Concerning that measure which has prompted so much
past discussion, the percentage REM within total sleep,
our findings are at the same time in agreement and
disagreement with all previous ones relating to sleep in
depressives. To the extent that total sleep is shortened
in psychotic depressives total REM time tends to be also,
so that average percentage REM is essentially the same
or only slightly higher than it is in non-psychotic
controls or age matched normals. Quite different conclusions from smaller samples are understandable, however, since proportions of REM from individual patients
range from practically none to levels almost twice those
found in the longer sleep or normals. It is this great

range of REM percentages among psychotic depressives, so
reminiscent of the variability of so many other biological
measures found in the mentally ill, that we consider the
most significant aspect of their EEG sleep records, but
what does it mean? While the ultimate significance of
this striking variability found in the REM portion of
sleep among psychotic depressives remains conjectural, we
believe we have established one point concerning it---
that the variability among patients is no greater than
that found in the same patient over time and in predictable relationships to phases in the natural history of
illness.

LONGITUDINAL STUDIES OF SLEEP IN DEPRESSION

Perhaps because EEG sleep studies are so laborious
and expensive most studies thus far have rested upon
implicit assumptions that would be summarily rejected in
any other field of medicine, i.e., that our patient
groups represent static pathological entities, and therefore, that the abnormal psychobiological patterns we might
hope to find in them would be equally unchanging. A few
studies already cited comparing patients within the same
diagnostic rubric but at different phases of illness
have pointed to important differences in a number of EEG
sleep parameters, and we have demonstrated how marked
these can be by means of extended longitudinal observations of individual patients over intervals ranging from
25 to 250 consecutive nights.

The case study illustrated in Fig. 2 is an example
from among nine we have so far completed, including five
psychotic depressed patients. Daily ratings on a
dimension of 'psychosis', independently provided by our
nursing staff, are plotted in the upper graphs, while

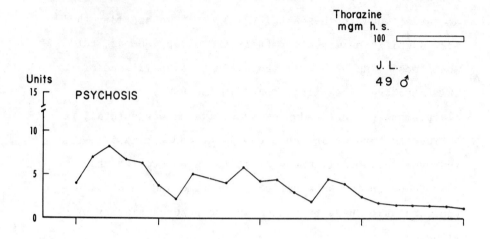

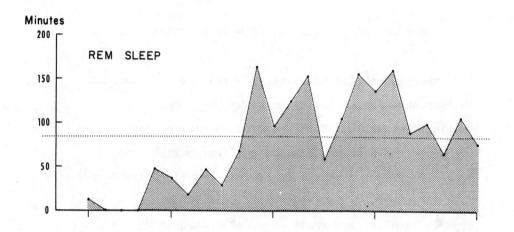

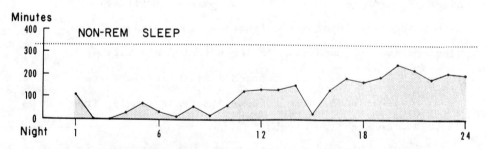

Figure 2 – Longitudinal Study of REM and Non-REM Sleep in Relation to Clinical Status in a Psychotic Depressive Patient.

Daily nursing ratings of 'psychotic behavior' are graphed at the top on a 15 point scale. REM and non-sleep measures are graphed on the two lower graphs in relation to 'standard' levels indicated by the dotted horizontal lines.

levels of REM and non-REM sleep for the corresponding
nights are plotted in the lower graphs, each against a
different scale of minutes in relation to what might be
thought of as standard levels in seven hours of normal
sleep.

This is one of the shortest of these studies which
we had the opportunity to do on a 49 year old man going
through a very transient psychotic depressive episode.
He had come to the National Heart Institute a week
before because of incapacitating cardiac concerns over
many years, apparently without organic basis, and his
history also included a brief course of electroshock
for a 'nervous breakdown' several years earlier. From
his first arrival on the medical ward he appeared very
tense, dejected and preoccupied with the separation
from his family, and was noted to have slept very little
for the first five hospital nights. On the night prior
to this study he was panicky and completely insomniac,
insisting that his family had all been killed in an
automobile accident, that he was about to be sacrificed
to medical research, and that his wife was talking to
him through the air conditioning ducts. As the graphs
indicate during the interval of increasing agitation
and psychosis after he was first transferred to the
psychiatric ward sleep was almost entirely lacking.
Then non-REM sleep gradually returned to nearly normal
levels over the next three weeks in parallel with the
remission of psychotic symptoms. Much more striking,
however, was the variation in REM sleep, which was
almost totally absent initially during the phase of
most acute disturbance and most severe sleep loss,
but then rose to very high levels as psychosis subsided
and sleep began to return.*

Fig. 3 attempts detailed diagrams of alternate
nights from this same patient in order to emphasize

---

*The falling off of REM on the last five nights may have
been due to the small doses of Thorazine he was given then
in the effort to allay his continuing anxiety prior to
his transfer to another hospital closer to home.

J.L.
49 ♂

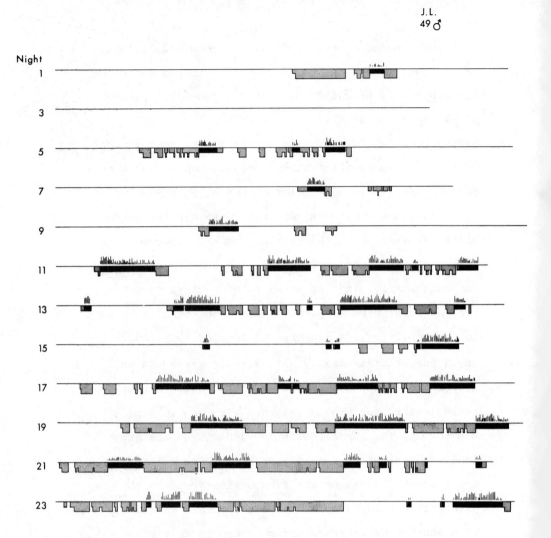

Figure 3 - <u>Diagrammatic Presentation of Alternate Nights</u>
<u>from the Same Patient as in Fig. 2.</u>

The code is the same as that in Fig. 1.

variations other than those in total REMor non-REM sleep.
REM latency and REM intensity are also highly variable,
but the shortest latencies and the most intense REM
occur during the interval just after sleep has begun to
return. Night 15 was one when this patient had little
sleep beside REM, going directly from waking to REM and
back to waking again, and there were many nights when
long stretches of REM were the least interrupted intervals
of this man's sleep.

Not all of the depressed patients we have studied
in this manner have shown such clear changes in terms of
clinical status or such dramatic changes in sleep patterns,
but all have exhibited widely varying amounts of REM at
different times, phases of most severe or developing
psychosis being consistently associated with low levels
of total REM, while phases of waning symptoms have been
accompanied by levels of REM well above normal values.*
Similarly there are wide swings in REM latency and REM
intensity, but while latency is generally minimal and
intensity maximal during the phase when REM levels are
highest, marked trends in the same directions are usually
evident even during the phase when total REM duration is
least.

THE REM DEPRIVATION HYPOTHESIS

Thus, I believe we have established that the sleep
patterns of severe depression are by no means static, but
undergo a dynamic progression pari passu with the course

---

*The same relationships apply to the only other case of
psychotic depression studied in a comparable manner by
Hawkins and his co-workers (33). Low levels of total
sleep and especially low REM levels were found before
electroshock treatment, while restored sleep with extremely
high REM levels accompanied clinical improvement. In our
experience that change reflects clinical improvement
regardless of treatment modality. We have seen similar
changes after successful drug treatment, even though the
particular drugs are known to have REM suppressive
tendencies in normal subjects.

of illness, and indeed, are remarkably sensitive indicators of its progression. Nevertheless, explanation for these changes in EEG sleep or their interpretation in relation to psychopathology remain matters of conjecture. A rapidly growing body of evidence insists that the REM phenomenon arises out of complex and intrinsic neurophysiological mechanisms of which neurohumoral processes are important links (34). It seems to follow, therefore, that these wide but relatively slow shifts in REM during the course of psychotic depression must mirror some variety of corresponding changes in central nervous functioning.

One school of thought suggests that C.N.S. alterations presumably reflected by varying REM parameters are primary manifestations of depressive illness itself, and this ties in well with current efforts to implicate altered indole metabolism as the crucial factor in depression (18, 29). While this is a plausible and provocative line of inquiry, to my knowledge there has been little progress thus far in explaining why these hypothetical changes in brain chemistry might arise. My own point of view, elaborated elsewhere (17, 20) does not discount the possible importance of such biochemical changes to sleep patterns or to the psychopathology of depression, but does imply that the altered sleep patterns found are inevitable consequences of more apparent elements in depressive illness.

Perhaps the most remarkable characteristic of the REM phenomenon is that when it is prevented from taking place over a series of nights the propensity for its occurrence seems to become more and more urgent and intense, as evidenced by its decreasing latency at the beginning of sleep, the increased percentage of sleep it occupies,

and in very protracted animal studies, by markedly
heightened intensity of its phasic elements, such as
the eye movements themselves (35, 36).

These are precisely the characteristics we do find
in the EEG sleep of psychotic depressives, even though
the increased proportion of REM is not evident until the
depression itself begins to abate. Since anything that
seriously troubles sleep tends to have such a suppressive
influence upon REM, I believe the short REM latencies,
increased REM intensity and eventually the extraordinary
abundance of REM we find in the sleep of psychotic
depressives can be most parsimoniously interpreted as
stigmata of the degree and duration of troubled sleep
they have experienced. Undoubtedly somatic processes
are involved in these slow changes, and quite possibly
such might effect the delicate balance of brain functioning upon which sanity depends, but the latter possibility
must still be substantiated.

While it would seem most likely that the common
source of the troubled sleep of severely depressed
persons is simply their troubled spirits, we might expect
to find the same dynamic pattern of REM suppression and
compensation under any circumstances of greatly altered
sleep. In fact, the same manifestations have been
described after drug suppression of REM in alcoholics
(30, 32), as well as in amphetamine or barbiturate
addicts (37 , 38).

To arrive finally at the central interest of this
conference, I hope it has now been made cogent to inquire
about the existence or nature of sleep disturbance
accompanying the development of acute schizophrenic
psychosis.

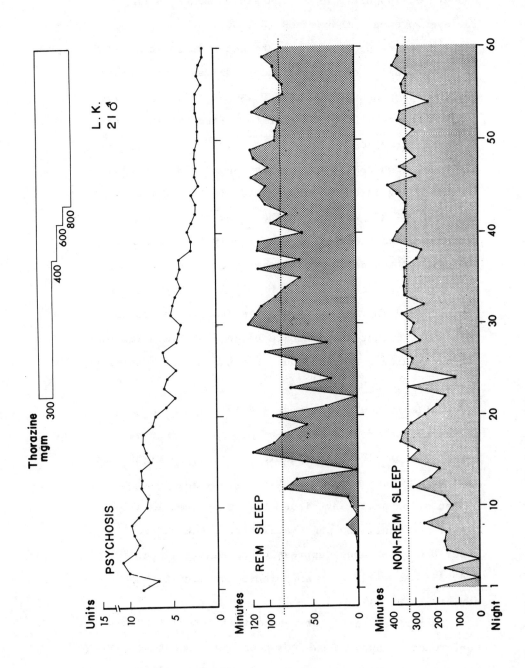

Figure 4 – Longitudinal Study of an Acute, Initial Schizophrenic Psychotic Episode – The First 60 Days
and Nights.

LONGITUDINAL STUDIES OF EEG SLEEP IN ACUTE SCHIZOPHRENIC PSYCHOSIS

As will soon be reported much more adequately, (39) over the past two years my colleagues and I have managed to obtain extended longitudinal studies of EEG sleep encompassing ten acute schizophrenic episodes in six patients. Fig. 4 illustrates the one example we have been able to study in this manner during an initial psychotic episode. History indicated that this young man had complained of difficulty with sleep over several months previously and that he had not slept at all from thetime when psychosis emerged several days before admission. As the graphs reveal, this patient averaged no more than two hours total sleep per night over the first two weeks of hospitalization, and REM was almost entirely absent for the first eleven nights. Non-REM sleep gradually returned with the first waning of psychotic behavior during the second week, while REM abruptly appeared after the rest of sleep approached normal levels, but was lost on several later nights when sleep was particularly disturbed.

To a greater or lesser degree, the marked insomnia we documented in this patient was also conspicuous in all of the ten psychotic episodes we have so far studied in this manner, and in each instance the attrition of REM has been particularly severe. In terms of the REM deprivation model and our previous observations of psychotic depression we would, therefore, expect to see compensatory excesses of REM after sleep began to improve. In this case, there was no immediate or conspicuous rebound of REM levels, although high REM times did appear sporadically. Other of these patients have had one or two nights of moderately high REM levels immediately after restoration of sleep, but none have shown sustained high REM levels like those of psychotic

768

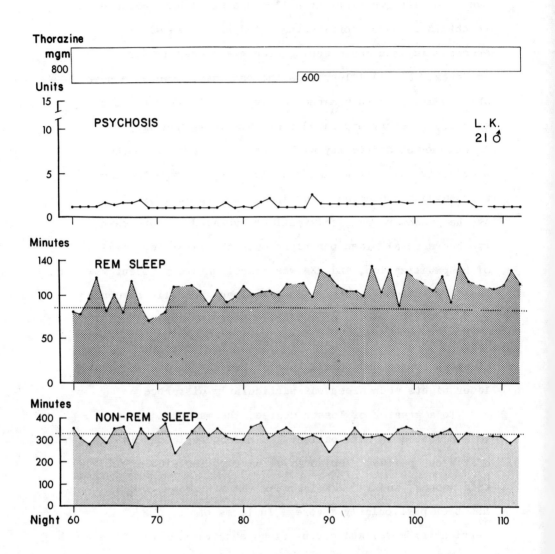

Figure 5 – Continuation of Study Shown in Fig. 4 –
The Last 50 Days and Nights.

depressives. As shown in Fig. 5, we continued to study
this same patient considerably longer than any other
after improvement, and it can be seen from the graph
that over the fifty night period prior to his discharge
he did display generally high REM levels. The possibility
that REM compensation in schizophrenics tends to be
especially delayed and gradual is in keeping with the
high levels found by other investigators in newly
remitted patients (26), but we cannot be sure of that
interpretation so long as we have no way of knowing what
the normal REM level might be for this individual.
Extremely little delta sleep appeared at any point in
this patient's hospitalization, and that has been true
of all the schizophrenics we have studied.

The previous example does not offer any good
estimate of how protracted or severe sleep disturbance
may have been before psychotic decompensation, but we
have some idea about this from three patients studied
during remitted intervals after initial psychotic
illness and then continuously throughout recurrent
psychotic episodes. Fig. 6 covers a span of 49 out
of the more than 140 nights of study for one of those
patients during which he went through five transient
psychotic episodes, each lasting from one to two weeks,
but successively diminishing in severity and duration.
This was the third studied and the fourth he had
experienced. The pattern of sleep changes is typical
of all, except that in the earlier ones insomnia had
been somewhat more severe, and the disproportionate
loss of REM more evident. In this instance, as in all
we have seen in any of the patients, restitution of
non-REM sleep slightly preceded REM restitution, and
the return of both preceded the waning of psychotic
symptoms, but there is only a transient suggestion of

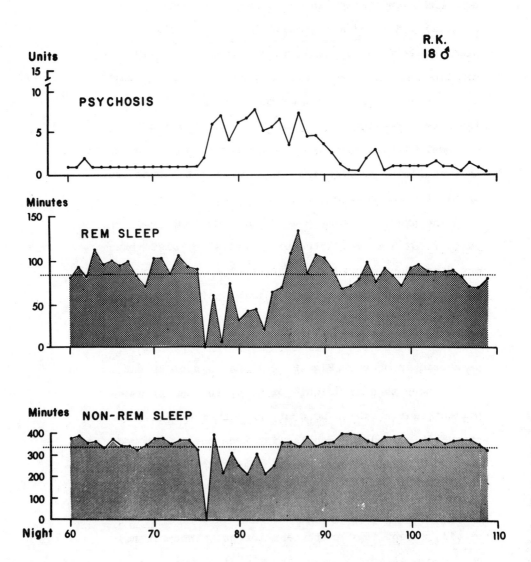

Figure 6 – Longitudinal Study of A Recurrent Schizophrenic Exacerbation.

compensatory REM levels immediately after. Perhaps
most significant in no instance did we see evidence of
serious sleep disturbance until one or two nights
before the recurrent breakthough of psychosis.

If further evidence confirms our present impressions
about the curious deficiency of REM compensation, so
similar to the findings after experimental REM deprivation in schizophrenics (40), additional explanation
may be required.* For the present, however, it is
cautious to assume that while insomnia accompanying acute
schizophrenic episodes may further weaken the already
overwhelmed ego capacities, perhaps its greatest significance is merely as an indicator of the degree of inner
turmoil. Needless to say, possibly there is still a
great deal we might learn from such objective indications
with regard to the natural history of psychosis.

---

*The interpretation offered by Zarcone and Dement in this
volume applies equally well to the findings described here.

REFERENCES

1. Snyder, F. The new biology of dreaming. Arch.
    gen. Psychiat. 8, 381, 1963.

2. Diaz-Guerrero, R., Gottlieb, J.S. and Knott, J.R.
    The sleep of patients with manic-depressive
    psychosis, depressive type: An electroencephalo-
    graphic study. Psychosom. Med. 8, 399, 1946.

3. Fisher, C. and Dement, W.C. Studies on the
    psychopathology of sleep and dreams. Amer. J.
    Psychiat. 119, 1160, 1963.

4. Koresko, R.L., Snyder, F. and Feinberg, I. "Dream
    time" in hallucinating and non-hallucinating
    schizophrenic patients. Nature 199, 1118, 1963.

5. Feinberg, I., Koresko, R.L., Gottlieb, F. and
    Wender,P.H. Sleep electroencephalographic and
    eye-movement patterns in schizophrenic patients.
    Compr. Psychiat. 5, 44, 1964.

6. Onheiber, P., White, P.T., Demyer, M.K. and
    Ottinger, D.R. Sleep and dream patterns of child
    schizophrenics. Arch. gen. Psychiat. 12, 568,
    1965.

7. Ornitz, E.M., Ritvo, E.R. and Walter, R.D. Dreaming
    sleep in autistic twins. Arch. gen. Psychiat.
    12, 77, 1965.

8. Azumi, K. A polygraphic study of sleep in
    schizophrenics. Psychiat. neurol. Jap. 68,
    1222, 1966.

9. Caldwell, D.R. and Domino, E.F. Electroencephalo-
    graphic and eye movement patterns during sleep
    in chronic schizophrenic patients. Electroenceph.
    clin. Neurophysiol. 22, 414, 1967.

10. Zarcone, V., Gulevitch, G., Pivik, T. and Dement, W.C.
    Partial REM phase deprivation and schizophrenia.
    Arch. gen. Psychiat. 18, 194, 1968.

11. Wilczak, H., Kubacki, A., Rzepecki, J., Kiljan, A.,
    Jus, A. and Jus, K. Badania poligraficzne nad
    snem nocnym u nieleczonych chorych na schizofrenie
    (korelacje elektrokliniczne). Psychiat. Pol. 2,
    175, 1968.

12. Dement, W.C. Psychophysiology of sleep and dreams.
    Amer. Handbook of Psychiat. Arieti, S. (ed.)
    3, 290, 1966.

13. Hawkins, D.R. and Mendels, J. Sleep disturbance
    in depressive syndromes. Amer. J. Psychiat.
    123, 682, 1966.

14. Oswald, I., Berger, R.J., Jaramillo, R.A.,
    Keddie, K.M., Olley, P.C. and Plunkett, G.B.
    Melancholia and barbiturates: A controlled EEG,
    body and eye movement study of sleep. Brit.
    J. Psychiat. 109, 66, 1963.

15. Gresham, S.C., Agnew, H.W., Jr. and Williams, R.L. The sleep of depressed patients. Arch. gen. Psychiat. 13, 503, 1965.

16. Castellotti, V. and Pittaluga, E. EEG study of spontaneous nocturnal sleep in depressive states. Riv. Neurol. 36, 417, 1966.

17. Snyder, F. Electrographic studies of sleep in depression. In Kline, N.W. and Laska, E. (eds.) Computers and Electronic Devices in Psychiatry. New York, Grune & Stratton, 1968, pp. 272-301

18. Hartmann, E. Longitudinal studies of sleep and dream patterns in manic-depressive patients. Arch. gen. Psychiat. 19, 312, 1968.

19. Zung, W.K., Wilson, W.P. and Dodson, W.E. Effect of depressive disorders on sleep EEG arousal. Arch. gen. Psychiat. 10, 439, 1964.

20. Snyder, F. Dynamic aspects of sleep disturbance in relation to mental illness. Presented at the Annual Meeting of the Society of Biological Psychiatry, Washington, D.C., June 14-16, 1968. To be published in the Societies Annual Volume, Recent Advances in Biological Psychiatry.

21. Blake, H. and Gerard, R.W. Brain potentials during sleep. Amer. J. Physiol. 119, 692, 1937.

22. Berger, R.J. and Oswald, I. Effects of sleep deprivation on behaviour, subsequent sleep, and dreaming. J. ment. Sci. 108, 457, 1962.

23. Baekeland, F. and Lasky, R. Exercise and sleep patterns in college athletes. Percept. motor Skills 23, 1203, 1966.

24. Lester, B.K., Burch, N.R. and Dossett, R.C. Nocturnal EEG-GSR profiles: The influence of presleep states. Psychophysiology 3, 238, 1967.

25. Feinberg, I., Koresko, R.L. and Gottlieb, F. Further observations on electrophysiological sleep patterns in schizophrenia. Compr. Psychiat. 6, 21, 1965.

26. Gulevitch, G., Dement, W.C. and Zarcone, V. All-night sleep recording of chronic schizophrenics in remission. Compr. Psychiat. 8, 141, 1967.

27. Lairy, G.C., Barte, H., Golsteinas, L. and Ridjanovic, S. IV - Sommeil de Nuit des Malades Mentaus. Le Sommeil de Nuit normal et pathologique etudes electroencephalographiques. Masson & Cie (eds.), Paris (VI) Nouvelle Serie, 2, 354, 1965.

28. Green, W.J. and Stajduhar, P.P. The effect of ECT on the sleep-dream cycle in psychotic depression. J. nerv. ment. Dis. 143, 123, 1966.

29. Mendels, J. and Hawkins, D.R. Sleep and depression. Further considerations. Arch. gen. Psychiat. 19, 445, 1968.

30. Snyder, F. Progress in the new biology of dreaming. Amer. J. Psychiat. 122, 377, 1965.

31. Gross, M., Goodenough, D., Tobin, M., Halpert, E., Lepore, D., Perlstein, A., Sirota, M., Dibianco, J., Fuller, R. and Kriskmer, I. Sleep disturbances and hallucinations in the acute alcoholic psychoses. J. nerv. ment. Dis. 142, 493, 1966.

32. Greenberg, R. and Pearlman, C. Delirium tremens and dreaming. Amer. J. Psychiat. 142, 133, 1967

33. Hawkins, D.R., Mendels, J., Scott, J., Bensch, G. and Teachy, W. The psychophysiology of sleep in psychotic depressives: A longitudinal study. Psychosom. Med. 29, 329, 1967.

34. Jouvet, M. Neurophysiology of the states of sleep. Physiol. Rev. 47, 117, 1967.

35. Dement, W.C. The effect of dream deprivation. Science 131, 1705, 1960.

36. Dement, W.C., Henry, P., Cohen, H. and Ferguson, J. Studies on the effect of REM deprivation in humans and in animals. In Kety, S.S., Evarts, E.V. and Williams, H.L. (eds.) Sleep and Altered States of Consciousness. ARNMD, Vol. XLV, Williams and Wilkins, Baltimore, 1967, p. 456.

37. Oswald, I. and Thacore, V.R. Amphetamine and phenmetrazine addiction. Physiological abnormalities in the abstinence syndrome. Brit. med. J. 2, 427, 1963.

38. Oswald, I. and Priest, R.G. Five weeks to escape the sleeping-pill habit. Brit. med. J. 2, 1093, 1965.

39. Kupfer, D.J., Wyatt, R.J., Snyder, F. and Scott, J. Sleep disturbance in acute schizophrenic patients. To be presented at the Annual Meeting of the American Psychiatric Association, Bal Harbour, Florida, May 5-9, 1969.

40. Zarcone, V., Gulevich, G., Pivik, T. and Dement, W.C. Partial REM phase deprivation and schizophrenia. Arch. gen. Psychiat. 18, 194, 1968.

F. Snyder, M.D., National Institute of Mental Health, Bethesda, Maryland 20014

SOME PARALLEL FINDINGS IN SCHIZOPHRENIC PATIENTS AND SEROTONIN-DEPLETED CATS*

WILLIAM DEMENT, VINCENT ZARCONE, JAMES FERGUSON,
HARRY COHEN, TERRY PIVIK, and JACK BARCHAS

The possibility that the findings of sleep research might be fruitfully applied to the problems of mental illness continues to inspire countless nocturnal vigils. In this presentation, we will summarize some results obtained from all-night recordings in schizophrenic patients and some related studies in experimental animals which may enable us to suggest that REM sleep mechanisms play a role in the pathogenesis of the psychotic state.

It has always been an attractive hypothesis that the processes underlying the production of dreams may also be involved in the genesis of psychotic illnesses simply because of the obvious phenomenological similarities[1-3]. Without claiming absolute veridicality, some of the features that characterize both dreaming and psychosis may be mentioned for the purpose of illustrating this principle. Thus, hallucinations or perceptions without a basis in reality may occur in both conditions. There is often a sense of depersonalization in that the self may be observed as though events were happening in the life of someone else. Time sense may be altered so that there is a feeling of timelessness - that time has stopped - or that it has speeded up or slowed down. Feelings or affects are more variable in intensity than in waking life and may be, at times, quite inappropriate to what is going on. Objects or other people often seem to be either incompletely recognized or incompletely represented, and may be involved in episodes that would not occur in normal circumstances. At times, thinking has a bizarre, fractured quality. Judgment may be partially suspended so that events which have an aura of strangeness are believed.

The possibility of a relationship between dreaming and psychosis has become even more attractive since it has become known that dreaming is but one

---

Supported by Grant MH 13860 from the National Institutes of Mental Health; Research Career Development Award 3 K3-MH 5804 from U.S.P.H.S.; Grant NGR 05-020-168 from N.A.S.A.; a grant from the Epilepsy Foundation; and VA Research Grant Funds.

aspect of a unique biological process universally distributed among all mammals, a process with its own neuroanatomical substrate and biochemical regulatory mechanism[4,5,6,7]. Thus, although many factors obviously contribute to the schizophrenic psychosis, we now know that some of the most puzzling manifestations of this illness are also the normal by-products of a functional process in the brain, and are routinely generated during its regularly occurring periods of activity every night in every human being. If we can, at least for the purposes of argument, assume that there is a correspondence between dreaming, REM sleep, and some of the psychotic symptoms such as hallucinations, then we might consider the quantity and universality of REM sleep and its urgent response to deprivation, and suggest that the major puzzle nowadays is not why or how hallucinations and other symptoms occur, but rather why they don't occur. In other words, what is it that so effectively prevents most people from "dreaming while awake"? From this point of view, certain aspects of the schizophrenic psychosis could be seen as the result of a malfunction in whatever process ordinarily confines dream experiences to the obscurity and safety of sleep. Recent work in our laboratories[8,9,10,11] has suggested that such a malfunction, or something close to it, can be produced in experimental animals by the chronic administration of para-chlorophenyl-alanine (PCPA), a selective depletor of brain serotonin[12]. The degree of relevance that such a "preparation" might have for those interested in the psychotic state in humans will be left to individual judgment. Our task in this presentation will be merely to summarize pertinent experimental data in both conditions and to point out the intriguing correspondences that this data has revealed.

Before proceeding further, we must define an important distinction with regard to the physiological concomitants of REM sleep. These concomitants may be divided into two classes which have been termed phasic events and tonic events[13,14]. Tonic events are those changes or physiological characteristics which more or less define the REM period, and which are maintained continuously throughout its duration. Examples of tonic events would be EEG activation, EMG suppression, brain temperature elevation, etc. Phasic events are those activities which are short-lasting and discontinuous. In addition to rapid eye movements themselves, a number of other activities have been described that fall into this category - for example, middle ear muscle contractions, cardiovascular irregularities, respiratory chances, muscular twitching, phasic changes in pupil diameter, phasic fluctuations in penile tumescence, and finally, the unique bursts of monophasic sharp waves that characterize the electrical activity of the pons oculomotor nuclei, lateral geniculate nuclei, and visual cortices [15,16,17].

It is our feeling that these monophasic sharp waves, hereafter referred to as PGO (pontine-geniculate-occipital) spikes, represent some sort of primary triggering process for all other phasic events, particularly eye movements. Attesting to their primacy in the triggering of phasic events in general is the fact that PGO spikes nearly always appear some time before the actual onset of the REM period. This and other properties of PGO spikes are illustrated in Figures 1 and 2.

Besides being a helpful taxonomic refinement, the distinction between tonic events and phasic events is important because under certain conditions, these two classes of activity may be dissociated. The first clear-cut demonstration of such a dissociation was accomplished by Delorme and Jouvet [18], who showed that REM periods were abolished by high doses of reserpine in the cat, but that phasic events (PGO spikes) continued to discharge throughout the period of suppression. An important principle is suggested by these and similar results, to wit: that at least two distinct neurological systems and/or mechanisms are involved in the REM phenomenon - the first a system which functions to produce REM periods, in effect a tonic events system; and the second, a system which generates or triggers the phasic events.

Finally, if we had to make a choice, it would seem that the subjective experience associated with REM periods should also be classified as a kind of phasic activity. The fact that some dream experiences appear to take place in NREM sleep [19,20,21] is not contradictory since a portion of the PGO spike activity is also associated with this phase of the sleep cycle.

THE EFFECT OF CHRONIC PCPA ADMINISTRATION IN CATS

A theory regarding the function of serotonin in brain has been developed by Jouvet [6,22,23,24] in which the amine is viewed as the transmitter or neuromodulator substance of a NREM sleep-inducing system whose cell bodies lie in

the raphe system, a group of nine midline cellular aggregations extending
from the medulla oblongata to the posterior diencephalon. Recent studies utilizing fluorescence microscopy have demonstrated that nearly all the serotonergic neurons of the brain are located in these nuclei and that serotonin in
other portions of the brain lies mainly in the axonal terminals of raphe neurons[25,26]. In an extensive series of ablation experiments in cats, Jouvet found
that loss of raphe tissue was associated with the development of insomnia which,
in turn, was correlated with a fall in brain serotonin. This result was buttressed by the additional finding that depletion of serotonin by administration of PCPA also produced a drastic reduction in sleep time. Finally, it
was noted that both PCPA and lesions in the raphe system were followed by
the appearance of PGO spikes in the waking state.

We have confirmed and extended these results with PCPA and have been led
to a somewhat different notion about the role of serotonin in brain[8,9,10,11,27].
Our studies involved continuous polygraphic and behavioral observations of
cats, 24 hours a day, 7 days a week, for long periods of time, up to two or
more months. The mean normative values for PGO spike densities in REM periods as well as daily NREM and REM sleep times were first established during
extended baseline periods. The polygraphic observations together with extensive behavioral observation and behavioral testing were continued throughout the subsequent period of chronic PCPA administration during which each
cat received daily subcutaneous injections of the drug in doses ranging from
75mg/kilo to 300mg/kilo.

Very little change was noted during the first 48 hours of PCPA administration. However, at some specific point in time, monophasic sharp waves bearing
an exact resemblance to PGO spikes began to appear during wakefulness in every
cat. The development of this particular change is illustrated in Figure 3.
Nearly all other important changes seemed to occur in close association with
the appearance of spike activity in the waking animal. There was a precipitous drop in sleep time (both REM and NREM fractions) and one had the impression of a profound internal disturbance. Indeed, the animals often seemed to
respond to the internally generated bursts of PGO spike activity as if they
were external stimuli. These responses most frequently took the form of

alerting and very often included searching movements of the head and eyes. Occasionally, the behavior associated with bursts of spikes suggested the possibility of fullblown hallucinations. In addition to the development of insomnia and "hallucinations," the PCPA animals underwent a profound and previously undescribed behavioral change which included the emergence of hypersexuality, hyperphagia, profound irritability, as well as a number of alterations peculiar to individual animals. These changes were exceedingly dramatic and it is difficulty to do them justice with mere words. For example, previously indifferent male cats would not only compulsively mount anesthetized male cats and passive male cats, but also would relentlessly stalk a fully awake, raging, clawing normal tomcat with sexual intent for as long as we would allow. Cats who normally ignored laboratory rats began to kill them with a rapidity and concentrated savagery that evoked images of the jungle. A good analogy to the emergence of these behavioral and electrophysiological changes in association with PCPA administration is the flood produced by destroying a dam. In this instance, the dam might be the serotonergic neurons of the raphé system.

Although the fullblown PCPA effect took several days to develop (which may simply represent the time required to reach a critical threshold of serotonin depletion), a nearly instantaneous reversal of both the electrophysiological and behavioral changes was accomplished by administering very small amounts of 5-hydroxytryptophan, the metabolic precursor of serotonin.

After several days in the state of insomnia and drive accentuation described above, a reversal of varying degrees took place even though the PCPA dosage was always maintained. The animals became more and more lethargic and sleep periods were both longer and more frequent. PGO spike bursts were less intense and appeared to lose their power to disturb the animal. By the seventh or eighth day of PCPA administration, both NREM and REM sleep times had returned to maximum values which were often within the baseline range. Figure 4 illustrates a typical sequence in one cat.

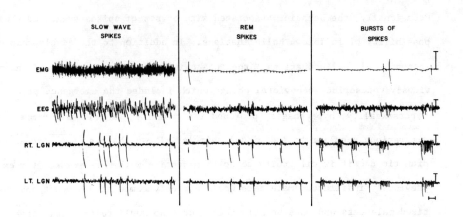

Figure 1. PGO spikes: the primary phasic event. The large amplitude, isolated spikes characteristically associated with NREM sleep are shown on the left, while the low amplitude bursts characteristic of REM sleep are shown on the right. The middle tracing shows an intermediate example most typical of the final moments of REM periods, or immediately after the REM onset. Calibrations: 50 microvolts, one second.

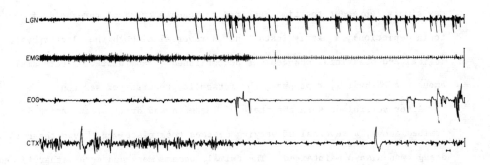

Figure 2. PGO spikes at onset of a REM period in the cat. Derivations: LGN, lateral geniculate nucleus; EMG, electromyogram from posterior neck muscles; EOG, electro-oculogram: CTX, cortical brain waves. Note high amplitude (polarity is irrelevant) single PGO spikes in LGN about 20 seconds before onset of REM period (EMG suppression and EEG activation). Bursts of eye movements and PGO spikes occur simultaneously with EEG activation. EMG suppression is not complete for another few seconds. PGO spikes continue to occur in bursts with or without eye movements for remainder of sample. Calibrations: one second and 50 microvolts.

Interesting changes took place in the pattern of PGO spike discharge. When the spikes appeared in the waking state, the frequency <u>within</u> REM periods showed a rapid fall to a substantially lower value in all cats (see Figure 5). Initially, only occasional spikes were seen in the waking state, but the frequency increased very quickly to a plateau which was always less than the discharge rate within REM periods. PGO spikes began to occur almost continuously in NREM sleep - that is, there were no prolonged periods of NREM sleep without spikes. As the PCPA treatment continued, it was as if all regulation of PGO activity had vanished allowing the spike discharge to disperse itself more or less equally regardless of background state.

We maintained cats on PCPA for up to 37 days. When the drug was withdrawn, there was a gradual return to normalcy over a three to five day period.

REM SLEEP DEPRIVATION STUDIES IN SCHIZOPHRENIC PATIENTS

A number of studies have described the all-night sleep patterns of various populations of schizophrenic patients[28-35]. Although there has been little consistency among the studies with regard to therapy (drug administration), diagnosis, and clinical state, there have been a few reasonably consistent, if somewhat undramatic, findings in what are otherwise essentially normal data. The first finding is that the schizophrenic populations appear to have a shorter latency for the onset of the first REM period compared to most normal control groups. Secondly, the overall sleep patterns of schizophrenics appear to be significantly unstable in that the NREM-REM cycle is extremely variable in length and the various sleep stages appear to be easily and frequently interrupted. In addition, the overall amounts of time devoted to the different stages appear to be highly variable from patient to patient.

In our own work[36,37,38,39], we have attempted to reduce some of the confounding variables by keeping phenothiazine medications constant throughout the periods of study and by carefully delineating the clinical state of the patient population. Our observations have been focused on two groups. Both groups were composed of chronic process schizophrenics with evidence of deterioration in occupational and social functioning. The patients in one group were experiencing active symptomatology - hallucinations, delusions, thought disorder, bizarre motor activity, and affective abnormalities. The continuing symptomatology was accepted by these men and served to explain their position in life for them. This was probably a factor that mitigated anxiety. The second group was as clinically differentiated as possible, consisting of patients with no active symptomatology whatsoever. In other words, they appeared to be in complete remission. These two patient populations were subjected to two consecutive nights of selective REM sleep deprivation. Each patient had baseline, deprivation, and recovery recordings.

Nine patients were studied in the actively ill group, and all nine <u>failed</u> to show a post-deprivation rise in total REM sleep time (REM rebound). Over the entire five night recovery period, they averaged only a 5 percent make-up of the REM time lost on the two deprivation nights. One patient was also REM deprived for an extended period of eight consecutive nights and he too failed to show the usual compensatory REM rebound.

On the other hand, patients in remission, including some patients who had also been studied while actively ill, all showed substantial rebounds averaging over 200 percent makeup following the deprivation. The percent makeup can be contrasted to the 50%-60% level characteristic of normal subjects, or non-schizophrenic patient control subjects over a five night recovery period following two deprivation nights. None of the patients showed any increase

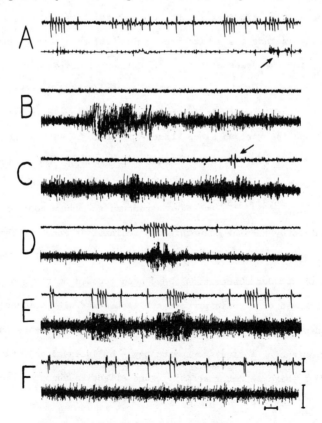

Figure 3.

Figure 3. Development of PGO spikes in the waking state during administration of PCPA. All tracings are from the same cat on the same day and were
selected from a single four hour time period (0400 to 0800) during which the
major changes happened to occur. The top tracing of each pair is a bipolar
recording from the left lateral geniculate nucleus (LGN) and the bottom
tracing is the simultaneous electromyogram from the posterior neck muscles.
Calibrations: 50 uV, 1 sec. <u>A</u>. At 0410, the animal was in a REM period and
the sample tracings show the typical PGO spike activity along with the characteristic EMG suppression. There is a miniscule bit of activity toward the
end of the EMG sample (arrow) which is concomitant with a flurry of muscular
twitching. <u>B</u>. This sample was taken from a period of wakefulness at around
0420. It was exactly like all other recordings seen during wakefulness in
a month of continuous baseline observation. The particular LGN derivation
shown in these samples remained flat even during body movements. The brief
but marked increase of EMG discharge in this tracing indicates gross bodily
movement. The overall high level of EMG activity is more or less unique
to the waking state. <u>C</u>. At 0437, which was approximately 45 hours after
PCPA administration was begun, the first unequivocal PGO spike during wakefulness was seen (arrow). <u>D</u>. The first good burst of spike activity occurred
at 0449 and was accompanied by searching movements of the head and eyes (note
EMG upsurge). <u>E</u>. By 0630, the PGO spike discharge was virtually continuous
and the cat remained fully awake for several hours. <u>F</u>. This sample was selected to illustrate some of the variability in the discharge pattern of PGO
spikes. It also shows that a less intense, non-bursting level of PGO spike
activity was apparently insufficient for the production of "hallucinatory"
behavior. The steady EMG level indicates lack of gross body movement.

---

in symptomatology during or after the deprivation periods. In a related
study, Luby and Caldwell[40] failed to see either an immediate or a delayed
REM sleep rebound following a period of <u>total</u> sleep deprivation in a group
of chronic schizophrenics.

There are only two other reported studies of selective REM sleep deprivation in schizophrenics. In one, Azumi <u>et al.</u>[41] found little or no REM rebound during recovery sleep following three nights of deprivation in three
patients. However, in the other study, Vogel and Traub[42] obtained substan-

tial REM sleep rebounds following five to seven nights of selective REM sleep deprivation in five schizophrenic patients. These patients were described as follows:

"In the last few years, all subjects had several acute episodes of floridly psychotic symptoms which included delusions, assaultive behavior, auditory and visual hallucinations, fecal smearing, catatonia, and word salad speech. During the baseline period of the experiment, the subjects were free of these florid symptoms." A variety of tests were repeatedly administered to the patients to help define their clinical state at different times during the experimental period. REM deprivation produced no change on the tests, but the initial levels or scores were not reported by Vogel and Traub. It seems to us that their patients were more similar to the patients in our second group who were essentially in complete remission with no active symptomatology. Accordingly, the observation of REM rebounds by Vogel and Traub is consistent with the observations reported by us on this second group.

In terms of a possible obligatory "quota" of REM sleep, we have considered the failure to rebound in actively ill patients a finding of great importance with far-reaching implications for understanding the actively psychotic state. In view of this, we have aimed our studies in experimental animals (see earlier sections) toward the goal of producing a laboratory model of the clinical situation and reproducing as many of the clinical findings as possible. In this sense, and in this sense only, we have regarded the cat treated chronically with PCPA as a laboratory model of the psychotic state.

SPECIFIC PARALLELS BETWEEN CHRONIC PCPA CATS AND SCHIZOPHRENIC PATIENTS

There is a great deal of resistance to the concept of "psychosis" in experimental animals, particularly in non-primate species. This is presumably because so many aspects of psychotic illnesses, indeed the essential defining characteristics, involve disturbances of functions that are uniquely human - such as symbol formation, associative processes, language and communication. On the other hand, these overt symptoms occupy the exclusive focus of our attention only because we have no information that definitely implicates changes on other levels of function. If we are willing to assume - at least for the sake of argument - that the presence of a biochemical abnormality is a <u>necessary</u> factor in the pathogenesis of the schizophrenic psychosis, it should then be completely obvious that reproducing the exact same biochemical abnormality in an experimental animal, such as the dog, cat, or rat, would never give us a condition resembling the human illness in all respects. The important question is, if we <u>knew</u> the basic cause of schizophrenia (recognizing, of course, the possibility of multiple causes and multiple syndromes) and could reproduce it in an animal, what would we get? First of all, we might get nothing. A biochemical defect that would produce schizophrenia in a human might have no significant consequence for a rat, or even a monkey. The best one could hope is that any disturbances seen in experimental animals would be recognizable members of the schizophrenic syndrome (inappropriate emotional behavior would be an example), and that no changes would be totally unrelated.

If we really knew the basic cause of schizophrenia, the foregoing discussion would be academic. No one would care the least whether or not reproducing the basic abnormality in experimental animals also reproduced the clinical syndrome. All our interest and concern would be directed toward reversal. Behavioral change would be of interest only if an independent measure of such a reversal were needed. Unfortunately, we know nothing about the basic cause of schizophrenia, or at least very little, and we are still searching for a good prospect. For this reason alone, while recognizing the many difficulties and logical inconsistencies, we cannot afford to ignore any experimentally produced change in animals that bears a reasonable resemblance to the schizophrenic syndrome or any of its parts. At the moment, the promise of such a resemblance - its relevance - can be judged only on the basis of whatever demonstrable physiological and behavioral parallels are present.

It is from this point of view that we would like to describe some intriguing similarities between the chronic PCPA syndrome in the cat and the schizophrenic psychosis in the human. We will judge this endeavor worthwhile if it stimulates any further attempt to evaluate the functional status of serotonergic systems in patients or any new approaches to the problem of measurement. Whether or not the chronic PCPA cat is the best model, or even a good model, has little meaning since, as far as we know, in the whole realm

of experimental psychopathology there is no other condition or preparation
that has been advanced as an animal model of the schizophrenic psychosis.

Before proceeding further, we should mention one possible parallelism
which cannot be conclusively evaluated at the present time, but which we do
not think exists. Biochemical analysis of brain tissue from cats receiving
150mg/kilo per day of PCPA has revealed that brain serotonin falls to undetectable levels within five days and remains undetectable throughout the period of drug administration. The maximum period of treatment in our cats
was 37 days. We do not believe that comparable results would be uniformly
obtained if schizophrenic brains were available for analysis. The basic abnormality in the PCPA cat may be defined or conceptualized as a functional
ablation of the serotonergic neurons of the raphe system, since we assumed
that chronic serotonin depletion of this magnitude must interfere with normal
transmission in these neurons. Accordingly, if the PCPA cat was the true and
valid model of the schizophrenic psychosis, we would expect to find abnormal
function of serotonin neurons in all patients, but we could not predict the
specific defect. A number of possibilities exist including abnormal synthesis of false transmitters, abnormal release, abnormal receptor sites, etc.,
any one of which could probably produce the required functional deficit in
serotonergic neurons.

1. Overall sleep patterns in PCPA cats and schizophrenic patients.

It is not the purpose of this discussion to evaluate the role of serotonin
in the regulation of sleep per se, although there can be little doubt that such
a role does exist. However, one issue must be clarified. The excellent and
extensive work of Jouvet as well as others[43,44,45] has led some people to
conclude that without serotonin there can be no sleep. Since schizophrenic
patients seem, for the most part, to obtain essentially normal amounts of
sleep, a serotonin depletion model in any species would be immediately suspect.
The answer to this objection is twofold. In the first place, in the hands
of some investigators, PCPA has been administered without producing insomnia[46,47], and in the second place, the studies showing that selective serotonin depletion leads to insomnia all involve single doses or very limited
periods of treatment with PCPA. We believe that our own studies involving

787

prolonged treatment with PCPA in cats have satisfactorily resolved any apparent conflict among other investigators. All of our cats have shown an early period of severe insomnia lasting several days, followed by a two or three day long recovery to more or less low normal amounts of both REM and NREM sleep. We have also observed a similar pattern of sleep reduction and recovery in two monkeys that we treated with PCPA for several weeks. Accordingly, we may assert that the finding of normal amounts of sleep in schizophrenic patients is no objection to regarding the chronic PCPA cat as a laboratory model of this condition.

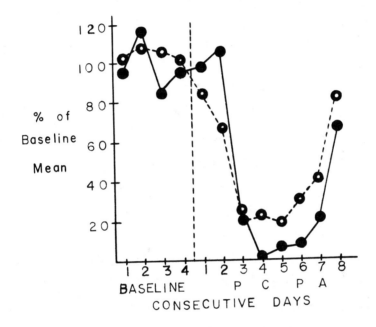

Figure 4. Changes in daily amounts of REM sleep and NREM sleep in cat receiving p-chlorophenylalanine (PCPA) and recorded 24 hours per day. All the recordings were carefully scored through a baseline period and 8 consecutive 24 hour periods on the serotonin depleting drug. The daily values for REM and NREM sleep are expressed as per cent of the baseline mean. Note that no significant change occurs on the first two days of PCPA administration except possibly a modest rise in total REM time. On the third PCPA day, there is a precipitous drop in both kinds of sleep which reaches its trough on the fifth day. Essentially normal levels of sleep are achieved by the eighth PCPA day (although still substantially below the baseline values). Brain serotonin is approximately zero at this point suggesting that it is not a crucial agent in the production of either NREM sleep or REM sleep.

The most striking parallelism between patients and PCPA cats in terms
of overall sleep patterns can be seen only when we examine schizophrenic
data derived from longitudinal studies. Such data is hard to come by because it requires the rarely encountered combination of opportunity and
industry. The only good longitudinal data that we have seen was reported
by Snyder[48], who showed that the acute onset of a prolonged psychotic episode in a schizophrenic patient was accompanied by severe insomnia of several days' duration followed by a return to more normal amounts of sleep.
A representative figure in Snyder's report bears a striking resemblance to
Figure 4 in this report, which illustrates the day by day sleep changes in
a representative cat.

Although we cannot properly define a value for REM sleep latency when
cats are allowed to sleep ad lib with round-the-clock polygraphic monitoring,
the measure can be evaluated in cats whose sleep is rigidly scheduled by en-
forcing wakefulness at all other times with a treadmill[49]. As with human
subjects, REM latency in cats is essentially the amount of NREM sleep that
intervenes between the first onset of sleep and the onset of the first REM
period. In five cats who were placed on a daily schedule of 12 hours on the
treadmill (awake) and 12 hours in the recording cage (mostly asleep), the initiation of PCPA treatment was followed by marked reductions in REM latencies
that ranged from about 60 percent to as little as 10 percent of the baseline
values. Similarly, several studies of schizophrenic patients have noted the
unusually early occurrence of first REM periods on certain nights. However,
a more systematic evaluation in the recent study of Stern et al.[50] which included data from 56 nights of sleep in eight untreated acute schizophrenics
showed a highly significant reduction in mean REM sleep latency as compared
to normal control subjects (53.3 min. vs. 93.7 min.).

Finally, without attempting an exhaustive description of data, we will
merely assert that chronic PCPA administration in cats increases individual
variability in amount of time spent in REM and NREM sleep and this, of course,
is the most commonly noted observation among all the studies of sleep in
schizophrenics.

2. Dreaming during wakefulness: psychotic symptomatology

There is little doubt that serotonin depletion in the cat has the effect
of "releasing" something to occur during wakefulness that ordinarily is con-

fined almost entirely to REM periods. If this something, specifically PGO
spike activity, is what triggers or instigates dream experiences, then the
PCPA cat might qualify as a waking dreamer. If the actively ill schizophrenic
is also a waking dreamer, as some have postulated[1,2,3], then the obvious
parallel may be drawn. However, lest we become too sanguine about this simple
metaphorical comparison, we should mention some qualifications. The truth of
the matter is that we really do not know enough about the essential phenomenology of either psychosis or dreaming to postulate their fundamental identity
with any degree of certainty. As Carney Landis has pointed out," very few persons have had the opportunity to study an autobiographical account by anyone
who has lived through a period of insanity"[51]. In recent years, the psychiatric literature has stressed interpretation and there has been a tendency
to ignore the literal meaning of what psychotic persons say about themselves.
The same tendency has existed to a somewhat lesser extent with regard to
dreaming where, again, we have focused on meaning and interpretation at the
expense of understanding the essential quality of the experience, as well as
the intricacies and determinants of specific dream content.

A second qualification has to do with the possible consequences of combining, or attempting to combine, waking and dreaming functions. While it
may be quite all right to generate a dream experience during sleep, when
there is presumably no competition for the perceptual equipment, it might be
quite different to inject dream images into the ongoing stream of waking perceptions being generated by sensory inputs from the environment. Some years
ago, one of us (WD) proposed a simple model of the neural substrate of
dreaming. "During REM sleep, dream images are, in effect, being substituted
for retinal stimulation at some point in the stimulus-response process"[52]. A
later study by Bizzi and Brooks[53] suggested a unique functional neural change
during REM sleep which involved an internally generated input to the visual
system at the level of the lateral geniculate nucleus via the pontine reticular formation. Specifically, they found that single shock stimulation at
pontine sites from which they were able to record PGO spike activity caused
an evoked response in the LGN, but only during periods of REM sleep. At
other times, identical stimuli yielded no response. Thus, an alternative
pathway for input to the visual system appeared to open up during REM sleep
through which discrete bursts of activity generated by REM sleep mechanisms

could be funneled into the perceptual apparatus. At the present time, it is parsimonious to assume that these intrusive stimuli in some way give rise to the perceptual imagery of the dream experience. If this is true, then to experience a waking dream would require that these bursts of activity impinge upon the visual system during periods of wakefulness. The appearance of bursts of REM-type spike activity at geniculate and cortical levels during wakefulness, well documented in the PCPA cat, supports the validity of this argument. However, we cannot presume to know what happens when retinal and pontine inputs collide at the lateral geniculate receptors. Does one or the other, presumably the more intense, win out? Does first one, then the other predominate? Is there a gating mechanism that cannot pass more than one input at a time? The present state of our knowledge allows us to say almost nothing about these and other possibilities. We can only conclude that if the processes that ordinarily give rise to the normal REM-type dream experience, whatever they may be, were "released" into the waking state, they would not necessarily produce a fullblown dream or hallucination in every instance. Such clearcut perceptual intrusions might require that certain other conditions be fulfilled, and hallucinatory activity might be intermittent, even though the basic instigators might be continuously present.

A third qualification would involve individual reactions to a waking dream. If such intrusive experiences were to be accepted as "real," therefore constituting psychotic symptoms, they would have to be virtually continuous, allowing an individual no chance for comparative reflection, or, they could have intruded from the very beginning of life, in which case, the real world would never have been properly learned. It is difficult to imagine what the "world view" of someone would be like if his experience of it had been continually intruded upon by his dreams. Such a defect might not announce itself in an unequivocal manner for many years. The occurrence of intrusive mental processes at all ages, and long before the onset of clinical symptoms, is detailed in at least one autobiographical account[54] by a recovered schizophrenic.

Finally, we must ask what aspects of REM sleep would be the minimum substrate required to generate dream experiences outside of REM periods. This is tantamount to asking for a description of the neurophysiology of the waking dream. Is the crucial process REM sleep, or is it merely something that oc-

curs _in_ REM sleep? It has often been pointed out that the most striking feature of the dreaming brain is its close resemblance to the waking brain[55,56,57].
Studies of many physiological variables during REM sleep uniformly suggest
the presence of a high level of arousal, in no way different from that seen
during active wakefulness. There are, in fact, only three differences between REM sleep and wakefulness that are worth mentioning - two have been
objectified and one has been inferred. Concretely, REM sleep is characterized first by a powerful inhibitory process[58,59,60] which presumably
prevents peripheral motor responses to the output of the dreaming brain,
thereby maintaining sleep, and second, by the previously described PGO spike
activity. The third characteristic is the lack of awareness of the environment - we infer a shutting out of environmental stimuli although evoked potentials can still be easily elicited.

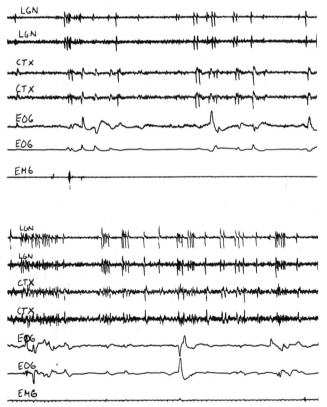

Figure 5. Polygraphic samples from periods of REM sleep before (lower
sample) and after (upper sample) treatment with parachlorophenylalanine.
LGN, right and left lateral geniculate nuclei; CTX, transcortical recordings
from right and left visual cortex; EOG, right and left electro-oculogram;
EMG, electromyogram from the posterior neck muscles. The discharge rate of
PGO spike activity is about one third normal in the serotonin-depleted cat,
although total daily REM time is within normal limits.

It is our working hypothesis that PGO spike activity, or rather, its human analog (as yet undemonstrated), is the minimum neural substrate of dream images. The continual occurrence of such activity in the waking state, as exemplified by the PCPA cat (see Figure 3), would not necessarily mean an endless sequence of waking dreams. Rather, it would mean the more or less continual operation of an intrusive process that might produce different things at different times, depending upon what else was going on. Thus, the essential quality of the experiential world produced by administration of PCPA would probably be an unpredictable mixture of externally and internally generated perceptions.

By contrast, the phrase, "dreaming while awake," which might imply a sensorium almost completely dominated by dream images, probably applies more aptly to the "locus coeruleus" preparation of Jouvet and Delorme[61]. Bilateral destruction of this nucleus appears to accomplish a selective disruption of the motor inhibitory process while all other aspects of REM periods are left more or less intact. The result is a cat that goes from wakefulness to NREM sleep in a normal fashion and shows the onset of REM periods at the proper times. These REM periods show normal PGO spike activity, but there is no EMG suppression and behavior, presumably the typical "behavior" of REM sleep, occurs. The locus coeruleus cat is completely oblivious to his environment during these "REM episodes," but he can be "aroused" by moderately intense stimuli in which case the episode is terminated and a period of completely normal wakefulness ensues. Although these two preparations are related, the essential difference between the locus coeruleus cat and the PCPA cat is that in the former, REM sleep intrudes into the waking state, whereas in the latter, something that ordinarily occurs only within REM sleep intrudes into the waking state. The intrusion of PGO spike activity during wakefulness in the PCPA cat is also far more pervasive.

Although we have spoken a great deal about "dreaming" in the cat, we have not yet directly confronted the question of whether or not the cat actually dreams. It is tempting to conclude that the relatively primitive nervous system of the cat lacks the capacity to elaborate complex imagery in response to PGO spikes and let the issue rest. This position would be compatible with the precise nature of the oculomotor activity during REM periods in the cat which, in contrast to the human, does not suggest that the cat is looking at

something. Rather, the eye movement typically occurs in intermittent clusters of small, rapid nystagmoid jerks with little or no variation in the
plane of movement.

On the other hand, we have accumulated some anecdotal evidence which mili-
tates against a categorical denial of the existence of dreaming in the cat.
We have noted, on occasion, marked variations in behavior immediately after
arousal from a REM period, particularly if the arousal occurs just after the
onset of the REM period. For the most part, cats awaken in a casual and unremarkable fashion. However, they occasionally appear very startled and show
pilo-erection, pupillary dilation, and other signs of either anger or fear.
Since the arousing stimuli are essentially constant, such variation could be
due to some unusual "dream" activity in the REM sleep just preceding arousal.
The same kind of behavior has been observed with spontaneous arousals on a
few occasions. Such evidence certainly does not suggest that the cat dreams
throughout every REM period. Rather, it is more compatible with the notion
that the PGO spike activity is occasionally intense enough to elicit a complex perceptual response.

By the same token, we are not sure that bursts of PGO spikes during wakefulness in PCPA cats are accompanied by hallucinations. The answer to this
question depends entirely upon what one is willing to infer from the associated behavior of the cat. Our own conclusions were based mainly upon careful
scrutiny of the videotape records upon which the PGO spikes and the cats'
behavior were simultaneously displayed. In general, behavioral responses were
associated with bursts of spikes (see Figure 6), while single spikes had no
behavioral correlate at all. By far the most frequent behavioral correlate
of spike bursts was a sequence of searching movements of the head and eyes.
In other words, the cat looked around. Our current feeling is that the PGO
spike activity does not instigate fullblown hallucinations (waking dream images) in the cat. In the first place, the behavior is not ordinarily accompanied by signs of emotion - anger, fear, or affection. In the second place,
the animals rarely exhibit visual fixation - rather, the behavior more properly suggests alerting, searching, and/or expectancy. The best inference
is that a burst of PGO spikes in the waking state is perceived by the cat as
a barrage of simple stimuli, like knocking on a door or flashing a light.
Occasionally, the cat does respond to waking spike bursts with behavior that

could be termed hallucinatory. However, we are willing to stipulate that although PGO spikes may be a necessary ingredient in the production of hallucinations, they are not sufficient, and that the ability to respond to their occurrence with the elaboration of complex imagery might require more brain than the cat possesses.

Assuming that PGO spikes do exist in the human, we would therefore expect that the most definitive information could only be obtained from a study of PCPA administration with human volunteers. One study has been reported in which patients with malignant carcinoid were treated with PCPA to control the high levels of peripheral serotonin[47]. Although it is uncertain that

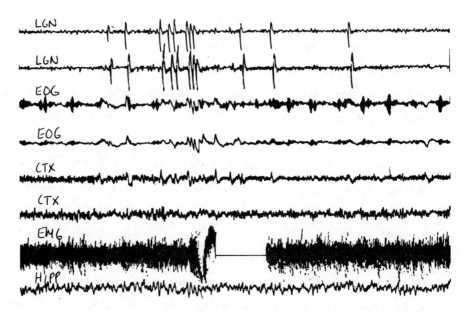

Figure 6. Example of correlative evaluation of "hallucinations" and PGO spike bursts in cat treated with parachlorophenylalanine. LGN, left and right lateral geniculate nuclei; EOG, electro-oculogram from electrodes in vertical (upper tracing) and horizontal planes; CTX, electroencephalogram from left and right visual cortex; EMG, electromyogram from posterior neck muscles; HIPP, dorsal hippocampus. An observer who is watching the cat presses a button which shorts out EMG whenever he judges that cat is "hallucinating." These "hallucinatory" episodes are, most typically, brief periods (about 3 sec in this example) during which the cat looks around in a searching or seeking manner. The lag time between spike burst in the LGN tracings and observer's signal is due to a fairly substantial reaction time which includes, on occasion, a rather complex decision making process.

an effective depletion of brain serotonin was accomplished, <u>patients re-</u>
<u>ceiving the maximum doses developed florid psychotic symptomatology, in-</u>
<u>cluding hallucinations, which necessitated discontinuation of treatment.</u>

We have obtained additional evidence on this issue from pilot observations on a pair of adult male rhesus monkeys. The monkeys were not implanted
for polygraphic recordings, but were observed continuously day and night in
their cages during a course of treatment with PCPA at a daily dose of 150-
250mg/kg. After about eight to ten days on the drug, both monkeys showed
behavior that all observers emphatically agreed was hallucinatory. In other
words, both monkeys appeared to be experiencing and responding to internally
generated visual images that were projected into the outer world. A representative example of such occurrences involved the stereotyped threat behavior performed by the monkeys whenever the experimenters approached too near
the cages. After the PCPA effect had developed, this behavior was often e-
mitted with a definite affective component (recorded on videotape) when no
one was in the vicinity.

It would appear that PCPA, through the mechanism of selective depletion of
brain serotonin, causes the development of hallucinations or closely related
behavioral responses in cats, monkeys, and humans. In cats, the basis of the
hallucinatory or searching responses appears to be the occurrence of bursts
of PGO spikes in the waking state. It is simply more parsimonious to assume
that the same process gives rise to both dreams and hallucinations than to
posit two entirely different mechanisms; assuming a single process, it follows
that the occurrence of any fullblown hallucinatory experience in the waking
state must involve an abnormal discharge of REM events, and the easiest, if
not the only way, to accomplish such an abnormal discharge is to interfere
with the normal function of serotonergic neurons. That serotonin is
definitely implicated seems absolutely certain. All the serotonin depletors -
reserpine, tetrabenazine, para-chloromethemphetamine, PCPA, etc. - bring on an
uncontrolled discharge of PGO spikes. Manipulations that directly damage the
serotonergic neurons also "release" PGO spikes, as for example, raphé lesions, and a similar intervention, the "split brain stem preparation" of
Michel and Roffwarg[62]. No other procedures or pharmacological treatments
have yielded a like result.

With regard to the postulated relationship between PGO spikes and dream images, the objection might be raised that while spikes occur in REM sleep, some dreaming is known to take place in NREM sleep. In the first place, substantial numbers of feline PGO spikes actually occur in NREM sleep (see Figures 1 and 2). Secondly, there is now good evidence, obtained by Pivik et al.[63] in our laboratories, that phasic events are discharged in human NREM periods, and by inference, PGO spike activity. Pivik has described a phasic (very brief) suppression of the tonic electromyographic activity during NREM sleep and has noted that a similar suppression may be seen occasionally in cats in association with single or double NREM PGO spikes. Examples of phasic EMG suppressions in both man and cat are shown in Figure 7. In addition to the well-known tonic motor inhibition associated with REM sleep, Pompeiano[58] has described a phasic inhibition that comes into play briefly _during_ REM periods in conjunction with spike bursts. The existence of an active phasic motor inhibitory process during NREM sleep in humans has just been demonstrated by Pivik who showed that the electrically elicited "H" reflex was transiently suppressed at the exact moment of the spontaneous EMG suppression. Accordingly, there is a strong inference that activity analogous to the feline PGO spike occurs during NREM sleep in humans and, in line with our postulated relationship, we may assume that this activity gives rise to NREM dreaming. Obviously, if we grant that PGO spikes occur in NREM sleep in humans, we must also assume their occurrence in REM sleep.

3. The response to selective REM sleep deprivation in PCPA cats.

Although its basic significance is still a puzzle, the existence of the REM sleep deprivation-compensation phenomenon has been conclusively established in a variety of species[64,65,66,67,68]. The simplest explanation for its occurrence has been in terms of some sort of need for REM sleep which requires that it must be at least partially "made up" after any sizable loss. Aside from the very fact of its existence, the assumption that there is a "need" for REM sleep is based almost exclusively on the consistent occurrence of this post-deprivation rebound. When we attempted to get a clearer idea about why REM sleep might be necessary by studying the effect of long-term selective REM deprivation in cats, we found that the procedure produced no impairment whatsoever[69,70]. Although we _did_ find a rather dramatic and characteristic alteration of behavior in REM-deprived cats, a result that we

subsequently confirmed in REM-deprived rats[71,72], we were still forced to
conclude that cats could dispense with REM sleep for long periods, and suffer only the consequence of an enhanced drive state. This conclusion did
not seem compatible with the universal occurrence of REM sleep in adult mammals, nor with its vigorous compensatory response to deprivation. Indeed,
the lack of deprivation associated impairment led us to propose that the
crucial role of the REM state was fulfilled in utero[56] in terms of ensuring
maximal activity during a developmental stage when the nervous system is isolated from external sources of stimulation. We also suggested that no important role for REM sleep existed in the adult organism.

In addition, our long-term REM deprivation studies also undermined the
notion of an obligatory quota of REM sleep. It was clearly shown that after
some duration of deprivation had been accomplished, usually around 20 - 30
days, the cats seemed to achieve some sort of equilibrium where further deprivation yielded no additional change, either in drive-oriented behavior
or in the size of the recovery rebound. At the time, it seemed possible
that this equilibrium was achieved through the mechanism of an intensity
change by which the small amounts of REM sleep that occasionally eluded the
deprivation procedure became collectively sufficient to forestall the further
accumulation of REM sleep loss. In addition to evidence of an increased frequency of phasic events within the REM fragments, the phasic events were also
occurring with a greater intensity in NREM sleep, i.e., just before the onset
of REM periods[73]. These changes in intensity in turn suggested the possibility that the presumed obligatory aspect of REM sleep might involve only the
phasic events, in particular, the PGO spikes, and that the REM periods might
function solely as a time in which maximal discharge of this activity could
be achieved without endangering the organism or intruding upon - thereby possibly disrupting - the functions of the waking state.

We recently have tested the functional equivalence of NREM and REM PGO
spikes, and also the possibility that the NREM spike discharge provides some
reduction of the need for REM periods. Our method was to deprive cats of
REM periods plus NREM PGO spikes by arousing them immediately after the occurrence of the first detectable PGO spike in NREM sleep. This procedure was
called "spike deprivation." The results showed that the spike deprivation
procedure led to a more rapid deprivation effect and a larger REM sleep rebound than the same amount of classical REM sleep deprivation. Conversely,

if we were able to maximize the occurrence of PGO spikes in NREM sleep while
at the same time eliminating REM periods, the manipulation would be followed
by little or no behavioral change and little or no compensatory REM rebound.
These results suggested that the crucial factor in the REM sleep deprivation-
compensation phenomenon might actually be the deprivation of PGO spike discharge, and further suggested that REM sleep loss would elicit no rebound if
this unique neural discharge were achieved in some alternative manner.

The foregoing results were obviously highly relevant to our consistent
findings of rebound failure after selective REM sleep deprivation in actively ill schizophrenic patients, described in an earlier section. The
first suggestion was that the lack of REM rebound in the patients was due to
enhanced phasic activity at some other time, possibly in NREM sleep periods.
We then realized that the postulated discharge was more likely to be occurring during wakefulness, which would explain not only the rebound failures,
but the active psychotic symptomatology as well. This line of thought received great impetus when the PGO spike releasing effect of PCPA in cats became known, and a situation that paralleled the postulated daytime phasic
event discharge in psychotic patients was hence available for study.

We decided to test the accuracy of our reasoning by REM-depriving chronic
PCPA cats. For this study, we concentrated our efforts on cats who were on
a sleep-wakefulness (treadmill) schedule analogous to humans. The first step
was to REM-deprive the animals for two days by arousals at the onset of each
REM period, commencing immediately after the end of the baseline period, and
before the PCPA treatment was started. After the initial period of severe
insomnia had passed and daily REM sleep time had returned to more normal
amounts and had stabilized (around 10th PCPA day), we repeated the deprivation. Thus, each cat served as its own control with three or four recovery
days following each procedure. Two cats survived to be deprived a third
time after the withdrawal of PCPA. Figure 8 depicts a typical result in one
cat. All cats showed similar results and provided a striking demonstration
of yet another parallel between the actively ill schizophrenic and the chronic PCPA cat. It should be noted that a very slight upward adjustment of the
rate of spike discharge in wakefulness would have been sufficient to accomo-
date the activity that would ordinarily have been discharged during REM

periods. This is because the total daily REM time in scheduled PCPA cats was around one half to two hours and wakefulness was often as much as 16 - 18 hours. Needless to say, when the animals had recovered from the effects of PCPA to the extent that no PGO spikes were seen during wakefulness, the additional episode of deprivation elicited a substantial REM rebound.

We have results from only one cat, but a striking parallel to the occurrence of exaggerated post-deprivation REM sleep rebounds in remissed schizophrenics should be mentioned. In this experiment, a cat on a 12-hour treadmill - 12-hour recording cage, sleep-wakefulness schedule was deprived of REM periods for two days. At the end of the second deprivation, the PCPA treatment was started. The results are shown in Figure 9. Instead of no REM rebound, an exaggerated REM rebound was observed. This suggested that

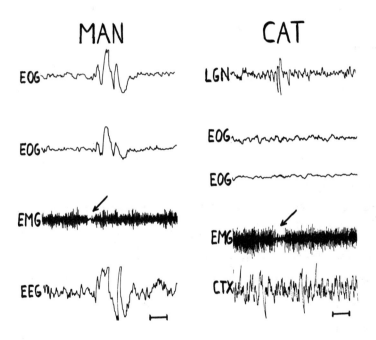

Figure 7. Phasic electromyographic suppressions during NREM sleep in man and cat. EOG, electrooculographic derivations; EEG, brain waves from C3/A2 derivation; CTX, electrocorticogram; LGN, lateral geniculate nucleus; EMG, electromyogram from posterior neck muscles. In the human sample, the suppression (arrow) is closely followed by a "K" complex in the EEG which spreads to the eye leads. In the cat, the EMG suppression is coincident with two spikes in the lateral geniculate nucleus. Calibration: 1 second.

even before the marked reduction of sleep time and the loss of control or containment of PGO spikes are seen, an earlier effect of slowly weakening or disrupting the function of the serotonergic neuronal systems is a "loosening up" or partial release of REM sleep itself. Such a mechanism would explain the finding in several cats that values for total REM time on the

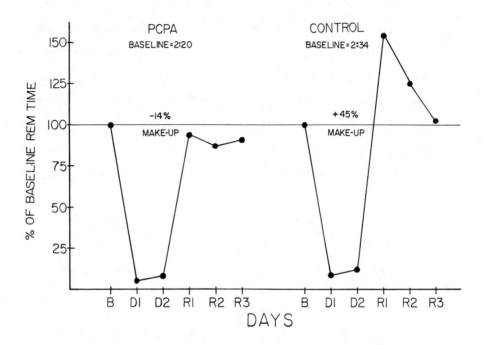

Figure 8. Rebound failure in a cat chronically treated with p-chlorophenylalanine (PCPA). The daily REM time values in this cat during the two deprivation periods are expressed in per cent of the baseline REM sleep time. Since there is usually a small reduction in the daily REM time after an animal has been stabilized on PCPA, 100 per cent of baseline actually represents a different value in the PCPA condition versus the control condition. These values are indicated on the graph in hours and minutes. As can be seen, although this cat was averaging 2 hours, 20 minutes of REM sleep per day on a 12-12 schedule (12 hours on treadmill-12 hours in recording cage) in the PCPA condition, two days of deprivation resulted in no makeup at all. The REM rebound following the similar period of deprivation prior to the administration of PCPA was of normal size. The failure to rebound while on PCPA is to all intents and purposes an exact duplication of the results of REM sleep deprivation in actively ill schizophrenic patients. It is possible that the chronic PCPA animal may serve as a useful model of the actively psychotic condition in humans.

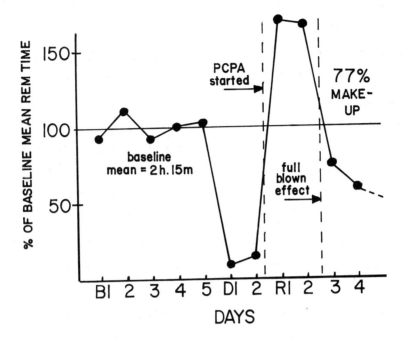

Figure 9. Unusually high REM rebound associated with the initiation of the PCPA treatment in one cat. This animal spent 12 hours each day on a treadmill throughout the study and slept _ad lib_. in his recording cage during the other 12. The first dose of PCPA was administered immediately after the second deprivation recording period. Twelve hours later, the animal started on his first day of uninterrupted recovery sleep, during which REM time was 69 percent above the baseline mean, a very respectable but not unique amount. However, the second recovery day was completely unique in that the REM sleep level was still strikingly elevated. By recovery day 3, the fullblown PCPA effect with waking PGO spikes and insomnia had emerged, which also affected total REM time. In spite of this, the "extra" REM sleep on the first two recovery days was nearly twice as great as the 3 day rebound that typically follows two days of deprivation in cats. Therefore, the value on this 3rd day was not included in the "makeup" calculation. On the abscissa, B stands for baseline; D for deprivation; and R for recovery.

first two days of PCPA administration were slightly in excess of the maximum baseline totals. It might also mean that a "sub-clinical" impairment of the serotonergic neurons could be uncovered by an exaggerated response to REM sleep deprivation, which would be a plausible explanation for the exaggerated REM sleep rebounds that were obtained from schizophrenic patients who were without active symptomatology, i.e. in remission[36].

Finally, Snyder[48] has pointed out that a REM deprivation effect does not appear to be a likely factor in the development of an acute schizophrenic psychosis because there is often a drastic reduction of REM sleep time for a few days at the onset of the psychotic episode, but no rebound occurs a few days later when the sleep times return to normal levels. This sequence of events is exactly the same as the changes over time in chronic PCPA cats (see Figure 4), who also show no compensatory rebound when REM times are restored after the initial period of insomnia. The mechanism of these post-insomnia rebound failures is probably the same as has been suggested for the specific REM deprivation studies- a complete release of phasic activity as a result of serotonin depletion so that no need for additional opportunity to discharge accumulates as a result of lost REM sleep.

4. The response of chronic PCPA cats to chlorpromazine (CPZ).

Because the above parallels between actively ill schizophrenics and chronic PCPA cats were so intriguing, we decided to try for yet another.[27] Since the most effective compound for reversing the psychotic state is CPZ or one of its derivatives, we decided to give the drug to five cats who had been receiving 150mg/kg PCPA for 5 to 20 consecutive days. These cats all displayed typical PGO spikes during wakefulness and the reduced fragmented sleep which accompany the daily administration of PCPA. Two of these cats exhibited compulsive sexual mounting of another male cat while on PCPA.

In every cat, waking spike activity was reduced and long periods of uninterrupted sleep returned after CPZ. This return to baseline-like patterns varied with both the dose of CPZ and the number of days of prior PCPA admini-stration. For example, in one cat who had received PCPA for 8 days and was then given a single 5mg/kg injection of CPZ, the results were dramatic. There was a 90 percent reduction in the number of waking spikes per hour of wakefulness, followed by 42 minutes of continuous sleep. The fall in the number of waking spikes and return of sleep was evident within 30 minutes after the injection and lasted about 36 hours. In cats getting smaller doses of CPZ, the effect was of shorter duration.

One cat was REM deprived before and after CPZ administration while on PCPA. Recovery REM time was not elevated after two days of deprivation while on PCPA alone. However, when deprived only one day and given both PCPA and CPZ, the cat showed a 50 percent increase in REM sleep time on the first recovery day. The two cats in this series who had displayed vigorous mounting of other male cats ceased this behavior temporarily (about 24 hours) after a single dose of CPZ.

Biochemical analysis of the brain of one CPZ treated PCPA cat was done to be sure that CPZ did not reverse the serotonin depletion. No serotonin was detected in any of the brain samples that were assayed.

Thus, in both actively ill schizophrenic patients and chronic PCPA cats, a reversal of abnormal behavior can be achieved by administration of CPZ. In the cat, this reversal is correlated with the return to a normal distribution of PGO spike discharge. The simplest interpretation would be that CPZ takes over the normal functions of serotonin and/or facilitates the function of any small amounts that might be present.

5. <u>Drive changes in actively ill schizophrenics and chronic PCPA cats.</u>

This is the final parallel we wish to mention, and because it involves areas of behavior that are fraught with difficulties (problems of conceptualization, definition, description, measurement, etc.), we wish only to point it out without making any claim at all as to its promise or authenticity. The real problem, of course, is how to specify or define drive behavior and drive functions in schizophrenic patients. Suffice it to say that the drive functions are surely severely disrupted in one way or another during, and perhaps even before and after, psychotic episodes. As was detailed in an earlier section, by far the most dramatic behavioral changes in PCPA cats were alterations, usually intensifications, in the overt drive oriented behaviors- sexual behavior, eating behavior, aggressive behavior, exploratory behavior, etc.

Furthermore, there was marked variability in these behaviors depending upon the duration of serotonin. Thus, the early changes suggested drive enhancement and the later behavior suggested drive depression. In the latter situation, the behavior was easily elicited, but was difficult to sustain.

SUMMARY AND CONCLUSIONS

We have described the effects of chronic PCPA administration in adult cats together with some recent observations on selective REM sleep deprivation in schizophrenic patients. We then attempted to draw significant parallels between actively ill schizophrenics and PCPA cats in the following areas:

1. Similar departures from the normal manifestations of sleep appear to exist in both conditions. A reduction in latency to the first REM period was one of the most obvious changes.

2. It was inferred that REM events intrude into the waking state in both conditions. A large cluster of substantive findings support this inference although the overall formulation still remains hypothetical.

3. Two days of REM sleep deprivation are <u>not</u> followed by a REM rebound in either actively ill schizophrenics or PCPA cats even when pre-deprivation (baseline) REM times are essentially normal.

4. It appears that CPZ has the capacity to reverse nearly all abnormalities in both conditions.

5. Drive functions are severely and globally disrupted or disturbed in both conditions.

Whether or not these parallels are sufficient justification for regarding the chronic PCPA cat as an animal model of the actively ill schizophrenic was not at issue in this presentation. Rather, in the course of describing experimental results and pointing out certain relationships, we have obtained a clearer notion of the consequences of a presumptive disruption in the functional capacity of serotonergic neurons in the brain. For example, at the beginning of this presentation we posed the half-serious question, what is it that prevents us from dreaming while we are awake? The effects of prolonged PCPA administration suggest that this is a valid question, and that the answer is a normally functioning serotonin system. This system must also play a role in the normal regulation of sleep and certain behaviors. Thus, it might be reasonable to conclude that sleep research and the study of sleep mechanisms has been and will be a fruitful approach to some of the problems of mental illness. The information presented here plus that which is relevant from other fields such as the neuropharmacology of psychotomimetic compounds may stimulate a more intensive effort to evaluate serotonin functions in schizophrenic patients. Even in the unlikely event that important portions of the psychotic syndromes are proven to be unrelated to dream processes, we can expect that such investigations will yield sufficient clarification of the issue to be well worth the effort.

REFERENCES

1. JACKSON, H.J. Selected Writings, in Taylor, J. (Editor), Basic Books, Vol. II, New York, 1958.

2. FREUD, S. The Interpretation of Dreams. Basic Books, New York, 1955.

3. JUNG, C. The Psychology of Dementia Praecox. Journal of Nervous and Mental Disease Publishing Co., New York, 1944.

4. DEMENT, W. An essay on dreams: the role of physiology in understanding their nature. In New Directions in Psychology, Vol. II, Newcomb, T. (Editor), Holt, Rinehart and Winston, New York, 1965.

5. KOELLA, W. Sleep: Its Nature and Physiological Organization. Charles C. Thomas, Publisher, Springfield, Ill., 1967.

6. JOUVET, M. Biogenic amines and the states of sleep. Science 163, 32, 1969.

7. KALES, A. Sleep: Physiology and Pathology. (Editor). J. P. Lippincott Co., Philadelphia (in press).

8. DEMENT, W. The biological role of REM sleep (circa 1968). In Sleep: Physiology and Pathology, Kales, A. (Editor), J. P. Lippincott Co., Philadelphia (in press).

9. FERGUSON, J., COHEN, H. HENRIKSEN, S., McGARR, K., MITCHELL, G., HOYT, G., BARCHAS, J., and DEMENT, W. The effect of chronic administration of PCPA on sleep in the cat. Paper presented at 9th Ann. Mtg. of Assoc. for Psychophysiol. Study of Sleep, Boston, March, 1969.

10. FERGUSON, J., HENRIKSEN, S., COHEN, H., HOYT, G., MITCHELL, G., McGARR, K., RUBENSON, D., RYAN, L., and DEMENT, W. The effect of chronic administration of PCPA on the behavior of cats and monkeys. Paper presented at 9th Ann. Mtg. of Assoc. for Psychophysiol. Study of Sleep, Boston, March, 1969.

11. DEMENT, W., HALPER, C., PIVIK, T., FERGUSON, J., COHEN, H., HENRIKSEN, S., McGARR, K., GONDA, W., HOYT, G., RYAN, L., MITCHELL, G., AZUMI, K., BARCHAS, J., and ZARCONE, V. Hallucinations and dreaming. In Perception and Its Disorders, Hamburg, D. (Editor), Williams & Wilkins, Baltimore (in press).

12. KOE, B. and WEISSMAN, A. Para-chlorophenylalanine: a specific depletor of brain serotonin. J. Pharm. Exp. Therap. 154, 499, 1966.

13. MORUZZI, G. Active processes in the brain stem during sleep. The Harvey Lectures. 58, 233, 1963.

14. DEMENT, W., FERGUSON, J., COHEN, H., and BARCHAS, J. Nonchemical methods and data using a biochemical model: The REM quanta. In Some Current Issues in Psychochemical Research Strategies in Man, Mandell, A. (Editor), Academic Press (in press).

15. BROOKS, D. and BIZZI, E. Brain stem electrical activity during deep sleep. Arch. ital. Biol. 101, 648, 1963.

16. MICHEL, F., JEANNEROD, M., MOURET, J., RECHTSCHAFFEN, A., and JOUVET, M. Sur les mécanismes de l'activité-de pointes au niveau du système visuel. C.R. Soc. Biol. 158,103, 1964.

17. CALVET, J., CALVET, M., and LANGLOIS, J. Diffuse cortical activation waves during so-called desynchronized EEG patterns. J. Neurophysiol. 28, 893, 1965.

18. DELORME, F., JEANNEROD, M., and JOUVET, M. Effets remarquables de la réserpine sur l'activité EEG phasique ponto-geniculo-occipitale. C.R. Soc. Biol. 159, 900, 1965.

19. FOULKES, D. Dream reports from different stages of sleep. J. abn. soc. Psychol. 65, 14, 1962.

20. MONROE, L. Psychological and physiological differences between good and poor sleepers. J. Abnorm. Psychol. 72,255, 1967.

21. RECHTSCHAFFEN, A., VERDONE, P., and WHEATON, J. Reports of mental activity during sleep. Canad. Psychiat. Assoc. J. 8, 409, 1963.

22. JOUVET, M. Mechanisms of the states of sleep: a neuropharmacological approach. In Sleep and Altered States of Consciousness, Kety, S., Evarts, E., and Williams, H. (Editors), Williams & Wilkins, Baltimore, 1967.

23. JOUVET, M. Neurophysiology of the states of sleep. Physiol. Rev. 47, 117, 1967.

24. JOUVET, M. Neurophysiological and biochemical mechanisms of sleep. In Sleep: Physiology and Pathology, Kales, A. (Editor), J. P. Lippincott Co., Philadelphia (in press).

25. DAHLSTROM, A. and FUXE, K. Evidence for the existence of monoamine-containing neurons in the central nervous system. I. Demonstration of monoamines in the cell bodies of brain stem neurons. Acta Physiol. Scand. 62, Suppl. 232, 1964.

26. DAHLSTROM, A. and FUXE, K. Evidence for the existence of monoamine-containing neurons in the central nervous system. II. Experimentally induced changes in the intraneuronal amine levels of bulbospinal neuron systems. Acta Physiol. Scand. 64, Suppl. 247, 1965.

27. COHEN, H., FERGUSON, J., HENRIKSEN, S., BARCHAS, J. and DEMENT, W. Reversal of para-chlorophenylalanine (PCPA) effects with chlorpromazine. Paper presented at 9th Ann. Mtg. of Assoc. for Psychophysiol. Study of Sleep, Boston, March 1969.

28. DEMENT, W. Dream recall and eye movements during sleep in schizophrenics and normals. J. Nerv. Ment. Dis. 122, 263, 1955.

29. KORESKO, R., SNYDER, F., and FEINBERG, I. "Dream Time" in hallucinating and non-hallucinating schizophrenic patients. Nature 199, 1118, 1963.

30. FEINBERG, I., KORESKO, R., GOTTLIEB, F., and WENDER, P. Sleep electroencephalographic and eye movement patterns in schizophrenic patients. Comp. Psychiat. 5, 44, 1964.

31. ONHEIBER, P., WHITE, P., DeMYER, M., and OTTINGER, D. Sleep and dream patterns of child schizophrenics. Arch. gen. Psychiat. 12, 568, 1965.

32. LAIRY, G., BARTE, H., GOLSTEINAS, L., and RIDJANOVIC, S. Sommeil de nuit des malades mentaux. In Le Sommeil de Nuit Normal et Pathologiques: Etudes Electroencephalographiques. Masson et Cie, Paris, 1965.

33. GULEVICH, G., DEMENT, W., and ZARCONE, V. All night sleep recordings of chronic schizophrenics in remission. Comp. Psychiat, 8, 241, 1967.

34. CALDWELL, D. and DOMINO, E. Electroencephalographic and eye movement patterns during sleep in chronic schizophrenic patients. Electroenceph. clin. Neurophysiol. 22, 414, 1967.

35. FEINBERG, I., KORESKO, R., and GOTTLIEB, F. Further observations on electrophysiological sleep patterns in schizophrenia. Comp. Psychiat. 6, 21, 1965.

36. ZARCONE, V., GULEVICH, G., PIVIK, T., and DEMENT, W. Partial REM phase-deprivation and schizophrenia. Arch. gen. Psychiat. 18, 194, 1968.

37. ZARCONE, V. and DEMENT, W. Sleep studies with schizophrenic patients. In Sleep: Physiology and Pathology, Kales, A. (Editor), J. P. Lippincott Co., Philadelphia (in press).

38. ZARCONE, V., GULEVICH, G., PIVIK, T., and DEMENT, W. REM Deprivation and Schizophrenia. In Recent Advances in Biologic Psychiatry, Wortis, J. (Editor), Plenum Press, New York, (in press).

39. ZARCONE, V., PIVIK, T., GULEVICH, G., AZUMI, K., and DEMENT, W. Partial deprivation of the REM state in schizophrenics with active symptomatology. Psychophysiol. 5, 239, 1968.

40. LUBY, E. and CALDWELL, D. Sleep deprivation and EEG slow wave activity in chronic schizophrenia. Arch. gen. Psychiat. 17, 361, 1967.

41. AZUMI, K., TAKAHASHI, S., TAKAHASHI, K., MARUYAMA, N., and KIKUTI, S. The effects of dream deprivation on chronic schizophrenics and normal adults: A comparative study. Folia Psychiat. Neurol. Jap. 21, 205, 1967.

42. VOGEL, G. and TRAUB, A. REM deprivation: I. The effect on schizophrenic patients. Arch. gen. Psychiat. 18, 287, 1968.

43. KOELLA, W., FELDSTEIN, A., and CZICMAN, J. The effect of para-chlorophenylalanine on the sleep of cats. Electroenceph. clin. Neurophysiol. 25, 481, 1968.

44. WEITZMAN, E., RAPPORT, M., McGREGOR, P., and JACOBY, J. Sleep patterns of the monkey and brain serotonin concentration: effect of p-chlorophenylalanine. Science 160, 1361, 1968.

45. MOURET, J., BOBILLIER, P., and JOUVET, M. Effets de la para-chlorophenylalanine sur le sommeil du rat. C.R. Soc. Biol. 161, 1600, 1967.

46. RECHTSCHAFFEN, A., LOVELL, R., FREEDMAN, D., WHITEHEAD, P. and ALDRICH, M. Effect of para-chlorophenylalanine (PCPA) on sleep in rats. Paper presented at 9th Ann. Mtg. of Assoc. for Psychophysiol. Study of Sleep, Boston, 1969.

47. ENGELMAN, K., LOVENBERG, W., and SJOERDSMA, A. Inhibition of serotonin synthesis by para-chlorophenylalanine in patients with carcinoid syndrome. N.E. J. Med. 277, 1103, 1967.

48. SNYDER, F. Sleep disturbance in relation to acute psychosis. In Sleep: Physiology and Pathology, Kales, A. (Editor), J. P. Lippincott Co., Philadelphia (in press).

49. FERGUSON, J. and DEMENT, W. The effect of variations in total sleep time on the occurrence of rapid eye movement sleep in cats. Electroenceph. clin. Neurophysiol. 22, 109, 1966.

50. STERN, M., FRAM, D., WYATT, R., GRINSPOON, L., and TURSKY, B. All-night sleep studies of acute schizophrenics. Arch. gen. Psychiat. 20, 470, 1969.

51. LANDIS, C. In Varieties of Psychopathological Experience. Mettler, F. (Editor), Holt, Rinehart & Winston, New York, 1964.

52. DEMENT, W. Perception during sleep. In The Psychopathology of Perception. Zubin, J. (Editor) Grune and Stratton, New York, 1965.

53. BIZZI, E. and BROOKS, D. Functional connections between pontine reticular formation and lateral geniculate nucleus during sleep. Arch. ital. Biol. 101, 666, 1963.

54. GREEN, H. I never promised you a rose garden. Signet Book, 1964.

55. DEMENT, W. Psychophysiology of sleep and dreams. Am. Handbook of Psychiatry, Vol. III, Arieti, S. (Editor), Basic Books, New York, 1966.

56. ROFFWARG, H., MUZIO, J., and DEMENT, W. Ontogenetic development of
    the human sleep-dream cycle. _Science_ 152, 606, 1966.

57. SNYDER, F. In quest of dreaming. In _Experimental Studies of Dreaming_.
    Witkin, H. and Lewis, H. (Editors), Random House, New York 1967.

58. POMPEIANO, O. Supraspinal control of reflexes during sleep and wakeful-
    ness. In _Aspects Anatomo-Fonctionnels de la Physiologie du Sommeil_.
    Jouvet, M. (Editor), Centre National de la Recherche Scientifique,
    Paris, 1965.

59. HODES, R. and DEMENT, W. Depression of electrically induced reflexes
    ("H"reflexes") in man during low voltage EEG "sleep". _Electroenceph._
    clin. Neurophysiol. 17, 617, 1964.

60. POMPEIANO, O. The neurophysiological mechanisms of the postural and
    motor events during desynchronized sleep. In _Sleep and Altered_
    States of Consciousness. Kety, S., Evarts, E., and Williams, H.
    (Editors), Williams and Wilkins, Baltimore, 1967.

61. JOUVET, M. and DELORME, F. Locus coeruleus et sommeil paradoxal.
    C.R. Soc. Biol. 159, 895, 1965.

62. MICHEL, F. and ROFFWARG, H. Chronic split brain stem preparation:
    Effect on the sleep-waking cycle. _Experientia_ 23, 1, 1967.

63. PIVIK, T., HALPER, C., and DEMENT, W. NREM phasic EMG suppressions
    in the human. Paper presented at 9th Ann. Mtg. of Assoc. for Psycho-
    physiol. Study of Sleep, Boston, 1969.

64. KHAZAN, N. and SAWYER, C. "Rebound" recovery from deprivation of
    paradoxical sleep in the rabbit. _Proc. Soc. Exp. Biol. Med._ 114,
    536, 1963.

65. JOUVET, D., VIMONT, P., DELORME, F., and JOUVET, M. Etude de la
    privation selective de la phase paradoxale de sommeil chez le chat.
    C.R. Soc. Biol. 158, 756, 1964.

66. BERGER, R. and MEIER, G. The effects of selective deprivation of
    states of sleep in the developing monkey. _Psychophysiol._ 2, 354, 1966.

67. MORDEN, B., MITCHELL, G., and DEMENT, W. Selective REM sleep depriva-
    tion and compensation phenomena in the rat. _Brain Res._ 5, 339, 1967.

811

. DEMENT, W. The effect of dream deprivation. Science 131, 1705, 1960.

69. DEMENT, W. Recent studies on the biological role of rapid eye move-
    ment sleep. Am. J. Psychiat. 122,404, 1965.

70. DEMENT, W., HENRY, P., COHEN, H., and FERGUSON, J. Studies on the effect
    of REM deprivation in humans and in animals. In Sleep and Altered
    States of Consciousness, Kety, S., Williams, H., and Evarts, E.,
    (Editors), Williams and Wilkins, Baltimore, 1967.

71. MORDEN, B., CONNER, R., MITCHELL, G., DEMENT, W., and LEVINE, S.
    Effects of rapid eye movement (REM) sleep deprivation on shock-in-
    duced fighting. Physiol & Behav. 3,425, 1968.

72. MORDEN, B., MULLINS, R., LEVINE, S., COHEN, H., and DEMENT, W. Effect
    of REMS deprivation on the mating behavior of male rats. Psychophysiol.
    5, 241, 1968.

73. FERGUSON, J. and DEMENT, W. Changes in intensity of REM sleep with
    deprivation. Presented at 6th Ann. Mtg. of Assoc. for Psychophysiol.
    Study of Sleep, Gainesville, Fla., 1966.

W. C. Dement, M.D., Ph.D., V. Zarcone, M.D., et. al., Stanford University School of Medicine, Department of Psychiatry, Palo Alto, California 94304

MICRO LINGUISTIC-KINESIC EVENTS IN

SCHIZOPHRENIC BEHAVIOR

WILLIAM S. CONDON and HENRY W. BROSIN

This paper focusses on some recent findings from the
micro analysis of sound films of "schizophrenic" behavior.
The major tentative finding concerns a self-dyssynchrony
which was found to occur in many of the cases examined.
This dyssynchrony may not be of the same "kind" in every
patient and only the existence of such dyssynchrony in
some patients can be postulated at this time. In several
instances the dyssynchrony seemed to abate as the patients
improved.

The finding of dyssynchrony resulted, to some degree,
from the intensive micro analyses of normal behavior. Thus
some clarifying statements concerning how normal behavior
behaves are presented prior to the discussion of dyssynchrony. A basic concept of long range research strategy
held that the discovery of the order pervading normal behavior, from micro to macro organizations, would provide
a valuable contrastive basis for the investigation of
pathological behaviors. Normal speech and body motion
(kinesics) were found to be markedly self-harmonious and
the characteristics of that harmony is specifiable. The
body moves in "configurations-of-change" which are isomor-

The following paper is dependent upon the pioneering explorations of the forthcoming book, The Natural History of an Interview; authored by Bateson, G., Birdwhistell,
R., Brosin, H.W., Hockett, C., and McQuown, N.A., (Ed.) To
be published 1969 by Grune & Stratton.[1] We are also deeply
indebted to the work of Albert E. Scheflen.

phic with the articulated segments of speech as they are
(2)
articulated.

This self-harmony of a speaker occurs across a wide
organizational field and seems to be characteristic of normal behavior. The body organizationally accompanies the
expression of speech in complex ways. It is a highly unified and integrated organism (as a totality) which is be-
having at any given moment. Many changes occur in relation to many other changes which are in turn part of still
other changes and happening all at once and sequentially;
yet all these changes participate in an integrated organization of change. Behavior is not a "thing" which can be
reduced to minimal segments of which it can then be said
to be composed. The concept of "whiles" has been utilized
as a heuristic, explanatory analog. Behavior is not composed of arms, legs, etc. as discrete units or elements of
behavior. Behavior is the ordered yet varying relationships of change these aspects of the body sustain to each
other during movement and through on-going sequences of
movement.

II. Method

A "unit-of-behavior" is observationally described in
terms of the sustaining and change of direction and speed
of the body parts in relation to each other as this is detectable using a time-motion analyzer to scan change as
stored on the series of still pictures which compose film.
Other special instrumentation permits the segmentation of
sound to a level commensurate with that of body motion.

The use of sound film, while failing to record many
aspects of behavior and communication, does provide audio-
visual data storage for much of overt behavior which can

then be re-viewed as often as desired. It offers the possibility of varying and correcting observer perspective in manifold ways in relation to the same behavior in the search for the regularities which may be hidden in that behavior.

Standard filming occurs at 24 frames per second, although high speed sound films have been taken at 48, 64, and 96 frames per second. The Time-Motion Analyzer, a manually operated, silent 16mm projector, permits the frame by frame analysis of film. It also permits variable sequence scanning whereby two frames can be contrasted with the following three frames, or four frames with one, or other sequence combinations, in the search for the change points in behavior. In a sense the observer infers that change has occurred. We observe a series of still photographs which were taken serially of behavior at 1/24 of a second intervals. When these are projected back at the same speed we see continuous motion. With the Time-Motion Analyzer, however, we are interested in what happens from frame to frame or in the contrast of one series of frames with another. Thus, if a wrist is flexing and continues to show a decreasing angle between hand and forearm through a series of these still pictures we infer that the wrist had been continuously flexing during that time. If in going from one frame to the next we keep seeing the angle decrease we assume the wrist is still sustaining its previous direction of movement. If, however, at one point we suddenly see the angle reverse and begin to increase we assume that the wrist has changed direction and is now beginning to extend. Since each frame is numbered we can then notate that flexion changes to extension at the frame where we have seen this change occur.

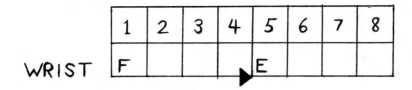

Thus the wrist flexes beginning with frame one and
continues flexion through frame four. Extension then begins at frame five. Each body part is carefully examined
in this fashion, giving rise to a transcription which resembles figure one which is presented below. The method,
in essence, involves repeated viewings of films at various
levels until order and pattern are seen. It is an analysis of the micro history of change of the body parts as
these have been recorded on film. It is from this history
of past regularities that we seek to predict the nature of
future regularities. The film is treated as if it were a
relatively unknown system which is then permitted, by variable scanning, to reveal its order. As order is detected
it can then be sought for in other films, including films
of other cultures, to see if it is a general characteristic of human behavior. The method is, perhaps, most nearly akin to that of the ethologist in the field where animals are observed hour after hour until some sense of order
and pattern emerges.

III. <u>Normal Behavior</u>

Figure 1, illustrates both self and interactional synchrony. *

---

* The body of a listener was found to move in configurations of change which were synchronous with the speech/
body configurations of the speaker. This often occurs up
to and including the phrasal level. The tempo or rhythmicity is also often shared by the interactants. However,
since the emphasis is on self-synchrony this interactional-
synchrony will not be discussed. Over 100 films of normal
behavior have been analyzed fame by frame and self and
interactional synchrony have been found to occur consistently. Interactional-synchrony is also illustrated in
Figure 1.

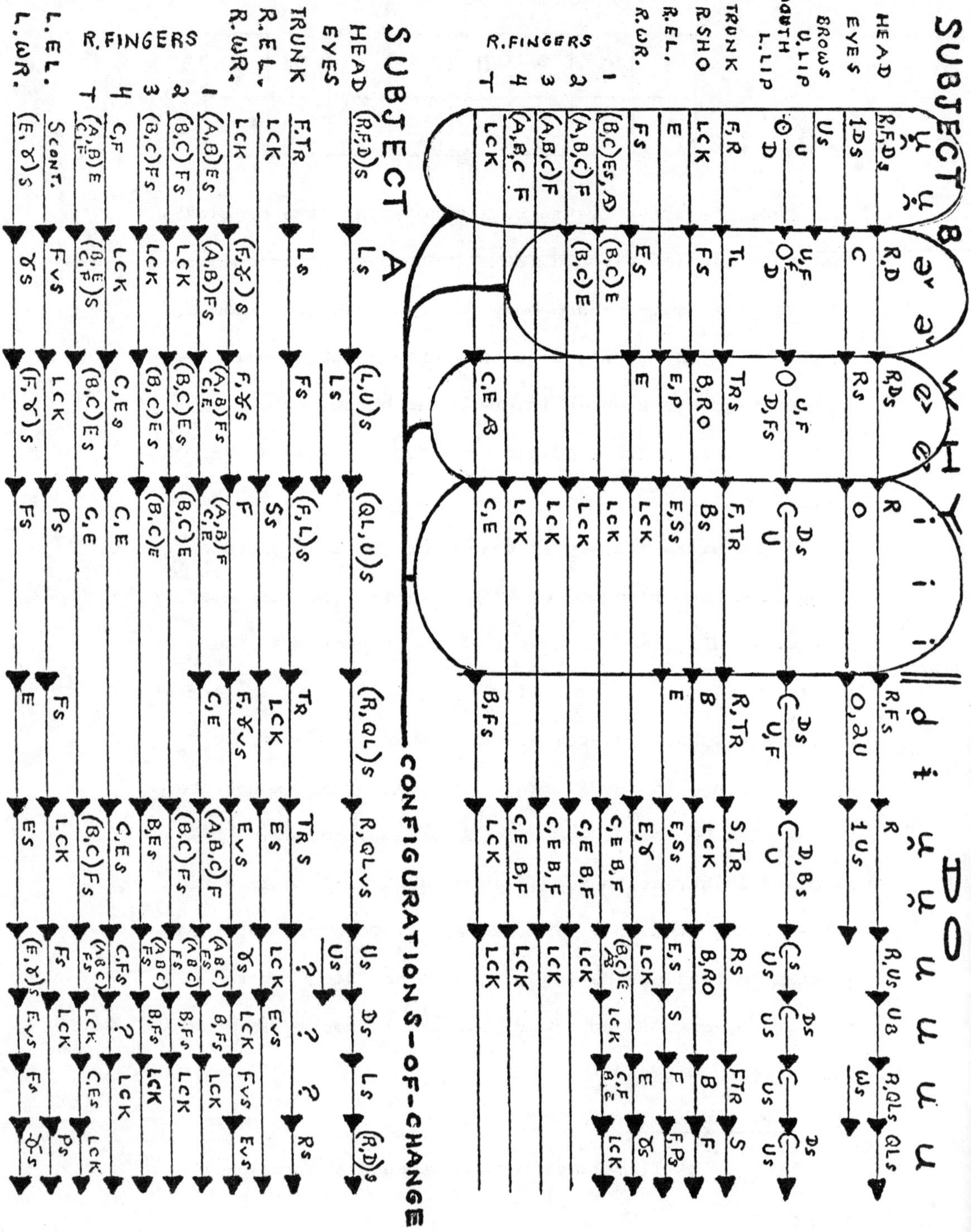
SUBJECT B
WHY DO
SUBJECT A
CONFIGURATIONS-OF-CHANGE
R. FINGERS
R. FINGERS

FIG. 1

Subject B says, "I was gon to ask you <u>why do</u> you um..." The linguistic-kinesic transcription of the two words "why do" is presented in figure 1. The film was taken at 48 frames per second, twice the speed of standard filming. The concept of "whiles" is utilized in the description.

Subject B's body moves in configurations-of-change which are isomorphic with the articulated segmentation of his speech. As he articulates the / ʬ ʬ /, a voiceless, high back vocoid which is the syllabic consonant / W / of "why", his head moves right, forward and down slightly; "while" his eyelid begins to come down very slightly at the onset of the eye blink; "while" his brows go up slightly; "while" his mouth opens; "while the trunk moves forward and right;"while" his right shoulder is locked, i.e., remains relatively still; "while" his right elbow extends; "while" his right wrist flexes slightly; "while" joints B and C of the first or index finger extend slightly and the finger adducts slightly; "while" joints A, B and C of fingers 2, 3 and 4 flex;"while" the thumb remains relatively still. Almost all of the above body parts sustain their direction of movement precisely across the emission of / ʬ ʬ / then change to a new direction together at the onset of /ə̆ə̆/. The right elbow, however, sustains its extension across both / ʬ ʬ / and /ə̆ə̆/ where it then pronates. Fingers 3 and 4 sustain their flexion across the first aspect of the word "why"---/ʬ ʬ ə̆ə̆ĕĕ/. When some body elements sustain direction of change longer than the rest of the body, they are accompanying a wider segment. This sustaining then coincides with the occurrence of two or more minimal configurations. The point to be made is that a wider or higher order sustaining movement does not begin or terminate interstitially to a lower order unit, but occurs synchronously with their boundaries.

The word "why" is, in this fashion, composed of four relatively minimal articulatory segments which are accompanied by four body-change configurations. A "unit" of behavior is in a sense a form of order within a process. The unit is not defined by the recurrence of the same content or identity. What recurs is predictable relationship-of-change. The body parts moving, whatever these might be at any given time, will tend to sustain and change directions of movement together, forming a configuration of change which will be isomorphic with the articulatory structure of the speech being emitted at that time. It is expected that in time classes of these configurations will be describable. What is postulated is that certain ordered relationships of change occur during behavior, not the content of those changes. Behavior can be analyzed into a serial emergence of such configurations of change. The body moves in an intricate harmony with the articulatory apparatus.

All linguistic kinesic transcriptions of normal behavior thus far have resembled those of figure 1. There tends to be a vertical alignment of the arrow points (which are points of change of direction of movement, not cessation of movement) which is a graphic representation of body parts changing synchronously together.

The body also tends to accompany the emission of speech across wider dimensions. This is illustrated in figure 2 by the word "ask" which is also from the above utterance, "I was gon to ask you why do you um..." The word has four minimal articulatory and kinesic configurations similar to "why." "Ask" can also be segmented into two articulatory aspects /æææɛɛ/ and /ssskk/ without contradiction,

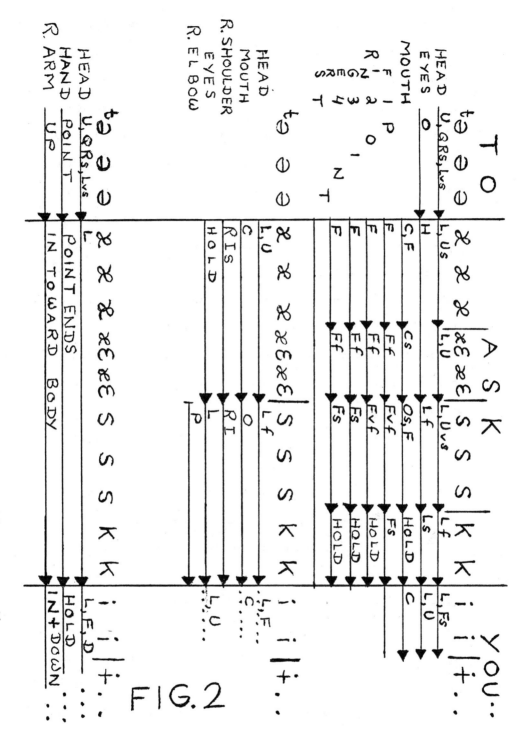

FIG. 2

3 CONTRASTS OF "ASK"

but a different contrastive perspective is required. The
five frames of the first aspect are contrasted with the five
frames of the second aspect by manually transporting the
film across the first five frames and then the second five

frames. In this contrast, which differs from the contrasts that led to the segmentation of the word into four aspects, a higher order segmentation can be distinguished. The lower order contrasts tend to smooth out and are not attended to while the relationships of change at the higher level dominate attention. The head moves primarily left and up across the first part and left fast across the second aspect. The mouth closes across the first and opens slightly across the second. The right shoulder rotates inwardly slightly across the first and then more rapidly across the second. The eyes hold their position across the first and then move left across the second. The right elbow begins to pronate with the onset of the second aspect. These body configurations thus accompany the higher order aspects of the articulation of the word.

The word "ask" also occurs as a lexical unity. The head had been moving up, inclining right slightly and moving slightly left across the word "to;" it then moves primarily left with some upward tendency across "ask;" and then moves left, forward and down across "you." The hand which had been sustaining a pointing gesture, relaxes this gesture across "ask" and holds the new position reached across "you." The right arm which had been moving upward, moves horizontally inward toward the body across "ask" and then continues inward but also down across "you." Body motion configurations are organizationally isomorphic with speech across a multiplicity of emergent levels. Several full utterances of three different people in three separate films were exhaustively examined. Sixty (60) words were analyzed and all the words were found to be accompanied across several organizational levels by the body with a precision equal to that described for the word "ask."

This same isomorphism has been detected at phrasal and
utterance levels as well. For example, the total utterance
above is accompanied by Subject B's hand moving upward, a-
cross and then down to his leg. This total utterance is
separated into two major aspects "I was gon to ask you" which
is accompanied by a hand point forming and ending and "why
do you um" where the hand moves right and holds. The first
aspect is then further distinguishable into two phrases "I
was gon" where the head moves primarily right and up and "to
ask you" where the direction of the head movement is primarily left. This also held true of the phrasal structure in
the three utterances of the three people in the films previously mentioned.

These organizational discriminations or distinctions are
the result of the adoption of diverse contrastive perspectives. The configurational-units so distinguished legitimately emerge from the behavior under investigation. A
factor supporting the adequacy of these segmentations is
that the multiple levels of units which were derived from
diverse contrastive perspectives are yet systematically
integrated with each other.

There does not appear to be a privileged perspective
for the discrimination of these regularities. They are, in
a sense, reciprocally defining as they participate together
to form the complex interweaving of the total behavior. The
boundary-forming, "clusters-of-change" emerge phenomenolo-
gically as a function of instrumental contrastive procedures which rely on the total behavior as the wider organized and sustaining matrix for contrast decisions. The pre-
ceeding sentence is an assumption of this segmental logic.
Each constellation-of-change thus seems to participate in

defining the boundaries of the others and they in turn reciprocally define it as they emerge in the on-going organizations of behavior.

There is some tentative evidence that the body may also
move in ensembles. At the present time there appear to be
at least three: (1) the head ensemble which includes the
eyes, mouth, nose, brows, etc.; (2) the shoulder-arm-hand
ensemble which also includes the fingers and; (3) the leg
and foot ensemble. (It is difficult to determine to which
ensemble the trunk belongs or whether it constitutes a separate system.) These ensembles may all act together, separately, or with different yet proportionate speeds in relation to each other. For example, the hands may be at rest
in the lap while the head (with facial changes) may be moving. Then the right hand may join the movement, then a
little later a foot may begin to move. All of these will
begin or stop rhythmically and synchronously with each other
during the on-going behavior.

IV. Pathological Behavior.

The intricate harmony of normal behavior has been presented in detail to provide a background for the examination of pathological behavior. Pathological behavior of
various kinds was found to be self-dyssynchronous in contrast to the self-synchrony of normal behavior. It was as
a contrast to the harmony of normal behavior that variations
from the order became detectable. The first instance of
self-dyssynchrony was observed in a film of an aphasic patient studied frame by frame. This was the first indication that such a phenomenon as dyssynchrony might exist. It
was not observable as such at standard film-projection speed.
The voice tended to delay 1/24 of a second behind the body
motion. The film itself was in proper "sound-sync" because

the speech of the female speech therapist interacting with the patient in the same film was synchronous with her body motion.

Dyssynchrony was next observed in a stutterer, primarily at the points of stutter. There was a left-right disharmony observable in the film at these moments which resembled that of the aphasic patient.

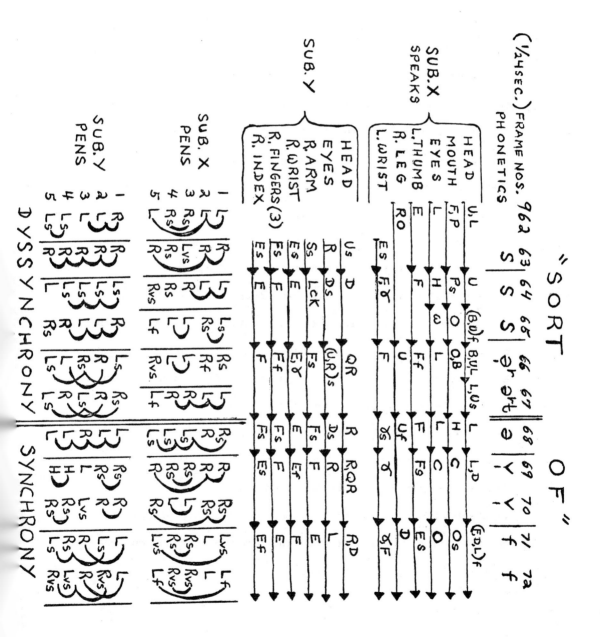

FIG. 3

Subject X, the stutterer, says, "That's sort of like..."
He stutters at the onset of "sort" but articulates "of"
correctly. Figure 3 illustrates a linguistic-kinesic micro
analysis of the words "sort of." The left thumb and wrist
are out of phase with the head, mouth and eyes. The body
begins to move prior to the onset of speech. The voice exhibits a constricted quality in the release of the initial
/S/ which resembles that of the aphasic patient. The left
wrist begins to extend slightly in synchrony with the onset
of the /S/. It thus moves interstitially to the first body
configuration. Body parts seldom if ever move independently
of the mouth, but this occurs across frames 66 and 67 where
the head changes direction rapidly.

Another aspect of the transcriptions of dyssynchrony or
perhaps another way of describing them is that there is a
change of some form at almost every frame. Thus the major
movement begins with frame 962, the wrist moves at 963, and
there are changes at every frame until the end of the word.
The word "of" displays speech and body motion synchrony.

The following dyssynchrony was found in the behavior of
a depressed, chronic, schizophrenic patient. A _part_ of his
body appeared to be "out-of-phase" with the rest of the body
(3)
and his speech. It seemed to be of a different type from
that of the stutterer and the aphasic.

Figure 4 displays the utterance, "I admitted into the hospital" spoken by this schizophrenic patient. The right index finger, represented by the open arrow point, moves out-
of-phase with the rest of the body and speech. The patient
and the doctor who is interviewing him are in synchrony except for the right index finger.

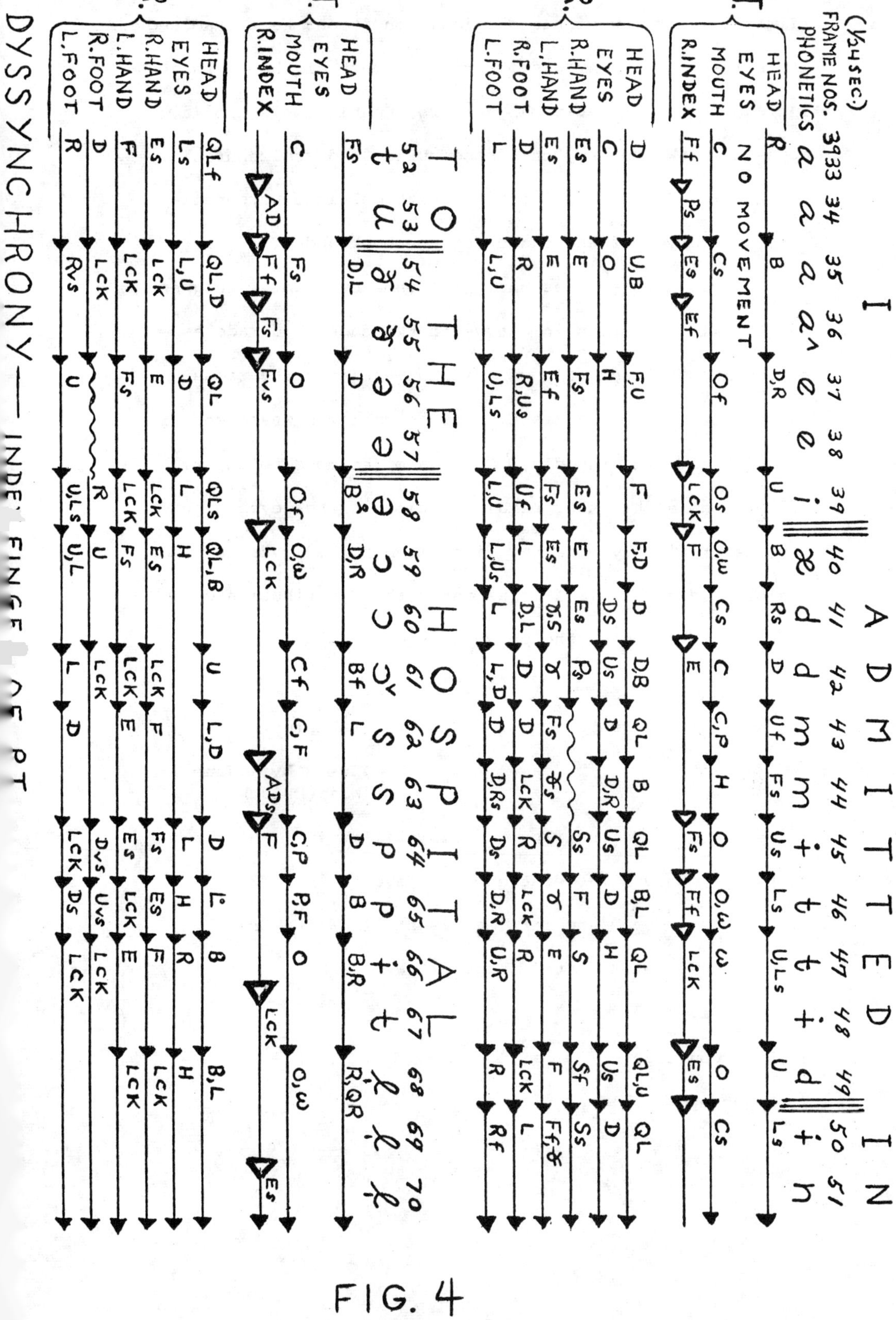
(1/24 SEC.)
FRAME NOS.
PHONETICS
PT.
DR.
HEAD
EYES
MOUTH
R.INDEX
R.HAND
L.HAND
R.FOOT
L.FOOT
NO MOVEMENT
I ADMITTED IN
TO THE HOSPITAL

FIG. 4

As a result of these observations a deliberate search for further self-disharmony was undertaken. A series of films of a variety of pathological conditions were examined and self-dyssynchrony was observed in most of them. These included films of petit mal seizure, Huntington's Chorea, aphasia, Parkinsonism, childhood autism and schizophrenia.

A film of the actual patient with multiple personalities who served as the basis for the book and film "The Three Faces of Eve," was analyzed frame by frame. Thigpen and Cleckley, the men in charge of the case, had made a thirty minute sound film of this patient in her various personalities. A transient, micro strabismus was discovered which occurred rapidly. One eye might move to the right or left while the other remained still; or the eyes might diverge or finally; one eye might move markedly faster than the other eye. Table I illustrates the distribution of these in relation to the personalities.

TABLE I

Frequency of Types of Strabismus

	Eve White	Eve Black	Jane I
1. Left eye moves and right eye is still	7	6	
2. Left eye moves faster than right eye	2	2	
3. Right eye moves and left eye is still		29	1
4. Right eye moves faster than left eye		6	1
5. Eyes diverge	1	9	
6. Eyes converge	1	4	
7. Right eye bobble			4
	11	56	6

Jane II (a later version of Jane I) was filmed two years later in her home and displayed no instances of micro strabismus. This, plus the distribution in the table, suggests that the strabismus may have abated as the patient became "more integrated."

Two films were made of a non verbal, $3\frac{1}{2}$ year old girl who was diagnosed as "autistic" by two child psychiatrists. The child was felt to be partially or totally deaf; an audiological examination had proven inconclusive. It was theorized that _if_ a listener dances in synchrony with a speaker, and _if_ this girl could hear, she would probably move synchronously with the voice of someone speaking to her. Surprisingly, she was found to move synchronously with many of the inanimate sounds in her environment and seemed to ignore sounds of the human voice. She would give what almost amounted to a startle reaction at the onset of even slight sounds, often displaying a "posture crumbling." She also became self-dyssynchronous at the onset of these sounds, although this abated and may have been part of the startle reaction. She moved in rhythmic harmony with the "structure" of these inanimate sounds -- changing posture as the sound changed.

The scattering of change points across the first four frames after the onset of the sound (frames 10689, 90, 91, 92) indicates the self-disharmony at this point. It abates rapidly and the rest of the behavior looks relatively synchronous. Transcriptions of several of her reactions to sound display a pattern similar to that illustrated in figure 5, having a similar scatter pattern at the onset of sound.

828

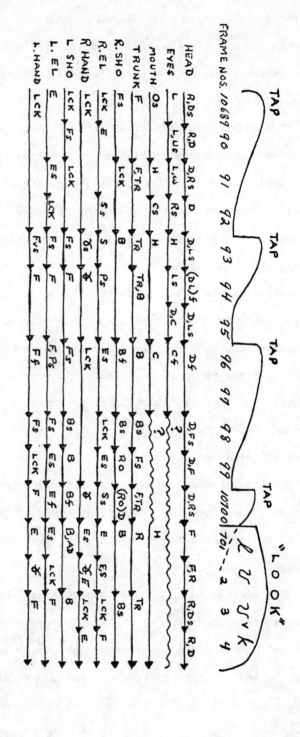

FIG. 5

AUTISTIC GIRL 3½/a
MARKED SYNCHRONY WITH INANIMATE
SOUND — THERAPIST TAPPING ON OBJECT

The present paper will focus on the findings from a frame by frame analysis of films of schizophrenic behavior. The self-disharmony or self-dyssynchrony in schizophrenia is very complex and may involve a variety of organizational levels simultaneously. The disharmony also seemed to have some relation to stressful verbal content.

Eighteen of 48 schizophrenic patients displayed moderate to marked dyssynchrony. Three cases will be presented to illustrate the nature of the self-disharmony. Figure 6 below shows a small segment of the behavior of a patient diagnosed as schizophrenic-catatonic. In the film, three male catatonic patients are shown seated side by side. The patient on the left appeared to be self-dyssynchronous: his eyes and mouth seemed out of phase. This is illustrated in figure 6.

FIG. 6

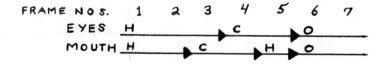

The second case to be illustrated is that of a young woman diagnosed as schizophrenic-paranoid. She was admitted several months prior to the date of filming in a state of agitation, sleeplessness and not eating. She is shown talking with her physician.

Her eyes, in the film, displayed some micro strabismus. There was also a temporal dyssynchrony in the way the body parts moved in relation to each other as contrasted with the normal, temporal organization of movement. Her left arm, with the hand held flexed and limp, moved slowly in a sustained direction for approximately 1/3 of a second and was disharmonious with the rhythm of her speech. While the left arm was moving in this fashion the right arm moved and changed in harmony with the speech. When this is projected at normal speed one gets a sense of a fleeting awkwardness in the behavior.

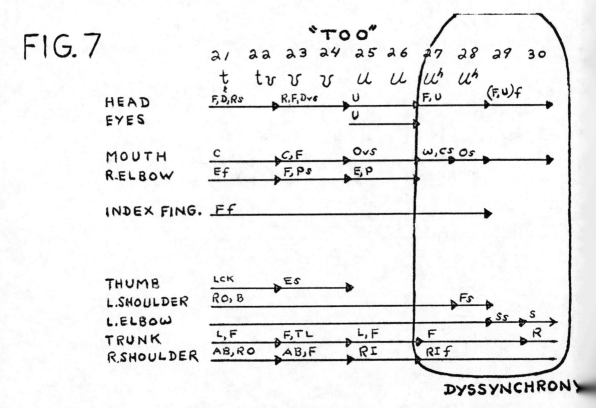

FIG.7

YOUNG WOMAN — PARANOID

Dyssynchrony occurs during her stressful utterance, "A real meth...*too*...of my life...at that time." The word "too" is shown in the figure. She lisps as she says "mess" (meth); her tongue is visible. This is the only occurrence of the lisp. She articulates the terminal /S/ normally in other instances.

Figure 7 illustrates this self-disharmony, particularly at the termination of the word "too." The vertical alignment of the arrow points which is characteristic of normal transcriptions is absent. There is some suggestion that certain parts of the body (index finger, left shoulder and left elbow) move at different change-rate than the rest of the body.

The third illustration is taken from a film showing seventeen patients with severe depressions. The patient described in figure 8 is an elderly woman who is seen talking with her physician.

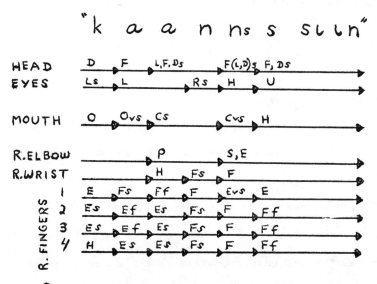

FIG. 8   ELDERLY WOMAN—DEPRESSED
"CONCEN" OF CONCENTRATED

832

There appears to be a temporal dyssynchrony between the fingers and the rest of the body. Also the head and eyes are
dyssynchronous. This occurs several times during her stressful utterance, "Just concentrated...on one thing...what's
going to happen to me?"

The fingers of the right hand move quite rapidly during
the articulation of the word "concentrated." There is some
change of direction of movement at every frame across
/ka a nh s / in contrast to the rest of the body. The
fingers appear to be moving in a temporal disharmony with
the rest of the body.

In another film, a schizophrenic patient is shown during
her hospitalization. Her treatment and gradual improvement
are depicted. When she is first seen, early in the film, a
marked and clearly detectable micro strabismus occurs. (Eve
Black and this patient revealed the most marked instances of
micro strabismus thus far observed.) The strabismus is not
observable later when the patient is improved, suggesting
that it may have abated as the improvement occurred.

V. Summary

The phenomenon of dyssynchrony, particularly as observed
in the behavior of schizophrenic patients is still in the
exploratory stages and much further work needs to be done.
Only a tentative and descriptive definition of dyssynchrony
can be offered at this time. It appears to be primarily an
"out-of-phase" phenomenon. Complex rhythmic regularities
were found to be salient features of normal personal and
interactional behavior. Dyssynchrony, in contrast, exhibits

some of the following features:

1. An aspect of the body sustains and changes direction of movement at different points than the rest of the body. Metaphorically, it is as if this part were operating on a different cycle than the rest of the body.

2. Quite often one eye appears to move faster than the other; or one eye moves and the other remains relatively still; or both eyes may diverge. This often occurs in two or three frames and is difficult to detect at normal projection speeds. Normal eye movements appear to be well coordinated in relation to moving together and speed of movement together.

3. The tempo of change of some parts of the body seem to be out of phase with the rest of the body. This is related to the speed with which parts of the body move with respect to each other.

There is also some indication that schizophrenic self-dyssynchronies may occur at points of stressful subject matter.

The following considerations are speculative. There are times when an observer senses an awkwardness in a patient's behavior, almost as if a part of the body belonged to someone else. This may be the effect on the observer of one part of the body being out-of-phase with another part. This proposition thus seeks to relate a clinical impression to a tentative, empirical observation.

The autistic child mentioned earlier displayed a repertoire of bizarre gestures. These gestures seemed to be representative of retained bits and pieces of the child's relation to her mother. For example, the mother would hold the child tightly by the forearm so that the child's wrist dangled limply. Later, when not with the mother, the child would hold her arm at the same angle and let the wrist hang limply. There were approximately fifteen of these gestures comprising her repertoire. These would repeat in various patterns. All of them seemed to have an analog in aspects of the relationship of the child and the mother.

One might wonder whether or not a similar relationship might not be involved in the "loss" of a body part in schizophrenic behavior; where a body part is out-of-phase with the rest of the body. The out-of-phase quality is also suggestive of a possible break-up of the ensembles of behavior. Schizophrenic dyssynchrony appears to occur at a higher organizational level (possibly at some semantic-emotive level) than aphasia. In aphasia and many of the other organic disabilities studied the disharmony seemed to occur at a relatively more micro level, namely below the level of the emergence of words.

The following study involving high speed sound films (48 frames per second) taken of subjects undergoing delayed auditory feedback supports the hypothesis of dyssynchrony.(4)

Six (6) "normal" subjects (student nurses) were filmed. Each subject wore ear phones and said paradigms and spoke spontaneously while hearing her own voice normally and tapping her fingers. This last item was introduced to provide an easily describinable behavior for kinesic analysis. Then each subject said paradigms and spoke spontaneously while tapping her fingers and undergoing delayed auditory feedback. All six subjects were self-synchronous under the normal condition. (Each subject had her own style of tapping her fingers in relation to the paradigms. This style repeated almost identically for the same paradigms even though separ-

ated by several minutes.) All six subjects displayed a
marked, left-right self-dyssynchrony during delayed auditory
feedback which resembled a mild aphasia. This dyssynchrony
was characterized (among other things) by out-of-phase movements between the right and left hand tapping movements.
There was also some tentative evidence of a displacement or
disorganization of the syllabic structure of the speech.

VI. Epilogue

The major, although not explicit, intent of the present
paper was to suggest and try to illustrate that the organizational complexity of human behavior is becoming amenable
to description and analysis. While we could not predict
when a re-viewing of a segment of film (perhaps for the
thousandth time) would lead to the discovery of a regularity,
after a time we became assured that this would occur.

The complexity of the multiple changes of multiple
changes became comprehensible and cognitively manageable in
terms of the precise order discoverable within those transformations. A predictability seemed to emerge as a function
of the determinable order in the behavior rather than as a
specification of causes and effects.

It seemed, as well, that pathological behavior was just
as ordered (in its "disorder") as normal behavior and was as
amenable to description.

References

1. McQuown, N.A. (Ed.) <u>The Natural History of an Interview</u>.
    To be published. Grune & Stratton
    1969.

2. Condon, W.S. and Ogston, W.D. A Segmentation of Behavior.
    <u>J. Psychiatric Research Vol. 5</u>
    pp. 221-235, 1967.

3. Condon, W.S. and Ogston, W.D. <u>Sound film analysis of
    normal and pathological behavior
    patterns</u>.
    J. Nerv. Ment. Dis. 143,338, 1966.

4. Pacoe, L.V.   Micro-kinesic analysis of the effects
                           of delayed auditory feedback using
                           sound film. (Read as "Micro-segmen-
                           tation of sound films: reliability
                           and control" at the American Psycho-
                           logical Association Meetings
                           August 30, 1968 in San Francisco.)

    The following is a list of the films from which the 48
    patients were analyzed.

5. Schizophrenia: Catatonic. Produced for the Mental
                           Health Division, Dept. of National
                           Health and Welfare by The National
                           Film Board of Canada, 1938.

6. Schizophrenia: Simple Type Deteriorated. Produced,
                           as above, by the National Film Board
                           of Canada, 1938.

7. Schizophrenia: Hebephrenic. Produced, as above, by
                           the National Film Board of Canada,
                           1938.

8. Schizophrenia: Paranoid Conditions. Produced by
                           the National Film Board of Canada,
                           1938.

9. The Faces of Depression: A phenomenological approach to
                           the depressive syndrome. Produced at
                           McGill University, 1940.

10. Prefrontal Lobotomy in Chronic Schizophrenia. Produced
                           by H.E.Bennett, M.D., Bishop Clarkson
                           Memorial Hospital, Omaha, Nebraska.
                           1943-44. (Our interest resided
                           primarily in those portions of the
                           film showing the patients' behavior
                           prior to the operation.)

11. Symptoms of Schizophrenia. Produced by J.D.Page, M.D.
                           New York, 1938.

12. Out of Darkness.   Parts I and II. Produced by Wyeth
                           Laboratories in consultation with
                           the American Psychiatric Association
                           and the National Association for
                           Mental Health. William C. Menninger
                           is narrator.

13. Depressed Schizophrenic Patient and Doctor. Produced
                    by Western Psychiatric Institute
                    and Clinic, University of Pittsburgh,
                    1965.

W. S. Condon, Ph.D., and H. W. Brosin, M.D., University of Pittsburgh School of Medicine,

Western Psychiatric Institute and   Clinic, 3811 O'Hara Street, Pittsburgh, Pa. 15213

PSYCHOTIC PATTERNS AND PHYSICAL CONSTITUTION

A THIRTY YEAR FOLLOW-UP OF THIRTY-EIGHT HUNDRED PSYCHIATRIC PATIENTS IN NEW YORK STATE

PSYCHIATRIC RESEARCH FOUNDATION LECTURE

WILLIAM SHELDON, NOLAN D.C. LEWIS, and ASHTON M. TENNEY

1. The Project and Its Background

As a college undergraduate, I enjoyed the privilege of attending a seminar given by Dr. Martin Peck at the Harvard medical school. Peck had been referred to Freud by William James and, as he put it, had "come to scoff but remained to pray." He had become one of the first practitioners of psychoanalysis to offer a seminar on the subject at an American medical school. He considered Freud the foremost emancipator of mankind but emphasized that the job was still only half done; that somebody now must bring descriptive order to comprehending the constitutional patterns underlying the psychiatric patterns.

As a graduate student in psychology, I met Dr. Sante Naccarati who, following the methodology of Viola and Di Giovanni, had found relatively high correlations between "morphological index" and mental characteristics. The morphological index turned out to be an anthropometrically derived radio between trunk mass and length of limbs. Viola's microsplanchnics had higher IQ's. For a doctor's thesis at the University of Chicago I repeated this work, finding similar although lower correlations. Something was there, all right, but clearly not yet in focus.

Later, in medical school, my attention was called to the fact that a number of investigators — notably Bean, Bryant and Goldthwait — had reported that both intestinal mass and total length of the gut tended to vary greatly in different people. Some persons, often called herbivorous types, had been found at autopsy to have a total gut length of forty feet or more; while others, called carnivorous types, measured around fifteen feet. I was permitted to test this observation by assisting as "measurer" at thirty autopsies. We had seventeen "herbivorous" and thirteen "carnivorous" cases. The mean total length for the former turned out to be 32 feet; for the latter, 19 feet. The longest gut was 43 feet; the shortest, 14 feet. Better than a three to one ratio. Again, something was there. This time, something pleasingly substantial. Forty three feet of it. The constitution problem began to seem worth looking into.

In 1934 I was awarded a two-year travelling fellowship to study constitutional and social psychiatry in Europe. One of the highlights emerging from this assignment was the contact with Dr. Ernst Kretschmer of the University of Tuebingen. He had collected references to the work of more than two hundred writers, ranging from Hippocrates (about 400 B.C.) to the twentieth century. Virtually all of them had described human physical or temperamental variation against the basic pattern of a threefold typology. Kretschmer had named his own focal types pyknic, athletic and leptosomic.

In those days Kretschmer held what were called interview clinics, at which psychiatric patients were presented for diagnostic study before a small group of doctors and students. The patient was led to a small platform, was then divested of his robe, and asked a few questions pertaining to his medical, behavioral and psychiatric history. Kretschmer had an excellent presence. He was gracious, sympathetic, provocative of confidence. He had the rare gift of being both helpful to the patient and instructive to the students. During the interview and examination, each student made physical ratings by underlining the appropriate items on a five-page form called the Constitution Schema. Later the psychiatric diagnosis was to be discussed against the background of the physical constitution. Most of the patients called pyknic were diagnosed circular psychosis (manic-depressive); most of the leptosomes, who were also called asthenics, were diagnosed schizophrenia. Most of the athletics were given hyphenated diagnoses, indicating diagnostic mixtures — one element usually being called either catatonic or paranoid schizophrenia.

Kretschmer was well aware that polar types are comparatively rare, both morphologically and psychiatrically. He knew that human constitutional morphology expresses a blending not of polar types but of primary components, with secondary components also blending at many levels — all the way from andric-gynic traits to molecular chemistry. Privately, he predicted, at least as early as 1934, that a standardizable quantification of primary components would eventually replace both the adjectival hyphenation and the fragmented segmental anthropometry which then still prevailed in the field of constitutional research. He liked the *idea* of somatotypic quantification as a constitutional frame of reference — a possibility which I had already begun to think out loud about. But Kretschmer felt that the necessary standardizing ground work would require the better part of a lifetime before it could provide the objective biological underpinning that he himself, perhaps in a less comprehensive way, was trying to give to psychiatry.

So Kretschmer continued to describe his constitutional patterns adjectivally, without taking substantial steps toward objective somatotyping. But Kretschmer had great insight into different types of psychotic performance, and it was while listening to his brilliant presentations that the plan of standardizing a somatotypic and also a psychiatric foundation for general epidemiologic record-keeping began to take shape in my own thought.

On returning to this country I set in motion some explorations which have been rather fully reported in the first four volumes of The Human Constitution series, all published by Harper, New York and London. These were *The Varieties of Human Physique, Varieties of Temperament, Varieties of Delinquent Youth* and *Atlas of Men*.

Hitherto unpublished, however, are The Basic Tables for Objective Somatotyping in their final form. These, together with instructions for their use, are included as a special supplement to this paper. I will try to tell you more about them shortly. But first I would like to report on the New York psychiatric follow-up project.

This will be really a preliminary field report on an epidemiologic study begun at the New York Psychiatric Institute in collaboration with Dr. Nolan Lewis in the spring of 1938. At that time the general framework of a practicable *constitutional* epidemiology was only just beginning to emerge into academic consciousness. We had only vague typologies, resting partly on subjective impressions and partly on fragmented phenotypic anthropometry. Somatotyping had been born, but was not yet grown to ambulatory stature. Its parents and a few of its godparents had voiced the hope that here was an operational scaffolding on which a *normative* human epidemiology could grow up.

Many of us realized that if once a normative epidemiology of human constitutional patterning were brought to full stature, then medical, psychiatric, criminologic, human developmental, and various other epidemiologies might before long begin to bear fruit. That was a major thesis of Carl Jung, with whom I had worked only four years previously; and it was in substance a favorite idea of Dr. Nolan Lewis, with whom I was now to give it a trial run. Dr. Lewis had already made major contributions to a biologically oriented psychiatry. He had pointed out that until we put psychiatry and biology on the same basic frame of reference — that is, until we can describe both the psychiatric pattern and the measurable organic constitution in terms of a normative epidemiology which *holds* at both levels — psychiatry will continue to operate blindly.

The New York Psychiatric Institute study, then, was planned as a two-level epidemiologic short term follow-up. Short term in the sense that we planned to follow these patients only through their one lifetime. Two level in the sense of including a psychiatric *and* a somatotypic or constitutional level of description. Epidemiology is defined as a field of science dealing with the distribution of disease states or normative states, within a human population. If our epidemiologic study was to be worth reporting it was necessary, obviously, to quantify both levels of variation — the psychiatric and the morphologic levels — in terms of comparable component units. The first major problem was, then, how to identify and quantify the primary psychiatric components. It was already clear that somatotyping could be handled with an operational matrix of only three primary components, and we had a plan for an ultimately objective quantification of these components. Could comparable *psychiatric* primary components be identified, and quantified? That was a question which had haunted me for years. And just one man had published findings which looked as if they might contain a constructive answer. Dr. Nolan Lewis, in a series of more than 2000 autopsies of psychotic patients had shown that wherever the diagnosis *hebephrenic* dementia praecox (schizophrenia) occurred, vascular hypoplasia, especially in the terminal vessels, was a constant finding. The paranoid schizophrenes almost never showed this characteristic. The manic and paranoid psychotics showed rather an antithesis — hyperplastic vascular structure —— as do most athletes. Dr. Lewis's catatonic schizophrenes tended toward the hebephrenic pole or toward an intermediate position.

In medical school I had been given an opportunity to observe some fifty autopsies of psychiatric patients. What I saw seemed not only to confirm the Dr. Lewis findings but to extend them. It seemed to me that in the clearly hebephrenic cases, the hypoplastic characteristic tended also to involve the whole mesodermal endowment — bone, muscle and connective tissue. Also that paranoia tended to reverse this finding, while the manic and manic-depressive patterns were accompanied by large viscera and a long, massive intestine even in cases where the patient had fallen fifty or seventy-five pounds below his maximal weight.

In short, it had seemed to me, even before I met Dr. Lewis in 1938, that he had given us not only a clue but possibly a *key* — to quantitative psychiatry. By 1938 I had been wondering whether Dr. Lewis had not perhaps been seeing, in his 2000 autopsies, another level of expression of the same three primary components that I by then had found clearly manifest at the somatotype level. The psychiatric entities appeared to derive from negative expression — lack of normal strength — somewhere.

In the normative epidemiological taxonomy which I called the somatotype distribution, expression of each of the primary components was positive. Endomorphy meant that the tissues derived from the endoderm were flourishing mightily in this organism. Viscera were in the ascendancy, perhaps with a forty foot gut. Mesomorphy meant the same for the mesodermal tissues, possibly with a Herculean chest, heart, and great vessels. Ectomorphy meant that the dangerous adventure of extension into space had taken over, with resulting dominance of surface over mass, and therefore with ectodermal tissues prevailing over both varieties of mass.

But all of the psychotics described by Dr. Lewis, as well as those shown by Kretschmer, had seemed to demonstrate clear failure at the expressive level – the temperamental level – in one or more of the three primary constitutional components. The hebephrenes were manifestly lacking in conative mesotonia; the paranoids in affective endotonia; the manics in inhibitory ectotonia; with catatonics inclined at different times to show all three of these primary temperamental disabilities in varying proportion.

So we had a clue, which might turn into a key. And we went to work. During the late spring of 1938 – I was at Harvard then – we worked on a device for scaling psychotic behavior reactions, and on standardization of a procedure we called the Somatotype Performance Test. Both were later published in detail in the book, *Varieties of Delinquent Youth*. The problem now was to try to scale the three primary psychiatric components quantitatively – in somewhat the same way that we were quantifying the somatotype – and to see what relationships might exist between these two levels of personality.

In June I moved to an office which Dr. Lewis provided in the Psychiatric Institute, and working out from there, began the job which now obviously is not finished but, we hope, is well begun. The object was to study – and ultimately to report – relationships between constitutional patterning and the primary psychiatric components in a sizeable sample, all of them to be followed through the life of the patient insofar as possible.

Dr. Lewis arranged a program including a visit to each of the twenty New York State Hospitals then treating committed psychotic patients who had not yet been designated chronic or "custodial". The team included myself, Dr. C. W. Dupertuis, and other assistants to handle the photography. Dr. Lewis was able to precede the team at most of the hospitals and to make the necessary selective arrangements in advance. In five months we photographed, interviewed, and assigned psychiatric index evaluations to all available ambulatory men found within one of the following groups: 1) Diagnosis dementia praecox in any of its subgroups, under age thirty, and total commitment less than two years; 2) diagnosis manic or manic-depressive, under 45, and total commitment less than two years.

In the twenty hospitals we found and processed 2800 men who met the criteria. Almost exactly 90% of these were in the dementia praecox (schizophrenia) categories. Another 1000 were then added to the series as an age factor control. They were DP cases who were between thirty and forty and had been held for two years or more; and M-D cases between forty-five and fifty-five who had been held for two years or more.

During the intervening 30 years I have visited each of the hospitals at least four times to read the charts. We have had splendid cooperation on this project all the way. Albany has kept us posted on the whereabouts of men who have been moved about, from one hospital to another. We are following outside death reports through the Board of Health.

Since 1948 there has been some able collaboration on the project. Two young men who in 1939 were in a course of mine at Harvard have continued their interest in constitutional research, as well as in other activities. Nathan Kline and Ashton Tenney have also carried out additional constitutional studies in three major hospitals, and have published papers in the field. In this New York State follow-up study, and in the necessary statistical work involved in standardizing objective somatotyping, Kline and Tenney have lent able collaboration at many points.

The real purpose of this preliminary report is to lay a foundation for publishing before long now, a sound epidemiologic study of the whole 3800 cases. Both the morphologic and psychiatric patterns need to be described against a meaningful frame of reference possessing objective scaffolding. Since the early books in The Human Constitution series were published, the somatotyping procedure has come of age in the sense that it has been made entirely objective, and at the same time operable. Now it needs to be made *available* — perhaps first of all to psychiatrists since its first major employment has been in a project aimed at bringing taxonomic order to psychiatric epidemiology.

2. Final Objectification of Somatotyping

There is one apparently urgent need common to all doctors. Whether physician, surgeon or psychiatrist, the doctor needs to comprehend the distinctive, characteristic and persisting individuality of the person with whom he is confronted. Against some familiar frame of reference with which he is as intimately at home as a rat must be at home with his immediate geography, a doctor needs to be alertly aware of the underlying biological predisposition of his patient. It may be the psychiatrist's main job to promote and use this awareness. If so, he has a primary need to be grounded in a constitutional taxonomy.

The first imperative for such a taxonomy was that of discovering first order criteria for the classification of human physiques. We had obvious criteria for differentiating man from the rest of the animal kingdom and for separating one sex from the other. All members of the same sex are not alike, however. They differ in innumerable ways, and in terms of a host of indices they could be sorted and classified. The challenge lay in finding those variable for sorting physiques which would produce the most fruitful and meaningful schema. These would be our first order variables.

Three primary aspects of bodily constitution were selected for study because they behave in bodily morphology as though each were a *component* of structure — something which enters universally but in different amounts into the making of every organism. Identification of these three is simple and straightforward. In order to facilitate the procedure and standardize the technique, the subjects are photographed from three angles — front, back and side. From a series of several thousand photographs of young men of college age it thus became an easy task to select those which showed the most extreme variations in the components under examination. Study of these extreme examples led to objective measurements which ultimately set each polar group apart from the other poles.

Three primary components were identified. The name of the first component, endomorphy, is derived from the fact that the digestive viscera, which (in endomorphs) tend to dominate the bodily economy, develop essentially from the *endodermal* embryonic layer. The second component, mesomorphy, means predominance of bone, muscle and connective tissue — the three principal *mesodermal* tissues. The third component, *ectomorphy*, appears to define a radical biological departure involving sacrifice of bodily mass in favor of surface. In proportion to his mass, an ectomorph has the greatest surface area and hence the greatest exposure to the outside world. Relative to his mass he therefore has the largest investment in skin and in sensory exteroceptors together with central nervous system and brain — all of which come from the *ectodermal* embryonic layer.

The somatotype is simply a three digit formula expressing the strength of each of these three primary components on a 7 point scale. The somatotypes 1 1 7, 1 7 1 and 7 1 1 are excessively rare polar extremes. The 4 4 4, a common somatotype in the male, is near the midpoint in all components.

It will readily be seen that both endomorphy and mesomorphy describe compactness of body (the pyknic physique in Kretschmer's terms), but two *very different kinds* of compactness. For an endomorph, the abdominal segment — the boiler room, as we sometimes say, seems to be dominant and to overshadow the thoracic segment, or engine room. Endomorphs are digestive athletes, as it were. They are champion processors of food, easily producing surplus fat for storage throughout the body. Therefore they tend to assume roundness of form, and to become spherically compact when they are overly nourished. The abdominal segment is king. Mesomorphs, on the other hand, are compact because they invest heavily in the supportive framework of the body — the somatic hard substance. Bone and muscle, with connective tissue. The mesomorphic extremities become powerfully developed, and the thoracic segment is king, prevailing strongly over the boiler room. Mesomorphy means athletic potential in the conventional sense, and the suggestion of squareness, cuboidal ruggedness, chestiness.

Ectomorphy defines an opposite to both kinds of compactness. This condition is really stretched-outness. An ectomorphic creature, of any kind, appears to be one who has abandoned the obvious biological securities of compact massiveness in favor of a pursuit, presumably, of some other kind of advantage which may accrue from an adventurous extension into what, for the growing organism, is unknown space and danger. The ectomorphic way would seem to be a dangerous way, perhaps like the danger of falling from a height. This may be why ectomorphs, when they break mentally, tend to break irreparably. One of the oldest and most constant observations in constitutional psychiatry emphasizes the tendency of ectomorphs toward that pattern of schizophrenia which used to be called hebephrenic — and almost always with a poor prognosis. It has been suggested that for ectomorphs the term schizophrenia should be translated, not split mind but fractured mind. Ectomorphy may be a high priced luxury, with fracturability a part of the cost. But such a luxury may be worth its cost. In the field of constitutional *values* we are appallingly ignorant.

The method of somatotyping, when first presented in *Varieties of Human Physique*, in 1940, involved four rather simple steps. First, calculate the ratio height over the cube root of weight, using a nomograph prepared for the purpose. Second, record 17 transverse measurements, each expressed as a ratio to stature.

The first four measurements are of the head and neck; the next three thoracic; the third group of three are arm measurements; the fourth group are abdominal; and the last group of four are leg measurements. Third, inspect the photograph and, referring to your table on which all the known somatotypes are distributed against the criterion height over the cube root of weight, make your estimate as to the somatotype. Normally you have available a file of correctly somatotyped photographs for comparison. Fourth, now turn to the 17 transverse measurements which you have recorded under the five appropriate bodily regions, and for each of the 17 consult your table on which the distribution of known somatotypes is plotted against the range of scores for that measurement. What you actually are doing, in each of these 17 instances, is measuring any deviation from your tentative somatotype estimate which you just recorded (step three).

At Harvard, in 1940, Professor S. S. Stevens built a machine which greatly facilitated this process by wiring into an illuminated switchboard the measurement patterns for each of the known somatotypes. With this machine, after the measurements were available, it was possible to determine the nearest somatotype in two or three minutes. The Harvard somatotyping machine also eliminated the need for step three, as presented above, since the switchboard included the height over cube root of weight ratio as an eighteenth measurement.

However, as matters turned out, this method of somatotyping from 17 measurements and a ponderal index was eventually to be superseded by a much simpler although more comprehensive procedure.

Some recurrent objections to somatotyping, and further objectification

As the theory of somatotyping was published in the first volume of the Human Constitution series, a number of major problems were doubtless over-simplified and some were left unexplored — or even worse, unmentioned. Hundreds of critical papers have resulted, some excellent and constructive; a few voicing mere emotional protest at the vulgar corruption of psychiatry with organic considerations. Space does not permit a review of this commentative literature here, but there are at least four specific objections which have been so cogently expressed or so widely discussed that it is almost mandatory for a serious presentation of the somatotyping idea to mention them. These are the main objections: (1) The somatotype changes. (2) Somatotyping is not objective. (3) There are only two, not three primary components. (4) Somatotyping omits the factor of size.

The objection that the somatotype changes has been regarded academically as a most damaging criticism. It has been possible to test this objection only by longitudinal studies carried out over respectably long periods. The real problem, of course, lies in the definition of the somatotype, and in the selection of the determining criteria. It will be recalled that in the very earliest beginnings somatotypes were determined by subjective inspection of photographs. This appeared to be the only possible way to make a sensible start. At the University of Chicago, with the help and guidance of Dr. L. L. Thurstone, who was mentor to my Ph.D. thesis, we had tried to use cluster analysis — later called factor analysis — in half a dozen attempts to identify primary factors in physical constitution. The results varied remarkably with different sets of measurements, although when I finally tried transverse measurements only — 32 of them — Thurstone decided that four primary factors were demonstrated, and that one of these factors was size. When we expressed all the measurements as ratios to stature, thus eliminating size, three factors remained. These apparently were expressions of the same three primary components that were later used in somatotyping. At any rate, the 17 measurements which were later used were selected from the original 32.

In the first "laying out" of the somatotypes, with 4000 sets of pictures, after deciding to try a 7 point scale and three primary components, we were confronted with the question, how many somatotypes shall there be? That would have been easy to answer if at the outset there had been available objective and unchanging criteria for determining the somatotype. But, of course, the purpose of the study was to find precisely those criteria. The question would have been self-answering if I could have assumed that the three primary components were completely orthogonal - zero correlations with one another. Then there could be 343 somatotypes, the cube of 7. At the other extreme, a critical threshold of high negative correlations would demand that the three components add up to a constant. This would be a *reductio ad absurdum*, for then the somatotypes would be plottable only on a plane surface, would have no third dimensional existence, and in fact would not exist as three structural components at all, but as only two. For if the sum of three units is a constant the third has no independent existence; and in that case the outcome of our experiment in three dimensional description of the human organism would simply have been a paper-thin man, two-dimensional. Since I had never encountered a two-dimensional man it seemed reasonable that a scientific classification of men had better rest its case on at least three primary structural dimensions.

Clearly it was necessary to steer between the Scylla of complete dependence and the Charybdis of complete independence among the primary dimensions. After a series of soul-searching discussions with Dr. Thurstone, who still played the kindly role of statistical mentor for my project, it was decided that in the absence of any advance knowledge of the probable correlations among our presumptive three primary dimensions, there could be no way of setting up *a priori* a correct set of boundaries for the somatotype matrix. It was like cutting a suit of clothes for a man you couldn't see, and whose measurements had never been taken. The only thing to do was to cut the suit by guess and common sense, try it out, and remodel — perhaps repeating the process many times.

At this point I recalled my first conversation with Kretschmer, and his patient answers to my then youthfully impatient academic insistence that *his* primary components of human constitutional variation ought to be mathematically objectified. "Yes, I would like that too," he said, "but that may be a long way off yet. Perhaps it will be done in another generation. Now it would be like dressing a baby in men's clothes".

Well, by 1940 it seemed time to try out a suit for the somatotype matrix, and we made up one. By then we had for years been "recognizing" such somatotypes as 7 1 1 and 4 4 4 — 9-totals and 12-totals, as well as tens and elevens. Thurstone had agreed that since men are structurally three-dimensional, surely *that* much "thickness" must be present in the somatotype matrix — *that* much independence among the components. So I postulated a matrix of 76 somatotypes, almost immediately added three more in the endomorph-mesomorph "Northwest", and *Varieties of Human Physique* went to press with 9-totals, 10-totals, 11-totals, and 12-totals. (No 8-totals and no 13-totals.)

For our purpose this matrix "worked" in the sense that it seemed feasible and fitting — by subjective criteria at this stage — to include all of the available cases within the 79 categories. And the distribution was 3-dimensionally continuous. There were examples for each category. The garment *appeared* to fit the contours, so far as a sizable population of college youths was concerned. I was well aware, as were several of my associates, that there were problems. The intuition grew that the material in that garment just might be more suggestive of stretchable elastic than of good English worsted, and by the mid-nineteen fifties that intuition had become a certainty. But more of this in a few minutes.

In laying out the original schema, we had of course visualized the somatotype as a dynamic, not a static concept. The height-weight ratio constituted one of the principal determining criteria, but this ratio travels through time as a trajectory, not as a straight line. From the data of the Actuarial Society of America, we had the "normal curve" for height over cube root of weight, from age 18 to 65, for 221,819 men who had been accepted for life insurance. From many cross-sectional (non-longitudinal) somatotype studies of men and women of various ages I had been able to construct approximately accurate trajectories of this sort for all of the common somatotypes, and for the rare ones by interpolation or extrapolation.

In 1954, in *Atlas of Men* we published these trajectories for each of the 88 somatotypes which by then had been included in the putative somatotype matrix. Also by 1954, all of my associates had for more than a decade been teaching that for somatotyping purposes, just as a person's height is the maximal height of record, the somatotyping ponderal index (SPI) must likewise be based on the heaviest ponderal index of record. By this rule, for somatotypic purposes, just as a person gets credit for his greatest achieved investment in linearity, so also he gets credit for his greatest achieved investment in mass. Otherwise the somatotype would indeed be a mere phenotypic concept, subject to change with any change in nutritional status.

By 1956 several normal, clinical and psychiatric populations had been followed, some of them for nearly 20 years. It had become very clear that despite nutritional changes the fundamental constitutional pattern remains stubbornly constant through life. We were searching for a set of parameters which both reflect the basic pattern accurately and remain constant. Certainly more than one hundred anthropometric measurements, ratios and indices had been explored — only to be found inadequate to that assignment. However, working with the Berkeley Growth Study at the University of California, we turned up an index that looked promising.

This was simply the area of the thoracic trunk over the area of the abdominal trunk, measured with a planimeter on a standard somatotype photograph. The trunk was divided at the nearest possible approximation to the plane of the anatomical waist — this is the plane midway between the lowermost plane of the ribs and the uppermost plane of the pelvis, with the individual standing fully erect. For the purposes of deriving and standardizing this index — now called the *Trunk index* — the TT (thoracic trunk) is the numerator and the AT (abdominal trunk) the denominator. The upper limit of the TT is defined by a line connecting the points where the sterno-cleido-mastoids cross the trapezii. The lower limit of AT is at the photographic center of the angle of the sub-gluteal fold. A specially constructed rectangular frame is used for holding the three photographs — frontal, lateral and dorsal — at exactly the same level with reference to one another while the areas are marked off.

The trunk index turned out to be a singularly valuable ratio, solving three of our difficult somatotyping problems. First, it provided an apparently dependable parameter for differentiating quantitatively between endomorphy and mesomorphy. Second, it has proved to be a constant, at least from the third year of life to old age, and is completely independent of nutritional state. That is to say, it is unaffected even by extreme variations in fatness or leanness, and in this last characteristic is unique among the almost countless measurements and ratios with which I have experimented. Third, it opened the way to a complete objectification of somatotyping.

At the University of California in 1929, a long term growth study and follow-up study of almost 1,000 children was initiated. The subjects were about equally divided between the two sexes. Nearly half of them were born during the year 1928-29. For approximately 400 of this series, somatotype photographs were taken at least once a year until the subjects were fully grown. Many of them were followed through their twenties, and some through their thirties. The 400 who stayed with the California project until they were fully grown are being studied intensively in connection with our project on the development of the somatotype in children. For all of the 400 the trunk index remained constant from the first photograph to the last. The TI may not be altogether a genetically determined characteristic, but it certainly is a pattern which stays constant through childhood, except for cases developing major pathology.

At the University of Minnesota, during World War II, a "starvation experiment" was carried out on a group of 34 students. Under mild starvation conditions these men lost from 25% to 40% of their total weight. Somatotype photographs of them were taken before and after the weight loss. All of these photographs were somatotyped during 1958 at the Texas Instruments Branch of the Constitution Laboratory, and at this time the trunk indices were calculated. The starvation changed none of the trunk indices (and, therefore, actually, none of the somatotypes.)

Somatotype photographs were taken of the class entering the United States Military Academy at West Point in 1946, and again on graduation in 1950. These boys had the advantages of closely supervised body conditioning and muscle developing exercises for four years at West Point. Many of them changed remarkably in their general appearance of physical competence and in the surface manifestations of muscular definition. But for all of them the trunk index remained a constant.

At Columbia University, somatotype photographs of the entering freshmen were taken regularly in the years between 1912 and 1917. In 1955 we photographed 208 of these Columbia graduates at the Constitution Laboratory in the Columbia Medical Center. None of the trunk indices had changed, although weight in a few instances had nearly doubled, and in a few other cases had decreased.

In a series of 46 pairs of identical twins of both sexes studied at the Constitution Laboratory during the same period, the trunk indices were identical within each pair, although in a few cases there were dramatic nutritional differences.

At this time we were running a follow-up study of 412 women and 22 men who had been attending the Columbia Medical Center Nutrition Clinic for purposes of supervised weight reduction. Some of the women succeeded in shedding — very temporarily — as much as 150 pounds. But the photographs at maximal and at minimal weight showed no detectable changes in trunk index. This remained constant despite nutritional changes.

In brief, then, the trunk index appears to remain unchanged from early childhood through late middle life — in both sexes. From the point of view of both objectification and standardization of somatotyping, this was news of some importance.

The next experiment was that of running the trunk index on a sample of 2000 young men and 2000 young women from our file of "standard examples" of all of the "recognized common somatotypes". It will be recalled that these collections had necessarily been built up from photographs somatotyped by the older partially objective — partially subjective procedure. It was soon discovered that in somatotyping, one thing we had learned to do was in large measure to make a surprisingly accurate subjective estimate of the trunk index — long before this index had been "discovered".

When the trunk indices for all the then available somatotypes were plotted, three facts almost literally jumped out from the page. (1) This ratio was manifestly a constant for those somatotypes in which endomorphy and mesomorphy were in balance. (2) Its variation was completely independent — zero correlation, in fact, for both sexes — with ectomorphy. (3) There was strongly positive correlation with mesomorphy, strongly negative correlation with endomorphy. In mesomorphy the thoracic segment really *is* king, and in endomorphy the abdominal segment is king.

Even more remarkable was the fact that the progression from endomorphic dominance to mesomorphic dominance, in both sexes, advanced in a series of progressive increments in trunk index. In somatotypes with the first component (endomorphy) at 7 and the second component (mesomorphy) at 1, the TI (trunk index) falls at 0.85 — and in those rare extreme asymptotic endomorphs who may weigh 600 pounds or more, at an even lower level (I have one case of a 700 pound woman with a TI of .65, but in our experience only one in about 4500 women, and one in about 13,000 men reaches this asymptotic tail of the distribution on TI).

In somatotypes with both of the first two components at 4, or at any other level, from 1 to 7, the TI falls at 1.45. When the first component is at 1, and the second at 7, the TI is 2.05. Here again there is an extreme asymptotic tail where the TI reaches still higher levels. We have two cases at 2.25 and one at 2.35. These men look like comic strip characters with gigantic chests and shoulders, and beanpole abdominal segments. They suggest Al Capp's L'il Abner.

We now had an operational procedure for objectively fixing the relative strengths of endomorphy and mesomorphy; and also, in the ponderal index taken at maximal mass, a second objective parameter — if we could just find a way to make effective use of it. But a third such parameter was needed. By definition the somatotype is a point in three-dimensional space. Such a point is actually the crossing point for three distributions, or three parameters.

I finally woke up, after twenty years of somewhat feeblemindedly making a hobby of this problem. The third parameter was, of course, stature. Maximal height is simply the degree of extension into space. When the other two parameters are known, that is precisely what ectomorphy is. First we have to have a measure of massiveness (SPI); then a separator for the two kinds of mass (TI); finally, a measure of the degree of stretched-outness into space (MH or maximal height).

Even back in 1954 I had published, in *Atlas of Men*, a table listing the mean height we had found for each somatotype in the male. For many years I had *used* height in somatotyping, but had not standardized its use as a determining parameter. The final move was just that step of standardization. We found that, as in the case of TI, the old subjective somatotyping had also made remarkably systematic use of this third parameter without fully appreciating what it was doing. The final step was to work out the systematic and realistic distribution of somatotypes on maximal stature. This was done, and a final set of basic tables for somatotyping was prepared.

In studies carried out since these tables have been available, it has been found that the matrix of somatotypes which I originally set up, and published in 1940, was almost shockingly too conservative. In this later work, by letting our three objective parameters *themselves* determine what somatotypes exist, we have now found it necessary to deal with a matrix far thicker than that originally postulated. Previously we had assigned somatotypes totalling 10, 11 and 12, with a few 9s. With the now fully objective procedure we find, in addition, somatotypes totalling 7 and 8, with all of the 9s; also 13, 14 and 15. Instead of the original matrix of 76 somatotypes, gradually expanded to 88, we now have a matrix of 267 7-point scale somatotypes, or 1713 13-point scale somatotypes. This results, of course, from the fact that the inter-correlations among the three objectively determined components are far lower than we originally dared suppose. TI yields zero correlations — orthogonality — with stature and with ectomorphy. The correlations between endomorphy and mesomorphy approach zero in both sexes. In males the mean for this correlation hovers around −.05; in females, around +.05. The ectomorphy − endormorphy correlations, and the ectomorphy − mesomorphy correlations, always negative, now average about −.40 in both instances.

Return now to the four critical objections regarding the somatotype:

1) The somatotype changes. It cannot change, since maximal stature and maximal massiveness are simply items of historical fact, and TI is constant through life.
2) Is not objective. Now it is completely objective. Can be derived on a computer as a function of three parameters, thus providing an operational definition of the procedure.
3) There are only two, not three primary components. This difficulty no longer exists. It

arose from the fact that the negative correlations among the primary components were too high. That condition has been corrected, thus permitting us to live and operate in three spatial dimensions again.

4) Omits the factor of size. Size has been restored by using stature as a determining parameter.

3. Quantification of the Psychiatric Variables

Bleuler had exerted a constructive influence on psychiatric classification. For more than a generation, psychiatrists had shown a tendency to rely on some variation of a three-pole typology for a diagnostic frame of reference. At the "psychotic" level, for example, it was already common to hear that in general three kinds of psychotic personality – together with mixtures – were to be encountered: cases showing *affective exaggeration*; or *paranoid projection*; or *hebephrenic regression*. Also at the "psychoneurotic" level a similar tripolar typology was usually assumed to exist, and was embraced within the concepts *hysterical, psychaesthenic* and *neuraesthenic psychoneurosis.*

Kraepelin, by including both mania and melancholia under the heaging *manic-depressive* psychosis, and by setting this new entity off against *dementia praecox*, had postulated a primary dichotomy which almost immediately unfolded to the primary trichotomy which Bleuler further refined.

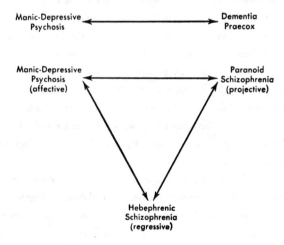

Figure 1. Illustrating the Kraepelinian Typology

A distinction is made between schizophrenic patterns in which a hostile or harsh reaction *against* seems to be the pre dominant temperamental set of the patient, and patterns characterized by reactions *away from* – by apathy, withdrawal from social contact, failure to participate or "take an interest." The reaction against is often buttressed by systematized delusions in support of a central fixed idea. The subject distorts his world of actual experience to fit the primary attitude. Hence the term *paranoid*. The patient is "in there fighting" against something. He has not given up; he has not jettisoned his cargo. There is a mesotonic drive, aimed at something.

The reaction *away from* is of an entirely different nature. The essential difference lies in the fact that the mesotonic drive is absent. The drive to compete and to fight — to participate — is simply not there. If any of this component ever was present, it has been jettisoned, thrown overboard. The essential fact in the picture is the mesopenia. The patient seems to have "regressed;" to have fallen back to what is in some respects an apparently infantile level of behavior, or a *hebephrenic* state.

To use the concept of infant-like, or infant-mind, as a description of the most extreme and helpless form of mental pathology, even it is said in Greek, is not very good semantics. These patients have not regressed. You can't "go back" in this life. They have reacted away from the problems and competitions of existence. They have jettisoned expression of their second component. What they show is an utter mesopenia.

The distinction between the mental aberration in which the against reaction is predominant, and that in which the away from reaction predominates presents as sharp a polarity of behavior as can be found in psychiatry. The psychiatrically conventional single-word symbols for the two temperamental reaction patterns are, respectively, paranoid and hebephrenic (endopenic and mesopenic).

Thus one end point of the original Kraepelinian dichtomy has grown apart into two end points. Figure 1 A grows into 1 B, and a tripolar orientation replaces a bipolar one. Hebephrenia makes operational sense as mesopenia, a concept with biological meaning. Meanwhile the reaction patterns that psychiatrists call paranoid, the reaction against, shows as a constant characteristic a singular lack of *compassion*, or affective warmth. The subject is without any bowels of mercy. According to his temperament and his strength he may look upon his world and his contemporaries as his persecutors or as legitimate objects of his own destructive fury. In either case his bond with his kind is one of hate, scorn, resentment, defiance; and all of this he "projects" against his environment. If he is weak, his reaction pattern has to be more covert than overt. It then takes the form of delusional ideation centered particularly around the central theme of his persecution. If he is strong — mesotonic — overt aggression and an arrogant manner will combine with opinionated superciliousness to produce a *dangerous* psychotic. The *strong* paranoids are ugly customers; the physically weak ones elaborate complex ideas of "reference," built around the central theme of their persecution. In both cases the constant in the picture is lack of "bowels of compassion." As hebephrenes are mesopenic, paranoids are endopenic. They lack participant compassion.

The affective psychotic, on the other hand, is one vast bowel of embracement. He seems to enfold his world in a cosmic Dionysian extrovertive embrace, tending to be so participant in *everything* that the focus of his energy is lost in ubiquity. He is compassionate with everything — as the paranoid is compassionate with nothing. The outstanding characteristic is a low threshold of reaction — somatic when mesomorphy prevails, and affective or emotive when endomorphy is dominant. The constant characteristic is enfeeblement of the constraint component, failure of inhibitory ectotonia — the temperament level of ectomorphy. He is feebly inhibited. The threshold of reaction is maladaptively low. In the *manic* state, which may be chronic or intermittent, he expresses elation or euphoria, or overactive participation, often without any apparent provocation at all. In the *"depressed"* state, which also may be chronic or intermittent, he similarly expresses uncontrolled emotional sorrow or extreme dejection without externally apparent provocation. The constant feature is maladaptive hyperactivity, somatic or emotive or both. Failure of inhibition. Pathological ectopenia. The inhibitory function of the brain seems somehow short-circuited, as if in reenforcement of effector functions.

In the manic phase the constant feature is lack of normal constraint in both emotional and somatic expression. The patient is maladaptively hyperactive, like a high-spirited dog in a forest of telephone poles. There may be euphorial emotionalism, motor overactivity, flight of ideas, press of speech, wild somatic and emotive commingling. Inhibitory failure, with both endotonic and mesotonic expression out of control — that is to say, a state of either commingled or alternating endorosis and mesorosis. Affective over-reaction and somatic over-reaction. In the "depression" phase there is also a pathologically uncontrolled overexpression of affect, but in this case it is melancholy affect rather than ebullience — still an uncontrolled expression of feeling (an endorosis) but in the mood of sadness and disappointment.

The terms manic, depressive, and manic-depressive psychosis, like the term schizophrenia, do not describe disease entities, then, but patterns of reaction in which a constant feature is readily recognizable — in this case pathological absence of inhibition, or failure of ectotonia. The expressed effect of the ectopenic condition depends of course on the underlying temperamental endowment of the individual. If he is mesotonic and vigorous, strong and somatically healthy, capable of sustained violent exertion without recourse to rest — if he is all this *and* temperamentally ectopenic, he will sustain a manic or hypomanic level of activity for long periods without rest. There are some who remain hypomanic all through life. These are athletes of a kind. One of them may exhaust a whole generation of contemporaries and two or three generations of wives or husbands, although they generally go out pleasantly enough in the end by way of a cerebral or cardiac "accident."

Such is the "pure manic," who of course is rare. Similarly rare are cases of pure depression, or "permanent aggressive melancholy." Far more common are the mixtures. There are about as many variants of these as there are individuals. Typically, some alternation occurs between the endorotic and the mesorotic ectopenia. Sometimes there seems to be regular alternation, a rhythm or cycle of the two phases, as if rest were needed for recovery from the manic phase. But in my experience clear-cut examples of such a rhythmic cycle are far less common than the term *cycloid psychosis* would seem to imply. What we characteristically find is not a patterned disease entity but a more or less maladaptive reaction pattern involving a) overly vigorous response which is either somatic or visceral-emotional or both; and b) pathologically feeble inhibition — failure of ectotonia.

The three operational end points seen in Figure 1 B appear to offer at least a beginning, then, for psychiatric orientation. In practice, we find psychiatric patients everywhere described — or perhaps "diagnosed" — against a frame of reference within which three primary components appear to be basic. The primary psychiatric components apparently measure decremental expression — failure of adaptive function in the normal expression of the primary components of temperament. The first psychiatric component (least maladaptive and commonest of the three) is really an overresponse — failure of the inhibitory function of the brain; insufficient ectotonia.

The second psychiatric component (less common and more maladaptive although not necessarily of lethal consequence) appears to involve a dissociative cutting off of the endotonic function of tempering compassion, resulting in "narrow" mindedness or paranoia. Insufficient endotonia. The third psychiatric component (comparatively more rare in the general population but almost fatally maladaptive) is apparent failure of the conative function itself — the mesotonic function of *doing* something, of making an active response to the presenting situation.

Morphologically, the three primary components are endomorphy, mesomorphy, and ectomorphy. Expressively (temperamentally) they are endotonia, mesotonia and ectotonia. Normative constitutional epidemiology is first concerned with quantification of these underlying components, and with recording the patterns of their distribution through the human population. Psychiatric epidemiology has an obvious first function of quantifying the primary psychiatric components and of recording their distribution — at least through the psychiatric population.

In the normative studies of morphology and temperament we had made no progress beyond quibbling over the polar types of Hippocrates and Aristotle (and Kretschmer) until we emerged from the idea of typologies and substituted the conception of continuous distribution of primary (and also secondary and more remotely derived) components which the familiar biological distribution curves would fit, multidimensionally. The first two volumes of the Human Constitution Series describe the steps leading to a description of the primary temperament taxonomies. The question now was: Could we take the same step in psychiatry, at last emerging from the Laocoön-like struggle to describe the mentally aberrant in terms of biologically unreal disease entities or "types" of reaction: could we emerge from this and substitute for it a polydimensional taxonomy which would be both operational and biologically true to life? In short, could mental aberrancy be described and diagnosed in terms of demonstrable, quantifiable components falling within a continuum with other measurable biological phenomena? If it could, there would be a bridge between psychiatry and the physical constitution, and it might open a road to biological humanics — incidentally, bringing scaffolding for the edifice in biological psychiatry that Dr. Lewis had already envisioned, and for which he had broken ground.

The polydimensional psychiatric taxonomy for which Dr. Lewis had long felt an urgent need now began to take shape in consciousness. We knew that the somatotyping edifice was basically sound; that had been tested against epidimiologic samplings which by 1938 included about 4,000 cases (and was destined to include, by 1968, more than 100,000 men, women and children). For several years some of us had been using a triangulation figure for illustrating the three-dimensional distribution of somatotypes. The next step was simply to superimpose the Kraepelinian psychiatric triangle on our now conventional somatotype triangle — resulting in Figure 2.

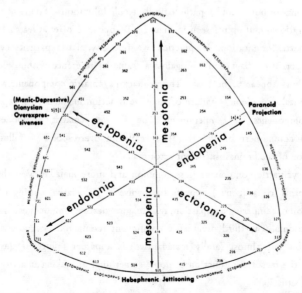

Figure 2. A Tripolar Psychiatric Orientation

Hypothetically the three psychiatric poles fell respectively opposite the three somatotypic poles; the Dionysian-affective pole opposite ectomorphy-ectotonia, the paranoid pole opposite endomorphy-endotonia, and the hebephrenic pole opposite mesomorphy-mesotonia.

Parenthetically, it might be of interest to mention that several years before starting the New York study I had shown Freud an early draft of this same diagram, on which I had called the three psychiatric poles *nach, gegen* and *ab* (toward, against and away from). Freud felt that the three polar psychiatric reaction patterns were almost certainly sound (as he and some of his followers had noted in published work) He felt that "someday" corresponding biological components will probably be demonstrable — but that so far as he was concerned that day lay well in the future. He was already having enough fun, and enough trouble, he said, as things were. But he liked the framework of three primary components, at both levels; felt that the psychiatric components probably corresponded with his own polar temperamental orientation (oral-erotic, urethral-erotic and anal-erotic). One might add that the inhibitory ectotonic temperament ("anal-erotic") never did enjoy any great popularity among Freudians — as Freud's name for it implies.

Figure 2 suggested a scaffolding from which quantitative bio-psychiatric description and diagnosis might emerge. The purpose of the New York study, which is still in progress, has been to give that idea a try. One clear objective was to effect a move-over from the rudimentary psychiatric typology to continuous multidimensional distributions along quantifiable parameters.

Keeping up with the diagnostic histories of these 3800 cases has provided a fascinating exercise. The nature and frequency of the diagnostic corrections have been highly instructive. In very few cases, less than five percent, has one diagnosis remained constant through the whole follow-up. In a much greater number of cases there have been six or more changes of diagnosis — often as many as there were changes in diagnosing officer. In many instances the patient has been assigned, through the years, all four of the conventional sub-varieties of schizophrenia (paranoid, hebephrenic, catatonic and "simplex"), together with, in some instances, one or more of the Dionysian-ectopenic labels (manic, manic-depressive, depressed).

In this connection, one early observation was of particular interest. It is the patients who fall in a particular range of somatotypes whose diagnoses get changed the most. These are of two groups: (1) the midrange somatotypes; and (2) those falling near the morphologic poles. Near the center of the somatotypic distribution, and near the polar somatotypes, there is great diagnostic uncertainty — almost a diagnostic turmoil. But when the somatotype falls near one of the psychiatric poles there is a clearly discernible tendency toward greater diagnostic agreement. Here it should be remembered that none of the diagnosing psychiatrists knew anything about somatotypes. Most of them were unaware of the nature of the study. Among midrange somatotypes, the diagnosis catatonic psychosis (usually catatonic schizophrenia) tends to prevail, but these are the patients who also get called everything else, all the way around the diagnostic clock. That diagnostic agreement should fall off in the middle of the somatotype distribution we did not find very surprising. But the same state of affairs was soon noted at all three of the somatotype poles. Polar endomorphs were found to oscillate between affective (or depressive) psychosis and hebephrenia; polar mesomorphs between the manic and the paranoid labels; polar ectomorphs between the paranoid and the hebephrenic labels. It was almost as if the psychiatrist *knew* the layout of Figure 2, and also knew how to somatotype. At first this seemed a somewhat shocking idea, but gradually, over a period of years, it began to dawn in my mind that there is a considerable modicum of truth in the idea. Most psychiatrists — and anybody else who really *looks* at people — *do* know how to somatype, at least in a vague, intuitive manner.

Near the somatotypic poles the hesitation is usually between just two different diagnoses, but near the middle of the somatotypic distribution all of the conventional typological psychiatric diagnoses tend to be about equally favored. In our series there are many patients of midrange somatotype whose diagnosis has been changed a dozen times or more. But these multiple diagnosis cases show one very interesting characteristic. List all of the diagnoses that one of them has been given, and plot these with dots on a spherical triangle similar to that used in Figure 2. You will find in four cases out of five that the average position for these dots is near the center of the figure. And most psychiatrists of the present generation use the term catatonic as about synonymous with mixed. Mixed psychosis. They describe patients labelled catatonic as evincing, at different times and under varying conditions, behavior suggestive of all three of the psychiatric poles. This has been so consistently noted, in all of the hospitals where we have worked, that on our diagrams of the psychotic reaction patterns, the central area of the triangle is usually referred to as the catatonic, or mixed psychosis, area.

The somatotypically midrange people, with all three of the primary biological components more or less equally represented, tend naturally enough under varying circumstances to manifest all three of the primary psychiatric components. At times a psychotic with somatotype 4 4½ 4 is very likely to behave like a manic-depressive; at times he may be singularly paranoid; at times he may elicit the diagnosis "clearly hebephrenic;" often he may be simply stuporous. His most common diagnosis usually turns out to be catatonic schizophrenia. Actually, the term catatonic has been defined in almost every way psychiatrically imaginable. Henderson and Gillespie, in their Textbook of Psychiatry (a classic in the field) defined catatonia as "an alternating state characterized by a stage of depression, a stage of excitement and a stage of stupor." Most psychiatrists follow Kraepelin in applying the term catatonic schizophrenia to virtually all cases of functional psychosis that show a mixture or alternation of all three of the primary psychiatric components. Kraepelin pointed out that this mixed picture is by far the commonest pattern of functional psychosis, and that many of these patients spend much of their time in a state of sustained (cataleptic) immobility.

Figure 3 is a diagrammatic summary of the apparent quantitative relationship among the primary psychiatric components plotted against a background of the somatotype matrix. Here the psychiatric index is expressed in the same way as the morphologic index (somatotype), with the poles for the psychiatric components opposite those of the morphologic components. The Greek letter ψ here stands for psychiatric. This symbol placed in front of the three familiar numerals used for the somatotype indicates a psychiatric rather than a morphologic index.

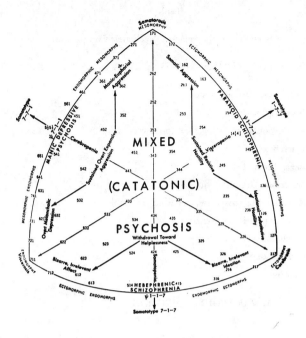

Figure 3. Diagram for the Psychotic Reaction Patterns

Table 1

Check list for the Primary Psychiatric Components

I AFFECTIVE-CONATIVE OVER-RESPONSE

1. Sustained overt expansive aggression.
2. Manic-euphorial aggression.
3. Conative over-response. Overly active, too energetic.
4. Distractible attention.
5. Flight of Ideas. Press of speech.
6. Expansive ideation. Grandiose outlook.
7. Exaggerated emotional response, whether in euphoric expansion or in depressive constriction.
8. Extroverted, lugubrious melancholy.
9. Overt melancholic depression.
10. Dionysian ectopenia.

II PARANOID PROJECTION

1. Sustained resistive hostility.
2. Ruthless somatic aggression.
3. Overt vindictive truculence, with systematic projection of blame.
4. Overt or covert obsession with own superiority.
5. Consistently self centered judgments and manifestations.
6. Opinionated, pedantic, conceited.
7. Critical, sarcastic.
8. Persistently subjective frame of reference.
9. Ideational-substitutive hostility.
10. Paranoid endopenia.

III SCHIZOID REGRESSION

1. Bizarre, irrelevant affect.
2. Bizarre, irrelevant ideation.
3. Apathetic withdrawal from social contact.
4. Listless, lethargic inertia.
5. Paucity of apparent emotion.
6. Paucity of thought content.
7. Incongruity of emotion and ideation.
8. Unkempt, dilapidated presentation.
9. Regression toward helplessness.
10. Hebephrenic mesopenia.

Note: Numerical values from 1 to 7 are assigned as follows for the traits evaluated:

1. Extreme lack	5. Marked degree
2. Slight evidence	6. Very marked degree
3. Present but not marked	7. Extreme degree
4. Noticeable degree	

One other point of great interest will doubtless have occured to anyone who in his thinking has begun to substitute the three-dimensional psychiatric index for the Kraepelinian typology. Psychotic personalities falling in the northwest sector of the distribution are frequently referred to as "cycloid," or manic-depressive. Actually, the same cycloid phenomenon is just as conspicuous in the northeast and in the south, as in the northwest sector of the diagram. Among paranoid schizophrenes presenting about the same strength in mesomorphy as in ectomorphy, there is very much the same alternation between somatic aggression and ideational substitutive hostility as is seen between euphorial and melancholic expressiveness in the northwest when endomorphy and mesomorphy are more or less in balance. And the same phenomenon is seen in the south among hebephrenic patients who show about the same strength in endomorphy and ectomorphy; these patients tend to alternate between bizarre, irrelevant affect and bizarre, irrelevant ideation.

When psychiatric behavior is described against a quantitative operational frame of reference the cycloid or alternational pattern is seen to be general — not specific to the manic-depressive corner of the picture. Also the same alternation is observed across the morphologic poles just as conspicuously as across the psychiatric poles — that is to say, you encounter endorotic, mesorotic and ectorotic cycloid alternation as conspicuously as you see the endopenic, mesopenic and ectopenic alternation. Among psychiatric patients of midrange somatotype the alternations of mood and behavior tend to become complex. Some of these patients show, at different times, the definitive criteria of *all* of the Kraepelinian typologic diagnoses. These are the people who almost universally get labelled catatonic.

In fairness to psychiatrists who have fallen into the conventional habit of applying the term cycloid only to the northwest sector, it is perhaps worth pointing out that the observable outward behavior is of course more violent and more dramatic in that quarter than in any other. This is because all expressiveness reaches its maximal volume at the pole of extreme ectopenia — the pole of pathological failure of the constraint (inhibitory) function. Doubtless it was to be expected that the phenomenon of cycloid swing would first be noted in the sector where overt behavior is most uninhibitedly accentuated.

With the polar scaffolding for a psychiatric frame of reference conceptually indicated, it was possible to take a step in the direction of quantification of the psychiatric components. First, a check list was worked out as a substitution of 7-point scale quantification for the traditional adjectival description still prevailing in psychiatric diagnosis. It was found that by using the scale, psychiatrists were able readily to translate their adjectival diagnoses into psychiatric indices corresponding to the morphological indices (somatotypes).

Figure 4 is really just an orderly arrangement of these resulting psychiatric indices, now substituting for the adjectival typologies used in Figure 3. Here ψ 7 1 1 is simply a form of mathematical shorthand for the most extreme degree of affective-conative over-response (Dionysian ectopenia), with no trace of either paranoid endopenia or hebephrenic mesopenia; ψ 1 7 1 represents the most extreme degree of paranoid projection, without any trace of Dionysian ectopenia or hebephrenic mesopenia; and ψ 1 1 7 indicates an extreme hebephrenic mesopenia with no signs of either Dionysian ectopenia or paranoid endopenia. At the center of catatonic territory, ψ 4 4 4 stands for a balanced mixture, at psychotic level, of all three of the primary psychiatric components.

At Elgin State Hospital, Illinois, in 1945, Dr. Phyllis Wittman, together with the writer

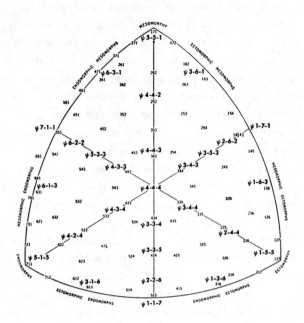

Figure 4. Hypothetical Psychiatric Indices for a Psychotic Population. (Skeletal or Incomplete Pattern.)

and several members of the Elgin staff, ran a pilot study to test the usefulness of this sort of quantitative psychiatric diagnosis.* First, 155 male patients, selected because of availability, were somatotyped. The somatotypes were turned over to a statistician, Dr. R. L. French at Northwestern University. Dr. Wittman and Dr. Charles Katz then independently scored the psychiatric index for each of the 155 cases, and turned these data over to Dr. French. The correlations between the Wittman and Katz psychiatric indices are shown in Table 2.

Table 2

Correlations between Wittman and Katz
Psychiatric Indices. Elgin Study

(N = 155)

Component I (Manic-depressive)	Component II (Paranoid)	Component III (Heboid)	Mean (3 Components)
r +.89	+.78	+.91	+.86

*For Dr. Wittman's report on this study, see *The Journal of Nervous and Mental Disease*, Vol. 108, No. 6, Dec. 1948, pp. 470-476.

In this study neither Wittman nor Katz had any knowledge of the somatotpyes, or of each other's psychiatric indices. The correlations seemed high enough to establish the probability that the Elgin Check List does usefully quantify the primary psychiatric components *as psychiatrists actually use these components.* The next step in this pilot study was carried out by Dr. Wittman. Using the hospital records, she very carefully determined the current prevailing diagnosis for each of the 155, still with no knowledge whatever of the somatotypes. She found that 12 were being carried as manic or manic-depressive psychosis;

27 as paranoid schizophrenia; 85 as hebephrenic schizophrenia; and 31 as catatonic schizophrenia. The somatotypes of the entire 155 were then plotted on the standard somatotype graph (Figure 5), and the somatotype distributions for the four diagnostic groupings follow (Figures 6-9).

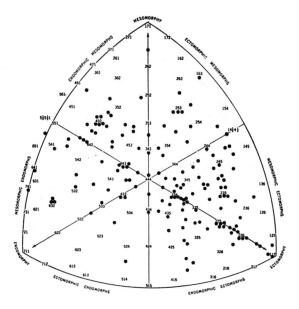

Figure 5. Distribution of Somatotypes for 155 Psychotic Patients. Elgin Series.

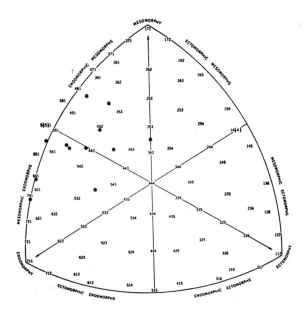

Figure 6. Distribution of Somatotypes for 12 Psychotic Patients. First Psychiatric Component Predominant. According to Hospital Records. Elgin Series.

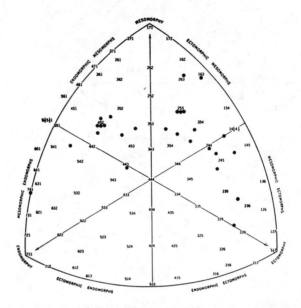

Figure 7. Distribution of Somatotypes for 27 Psychotic Patients. Second Psychiatric Component Predominant. According to Hospital Records. Elgin Series.

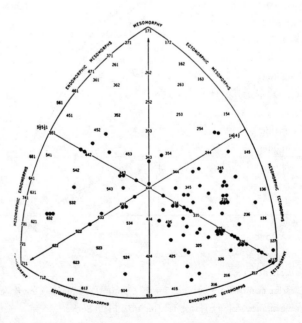

Figure 8. Distribution of Somatotypes for 85 Psychotic Patients. Third Psychiatric Component Predominant. According to Hospital Records. Elgin Series.

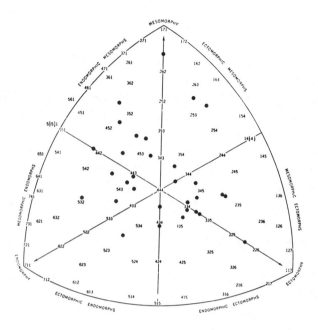

Figure 9. Distribution of Somatotypes for 31 Psychotic Patients. Mid-range Strength in All Three Primary Psychiatric Components According to Hospital Records. Elgin Series.

It is evident enough that at the primary structural level (somatotype level) variations of pattern are to be found which are also reflected at the behavioral level with which psychiatrists have to be concerned. Compare Figures 5 - 9 with Figure 10, which defines the (presumably normal) somatotype distributions for 4000 college boys photographed in seven universities. Then compare these patterns with Figure 11, presenting the somatotypes of the 200 delinquent young men of Boston whose careers were presented in the book, *Varieties of Delinquent Youth* (Harper, 1949). Note that if you (imaginatively) superimpose Figure 6 on Figure 9, the result will be a somatotype distribution rather closely resembling that of Figure 11. About ten percent of those 200 delinquent boys were markedly manic (ψ1) in the psychiatric sense, with most of the other 90 percent showing varying degrees of more or less evenly balanced catatonic mixtures of the three primary psychiatric components. Actually, polar manic personalities are found with very nearly the same frequency among criminal and delinquent men as among psychotic men, while polar paranoids (ψ2) are scarce and polar hebephrenes (ψ3) are almost unknown among the criminally delinquent. The third psychiatric component is apparently a fatal handicap to successful survival in criminality.

Returning now to our 3800 New York psychotics, whose careers have as yet been followed for only three decades, we find that among them also a predominant third psychiatric component seems to be fatal to long survival. Each of these patients was given a psychiatric index at the time of being posed for his photograph — a procedure called the somatotype performance test. (See Table 3). Figure 12 is an almost perfectly posed somatotype photograph — no trace of psychotic performance (ψ 1 1 1). Figure 13 shows ψ 1 predominance (ψ 5 3 1½). Figure 14 reveals ψ 2 predominance (ψ 2 ½ 5 2½). Figure 15 presents an obvious ψ 3 problem (ψ 1 1½ 5½). Figure 16 is a catatonic case with the three psychiatric components nearly balanced — (ψ 3 3½ 3).

Table 3

Instructions for Posing in Somatotype Photography

1. Frontal Picture.

Stand in front of the subject. Demonstrate the position of attention. Tell him to take that position. Demonstrate forced extension of the arms. Tell him to do the same. Take hold of his wrists firmly and bring the shoulders down. Center the shoulder points in the mid-frontal plane (shoulders are not to be rolled forward or backward). Make certain that the chest is relaxed, relaxing it manually if necessary.

Making certain that the arms are as forcibly extended as possible, with the elbows locked so that the triceps muscles stand out if they will. See that the subject's fingers are together, with the thumbs along the forefingers, and hyperextend his fingers manually by bringing your own inside hand down across his fingertips while your outside hand holds his hand in position. Bend his wrists inward so that his fingers point perpendicularly to the floor. Place his hands so that his wrists are five inches out from his thighs and so that the middle fingers are in the same frontal plane with the centers of his external malleoli.

Be sure that the subject's face is straight toward the camera, with the head held on the eye-ear plane. The head is centered on a center mark at the top of the beaded screen.

Before turning the pedestal for the next picture, tell the subject that you are about to turn him, and hold him firmly by the shoulders.

2. Profile Picture

Make certain again that the chest is relaxed and that the shoulder points are in the mid-frontal plane.

Right arm out of sight. Left arm in forced hyperextension, locked at the elbow. Make certain that the triceps muscle stands out if it can be made to do so. Hand and fingers as in the frontal picture, with the middle finger in the plane with the center of the external malleolus. Left arm as a whole in the center of the body. The arm must not cut the back line or front line of the body. Body and face in perfect profile. The two legs in perfect alignment with no flexion or hyperextension at the knees.

Center points of the shoulder, hip, knee, and external malleolus to define a straight line if possible.

3. Dorsal Picture

Same position as frontal picture. Check center position of the shoulder and level position of head. Make certain that the shoulders have not lifted.

Note: When the subject to be photographed is a psychiatric patient, to be given a psychiatric index based on his/or her performance in this test situation, and when the posture is not perfectly maintained after the first posing, the patient is to be posed a second time — and a third time if the second performance is also imperfect. The procedure of posing a psychiatric patient for somatotype photography is referred to as the Somatotype Performance Test.

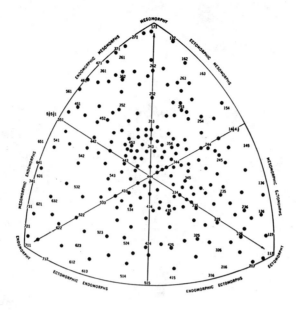

Figure 10. The Distribution of Somatotypes for a Male College Population of 4000. Each Black Dot Represents 20 Cases.

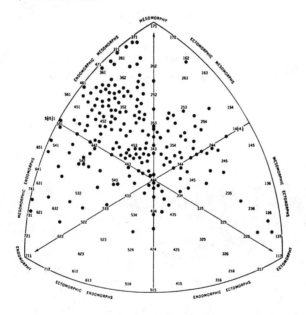

Figure 11. Distribution of Somatotypes for 200 Delinquent Boys. Boston Study.

Among the New York 3800, thirty years after initiation of the study, 128 had been released to private psychiatric care, usually under the care of relatives or of private institutions — with no claim of recovery or "cure;" 43 individuals had made a successful "escape" and had disappeared from the picture; 19 had been deported, all with poor prognosis; and 36 had been discharged as improved, usually with an implied favorable prognosis. The remainder of the series, 3574, had died or had been put under permanent custodial care with no expectation of recovery and no further claims of improvement, although about 55 percent of these had on earlier occasions been discharged as improved —

864

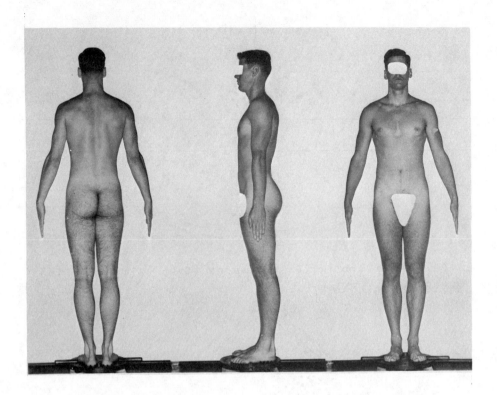

Figure 12A.   An Almost Perfectly Posed Somatotype Photograph. No trace of Psychotic Performance. (ψ 1 1 1)

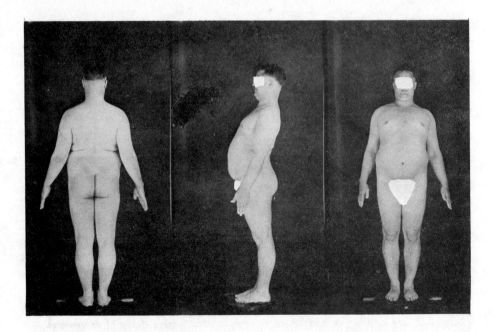

Figure 13. ψ 1 Predominance (ψ 5½ 1½ 1½) Affective — Manic

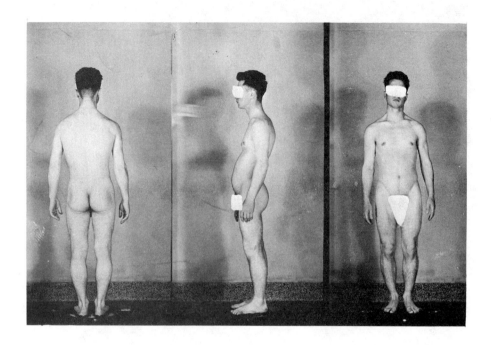

Figure 14. ψ 2 Predominance (ψ 1½ 5 2½) Paranoid

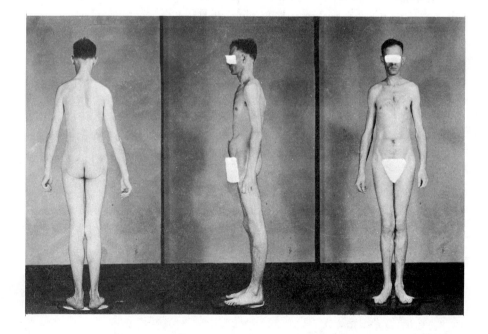

Figure 15.   ψ 3 Predominance (ψ 1 1½ 5½) Hebephrenic

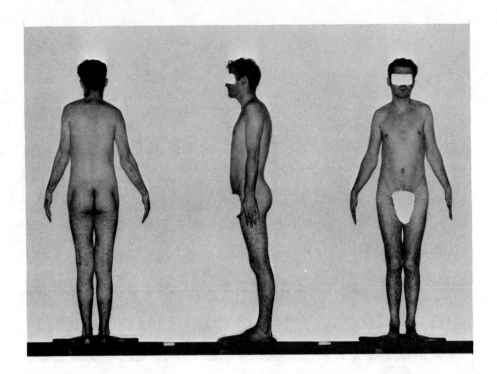

Figure 16. Catatonic. Three Psychiatric Components Nearly Balanced. (ψ 3 3½ 3)

some of them as many as seven or eight times. About 15 percent of this group had been discharged on at least one occasion as recovered.

It is with the group of 36 — less than one percent of the series, who according to our current information had somehow really benefitted from treatment, or perhaps had actually recovered, that we have most recently been concerned. It has seemed an epidemiologic imperative to call descriptive attention to this small group of men who appear to have responded well to psychiatric care. First, we might look at their somatotypes (Figure 17).

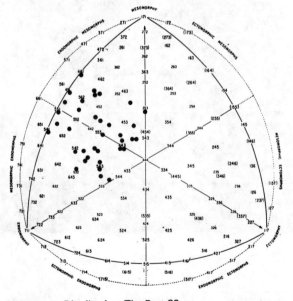

Figure 17. Somatotype Distribution. The Best 36.

Table 4

The Best 36. Somatotypes and Psychiatric Indices.

	Somatotypes			Psychiatric Index		
1.	3	5	2½	3	5	2
2.	5	4	2½	4	4	1½
3.	4	4½	1½	3	4½	1½
4.	5	4½	2	5½	3	1½
5.	4½	3½	2	4	4	1½
6.	4	4½	1	2½	5	1½
7.	4½	5	2½	2½	5½	2
8.	4½	4½	2½	4	3	2
9.	3½	5	1½	3½	5	1½
10.	4	6½	1	3	6	1
11.	4	4½	2	2	4	1½
12.	4½	4	2½	4	2½	1½
13.	4½	4	1½	4	1½	1½
14.	4	4½	3½	2	4½	1½
15.	5	3½	4	4	1½	2
16.	5	3½	3	3½	2½	1
17.	4	4½	1½	3	4	1
18.	4	5½	2	4½	2	1
19.	4½	4½	1	3	2½	1½
20.	4½	4½	3½	3	3½	1
21.	5½	5	1½	3½	3	1½
22.	3½	5	1½	2½	3½	1
23.	2½	5	3	1	4	2
24.	4	4	3	1½	4	1½
25.	3½	4	2½	1½	4	1
26.	3½	4½	3	3	2	1½
27.	5	4	2½	4	2½	1½
28.	4	5	1	2½	4	1
29.	4½	4	2½	3	3½	1½
30.	5½	4½	1	3½	3½	1
31.	4	4	3	3	2	1
32.	5	4	3	3	3½	1½
33.	5	4	3	3	2	1½
34.	4½	3½	2	3½	2	1½
35.	4	4½	2½	1½	3	1½
36.	4	4½	3½	2	3½	1
Mean values	4.3	4.4	2.3	Mean: 3.1	3.4	1.4

This is a remarkably concentrated cluster of 36 somatotypes. There are no ectomorphs here, no mesopenes, and but one endopene — a 2½ 5 3 (no.23). Table 4 compares the somatotypes of the 36 with the psychiatric indices assigned at the time of the original somatotype performance tests. The somatotypes indicate that ectomorphy, at 2.3, is singularly low — more than a standard deviation below the mean for the American male population. Our small nucleus of 36 ectopenic men, though unquestionably psychotic, have been outstandingly successful in resisting deteriorative progression of their mental dysfunction. The mean endomorphy at 4.3, and the mean mesomorphy at 4.4, are both approximately half a sigma *higher* than in the general male population. In our normative studies, now based on three decades of data gathering, the average American male somatotype — as attributed from the Basic Tables for Somatotyping that accompany this paper — falls at about 4 4 3½. In the general population the sigmas for endomorphy and mesomorphy fluctuate narrowly at approximately .70 to .75. The sigma for ectomorphy is always higher, usually falling between 1.00 and 1.10.

Our group successfully resistive to psychotic deterioration are then about a half sigma up in the first two primary somatotype components, and better than a full sigma down in the third. Yet for the series as a whole, for the entire 3800, ectomorphy is *above* the normative mean, and the other two components are below their normative means. These data will follow later in a more detailed publication.

The psychiatric indices are worth looking at. These are not based on shifting diagnostic opinions, which in the hospital records often change from year to year, and sometimes from month to month, but on an objective performance test with a photographically recorded outcome. Bearing this in mind, the uniformly low level of the third (hebephrenic) psychiatric component among our 36 most successful cases raises interesting questions. The mean psychiatric index for the group is ψ 3.1 3.4 1.4. This index is a quantified measure of the subject's response to the process of being posed in a position of military attention, as that process has been taught at West Point and elsewhere for more than a century. The index ψ 1 1 1 signifies that the subject assumed the military position perfectly in all three poses, and in each instance held it steadfastly for an intervening few seconds until the picture was snapped. ψ 1 1 1 means normal, pleasant, unstrained, adaptive readiness for competent performance

(1) No manic trace of conative or emotive overextension (or of depressive reaction) in bodily posture or in the face, arms or hands;
(2) no trace of resistive paranoic hostility or expression of suspiciousness, no harsh rigidity in the posture, hands or countenance;
(3) no suggestion of hebephrenic flaccidity or lack of alert competence and readiness for effective action, either in bodily posture or in the position of the head and extremities, or especially in the firm extension of arms and fingers. (Where the third psychiatric component is dominant, there is apparently *always* notable failure to maintain purposeful extension of the arms and fingers, even in early childhood many years before other ψ 3 signs are noted and the individual is thereby brought to psychiatric attention).

For a normal individual, in good health and free of psychotic dysfunction in all three directions (or dimensions), the somatotype performance test yields a psychiatric (ψ) index of 1 1 1. In a series of 17,000 college undergraduates, about equally divided between boys and girls — this was a series used for establishing normative somatotyping distributions — we found that between six and seven percent "flunked" the somatotype performance test in the sense that they showed psychiatric indices variant from the normal ψ1 1 1. This does not mean that all the flunkers will eventually be tagged as psychotic, but probably it does mean that most of them are *potentially* psychotic.

When it had become clear that the outstanding overt characteristic of our 36 long-surviving psychotics is a psychiatric index relatively free of ψ 3 (hebephrenia), and some of my associates had begun to call them hebepenes or cases lacking in (literally, cases with poverty of) this third psychiatric component, we looked at the psychiatric indices of the first 36 of the 3800 whom we knew to have died before age 40 or by then to have been transferred to permanent custodial care with no prospect of improvement. For this group, the psychiatric index turned out to be 2.3 1.2 5.8. Perhaps we can label these unfortunate ones, as a group, the hebephrenic platoon, in contrast with the sturdier soldiers of the hebepenic platoon.

Let me try to summarize in three simple suggestions.

1. Psychiatrists, as well as epidemiologists and clinicians in other fields, might find the Somatotype Performance Test, with its resulting Psychiatric Index, a useful tool first for diagnosis and prognosis, and then as a navigational help toward therapeutic orientation.

2). Kretschmer might be astonished to know it, but he was a principal architect for the scaffolding of both the somatotype and the psychiatric index. Things of this nature are ideas first; then they take shape as verbal scaffolding; later, perhaps much later, they emerge as durable objective structure.

3). When Dr. Nolan Lewis made known the amazingly clear relationship he had found between peripheral-vascular hypoplasia and what we in this lecture have been calling the third psychiatric component, he laid down the scaffolding for the bridge we so badly need, between structure and function in psychiatry. The next step, almost surely, will be establishment of free therapeutic traffic across that bridge.

APPENDIX ON SOMATOTYPING

How to Use the Basic Tables

The somatotype is simply a point within cubical or three-dimensional space, where three distributions cross. The three are: trunk index, height, and somatotyping ponderal index. The procedure for measuring the trunk index, with a planimeter, is outlined in Table 5. This is the photographic area of the thoracic trunk over the abdominal trunk. Height, for somatotyping purposes, is maximal adult height, usually measured in inches and tenths. The somatotyping ponderal index (SPI) is height over the cube root of weight taken at that point in the individual's history (after early childhood) when the heaviest phenotype (maximal mass) is achieved. Thus height insures recognition of maximal ectomorphy, and SPI insures recognition of maximal endomorphy plus mesomorphy. We have seen that trunk index provides the necessary differentiation between the two kinds of mass — between endomorphy and mesomorphy.

Assume now that for a 19 year old boy you have correctly determined the three somatotyping parameters; that the trunk index falls nearest to 1.45, height nearest to 70.8 inches, and SPI nearest to 13.15. You are inexperienced at somatotyping, and want all of the help you can get. So you turn first to Table 6. There you note that the crossing point for your two parameters (1.45 and 70.8) gives you three possible somatotypes to choose among: 2 2 6, 3 3 5, and 4 4 4. Turn now to the basic tables and look up the SPI's for these three somatotypes in the →20 column. You find 2 2 6 at 14.20, 3 3 5 at 13.70, and 4 4 4 at 13.15. You now have found your boy correctly somatotyped at 4 4 4, and are on your way to become a somatotyping expert. Had it been a girl, with exactly the same data except for height, and had she been nearer to 65.6 than to any other height listed in the table, then *she* would have been a 4 4 4.

For a beginner, the most difficult step in somatotyping is that of getting an accurate weight history. If a person is older than 20, it is of the first order of importance to know his maximal weight *before* 20, between 20 and 30, between 30 and 40, and between 40 and his present age. With the three parameters reliably determined, somatotyping is not much more difficult than looking up squares and cube roots in Barlow's Tables.

Table 5

Procedure for Measuring the Trunk Index

Frontal Picture

1. Lay a straight edge along the line running from the pubic tubercle, through the anterior superior spine, and to the surface of the body. Mark the intersection of this line with the surface. Both sides, right and left.

You have now located the approximate plane of the tops of the iliac crests.

2. Mark the two points of maximal indentation that are seen immediately below the ribs — right and left.

You have now located the approximate plane of the bottom of the ribs, as seen frontally (or dorsally) in the photographic presentation.

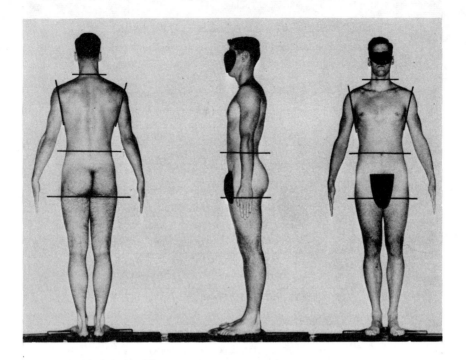

Figure 12B. Illustrating the Trunk Index for Figure 12A.

Call your points marking the bottom of the ribs the BR points. Call the points marking the tops of the iliac crests the TC points.

3. Bisect the distance between the BR and the TC, on both sides of the body, and mark these half way points. You have determined the tentative location of the plane you are seeking, *if* the lateral picture shows the lumbar angle at exactly this same level. This is the Trunk Index plane (TIP).

Lateral Picture

The problem now is to check, and if necessary to correct your tentative TIP. To do this, turn to the lateral picture.

4. Lay your pointer needle at the center of the lumbar angle. If you are working with a pronounced mesomorph this is easy. The long thoracic segment then may extend nearly to the buttocks and results in a low, narrow, lumbar angle. Mesopenes, especially mesopenic women, sometimes present a very wide angle. In such a case the notching of your pointer needle is a bit like notching an arrow on a long bow. Now mark the center of the lumbar angle (CLA).

If CLA is the same level as your previously marked tentative TIP, you have your final TIP. If not, then bisect the difference between these two levels, and draw your division line across all three pictures at that level, which is your final TIP.

Demarkation of the Trunk from the Distal Segments

On each side of the neck, mark the center of the angle formed at the point where the trapezius muscle crosses the sterno-cleido-mastoid. Cut off the head by connecting these two marks. (Frontal or dorsal picture, or both).

On the lateral picture, mark the center of the angle formed by the buttock and the thigh

Table 6

Table S-TI. The 267 Whole Somatotypes (7-Point Scale)
Distributed on Male and Female Stature, and on Trunk Index.

Stature M	F	85	95	105	115	125	135	145	155	165	175	185	195	205
852	789	717		627		537		447		357		267		177
840	778		726		636		546		456		366		276	
828	767			735		645		555		465		375		
816	756				744		654		564		474			
804	744		617		527	753	437	663	347	573	257		167	
792	733		716		626		536	762	446	672	356	266		176
780	722		725		635		545	771	455		365		275	
768	711			734		644		554		464		374		
					517		427		337		247		157	
756	700		616		743		653		563		473		166	
						526		436		346		256		
744	689	715		625	417	752	327	662	237	572	147	265		175
						535		445		355				
732	678			724	516	634	426	761	336	671	246	364	156	274
							317	544	227	454	137			
720	667		615	733	525	643	435	553	345	463	255	373	165	
					416		326		236		146			
							217		127					
708	656	714		624	742	534	652	444	562	354	472	264		174
					515		425		335		245		155	
							316		226		136			
696	644		723		633	751	543	661	453	571	363		273	
				614		524		434	117	344		254		164
					415		325		235		145			
684	633	713		732		642	216	552	126	462		372		173
					623		533		443		353		263	
				514		424		334		244		154		
672	622		722		741	315	651	225	561	135	471		272	
				613		632		542		452		362		163
					523		433		343		253			
660	611	712		731	414	641	324	551	234	461	144	371		172
				622		532		442		352		262		
648	600			721	513	631	423	541	333	451	243	361	153	271
								116						
636	589			612		522		432		342		252		162
								215		125				
624	578	711		621		531		441		351		261		171
							314		224		134			
612	567				413		323		233		143			
600	556			512		422		332		242		152		
588	544			611		521		431	115	341		251		161
576	533						214		124					
564	522				313		223		133					
552	511			412		322		232		142				
540	500			511		421		331		241		151		
Trunk Index		85	95	105	115	125	135	145	155	165	175	185	195	205

Table 7

Distribution of the Possible Combinations of Endomorphy – Mesomorphy
on Trunk Index. Full Matrix of 1713 Somatotypes (13-point scale)
Men and Women.

T. I.

205	1-7
200	1-6½; 1½-7
195	1-6; 1½-6½; 2-7
190	1-5½; 1½-6; 2-6½; 2½-7
185	1-5; 1½-5½; 2-6; 2½-6½; 3-7
180	1-4½; 1½-5; 2-5½; 2½-6; 3-6½; 3½-7
175	1-4; 1½-4½; 2-5; 2½-5½; 3-6; 3½-6½; 4-7
170	1-3½; 1½-4; 2-4½; 2½-5; 3-5½; 3½-6; 4-6½; 4½-7
165	1-3; 1½-3½; 2-4; 2½-4½; 3-5; 3½-5½; 4-6; 4½-6½; 5-7
160	1-2½; 1½-3; 2-3½; 2½-4; 3-4½; 3½-5; 4-5½; 4½-6; 5-6½; 5½-7
155	1-2; 1½-2½; 2-3; 2½-3½; 3-4; 3½-4½; 4-5; 4½-5½; 5-6; 5½-6½; 6-7
150	1-1½; 1½-2; 2-2½; 2½-3; 3-3½; 3½-4; 4-4½; 4½-5; 5-5½; 5½-6; 6-6½; 6½-7
145	1-1; 1½-1½; 2-2; 2½-2½; 3-3; 3½-3½; 4-4; 4½-4½; 5-5; 5½-5½; 6-6; 6½-6½; 7-7
140	1½-1; 2-1½; 2½-2; 3-2½; 3½-3; 4-3½; 4½-4; 5-4½; 5½-5; 6-5½; 6½-6; 7-6½
135	2-1; 2½-1½; 3-2; 3½-2½; 4-3; 4½-3½; 5-4; 5½-4½; 6-5; 6½-5½; 7-6
130	2½-1; 3-1½; 3½-2; 4-2½; 4½-3; 5-3½; 5½-4; 6-4½; 6½-5; 7-5½
125	3-1; 3½-1½; 4-2; 4½-2½; 5-3; 5½-3½; 6-4; 6½-4½; 7-5
120	3½-1; 4-1½; 4½-2; 5-2½; 5½-3; 6-3½; 6½-4; 7-4½
115	4-1; 4½-1½; 5-2; 5½-2½; 6-3; 6½-3½; 7-4
110	4½-1; 5-1½; 5½-2; 6-2½; 6½-3; 7-3½
105	5-1; 5½-1½; 6-2; 6½-2½; 7-3
100	5½-1; 6-1½; 6½-2; 7-2½
95	6-1; 6½-1½; 7-2
90	6½-1; 7-1½
85	7-1

(sub-gluteal fold). Cut off the legs at this exact level, with a continuous line passing through all three pictures.

On the frontal or dorsal picture (or both) mark the center of the external arc formed by the deltoid muscle at the shoulder, right and left. In each instance connect, with a straight line, the resulting mark with the adjacent top of the axillary fold. You have now cut off the arms, and are ready to use the planimeter. The Trunk Index is a fraction; the thoracic area divided by the abdominal area. These areas can be measured equally well on the dorsal or the frontal picture – or on both, then taking the average of the two.

Finally, now, a brief look at one more somatotype. Consider Figure 12 again (now 12 B). For this 22 year-old the three somatotyping parameters are: TI 155, HT 75.3, SPI 12.74 at 21. A glance at Table 7 ("Beginner's Trunk Index Finding Table") tells you that, with TI at 155, his mesomorphy exceeds his endomorphy by one full degree. Now a glance at Table 6 reveals that, at this TI and at height 75.3, he might have an endomorphy – mesomorphy ratio of 3-4, 4-5, or 5-6. A casual *look* at Figure 12 B should suggest 4-5 as the most likely possibility. Turn now to the Basic Tables, page 22, and check the SPI's in the →30 column. There you find an almost perfect fit, for the three parameters, in somatotype 4 5 4½ (40 50 45). SPI 12.70, between ages 20 and 30.

Summary. 1. With standardized somatotyping available, it is almost as easy to record the somatotype correctly as to ignore it. This done, the dysplasias, the andric and gynic levels, the manifest ethnic ingredients, and especially the psychiatric index as shown at the somatotype performance test – are then also almost as easily recorded as ignored. 2. When these constitutional data are ignored, or thrown away, research data in psychiatry may become, let us say, somewhat carelessly expended ammunition.

This paper was supported in part by grants MH 14934 and MH 07292
from the National Institute of Mental Health, and by the New York
State Department of Mental Hygiene.

W. H. Sheldon, M.D., and A. Tenney, Ph.D., Rockland State Hospital, Research Center, Orangeburg, N.Y.

N. D. Lewis, M.D., N. J. Neuropsychiatric Institute, Princeton, N.J.

SOMATOTYPE	T I	HEIGHT (M)	(F)	SPI →20	WEIGHT (M)	(F)	SPI →30	WEIGHT (M)	(F)	SPI →40	WEIGHT (M)	(F)	SPI →50+	WEIGHT (M)	(F)
) 10 50	145	588	544	1440	68	54	1430	70	55	1425	70	56	1425	70	56
) 10 55	145	618	572	1448	78	62	1438	79	63	1435	80	63	1435	80	63
) 10 60	145	648	600	1455	88	70	1445	90	72	1445	90	72	1445	90	72
) 10 65	145	672	622	1465	97	77	1458	98	78	1458	98	78	1458	98	78
) 10 70	145	696	644	1475	105	83	1470	106	84	1470	106	84	1470	106	84
) 15 45	150	582	539	1425	68	54	1413	70	56	1405	71	56	1405	71	56
) 15 50	150	612	567	1433	78	62	1423	80	63	1415	81	64	1415	81	64
) 15 55	150	642	594	1440	89	70	1430	90	72	1425	91	72	1425	91	72
) 15 60	150	666	617	1448	97	77	1438	99	79	1435	100	79	1435	100	79
) 15 65	150	690	639	1458	106	84	1448	108	86	1448	108	86	1448	108	86
) 15 70	150	708	656	1468	112	89	1460	114	91	1460	114	91	1460	114	91
) 20 40	155	576	533	1410	68	54	1395	70	56	1385	72	57	1385	72	57
) 20 45	155	606	561	1418	78	62	1405	80	64	1395	82	65	1395	82	65
) 20 50	155	636	589	1425	89	71	1415	91	72	1405	93	74	1405	93	74
) 20 55	155	660	611	1433	98	78	1423	100	79	1415	101	81	1415	101	81
) 20 60	155	684	633	1440	107	85	1430	109	87	1425	111	88	1425	111	88
) 20 65	155	702	650	1450	113	90	1440	116	92	1438	116	92	1438	116	92
) 20 70	155	720	667	1460	120	95	1450	122	97	1450	122	97	1450	122	97
) 25 35	160	570	528	1393	69	54	1378	71	56	1368	72	57	1368	72	57
) 25 40	160	600	556	1400	79	63	1385	81	65	1375	83	66	1375	83	66
) 25 45	160	630	583	1408	90	71	1395	92	73	1385	94	75	1385	94	75
) 25 50	160	654	606	1415	99	79	1405	101	80	1395	103	82	1395	103	82
) 25 55	160	678	628	1423	108	86	1413	110	88	1405	112	89	1405	112	89
) 25 60	160	696	644	1430	115	91	1420	118	93	1415	119	94	1415	119	94
) 25 65	160	714	661	1440	122	97	1430	124	99	1428	125	99	1428	125	99
) 25 70	160	726	672	1450	126	100	1440	128	102	1440	128	102	1440	128	102
) 30 30	165	564	522	1375	69	55	1360	71	57	1350	73	58	1350	73	58
) 30 35	165	594	550	1383	79	63	1368	82	65	1358	84	66	1358	84	66
) 30 40	165	624	578	1390	90	72	1375	93	74	1365	96	76	1365	96	76
) 30 45	165	648	600	1398	100	79	1385	102	81	1375	105	83	1375	105	83
) 30 50	165	672	622	1405	109	87	1395	112	89	1385	114	91	1385	114	91
) 30 55	165	690	639	1413	116	92	1403	119	94	1395	121	96	1395	121	96
) 30 60	165	708	656	1420	124	99	1410	127	101	1405	128	102	1405	128	102
) 30 65	165	720	667	1430	128	101	1420	130	104	1418	131	104	1418	131	104
) 30 70	165	732	678	1440	131	104	1430	134	107	1430	134	107	1430	134	107
) 35 25	170	558	517	1358	69	55	1340	72	57	1330	74	59	1330	74	59
) 35 30	170	588	544	1365	80	63	1350	83	65	1340	84	67	1340	84	67
) 35 35	170	618	572	1373	91	72	1358	94	75	1348	96	76	1348	96	76
) 35 40	170	642	594	1383	100	79	1368	103	82	1358	106	84	1358	106	84
) 35 45	170	666	617	1390	110	87	1375	114	90	1365	116	92	1365	116	92
) 35 50	170	684	633	1398	117	93	1385	120	95	1375	123	98	1375	123	98
) 35 55	170	702	650	1405	125	99	1393	128	102	1385	130	103	1385	130	103
) 35 60	170	714	661	1413	129	102	1400	133	105	1395	134	106	1395	134	106
) 35 65	170	726	672	1423	133	105	1410	137	108	1405	138	109	1405	138	109

SOMATOTYPE	T I	HEIGHT (M)	HEIGHT (F)	SPI →20	WEIGHT (M)	WEIGHT (F)	SPI →30	WEIGHT (M)	WEIGHT (F)	SPI →40	WEIGHT (M)	WEIGHT (F)	SPI →50+	WEIGHT (M)	WEIGHT (F)
10 35 70	170	738	683	1433	137	108	1420	140	111	1405	145	115	1405	145	115
10 40 20	175	552	511	1340	70	55	1320	73	58	1310	75	59	1310	75	59
10 40 25	175	582	539	1348	80	64	1330	84	67	1320	86	68	1320	86	68
10 40 30	175	612	567	1355	92	73	1340	95	76	1330	97	77	1330	97	77
10 40 35	175	636	589	1365	101	80	1350	105	83	1340	107	85	1340	107	85
10 40 40	175	660	611	1375	111	88	1360	114	91	1350	117	93	1350	117	93
10 40 45	175	678	628	1383	118	94	1368	122	97	1358	124	99	1358	124	99
10 40 50	175	696	644	1390	126	99	1375	130	103	1365	133	105	1365	133	105
10 40 55	175	708	656	1398	130	103	1383	134	107	1375	137	109	1375	137	109
10 40 60	175	720	667	1405	135	107	1390	139	110	1385	140	112	1385	140	112
10 40 65	175	732	678	1415	138	110	1400	143	114	1395	144	115	1395	144	115
10 40 70	175	744	689	1425	142	113	1410	147	117	1405	148	118	1405	148	118
10 45 15	180	546	506	1323	70	56	1300	74	59	1288	76	61	1285	77	61
10 45 20	180	576	533	1333	81	64	1310	85	67	1300	87	69	1298	87	69
10 45 25	180	606	561	1340	92	73	1320	97	77	1310	99	79	1308	99	79
10 45 30	180	630	583	1348	102	81	1330	106	84	1320	109	86	1318	109	87
10 45 35	180	654	606	1355	112	89	1340	116	92	1330	119	95	1328	119	95
10 45 40	180	672	622	1365	119	95	1350	123	98	1340	126	100	1338	127	100
10 45 45	180	690	639	1373	127	101	1358	131	104	1348	134	107	1345	135	107
10 45 50	180	702	650	1380	132	104	1365	136	108	1355	139	110	1355	139	110
10 45 55	180	714	661	1388	136	108	1373	141	112	1365	143	114	1363	144	114
10 45 60	180	726	672	1398	140	111	1383	145	115	1375	147	117	1373	148	117
10 45 65	180	738	683	1405	145	115	1393	149	118	1385	151	120	1383	152	120
10 45 70	180	756	700	1415	153	121	1403	156	124	1395	159	126	1395	159	126
10 50 10	185	540	500	1305	71	56	1280	75	60	1265	78	62	1260	79	62
10 50 15	185	570	528	1315	81	65	1290	86	69	1278	89	71	1273	90	71
10 50 20	185	600	556	1325	93	74	1300	98	78	1290	101	80	1285	102	81
10 50 25	185	624	578	1333	103	82	1310	108	86	1300	111	88	1295	112	89
10 50 30	185	648	600	1340	113	90	1320	118	94	1310	121	96	1305	122	97
10 50 35	185	666	617	1348	121	96	1330	126	100	1320	128	102	1315	130	103
10 50 40	185	684	633	1355	129	102	1340	133	105	1330	136	108	1325	138	109
10 50 45	185	696	644	1363	133	105	1348	138	109	1338	141	112	1335	142	112
10 50 50	185	708	656	1370	138	110	1355	143	113	1345	146	116	1343	147	117
10 50 55	185	720	667	1380	142	113	1365	147	117	1355	150	119	1353	151	120
10 50 60	185	732	678	1390	146	116	1375	151	120	1365	154	123	1363	155	123
10 50 65	185	750	694	1398	154	122	1385	159	126	1375	162	129	1373	163	129
10 50 70	185	768	711	1405	163	130	1395	167	132	1385	171	135	1385	171	135
10 55 10	190	564	522	1295	83	65	1268	88	70	1250	92	73	1243	93	74
10 55 15	190	594	550	1305	94	75	1278	100	80	1263	104	83	1255	106	84
10 55 20	190	618	572	1315	104	82	1290	110	87	1275	114	90	1268	116	92
10 55 25	190	642	594	1323	114	91	1300	120	95	1285	125	99	1278	127	100
10 55 30	190	660	611	1333	121	96	1310	128	101	1298	131	104	1290	134	106
10 55 35	190	678	628	1340	130	103	1320	136	108	1308	139	111	1300	142	113
10 55 40	190	690	639	1348	134	107	1330	140	111	1320	143	113	1313	145	115
10 55 45	190	702	650	1355	139	110	1338	144	115	1328	148	117	1323	149	119
10 55 50	190	714	661	1363	144	114	1345	150	119	1335	153	121	1330	155	123

SOMATOTYPE	T I	HEIGHT (M)	HEIGHT (F)	SPI →20	WEIGHT (M)	WEIGHT (F)	SPI →30	WEIGHT (M)	WEIGHT (F)	SPI →40	WEIGHT (M)	WEIGHT (F)	SPI →50+	WEIGHT (M)	WEIGHT (F)
					SPI WITH MAXIMAL WEIGHTS AT PROGESSIVE AGES										
10 55 55	190	726	672	1370	149	118	1355	154	122	1345	157	125	1340	159	126
10 55 60	190	744	689	1380	157	124	1365	162	129	1355	166	131	1350	167	133
10 55 65	190	762	706	1388	165	132	1375	170	135	1365	174	138	1360	176	140
10 55 70	190	786	728	1398	178	141	1385	183	145	1375	187	148	1373	188	149
10 60 10	195	588	544	1285	96	76	1255	103	81	1235	108	85	1225	111	88
10 60 15	195	612	567	1295	106	84	1268	112	89	1248	118	94	1238	121	96
10 60 20	195	636	589	1305	116	92	1280	123	97	1260	129	102	1250	132	105
10 60 25	195	654	606	1315	123	98	1290	130	104	1273	136	108	1263	139	110
10 60 30	195	672	622	1325	130	103	1300	138	110	1285	143	113	1275	146	116
10 60 35	195	684	633	1333	135	107	1310	142	113	1298	146	116	1288	150	119
10 60 40	195	696	644	1340	140	111	1320	147	116	1310	150	119	1300	153	122
10 60 45	195	708	656	1348	145	115	1328	152	121	1318	155	123	1310	158	126
10 60 50	195	720	667	1355	150	119	1335	157	125	1325	160	128	1320	162	129
10 60 55	195	738	683	1363	159	126	1345	165	131	1335	169	134	1330	171	135
10 60 60	195	756	700	1370	168	133	1355	174	138	1345	178	141	1340	180	143
10 60 65	195	780	722	1380	181	143	1365	187	148	1355	191	151	1350	193	153
10 60 70	195	804	744	1390	194	153	1375	200	158	1365	204	162	1360	207	164
10 65 10	200	606	561	1275	107	85	1243	116	92	1223	122	97	1213	125	99
10 65 15	200	630	583	1285	118	93	1255	126	100	1235	133	105	1225	136	108
10 65 20	200	648	600	1295	125	99	1268	133	106	1248	140	111	1238	143	114
10 65 25	200	666	617	1305	133	106	1278	142	113	1260	148	117	1250	151	120
10 65 30	200	678	628	1315	137	109	1288	146	116	1273	151	120	1263	155	123
10 65 35	200	690	639	1323	142	113	1298	150	119	1285	155	123	1275	158	126
10 65 40	200	702	650	1330	147	117	1308	155	123	1298	158	126	1288	162	129
10 65 45	200	714	661	1338	152	121	1315	160	127	1305	164	130	1298	166	132
10 65 50	200	732	678	1348	160	127	1325	169	134	1315	172	137	1310	174	139
10 65 55	200	750	694	1355	170	134	1335	177	140	1325	181	144	1320	183	145
10 65 60	200	774	717	1363	183	146	1345	191	151	1335	195	155	1330	197	157
10 65 65	200	798	739	1370	198	157	1355	204	162	1345	209	166	1340	211	168
10 65 70	200	828	767	1380	216	172	1365	223	177	1355	228	181	1350	231	183
10 70 10	205	624	578	1265	120	95	1230	131	104	1210	137	109	1200	141	112
10 70 15	205	642	594	1275	128	101	1243	138	109	1223	145	115	1213	148	117
10 70 20	205	660	611	1285	135	108	1255	145	115	1235	153	121	1225	156	124
10 70 25	205	672	622	1295	140	111	1265	150	119	1248	156	124	1238	160	127
10 70 30	205	684	633	1305	144	114	1275	154	122	1260	160	127	1250	164	130
10 70 35	205	696	644	1313	149	118	1285	159	126	1273	163	129	1263	167	133
10 70 40	205	708	656	1320	154	123	1295	163	130	1285	167	133	1275	171	136
10 70 45	205	726	672	1330	163	129	1305	172	137	1295	176	140	1288	179	142
10 70 50	205	744	689	1340	171	136	1315	181	144	1305	185	147	1300	187	149
10 70 55	205	768	711	1348	185	147	1325	195	155	1315	199	158	1310	201	160
10 70 60	205	792	733	1355	200	158	1335	209	166	1325	214	169	1320	216	171
10 70 65	205	822	761	1363	219	174	1345	228	181	1335	233	185	1330	236	187
10 70 70	205	852	789	1370	241	191	1355	249	197	1345	254	202	1340	257	204
15 10 45	140	582	539	1423	68	54	1408	71	56	1400	72	57	1400	72	57
15 10 50	140	612	567	1430	78	62	1418	80	64	1410	82	65	1410	82	65

SOMATOTYPE	T	I	HEIGHT (M)	HEIGHT (F)	SPI →20	WEIGHT (M)	WEIGHT (F)	SPI →30	WEIGHT (M)	WEIGHT (F)	SPI →40	WEIGHT (M)	WEIGHT (F)	SPI →50+	WEIGHT (M)	WEIGHT (F)
15 10 55	140	642	594	1438	89	70	1425	91	72	1420	92	73	1420	92	73	
15 10 60	140	666	617	1445	98	78	1433	100	80	1430	101	80	1430	101	80	
15 10 65	140	690	639	1455	107	85	1443	109	87	1440	110	87	1440	110	87	
15 10 70	140	708	656	1465	113	90	1455	115	92	1453	116	92	1453	116	92	
15 15 40	145	576	533	1408	68	54	1390	71	56	1380	73	58	1380	73	58	
15 15 45	145	606	561	1415	79	62	1400	81	64	1390	83	66	1390	83	66	
15 15 50	145	636	589	1423	89	71	1408	92	73	1400	94	74	1400	94	74	
15 15 55	145	660	611	1430	98	78	1418	101	80	1410	103	81	1410	103	81	
15 15 60	145	684	633	1438	108	85	1425	111	88	1420	112	89	1420	112	89	
15 15 65	145	702	650	1448	114	90	1435	117	93	1430	118	94	1430	118	94	
15 15 70	145	720	667	1458	120	96	1445	124	98	1443	124	99	1443	124	99	
15 20 35	150	570	528	1390	69	55	1373	72	57	1363	73	58	1358	74	59	
15 20 40	150	600	556	1400	79	63	1383	82	65	1373	83	66	1368	84	67	
15 20 45	150	630	583	1408	90	71	1390	93	74	1380	95	75	1378	96	76	
15 20 50	150	654	606	1415	99	79	1400	102	81	1390	104	83	1390	104	83	
15 20 55	150	678	628	1423	108	86	1408	112	89	1400	114	90	1400	114	90	
15 20 60	150	696	644	1430	115	91	1418	118	94	1410	120	95	1410	120	95	
15 20 65	150	714	661	1440	122	97	1428	125	99	1420	127	101	1420	127	101	
15 20 70	150	726	672	1450	126	100	1438	129	102	1433	130	103	1433	130	103	
15 25 30	155	564	522	1373	69	55	1355	72	57	1345	74	58	1340	75	59	
15 25 35	155	594	550	1383	79	63	1365	82	65	1353	85	67	1348	86	68	
15 25 40	155	624	578	1390	90	72	1373	94	75	1360	97	77	1358	97	77	
15 25 45	155	648	600	1398	100	79	1380	104	82	1370	106	84	1368	106	84	
15 25 50	155	672	622	1405	109	87	1390	113	90	1380	115	92	1378	116	92	
15 25 55	155	690	639	1413	116	92	1398	120	95	1390	122	97	1388	123	98	
15 25 60	155	708	656	1420	124	99	1408	127	101	1400	129	103	1398	130	103	
15 25 65	155	720	667	1430	128	101	1418	131	104	1410	133	106	1410	133	106	
15 25 70	155	732	678	1440	131	104	1428	135	107	1423	136	108	1423	136	108	
15 30 25	160	558	517	1355	70	56	1338	73	58	1325	75	59	1320	76	6C
15 30 30	160	588	544	1365	80	63	1348	83	66	1335	85	68	1330	86	6?
15 30 35	160	618	572	1373	91	72	1355	95	75	1343	97	77	1338	99	7?
15 30 40	160	642	594	1380	101	80	1363	105	83	1350	108	85	1348	108	8?
15 30 45	160	666	617	1388	110	88	1370	115	91	1360	117	93	1358	118	9?
15 30 50	160	684	633	1395	118	93	1380	122	97	1370	124	99	1368	125	9?
15 30 55	160	702	650	1403	125	99	1388	129	103	1380	132	104	1378	132	10?
15 30 60	160	714	661	1413	129	102	1398	133	106	1390	136	108	1388	136	10?
15 30 65	160	726	672	1420	134	106	1408	137	109	1400	139	111	1400	139	11?
15 30 70	160	738	683	1430	137	109	1418	141	112	1413	142	113	1413	142	11?
15 35 20	165	552	511	1338	70	56	1318	73	58	1305	76	60	1300	77	6?
15 35 25	165	582	539	1348	80	64	1328	84	67	1315	87	69	1310	88	7?
15 35 30	165	612	567	1355	92	73	1338	96	76	1323	99	79	1320	100	7?
15 35 35	165	630	583	1363	99	78	1345	103	81	1333	106	84	1330	106	8?
15 35 40	165	660	611	1373	111	88	1355	116	92	1340	119	95	1338	120	9?
15 35 45	165	678	628	1380	119	94	1363	123	98	1350	127	101	1348	127	10?
15 35 50	165	696	644	1388	126	100	1370	131	104	1360	134	106	1358	135	10?

ATOTYPE	T I	HEIGHT (M)	(F)	SPI →20	WEIGHT (M)	(F)	SPI →30	WEIGHT (M)	(F)	SPI →40	WEIGHT (M)	(F)	SPI →50+	WEIGHT (M)	(F)
35 55	165	708	656	1395	131	104	1380	135	107	1370	138	110	1368	139	110
35 60	165	720	667	1405	135	107	1388	140	111	1380	142	113	1378	143	113
35 65	165	732	678	1413	139	110	1398	144	114	1393	145	115	1390	146	116
35 70	165	744	689	1423	143	114	1408	148	117	1403	149	118	1400	150	119
40 15	170	546	506	1323	70	56	1298	74	59	1283	77	61	1275	79	63
40 20	170	576	533	1330	81	64	1308	85	68	1293	88	70	1288	89	71
40 25	170	606	561	1338	93	74	1318	97	77	1303	101	80	1298	102	81
40 30	170	630	583	1345	103	81	1328	107	85	1313	110	88	1310	111	88
40 35	170	654	606	1355	112	89	1338	117	93	1323	121	96	1320	122	97
40 40	170	672	622	1365	119	95	1348	124	98	1333	128	102	1330	129	102
40 45	170	690	639	1373	127	101	1355	132	105	1340	137	108	1338	137	109
40 50	170	702	650	1380	132	104	1363	137	108	1350	141	112	1348	141	112
40 55	170	714	661	1388	136	108	1370	142	112	1360	145	115	1358	145	115
40 60	170	726	672	1395	141	112	1380	146	115	1373	148	117	1370	149	118
40 65	170	738	683	1405	145	115	1390	150	119	1383	152	120	1380	153	121
40 70	170	756	700	1415	153	121	1400	157	125	1393	160	127	1390	161	128
45 10	175	540	500	1305	71	56	1278	75	60	1260	79	62	1250	81	64
45 15	175	570	528	1313	82	65	1288	87	69	1270	90	72	1263	92	73
45 20	175	600	556	1323	93	74	1298	99	79	1283	102	81	1275	104	83
45 25	175	624	578	1330	103	82	1308	109	86	1293	112	89	1285	115	91
45 30	175	648	600	1338	114	90	1318	119	94	1303	123	98	1295	125	99
45 35	175	666	617	1345	121	97	1328	126	100	1313	131	104	1308	132	105
45 40	175	684	633	1355	129	102	1335	135	107	1323	138	110	1318	140	111
45 45	175	696	644	1363	133	105	1345	139	110	1330	143	114	1328	144	114
45 50	175	708	656	1370	138	110	1353	143	114	1340	147	117	1338	148	118
45 55	175	720	667	1380	142	113	1363	147	117	1350	152	121	1348	152	121
45 60	175	732	678	1388	147	117	1370	153	121	1360	156	124	1358	157	124
45 65	175	750	694	1398	154	122	1380	161	127	1373	163	129	1370	164	130
45 70	175	768	711	1405	163	130	1390	169	134	1383	171	136	1380	172	137
50 10	180	564	522	1295	83	65	1265	89	70	1248	92	73	1238	95	75
50 15	180	594	550	1305	94	75	1275	101	80	1260	105	83	1250	107	85
50 20	180	618	572	1315	104	82	1288	110	88	1273	114	91	1263	117	93
50 25	180	642	594	1323	114	91	1298	121	96	1283	125	99	1273	128	102
50 30	180	660	611	1330	122	97	1308	128	102	1293	133	106	1283	136	108
50 35	180	678	628	1338	130	103	1315	137	109	1303	141	112	1293	144	115
50 40	180	690	639	1345	135	107	1325	141	112	1313	145	115	1305	148	117
50 45	180	702	650	1353	140	111	1333	146	116	1320	150	119	1315	152	121
50 50	180	714	661	1363	144	114	1343	150	119	1330	155	123	1325	156	124
50 55	180	726	672	1370	149	118	1353	154	123	1340	159	126	1335	161	128
50 60	180	744	689	1380	157	124	1363	163	129	1350	167	133	1345	169	134
50 65	180	762	706	1388	165	132	1373	171	136	1360	176	140	1355	178	141
50 70	180	786	728	1398	178	141	1383	184	146	1373	188	149	1368	190	151
55 10	185	588	544	1285	96	76	1253	103	82	1233	108	86	1220	112	89
55 15	185	612	567	1295	106	84	1265	113	90	1245	119	94	1233	122	97
55 20	185	636	589	1305	116	92	1275	124	99	1258	129	103	1245	133	106
55 25	185	654	606	1313	124	98	1285	132	105	1268	137	109	1255	142	113

SPI WITH MAXIMAL WEIGHTS AT PROGESSIVE AGES

SOMATOTYPE	T	I	HEIGHT (M)	(F)	SPI →20	WEIGHT (M)	(F)	SPI →30	WEIGHT (M)	(F)	SPI →40	WEIGHT (M)	(F)	SPI →50+	WEIGH (M)	(F)
15 55 30	185	672	622	1323	131	104	1295	140	111	1280	145	115	1268	149	1	
15 55 35	185	684	633	1330	136	108	1305	144	114	1290	149	118	1280	153	1	
15 55 40	185	696	644	1338	141	112	1315	148	117	1303	152	121	1293	156	1	
15 55 45	185	708	656	1345	146	116	1325	153	121	1310	158	126	1303	160	1	
15 55 50	185	720	667	1355	150	119	1333	158	125	1320	162	129	1315	164	1	
15 55 55	185	738	683	1363	159	126	1343	166	132	1330	171	135	1325	173	1	
15 55 60	185	756	700	1370	168	133	1353	174	138	1340	180	143	1335	182	14	
15 55 65	185	780	722	1380	181	143	1363	187	149	1350	193	153	1345	195	15	
15 55 70	185	804	744	1390	194	153	1373	201	159	1360	207	164	1355	209	16	
15 60 10	190	606	561	1275	107	85	1240	117	93	1218	123	98	1205	127	10	
15 60 15	190	630	583	1285	118	93	1253	127	101	1230	134	106	1218	138	1	
15 60 20	190	648	600	1295	125	99	1265	134	107	1243	142	112	1230	146	1	
15 60 25	190	666	617	1305	133	106	1275	143	113	1255	149	119	1243	154	12	
15 60 30	190	678	628	1315	137	109	1285	147	117	1268	153	121	1255	158	12	
15 60 35	190	690	639	1323	142	113	1295	151	120	1280	157	124	1268	161	12	
15 60 40	190	702	650	1330	147	117	1308	155	123	1293	160	127	1280	165	13	
15 60 45	190	714	661	1338	152	121	1315	160	127	1300	166	131	1290	170	13	
15 60 50	190	732	678	1348	160	127	1325	169	134	1310	174	139	1303	177	14	
15 60 55	190	750	694	1355	170	134	1335	177	140	1320	183	145	1313	186	14	
15 60 60	190	774	717	1363	183	146	1345	191	151	1330	197	157	1323	200	15	
15 60 65	190	798	739	1370	198	157	1353	205	163	1340	211	168	1333	215	17	
15 60 70	190	829	767	1380	216	172	1363	224	178	1350	231	183	1343	234	18	
15 65 10	195	624	578	1265	120	95	1225	132	105	1203	140	111	1190	144	11	
15 65 15	195	642	594	1275	128	101	1238	139	110	1215	148	117	1203	152	12	
15 65 20	195	660	611	1285	135	108	1250	147	117	1228	155	123	1215	160	12	
15 65 25	195	672	622	1295	140	111	1263	151	119	1243	158	125	1230	163	12	
15 65 30	195	684	633	1305	144	114	1273	155	123	1255	162	128	1243	167	13	
15 65 35	195	696	644	1313	149	118	1283	160	126	1268	165	131	1255	171	13	
15 65 40	195	708	656	1320	154	123	1295	163	130	1280	169	135	1268	174	13	
15 65 45	195	726	672	1330	163	129	1305	172	137	1290	178	141	1280	182	14	
15 65 50	195	744	689	1340	171	136	1313	182	144	1298	188	150	1290	192	15	
15 65 55	195	768	711	1348	185	147	1323	196	155	1308	202	161	1300	206	16	
15 65 60	195	792	733	1355	200	158	1333	210	166	1318	217	172	1310	221	17	
15 65 65	195	822	761	1363	219	174	1343	229	182	1330	236	187	1323	240	19	
15 65 70	195	852	789	1370	241	191	1353	250	198	1340	257	204	1333	261	20	
15 70 10	200	636	589	1255	130	103	1213	144	114	1190	153	121	1178	157	12	
15 70 15	200	654	606	1265	138	110	1225	152	121	1203	161	128	1190	166	13	
15 70 20	200	666	617	1275	143	113	1238	156	124	1215	165	131	1203	170	13	
15 70 25	200	678	628	1285	147	117	1248	160	127	1228	168	134	1215	174	13	
15 70 30	200	690	639	1295	151	120	1260	164	130	1243	171	136	1230	177	14	
15 70 35	200	702	650	1303	156	124	1270	169	134	1255	175	139	1243	180	14	
15 70 40	200	720	667	1310	166	132	1283	177	141	1268	183	146	1255	189	15	
15 70 45	200	738	683	1320	175	139	1293	186	147	1278	193	153	1265	199	15	
15 70 50	200	762	706	1330	188	150	1303	200	159	1288	207	165	1278	212	16	
15 70 55	200	786	728	1338	203	161	1313	215	170	1298	222	176	1288	227	18	
15 70 60	200	816	756	1348	222	176	1323	235	187	1308	243	193	1300	247	19	
15 70 65	200	846	783	1355	243	193	1333	256	203	1318	264	210	1310	269	21	

SPI WITH MAXIMAL WEIGHTS AT PROGESSIVE AGES

SOMATOTYPE	T	I	HEIGHT (M)	HEIGHT (F)	SPI →20	WEIGHT (M)	WEIGHT (F)	SPI →30	WEIGHT (M)	WEIGHT (F)	SPI →40	WEIGHT (M)	WEIGHT (F)	SPI →50+	WEIGHT (M)	WEIGHT (F)
20 10 40	135	576	533		1405	69	55	1385	72	57	1375	74	58	1375	74	58
20 10 45	135	606	561		1413	79	63	1395	82	65	1385	84	66	1385	84	66
20 10 50	135	636	589		1420	90	71	1405	93	74	1395	95	75	1395	95	75
20 10 55	135	660	611		1428	99	78	1413	102	81	1405	104	82	1405	104	82
20 10 60	135	684	633		1435	108	86	1420	112	89	1415	113	90	1415	113	90
20 10 65	135	702	650		1445	115	91	1430	118	94	1425	120	95	1425	120	95
20 10 70	135	720	667		1455	121	96	1440	125	99	1435	126	100	1435	126	100
20 15 35	140	570	528		1388	69	55	1368	72	57	1358	74	59	1353	75	59
20 15 40	140	600	556		1398	79	63	1378	83	66	1368	84	67	1363	85	68
20 15 45	140	630	583		1405	90	71	1385	94	75	1375	96	76	1373	97	77
20 15 50	140	654	606		1413	99	79	1395	103	82	1385	105	84	1385	105	84
20 15 55	140	678	628		1420	109	86	1403	113	90	1395	115	91	1395	115	91
20 15 60	140	696	644		1428	116	92	1413	120	95	1405	122	96	1405	122	96
20 15 65	140	714	661		1438	122	97	1423	126	100	1415	128	102	1415	128	102
20 15 70	140	726	672		1448	126	100	1433	130	103	1425	132	105	1425	132	105
20 20 30	145	564	522		1370	70	55	1350	73	58	1340	75	59	1330	76	60
20 20 35	145	594	550		1380	80	63	1360	83	66	1350	85	68	1340	87	69
20 20 40	145	624	578		1390	90	72	1370	94	75	1360	97	77	1350	99	78
20 20 45	145	648	600		1398	100	79	1378	104	83	1368	106	84	1363	107	85
20 20 50	145	672	622		1405	109	87	1385	114	91	1375	117	93	1375	117	93
20 20 55	145	690	639		1413	116	92	1395	121	96	1385	124	98	1385	124	98
20 20 60	145	708	656		1420	124	99	1405	128	102	1395	131	104	1395	131	104
20 20 65	145	720	667		1430	128	101	1415	132	105	1405	135	107	1405	135	107
20 20 70	145	732	678		1440	131	104	1425	136	108	1415	138	110	1415	138	110
20 25 25	150	558	517		1353	70	56	1333	73	58	1320	76	60	1310	77	61
20 25 30	150	588	544		1363	80	64	1343	84	66	1330	86	68	1320	88	70
20 25 35	150	618	572		1370	92	73	1350	96	76	1338	99	78	1330	100	80
20 25 40	150	642	594		1380	101	80	1360	105	83	1348	108	86	1340	110	87
20 25 45	150	666	617		1388	110	88	1368	115	92	1355	119	94	1350	120	95
20 25 50	150	684	633		1395	118	93	1375	123	98	1365	126	100	1363	126	100
20 25 55	150	702	650		1403	125	99	1385	130	103	1375	133	106	1373	134	106
20 25 60	150	714	661		1413	129	102	1395	134	106	1385	137	109	1383	138	109
20 25 65	150	726	672		1420	134	106	1405	138	109	1395	141	112	1393	142	112
20 25 70	150	738	683		1430	137	109	1415	142	112	1405	145	115	1405	145	115
20 30 20	155	552	511		1335	71	56	1315	74	59	1300	77	61	1290	78	62
20 30 25	155	582	539		1345	81	64	1325	85	67	1310	88	70	1300	90	71
20 30 30	155	612	567		1355	92	73	1335	96	77	1320	100	79	1310	102	81
20 30 35	155	636	589		1363	102	81	1343	106	84	1328	110	87	1320	112	89
20 30 40	155	660	611		1370	112	89	1350	117	93	1335	121	96	1330	122	97
20 30 45	155	678	628		1378	119	95	1358	124	99	1345	128	102	1340	130	103
20 30 50	155	696	644		1385	127	101	1365	133	105	1355	136	107	1350	137	109
20 30 55	155	708	656		1395	131	104	1375	137	109	1365	140	111	1360	141	112
20 30 60	155	720	667		1405	135	107	1385	140	112	1375	144	114	1370	145	115
20 30 65	155	732	678		1413	139	110	1395	144	115	1385	148	117	1383	148	118

SOMATOTYPE	T I	HEIGHT (M)	HEIGHT (F)	SPI →20	WEIGHT (M)	WEIGHT (F)	SPI →30	WEIGHT (M)	WEIGHT (F)	SPI →40	WEIGHT (M)	WEIGHT (F)	SPI →50+	WEIGHT (M)	WEIGHT (F)
20 30 70	155	744	689	1420	144	114	1405	148	118	1395	152	120	1395	152	120
20 35 15	160	546	506	1320	71	56	1295	75	60	1278	78	62	1265	80	64
20 35 20	160	576	533	1328	82	65	1305	86	68	1288	89	71	1278	92	73
20 35 25	160	606	561	1335	94	74	1315	98	78	1298	102	81	1288	104	83
20 35 30	160	630	583	1345	103	81	1325	107	85	1308	112	89	1300	114	90
20 35 35	160	654	606	1353	113	90	1333	118	94	1315	123	98	1310	124	99
20 35 40	160	672	622	1363	120	95	1343	125	99	1325	130	103	1320	132	105
20 35 45	160	690	639	1370	128	101	1350	134	106	1335	138	110	1330	140	111
20 35 50	160	702	650	1378	132	105	1358	138	110	1345	142	113	1340	144	114
20 35 55	160	714	661	1385	137	109	1368	142	113	1355	146	116	1350	148	117
20 35 60	160	726	672	1395	141	112	1378	146	116	1368	149	119	1363	151	120
20 35 65	160	738	683	1403	146	115	1388	150	119	1378	154	122	1373	155	123
20 35 70	160	756	700	1413	153	122	1398	158	126	1388	162	128	1383	163	130
20 40 10	165	540	500	1305	71	56	1275	76	60	1255	80	63	1240	83	66
20 40 15	165	570	528	1313	82	65	1285	87	69	1265	91	73	1253	94	75
20 40 20	165	600	556	1320	94	75	1295	99	79	1275	104	83	1265	107	85
20 40 25	165	624	578	1328	104	82	1305	109	87	1285	115	91	1278	116	93
20 40 30	165	648	600	1335	114	91	1315	120	95	1295	125	99	1290	127	101
20 40 35	165	666	617	1345	121	97	1325	127	101	1305	133	106	1300	134	107
20 40 40	165	684	633	1355	129	102	1335	135	107	1315	141	112	1310	142	113
20 40 45	165	696	644	1363	133	105	1343	139	110	1325	145	115	1320	147	116
20 40 50	165	708	656	1370	138	110	1350	144	115	1335	149	119	1330	151	120
20 40 55	165	720	667	1378	143	113	1360	148	118	1348	152	121	1343	154	123
20 40 60	165	732	678	1385	148	117	1370	153	121	1360	156	124	1355	158	125
20 40 65	165	750	694	1395	155	123	1380	161	127	1370	164	130	1365	166	131
20 40 70	165	768	711	1405	163	130	1390	169	134	1380	172	137	1375	174	138
20 45 10	170	564	522	1295	83	65	1263	89	71	1243	93	74	1228	97	77
20 45 15	170	594	550	1303	95	75	1273	102	81	1253	107	85	1240	110	87
20 45 20	170	618	572	1313	104	83	1285	111	88	1265	117	92	1253	120	95
20 45 25	170	642	594	1320	115	91	1295	122	97	1275	128	101	1263	131	104
20 45 30	170	660	611	1328	123	97	1305	129	103	1285	135	108	1275	139	110
20 45 35	170	678	628	1335	131	104	1313	138	109	1295	144	114	1285	147	117
20 45 40	170	690	639	1345	135	107	1323	142	113	1305	148	117	1298	150	119
20 45 45	170	702	650	1353	140	111	1330	147	117	1315	152	121	1308	155	123
20 45 50	170	714	661	1363	144	114	1340	151	120	1325	156	124	1320	158	126
20 45 55	170	726	672	1370	149	118	1350	156	123	1335	161	128	1330	163	129
20 45 60	170	744	689	1378	157	125	1360	164	130	1348	168	134	1343	170	135
20 45 65	170	762	706	1388	165	132	1370	172	137	1358	177	141	1353	179	142
20 45 70	170	786	728	1398	178	141	1380	185	147	1370	189	150	1365	191	152
20 50 10	175	588	544	1285	96	76	1250	104	82	1230	109	87	1215	113	90
20 50 15	175	612	567	1295	106	84	1263	114	90	1243	119	95	1228	124	98
20 50 20	175	636	589	1305	116	92	1275	124	99	1255	130	103	1240	135	107
20 50 25	175	654	606	1313	124	98	1285	132	105	1265	138	110	1250	143	114
20 50 30	175	672	622	1320	132	105	1295	140	111	1275	146	116	1260	152	120
20 50 35	175	684	633	1328	137	108	1302	145	115	1285	151	120	1273	155	123
20 50 40	175	696	644	1335	142	112	1310	150	119	1295	155	123	1285	159	126

SOMATOTYPE	T	I	HEIGHT (M)	HEIGHT (F)	SPI →20	WEIGHT (M)	WEIGHT (F)	SPI →30	WEIGHT (M)	WEIGHT (F)	SPI →40	WEIGHT (M)	WEIGHT (F)	SPI →50+	WEIGHT (M)	WEIGHT (F)
20 50 45	175	708	656	1345	146	116	1320	154	123	1305	160	127	1298	162	129		
20 50 50	175	720	667	1355	150	119	1330	159	126	1315	164	130	1310	166	132		
20 50 55	175	738	683	1363	159	126	1340	167	132	1325	173	137	1320	175	139		
20 50 60	175	756	700	1370	168	133	1350	176	139	1335	182	144	1330	184	146		
20 50 65	175	780	722	1380	181	143	1360	189	150	1348	194	154	1343	196	155		
20 50 70	175	804	744	1390	194	153	1370	202	160	1360	207	164	1355	209	166		
20 55 10	180	606	561	1275	107	85	1238	117	93	1215	124	98	1200	129	102		
20 55 15	180	630	583	1285	118	93	1250	128	101	1228	135	107	1213	140	111		
20 55 20	180	648	600	1295	125	99	1263	135	107	1240	143	113	1225	148	118		
20 55 25	180	666	617	1303	134	106	1273	143	114	1250	151	120	1235	157	125		
20 55 30	180	678	628	1313	138	109	1283	148	117	1263	155	123	1248	160	127		
20 55 35	180	690	639	1320	143	113	1293	152	121	1273	159	126	1260	164	130		
20 55 40	180	702	650	1328	148	117	1303	156	124	1285	163	129	1273	168	133		
20 55 45	180	714	661	1338	152	121	1313	161	128	1295	168	133	1285	172	136		
20 55 50	180	732	678	1348	160	127	1323	169	135	1305	176	140	1298	179	143		
20 55 55	180	750	694	1355	170	134	1333	178	141	1315	186	147	1308	189	149		
20 55 60	180	774	717	1363	183	146	1343	191	152	1325	199	158	1318	203	161		
20 55 65	180	798	739	1370	198	157	1350	207	164	1335	214	170	1328	217	172		
20 55 70	180	828	767	1380	216	172	1360	226	179	1348	232	184	1340	236	188		
20 60 10	185	624	578	1265	120	95	1225	132	105	1200	141	112	1185	146	116		
20 60 15	185	642	594	1275	128	101	1238	139	110	1213	148	117	1198	154	122		
20 60 20	185	660	611	1285	135	108	1250	147	117	1225	156	124	1210	162	129		
20 60 25	185	672	622	1295	140	111	1260	152	120	1238	160	127	1223	166	132		
20 60 30	185	684	633	1305	144	114	1270	156	124	1250	164	130	1235	170	135		
20 60 35	185	696	644	1313	149	118	1283	160	126	1263	167	133	1248	173	137		
20 60 40	185	708	656	1320	154	123	1295	163	130	1275	171	136	1260	177	141		
20 60 45	185	726	672	1330	163	129	1305	172	137	1285	180	143	1273	185	147		
20 60 50	185	744	689	1340	171	136	1315	181	144	1295	190	151	1285	194	154		
20 60 55	185	768	711	1348	185	147	1325	195	155	1305	204	162	1295	209	166		
20 60 60	185	792	733	1355	200	158	1335	209	166	1315	218	173	1305	224	177		
20 60 65	185	822	761	1363	219	174	1343	229	182	1325	239	189	1315	244	194		
20 60 70	185	852	789	1370	241	191	1350	251	200	1335	260	206	1325	266	211		
20 65 10	190	636	589	1255	130	103	1210	145	115	1185	155	123	1170	161	128		
20 65 15	190	654	606	1265	138	110	1223	153	122	1198	163	129	1183	169	134		
20 65 20	190	666	617	1275	143	113	1235	157	125	1210	167	133	1195	173	138		
20 65 25	190	678	628	1285	147	117	1245	162	128	1223	170	135	1208	177	141		
20 65 30	190	690	639	1295	151	120	1258	165	131	1238	173	138	1223	180	143		
20 65 35	190	702	650	1303	156	124	1270	169	134	1250	177	141	1235	184	146		
20 65 40	190	720	667	1310	166	132	1283	177	141	1263	185	147	1248	192	153		
20 65 45	190	738	683	1320	175	139	1293	186	147	1273	195	154	1258	202	160		
20 65 50	190	762	706	1330	188	150	1303	200	159	1283	210	167	1270	216	172		
20 65 55	190	786	728	1338	203	161	1313	215	170	1293	225	178	1280	232	184		
20 65 60	190	816	756	1348	222	176	1323	235	187	1303	246	195	1293	251	200		
20 65 65	190	846	783	1355	243	193	1330	257	204	1313	267	212	1303	274	217		
20 70 10	195	648	600	1245	141	112	1195	159	127	1170	170	135	1155	177	140		
20 70 15	195	660	611	1255	145	115	1208	163	129	1183	174	138	1168	180	143		

SOMATOTYPE	T	I	HEIGHT (M)	(F)	SPI →20	WEIGHT (M)	(F)	SPI →30	WEIGHT (M)	(F)	SPI →40	WEIGHT (M)	(F)	SPI →50+	WEIGHT (M)	(F)
20 70 20	195		672	622	1265	150	119	1220	167	133	1195	178	141	1180	185	1
20 70 25	195		684	633	1275	154	122	1233	171	135	1210	181	143	1195	188	1
20 70 30	195		696	644	1285	159	126	1245	175	138	1225	183	145	1210	190	1
20 70 35	195		714	661	1293	168	134	1258	183	145	1238	192	152	1223	199	1
20 70 40	195		732	678	1300	179	142	1270	191	152	1250	201	160	1235	208	1
20 70 45	195		756	700	1310	192	153	1280	206	164	1260	216	171	1245	224	1
20 70 50	195		780	722	1320	206	164	1290	221	175	1270	232	184	1255	240	1
20 70 55	195		810	750	1330	226	179	1300	242	192	1280	253	201	1268	261	2
20 70 60	195		840	778	1340	246	196	1310	264	209	1290	276	219	1280	283	2
25 10 35	130		570	528	1388	69	55	1365	73	58	1350	75	60	1348	76	
25 10 40	130		600	556	1395	80	63	1373	83	66	1360	86	68	1358	86	
25 10 45	130		630	583	1403	91	72	1380	95	75	1370	97	77	1368	98	
25 10 50	130		654	606	1410	100	79	1390	104	83	1380	106	85	1378	107	
25 10 55	130		678	628	1418	109	87	1398	114	91	1390	116	92	1388	117	
25 10 60	130		696	644	1425	117	92	1408	121	96	1400	123	97	1398	123	
25 10 65	130		714	661	1435	123	98	1418	128	101	1410	130	103	1408	130	1
25 10 70	130		726	672	1445	127	101	1428	131	104	1420	134	106	1418	134	1
25 15 30	135		564	522	1370	70	55	1348	73	58	1333	76	60	1325	77	
25 15 35	135		594	550	1380	80	63	1355	84	67	1343	87	69	1335	88	
25 15 40	135		624	578	1388	91	72	1365	96	76	1350	99	78	1345	100	
25 15 45	135		648	600	1395	100	80	1373	105	83	1360	108	86	1358	109	
25 15 50	135		672	622	1403	110	87	1380	115	92	1370	118	94	1368	119	
25 15 55	135		690	639	1410	117	93	1390	122	97	1380	125	99	1378	126	1
25 15 60	135		708	656	1418	124	99	1398	130	103	1390	132	105	1388	133	1
25 15 65	135		720	667	1428	128	102	1408	134	106	1400	136	108	1398	137	1
25 15 70	135		732	678	1435	133	105	1418	138	109	1410	140	111	1408	141	1
25 20 25	140		558	517	1353	70	56	1328	74	59	1313	77	61	1303	79	
25 20 30	140		588	544	1363	80	64	1338	85	67	1323	88	70	1313	90	
25 20 35	140		618	572	1370	92	73	1349	96	76	1333	100	79	1323	102	8
25 20 40	140		642	594	1380	101	80	1358	106	84	1343	109	87	1335	111	8
25 20 45	140		666	617	1388	110	88	1365	116	92	1350	120	95	1345	121	9
25 20 50	140		684	633	1395	118	93	1373	124	98	1360	127	101	1358	128	10
25 20 55	140		702	650	1403	125	99	1380	132	104	1370	135	107	1368	135	10
25 20 60	140		714	661	1410	130	103	1390	136	108	1380	139	110	1378	139	11
25 20 65	140		726	672	1418	134	106	1400	139	111	1390	142	113	1388	143	11
25 20 70	140		738	683	1428	138	109	1410	143	114	1400	146	116	1400	146	11
25 25 20	145		552	511	1335	71	56	1310	75	59	1293	78	62	1283	80	6
25 25 25	145		582	539	1345	81	64	1320	86	68	1303	89	71	1293	91	7
25 25 30	145		612	567	1355	92	73	1328	98	78	1313	101	81	1303	104	8
25 25 35	145		636	589	1363	102	81	1338	107	85	1323	111	88	1313	114	9
25 25 40	145		660	611	1370	112	89	1348	117	93	1330	122	97	1323	124	
25 25 45	145		678	628	1378	119	95	1355	125	100	1340	130	103	1335	131	10
25 25 50	145		696	644	1385	127	101	1363	133	105	1350	137	109	1345	139	11
25 25 55	145		708	656	1395	131	104	1373	137	109	1360	141	112	1355	143	11
25 25 60	145		720	667	1403	135	107	1380	142	113	1370	145	115	1365	147	11

SPI WITH MAXIMAL WEIGHTS AT PROGESSIVE AGES

				SPI WITH MAXIMAL WEIGHTS AT PROGESSIVE AGES										
SOMATOTYPE	T I	HEIGHT		SPI →20	WEIGHT		SPI →30	WEIGHT		SPI →40	WEIGHT		SPI →50+	WEIGHT
		(M)	(F)		(M)	(F)		(M)	(F)		(M)	(F)		(M) (F)
5 25 65	145	732	678	1410	140	111	1390	146	116	1380	149	119	1378	150 119
5 25 70	145	744	689	1418	144	115	1400	150	119	1390	153	122	1388	154 122
5 30 15	150	546	506	1320	71	56	1293	75	60	1270	79	63	1260	81 65
5 30 20	150	576	533	1328	82	65	1300	87	69	1283	90	72	1273	93 73
5 30 25	150	606	561	1335	94	74	1310	99	79	1293	103	82	1283	105 84
5 30 30	150	630	583	1345	103	81	1320	109	86	1303	113	90	1293	116 92
5 30 35	150	654	606	1353	113	90	1328	119	95	1310	124	99	1303	126 101
5 30 40	150	672	622	1360	121	96	1338	127	100	1320	132	105	1313	134 106
5 30 45	150	690	639	1368	128	102	1345	135	107	1330	140	111	1323	142 113
5 30 50	150	702	650	1378	132	105	1355	139	110	1340	144	114	1333	146 116
5 30 55	150	714	661	1385	137	109	1363	144	114	1350	148	117	1343	150 119
5 30 60	150	726	672	1395	141	112	1373	148	117	1360	152	121	1355	154 122
5 30 65	150	738	683	1403	146	115	1383	152	120	1370	156	124	1365	158 125
5 30 70	150	756	700	1410	154	122	1393	160	127	1380	164	131	1378	165 131
5 35 10	155	540	500	1305	71	56	1273	76	61	1248	81	64	1235	84 66
5 35 15	155	570	528	1313	82	65	1283	88	70	1260	93	74	1248	95 76
5 35 20	155	600	556	1320	94	75	1290	101	80	1270	105	84	1260	108 86
5 35 25	155	624	578	1328	104	82	1300	111	88	1280	116	92	1270	119 94
5 35 30	155	648	600	1335	114	91	1310	121	96	1290	127	101	1280	130 103
5 35 35	155	666	617	1345	121	97	1320	128	102	1300	134	107	1293	137 109
5 35 40	155	684	633	1353	129	102	1328	137	108	1310	142	113	1303	145 115
5 35 45	155	696	644	1360	134	106	1338	141	112	1320	147	116	1313	149 118
5 35 50	155	708	656	1370	138	110	1345	146	116	1330	151	120	1323	153 122
5 35 55	155	720	667	1378	143	113	1355	150	119	1340	155	123	1333	158 125
5 35 60	155	732	678	1385	148	117	1365	154	123	1350	159	127	1345	161 128
5 35 65	155	750	694	1395	155	123	1375	162	129	1360	168	133	1355	170 134
5 35 70	155	768	711	1403	164	130	1385	171	135	1370	176	140	1365	178 141
5 40 10	160	564	522	1295	83	65	1263	89	71	1238	95	75	1223	98 78
5 40 15	160	594	550	1303	95	75	1273	102	81	1248	108	86	1235	111 88
5 40 20	160	618	572	1313	104	83	1283	112	89	1258	119	94	1248	121 96
5 40 25	160	642	594	1320	115	91	1290	123	98	1268	130	103	1258	133 105
5 40 30	160	660	611	1328	123	97	1300	131	104	1280	137	109	1270	140 111
5 40 35	160	678	628	1335	131	104	1310	139	110	1290	145	115	1280	149 118
5 40 40	160	690	639	1345	135	107	1320	143	113	1300	150	119	1293	152 121
5 40 45	160	702	650	1353	140	111	1328	148	117	1310	154	122	1303	156 124
5 40 50	160	714	661	1363	144	114	1338	152	121	1320	158	126	1313	161 128
5 40 55	160	726	672	1370	149	118	1348	156	124	1330	163	129	1323	165 131
5 40 60	160	744	689	1378	157	125	1358	164	131	1343	170	135	1335	173 137
5 40 65	160	762	706	1385	167	132	1368	173	137	1353	179	142	1345	182 145
5 40 70	160	786	728	1395	179	142	1378	186	147	1363	192	152	1355	195 155
5 45 10	165	600	556	1285	102	81	1248	111	88	1225	118	94	1208	123 98
5 45 15	165	612	567	1295	106	84	1260	115	91	1235	122	97	1220	126 100
5 45 20	165	636	589	1305	116	92	1270	126	100	1248	132	105	1233	137 109
5 45 25	165	654	606	1313	124	98	1280	133	106	1258	141	112	1245	145 115
5 45 30	165	672	622	1320	132	105	1290	141	112	1268	149	118	1255	154 122
5 45 35	165	684	633	1328	137	108	1300	146	115	1280	153	121	1268	157 124

SOMATOTYPE	T I	HEIGHT (M)	(F)	SPI →20	WEIGHT (M)	(F)	SPI →30	WEIGHT (M)	(F)	SPI →40	WEIGHT (M)	(F)	SPI →50+	WEIGHT (M)	(F)
25 45 40	165	696	644	1335	142	112	1308	151	119	1290	157	124	1280	161	127
25 45 45	165	708	656	1345	146	116	1318	155	123	1300	162	128	1290	165	132
25 45 50	165	720	667	1355	150	119	1328	159	127	1310	166	132	1300	170	135
25 45 55	165	738	683	1363	159	126	1338	168	133	1320	175	139	1313	178	141
25 45 60	165	756	700	1370	168	133	1348	176	140	1330	184	146	1323	187	148
25 45 65	165	780	722	1378	181	144	1358	189	150	1343	196	155	1335	199	158
25 45 70	165	804	744	1388	194	154	1368	203	161	1353	210	166	1345	214	169
25 50 10	170	606	561	1275	107	85	1235	118	94	1213	125	99	1195	130	103
25 50 15	170	630	583	1285	118	93	1248	129	102	1225	136	108	1208	142	112
25 50 20	170	648	600	1295	125	99	1260	136	108	1238	143	114	1220	150	119
25 50 25	170	666	617	1303	134	106	1270	144	115	1248	152	121	1230	159	126
25 50 30	170	678	628	1313	138	109	1280	149	118	1258	157	124	1243	162	129
25 50 35	170	690	639	1320	143	113	1288	154	122	1268	161	128	1255	166	132
25 50 40	170	702	650	1328	148	117	1298	158	126	1280	165	131	1268	170	135
25 50 45	170	714	661	1335	153	121	1308	163	129	1290	170	135	1278	174	138
25 50 50	170	732	678	1345	161	128	1318	171	136	1300	179	142	1290	183	145
25 50 55	170	750	694	1353	170	135	1328	180	143	1310	188	149	1300	192	152
25 50 60	170	774	717	1363	183	146	1338	194	154	1320	202	160	1313	205	163
25 50 65	170	798	739	1370	198	157	1348	207	165	1330	216	172	1323	219	174
25 50 70	170	828	767	1380	216	172	1358	227	180	1343	234	186	1335	239	190
25 55 10	175	624	578	1265	120	95	1223	133	106	1198	141	112	1180	148	118
25 55 15	175	642	594	1275	128	101	1235	140	111	1210	149	118	1193	156	123
25 55 20	175	660	611	1285	135	108	1248	148	117	1223	157	125	1205	164	130
25 55 25	175	672	622	1295	140	111	1258	152	121	1233	162	128	1215	169	134
25 55 30	175	684	633	1305	144	114	1268	157	124	1245	166	131	1228	173	137
25 55 35	175	696	644	1313	149	118	1278	162	128	1258	169	134	1240	177	140
25 55 40	175	708	656	1320	154	123	1288	166	132	1268	174	138	1253	180	144
25 55 45	175	720	667	1328	159	127	1298	171	136	1280	178	141	1265	184	147
25 55 50	175	744	689	1338	172	137	1308	184	146	1290	192	152	1278	197	157
25 55 55	175	768	711	1345	186	148	1318	198	157	1300	206	164	1288	212	168
25 55 60	175	792	733	1355	200	158	1328	212	168	1310	221	175	1300	226	179
25 55 65	175	822	761	1363	219	174	1338	232	184	1320	241	192	1310	247	196
25 55 70	175	852	789	1370	241	191	1348	252	201	1330	263	209	1323	267	212
25 60 10	180	636	589	1255	130	103	1210	145	115	1183	155	123	1165	163	129
25 60 15	180	654	606	1265	138	110	1223	153	122	1195	164	130	1178	171	136
25 60 20	180	666	617	1275	143	113	1235	157	125	1208	168	133	1190	175	139
25 60 25	180	678	628	1285	147	117	1245	162	128	1220	172	136	1203	179	142
25 60 30	180	690	639	1295	151	120	1255	166	132	1233	175	139	1215	183	145
25 60 35	180	702	650	1303	156	124	1268	170	135	1245	179	142	1228	187	148
25 60 40	180	720	667	1310	166	132	1280	178	141	1258	187	149	1240	196	156
25 60 45	180	738	683	1320	175	139	1290	187	148	1268	197	156	1253	204	162
25 60 50	180	762	706	1330	188	150	1300	201	160	1280	211	168	1265	219	174
25 60 55	180	786	728	1338	203	161	1310	216	172	1290	226	180	1275	234	186
25 60 60	180	816	756	1348	222	176	1320	236	188	1300	247	197	1288	254	202
25 60 65	180	846	783	1355	243	193	1328	259	205	1310	269	214	1298	277	220
25 65 10	185	648	600	1245	141	112	1195	159	127	1168	171	136	1148	180	143

SPI WITH MAXIMAL WEIGHTS AT PROGESSIVE AGES

ATOTYPE	T I	HEIGHT (M)	HEIGHT (F)	SPI →20	WEIGHT (M)	WEIGHT (F)	SPI →30	WEIGHT (M)	WEIGHT (F)	SPI →40	WEIGHT (M)	WEIGHT (F)	SPI →50+	WEIGHT (M)	WEIGHT (F)
65 15	185	660	611	1255	145	115	1208	163	129	1180	175	139	1163	183	145
65 20	185	672	622	1265	150	119	1220	167	133	1193	179	142	1175	187	148
65 25	185	684	633	1275	154	122	1230	172	136	1205	183	145	1188	191	151
65 30	185	696	644	1285	159	126	1243	176	139	1218	187	148	1200	195	155
65 35	185	714	661	1293	168	134	1255	184	146	1230	196	155	1213	204	162
65 40	185	732	678	1300	179	142	1268	192	153	1243	204	162	1225	213	170
65 45	185	756	700	1310	192	153	1278	207	164	1255	219	174	1238	228	181
65 50	185	780	722	1320	206	164	1288	222	176	1265	234	186	1250	243	193
65 55	185	810	750	1330	226	179	1298	243	193	1278	255	202	1263	264	209
65 60	185	840	778	1340	246	196	1308	265	210	1288	277	220	1275	286	227
70 10	190	654	606	1230	150	120	1180	170	135	1153	182	145	1133	192	153
70 15	190	666	617	1240	155	123	1193	174	138	1165	187	149	1145	197	156
70 20	190	678	628	1253	158	126	1205	178	142	1178	191	152	1158	201	159
70 25	190	690	639	1263	163	130	1218	182	144	1190	195	155	1170	205	163
70 30	190	708	656	1273	172	137	1230	191	152	1205	203	161	1185	213	170
70 35	190	726	672	1280	182	145	1243	199	158	1218	212	168	1198	223	176
70 40	190	750	694	1290	197	156	1255	213	169	1230	227	180	1210	238	189
70 45	190	774	717	1300	211	168	1265	229	182	1240	243	193	1223	253	202
70 50	190	804	744	1310	231	183	1275	251	199	1253	264	209	1235	276	219
70 55	190	834	772	1320	252	200	1285	273	217	1263	288	228	1248	298	237
10 30	125	564	522	1370	70	55	1345	74	58	1325	77	61	1320	78	62
10 35	125	594	550	1378	80	64	1353	85	67	1335	88	70	1330	89	71
10 40	125	624	578	1385	91	73	1360	97	77	1345	100	79	1340	101	80
10 45	125	648	600	1393	101	80	1368	106	84	1355	109	87	1350	111	88
10 50	125	672	622	1400	111	88	1375	117	93	1365	119	95	1360	121	96
10 55	125	690	639	1408	118	93	1385	124	98	1375	126	100	1370	128	101
10 60	125	708	656	1415	125	100	1395	131	104	1385	134	106	1380	135	107
10 65	125	720	667	1425	129	103	1405	135	107	1395	137	109	1390	139	110
10 70	125	732	678	1435	133	105	1415	138	110	1405	141	112	1400	143	114
15 25	130	558	517	1353	70	56	1325	75	59	1305	78	62	1298	79	63
15 30	130	588	544	1363	80	64	1335	85	68	1315	89	71	1308	91	72
15 35	130	618	572	1370	92	73	1343	97	77	1325	101	80	1318	103	82
15 40	130	642	594	1378	101	80	1353	107	85	1335	111	88	1330	112	89
15 45	130	666	617	1385	111	88	1360	117	93	1345	121	97	1340	123	98
15 50	130	684	633	1393	118	94	1368	125	99	1355	129	102	1350	130	103
15 55	130	702	650	1400	126	100	1375	133	106	1365	136	108	1360	138	109
15 60	130	714	661	1408	130	103	1385	137	109	1375	140	111	1370	142	112
15 65	130	726	672	1415	135	107	1395	141	112	1385	144	114	1380	146	115
15 70	130	738	683	1425	139	110	1405	145	115	1395	148	117	1393	149	118
20 20	135	552	511	1335	71	56	1305	76	60	1285	79	63	1275	81	64
20 25	135	582	539	1345	81	64	1315	87	69	1295	91	72	1285	93	74
20 30	135	612	567	1355	92	73	1325	99	78	1305	103	82	1295	106	84
20 35	135	636	589	1363	102	81	1335	108	86	1315	113	90	1308	115	91
20 40	135	660	611	1370	112	89	1345	118	94	1325	124	98	1320	125	99
20 45	135	678	628	1378	119	95	1353	126	100	1335	131	104	1330	132	105

SPI WITH MAXIMAL WEIGHTS AT PROGESSIVE AGES

SOMATOTYPE	T	I	HEIGHT (M)	(F)	SPI →20	WEIGHT (M)	(F)	SPI →30	WEIGHT (M)	(F)	SPI →40	WEIGHT (M)	(F)	SPI →50+	WEIGHT (M)	(F)
30 20 50	135	696	644		1385	127	101	1360	134	106	1345	139	110	1340	140	111
30 20 55	135	708	656		1393	131	104	1368	139	110	1355	143	113	1350	144	115
30 20 60	135	720	667		1400	136	108	1375	144	114	1365	147	117	1360	148	118
30 20 65	135	732	678		1408	141	112	1385	148	117	1375	151	120	1373	152	120
30 20 70	135	744	689		1415	145	115	1395	152	120	1385	155	123	1385	155	123
30 25 15	140	546	506		1320	71	56	1288	76	61	1263	81	64	1253	83	66
30 25 20	140	576	533		1328	82	65	1295	88	70	1275	92	73	1265	94	75
30 25 25	140	606	561		1335	94	74	1305	100	79	1285	105	83	1275	107	85
30 25 30	140	630	583		1345	103	81	1315	110	87	1295	115	91	1285	118	93
30 25 35	140	654	606		1353	113	90	1325	120	96	1305	126	100	1295	129	102
30 25 40	140	672	622		1360	121	96	1335	128	101	1315	133	106	1308	136	108
30 25 45	140	690	639		1368	128	102	1343	136	108	1325	141	112	1318	143	114
30 25 50	140	702	650		1378	132	105	1353	140	111	1335	145	115	1328	148	117
30 25 55	140	714	661		1385	137	109	1360	145	115	1345	150	119	1338	152	121
30 25 60	140	726	672		1393	142	112	1368	149	119	1355	154	122	1350	156	123
30 25 65	140	738	683		1400	146	116	1378	154	122	1365	158	125	1360	160	127
30 25 70	140	756	700		1408	155	123	1388	162	128	1375	166	132	1373	167	133
30 30 10	145	540	500		1305	71	56	1270	77	61	1240	83	66	1230	85	67
30 30 15	145	570	528		1313	82	65	1278	89	71	1253	94	75	1243	96	77
30 30 20	145	600	556		1320	94	75	1285	102	81	1265	107	85	1255	109	87
30 30 25	145	624	578		1328	104	82	1295	112	89	1275	117	93	1265	120	95
30 30 30	145	648	600		1335	114	91	1305	122	97	1285	128	102	1275	131	104
30 30 35	145	666	617		1343	122	97	1315	130	103	1295	136	108	1285	139	111
30 30 40	145	684	633		1350	130	103	1325	138	109	1305	144	114	1295	147	117
30 30 45	145	696	644		1360	134	106	1335	142	112	1315	148	117	1305	152	120
30 30 50	145	708	656		1370	138	110	1345	146	116	1325	153	121	1315	156	124
30 30 55	145	720	667		1378	143	113	1353	151	120	1335	157	125	1328	159	127
30 30 60	145	732	678		1385	148	117	1360	156	124	1345	161	128	1340	163	130
30 30 65	145	750	694		1393	156	124	1370	164	130	1355	170	134	1350	171	136
30 30 70	145	768	711		1400	165	131	1380	172	137	1365	178	141	1360	180	143
30 35 10	150	564	522		1295	83	65	1260	90	71	1230	96	76	1218	99	79
30 35 15	150	594	550		1303	95	75	1268	103	82	1240	110	87	1230	113	89
30 35 20	150	618	572		1313	104	83	1278	113	90	1253	120	95	1243	123	97
30 35 25	150	642	594		1320	115	91	1285	125	99	1263	131	104	1253	135	107
30 35 30	150	660	611		1328	123	97	1295	132	105	1275	139	110	1265	142	113
30 35 35	150	678	628		1335	131	104	1305	140	111	1285	147	117	1275	150	119
30 35 40	150	690	639		1343	136	108	1315	144	115	1295	151	120	1285	155	123
30 35 45	150	702	650		1353	140	111	1325	149	118	1305	156	124	1295	159	126
30 35 50	150	714	661		1363	144	114	1335	153	121	1315	160	127	1305	164	130
30 35 55	150	726	672		1370	149	118	1343	158	125	1325	164	130	1318	167	133
30 35 60	150	744	689		1378	157	125	1353	166	132	1335	173	137	1330	175	139
30 35 65	150	762	706		1385	167	132	1363	175	139	1345	182	145	1340	184	146
30 35 70	150	786	728		1393	180	143	1373	188	149	1355	195	155	1350	197	157
30 40 10	155	588	544		1285	96	76	1250	104	82	1220	112	89	1205	116	92
30 40 15	155	612	567		1295	106	84	1260	115	91	1230	123	98	1218	127	101
30 40 20	155	636	589		1305	116	92	1270	126	100	1240	135	107	1230	138	110

SPI WITH MAXIMAL WEIGHTS AT PROGESSIVE AGES

SOMATOTYPE	T I	HEIGHT (M)	(F)	SPI →20	WEIGHT (M)	(F)	SPI →30	WEIGHT (M)	(F)	SPI →40	WEIGHT (M)	(F)	SPI →50+	WEIGHT (M)	(F)
30 40 25	155	654	606	1313	124	98	1278	134	107	1253	142	113	1243	146	116
30 40 30	155	672	622	1320	132	105	1285	143	113	1265	150	119	1255	154	122
30 40 35	155	684	633	1328	137	108	1295	147	117	1275	154	122	1265	158	125
30 40 40	155	696	644	1335	142	112	1305	152	120	1285	159	126	1275	163	129
30 40 45	155	708	656	1345	146	116	1315	156	124	1295	163	130	1285	167	133
30 40 50	155	720	667	1355	150	119	1325	160	128	1305	168	134	1295	172	137
30 40 55	155	738	683	1363	159	126	1335	169	134	1315	177	140	1308	180	142
30 40 60	155	756	700	1370	168	133	1345	178	141	1325	186	147	1320	188	149
30 40 65	155	780	722	1378	181	144	1355	191	151	1335	199	158	1330	202	160
30 40 70	155	804	744	1385	196	155	1365	204	162	1345	214	169	1340	216	171
30 45 10	160	606	561	1275	107	85	1235	118	94	1208	126	100	1190	132	105
30 45 15	160	630	583	1285	118	93	1245	130	103	1218	138	110	1203	144	114
30 45 20	160	648	600	1295	125	99	1258	137	108	1230	146	116	1215	152	120
30 45 25	160	666	617	1303	134	106	1265	146	116	1240	155	123	1225	161	128
30 45 30	160	678	628	1313	138	109	1275	150	119	1253	158	126	1238	164	131
30 45 35	160	690	639	1320	143	113	1285	155	123	1263	163	130	1250	168	134
30 45 40	160	702	650	1328	148	117	1295	159	126	1275	167	132	1263	172	136
30 45 45	160	714	661	1335	153	121	1305	164	130	1285	172	136	1273	176	140
30 45 50	160	732	678	1345	161	128	1315	172	137	1295	181	144	1283	186	148
30 45 55	160	750	694	1353	170	135	1325	181	144	1305	190	150	1295	194	154
30 45 60	160	774	717	1363	183	146	1335	195	155	1315	204	162	1308	207	165
30 45 65	160	798	739	1370	198	157	1345	209	166	1325	218	173	1318	222	176
30 45 70	160	828	767	1378	217	172	1355	228	181	1335	239	190	1330	241	192
30 50 10	165	624	578	1265	120	95	1220	134	106	1195	142	113	1175	150	119
30 50 15	165	642	594	1275	128	101	1233	141	112	1208	150	119	1188	158	125
30 50 20	165	660	611	1285	135	108	1245	149	118	1220	158	126	1200	166	132
30 50 25	165	672	622	1295	140	111	1255	154	122	1230	163	129	1213	170	135
30 50 30	165	684	633	1305	144	114	1265	158	125	1240	168	133	1225	174	138
30 50 35	165	696	644	1313	149	118	1275	163	129	1253	171	136	1238	178	141
30 50 40	165	708	656	1320	154	123	1285	167	133	1265	175	139	1250	182	145
30 50 45	165	726	672	1328	163	130	1295	176	140	1275	185	146	1260	191	152
30 50 50	165	744	689	1335	173	137	1305	185	147	1285	194	154	1270	201	160
30 50 55	165	768	711	1345	186	148	1315	199	158	1295	209	166	1283	214	170
30 50 60	165	792	733	1355	200	158	1325	214	169	1305	224	177	1295	229	181
30 50 65	165	822	761	1363	219	174	1335	233	185	1315	244	194	1308	248	197
30 50 70	165	852	789	1370	241	191	1345	254	202	1325	266	211	1320	269	214
30 55 10	170	636	589	1255	130	103	1208	146	116	1180	157	124	1160	165	131
30 55 15	170	654	606	1265	138	110	1220	154	123	1193	165	131	1173	173	138
30 55 20	170	666	617	1275	143	113	1233	158	125	1205	169	134	1185	178	141
30 55 25	170	678	628	1285	147	117	1243	162	129	1215	174	138	1198	181	144
30 55 30	170	690	639	1295	151	120	1253	167	133	1228	177	141	1210	185	147
30 55 35	170	702	650	1303	156	124	1263	172	136	1240	181	144	1223	189	150
30 55 40	170	720	667	1310	166	132	1275	180	143	1253	190	151	1235	198	158
30 55 45	170	738	683	1318	176	139	1285	189	150	1263	200	158	1245	208	165
30 55 50	170	762	706	1328	189	150	1295	204	162	1275	213	170	1258	222	177
30 55 55	170	786	728	1338	203	161	1305	218	174	1285	229	182	1270	237	188
30 55 60	170	816	756	1348	222	176	1315	239	190	1295	250	199	1283	257	205

SOMATOTYPE	T	I	HEIGHT (M)	HEIGHT (F)	SPI →20	WEIGHT (M)	WEIGHT (F)	SPI →30	WEIGHT (M)	WEIGHT (F)	SPI →40	WEIGHT (M)	WEIGHT (F)	SPI →50+	WEIGHT (M)	WEIGHT (F)
30 55 65	170		846	783	1355	243	193	1325	260	206	1305	272	216	1295	279	221
30 60 10	175		648	600	1245	141	112	1195	159	127	1165	172	137	1145	181	144
30 60 15	175		660	611	1255	145	115	1208	163	129	1178	176	140	1158	185	147
30 60 20	175		672	622	1265	150	119	1220	167	133	1190	180	143	1170	189	150
30 60 25	175		684	633	1275	154	122	1230	172	136	1203	184	146	1183	193	153
30 60 30	175		696	644	1285	159	126	1240	177	140	1215	188	149	1195	198	157
30 60 35	175		714	661	1293	168	134	1253	185	147	1228	197	156	1208	206	164
30 60 40	175		732	678	1300	179	142	1265	194	154	1240	206	163	1220	216	172
30 60 45	175		756	700	1310	192	153	1275	208	165	1253	220	174	1233	231	183
30 60 50	175		780	722	1320	206	164	1285	224	177	1265	234	186	1245	246	195
30 60 55	175		810	750	1330	226	179	1295	245	194	1275	256	204	1258	267	212
30 60 60	175		840	778	1340	246	196	1305	267	212	1285	279	222	1270	289	230
30 65 10	180		654	606	1230	150	120	1180	170	135	1150	184	146	1128	195	155
30 65 15	180		666	617	1240	155	123	1193	174	138	1163	188	149	1140	199	159
30 65 20	180		678	628	1253	158	126	1205	178	142	1175	192	153	1155	202	161
30 65 25	180		690	639	1263	163	130	1215	183	145	1188	196	156	1168	206	164
30 65 30	180		708	656	1273	172	137	1228	192	152	1200	205	163	1180	216	172
30 65 35	180		726	672	1280	182	145	1240	201	159	1213	214	170	1193	225	179
30 65 40	180		750	694	1290	197	156	1253	214	170	1225	229	182	1205	241	191
30 65 45	180		774	717	1300	211	168	1263	230	183	1238	244	194	1218	257	204
30 65 50	180		804	744	1310	231	183	1273	252	200	1250	266	211	1230	279	221
30 65 55	180		834	772	1320	252	200	1283	275	218	1260	290	230	1243	302	240
30 70 10	185		660	611	1218	159	126	1165	182	144	1135	197	156	1110	210	167
30 70 15	185		672	622	1228	164	130	1178	186	147	1148	201	159	1125	213	169
30 70 20	185		684	633	1240	168	133	1190	190	151	1160	205	162	1140	216	171
30 70 25	185		702	650	1250	177	141	1203	199	158	1173	214	170	1153	226	179
30 70 30	185		720	667	1260	187	148	1215	208	165	1185	224	178	1165	236	188
30 70 35	185		744	689	1270	201	160	1228	222	177	1198	240	190	1178	252	200
30 70 40	185		768	711	1280	216	171	1240	238	189	1210	256	203	1190	269	213
30 70 45	185		798	739	1290	237	188	1250	260	207	1223	278	221	1203	292	232
30 70 50	185		828	767	1300	258	205	1260	284	226	1235	301	240	1215	316	252
35 10 25	120		558	517	1350	71	56	1323	75	60	1303	79	62	1293	80	64
35 10 30	120		600	556	1360	86	68	1333	91	73	1313	95	76	1305	97	7
35 10 35	120		630	583	1368	98	77	1340	104	82	1323	108	86	1315	110	8
35 10 40	120		642	594	1375	102	81	1350	108	85	1333	112	88	1325	114	9
35 10 45	120		666	617	1383	112	89	1358	118	94	1343	122	97	1335	124	9
35 10 50	120		684	633	1390	119	94	1365	126	100	1353	129	102	1345	132	10
35 10 55	120		702	650	1398	127	101	1373	134	106	1363	137	108	1355	139	11
35 10 60	120		714	661	1405	131	104	1383	138	109	1373	141	112	1365	143	11
35 10 65	120		726	672	1413	136	108	1393	142	112	1383	145	115	1375	147	11
35 10 70	120		738	683	1423	139	111	1403	146	115	1393	149	118	1385	151	12
35 15 20	125		552	511	1333	71	56	1303	76	60	1283	80	63	1270	82	6
35 15 25	125		582	539	1343	81	65	1313	87	69	1293	91	72	1280	94	7
35 15 30	125		612	567	1350	93	74	1323	99	79	1303	104	82	1293	106	8

ATOTYPE	T I	HEIGHT (M)	HEIGHT (F)	SPI →20	WEIGHT (M)	WEIGHT (F)	SPI →30	WEIGHT (M)	WEIGHT (F)	SPI →40	WEIGHT (M)	WEIGHT (F)	SPI →50+	WEIGHT (M)	WEIGHT (F)
					SPI WITH MAXIMAL WEIGHTS AT PROGESSIVE AGES										
15 35	125	636	589	1360	102	81	1333	109	86	1313	114	90	1303	116	92
15 40	125	660	611	1368	112	89	1340	119	95	1323	124	99	1313	127	101
15 45	125	678	628	1375	120	95	1348	127	101	1333	132	105	1325	134	106
15 50	125	696	644	1383	127	101	1355	136	107	1343	139	110	1335	142	112
15 55	125	708	656	1390	132	105	1365	140	111	1353	143	114	1345	146	116
15 60	125	720	667	1398	137	109	1373	144	115	1363	147	117	1355	150	119
15 65	125	732	678	1405	141	112	1383	148	118	1373	152	120	1365	154	123
15 70	125	744	689	1413	146	116	1393	152	121	1383	156	124	1375	158	126
20 15	130	546	506	1315	72	57	1285	77	61	1260	81	65	1245	84	67
20 20	130	576	533	1325	82	65	1295	88	70	1270	93	74	1258	96	76
20 25	130	606	561	1333	94	75	1303	101	80	1280	106	84	1268	109	87
20 30	130	630	583	1343	103	82	1313	110	88	1293	116	92	1280	119	94
20 35	130	654	606	1350	114	90	1323	121	96	1303	126	101	1290	130	104
20 40	130	672	622	1360	121	96	1333	128	102	1313	134	106	1303	137	109
20 45	130	690	639	1368	128	102	1340	137	108	1323	142	113	1313	145	115
20 50	130	702	650	1375	133	106	1348	141	112	1333	146	116	1325	149	118
20 55	130	714	661	1383	138	109	1355	146	116	1343	150	119	1335	153	121
20 60	130	726	672	1390	142	113	1365	150	119	1353	154	123	1345	157	125
20 65	130	738	683	1398	147	117	1373	155	123	1363	159	126	1355	162	128
20 70	130	756	700	1405	156	124	1383	163	130	1373	167	133	1368	169	134
25 10	135	540	500	1300	72	57	1268	77	61	1238	83	66	1223	86	68
25 15	135	570	528	1308	83	66	1275	89	71	1250	95	75	1235	98	78
25 20	135	600	556	1318	94	75	1285	102	81	1260	108	86	1245	112	89
25 25	135	624	578	1325	104	83	1293	112	89	1270	119	94	1258	122	97
25 30	135	648	600	1333	115	91	1303	123	98	1280	130	103	1268	133	106
25 35	135	666	617	1343	122	97	1313	131	104	1290	138	109	1280	141	112
25 40	135	684	633	1350	130	103	1323	138	110	1300	146	115	1290	149	118
25 45	135	696	644	1358	135	107	1330	143	114	1310	150	119	1300	153	122
25 50	135	708	656	1368	139	110	1340	147	117	1320	154	123	1313	157	125
25 55	135	720	667	1375	144	114	1348	152	121	1330	159	126	1323	161	128
25 60	135	732	678	1383	148	118	1355	158	125	1340	163	130	1333	166	132
25 65	135	750	694	1390	157	124	1365	166	131	1353	170	135	1345	173	137
25 70	135	768	711	1398	166	132	1375	174	138	1363	179	142	1355	182	144
30 10	140	564	522	1293	83	66	1258	90	71	1228	97	77	1213	101	80
30 15	140	594	550	1300	95	76	1265	104	82	1238	110	88	1223	115	91
30 20	140	618	572	1310	105	83	1275	114	90	1250	121	96	1235	125	99
30 25	140	642	594	1318	116	92	1283	125	99	1260	132	105	1245	137	109
30 30	140	660	611	1325	124	98	1293	133	106	1270	140	111	1258	144	115
30 35	140	678	628	1333	132	105	1303	141	112	1280	149	118	1268	153	121
30 40	140	690	639	1340	137	108	1313	145	115	1290	153	122	1278	157	125
30 45	140	702	650	1350	141	112	1323	149	119	1300	157	125	1288	162	129
30 50	140	714	661	1360	145	115	1333	154	122	1310	162	128	1300	166	131
30 55	140	726	672	1368	149	119	1340	159	126	1320	166	132	1310	170	135
30 60	140	744	689	1375	158	126	1348	168	134	1330	175	139	1323	178	141
30 65	140	762	706	1383	167	133	1358	177	141	1340	184	146	1333	187	149
30 70	140	786	728	1390	181	144	1370	189	150	1353	196	156	1345	200	159
35 10	145	588	544	1283	96	76	1245	105	83	1215	113	90	1198	118	94

SOMATOTYPE	T I	HEIGHT (M)	(F)	SPI →20	WEIGHT (M)	(F)	SPI →30	WEIGHT (M)	(F)	SPI →40	WEIGHT (M)	(F)	SPI →50+	WEIGHT (M)	(F)
35 35 15	145	612	567	1293	106	84	1255	116	92	1225	125	99	1210	129	10
35 35 20	145	636	589	1300	117	93	1265	127	101	1235	137	108	1220	142	11
35 35 25	145	654	606	1310	124	99	1273	136	108	1248	144	114	1233	149	11
35 35 30	145	672	622	1318	133	105	1283	144	114	1258	152	121	1243	158	12
35 35 35	145	684	633	1325	138	109	1293	148	117	1270	156	124	1255	162	12
35 35 40	145	696	644	1333	142	113	1303	152	121	1280	161	127	1265	167	13
35 35 45	145	708	656	1343	147	117	1313	157	125	1290	165	132	1278	170	13
35 35 50	145	720	667	1350	152	121	1323	161	128	1300	170	135	1288	175	13
35 35 55	145	738	683	1360	160	127	1330	171	135	1310	179	142	1300	183	14
35 35 60	145	756	700	1368	169	134	1340	180	143	1320	188	149	1313	191	15
35 35 65	145	780	722	1375	183	145	1350	193	153	1330	202	160	1323	205	16
35 35 70	145	804	744	1383	196	156	1360	207	164	1343	215	170	1335	218	17
35 40 10	150	606	561	1273	108	86	1235	118	94	1203	128	101	1185	134	10
35 40 15	150	630	583	1283	118	94	1245	130	103	1213	140	111	1198	145	11
35 40 20	150	648	600	1293	126	100	1255	138	109	1223	149	118	1208	154	12
35 40 25	150	666	617	1300	134	107	1263	147	117	1235	157	125	1220	163	12
35 40 30	150	678	628	1310	139	110	1273	151	120	1248	160	127	1233	166	13
35 40 35	150	690	639	1318	143	114	1283	156	124	1258	165	131	1243	171	13
35 40 40	150	702	650	1325	149	118	1293	160	127	1270	169	134	1255	175	13
35 40 45	150	714	661	1333	154	122	1303	165	131	1280	174	138	1265	180	14
35 40 50	150	732	678	1343	162	129	1313	173	138	1290	183	145	1278	188	14
35 40 55	150	750	694	1350	171	136	1323	182	144	1300	192	152	1290	197	15
35 40 60	150	774	717	1360	184	147	1333	196	156	1310	206	164	1303	210	16
35 40 65	150	798	739	1368	198	158	1343	210	167	1320	221	175	1313	224	17
35 40 70	150	828	767	1375	218	174	1353	229	182	1333	240	191	1325	244	19
35 45 10	155	624	578	1263	121	96	1220	134	106	1188	145	115	1170	152	12
35 45 15	155	642	594	1273	128	102	1230	142	113	1200	153	121	1183	160	12
35 45 20	155	660	611	1283	136	108	1243	150	119	1210	162	129	1195	168	13
35 45 25	155	672	622	1293	140	111	1253	154	122	1223	166	132	1208	172	13
35 45 30	155	684	633	1303	145	115	1263	159	126	1235	170	135	1220	176	14
35 45 35	155	696	644	1310	150	119	1273	163	129	1248	173	137	1233	180	14
35 45 40	155	708	656	1318	155	123	1283	168	134	1258	178	142	1243	185	14
35 45 45	155	726	672	1325	164	130	1293	177	140	1268	188	149	1253	195	15
35 45 50	155	744	689	1333	174	138	1303	186	148	1278	197	157	1265	203	16
35 45 55	155	768	711	1343	187	148	1313	200	159	1290	211	167	1278	217	17
35 45 60	155	792	733	1350	202	160	1323	215	170	1300	226	179	1290	231	18
35 45 65	155	822	761	1360	221	175	1333	234	186	1310	247	196	1303	251	19
35 45 70	155	852	789	1368	242	192	1343	255	203	1323	267	212	1315	272	21
35 50 10	160	636	589	1255	130	103	1205	147	117	1175	159	126	1155	167	13
35 50 15	160	654	606	1265	138	110	1218	155	123	1188	167	133	1168	176	14
35 50 20	160	666	617	1275	143	113	1230	159	126	1200	171	136	1180	180	14
35 50 25	160	678	628	1285	147	117	1240	163	130	1210	176	140	1193	184	14
35 50 30	160	690	639	1295	151	120	1253	167	133	1223	180	143	1205	188	14
35 50 35	160	702	650	1303	156	124	1263	172	136	1235	184	146	1218	191	15
35 50 40	160	720	667	1310	166	132	1273	181	144	1248	192	153	1230	201	15
35 50 45	160	738	683	1318	176	139	1283	190	151	1258	202	160	1240	211	16
35 50 50	160	762	706	1325	190	151	1293	205	163	1268	217	173	1253	225	17

						SPI WITH MAXIMAL WEIGHTS AT PROGESSIVE AGES										
MATOTYPE	T	I	HEIGHT (M)	(F)	SPI →20	WEIGHT (M)	(F)	SPI →30	WEIGHT (M)	(F)	SPI →40	WEIGHT (M)	(F)	SPI →50+	WEIGHT (M)	(F)
5 50 55			160	786	728	1333	205	163	1303	219	174	1278	233	185	1265	240	191
5 50 60			160	816	756	1343	224	178	1313	240	191	1290	253	201	1278	260	207
5 50 65			160	846	783	1350	246	195	1323	261	207	1300	276	219	1290	282	224
5 55 10			165	648	600	1245	141	112	1190	161	128	1160	174	138	1138	185	147
5 55 15			165	660	611	1255	145	115	1203	165	131	1173	178	141	1153	188	149
5 55 20			165	672	622	1265	150	119	1215	169	134	1185	182	145	1165	192	152
5 55 25			165	684	633	1275	154	122	1228	173	137	1198	186	148	1178	196	155
5 55 30			165	696	644	1285	159	126	1238	178	141	1210	190	151	1190	200	158
5 55 35			165	714	661	1293	168	134	1250	186	148	1223	199	158	1203	209	166
5 55 40			165	732	678	1300	179	142	1260	196	156	1235	208	165	1215	219	174
5 55 45			165	756	700	1308	193	153	1273	209	166	1245	224	178	1228	233	185
5 55 50			165	780	722	1318	207	164	1283	225	178	1258	238	189	1240	249	197
5 55 55			165	810	750	1328	227	180	1293	246	195	1268	261	207	1253	270	214
5 55 60			165	840	778	1335	249	198	1303	268	213	1280	283	225	1265	293	233
5 60 10			170	654	606	1233	149	119	1178	171	136	1145	186	148	1123	198	157
5 60 15			170	666	617	1243	154	122	1190	175	139	1158	190	151	1135	202	161
5 60 20			170	678	628	1253	158	126	1203	179	142	1173	193	153	1150	205	163
5 60 25			170	690	639	1263	163	130	1213	184	146	1185	197	157	1163	209	166
5 60 30			170	708	656	1273	172	137	1225	193	154	1198	206	164	1175	219	174
5 60 35			170	726	672	1280	182	145	1238	202	160	1210	216	171	1188	228	181
5 60 40			170	750	694	1290	197	156	1250	216	171	1223	231	183	1200	244	193
5 60 45			170	774	717	1300	211	168	1260	232	184	1235	246	196	1213	260	207
5 60 50			170	804	744	1310	231	183	1273	252	200	1248	267	212	1225	283	224
5 60 55			170	834	772	1320	252	200	1283	275	218	1258	291	231	1238	306	242
5 65 10			175	660	611	1220	158	126	1160	184	146	1128	200	159	1105	213	169
5 65 15			175	672	622	1230	163	129	1175	187	148	1143	203	161	1120	216	171
5 65 20			175	684	633	1240	168	133	1188	191	151	1155	208	165	1133	220	174
5 65 25			175	702	650	1250	177	141	1200	200	159	1170	216	171	1148	229	182
5 65 30			175	720	667	1260	187	148	1210	211	168	1183	225	179	1160	239	190
5 65 35			175	744	689	1270	201	160	1223	225	179	1195	241	192	1173	255	203
5 65 40			175	768	711	1280	216	171	1235	240	191	1208	257	204	1185	272	216
5 65 45			175	798	739	1290	237	188	1248	261	208	1220	280	222	1198	296	235
5 65 50			175	828	767	1300	258	205	1260	284	226	1233	303	241	1210	320	255
5 70 10			180	666	617	1205	169	134	1145	197	156	1113	214	170	1088	229	182
5 70 15			180	678	628	1215	174	138	1158	201	159	1125	219	174	1103	232	185
5 70 20			180	696	644	1228	182	144	1173	209	165	1140	228	180	1118	241	191
5 70 25			180	714	661	1238	192	152	1185	219	174	1153	237	188	1130	252	200
5 70 30			180	738	683	1250	206	163	1198	234	185	1168	252	200	1145	268	212
5 70 35			180	762	706	1260	221	176	1210	250	199	1180	269	214	1158	285	227
5 70 40			180	792	733	1270	243	192	1223	272	215	1193	293	232	1170	310	246
5 70 45			180	822	761	1280	265	210	1233	296	235	1205	317	252	1183	335	266
0 10 20			115	552	511	1330	71	57	1300	77	61	1280	80	64	1265	83	66
0 10 25			115	582	539	1340	82	65	1310	88	70	1290	92	73	1278	94	75
0 10 30			115	612	567	1350	93	74	1320	100	79	1300	104	83	1290	107	85

SOMATOTYPE	T	I	HEIGHT (M)	HEIGHT (F)	SPI →20	WEIGHT (M)	WEIGHT (F)	SPI →30	WEIGHT (M)	WEIGHT (F)	SPI →40	WEIGHT (M)	WEIGHT (F)	SPI →50+	WEIGHT (M)	WEIGHT (F)
							SPI WITH MAXIMAL WEIGHTS AT PROGESSIVE AGES								
40 10 35	115		636	589	1358	103	82	1330	109	87	1310	114	91	1300	117	93
40 10 40	115		660	611	1365	113	90	1340	119	95	1320	125	99	1310	128	101
40 10 45	115		678	628	1372	121	96	1348	127	101	1330	132	105	1320	136	108
40 10 50	115		696	644	1380	128	102	1355	136	107	1340	140	111	1330	143	114
40 10 55	115		708	656	1388	133	106	1363	140	111	1350	144	115	1340	147	117
40 10 60	115		720	667	1395	137	109	1370	145	115	1360	148	118	1350	152	121
40 10 65	115		732	678	1403	142	113	1380	149	119	1370	153	121	1360	156	124
40 10 70	115		744	689	1410	147	117	1390	153	122	1380	157	124	1370	160	127
40 15 15	120		546	506	1313	72	57	1283	77	61	1258	82	65	1240	85	68
40 15 20	120		576	533	1323	83	65	1293	88	70	1268	94	74	1253	97	77
40 15 25	120		606	561	1330	95	75	1300	101	80	1278	107	85	1265	110	87
40 15 30	120		630	583	1340	104	82	1310	111	88	1290	116	92	1278	120	95
40 15 35	120		654	606	1348	114	91	1320	122	97	1300	127	101	1288	131	104
40 15 40	120		672	622	1358	121	96	1330	129	102	1310	135	107	1298	139	110
40 15 45	120		690	639	1365	129	103	1338	137	109	1320	143	113	1308	147	117
40 15 50	120		702	650	1373	134	106	1345	142	113	1330	147	117	1320	150	119
40 15 55	120		714	661	1380	139	110	1353	147	117	1340	151	120	1330	155	123
40 15 60	120		726	672	1387	143	114	1363	151	120	1350	156	123	1340	159	126
40 15 65	120		738	683	1395	148	117	1370	156	124	1360	160	127	1350	163	129
40 15 70	120		756	700	1403	156	124	1380	164	131	1370	168	133	1360	172	136
40 20 10	125		540	500	1295	73	58	1265	78	62	1235	84	66	1215	88	70
40 20 15	125		570	528	1305	83	66	1275	89	71	1245	96	76	1228	100	79
40 20 20	125		600	556	1315	95	76	1285	102	81	1255	109	87	1240	113	90
40 20 25	125		624	578	1323	105	83	1293	112	89	1268	119	95	1253	124	98
40 20 30	125		648	600	1330	116	92	1300	124	98	1280	130	103	1265	134	107
40 20 35	125		666	617	1340	123	98	1310	131	104	1290	138	109	1275	143	113
40 20 40	125		684	633	1350	130	103	1320	139	110	1300	146	115	1285	151	120
40 20 45	125		696	644	1358	135	107	1328	144	114	1310	150	119	1298	154	122
40 20 50	125		708	656	1365	140	111	1335	149	119	1320	154	123	1310	158	126
40 20 55	125		720	667	1373	144	115	1345	153	122	1330	159	126	1320	162	129
40 20 60	125		732	678	1380	149	119	1355	158	125	1340	163	130	1330	167	132
40 20 65	125		750	694	1388	158	125	1363	167	132	1350	171	136	1340	175	139
40 20 70	125		768	711	1395	167	132	1370	176	140	1360	180	143	1350	184	146
40 25 10	130		564	522	1288	84	67	1255	91	72	1225	98	77	1205	103	81
40 25 15	130		594	550	1298	96	76	1265	104	82	1235	111	88	1215	117	93
40 25 20	130		618	572	1308	105	84	1275	114	90	1245	122	97	1228	127	101
40 25 25	130		642	594	1315	116	92	1283	125	99	1255	134	106	1240	139	110
40 25 30	130		660	611	1323	124	99	1290	134	106	1268	141	112	1253	146	116
40 25 35	130		678	628	1330	132	105	1300	142	113	1278	149	119	1263	155	123
40 25 40	130		690	639	1340	137	108	1310	146	116	1288	154	122	1273	159	126
40 25 45	130		702	650	1348	141	112	1318	151	120	1298	158	126	1285	163	129
40 25 50	130		714	661	1358	145	115	1328	155	123	1308	163	129	1298	166	132
40 25 55	130		726	672	1365	150	119	1335	161	128	1318	167	133	1308	171	136
40 25 60	130		744	689	1373	159	126	1345	169	134	1328	176	140	1318	180	143
40 25 65	130		762	706	1380	168	134	1355	178	141	1338	185	147	1328	189	150
40 25 70	130		786	728	1388	182	144	1365	191	152	1350	197	157	1340	202	160
40 30 10	135		588	544	1280	97	77	1245	105	83	1215	113	90	1195	119	94

SOMATOTYPE	T	I	HEIGHT (M)	(F)	SPI →20	WEIGHT (M)	(F)	SPI →30	WEIGHT (M)	(F)	SPI →40	WEIGHT (M)	(F)	SPI →50+	WEIGHT (M)	(F)
0 30 15	135		612	567	1290	107	85	1255	116	92	1225	125	99	1205	131	104
0 30 20	135		636	589	1300	117	93	1265	127	101	1235	137	108	1215	143	114
0 30 25	135		654	606	1308	125	99	1273	136	108	1245	145	115	1228	151	120
0 30 30	135		672	622	1315	133	106	1280	145	115	1255	154	122	1240	159	126
0 30 35	135		684	633	1323	138	110	1290	149	118	1265	158	125	1250	164	130
0 30 40	135		696	644	1330	143	114	1300	153	122	1275	163	129	1260	169	134
0 30 45	135		708	656	1340	147	117	1310	158	126	1285	167	133	1273	172	137
0 30 50	135		720	667	1350	152	121	1320	162	129	1295	172	137	1285	176	140
0 30 55	135		738	683	1358	160	127	1328	172	136	1305	181	143	1295	185	147
0 30 60	135		756	700	1365	170	135	1335	182	144	1315	190	151	1305	194	154
0 30 65	135		780	722	1373	183	145	1348	194	154	1328	203	161	1318	207	164
0 30 70	135		804	744	1380	198	157	1360	207	164	1340	216	171	1330	221	175
0 35 10	140		606	561	1270	109	86	1233	119	94	1200	129	102	1180	135	107
0 35 15	140		630	583	1280	119	94	1243	130	103	1210	141	112	1190	148	118
0 35 20	140		648	600	1290	127	101	1253	138	110	1220	150	119	1203	156	124
0 35 25	140		666	617	1298	135	107	1260	148	117	1230	159	126	1215	165	131
0 35 30	140		678	628	1308	139	111	1270	152	121	1243	162	129	1228	168	134
0 35 35	140		690	639	1315	144	115	1280	157	124	1253	167	133	1238	173	138
0 35 40	140		702	650	1323	149	119	1290	161	128	1265	171	136	1250	177	141
0 35 45	140		714	661	1330	155	123	1300	166	131	1275	176	139	1260	182	144
0 35 50	140		732	678	1340	163	130	1310	174	139	1285	185	147	1273	190	151
0 35 55	140		750	694	1348	172	136	1318	184	146	1295	194	154	1283	200	158
0 35 60	140		774	717	1358	185	147	1328	198	157	1305	209	166	1295	214	170
0 35 65	140		798	739	1365	200	159	1338	212	168	1318	222	176	1308	227	180
0 35 70	140		828	767	1373	219	174	1350	231	183	1330	241	192	1320	247	196
0 40 10	145		624	578	1260	121	97	1220	134	106	1185	146	116	1165	154	122
0 40 15	145		642	594	1270	129	102	1230	142	113	1195	155	123	1178	162	128
0 40 20	145		660	611	1280	137	109	1240	151	120	1205	164	130	1190	171	135
0 40 25	145		672	622	1290	141	112	1250	155	123	1218	168	133	1203	174	138
0 40 30	145		684	633	1300	146	115	1260	160	127	1230	172	136	1215	178	141
0 40 35	145		696	644	1308	151	119	1270	165	130	1243	176	139	1228	182	144
0 40 40	145		708	656	1315	156	124	1280	169	135	1255	180	143	1240	186	148
0 40 45	145		726	672	1323	165	131	1290	178	141	1265	189	150	1250	196	155
0 40 50	145		744	689	1330	175	139	1300	187	149	1275	199	158	1260	206	164
0 40 55	145		768	711	1340	188	149	1310	201	160	1285	213	169	1273	220	174
0 40 60	145		792	733	1350	202	160	1320	216	171	1295	229	181	1285	234	186
0 40 65	145		822	761	1358	222	176	1330	236	187	1308	248	197	1298	254	202
0 40 70	145		852	789	1365	243	193	1340	257	204	1320	269	214	1310	275	218
0 45 10	150		636	589	1253	131	104	1205	147	117	1170	161	128	1150	169	134
0 45 15	150		654	606	1263	139	110	1215	156	124	1180	170	135	1163	178	141
0 45 20	150		666	617	1273	143	114	1228	160	127	1193	174	138	1175	182	145
0 45 25	150		678	628	1283	148	117	1238	164	131	1205	178	142	1188	186	148
0 45 30	150		690	639	1293	152	121	1250	168	134	1218	182	144	1200	190	151
0 45 35	150		702	650	1300	157	125	1260	173	137	1230	186	148	1213	194	154
0 45 40	150		720	667	1308	167	133	1270	182	145	1243	194	155	1225	203	161
0 45 45	150		738	683	1315	177	140	1280	192	152	1253	204	162	1235	213	169
0 45 50	150		762	706	1323	191	152	1290	206	164	1263	220	175	1248	228	181

						SPI WITH MAXIMAL WEIGHTS AT PROGESSIVE AGES										
SOMATOTYPE	T	I	HEIGHT (M)	(F)	SPI →20	WEIGHT (M)	(F)	SPI →30	WEIGHT (M)	(F)	SPI →40	WEIGHT (M)	(F)	SPI →50+	WEIGHT (M)	(F)
40 45 55	150		786	728	1330	206	164	1300	221	176	1273	235	187	1260	243	193
40 45 60	150		816	756	1340	226	180	1310	242	192	1285	256	204	1273	263	209
40 45 65	150		846	783	1348	247	196	1320	263	209	1298	277	220	1285	285	226
40 50 10	155		648	600	1245	141	112	1190	161	128	1155	177	140	1135	186	148
40 50 15	155		660	611	1255	145	115	1203	165	131	1168	180	143	1148	190	151
40 50 20	155		672	622	1265	150	119	1215	169	134	1180	185	146	1160	194	154
40 50 25	155		684	633	1275	154	122	1228	173	137	1193	188	149	1173	198	157
40 50 30	155		696	644	1285	159	126	1240	177	140	1205	193	153	1185	203	161
40 50 35	155		714	661	1293	168	134	1250	186	148	1218	201	160	1198	212	168
40 50 40	155		732	678	1300	179	142	1260	196	156	1230	211	167	1210	221	176
40 50 45	155		756	700	1308	193	153	1270	211	167	1240	227	180	1223	236	188
40 50 50	155		780	722	1315	209	166	1280	226	179	1250	243	193	1235	252	200
40 50 55	155		810	750	1323	229	182	1290	248	197	1263	264	209	1248	273	217
40 50 60	155		840	778	1330	252	200	1300	270	214	1275	286	227	1260	296	235
40 55 10	160		654	606	1233	149	119	1175	172	137	1140	189	150	1118	200	159
40 55 15	160		666	617	1243	154	122	1188	176	140	1153	193	153	1130	205	163
40 55 20	160		678	628	1253	158	126	1200	180	143	1168	196	155	1145	208	165
40 55 25	160		690	639	1263	163	130	1213	184	146	1180	200	159	1158	212	168
40 55 30	160		708	656	1273	172	137	1225	193	154	1193	209	166	1170	222	176
40 55 35	160		726	672	1280	182	145	1235	203	161	1205	219	173	1183	231	183
40 55 40	160		750	694	1290	197	156	1248	217	172	1218	233	185	1195	247	196
40 55 45	160		774	717	1298	212	169	1258	233	185	1228	250	199	1208	263	209
40 55 50	160		804	744	1308	232	184	1270	254	201	1240	273	216	1220	286	227
40 55 55	160		834	772	1315	255	202	1280	277	219	1253	295	234	1233	309	245
40 60 10	165		660	611	1220	158	126	1160	184	146	1125	202	160	1100	216	171
40 60 15	165		672	622	1230	163	129	1173	188	149	1140	205	162	1115	219	174
40 60 20	165		684	633	1240	168	133	1185	192	152	1155	208	165	1130	222	176
40 60 25	165		702	650	1250	177	141	1198	201	160	1168	217	172	1143	232	184
40 60 30	165		720	667	1260	187	148	1210	211	168	1180	227	181	1155	242	193
40 60 35	165		744	689	1270	201	160	1223	225	179	1193	243	193	1168	258	205
40 60 40	165		768	711	1280	216	171	1235	240	191	1205	259	205	1180	276	219
40 60 45	165		798	739	1290	237	188	1248	261	208	1218	281	223	1193	299	238
40 60 50	165		828	767	1300	258	205	1260	284	226	1230	305	242	1205	324	258
40 65 10	170		666	617	1205	169	134	1143	198	157	1108	217	173	1083	233	185
40 65 15	170		678	628	1215	174	138	1155	202	161	1123	220	175	1098	235	187
40 65 20	170		696	644	1228	182	144	1170	211	167	1138	229	181	1113	245	194
40 65 25	170		714	661	1238	192	152	1183	220	174	1150	239	190	1125	256	203
40 65 30	170		738	683	1250	206	163	1195	236	187	1165	254	202	1140	271	215
40 65 35	170		762	706	1260	221	176	1208	251	200	1178	271	215	1153	289	230
40 65 40	170		792	733	1270	243	192	1220	274	217	1190	295	234	1165	314	249
40 65 45	170		822	761	1280	265	210	1233	296	235	1203	319	253	1178	340	270
40 70 10	175		672	622	1190	180	143	1125	213	169	1090	234	186	1065	251	199
40 70 15	175		690	639	1203	189	150	1140	222	176	1105	243	193	1080	261	207
40 70 20	175		708	656	1215	198	157	1155	230	183	1120	253	201	1095	270	215
40 70 25	175		732	678	1228	212	168	1168	246	196	1135	268	213	1110	287	228

						SPI WITH MAXIMAL WEIGHTS AT PROGESSIVE AGES									
SOMATOTYPE	T I	HEIGHT		SPI	WEIGHT		SPI	WEIGHT		SPI	WEIGHT		SPI	WEIGHT	
		(M)	(F)	→20	(M)	(F)	→30	(M)	(F)	→40	(M)	(F)	→50+	(M)	(F)
40 70 30	175	756	700	1240	227	180	1180	263	209	1150	284	226	1125	303	241
40 70 35	175	786	728	1250	249	198	1193	286	227	1163	309	245	1138	329	262
40 70 40	175	816	756	1260	272	216	1205	311	247	1175	335	266	1150	357	284
45 10 15	110	546	506	1308	73	58	1273	79	63	1248	84	67	1233	87	69
45 10 20	110	576	533	1315	84	67	1280	91	72	1258	96	76	1245	99	78
45 10 25	110	606	561	1322	96	76	1290	104	82	1268	109	87	1258	112	89
45 10 30	110	630	583	1333	106	84	1300	114	90	1278	120	95	1270	122	97
45 10 35	110	654	606	1340	116	92	1310	124	99	1288	131	104	1280	133	106
45 10 40	110	672	622	1348	124	98	1320	132	105	1298	139	110	1290	141	112
45 10 45	110	690	639	1355	132	105	1328	140	111	1308	147	117	1300	150	119
45 10 50	110	702	650	1363	137	108	1335	145	115	1320	150	119	1313	153	121
45 10 55	110	714	661	1370	142	112	1343	150	119	1330	155	123	1323	157	125
45 10 60	110	726	672	1380	146	115	1353	154	123	1340	159	126	1333	162	128
45 10 65	110	738	683	1388	150	119	1363	159	126	1350	163	129	1343	166	132
45 10 70	110	756	700	1398	158	126	1373	167	133	1360	172	136	1353	174	138
45 15 10	115	540	500	1290	73	58	1255	80	63	1225	86	68	1208	89	71
45 15 15	115	570	528	1298	85	67	1263	92	73	1235	98	78	1220	102	81
45 15 20	115	600	556	1308	97	77	1273	105	83	1245	112	89	1233	115	92
45 15 25	115	624	578	1315	107	85	1280	116	92	1258	122	97	1245	126	100
45 15 30	115	648	600	1323	118	93	1290	127	101	1268	133	106	1258	137	108
45 15 35	115	666	617	1333	125	99	1300	134	107	1278	142	113	1268	145	115
45 15 40	115	684	633	1340	133	105	1310	142	113	1288	150	119	1278	153	122
45 15 45	115	696	644	1348	138	109	1318	147	117	1298	154	122	1288	158	125
45 15 50	115	708	656	1355	143	113	1325	153	121	1308	159	126	1298	162	129
45 15 55	115	720	667	1363	147	117	1335	157	125	1318	163	130	1310	166	132
45 15 60	115	732	678	1373	152	120	1345	161	128	1328	167	133	1320	171	136
45 15 65	115	750	694	1380	161	127	1355	170	134	1338	176	140	1333	178	141
45 15 70	115	768	711	1390	169	134	1363	179	142	1348	185	147	1343	187	148
45 20 10	120	564	522	1280	86	68	1245	93	74	1213	101	80	1195	105	83
45 20 15	120	594	550	1290	98	78	1255	106	84	1223	115	91	1208	119	94
45 20 20	120	618	572	1300	107	85	1265	117	92	1235	125	99	1220	130	103
45 20 25	120	642	594	1308	118	94	1273	128	102	1245	137	109	1233	141	112
45 20 30	120	660	611	1315	126	100	1280	137	109	1258	144	115	1245	149	118
45 20 35	120	678	628	1323	135	107	1290	145	115	1268	153	121	1255	158	125
45 20 40	120	690	639	1333	139	110	1300	150	119	1278	157	125	1265	162	129
45 20 45	120	702	650	1340	144	114	1308	155	123	1288	162	129	1275	167	132
45 20 50	120	714	661	1348	149	118	1318	159	126	1298	166	132	1288	170	135
45 20 55	120	726	672	1355	154	122	1328	163	130	1308	171	136	1298	175	139
45 20 60	120	744	689	1365	162	129	1338	172	137	1318	180	143	1310	183	145
45 20 65	120	762	706	1373	171	136	1345	182	145	1328	189	150	1320	192	153
45 20 70	120	786	728	1383	184	146	1355	195	155	1338	203	161	1333	205	163
45 25 10	125	588	544	1270	99	79	1233	108	86	1200	118	93	1183	123	97
45 25 15	125	612	567	1280	109	87	1245	119	94	1213	128	102	1195	134	107
45 25 20	125	636	589	1290	120	95	1255	130	103	1223	141	112	1208	146	116
45 25 25	125	654	606	1300	127	101	1263	139	110	1235	149	118	1220	154	123

SPI WITH MAXIMAL WEIGHTS AT PROGESSIVE AGES

SOMATOTYPE	T	I	HEIGHT (M)	HEIGHT (F)	SPI →20	WEIGHT (M)	WEIGHT (F)	SPI →30	WEIGHT (M)	WEIGHT (F)	SPI →40	WEIGHT (M)	WEIGHT (F)	SPI →50+	WEIGHT (M)	WEIGHT (F)
45 25 30	125	672	622		1308	136	108	1270	148	117	1245	157	125	1230	163	129
45 25 35	125	684	633		1315	141	112	1280	153	121	1255	162	128	1243	167	132
45 25 40	125	696	644		1323	146	115	1290	157	124	1265	167	132	1253	171	136
45 25 45	125	708	656		1333	150	119	1300	162	128	1275	171	136	1265	175	139
45 25 50	125	720	667		1340	155	123	1308	167	133	1285	176	140	1275	180	143
45 25 55	125	738	683		1348	164	130	1318	176	139	1295	185	147	1288	188	149
45 25 60	125	756	700		1358	173	137	1328	184	146	1305	194	154	1298	198	157
45 25 65	125	780	722		1365	187	148	1338	198	157	1315	209	166	1310	211	167
45 25 70	125	804	744		1375	200	158	1348	212	168	1328	222	176	1323	224	178
45 30 10	130	606	561		1263	110	88	1223	122	97	1190	132	105	1173	138	109
45 30 15	130	630	583		1273	121	96	1233	133	106	1200	145	115	1183	151	120
45 30 20	130	648	600		1283	129	102	1245	141	112	1213	152	121	1195	159	127
45 30 25	130	666	617		1290	138	109	1253	150	119	1223	161	128	1205	169	134
45 30 30	130	678	628		1300	142	113	1263	155	123	1233	166	132	1218	172	137
45 30 35	130	690	639		1308	147	117	1270	160	127	1243	171	136	1228	177	141
45 30 40	130	702	650		1315	152	121	1280	165	131	1253	176	140	1240	181	144
45 30 45	130	714	661		1323	157	125	1290	170	135	1263	181	143	1253	185	147
45 30 50	130	732	678		1333	166	132	1300	179	142	1273	190	151	1265	194	154
45 30 55	130	750	694		1340	175	139	1308	189	149	1283	200	158	1275	204	161
45 30 60	130	774	717		1350	188	150	1318	203	161	1293	214	171	1285	219	174
45 30 65	130	798	739		1358	203	161	1328	217	172	1305	229	182	1298	232	185
45 30 70	130	828	767		1368	222	176	1340	236	188	1318	248	197	1310	253	201
45 35 10	135	624	578		1253	124	98	1210	137	109	1175	150	119	1155	158	125
45 35 15	135	642	594		1263	131	104	1220	146	115	1188	158	125	1168	166	132
45 35 20	135	660	611		1273	139	111	1233	153	122	1198	167	133	1180	175	139
45 35 25	135	672	622		1283	144	114	1243	158	125	1210	171	136	1193	179	142
45 35 30	135	684	633		1290	149	118	1250	164	130	1220	176	140	1203	184	146
45 35 35	135	696	644		1300	153	122	1260	169	134	1233	180	142	1215	188	149
45 35 40	135	708	656		1308	159	126	1270	173	138	1243	185	147	1225	193	154
45 35 45	135	726	672		1315	168	133	1280	182	145	1253	195	154	1238	202	160
45 35 50	135	744	689		1323	178	141	1290	192	152	1263	204	162	1250	211	167
45 35 55	135	768	711		1333	191	152	1300	206	164	1273	220	174	1263	225	178
45 35 60	135	792	733		1343	205	163	1308	222	176	1283	235	186	1273	241	191
45 35 65	135	822	761		1350	226	179	1320	241	192	1295	256	203	1288	260	206
45 35 70	135	852	789		1360	246	195	1330	263	209	1308	276	219	1300	282	224
45 40 10	140	636	589		1243	134	106	1198	150	119	1163	164	130	1140	174	138
45 40 15	140	654	606		1253	142	113	1208	159	126	1173	173	138	1153	182	145
45 40 20	140	666	617		1263	147	117	1220	163	129	1185	178	141	1168	185	147
45 40 25	140	678	628		1273	151	120	1230	167	133	1198	181	144	1180	190	151
45 40 30	140	690	639		1283	156	124	1240	172	137	1210	185	147	1193	193	154
45 40 35	140	702	650		1290	161	128	1250	177	141	1220	191	151	1203	199	158
45 40 40	140	720	667		1300	170	135	1260	187	148	1233	199	158	1215	208	165
45 40 45	140	738	683		1308	180	142	1270	196	156	1243	209	166	1225	219	173
45 40 50	140	762	706		1315	195	155	1280	211	168	1253	225	179	1238	233	185
45 40 55	140	786	728		1325	209	166	1290	226	180	1263	241	192	1250	249	198
45 40 60	140	816	756		1335	228	182	1300	247	197	1273	263	209	1263	270	214
45 40 65	140	846	783		1343	250	198	1310	269	214	1285	285	226	1275	292	232

SOMATOTYPE	T I	HEIGHT		SPI	WEIGHT		SPI	WEIGHT		SPI	WEIGHT		SPI	WEIGHT	
		(M)	(F)	→20	(M)	(F)	→30	(M)	(F)	→40	(M)	(F)	→50+	(M)	(F)
45 45 10	145	648	600	1233	145	115	1183	164	130	1145	181	144	1123	192	153
45 45 15	145	660	611	1243	150	119	1195	168	134	1158	185	147	1138	195	155
45 45 20	145	672	622	1253	154	122	1205	173	138	1170	189	150	1150	200	158
45 45 25	145	684	633	1263	159	126	1218	177	140	1183	193	153	1163	203	161
45 45 30	145	696	644	1273	163	129	1228	182	144	1195	198	157	1175	208	165
45 45 35	145	714	661	1283	172	137	1240	191	151	1208	206	164	1188	217	172
45 45 40	145	732	678	1290	183	145	1250	201	160	1220	216	172	1200	227	180
45 45 45	145	756	700	1300	197	156	1260	216	171	1230	232	184	1210	244	194
45 45 50	145	780	722	1308	212	168	1270	232	184	1240	249	197	1223	259	206
45 45 55	145	810	750	1318	232	184	1280	253	201	1250	272	216	1238	280	222
45 45 60	145	840	778	1325	255	202	1290	276	219	1263	294	234	1250	303	241
45 50 10	150	654	606	1223	153	122	1168	176	140	1130	194	154	1108	206	164
45 50 15	150	666	617	1233	158	125	1180	180	143	1143	198	157	1120	210	167
45 50 20	150	678	628	1245	162	128	1193	184	146	1158	201	159	1135	213	169
45 50 25	150	690	639	1255	166	132	1205	188	149	1170	205	163	1148	217	172
45 50 30	150	708	656	1265	175	139	1218	196	156	1183	214	171	1160	227	181
45 50 35	150	726	672	1273	185	147	1228	207	164	1195	224	178	1173	237	188
45 50 40	150	750	694	1283	200	158	1240	221	175	1208	239	190	1185	254	201
45 50 45	150	774	717	1290	216	172	1250	237	189	1218	257	204	1198	270	214
45 50 50	150	804	744	1300	237	187	1260	260	206	1228	281	222	1210	293	232
45 50 55	150	834	772	1308	259	206	1270	283	225	1240	304	241	1223	317	252
45 55 10	155	660	611	1210	162	129	1150	189	150	1113	209	165	1090	222	176
45 55 15	155	672	622	1220	167	133	1165	192	152	1128	211	168	1105	225	178
45 55 20	155	684	633	1233	171	135	1178	196	155	1143	214	170	1120	228	181
45 55 25	155	702	650	1243	180	143	1190	205	163	1155	225	178	1133	238	189
45 55 30	155	720	667	1253	190	151	1203	214	170	1168	234	186	1145	249	198
45 55 35	155	744	689	1263	204	162	1215	230	182	1180	251	199	1158	265	211
45 55 40	155	768	711	1270	221	175	1225	246	196	1193	267	212	1170	283	224
45 55 45	155	798	739	1280	242	192	1238	268	213	1205	290	231	1183	307	244
45 55 50	155	828	767	1293	263	209	1250	291	231	1218	314	250	1195	333	264
45 60 10	160	666	617	1198	172	137	1135	202	161	1098	223	177	1075	238	189
45 60 15	160	678	628	1208	177	141	1148	206	164	1113	226	180	1090	241	191
45 60 20	160	696	644	1220	186	147	1163	214	170	1128	235	186	1105	250	198
45 60 25	160	714	661	1230	196	155	1175	224	178	1140	246	195	1118	260	207
45 60 30	160	738	683	1240	211	167	1188	240	190	1153	262	208	1130	279	221
45 60 35	160	762	706	1250	227	180	1200	256	204	1165	280	223	1143	296	236
45 60 40	160	792	733	1260	248	197	1213	278	221	1178	304	241	1155	322	256
45 60 45	160	822	761	1270	271	215	1225	302	240	1190	330	262	1168	349	277
45 65 10	165	672	622	1183	183	145	1118	217	172	1080	241	191	1058	256	203
45 65 15	165	690	639	1195	193	153	1133	226	179	1095	250	199	1073	266	211
45 65 20	165	708	656	1208	201	160	1148	235	187	1110	259	206	1088	276	219
45 65 25	165	732	678	1218	217	172	1160	251	200	1125	275	219	1103	292	232
45 65 30	165	756	700	1230	232	184	1173	268	213	1138	293	233	1115	312	247
45 65 35	165	786	728	1240	255	202	1185	292	232	1150	319	254	1128	338	269
45 65 40	165	816	756	1250	278	221	1198	316	251	1163	345	275	1140	367	292

SOMATOTYPE	T	I	HEIGHT (M)	(F)	SPI ➞20	WEIGHT (M)	(F)	SPI ➞30	WEIGHT (M)	(F)	SPI ➞40	WEIGHT (M)	(F)	SPI ➞50+	WEIGHT (M)	(F)
						SPI WITH MAXIMAL WEIGHTS AT PROGESSIVE AGES										
45 70 10			170	684	633	1168	201	159	1103	238	189	1065	265	210	1043	282	224
45 70 15			170	702	650	1180	211	167	1118	248	197	1080	275	218	1058	292	232
45 70 20			170	726	672	1195	224	178	1133	263	209	1095	291	231	1073	310	246
45 70 25			170	750	694	1208	239	190	1145	281	223	1108	310	246	1085	330	262
45 70 30			170	780	722	1220	261	207	1158	306	242	1123	335	266	1100	357	283
45 70 35			170	810	750	1230	286	227	1170	332	263	1135	363	289	1113	385	306
50 10 10			105	540	500	1285	74	59	1245	82	65	1215	88	70	1200	91	72
50 10 15			105	570	528	1293	86	68	1253	94	75	1225	101	80	1213	104	82
50 10 20			105	600	556	1300	98	78	1260	108	86	1235	115	91	1225	118	94
50 10 25			105	624	578	1308	109	86	1270	119	94	1245	126	100	1238	128	102
50 10 30			105	648	600	1315	120	95	1280	130	103	1255	138	109	1250	139	111
50 10 35			105	666	617	1323	128	101	1290	138	109	1265	146	116	1260	148	117
50 10 40			105	684	633	1330	136	108	1300	146	115	1275	154	122	1270	156	124
50 10 45			105	696	644	1338	141	112	1308	151	119	1288	158	125	1283	160	126
50 10 50			105	708	656	1345	146	116	1315	156	124	1300	162	128	1295	163	130
50 10 55			105	720	667	1355	150	119	1325	160	128	1310	166	132	1305	168	134
50 10 60			105	732	678	1365	154	123	1335	165	131	1320	171	136	1315	172	137
50 10 65			105	750	694	1375	162	129	1345	173	137	1330	179	142	1325	181	144
50 10 70			105	768	711	1385	171	135	1355	182	144	1340	188	149	1335	190	151
50 15 10			110	564	522	1275	87	69	1235	95	76	1203	103	82	1188	107	85
50 15 15			110	594	550	1283	99	79	1243	109	87	1213	117	93	1200	121	96
50 15 20			110	618	572	1293	109	87	1253	120	95	1225	128	102	1213	132	105
50 15 25			110	642	594	1300	120	95	1260	132	105	1235	140	111	1225	144	114
50 15 30			110	660	611	1308	128	102	1270	140	111	1245	149	118	1238	152	120
50 15 35			110	678	628	1315	137	109	1280	149	118	1255	158	125	1248	160	127
50 15 40			110	690	639	1323	142	113	1290	153	122	1265	162	129	1257	165	131
50 15 45			110	702	650	1330	147	117	1298	158	126	1275	167	132	1268	170	135
50 15 50			110	714	661	1338	152	121	1308	163	129	1288	170	135	1280	174	138
50 15 55			110	726	672	1348	156	124	1318	167	133	1298	175	139	1290	178	141
50 15 60			110	744	689	1358	164	131	1328	176	140	1308	184	146	1303	186	148
50 15 65			110	762	706	1368	173	137	1338	185	147	1318	193	154	1313	195	155
50 15 70			110	786	728	1378	186	147	1348	198	158	1328	207	165	1325	209	166
50 20 10			115	588	544	1265	100	80	1225	111	88	1190	121	96	1175	125	99
50 20 15			115	612	567	1275	111	88	1235	122	97	1203	132	105	1188	137	109
50 20 20			115	636	589	1285	121	96	1245	133	106	1215	143	114	1200	149	118
50 20 25			115	654	606	1293	129	103	1253	142	113	1225	152	121	1213	157	125
50 20 30			115	672	622	1300	138	110	1260	152	120	1235	161	128	1225	165	131
50 20 35			115	684	633	1308	143	113	1270	156	124	1245	166	131	1235	170	135
50 20 40			115	696	644	1315	148	117	1280	161	127	1255	171	135	1245	175	138
50 20 45			115	708	656	1323	153	122	1290	165	132	1265	175	139	1255	180	143
50 20 50			115	720	667	1330	159	126	1300	170	135	1275	180	143	1265	184	147
50 20 55			115	738	683	1340	167	132	1310	179	142	1285	189	150	1278	193	153
50 20 60			115	756	700	1350	176	139	1320	188	149	1295	199	158	1290	201	160
50 20 65			115	780	722	1360	189	150	1330	202	160	1305	214	169	1303	215	170
50 20 70			115	804	744	1370	202	160	1340	216	171	1315	229	181	1315	229	181

SPI WITH MAXIMAL WEIGHTS AT PROGESSIVE AGES

SOMATOTYPE	T I	HEIGHT (M)	(F)	SPI →20	WEIGHT (M)	(F)	SPI →30	WEIGHT (M)	(F)	SPI →40	WEIGHT (M)	(F)	SPI →50+	WEIGHT (M)	(F)
50 25 10	120	606	561	1255	113	89	1213	125	99	1178	136	108	1163	141	112
50 25 15	120	630	583	1265	124	98	1223	137	108	1190	148	118	1175	154	122
50 25 20	120	648	600	1275	131	104	1235	144	115	1203	156	124	1188	162	129
50 25 25	120	666	617	1283	140	111	1243	154	122	1213	166	132	1198	172	137
50 25 30	120	678	628	1293	144	115	1253	158	126	1223	170	135	1210	176	140
50 25 35	120	690	639	1300	150	119	1260	164	130	1233	175	139	1220	181	144
50 25 40	120	702	650	1308	155	123	1270	169	134	1243	180	143	1233	185	147
50 25 45	120	714	661	1315	160	127	1280	174	138	1253	185	147	1243	190	150
50 25 50	120	732	678	1323	169	135	1290	183	145	1263	195	155	1255	198	158
50 25 55	120	750	694	1333	178	141	1300	192	152	1273	205	162	1265	208	165
50 25 60	120	774	717	1343	191	152	1310	206	164	1283	220	175	1278	222	177
50 25 65	120	798	739	1353	205	163	1320	221	175	1293	235	187	1290	237	188
50 25 70	120	828	767	1363	224	178	1330	241	192	1305	255	203	1303	257	204
50 30 10	125	624	578	1245	126	100	1200	141	112	1165	154	122	1150	160	127
50 30 15	125	642	594	1255	134	106	1213	148	117	1178	162	128	1163	168	133
50 30 20	125	660	611	1265	142	113	1225	156	124	1190	171	135	1175	177	141
50 30 25	125	672	622	1275	146	116	1235	161	128	1200	176	139	1185	182	145
50 30 30	125	684	633	1285	151	120	1245	166	131	1210	181	143	1195	188	149
50 30 35	125	696	644	1293	156	124	1253	171	136	1220	186	147	1208	191	152
50 30 40	125	708	656	1300	162	128	1260	177	141	1230	191	152	1220	195	155
50 30 45	125	726	672	1308	171	136	1270	187	148	1240	201	159	1233	204	162
50 30 50	125	744	689	1315	181	144	1280	196	156	1250	211	167	1245	213	169
50 30 55	125	768	711	1325	195	155	1290	211	167	1260	226	180	1255	229	182
50 30 60	125	792	733	1335	209	166	1300	226	179	1270	243	192	1265	245	195
50 30 65	125	822	761	1345	228	181	1310	247	196	1283	263	209	1278	266	211
50 30 70	125	852	789	1355	249	197	1320	269	214	1295	285	226	1290	288	229
50 35 10	130	636	589	1235	137	108	1188	153	122	1153	168	133	1133	177	140
50 35 15	130	654	606	1245	145	115	1200	162	129	1165	177	141	1145	186	148
50 35 20	130	666	617	1255	149	119	1213	166	132	1178	181	144	1160	189	150
50 35 25	130	678	628	1265	154	122	1223	170	135	1188	186	148	1170	195	155
50 35 30	130	690	639	1275	158	126	1233	175	139	1200	190	151	1183	198	158
50 35 35	130	702	650	1283	164	130	1240	181	144	1210	195	155	1193	204	162
50 35 40	130	720	667	1293	173	137	1250	191	152	1220	206	163	1205	213	170
50 35 45	130	738	683	1300	183	145	1260	201	159	1230	216	171	1218	222	176
50 35 50	130	762	706	1308	198	157	1270	216	172	1240	232	185	1230	238	189
50 35 55	130	786	728	1318	212	169	1280	232	184	1250	249	198	1240	255	202
50 35 60	130	816	756	1328	232	184	1290	253	201	1260	272	216	1253	276	220
50 35 65	130	846	783	1338	253	200	1300	276	219	1273	294	233	1265	299	237
50 40 10	135	648	600	1225	148	118	1175	168	133	1140	184	146	1115	196	156
50 40 15	135	660	611	1235	153	121	1188	171	136	1153	188	149	1130	199	158
50 40 20	135	672	622	1245	157	125	1200	176	139	1165	192	152	1145	202	160
50 40 25	135	684	633	1255	162	128	1210	181	143	1178	196	155	1158	206	163
50 40 30	135	696	644	1265	167	132	1220	186	147	1190	200	158	1170	211	167
50 40 35	135	714	661	1275	176	139	1230	196	155	1200	211	167	1180	222	176
50 40 40	135	732	678	1285	185	147	1240	206	163	1210	221	176	1190	233	185
50 40 45	135	756	700	1293	200	159	1250	221	176	1220	238	189	1203	248	197

SPI WITH MAXIMAL WEIGHTS AT PROGESSIVE AGES

SOMATOTYPE	T I	HEIGHT (M)	(F)	SPI →20	WEIGHT (M)	(F)	SPI →30	WEIGHT (M)	(F)	SPI →40	WEIGHT (M)	(F)	SPI →50+	WEIGHT (M)	(F)
50 40 50	135	780	722	1300	216	171	1260	237	188	1230	255	202	1215	265	210
50 40 55	135	810	750	1310	236	188	1270	259	206	1240	279	221	1228	287	228
50 40 60	135	840	778	1320	258	205	1280	283	225	1250	303	241	1240	311	247
50 45 10	140	654	606	1213	157	125	1160	179	143	1123	198	157	1098	211	168
50 45 15	140	666	617	1223	161	128	1173	183	146	1135	202	161	1113	214	170
50 45 20	140	678	628	1235	165	131	1185	187	149	1150	205	163	1128	217	173
50 45 25	140	690	639	1245	170	135	1195	193	153	1163	209	166	1140	222	176
50 45 30	140	708	656	1255	180	143	1208	201	160	1175	219	174	1153	232	184
50 45 35	140	726	672	1265	189	150	1218	212	168	1185	230	182	1163	243	193
50 45 40	140	750	694	1275	204	161	1230	227	180	1198	245	194	1175	260	206
50 45 45	140	774	717	1283	220	175	1240	243	193	1208	263	209	1188	277	220
50 45 50	140	804	744	1293	240	191	1250	266	211	1218	288	228	1200	301	238
50 45 55	140	834	772	1303	262	208	1260	290	230	1228	313	248	1213	325	258
50 50 10	145	660	611	1200	166	132	1145	192	152	1105	213	169	1080	228	181
50 50 15	145	672	622	1213	170	135	1158	195	155	1120	216	171	1095	231	183
50 50 20	145	684	633	1225	174	138	1170	200	158	1135	219	173	1110	234	185
50 50 25	145	702	650	1235	184	146	1183	209	166	1148	229	182	1123	244	194
50 50 30	145	720	667	1245	193	154	1195	219	174	1160	239	190	1135	255	203
50 50 35	145	744	689	1255	208	165	1208	234	186	1173	255	203	1148	272	216
50 50 40	145	768	711	1265	224	178	1220	249	198	1185	272	216	1160	290	230
50 50 45	145	798	739	1275	245	195	1230	273	217	1195	298	236	1173	315	250
50 50 50	145	828	767	1285	268	213	1240	298	237	1205	324	258	1185	341	271
50 55 10	150	666	617	1188	176	140	1128	206	164	1088	229	182	1065	245	194
50 55 15	150	678	628	1200	180	143	1140	210	167	1103	232	185	1080	247	197
50 55 20	150	696	644	1213	189	150	1155	219	173	1118	241	191	1095	257	203
50 55 25	150	714	661	1223	199	158	1168	228	181	1130	252	200	1108	268	212
50 55 30	150	738	683	1233	214	170	1180	245	194	1143	269	213	1120	286	227
50 55 35	150	762	706	1243	230	183	1193	261	207	1155	287	228	1133	304	242
50 55 40	150	792	733	1253	253	200	1205	284	225	1168	312	247	1145	331	262
50 55 45	150	822	761	1263	276	219	1215	310	246	1178	340	270	1158	358	284
50 60 10	155	672	622	1175	187	148	1110	222	176	1070	248	196	1050	262	208
50 60 15	155	690	639	1188	196	156	1125	231	183	1085	257	204	1065	272	216
50 60 20	155	708	656	1200	205	163	1140	240	191	1100	267	212	1080	282	224
50 60 25	155	732	678	1210	221	176	1153	256	203	1113	284	226	1093	300	239
50 60 30	155	756	700	1220	238	189	1165	273	217	1125	303	241	1105	320	254
50 60 35	155	786	728	1230	261	207	1178	297	236	1138	329	262	1118	347	276
50 60 40	155	816	756	1240	285	227	1190	322	256	1150	357	284	1130	377	299
50 65 10	160	684	633	1160	205	162	1095	244	193	1055	273	216	1033	290	230
50 65 15	160	702	650	1173	214	170	1110	253	201	1070	282	224	1048	301	239
50 65 20	160	726	672	1188	228	181	1125	269	213	1085	300	238	1063	319	253
50 65 25	160	750	694	1198	245	194	1138	286	227	1098	319	253	1075	340	269
50 65 30	160	780	722	1210	268	212	1150	312	247	1110	347	275	1090	366	291
50 65 35	160	810	750	1220	293	232	1163	338	268	1123	375	298	1103	396	314
50 70 10	165	696	644	1145	225	178	1080	268	212	1040	300	237	1015	322	255

SPI WITH MAXIMAL WEIGHTS AT PROGESSIVE AGES

SOMATOTYPE	T	I	HEIGHT (M)	(F)	SPI →20	WEIGHT (M)	(F)	SPI →30	WEIGHT (M)	(F)	SPI →40	WEIGHT (M)	(F)	SPI →50+	WEIGHT (M)	(F)
70	15	165	720	667	1160	239	190	1095	284	226	1055	318	253	1030	342	272
70	20	165	744	689	1175	254	202	1110	301	239	1070	336	267	1045	361	287
70	25	165	774	717	1188	277	220	1123	327	260	1083	365	290	1060	389	309
70	30	165	804	744	1200	301	238	1135	355	282	1095	396	314	1075	418	332
5 10	10	100	564	522	1258	90	71	1218	99	79	1188	107	85	1173	111	88
5 10	15	100	594	550	1265	104	82	1225	114	91	1198	122	97	1185	126	100
5 10	20	100	618	572	1275	114	90	1235	125	99	1208	134	106	1198	137	109
5 10	25	100	642	594	1283	125	99	1245	137	109	1218	146	116	1208	150	119
5 10	30	100	660	611	1293	133	106	1255	145	115	1228	155	123	1220	158	126
5 10	35	100	678	628	1300	142	113	1263	155	123	1238	164	131	1230	167	133
5 10	40	100	690	639	1308	147	117	1273	159	126	1248	169	134	1240	172	137
5 10	45	100	702	650	1315	152	121	1280	165	131	1258	174	138	1250	177	141
5 10	50	100	714	661	1323	157	125	1290	170	135	1270	178	141	1263	181	143
5 10	55	100	726	672	1333	162	128	1300	174	138	1280	182	145	1273	185	147
5 10	60	100	744	689	1343	170	135	1310	183	145	1290	192	152	1285	194	154
5 10	65	100	762	706	1353	179	142	1320	192	153	1300	201	160	1295	204	162
5 10	70	100	786	728	1363	192	152	1330	206	164	1313	215	170	1308	217	172
5 15	10	105	588	544	1248	105	83	1205	116	92	1173	126	100	1158	131	104
5 15	15	105	612	567	1258	115	92	1215	128	102	1185	138	110	1170	143	114
5 15	20	105	636	589	1265	127	101	1225	140	111	1195	151	120	1183	155	123
5 15	25	105	654	606	1275	135	107	1235	149	118	1205	160	127	1195	164	130
5 15	30	105	672	622	1283	144	114	1243	158	125	1215	169	134	1205	173	138
5 15	35	105	684	633	1290	149	118	1253	163	129	1228	173	137	1218	177	140
5 15	40	105	696	644	1298	154	122	1263	167	133	1238	178	141	1228	182	144
5 15	45	105	708	656	1308	159	126	1273	172	137	1248	183	145	1238	187	149
5 15	50	105	720	667	1315	164	130	1280	178	141	1258	187	149	1250	191	152
5 15	55	105	738	683	1325	173	137	1290	187	148	1268	197	156	1263	200	158
5 15	60	105	756	700	1335	182	144	1300	197	156	1278	207	164	1273	209	166
5 15	65	105	780	722	1345	195	155	1310	211	167	1290	221	175	1285	224	177
5 15	70	105	804	744	1353	210	166	1320	226	179	1300	237	187	1298	238	188
5 20	10	110	606	561	1238	117	93	1193	131	104	1160	143	113	1145	148	118
5 20	15	110	630	583	1248	129	102	1203	144	114	1173	155	123	1158	161	128
5 20	20	110	648	600	1258	137	108	1215	152	120	1185	164	130	1170	170	135
5 20	25	110	666	617	1265	146	116	1223	161	128	1195	173	138	1183	178	142
5 20	30	110	678	628	1275	150	119	1233	166	132	1205	178	142	1195	183	145
5 20	35	110	690	639	1283	156	124	1243	171	136	1215	183	145	1205	188	149
5 20	40	110	702	650	1290	161	128	1253	176	140	1228	187	148	1218	191	152
5 20	45	110	714	661	1298	166	132	1263	181	143	1238	192	152	1228	197	156
5 20	50	110	732	678	1308	175	139	1273	190	151	1248	202	160	1238	207	164
5 20	55	110	750	694	1318	184	146	1283	200	158	1258	212	168	1250	216	171
5 20	60	110	774	717	1328	198	157	1293	214	171	1268	227	181	1263	230	183
5 20	65	110	798	739	1335	214	170	1303	230	182	1278	243	193	1275	245	195
5 20	70	110	828	767	1345	233	185	1313	251	199	1290	264	210	1288	266	211
5 25	10	115	624	578	1228	131	104	1180	148	118	1148	161	128	1130	168	134
5 25	15	115	642	594	1238	139	110	1193	156	123	1160	170	134	1143	177	140

						SPI WITH MAXIMAL WEIGHTS AT PROGESSIVE AGES									
SOMATOTYPE	T I	HEIGHT		SPI →20	WEIGHT		SPI →30	WEIGHT		SPI →40	WEIGHT		SPI →50+	WEIGHT	
		(M)	(F)		(M)	(F)		(M)	(F)		(M)	(F)		(M)	(F)
55 25 20	115	660	611	1248	148	117	1205	164	130	1173	178	141	1155	187	148
55 25 25	115	672	622	1258	152	121	1215	169	134	1183	183	145	1168	190	151
55 25 30	115	684	633	1265	158	125	1223	175	139	1193	188	149	1180	195	154
55 25 35	115	696	644	1275	163	129	1233	180	142	1205	193	153	1193	199	157
55 25 40	115	708	656	1283	168	134	1243	185	147	1215	198	157	1203	204	162
55 25 45	115	726	672	1290	178	141	1253	195	154	1225	208	165	1215	213	169
55 25 50	115	744	689	1300	187	149	1263	204	162	1235	219	174	1225	224	178
55 25 55	115	768	711	1310	201	160	1273	220	174	1245	235	186	1238	239	188
55 25 60	115	792	733	1318	217	172	1283	235	186	1255	251	199	1250	254	202
55 25 65	115	822	761	1328	237	188	1293	257	204	1268	272	216	1263	276	218
55 25 70	115	852	789	1338	258	205	1303	280	222	1280	295	234	1275	298	237
55 30 10	120	636	589	1218	142	113	1170	161	128	1135	176	140	1118	184	146
55 30 15	120	654	606	1228	151	120	1183	169	134	1148	185	147	1130	194	154
55 30 20	120	666	617	1238	156	124	1195	173	138	1160	189	150	1143	198	157
55 30 25	120	678	628	1248	160	127	1205	178	142	1170	195	155	1153	203	162
55 30 30	120	690	639	1258	165	131	1215	183	145	1183	198	158	1165	208	165
55 30 35	120	702	650	1265	171	136	1223	189	150	1193	204	162	1178	212	168
55 30 40	120	720	667	1275	180	143	1233	199	158	1203	214	170	1190	221	176
55 30 45	120	738	683	1283	190	151	1243	209	166	1213	225	179	1203	231	183
55 30 50	120	762	706	1293	205	163	1253	225	179	1225	241	191	1215	247	196
55 30 55	120	786	728	1300	221	176	1263	241	192	1235	258	205	1225	264	210
55 30 60	120	816	756	1310	242	192	1273	263	209	1245	282	224	1238	286	227
55 30 65	120	846	783	1320	263	209	1283	287	227	1258	304	241	1250	310	244
55 35 10	125	648	600	1205	156	123	1158	175	139	1120	194	154	1100	204	162
55 35 15	125	660	611	1218	159	126	1170	180	142	1135	197	156	1115	207	165
55 35 20	125	672	622	1228	164	130	1183	183	145	1148	201	159	1128	211	167
55 35 25	125	684	633	1238	169	134	1193	188	149	1160	205	162	1140	216	171
55 35 30	125	696	644	1248	173	137	1203	194	153	1170	211	167	1153	220	174
55 35 35	125	714	661	1258	183	145	1213	204	162	1183	220	174	1165	230	182
55 35 40	125	732	678	1265	194	154	1223	214	170	1193	231	184	1175	242	192
55 35 45	125	756	700	1275	208	165	1233	231	183	1203	248	197	1188	258	205
55 35 50	125	780	722	1283	225	178	1243	247	196	1213	266	211	1200	275	218
55 35 55	125	810	750	1293	246	195	1253	270	214	1225	289	229	1213	298	236
55 35 60	125	840	778	1303	268	213	1263	294	234	1235	315	250	1225	322	256
55 40 10	130	654	606	1195	164	130	1145	186	148	1108	206	164	1085	219	174
55 40 15	130	666	617	1205	169	134	1158	190	151	1120	210	167	1100	222	177
55 40 20	130	678	628	1218	172	137	1170	195	155	1135	213	169	1115	225	179
55 40 25	130	690	639	1228	177	141	1180	200	159	1148	217	172	1128	229	182
55 40 30	130	708	656	1238	187	149	1193	209	166	1160	227	181	1140	240	191
55 40 35	130	726	672	1248	197	156	1203	220	174	1170	239	189	1150	252	200
55 40 40	130	750	694	1258	212	168	1213	236	187	1183	255	202	1163	268	213
55 40 45	130	774	717	1265	229	182	1223	253	202	1193	273	217	1175	286	227
55 40 50	130	804	744	1275	251	199	1233	277	220	1203	299	237	1188	310	247
55 40 55	130	834	772	1285	273	217	1243	302	240	1213	325	258	1200	336	267
55 45 10	135	660	611	1183	174	138	1130	199	158	1090	222	176	1068	236	187
55 45 15	135	672	622	1195	178	141	1143	203	161	1105	225	178	1083	239	189

SPI WITH MAXIMAL WEIGHTS AT PROGESSIVE AGES

SOMATOTYPE	T	I	HEIGHT (M)	(F)	SPI →20	WEIGHT (M)	(F)	SPI →30	WEIGHT (M)	(F)	SPI →40	WEIGHT (M)	(F)	SPI →50+	WEIGHT (M)	(F)
55 45 20	135		684	633	1205	183	145	1155	208	165	1120	228	181	1098	242	192
55 45 25	135		702	650	1218	191	152	1168	217	172	1133	238	189	1110	253	201
55 45 30	135		720	667	1228	202	160	1180	227	181	1145	249	198	1123	264	210
55 45 35	135		744	689	1238	217	172	1190	244	194	1158	265	211	1135	282	224
55 45 40	135		768	711	1248	233	185	1203	260	206	1168	284	226	1148	299	238
55 45 45	135		798	739	1258	255	203	1213	285	226	1180	309	246	1160	326	259
55 45 50	135		828	767	1268	278	221	1223	310	247	1190	337	268	1173	352	280
55 50 10	140		666	617	1170	184	147	1115	213	169	1075	238	189	1050	255	203
55 50 15	140		678	628	1183	188	150	1128	217	173	1090	241	191	1065	258	205
55 50 20	140		696	644	1195	198	157	1143	226	179	1105	250	198	1080	268	212
55 50 25	140		714	661	1205	208	165	1155	236	187	1118	260	207	1093	279	221
55 50 30	140		738	683	1218	222	176	1168	252	200	1130	279	221	1108	295	234
55 50 35	140		762	706	1228	239	190	1180	269	214	1143	296	236	1120	315	250
55 50 40	140		792	733	1238	262	208	1193	293	232	1155	322	256	1133	342	271
55 50 45	140		822	761	1248	286	227	1203	319	253	1165	351	279	1145	370	294
55 55 10	145		672	622	1158	195	155	1098	229	182	1058	256	203	1033	275	218
55 55 15	145		690	639	1170	205	163	1113	238	189	1073	266	211	1048	285	227
55 55 20	145		708	656	1183	214	171	1128	247	197	1088	276	219	1063	295	235
55 55 25	145		732	678	1193	231	184	1140	265	210	1103	292	232	1078	313	249
55 55 30	145		756	700	1205	247	196	1153	282	224	1115	312	247	1090	334	265
55 55 35	145		786	728	1215	271	215	1165	307	244	1128	338	269	1105	360	286
55 55 40	145		816	756	1225	296	235	1178	332	264	1138	369	293	1118	389	309
55 60 10	150		684	633	1145	213	169	1083	252	200	1043	282	224	1018	303	240
55 60 15	150		702	650	1158	223	177	1098	261	207	1058	292	232	1033	314	249
55 60 20	150		726	672	1170	239	189	1113	278	220	1073	310	246	1048	332	264
55 60 25	150		750	694	1180	257	203	1125	296	235	1085	330	262	1060	354	281
55 60 30	150		780	722	1193	279	222	1138	322	255	1100	357	283	1075	382	303
55 60 35	150		810	750	1203	305	242	1150	349	277	1113	385	306	1088	413	328
55 65 10	155		696	644	1130	234	185	1068	277	219	1028	310	246	1000	337	267
55 65 15	155		720	667	1145	249	198	1083	294	234	1043	329	262	1015	357	284
55 65 20	155		744	689	1158	265	211	1098	311	247	1058	348	276	1030	377	299
55 65 25	155		774	717	1170	290	230	1110	339	270	1070	379	301	1045	406	323
55 65 30	155		804	744	1183	314	249	1123	367	291	1085	407	322	1060	436	346
55 70 10	160		714	661	1118	260	207	1055	310	246	1013	350	278	983	383	304
55 70 15	160		738	683	1130	279	221	1068	330	262	1028	370	293	998	404	321
55 70 20	160		768	711	1145	302	239	1083	357	283	1043	399	317	1013	436	346
55 70 25	160		798	739	1158	327	260	1095	387	307	1055	433	344	1028	468	371
60 10 10	95		588	544	1230	109	87	1190	121	96	1160	130	103	1145	135	107
60 10 15	95		612	567	1240	120	96	1200	133	105	1170	143	114	1158	148	117
60 10 20	95		636	589	1250	132	105	1210	145	115	1180	157	124	1170	161	128
60 10 25	95		654	606	1260	140	111	1220	154	123	1190	166	132	1180	170	135
60 10 30	95		672	622	1270	148	117	1230	163	129	1200	176	139	1190	180	143
60 10 35	95		684	633	1278	153	122	1238	169	134	1210	181	143	1200	185	147

SPI WITH MAXIMAL WEIGHTS AT PROGESSIVE AGES

SOMATOTYPE	T	I	HEIGHT (M)	(F)	SPI →20	WEIGHT (M)	(F)	SPI →30	WEIGHT (M)	(F)	SPI →40	WEIGHT (M)	(F)	SPI →50+	WEIGHT (M)	(F)
60 10 40	95		696	644	1285	159	126	1245	175	138	1220	186	147	1210	190	151
60 10 45	95		708	656	1293	164	131	1255	180	143	1230	191	152	1223	194	154
60 10 50	95		720	667	1300	170	135	1265	184	147	1240	196	156	1235	198	158
60 10 55	95		738	683	1310	179	142	1275	194	154	1250	206	163	1245	208	165
60 10 60	95		756	700	1320	188	149	1285	204	162	1260	216	171	1255	219	174
60 10 65	95		780	722	1330	202	160	1295	219	173	1273	230	182	1268	233	185
60 10 70	95		804	744	1340	216	171	1305	234	185	1285	245	194	1280	248	196
60 15 10	100		606	561	1220	123	97	1175	137	109	1145	148	118	1130	154	122
60 15 15	100		630	583	1230	134	106	1185	150	119	1155	162	129	1143	167	133
60 15 20	100		648	600	1240	143	113	1198	158	126	1168	171	136	1155	177	140
60 15 25	100		666	617	1250	151	120	1208	168	133	1178	181	144	1165	187	149
60 15 30	100		678	628	1260	156	124	1218	172	137	1188	186	148	1178	191	152
60 15 35	100		690	639	1268	161	128	1225	179	142	1198	191	152	1188	196	156
60 15 40	100		702	650	1275	167	132	1235	184	146	1210	195	155	1200	200	159
60 15 45	100		714	661	1283	172	137	1245	189	150	1220	200	159	1210	205	163
60 15 50	100		732	678	1293	181	144	1255	198	158	1230	211	167	1223	214	170
60 15 55	100		750	694	1303	191	151	1265	208	165	1240	221	175	1233	225	178
60 15 60	100		774	717	1313	205	163	1275	224	178	1250	237	189	1245	240	191
60 15 65	100		798	739	1320	221	175	1285	239	190	1263	252	200	1258	255	203
60 15 70	100		828	767	1330	241	192	1295	261	208	1275	274	218	1270	277	220
60 20 10	105		624	578	1210	137	109	1160	156	124	1130	168	134	1115	175	139
60 20 15	105		642	594	1220	146	115	1173	164	130	1143	177	140	1128	184	146
60 20 20	105		660	611	1230	154	123	1185	173	137	1155	187	148	1140	194	154
60 20 25	105		672	622	1240	159	126	1195	178	141	1165	192	152	1153	198	157
60 20 30	105		684	633	1250	164	130	1205	183	145	1175	197	156	1163	203	161
60 20 35	105		696	644	1258	169	134	1215	188	149	1188	201	159	1175	208	165
60 20 40	105		708	656	1265	175	139	1225	193	154	1200	205	163	1188	212	168
60 20 45	105		726	672	1275	185	146	1235	203	161	1210	216	171	1198	223	176
60 20 50	105		744	689	1285	194	154	1245	213	169	1220	227	180	1210	232	185
60 20 55	105		768	711	1295	209	166	1255	229	182	1230	243	193	1223	248	196
60 20 60	105		792	733	1305	224	177	1265	245	195	1240	261	207	1235	264	209
60 20 65	105		822	761	1313	245	195	1275	268	213	1253	282	224	1248	286	227
60 20 70	105		852	789	1320	269	214	1285	291	231	1265	306	243	1260	309	246
60 25 10	110		636	589	1200	149	118	1150	169	134	1118	184	146	1100	193	154
60 25 15	110		654	606	1210	158	126	1163	178	141	1130	194	154	1113	203	161
60 25 20	110		666	617	1220	163	129	1175	182	145	1143	198	157	1125	207	165
60 25 25	110		678	628	1230	167	133	1185	187	149	1153	203	162	1138	211	168
60 25 30	110		690	639	1240	172	137	1195	193	153	1165	208	165	1150	216	172
60 25 35	110		702	650	1248	178	141	1205	198	157	1175	213	169	1160	222	176
60 25 40	110		720	667	1258	187	149	1215	208	165	1188	223	177	1173	231	184
60 25 45	110		738	683	1268	197	156	1225	219	173	1198	234	185	1185	242	191
60 25 50	110		762	706	1278	212	169	1235	235	187	1210	250	199	1198	257	205
60 25 55	110		786	728	1285	229	182	1245	252	200	1220	267	212	1210	274	218
60 25 60	110		816	756	1295	250	199	1255	275	219	1230	292	232	1223	297	236
60 25 65	110		846	783	1303	274	217	1265	299	237	1243	315	250	1235	321	255
60 30 10	115		648	600	1190	161	128	1140	184	146	1105	202	160	1085	213	169

SOMATOTYPE	T I	HEIGHT (M)	HEIGHT (F)	SPI →20	WEIGHT (M)	WEIGHT (F)	SPI →30	WEIGHT (M)	WEIGHT (F)	SPI →40	WEIGHT (M)	WEIGHT (F)	SPI →50+	WEIGHT (M)	WEIGHT (F)
50 30 15	115	660	611	1200	166	132	1153	188	149	1118	206	163	1098	217	172
50 30 20	115	672	622	1210	171	136	1165	192	152	1130	210	167	1110	222	176
50 30 25	115	684	633	1220	176	140	1175	197	156	1143	214	170	1123	226	179
50 30 30	115	696	644	1230	181	144	1185	203	161	1155	219	173	1135	231	183
50 30 35	115	714	661	1240	191	151	1195	213	169	1165	230	183	1148	241	191
50 30 40	115	732	678	1250	201	160	1205	224	178	1175	242	192	1160	251	200
50 30 45	115	756	700	1260	216	171	1215	241	191	1188	258	205	1173	268	213
50 30 50	115	780	722	1270	232	184	1225	258	205	1200	275	218	1185	285	226
50 30 55	115	810	750	1278	255	202	1235	282	224	1210	300	238	1198	309	245
50 30 60	115	840	778	1285	279	222	1245	307	244	1220	326	259	1210	335	266
50 35 10	120	654	606	1178	171	136	1128	195	155	1090	216	172	1070	228	182
50 35 15	120	666	617	1188	176	140	1140	199	159	1103	220	175	1083	233	185
50 35 20	120	678	628	1200	180	143	1153	203	162	1118	223	177	1098	235	187
50 35 25	120	690	639	1210	185	147	1163	209	166	1130	228	181	1110	240	191
50 35 30	120	708	656	1220	195	155	1175	219	174	1143	238	189	1123	251	199
50 35 35	120	726	672	1230	206	163	1185	230	182	1153	250	198	1135	262	208
50 35 40	120	750	694	1240	221	175	1195	247	196	1165	267	211	1148	279	221
50 35 45	120	774	717	1250	237	189	1205	265	211	1175	286	227	1160	297	236
50 35 50	120	804	744	1260	260	206	1215	290	230	1188	310	246	1173	322	255
50 35 55	120	834	772	1268	285	226	1225	316	250	1198	337	268	1185	349	277
50 40 10	125	660	611	1165	182	144	1115	207	165	1075	231	184	1055	245	194
50 40 15	125	672	622	1178	186	147	1128	211	168	1090	234	186	1070	248	196
50 40 20	125	684	633	1190	190	151	1140	216	171	1105	237	188	1085	251	199
50 40 25	125	702	650	1200	200	159	1153	226	179	1118	248	197	1098	261	207
50 40 30	125	720	667	1210	211	168	1165	236	188	1130	259	206	1110	273	217
50 40 35	125	744	689	1220	227	180	1175	254	202	1143	276	219	1123	291	231
50 40 40	125	768	711	1230	243	193	1185	272	216	1155	294	233	1135	310	246
50 40 45	125	798	739	1240	267	212	1195	298	236	1165	321	255	1148	336	267
50 40 50	125	828	767	1250	291	231	1205	324	258	1175	350	278	1160	364	289
50 45 10	130	666	617	1153	193	153	1100	222	176	1060	248	197	1038	264	210
50 45 15	130	678	628	1165	197	157	1113	226	180	1075	251	199	1053	267	212
50 45 20	130	696	644	1178	206	163	1128	235	186	1090	260	206	1068	277	219
50 45 25	130	714	661	1188	217	172	1140	246	195	1103	271	215	1080	289	229
50 45 30	130	738	683	1200	233	184	1153	262	208	1115	290	230	1095	306	243
50 45 35	130	762	706	1210	250	199	1163	281	224	1128	308	245	1108	325	259
50 45 40	130	792	733	1220	274	217	1175	306	243	1140	335	266	1120	354	280
50 45 45	130	822	761	1230	298	237	1185	334	265	1150	365	290	1133	382	303
50 50 10	135	672	622	1140	205	162	1085	238	188	1045	266	211	1020	286	227
50 50 15	135	690	639	1153	214	170	1100	247	196	1060	276	219	1035	296	235
50 50 20	135	708	656	1165	224	179	1115	256	204	1075	286	227	1050	307	244
50 50 25	135	732	678	1178	240	191	1128	273	217	1088	305	242	1065	325	258
50 50 30	135	756	700	1190	256	204	1140	292	232	1100	325	258	1080	343	272
50 50 35	135	786	728	1200	281	223	1153	317	252	1113	352	280	1093	372	295
50 50 40	135	816	756	1210	307	244	1165	344	273	1125	382	303	1105	403	320
50 55 10	140	684	633	1128	223	177	1070	261	207	1030	293	232	1003	317	251

SOMATOTYPE	T	I	HEIGHT (M)	(F)	SPI →20	WEIGHT (M)	(F)	SPI →30	WEIGHT (M)	(F)	SPI →40	WEIGHT (M)	(F)	SPI →50+	WEIGH (M)	(F)
60 55 15	140		702	650	1140	234	185	1085	271	215	1045	303	241	1018	328	26
60 55 20	140		726	672	1153	250	198	1100	287	228	1060	321	255	1033	347	27
60 55 25	140		750	694	1165	267	211	1113	306	242	1073	341	271	1048	367	29
60 55 30	140		780	722	1178	290	230	1125	333	264	1088	368	292	1063	395	31
60 55 35	140		810	750	1188	317	252	1138	361	286	1100	399	317	1075	428	34
60 60 10	145		696	644	1115	243	193	1055	287	227	1015	322	255	985	353	27
60 60 15	145		720	667	1128	260	207	1070	305	242	1030	342	272	1000	373	29
60 60 20	145		744	689	1140	278	221	1085	322	256	1045	361	287	1015	394	31
60 60 25	145		774	717	1153	303	240	1098	350	278	1060	389	309	1030	424	33
60 60 30	145		804	744	1165	329	260	1110	380	301	1075	418	332	1045	455	36
60 65 10	150		714	661	1103	271	215	1043	321	255	1000	364	289	968	401	31
60 65 15	150		738	683	1115	290	230	1055	342	271	1015	384	305	983	423	33
60 65 20	150		768	711	1128	316	250	1070	370	293	1030	415	329	998	456	36
60 65 25	150		798	739	1140	343	272	1083	400	318	1045	445	354	1013	489	38
60 70 10	155		732	678	1090	303	241	1030	359	285	985	410	326	950	457	36
60 70 15	155		762	706	1103	330	262	1043	390	310	1000	442	352	965	492	39
60 70 20	155		792	733	1115	358	284	1055	423	335	1015	475	377	980	528	41
65 10 10	90		606	561	1190	132	105	1130	154	122	1098	168	133	1090	172	13
65 10 15	90		630	583	1200	145	115	1140	169	134	1108	184	146	1103	186	14
65 10 20	90		648	600	1210	154	122	1153	178	141	1120	194	154	1115	196	15
65 10 25	90		666	617	1220	163	129	1163	188	149	1130	205	163	1125	207	16
65 10 30	90		678	628	1230	167	133	1173	193	153	1140	210	167	1135	213	16
65 10 35	90		690	639	1238	173	138	1180	200	159	1150	216	172	1145	219	17
65 10 40	90		702	650	1248	178	141	1190	205	163	1163	220	175	1158	223	17
65 10 45	90		714	661	1255	184	146	1200	211	167	1173	226	179	1168	228	18
65 10 50	90		732	678	1265	194	154	1213	220	175	1183	237	188	1180	239	19
65 10 55	90		750	694	1275	204	161	1223	231	183	1193	248	197	1190	250	19
65 10 60	90		774	717	1285	219	174	1233	247	197	1203	266	212	1200	268	21
65 10 65	90		798	739	1295	234	186	1243	265	210	1215	283	225	1213	285	22
65 10 70	90		828	767	1305	255	203	1255	287	228	1228	307	244	1225	309	24
65 15 10	95		624	578	1178	149	118	1115	175	139	1080	193	153	1073	197	15
65 15 15	95		642	594	1190	157	124	1128	184	146	1093	203	161	1085	207	16
65 15 20	95		660	611	1200	166	132	1140	194	154	1105	213	169	1098	217	17
65 15 25	95		672	622	1210	171	136	1150	200	158	1118	217	172	1110	222	17
65 15 30	95		684	633	1220	176	140	1160	205	162	1128	223	177	1120	228	18
65 15 35	95		696	644	1228	182	144	1170	211	167	1140	228	180	1133	232	18
65 15 40	95		708	656	1238	187	149	1180	216	172	1150	233	186	1143	238	18
65 15 45	95		726	672	1248	197	156	1190	227	180	1160	245	194	1155	248	19
65 15 50	95		744	689	1255	208	165	1200	238	189	1170	257	204	1168	258	20
65 15 55	95		768	711	1265	224	178	1210	256	203	1180	276	219	1178	277	22
65 15 60	95		792	733	1275	240	190	1220	274	217	1190	295	234	1188	296	23
65 15 65	95		822	761	1285	262	208	1233	296	235	1205	317	252	1203	319	25
65 15 70	95		852	789	1295	285	226	1245	320	255	1218	342	272	1215	345	27
65 20 10	100		636	589	1168	161	128	1103	192	152	1065	213	169	1055	219	17

SPI WITH MAXIMAL WEIGHTS AT PROGESSIVE AGES

SOMATOTYPE	T	I	HEIGHT (M)	HEIGHT (F)	SPI →20	WEIGHT (M)	WEIGHT (F)	SPI →30	WEIGHT (M)	WEIGHT (F)	SPI →40	WEIGHT (M)	WEIGHT (F)	SPI →50+	WEIGHT (M)	WEIGHT (F)
65 20 15	100		654	606	1178	171	136	1115	202	161	1078	223	178	1068	230	183
65 20 20	100		666	617	1190	175	139	1128	206	164	1093	226	180	1083	233	185
65 20 25	100		678	628	1200	180	143	1138	211	168	1103	232	185	1093	239	190
65 20 30	100		690	639	1210	185	147	1150	216	172	1115	237	188	1105	243	193
65 20 35	100		702	650	1218	191	152	1160	222	176	1128	241	191	1118	248	197
65 20 40	100		720	667	1228	202	160	1170	233	185	1140	252	200	1130	259	206
65 20 45	100		738	683	1238	212	168	1180	245	194	1150	264	209	1143	269	213
65 20 50	100		762	706	1248	228	181	1190	263	209	1160	283	225	1155	287	228
65 20 55	100		786	728	1258	244	194	1200	281	223	1170	303	241	1165	307	244
65 20 60	100		816	756	1268	267	212	1210	307	244	1180	331	263	1178	332	264
65 20 65	100		846	783	1275	292	232	1220	333	264	1193	357	283	1190	359	285
65 25 10	105		648	600	1155	177	140	1090	210	167	1053	233	185	1040	242	192
65 25 15	105		660	611	1168	180	143	1103	214	170	1065	238	189	1053	246	195
65 25 20	105		672	622	1178	186	147	1115	219	174	1078	242	192	1065	251	199
65 25 25	105		684	633	1188	191	151	1128	223	177	1090	247	196	1080	254	201
65 25 30	105		696	644	1198	196	155	1138	229	181	1103	251	199	1093	258	205
65 25 35	105		714	661	1208	206	164	1148	241	191	1115	263	208	1105	270	214
65 25 40	105		732	678	1218	217	172	1158	253	201	1128	273	217	1118	281	223
65 25 45	105		756	700	1228	233	185	1170	270	214	1138	293	233	1128	301	239
65 25 50	105		780	722	1238	250	198	1180	289	229	1150	312	247	1140	320	254
65 25 55	105		810	750	1248	273	217	1190	315	250	1160	340	270	1153	347	275
65 25 60	105		840	778	1258	298	237	1200	343	273	1170	370	294	1165	375	298
65 30 10	110		654	606	1145	186	148	1080	222	177	1040	249	198	1025	260	207
65 30 15	110		666	617	1155	192	152	1093	226	180	1053	253	201	1038	264	210
65 30 20	110		678	628	1168	196	155	1105	231	184	1065	258	205	1050	269	214
65 30 25	110		690	639	1178	201	160	1115	237	188	1078	262	208	1063	273	217
65 30 30	110		708	656	1188	212	168	1125	249	198	1093	272	216	1078	283	225
65 30 35	110		726	672	1198	223	176	1135	262	208	1103	285	226	1090	295	234
65 30 40	110		750	694	1210	238	189	1148	279	221	1115	304	241	1103	314	249
65 30 45	110		774	717	1220	255	203	1158	299	237	1128	323	257	1115	335	266
65 30 50	110		804	744	1230	279	221	1170	324	257	1140	351	278	1128	362	287
65 30 55	110		834	772	1238	306	242	1180	353	280	1150	381	303	1140	392	311
65 35 10	115		660	611	1133	198	157	1065	238	189	1025	267	212	1010	279	221
65 35 15	115		672	622	1145	202	160	1078	242	192	1038	271	215	1023	283	225
65 35 20	115		684	633	1155	208	165	1090	247	196	1050	276	219	1035	289	229
65 35 25	115		702	650	1168	217	172	1103	258	205	1065	286	227	1050	299	237
65 35 30	115		720	667	1178	228	182	1115	269	214	1078	298	237	1063	311	247
65 35 35	115		744	689	1188	246	195	1125	289	230	1090	318	253	1075	332	263
65 35 40	115		768	711	1200	262	208	1138	307	244	1103	338	268	1088	352	279
65 35 45	115		798	739	1210	287	228	1148	336	267	1115	367	291	1103	379	301
65 35 50	115		828	767	1220	313	248	1160	364	289	1128	396	314	1115	410	326
65 40 10	120		666	617	1120	210	167	1053	253	201	1010	287	228	995	300	238
65 40 15	120		678	628	1133	214	170	1065	258	205	1023	291	231	1008	304	242
65 40 20	120		696	644	1145	225	178	1078	269	213	1038	301	239	1023	315	249
65 40 25	120		714	661	1155	236	187	1090	281	223	1050	314	249	1035	328	260
65 40 30	120		738	683	1168	252	200	1105	298	236	1063	335	265	1048	349	277

SOMATOTYPE	T I	HEIGHT (M)	HEIGHT (F)	SPI →20	WEIGHT (M)	WEIGHT (F)	SPI →30	WEIGHT (M)	WEIGHT (F)	SPI →40	WEIGHT (M)	WEIGHT (F)	SPI →50+	WEIGHT (M)	WEIGHT (F)
							SPI WITH MAXIMAL WEIGHTS AT PROGESSIVE AGES								
65 40 35	120	762	706	1178	271	215	1115	319	254	1075	356	283	1060	371	295
65 40 40	120	792	733	1190	295	234	1128	346	274	1090	384	304	1075	400	317
65 40 45	120	822	761	1200	321	255	1138	377	299	1100	417	331	1088	431	342
65 45 10	125	672	622	1108	223	177	1038	271	215	995	308	244	978	324	257
65 45 15	125	690	639	1120	234	186	1050	284	225	1008	321	255	990	339	269
65 45 20	125	708	656	1133	244	194	1063	295	235	1023	331	264	1005	350	278
65 45 25	125	732	678	1145	261	208	1078	313	249	1035	354	281	1020	370	294
65 45 30	125	756	700	1155	280	223	1090	334	265	1048	375	298	1033	392	311
65 45 35	125	786	728	1168	305	242	1103	362	288	1060	408	324	1045	426	338
65 45 40	125	816	756	1180	331	263	1118	389	309	1075	437	348	1060	456	363
65 50 10	130	684	633	1095	244	193	1023	299	237	980	340	269	963	358	284
65 50 15	130	702	650	1108	254	202	1035	312	248	993	353	280	975	373	296
65 50 20	130	726	672	1120	272	216	1050	331	262	1008	374	296	990	394	313
65 50 25	130	750	694	1133	290	230	1063	351	278	1020	398	315	1003	418	331
65 50 30	130	780	722	1145	316	251	1078	379	300	1033	431	341	1018	450	357
65 50 35	130	810	750	1155	345	274	1090	410	326	1045	466	370	1030	486	386
65 55 10	135	696	644	1083	265	210	1008	329	261	965	375	297	945	400	316
65 55 15	135	720	667	1095	284	226	1023	349	277	980	397	315	960	422	335
65 55 20	135	744	689	1108	303	240	1035	371	295	993	421	334	973	447	355
65 55 25	135	774	717	1120	330	262	1050	401	318	1008	453	360	988	481	382
65 55 30	135	804	744	1133	357	283	1063	433	343	1020	490	388	1000	520	412
65 60 10	140	714	661	1070	297	236	993	372	295	950	425	337	928	455	361
65 60 15	140	738	683	1083	316	251	1008	392	311	965	447	355	943	479	380
65 60 20	140	768	711	1098	342	272	1023	423	336	980	481	382	958	515	409
65 60 25	140	798	739	1110	372	295	1035	458	364	995	516	410	973	552	438
65 65 10	145	732	678	1058	331	263	978	419	333	935	480	381	910	520	414
65 65 15	145	762	706	1070	361	287	993	452	359	950	516	410	925	559	445
65 65 20	145	792	733	1085	389	308	1008	485	385	965	553	438	940	598	474
65 70 10	150	756	700	1045	379	301	965	481	382	920	555	440	895	603	478
65 70 15	150	786	728	1058	410	326	978	519	412	935	594	472	910	644	512
70 10 10	85	624	578	1150	160	127	1070	198	158	1035	219	174	1035	219	174
70 10 15	85	642	594	1160	170	134	1083	208	165	1048	230	182	1048	230	182
70 10 20	85	660	611	1170	180	142	1095	219	174	1060	241	192	1060	241	192
70 10 25	85	672	622	1180	185	146	1105	225	178	1070	248	196	1070	248	196
70 10 30	85	684	633	1190	190	151	1115	231	183	1080	254	201	1080	254	201
70 10 35	85	696	644	1200	195	155	1125	237	188	1093	258	205	1093	258	205
70 10 40	85	708	656	1210	200	159	1135	243	193	1105	263	209	1105	263	209
70 10 45	85	726	672	1220	211	167	1148	253	201	1115	276	219	1115	276	219
70 10 50	85	744	689	1230	221	176	1160	264	210	1125	289	230	1125	289	230
70 10 55	85	768	711	1240	238	189	1170	283	224	1135	310	246	1135	310	246
70 10 60	85	792	733	1250	254	202	1180	302	240	1145	331	262	1145	331	262
70 10 65	85	822	761	1260	278	220	1193	327	260	1158	358	284	1158	358	284

SOMATOTYPE	T I	HEIGHT (M)	(F)	SPI →20	SPI WITH MAXIMAL WEIGHTS AT PROGESSIVE AGES WEIGHT (M) (F)		SPI →30	WEIGHT (M) (F)		SPI →40	WEIGHT (M) (F)		SPI →50+	WEIGHT (M) (F)	
70 10 70	85	852	789	1270	302	240	1205	353	281	1170	386	307	1170	386	307
70 15 10	90	636	589	1138	175	139	1058	217	173	1018	244	194	1015	246	195
70 15 15	90	654	606	1148	185	147	1070	228	182	1030	256	204	1028	257	205
70 15 20	90	666	617	1160	189	150	1083	233	185	1045	259	206	1043	260	207
70 15 25	90	678	628	1170	195	155	1093	239	190	1055	265	211	1053	267	212
70 15 30	90	690	639	1180	200	159	1105	243	193	1068	270	214	1065	272	216
70 15 35	90	702	650	1190	205	163	1115	250	198	1080	275	218	1078	276	219
70 15 40	90	720	667	1200	216	172	1125	262	208	1093	286	227	1090	288	229
70 15 45	90	738	683	1210	227	180	1135	275	218	1103	300	237	1100	302	239
70 15 50	90	762	706	1220	244	194	1148	292	233	1113	321	255	1113	321	255
70 15 55	90	786	728	1230	261	207	1158	313	248	1123	343	272	1123	343	272
70 15 60	90	816	756	1240	285	227	1168	341	271	1133	374	297	1133	374	297
70 15 65	90	846	783	1250	310	246	1180	369	292	1145	403	320	1145	403	320
70 20 10	95	648	600	1125	191	152	1045	238	189	1000	272	216	995	276	219
70 20 15	95	660	611	1138	195	155	1058	243	193	1015	275	218	1010	279	221
70 20 20	95	672	622	1150	200	158	1070	248	196	1030	278	220	1025	282	223
70 20 25	95	684	633	1160	205	162	1083	252	200	1043	282	224	1038	286	227
70 20 30	95	696	644	1170	211	167	1095	257	203	1055	287	227	1050	291	231
70 20 35	95	714	661	1180	222	176	1105	270	214	1068	299	237	1063	303	240
70 20 40	95	732	678	1190	233	185	1115	283	225	1080	311	247	1075	316	251
70 20 45	95	756	700	1200	250	198	1125	303	241	1090	334	265	1088	335	266
70 20 50	95	780	722	1210	268	212	1135	325	257	1100	357	283	1100	357	283
70 20 55	95	810	750	1220	293	232	1145	354	281	1110	389	308	1110	389	308
70 20 60	95	840	778	1230	319	253	1155	385	306	1120	422	335	1120	422	335
70 25 10	100	654	606	1113	203	161	1033	254	202	988	290	231	980	297	236
70 25 15	100	666	617	1125	207	165	1045	259	206	1000	295	235	993	302	240
70 25 20	100	678	628	1138	211	168	1058	263	209	1015	298	237	1008	304	242
70 25 25	100	690	639	1148	217	172	1068	270	214	1028	302	240	1020	310	246
70 25 30	100	708	656	1158	229	182	1080	282	224	1043	313	249	1035	320	255
70 25 35	100	726	672	1168	240	190	1090	295	234	1055	326	258	1048	332	264
70 25 40	100	750	694	1180	257	203	1103	314	249	1068	346	274	1060	354	281
70 25 45	100	774	717	1190	275	219	1113	336	267	1078	370	294	1073	375	298
70 25 50	100	804	744	1200	301	238	1125	365	289	1090	401	318	1085	407	322
70 25 55	100	834	772	1210	327	260	1135	397	315	1100	436	346	1095	442	350
70 30 10	105	660	611	1100	216	171	1020	271	215	975	310	246	965	320	254
70 30 15	105	672	622	1113	220	175	1033	275	218	988	315	250	978	324	257
70 30 20	105	684	633	1125	225	178	1045	280	222	1000	320	254	990	330	261
70 30 25	105	702	650	1135	237	188	1055	295	234	1015	331	263	1005	341	271
70 30 30	105	720	667	1145	249	198	1065	309	246	1030	342	272	1020	352	280
70 30 35	105	744	689	1158	265	211	1078	329	261	1043	363	288	1033	374	297
70 30 40	105	768	711	1170	283	224	1090	350	278	1055	386	306	1045	397	315
70 30 45	105	798	739	1180	309	246	1103	379	301	1068	417	331	1058	429	341
70 30 50	105	828	767	1190	337	268	1115	410	326	1080	451	358	1070	463	368
70 35 10	110	666	617	1088	229	182	1005	291	231	960	334	265	950	345	274
70 35 15	110	678	628	1100	234	186	1018	295	235	973	338	269	963	349	277

SPI WITH MAXIMAL WEIGHTS AT PROGESSIVE AGES

SOMATOTYPE	T	I	HEIGHT (M)	HEIGHT (F)	SPI →20	WEIGHT (M)	WEIGHT (F)	SPI →30	WEIGHT (M)	WEIGHT (F)	SPI →40	WEIGHT (M)	WEIGHT (F)	SPI →50+	WEIGHT (M)	WEIGHT (F)
70 35 20	110		696	644	1113	245	194	1030	309	244	985	353	279	975	364	288
70 35 25	110		714	661	1123	257	204	1043	321	255	998	366	291	988	377	299
70 35 30	110		738	683	1135	275	218	1055	342	271	1013	387	307	1003	398	316
70 35 35	110		762	706	1148	292	233	1068	363	289	1025	411	327	1015	423	337
70 35 40	110		792	733	1160	318	252	1080	394	313	1040	442	350	1030	455	360
70 35 45	110		822	761	1170	347	275	1093	425	338	1053	476	377	1043	490	388
70 40 10	115		672	622	1075	244	194	990	313	248	945	360	285	935	371	294
70 40 15	115		690	639	1088	255	203	1003	326	259	958	374	297	948	386	306
70 40 20	115		708	656	1100	267	212	1015	339	270	970	389	309	960	401	319
70 40 25	115		732	678	1113	284	226	1030	359	285	983	413	328	973	426	338
70 40 30	115		756	700	1125	303	241	1045	379	301	995	439	348	985	452	359
70 40 35	115		786	728	1138	329	262	1058	410	326	1010	471	374	1000	486	386
70 40 40	115		816	756	1150	357	284	1070	444	353	1025	505	401	1015	520	413
70 45 10	120		684	633	1063	266	211	975	345	274	930	398	315	920	411	326
70 45 15	120		702	650	1075	278	221	988	359	285	943	413	327	933	426	338
70 45 20	120		726	672	1088	297	236	1000	383	303	955	439	348	945	453	360
70 45 25	120		750	694	1100	317	251	1015	403	320	968	465	369	958	480	380
70 45 30	120		780	722	1113	344	273	1030	434	344	980	504	400	970	520	412
70 45 35	120		810	750	1125	373	296	1043	468	372	995	539	428	985	556	441
70 50 10	125		696	644	1050	291	231	960	381	302	915	440	349	905	455	360
70 50 15	125		720	667	1063	311	247	973	405	322	928	467	371	918	482	384
70 50 20	125		744	689	1075	332	263	985	431	342	940	496	394	930	512	407
70 50 25	125		774	717	1088	360	286	1000	464	369	953	536	426	943	553	440
70 50 30	125		804	744	1100	390	309	1015	497	394	965	578	458	955	597	473
70 55 10	130		714	661	1038	325	258	945	431	342	900	499	396	888	520	412
70 55 15	130		738	683	1050	347	275	958	457	362	913	528	419	900	551	437
70 55 20	130		768	711	1065	375	298	973	492	390	928	567	450	915	591	469
70 55 25	130		798	739	1078	406	322	988	527	418	940	612	486	928	636	505
70 60 10	135		732	678	1025	364	289	930	488	387	885	566	450	870	596	473
70 60 15	135		762	706	1040	393	313	945	524	417	900	607	483	885	638	508
70 60 20	135		792	733	1055	423	335	960	562	445	915	649	514	900	681	540
70 65 10	140		756	700	1013	416	330	915	564	448	870	656	521	855	691	549
70 65 15	140		786	728	1028	447	355	930	604	480	885	701	557	870	737	586
70 70 10	145		780	722	1000	475	376	900	651	516	855	759	602	840	801	635

COMPARATIVE STUDIES IN THE PSYCHOMORPHOLOGICAL CONSTITUTION OF SCHIZOPHRENICS AND OTHER GROUPS: A SURVEY.

DETLEV VON ZERSSEN

CONSTITUTIONAL RESEARCH deals with the inter-individual variations of relatively constant traits of the human being - called constitutional variables - and with correlations (see 1) of these traits (2). Since KRETSCHMER's pioneer work, (3), psychomorphologic correlations have become the domain of psychiatric investigations (4, 5). During the last decades more refined techniques for measuring constitutional variables and analyzing the data statistically have been introduced into research of this sort(2). The present report is a survey of various results obtained by use of these methods.

As a frame of reference for describing variations in human physique I emply SHELDON's original system of somatotypes (6, 7, 8, 9). According to this system the individual somatotype consists of a combination of three complex variables, namely

I.   endomorphy, corresponding to the degree of obesity
            or fatness (10, 11)

II   mesomorphy, corresponding to the degree of muscularity (11) and

III   ectomorphy, characterized by slenderness or linearity
            as opposed to stoutness, called ectopenia.
            Ectomorphy is equal to an extreme degree
            of leptomorphy, whereas ectopenia is equal
            to euromorphy (12, 13). Pyknics as described
            by KRETSCHMER (3) are thus ectopenes (and
            are not pure endomorphs, as many authors assume).

An individual's somatotype may be plotted graphically in a "somatotype distribution chart" (8, 9). This is a two-dimensional projection, as seen in Fig. 1. Therefore, it is quite obvious that - instead of relating the plotted individuals to three oblique axes which indicate the

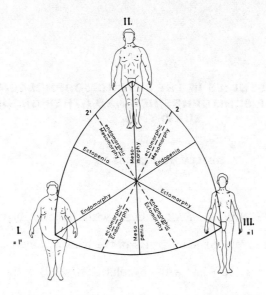

Fig. 1   SHELDON's somatotype distribution chart
(simplified) with examples of three extreme
types of physique and with two additional axes
of reference (2 and 2).

degree of the three components of somatotype - two orthogonal axes

suffice for describing the underlying distribution, no information being

lost (12, 14, 15).   The new axes would represent two independent dimen-

sions of variations in physique (instead of three interdependent ones

as originally assumed by SHELDON)*.

The axes' spacial orientation in the plane in which the distribution

is located may be chosen arbitrarily.   However, from a semantic

point of view those solutions are to be preferred which can most easily

be interpreted within the framework of known facts or well-accepted

theories.   In an attempt to achieve a biologically meaningful descrip-

tion of variations in physique on the basis of two independent dimensions,

we took into account the well-known influence of sex (9, 11) and of age (17)

- -

*   A third dimension of skeletal size can be represented as an axis
vertical to this coordinate system.   The whole three-dimensional
system would then be comparable to SHELDON's new version of
somatotypology, reported in this volume.   It consists of three nearly
independent components of physique represented by the ponderal
index (related to our dimension 1), the trunk index (related to our
dimension 2) and height (related to skeletal size).

on the distribution of somatotypes in SHELDON's system, obtaining

the following solution (5, 12, 16):

dimension 1 (age-dependent) = ectomorphy versus ectopenia;

dimension 2 (sex-dependent) = ectomorphic mesomorphy
(or athletic-andromorphic
build) versus ectomorphic
endomorphy (or gynecomorphic
build).

As can be easily recognized, the first dimension of this solution is

identical with the third component within SHELDON's system, whereas

our second dimension is a combination of SHELDON's first and second

components.

When we consider the physical structure alone, disregarding

the determinants of the variations in question, another solution seems

to provide a more adequate frame of reference*:

dimension 1' = endomorphy (or obesity) versus endopenia (or leanness);

dimension 2' = endomorphic mesomorphy (or somatic robustness)
versus endomorphic ectomorphy (lack of robustness).

Fig. 2 shows the distribution of the individual somatotypes of

psychotics with a predominantly non-paranoid schizophrenic symptom

pattern. The relative slenderness of this group, as described by

KRETSCHMER (3), becomes evident from the distribution of plots.

Also in accordance with KRETSCHMER's concept of psychomorpho-

logical correlations is the distribution of the somatotypes of a group

of psychotics with predominantly affective disorders at the opposite

side of the ectomorphic-ectopenic dimension (Fig. 3).

- -

* Both versions of the two-dimensional system of somatotypes can
  be derived not only on the basis of topological and biological considerations concerning SHELDON's primarily subjective taxonomy
  of variations in physical appearance, but also by means of factor
  analyses (see 18) of objective somatometric and photometric measurements (5, 16) (see also 19).

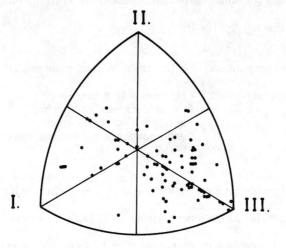

Fig. 2 Distribution of somatotypes for 85 psychotic patients
with predominantly non-paranoid schizophrenic symptomatology (according to SHELDON)

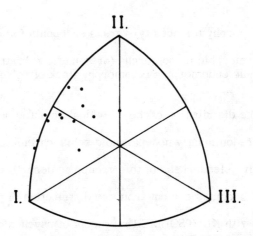

Fig. 3 Distribution of somatotypes for 12 psychotic patients
with predominantly affective symptomatology (according to SHELDON)

However, after matching manic-depressives and schizophrenics
exactly according to sex, age and distribution of verbal intelligence,
we were not able to demonstrate anthropometrically any definite morphological difference between the two groups of psychotics (Tab. 1,
$u_{md/sch}$).

No of test		Morphological variables	Sex	$u_{md/sch}$	$u_{old/young}$	
1	a	Subcutaneous fat	m	2,05*	- 1,32(*)	+
1	b	(subscapular)	f	0,17	+ 2,86**	+
2	a	Bicristal diameter	m	0,90	+ 1,44(*)	+
2	b		f	1,04	+ 0,78	+
3	a	Breast depth	m	0,29	+ 1,39(*)	+
3	b		f	2,14*	+ 2,31**	+
4		Type index (Rees/Eysenck)	m	0,00	+ 2,17*	+
5		Strömgren index	m	0,35	- 2,54**	+
6		Relative chest width	m+f	0,33	+ 3,11***	+
7		Kretschmer index	m	0,69	- 0,52	+
8		Pignet index	m	0,75	-0,87	+
9		Ponderal index	m+f	0,03	- 2,92**	+

Tab. 1 Mann-Whitney u-test (20) of morphological group differences in 48 psychotic patients (age 20-60) (see 21)

$u_{md/sch}$ = u-value of comparison between manic-depressivs and schizophrenics

$u_{old/young}$ = u-value of comparison between patients of older and younger age group
(*) $p < 0.10$; * $p < 0.05$; ** $p < 0.01$; *** $p < 0.001$
+ difference in basic accordance with hypothesis
- difference in basic contradiction with hypothesis

By dividing the whole group of psychotics according to age, the differences in body build expected for the diagnostic groups were found for the age groups, the younger patients being more ectomorphic than the older ones, who turned out to be relatively ectopenic or pyknic (Tab. 1, $u_{old/young}$).

As groups of manic-depressivs are on the average about one or two decades older than groups of schizophrenics(4), it can be concluded that morphological differences between the two groups are mainly due to this age difference (21).

Nevertheless, psychomorphological relations exist in respect to some abnormal reaction types as well as to normal character traits. The latter are to a certain extent in accordance with KRETSCHMER's and with SHELDON's concepts of such relations, but seem to be of a simpler kind than those proposed by these authors.

Emotional correlates of variations in body build form a single complex dimension, which may be called "mental vitality" (5, 21). It has two poles, the one consisting of extroverted activity and a low tendency to certain neurotic traits (especially anxiety, depression and signs of autonomic imbalance), and the other one comprising introversion, inhibition and irritability (Tab. 2).

Test items	Coefficient of correlation with		
	type-index,	pond.-index,	biceps girth
1.) active	-.29*	-.46***	.38**
2.) stubborn	-.28*	-.24(*)	.13
3.) sociable	-.08	-.13	.26*
4.) somewhat curious	-.25*	.00	-.05
5.) self-reliant	-.17	-.35**	.31*
6.) athletic	-.26*	-.40**	.39**
7.) mentally robust	-.15	-.23(*)	.31*
8.) fearless	-.19	-.34**	.27*
9.) easy-going	-.26*	-.20	.14
10.) confiding	-.07	-.25*	.14
11.) warm-hearted	-.25*	-.30*	.27*
12.) assured	-.38**	-.32*	.33**
13.) dependent	.08	.17	-.40**
14.) timid	.09	.24(*)	-.27*
15.) sensitive	.11	.29*	-.27*
16.) reserved	.31*	.18	-.10
17.) moody	.37**	.41**	-.31*

Tab. 2   Matrix of psychomorphological correlations in a sample of 61 male students. The underlined items form a bipolar general factor of emotional traits.

(*) p .10; * p .05; ** p .01; *** p .001

Criteria of this complex dimension of personality traits are correlated with criteria of both the ectomorphic-ectopenic and the andromorphic-gynecomorphic dimensions of physique: Mentally more vital persons are on the average more ectopenic and more mesomorphic than less vital ones, who tend to be more ectomorphic and more gynecomorphic.

By a rotation of the axes of reference in SHELDON's system of somatotypes the description of this psychomorphological relationship can be simplified still further (Fig. 1). Our second version of reducing SHELDON's trifold typological system to a two-dimensional one enables us to describe "mental vitality" as the correlate of a single morphological dimension, namely robustness, placing endomorphic mesomorphy and endomorphic ectomorphy opposite to one another. (According to our findings the endomorphic-endopenic dimension as such has no systematic relation to mental vitality*).

We found psychomorphological correlations of this kind in various groups of normal male individuals. The coefficients of correlation, however, were usually rather low, seldom exceeding the value of 0.4 (5, 13, 22). In females the respective coefficients did not even reach this value (5).

These findings fit well into the picture one gains from most of those studies in which similar objective biometric techniques have been employed, e. g. from the investigations of REES and EYSENCK (23) in England, of SELTZER (24, 25) and of CHILD (26) in the U. S. A., and to some extent those of KNUSSMANN (27) in Germany and of LINDEGARD and NYMAN (28) in Sweden.** On this basis various relations between morphological and abnormal behavioral types may be explained:

Whereas the correlation of psychotic reaction types to body build are largely spurious, caused by the influence of age upon habitus and type of psychosis (Tab. 1), other psychomorphological relations - besides those between physique and normal personality (Tab. 2) - are independent of the age factor.

Fig. 4 shows a comparison of somatotypes which according to PARNELL (11) are commonly found in male students in need and not in need of psychiatric care (part b) and a) of the figure respectively). It can be supposed that the first group consists almost entirely of neurotics. The somatotypes of this group are predominantly endomorphic ectomorphs.

_____

* This holds true for skeletal size as well.

** Findings at variance with those mentioned here were published by CORTES and GATTI (29).

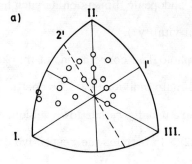

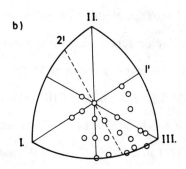

Fig. 4   Somatotypes which appeared more often
           among Oxford male students not under
           psychiatric care (a) or under psychiatric
           care (b) respectively (according to PARNELL) (11)

This is in basic accordance with results concerning the physical

constitution of male neurotics (4, 23). In an unpublished series we

could support these findings. Moreover, from our psychometric

studies with various groups of psychiatric patients it can be con-

cluded that neurotics are mentally less vital than normals, whereas

the premorbid personalities of psychotics of the manic-depressive

and of the schizophrenic type do not systematically differ from each

other, deviating only slightly from the personalities of normal indi-

viduals in respect to the mental correlates of variations in body build

(5). However, they do show deviations in other personality traits (30).

The predominant somatotypes of the more stable group of students

in Fig. 4 a) show a marked tendency towards endomorphic meso-

morphy: The mentally more vital individuals with a robust physique

are less inclined to neurotic breakdown than those with reduced vital

strength and a generally less stout and less muscular build.

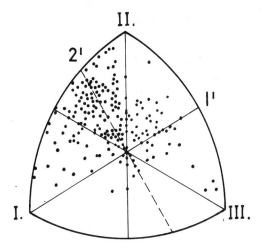

Fig. 5   Distribution of somatotypes for 200
delinquent boys (according to SHELDON) (8)

Nevertheless, under unfavorable social conditions, mental robustness and impulsiveness (as the emotional correlates of physical robustness) may contribute to the development of active antisocial behavior: The somatotypes of delinquent youths (Fig. 5), and even more those of adult criminals (Fig. 6), show a similar tendency towards endomorphic mesomorphy (or robustness), as found among the mentally healthy students. This relationship was described by SHELDON et al. (7) and SELTZER (31) in the U.S.A. and by PARNELL (11) and other authors in England (see 32). It seems to be independent of age and to some extent at least of the level of intelligence (31). Thus, crime and delinquency are constitutionally opposed to certain types of neurotic inadequacy.

Within the framework of a general theory of individual methods for handling aggressive impulses - a more extrapunitive one, leading to criminal acting out, and a more intrapunitive one, resulting in neurotic symptom formation in terms of anxiety, depression and autonomic dysfunction - one may describe certain neurotic disorders as the negative of criminality.

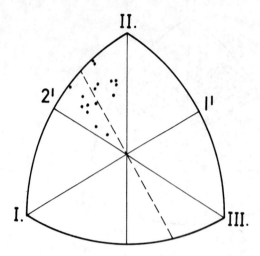

Fig. 6   Distribution of somatotypes for 16 male
criminals (according to SHELDON) (8)

This is a basic modification of FREUD's (33) concept of neu-

rosis as the negative of perversion, a concept which originated

from libido theory at a time when an explicit theory of aggression

did not yet exist. Such a theory appears necessary for a thorough

understanding of the psychomorphological correlations which more

recent constitutional research within psychiatry and related fields

has revealed.

ACKNOWLEDGEMENT: The author thanks the Deutsche Forschungs-

gemeinschaft, Bad Godesberg/Germany, for financial support of his

investigation, Dipl. Psych. Huneke, Dr. Netter-Munkelt, Prof. Othmer,

Dr. Unger (34), Dr. Wilde (35), and others for their cooperation,

and Dr. Parnell and Dr. Sheldon for their permission to replicate

figures from their publications.

REFERENCES

1. FISHER, R. A. Statistical Methods for Research Workers, 13th ed., Hafner, New York, 1963.

2. ZERSSEN, D. v. Methoden der Konstitutions- und Typenforschung, in Enzyklopadie der geisteswissenschaftlichen Arbeitsmethoden, Thiel, M. (Editor), Oldenbourg, Munich (in press).

3. KRETSCHMER, E. Korperbau und Charakter, 25th ed., Springer, Berlin-Gottingen-Heidelberg, 1967.

4. REES, L. Constitutional Factors and Abnormal Behaviour, in Handbook of Abnormal Psychology, Eysenck, H. J. (Editor), Basic Books, New York, 1961.

5. ZERSSEN, D. v. Korperbau, Personlichkeit und seelisches Kranksein, Thieme, Stuttgart (to be published).

6. SHELDON, W. H., STEVENS, S. S., TUCKER, W. B. The Varieties of Human Physique, Harper Bros., New York-London, 1940.

7. SHELDON, W. H., STEVENS, S. S. The Varieties of Temperament, Harper Bros., New York-London, 1942.

8. SHELDON, W. H., HARTL, E. M. and McDERMOTT, E. Varieties of Delinquent Youth, Harper Bros., New York, 1949.

9. SHELDON, W. H. DUPERTUIS, C. D. and McDERMOTT, E. Atlas of Men, Harper Bros., New York, 1954.

10. LINDEGARD, B. Variations in Human Body-Build, Munksgaard, Copenhagen, 1953.

11. PARNELL, R. W. Behaviour and Physique, Arnold, London, 1958.

12. ZERSSEN, D. v. Dimentionen der morphologischen Habitusvariationen und ihre biometrische Erfassung. Z. menschl. Vererb. -u. Konstit. -Lehre 37, 611-625, 1964.

13. ZERSSEN, D. v. Eine Biometrische Uberprufung der Theorien von Sheldon uber Zusammenhange zwischen Korperbau und Temperament. Z. exp. angew. Psychol. 12, 521-548, 1965.

14. EKMAN, G. On the Number and Definition of Dimensions in Kretschmer's and Sheldon's Constitutionsl Systems, in Essays in Psychology Dedicated to David Katz, Ekman, G., Husen, T., Johansson, G. and Sandstrom, C. I. (Editors), Almqvist & Wiksells, Uppsala, 1951.

15. HUMPHREYS, L. C. Characteristics of type concepts with special reference to Sheldon's typology. Psychol. Bull. 54, 218-228, 1957.

16. ZERSSEN, D. v. Habitus und Geschlecht. Homo 19, 1-27, 1968.

17. NEWMAN, R. W. Age changes in body build. Amer. J. phys. Anthropol., N. S. 10, 75-90, 1952.

18. HARMAN, H. H. Modern Factor Analysis, 2nd ed., Chicago University Press, Chicago, 1967.

19. TANNER, J. M. Human Growth and Constitution, in Human Biology, Harrison, G. H., Weiner, J. S., Tanner, J. M. and Barnicot, N. A. (Editors), Clarendon, Oxford, 1964.

20. SIEGEL, S. Nonparametric Statistics for the Behavioral Sciences, McGraw-Hill, New York-Toronto-London, 1956.

21. ZERSSEN, D. v. Korperbau, Psychose und Personlichkeit. Nervenarzt 37, 52-59, 1966.

22. ZERSSEN, D. v. Biometrische Studien uber "Korperbau und Charakter". Fortschr. Neurol. Psychiat. 33, 455-471, 1965.

23. REES, L. and EYSENCK, H. J. A factorial study of some morphological and psychological aspects of human constitution. J. ment. Sci. 91, 8-21, 1945.

24. SELTZER, C. C. The relationship between the masculine component and personality. Amer. J. phys. Anthropol., N. S. 3, 33-47, 1945.

25. SELTZER, C. C., WELLS, F. L. and McTERNAN, E. B. A relationship between Sheldonian somatotype and psychotype. J. Personal. 16, 431-436, 1948.

26. CHILD, I. L. The relation of somatotype to self-ratings on Sheldons temperamental traits. J. Personal. 18, 440-453, 1950.

27. KNUSSMANN, R. Konstitution und Partnerwahl. Homo 11, 133-152, 1960.

28. LINDEGARD, B. and NYMAN, G. E. Interrelations between Psychologic, Somatologic and Endocrine Dimensions, Gleerup, Lund, 1956.

29. CORTES, J. B. and GATTI, F. M. Physique and self-description of temperament. J. consult. Psychol. 29, 432-439, 1965.

30. ZERSSEN, D. v., in collaboration with KOELLER, D. M. and REY, E. R. Objektivierende Untersuchungen zur pramorbiden Persönlichkeit endogen Depressiver, in Das depressive Syndrom, Hippus, H. and Selbach, H. (Editors), Urban und Schwarzenberg, Munich-Berlin-Vienna (in press).

31. SELTZER, C.C. A Comparative Study of the Morphological
    Characteristics of Delinquents and Non-Delinquents,
    in Unraveling Juvenile Delinquency, Glueck, S. and
    Glueck, E.T., Harvard University Press, Cambridge/
    Mass., 1950.

32. EYSENCK, H.J. Crime and Personality, Routledge & Paul,
    London, 1964.

33. FREUD, S. Drei Abhandlungen zur Sexualtheorie, in
    Gesammelte Werke, Bd. V: Werke aus den Jahren
    1904 - 1905, Imago, London, 1949.

34. UNGER, C. Experimenteller Beitrag zum Problem psycho-
    morphologischer Zusammenhange. Med. Thesis, Univ.
    Heidelberg, 1967.

35. WILDE, K. Eine Uberprufung verschiedener Konstitutions-
    typologien mit objektiven anthropometrischen und
    psychometrischen Methoden. Med. Thesis, Univ.
    Hamburg, 1964.

D. von Zerssen, M.D., Max-Planck Institute für Psychiatrie, 8 München, 23,

Kraepelinstrasse 10, Munchen, Germany.

POWER SPECTRAL DENSITY: A METHODOLOGY FOR THE RHYTHM ANALYSIS OF DISORDERED SPEECH

JOHN J. DREHER, AND ARTHUR J. BACHRACH

The purpose of this report is to describe a methodology of speech analysis that has proved valuable in the study of features of normal speech patterning and which appears to hold promise as an approach to disordered speech as well. This methodology, to be detailed in later sections of this report, is an analysis of vocal rhythms in speech, a structural aspect of vocal behavior that represents the repetitive patterning of talking and silence that make up spoken expression. During the course of the research noted above it was observed that clearly defined vocal rhythms attach to individuals, a fact to be considered later on in this report.

The structural analysis of speech in populations considered disordered within a psychopathological classification has been relatively neglected in favor of content analysis, largely a function of an underlying psychodynamic conceptualization of language as an expression of ideas, feelings (conscious or "unconscious") and thoughts. Content, then, for a large number of psychologists and psychiatrists is "symbolic" of "inner" events and the majority of research in the area of psychotic speech has been content oriented rather than structural (Brady, 1958; Pavy, 1968). Some investigators such as Skinner (1958) and Greenspoon (1955, 1962) have treated verbal behavior as subject to the same control as other types of motor behavior. Work in group verbal conditioning (Bachrach, Candland and Gibson, 1961; Witters and Bachrach, 1967) has demonstrated similar results. Other researchers, such as Chapple (1939), Starkweather (1956, 1960), Hargreaves (1960), Matarazzo (1962), Webb (1968), and Dinoff et al (1967) have been interested in relating some structural aspects of speech to diagnostic grouping or to "emotional" components of behavior. Chapple and Lindemann (1942), for example, using speech duration and silence duration as variables found some differences between psychiatric and normal populations. All of these studies have approached non-content aspects of speech by analyzing such variables as pause length or utterance duration either averaged or summed over one or more interview sessions. Time series analyses have not been made and there seems to be profit in a sensitive sequential analysis of structure that is reliable, quantifiable, repeatable and sensitive. In particular, sequential segments analyses as time series data can provide the crucial data of assessing change, so important in evaluating treatment procedures.

The vocal rhythm analysis methodology we believe offers such a possibility for an optimally effective and sensitive measure. It has been applied to presumably disordered speech samples from schizophrenics and aphasics as well as to samples of helium speech taken from deep sea divers (Bachrach, Hegge, & Dreher, study in progress).

In the above paragraphs we have been implicitly critical of an overemphasis on content as a variable in studying disordered speech. The authors believe that an illustration of this problem of content analysis may be drawn from a classic example of psychotic speech taken from a standard textbook on psychopathology (Cameron, 1947) in which the following exchange was presented between an interviewer and a patient:

To the question, "Why are you in the hospital?" the patient replied:

> "I'm a cut donator, donated by double sacrifice. I get two days for every one. That's known as double sacrifice; in other words, standard cut donator. You know, we considered it. He couldn't have anything for the cut, or for these patients. All of them are double sacrifice because it's unlawful for it to be donated anymore. (Well, what do you do here?) I do what is known as the double criminal treatment. Something that he badly wanted, he gets that, and seven days criminal protection. That's all he gets, and the rest I do for my friend. (Who is the other person that gets all this?) That's the way the asylum cut is donated. (But who is the other person?) He's a criminal. He gets so much. He gets twenty years' criminal treatment, would make forty years; and he gets seven days' criminal protection and that makes fourteen days. That's all he gets. (And what are you?) What is known as cut donator Christ. None of them couldn't be able to have anything; so it has to be true works or prove true to have anything, too. He gets two days, and that twenty years makes forty years. He loses by causing. He's what is known as a murder. He causes that. He's a murder because he causes that. He can't get anything else. A double sacrifice is what is known as where murder turns, turns the friend into a cut donator and that's what makes a daughter-son. (A daughter-son?) Effeminate. A turned Christ. The criminal is a birth murder because he makes him a double. He gets two days' work for every one day's work because after he's made a double, he gets twice as much as it is. He's considered worth twice that much more. He has to be sacrificed to be a double."

From the standpoint of content, this is a typical example of bizarre speech found in psychopathology books. What is particularly striking and not commented upon, however, is the structure of the material. For example, responding to the question "Why are you in the hospital?", the patient replied, "I'm a cut donator, donated by double sacrifice." Syntactically, this is structurally identical to a sentence such as "I'm an accident victim, run over by a truck." The responsiveness of the patient to questions throughout, and some structural aspects of his response would seem to be clearly within the realms of "normal" speech, although the linguist would classify its syntax as perhaps a seventh order approximation to

English. We cannot overestimate the importance of the
interactive aspects--bizarre or not , the patient is
communicating in an understandable linguistic interchange. It is in the area of content that the unusual
quality of the speech sample most strikingly appears
and, even here it is possible, as one of us has suggested elsewhere (Bachrach, 1953) that "delusional" communication may have allegorical or testing operations for
a patient in his interactions. Content is undoubtedly
an interesting variable but we believe that structural
analysis, long neglected, may be of greater profit in
examining disordered speech.

PROCEDURE

It can be shown that clearly defined vocal rhythms
attach to individuals. Rhythm, in this context, refers
to the repetitive patterning of talking and silence that
make up spoken expression. There are, of course, various
ways of representing these sequences, depending upon the
aspects of interest.

Perhaps the easiest method of making a visual record
of these sequences is to run a given amount of connected speech through a graphic level recorder, which pays
attention only to speech power and produces a trace of
time vs. intensity, resembling a string of "hills and
valleys."

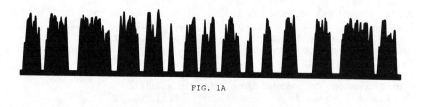

FIG. 1A

FIG. 1B

Fig. 1. Transformation of speech segments into
equivalent duration lengths.

Figure 1A shows such a trace of the voice during running
speech. Each time the recording stylus returns to the
baseline, the voice has dropped to silence. Thus, the
time measurement along the base of the "hills" is a measure of how long the voice was "on." The intervening
blank areas denote the amount of time the voice was
"off." Because the display of voiced and silent periods
depends upon the time constants of the writing instrument, its controls were so adjusted that the stylus returned to the baseline when human listeners agreed that
a "pause" had occurred. The minimum time for "pause" in
this study was finally set at .350 second, arrived at by
listener agreement after considering both spontaneous
and reading speech production in two languages. Normals,

obviously, furnished this base. We again point out that
this value is a minimum, and that pauses connecting phonated segments can often be inordinately long under some
circumstances. As a matter of fact, it is quite possible that important information might be inferred from
the magnitude and distribution of pauses along, although
our attention here will be focused only on the phonation
duration sequences. Because of this latter consideration, the record in Figure 1A, which still contains amplitude (stress) information not usable under our present
concept of rhythm, needs suitable transformation into
the simpler display of Figure 1B. This was accomplished
by using each phonated period to generate a series of
square pulses subject to integration, and interrupted by
the .350 sec. time constant. Since the number of these
pulses is proportional to duration and can easily be
counted, our data can now be handled in various ways.
Circuitry for this transformation is shown in Figure 2.

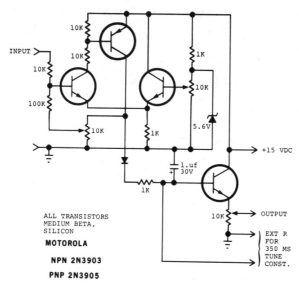

Fig. 2.   Transformation circuit for quantifying
          durations of phonated segments.

Although a general distribution can be made of the
resulting lengths, as shown in the 17-minute sample of
a Taiwan legislator (Fig. 3), the possibility exists
that the feature of sequencing could be an individual
characteristic.

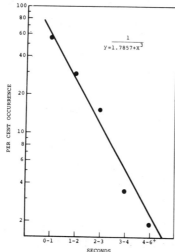

$$y = \frac{1}{1.7857 + x^3}$$

Fig. 3.   Distribution of segment durations of 17 min-
          utes of discourse by Taiwan legislator, 1966.

The experimental hypothesis pursued here is a possible basic difference between the voice rhythms of schizophrenics and normal subjects. First, let us make some observations about normal speech. Without attempting to assign causality, it is apparent that by sequentially plotting phonation segments as a sequential histogram we can identify this display as similar to the waveform of a nonstationary noise process. As we shall see later on, this is a valid observation and that hidden periodicities are, indeed, present in this noisy wave. The search, basically springs from the question, does a talker show random programming in his utterances, or is there an underlying pattern? At this point, assuming that patterns exist, "normality" would imply some invariances that could serve as comparators for psychiatric patients.

The equipment we employed in this phase was the Computer of Average Transients (CAT). This model was by Technical Measurements Corporation of Connecticut. Basically, this small computer is an averaging circuit, scanning a noisy signal many times and pulling out repetitive phenomena by virtue of the fact that on successive scans a real signal will add arithmetically, while noise will increase only by its square root. One of the accessories is a correlation circuit for comparing aspects of the same or different signals. This latter accessory was used here. (See Fig. 4).

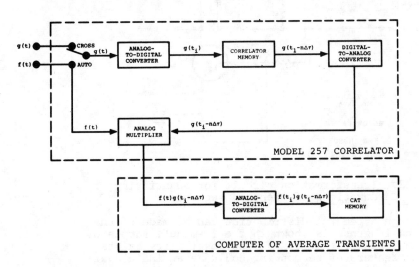

Fig. 4. CAT correlation schema.

Classically, the autocorrelation function applies to a stationary process and is defined as follows:

$$\phi_{ff}(\tilde{\tau}) = \lim_{T \to \infty} \frac{1}{2T} \int_{-T}^{T} f(t) \, f(t \pm \tilde{\tau}) \, dt$$

where:

ϕ_{ff} = autocorrelation function
$f(t)$ = a waveform that is a function of time
$\tilde{\tau}$ = an incremental delay in the signal train
T = period of integration

The resulting autocorrelograms allow us to assess the presence and nature of any periodic components of the

signal. If only random components (noise) are present,
the autocorrelation function will approach zero as T
increases. However, if a real periodicity is buried in
the signal, as in the case of a sine wave overlaid by
wideband noise (See Fig. 5), the function, which has a
maximum at t = o and at this point has the value $\frac{A^2}{2} + K$

(or one-half the squared voltage of the signal plus the
mean square value of the noise), will be asymptotic to
$\frac{A^2}{2}$, since the noise value will eventually approach zero.

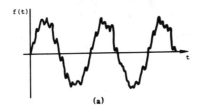

(a)

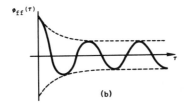

(b)

Fig. 5. Autocorrelation of sine wave buried in
wide band noise (b and a).

To start, the voice signals (running speech) were pre-
processed to convert the phonation period into a standard format of smoothed envelopes differing from each
other only in duration. The pulse trains, triggered on
and off by a threshold-detecting multivibrator, are individually integrated by the pre-processing circuit (Fig.
2), led into the computer's circuit, and stored in successive addresses of its memory. Thus, to store a speech
sample of 32 seconds, sampling is carried on at a rate
of 128 milliseconds per address for a total of 256 addresses.

Now that the speech is converted into a form usable
by the CAT, autocorrelations of the phonation sequences
can be performed.

Obviously, any speech sample occupies only a finite
time, and the theoretical autocorrelation function must
be approximated, with accuracy dependent upon the length
of record T. With various sample lengths it can be considered a quasi-stationary process and subjected to the
CAT's digital computation. Thus, for digital conversion,
Eq. 1 may be rewritten

$$\phi ff(n\Delta\tau) \approx \frac{1}{K+1} \sum_{i=o}^{K} f(t_i)f(t_i - n\Delta\tau)$$

where $K = \frac{T}{t}$ is the number of sample intervals in T
extent, and n = 0, 1, 2, ... N intervals of t. The output, an autocorrelogram, may be graphically produced by
an associated X-Y plotter.

From the displays we may extract periodicity information. If, for example, a total signal lasting 65 seconds

is fed into the CAT, its 256-address display can be time-divided into equal intervals, and the occurrence of reg-ular events can be measured as a function of their period in the 65-second sample. Thus, one maximum in the center of the display would indicate a period of 32.5 seconds; four equally spaced humps would stand for 65/4, or 16.25 seconds per occurrence of the phenomenon.

The same reasoning can be applied to any of the total integration lengths fed into the system. In Figure 6, below, are shown the basic rhythms of John F. Kennedy, first in his inaugural address of 1961, and next in his address on the occasion of the Cuban crisis of 1962.

PERIODIC COMPONENTS OF DELIVERY

KENNEDY

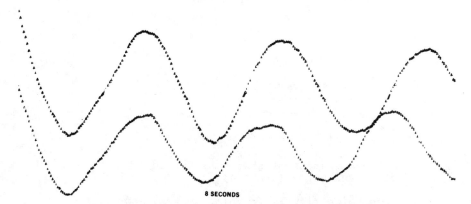

8 SECONDS

Fig. 6.   Top trace is Inaugural Address; bottom
          trace represents Cuban Crisis speech.

Because the total sample length here was 8.192 sec-onds, the periodicity in his inaugural may be computed as 2.73 seconds, and that of the Cuban crisis address as 2.20 seconds. Although this nominal 8-second sample is actually the average/correlation of several sequent-ial periods of this length, Kennedy's consistency and precision in hitting these rhythms have produced almost pure sine wave charts.

Increasing the sampling time to 32 seconds in the Cu-ban crisis address, we detect that this basic 2.2-second period can show a deviation from 1.44 to 2.58 seconds. Despite the rather obvious inference that these rhythms may be dictated by rigorous adherence to a written text, it seems equally obvious that a speaker's periods are al-so a mirror of his systemic rhythms. In a different sit-uation, shown in Figure 7, Kennedy employs a similar phonation periodicity. This record was taken from a pre-election, enthusiastic crowd-rousing speech given at a political convention in 1960. Using several 32.8-second samples, we here may observe that it contains a mean per-iod of 2.20 seconds, with fluctuations from 2.05 to 2.62 seconds.

PERIODIC COMPONENTS OF DELIVERY

JOHN F. KENNEDY
PRE-ELECTION SPEECH

32 SECONDS

TOTAL TIME *1½ MINUTES*

Fig. 7

Fortunately, the spotlight of history has been focused upon our great leaders, and in some cases we have
voice records over rather considerable periods of their
lives.   In the case of Franklin D. Roosevelt we have a
voluminous record of his·utterances from his accession
to office until his death.   Figure 8 depicts the rhythms
associated with two of FDR's speeches, first, his famous
"nothing to fear but fear itself" fireside chat and second, his last public pronouncement, the Yalta address.
As history has recorded, it was only a matter of hours
after the Yalta Conference before the demise of the American leader.   Quite apparent to the listener is the
word-slurring accompanying the Yalta speech, an apparent
result of brain injury.   In respect to delivery, Roosevelt's early "fireside chat" exhibits a mean period of
2.82 seconds with excursions from 2.25 to 3.85 seconds.
In comparison, his last address at Yalta showed a mean
of 3.00, varying from as short as 2.24 to as long as
3.97 seconds (See Fig. 8).

PERIODIC COMPONENTS OF DELIVERY
FRANKLIN D. ROOSEVELT

65.6 SECOND INTEGRATION

FIRESIDE CHAT

YALTA ADDRESS

Fig. 8.   Rhythms from beginning and end of
Roosevelt's terms.

934

These examples, however, although interesting in their own right, point up a fundamental weakness of the correlogram--that its own sometimes irregular form is difficult to interpret in terms of component periodicities. The most obvious remedy is simply a Fourier transform yielding, in this instance, a power spectral density plot of component frequencies (or periods) of the autocorrelation function.

Cooley and Tukey (1965) pioneered a numerical computation of this previously formidable operation that can be adapted to a digital computer. Results of such an analysis is shown in Figure 9, where the regularly oscillating autocorrelogram of the series 0000101010100000 shows, predictably, a cycle of 8 elements (4 zeros, 4 tens, repeat).

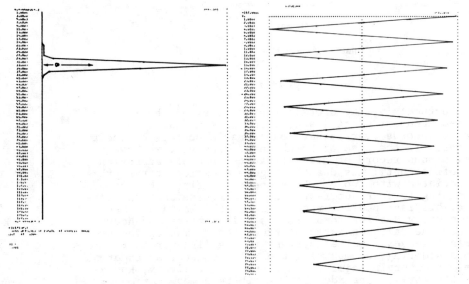

Fig. 9. Fourier power transform of four 10's,
         four zeros, etc.

The accompanying spike of the Fourier transform unequivocally indicates that the dominant (in this case, the only) period is 8. The advantage of this second step lies in the fact that were the autocorrelogram an uneven wave, all component periods and their relative importance would be so displayed. We thus adopt this analysis for our comparisons.

Test data were derived from voice recordings of 14 normal and 30 psychiatrically classified subjects. Normal simply recounted a three-minute sample of familiar recollections.Aberrant subjects were recorded at the Arizona State Hospital and at Barrow Neurological Institute, Phoenix. A different, but we believe defensible, procedure was followed to elicit the schizophrenic utterances. This involved general (and consistently the same) questioning of the patient by a clinician, who allowed the subject free rein to converse uninterrupted if he were able. Since pause durations were not measured, the clinicians interjections were deleted from the final tapes and replaced by a pause. In this manner the computer could see only a series of patient talk-and-pause sequences backed end-to-end, the clinician's contribution being elicited by a pause in the first place.

In all instances, various lengths of speech sample were integrated by continuous autocorrelation, stored outputs being read from the CAT's memory to a digital printer, and these data transferred to IBM punched cards. Data cards were then treated with a Fast Fourier Transform program in the CDC #6600 Computer according to the schema in Figure 10.

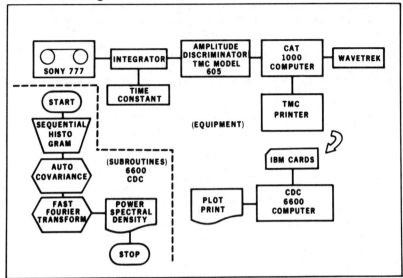

Fig. 10

At the moment we shall confine our attention to one case, which may hold some interesting inferences. A female patient at Barrow Neurological Institute furnished two oral interviews. The first was taken prior to the performance of a frontal lobectomy intended to decrease grand mal seizure frequency. The second was taken following the operation, at which time the seizures were absent. The initial Fourier power transforms are shown in Figure 11.

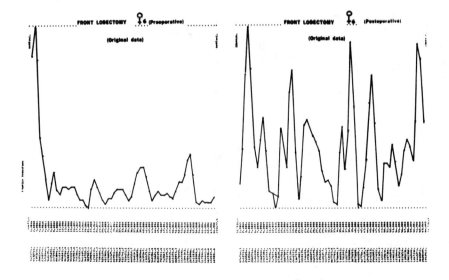

Fig. 11

To the ear, the pre-operative speech rhythms, shown on the left, were stumbling, disjointed, and halting. This impression is visually reinforced by the relatively uniform power distribution up-and-down the spectrum, and by the lack of definitely defined peak regions. On the

other hand, the post-operative speech pictured on the
right sounded crisp, chatty, and much closer to "normality." We notice in this trace a vigorous and pronounced
periodic structure in the definite and powerful peaks.

While these contrasts themselves might eventually constitute some sort of therapy metric (and this aspect has
yet to be evaluated), they raise some equally interesting questions regarding the organism under examination:
Do the data contain any invariances that carry over from
the pre- to post-operative condition? If so, what sort
of data transformation will reveal them? If such invariances (the same rhythm properties) can be found, are
they short- or long-period in nature? This is to say,
did the therapy more markedly affect the short-term or
long-term rhythms?

Speaking philosophically, the whole problem is open-
ended. There are, of course, many kinds of legitimate
transform operations that can be applied to data to emphasize certain relationships and minimize others. If
a certain transform succeeds in revealing similarities
in different sets of data, the problem is ended -- it
positively emerges. If, however, like relationships
cannot be shown, it may simply mean that our transform
was not effective for the job, and that the invariances
are still there but hidden. In this particular case the
answer is quickly arrived at by treating the raw data
values by a smoothing average of 3. Although the original input curves are thus rendered visually quite different, the Fourier analysis of their respective correlo-
grams show that two periodic regions present in the pre-
operative situation have perseverated into the post-operative condition. Inasmuch as a smoothing average acts
as a filter, we have effectively removed the high-frequen-
cy regions from both spectra and may observe, in Figure
12, two low-frequency (long period) rhythms that were relatively unaffected by the frontal lobectomy.

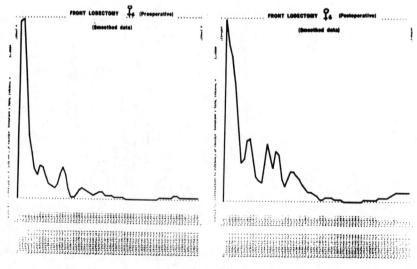

Fig. 12

The proposed methodology for analysis of vocal rhythm is considered, as in the case reported, to be a potentially valuable one for assessing change such as may occur in surgical intervention, psychotherapy and drug therapy. The groups studied at Barrow Neurological Institute and Arizona State Hospital*were analyzed to see if any structural entities might appear to offer leads toward consideration of specific disorders. While we recognize that diagnosis, using ill-defined terms such as "chronic undifferentiated schizophrenia," remains a methodological problem and does not lend itself to optimal evaluation, we grouped the patients according to speaker component periodicities (oral segment rhythms) illustrated in Figure 13.

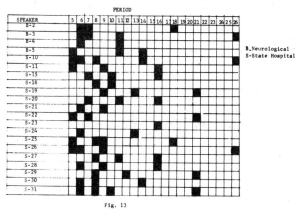

Fig. 13

The blocked out squares mean that the speaker had a certain length-combination pattern extending over n segments; a pattern of segment length is such that it takes n of these to make this particular pattern. So, for example, a pattern of segment length 5 requires 5 of these to make the pattern. The Tau measure referred to previously= 1 segment.

A preliminary analysis of grouping among the patient samples indicates the following:

Patients B-3, S-10, S-26 all showed maximum power long periods. This group consisted of one neurological patient, a 75 year old male stroke victim, a 27 year old female chronic undifferentiated schizophrenic, and a 28 year old female schizophrenic diagnosed also as chronic brain syndrome with convulsions.

Patients B-2, B-3, S-10, S-26 (which included three of the above group) had common short periods. B-2 is a 26 year old male stroke victim.

Patients B-3, B-4, and B-5 shared a common period. These patients were diagnosed respectively as a 75 year old male stroke patient, a male glioblastoma patient (left temporal and deep posterior frontal, post-operative) and a male stroke victim.

*The authors wish to express their gratitude to Dr. Joseph T. White, Head, Division of Neurology, Barrow Neurological Institute and to Dr. Willis Bower, Superintendent, Arizona State Hospital for their help in obtaining subjects.

Patients S-10, S-25, S-26, and S-31 showed at least
four periods, and four different types of rhythm. The
patients were diagnosed as scizophrenic, with S-10 being
diagnosed as chronic brain syndrome, convulsions and S-31
having a diagnosis of diabetes. All four patients were
described on charts as being "loud and combative."

Patients S-16, S-23 and S-24 had the fewest periods
(S-23 had one only, the sole subject so ordered). These
patients, a 59 year old female, a 27 year old male and a
35 year old female were all diagnosed as paranoid schizophrenic. S-25, the 27 year old male was also diagnosed
as chronic brain syndrome with convulsions.

Given the problem of clearcut diagnostic categories we
can only start to order the data with regard to patterns
of speech analysis for groups and, indeed, as we have suggested, this might not be the most fruitful avenue to
pursue. The illustrations of individual patterning such
as may be found in the speech samples of Kennedy and
Roosevelt and the analysis of change, structurally deline-
ated, in the lobectomy patient at Barrow Neurological
Institute described pre- and post- operative may be a more
successful approach. In any case the analysis of structure,
objectively defined, offers a promising methodology for
assessment. A collection of normal samples as well as
disordered speech is a necessary normative base.

The authors are grateful to Mrs. Elaine Young,
Mr. Scott Lawrence, and Mr. Robert Norton for
their aid in data collection and analysis.

Dr. Dreher is Director, Life Sciences at the
Douglas Advanced Research Laboratories, and
Technical Consultant to Hoover Institution,
Stanford.

Dr. Bachrach is Director, Behavioral Sciences
Department, Naval Medical Research Institute,
National Naval Medical Center. He is also
Technical Consultant to the Douglas Advanced
Research Laboratories and Consultant in Neuro-
psychology, Barrow Neurological Institute.

REFERENCES

Bachrach, A. J. Notes on the psychopathology of delusions. Psychiatry: Journal for the Study of Interpersonal Processes, 1953, 16, 375.

Bachrach, A. J., Candland, D. K., & Gibson, J. T. Group reinforcement of individual response: Experiments in verbal behavior. In I. A. Berg & B. Bass (Eds.) Conformity and Deviation. New York: Harper and Brothers, 1961.

Brady, J. P. Language in schizophrenics: Review of several approaches to the problem. Amer. J. Psychother., 1958, 12, 473-487.

Cameron, N. The Psychology of Behavior Disorders: A Biosocial Interpretation. New York: Houghton Mifflin, 1947, pp. 466-467.

Chapple, E. D. Quantitative analysis of the interaction of individuals. Proceedings of the National Academy of Sciences, 1939, 25, 58-67.

Chapple, E. D., & Lindemann, E. Clinical implications of measurements of interaction rates in psychiatric interviews. Applied Anthropology, 1942, 1, 1-11.

Cooley, J. W., & Tukey, T. W. An algorithm for the machine calculation of complex Fourier series. Mathematics of Computations, 1965, 19, 297-301.

Dinoff, M., Patterson, W. E., Hannon, J. E., & Morris, J. R. Standardized interview performances of regressed schizophrenics, and normals. Psychol. Reports, 1967, 20, 119-123.

Greenspoon, J. The reinforcing effect of two spoken sounds on the frequency of two responses. American Journal of Psychology, 1955, 68, 409-417.

Greenspoon, J. Verbal conditioning and clinical psychology. In A. J. Bachrach (Ed.) Experimental Foundations of Clinical Psychology. New York: Basic Books, 1962. Chap .15, pp. 510-553.

Matarazzo, J. D. Prescribed behavior therapy: Suggestions from interview research. In A. J. Bachrach (Ed.) Experimental Foundations of Clinical Psychology. New York: Basic Books, 1962. Chapt. 14, pp. 421-510.

Pavy, D. Verbal behavior in schizophrenics: A review of recent studies. Psychological Bulletin, 1968, 70, 164-178.

Skinner, B. F. Verbal Behavior. New York: Appleton-Century-Crofts, 1957.

Starkweather, J. A. The communication value of content free speech. American Journal of Psychology, 1956, 69, 121-123.

Starkweather, J. A. A speech rate meter for vocal behavior analysis. Journal for the Experimental Analysis of Behavior, 1960, 3, 111-114.

Webb, J. T. Automated standardized interviews. Presented at Research Conference on Interview Behavior, The Psychiatric Institute, University of Maryland, Baltimore, April 22, 1968.

Witters, D., & Bachrach, A. J. The effects of competing contingencies upon fixed ratio baselines in a small group situation. Psychological Record, 1965, 15, 103-110.

SUMMATION AND EPILOGUE

D. V. SIVA SANKAR

The several studies reported in this monograph point out the
diversity of the different factors involved in the etiology and/or
characterization of schizophrenia. Schizophrenia may be the
outcome (product or even byproduct) and may be only symptomatic of compensation and defense against both the internal
lack of homeostasis and the external psychophysiological and
socio-economic factors. The present monograph portrays the
several aspects - epidemiological, electrophysiological, biological, pharmacological, psychological, etc. - of schizophrenia. The relevant areas of somatotyping, and psychobiological aspects of sleep have also been indicated.

The inability of biological experimentation to pin point the
etiological mechanisms in schizophrenia, as has been fondly
expected from the beginning, has become more common place
knowledge. This does not imply the fruitlessness of biological
research, but only its application to the elucidation of the mechanisms that result in schizophrenia. This may be due to two
factors : (a). The biological areas of investigation may not be
directed to the more ordinary metabolic studies, but to a
study of the dynamic alteration and control of metabolism in
carefully controlled setups. These are very difficult to come by
in experimentation involving humans. (b). While the whole
given population of patients under study may have the psychiatric
label "schizophrenia", this population may be heterogeneous
in its characteristic pathobiology. Perhaps, this is one of the more
important services of biology to this area of psychobiology,
namely the diversity of the etiological factors that may lead to
psychiatric deviation. The disease involves a total personality and its entire inventory of neuro- and psychobiology.

Figure 1 indicates several events arbitrarily designated as
primary, secondary and acute. All these factors may be directly or indirectly related in the final manifestation of psychiatric

deviation. The main problem here is one of feedback and inter-group effector mechanisms, and the effect of secondary events on the primary events especially in so far as embryogenesis and morphogenesis. The several biochemical and metabolic factors shown in Fig. 1, have been reviewed in several publications, including some in this monograph. These areas include the metabolism of carbohydrates, lipids, glycolipids, amino acids, proteins, hormones etc. Transmethylation has been reported to be involved in schizophrenia. Permeability and membrane barriers may also be involved. The role of amines is perhaps one of the most important areas as it may be related to the acute events that may either precipitate or accompany an acute breakdown. But, it may be pointed out, that the word 'acute' may also be relative. These amines include indoleamines, catecholamines and their metabolites, with their close metabolic linking to blood pressure, carbohydrate and hormone metabolism, and their integration into the control of metabolism.

Some of the physiological events are also shown in Fig. 1, as secondary events. Another important aspect of this disease is perhaps altered " transducer functions" of the cell. These functions include generation of energy, in all its forms (heat, chemical, electric, potential, kinetic etc.), and their interconversion to each other. This would also involve the interconversion of environmental details and factors into molecular mechanisms in the neurobiological substrates. It is the testing of these transducer functions that has given us most of our concepts about the dynamic aspects of schizophrenia (eg. visual motor tests). The concept of body image may not necessarily be limited to three dimensions only, but may also be incorporated into time as its fourth dimension. Altered homeostatic mechanisms may also express themselves in psychophysiological and psychochemical aberrations (cf. Fig. 1).

The extent of damage and its uncompensated occurrence in these several areas may delineate the extent and depth of biochemical deviation. The proportionality between the extent of psychiatric deviation and biological deviation may stand more careful scrutiny.

F I G U R E I

PRIMARY EVENT OF QUESTIONABLE CERTAINTY

Inherited disability to resist stress (of varying types and degrees) influenced by learning and congenital defects (eg. PKU, lipidoses etc.)

Pregnancy accidents of known and unknown etiology, course and extent of damage. Defective embryogenesis and morphogenesis, not necessarily determined by genetic mechanisms of inheritance; and stress. Birth Factors ETC.

METABOLIC carbohydrate, lipid, amino acid, protein, transmethylation, amines, and their metabolism. Membrane structures ETC.

PHYSIOLOGIC Homeostasis. Vestibular, reticular, thalamic, neuroregulatory, autonomic, & electrobiologic functions. Growth, ETC.

TRANSDUCER functions. Emotional behavior, visual motor function, Regulation of temperature, blood pressure, pupillary size, and electron transport. Immunobiological and allergy reactions. ATP production. Hallucinations, ETC.

GROSS defects like mental retardation, brain damage, chromosomal defects, ETC.

ENVIRONMENTAL sociologic, psychophysiologic factors. Mood control, behavior, rage reactions, group behavior, artistic abilities, pursuit of 'pleasure' and goal directed activities. Body image, space-time orientation, intelligence, learning, ETC.

UNKNOWN damage to neurobiological substrate that future research has to unveil.

Acute Breakdown Characteristics
Neuroendocrine Functions
Biogenic Amines
Hormones
ETC?

943

The result of these several interacting etiological factors may be manifested as a large group of biological disorders, referred to under the limited number of diagnostic categories of schizophrenia. The extent of psychiatric deviation in known cases of biological deviation (or disease, eg. pellagra) may be given more attention in future studies. Certainly, more weight should be given to testing transducer functions in dynamic settings of well controlled, well diagnosed and "homogeneous" patient populations.

The lack of apparent chromosomal defects in schizophrenia has been documented. However, there are many cases of psychiatric deviations in persons with chromosomal deviations. But, we do not refer to these cases as "chromosomal schizophrenias". Similarly, Dr. Dohan brings out a possible relation between celiac disease and schizophrenia. Again, we do not refer to pellagra psychosis as "niacinamide schizophrenia". These are examples of how any given kind of aberration may affect the psychiatric health of human beings, without being considered as monofactorial, monogenetic, etiological aberrations. The following Table attempts to point out some of these considerations, where a clinical or subclinical dysfunction may lead to schizophrenia, either as a primary result through acting on the nervous system, or as a secondary result through acting on other areas of the body.

T A B L E I

Possible etiological types of schizophrenia*

I. Overt biological disease :
    Leading primarily to psychobiological dysfunction
    Leading secondarily to psychobiological dysfunction

II. Subclinical abnormalities
    Ordinary stress leads to psychiatric dysfunction
    Abnormal stress leads to psychiatric dysfunction

III. Genetic abnormalities

IV. Defective embryogenesis

* Genetic predisposition on a polygenic basis is tacitly assumed in all these cases.

Final equilibrium in personality is a delicate state depending on a multitude of variables. Can variation in any of these variables give rise to a disruption in this delicate psychobiological balance? - and result in a gamut of aberrations from schizophrenia, schizoid, psychotic, neurotic, or odd behavior ? Whatever the primary or secondary biogenetic mechanism may be, the biochemical events in an acute breakdown may consist of a funnelling of these abnormalities through a metabolite of biogenic amines. Several genetic abnormailities are known in the metabolism of aromatic amino acids. It is conceivable that there may be other defects (subclinical or clinical, homozygous or heterozygous, genotypic or phenotypic) in the metabolism of aromatic substances in, at least some cases of, schizophrenia. The studies on periodic catatonia are specially fortunate as the periodic recurrences afford an opportunity to study acute events in this disease. Here again, the recurrences after sometime may not be strictly comparable to the initial ones, as psychobiological compensating mechanisms may have set in.

The research on schizophrenia stimulated our interest in several biochemical and biological systems. However, the basic defect still eludes us, perhaps due to the nature of our concept of what schizophrenia is. The situation, in some ways, is comparable to research on cancer. It was felt in the beginning that an answer to the problem of cancer was round the corner; only to realize later that the problem of growth is a lot more enormous than can be answered by the early findings. Similarly, in the field of schizophrenia, the early torrent of biological treasure hunts has begun to lose its irradiance. The multiplicity of conflicting reports points out clearly that we may need to change our concepts of psychiatric disease (at least in its biological coordinates) and that we may investigate basic neurobiology before we can write the final word on the biology of schizophrenia and its classification. It is with the fervent hope that more basic research in neurobiology (in a field of human experimentation) will be facilitated in the future, that I terminate my final comments.